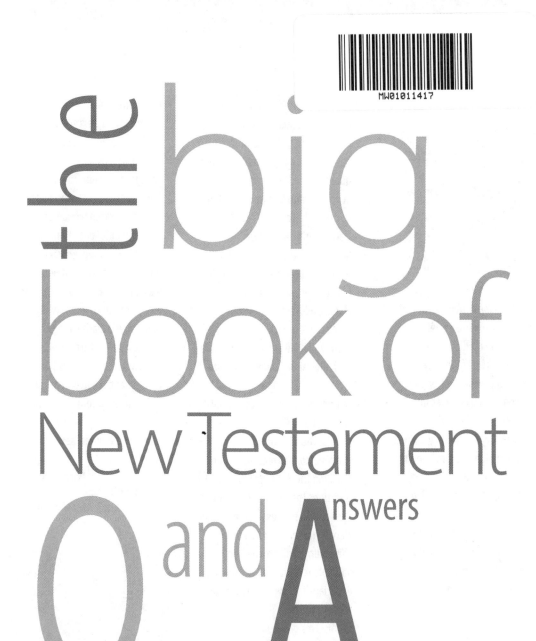

the big book of New Testament Q and Answers

MICHAEL ESCHELBACH

The Big Book of New Testament Questions and Answers is a compelling read and vital new resource. I found myself captivated as page after page Dr. Eschelbach provides insight into the "story behind the story" of God's Word in an easy-to-read format. I highly recommend this book for Bible study leaders, teachers, students and all who desire to experience the richness that comes with the Spirit-filled discernment of the Gospel message and its impact on our own personal faith fused journey.

—Dr. Kurt Senske
Author, *The Calling:
Live a Life of Significance*
(Concordia, 2010)
President & CEO,
Lutheran Social Services
of the South

Michael Eschelbach is known among students on the campuses where he has taught as having the ability to address their questions and concerns about the Scriptures and God in a way that both speaks to them and also clarifies difficult matters. This book, compiled from questions he has received over the years in his New Testament introduction classes, addresses questions many readers of the New Testament will have and answers them with precision and intelligibility while also helping readers come to grips with the great theological themes of God's Word. These are just the type of questions every pastor has received when teaching the Bible, exactly the questions that are on the mind of thoughtful, serious readers of the New Testament. For this reason, this volume will prove to be a valuable resource for anyone, but especially for laypersons who are reading the New Testament for themselves or preparing to teach it to others.

—Rev. Andrew Steinmann, PhD
Distinguished Professor
of Theology and Hebrew
Concordia University Chicago

As a former student of Dr. Eschelbach, his excellent teaching comes through in this book as clearly as it did in the college classroom. The questions are extensive, capturing many things I've often wondered, but also including ideas I'd never before considered, which helped me read the text in a deeper way. In his responses, Eschelbach answers with wisdom, while maintaining clarity and simplicity. Explanations are based solidly in Scripture and always point the reader back to Christ. This is a wonderful companion book for biblical study, whether it is a group or individual setting.

—Bethany Regan
Former Student
Concordia University Chicago
class of 2006

Bible-believing Christians are aware that we live in a time in which the world has painted a target on God's Holy Word. Skeptics, cynics, global religions, and even some Christian denominations compete with each other in taking pot-shots at Scripture's truths. The faithful who wish to make an educated response to the questions they hear often feel ignorant and ill-prepared to do so. Which is why Dr. Eschelbach's volume, *The Big Book of New Testament Questions and Answers* is necessary. He has done the research which allows us to make educated and evangelical replies to common challenges about God's Word.

—Rev. Kenneth R. Klaus
Speaker Emeritus
of *The Lutheran Hour*®

Martin Luther left us a legacy that to this day reminds us of the powerful and intimate nature of question-asking in the formation of the faith. Father and mother sit with children who learn the faith through the recitation of the chief articles of faith, and through the simple question: "What does this mean?" And to this question the Word of God in Christ gives answer. Here, too, Dr. Eschelbach reminds us of the joy of asking good questions, and being guided in God's Word to receive faithful answers. Readers will find here answers to real questions that are being asked about the New Testament. And they will find also a faithful model for how to approach the many questions that are yet to be asked.

—Rev. David Rufner
Pastor of New Hope Lutheran
Church, Hudsonville, MI

Dr. Eschelbach's book is a valuable resource for anyone studying or teaching the Bible. Not only are the answers insightful, but the questions themselves help one realize what others wonder when they read these texts. Bible study leaders will benefit from seeing what questions may arise, even if people don't voice them. Everyone will appreciate Dr. Eschelbach's responses, which reference other Bible passages.

—Ted Kober
President, Ambassadors
of Reconciliation

Published 2015 by Concordia Publishing House
3558 S. Jefferson Ave., St. Louis, MO 63118-3968
1-800-325-3040 • www.cph.org

Manufactured in the United States of America

Library of Congress Cataloging-in-Publication Data

Eschelbach, Michael A., 1957-

The big book of New Testament questions and answers / Michael Eschelbach.

pages cm

Includes index.

ISBN 978-0-7586-4919-5

1. Bible. New Testament—Criticism, interpretation, etc.—Miscellanea. I. Title.

BS2361.3.E83 2015

225.6—dc23

2014047209

1   2   3   4   5   6   7   8   9   10   24   23   22   21   20   19   18   17   16   15

Contents

Introduction

"Students are required to submit two questions on the reading from the New Testament for each class meeting" is what the syllabus said. The queries that form the basis of this book were collected from more than forty sections of a course I teach called "New Testament Introduction." Once collected, the questions were collated so that duplicates could be removed and similar questions on a set of verses could be combined. The questions have been lightly edited so the reader might see not just what the students asked but how they asked it.

Unlike commentaries on books of the New Testament, this work only responds to questions that the content of the New Testament generates in the minds of college students. Some questions are more objective in nature and simple to answer; most questions indicate a difficulty in the text or a concept addressed in the text. The questions these students asked are significant. With few exceptions, each time I would read what the student submitted, I found myself thinking, "That's a good question." Inviting students to ask their questions committed me to finding a way to explain the theology of the New Testament that would solve the puzzles it so often presents to its readers. There was no way to hurry through the writing of this manuscript since every question came from a student of mine, all of whom I came to know and care about during the course of a semester. I have endeavored to be as focused and brief as possible yet equally committed to making sure that the questions have been answered clearly, effectively, and faithfully.

Answering questions requires a different approach to writing. I was not the guide or architect of this work. I was committed to following where the questions led. I also had to start anew with each question, taking time to hear what was being asked and why the text generated the question it did. Some questions required research regarding grammar, syntax, and the meaning of particular words. Questions from the four Gospels drew upon many years of previous work on harmonizing the Gospels. This research yielded great benefits for me besides just the answers to the questions.

Like any work that is a product of research, this one will never be finished. Reading the New Testament, the questions, and my answers are bound to lead to further questions as well as the discovery of new observations, better explanations, and more references within and outside of the New Testament itself. This text is intended to serve as a resource to those who read the New Testament but may also be a basis for individual or group Bible studies.

The questions and answers appear in the same order as the New Testament in your Bible. Thus, if you are reading your Bible and have a question on Luke 3:5, for example, you can browse the section of Luke 3 to see if there might be a similar question. When checking for a question on a particular chapter and verse, be careful to note that a verse or set of verses may be included in a larger portion of the text.

ACKNOWLEDGMENTS

I am forever grateful to the students who asked the questions that have provided so many years of wonderful theological exercise, both in researching answers and in articulating them. Many thanks also to Adina Archan, Jackie Scarborough, and Bethany Richeson, who helped with collating and proofreading.

ABBREVIATIONS

OLD TESTAMENT

Gn	Genesis
Ex	Exodus
Lv	Leviticus
Nu	Numbers
Dt	Deuteronomy
Jsh	Joshua
Jgs	Judges
Ru	Ruth
1Sm	1 Samuel
2Sm	2 Samuel
1Ki	1 Kings
2Ki	2 Kings
1Ch	1 Chronicles
2Ch	2 Chronicles
Ezr	Ezra
Ne	Nehemiah
Est	Esther
Jb	Job
Ps	Psalms
Pr	Proverbs
Ec	Ecclesiastes
Sg	Song of Solomon
Is	Isaiah
Jer	Jeremiah
Lm	Lamentations
Ezk	Ezekiel
Dn	Daniel

Hos	Hosea
Jl	Joel
Am	Amos
Ob	Obadiah
Jnh	Jonah
Mi	Micah
Na	Nahum
Hab	Habakkuk
Zep	Zephaniah
Hg	Haggai
Zec	Zechariah
Mal	Malachi

NEW TESTAMENT

Mt	Matthew
Mk	Mark
Lk	Luke
Jn	John
Ac	Acts
Rm	Romans
1Co	1 Corinthians
2Co	2 Corinthians
Gal	Galatians
Eph	Ephesians
Php	Philippians
Col	Colossians
1Th	1 Thessalonians
2Th	2 Thessalonians
1Tm	1 Timothy
2Tm	2 Timothy
Ti	Titus
Phm	Philemon
Heb	Hebrews
Jas	James
1Pt	1 Peter
2Pt	2 Peter
1Jn	1 John
2Jn	2 John
3Jn	3 John
Jude	Jude
Rv	Revelation

Matthew

Q 1:1–17 Why is Jesus' genealogy listed?

Both Matthew and Luke provide genealogies of Jesus, but for different reasons. Matthew records the genealogy in order to demonstrate two things. First, Matthew wants the reader to understand that God, not Joseph, is the father of Jesus. God has provided what no human father ever could. Second, Matthew wants to remind the Jews that they are not a "super" race that generated a "super" man (Messiah) from superior genetic material. Note how the text would draw in a Jewish reader by mentioning first two "super" men from Israel's past: Abraham and David. Then the text lays out a genealogy that is full of foreigners and embarrassments: Judah, who raised wicked sons and was the mastermind behind the mistreatment of Joseph; Tamar, who bore sons to her father-in-law; Rahab, the harlot of Jericho; and Ruth, the Moabite.

Note how the text highlights both the failure of men and the virtue of women in contrast to the men. "Judah and his brothers" (1:2) brings to mind the Lord's dealings with Joseph (cf. Gn 37:12–36). That David begot Solomon "by the wife of Uriah" (1:6) points to David's adultery, murder, and disrespect for God. Josiah begot Jechoniah "at the time of the deportation to Babylon" (1:11), which reminds the reader of how foolish it was for Judah to follow the wicked example of Israel and so fall, needlessly, into captivity.

Q 1:2–16 In Matthew's genealogy, it says Joseph is from the line of Judah, but he's not the biological father of Jesus. Is Mary related and also from that lineage?

Mary's lineage is recorded in Lk 3:23–38. There Luke reveals that Jesus was thought to be of Joseph ("as was supposed" [v. 23]) but was really of Heli, Mary's father. Joseph and Mary's genealogies are identical from Adam to Solomon, at which point they separate until Shealtiel and Zerubbabel (at the time of the Babylonian captivity of Judah), and then they separate again.

Q 1:17 Is there significance in the fact that there were fourteen generations from Abraham to David, fourteen from David to the Babylonian exile, and fourteen from the exile to Christ?

There is much speculation about significance, especially because of Jewish traditions having to do with numbers. Some say fourteen names are given in order to make the list easier to remember. The number 7 has to do with completion in time (seven days in a week) and 2 has to do with things being certain (Pharaoh had the same dream twice, cf. Gn 41:32). Although we cannot say for certain if there is a deeper intention in using the number 14, what the apostle Paul says is certain: "When the *fullness of time* had come, God sent forth His Son . . ." (Gal 4:4, italics added).

Q 1:19 Why did Joseph decide to divorce Mary since they were not married at this point?

In biblical times, a man's public declaration that he would be husband to a woman was absolutely binding. A marriage worked in this way: (1) A man received permission from the woman's father. (2) The man declared his intent to be husband to that woman. (3) For a period of time, the man demonstrated to everyone his ability and faithfulness in providing for her. All this took place before they engaged in any physical intimacy. (4) When the man's ability to husband the woman was evident, there was a party, and following that the man and woman consummated the marriage by intercourse and cohabitation. Consider how women and children would benefit from this practice, in contrast to the consequences of sexual promiscuity practiced and urged upon young people in this day and age.

Q 1:20 Why are Joseph's dreams told? Didn't Mary have any dreams?

Joseph's dreams are told to explain his actions. Joseph learned from "an angel of the Lord" in his dream that he did not need to divorce Mary because she had not been unfaithful. He needed to flee to Egypt because Herod sought to destroy the child. Joseph, as the one responsible for the care and well-being of his family, is directed by

God through dreams. Unless the text tells us, we cannot know if Mary had any dreams.

• • • • • • • • • • • • • • • • • •

Q **1:23 Why was Jesus called "Immanuel"?**
The baby Jesus was given many names by direction of God. One of His names is "Immanuel," which is a Hebrew name meaning "God with us" (Is 7:14). The name is fitting because God the Son had come among His people by taking upon Himself human nature. The reality of God being among His people in human nature makes certain God's promise that He would continue to be with us.

• • • • • • • • • • • • • • • • • •

Q **1:25 The end of Mt 1 leaves us at Jesus' birth and leads right into the beginning of the visit of the Magi in the second chapter. Why is that?**
Matthew is giving as much of Jesus' background as possible while hurrying to the work of Jesus during His adult ministry. Matthew focuses on Jesus' fulfillment of the Old Testament in several ways. First, Jesus fulfills specific prophecies from the Old Testament (Mt 1:23; 2:6, 15, 18, 23). Second, Jesus is re-living the life of Israel in order to fulfill all that was expected of them (and us) according to the Law: Jesus is the promised Seed of Abraham; He is the perfect King that David failed to be; He went to Egypt and then came back to the land of Canaan in perfect obedience to the Word of the Lord. Third, just as the Old Testament

> ## Why was Jesus called "Immanuel"?

is full of examples of Gentiles being more faithful than Jews (as is noted by Matthew in the genealogy, vv. 1:3, 5), so also now it was the Wise Men from the East who came to worship the child while the religious and civil leaders of Israel were "troubled" (Mt 2:3).

• • • • • • • • • • • • • • • • • •

Q **2:1–2 How did the Wise Men know that the star represented the birth of the Messiah?**
Matthew tells us that these men came from the East. Five hundred years before this, the Babylonians had come from the East and carried the children of Judah away captive. During the Babylonian captivity, Daniel, Ezekiel, and other faithful Jews (Dn 1:3–4) were active witnesses to God's revelation, which surely would have included prophecies about the coming of the Messiah. These prophecies and teachings of the Old Testament remained among the people of the East, even after the Jews returned from there. Compare also the numbers of foreigners who sought out Jesus (Mt 8:5; Mk 7:24–30; Jn 12:20–21) and those who came to Jerusalem regularly looking for the Messiah (Ac 2:5–11; 8:26–39).

Q 2:5, 15, 23 Who is "the prophet" referred to throughout the chapter?

In 2:5, the prophet quoted is Micah (5:2); in 2:15, the prophet is Hosea (11:1); and in 2:23, the prophet is Isaiah (11:1; 53:3). Sometimes the prophet is mentioned in the text (as in Mt 2:17), and some Bibles will give you the name of the prophet in a reference. At the time of Jesus, most Jews would have been very familiar with these quotations and would have known which prophet had spoken them. Matthew appeals to this common knowledge of the message of the prophets in order to prove that Jesus is in fact the Messiah they predicted.

Q 2:8 Why didn't Herod just follow the Magi?

There is no explanation provided in the biblical text, but we might consider a few reasonable possibilities:

1. Herod was busy and influential and so could not spend time looking for Jesus.

2. When people have devious motives and are deceitful, they often think that everyone around them is suspicious. Herod was intensely paranoid; he killed many of his own family members, suspecting that they were plotting against him. Perhaps Herod did not want the Magi to suspect him.

3. Herod was a vain man; perhaps he thought it would be beneath him to go searching about for an infant.

Q 2:11 How long was it between Jesus' birth and the visit of the Wise Men?

Many assume that a long time passed between Jesus' birth and the visit of the Wise Men because Herod had all children two years old or younger put to death. What we know for certain is that at least forty days after Jesus' birth must have passed before the Wise Men visited. We know this because Mary and Joseph went to the temple in Jerusalem to offer the required sacrifice for a newborn. They could not have done this until Mary was ceremonially clean after giving birth, which would be forty days (Lv 12:1–6). At the time they gave the sacrifice, they were still poor, since Joseph offered doves instead of a lamb. Also, after the Wise Men visited, the holy family fled immediately to Egypt. So, it can be assumed that the holy family moved to a house as soon as possible after the birth of Jesus, circumcised Him on the eighth day, took Him to Jerusalem for the sacrifice after forty days, and then the Wise Men visited. This could have been as long as two years after Jesus' birth.

Q 3:1 Why is John the Baptist suddenly discussed in ch. 3? And why does it mention him only as an adult, instead of introducing him as an infant born before Christ?

Each of the Gospels has a particular focus. Matthew, as the first Gospel written, is interested in quickly connecting Jesus with the "essential people" of Israel's past. Note how Matthew does not trace Jesus back to the beginning (Adam), but traces Jesus to the great fathers of Israel—Abraham and David. Once Jesus' beginnings are in place, Matthew moves on to the work that Jesus was born to do, which is highlighted in His three and a half years of public ministry, beginning with His Baptism by John the Baptist. Consider also how Mark skips all of Jesus' beginnings, while Luke backs all the way up to the origin of John the Baptist—each because of a particular focus or audience to whom they were responding.

• • • • • • • • • • • • • • • • • • •

Q 3:5–6 People were going out to John confessing their sins. Does this support the idea of adult-only Baptism?

The issue of infant or adult Baptism cannot be answered in this text. We don't know if both children and adults were seeking out John. What this text highlights is the fact that people were looking for help ("going out") and admitting they had problems they could not solve ("confessing their sins"). This is in stark contrast to the leaders of the Jews, who only came out to argue for their own self-righteousness. Of course, their argument failed with Jesus, and it failed again when they died. (If they were righteous, why would they age and die? [See Gal 3:12.]) Interestingly, Matthew identifies the Jewish leaders as the "brood of vipers" (3:7), while Luke does not identify them.

• • • • • • • • • • • • • • • • • • •

Q 3:7–10 This passage speaks of faith without works being dead. Does this still apply to the present day?

John the Baptist makes at least four points in this passage. (1) John addresses people who were coming to him not because they sought the truth but because they wanted to see if they needed to be concerned about a certain man's activity. (2) John impresses upon the listener that truth is the absolute issue, especially concerning repentance and the life that is consistent with repentance. Repentance is God's activity in people that turns them from lives of their own making, devoted to destructive ways, to lives provided by God, which are devoted to the way of life. Faith, produced by God's Word, motivates both the turning and movement in the right direction. Faith always works itself out through deeds. (3) John highlights the re-creative power of God, remembering how God created Isaac when it was impossible for Abraham and Sarah to bear a child and the fact that God can and does make believers out of stone (Ezk 36:26; 37). (4) John issues the most severe of warnings, hoping to silence their arrogant human natures to make room for the Gospel to prevail in their lives (Rm 3:19–26). Our human nature is no different than that of the people to whom John was speaking, and our need for truth and grace is just as great.

How are pastors able to baptize with the Holy Spirit?

Q **3:11–12 When John the Baptist says, "I baptize you with water," does he mean that he is not able to baptize with the Holy Spirit? If so, then how are pastors today able to baptize with the Holy Spirit?**

John the Baptist is making a distinction between himself, as one who administers Baptism ("I baptize you with water"), and Jesus, who makes the Baptism happen ("He will baptize you with the Holy Spirit and fire"). John's Baptism was certainly accompanied by the Holy Spirit, since this is when the Spirit descended on Jesus in the form of a dove. (Paul makes these same two points in Ac 19:1–6.) John is also directing the listener's attention ahead to Pentecost, when the Holy Spirit will make His presence known by placing a tongue of fire on each apostle's head. Acts consistently distinguishes between the normal means of receiving the Holy Spirit through the preaching of the Word and Baptism (2:38) and the special manifestation of the Holy Spirit to confirm the application of the Gospel apart from works of the Law, through the laying on of the apostles' hands (5:12; 8:14–19; 10:44–48; 14:3; 15:7–10; 19:6). Ever since the time of Christ, anyone baptized according to the Word of God is baptized with the Holy Spirit because the Word and Spirit of God are inseparable.

Q **3:12 "Winnowing fork" and "threshing floor"? What does this verse mean?**

This verse uses terms associated with harvesting wheat. During the harvest, grain would be gathered (stalk and all) from the field and threshed, a process where it was beaten with sticks to separate the grain from the head of the plant. Then a winnowing fork would be used to throw the mass up in the air so the wind would take away everything but the heavy grain, which would fall back to the floor. With this metaphor, John warned the Jewish leaders that God would be coming in judgment to separate what was valuable (people of faith) from what was worthless (people who despised the faith). Reference to the harvest as a means of explaining the final judgment is common in the Bible (cf. Jer 8:20; Mt 13:30; Rv 14:15).

Q **3:15 Why did Jesus have to be baptized? He was the Son of God and had done nothing that merited repentance.**

Jesus came to be baptized because it was necessary for Him to live every moment of our lives for us. Consider how the Bible comments on the completeness of His obedience: His childhood in Lk 2:51–52 and His temptation in Lk 4:13 (cf. Heb 4:15). John himself recognized that Jesus had no need, for His own sake, to be baptized and would have prevented Him. But Jesus answered that it was necessary for Him to "fulfill all righteousness" not for Himself but on our behalf. The beauty of this is that God does not want there to be any moment or event in our lives where we are left to fulfill what the Law requires with our own abilities, for this would put our salvation and peace in jeopardy. So in the case of Baptism, it is effective and saves entirely by God's own activity. Jesus declares His entire life to be ours in the Gospel, and this gift is confirmed in our Baptism. If our conscience wanted to accuse us of not having the benefit of Baptism because we did not receive it with a pure heart or with pure thoughts, Jesus would contend that He has already accepted it for us in perfection and now declares that perfection to be ours (Jn 16:14–15).

● ● ● ● ● ● ● ● ● ● ● ● ● ● ● ● ● ● ● ●

Q 3:17 Could everyone hear the Father's voice when He said He was pleased with Jesus?

This text does not tell us who heard and did not hear these words that God spoke. The Book of John does state that those who heard it did not understand. In John 12:28, when the Father speaks, the crowd wasn't sure what they heard—some said it had thundered and some said an angel had spoken. Similarly, when Paul was met by the Lord on the way to Damascus, those with him heard something (Ac 9:7) but could not understand what was being said (22:9). These examples give the impression that people typically did not understand what God said from heaven, but this cannot be applied to Jesus' Baptism with certainty.

● ● ● ● ● ● ● ● ● ● ● ● ● ● ● ● ● ● ● ●

Q 4:1–11 Why was Jesus led into the desert to be tempted?

Satan wants to destroy God's life-giving activity at all times (Jn 8:44). Satan failed to destroy Jesus as an infant (Mt 2:1–12). Apparently the next opportunity that Satan had was after Jesus' Baptism. If God had declared that He was well pleased with His Son, perhaps Satan could destroy His plan by tempting the Son to do something that would displease the Father, so Satan tempts Jesus.

● ● ● ● ● ● ● ● ● ● ● ● ● ● ● ● ● ● ● ●

Q 4:2 Why was Jesus fasting for forty days and forty nights?

All of Jesus' life is a "re-living" of every human life and, in particular, the life of the children of Israel (Israel is called God's "son" in Ex 4:22–23, and Jesus is God's Son). Remember how the children of Israel gave in to their cravings in the wilderness, which climaxed in idolatry and sexual immorality (Ex 32; 1Co 10:1–11; Heb 3:12–4:1). Jesus fasts to demonstrate how completely His human nature lives in service of His Spirit, not only avoiding self-indulgence, but also fasting so that He might concentrate more completely on resisting every temptation (Lk 4:13). The time was forty days, corresponding to the number of days the spies were in the land of Canaan, which corresponds to the number of years Israel wandered in the desert.

Q **4:3 Was the devil visible to Jesus? Could Jesus see any spiritual figure, as He was true God as well as true man?**

Since Jesus is true God, He knows and sees all things (Ps 139:11–16). We cannot know from the text what form the devil took when he appeared to Jesus, and that is part of the point. If the devil's only form was a visible figure in a red suit with horns, tail, and pitchfork, we could easily beware of him. The problem is that we don't know what form the devil will take or how his temptations will come to us. Thus the Bible instructs us to be sober and vigilant (1Pt 5:8), to beware that the devil disguises himself as an angel of light (2Co 11:14), and to put on the whole armor of God (Eph 6:11–18).

Q **4:8 Why did Satan tempt Jesus with all the kingdoms of the earth? Aren't they already His?**

First, Satan is limited in what he knows and, apparently, what he is capable of understanding. He sees Jesus of Nazareth, the man, and assumes He can be tempted as any other man. Second, it was necessary for Jesus to fulfill all righteousness (Mt 3:15). This means that He had to successfully overcome every temptation (Lk 4:13). Clearly this temptation is the most comprehensive and threatening of all (consider the consistent theme throughout literature and film of possessing everything).

Q **4:10 Did Satan know that Jesus would not give in to temptation?**

It appears that Satan's knowledge is limited. We know that the Word of God cannot be broken (Jn 10:35). Since Jesus is that Word of God in human nature, He cannot fail, though the temptations are real. Satan does not know everything the Bible says, for while he can quote it (Mt 4:6), he obviously did not know what is said about the crucifixion of Jesus and what that would accomplish for us. If he had, he would not have put it into Judas's heart to betray Jesus.

Q **4:12 Why was John put into prison?**

King Herod arrested John because he didn't like what John said about his marriage to Herodias, his brother Phillip's wife (Mk 6:17–20). While Herod held John in prison, he did not execute him because he was afraid of him and, surprisingly, "heard him gladly" (Mk 6:20). We should be careful to remember that Herod was part Jew and had at least some fear of the Lord.

Q **4:17 Is it significant that Jesus uses the same words John the Baptist spoke, "Repent, for the kingdom of heaven is at hand," to preach in Capernaum after John is imprisoned?**

The continuity between Old Testament prophets (Ezk 18), John the Baptist (Mt 3:2), and Jesus is absolutely significant. The Bible articulates one singular message of truth from

God the Father so that no one, not even Jesus (Jn 14:11) nor the Holy Spirit (16:13), speak words of their own invention. Repentance is a theme present throughout the Bible because fallen human nature is always determined to move away from God, in the direction of self-destruction. The beauty of John's message is that the long-awaited Kingdom is now present with the incarnation of Jesus. The message of John gives way to Jesus speaking for Himself, just as artificial light is no longer noticeable in the bright light of the sun.

· ·

Q 4:18 Had Jesus ever talked to these men before calling them to follow Him?

The Gospel of John makes it clear that John the Baptist told the disciples about Jesus, and they had spent time with Him before what appears to be their first encounter in the Synoptic Gospels (Jn 1:29–51). The people of Israel were eagerly anticipating the appearance of the Messiah. The anticipation, along with John's testimony and the early encounter between Jesus and the disciples, makes their response to His calling here much more understandable.

· ·

Q 4:20 When the brothers followed Jesus, what were they forced to leave behind?

The disciples were not forced to leave anything behind. They were inspired to follow Jesus in order to obtain what is of incomparably greater value than their material belongings (Php 3:7–21). So, they left behind both everything and nothing. On the one hand, Jesus

said that being a disciple would mean losing everything, even your family and your own life (Mt 10:34–39). On the other hand, the disciples still had homes, families, and tools by which they earned money for material necessities (1Co 9:4–5; Jn 21:3–8).

· ·

Q 4:23 Why is it that Jesus could heal the sick, but we still have no cure for some diseases today?

First of all, Jesus is the Creator of all things and has absolute power over all His creation, even those elements that are destructive (Lk 4:36). Second, remember these two features about Jesus' healings: (1) He did not say "your faith has made you healthy" but rather "your faith has saved you" (e.g., Lk 7:50), and (2) these people eventually experienced disease or illness again and died. The point of healings was to demonstrate that Jesus was the Savior, the Son of the living God. The human nature of the people He healed would have to die at some point because "the wages of sin is death" (Rm 6:23). The real cure for diseases and illnesses then is the same as now; faith that provides eternal life for the soul and the promise of the resurrection of an immortal body (1Co 15:50–58).

· ·

Q 4:24 Are there still demon-possessed people today?

The soul of a human being is a space to be inhabited by a spirit. If the Holy Spirit is not filling that soul, then demons will (Mt 12:43–45; Jn 8:44). The difficulty today is distinguishing between demon possession, physiological imbalances, and the wicked orientation of fallen human nature (Mk 7:21–23). Demon possession today may also come in more subtle ways, since it is more effective. That is to say, people are fearful of the kind of demoniac described in the Bible, but no one pays any attention to a person who is self-righteous, atheistic, or self-indulgent.

Q 5:3 What does it mean to be poor in spirit? Further explain "the happy" and "the blessed."

This verse actually says, "Blessed [happy] are the poor in spirit." The Bible has two words that are translated "bless." The word used here is *makarios*, which means, "to be happy in spite of your circumstances because of what lies ahead." (Contrast that with "joy," which means to be happy because of your circumstances.) Christians are happy to be materially poor, not because they endure physical poverty, but because of their recognition that the true riches and love of God leads them to pursue the things of God and leave behind the things of men. Consider the examples Jesus gives in this same discourse (Mt 6:19–34). Compare also the response of early Christians (Ac 2:44–45; 4:36–37) and Paul (Php 3:7ff.). Thus, Christians are not forced to be poor, nor do they try to be poor. Rather, by means of their relationship with God, who freely gives His love, and by a life of loving relationships toward people whom God freely provides, Christians have little use for what

the world calls riches, and they are happier without them.

Q 5:13 What does saltiness mean?

Jesus uses the term *salt* to describe Christians because their life and words enhance people's thirst for God's living water. We listen to people, observe them, then ask questions and relate to them in a way that causes them to wonder if there's more to life than material and temporary things. When we explain the truth of God's absolute Law in a caring way, people experience a thirst for what would truly satisfy their longing or accusing conscience (cf. Jn 4).

Q 5:13 If you lose sight of God, does that mean you are forever damned?

First of all, Jesus' main point here is that Christians who would keep the name or outward association of "Christian" but replace its content with worldly thinking are despised ("trampled under people's feet") by the worldly. Second, a person is only forever damned if he or she continually insists on losing sight of God. We must be careful never to make this judgment on a person. However, the warning and danger are real, since we have a human nature that would do just this. So Jesus speaks severe warnings to keep us from carelessly letting go of the Word and Spirit of God. Consider the following passages on this subject: Mt 12:31–32; 19:23–26; Heb 2:1–4:11; 6:4–9; 10:26–31.

Q 5:20 Do people go to heaven based on the amount of faith they have?

Jesus deals with this issue when He responds to the apostles' request for increased faith. Jesus said, "If you had faith like a grain of mustard seed" (Lk 17:6). Besides this, Paul explains that the size of a person's faith is determined by God (Rm 12:3). On this occasion, Jesus is exposing the hypocrisy of the Jewish leaders. People had become convinced that the Jewish leaders had the greatest of faith because they were so "religious," so consumed with laws and rules. Here, Jesus wishes to destroy the notion that we can obtain heaven by pious conduct of our own invention or that we can earn God's favor by keeping the Law. No, salvation requires infinitely greater faith than that of the Jewish leaders, who in fact had thrown away faith in favor of works (Rm 10:1–9). Salvation requires the faith Jesus demonstrated throughout His life and death. That faith and faithfulness is credited to us in its entirety when the promises and Spirit of God work faith in us.

Q 5:21–48 Jesus says to the people, "You have heard that it was said," before each topic He is talking about. From whom have the people heard this before? Is Jesus contradicting the Old Testament by saying these things?

Jesus uses this phrase about six times in this chapter, but most of the sermon is spent correcting false understandings that the people held because of the false teachers among the Jewish leaders. Notice that this is the beginning of Jesus' public ministry and that He begins this section by saying, "Do not think that I have come to abolish the Law and the Prophets" (5:17). Jesus was not contradicting the Old Testament; rather, He was clearly distinguishing between what the people had been taught and what God's Law actually said and intended. Jesus could do the same today. There remains a serious difference between religious opinion and tradition and what Jesus taught in the New Testament.

Q 5:21–22 Are humans subject to judgment by other humans only after murder, or is this referring to divine judgment?

Murder is a "capital crime," which the Bible requires men in authority to punish with death (Gn 9:5–6; Rm 13:4). In any case, civil authority and church authority act as God's agents to minimize the destructive activity of people. This judicial activity is also meant to serve the mission of the Church by teaching people the fear of God, which prepares them for the Word that works repentance and faith—so that a human might not come under divine judgment.

Q 5:22 What is the meaning of, "Whoever insults his brother will be liable to the council; and whoever says, 'You fool!' will be liable to the hell of fire"?

The Aramaic word *raca* that is translated "insults" here means "vain or empty," comparable to our word *stupid*. The word *fool* in the Bible does not mean "stupid," but "unbeliever," as Ps 53:1 makes clear: "The fool says in his heart, 'There is no God.'" This is the kind of condemning judgment that Jesus forbids in Mt 7:1: "Judge not, that you be not judged." The eternal condemnation of an individual belongs to God, not to us. Jesus forbids us to think such of another person, so that we never give up hope for sharing the Word with anyone, no matter how contrary to God they may seem at a given time.

Q 5:25–30 Why do these verses sound so literal and we don't ever seem to take them seriously?

The words of Jesus are clear and sure. The problem is that our human nature, which worries about all these material things, is incapable of faith in God, who promises to provide (1Co 15:50). What is worse, our human nature, having rejected God, must prove to itself that it has a blessed life apart from God. So, fallen human beings spend their whole lives trying to accumulate material things that give us a sense of power, worth, security, and well-being. (See Lk 12:16–21, and notice what follows the example Jesus gives here!) The problem is that no material goods can fulfill the absence of the infinite living God, so nothing is ever enough. The only way to live by these words of Jesus is according to the soul that is filled with the Spirit of God, which works

faith and longs for eternal relationships with God and others (Php 4:11–13).

Q 5:30 What does "lose one of your members" mean?

Jesus speaks of losing an eye, arm, or foot in order to help us understand how hard it is for our human nature to give up its wicked behavior. If we were to literally cut off the parts of our body that cause us to sin, where would we stop? The point is that we make the comparison that Jesus provides for us. When we would cling to selfish thinking or pride, when we would refuse to give up a bad habit or repent of wrongdoing, this is when we should remember that it's better to cut off something you think is integral to your life—one of your own limbs—than to stubbornly defend and maintain your ways that will hold you under the wrathful judgment of God.

Q 5:31–32 How does divorcing a woman cause her to commit adultery? Why is the woman the only one committing adultery? What happens if a man divorces his wife for reasons other than adultery—is she never allowed to marry again because of her husband's sin? When people are divorced for a reason other than marital infidelity and one gets remarried, are that person and the new spouse living in sexual immorality?

To understand these verses, it is helpful to read Jesus' response to the Pharisees' question about divorce in Mt 19. There, Jesus appeals to creation for the model of the marriage relationship. Next, remember that Jesus is speaking to a culture where women could not divorce at all and where men were often callous about divorcing their wives and taking divorced women as wives. (Mark records Jesus' words regarding the Gentile practice where women could also sue for divorce in 10:12.) The union of one man and one woman is sacred because it reflects the union between the one true God and His people. Also, children and society need stable families with faithful parents at the head. If one person in a marriage commits adultery, the union is broken. This does not mean, though, that the marriage cannot be sustained (reconciliation is always the most desirable solution); divorce is not required of the "innocent" party.

If a woman is divorced by her husband apart from adultery, she is forced to seek another man to be responsible for her through marriage. The problem is that her first marriage is still binding in God's sight. Therefore, if she remarries, she is committing adultery. The point that Jesus is making here is that the divorcing husband is causing her to commit adultery (consider Jesus' words about those who cause others to sin in Mt 18:6–9).

Finally, we must remember the principles of grace and repentance. A Christian would always seek to restore marriage if it is possible. To whatever extent that is no longer possible (because of adultery or because a person has already remarried), Christians still repent of past errors, seek reconciliation in whatever ways are possible, and seek to uphold virtue and marriage in the future. While a person should never divorce (or contradict God's design in any way), because he or she knows there is forgiveness (Rm 6:1–2), there is always repentance and grace to restore people to God and, as much as possible, to one another.

● ●

Q 5:33–37 Jesus commands never to enter into an oath. What is meant by this? Some people, such as notary publics, are under oath to uphold the laws of the state and are duly authorized to administer oaths. Are these people sinning and causing others to sin?

The government that asks you to take an oath also protects your religious convictions. Jesus forbids the taking of oaths for two reasons: (1) We cannot assure absolute faithfulness. (2) People often make oaths in order to deceive others. For example, if we are asked to "solemnly swear to tell the truth, the whole truth, and nothing but the truth, so help us God," in honesty we would have to respond that we cannot possibly tell the whole truth because we only know what we have seen and heard. If the government asks us to "swear" to do or not do something, we must respectfully inform them that our Lord has forbidden this. If the question is restated in a simple form ("Will you tell the truth?" or "Will you perform the duties of . . ."), we may confidently answer, "Yes!" In fact, courts no longer ask for people to take an oath on the Bible. They simply ask, "Will you tell the truth . . . ?" to which we may answer simply, "Yes." Marriage is another example. There are no vows or oaths in the marriage service, only questions: "Will you have this woman . . . will you have this man?"

* *

Q 5:33 Do these verses mean something like "I swear to God"? What about swear words or even words we don't really consider swear words, such as "crud" or "darn"? If it does only mean that, what does the Bible say about swear words?

Properly speaking, to "swear" means to take an oath before God. If someone says the words as a meaningless expression, they are taking God's name in vain. To "curse" means to call down a curse from God upon someone or something (Mk 11:13–14, 20–21). Other words fall under the category of taking God's name in vain or simply bad, coarse, or crass language, which is also forbidden for Christians (Eph 5:3–4).

* *

Q 5:38–39 The Bible says, "An eye for an eye," but Jesus says, "Turn . . . the other [cheek]." When is one or the other applicable?

How can we be perfect when we are by nature sinful?

The instructions for punishment that include "an eye for an eye and a tooth for a tooth" were given to the governing authorities in Old Testament society (Ex 21:24; Lv 24:20), never to individuals. God wants to provide justice and protection (especially to the helpless; notice that the Ex 21:24 context has to do with harming an unborn infant!) but wants that justice and protection to exist in a context of love. Civil authorities do not seek vengeance; neither may an individual. Civil authorities do not execute judgment out of hatred but out of duty. Individuals, whether simple citizens or those in positions of authority, still love their enemies and pray for those who spitefully use and abuse them. The overarching reason for this is our perspective on eternity. If Jesus did not love His enemies, where would we be? Now that we are reconciled to Him, our life's work is to be advocates for others, especially our enemies, as they are most in need of spiritual advocates (2Co 5:14–21).

* *

Q 5:48 How can we be perfect when we are by nature sinful?

God would not be helping us at all if He lowered His standard of life to match our ability. Holding up and holding fast to His ideal creation is imperative if we are going to pursue life as He intends us to know it. Life requires perfection. Jesus' life proves this in a positive way; our disintegration and death prove it in the negative way. So how to meet this imperative: "Be perfect"? God provides for us to meet this in three ways. (1) We are perfect because Jesus provides His perfect life for us (Jn 16:14–15). (2) We are perfect because Jesus has taken away our sins (Rm 8:1). (3) With all shortcomings forgiven and the Holy Spirit at work in us, we do in fact begin to live according to God's intent more and more each day, though humble Christian self-perception would argue the opposite. When I look worse to myself, I cling more necessarily to God's grace, and God's grace provides abundant forgiveness and the imputation of Christ's perfect life, so God's grace works a better life in me. (See Mt 25:31–46 and note how the unbelievers dispute their guilt and the believers are seemingly unaware of their righteousness.)

• • • • • • • • • • • • • • • • • • •

Q **6:1–4 If we give to the needy, and we know that they will do wrong with it, should we still give to them?**

When thinking of the "needy," we do well to remember two things. First, "needy" people in the first century AD were in much more essential and desperate need than many people who claim to be needy today. The needy people of Jesus' day actually had nothing: no way to earn money, no welfare system, no assets. When someone gave to the needy, it was food, clothing, or shelter, which was essential. Second, we should consider what any given person really needs. For example, when the four men brought the paralytic to Jesus, Jesus first forgave his sins. Only in response to the objections of the Jews did Jesus also heal him (Mk 2:3–12). "Charity" today often means

giving whatever relieves feelings of guilt or responsibility in the easiest and quickest way. What people usually need most is the kind of time it takes to work with them to correct the problems that make them needy. So, we would surely not give anything that we knew would work harm. We would rather seek a means to provide what would genuinely help a person in need. This is time-consuming, usually requires a great personal investment, and is in fact truly loving one's neighbor (Lk 10:25–37).

• • • • • • • • • • • • • • • • • • •

Q **6:3 How can you keep your right hand from knowing what your left hand is doing?**

Jesus clarifies this expression when He speaks about doing charitable deeds "in secret" in this passage. The problem Jesus is addressing has to do with fallen human nature's determination to ruin God's work in us. If our selfishness is not able to prevent us from doing a charitable deed, then our pride still seeks opportunities to ruin the deed by boasting about it. Jesus speaks of the right hand as representing the believer's will directed by the Spirit of God. The left hand is what is foreign or contrary to God's work—our fallen human nature. Thus Jesus is essentially saying, "Do not let your proud/selfish human nature get in the way of what your loving and charitable divine nature is doing." Practically speaking, Christians seek to respond positively to needs before their human nature has a chance to think about it. Once the good is done, Christians withdraw in order to avoid recognition and to be available for the next opportunity to help. This is precisely what Jesus did during His ministry (Is 42:2–3; Mk 1:40–45).

Q 6:4 Why is it so important to do charitable deeds in secret? If people find out, do the works no longer have meaning in the eyes of God?

"Good works," including charitable deeds, are only good before God if they are done completely out of gratitude for God's love toward us (1Jn 4:19) and completely out of selfless, loving service to others (1Jn 4:11). If we do something in order to get something from God or from the world around us, the deed is really about us, and therefore no longer "good."

Q 6:5–6 Are we not allowed to pray out in the open? Why would this be so displeasing to God?

The problem is not praying in the open, for there are many examples in the Bible of people praying in full view of others (e.g., Solomon in 2Ch 6; Paul in Ac 20:36). In the previous verse, Jesus explains that hypocrites pray in order to be seen by people, not because they want to serve other people by interceding for them or praying with them. As was the case with good works, so with prayer: Christians seek less attention for themselves in order to draw more attention to God.

Q 6:5–14 How does this relate to the Prayer of the Church we do corporately every Sunday? If God already knows what we need and Jesus gave us this prayer, should we pray with any other words about anything else?

Acts 2:42 records that the first Christians continued steadfastly in the apostles' doctrine, the fellowship, the breaking of bread, and the prayers. Notice the definite article with "prayers." From its beginning, the Christian Church did in public assembly the very thing its members did in private. In fact, the Collects found in many hymnals were written and recorded to avoid negative attention and vain repetition, which public prayer is prone to do. Paul commands us to pray for people in authority (1Tm 2:1–3) and invites us to bring every need to God in prayer (Php 4:6). The prayer recorded here (commonly known as the Lord's Prayer) is a condensed version of what the Lord prayed on Holy Thursday evening in the Upper Room (Jn 17). Paul also provides models and content of prayer throughout his Epistles, where we often read variations of "My prayer to God is that . . . " (Rm 10:1; Eph 1:16; Php 1:4–9; 4:6; Col 1:9–12; 2Th 1:11–12). Prayer should not be intended to inform God or to change His mind. Prayer is a means by which God draws us into His will as active participants. When we remain in His Word (Jn 8:31), it inspires us and directs our prayers in accordance to God's expressed will. As we pray, we are all the more inspired to think and act according to the

Word of God, thus becoming a still more active part of God's work.

● ● ● ● ● ● ● ● ● ● ● ● ● ● ● ● ● ●

Q 6:9–13 Why is the last part of the Lord's Prayer not here?

The Bible is recorded in many ancient manuscripts, from many times and places where it was copied. Because it was copied by hand, even though painstaking efforts were made for accuracy, changes occurred as manuscripts were copied. Some ancient manuscripts include the ending of the Lord's Prayer; others do not. Scholars follow important principles regarding how to determine what is most likely the original text, but still there is disagreement. Luke records this prayer from a later time in Jesus' ministry, and on that occasion, some manuscripts omit the last petition, "But deliver us from evil" (Lk 11:2–4). When thinking about the significance of this, remember that most texts in the Bible have no variations, and the variations that do exist do not affect the teachings of the Bible. So also here, many texts teach us that the Kingdom, power, and glory belong to God forever, and many other texts teach us to appeal to God to deliver us from evil.

● ● ● ● ● ● ● ● ● ● ● ● ● ● ● ● ● ●

Q 6:14 Why is it so easy to ask God for forgiveness but difficult to grant others forgiveness?

Jesus deals with this issue often in the Gospels—for example, with Peter (Mt 18:21–35) and with Simon the Pharisee (Lk 7:36–50). It really has to do with our pride and selfishness. Pride makes us think that we deserve to be forgiven by God (a glaring contradiction in terms) and that no one else deserves to be forgiven by us. Selfishness makes us glad to know God forgives freely, while at the same time feeling glad to hold others' guilt against them so we can more easily manipulate them for our own purposes.

● ● ● ● ● ● ● ● ● ● ● ● ● ● ● ● ● ●

Q 6:15 Why won't God forgive us if we won't forgive others? Doesn't God forgive everything?

God has indeed forgiven all sins because Jesus took them and their penalty upon Himself in His crucifixion and death. But fallen human nature is opposed to God, even to all His efforts for our good. When a person refuses to forgive others, it really demonstrates a refusal to accept that person's own dependency upon God's forgiveness. Another aspect of the problem is described by Paul (Rm 1:18ff.), where he describes the depravity of fallen human nature and how God responds by giving people over to their own stubborn way of thinking, which results in their being unloving and unforgiving.

● ● ● ● ● ● ● ● ● ● ● ● ● ● ● ● ● ●

Q 6:16–18 What is fasting really supposed to be, and is that something we as Christians should be doing?

Fasting was a common practice in the Old Testament, during Jesus' ministry, and in apostolic times. Jesus fasted for forty days in the wilderness while He was tempted by the devil. He once explained to His disciples that a certain kind of demon can only be cast out by fasting and prayer (Mk 9:29). On the other hand, fasting as a matter of hypocritical religious practice is despised by God (Is 58:3–4; Jer 14:12; Zec 7:5), and Jesus warned about the same in this text. Fasting does provide health benefits with proper supervision, but more important, denying the appetites of the body allows us to concentrate on issues of the soul. When our human appetites are filled, we have little concern with larger, spiritual concerns (Lk 16:19–31; Dt 6:10–12; Jer 5:7–9). Note that if you are diabetic, fasting could be hazardous. Always check with your doctor.

- - - - - - - - - - - - - - - - - -

Q 6:19–20 Is this passage saying that we are saved by our good works and that better works make a better place for us in heaven?

Be careful to distinguish between God's counsel on how to live well in this world and how to live forever. Notice that Jesus is not speaking in a context of "how we are saved." Jesus is talking about the fundamentals of how we live in this world. His point is made in v. 21: "For where your treasure is, there your heart will be also." If the substance of our living is to accumulate material things, we will be disappointed now and in eternity, because material things do not provide a life for us but require our life of us. Relationships of love toward other people can only

be provided for by a steady attachment to God and His Means of Grace. As He provides eternal life/union with us, we are enabled to share that life/union with others, which will also last forever. Best of all, the life God provides and that we share is comprehensive and invulnerable—it cannot be stolen, disintegrate, or spoil. This is a reason to get up in the morning and sleep well at night.

- - - - - - - - - - - - - - - - - - -

Q 6:22 What does this verse mean? What is the connection to the other verses in context?

This verse is a summary of the counsel that Jesus is giving: how do you look at life? The way you see things is the "lamp of the body"—how your human nature sees, understands, and functions in this world. If your eye is good—you see things by the Creator's insight and wisdom—then everything will make sense and you will know what to do, when to do it, and how to do it. Note that Jesus said this about Himself (Jn 5:19–20). Consider in this regard Paul's immense insight into human suffering and difficulties (2Co 1:8–11; 4:1–5:21).

- - - - - - - - - - - - - - - - - - -

Q 7:6 This verse seems out of place in this section. Why is it included? What exactly are we not to give to "dogs" and "pigs"?

One explanation is as follows: if you read all of Mt 5–7 (the Sermon on the Mount) and consider what John said about writing down only a representative sample of what Jesus said and did (Jn 21:25), then it is possible to see that Matthew wrote only the important points of Jesus' discourse. On the other hand, it is possible that Jesus was following a pattern like Proverbs where principles are given one after another (cf. Pr 9:7–9). What they have in common is truth. Yet another possibility is to see this verse as a "hinge." The first five verses deal with the intense hypocrisy of people who condemn others (this is not the same as telling someone that what they are doing is wrong). Jesus warns of speaking words of grace and forgiveness to such people, since they despise it (for example, the unforgiving servant in Mt 18:21–35). After this verse, Jesus begins to speak to people who are still sinners, but not hypocrites about it.

"What is holy" calls to mind the offerings that were brought into the tabernacle in the Old Testament. Every part of a sacrifice was to be properly disposed of, either by consumption or by fire. "Pearls" occurs eight times in the New Testament, almost exclusively in Matthew and Revelation. In Mt 13:45–46, the "pearl of great value" is the one for which the merchant gladly sells all his others to possess. What is most holy is the sacrifice of Jesus' life and body on the cross, which provides God's grace to us. The pearl of great value is the Word of God itself, particularly the Gospel or promises. "Dogs" is a word used by Paul (Php 3:2) and John (Rv 22:15) to speak of those who wickedly oppose the Gospel of salvation. "Pigs" were considered unclean and detestable. Pigs (or swine) are mentioned only in the Gospels when Jesus casts demons out of a man and into the herd of swine (Mt 8:30) and in the parable of the lost sons (Lk 15:15–16). In summary, Jesus warns against speaking words of grace and forgiveness to people who are secure in their own arrogant human nature, because they will despise and oppose that grace and even attack those who would share it with unbelievers. Compare this with Jesus' warning to the disciples regarding mission work and people who resist their preaching (Mt 10:14ff.).

. . . .

Q **7:15 Would church bodies who don't believe in salvation by grace alone fall into the category of "false prophets"?**

No church can be considered a "false prophet," because prophets are individuals, though a church body can publicly confess the false teaching of its leaders/members. Here Jesus is being much more comprehensive in warning us of false teachers who can be found anywhere and everywhere (see also Jn 10). We want to be careful to distinguish between a Christian church body that clearly adheres to the Bible in all its teachings and those individuals within that church who are false teachers.

. . . .

Q **7:19 Why cut down a bad tree when there could be good fruit on that tree?**

The answer is provided in the context here and in two other explanations by Jesus. V. 17 says a bad tree bears bad fruit and is incapable of bearing good. In both

How do we know our Father's will?

Lk 13:6–9 and Jn 15, Jesus describes the Father's patience and care with trying to make a plant fruitful. The judgment to cut a tree down never comes until there is no hope for the individual (Heb 6:4–6). Such severe language is necessary to silence the arrogance of human pride, which refuses God's saving work (Rm 3:19ff.). Nevertheless, this is a judgment that belongs only to God (Mt 5:22; 7:1).

Q 7:21 How do we know our Father's will?

This question is best answered by listening to God express His will throughout the Scriptures. For example: "[God] desires all people to be saved and to come to the knowledge of the truth" (1Tm 2:4). Also consider 1Th 4:3: "For this is the will of God, your sanctification . . ." The will of God is also expressed in imperative language as found in Rm 12, which contains forty-six imperatival statements in twenty-one verses. The Bible does address many particular situations, but it also consistently reminds us of the principles of God's will that may always be applied (Rm 13; Eph 4–6).

Q 7:29 Doesn't Jesus have the undisputed authority, being God and man?

Jesus does have absolute authority, because He is the Son of God (Mt 16:16–17;

Lk 22:70; Jn 10:24–30; Rm 1:1–4). Because Jesus *is* the Word of God in human flesh, He speaks that Word authoritatively. What the text reveals is the contrast between the teaching they were used to and what Jesus was offering. God's Word is truth, and truth is reflected in reality. Therefore, false teaching always lacks real authority because it does not correspond with reality. Why should we submit to teaching that cannot affect our lives positively because it has no basis in reality?

Q 8:2 Why does the man with leprosy ask Jesus if He is willing to heal instead of just asking Him to heal his leprosy?

Most, if not all, of the people who ask Jesus for help come to Him knowing they have no right to ask and He has no obligation to act for them. The leper demonstrates his faith by his humility and by clearly expressing that the issue is not Jesus' ability to heal (since He is true God) but His willingness, since God has a right to execute judgment on sinners but chose instead to act according to His gracious nature.

Q 8:3 Jesus physically does the healing, but is it truly Him performing the miracles or God the Father working through Jesus? What would happen if people just touched Jesus without Him knowing?

As the Son of God, Jesus is inseparable from the Father; He is a physical expression of Him (Jn 14:9–11, Col 1:15–16). The

Father does not act except by the agency of the Son (consider the Son's activity in creation itself, Pr 8:12–31). We do have an example of someone touching Jesus with Jesus giving the impression that He did not know who (Mk 5:27–31, though Jesus as true God must have known, but asked for purposes of instructing His disciples), but we have no examples of anyone touching Jesus accidentally. Proximity with God does a person no good (Mt 7:21–23; 1Co 10:1–13; Heb 3:16–19). It is the faith, first inspired by the Word of God, that draws a person to Christ with a connection that will not be disappointed, whether by touch or word alone (8:5–13).

Q 8:4 Why did Jesus not want the man He healed of leprosy to go tell anyone about it? What was the gift that Moses commanded?

Jesus issues this warning for at least two reasons. First, He wants to avoid the kind of wild popularity that would make Him inaccessible to average people. As it was, the men who brought the paralytic on the mat could not gain access to Jesus except through the roof (Lk 5:18ff.). Second, Jesus did not want people to miss the point of His mission; healing was temporary and indicative of His divine nature, but His real purpose was to reconcile people to God by forgiving their sins. Notice in Lk 5 that Jesus responds to the paralytic by forgiving his sins. Only after the Pharisees object does Jesus heal the man in order to prove His authority. Isaiah prophesied about this quiet, accessible nature of Jesus (Is 42:1–4).

The Law of Moses regarding leprosy is recorded in Lv 13 and 14. When a leper was healed, he was to bring two birds. One bird was killed as a sacrifice, the other bird was sprinkled with the blood of the dead bird and set free. This is an indication of how the blood of Jesus' sacrifice would cleanse us from sin and set us free to live before God.

Q 8:5 Why does the centurion not feel like Jesus can come into his house?

The Centurion himself (a Roman military officer of one hundred ["cent . . ."] soldiers) admits that he is not worthy to have Jesus in his home. This is a consistent theme among those who come to Jesus for help and find help. Knowing how unworthy we are of any favor from God and knowing that there is no help anywhere else provides the setting where grace and faith can work. (Consider this theme in the songs of Hannah and Mary [1Sm 2:7–8; Lk 2:52–53].) People who refuse to admit their need found no help in the Son of God, though He was right in front of them (Mt 13:58).

Q 8:10 Jesus sees the faith of the centurion and is amazed. Doesn't He know all?

Knowing about something does not necessarily eliminate the emotion of amazement. We know about re-creative powers in nature and the magnificence of mountains and oceans, yet we are no less amazed when observing these time after time. Jesus is also fully human in His nature and from that perspective could also be amazed. The word translated "amazed" (*thaomadzo*) has to do with seeing something that gives you reason to pause, take notice, and be impressed in some way (not necessarily surprised).

• • • • • • • • • • • • • • • • • • •

Q **8:10 When Jesus says "Israel" here, does He mean "the land of Israel" or "the chosen people of God"?**

Jesus cannot mean "the chosen people of God" in reality, because these are the people that Matthew is highlighting; Gentiles, foreigners, widows, centurions—every kind of low, despised, rejected person is found demonstrating by their faith that they are the genuine children of Abraham, Isaac, and Jacob (Rm 2:28–29; Gal 4:28–31). Jesus probably does not mean the "land of Israel" either, since most of these outcast people were living there. Thus, Jesus must mean that He has not found such faith among the ethnic nation of Israel. Those who *ethnically* and *religiously* should have been most ready to receive Jesus in faith rejected Him (Jn 1:11–13).

• • • • • • • • • • • • • • • • • • •

Q **8:12 When Jesus says that the sons of the kingdom will be thrown into outer darkness, what kingdom is He referring to? How does this relate to the whole of the section from vv. 5–13?**

Jesus is referring to the sons of the kingdom of Israel. The problem is that the sons of the kingdom had no appreciation for the kingdom itself or for its King. Jesus speaks to this same problem in the parables in Matthew (21:28–22:14) and in Lk 14–17. Jesus' words here relate to the whole section as He observes the consistent reality that foreigners are more faithful than the people who should have been His own. Note in this chapter that Jesus heals a leper, a centurion, and a mother-in-law—three kinds of people that the Jewish leaders despised most.

• • • • • • • • • • • • • • • • • • •

Q **8:13 Does God empower men and women today to heal as Jesus did?**

Remember the purpose of healing throughout the Bible: to authenticate someone as an agent of God. Clearly the purpose of healing is not to solve a problem, since everyone who was healed eventually died anyway. Jesus grants the apostles power to heal in order to authenticate them in Mt 10:8 and Mk 16:18 (notice explicit mention of authentication as purpose in Mk 16:20). After Pentecost and the time of the apostles, we do not see divine activity in such impressive forms, but we do have the inspired Word to which that activity pointed. Nevertheless, God still empowers people with extraordinary talents in the fields of medicine.

• • • • • • • • • • • • • • • • • • •

Q **8:14–17 Why does Matthew jump so quickly from one miracle to the next?**

Actually Matthew does many things quickly, all having to do with the fact that God is God of all people, not just the Jews; nor do the Jews have some favored status because they are genetically superior.

Matthew gets right at this already in the genealogy (see questions and answers in ch. 1). Matthew records Jesus' public ministry beginning with the Sermon on the Mount, three chapters of Jesus pounding established Jewish teaching. Then Matthew clicks right into Jesus healing people whom Jews would have nothing to do with. Those who arrogantly thought they were on the inside found themselves left out, and those who were made to feel cast out were brought near by the grace and love of Jesus for those in need.

Q 8:14–22 Did Jesus' disciples leave their families, including wives and children, or did their families travel with them?

The Bible doesn't answer this question directly. However, the culture of the time, needs of children at home for their mother, and eventually danger associated with discipleship make it unlikely that families traveled with the apostles. For a quick perspective, read Pr 31 and 1Co 7.

Q 8:16 Did Jesus ever use His power by bringing people back from the dead? How did Jesus decide whether or not to perform a requested miracle?

Yes, see Mk 5:35–43; Lk 7:11ff.; and Jn 11:43–44. The Bible suggests that Jesus did not "decide" but simply recognized when a miracle would be in harmony with the Father's will and purpose (Mt 13:58; Jn 2:4, 5:30).

Q 8:16 Was "demon possession" just a catchall explanation for people exhibiting symptoms of an unknown ailment? In our day and time, is it still possible to be demon possessed, and would you then rid yourself of demons with the Word? What were the demon-possessed people like?

We have no certainty of exactly what was wrong with people at this time, nor what they might have called these maladies. What we do know is that (1) people have often misjudged a physiological problem as a spiritual one and (2) demon possession is real.

Demon possession is possible when a human soul is not inhabited already by the Holy Spirit (Mt 12:43–45; 1Co 6:19). Demon possession can be obvious/grotesque (as in the case of the man in Lk 8:27ff.) or more subtle, as in the case of Judas Iscariot (Jn 12:4; 13:2).

As long as there are human beings with a soul, demon possession is possible. Because the Word of the Lord is truth (Jn 17:17), inspired by the Holy Spirit (Jn 6:63; 2Tm 3:16), and endures forever (Mt 24:35), it will always provide the remedy for and protection from demon possession.

The Bible offers examples from people who were apparently normal except for special abilities (such as the fortune teller in Ac 16:12–19) to people who were violent (Ac 19:14–17) and uncontrollable (Mk 5:2–5). Today it may well be impossible to recognize a demon-possessed person since the devil has learned that being subtle is more effective in leading people to their own destruction.

Q 8:17 How does Isaiah's prophecy relate to Jesus' healing powers?

The sacrifice of Christ for us is all-inclusive. As a man, Christ bore the burden of obeying every law plus the burden of consequence and punishment for every failure of ours to keep the Law. He sacrificed Himself by taking our sins and infirmities upon Himself. Thus the picture of Christ suffering during Good Friday is really only a small picture of what He endured during His entire life, but especially during the three and a half years of His public ministry.

Q 8:18–22 Why were people fearful of following Jesus?

Most (if not all) people seek a leader in the interest of the comfort, safety, and well-being of their own human nature. People would naturally want to follow Jesus because they thought He was going to be a winner politically (Ac 1:6) or because He relieved their physical needs (Jn 6:26–27). However, the treatment of John by Herod, the treatment of Jesus by the Jewish and Roman leadership, and the experience of the Christian Church recorded in Acts tells us that the world was intensely hostile toward Christians.

Q 8:20 What does Jesus mean by this answer?

Jesus is warning the scribe that following Jesus will not mean a safe, comfortable life. If the scribe would follow Jesus, he must know that he will follow Jesus through every conceivable discomfort for the sake of eternal, spiritual life. The Son of Man cannot rest in this world because it is completely contrary to Him and because He is never free, even for a moment, from the burden of saving it.

Q 8:21–22 Why wouldn't Jesus let one of His disciples go and bury his dead father? Is Jesus saying we shouldn't try to witness to those who are not in Christ? Are there people who are spiritually "dead" with no hope for salvation?

Jesus is using the term "dead" in two ways. He is telling the young man to let people who are "spiritually dead" take care of matters where no *life* is concerned, meaning the burying of "dead" human corpses. Jesus' intent may be compared to the practice of medical triage, where the wounded are separated into three groups: (1) those who can clearly not be saved, (2) those who are injured but in little danger of dying, and (3) those who will surely die unless treated immediately. Jesus wants His disciples to focus their attention on the people who might be helped if they spent time with them now. His words certainly raise questions about Christian funeral practices. At the time of the death of a loved one, Christians maintain their focus on life, being conscious of the time as an opportunity to make a clear and compelling witness to all concerned.

There are people who are spiritually dead and have no hope of salvation, but we are in no position to make such a judgment (Mt 7:1). Rather, we look for the fields that are ripe for harvest (Jn 4:35), serving as ambassadors for Christ (2Co 5:14–21) to those who are hungry for the Word (1Pt 3:15).

● ●

Q 8:23–27 Why did the disciples not believe that the Son of God could control everything, including the wind and waves?

The disciples did not believe for the same reason we don't. Fallen human nature is not capable of what should be the natural relationship of faith in God, who is absolutely reliable.

Notice that Jesus has already lamented and positively addressed the faithlessness of fallen human nature in the Sermon on the Mount, especially in Mt 6:25–34. Immediately following the Sermon on the Mount, Matthew records three examples of Jesus' will and ability. Jesus healed those who, in the eyes of the Jewish religious establishment, would be least able: a leper, a centurion's servant, and Peter's mother-in-law. Matthew concludes that narrative with an absolute statement: "He cast out the spirits with a word and healed all who were sick" (8:16).

Paul addresses this inability of fallen

human nature in 1Co 2:14: "the natural person does not accept the things of the Spirit of God, for they are folly to him, and he is not able to understand them because they are spiritually discerned." God provides a remedy for this fallen condition in regeneration, which is explained beautifully in Ezk 36 and Ti 3. See also Jn 3, where the contrast between human disability in matters of faith and Jesus' remedy for the same is precisely the point.

John offers profound encouragement for us in his First Epistle. Our regenerate soul (or "new man" as Paul puts it) is absolutely faithful even as our fallen nature is not. John says that those who are anointed by God "have all knowledge" (1Jn 2:20, 27) and "cannot keep on sinning" (3:9; 5:18).

Notes: (1) This occasion was prophesied in Ps 107:23–31. (2) The storms of nature and God's remedy are a physical indication of all kinds of events in our lives that feel like storms, raging against us, making us fearful, challenging our faith in God.

● ●

Q 8:27 What did the people feel when Jesus calmed the storm? Why did they ask who He was when they had already professed Him as Lord?

Unless the text tells us what the people thought and felt, we can only speculate, which is perilous and unfruitful. This verse is an account of specific people, the disciples. We know from many accounts in the Gospel narrative and even after Pentecost that the disciples had the same trouble with their human natures as everyone else. The disciples were at times amazed, confused, uncertain, or even mistaken (Jn 13:27–29; 14:5, 8, 22; Ac 10:9–15; Gal 2:11–13).

Many more texts report that people in general were amazed. We know from Exodus and from Jn 6 that human nature is very fickle, selfish, and shortsighted. Jesus exposes and laments these fallen aspects of our nature in Jn 6:26–71. Questioning who Jesus was highlights the need to recognize and distinguish between fallen human nature and a regenerate soul. As long as we are composed of both, we will experience both understanding and misunderstanding, faith and doubt at the same time.

• •

Q **8:28 It seems the men in this text truly were demon possessed. How can we distinguish between possession and a medical disease? (See demon possession also in Mt 12:22.)**

See a discussion of this under 8:16 above. Jesus, as the Son of God, could certainly distinguish between demon possession and severe diseases. From our perspective this might not be so obvious. We do seem to recognize seizures as having physiological origins, such as epilepsy. On the other hand, psychological maladies are not so easily diagnosed; perhaps they are the product of injuries, chemical imbalances, or tumors, or perhaps there is demon possession. The good news is that modern medicine is greatly effective in diagno-

sis and treatment of all kinds of diseases, though temporary. On the other hand, the Gospel provides a permanent remedy for every trouble. This remedy provides a foundational measure of peace and conviction that enhances also medical treatment.

• •

Q **8:30 Why do the demons beg Jesus to send them to a herd of pigs?**

First, the demons are fearful of being tormented by Jesus (8:29). We really have no record of what God has said to the devil or his demons, but they clearly have knowledge of the doom that awaits them at the end. Revelation 12:12 tells us that the devil is enraged because he knows that his time is short. Revelation 19–20 also describe how the harlot, the beasts, the dragon, and even death and Hades will be thrown into the lake of fire. Second, demons apparently hate to be without a host. In Mt 12:43–45, Jesus explains how demons who have been cast out wander through waterless places, seeking rest but finding none. Perhaps the demons realize that Jesus, as He was physically present in that place, would never allow the demons to possess any living soul, but He might at least let them find a home in the herd of swine. Third, don't miss the fact that demonic forces cannot do anything without the consent of God. Our world is not "dualistic," meaning there are competing forces of good and evil, no one knowing which will prevail. The created universe is God's creation, and the one living God is the only one who has knowledge and control of all things. Fourth, while the demons seem to know some things (like who Jesus is), they don't know when or what exactly God is going to do. Finally, a general note on demon possession: according to Mt 12:43–45, demons can and do inhabit empty houses, meaning human souls that are not already filled with the Spirit of God. John 6:63 makes clear that our source for God's Spirit is His Word. Thus Jesus said, "If you abide in My Word, you are truly My disciples, and you will know the truth, and the truth will set you free" (Jn 8:31–32).

● ● ● ● ● ● ● ● ● ● ● ● ● ● ● ● ● ●

Q 8:34 Why did the people of Gadarenes plead with Jesus to leave? Are they fearful of Him?

It is common for honest people to express fear and discomfort in the presence of God. Isaiah exclaimed, "Woe is me! For I am lost; for I am a man of unclean lips" (Is 6:5). Similarly, Peter asked the Lord to depart from him because he was a sinner (Lk 5:8). Perhaps the most enlightening example of all is found in the widow of Zarephath. Elijah had come to stay with this widow and her son during the three-and-a-half-year drought in Israel. During that time, the widow's only son died, so "she said to Elijah, 'What have you against me, O man of God? You have come to me to bring my sin to remembrance and to cause the death of my son!'" (1Ki 17:18). We know we justly deserve God's wrath and punishment for our contradiction to His design for us, yet we also somehow believe that we can hide

from Him (as Adam and Eve tried but also failed to do). When God makes His presence known, it is not surprising that people fear He will see or know things He would not have otherwise and will punish people accordingly. This human fear serves to highlight the gracious nature of God in the person of Jesus Christ. Whatever He learns or finds out about (as if He didn't already know everything), He provides the remedy for, suffering the punishment instead of us.

The people might have been curious as to what Jesus would do next, but the desire to "find out" is often overwhelmed by the fear of "being found out." However, to fear God but not love and trust in Him is to miss the essential character of His nature. God is just and fearsome, but more than anything He is love. His love is what moved Him to reconcile and justify us through the vicarious atonement of His own Son.

● ● ● ● ● ● ● ● ● ● ● ● ● ● ● ● ● ●

Q Jesus did a whole lot of walking. About how many miles did He cover?

Everyone did a lot of walking for most of the world's history, as very few could afford animals to carry them and there were no other means until the last 120 years or so. You can check distances on any good Bible atlas, but here are a few examples: Jerusalem to Bethlehem is less than five miles, Jerusalem to Jericho is about twenty miles (I have made most of that walk), and the southern end of the Sea of Galilee is about sixty miles from the northern end of the Dead Sea. Most people can easily walk three miles an hour. If you are a traveling teacher, as Jesus was, you might cover fifteen thousand miles or more in the course of three and a half years.

. . . .

Q **9:1–8 It appears that Jesus wants us to know that He has the power to forgive sins, but after the scribes question Him, He seems to change what He says. Why?**

When the scribes challenge Jesus' authority, He shifts His focus from His *will* to forgive sins to His *authority* to forgive sins. Clearly it is easier to say something than it is to do something—therefore Jesus demonstrates His authority by healing the paralytic. This is particularly powerful for these people and many others today who think that illness in general is always a result of some sin in particular. Thus, healing the man, in the minds of that audience, was absolute proof that the paralytic had, in fact, been forgiven by Jesus' authority.

. . . .

Q **9:2 Why does Jesus first forgive the sins of the paralytic?**

Jesus may surprise everyone not only by forgiving sins first but by appearing to be concerned only with forgiving sins and not at all concerned with healing the paralytic. People who see their life as consisting of what they do with their physical body in a physical world are bound to misunderstand God's intent and salvation. Materialism makes people think that God's purpose is to forever "fix" what goes wrong in their

physical lives. In fact, if God were to provide for people who are materialistic according to their wishes, there would be no need for faith and no interest in redemption. In fact, the healing that Jesus did had little to do with the material life of the people healed since they would all surely become ill again and eventually die (the end of materialism!). The real purpose of healing was to demonstrate, as Jesus does in this narrative, that forgiveness, redemption, and regeneration are the real solution to our disintegrating condition of body and soul. As God redeems us through the forgiveness of sins, He regenerates our soul, giving us a life that endures forever and the promise of a body resurrected in perfection in a new earth and heaven (Jer 31; Jn 11:25–26; 1Co 15).

. . . .

Q **9:9 Is Matthew, the author of this book, the one spoken about here, and if so, why does he refer to himself in that way? Is he the only one who refers to following Jesus as being called?**

This is the Matthew who is the author of this Gospel. Lk 5:27 reveals Matthew's previous name, Levi. Presumably he changed it to Matthew after his conversion. My suggestion is that Matthew would never refer to himself as Levi after his calling because he took seriously his redemption. "Levi, the tax collector" was no more; that life was forgiven, separated from him as far as the East is from the West. Matthew, a called apostle of the Lord Jesus Christ, was regenerated in his Lord's image, living the new life that

God had provided by grace. Mark does not refer to himself by name in his Gospel, but many suspect he is the young man who ran away naked in the Garden of Gethsemane (Mk 14:51–52). John never refers to himself in his Gospel except as "the disciple whom Jesus loved." You may recall that Saul was referred to as Paul after his conversion (Ac 13:9). In the Early Church, Baptism held this very powerful sense of new beginning, and in many instances that was when the child was named, at its "Christening" ("christen" from the Greek word for "to anoint" or "pour").

Matthew records that Jesus called Peter and his brother Andrew, then James and John (Mt 4:18, 21). The term *called* is fairly common in the New Testament. Jesus said that "many are called, but few are chosen" (Mt 22:14). The commissioning of certain "called" men as apostles is distinct from a general calling (10:1ff, Lk 6:13).

● ● ● ● ● ● ● ● ● ● ● ● ● ● ● ● ● ● ●

Q 9:13 What does it mean to want "mercy, and not sacrifice"?

First of all, you may note that Jesus responds to the issue of Sabbath law again in Mt 12 and quotes Hosea for a second time.

Second, you may imagine that Jesus' teaching of God's mercy would mean everything to a man who was formerly accepted by no one—to the Romans, Matthew was a Jewish barbarian who sold out his own people to collect taxes; to the Jews, he was a traitor who worked for the Romans. But to

God, he was redeemed, accepted by God for Jesus' sake. And as if that were not enough, he was also called to be an apostle.

My third point addresses the heart of what Jesus says about mercy and not sacrifice. Clearly God wanted sacrifice, because He is the one who sacrificed the first animals in Gn 3 to make coverings for Adam and Eve. He is also the one who instituted the sacrificial system through Moses. Yet, it was not the blood of bulls and goats that God wanted, as Hebrews makes very clear. God ordained the sacrifices because He is merciful and was willing to provide a substitute. The innocent animals were meant to do two things. One, the sacrifices reminded the people of the consequences of their rebellion against the Law—our hatred of God and others really does cause death. We may hide our eyes, we may blame others, people may not show us the damage we do, but the damage is done and everyone suffers for it. Knowing this should teach us to repent and turn toward a life of mercy to others. And two, the sacrifices reminded the people about God's promises to send one, single, perfect sacrifice who would redeem all people of all time, once and for all. Hebrews speaks to this as well.

I often hear people talk about the sacrifices they make—for a spouse, for their children, for charitable giving or service to others. This kind of talk makes me embarrassed and ashamed. God's Son sacrificed His prerogatives as God (Php 2:5–11) to become a man and suffer the most horrible condemnation of the Law for all people for all eternity. That is a sacrifice. On the basis of that sacrifice, God accepts us all back as His own, regenerates us in the image of His Son with an eternal and invulnerable life, and provides for us superabundantly beyond all we can think or ask. So how could we ever even begin to claim that we make sacrifices? We live in God's inexhaustible mercy, and thus have the calling, high privilege, and freedom to be merciful to others with no cost to ourselves, since we and all we have are God's.

Finally, "mercy, and not sacrifice" can help us keep our perspective on the things to which we devote ourselves and how we go about doing those things. For example, if mercy toward others is our purpose, then we will be careful not to make ourselves busy with activity that does not really advance God's mercy in the lives of others. We will be careful not to let formalities (formal arrangements, organizations, meetings, even church services) eclipse the mercy they were established to promote. Is it possible that mercy is the "love you had at first" that the congregation in Ephesus had left, to which God warned them to return (Rv 2:4–5)?

The Sabbath law of the Old Testament is based on at least three things. First, even before the fall, the seventh day was to be a Sabbath because God Himself rested on that day. It makes no sense to suppose that God rested because He was tired, but it does make sense that He rested because

rest is itself good, and because rest from our labor—no matter how much we love it—helps us keep a healthy awareness of how much we love our work. Second, after the Exodus, God's commands to keep the Sabbath include reference to Israel's bondage in Egypt and His deliverance of them. When Israel was in Egypt, they could never rest but had to work all day long, every day. What sense would it make for them, having been set at liberty again, to return to a life of bondage to their work? The Sabbath for Israel was a celebration of their redemption. Third, Israel's history of breaking the Sabbath makes it clear that our human nature is contrary to God, nature, and good sense in every way. Addictions, I believe, are evidence of our fallen human nature's determination to live in bondage. Thus, the Sabbath is an important practice or exercise in living at liberty, as Paul commands in Gal 5:1, "For freedom Christ has set us free; stand firm therefore, and do not submit again to a yoke of slavery." So, by way of review, there is a Sabbath law because:

1. God rested.

2. Rest helps us keep a fresh, clear perspective on love of our work and on our life as a whole.

3. God redeemed Israel from bondage in Egypt.

4. Rest is important as a time for recovery from serious labor.

5. Our fallen human nature must practice and exercise rest if we are to retain the good of it.

Now, in the New Testament, you will notice that the Sabbath law appears to be missing. Whenever Jesus or Paul recount the Ten Commandments, the third one is always missing (Mt 19:18–19; Rm 13:9). I suggest this is because with the redemption of Jesus, every day is Sabbath. If Jesus redeemed us from the curse of the Law, as Paul argues in Gal 3, then Christians do all things from love, not obligation. Love of God for us regenerates, reorients, inspires, and provides super-abundantly for us. How could we possibly "have to do" anything when God provides for us beyond all we could ask or think (Eph 3:20) and when all things are already ours, whether in heaven or on earth (1Co 3:21)? How could we possibly "have to do" anything for others when God has liberated us to a life free from concerns for ourselves and free to help others realize God's potential for them?

The next section of the text has to do with wine and wineskins. There we will have a chance to consider how human nature has turned the Gospel and New Testament into Law. Interestingly, this rebellion of fallen human nature to the Gospel is precisely what the apostles had to fight off in two successive councils in Jerusalem (Ac 11; 15).

● ●

Q **9:14–17 Is this "John" John the Baptist?**

Yes, as there are no other "Johns" mentioned in the New Testament who had disciples.

● ●

Q **9:15 Who is the bridegroom? What is this parable about?**

Jesus is the Bridegroom; the Body of believers, collectively, is the Bride of Christ (Mt 25:1–15). Compare this with Paul's description of the proper relationship between a husband and wife in Eph 5:21–33.

This parable is another occasion where Jesus clarifies the intent of the Old Testament—our composition as people made in God's image but fallen—and the New Testament, which He was setting in motion.

First, as Paul said, the Law was our tutor to bring us to Christ (Gal 3:24). The Law of Moses was like a fast with all of its requirements and threats toward those who fail. Watching diligently for the master of the house or bridegroom to come required the kind of focus and self-denial that a fast is intended to promote (Is 21:11–12; Ezk 33; Mt 24:42–51).

However, Israel in the Old Testament (and Christians in the New Testament) tends to revere the form rather than the content of God's institutions. Thus, when the bridegroom or master of the house came, he found the watchmen committed to their formalities of watching rather than the object of their watch. This misplaced commitment to formality rather than to the Word in Scripture (and then incarnate) is what is meant by the foolish virgins having no oil for their lamps (Mt 25:1–15).

Now, in the presence of the One we have been waiting, hoping, watching, and fasting for, there can only rightly be joy and celebration. This is the reason Sundays could never be a part of Lent; it is simply impossible to refrain from celebration on the day of the Lord's resurrection from the dead!

Second, Jesus provides clarity and certainty for His paradigm of bridegroom and friends by adding a second and third example. Note how God's creation was designed to provide multitudes of examples to how the more essential, spiritual dimension of life works (Ps 19; Rm 1). The second example is simple; you cannot "patch" something new on something old. The Jewish religious leaders of Jesus' day simply could not accept who Jesus was. Many of these leaders did believe that Jesus was the Messiah after His resurrection but still could not accept the fulfillment of the Old Testament with the New Testament. So they tried to keep the Old Testament system with Jesus patched onto it, as is evident in Ac 11 and 15.

The third example shifts from two to four elements. As is the case with any parable, the key is to properly identify what the elements are indicating. I suggest that the old wine skins indicate our human nature—our "old skin," if you will. The new skin indicates our regenerate soul. The old wine is the Mosaic Law, and the new wine is the Gospel. We can check this suggestion of elements against Jesus' description of the dynamics involved. Our human nature can accept the Law because it has no life or energy of its own. We have the Law in us, but

we are unable to obey it; old wine just sits in old skins. By way of contrast, new wine has lots of energy, which is why you have to put it in new skins that are able to stretch to the dynamics of the new wine. The new wine, like the Gospel, is its own force, doing what God intends by God's inspiration and Spirit. (Don't miss the connection where "spirits" equal alcohol, which makes the heart glad—Ps 104:15—and God's "Spirit," which is His force to give us a new heart that overflows with joy).

Note Jesus' warning that you cannot put new wine in old skins, because in so doing you will lose both. If you think that our fallen human nature can adopt the Gospel as a way of life, you will suffer loss in one of two ways. Some people see the Gospel as offering the freedom to do whatever the lusts of the flesh desire because God will forgive us. By following the lusts of the flesh, we will suffer the loss of our bodies (both in time as a consequence of contradicting God's design and in eternity because of faithlessness), and the Gospel, which not only confirms forgiveness, but regenerates us into a life of faithfulness and eager compliance with God's design for us.

On the other hand, some people lose body, soul, and Gospel because they make the Gospel a new Law. Listen to people talk about their life in the Church: they "have to" tithe, attend church, go to Communion, be baptized, go to confirmation classes, and attend meetings, potlucks, and all the rest. The language of "have to" reveals that fallen human nature, in its pride and arrogance, has made the gifts of God's grace in Christ a new set of formalities to be obeyed.

Third, Jesus is clarifying again, as He does throughout the Gospels, the comprehensive nature of the New Testament. The Law cannot save us and never could, nor was it given to do so. Our fallen human nature cannot save us nor keep the Law. But these elements are distinct from the Gospel of Jesus fulfilling the Law for us and conveying the blessings of perfection to us in His Word and Sacraments. One of the very first blessings is the regeneration of our souls. The Lord re-creates us now so that our inner person is always eager for and responsive to His Word (Ti 3).

• •

Q 9:15b What was the point in fasting for the disciples?

The point of fasting for anyone has to do with feeding our soul rather than our body. Jesus commanded the crowds, "Do not work for the food that perishes, but for the food that endures to eternal life, which the Son of Man will give to you" (Jn 6:27). Paul instructs Christians to put to death the passions and desires of our flesh (Rm 8:13; Col 3:5). If we can remember that our flesh wars against our spirit and is contrary to it (Gal 5:16–26), then it makes sense to deny those appetites in order to weaken the flesh so the Spirit may have dominion with us. In a way, fasting is like tithing and the Sabbath (rest). It helps to practice living in the liberty for which Christ has set us free. Tithing is a practice in freedom from concern

for material providence, supported and inspired by God's Word and history of providence (Mt 6:25–34; Rm 8:32; Eph 3:20). Living at rest even while we serve one another with great vigor is a practice in living under God's grace rather than the Law (Rm 8:1–17; 12:1–2). So, fasting is the practice of living in our God-given freedom from concerns for our own physical well-being. Life and freedom are found not in one's ability to satisfy carnal desires but in living without satisfying them. The life God gives us transcends carnal desires and threats. We are invulnerable; we are regenerated in the image of the Son of God, who lives and reigns to all eternity.

Fasting also has physiological benefits, which are not to be ignored. Fasting provides for detoxification, healing, reduction of core body temperature, a feeling of rejuvenation, and greater life expectancy, to name a few. You should consult your doctor before starting any fast.

• • • • • • • • • • • • • • • • • • • •

Q 9:16–17 What is the significance of the "patch"?

The patch is the New Testament; the old garment is the Old Testament. As you can see in Ac 11 and 15, the Jewish religious leaders were attempting to "patch" Christ into their system of legalism. But Christ cannot be patched on to legalism for He is the "end of the law for righteousness to everyone who believes" (Rm 10:4). Most of Rm 10 and practically all of Galatians is a record of Paul making this case against trying to add Christ to the Old Testament. Sadly, for many people who claim a Christian confession, Christ is the new Moses, while a life in the Word and Sacraments are the new sacrifices required of us.

● ● ● ● ● ● ● ● ● ● ● ● ● ● ● ● ● ●

Q **9:17 What did the old skin/new skin represent?**

The old skin is indicative of our old skin, our human nature (Rm 5:6–10). The new skin is our regenerate soul (Ti 3:3–5). The old wine is the Old Testament. The new wine is the New Testament. See Mt 9:14–17 above for a more complete explanation.

● ● ● ● ● ● ● ● ● ● ● ● ● ● ● ● ● ●

Q **9:18–26 It is interesting that Matthew highlights the importance Jesus puts on women, especially since the time period held a lower social status for women.**

This is an interesting comment because the same could be said of Luke and John as well. Luke records details about Elizabeth and Mary, Anna, the widow of Zeraphath, the widow of Nain, and Mary and Martha. John records details about Mary at the wedding in Cana, the woman at the well in Samaria, Mary and Martha at the raising of Lazarus, and Jesus giving Mary into the care of John at His crucifixion. On the one hand, it appears that as soon as something particular is claimed for one Gospel, the others reveal similar emphases. On the other hand, interest in peculiarities in biblical books and claims that they are unique tend to make us more interested readers.

We may also want to use caution when suggesting that Jesus puts importance on one group or another. Both the Old and New Testaments are full of examples and clear articulation of the fact that God does not show partiality (Ac 10:28, 34). However, God does oppose the proud and defend the humble (1Sm 2:8; 1Pt 3:5). Jesus is not putting importance on anyone. He is demonstrating the need of people and the importance of Himself as the fulfiller of all need.

Jesus demonstrates awareness of and care for all of the lowly, outcast people of His time—the blind, lame, deaf, mute, leprous, tax collectors, soldiers, prostitutes, adulteresses, Romans, Samaritans, and Ethiopians (Mt 8:1–17; Mk 5:21–43; Lk 3:10–14; 4:24–27; Jn 4:1–26; 8:1–12; Ac 8:1–40). People from anywhere who have done anything, but who still come penitently seeking reconciliation from Jesus, find exactly that.

The time has come long ago for us to stop seeing divisions or making distinctions on the basis of formalities (the external but trivial realities about people). What binds us together or divides us has to do with souls that are arrogant or humble, self-deceptive or honest. This is Paul's argument with the Corinthians (1Co 1:10–31).

● ● ● ● ● ● ● ● ● ● ● ● ● ● ● ● ● ●

Q **9:20 Why did bleeding make the woman unclean? What kind of a disease can make a person bleed for twelve years?**

I suggest that the issue with blood starts at the beginning. In God's creation, nothing was supposed to die, thus blood was never meant to be shed. God's intent was for no loss of life, ever (Gn 1:29–31). So, why does this make a woman with a hemorrhage unclean? Isn't the ailment itself hardship enough?

The life we lead is supported by our blood. Thus, our life is an extension of our life's blood. Adam's blood supported his life, which was supposed to be invested in the care of his wife, along with the rest of God's creation (Gn 2:15, 18–24). However, Adam contradicted that design, using his life against God's will and against his wife.

I have suggested that Adam's contradiction to design consisted of usurping authority while at the same time abandoning responsibility. This suggestion is based on the following evidence: First, Adam was alone when God instructed him about his life and the garden. He was with Eve when the serpent spoke with her, yet he said nothing. Where did Eve get the extra prohibition from if not from Adam? Second, the religious leaders of Jesus' day had also sought to usurp authority by adding to God's Law while abandoning it themselves (Mt 23). Third, God calls Adam, not Eve, to account after the fall. Fourth, Adam blames God and Eve for the fall rather than himself. Contrast this with the Second Adam, Jesus, who is innocent but accepts all guilt (Gn 3:12; Lk 23:13–18; 2Co 5:21). In using, or misusing, his life in this way, Adam is shedding or wasting his blood (life).

Does this make sense, then, of the Old Testament laws about blood, and would it surprise us if the shedding of blood brought with it various negative physical consequences? This would also seem to explain why, over time, religious leaders added a severe sense of condemnation that overshadowed the original laws from the Torah.

Many kinds of ailments can afflict a person with loss of blood for long periods of time: bleeding ulcers for example. It is certainly possible that this woman had some sort of illness or injury in her reproductive organs that caused her to bleed through her uterus. The Torah prohibits intercourse while a woman is bleeding in her menstrual cycle and requires forty or eighty days for a woman to be clean after she delivers a male or female baby, respectively. Is it possible that these laws have at least two intentions? One, laws regarding the flow of blood reminded the people that loss of blood, like loss of life in any form, is contrary to God's intent. Two, in the case of women's flow of blood, God's intent would be to provide prohibitions so they might rest. If they were unclean, then contact with them would be avoided, which would keep them convalescing in their homes.

Note then the significance, on many levels, of Jesus' healing the woman with the flow of blood. God incarnate is correcting the consequences of Adam's rebellion. In particular, the loss of blood for women because of their potential for childbearing is being reversed by this One Son, born of a woman (Gal 4:4). Our redemption was accomplished by the loss of God's blood on our behalf and in our stead (Ac 20:28). As redeemed children of God, we are free and inspired to "shed our blood" in service to others. This is still true of women who bear children and of men in the armed forces or law enforcement services who protect the lives of others.

● ● ● ● ● ● ● ● ● ● ● ● ● ● ● ● ● ● ●

Q **9:20–22 It seems that the woman here believed that Jesus' cloak—not Jesus Himself—would heal her. Why did Jesus heal her? Why is the story about the woman in the middle of the story about the girl?**

The woman believed that Jesus would do the healing but that she was unworthy of approaching Him directly and immediately (note that she "came up behind Him"). Other accounts of healing make this explicit. For example, the centurion who pleads for the healing of his servant would not ask Jesus to come to his home (Mt 8:8). The woman's conviction about the person of Jesus not only produced in her deep humility but at the same time convinced her that the power and divine nature of Jesus was of a nature so powerful that it could be communicated through means, in this case Jesus' cloak. The significance of this reality supports and is consistent with God's practice of working through means: His ministry through His regenerate people (2Co 5:20) and His ordaining of the Sacraments.

Jesus healed her, as He did in every case, to demonstrate that He was God incarnate, the fulfillment of all the prophecies

and promises of God, *and* to show that the essence of His work was the restoration of His creation. His redemption would provide spiritual healing and, in time, deliver us from all the ailments of our fallen human nature.

The narrative indicates two other reasons for this healing at this time. First, Jesus uses the woman as an example of faith, as He often does (Mt 8:5–13). Note well the questions of Jesus and the interaction with the disciples in Mk 5:30–34. Is it possible that we are meant to consider why this woman was affected by Jesus so when many, many others were also making contact with Him (Mk 5:31)? Has anything changed? Lots of people spend time "around" Jesus but seem to accrue no benefit (Mt 7:21–23). Truth evident in one's need, humility generated by the fear of the Lord, and faith that seeks and clings to the mercy of God is what connects human beings with the Word and benefits of God. Second, this event took place in the middle of Jesus' coming to heal Jairus's daughter. Could it be that Jesus wants to spend this time with the woman to allow time for Jairus's daughter to die and for his servants to come with the news? Note the significance of this in the narrative—the servants not only come with the report but add, "Why trouble the Teacher any further?" which provides for Jesus' response, "Do not fear, only believe" (Mk 5:35–36). Jesus took time like this when the news came of Lazarus' death (Jn 11).

Q **9:29–30 Throughout Jesus' ministry in Matthew, He heals many, but why does He not want the blind man to tell anyone about His miracle?**

What we know for certain is that Jesus did not want people to misunderstand Him or His purpose. The feeding of the five thousand according to John's account makes clear that people's material, selfish interests blind them to their real needs and the real significance of the Christ (Jn 6:26–29). Miracles do not convert people into believers; the history of Israel in the exodus provides forty years of evidence for this. However, miracles do authenticate the Word of God's messengers and the fact that the Word itself became flesh. Miracles point to the One upon whom faith rightly depends. What we may not know for certain is why Jesus forbids some people from telling and not others. One possibility might be location. After Jesus healed the man with the demon called "Legion," He commanded the man to go and tell people in the surrounding area what had been done for him. This was in the region called "the Decapolis" or "ten cities," north and east of the Sea of Galilee. This was a region of Gentiles (hence the herd of swine), where Jesus spent very little time. Contrast this to Jesus' activity in the cities of Galilee or Judea, where large populations spread news (and the wrong import of that news) very quickly. Compounding the problem of mistaken yet excited populations was the threat of Jewish religious leaders. Jesus needed to guard against these authorities becoming too jealous and too threatened by Jesus' ministry too soon.

Q **9:34 Why does Jesus not confront the Pharisees again?**

Let's consider a parallel account: Lk 11:14–26. Here, Jesus does confront the Pharisees for their accusation. It could be that Matthew simply omitted that part of the encounter for the sake of emphasis or in order to move on to another part of the narrative. However, research indicates that Lk 11 is a different occasion than Mt 9 (Judea, not Galilee; and after the transfiguration, not before).

There are two important lessons on the basis of this question: First, we can never be certain that we know absolutely everything Jesus said or did on any given occasion, since the Gospels are not exhaustive nor do they claim to be (Jn 20:30). Rather, the Gospels include what they do to fulfill their purpose (20:31). Second, we might suspect, as we do with the cleansing of the temple, that Jesus was very consistent and faithful in His response to human need, especially our need, to know the truth and to see the truth defended. Thus, we might suspect that Jesus always confronted the Pharisees, but we cannot make claims beyond what the texts provide for us.

Perhaps the point of variation in the accounts is to encourage us to "pick our battles," as prudence dictates. Sometimes it may be necessary or an opportune time to confront an issue; other times it may be wise to "hold our peace." Proverbs speaks a great deal about time, advising us regarding timing and the tongue (15:28; 26:4–5).

• • • • • • • • • • • • • • • • • • • •

Q 10:1 Jesus sends out the Twelve into the mission field, but for how long? Did they go individually or in groups? Do we have any further mention anywhere concerning their mission journeys?

We might begin by considering that the Twelve went into the mission field for less than three years (the whole of Jesus' public ministry). We might reduce the time frame further by considering the time that all the other activity in the Gospels must have taken. We might reduce the time further still by observing that the disciples are back in the company of Jesus at Mt 12:1. The parallel reports in Mk 3:1ff. and Lk 9:1ff. agree. Interestingly, after the transfiguration and Jesus' move from Galilee in the north to Judea in the south, Jesus sends disciples out again and Luke records their return (Lk 10:1–17ff.).

While the text does not say if they went individually or in groups on this occasion, the sending recorded in Lk 10 suggests pairs might have been Jesus' custom. Sending disciples in pairs provides many benefits and arguably no drawbacks.

The mission work reported in Mt 10 and its parallels in Mk 3 and Lk 9 are not referred to in any other places of which I am aware. However, the Gospel accounts of Jesus' ministry and the Acts of the Apostles provide a very comprehensive review of and instruction in mission work. Note, for example, that the missionaries in Acts apparently never traveled alone (Ac 15:39–40).

• • • • • • • • • • • • • • • • • • • •

Q 10:4 Why does Matthew note in this verse that Judas Iscariot is the one who betrayed Jesus?

The simple answer is because he wants you to know. A little research reveals that Judas is referred to by name only in the Gospels and Acts, but not uniformly, as follows: six times in Matthew, four times in Mark, five times in Luke, nine times in John, and eight times in Acts. Of the six times Matthew refers to Judas, he includes the reference to betrayal in three of those (10:4; 26:25; 27:3). Mark, Luke, and John also refer to Judas as a betrayer, but in varying degrees. Could it be that Jesus' redemption of Matthew from his condemnation as a "tax collector and sinner" make him especially sensitive to anyone or anything that meant to do his Redeemer harm?

• • • • • • • • • • • • • • • • • • • •

Q 10:5 Were the disciples sent out by Jesus able to do most of the things that He was doing?

Matthew 10:1 and its parallels (Mk 3:15; Lk 9:2, 6) record what the disciples were empowered to do. The second recorded occasion of the disciples being sent (Lk 10:9, 17) includes the casting out of demons. Mark 16:17–20 adds miraculous means given to the apostles *and* their purpose: to authenticate their teaching as the very Word of God. Acts demonstrates this authorization of the apostles and the veracity of their teaching.

● ● ● ● ● ● ● ● ● ● ● ● ● ● ● ● ● ● ● ●

Q **10:5–6 Why was the Good News about the Kingdom to be proclaimed first only to the Jews?**

First, historically, the fulfillment of God's promise to send a Savior has come through all humanity (Adam) through the children of Israel to Jesus then works back out again to Jerusalem, Judea, Samaria, and the ends of the earth (Ac 1:8). Second, it may simply be a reasonable place to start proclaiming the fulfillment of the Old Testament, as Paul was accustomed to do in his ministry (Ac 17:2). Note that, while it may make sense to begin with people already familiar with the Old Testament (Rm 3:1–3), these people were not at all the most receptive to the Good News (Jn 1:11). Third, Gregory the Great (540–604; pope in Rome) observed that the resistance of the Jews would ultimately open the door of the Gospel to the Gentiles (*Gospel Homilies*, 40). Paul makes a similar argument in Rm 11:12, 15–16. On the other hand, Jesus (Mt 8), Philip (Ac 8), Peter (Ac 10), and Paul (Ac 17) all had plenty of interaction with Gentiles, even so much contact and success as to highlight the receptivity of the "outcasts" and the hardness of the hearts of the "in crowd." Fourth, I would like to suggest a synthesis of the possible answers, as follows:

a. God remains true to His promises and does not forsake His people, even though they forsake Him (Rm 3:1ff.; note also 2Tm 2:12–13).

b. God is just and His ways demonstrate His justice. The Jews who remained unbelieving would have no excuse since they were the first to receive the Good News yet renounced that news from the first to the end of their days.

c. The example of the Jews' hard hearts would serve as an additional reminder (add it to the Pharaoh's example) that fallen human nature is exceedingly contrary to God and must be guarded against (Rm 5:6–10; 9:1–11:36; Heb 2:1–3:19).

d. Knowing these things would make believers both careful and so very grateful for the grace of God extended in and accomplished through Jesus Christ.

● ● ● ● ● ● ● ● ● ● ● ● ● ● ● ● ● ● ● ●

Q **10:8 If Jesus gave disciples the power to drive out demons, why does the Church make little mention of them today? Were the twelve disciples given the same authority to drive out evil spirits and to heal every disease and sickness that Jesus healed? Was this authority temporary?**

There could be many reasons for the Church not mentioning the driving out of demons much in our day. First, history records widespread superstition among people, especially religious people, and many horrible practices as a consequence of that superstition—the Salem witch trials, for example. If you talked about demons today, many people would react negatively and understandably so.

Second, now that everyone is used to "scientific" explanations and the advances of the medical arts, it seems absurd to call something demon possession when it might be a chemical imbalance or psychological phenomenon.

Third, I would like to suggest the possibility that there is little or no demon possession in our day because (a) the devil has learned to be more effective by being more subtle, and (b) so many people in our culture have romanticized and/or popularized demon possession. For all these reasons, it is not surprising that some churches prefer to apply their efforts to matters more certain and with less negative "baggage."

While Jesus gave His disciples power over evil spirits and sicknesses, it would seem impossible for them to possess or apply these powers in the same way as He, the Son of God, did. One example makes this evident in Mt 17:14–21.

No text that I know of tells us whether the apostles possessed this special authority all their lives or only for a time. What we do know is that Jesus gave them these abilities to demonstrate and make inarguable that (1) God's grace and salvation is universal and accomplished in the work of Jesus, (2) this Gospel of Jesus Christ is for all people and comes immediately with the preaching of the Word, and (3) the apostles

are authorized to declare the Word of God and set it in writing (Jn 14:26; Mk 16:17–20; Ac 11, 15; 2Pt 1:12–21).

● ● ● ● ● ● ● ● ● ● ● ● ● ● ● ● ● ● ● ●

Q **10:8–10 It seems like these verses are contradicting each other regarding whether or not the disciples should be paid. What's really going on?**

In v. 8, Jesus would prevent the apostles from charging people for their exercise of the special authority He has given them. I suspect at least two reasons for this: (1) to authenticate the apostles as agents (spokesmen and writers) of God through the particular gifts given them and (2) to prevent the people from confusing the witness of these gifts with those who deceive in their own interest (Ac 8:18–24; 13:6–12; 16:16–19).

In vv. 9–10, Jesus is preventing the apostles from taking their own provisions as they go out according to His command. Perhaps the hardest lesson for us to learn is trusting the Lord to provide for us as we serve Him. You may recall that Jesus addressed the same message to everyone in the Sermon on the Mount (Mt 6:19–34).

Perhaps the next hardest lesson is how to love others. What does it mean to know God as He reveals Himself to us and to know that real life consists of loving our neighbor if we are going to devote ourselves to getting what we think we need to live from those around us? What do you learn if you compare the life of "getting for oneself by one's own efforts" with "giving ourselves freely for the sake of others because God gives

Himself freely to us"? The Old and New Testaments are overflowing with records of God providing for His agents and His people, especially in the most unlikely of circumstances. For example: Noah's ark (Gn 6); the exodus, wandering, and conquest of the Promised Land (Exodus–Joshua); Elijah (1Ki 17); the challenge of Haggai (Hg 1); the feeding of the multitudes in the wilderness (Mt 14–15, and note Jesus' reference to these in Mt 16!); and during Paul's voyage to Rome (Ac 27–28). Note also Paul's argument for God's providence as he compares the greater to the lesser: "He who did not spare His own Son but gave Him up for us, how will He not also with Him graciously give us all things?" (Rm 8:32).

Martin Luther rightly focused on the Second Article of the Creed in order to combat the insidious teaching of works righteousness, much as Paul does in Galatians. On the other hand, if we do not live in the light and firm foundation of the First Article of the Creed, we will essentially never get to the Second Article. Remaining in the Word depends in part on believing that you have liberty to do so. In fact, we don't have time to not have time to remain in the Word.

● ●

Q 10:13 What does Christ mean by "Let your peace return to you"? What is the difference between giving a greeting, peace, and a blessing?

"Peace" in the Old Testament has to do with being in a broad or wide-open space (Pss 18:19; 31:8). In the New Testament, "peace" has to do with a similar idea. Consider Jesus' first words to the apostles who were meeting in private with the doors locked: "Peace to you" (Lk 24:36). Spiritually speaking, we might consider how contradicting God's design continually narrows and restricts our life (Adam and Eve *hid* when they heard the Lord approaching). Living under the curse of the Law bears down on a guilty conscience with the ultimate confinement: condemnation under the wrath of God.

"Worthy" in the New Testament has to do with one thing matching another. Thus, when the apostles entered a village, they would look for people who were God-fearing, humble, and seeking mercy (see Cornelius [Ac 10]). Upon entering the homes of such people, the apostles would explain the person and work of Jesus, who delivers from condemnation and puts us at liberty to live in the love of God and for the love of neighbor (Rm 8:1; Gal 5:1). However, if the apostles were mistaken and a person was self-righteous, the proclamation of God's grace would find no place, like seed upon stony ground. This is related to Jesus' warning that we not cast our pearls before swine nor give what is holy to the dogs (Mt 7).

A "greeting" has more to do with the action than the content; when you meet someone, you speak to them. Extending peace to someone, in the biblical sense, has to do with bearing witness to the grace of God that delivers from condemnation and the bondage of the flesh (Heb 2:14–15).

A "blessing" is, in one way, a form of prayer, as in the Aaronic blessing: "The LORD bless you and keep you" (Nu 6:24). Depending on the authority of the source, a blessing can actually affect what is spoken, as when Jesus blessed the loaves and fish so that the multitude could eat. This is also what Jesus did with bread and wine on Holy Thursday evening. Paul used this same word also when he wrote, "The cup of blessing that we bless, is it not a participation in the blood of Christ?" (1Co 10:16).

. . . .

Q 10:14 Why does He tell them to shake the dust off their feet?

I suspect this has to do with making clear that there is *no* connection between people—not even the least of all elements on the least esteemed part of their body. Those who offer the grace of God have nothing to do with those who reject that grace.

. . . .

Q 10:16 Could you explain how to be shrewd as snakes yet innocent as doves?

This does seem like risky advice, given the serpent's history. However, the key is not with the snake but with his disposition. First of all, the term translated here as "shrewd" or "wise" has to do with thinking: being observant, paying attention, understanding how things are, having insight (even wisdom).

Second, like many words, this term is not inherently negative or positive. According to the Greek translation of Gn 3:1, the serpent in the garden was shrewd. In contrast, Jesus urges us to be like the shrewd man who built his house on the rock (not the sand). The shrewd servant is watchful, prepared always for the master's return (Mt 24:45). Therefore, given the dangers presented by the deceptive ways of the devil and world, plus the wicked and careless tendencies of our own fallen nature (Rm 5:6–10; Eph 2:1–7), it is imperative that we be *more* thoughtful, alert, careful, wise, prudent, and discerning than they.

Third, another aspect of the key is the innocence factor. You are, no doubt, acquainted with the appearances and character of doves in the Bible. A dove returning with an olive branch proved that the flood was over and was understood to mean that God was now at peace again with the world (Gn 8:8–12). The Holy Spirit in the form of a dove rested upon Jesus at His Baptism (Jn 1:29–34).

Finally, if you think about it, the entire Bible is either (a) addressing the necessary conversion from wickedness to innocence, (b) addressing the watchfulness necessary for preserving that innocence, or (c) testifying to the One who provides and works innocence in His people—the Lord Jesus. The Book of Hebrews (especially chs. 2–4) is doing exactly what Jesus is concerned with here.

● ● ● ● ● ● ● ● ● ● ● ● ● ● ● ● ● ● ●

Q 10:23 What did Jesus mean when He told His disciples that they would not finish going through the cities of Israel before the Son of Man comes?

If we read all of Mt 10, especially the verses that lead up to and come after v. 23, Jesus appears to prophesy increasing resistance to His kingdom and those who serve it. Jesus' prophecy climaxes with His assurance in the face of all this opposition: "But the one who endures to the end will be saved" (v. 22).

If we focus on Jesus' reference to the "end" and consider that to mean Judgment Day, then we might argue that "going through the cities of Israel" refers to wherever in the world the Jews might be living before Judgment Day.

Another possibility is that Jesus is referring to His own coming, specifically into Jerusalem on Palm Sunday, especially as it leads to Good Friday. It is possible that the apostles had not finished going through all the cities of the geographical Israel between this first commissioning/sending of the apostles and Palm Sunday.

Jesus makes another prophecy that is related and parallel to this one. In Mt 23:39, Jesus says, "For I tell you, you will not see Me again until you say, 'Blessed is He who comes in the name of the Lord.'" Indeed, the people did say that, but it was on Palm Sunday, earlier in the week (Mt 21:9).

Is it possible that in both cases Jesus is referring to His appearances after His resurrection? We have no account of people calling Jesus blessed, but the people did see Him again, and the disciples had gone through no villages of Israel in the meantime (they were hiding behind locked doors). Is it possible that Jesus is referring to Pentecost and His coming and appearing is a spiritual one?

Perhaps the best answer to the question about v. 23 is a combination. One could argue that Jesus, the Son of Man, came to Jerusalem on Palm Sunday, again after His resurrection, and again by the Spirit's outpouring on Pentecost *and* that these "comings" are indicative, though not the ultimate fulfillment, of Jesus' prophecy. These early indications point us toward the promise of His second and final coming with hope, anticipation, watchfulness, and a certain diligence to try to get to all the cities of every human being before the end of days.

● ● ● ● ● ● ● ● ● ● ● ● ● ● ● ● ● ● ●

Q 10:25 What does the word *Beelzebul* mean?

The word means "Lord" (*beel*, similar to *baal*) of something, either of a place (*zebul*) or of "the flies" (*zebub*). The term refers to a Philistine deity, to whom King Ahaziah sent messengers to inquire about his recovery from a fall (2Ki 1:2–3). In the New Testament, Matthew (12:24), Mark (3:22), and Luke (11:15) all record the occasion when the religious leaders accuse Jesus of casting out demons by Beelzebul, the "prince of demons."

Q 10:28–31 What is the connection here between sparrows and human nature?

The Bible uses comparisons of many kinds. For example, parables are comparisons: "The kingdom of heaven is like treasure hidden in a field" (Mt 13:44). Other comparisons are from lesser to greater (Mt 7:11; Rm 8:32). In this case, note how the examples of sparrows and hair in vv. 29–30 are preceded and followed by imperatives (commands) not to fear anyone or anything but God alone (vv. 28, 31). It appears that God never issues a command or imperative without providing the means whereby we might obey. Why shouldn't we be afraid? Well, consider a creature of as little value as a sparrow or something as abundant and superficial as the hairs of your head. If no sparrow falls apart from God's will and even the hairs of your head are numbered, then of how much more value are you to God? God's undefeatable and gracious will for us is the foundation of our love for Him and our liberty to serve others.

Q 10:29 How much value today is that penny equivalent to?

This "copper coin" was called an "assarion" and was worth one-sixteenth of a denarius. A denarius was equivalent to a day's wages (Mt 20:2–13). Thus, in Matthew's account, two sparrows are sold for the cost of a half hour's labor, or in Luke's account, five sparrows for one hour's labor (interestingly, they seemed to have volume discounts in Jesus' day as in ours!).

Q 10:34 Why does Jesus speak so harshly?

The relationship between Jesus and peace may be clarified best in His words to the apostles on Holy Thursday evening, "Peace I leave with you, My peace I give to you. Not as the world gives do I give to you" (Jn 14:27). Fallen human nature tends to see its own immediate, carnal interests above all things; therefore, people have and continue to expect and even demand that God grant them peace now. This peace is characterized by selfish interests, the desire for a life without challenge, conflict, struggle, or self-denial. Jews and disciples of Jesus' day looked for a Messiah who would re-establish the power and privilege of people who considered themselves favored by God. Since that time, people who feel entitled and make claims to privilege before God still expect Him to play the role of the genie in the bottle. This is the kind of expectation that Jesus is confronting and why He may sound harsh. The peace Jesus came to establish is comprehensive and enduring. Jesus made peace with God on our behalf, having done all that the Law requires of us and having suffered all that the Law threatens for those who fail. Jesus makes peace between people by restoring us

> Why does Jesus speak so harshly?

to an honest humility about our nature and by providing us with a regenerate nature in His image. The sword Jesus advances is the sword of the Spirit and truth. The truth always finds intense opposition from fallen humanity in a fallen world, so by necessity the sword of God's Word clashes as it advances.

• • • • • • • • • • • • • • • • • •

Q 10:38 In this verse, Jesus states, "Whoever does not take his cross and follow Me is not worthy of Me." Was He alluding to His own death on the cross, or was this a common phrase that anyone might have used and understood?

It could have been both, so the main question is this: would this statement have been easily understood by His disciples? Christ is certainly referring to His own impending death with these words. Research of other literature of that time would be required to determine if this phrase about carrying one's cross was common. The cross was known, both from the Old Testament and from Roman law, as an accursed way to die (Gal 3:13). It is possible that Jesus suspected that His listeners were not grasping the importance of His statement, because He continued with an explanation about saving or losing one's life (v. 39).

I could say it was common in my day, but that was among Christians who applied this notion to their lives: "That's just a cross I'll have to bear." I don't know if I have ever heard non-Christians use the expression.

Please note also that the word *worthy* means "to be consistent with" or "to match" rather than "to earn." Taking up one's cross and following Jesus is not what we do to make ourselves disciples, but what God does in us that flows from our regeneration (Jn 1:11–13; 15:16). While many people would and continue to claim Jesus as their Lord, they refuse to follow Jesus' example of sacrificing self for the sake of others (Mt 7:21–23). The "cross" of Jesus refers not only to the climax of His suffering in the crucifixion but also to His entire life of service and humiliation (Php 2:4–8).

• • • • • • • • • • • • • • • • • •

Q 10:39 What does it mean when Jesus says, "Whoever finds his life will lose it"?

It is impossible to make sense of these verses until we distinguish between the natures that make up a human being. We tend to think of ourselves as one dimensional; there is just me, that person I see in the mirror, the person that gets hungry and eats and gets sleepy and sleeps (or cannot sleep). The truth is that our outward, physical nature is only an extension of who we really are. The essence of our being is our soul, and that soul is animated by a spirit, either of God or of the devil (Mt 12:43–45). Once we recognize our composition and the antagonism between our regenerate soul and our fallen flesh, Jesus' words make perfect sense (Gal 5:19–25).

Q 11:2 Why did John send messengers questioning Jesus' identity when he knew that Jesus was the Christ?

John clearly knew who Jesus was from the beginning—this is evident in the narratives about Jesus' Baptism (Mt 3; Lk 3) and especially in John's Gospel (Jn 1:19–34). The answer to this question is evident in the phrase "When John heard in prison." Now, remembering that John the Baptist was still a real human being, what would you be wondering if you were languishing in prison while the Son of God was free and actively doing all sorts of miracles? Like anyone, John might certainly have been wondering why the Lord did not use His power and wisdom to gain John's release from prison.

The answer to that question, I believe, is related to the reason for Jesus waiting four days before he came to Lazarus's tomb. The Word and promises of God to us are not fragile or something to be nervous and worry about. The life that God gives us and intends us to live is *invulnerable* because it flows from the life of Christ Himself—a life that was crucified, dead, and buried, yet rose the third day. How could we possibly love others as Christ loves us if we must always have an eye toward protecting our own life?

The life that God had given John the Baptist was a life of faith, the life of John's eternal soul. That life could not be imprisoned or beheaded (note Paul's reference along these lines while he was in prison [2Tm 2:9]). John had to come to terms with the difference between his soul and body,

between temporal life and eternal life. We must do the same and can benefit from John's experience. He struggled to keep his eternal soul in perspective and so will we.

Now look at Jesus' remedy. What should we do when a particular hardship we're enduring causes us to wonder if Jesus is the Christ? Jesus directed the disciples of John to report what they saw Jesus doing. We have the record of what Jesus did in the Gospels; there we will find both the remedy for our human nature's unrest and further inspiration for the dauntless faith of our regenerate souls.

Q 11:2 How is it that John can doubt after having seen the Baptism of Christ?

This is a great question, not because of the answer it invites, but because it exposes our own human nature. So, let me answer this question with another question: "How is it that we can doubt after having known the Scriptures and seeing so clearly the gracious working of God in nature and in our lives?"

We not only can doubt, but we cannot help but doubt since the natural man receives not the things of the Spirit (1Co 2:14). Thank God for regenerating our souls in the image of Christ—a regenerate soul that absolutely believes, though it does not always succeed in dominating our thoughts or actions (Gal 5; Col 3). God has countered our fallen nature by raising us up as new people, united with Christ through a life in His Word and Spirit. He has also made readily and inexhaustibly available the Means of Grace by which we might subdue the doubts of our flesh until the actual physical death of that human nature sets us free.

●●●●●●●●●●●●●●●●●●●●●●

Q **11:11 Why is the lowliest angel in heaven greater than John the Baptist? Is there rank in heaven?**

The term *angel* does not occur in this verse, though the previous verse, quoting Mal 3:1, refers to John as an "angel" (Greek) or "messenger" (English) who will prepare the way for Jesus. In this verse, Jesus says the lowliest person in the kingdom of heaven is greater than John. Jesus' words are a part of His long response to the disciples of John the Baptist. First, Jesus affirms John's special role as a messenger who was chosen and sent by God. Second, Jesus denies that John has or could ever achieve the righteousness that the Law requires. Third, this affirmation and then denial make sense if we keep in mind the composition of human beings, including John. Notice that Jesus affirms John's greatness among "those born of women." As a fallen human being in a world of the same, John was the best. On the other hand, as wonderful and righteous as John may have been, he was still born of fallen human parents and so had a fallen human nature himself. That's why John had doubts about Jesus (Mt 11:1–19; Jn 3:6; 1Co 2:14; 15:50). Finally, Jesus moves forward to a comparison between fallen human nature, even at its best, and a regenerate soul: "one who is . . . in the kingdom of heaven." Jn 1:11–13; 3:1–6; and Ti 3:5–7 make it clear

that only a regenerate soul can live in real communion with God. The First Epistle of John makes it clear that because this soul is generated by God, it is without sin, loves God, and believes in God (3:9; 4:7; 5:1, 4, 18). Thus, according to the human ability to be righteous, John is the very best of all time. But, according to the righteousness that comes by faith, even the lowliest believer is greater than John because that lowliest believer has been perfected in Christ.

Regarding "rank" in heaven, there is and isn't. There are passages that speak of levels of heaven (2Co 12:2). Jesus spoke of those who would receive greater punishment in eternity (Mt 11:22; 18:6ff.). James also speaks of a stricter judgment (Jas 3:1). Revelation describes the Lord on His throne surrounded by the twenty-four thrones of elders (4:4; 11:16; 20:4). When James and John asked for a place of priority in heaven, Jesus affirms that there are such places but they are prepared for those whom the Father chooses (Mt 20:21–23). Even King David hints at "rank" in heaven and perhaps also provides the key for our understanding: "I would rather be a doorkeeper in the house of my God than dwell in the tents of wickedness" (Ps 84:10). Whether there are ranks or not, heaven will still be paradise and hell will still be no place anyone wants to be.

Q 11:16–19 Is Jesus saying that this generation is like a bunch of bratty kids who want only their way, even when that way can change on a whim?

To begin with, yes, Jesus is saying something like that, but let's take a more careful look at the passage and this question. First of all, are these "bratty" kids or adults? Adults of this generation are like children who refuse to be satisfied, no matter what is offered. Yet, in Mt 18, Jesus says that unless you repent and become as a child, you cannot enter the kingdom of heaven. Perhaps it is the self-righteous judgment and opinion of the children in the marketplace that marks the transition from faithful child to faithless adult.

Second, "this generation" is referring to fallen human nature, not this particular group of people. The Bible is very consistent and clear in its description of the wicked, contrary disposition of human nature toward God (Jn 3:18–20; 1Co 2:14; Gal 5:19–21). The condition of human nature since Adam's fall explains why the Bible does not talk about reforming or improving our nature but of putting it to death while God regenerates our souls in the image of His Son (Ti 3:4–5; 1Jn 3–5).

Third, the lust of the flesh is one "whim" after another, none of which satisfy. Thus Jesus offered living water to the Samaritan woman at the well so that she would never thirst again. This living water is nothing else than Jesus Himself—the way, the truth, and the life, the very Word of God incarnate. He is, in fact, the only hope for our human nature. He has redeemed us from the guilt of our sin. He works out His will in us, even while our human nature would resist. He has promised us relief from this human nature in death and a perfect replacement in the resurrection (2Co 5; 1Co 15). Finally, as is the case throughout the Bible, we understand the text correctly when we see ourselves in it. The point is not so much that the Pharisees and Scribes of that place and time rejected Jesus and His prophets, but that we are of the same nature as those who rejected Jesus. Recognizing this part of our nature prepares us for the promises and effective workings of grace that follow: "Come to Me, all who labor and are heavy laden, and I will give you rest" (Mt 11:28).

Q 11:19 What is meant by the phrase "eating and drinking"?

John was known for his eccentric ways—camel's hair clothing, diet of wild locusts and honey, and fasting (Mt 3:4; 9:14; Lk 5:33). Jesus was not known for His fasting, and when questioned about it, He explained that His nature and presence should rightly produce celebration, not self-denial (Mt 9:15; Jn 12:35–36). So there is a contrast between a believer's conduct in anticipation/preparation for the Lord and a believer's conduct in the presence of the Lord. The Early Church's recognition of this is evident in the fact that Sundays, the day of the Lord's resurrection and presence among

His disciples (Jn 20), were not included in the penitential season of Lent. Fasting was/is appropriate during Lent and Advent, but never on the Lord's Day. When the Lord is present we celebrate His Supper!

. . . .

Q 11:20 How can people, after seeing with their own eyes and experiencing firsthand, still not follow God's way of life? Is this not what happened already with the Jews even though God had delivered and led them to the Promised Land?

See the answer on Mt 11:2.

. . . .

Q 11:21–22 What does Jesus mean when He says, "They would have repented . . . in sackcloth and ashes"? Is that an allusion to death, meaning they would have repented even to the moment they died or were in their lowliest state? Why are Tyre and Sidon called condemned cities?

Jesus continues this discourse with a parallel comparison between Capernaum and Sodom (11:23–24). The significance of these comparisons has three parts. First, Jesus chooses cities that are remembered for their relentless wickedness (Is 23; Jer 25; Ezk 26–28). Second, Jesus is comparing the means available that might have worked repentance and restoration. The Old Testament prophets spoke about Tyre and Sidon—and Lot warned Sodom (Gn 19:9)—but the cities of Israel, such as Chorazin, Bethsaida, and Capernaum had the Son of

God Himself dwelling among them, performing miracles and signs that had never been heard of (Jn 9:32). Third, these cities of Israel were exceedingly proud and self-righteous even while they were contradicting and opposing God's Son at every turn.

This three-part comparison is intentionally shocking in its inversion. Ancient cities that were destroyed by God for their wicked ways would have been the model of repentance if they'd had the opportunities that the cities of Israel spurned. The magnitude of the comparison suggests that the only chance left of getting through to the hard hearts of these Israelites is to jar them out of their high self-opinion (cf. Mt 23). Jesus makes similarly shocking comparisons in the parable of the wicked tenants (Lk 20:9–19), the prodigal sons (15:11–32), and the Pharisee and publican (18:9–14).

What happened to Tyre and Sidon is a long history. Isaiah, Jeremiah, Joel, and Zechariah all denounced Tyre and Sidon (Jer 25:22; 27:3; Jl 3:4; Zec 9:2) for their unfaithfulness.

. . . .

Q 11:26 Is this verse referring to God's sense of humor?

I don't see anything in this verse that would suggest humor. Actually, it's quite the contrary. In the verse preceding, Jesus makes a very important observation about how revelation works and who (in general) gets it and who doesn't.

I'm providing the following translation for clarity and accuracy: "At that time Jesus answered and said, 'I agree with You, Father, Lord of heaven and earth, that You have hidden these things from the wise and understanding and revealed them to babes.'" Why did it seem good in God's sight to do so? Paul answers exactly this question in 1Co 1:18–31. God inevitably brings down the proud because their pride has no foundation, no substance in reality. What can a person claim for himself or herself in pride for which God should not get all the credit? God promises to raise up the humble, since they are empty vessels looking to God and grateful to God for His providence, the way babes are content with the simplest and most basic providence of their parents.

. . . .

Q 11:27 Doesn't the Spirit reveal the Father and Son? Why isn't He mentioned?

Begin by remembering that God is One, though Scripture reveals that God exists as three distinct persons. Father, Son, and Holy Spirit appear to have some distinct activities, yet it is still one God at work. The Athanasian Creed takes great pains to make this clear. When it comes to revealing the Father, this is a task that Jesus describes as His own (Jn 1:18; 14:6–11). Yet, Paul tells us that the Spirit searches everything, even the depths of God (1Co 2:10). Jesus resolves any apparent tension by explaining how His work is really inseparable from the Spirit's (Jn 6:63; 14:26; 15:26; 16:13). Words communicate what is in the mind and spirit of a person; Jesus is the Word of God. Nevertheless, words cannot be expressed without the breath of the one speaking; the Holy Spirit is the breath and Spirit of God.

The Spirit is mentioned in some particular contexts in the Bible: Gn 1:2; Ezk 37; Lk 1:35; Jn 14–16; 1Co 12:3. The obvious answer to the question of the Spirit being seldom mentioned is because God wills it so. Perhaps this is so because the Spirit is always with the Son, the Word of God, and so needs no mention. Consider, for example, Jn 3. Jesus' first explanation to Nicodemus is that believers are generated from above (where God the Father resides). In Jesus' second response to Nicodemus, He further describes this generation of a believer as being from water and the Spirit. (In the very next chapter, Jesus refers to Himself as "living water.") This text, coupled with Jn 6:63, gives plain evidence that the Word of God is inseparable from the Spirit of God.

Note: It seems fascinating, but not surprising, that water is composed of gases ("spirits") and that it can take the form of clouds, be crystal clear, and be profoundly soft or hard, depending on how you meet it.

. . . .

Q 11:28–30 What about this idea of being joyful sufferers—finding joy in the trials of being Christians? What does "take My yoke upon you" mean? Is "rest for your souls" referring to heaven?

Understanding this text begins with identifying key elements. What is laborious that makes us heavy laden? What kind of rest is Jesus talking about? What is Jesus' yoke? Of these three, the yoke of Jesus can be identified with the greatest certainty. One might jump to the conclusion that the yoke of Jesus is His suffering and death. But how can this be if Jesus says, "My yoke is easy, and My burden is light"? Is there a yoke and burden that Jesus bears that is more substantive or essential to His person, which is light in itself, but necessitates His suffering and death?

Jesus humbled Himself to be born of a virgin. Jesus is honest in every encounter we observe in the Gospels, because He is the truth. Thus, I suggest that Jesus' yoke and burden—light and easy—is honesty and humility. What then, is laborious and makes us heavy laden? How about claiming to be what we are not? Fallen human nature labors endlessly to put itself in double jeopardy; we avoid the gracious providence of God and we insist on trying to provide for ourselves. Jesus spoke to this with the crowd of more than five thousand He had just fed the day before: "Do not work for the food that perishes, but for the food that endures to eternal life, which the Son of Man will give to you" (Jn 6:27).

Worse than laboring for food is the human ego's insistence on justifying itself, the most absurd and self-defeating of all human follies. Here consider Paul's response to this matter in Gal 2–3. Honesty and humility bring absolute rest, for "if we confess our sins, [God] is faithful and just to forgive us our sins and to cleanse us from all unrighteousness" (1Jn 1:9). Honesty and humility give us rest in our relationships with others as well as with God. Great rest comes from admitting our failures and limitations, while at the same time accepting the confessions and limitations of others.

● ● ● ● ● ● ● ● ● ● ● ● ● ● ● ● ● ● ●

Q **12:2 The disciples broke the Law by picking heads of grain to eat on the Sabbath. Is it right that Jesus allows them to break the Law in the eyes of others when He is the Lord?**

The particular meaning of "law" in any particular text is very important. In general, "law" means something like "the way things have to be." Some laws are very long lasting, if not eternal, like the moral law or the laws of nature. Other laws, like the Old Testament ceremonial laws, were established for a specified time and purpose and were fulfilled by Christ (Gal 3:24; Mk 7:5, 17–19; Rm 10:4). Civil law teaches us how to get along with one another (Rm 13; Eph 6:5–9; Lv 19:14). Finally, there are the laws created by people. If these laws are faithful applications of moral law and to the extent they are enacted by legitimate governments, we are bound to obey them as Jesus did (Mt 17:24–27; Rm 13:7). On the other hand, when the laws of people contradict God's Law, we must obey God rather than men (Ac 5:29; Gal 2:5).

Sabbath law forbade work on the seventh day (Saturday) for two reasons: because God rested from His work on the seventh day and because God had delivered

Israel from bondage to the Egyptians. The Sabbath law, as with all of God's Law, was a gift, not a burden. The Sabbath law was a way to practice faith in God and to have that faith confirmed by His providence. The Jewish religious leaders, over time and consistent with typical human determination, turned blessing into curse by making the Law a useless and bitter obligation. This is why Jesus confronts the teaching of the religious leaders both in word (Mt 5–7; 12; 15; 23) and in deed (Mt 12; Mk 3; Jn 9). Jesus addresses the issue of the "spirit" or "intent of the law" here, and in examples that include the average person's need to perform circumcision, leading an animal to water, or lifting one out of a pit. In fact, if you read the Gospels with this issue in mind, it may seem like Jesus only worked on the Sabbath! Or at least those are the only occasions that the apostles recorded.

So, the answer is "no," eating what God so readily provided as they walked through fields of grain was not sinful according to the Law *and* a qualified "yes," it is not only right for Jesus but necessary for Him (the light of the world) to expose the hypocrisy and tyranny of laws invented by humans. Jesus truly did come to deliver us from the curse of the Law. The reassertion and affirmation of the intent of His Law released the people from the tyranny of self-serving, hypocritical leaders. His substitutionary atonement redeemed us from the curse of the real and binding Law of God (Rm 8:1ff.; Gal 3).

Q 12:7 Why did Jesus ask them again if they knew the meaning of "I desire mercy, and not sacrifice?"

This is an imperative, issuing a challenge rather than a question, occurring in Mt 9:13 as well. In ch. 9, the Jewish religious leaders objected because Jesus had dinner with tax collectors and sinners at Matthew's house, following Matthew's calling by Jesus. In ch. 12, the Jewish religious leaders complain about plucking grain to eat as Jesus' disciples walked through the fields.

Why does God repeat things in history and in biblical texts? In general, I suspect it has to do with the reluctance and even the opposition of our human nature to the thoughts and ways of God (Is 55; 1Co 1:18–25; 2:14). In particular, you may consider how important this quote from Hosea was to someone like Matthew. As a tax collector, Matthew was despised by the Jews, and no amount of sacrifices could have overcome this. As a Jew, Matthew could never be accepted by the Romans. Along came Jesus, and with a word Matthew was reconciled to God. You may also consider the parallel between Matthew and Paul in this regard. Paul was a fierce defender of the pure Gospel because he could never have forgotten for a moment how absolutely his life depended upon it, as the first of his letters to the Corinthians makes evident. Contrast Paul with Peter, who sounded good at times (Mt 16:16; Ac 2; 10; 11; 15) but often abandoned the Gospel (Mt 16:22; Gal 2:11ff—note that this incident in Antioch happened *after* Peter's defense of the Gospel at the first Jerusalem Council [Ac 11]!).

What a marvelous characteristic of God: that He not only desires mercy rather than sacrifice, but He is patient and steadfast in making that known to us.

● ● ● ● ● ● ● ● ● ● ● ● ● ● ● ● ● ● ●

Q **12:14 Why were the Pharisees so upset by Jesus working on the Sabbath that they wanted to kill Him?**

The Sabbath was just one of many issues that infuriated the Pharisees. They often objected violently to His teaching (Lk 4:28–29), especially when He testified to His nature as the Son of God (Jn 10:31–33). The root of such violent reaction is really man's ego and vain insistence on claiming power and ability that are not ours. Consider King Herod's reaction to the Wise Men's inquiry, "Where is He who has been born king of the Jews" (Mt 2:2), or the rage of the devil because he is fallen and can never recover (Rv 12:13–17). The only remedy for such a negative and violent opposition to God comes when we are brought to an honest admission of the truth about ourselves; we are failures under the Law and deserve to die (in the fullest sense of that word). But we are also God's creation and the object of His redemptive Word in Christ and through the Spirit. If we live in the truth about ourselves, then we are overjoyed to meet, learn about, hear from, and live in communion with the Christ (cf. Mt 9:11–13; Rm 5).

● ● ● ● ● ● ● ● ● ● ● ● ● ● ● ● ● ● ●

Q **12:15 Why does Jesus tell the people He's healed not to tell anyone who He is?**

If you read Jn 6:15ff, you will note that the crowds of people really missed the point of Jesus' miracle. Fallen human nature is driven and possessed by an appetite for material things with self-destructive concentration. While Jesus does heal people as evidence of His divine nature, He is really interested in the eternal souls of everyone and in regenerating those souls through His teaching (Jn 6:27ff.). Jesus wanted those He healed to be silent so the crowds who missed the point would be less likely to seek Him for the wrong reasons. Then He would be free and unmolested in His work of visiting many people and villages with the Word.

● ● ● ● ● ● ● ● ● ● ● ● ● ● ● ● ● ● ●

Q **12:19 Did Jesus contradict this prophecy when He overturned tables and yelled in the temple court?**

Jesus fulfilled all that the Law and Prophets said about Him perfectly; this is one of the ways we know He is truly the Son of God. Sometimes mistranslations of texts, or our inaccurate recollection of them, suggest contradictions that do not really exist. For example, none of the accounts of Jesus cleansing the temple (Mt 21:12–13; Mk 11:15–17; Lk 19:45–46; Jn 2:13–17) record Him yelling—only saying and teaching. A second key for understanding is in the suggestion of a different context. Jesus was not in the streets but in the temple. This observation leads us to a

> ## What does it mean to be demon possessed?

third key, also related to context. Isaiah's prophecy about the Messiah not lifting up His voice in the streets sets Jesus in contrast to self-serving, self-appointed individuals who wanted attention and the attraction of people for their own purposes or sense of power. Jesus consistently took people aside from the crowd to heal and then commanded such a person to keep silent about it. Finally, the context of Isaiah's prophecy has much to do with the overall disposition of the Son of God in the person of Jesus: "A bruised reed He will not break, and a faintly burning wick He will not quench" (Is 42:3). Jesus does not strike terror into people in order to get selfish and external control. Jesus loves patiently and kindly, knowing our weaknesses, communicating His Word, grace, and Spirit to us in order to bind up the broken and strengthen the flame of faith.

Q 12:22 In the New Testament, there is much talk of demon possession. Why do we not hear anything about them today? What does it mean to be demon possessed?

Paul once wrote that your body is the temple of the Holy Spirit who is in you (1Co 6:19). It appears, then, that being made in the image of God includes three aspects to our nature: body, soul, spirit. Our body is

dying under the Law but will be resurrected in perfection (1Co 15:35ff.). Our souls are regenerated by the Word and Spirit of God (Ti 3:5) and are at war with our bodies (Gal 5:17ff.; Rm 7:14–25). Body and soul are animated by either the Spirit of God or the devil. So, to be demon possessed is to be inhabited by and driven by the devil (or demonic spirits, Mt 8:30ff.). The Bible doesn't tell us why they were so prevalent then and not now. I suspect that while demon possession is just as prevalent today as in the past, the devil has learned the advantages of being subtle. Revelation 12 explains how the dragon/devil, having been defeated by Christ, went off to make war with His offspring, the Church. Could it be that this war of the dragon or devil has to do with the patient, unpretentious undermining of values, distraction with material things, and addiction to entertainment and self-gratification that we see today? Perhaps selfish materialism *is* demon possession, and we've just become used to it. This possibility makes it all the more essential that we heed Jesus' instruction to remain in His Word (Jn 8:31) and Paul's admonition that the Word of Christ dwell in us richly (Col 3)!

Q 12:24 Are the Pharisees saying that Jesus is curing demon-possessed people because He is of demons?

Yes, that is exactly what they are saying. The Jewish religious leaders said something similar to Jesus in Jn 8:48: "Are we not right in saying that You are a Samaritan and have a demon?" These are examples of occasions in life that reveal the stubborn, dishonest nature of humanity since the fall of Adam. When people who adamantly oppose the truth are confronted with truth they cannot escape, they attack the speaker in order to dismiss the speech. But the speaker, in this case Jesus Christ, could not be overcome even by crucifixion and the grave because He is the way, the truth, and the life.

● ●

Q 12:31 If no one sin is greater than another, how come one is pointed out as the greatest?

First of all, the text does not use the language of lesser and greater. The text says that all sins will be forgiven with one and only one exception: blasphemy against the Holy Spirit. Second, the reason that blasphemy against the Holy Spirit is unforgivable is because the Holy Spirit is the agent or means by which forgiveness is applied to the sinner (Jn 20:22–23). Blasphemy against the Holy Spirit is the stubborn, relentless contradiction of God's redemption in Christ as can be seen in the "goats" of judgment day (Mt 25:41–45) or the elder son who refused to come into his father's house (Lk 15:25–28). The expression "the unforgivable sin" is like saying, "The only person who cannot benefit from water is the person who refuses water." Third, this text requires us to consider the distinction and relationship between forgiveness as an accomplished reality in Jesus' Passion, death, and resurrection and the application or realization of that forgiveness in the life of an individual. Texts that give us

the authority and responsibility to express forgiveness usually fail to convey the significance of tense in the original text. Jesus said, "The sins of whomever you forgive *have been* forgiven and the sins of whomever you bind *have been bound*" (cf. Jn 20:22–23; Mt 18:18). The perfect passive "have been bound" emphasizes the enduring nature of a past accomplishment—Jesus' vicarious atonement for all. This accomplishment is the reason we not only can but must confirm this accomplishment for the comfort of the penitent or refuse this comfort to those whose impenitence blasphemes the Holy Spirit.

● ●

Q 12:31–32, 37 Why does Jesus say all sins except those committed against the Spirit will be forgiven? What about v. 37, where He says that by our words we will be acquitted or condemned? What would be a sin against the Spirit, and how is it different from any other sin?

Perhaps the best way toward a certain answer to this question is to consider texts that describe a condemnation or fear of condemnation from which a person cannot be restored. Before looking at such texts, it would seem prudent to remember that we cannot know, for certain, the spiritual condition or future of any person. We have instructions about speaking the truth in love (Eph 4:15) and about dealing with an erring brother (Mt 18:15ff.). We also have a clear prohibition from Jesus against condemning anyone (7:1).

Paul reacts in shock and horror upon learning that the Galatians have abandoned the grace of God in the Gospel in order to return to pursuing justification by obedience to the Law (Gal 1:6–10). The question Paul asks in response has to do with how the Galatians received the Spirit: by works of Law or the hearing of faith? It is evident here that without the Holy Spirit, the Galatians would remain under the Law. This is parallel to Paul's positive statement in Rm 8:1: "there is therefore now no condemnation for those who are in Christ Jesus." Even more powerfully in Hebrews, we learn that "it is impossible in the case of those who have once been enlightened, who have tasted the heavenly gift, and have shared in the Holy Spirit, and have tasted the goodness of the word of God and the powers of the age to come, and then have fallen away, to restore them again to repentance, since they are crucifying once again the Son of God to their own harm and holding Him up to contempt" (6:4–6) and of "how much worse punishment, do you think, will be deserved by the one who has trampled underfoot the Son of God, and has profaned the blood of the covenant by which he was sanctified, and has outraged the Spirit of grace" (10:29). In both cases, we can see that it is neither any particular sin nor the breaking of any particular commandment that is the issue. The problem has to do with a determined, persistent renunciation, rejection, and despising of the means by which God provides the remedy for sin—the realization of the redemptive work of Christ. So, it is not sin that is unforgivable, but the refusal of forgiveness itself by which a person forces himself or herself back under the curse of the Law from which Christ has set us free. This is apparent when we compare the lives of Saul, David, Judas, and Peter. All four of these men were sinners. David and Peter acted in ways that are shocking, yet surrounded by the Word and Spirit of God, they were restored and died in faith. Saul and Judas, by contrast, rejected the very Word and Spirit of God, leaving no source of help or hope. The last few verses about being justified or condemned by our words simply remind us that the mouth speaks what the heart is full of (or void of). People who are guilty of this sin against the Holy Spirit will make it abundantly clear by what they have to say.

Fallen human nature does not receive the things of the Spirit (1Co 2:14) and cannot be reformed/restored to perfection in this life. This nature of ours presents a real and constant threat that God responds to with the most severe of language. Nevertheless, the purpose of that language, as in all that God says and does, is to work salvation—to crucify and silence our noisy, contradictory human nature so that the Gospel can be heard and so that it can work redemption and regeneration. While we may have to leave a person (or village) alone for a time because he or she refuses to hear, we would never stop looking or praying for the time when such a person's disposition would change, allowing us to reaffirm the truth and grace of God to them by the power of the Spirit of Christ through the Word.

● ●

Q **12:32 What does it mean to "speak against the Holy Spirit"?**

Think first of the essence or nature of the Holy Spirit, for example, according to Gn 2:7 and Jn 16:14. The Holy Spirit is the "life maker" according to Jn 6:63. Blasphemy, then, would have to do with denying, rejecting, resenting, contradicting, mocking, and despising the Holy Spirit according to His essential nature. Thus we can see that blaspheming the Holy Spirit is unforgivable because it disallows the very source and agent of forgiveness.

● ●

Q **12:39–40 What is the significance of the sign of Jonah? When Jesus goes to the heart of the earth, is this referring to Judgment Day? It doesn't seem as if Jesus was gone for three days and three nights as the Scripture says.**

The "evil and adulterous generation" Jesus is speaking to here actually has to do with fallen human nature rather than a particular group of people in time or place. Jesus describes the hearts of fallen humans in just such terms (Mk 7:20–23), and Paul also reports that "the natural person does not accept the things of the Spirit of God, for they are folly to him, and he is not able to understand them because they are spiritually discerned" (1Co 2:14). The "sign" of Jonah has to do with the refusal of fallen human nature to recognize the truth, the need for repentance, and the necessity of God's grace for redemption. Jonah is indicative of all Israel at that time—running away from God's call to serve others on His behalf, a desire to die (once by drowning and once under the heat of the sun) rather than be an ambassador of God's mercy, and only ever a measured, unhappy, outward compliance with God's command. If a people cannot see their own condition in Jonah or in Jesus' death and burial, they won't understand anything else God has to say. This is one of the points of the conversation between Abraham and the rich man after he had died, "'No, father Abraham, but if someone goes to them from the dead, they will repent.' He said to him, 'If they do not hear Moses and the Prophets, neither will they be convinced if someone should rise from the dead'" (Lk 16:30–31). The truth of Abraham's response can be witnessed in the Pharisees' response to the raising of Lazarus (Jn 11) and Jesus' own resurrection (Mt 28:11–15).

Jesus says He will be three days and nights in the heart of the earth. This presents some difficulty, both because Jesus was three days but only two nights in the tomb and because Jesus said to the thief, "Truly, I say to you, today you will be with Me in Paradise" (Lk 23:43). Ancient people considered any portion of time as a whole. This is why chronologies of kings, for example, have to remember that two kings often claimed the same year as part of their reign because they had reigned for part of it, even if only a day. Thus the promise that Jesus would rise on the third day means that you can count all of Friday, Saturday, and Sunday (three days and three nights) in your reckoning. Perhaps this understanding also resolves the question of Jesus' location during this time. We do know that Jesus was left in the tomb on Good Friday, that He descended into hell (1Pt 3:19), and that He was in paradise (Lk 23:48).

. . . .

Q **12:42 Who is the queen of the South?**

She is also known as the queen of Sheba. Various suggestions have been made as to the location of this kingdom: Egypt, Ethiopia, or Yemen. The Old Testament (1Ki 10:1–13) records the visit of this queen to King Solomon, which would date her and her visit to somewhere in the tenth century BC.

. . . .

Q **12:43–45 What does this analogy mean?**

To begin with, this is not an analogy, though it contains some nonliteral language. Unclean spirits are real, and their effects on the person possessed are well attested in the Gospels. Demons seem to need or at least prefer to dwell within a human being or an animal (Mt 8:30ff.). The Word of the Lord casts demons out of a person possessed by them (7:22; cf. 17:14–21, where Jesus adds prayer and fasting to the forces that drive demons out). Once a demon is cast out of a person, Jesus describes the person as a house that is now uninhabited by demonic forces but is also not inhabited by the Spirit of God, as God intended (Gn 2:7; 1Co 6:19). Apparently, demons without a host find no place to rest as they roam about the earth. Restless demons then return to the person they were cast out of, and if they find that person without the Spirit of God dwelling in them, they not only repossess the person but gather other demons to join them, and the last state is worse than the first. This description parallels the words of Jesus and Paul regarding the condition of a person who rejects the Holy Spirit (Mt 12:31–32; Heb 6:4–6; 10:26–29). Thus, if the Word of God dwells in us richly (Col 3:16) because we are remaining in the Word (Jn 8:31; Ac 2:42), then we have the armor of God (Eph 6:11ff.) and are impregnable to demonic forces (Mt 8:24–25; 1 Jn 5:18). Apart from the Word of God. we are not only empty and devoid of life, but also completely subject to the work and ways of the devil (Eph 2:1–3).

. . . .

Q **12:46–50 Why did Jesus not recognize His brothers and mother but refer to His disciples as His family? Could not His mother and brothers also be doing the will of His Father? Was there a deeper reason why Jesus wouldn't see His mother and brothers? Was this rude? What point is He trying to make?**

Jesus surely recognized His brothers and mother and would have known that they stood outside, but there is the key word: *outside*. From the very beginning, the Bible distinguishes between simple physical/biological relationships and spiritual relationships. Consider the significance of Isaac in relation to Ishmael, which Paul addresses in Gal 4. Note the significance of David being chosen king rather than any of the older sons of Jesse. What matters most to the Lord is the relationship that endures forever, that has to do with the essence of our being, our soul. Two other texts reveal that Jesus' mother and brothers did not understand nor accept who He was: Jn 7:5 and Mk 3:21. Jesus is no more rude in this instance than He was at the wedding of Cana where He said to Mary, "Woman, what does this have to do with Me?" (Jn 2:4). Whenever anyone would assert themselves and/or their ideas of what matters over against Jesus' fulfillment of His work or redemption, Jesus rightly questions their purpose and commitments. Perhaps the best example of this is in Mt 16:13–23. One moment Peter is blessed because he knows that Jesus is the Christ, the Son of the Living God, and the next moment he is Satan, because he would prevent Jesus from fulfilling the work of redemption that is essential for the Christ to accomplish.

● ●

Q **13:14 When it speaks of the prophecy of Isaiah, I have often wondered why it seems as if God doesn't want people to understand.**

There are several places in the Bible where we have a chance to see that Judgment Day comes sooner or later or, for those covered by the righteousness of Christ, not at all. For example, in Ex 4:22–23, God tells Moses what to say to Pharaoh but goes on to reveal that Pharaoh will refuse and lose his firstborn son as a consequence.

Vv. 7–8 of 1Pt 2 describe how those who reject Christ, the cornerstone, are destined to stumble and disobey. Judas Iscariot and King Saul are both examples of condemnation evident already during the physical life of the individual. The problem for both Saul and Judas (in contrast to David and Peter) was their consistent and determined rejection of the Word of the Lord (1Sm 15:26; Jn 12:6). The prophecy of Isaiah, repeated by Jesus in the company of so many who refused to listen to His simple, gracious message, is not saying that God doesn't want people to understand but is a condemnation of their refusal to listen so that they might understand. The biblical accounts of human refusal to listen and the serious consequences of that are a help to us in body and soul. The impending judgment of God is a powerful and needed force to keep our fallen human nature humble and submissive. Our redemption from that judgment by Christ is the most powerful of all forces, and it regenerates us and inspires faith (Jn 5:19–30; Rm 8:1ff.; 1Jn 3:1ff.).

● ●

Q **13:24–30 Can Satan place people on earth?**

The parable, as explained by Jesus in 13:36–43, describes the life of the "sons of the kingdom" with the "sons of the evil one" together in this world. The term "sons of" does not refer to the creation of people (body and soul) but refers to the difference in their condition due to the influences of the Word of God on the one hand or the deceit of the devil on the other. Satan constantly prowls about seeking someone to devour, making such a person his child by making such a person an agent of lies and murder (Jn 8:31–59).

• • • • • • • • • • • • • • • • • • •

Q 13:31–33 Why doesn't Matthew explain these parables? What do they mean?

I don't think we have a way of knowing why the Gospels record Jesus explaining some parables but not others. I do know that the explanations that Jesus provides in the Gospels and elsewhere in the Bible are invaluable for knowing how to approach the parables without explanations. You may also note that there is teaching in plain language and often historical accounts that make the same point as a parable. Paul refers to the way the Bible interprets itself in Rm 12:6, "If prophecy, in proportion to our faith."

The first parable, about the mustard seed, is raising a question of perception and judgment. Some might look at a mustard seed and conclude, "It is too small to be of any real importance," just as people look at children, Jesus, or the Word of God and despise them (Mk 10:13–14; Lk 4:22 [Is 53]; Rv 11). However, the Word of God entered the world as God's Seed in the Virgin Mary

and grew and provided universal redemption and fulfilled all of God's promises to restore His creation. The Word of God produces a refuge that is inexhaustible. Consider Jesus' teaching in the Sermon on the Mount, where He refers to birds and how God provides for them, so how much more will He provide for you (Mt 6:26).

The second parable compares the properties of leaven (yeast) with the kingdom of God. The Word of God is a powerful force that continues to affect everything around it. Like a spring that continues to pour forth water, that water will continue to flow, accumulate, and saturate. Thus Is 55 describes the powerful and pervasive character of God's Word. On the other hand, Jesus (Mt 16) and Paul (1Co 5) warn about the leaven of lies, false teaching, and wicked practices.

• • • • • • • • • • • • • • • • • • •

Q 13:36–58 To fully understand Jesus' messages in the parables, one needs to know and understand why He used parables. If Jesus called His disciples to spread the Word, why do they have a hard time understanding the parables?

Given the nature of our condition since the fall of Adam, our inability to understand what the good Lord is saying to us is to be expected. Both Jesus in Mt 16 and Paul in Col 3 remind us that we are not thinking the thoughts of God but the thoughts of sinful humankind. Fallen human nature is at the same time proud and selfish, and to justify ourselves in both requires dishonesty, gross dishonesty. Therefore, when we hear Jesus (or anyone else) telling us the truth, we typically "don't get it." This is why God gives the Law in clear, literal language that has the power to crush our pride, condemn our selfishness, and silence our contradicting thoughts/words (Rm 3:19). Those who had been crushed by the Law recognized themselves in the parables and tended to understand. Compare the two groups of people that Luke clearly describes as the audience for Jesus' parables about the lost (i.e., sheep, coin, sons). They would have freely admitted that they were the one lost sheep or coin. Consequently, they would have loved to know that the Lord looked so diligently for them and that there was such rejoicing in heaven because they had been found. The humble and honest listener would readily identify with the younger son whose conduct was reprehensible yet who came to repentance and was welcomed back into his father's home with much rejoicing.

● ● ● ● ● ● ● ● ● ● ● ● ● ● ● ● ● ● ● ●

Q 13:52 What did Christ mean in this verse? Are there any eschatological relations to Revelation, or are they just literal "kingdom of heaven" sayings?

The term "kingdom of heaven" occurs thirty-two times in the New Testament, all of them in Matthew. The term "kingdom of God" is parallel and occurs sixty-eight times in the New Testament, five of them in Matthew. Perhaps the most simple and clear explanation of this Kingdom is to associate it with Jesus Himself. At the beginning of His public ministry, Jesus said the kingdom of God was "at hand" (Mk 1:15). The expression "at hand" does not mean it will come soon, but rather that it has come and will endure *in the person of Jesus*. Immediately after that proclamation, Mark records Jesus healing the sick and forgiving sins—essentially Jesus is restoring God's creation according to God's will. This Kingdom is realized by believers in part during this life and then fully in the resurrection of the dead and God's recreation of the universe. Here it is critical to make sure we always remember that the Kingdom is bound up in Christ, rather than thinking of the Kingdom as a place or in a distant time with Christ somehow absent or left behind. Jesus confessed to Pontius Pilate, "My kingdom is not of this world" (Jn 18:36). When Peter offered to build shelters for Jesus, Moses, and Elijah at the transfiguration, God interrupted him to say, "This is My beloved Son, *listen* to Him" (Mk 9:7, emphasis added). Fallen human beings have a bad habit of trying to turn Christ's kingdom into one of their own, in time and in a material way. This was the case also in the Old Testament with the ark and then with the temple. If God is not present, then neither is His kingdom. Once again, let me say: the kingdom of heaven/God is evident in Christ and comes to us in His Word and Spirit. To know more about this Kingdom, we need only read the Gospels and watch Jesus establish it wherever He is.

Why was John the Baptist beheaded?

Q 13:53–58 With all of Jesus' success with other people, why did the Nazarenes reject Him?

Jesus addresses this directly in Lk 4:15–37. You see the turning point in the people's thinking, especially in v. 22. We tend assume that the people "marveling" at Jesus is a good thing, but here it betrays human arrogance that rejects what is above and beyond itself. John addresses the issue of Jesus being rejected by His own people in Jn 1:11. What the life of Christ challenges us to consider is the real nature of our identity. Paul teaches that being children of God and descendants of Abraham is not a matter of physical procreation but a product of the Word and will of God alone (Rm 2:28–29; Gal 3:7; Lk 3:7–8; Jn 1:12–13). Fallen human pride and jealousy make enough trouble when confronted with someone "better," so we ought not be surprised when people are even more opposed when a man demonstrates that He is the Son of God, the one and only Redeemer, and He who will judge the living and the dead. Consider the opposition and often hostility of the Romans, Jews, Muslims, and Mormons against the unique and unparalleled truth of Christ. In our day, as was the case with some Jewish leaders in Jerusalem (Ac 4:1–2) and with many Greeks in Athens (17:32), the sophisticated but fallen human ego does not want to admit either its limitations or that it is subject to and dependent upon God now and eternally, body and soul (Pss 2; 14; 53). The good news is that God is patient and knows how to humble our human nature and regenerate our soul—a regenerate soul that both recognizes and rejoices in the exclusive magnificence of the Redeemer of all the world.

Q 14:1–11 Why was John the Baptist beheaded? Did the leaders fear that someone with his influence would create an uprising among the people? Why would the mother want the head of John? Why was he put into prison to begin with?

Let's begin with the easiest question. John was put into prison because he spoke publicly against the sexual immorality of Herod (Mt 14:3–5; Lk 3:19–20). Mark 6:17–20 gives more detail, mainly that it was Herodias who wanted to silence John's condemnation by putting him to death, but Herod protected him, sent for him often, and heard him gladly. Remember that Herod was half Jewish and for this reason advocated for the Jews under the Roman Empire in many ways.

Next, Herodias, the mother, wanted the head of John as a demonstration of her power over John. "Head" has to do with power and authority, as in the term "heads of state." Rulers used to always be at the "head" of the army in battle. Capital punishment was final because it decapitated the person, which demonstrated the power of the one to permanently eliminate the power and life of the other. Notice how a person could deceive himself into believing he possessed real power inasmuch as he could extinguish the life of another. So it was all through history with the prophets, apostles, and Jesus. However, one's ability to silence and extinguish the lives of the opposition does not eliminate the forces of truth, which we are all always subject to.

Finally, Herod had John beheaded for at least two reasons. First, John condemned Herod's adultery with Herodias. Herod's lust for her and fear of her made Herod comply with her wicked will. Second, Herod's lust (again), carelessness in drinking, and pride made him swear an oath to something in the presence of his guests that no one should ever make. Wickedness is never idle, and that of Herod, Herodias, and Herodias's daughter all combined eventually to the martyrdom of John. But when has this not been the case? Adam, in effect, decapitated Eve when he blamed her for the fall. Thus, it was necessary for the Son of God to take our nature and suffer the humility of capital punishment under the Law because He is our head, and in this way He redeemed us to Himself. "The fear of man lays a snare, but whoever trusts in the LORD is safe" (Pr 29:25). The imprisonment of John and his execution makes an essential point about God's providence for those who serve and trust in Him; even John was troubled about this (Jn 11:2–6). Human nature is prone to thinking that the purpose of our relationship with God

is to satisfy and protect that part of us. On the contrary, the hardships and, ultimately, death of our human nature is part of God's work to liberate us from our fallen, corrupt nature. (See 2Co 1:8–9; 4:1–5:21; 12:1–10.)

Q **14:19 This text doesn't say that the fish were shared with the crowds. Do we know for sure that fish were shared?**

This text says that Jesus blessed both bread and fish but only mentions the loaves in the distribution. In Mt 15:36 and Lk 9:14, neither bread nor fish are identified in the distribution. However, Mk 6:43 says that the fragments collected afterward were of the loaves and the fish. Thus Mark makes clear what is ambiguous in Matthew and Luke.

Q **14:22 Why did Jesus send His disciples ahead in the boat?**

Certainly Jesus could have had His disciples wait for Him to travel together in the boat. The text suggests that Jesus wanted time to be by Himself to pray. There is at least one account of Jesus traveling in the boat from the start (Mk 4:35–41). There are several occasions where Jesus wanted to be alone to pray (Mk 1:35; Mt 26:39). Jesus even teaches us to pray alone (Mt 6:6). Jn 6:15 reveals that part of Jesus' concern in sending the disciples had to do with dealing with the crowds that intended to take Him by force and make Him king. Besides all this, Jesus coming across the sea on foot provided another remarkable proof of His divine nature.

Q 14:24 While walking on water, how far did Jesus actually go?

The same account in Jn 6:16–21 records that the disciples had rowed three or four miles when Jesus came to them. Like the twelve baskets full of leftover food from feeding the five thousand with five loaves and two fish, in this case also Jesus leaves no room to question His ability to rule His own creation.

Q 14:25–30 Why did Peter doubt when the winds came?

Interestingly, you ask the same question Jesus asked, "O you of little faith, why did you doubt?" The text says that Peter began to doubt when "he saw the wind, [and] he was afraid." Perhaps Jesus' parable of the houses built on sand or rock help answer (Mt 7:24–27). Peter was paying more attention to what he saw with his eyes than to what Jesus had told him. Our perceptions or assessments, in contrast to the Word of God, are like sand, leaving us to be demolished when challenged. Yet Jesus uses Peter to teach us both that our fallen human nature is utterly unbelieving (1Co 2:14) and that He has taken this into account. Thus, Jesus both invites Peter to come to Him and lifts Peter out of the water by taking his hand.

Q 15:2 What is the significance of washing hands before eating?

First, washing removes elements that would cause us harm. We are instructed nowadays to wash our hands all the time; we take baths and showers; we wash our clothes and clean our homes (Mk 7:4). Second, washing is indicative of the more essential but nonmaterial cleansing of our lives, souls, and relationships (1Pt 3:21). Please note the term *indicative* rather than *figurative* or *symbolic*, as the latter terms suggest what is not real or elements that have no substantive relationship. The term *indicative* suggests an essential relationship, as John's Gospel makes abundantly clear. The germs that infect and fight against our life point to the sin that infects our whole life, body and soul. The blood of Jesus Christ cleanses us from all sin and redeems us, body and soul (2Co 5).

Q 15:2–7 What was Jesus saying? How did the Pharisees break the Fourth Commandment?

God is concerned with truth and reality, not with lies and pretense. As in the Sermon on the Mount (Mt 5–7), Jesus makes clear the full intent of the Law. Fallen human nature continually tries to manipulate the Law in order to make it justify rather than condemn our ways. The Pharisees did not want to care for their parents. They wanted to spend the care and devotion due their parents on themselves and at the same time feed their pride and self-righteousness, so they "claimed" that they were giving what was due their parents to God. The Book of Malachi focuses on this problem of self-righteousness and self-deception. God needs nothing from us but is served by us as we serve others on His behalf (Mt 10:40; 25:40, 45).

• • • • • • • • • • • • • • • • • • • •

Q 15:13 What does Jesus mean when He states, "Every plant that My heavenly Father has not planted will be rooted up"? What does the plant represent?

Plants are indicative of people in many ways. Is 5:7 describes God's people as His planting. Jesus uses the relationship between vine and branch to make clear our complete dependence upon union with Him (Jn 15). Jesus also tells a parable of severe warning about a fig tree that has not borne figs for three years. The gardener pleads for the tree and begs permission to cultivate the tree. Though the master grants another year to see if the fig tree will bear, if there is no fruit after the next year, the tree is to be cut down. Finally, in Mt 3:10 and 7:17–19, Jesus explains that good trees bear good fruit and bad trees bear bad fruit. This explanation is profound in at least two ways. First, Jesus emphasizes that the fruit is the product of the tree. We are "bad" trees since the fall of Adam and so bear nothing but bad fruit (Rm 3:10–18; 5:6–11), but we are also "good" trees because the Lord has regenerated us in His image and therefore bear only good fruit (Jn 1:12–13; 1Jn 3–5). Second,

the fruit bears witness to the tree, despite our fallen nature's attempt at self-righteous claims or our regenerate nature's genuine humility (Mt 25:31–46).

• • • • • • • • • • • • • • • • • • • •

Q 15:18–20 Jesus states that what comes from a man's heart makes him unclean. How are we supposed to spread the Word of God then? From the soul, stomach, mind? This does not make sense to me.

As in so many cases, distinguishing the natures of which we are composed is the key. The heart of our fallen human nature is "deceitful above all things, and desperately sick" (Jer 17:9). This heart is one piece and nature with our flesh, which is full of everything bad, as Jesus says here and as Paul says in Gal 5:19–21. This heart or nature cannot be reformed, which is why death is the only permanent remedy for us. On the other hand, God regenerates us in the image of His Son, which includes heart, mind, and disposition (Ezk 36:26–27; Php 2:5; 1Jn 5:4–5). This is the nature that lives and thrives by the Word of God and which seeks to share that Word of God with others (2Co 5:14–21).

• • • • • • • • • • • • • • • • • • • •

15:21–28

I have provided a single explanation for this whole section at the end of this series of questions; you may want to read that first. I have taken portions of that explanation as answers to the particular questions that follow.

• •

Q 15:21 Why did Jesus not help the Canaanite woman right away?

Jesus, knowing the woman's faith and purpose, wants to expose the truth about her, her faith, and His own nature in a profound and powerful way on this occasion. Compare this encounter with God's similar purpose in Job's life (Jas 5:11), with a blind man (Jn 9), and with Paul (2Co 12:7–10).

• •

Q 15:22 Why did a Canaanite woman refer to Jesus as the "Son of David"? In other words, how and why did she know this?

As you read through the Gospels, you will notice that many, many foreigners seem to know a lot about the promises of God in the Old Testament. Apparently, but not surprisingly, when God's faithful people of the Old Testament traveled, they shared the Word of God! How else would the Wise Men from the East have known about the King of the Jews? People move about, especially when persecuted, and God uses this movement to bring His Word and kingdom to those who sat in darkness. Regarding the particular term "Son of David," there are a few key references in the Old Testament to the coming Savior or Messiah. One of them is the "Son of David," which comes from 2Sm 7, where David wants to build a house

for God but God says He will build David's house through His Son.

• •

Q 15:22 Could some instances of demon possession in the Bible be schizophrenia or other mental disorders and not truly demon possession?

Every human trouble could be demon possession, from mental illness to computer viruses. On the other hand, the devil could be completely absent and a fallen world just won't work as it was created to. Jesus cared for people in body and soul and teaches us in the New Testament to do the same (Lk 10:25–37; Jas 2:15–17).

• •

Q 15:24 Romans 1:16 says, "I am not ashamed of the gospel, for it is the power of God for salvation to everyone who believes, to the Jew first and also to the Greek." Why does Jesus say then in Mt 15:24, "I was sent only to the lost sheep of the house of Israel"? It surprises me that Jesus would refuse to help anyone.

Both Romans (2:28–29) and Galatians (3:8–9) confirm that the "lost sheep of . . . Israel" are people of faith, like Abraham. Jesus made the same point in the parable of the lost sheep (Mt 18:12–13). As you will see below, Jesus is not refusing to help. He is taking advantage of an opportunity to reveal who receives and who doesn't receive the help that is ever present with God and why or why not.

Q **15:24–28 What is important about dogs here, and how does it connect to the woman's faith?**

The term *dog* is only used in a negative sense in the New Testament (Mt 7:6; Rv 22:15). The point that Jesus is using the woman to make is that dogs have more sense than the proud, self-righteous Jews who were following Jesus in body but not at all in spirit or in truth. The woman, in contrast to the crowd, cares only for the daughter who needs help. She is focused on Jesus, who brings help. She cares nothing for her pride but willingly and eagerly claims the lowest of places, that of a little dog. The woman knows very well that even the little dogs benefit from the Master's table.

We tend to read over simple teachings because it is so easy for us to assume we already know the point or to "convert" the teaching in support of our own way of thinking. Jesus used parables and unusual circumstances to shock people out of self-deception and into honesty and grace.

Q **15:26 What does Jesus mean when He says, "It is not right to take the children's bread and throw it to the dogs"? Why does Jesus say that so harshly to the woman?**

Jesus is using this woman to correct the prevalent but inverted notion of who is close to, beloved by, helped by, and in communion with God. Popular opinion equates vain, superficial, material values with what commends us before God. The wealthy, powerful, pedigreed Jews assumed they were the children of Abraham and also God and expected the Messiah to honor them and grant them every privilege. These same people considered the lower classes of Jews and Gentiles as all dogs (ancient rabbinic literature makes this exceedingly clear). Jesus explodes such notions by avoiding popularity and the crowds in order to make intimate and helpful connections with lowly, despised individuals.

Q **15:21–28 A more comprehensive explanation:**

First, note that Mark also includes this narrative (7:24–30), but Luke and John don't. That is interesting but invites speculation, which is not usually helpful.

Second, note that this encounter between Jesus and a woman is similar to the event recorded in Mt 9:20–22; Mk 5:25–34; and Lk 8:43–48 but is not in John. Notice also, in the case of that narrative, that Matthew spends only three verses on it, Luke spends six, but Mark spends ten. The significance of these differences will be discussed in Mk 5.

Third, consider the audience. According to Matthew, Jesus had just finished responding to objections and issues forced by the Pharisees and scribes (15:1) who had come to Him from Jerusalem while He was in the land of Gennesaret (14:34). Now Jesus is in the region of Tyre and Sidon

(15:21). To understand the meaning and intent of Jesus' interaction with this woman, it is imperative that we recognize the contrast between assumptions about people and places that all four Gospels emphasize. Popular assumptions were, and still are, that some people are favored by God because of physical descent and location. Yet such people are typically more opposed to God than faithful (Jn 1:11). On the other hand, the Gentiles time and again prove themselves to be more faithful and devout, as was also the case in the Old Testament (take Jonah for example, or see Jesus' articulation of this in Lk 4:24–30). In this text, Jesus is in a "foreign" land considered to be faithless, surrounded by a crowd of the proud (Lk 17:17–18; 18:9–14) that expects the favor of God, but in fact is foreign, if not opposed, to Christ (Mt 7:21–23). Jesus is going to use His encounter with this woman, foreign yet faithful, to expose the reality of what joins or separates us from God.

Fourth, though the text makes sure we know this person is both a woman and foreigner (Canaan), somehow she knows important facts. She knows that Jesus is the Son of David, the promised Savior and, I suspect, because of what she knew about the nature of that promised Savior, she cries to Him for mercy. Here, recognize that often foreigners were much more affected by the words and promises of God (note the Wise Men who come to see Jesus at Bethlehem, the "poor, dumb shepherds" of Lk 2, and the queen of Ethiopia in the days of Solomon (Mt 12:38–42).

Fifth, Jesus does not answer her because He knows her faith (He and His Word and His Spirit were the cause of it, after all), and He wants to highlight that faith for the benefit of the faithless in the crowd all around Him. Jesus' wisdom bears fruit. As Jesus ignores her, the woman continues to cry for mercy (like blind Bartimaeus in Mk 10:46–52), and the faithless in the crowd become annoyed and ask Jesus to send her away (as they ask Him to do regarding children in Mk 10:13–14). Now Jesus is going to make His point with even more power and clarity; He is going to reassert the truth about who does or does not belong to God. When Jesus says He was not sent except to the lost sheep of the house of Israel, the woman demonstrates that this is, in truth, who she is by pleading with Him yet again, "Lord, help me." This is the response of a lost yet faithful lamb (Ps 119:174–76). Those who are proud and hypocritical would never endure such an insult, which exposes their real, ungodly nature. A third time, Jesus raises the intensity of this revelation by offering a challenge He knows the woman's faith can meet. What is more, I suspect, Jesus is turning right-side-up everyone's notion of who are the children of God and who are the dogs: "It is not right to take the children's bread and throw it to the dogs." The average, proud, materialistic and therefore nationalistic- and ethnic-thinking person assumes that the Jews are the children and everyone else, especially foreigners and especially foreign women, are the dogs. But is this the case? What does the woman show us when she responds that "even the dogs eat the crumbs that fall from their masters' table"? By admitting her unworthiness, yet at the same time remaining steadfast in her knowledge of Jesus' identity and nature—and in unswerving devotion to another (she comes on behalf of her daughter, not herself)—this woman shows that she is, in fact, the child at the Father's table. At the Father's table, this woman has heard the words of God about the promised Son of David that have made her humble, faithful, and devoted to the life of another. At the same time, Jesus provides a thundering condemnation of the hypocrites who surround Him in physical space and make claims on the basis of national/ethnic ancestry, but who are unwilling to do what even the most pathetic, stupid creature would: at least eat the crumbs that fall from the table (Mt 7:21–23; Lk 13:22–35; Rm 2:28–29; Gal 3:8–9; Jer 8:4–7).

The woman's final response is the last, clear, and most powerful element of Jesus' teaching by way of this circumstance. The woman's unhesitating, immediate, humble, and true response proves the essential nature of her faith in contrast with the feigned and pretentious attitudes of those who "follow" Jesus while their hearts are far from Him. Jesus confirms that the woman is a child at the Master's table by certifying her nature (a child of promise and faith, just as Abraham, Isaac, and Jacob) and by answering her plea for help, which is true to His nature as the Son of God and David. Note that nothing contrary or unexpected took place in this encounter for Jesus or the woman. He is great; we are undeserving. He

is God, and we are poor, miserable reprobates. He is merciful, and we need mercy. We hold fast to our plea for mercy, and He never, ever disappoints but always grants mercy and restoration. The crowd and readers of all time are left to scratch their heads. As is the case with parables, will the truth about our need and humility allow us to see how things really are, or will pride, ego, and self-righteousness hold us in this contrary disposition, disgusted with Jesus' attentions to the undeserving?

● ●

Q **15:32–39 Why does Matthew tell the story of the four thousand and not the five thousand? Why does the feeding of the masses occur twice?**

Many similar events are recorded in the Bible, probably for emphasis. For example, the lives of all the judges reveal similarities between them, certain virtues and certain vices that undermine those virtues. The virtues of the judges point forward to the promised Savior, and the vices of the judges prove why that Savior must be the Son of God. Matthew records Jesus cleaning the temple on Palm Sunday, Mark records it on the next day, Luke may be suggesting that this happened every day of Holy Week, and John records this on Jesus' first visit to the temple. Why? God is never willing to let His temple be abused. So then, the feeding of the multitudes on different occasions proves God's diligent care for us. It is not possible to be neglected by God in the body while you are busy following and listening to Him for the good of your soul. These narratives prove what Jesus declared in 6:25–34.

Q 15:32–38 Does the feeding of four thousand somehow relate to Communion?

Yes, absolutely, and that is most clearly seen in John's record of the feeding of the five thousand (Jn 6). Since God created the material universe to bear witness to Himself (Ps 19:1–3; Rm 1:19–20), everything in our material life has spiritual significance. Jesus making water into wine at the wedding of Cana (Jn 2), Jesus' discussion with Nicodemus about washing and with the Samaritan woman at the well regarding living water (Jn 3; 4), and Jesus' discussion of true bread and true drink (Jn 6) turn our thinking from physical to spiritual, from temporal to eternal life (Col 3:1ff.). Jesus' providence for the crowds in the wilderness points to and illustrates the more comprehensive and profound way that God provides for us in every way for all eternity through Jesus. As God created grain to "embody" what we need from earth, rain, and sun, so the Son of God took on a human nature in order to fulfill the Law for us and thus, through that body, restore our lives. The Holy Bible is so important because it is the very Word of God, the living water, the bread of life, present and always available to give us life (Jn 6:63).

Q 15:34 Why is seven such a significant number?

All of the numbers from one to twelve (and a few others) have significance in the Bible. Beware of the notion that seven is the "number of completion," because ten and twelve are also such numbers. The issue is not "completion" in itself but the *content* of what is complete. Seven is the number of days in the week and seventy-seven is the number of times we should forgive a person who does us wrong (Mt 18:22). However, numbers of items in particular may not have any significance, as in this case. When Jesus fed the five thousand, He had five loaves and two fish, and they collected twelve baskets full of scraps afterwards. Here they have seven loaves and a few fish—there's no particular number—and collected seven basketfuls afterwards. Good principles of interpretation are careful to do two things at once: (1) watch carefully for significance and (2) do not assign significance if the text gives you no reason to do so. The very clear point here is that Jesus always provides and provides abundantly, especially in places where that seems impossible (consider the parallel of Israel in the wilderness).

Q 15:37 What is the importance of the disciples picking up the seven baskets of leftover pieces of bread?

The first matter of importance is evidence that Jesus provided abundantly from very little in the wilderness. Modern critical scholars who begin with the conviction that there is no such thing as miracles have tried to argue that each of the people in the crowd had just a very little to eat and later on the Gospel accounts were exaggerated. The fact that there was more food left over than they started with proves the miracle and the Lord's intent to convince us of His bounteous goodness towards us. Second, John's account (6:12) records Jesus commanding that the fragments be collected so "that nothing may be lost." This command is consistent with the Lord's will that we should be good stewards of His providence (1Co 7:31). Fallen human nature errs in contrast to both these matters. We worry and fear as though the Lord cannot or will not provide for us (Mt 16:5–12); then, when He does bless us with bounty, we tend to waste the extra (Lk 12:13–21).

Q 16:2–3 Does the color red have any significance when referring to the sky?

Meteorologists have explained the truth and cause of the condition referred to by Jesus. In middle latitudes, where the winds prevail from the west, the morning sun makes a red sky if storm clouds are approaching from the west. On the other hand, an evening sun makes a red sky if storms are past and their clouds are to the east. The saying "Red sky in morning, sailors take warning; red sky at night, sailor's delight" seems to have been well-known in Jesus' day, which is why He refers to it as

an example. God's creation has innumerable lessons to teach us, and we have learned some of them well. All creation is meant to teach us about the spiritual realities that parallel these, yet we are ever so slow to recognize or learn these lessons. You can see Jesus making this very point with the Pharisees and Sadducees—they know how to read the signs of storm or fair weather in nature, so how can they not see the spiritual trouble of their own time and place? Jesus says it is, at least in part, because they are hypocrites.

Q 16:4 What does Jesus mean by "except the sign of Jonah"? What was the sign of Jonah?

This is the second time Jesus responds to hypocrites demanding a sign from Jesus, even though they know very well that Jesus has been healing the sick, raising the dead, and doing a host of other miracles (note how Nicodemus, one of the Pharisees, says, "We know that You are a teacher come from God" [Jn 3:1–2]). An "evil and adulterous generation" refers to all human nature, which does not, indeed, cannot grasp the import of what Jesus is doing in His ministry (1Co 2:14; Jn 6:26ff.). The "sign of Jonah" is described by Jesus in Mt 12:38–42. If the religious leaders of the Jews cannot see the lesson God taught to and through Jonah, then they will never grasp the significance of Jesus' teaching or the miracles that authenticated that teaching. But hypocrites are always exposed by the light of God's truth. Pagan sailors, idolatrous Ninevites,

What was the sign of Jonah?

the king of Nineveh—all repented at the earliest sign of judgment from God, but Jonah, like Israel, refused to admit its unbelief and self-destructive self-indulgence. Jesus' response to the Jews here is similar to Abraham's response to the rich man (Lk 16:27–31).

- -

Q **16:5–12 Why does Jesus refer to yeast regarding the teachings of the Pharisees and Sadducees?**

False teaching, like yeast, is among the most powerful forces to infect, as Paul notes in 1Co 5:6. The infective nature of fallen human nature contrary to God is what explains Jesus' radical command about cutting off hand and foot or plucking out the eye that causes us to sin (Mt 18:8–9).

- -

Q **16:8 Why does Jesus respond to the disciples' misunderstandings with "you of little faith"? Is faith equated with wisdom?**

The disciples are preoccupied with two things: their physical appetite ("Oh my gosh, what if we might be hungry for a moment?") and their inflated sense of self-importance ("Oh my gosh, we forgot to bring bread, now what? Never mind that God fed Israel for forty years in the desert, gave them water out of a rock, or all the many

times already that Jesus has fed multitudes in the wilderness"). The dishonest claim of "mature" human ego is what makes us misunderstand or simply miss everything God's Word and creation would teach us. Faith has to do with our dependence upon God and clarity in our own minds about that dependence. Jesus points to children as the model of faith because they have not yet developed an ego that makes dishonest claims for itself. Children are dependent upon God, have no challenging thoughts to the contrary, and are never disappointed by God (Rm 10:11; 1Pt 2:6).

- -

Q **16:12 What is the difference in the teaching of the Pharisees and Sadducees and the real teachings of God? And why was it wrong?**

Matthew 5–7 and 23 are very clear, extended examples of the difference between the teaching of the Pharisees and Sadducees and God. The main difference is that the Jewish religious leaders, like all fallen human beings, reduced, diluted, and/or even reversed the Law of God in order to claim that they have kept the Law and were thus just before God and better than other people. This use of the Law is deadly in two ways. First, the Law always accuses so that, despite any attempts to make the Law justify us, it will always condemn us. Second, changing the Law to serve our fallen, contrary human nature means that we turn against our neighbor (to our neighbor's detriment and ours) instead of toward him or her in love, as the Law teaches. All that is ever wrong is always wrong because it undermines and destroys our life with God and neighbor—and there is no life apart from these.

● ● ● ● ● ● ● ● ● ● ● ● ● ● ● ● ● ● ●

Q 16:19 What does Jesus mean by "Whatever you bind on earth shall be bound in heaven"?

Mt 18:15–18 and Jn 20:23 make it clear that sins are bound or loosed. Jesus gives His disciples not only the authority to confirm forgiveness or the absence of forgiveness but also the responsibility to do so. Notice the expression "confirm" forgiveness or its absence. Jesus is the Lamb of God who bore away the sins of the world, all of them, in His own person in His crucifixion (2Co 5:21). What remains now is for us to realize the benefits of that grace or refuse to do so. The original language is very important here. Jesus said, "Whatever you bind on earth *has been bound* in heaven and whatever you loose on earth *has been loosed* in heaven." The emphasized portions reveal the perfect passive tense of these two verbs, to bind and to loose. The emphasis here is that our actions depend on realities that already exist in heaven. When we make clear to an impenitent person that his or her sins have not been forgiven, we are not making something happen that is not already the case; we are only confirming the truth on behalf of God and for the sake of the individual. Conversely, any time we make clear to a penitent sinner that he or she is forgiven, it is because he or she has already

been forgiven by God; we have the joy and pleasure of confirming that truth for such a person's well-being.

● ● ● ● ● ● ● ● ● ● ● ● ● ● ● ● ● ● ●

Q 16:20 Why did Jesus not want them to tell people who He was?

Isaiah 42:1–3 provides a helpful insight here. The Son of God became man in order to reconcile God and man and restore communion between us. Jesus did not want to promote His own popularity for at least three reasons. First, Jesus did not come to be popular by human standards but "to seek and to save the lost" (Lk 19:10). On several occasions, Jesus refused the demands of those who were committed to vain, material self-interest (Mt 16:1–4; Jn 6:15; 25ff.). Second, popularity would prevent the most faithful of people from gaining access to the Lord in whom they believed so profoundly. Consider the example of the woman with the flow of blood (Mk 5:27ff.) or the blind man who was rebuked by the crowd (Mk 10:48) or the women and children that the disciples would have sent away (Mt 19:13–14). Third, Jesus did not want to encourage any mistaken sense of what kind of help we really need. For example, Jesus waited until Lazarus was dead several days before going to him (Jn 11) in order to remove our sense of emergency and fear of physical vulnerability. Jesus forgave the sins of the paralyzed man and only afterward healed him, in order to demonstrate His authority to forgive (Mk 5:20ff.). Finally, Jesus' teaching in the Sermon on the Mount summarizes this all:

"But seek first the kingdom of God and His righteousness, and all these things will be added to you" (Mt 6:33; see also 1Co 1:18–31).

• •

Q 16:21–22 Why was Peter so upset about Jesus' proclamation?

First, it is possible that Peter is simply thinking the way anyone would: important and wonderful people should be protected from suffering and provided with comfort and luxury—just as we have seen through history and even in our day. Second, it is also possible that Peter's idea of the "Messiah" was the same as most other Jews. Thinking materially, the Jews were (and some still are) looking for a "Messiah" who would be a warrior like David and would re-establish Israel to the power, wealth, authority, and control of Solomon's time. As Paul argues in 1Co 1:18ff., kings and gods don't do the suffering; they inflict the suffering upon others. Third, life in the midst of death, love of enemies, and rising from the dead were (and still are) such foreign ideas, almost never experienced, that we can understand why virtually no one believed that Jesus would really rise from the dead (Lk 24:1–8, 21; Mk 16:14; Jn 20:15).

• •

Q 16:23 Was Satan in Peter in this verse?

Since Jesus turned to Peter and said, "Get behind me, Satan," this must be the case. Another possibility is that Jesus is addressing the words/thoughts of Satan that anyone might think or say without being possessed by the devil. What matters most is that the severity of Jesus' response reveals the severity of this error of human thinking, which Jesus goes on to address in 16:24–28. In a fallen world, nothing good comes easy, and love for others is the most difficult of all because it requires self-denial and faith in God. Paul (Col 3:1ff.), Peter (1Pt 1:3–9), and James (1:2ff.) all speak to the need for reversing our natural thoughts to recognize that "whoever saves his life will lose it and whoever loses his life for Jesus' sake will find it" (v. 25).

• •

Q 16:27 How can this verse be understood so as to avoid teaching works-righteousness?

The Bible is full of imperatives (commands) that reveal God's will for us and conditional statements that describe who will be saved or condemned. Rm 12 contains forty-six imperative statements in twenty-one verses. Rm 10 says that if we believe with our heart and confess with our mouth, we will be saved. James even argues that it is our works that prove our faith and the righteousness that flows necessarily from faith. The real question is how to become such a person. Here the biblical text is absolutely consistent and relentless in explaining that we cannot make ourselves into such people, even as we cannot make ourselves a person in the first place. It is the Word that works faith and produces the fruits of faith (Jn 6:63; 15:1ff.; Rm 10:17). It is God Himself who regenerates us by His Word and makes us His own children who do His will (Jn 1:12–13; 3:1–6; 1Jn 3–5; Ti 3:4–6).

Q **16:28 What is meant by "taste death," because surely no one from that day is still alive? Does that mean that the Son of Man has already come in His kingdom?**

First, let's define life and death. Life has to do with experiencing relationships by the power/presence of God. God formed Adam out of the dust of the ground, but he didn't live until God breathed into him the breath (Spirit) of life. God told Adam that in the day he disobeyed/ate the forbidden fruit he would surely die, yet Adam did not collapse when he ate the fruit. What Adam did experience immediately was the loss of his relationship with God and with Eve. So, death is the cessation of relationships, only partially revealed in the cessation of physical function. Many people who are "alive" physically are more dead than any corpse because they are isolated by selfishness and thus opposed to all others and to love. So, when Jesus says that those who believe in Him will never taste or see or experience death, He means that such people will never know what it is to be condemned to isolation from God and others. Jesus has saved everyone from the necessity of experiencing such death by enduring the condemnation of eternal isolation during His crucifixion—so He cried out, "My God, My God, why have You forsaken Me?" (Mt 27:46; Mk 15:34).

Q **17:1–13 Why does the transfiguration happen; what is the significance?**

This event took place just before Palm Sunday and Holy Week. Like Jesus' Baptism, this occasion has to do with God revealing and confirming the truth about His Son. Jesus' Baptism marks the beginning of His public ministry, includes the voice of the Father saying, "This is My beloved Son, with whom I am well pleased," and is immediately followed by a very serious trial in the desert. Jesus' transfiguration marks the end of His public ministry, also includes the approving voice of the Father, and is followed by the most serious trial of all, Jesus' suffering and death. Like the voice of the Father, Moses and Elijah are also there to confirm the identity of Jesus and the fact that He is fulfilling all that the Law and the prophets have written (more on this below). I suspect that this reconfirmation of Jesus' divine nature is especially important because the disciples will be sorely tempted to give up hope during Jesus' arrest, trial, suffering, and death.

Q **17:1 Why did Jesus only take three disciples with Him?**

I know of no place where the Bible provides a direct answer to this question. Paul mentions Peter, James, and John as "pillars" of the Church (Gal 2:9), and the Old Testament is full of examples of layers and subdivisions for the sake of good governance (Ex 18:21–25; Nu 31:48; Dt 16:18). The notion of these three apostles being pillars of the

Church is curious given the differing life spans of these men. James was executed by Herod relatively soon after Jesus' ascension. Peter was executed in Rome around AD 67. John lived to the end of the first century. So, perhaps Jesus chose these three to bear witness to extraordinary revelation from Jesus, to lead the group of apostles, to serve as pillars of the Church, and to represent the various lives, characteristics, and life spans of all the faithful people who would follow.

Q **17:3 Is Moses and Elijah's importance in the Old Testament the reason why they appeared with Jesus?**

Yes. God gave the Ten Commandments through Moses (Jn 1:17; 7:19) and Elijah was chief among all the prophets (Mal 4:5; Mt 11:14). Moses and Elijah appear with Jesus because He is about to finish His work of fulfilling all that the Law demands and all that God promised through the prophets. Interestingly, Moses and Elijah appear together again in Rv 11:3–6. Here they are described as olive trees. As olive oil was burned in lamps to make light, so also Moses and Elijah (the Law and Prophets) provided the light of God's Word. They are not mentioned by name but according to significant events in their history (Moses and the plagues, Elijah preventing the rain).

Q **17:11–12 What does Jesus mean by "Elijah does come, and he will restore all things"? Did the disciples think that John the Baptist was Elijah?**

I suspect that John was, in effect, Elijah and restored "all things" in two ways. First, John promoted the restoration of godly thinking inasmuch as he "will turn many of the children of Israel to the Lord their God, and he will go before Him in the spirit and power of Elijah, to turn the hearts of the fathers to the children, and the disobedient to the wisdom of the just, to make ready for the Lord a people prepared" (Lk 1:16–17). Second, yet related, John humbled the proud, comforted the lowly, and exposed the crooked ways of deceit with the proclamation of truth (Lk 3:3–18). The intense response of John to the hypocrites and people in Mt 3 and Lk 3 bears real similarities with Elijah's challenge to the prophets of Baal (1Ki 18:17–40).

Q **17:12 How does John the Baptist tie into the rejection of Elijah?**

Perhaps this answer can be found by examining comparable moments of rejection in the lives of the two prophets. In 1Ki 19:14, Elijah complains desperately, "I have been very jealous for the LORD, the God of hosts. For the people of Israel have forsaken Your covenant, thrown down Your altars, and killed Your prophets with the sword, and I, even I only, am left, and they seek my life, to take it away." Similarly, John sounds disappointed and disillusioned as he awaits his own beheading in Herod's prison and sends disciples to ask Jesus, "Are You the one who is to come, or shall we look for another?" (Lk 7:18–35).

• • • • • • • • • • • • • • • • • •

Q 17:20–21 **What does Jesus imply when He talks about having faith as small as a mustard seed and being able to move a mountain with that faith? If I have faith, why can't I move mountains?**

If you have faith, why would you want to move a mountain? Or does Jesus mean by "moving mountains" that faith makes a person able to overcome seemingly insurmountable challenges? Faithful interpretation begins by considering language in its most simple sense. If Jesus says a person with faith as small as a mustard seed can move mountains, this must be true. If we cannot move mountains, then our faith must be smaller than that. Add to this simple understanding the context of Jesus' lament over the disciples' "little faith" and the disciples' question about why they were unable to cast out a demon. Is it possible that the nature of faith rather than quantity of faith is the issue? If we define *faith* (or belief or trust; these are all translations of the same Greek word, *pistis*) as dependence, either actual or contended, then we might see the reason for the disciples' failure. If we would contend that faith is personal, having to do with our own ego and abilities, then we have excluded God to that extent and confined our potential by our own limitations.

Jesus is the truth and depended completely and absolutely on God, thus for Him nothing was impossible. Paul wrote that God has assigned to each one of us a measure of faith (Rm 12:3), so quantity is not a concern. What we can and must be concerned with is honesty about our complete and absolute dependence on God. God's truth and grace work honesty in us so that His Spirit might move us to serve Him in moving others toward genuine faith, which is more difficult than moving mountains—some might even say impossible, but not for God!

• • • • • • • • • • • • • • • • • •

Q 17:14–21 **Why, if the Bible makes so many references to demons, does the Church make no mention?**

The answer to this question depends on what is meant by "Church." The Roman Catholic Church has had a lot to say about demons and demon possession since ancient times and is still very active in validating and assisting people with recovery from demon possession. We hear little about demon possession today for a variety of reasons. First, modernism has rejected any idea of supernatural forces that cannot be explained or controlled by science, thus eliminating any recognition of demonic activity. Second, modern medicine has discovered physiological causes for some ailments that were thought to be demon possession in times past. Third, it is possible that the devil has learned that subtle activity in the lives of "normal" people is much more effective in promoting unbelief than extraordinary and shocking interference by way of possession. What is most important to remember is that the devil and demons are predators looking for empty souls to tempt or possess (Mt 12:43–45; 1Pt 5:8). Remaining in the Word daily keeps our body, the temple of the Holy Spirit, full of that Spirit and thus impenetrable to the devil (1Co 6:19).

- -

Q 17:24–27 Why does Jesus have Peter catch a fish to get money to pay the temple tax? Is Jesus just showing that it's a good thing to pay taxes? How are they sure that first fish will have a coin in it?

We know that God wants us to pay everyone what we ought: honor, respect, taxes, and the like (Rm 13:1–8). Here, as in many places, Jesus first reveals the truth, then deals with the fallen world as it is. The truth is Jesus owes no one anything, and all the taxes and collectors and rulers for whom they collect all belong to Jesus and owe Him their very lives. But being God indeed and a true King means serving, not being served, so Jesus provides Peter with a means of paying the tax. What about the peculiar means, in the mouth of a fish? Perhaps Jesus is making a couple of points by providing for the tax in this way. First, His knowledge of this fish with the coin and the fact that it will be the first to bite Peter's hook just emphasizes the fact that Jesus, as God, owes no one anything. Second, God provided Peter with a living by way of the fish that Peter caught and ate/sold. So, in reality, the means of paying what Peter owes has always been in

the mouth of the fish. See Mt 22:15–22 for a parallel example of Jesus dealing with truth and ideals while supporting the legal system at work in a fallen world.

- -

Q 18:3 Why does Jesus want us to be like little children to enter heaven? What does the Bible say about children understanding their own faith?

The answer to this question might begin with consideration of adults in contrast to children. The exodus account reveals how none of the adults (except Caleb and Joshua) of Israel entered the Promised Land—only those who were children at the time of the Red Sea crossing (Heb 3:16–19). Paul contrasts the ego of adults, both Jews and Greeks, with those whom God saves by grace (1Co 1:18–31). Children, especially the younger, lack the developed sense of self that fallen, adult human nature has. Adults tend to be opinionated, contrary, suspicious, and judgmental of others, yet self-righteous and self-indulgent. Adults are dishonest with themselves and others about the truth of their condition and their utter dependence upon God and others (consider the description, "a self-made man"). Children, immature and undeveloped according to their fallen human nature, especially their minds, simply are dependent with no contentions to the contrary (though they are lurking and will come all too soon). Please note the other verses in this context where Jesus points to children as the model of faith (honesty about dependence): Mt 18:4, 6, 10, 14; 19:14.

Q **18:6–9 Could this section be taken to mean it is better to let go of people you feel are important to you but who could cause you to divert from your spiritual path?**

What you suggest is true, and Paul says exactly that in 1Co 7:12–15 and 15:33 (cf. Pr 12:26). However, in this passage Jesus is speaking about our own person and not that of others; see question on Mt 18:8.

Q **18:8 What does cutting off our hands and feet have to do with sin? Is this to be taken literally?**

If it is *your* hand, foot, or eye that causes you to sin, remove it far from you so that you do not forfeit your whole life for the sake of that part of you. Many suggest that Jesus is speaking figuratively, not literally, meaning that we should rid ourselves of those habits or temptations that lead to sin. But what if Jesus is being literal? Does our hand or foot or eye cause us to sin? Jesus said, "For from within, out of the heart of man, come evil thoughts, sexual immorality, theft, murder, adultery, coveting, wickedness, deceit, sensuality, envy, slander, pride, foolishness. All these evil things come from within, and they defile a person" (Mk 7:20–23; cf. Jer 17:9). So, the heart is the part we must cut out and cast away, yet this is not the muscle that pumps our blood, but the very essence of our fallen nature, which God promised to provide by way of transplant (Ezk 36:26–27; cf. Rm 6:12–14; Gal 5:24).

Aren't we supposed to forgive and forget?

Q **18:12–14 Who are the "lost sheep"?**

This is the all-important question for the text, for misidentifying the sheep means misapplying the text. This parable, like the parable of the lost sons (Lk 15:11–32), provides a surprising contrast between the temporarily and profoundly lost. Both parables begin with the one lost but then found who causes much rejoicing. The one lost but now found provides a contrast with the ninety-nine who are abandoned by the good shepherd or the older son who is "near to the house" (Lk 15:24), refusing to come in. Note the shocking nature of Jesus' question, "Who wouldn't leave the ninety-nine to search for the one?" In real life, no one would! But Jesus explains: the ninety-nine are those who "need no repentance" (Lk 15:7). This cannot refer to sinless people since there are none (Rm 3). Rather, Jesus is referring to those who contend for their own righteousness and in so doing reject God's grace and Savior (Lk 17:9–14; Rm 10:1–3). So, the lost are found, and those who consider themselves to never have been lost are so very lost. Those with faith like a child, humble, honest, penitent sinners, will always see themselves as the "bad" character who ends up redeemed and reconciled. Those who are arrogant, self-righteous, and opposed to God see themselves as the "good" character and end up outside (Mt 7:21–23; 25:31–46).

● ●

Q 18:15–20 Is this how Jesus intends for us to deal with quarrels in the Church still today? What if you are in the wrong? Aren't we supposed to forgive and forget?

Yes, this is how Jesus intends for us to deal with every trouble in every setting. This text tells us what to do if another person is wrong or does wrong. In Mt 5:23–26 and 18:6–9, Jesus tells us what to do if I am the one who is wrong. Together, these passages provide a universal remedy; everyone works together to make sure that wrongdoing does not persist but is repented of and forgiveness confirmed. Yes, we are supposed to forgive and forget, for this is how God deals with us for Jesus' sake (Pss 25:7; 79:8; 103:12). However, forgiveness and forgetfulness is for the penitent, not the impenitent. Gracious treatment of those who despise truth and mercy only feeds their contempt for God, neighbor, truth, and mercy. God calls us to treat the impenitent as a "Gentile or tax collector," that is, to have nothing to do with them so they might experience the isolation of judgment while there is still time to repent.

● ●

Q 18:18 Can you explain the full impact and authority this verse gives?

There are at least two essential elements for understanding Jesus' intent here. First, we are always acting as God's agents or means, never on our own authority (2Co 5:20). Second, the language here makes it clear that we are only "confirming" or mak-

ing clear to a person the situation that already exists. Jesus did not say, "*if* you forgive, *then* they are forgiven . . . *if* you retain, *then* they are retained" as if our actions determined the sinner's condition before God. Rather Jesus said, "Whatever you bind on earth *has been bound* in heaven and whatever you loose on earth *has been loosed* in heaven" (author's translation). In both cases, the verbs (to bind or to loose) are in the perfect tense and passive voice, emphasizing the fact that this action has already taken place with enduring consequences—this is the very truth that we are responsible to ascertain with regard to an individual and to confirm to that individual. Be careful to remember that in either case, whether loosing (confirming forgiveness) or binding (confirming that impenitence means the rejection of grace already extended), all is done for the benefit of the individual (see the example in 1Co 5:1–5 and 2Co 2:6–11).

● ●

Q 18:19 What happens when two or three people pray together and don't get what they asked for? Does that mean they are doing something wrong or do not have faith?

The key is in the next verse, "For where two or three are gathered in My name, there am I among them." This is the same as Jn 14:14: "If you ask Me anything in My name, I will do it." The phrase "in My name" is not a magic incantation that we can add to the end of any request, demanding God to grant it, like a genie in a bottle. The Word of God regenerates us (Ti 3:4–6), gives us the mind of Christ (Php 2:5), creates faith in us (Rm 10:17), and teaches us how and what to pray for (Mt 6:5–15; Jas 1:5–8, 4:3). God will grant whatever is asked in faith because faith acts and asks according to His will. You may also want to consider that these words about prayer fall within a discussion that is clearly focused on repentance and forgiveness, a prayer concern that God is exceedingly attentive to.

Q 18:19–20 Does that mean you have a better chance with God if you're not alone?

I suspect not since God pays close attention to the lonely and forsaken (Lk 7:12ff.; Pss 25:16; 68:5; Dt 10:18). The value of two or three gathered in the Word of God comes in the shared wisdom, insight, and correction (Pr 11:14; Gal 2:1–2). The more clearly we see the will of God in His Word, the more our prayers will be composed according to His will and answered with certainty.

Q 18:22 Why is the number "seventy-seven"? Is "seventy-seven times" literal?

As discussed briefly in Mt 15:34 above, most numbers in the Bible have some significance, though we must be careful not to force unintended meanings upon them, as is the case with those who try to use biblical numbers and dates to calculate the end of the world (Ac 1:6–7). The number 7 seems to be related to the passage of time—seven days in a week. Ten has to do with the Law (as in the Ten Commandments). Therefore, 70 x 7 is Jesus' way of saying that we forgiveness is accomplished and ready to be confirmed no matter how many offenses are committed. Jesus does not mean to say that we should keep track of how many times we have forgiven someone—refusing to forgive after the 490th time. This idea is that forgiving someone so many times would allow for more than enough time to pass for us to forget how many times we had forgiven or been wronged.

Sound principles of interpretation require us to take language in its most simple, literal sense, unless something clear requires us to do otherwise. There is some disagreement over Jesus' response in v. 22; is it 70 or 77 or 70 x 7 (490)? Whichever way, to think that Jesus intends us to keep track of how many times we forgive someone and refuse after 70 or 77 or 490 is to miss the point. I believe the idea here is that the number of times is big enough that we lose interest in counting and instead concentrate on being faithful stewards of God's grace on behalf of penitent sinners, which is precisely the point of the parable Jesus tells in further response to Peter (Mt 18:23–35).

Q **19:3–12 My parents are divorced and my dad remarried. His new wife has been married and divorced four times. What does the Bible say about this? Why did Jesus have to discuss divorce?**

In this text, Jesus discusses divorce because the Pharisees asked if it was lawful for a man to divorce his wife for any reason. Notice that Jesus responds with the ideal—the relationship between man and woman that God created them to enjoy—then answers their question on that basis: "What therefore God has joined together, let not man separate." The Pharisees, wanting to justify themselves, tried to use Moses as an excuse (see 19:8–9 below). At this point, Jesus clarifies that it is the hardness of the human heart that is the real cause of divorce and that any man who divorces his wife, except for fornication, commits adultery. Hardness of heart is a very serious condition to be in (remember Pharaoh) and is the root of all kinds of wrongdoing, some of which cause divorce. Certainly no one has benefited from the four previous divorces of your father's wife. However, it is not the division of families that is the worst of the wrong, but the selfishness, carelessness, and hardness of heart that spread and cause even more harm. This is why Jesus has to address the problem of divorce.

Q **19:3–9 Is divorce a sin? Is it okay to remarry if you've been divorced?**

Yes, divorce is a sin, except in three cases: fornication, abuse, or abandonment. Paul discusses abandonment or abuse (which forces the victim to abandon the home) in 1Co 7. The term *fornication* (*porneia* in Greek) is a broad term encompassing every kind of sexually related activity that is contrary to, apart from, or detrimental to the single union of a man and woman in marriage. If someone is divorced because his or her spouse forced it for one of these three reasons, then that person is free to remarry—only he or she must be careful to seek a marriage that will last. "She is free to be married . . . only in the Lord" (1Co 7:39).

Q **19:8–9 Jesus replied, "Because of your hardness of heart Moses allowed you to divorce your wives, but from the beginning it was not so. . . . Whoever divorces his wife, except for sexual immorality, and marries another, commits adultery." What is sexual immorality? And what will happen to the divorced people?**

"Sexual immorality" is a broad term for the Greek *porneia* or "fornication." The term refers to everything that is not part of the natural physical intimacy between a husband and a wife with a view toward procreation. What happens to divorced people is no different than what happens to anyone else; it depends on repentance and faith. Repentance is the continually turning away from sin that God's Word and Spirit work in us. Faith is what keeps us connected with the grace of God that regenerates us.

Q **19:9 Jesus says the only reason for divorce is sexual immorality; does this mean it's wrong to divorce in situations of domestic abuse?**

Jesus does not address the issue of abuse here, perhaps because He wants to stay focused on the Pharisee's question or because abuse is a cause for criminal prosecution that would result in separation. In 1Co 7, Paul explains causes for divorce, and they include abuse.

Q **19:9 How is someone committing adultery if he or she marries someone who has been divorced?**

Remember that any physically intimate activity outside of the natural, healthy relationship between a husband and wife is forbidden. Therefore, if a person is divorced without biblical cause, he or she is committing adultery by pursuing a marriage with another.

Q **19:11–12 Why does Jesus say some can't marry because they "have been so from birth"? What does this mean?**

First of all, remember that man and woman were created for each other so that marriage is natural and the norm. Both Jesus and Paul refute and warn against the notions that remaining single is something we can simply choose and that it commends us to God (Mt 19:11; 1Co 7:1–4; 1Tm 4:3).

On the other hand, Jesus also says that some people are born with a physiology and/or disposition free from those passions that would require marriage. Jesus and Paul only recommend remaining single because of the perilous nature of the times and in order that one may be more easily focused on service to others.

Q **19:13–15 Little children are very highly valued in today's Church. Many opportunities to learn about God and Jesus are open to them. Why did the disciples rebuke them?**

(See discussion above at 18:3.) Children are valued by some churches today, but not all churches, as is clear from the number of congregations that fail to support—then close—their grade schools. The disciples rebuked the women who were bringing their children to Jesus for the same reason they rebuked blind Bartimaeus: a tragic inversion of what the Lord is interested in. In a fallen world, where dominion means taking your life from all the people you force to support you, lords have nothing to do with people who have nothing substantial to offer. In God's kingdom, dominion is real and means that the Lord supports all and gives everything, especially to those who are not able to provide for themselves (1Co 1:18–31).

• • • • • • • • • • • • • • • • • • • •

Q **19:16–30 Jesus says that it is as hard for a rich man to enter heaven as it is for a camel to go through the eye of a needle. Why?**

Jesus answered this question in 6:24: "No one can serve two masters, for either he will hate the one and love the other, or he will be devoted to the one and despise the other. You cannot serve God and money." Paul explains that "the love of money is a root of all kinds of evil" (1Tm 6:10). John warns us not to "love the world or the things in the world. If anyone loves the world, the love of the Father is not in him. For all that is in the world—the desires of the flesh and the desires of the eyes and pride of life—is not from the Father but is from the world. And the world is passing away along with its desires" (1Jn 2:15–17).

• • • • • • • • • • • • • • • • • • • •

Q **19:17 Why would Jesus say, "If you would enter life, keep the commandments"?**

Consider the question that Jesus is answering and the nature of the person who asked. This chapter begins with Pharisees testing Jesus with a question about divorce; now a man asks Jesus, "What good deed must I do to have eternal life?" In the parallel accounts in Mark (10:17–22) and Luke (10:25–29), the young man says, "What must I do *to inherit* eternal life?" (emphasis added). Luke's account reveals the most obvious reason for Jesus' response: "But he, desiring to justify himself, said to Jesus,

'And who is my neighbor?'" So, the fact is, if you do want to work your way to life eternal by justifying yourself, there is only one way to do so: you must keep the whole Law perfectly. If, on the other hand, we recognize that we cannot begin to keep the least requirement of the Law in the least way and that it is absurd and impossible to think we can make ourselves heirs of another person (let alone God), then our question is that of Paul, "Wretched man that I am! Who will deliver me from this body of death? Thanks be to God through Jesus Christ our Lord" (Rm 7:24–25).

• • • • • • • • • • • • • • • • • • • •

Q **19:21 How are we to survive if we sell all we have? What exactly is God pointing at?**

There are two parts to this answer. First, Jesus was exposing the truth to this young man. While he may have done very well at keeping the commandments he listed according to what he *didn't do*, he still failed to keep these commandments by what he *did do*—especially in terms of love for neighbor versus self (see the account in Lk 10:25–29). A different rich man, the one who never gave even a scrap from his table to Lazarus, might also have argued that he had not broken any commandments (Lk 16:19–31). Second, is it possible to sell everything one has and follow Jesus and not survive? Consider Israel during the exodus and wilderness wandering (water, the manna, then meat—then a land with homes, vineyards, olive groves, and winepresses all prepared for them, which they refused to enter and possess); Elijah during the famine (1Ki 17); or David and his men during Saul's pursuit of them (1Sm 25). When Jesus sent His twelve apostles to extend His kingdom to others, He commanded them not to take anything with them except what they were wearing, "for the laborer deserves his food" (Mt 10:5–10). The first Christians clearly followed Jesus' teaching by selling their possessions, yet they did not sell everything, nor were they obligated to (Ac 4:32–5:11).

● ● ● ● ● ● ● ● ● ● ● ● ● ● ● ● ● ● ●

Q **19:24 What is the point of this verse?**

The apostles understood Jesus' point right away and said, "[W]ho then can be saved?" (v. 25). Jesus affirms their understanding by saying, "[W]ith men this is impossible." It is, in fact, impossible for us to save ourselves; this is the point of the term *save*. This also explains the necessity of God becoming man and taking our place under the Law—to do what it requires actively in obedience to God and love of neighbor and to suffer all that the Law threatens for those who fail. Remember that Jesus said you "cannot serve God and money" (Mt 6:24).

● ● ● ● ● ● ● ● ● ● ● ● ● ● ● ● ● ● ●

Q **20:1–16 Because the first set of workers worked longer, the parable seems unfair. What is the point of the parable?**

Many, if not all, of the parables tend to turn our thinking "right side up." Remember the parables of the lost? Those who are lost become found, and those who claim they are not lost remain lost forever. In the case of the vineyard workers, there is the main point then several related subpoints. The main point is that we ought never criticize or begrudge God's graciousness. The religious leaders of Israel wanted to claim God's favor on the basis of physical descent and despised everyone else. Jonah was the personification of Israel and exposed this attitude as he complained bitterly about God showing mercy to the people of Nineveh. In this parable, the master shows mercy by giving idle men good work to do with fair pay; why should they complain when that same gracious disposition benefits others? A second, related point has to do with our view of work or service. Why do we tend to share the idea of these men that it is better to stand around idle all day rather than working? Consider the work itself: beautiful weather, outdoors, sunshine, grapevines, all the grapes you want to eat, companionship while you work, conversation, physical exercise, and at the end of a great day, money with which the worker might buy the finished product of his labor, wine (and a little bread and cheese?). Remember that before the fall, God put Adam in the Garden of Eden to tend and keep it. It is a lie of the devil, world, and our fallen human nature that working is bad but being served while you do nothing is good. Thank God for being gracious, restoring our thinking, and for having prepared good work for us by which we might realize the fullness of life (Eph 2:10).

Q 20:16 How are we to understand this?

This has to do with the proud being brought down and the lowly being raised up (1Sm 2:1–10; Lk 1:46–55; 3:5). One of the features of God's perfect love is His justice. We have a sense of love and fairness as well. In the end, God will provide equity for everyone, as He demonstrates in the case of Lazarus and the rich man (Lk 16:19–31). With some exceptions (Lk 14:7–11), people are first because they make themselves so at the expense of or as a burden to those who become last. It is fundamentally unfair for gifted people to use their gifts selfishly, to take advantage of the less gifted, in order to amass riches and power for their own selfish appetites. It is fundamentally unfair for those who bear the burdens of labor to be robbed of fair compensation for their labor and the liberty to enjoy that compensation (Jer 22:13ff.; Jas 5:4). Therefore, God will provide equity in eternity for the inequities suffered in time.

Q 20:21 How is it this mother was so bold as to ask Jesus to grant her sons a place at His right and left hands?

Many people suffer from relentless ambition, including some mothers on behalf of their sons. The history of Joseph Kennedy (father of John F. Kennedy) and his family provides a powerful and tragic example. In this passage, we see a mother wanting a glorious and powerful position for her sons, not realizing or considering the infinite requirements of that place—requirements only the Son of God, crucified and risen, could fulfill. Read Lk 14 for more on the subject of self-seeking.

Q 21:7 How could Jesus ride on a donkey and a colt at the same time? What is the significance of the coats being laid on the ground?

The only explanation I can see is suggested by the quotation from Zec 9:9 where "colt" is a further description of the donkey upon which Jesus would sit (cf. Jn 12:15). Laying of coats upon Jesus' path seems to be a custom of respect from ancient times. I see further significance between the coats and the palm branches that people laid upon the ground before Jesus. After Adam and Eve disobeyed God, they hid from God and from each other, in part, by making coverings of fig leaves (Gn 3:7). Later, God made coverings for Adam and Eve from animal skins, indicating the necessity of the death of innocent life in order to cover their shame (3:21). When the Lamb of God that bore away the sin of the world entered Jerusalem to complete that work, the people laid before Jesus palm branches and their cloaks. This activity of the people reminds us that hiding behind coverings of fig leaves as Adam and Eve did or behind coverings of our design are no longer necessary since the Lamb of God has come to take away the sins of the world.

How can Jesus be angry?

Q **21:18–19 Why did Jesus curse the fig tree? If anger is a sin, how can Jesus be angry?**

Anger is not necessarily a sin (Ps 4:4). God is angry often in biblical texts and rightly so, for if there was not just cause, God would not be angry. The people, especially religious leaders, have given Jesus cause to be angry and frustrated for three and a half years. During this week, all of that conflict is coming to a head that will end with Jesus' arrest, trial, crucifixion, and (happily for all) resurrection. The fig tree, like all of creation, will suffer as a consequence and illustration of the failure of man (Rm 8:19–23). Jesus, like the master in the parable of the fig tree, has been coming to His people for three years looking for the fruits of faith (for any little shred of evidence of faith; Lk 13:6–9). Jesus also plainly warned people about the peril of their faithlessness (fruitlessness; Mt 23:37–39). So, as the people of Israel have been without the fruits of faith that were due, Jesus curses a fig tree as a warning to them before it is too late. The other text that helps make sense of Jesus cursing the fig tree is 2Tm 4:1–3: "I charge you in the presence of God and of Christ Jesus, who is to judge the living and the dead, and by His appearing and His kingdom: preach the word; be ready in season and out of season; reprove, rebuke, and exhort, with complete patience and teaching, . . . but having itching ears they will accumulate for themselves teachers to suit their own passions." With the advent of God's incarnation in Christ,

His redemption of all, and the New Testament came a new urgency and need for readiness. This urgency is increased by the rapidly declining condition of humanity (Rm 1:18–31) and because the devil, having been defeated by Jesus, has come down to earth to make war with the faithful (Rv 12).

Q **21:23–27 What were the Pharisees afraid of?**

The Pharisees were desperate for a means of rejecting Jesus. They could not deny that He was doing miraculous signs (Jn 11), and they could not defeat His teaching. They were grasping at straws by challenging His authority with a ridiculous question. Jesus, always the faithful teacher, exposed their error so they might repent, though they refuse. The Pharisees were powerful and numerous, but their power depended on the support of the people (in contrast to the political/military power of the Romans and the religious authority of the Sadducees). John also exposed the hypocrisy and wicked nature of the Pharisees (Mt 3), but they could do nothing about it because of the large crowds of people that came out to John and revered him *highly* as a prophet (Lk 3). Jesus often asked hypocrites questions that would force them to honesty (Mt 12:1–12; Mk 10:17–18). If they claimed disregard for John because he was not from

God, the people would revolt. If they admitted that John was from God, why didn't they believe John's witness to Jesus? Sadly, rather than admit the truth and benefit, the Pharisees refused to answer. Contrast a wicked hatred of the light of truth (Jn 3:18ff.) with the practice of the faithful walking in the light constantly (1Jn 1:7; Ps 119:105; Col 3:16).

Q 21:25 Would this be a good verse to use in ministering to those who believe in adult Baptism, such as the Anabaptists?

I doubt this passage would be much help with those who claim that Baptism is not effective unless a person is old enough to understand what he or she is doing and makes the decision to do so. In such conversations and in their writings, Anabaptist claim that only adults were baptized by Jesus. The real issue with Anabaptists is not primarily about Baptism but about how we are saved. If God, indeed, does the saving, then His illustration of children as the model makes sense because they are less able or interested in fighting off God's activity on their behalf. However, if God has only provided the opportunity to be saved and our salvation depends on our own decision, understanding, commitment, and understanding, then an adult would be more able to try, but the whole approach must fail (Gal 3).

Q 21:27 Why wouldn't Jesus tell them under what authority He was able to do these things?

Jesus has already warned us in the Sermon on the Mount not to cast our pearls before swine or give what is holy to the dogs (Mt 7:6). Similarly, Jesus refused to answer the questions of those who had no interest in the truth (here and Mt 26:63; Mk 14:61). In fact, God finally refused to say anything at all to the Israelites of the Old Testament because they refused to listen (1Sm 28:6 and the absence of revelation between Malachi [400 BC] and John).

Q 21:28–32 Is either son correct? Was Jesus telling the disciples they were wrong when they guessed the first son?

Once again, Jesus is exposing the truth in contrast to lies. The religious leaders made an outward show of obedience to God but disobeyed and rebelled against Him with the rest of their lives (Mt 15:8); they represent the son who immediately said he would go but did not. The religious leaders also despised the common people and especially foreigners because they had not obeyed God since the beginning, yet these people have since repented (Lk 3:10–14; cf. the parable of the lost sons in Lk 15, especially vv. 31–32).

Q 21:42 What does Jesus mean when He says, "The stone that the builders rejected has become the cornerstone?"

Here, again, Jesus points out absolute opposites. If the religious leaders were builders, a stone would have to be quite worthless before it was rejected. Yet Jesus, whom they steadfastly rejected, was the best and most important of all stones; Jesus is the cornerstone who oriented the rest of the building to perfection (Eph 2:20–22).

Q 22:1–14 This is a confusing parable. What is the significance?

This parable has an interesting parallel in Lk 14. The main point of both parables is the same: always come when God calls! Now we can look at some of the particular features that support that point. First, the king is having a celebration and graciously invites everyone to come, just as Jesus has redeemed everyone and provided a place for them in the kingdom of God. Second, people who are full of themselves, committed to the things of this world and deceived by the devil, ignore, make light of, make excuses to, and even mistreat and murder the messengers that bring invitation, just as people have treated the prophets, apostles, servants of God, and most of all, His Word. Third, the king is determined that the feast will fulfill its purpose, so he sends his servants to those who are humble, poor in the things of this world, and too much in need of necessities to be deceived by the devil, just as Jesus connected with the poor, sick, rejected (tax collectors and "sinners"), and foreigners who knew well their need of Him. Fourth, in this account the king noticed a man who was there without a wedding garment (v. 12). The wedding garment is analogous to the righteousness and grace of Christ, which forgives our sin (removes our filthy garments) and clothes us with Christ (Gal 3:27). Note carefully that the king doesn't begin with judgment but with a question: "Friend, how did you get in here without a wedding garment?" The man, like the enemies of Jesus, could not speak (he had no defense) and would not speak (too proud to repent and beg for a wedding garment). We cannot come before God on the basis of our own life and works (Is 64:6). The religious leaders tried to assert their own righteousness before Jesus but were always left exposed in shame and refusing to speak (unable to withstand the truth, unwilling to submit to it in humility; cf. Mt 21:26–27). Fifth, the man is bound and cast into outer darkness. This is hell, where the life-giving light of God does not shine. This is "outer," where there are no relationships that compose life. There is weeping and gnashing of teeth in the utter absence of the fullness of life that God intended us to know but which such people steadfastly refused. Finally, the expression "many are called, but few are chosen" reflects two significant truths. First, "many" refers to the fact that God desires all men to be saved and come to the knowledge of the truth (1Tm 2:4) and that God acted upon that desire by redeeming all people in the life of His Son (Jn 3:16). Second, "chosen" refers to the fact that God chooses us; we do not choose Him (Jn 15:16, 19).

● ● ● ● ● ● ● ● ● ● ● ● ● ● ● ● ● ● ● ●

Q 22:15–17 If the Pharisees were the leaders of the church, how did the church get so corrupted? Why didn't the Pharisees understand?

The Pharisees did not want to understand (Jn 9:40–41; 11:45–57). This is true of all fallen human nature (1Co 2:14; Rm 7) but is eternally perilous in those who have no regenerate soul (Lk 7:30ff.; Jn 1:11–13). This is why the conversion of anyone is miraculous (Mt 19:26) and the conversion of dire opponents of God even more remarkable (Ac 9). The religious leaders of Jesus' time had discovered the power and wealth of holding people in their guilt rather than conveying to them the truth and grace of God (Mt 23:2–4). The higher a person rises in human institutions, the more pressure the devil, world, and fallen human nature exert to corrupt that person.

● ● ● ● ● ● ● ● ● ● ● ● ● ● ● ● ● ● ● ●

Q 22:21 How is it decided what is Caesar's and what is God's?

In the end, all things belong to God, as He is the Creator and Source of all things (1Co 4:7). We have many ways of demonstrating ownership or belonging, from birth certificates to registrations to possessions within our home (which has its own deed). In this case, the image of Caesar was on the coin, just as our currency technically

belongs to the U.S. government. Yet, if all things belong to God, then our concern is not with ownership but with stewardship. God urges and expects us to give everyone around us their due (Rm 13), but what inspires and determines all our stewardship best is love (Rm 13:8).

● ● ● ● ● ● ● ● ● ● ● ● ● ● ● ● ● ● ● ●

Q 22:15–22 It appears that this section talks about the idolatry of Caesar's picture on the coin. Is our U.S. currency wrong to depict the past presidents?

The text does not directly speak of the idolatry of Caesar's picture, but Jesus does expose the crass idolatry and hypocrisy of the religious leaders. In the first place, they have no real question; they are not asking Jesus how to rightly live before God and within our civilization. Jesus has been teaching that true riches are found in God's abundant care for us and in our care for others (Lk 16:11; Mt:39; 19:29). In the second place, it is the religious leaders' love of money and the power it allows them to pretend that not only makes them idolize money but also makes them determined to justify their wickedness.

● ● ● ● ● ● ● ● ● ● ● ● ● ● ● ● ● ● ● ●

Q 22:15 Were there any Pharisees who followed Jesus?

Yes, Nicodemus followed Jesus (Jn 19:39). Joseph of Arimathea may have been a Pharisee, but the text does not say (Jn 19:38). After Jesus' ascension, other Pharisees believed that Jesus was the Christ, the

Son of God, but still rejected salvation by grace, insisting that we are saved by keeping the Law of Moses (Ac 15:5ff.).

• •

Q 22:29–30 Will we still be husbands, wives, dads, moms, sons, and daughters in heaven? Will we know one another and be in relationships with one another? Is Jesus saying that people in heaven will not remember people who were important in their life?

This text does not answer those questions, and it is not helpful to speculate. The account (not parable) of Lazarus and the rich man certainly suggests that we know one another and are in relationships (Lk 16:19–31). John writes that while we don't know much about our life after death, we know that we will be like the resurrected Jesus, who had distinguishing marks and who ate and drank (1Jn 3:2; Lk 24:36–43)

• •

Q 22:32 Is this verse saying that God is not God for everyone?

Jesus provides a particular response to the Sadducees' contention that there is no resurrection of the dead. Jesus appeals to text, history, and people that the Sadducees are absolutely committed to. So, what point is Jesus proving when He refers to God's words (actually, it was the pre-incarnate Jesus who spoke to Moses from the burning bush!), saying He is the God of Abraham, Isaac, and Jacob? Notice that all three of these

men were dead and buried at this time. Yet, when Abraham was too old to have a son by Sarah, God gave him Isaac. God did about the same thing with Isaac (Gn 25:21). Yet again, Jacob had trouble conceiving by Rachel (Gn 30:1–2). How else can you prove to someone that God provides life after death than to extend a person's life through his or her children, children that the couple found it impossible to conceive? God is for everyone and has provided eternal life for all in Christ. The evidence for that eternal life is provided in particular examples in history: the dead that Jesus raised, Jesus' resurrection itself, and God's gift of children.

• •

Q 22:34–40 Why is one commandment greater or more important than the rest of the Commandments?

There might be two reasons for wondering this. A hypocrite or one trying to justify himself or herself might want to argue that he or she has kept the most important commandments and that failing to keep the others shouldn't matter. James rejects this thinking (Jas 2:10), and Jesus exposed that the religious leaders had it backwards (Mt 23:23–24). On the other hand, because some commandments include others, it is possible to see the Law as interrelated by cause and effect. Jesus provided a simpler and more comprehensive version of the Ten Commandments: love God above all and neighbor as self. Yet, no one can truly love his neighbor if he does not love God.

In other words, love of God is the most important of all commandments because all the rest flow from it.

● ● ● ● ● ● ● ● ● ● ● ● ● ● ● ● ● ● ●

Q **22:36 How was the question "Which is the great commandment in the Law?" a test for Jesus?**

The religious leaders spent their time trying to justify themselves and, in so doing, devoted much time and effort to classifying the Law in ways that would allow them to claim innocence (Mt 15:1–9). Their hope was that Jesus would choose some part of the Law that they could prove was not as important as another part. This is the same approach they used with Jesus regarding paying taxes (Mt 22:17ff.) and what to do with a woman caught in adultery (Jn 8:3ff.).

● ● ● ● ● ● ● ● ● ● ● ● ● ● ● ● ● ● ●

Q **22:39 Jesus said, "You shall love your neighbor as yourself." Does this mean that if you don't respect yourself or love yourself, you don't love your neighbor? And if so, are you following the commandment?**

God's wisdom and will, like this commandment, always have in view the very best experience and life for all. Thus, the commandment is based on a healthy concern for one's own well-being. Perhaps part of the wisdom of this commandment is that love and respect for others are the makings of healthy love and respect for self? We can have ideals and know what is healthy for us because we are created by God with design and purpose that are intended to endure.

This means that love for others is good for them and us and is good in the moment and forever. Apparent conflict between our good and that of others or between what we want now versus eternally reveals mistaken thinking. It does not reveal opposition in relationships or between the present and future.

● ● ● ● ● ● ● ● ● ● ● ● ● ● ● ● ● ● ●

Q **22:41–46 Is Jesus saying that He is not of the line of David? What was the point of Jesus asking the Pharisees who the Christ was?**

The conflict between Jesus and the religious leaders is coming to a climax during the days after Palm Sunday. As you may have noticed, for more than three years the religious leaders have been asking Jesus questions, not because they seek help but because they want to justify the only real help there is. This text marks a turning point between Jesus' patient responses to the hard of heart and the unleashing of His just judgment against them in the next chapter. To turn this corner Jesus adopts the approach of His opponents: He asks two questions that seem impossible to answer on the basis of the Old Testament. If the Messiah or Christ is to be David's son, how can David call Him "Lord?" Their inability to answer means that either (a) they don't want to answer because it would mean admitting that Jesus IS exactly who He claims to be and they should worship rather than oppose Him, or (b) they really don't know the Scriptures nor the meaning of all the prophecies concerning the Savior. For us, the answer is simple: the Messiah or Christ is both true man and true God, as Paul says plainly in Rm 1:3–4.

• • • • • • • • • • • • • • • • • • • •

Q **22:43 Is the Pharisee's expectation that the Christ would be the Son of David an indication that they wanted the Messiah to be an earthly king?**

Certainly their focus on the Davidic prophecies and apparent ignorance of the divine nature of the Christ suggests their desire for an earthly king. If the Christ is true God, then they would have to repent of their own ideas for wealth and power in submission to Him. However, if the Christ were only another king in the line of David, they had reason to hope that they could manipulate Him for their own purposes, which is why Israel wanted a king in the first place (1Sm 8:5).

• • • • • • • • • • • • • • • • • • • •

Q **22:44 What does this verse mean?**

This is a quotation of Ps 110:1. David is reporting these words from God the Father to God the Son. I suspect David calls God the Father "the" Lord for His headship in the Trinity but includes the Son and Holy Spirit in that term and calls the Christ and Savior "my" Lord because Jesus is the personal means by which God reveals Himself and conveys His blessings to us (Jn 1:17–18). These words of the Father to the Son reflect the Father's recognition and acceptance of the Son's redeeming work for the life of the

world and His victory over all opposition. Paul explains this well in Php 2:5–11 (cf. Ps 2 and Rv 12:5).

• • • • • • • • • • • • • • • • • • • •

Q **23:1–36 What is the point of the seven woes parable?**

Rather than a parable, which makes a comparison between like things, Jesus is speaking clearly about the people and things themselves. Parables are used in mixed audiences, where the humble and needy recognize themselves as such and grasp the grace of God conveyed in the parable (the lost sheep now found, the younger son welcomed home; Lk 15). Proud, contradictory, and self-righteous hypocrites never could see the grace of God extended to them. On this occasion, the audience consists of these people alone and time is running out, so Jesus speaks in plain language about their dire need to repent—now.

• • • • • • • • • • • • • • • • • • • •

Q **23:2 Jesus says that the Pharisees "sit on Moses' seat," yet He goes on to say that what they teach is wrong. What does Jesus mean when He says this?**

"Moses' seat" refers to his authority and responsibility as one who communicates God's Word to the people. Remember that people at this time did not have access to the Scriptures except as communicated to them by the religious leaders. So, inasmuch as they would read and/or explain the Old Testament to the people, they should listen, but they ought not to act like these leaders.

Q 23:9–10 If Jesus said we aren't allowed to call anyone else "father" and "instructor" other than God, are we sinning when we use these words?

The short answer is "yes." Jesus said not to do this, and we do, so that is disobedience or sin. The longer answer begins with recognizing a general disregard among people who claim to be Christian for the simple teaching and prohibitions of Jesus. For example, Jesus said that "one's life does not consist in the abundance of his possessions" (Lk 12:15), yet many Christians possess material things in abundance. Jesus said of the Lord's Supper, "Do this often." Paul taught that the Lord's Supper is the central reason for gathering in public as the Body of Christ, and the Lutheran Confessions state that we should celebrate the Sacrament every Sunday, yet most congregations offer the Lord's Supper every other Sunday. Finally, Jesus said, "If you abide in My Word, you are truly My disciples" (Jn 8:31), yet few religious leaders or Christians actually do this. And there are significant consequences for all this disregard of Jesus' teaching. In the case of this text, dealing with calling someone "father" or "instructor," Jesus' point is that we not idolize someone or put them in the place of God, as is often the case. Note Jesus' warning about loving father or mother, son or daughter more than Him (Mt 10:37; even more powerfully in Lk 14:26). Our biological fathers and earthly teachers rightly bear those titles only inasmuch as they are acting on God's behalf to raise us in His nurture and admonition, grace and truth.

Q 23:25–26 Jesus says the Pharisees should clean the inside of the cup then the outside. Does He mean that we should cleanse our souls and minds first, then deal with the other parts?

This parallels His teaching about hand, foot, or eye causing us to sin (see answer for Mt 18:8–9). Jesus addresses the root of the problem in two ways. First, which is more important to our health: a cup that looks clean on the outside but is dirty inside or a cup that is clean on the inside but not so good looking on the outside? Jesus is always interested in the essence of things rather than appearances (Jn 7:24). Second, while this dynamic is not evident physically, Jesus describes the relationship of cause and effect. He says that if you take care of cleaning the inside of the cup, the outside will get cleansed as well. Jesus' example of trees and plants makes this relationship more obvious (see Mt 7:17–18).

Q 24:1–51 Did time pass in between the parables that Jesus taught in this chapter, or did He tell them all in one sitting?

It is impossible to answer this question with certainty. However, with the exception of v. 3 ("As He sat on the Mount of Olives"), there is no language that indicates any break or change of time.

● ● ● ● ● ● ● ● ● ● ● ● ● ● ● ● ● ● ● ●

Q **24:2 How does Jesus know that the temple is going to be destroyed? What does He mean by, "Truly, I say to you, there will not be left here one stone upon another stone that will not be thrown down"?**

He knows this because He is true God and knows all things, the only exception being the exact time of the end (Mt 24:36).

When the Roman army came, less than forty years after Jesus said this (AD 70), they destroyed Jerusalem. The temple was torn apart to the very last stone for at least two reasons. First, the Romans wanted to make clear the utter defeat of Israel and its God, for in these times the defeat of a nation and its god(s) were inseparable in the minds of people. Second, there was gold on the walls of the temple, and when it was burned, the molten gold made its way between the stones. Therefore, every stone was taken apart in order to recover the gold that was there. The most important message here is the reorientation of the disciples' thinking. They are impressed with stones hewn and assembled by men that make buildings that are hollow, unable to maintain themselves against support or give life to those within. Jesus is "opposite" these buildings on the Mount of Olives. He is the living stone, a rock of refuge, a mighty fortress, hewn from a mountain without hands (Dn 2:34, a reference to the virgin birth of Jesus), the very source of life, and unconquerable as His ministry, death, and resurrection demonstrate. Please note man's preoccupation with

building and God's consistent warning and rebuke (2Sm 7:1–17; Mt 17:4–5).

● ● ● ● ● ● ● ● ● ● ● ● ● ● ● ● ● ● ● ●

Q **24:3–31 How is the depiction of the end of days from Christ in the Gospel of Matthew related to John's in Revelation?**

There are many parallels between this depiction and those of Revelation. Jesus indicates here that many terrible and trying times will come, but the end is not yet. Revelation affirms this view of the times between Jesus' first and second coming, describing partial destructions in early visions, but not complete destruction until Judgment Day. Jesus warns of deceivers and deception, as does Rv 12:9; 13:14; 18:23; 19:20; 20:3, 8, 10. Jesus spoke of wars, famines, earthquakes, and pestilence, as does Rv 6:8; 12; 8:5; 11:13, 19; 16:18; 18:8. Tribulation is a very significant theme in both (Rv 1:9; 2:9–10, 22; 7:14). Trumpets are also a prevalent item in passages, occurring fifteen times in Revelation, and in 11:15 having to do with the gathering of the elect. The faithful are urged to patience as they await the end (Rv 6:10–11). Finally, the abomination that causes desolation is described in Rv 11, when the beast kills God's two witnesses (the Word itself) and people celebrate and make merry over their dead bodies for three and a half days. One possible way of viewing this is how the Enlightenment, Rationalism, modernism, and secular humanism have rejected the Bible as the Word of God.

Q **24:4 How will we know when Christ comes if we are never to believe anyone who says they've seen Him?**

The return of Christ on Judgment Day will be unmistakable. He will come in a moment (1Co 15:52), will include everyone (1Th 4:16–17), and will dissolve the whole universe with fire (2Pt 3:10). No one can be missed, nor can anyone miss the second, final coming of Christ.

Q **24:7–8 Why does Jesus mention birth pains in the description of the end?**

When people think about the end times and Judgment Day, most remember the language of vv. 6–7: "wars and rumors of wars . . . famines and earthquakes" and the like. What is commonly forgotten is Jesus' warning that these kinds of events are only the beginning—like a woman in labor. There have been wars and rumors of wars throughout history, but no Judgment Day yet. Just so, a woman's labor pains can go on and on without a delivery. What really matters is that we are prepared and preparing always by working to advance the kingdom of God in the lives of all.

Q **24:9 It says you will be handed over to be persecuted and put to death. Now does this mean everyday law or does it mean going to church and confessing?**

If I understand this question correctly, the answer is both. History reveals that governments and churches persecuted people and put them to death—often working together, as in the case of the Reformation or the Spanish Inquisition. Now that "religious tolerance" has been adopted by much of the "civilized" world and governments protect individual's rights, there is more often abandonment of the faith than persecution for it. However, there are still many nations (Communist or Islamic) where Christians are actively and violently persecuted.

Q **24:19 Why will Judgment Day be especially dreadful for pregnant women and nursing mothers? Why were they singled out for suffering?**

They are not singled out for suffering, but because of their condition were particularly vulnerable to the ravages of war, which they experienced brutally when the Romans destroyed Jerusalem in AD 70. The vulnerability of women and children in time of war directs our attention to an even worse situation for these—the assaults of fallen humanity, especially in our day. Selfish pursuits, greed, sexual self-indulgence, and a general disrespect for God's gift of life result in abortion, abuse of women and children, and abandonment.

Q **24:22 "But for the sake of the elect those days will be cut short." What does this mean in terms of the end times?**

This text means to emphasize how hard it will become to keep the Christian faith. Certainly God has known for all eternity what will happen and when the right time will be to end this world. Here Jesus is speaking about how well He knows that over time the opposition of devil, world, and flesh to truth and grace will become overwhelming. On the one hand, this is a warning about how bad things will become; on the other, it is an encouragement that God knows this and has made determinations for our well-being accordingly.

Q **24:30 What is "the sign of the Son of Man"?**

Rv 12 describes the sign of the first coming of Jesus, when He was born of the Virgin Mary. I suspect the "sign" referred to here is described in the second half of this verse, "The Son of Man coming on the clouds of heaven with power and great glory" (and consider including what is described in the verses that follow).

Q **24:35 Why does He say heaven will pass away?**

In the Bible, "heaven" can refer to paradise, where the souls of the faithful go to be with God, as in 1Pt 1:4, or it can be the sky

above, including outer space, as in Ps 19:1. Jesus says that heaven and earth will pass away, referring to the destruction of this created universe and the creation of new (2Pt 3:12–13).

> Are we experiencing the end times now?

Q **24:36 Are we experiencing the end times now? Why does Christ say the end is close when He doesn't know when it's coming? If Jesus is God, thus omniscient, why is it that He does not know when the end of the age is coming?**

People have considered themselves to be in the end times ever since Jesus ascended into heaven (1Jn 2:18ff.). Luther thought he was in the last times, and understandably so in view of the conflict between the Roman Church, the Empire, and the evangelical princes and leaders. The founders of the Seventh Day Adventist Church and many others have made predictions of the last day—the most recent being for 2012. Three things we can be certain of. First, we will not know the day or hour; Jesus made this abundantly clear (Ac 1:7). Second, God intends people of every age to recognize the signs of the end and respond accordingly (Mt 24:45–51). Third, we must be closer to the end times than anyone else in the past, not only because time has passed but because we are living in a time when the vanity and arrogance of human reason is sitting where it should not (rejecting truth, especially that conveyed in the Bible).

Isn't it interesting that people wonder about the end of the world rather than their own end? What difference does it make when the world will end if we die before then? Jesus, like so many of the prophets and apostles, is always urging us to consider our time, redeem it, act prudently, and be watchful (Ps 90:12; Lk 19:41–44).

People talk about the coming of Judgment Day and being prepared for it, especially because no one knows when it will come. Any text about Jesus, whether His own words or those of others, must be understood according to the nature of Jesus it is referring to. When Jesus raises the dead, heals the sick, or stills storms, He is acting according to His divine nature; He is true God. When Jesus is tired, thirsty, hungry, or when He doesn't know something, this would be according to His human nature; He is true man. This verse is especially curious because Jesus seems to be referring to His divine nature, the "Son" in contrast to the "Father," who alone knows the day and hour. Here is a mystery in the divine nature that must remain a mystery.

Q 24:36–51 How did the people of Jesus' day react to what He said in this passage?

A reliable and specific answer to this question would require eyewitness testimony from people of Jesus' day, of which we have almost none, except the Bible. Jesus Himself tells us that many will ignore His warning, for they will live without concern as people did in the days of Noah (v. 37). There will also be people like the "faithful and wise servant" (v. 45) and like the "wicked servant" (v. 48). If we consider how people are basically the same, I suspect that people in Jesus' day reacted the same way as people in ours.

Q 24:40–41 How does this passage not support the rapture?

End times passages in the Bible need to be considered together, in reference to one another. Notice how this verse does not specify what it means that "one will be taken and one left." What can we learn from consulting the passage where the word *rapture* (in Latin) is used? In 1Th, Paul explains that when Christ comes, the dead "in Christ" will rise first and then those who were already living and faithful will join them with Christ "in the clouds to meet the Lord in the air, and so will we always be with the Lord." Thus it is not just the faithful who are living that are "raptured" but also those who have passed away, who will be raised from the dead. Paul provides further explanation in 1Co 15:23ff. There is a sequence on the last day that has to do with priority and honor: Christ comes first (because He is the first-fruit of the resurrection), then those who are Christ's, then the end. Yet Paul says the end comes "in a moment, in the twinkling of an eye, at the last trumpet" (1Co 15:52; see also 1Jn 3:2). But what of the unbelievers who are dead or alive at the last day? Peter seems to say they will be destroyed with fire (2Pt 3:7–10). Peter also provides an essential clue for understanding the relationship between the order of events and the duration of time: "with the Lord one day is as a thousand years, and a thousand years as one day" (2Pt 3:8). While there is an order to events on the last day, including the judgment itself (Mt 25:31–46; Rv 20:11–15), it all takes place just once and in an instant.

· ·

Q **25:1–13 Why did Christ use virgins in His parable? Does this talk about "Christians" who really aren't at heart Christians?**

The fact that all ten women were virgins and were waiting is essential to the point of the parable. Jesus is neither contrasting good people with bad people, nor religious with pagan people. All ten were waiting and all ten were virgins, but only half brought oil for their lamps. If light is the evidence of faith (Mt 5:16) and the flame is faith (Jer 20:9), then oil would be the Word that produces faith (Jn 6:63; Rm 10:17). The five virgins who brought oil know that their life and faith depend upon God. The five virgins who brought no oil are religious, even virgins (spiritually devoted to the only true God), but their ego or self-righteousness leads them to believe that faith is their own work and that they can meet God on their own merits. Notice how this is similar to the man who came to the wedding feast without a wedding garment (Mt 22:11–14).

To be a "Christian," in fact, is to be the product of the Word of God as one remains in it (Jn 8:31). People who neglect or ignore the Word presume to have a relationship with God on their own terms, which brings wrath rather than compliments from God (Is 64:6; Mt 7:21–29).

· ·

Q **25:1 What were they actually doing here? Why were they waiting for a bridegroom to go to the wedding banquet?**

A parable means to clarify something about a parallel or similar situation. God's faithful people are regularly described as His betrothed who await the complete and permanent union with Christ, the Bridegroom. We are waiting for Christ to come and establish paradise eternal, yet many do not wait as God has instructed and warned us. They will find that without the Word of God their own life and merits condemn rather than commend them before God (vv. 41–46).

· ·

Q **25:3 Why couldn't the virgins share their lamp oil? Wasn't there enough?**

Fascinating, isn't it? If Jesus taught anything, it was to share—indeed, to give all and ourselves for the sake of others. How can the faithful, exemplary virgins in this parable be justified in their denial? The only answer I can suggest is to see the oil not as the Word of God itself, but the Word of God in the life and experience of the individual. We can and do share the Word of God with others;

this is our purpose and we do so without worry, as the Word of God is inexhaustible. In fact, the more we share it, the more there is for everyone. On the other hand, having a foundation on the Rock, with Christ as the cornerstone and the apostles and prophets as the foundation, takes time in the Word, and that cannot be shared.

Q 25:9 If we share the work, isn't that sharing oil with others?

This would be true if oil were indicative of works, and some might argue thus. The problem with identifying oil with works is that our works never begin to be sufficient to commend or justify us before God (Is 64:6; Rm 3:10–18). On the other hand, a life in the Word means that the Word is regenerating our soul, creating faith, and keeping us "in Christ," where there is no condemnation (Rm 8:1). While the Word can be shared, and we want to, one's own life in that Word cannot, which is the warning and point of this parable.

Q 25:28 Why was the one talent given to the servant who had ten instead of the servant who had five?

Jesus provides the answer to this question in v. 29: "For to everyone who has will more be given." The servant whose five talents made ten appears to be the best of the three. Giving the talent to the one who returned ten emphasizes Jesus' point.

Q 25:31–46 What is the significance of sheep and goats in this parable?

The Bible consistently describes the faithful as sheep—vulnerable by nature yet innocent (Ps 23; Jer 23; Jn 10:28–29). The Bible also describes the unfaithful as goats because they are contrary and aggressive (Dn 8:5; Pr 30:31). The best way to get the sense of the significance of these animals is to read the contexts in which they occur in the Bible. An exhaustive concordance makes this possible.

Q 26:1–5 Why did they put Jesus on trial instead of assassinating Him?

It is possible that the religious leaders were worried about being blamed if Jesus were assassinated, since the people were well aware of their opposition to Him. What is certain is that Jesus would be crucified, because this is the death appointed for those who are the accursed of God (Dt 21:23; 27:26; Gal 3:8–14). It is also certain that the religious leaders, while they knew who Jesus was, were determined as hypocrites to pretend that His death was the consequence of someone else's judgment (Jn 18:31–32).

Q 26:6–13 What significance is there to Jesus being anointed by the woman at Bethany?

In the Bible, anointing has to do with authenticating (2Sm 2:4), authorizing (Ex 28:41), healing (Lk 10:34; Jas 5:14), and caring for the remains of the dead (Mk 16:1). There are at least two main points of significance here. First, Jesus explains that this woman has anointed Him in advance for burial (Mt 26:12). The prophecy of Jesus' anointing for burial may be included with many other prophecies and explanations that Jesus gave about what redeeming the world would require of Him (Mt 16:21). Second, this woman is Mary, who is a powerful example of God's intended relationship between those in need and His Son who fulfills all need (Mk 14:8; 16:9; Lk 7:38–46; Jn 11:2; 12:3; note well that Jn 11 is the first time this woman is clearly identified).

Q 26:14–16 How much money is thirty silver coins equal to in these days, and why would Judas take that over Jesus and everlasting life in heaven?

Various ways of figuring this value give a range from one month's wages to a year's wages to the value of a slave for seven years. A good guess in today's dollars would be somewhere between $4,000 and $40,000. Judas took the money because he had come to love it, and this love is the root of all kinds of evil (1 Tm 6:10).

Q 26:18–19 When Jesus tells His disciples to find a man, do they just pick any random man on the street?

Your question is a great example of why the four Gospels are important for the details they each supply. This account in Mk 14:13–15 and in Lk 22:10–12 reveal that Jesus had also told them that this "certain man" would meet them carrying a pitcher of water. This is the man they should follow.

Q 26:25 Is there any particular reason why Jesus made it known that Judas was the betrayer? Why don't the other disciples react upon hearing that Judas will be the betrayer?

Jesus *is* the truth and always tells the truth. Judas asked Jesus a simple question, and Jesus answered. The real question is why Judas asked. I suspect the answer to that question has to do with the hypocrisy of a betrayer (Jn 12:6). The other disciples consistently have trouble understanding what seems simple to most of us who know the whole story. The disciples didn't understand Jesus' teaching about leaven (Mt 16:11), nor about the necessity of His suffering and crucifixion (16:21–23), nor about His resurrection (Lk 24:21ff.), nor about His words with Judas Iscariot (Jn 13:28–30).

Q 26:36–46 Why did the disciples fall asleep, other than the fact that they were tired? Was this vital to the plan God had?

The text does explain that the disciples' eyes "were heavy" (v. 43). Mark includes that they were speechless when Jesus rebuked them for sleeping (14:40), and Luke includes that they were sleeping from sorrow (22:45). The sleep of the disciples, like their many other failures, reveals that we all suffer from the failings of human nature and that God redeems us from these failures. When we sleep, Jesus remains awake (Ps 121). When we awaken, Jesus rebukes, forgives, and urges us to wakefulness. Jesus urged them to "watch and pray that you may not enter into temptation" (v. 41). But they simply could not, and neither can anyone else, which is why we need Jesus as our Redeemer. Only Jesus is attentive to what needs attention always and without fail in order to save us in our need and redeem us from all our failures. We find powerful warning in the example and consequences of the disciples, and we find great encouragement in Jesus toward determination to watchfulness in Word and prayer.

Q 26:38–44 What is the significance that Jesus prayed three times?

Things that have to do with God tend to come in threes. There are the three persons of the Trinity: Father, Son, and Holy Ghost. The heavenly beings sang to God, "Holy, holy, holy" in Isaiah's vision (Is 6:3). Paul asked the Lord three times to remove his thorn in the flesh (2Co 12:8). Perhaps, when it comes to prayer, asking two times is giving up too easily (Lk 18:1–8) and asking more than three times is vain repetition (Mt 6:7–8)?

Q 26:39, 42 Why does Jesus use the imagery of a cup? Is this possibly a reference to one of the "cups" of the Seder dinner?

As we have seen before, the best way to decipher biblical terms is to read them as they occur in context. A "cup" holds things, especially things to drink, and drinking is necessary for our life. But the significance of a "cup" is that it holds something, not that it is a material vessel that holds fluid. Pss 11:6; 23:5; and Mt 23:26 are examples of "cup" meaning the whole content of a person and his or her life. In Mt 20:22–23, Jesus responds to two disciples' interest in sharing His glory; Jesus asks if they are able to drink the cup He will drink. Here, as in ch. 26, "cup" refers to the whole of what Jesus is required to do according to the will of the Father as our substitute. In Jn 18:11, Jesus also describes what He must do to accomplish salvation as His cup.

Q 27:5 There are a lot of questions regarding Judas' death. What are your thoughts on it?

As is often the case in history, some reports are brief and others provide more detail. This text in Matthew is brief and clear—Judas "went and hanged himself." In Ac 1:18, Peter says that Judas purchased a field, fell headlong, burst open, and had all his intestines gush out. Some have argued that these two reports are contradictory, but this is not necessarily so. Judas had been stealing money from the disciples' treasury for some time; these were certainly "the wage for . . . wrongdoing" (2Pt 2:13) with which he would have bought the field, rather than the thirty pieces of silver that he returned. This explanation also makes more sense because Judas would have had much more time to consider and purchase a field before betraying Jesus than after. Regarding the hanging, Acts is providing more detailed information about what happened either during or after the hanging itself. Whatever elements were part of the hanging may certainly have given way so that he hanged, then fell, then burst open.

Q 27:14 Why didn't Jesus answer the charges brought against Him?

Jesus was silent here for the same reason He did not do many mighty works (Mt 13:58) nor provide a sign on demand (Mk 8:11–12). He refuses to reveal truth and mercy to those who have despised them, though He does answer direct questions for the sake of the truth (Jn 19:10).

Q 27:18 Why did the people turn on Jesus after He had helped them?

As you may already suspect, crowds of people can be fickle, loving you one minute and hating you the next (Ac 14:11–19; 28:3–6). Even those who were helped by Jesus could turn on Him in a moment (Lk 4:22–30; Jn 6:60–66). However, Matthew gives us reason to understand that this group was

not composed of the faithful whom Jesus had helped but of those He could not help because of their unbelief (Mt 27:1; Jn 9:40–41; see also Paul Maier's book *Pontius Pilate* [Grand Rapids: Kregel, 1968]).

Q 27:24–26 The section says that Pilate "washed his hands" of Jesus, but then flogged him. Why did he do this?

Lk 23:22 suggests that Pilate wanted to set Jesus free and hoped to accomplish this by humiliating Jesus before the crowd: "Why, what evil has He done? I have found in him no guilt deserving death. I will therefore punish and release Him."

Q 27:25 Is this why Jews have been persecuted for so many years, because they condemned themselves?

First, there has been persecution of one person by another since Adam blamed Eve for the fall (Gn 3:12) and Cain killed Abel (Gn 4:8). Second, there is also a history of God sending one nation to destroy another according to His righteous judgment (Dt 9:5; 1Ki 19:15–18; Is 45:1). Third, God sometimes gives the stubborn and rebellious what they demand (Nu 16:12–35; 1Sm 8:4–22). Fourth, while it seems exceedingly unwise to call down responsibility for someone's death upon yourself, God has also made it very clear that the children should not be punished for the sins of the fathers (Dt 24:16; Jer 31:29–30). Last of all,

113

the Lord declares that when He does punish to the third and fourth generation, it is to those who hate Him (Ex 34:7). It is never wise to demand the death of the innocent and demand responsibility for their blood. On the other hand, it is the very greatest of blessings that the Lord leads us to repent of abusing others and provides for us a life that not only survives persecution but actually thrives in the face of it (Ac 9:1–16; 1Tm 1:12–17; Jas 1:2ff.; 1Pt 1:6–9).

Q **27:32 Why in some Gospels does it say that Jesus carried the cross and in others it says Simon?**

Mt 27:32; Mk 15:21; and Lk 23:26 all agree that Simon, a man coming from his field, was compelled to carry Jesus' cross after Him. However, none of these three Gospels offer any details about Jesus carrying His cross but simply say they "led Him away to crucify Him" (Mt 27:31; Mk 15:20; Lk 23:26). John's Gospel offers the clarification that Jesus did carry His own cross from the place of His trial toward Golgotha (Jn 19:17). We suspect that the soldiers compelled Simon to carry Jesus' cross because Jesus could hardly do so after the abuses He had already suffered.

Q **27:34 What is the gall mixed with wine that the soldiers offered Jesus?**

The Greek word (*colh*) is translated either "gall" or "bile." I have seen an article that identified this as hemlock on the basis of a text in Hosea, but a different Greek word is used there. Articles on this verse do tend to agree that gall acted as an anesthetic, which would have offered some small relief of pain for those being crucified.

Q **27:48 Why did the soldiers put "sour wine" on the sponge for Jesus?**

The text does not say why this was done, but we have hints. First, it may be that this sour wine was the only drink available. Why not water? It may be that water was "too good" for those being executed thus. Sour wine would be bitter, as their death was intended. It could just be that this was a drink no one else wanted, so it was kept here rather than water, which might become contaminated over time (though who would worry about that if you are giving it to those about to die?). Second, it may be that the person going to get this drink for Jesus intended it to help Him, since the others said, "Wait, let us see whether Elijah will come to save Him."

Q **27:51 What is the significance of the temple curtain being torn in two?**

The short answer is that it means Christ has removed all that had separated people from God. The longer answer is provided by the Old Testament, which explains why there was a curtain in the first place, and by Hebrews, which declares the significance of Jesus' death for that curtain. Ex 26:31–34 describes the place of this curtain between the Holy and Most Holy Place in the tabernacle. Ex 30:1–10 describes that only the high priest may pass through that curtain—once a year and not without the blood of a sacrifice. All of this makes clear the separation that has taken place between humankind and Creator and is an indication of what is required to reunite the two. Heb 9:1–15 provides a wonderful review and summary of the curtain's function, while Heb 10:19–25 focuses on the elimination of the curtain and all the rest of this Old Testament architecture by the incarnate Son of God. The life of Jesus in our place, His vicarious atonement for us, removed all that separated us from God and provides us all with immediate access to and connection with God through His Word and Spirit (Jn 14–16).

● ● ● ● ● ● ● ● ● ● ● ● ● ● ● ● ● ● ●

Q 27:57–61 Why did Joseph of Arimathea bury Jesus?

Not all of the religious leaders in Israel were opposed to Jesus. Nicodemus and Joseph of Arimathea were both disciples of Jesus by the end of His ministry, though "secretly for fear of the Jews" (Jn 19:38–39). When Joseph went to ask for the body of Jesus, Mark and Luke both add that Joseph was waiting for the kingdom of God, and Luke adds that Joseph was a good and just man who had "not consented to [the council's] decision and action" (Lk 23:51).

● ● ● ● ● ● ● ● ● ● ● ● ● ● ● ● ● ● ●

Q 28:11–15 The story was spread that the disciples stole Jesus' body. Do Jews today still believe this? Why does this seem different than John's account of the resurrection morning?

Matthew says that this story was still reported among the Jews, at least until the time he wrote the Gospel, about AD 50. A quick Internet search on this subject yields plenty of results that indicate that this story is still being promoted. Happily, some people have provided very thorough and compelling arguments in response, demonstrating that stealing the body of Jesus was neither possible nor sensible. For example, why would the apostles accept execution rather than deny a resurrection that they knew never took place? As we have seen above, the differences between the Gospels' report of the same event has to do with different focus and the inclusion or exclusion of different details. Where one account is very specific about some things, it will also say nothing about other details that another Gospel reports. This is to our advantage, for as we consider the four Gospels together, we gain a much fuller picture of what took place.

Q **28:17 Is it true that Thomas wasn't the only person to doubt the resurrection?**

Absolutely. According to Mark's Gospel, not only did the apostles doubt but they were also rebuked by Jesus for their unbelief and hardness of heart (Mk 16:14). Luke reports Jesus' effort to help the apostles past their doubt by inviting them to handle His body and by eating something in front of them (Lk 24:36–43). John's Gospel also records Jesus giving extra assurances to the apostles (Jn 20:19–23; 21:4–14).

Q **28:19 When Jesus says "go," does that mean to take a mission trip and "go," or does it mean "as you go" on with your life to take the Gospel to everyone you encounter?**

There is only one imperative in this section: "make disciples." Jesus says we are to do this through the whole course of life "as we go about." Jesus also clarifies that we make disciples by immersing them in His Word. Notice how Jesus emphasizes this by saying it in slightly different language. First He says, "Baptizing them in the name of the Father and of the Son and of the Holy Spirit"; then He confirms His meaning by repeating this in other words, "teaching them to observe all that I have commanded you." The rite of Christian Baptism is certainly included in this command, as are the Lord's Supper and Absolution, but these are extensions of and confirmations of the Word, not to be separated from a life in that Word that makes the Sacraments effective. Yes, take the Gospel to everyone you encounter all through the course of your life.

Q **28:19 Does this verse suggest that infant Baptism is preferred, or does it suggest that people should be taught about Jesus before they are baptized?**

It would seem very odd not to baptize infants and children, since Jesus refers to them as the standard of faith (Mt 18:3, 4, 6, 10; 19:14). It would also be strange to make an exclusion when Jesus uses a universal, such as "all nations." The issue with infant Baptism seems to have two different but related causes. First, Baptism does take place in the context of instruction of the Word. It is a life in the Word that moves believers to seek Baptism for themselves and for their children (look carefully at Ac 2:39; 10:24ff.; 16:33), and the Word works faith in all, especially in children who are typically less resistant (1Co 2:14). Second, those who argue against baptizing infants do so because they see faith and salvation as a work of man rather than God. Faith and regeneration are God's work, which He effects through those who precede us in the faith (Ti 3:4–6; 1Pt 1:5; Jn 1:11–13; Eph 6:4; Dt 6:4ff.; Ex 12:24–27). Infancy is the most obvious place for Baptism when possible because, like birth, it confirms the reality of our new life in Christ (Jn 3).

Mark

Q **1:1 Why does Mark skip over Jesus' birth?**

Mark doesn't give us an answer, so we may only suggest possibilities. First, Matthew had already written about the birth of Jesus in his Gospel (AD 50). Mark, writing for Peter, may have considered that sufficient. Second, since this Gospel was written for a primarily Gentile audience, Peter may not have thought the genealogy of Jesus or His birth were as important as the public ministry of Jesus. Third, just as Matthew immediately captures the attention of Jewish readers with the genealogy, Peter may have wanted to get right to the action of Jesus' ministry for the sake of his Gentile readers. This suggestion is supported by the frequent use of the term *immediately* in Mark's Gospel (forty-two of fifty-nine times in the New Testament).

Q **1:2–6 Why does John the Baptist sound like he looks wild? Why is he eating locusts?**

The quick answer might be that John is fundamentally countercultural from the core of his being to his appearance and diet. The longer answer has two parts. First, John was the last of the prophets of whom Elijah was the first. Jesus explained to His disciples that John had come in the "spirit and power of Elijah" (Lk 1:17; cf. Mk 9:11–13). There is a description of Elijah in 2Ki 1:8 that describes John as well. Second, the great contrast between John's life in the wilderness and the life of the religious leaders in the cities is important. God's people are strangers and sojourners in the world. We are children of Abraham, who had lived in tents his whole life (Heb 11:8–10). We are disciples of Jesus, who had no place to lay His head (Mt 8:20). John lived and extended

117

Why was Jesus baptized?

the kingdom of God to people by the Jordan River, pointing constantly to the necessity of a life in the Word of God (Ps 1; Jn 4:6–14).

• • • • • • • • • • • • • • • • • • • •

Q 1:4–9 If Baptism is for repentance from sin, then why was Jesus baptized?

Jesus was baptized for the very same reason He did everything else, "to fulfill all righteousness" (Mt 3:15). A simple question puts the whole matter into perspective: is there any moment of our life that we do not want Christ to have lived for us and atoned for? How would we have any peace or hope of reconciliation with God if it were necessary for us to do even the smallest thing perfectly? So Paul explained that salvation "depends on faith, in order that the promise may rest on grace and be guaranteed" (Rm 4:16). Jesus lived every aspect and moment of our life in order to cover us with His righteousness and fulfill the Law for our failure. This is what the prophet means when he says the Lord will give us double for our sins (Is 40:2).

• • • • • • • • • • • • • • • • • • • •

Q 1:8 What does it mean to be baptized with the Holy Spirit? Is John talking about Pentecost? What is the history of baptizing with water before John?

Interestingly, the answer to this question is not found in the term *Holy Spirit* but in the term *baptized*. In Greek, *baptized* means "wash" or, better still, "awash" as in

"immersed constantly." The fulfillment of John's prophecy can be seen in three ways, though they are all, really, the same. First, those who followed Jesus, especially the apostles, were immersed in the Holy Spirit because Jesus was constantly communicating His Spirit with His Word (Jn 6:63). Second, those who were present at Pentecost would also be awash in the Holy Spirit as He came upon them in the preaching of Peter and in fulfillment of the prophecy of Jl 2:28–32. Third, anyone at any time who remains in the Word as Jesus calls us to (Jn 8:31–2; 15:1–7) is awash in the Holy Spirit.

An overview of the occurrences of the language of washing in the Bible is very helpful—perhaps essential—for understanding Baptism:

- Ex 19:10–14. All the people are instructed to wash their clothes before the Lord appeared to them.

- Ex 30:21. The people are to wash their hands and feet (consider the Islamic practice that likely has its origin here).

- Lv 19:7. The priests wash their clothes and their bodies before entering into service in the tabernacle.

- 2Ki 5:10–13. Naaman the Syrian leper is healed by washing in the Jordan according to the Word of the Lord.

- Ezk 36:25–27. God will sprinkle clean water on the people and fill them with His Spirit.

- Mk 7:3–4. Describes how the Jewish religious leaders washed almost everything.

Q 1:10 What does it mean for the heavens to be torn open?

One of the consequences of Adam's disobedience was that he and all his descendants were cast out of the garden paradise and the way was guarded by angels with flaming swords (Gn 3:24). Jesus' obedience to the Law opened again the way to paradise for all the world, and the Holy Spirit came again to bring the breath of God back for the life of the world. The word translated "torn" in your Bible occurs in three other important contexts. One, the temple curtain is torn in two from top to bottom (Mt 27:51; Mk 15:38). The reaction of the heavens at Jesus' Baptism is an early indication of what He will accomplish absolutely through the course of His life and especially in His death. Jesus has reopened the way to God and re-established our communion with Him. Two, Jesus warns that an unshrunk patch will tear the mended clothing (Lk 5:36). Jesus uses this example to show that the Law and grace cannot be mixed. If we attempt to use grace or forgiveness only to "patch" certain parts of our lives, the patch or grace of God will shrink, and a worse problem will result. Consider the significance of this result as described in Heb 6:4–8; 10:26–31. Only a life generated by and lived completely within the grace of God can respond to the life-giving activity of the Holy Spirit. Three, the soldiers did not want to tear Jesus' tunic because it was woven as one piece (Jn 19:24). This is one of many indications that the Word of God cannot be broken, nor can you tear off this or that part of the Bible to use for your own purposes. The Bible is a unified whole that interprets itself and is attested to by creation (Rv 22:18–19; Rm 1:18–20).

Q 1:12–13 Why did Jesus allow Himself to be tempted? What was the purpose of that?

As mentioned above in 1:4–9, Jesus lived every aspect and moment of our life in order to cover us with His righteousness and fulfill the Law for our failure. The history of Israel in captivity and during the exodus is insurmountable evidence of the fallen condition of our human nature. Even with God present as a pillar of cloud or fire, the people continually gave in to their own lusts, idolatry, adultery, and rebellion during the forty years they wandered (Heb 3:16ff.). Since we all constantly fail to overcome temptation by obedience to the will of God, it was necessary for Jesus to overcome every temptation for us during His forty days in the wilderness (Jas 1:13–15; 2Co 5:21; Gal 3:10–14). Jesus did all that the Law requires and then declared that this fulfillment of the Law accomplished life and perfection to us (Jn 16:14).

Q 1:13 What does it mean that the angels were ministering to Him?

There are three main subjects in this verse that reveal a spectrum in creation. First, there is the devil, who spent forty days trying to overcome Jesus with temptations. The devil was the first to fall and the worst of all the fallen. He is the instigator and agitator of opposition against God. Second, the text says that Jesus was with the wild beasts. The "wildness" of the beasts and the danger they present is also a consequence of the fall, for which Jesus would inaugurate a remedy (Is 11:1–9). Third, there are the angels who remained good and faithful to God. These angels serve (*diakoneo* = "serve" or "minister") according to God's purpose, delivering messages and rebukes (Lk 1:13–20). Jesus told His apostles that He could ask and the Father would send thousands of angels to fight on His behalf—though this would never be necessary (Mt 26:53). Luke records that while Jesus was in agony praying in the Garden of Gethsemane angels came and strengthened Him (Lk 22:43). Matthew's Gospel makes clear that the angels did not begin to minister to Jesus until the devil finished the temptations and departed from Jesus (Mt 4:11). Thus, the common, basic meaning of "serve" suggests that the angels attended to Jesus' physical needs according to His human nature.

- - - - - - - - - - - - - - - - - - - -

Q 1:20 What reasons did they have to follow Jesus? Had His word spread, or were they just going by faith?

Yes, the word about Jesus and the words of Jesus had spread (Jn 1:15ff.). John's Gospel reveals that Peter and Andrew were already followers of John the Baptist (Jn 1:35ff.).

In addition, the Roman occupation of and rule over Israel, coupled with the burdens imposed by the religious leaders, make it easy to understand why young men might be eager and ready to follow a rabbi who "taught them as one who had authority and not as the scribes" (Mk 1:22, cf. v. 27). If we define faith as "honesty about dependence," then "faith" is a good explanation for the response of those whom Jesus called. Most common people in Israel knew they were powerless and completely dependent on God for their life and hope. The miracles of Jesus bore powerful witness to the truth of His teaching about His kingdom, which was not of this world, and that liberated the oppressed and gave everlasting hope to the lowly (Lk 1:69–79).

- - - - - - - - - - - - - - - - - - - -

Q 1:24 Why would people in the synagogue ask Jesus if He came there to destroy them?

The preceding verse directs our attention to a particular man who had a demon. It is this demon that cried out, "Have You come to destroy us?" The plural "us" refers to the demon but also reveals that there are a multitude of demons in this man. A different encounter of Jesus with a demon named "Legion" confirms that numbers of demons do gather to possess one person (Mk 5:9). The destruction that the demon is worried about reveals three things. First, demons do not know God's plan in Christ nor His timing, only that their destruction is certain (Mt 8:29; Mk 5:10). Second, the destruction of the devil and his demons is already accomplished in Christ and will be final at Judgment Day (Rv 12:9, 17; 20:10). Third, Jesus always binds and constrains the devil because He is the Word and truth of God. Notice the single means by which Jesus defeats the devil's temptations: "It is written" (Lk 4:1–13). The Word and truth of God is what binds the dragon (Rv 20:2).

Q 1:26 Where do evil spirits go after they have been cast out? Are there evil spirits today?

Jesus said that demons pass through "waterless places" where they have no rest (Mt 12:43–45). Consider the significance of that language in contrast to Jesus Himself, who gives living water and perfect rest (Ps 23; Jn 4). Demons on another occasion begged Jesus not to send them "out of the country" (Mk 5:10), which may suggest their fear of the unknown and impending conclusion of God's judgment against them (see also Rv 12:17; 20:10).

I cannot think of any reason to believe there aren't demons or unclean spirits today. Some might argue that there are no demons in our time because we don't see demon possession today as in biblical times. However, it is possible that demons have learned that subtle, gradual undermining of truth and faith is more effective than the terrifying forms of possession from which Jesus relieved people.

Q 1:27 What are "unclean spirits"?

The term *unclean spirit* occurs twenty times in the New Testament, all of them in the Gospels—with the exception of two in Acts and two in Revelation. Mk 5:13–15 demonstrates that an "unclean spirit" and a "demon" are the same thing. Mk 5:5 and 13 show that the intent of unclean spirits/demons is to destroy a person's life. Rv 16:3 and Mk 9:25 together indicate that the devil is the one who sends out unclean spirits and that their chief purpose is to deceive with words, in contradiction with the truth provided in the Word of God. This is why Jesus forbids the unclean spirits/demons to speak (Mk 16:3).

Q 1:32 Why did they have to wait until the sun went down to start healing?

There is no indication that the people had to wait until evening to come themselves or bring others for healing. Once Jesus settled in a certain place at the end of a day, word would circulate of Jesus' location, and people would continue to come there for help. There are plenty of texts that record Jesus healing during the daytime. On the other hand, there may be some relationship between the coming of darkness, trouble in people's lives, and God's remedy/judgment in Jesus. The parable of the vineyard workers (Mt 20) indicates that the end of a day is like the end of all time, when God settles accounts with people. Jesus said that we must do the work of God during the day, before

121

night comes when no one can work (Jn 9:4). Jesus came to His disciples at the evening on the day of His resurrection, when they were meeting behind locked doors because of their fear (Jn 20:19). Finally, John's Gospel says that Jesus is the light who has come into the world, which the darkness is not able to overcome (Jn 1:5). Together, these passages suggest this verse and others like it bear historical witness in physical circumstances of the greater, absolute conflict between God and the devil, God's work and the devil's, and between Jesus' salvation and the inability of all opposition to stop Him.

Q 1:34 Why were there so many demon-possessed people? Does this still happen today? How did the demons know who Jesus was?

Demon possession is about the battle for the hearts and souls of human beings. Our essence is the soul that lives in relation to a physical world through a physical body and is animated by a spirit. If we are not animated by the Spirit of God, as God intended, then we are an empty place for demons to take over (Gn 2:7; Mt 12:43–44).

It is difficult to provide evidence proving a direct relationship between demon possession and human suffering today. On the other hand, there is no evidence suggesting that demons no longer exist or that they are no longer interested in the suffering and death of human beings, in time and in eternity.

Demons may well have known who Jesus was for at least two reasons. One, the life and work of Jesus clearly demonstrated that He was the promised Messiah, the Son of God and Son of Mary (Jn 3:1–2). Two, demons were bound by the presence of Jesus, an absolute effect that only God could have upon them (Mk 5:7–12).

Q 1:35 Jesus prays in a solitary place. Is the solitude significant?

The place where Jesus prays is an *eremos* or "desert" place, and there is great significance. First, the term *desert* occurs forty-eight times in the New Testament, mostly in the Gospels. Second, John the Baptist was preaching in the desert (Mk 1:3), and Jesus continued His ministry in the desert so that crowds of people would not limit access to Him or promote misunderstanding about His purpose (Mk 1:45; Jn 6:15, 26). Jesus also went into the desert and took His disciples there in order to be alone and rest (Mk 6:31). Third, the wilderness is indicative of a fallen world, a place where the living water of God's Word is scarce. Jesus was tempted in the desert (Mk 1:12) in order to atone for Israel's failure in the desert (Ex 13:18ff.; Heb 3:16–19; Ac 7:30–44). Fourth, Jesus demonstrates God's gracious will to redeem us by providing for our lives in the desert (Jn 6:31–49). Thus, on the one hand, our life in a fallen world, apart from the Word of God, is like life in the desert: hard, cold, perilous, deadly. On the other hand, God consistently provides for His people during our life in this world (desert place) and even provides rest and time for renewed spiritual focus, because desert places are also free from so much of what is popular, crowded, and contrary to faith in this world.

* *

Q 1:40–45 Why could Jesus not enter a town openly anymore after He healed the man with leprosy?

The text says that the leper, having been healed, disobeyed Jesus' command to be silent but "went out and began to talk freely about it." After this, Jesus could not openly enter the city because people would make such a crowd around Him that He could not move (Mt 13:2; Mk 3:9). People could not get to Him (Mk 2:4), and most important, people would miss the whole point of Jesus' ministry (Mt 9:23; 20:31; Mk 5:31; Jn 6:15, 26).

* *

Q 1:44 Why didn't Jesus want the healing of the leper to be known?

Jesus' feeding of the five thousand reveals that fallen human nature completely misses the point of miracles. Jesus' miracles prove that He is true God and true man, the Savior of the world. However, fallen human beings don't want God to save them from the world but to give them more of it (Jn 6:15, 23). Miracles don't bring anyone to faith, as any number of accounts show (Lk 17:17; Jn 11:45–50; 12:37). Miracles demonstrate the authority and authenticity of a messenger of God, the prophets (Dt 13:1–5; 18:15–22), the

apostles (Mk 16:16–20), and above all, Jesus (Jn 3:2; 7:31).

* *

Q 2:5–9 Originally, Jesus says the man's sins have been forgiven. It's only after Jesus discovers what is in the hearts of the scribes that He heals the man of his disease. Would Jesus have healed the man if He didn't want to prove anything to the scribes?

Notice that forgiveness is what the paralytic and his friends came for, as they do not appear to be shocked or disappointed at Jesus forgiving rather than healing. Jesus solves problems in the correct order: first soul, then body. He speaks to this in Lk 9:25: "What does it profit a man if he gains the whole world and loses or forfeits himself?" James wrote, "Confess your sins to one another and pray for one another, that you may be healed" (Jas 5:16). Paul wrote at length about the significance of the soul in relation to the body (2Co 1:7–9; 4:1–5:21; 12:1–10; Gal 5:16–25).

We cannot know for sure if Jesus would have healed the man of his paralysis or not, but we can be certain that because Jesus redeemed the world, this man would be healed of every infirmity of body and soul on the last day (1Co 15:50–57).

* *

Q 2:9–11 How does this passage relate to a pastor's authority to forgive sins in corporate worship?

The scribes were right to argue that

only God can forgive sins (Mk 2:7). Their mistake was refusing to accept that Jesus was God, as He so clearly and consistently demonstrated Himself to be. While the prerogative and ability to forgive sins belongs to God alone (who else can bear away the sins of the world?), God gives both authority and responsibility to confirm the reality of forgiveness to His people (Mt 18:15–22; Jn 20:21–23; 2Co 5:20). Consider two points of clarification. One, God alone forgives, and we confirm that forgiveness in our relationships with others. The parable of the unforgiving servant makes this clear in one way (Mt 18:23–35) and makes the precise language of His commission to us clear in another. Jesus said, "Whatever you bind on earth *has been bound* in heaven and whatever you loose on earth *has been loosed* in heaven" (Mt 18:18; Jn 20:23). Notice that people are not bound in their sin or forgiven because we bind or forgive. Rather, we recognize and then confirm that people are bound or forgiven because this is the fact of their condition. We are agents of God's activity in people's lives, bearing witness to the truth, having neither the authority nor the ability to act independently. Second, corporate or general Confession and Absolution as practiced by congregations in worship is not a practice that is established in the New Testament. There is nothing wrong with any group of believers confessing the truth of their sinfulness and of God's grace in public, but this is no substitute for private reflection, examination, confession, and absolution among individuals, spouses, and families.

Q 2:13–17 Is the Levi in the story the same as Matthew? If so, why is he called Levi instead of Matthew?

Levi in this narrative is Matthew, as you can see in Mt 9:9–13. We suppose that Matthew does not ever refer to himself as Levi because of the distinction he made between his old life as Levi the tax collector and his new life as Matthew. It has not been uncommon in history for people to take a new name when they became Christian in order to demonstrate and more fully appreciate how God forgives the past and regenerates us to be His children.

Q 2:16 Why do some Bible translations put the word "sinners" in quotes?

There are no quotes in the Greek manuscripts of this text. Some English translations put "sinners" in quotes to help the reader understand that the Jewish religious leaders were applying this term to others, as if it did not apply also to themselves. All human beings, except Jesus, are sinners, as the Bible and nature make very clear (Rm 3:10–20).

Q 2:18 Why were John's disciples and the Pharisees fasting?

First, we need to remember the struggle between the fallen human nature or our flesh ("old man") and the regenerate soul ("new man"). These are opposed to each other, and one or the other will dominate our whole life, depending on how strong and well-nourished it is (Gal 5:16–25; Rm 6). Second, consider what trouble the "appetite" of the flesh makes for us, both individually and collectively (Jas 4:1–4). Not only does our flesh want food in quantity and kind that is not good for us, but the lust of the flesh is an appetite for practically everything. Selfishness, pride, greed, adultery, and lust are all attempts by fallen human nature to replace an infinite emptiness caused by our rejection of God. Thus, even when the Jewish religious leaders denied their appetite for food by fasting, they were doing so to satisfy their pride and self-righteousness. Third, among the faithful, fasting has had two main purposes. On the one hand, denying the appetites of the body is part of repentance (Ne 9:1; Ps 35:13). Consider how and why Paul did not eat or drink anything for three days after the Lord appeared to him on the road to Damascus (Ac 9:3–9). On the other hand, it was common for faithful people to concentrate on spiritual matters, in part, by ignoring the desires of the body (Est 4:3; Ac 14:23). Fallen human nature and regenerate souls do many things that look the same on the surface. However, fallen human nature always acts selfishly and, in doing so, acts against itself and others at the same time. The regenerate soul always acts in response to God's love and grace, seeking to love and act graciously toward others, and in so doing, benefits itself and others at the same time.

· · · · · · · · · · · · · · · · · · · ·

Q **2:23–3:6 Please explain Jesus being the "Lord of the Sabbath."**

Sabbath means "rest." Genesis 2:2–3 explains that the Lord finished His work of creation and rested on the seventh day and established every seventh day as a Sabbath or rest for all creation (Ex 20:8–11). Israel's bondage in Egypt and their exodus provided a second reason for the Sabbath. While the Israelites were slaves, they could get no rest. God delivered them from bondage and gave them rest again; therefore, Israel was to honor and appreciate that deliverance of God by enjoying the Sabbath rest (Dt 5:13–18). However, one of the many problems of fallen human nature is its determination to reverse and contradict everything God does (Galatians records Paul's fight against this work of fallen human nature). The Jewish religious leaders, over time, had added and expanded the Ten Commandments to 616 laws. They created many new laws that forbade all kinds of different activities on the Sabbath. By making more laws with more detail, they could attempt to justify themselves by claiming to keep the new rules and at the same time appear better than others by condemning them for failing to keep the rules. This is the setting Jesus is battling. Jesus reminds the Jews that the Sabbath was made for people as a gift and benefit; people were not made for the Sabbath, to be enslaved under a burdensome law. Just as Jesus is Lord and Master over all creation so that it promotes and sustains life, so also Jesus is Lord of the Sabbath (both the day and the

Law), rescues it from being a burden imposed, and re-establishes it as a benefit that supports us.

• • • • • • • • • • • • • • • • • • •

Q 2:27 Does the Sabbath Day of rest still apply to people?

The answer is both yes and no. There are three types of law in the Bible: ceremonial, civil, and moral. The ceremonial law was established by God through Moses to point forward to Christ. Christ fulfilled all the promises of God that the ceremonial law pointed to; thus they are no longer in effect (Mk 7:19; Ac 10:9–16). The principles behind the civil law remain in effect since it reflects reason and supports cooperation; for example, the prohibition against moving landmarks. The moral law, expressed in the Ten Commandments, is still in effect with temporal and eternal consequences, though Jesus clarifies the intent of these Commandments by summarizing them: "Love the Lord your God with all your heart . . . soul . . . mind and . . . strength . . . and your neighbor as yourself" (Mk 12:30–31). Now to the Sabbath law in particular. There seems to be no imposition of any Sabbath law from the time of Christ forward. Some have noticed that when the moral law is rehearsed in the New Testament, the Third Commandment regarding the Sabbath is missing (Mt 19:18–19; Rm 13:9). The redemption Jesus provides from all burdens of the Law, and also His ministry recorded in the Gospels, all suggest that, in fact, every day is Sabbath from the time of Christ on. All of the Gospels record Jesus asserting the purpose of rest and mercy against the legalism and condemnation of the religious leaders (Mt 9:12–13; 12:1–8; Mk 3:2–5; Lk 13:10–17; Jn 7:22–24). The Books of Galatians and Hebrews are concentrated on protecting the rest that the Gospel provides against any re-imposition of the Law's condemnation of believers (Gal 3:10–14; Heb 4:4–11). The practice of the New Testament Church of meeting on Sunday affirms the priority of Christ and His redemption over the Law. We gather on the day of the sun (Sunday) at the rising of the sun in order to celebrate the resurrection of Jesus and His triumph over death.

• • • • • • • • • • • • • • • • • • •

Q 3:1–6 Does Jesus purposefully provoke the Pharisees?

Jesus always and only loves others, especially those who oppose Him (Jn 8). The Pharisees are provoked only because they insist on taking away life where God would freely give it (Gal 2:11–21). Any reader of the Gospels may get the impression that Jesus rested all week and worked only on the Sabbath. We must be careful to remember that the Gospel writers have not recorded all that Jesus did (Jn 21:25). Perhaps the apostles couldn't help recording Jesus' ministry on Sabbath days because the relief He brought in so doing was profound. For more on this matter, see Jesus' example of wine and wineskins (Mt 9:14–17).

How did Jesus decide who to call?

Q 3:11–12 Why wouldn't Jesus let the demon speak? Isn't that why He was there in the first place—to let people know about Him?

How would a person know when to believe what a demon says and when not to? There are at least two reasons why Jesus forbids the demons to speak about Him. First, demons are all about destroying lives by deceiving people, so it is not fitting for them to speak the truth about God. Second, Jesus has been commanding almost everyone to keep quiet about Him to prevent popularity and crowds from undermining His work among the humble and faithful (see Mk 7:36; 8:30; 9:9; and my answer at Mk 1:40–45).

Q 3:13 How did Jesus decide who to call?

Since Jesus is true God, knows how to make all thing work together for good (Rm 8:28), has prepared good works for each of us to walk in (Eph 2:10), and has assigned to each of us a measure of faith (Rm 12:3), it must have been perfectly clear to Him from all eternity who He would call. We know more about some apostles than others, but each had strengths and weaknesses that God would employ in the service of the Gospel. John 1:43–51 records when Jesus called Philip and Nathanael and details about them. Mark 2:13–17 records details about Matthew when Jesus called him. We know much about Paul from Ac 8–9 and even more about why God called him from

his own observations in his epistles (1Tm 1:13). Much of what is particular to each of the apostles is evident in their writing and serves to give us a fuller view of the truth God means to reveal to us. All of us can see ourselves in the apostles and be encouraged to know that as God used them, so He can use us. Finally, Ac 1:21–22 reveals that apostles had to be eyewitnesses of Jesus' ministry and resurrection (Paul is a special exception who was given the required revelation in an extraordinary way [2Co 12:1–7]).

Q 3:17 Why did Jesus give James and John the name Sons of Thunder?

Luke records an occasion where James and John asked Jesus if He wanted them to call fire down from heaven to consume a village that would not receive Jesus (Lk 9:52–55). This is most likely the aspect of their personality for which Jesus named them.

Q 3:21 Did Jesus' family think He was crazy?

Yes. There is a hint of this in the narrative that follows (Mk 3:31). The fact that Jesus' family was outside the house while He was inside teaching, as well as His response to their message, suggests that they didn't accept who He was. John provides clear

127

confirmation of this, reporting that "not even His brothers believed in Him" (Jn 7:5). Jesus' family realized the truth about Him only after His resurrection from the dead (Ac 1:14). Remember that Jesus' family is not alone. Paul says that any fallen human nature in its pride will reject God's mystery in Christ (1Co 1:18–31).

• • • • • • • • • • • • • • • • • • •

Q **3:24 Why do we have denominations?**

Paul provides a very simple answer in 1Co 11:9: "for there must be factions among you in order that those who are genuine among you may be recognized." There is only one Church because the true Church is the Body of Christ, made up of all believers of all times and places, genuine believers, children of God, known for certain only to God (Eph 4:4–6). What causes divisions and denominations is not so good. One cause for denominations is fallen human nature's pride, greed, and lust for power and control (1Co 1:10–25; Gal 6:12–13). Fallen human nature's love of this world, vanity, and dishonesty generates hypocrisy, which makes people want to create a church that will justify their wickedness (Ac 5:1–11; 15:5; Jas 4:1–6). Finally, denominations come into existence, persist, and multiply because people are more committed to their own opinions than to the truth, and they refuse to examine or have their opinions examined by the truth (Jn 3:19–21; 1Jn 2:15–19). Many will claim there are denominations because the Bible is unclear; some even claim that each person has a right to interpret the Bible

as he or she sees fit. But the Bible expressly denies these claims: "No prophecy of Scripture comes from someone's own interpretation. For no prophecy was ever produced by the will of man, but men spoke from God as they were carried along by the Holy Spirit" (2Pt 1:20–21). Truth is singular, and the grace of God is powerful to regenerate us as children of God and inspire us to a singular devotion to the truth and to walking together in that truth and grace.

• • • • • • • • • • • • • • • • • • •

Q **3:29 What is an eternal sin? How does one blaspheme against the Holy Spirit? What if you do it as a child? Will you be forgiven?**

There is only one eternal sin. This sin is eternal because it rejects the Holy Spirit, who conveys the grace and forgiveness of God to us. The only sin that is never forgiven is so only because it refuses forgiveness. To blaspheme means to be entirely opposed to, especially in every thought and word. The work of the Holy Spirit is to change our mind, our thoughts, and our ways and to communicate the love of Christ to us through His Word. How can a person know forgiveness if that person's every thought and word is opposed to and contradicts the Word of Christ that confirms forgiveness? The Letter to the Hebrews warns about this sin and gives more detail (Heb 6:4–8; 10:26–31). How old a person is does not matter as much as the person's disposition. It would seem impossible for a person who is concerned and fearful about this sin to be guilty of it. Children are at least less likely to be guilty of this sin since they have not yet come to the kind of arrogant and stubborn self-assertion and opinion that is characteristic of this sin (Mt 18:3; 1Co 1:27–29). This sin, according to the text, is never forgiven—but remember, this sin is never forgiven because it never repents, never has a second thought about its opposition to God. This sin is precisely the opposition to God that is arrogant, adamant, contrary, conscious, contradictory, and vicious, so that forgiveness is steadfastly refused.

We must be careful never to judge another person or even ourselves as being guilty of this sin (Mt 7:1). God's severe language against this sin works to keep us from carelessly falling prey to it, while His grace, love, and patience work to regenerate us as faithful souls that cling to Him in love and gratitude.

• •

Q 3:30 Do people today become possessed by evil spirits?

I am not sure how anyone could know for certain that a particular person was possessed by a demon. However, the instances of demon possession in biblical history are certain, and the Bible is clear that the devil is still at work in the world. Jesus warned that a demon cast out will return to the person if he or she is not inhabited by the Holy Spirit (Mt 12:43–44; 1Co 6:19). Paul warned that the devil and his ministers transform themselves into angels of light (2Co 11:13–15). Peter warns that the devil prowls about

seeking whom he may devour (1Pt 5:8–9). John warns that the devil has gone to make war with believers (Rv 12:17). The only way to be secure from the devil and his attacks is by remaining in the Word (Jn 8:31–47; Eph 6:10–18).

• •

Q 3:31–33 How do Roman Catholics defend Mary's lifelong virginity? Why is Jesus not happy to see His mother?

The best way to find out about any belief is to ask a person who is devoted to it or to read official documents from those who practice and/or defend the belief. It is a characteristic of fallen human nature to add and subtract from the Word of God, which is why the Bible forbids it (Dt 4:2; Jer 36:20–26; Mt 23:1–39; Rv 22:18–19). The text does not say Jesus was not happy to see His mother, but one may wonder why they are outside the house instead of being right there with Jesus. Jesus answered that question Himself in Lk 4:24. See also 3:21 above.

• •

Q 3:34–35 Why did Jesus denounce His mother and His brothers?

I wouldn't call this denouncing them (see 3:31–33 and 3:21 above). Compare these verses with Jesus' response to His mother in Jn 2:4: "Woman, what does this have to do with Me?" Mary and Jesus' siblings are, apparently, thinking of Him only according to His human nature and only according to their care in this world. Jesus must be about His Father's business, as He explained when He was twelve years old (Lk 2:49). Jesus is clarifying the nature of substantive relationships between people and God; whoever keeps hearing the Word of the Lord properly belongs to His family because it is the Word that generates and sustains us as His own (Jn 1:12–13; 3:3–8; 10:27–28).

• • • • • • • • • • • • • • • • • • •

Q 4:1–20, 30–32 The kingdom of God is described as both a growing seed and a mustard seed. Why?

The kingdom of heaven may be compared to a multitude of things because God made creation as a witness to all people of all times and places (Ps 19; Rm 1:20). The kingdom of God is the real substance—the essence, if you will—and the material world is indicative of these things or like them. In his Gospel, John makes this clear as he records Jesus saying things like "I am the door" (10:9), "I am the good shepherd" (10:11), and "I am the living bread that came down from heaven" (6:51). All other doors and shepherds and bread are like, but not equal to, Him.

Next, in one way the kingdom of heaven is like any seed that is scattered because of the effect the environment has on the seed. People often do not understand or care to understand the Word. People have misplaced priorities that choke out the Word in their lives. People sometimes eagerly accept the Word but then just as quickly abandon it when challenges come. The Word itself regenerates people to be good soil, soil that makes a good place for the Word and will of God to grow and flourish. On the other hand, the kingdom of God is like a mustard seed. In this case, we are not considering the effects of the environment on the seed but the ability of the seed to provide an environment. The kingdom of God takes up no space at all and yet includes and provides the best of places for everyone. Consider how you can read your Bible to yourself and to as many people as you like as often as you like without diminishing the Word in your Bible. All that is of God increases as it is given, and everyone benefits. What is not of God is lost, even when we try to keep it all to ourselves.

• • • • • • • • • • • • • • • • • • •

Q 4:11 Why did Jesus explain the parables only to His disciples and not to everyone else?

God has never been interested in speaking to those who have no interest in listening. This explains the roughly 430 years of silence between Malachi, the last of the Old Testament prophets (400 BC), and John the Baptist, who prepared people for the Christ (AD 30). Jesus refused to speak during most of His own trial because His accusers had steadfastly rejected the truth (Mt 26:63). Jesus allows for no hypocrisy, no self-deception, no pretense—nothing untrue. If you are a disciple of Jesus, you will follow Him, and in so doing will find answers to your questions (cf. Mk 4:33–34 with Jn 6:60–69). The same is true today: if we remain in the

Word, the Word will explain itself to us in time (2Pt 1:19; Is 55:10–11; Gn 32:26).

• • • • • • • • • • • • • • • • • • •

Q 4:12 The understanding of parables is conceivable today, isn't it?

King Solomon said, "What has been is what will be, and what has been done is what will be done, and there is nothing new under the sun" (Ec 1:9). The Bible is concerned with the substance of life, which is universal and unchanging. The parables use obvious and common physical relationships to teach us about more significant spiritual relationships. You don't have to be a shepherd to understand the relationship between a gate, a shepherd, a robber, a wolf, and the sheep (Jn 10; Jer 23). Even if you have electric lights, you recognize the folly in having no extra oil for your lamp (Mt 25:1–13). The problem with understanding parables is either that people don't care enough to listen long enough to understand (see second paragraph under 4:1–20, 30–32 above) or because they are too full of their own opinions to learn anything (Jn 8:43–44; Rm 1:16–21; 2Co 3:12–14).

• • • • • • • • • • • • • • • • • • •

Q 4:21 Would they use a special stand to put the lamp on?

Like the language of parables considered in the questions preceding this one, there is no reason to think the language is figurative or uncommon. We hang lights from the ceiling or elevate them with some kind of pole or post so that the light is dif-

fused over a larger area, making the light more effective. Simple people of humble means would use what might be readily available, as we would if we were camping. Wealthy people or servants in the temple would have more elaborate lampstands made of precious materials (Ex 25:31–39).

• • • • • • • • • • • • • • • • • • •

Q 4:25 "From the one who has not, even what he has will be taken away." What does this mean? It seems backward.

We are God's creation and completely dependent on Him, the universe He created, and the people around us. Therefore, as contingent beings, we can be only stewards and never possessors of things. Everything we have is a gift, including responsibility and opportunity. So we note two important features of the faithful stewards' report when Jesus tells a parable about them (Mt 25:14–29; Lk 19:12–26; 1Co 4:7). First, stewards are given different amounts with which to work, according to their ability (this is even true of faith; God assigns to each person a particular measure [Rm 12:3]). Second, in Luke's account, the faithful stewards report that it was not they but the master's goods that account for the increase: "Lord, your mina has earned five minas." On the other hand, a poor steward won't even allow the master's goods to do what they would naturally, for which he is rightly condemned (Lk 19:20–23). Good stewards take good care of what is given them, and so God gives them more to take good care of (Mt 25:21, 23). Bad stewards waste what is given them, so even that is taken away lest they lose it through waste (Mt 25:28–30). Life is not something we make for ourselves—God gives it to us in abundance every day. Life is not an obligation but an opportunity to see what we can make of what we have moment by moment, day by day. God has already forgiven our failures and mistakes. God has already provided for our lives in the resurrection and eternity. This makes stewardship interesting and joyful rather than burdensome and frightening.

Q 4:29 "He puts in the sickle." What does that mean?

Even if someone isn't familiar with farming or old farming tools such as a sickle, the context makes it clear that "putting in the sickle" has to do with a harvest. When something is at its maximum value, we take that something and put it in a safe place or put it to work according to its design. When a grain, vegetable, or fruit is ripe, we eat it or store it for our later needs. When opportunities in relationships are present, we respond to those opportunities in order to enjoy the "fruit" of good relationships. When this world has fulfilled God's purpose for it, and all people who are meant to live and come to faithfulness have done so, then Christ will come again and gather His people into the resurrection of life eternal (Jn 5:28–29; Rv 14:15).

Q 4:30–34 If faith the size of a mustard seed moves mountains, then what does that say about our faith, because I don't see any mountains moving?

The answer to this question comes in two parts. First, the point of comparing faith to a mustard seed is to reject thoughts about quantity in respect to faith. Faith is not a substance like gold, which increases the power of the person who possesses it (more gold = more power). Consider what happens to our understanding of this verse if we define faith as "honesty about dependence." The more honest we are about our dependence on God, His grace, and His creation, the more we live in wisdom and harmony with God's will, and much good is accomplished. Second, consider what the purpose would be in moving a mountain? Jesus chose an example of something practically impossible in order to reveal that faith does the impossible. This is exactly the point Jesus made so clearly with His disciples in Mt 19:23–26. Jesus said, "It is easier for a camel to go through the eye of a needle than for a rich person to enter the kingdom of God." When the disciples wondered if anyone could be saved, Jesus replied, "With man this is impossible, but with God all things are possible." Even a small amount of honesty begins to move the mountain of opposition that our fallen human nature, pride, and self-righteousness have established against the truth. The more truth that affects us, the more honest we are. The more honest we are, the more our mountain of opposition to God is removed, like casting it into the sea. Thus the Sacrament of Baptism indicates this accomplishment of God in our lives—the Word casts away and drowns the mountain of opposition from our human nature, and His Spirit and grace work faith—all impossible for us, but all accomplished by God (Mt 18:3; Rm 6:1ff.; 1Co 1:18–31; 2Co 10:3–5).

. . . .

Q **4:33–34 Why does Jesus speak in parables? Did the people understand the parables?**

Jesus speaks in parables for two reasons. On the one hand, speaking in parables protects the value of His Word from people who despise it. Jesus warns us, "Do not give dogs what is holy, and do not throw your pearls before pigs, lest they trample them under their feet and turn to attack you" (Mt 7:6). On the other hand, for humble, God-fearing people who come to Jesus to listen and for help, the parables use what is material and common to teach about things spiritual and divine. The proud don't get the point of the parables because they refuse to get it, just as they remain unforgiven—not because Christ has not provided forgiveness, but because they refuse it (see Mk 3:28–29 above). The humble recognize immediately that they are the lost, but in so doing, come to realize that they have been found and restored by God. Notice the two different groups of people with Jesus, who they are, and their disposition toward Him. Now notice that in the three parables He tells, what

> ## Why does Jesus speak in parables?

was lost is always found, but what was assumed not to be lost, like the older brother of the prodigal son, is so lost that it may never be recovered. People who live in honesty because their lives are based in necessity understand the parables because their teaching is based on the simple, necessary relationships in God's creation. People who are arrogant and vain, who deceive themselves about the real substance of life by living artificially, can't understand the parables because they refuse the truth about life in all aspects. See also Mk 4:1–20, 30–32 above.

. . . .

Q **4:40–41 Why did the disciples ask, "Who then is this?" Did they really not understand that Jesus was God?**

As we have seen above, fallen human nature has a very hard time accepting that God has become a true man in the person of Jesus Christ (Lk 4:22; Mk 3:21; Jn 7:5). Consider how many times Jesus explained how He would have to die but that He would rise from the dead on the third day. Yet even His apostles found it nearly impossible to accept (Mk 24:21ff.; Jn 20:24–25). With the fall of Adam, human nature replaced the ability to recognize the truth with a spirit of contradiction to the truth. Unless God disables the opposition of our human nature, we cannot understand anything He teaches or recognize anything that is true (Rm 1:18–31).

When God overcomes our opposition to the truth according to our human nature and regenerates our soul, then we know the truth and know how our life depends on remaining in the truth (Jn 3:1–8; 1Jn 2:20–27; Is 55).

Q 4:41 When do the disciples finally catch on that Jesus is the Messiah?

The disciples of Jesus were probably "catching on" little by little all during His ministry. Jesus made many profound and early impressions when He called disciples (Jn 1:49), when He did miracles (Mk 1:29–34), and when He taught (Lk 4:16ff.). Peter expressed direct opposition right after he confessed that Jesus was the Messiah (Mt 16:13–23). Even after His resurrection, Jesus had to explain again what the Messiah would accomplish and how (Lk 24:13–27). Peter did not seem to be fully convinced of the significance of God's salvation through the Messiah until the Second Jerusalem Council (cf. Ac 10:9–16; 11:1–18; Gal 2:11–16; and Ac 15:5–12). Our fallen human nature does not and will not ever grasp what God has done in the Messiah or Christ (1Co 2:14). This is why it is necessary for God to regenerate us through His Word, in the image of His own Son, so that we can, in the essence of our being, know and cling to Jesus, who is the Christ (Jn 1:11–13; 3:3–8).

Q 5:1–20 I find it interesting that the man who was demon possessed is

told by Jesus to tell his family and others what Jesus has done for him, in contrast to Jesus telling the people He has healed and those He has driven evil spirits out of to not tell anyone what He had done. Is there any significance in Jesus instructing the demon-possessed man to tell people what He has done?

Location and population are very important in Jesus' ministry. For example, Matthew spends most of his Gospel recording Jesus' ministry in Galilee (north), while Luke moves very quickly to Jesus' later ministry in Judea (south). When Jesus is in the populated cities of Galilee (Capernaum, Nazareth) and Judea (Jerusalem, Bethany), news travels fast and crowds confuse the significance of that news. Jesus restricts news about Himself in these Jewish, urban areas because that news turns into a kind of popularity that is contrary to Jesus' purpose (see Mk 1:44 above). The man who was healed in this narrative lived near the north-eastern shore of the Sea of Galilee, an area that was relatively remote and inhabited by many non-Jewish people. Since this area was remote and the people there non-Jewish, it makes sense that Jesus would direct the man, now healed and faithful, to stay and be a witness to Jesus there.

Q 5:7–9 Why does Jesus ask what the demon's name is?

Since Jesus is true God, we might wonder at many points about why He asks questions.

In the Garden of Eden, God called to Adam, "Where are you?" (Gn 3:9). When the woman with a flow of blood touched Jesus from behind in a crowd, Jesus stopped and asked, "Who touched My garments?" (Mk 5:30). One may also wonder why Jesus asks others to do things He could easily do Himself, like roll away the stone from Lazarus's tomb (Jn 11:39). The answer in every case is "for our benefit." By asking questions, Jesus is drawing our attention to the lesson to be learned. In this case, it is important for us to know the magnitude of trouble the demon-possessed man was in and yet why that trouble didn't destroy him. First, by the question, Jesus reveals that there is not just one demon in this man but many. Next, by allowing the demons to move to the herd of swine, Jesus shows us both the power and intent of the demons: absolute and immediate destruction. Finally, we come to the most important question, "Why wasn't the man destroyed by the demons?" The answer is because God is in control of all things. Neither the devil, nor demons, nor anyone or anything else is free to do as it pleases, but God orders, limits, and controls all things for the essential and eternal benefit of His people (Rm 8:28; 13:1–4; 2 Co 4:17–18; Col 1:13–18; Heb 1:1–14). There is only one God, and we are blessed to know that He sets limits on the harm evil can do and causes even what evil does to work for our good, just as He so clearly did with Job (Jb 1:6–2:8; 42:1–17).

● ●

Q **5:11–13 Why did the demons beg Jesus to "send us to the pigs" when all they did was jump into the lake and drown?**

Good question. Why would we expect demons to act reasonably or to have a point? What could possibly be the point of opposing God and His will for His creation? However, we oppose Him too. Consider how hard it is to convince anyone of the truth and then to act accordingly. We are slow to learn and quick to forget. Paul urges us to learn these lessons in general when he asks, "What fruit were you getting at that time from the things of which you are now ashamed? For the end of those things is death" (Rm 6:21). Despite this truth and our knowledge of it, according to our fallen human nature, we continue to contradict the truth and God's good will for us to the day we die. We are generally careless with most everything that is deadly for us, especially things that are deadly to our soul and eternity. Paul, with powerful language, urges the Ephesians to put on the whole armor of God as defense against the principalities and powers of the air, yet I know of no one who does this, not even pastors (Eph 6:11–13). So, biblical history, like our own experiences in this life, is very important, as it impresses upon us the truth and urges us to cling to the grace of God and the Means of Grace that make us wise, prudent, and faithful.

Q 5:13 Where did the demons go after they drowned?

Actually, only the pigs drowned; demons are eternal beings. We have reason to believe that the demons would move on, looking for some other person to possess (Mt 12:43–45). We also know, from the Matthew passage, that if the demons found no suitable host, they would try to return to the man Jesus healed. Ultimately, the devil, his demons, and all who steadfastly opposed God will be cast into the lake of fire for all eternity (Rv 20:10).

Q 5:19 Why does Jesus sometimes tell people to tell others about what has happened, but other times tells people not to tell anyone?

For an explanation of why Jesus forbade people to speak about Him, see Mk 1:44 above. For an explanation of why Jesus forbade demons to speak about Him, see Mk 3:11–12 above. The reason Jesus told this man to tell others is explained in Mk 5:1–20 above.

Q 5:31 Why does Jesus ask, "Who touched Me?"

Jesus asks questions for our benefit. Questions force us to face the truth—more than that, questions force us to see how these truths apply to us. In this particular case, Jesus wants the crowd around Him to notice, recognize, and learn from the exemplary faith of this woman. For further explanations to questions about this passage, see Mt 9:18–26 and 9:20. Compare this narrative with that of the woman who came to Jesus on her daughter's behalf (Mk 7:24–30; see Mt 15:21–28 for a more comprehensive explanation of this episode).

Q 5:41 Why does Mark use Aramaic?

Mark is recording something that Jesus said in Aramaic. In Palestine at this time, people spoke Aramaic and Greek; some also spoke Hebrew. Naturally, Jesus would have spoken to this little girl in her first or native language, and Mark is recording direct speech.

Q 5:43 How could the parents have kept the resurrection of their daughter a secret?

The reaction of the mourners to Jesus and Jesus' reaction to them (Mk 5:39–40) suggests that people are very hard to convince about the resurrection from the dead. While word of this resurrection may have spread among some, even people who want to believe in the resurrection of the dead tend to slip back into unbelief. Consider Jesus' own apostles who were with Him when He raised many different people from the dead, yet they didn't believe (Mk 15:9–14).

For Jesus' reasons to keep His work a secret, see answer above at Mk 5:1–20.

Q 6:4–6 Why was it that Jesus' hometown lacked so much in faith?

The rejection of Jesus by His own people is explained by Jesus Himself in v. 4. John comments on this rejection more generally: "He came to His own, and His own people did not receive Him" (Jn 1:11). Jesus marvels at many different points during His ministry at the unbelief of people: a man whose boy was plagued (Mk 9:24), the apostles about food (Mk 8:17–21), and an almost universal absence of faith near the end of time (Lk 18:8). Jesus explained in the parable of the sower why faith is lacking in His own people and in everyone else (Mk 4:14–19). This is why Jesus explains to Nicodemus that unless a person is regenerated by God through God's Word and Spirit, he or she cannot see or enter the kingdom of heaven (Jn 3:3–8). Jesus also has a very lengthy discussion with the crowds He had fed on the subject of faith and unbelief, which is recorded in Jn 6:26–68.

Q 6:5 If Jesus is all-powerful, why does this verse say He "could do no mighty work there"?

The answer to this question depends on both the next verse and on understanding the purpose of miracles and their relationship to faith. The next verse reports that Jesus "marveled because of their unbelief." Paul explains that "faith comes from hearing, and hearing through the word of Christ" (Rm 10:17). Jesus said that faith is

God's work in us (Jn 6:29; cf. 1Pt 1:5). If we define faith as "honesty about dependence," then it is clear how the Law makes us see the truth about our fallen condition and utter dependence, while the Gospel regenerates us and shows us how wonderfully and completely God has remedied our situation. All this is the product of the Word. So where do miracles come in? Miracles confirm and authenticate that Word (Mk 16:17–20; Jn 7:31; 10:38).

Next, we need to understand what it means for God to be all-powerful. Omnipotence is not the controlling aspect of God's nature—how could it be? John wrote that God is love (1Jn 4:16). It is the love of God and His wisdom that directs how He will or will not use His power. Thus Jesus does not speak or do miracles that would confirm His Word if that only leads people to ignore or oppose them with a harder heart (consider the example of Pharaoh or what Paul warns about in Rm 1:24–28).

Finally, we can see that this verse is not talking about what God is not powerful enough to do but what God is too wise and prudent to do. There is no waste with God, as He is perfectly wise and prudent and careful. God does not throw pearls before swine nor give what is holy to the dogs (Mt 7:6). Consider the remedy God supplied for those bitten by serpents during the exodus. Only those people who were honest about their dependence on God looked at the bronze serpent on the pole and were healed (they believed the Word of God;

Nu 21:9; Jn 3:14; 1Co 10:9). The best—perhaps the only—way to bring the faithless to faith is by leaving them to their own ways until emptiness and inability forces them to honesty. Then a person has ears to hear the Word and eyes to see how the life of Jesus confirmed this as truth.

● ● ● ● ● ● ● ● ● ● ● ● ● ● ● ● ● ● ●

Q 6:13 Why don't the followers of Christ still drive out demons and heal people today?

There are two reasons, both having to do with the purpose of miracles. The purpose of miracles is primarily to authenticate God's Word and those who speak it, as discussed in Mk 6:5 above. The Word of God always drives out demons. Healing of our bodies is always followed by subsequent illnesses and death. The only absolute and lasting remedy for the condition of our fallen human nature comes in the resurrection from the dead (1Co 15:42ff.). The first reason why the followers of Christ don't continue to drive out demons and heal people is because the purpose of doing so in a miraculous way is complete. Jesus' works authenticated Him; the miracles of the apostles authenticated them and the Gospel. Note how the immediate speaking of the languages of foreigners and the preaching of the Word always defeats opposition to the Gospel (Ac 2:14–46; 10:34–35, 44–47; 11:1–18; 15:1–12).

Second, God is always driving out demons and healing people—given His nature, how can this not be the case? Jesus

healed ten lepers but only one returned to thank Him (Lk 17:11–19). Almost every human being enjoys the benefits of an immune system and the "natural" healing properties of human physiology. But why should we heal? We heal as we do, even those most opposed to God, because God intends to provide a profound and indisputable witness to His love for us and His will that we should live and not die. At the same time, faithful followers of Christ seek to be good stewards of the gifts God has given us, including languages and the healing arts. God still drives out demons and heals both believers and unbelievers, in more or less time, sometimes for the present but always for the purpose of all eternity (Rm 2:4; 2Co 4:1–5:8; 12:7–10).

● ● ● ● ● ● ● ● ● ● ● ● ● ● ● ● ● ● ●

Q 6:17 What's the story with Herod, Herodias, and Philip?

The story is rather simple, and Mark has the most complete account (Mk 6:14–29; Mt 14:1–12; Lk 3:19–20; 9:7–9). Herod did not take his brother Philip's wife because Philip had died but took her as an adulterer too powerful for Philip to oppose. Note that the history of the family of Herod is difficult to trace because so many members adopted the same names, and intermarriages make relationships confusing. The information that Mark supplies is enough to report what happened to John the Baptist and why.

● ● ● ● ● ● ● ● ● ● ● ● ● ● ● ● ● ● ●

Q 6:22–23 Why would Herod give the girl up to half his kingdom for one dance?

This is why the proverb says, "It is not for kings, O Lemuel, it is not for kings to drink wine, or for rulers to take strong drink" (Pr 31:4). This is also why God warns us against swearing (Mk 6:23, 26; Mt 5:34–36). The combination of alcohol and swearing oaths is deadly, as we see here. The history of powerful people and their feasts suggests that there was plenty to drink (1Sm 25:36; 1Ki 16:9; Jl 3:3; Rv 17:2). The history of fallen human nature reveals arrogance, pride, and boasting, especially when intoxicated (1Co 1:18–25; Pr 11:2; 16:18). Herod, wanting to seem as almighty as God Himself, makes the presumptuous offer that he does, too drunk and self-impressed to consider the opportunity this would present for Herodias. Regarding the perils of considering oneself as almighty as God, read what happens to this Herod's son in Ac 12:21–23.

● ● ● ● ● ● ● ● ● ● ● ● ● ● ● ● ● ● ● ●

Q 6:25 Why did the daughter of Herod request John the Baptist's execution?

Herodias hated John and wanted to kill him because John said it was not lawful for her to be married to Herod. When Herod promised to give her daughter whatever she asked for, she consulted with her mother, who told her to ask for John's head (6:19, 24).

● ● ● ● ● ● ● ● ● ● ● ● ● ● ● ● ● ● ● ●

Q 6:41 Is there any connection between the feeding of the five thousand and Communion?

Yes—the same kind of connection as between all things physical and spiritual. Think of the soul and things spiritual as the essence but immaterial, and the material creation as indicative but material. This relationship is what makes the parables work.

All four Gospels record the feeding of the five thousand (Mt 14:13–22; Mk 6:30–44; Lk 9:10–17; Jn 6:1–14). John's Gospel includes a record of the interaction between Jesus and the crowds on the following day. Jesus explains that He is the true, living bread and drink that comes down from heaven. While we are acutely aware of our body's need for food and drink, Jesus warns that this food cannot sustain our bodies and our bodies cannot endure in their fallen condition ("Your fathers ate the manna in the wilderness and are dead" [Jn 6:49]). The connection is as follows:

1. In a general way, Jesus feeds the crowd because He is God, the author and provider for our lives in every way (Col 3:16–18).

2. More particularly, Jesus provides for their physical hunger in order to demonstrate that all things are provided for those who listen to and follow His teaching (Mt 6:25–33).

3. Jesus provides bread and fish for these people when it is impossible to do so, just as He offered living water to a woman when He had nothing with which to draw from the well (Jn 4:10–11). Miracles authenticate Jesus as the Son and Word of God.

4. Jesus goes on to talk about His body and blood, even though there was no drink provided and wine is not mentioned. Jesus makes this progression because His Word is God in a physical form, as bread bears nutrition and as blood carries life to all parts of the body.

5. So then, our whole life depends on God, and our physical life depends on our spiritual life. The Word is to our whole life, especially to our soul, as bread and wine are to our physical life. This is the connection between the feeding of the five thousand and Communion. See 1Co 10–11 for more on this subject.

Q 6:52 What was the real meaning of the bread?

This had to do with the apostles not understanding Jesus' teaching. This is an important witness to how uncomprehending and distracted fallen human nature is. Jesus had just finished feeding more than five thousand men, plus women and children, from five loaves of bread and two fish. Then, to make sure there was no mistake about what just happened, Jesus had the apostles gather up the leftovers—twelve basketfuls. Should this be lesson enough to take our concern for food off the plate for the rest of our lives? If Jesus provides food no matter what and walks on water, then why should we ever be afraid for any reason (Rm 8:32)? Mark 8:13–21 and Mt 16:5–12 record another occasion where the disciples

display their failure to grasp the import of Jesus' miracles. On this occasion, Jesus warns His apostles to beware of the leaven of the Jewish religious leaders. The apostles immediately begin talking about how they forgot to bring bread. Jesus responds by asking them how they could worry about bread (like worrying about their lives in a storm) when He had just fed the multitudes. Before we are too hard on the apostles, we might consider all the kinds of things we worry about, especially since we have a whole Bible's worth of history about how fully and faithfully God provides for His people.

Q 7:1–3 Why did the Pharisees confront Jesus?

According to the text, they confronted Jesus about issues of ceremonial washing. The Pharisees had numerous rules, including many about washing rites (Mk 7:4). This is the reason on the surface. The real issue has to do with what makes us righteous in the eyes of God. Fallen human nature cannot be perfect, yet it is proud. The only way for fallen human nature to sustain its pride is to claim a righteous life, and the only way to do that is to replace divine Law—which deals with the essentials of life—with man-made rules that deal with superficial matters (Mt 5:17–48). Jesus ignores their rules and their legalistic misapplication of God's Law, which not only exposed the uselessness of their system but also exposed their unrighteousness and guilt before God.

Jesus fulfills the Law of God by perfect obedience to the Father and by genuinely loving others, which sometimes requires dirty hands and often takes place on the Sabbath.

* *

Q 7:24–30 Was the girl with the unclean spirit possessed by a demon?

The passage makes it clear that the girl had an evil spirit because the woman kept asking Jesus to cast "the demon out of her daughter" (v. 26). Demons are like the devil but do not seem to share his priority (Mt 12:24; the devil is referred to as the "prince of demons"). Demon possession was certainly real in biblical times and there is no reason to think it does not still happen today. While there are always some who are interested in ailments that seem to lack physical definition, modern medicine generally treats every ailment as physical in nature, rather than a case of demon possession.

The relationship between demon possession and sickness is uncertain. For example, Mk 1:32 says that people brought to Jesus "all who were sick or oppressed by demons." It sounds as if these are two distinct groups, and so far I have been unable to find a text that ties sickness with demon possession.

Note that Mark and Matthew include this narrative (Mt 15:21–28), but Luke and John do not. Also note that this encounter between Jesus and a woman is similar to the event recorded in Mt 9:20–22; Mk 5:25–34; and Lk 8:43–48, but is not in John. See Mt 15:21–28 for a more comprehensive explanation.

* *

Q 8:12 Didn't Jesus show any miraculous signs? Why did He say none would be given?

Jesus did three and a half years of miraculous signs, so many that the world could not hold a record of them all (Jn 21:25). On this occasion, both Matthew (16:1–4) and Mark (8:10–12) record Jesus saying only that no sign will be given. However, Matthew records a similar conversation (12:38–42) with an explanation that Mark does not record (Matthew's account would have taken place between Mk 3:29 and 3:30). What should we make of all this?

First, we have considered in previous questions and answers that Jesus does not cast pearls before swine nor give what is holy to dogs (Mt 7:6; cf. Mk 4:33–34 and 6:5 above). While Jesus has done plenty of signs in public and for masses of people to demonstrate His divine nature (Jn 5:36), He refuses to do signs for those who steadfastly refuse to see what He is showing them (Jn 6:30–31, 49; 8:30–59).

Second, according to Mt 12:38–42, in response to the Jewish religious leaders' first demand for a sign, Jesus did offer an explanation. He told them that no sign would be given them except for the sign of Jonah. There are at least two aspects to the sign of

Jonah. One sign of Jonah has to do with how immediately and thoroughly the sailors and Ninevites repented in the presence of Jonah. The other sign has to do with Jonah and his stubbornness and refusal to understand, learn from, or accept what God was showing Him through these foreign people.

• • • • • • • • • • • • • • • • • • • •

Q **8:15 What is the yeast of the Pharisees and Herod?**

Yeast has two features that the New Testament uses for teaching. First, yeast always affects the whole of what it is introduced to (1Co 5:6–9). The fall of Adam in human nature is like yeast because it infects all of us. Paul describes this infection as malice and wickedness. Second, yeast has a chemistry that "puffs up" the lump of dough by filling it with pockets of air. Paul contrasts this being "puffed up" with the "unleavened" disposition of sincerity and truth (cf. 1Co 5:8; Mt 11:28–30; 1Co 4:6; 8:1).

• • • • • • • • • • • • • • • • • • • •

Q **8:22–25 Why does Jesus touch the blind man's eyes twice?**

Only Mark records this strange account. Mark's Gospel has a little more focus on the unbelief of people, which may be why Mark recorded it (notice Jesus' anger with the religious leaders in 3:5 and with His own apostles in 16:14). The problem cannot be a lack of power with the Son of God. It may be that Mark is highlighting one of the difficulties that a weak faith causes. This is precisely

the problem reported only in Mark with another case of difficulty with healing (9:24). On the positive side, this narrative may be another of many encouragements for us to be diligent and unwavering in our appeals to God for help (Lk 18:1–8; 2Co 4:1, 16). Remember that God uses the experiences we have as material people in a material and temporal world in the interest of our eternal soul. Having physical blindness healed is not nearly as important as healing spiritual blindness (Jn 9:41).

• • • • • • • • • • • • • • • • • • • •

Q **8:23–26 How do people always recognize Jesus?**

Isaiah prophesied that there would not be anything extraordinary or exceptionally beautiful about the Messiah that would attract people to Him (Is 53:2b). However, Jesus usually had His twelve apostles with Him, which would draw some attention. It is likely that people shared descriptions of Jesus and, after having seen Him once, would not be likely to forget what He looked like.

• • • • • • • • • • • • • • • • • • • •

Q **8:26 Why does Jesus tell the blind man not to go to the village?**

Some ancient Greek manuscripts include "nor tell anyone in the town," and different translations will include or exclude this depending on which manuscript traditions they follow. Whether these extra words were in the original text or not, from ancient times it is evident that people understood that the reason Jesus told the man not to go into the town was to keep him from telling people about what Jesus had done. Jesus' command for silence about His miracles has been discussed above at Mk 1:44.

● ● ● ● ● ● ● ● ● ● ● ● ● ● ● ● ● ● ●

Q 8:30 Why does Jesus warn Peter not to say anything?

See Mk 1:44 above.

● ● ● ● ● ● ● ● ● ● ● ● ● ● ● ● ● ● ●

Q 8:31 Why does Jesus refer to Himself as the Son of Man?

The expression "Son of Man" occurs 191 times in the Bible—including 93 times in Ezekiel and 86 times in the New Testament. Reading Ezekiel is an essential step for understanding the context in which Jesus used this expression (see Ezk 2:1–5; 21:6; 37:1–14). Jesus is called the Son of Man because He is fulfilling all that the Law requires of every human being of all time (2Co 5:21). He is the Son of Adam as promised to Adam and Eve (Gn 3:15; 4:1). Note how Eve thought God's promise had been fulfilled in her first child as she observes, "I have gotten a man, the Lord" (Gn 4:2, author's translation) Beware, as many English versions mistranslate this, "With the help of the Lord." Jesus is the Son promised to Abraham, Isaac, Jacob, and David (Gn 12:3; 2Sm 7:12–16; Gal 3:13–16).

Why does Jesus refer to Himself as the Son of Man?

● ● ● ● ● ● ● ● ● ● ● ● ● ● ● ● ● ● ●

Q 9:1 How do we know what context to take this verse in? What does this verse mean?

The context is that Jesus is about to complete His work of redemption through His crucifixion, death, and resurrection in Jerusalem. You will notice that right after Jesus says these words, He is transfigured (9:2ff.), and then comes Palm Sunday (11:1ff.), Holy Week, and Jesus' resurrection on Easter. Jesus' prophecy is fulfilled in at least two ways. First, there were indeed people present who would see the kingdom of God appear with power before they died. The apostles and others would see Jesus after He rose from the dead and would watch Him ascend into heaven, to the right hand of God (Jn 20:19–30; 1Co 15:3–6). Second, Jesus said that no one who believes in Him would ever taste death (Jn 8:52). Human beings consist essentially of an eternal soul. That soul, together with our body, was created to be in positive relationships with others, otherwise known as communion or fellowship. Even though our bodies decompose and cease to function, our souls live on in uninterrupted experience and consciousness (Lk 16:19–31; 23:42–43). Therefore, death means something like "the absence of positive relationships." We know that Jesus died, absolutely and for all, when He cried out, "My God, My God, why have You forsaken Me?" (Mt 27:46; Mk 15:34). To "taste" death means to experience it. Since Jesus bore away in His own body the sins of the world, He tasted death for everyone (Heb 2:9). Jesus speaks in even more comprehensive terms when He declares that no one who believes in Him will ever die (Jn 11:25–26). Some of those standing with Jesus in this passage would realize the fulfillment of Jesus' words in both ways: they would see Him after His resurrection and they would never experience death. From that time forward, no one who believes in Jesus would ever experience true, lasting death (Jn 8:52; 11:25–26; 2Co 5:1ff.).

• •

Q 9:2–13 Could you please explain the transfiguration, especially the part that involves Moses and Elijah? Is the transfiguration's sole purpose demonstrating resurrection? If so, why wasn't the resurrection of Lazarus and Christ and others enough? Was it an action of God to demonstrate His glory?

I will provide short answers here; please see questions at Mt 17:1ff. for more complete answers.

The term *transfiguration* is Latin for the Greek *metamorphosis*, which means, literally, "the action of changing form." The appearance of Jesus changes as He reveals His divine nature, which was normally hidden beneath an ordinary human nature (Is 53:2b; Heb 2:17). Moses is the one who communicated the Law from God to the people (Jn 1:17). Elijah was the first and foremost

of the prophets (1Ki 18–2Ki 10:17; Jas 5:17). As John the Baptist and God's voice from heaven pointed to Jesus as the Christ at the beginning of His public work, so now we realize that Jesus has fulfilled all that the Law requires and all that God promised through the prophets. Once again, the voice of God confirms Jesus as the Christ just before He suffers and dies in order to finish His work.

The point of the transfiguration is threefold. God the Father confirms that Jesus is His Son and that He is well pleased with Him. Jesus will suffer absolute rejection and die not because He has done wrong, but because He is the only one to have done all things absolutely right, out of perfect love. God the Father gives this profound witness to Peter, James, and John in order to strengthen their faith during the period of trial about to come. God gives us this witness to Jesus' nature. We live in constant temptation to forget that God is ever present in the ordinary form of the printed Word, water, bread, and wine. All the fullness of the Godhead was present with Jesus in a body, and that fullness is still present with us in the body of the Holy Scriptures (Col 1:19; 3:16).

While the appearance of Moses and Elijah does bear witness to the resurrection, the physical raising of many others and of Jesus is a much more powerful witness since these people had living families and friends, were resurrected bodily, and lived on for some time. Interestingly, no amount of resurrecting from the dead seems able to convince fallen yet proud human nature. When fallen human nature is disabled and crushed under the Law, the Spirit will regenerate us in the image of Christ. Then we don't need a resurrection at all; the Word of God will be more than sufficient (Lk 23:42–43; Jn 20:29). Compare the response of the Jewish religious leaders with that of Mary and Martha at the raising of Lazarus (Jn 11:17–53).

This was one of the many actions of God that demonstrate His glory—though His glory (to do what no one else can or would do) is most clearly demonstrated in His humiliation, suffering, and death as our substitute because of His love for us.

Q 9:6 My Bible translation puts this verse in parentheses. Why is that?

Some English translations put this verse in parentheses because it sounds like a thought that is "parenthetical" to the narrative. A parenthetical comment is the note of an editor or a thought that a person has in his or her own mind, reflecting on the content of the main narrative. In this case, the comment anticipates a question from readers: "Why would Peter ask permission to build shelters for Moses, Elijah, and Jesus?"

Q 9:10 Why did they discuss the rising of the dead?

We know that many people in Jesus' day vigorously opposed the resurrection of the dead (Mk 12:18). Most struggle with the idea of the resurrection of the dead because it is almost never experienced (Lk 24:5–7,

21–24). Others believed in the resurrection but didn't expect to experience it until the end of the world (Jn 11:24). We have the advantage of knowing the whole of biblical history containing many accounts of bodily resurrection and clear promises of the resurrection of all the faithful on the last day (1Co 15:35ff.).

Q 9:11–13 Is Jesus referring to John the Baptist in this passage? How is John the Baptist Elijah? Does he know that he is?

John the Baptist, like Elijah, was a focused and particular prophet who would turn the hearts of the people to the Lord (1Ki 18:21; Lk 1:16–17). The Spirit of the Lord made both men powerful, unconquerable, and faithful witnesses (2Ki 2:9; Lk 1:15). Both men had unusual diet and wardrobe (1Ki 17:4; 2Ki 1:8; Mk 1:6). I suspect John realized he had come in the power and spirit of Elijah as he was filled with the Holy Spirit from his mother's womb, leaped for joy at hearing Mary's voice, never drank alcohol, and ministered to people in the wilderness, baptizing them in the Jordan.

See questions at Mt 17:11–12 for more answers.

Q 9:14–32 How were the disciples able to perform miracles?

Mk 6:7–13 provides a record of Jesus setting apart twelve of His disciples as apostles and giving them authority to cast out demons and heal people. Mark's Gospel

145

concludes by reminding us that the apostles were authenticated by the authority Jesus gave them to do miracles (Mk 16:16–20). This narrative shows that a fallen human being, even one authorized by Jesus to heal, does not possess the ability as God Himself possesses it. The apostles failed to cast out this demon. The father of the demon-possessed boy cries to the Lord for help in his struggle against unbelief (9:24). Only Jesus, the true Son of God and Son of Man, never fails.

● ● ● ● ● ● ● ● ● ● ● ● ● ● ● ● ● ● ●

Q 9:14–29 Jesus seems to get angry that the people do not understand Him. Why does He not know of the ignorance of people?

The three Synoptic Gospels—Matthew, Mark, and Luke—each reveal a slightly different disposition of Jesus toward people in general. Matthew is the most balanced, Luke is more positive, and Mark more negative. Mark's Gospel alone reports that Jesus was angry in the synagogue (3:5). Mark alone reports that Jesus rebuked His apostles' unbelief and hardness of heart after the resurrection (16:14). There is a very important difference between knowing all about the fallen human condition and having to deal with it day after day. Jesus surely knows our faults and inabilities (Jn 2:24–25; Pss 14:1–3; 103:14). His frustration and anger flow not from our disabilities but from the way we stubbornly assert our own opinions and ways in opposition to the remedies He makes so readily and abundantly available (Ezk 18:1ff.; Is 55:1ff.; Jer 8:4–9; Mt 23:13–38). This is why Jesus points to the weak, helpless, and children as the model of faith and why He is so angry when people would prevent them from coming to Him (Mk 10:13–14; 1Co 1:18–31). We might also be careful to note that Jesus is much more patient with the average person than with those who claim to be teachers (compare the patience of Jesus in Jn 6:25–65 with the severity of His language in Jn 8:31–47. See also Jas 3:1; Jer 23).

● ● ● ● ● ● ● ● ● ● ● ● ● ● ● ● ● ● ●

Q 9:15 Does the people's reaction to seeing Jesus indicate something similar to how Moses still "glowed" when he went out to the people from the Lord's presence?

Moses' physical appearance glowed so that he put a veil over his face when he spoke with the people (Ex 34:32–35; 2Co 3:10–18). The people's reaction probably has more to do with their anticipation of what Jesus will do than anything having to do with His appearance (Is 53:2b). The people had come to expect great things from Jesus, and they would have been even more interested, now, to see if Jesus could succeed where the apostles had failed.

● ● ● ● ● ● ● ● ● ● ● ● ● ● ● ● ● ● ●

Q 9:19 Who is Jesus calling the faithless generation?

On the one hand, Jesus could be speaking with the generation of people who were with Him at the time, but this seems unlikely because the Bible records the unbelief of people from the beginning and predicts it to the end (Nu 14:33; Lk 18:8). When complaining about the unbelieving generation, He is surely talking about fallen human nature—all generated from Adam since Adam's disobedience and unbelief.

● ● ● ● ● ● ● ● ● ● ● ● ● ● ● ● ● ● ●

Q 9:28–29 How was this demon different from others? What does Jesus mean when He says this can only come by prayer?

The difference appears to be with those trying to cast out the demon, rather than the demon itself. Notice at first Jesus is taking time to talk with the father about the boy, but when Jesus sees a crowd coming together, He very quickly dispenses with the demon. Jesus, being true God, is always in control and never has any trouble commanding anything in creation (Mk 4:41). The disciples, authorized by Jesus but still weak in their faith, are the ones who have trouble with this demon; the father struggles with faith as well (Mt 17:20; Mk 9:24). Only Mark's account records Jesus saying this kind of demon requires prayer to cast out. Jesus connects the efficacy of prayer with faith (Mt 21:22); Paul says that faith comes from hearing the Word (Rm 10:17), and Jesus says if a person remains in His Word, what he or she asks will be granted (Jn 15:7). Now, perhaps we can make sense of Jesus' word about faith in Matthew's account, His mention of prayer here, why the apostles could not cast out the demon, and why Jesus never had trouble. Jesus is the

Word of God, has absolute, perfect faith, and is therefore always heard when He prays and always obeyed when He commands (Jn 11:22). The apostles, like anyone, inasmuch as there is an absence of the Word in our life, fail when faith is called upon—so God is the one we depend on and never ourselves (Mk 10:26–27).

● ● ● ● ● ● ● ● ● ● ● ● ● ● ● ● ● ● ●

Q 9:33–37 Who is the greatest?

Matthew's record of this same conversation provides the answer to this question: "Whoever humbles himself like this child is the greatest in the kingdom of heaven" (Mt 18:4). Later in Jesus' ministry, He adds that whoever would be the greatest must be servant of all (Mt 23:11). In Luke's Gospel, Jesus says the greatest must be as the younger (Lk 22:26). Jesus Himself demonstrates this truth in His own life by His incarnation and humiliation (Php 2:5ff.) and in many particular acts of service, like washing the disciples' feet (Jn 13:1–17).

● ● ● ● ● ● ● ● ● ● ● ● ● ● ● ● ● ● ●

Q 9:34 Why are the disciple arguing when they know they are nothing compared to Jesus?

If we follow Jesus' advice and take the log out of our own eye first, the answer to this question is simple. Like almost every other person in the Bible, the disciples have a fallen human nature. The history of fallen human nature in the Bible has at least three purposes. (1) Despite the failings of human nature since the fall, it is still incredibly proud. The whole history of man and biblical history as well show us the depth, universality, and magnitude of our fallen condition. Thus we can claim no more ability in matters of faith and life than a child. Such humility is a necessary condition for our salvation (Mt 18:4; Rm 3:19, 26–28). (2) The failings of the disciples allow us to see the depth, universality, and magnitude of God's grace (Rm 8:31–39). (3) The history of the disciples is evidence for the necessity of the Holy Spirit to regenerate and sustain the faithful soul and the failings of fallen human nature until the day we put it off (Rm 7:14–25; 1Co 15:53–58).

Q 9:38 Why do the disciples appear to be so arrogant and stupid?

Everything that is wrong is a consequence of the fall of Adam and is thus condemned (Pr 16:5; Mal 4:1; 2Tm 3:2; Ti 1:7). Perhaps in this verse the disciples are more possessive, territorial, or vain than arrogant—all these are also condemned by God. Then again, maybe the problem is fear (Heb 2:14–15). Since human beings are separated from God, we are possessed by a constant fear of loss. Fear of loss creates an acute sense of competition (think about how our culture today fosters and glorifies competition rather than cooperation and service). The disciples have been called by an impressive rabbi and, like the other religious leaders, are afraid of becoming unimportant and ignored (Jn 11:48). Stupidity is also

a consequence of rebellion against God (Jer 8:7–9). God's remedy for this is in Christ, who rebuked His disciples (as He does regularly) and who re-establishes communion between us and God (2Co 5:17–20). Communion with God provides forgiveness for arrogance and stupidity, replaces fear with love, and moves us to seek cooperation with others rather than competition against them (1Jn 4:18; 1Co 1:30–31; 3:21; Jn 13:12–17).

Q 9:42–50 How do you know when to interpret the Bible for its face value or to read into it? Is there a reason we keep encountering the same lessons? Are we really supposed to cut off body parts that sin?

Repetition is an ancient and proven method of teaching. Since our fallen human nature is opposed to God, it is necessary to constantly relearn and reapply the lessons He teaches us. Four Gospels in the New Testament give us perspective and a more complete view of the life and teaching of Jesus.

Principles of biblical interpretation are well-known and have a history that can be studied. Much of what the Bible means to say is made clear with access to the original languages. Much of what the Bible says may require application but not interpretation—for example, historical narrative or clear imperatives, such as "love your neighbor as yourself." The most important principle is "Scripture interprets Scripture" or "Scripture interprets itself." This means that the Bible itself will tell you if your understanding of a passage is correct, but this requires that we read and keep rereading the Bible in order to know how it comments on itself. Vv. 20–21 of 2Pt 1 explain that the Bible is not of any private interpretation because it is not the word of men. The second most important principle is that we take a passage in the most simple and literal sense unless we are forced to do otherwise. What happens if we apply these two principles to this passage? Does Jesus really mean that if our hand or foot causes us to sin, we should cut it off? Why not? His explanation makes sense—wouldn't it be better to enter heaven with one hand or foot than to spend eternity in hell (especially since in the resurrection our body will be restored to perfection)? Next, consider whether it is indeed our hands or feet that make us sin. What does the Bible say? The source of our trouble is the heart (Jer 17:9; Mk 7:21–23). Does Jesus mean we should cut out our heart? Absolutely—only not the muscle that pumps blood but that central aspect of our being for which the heart is named. God promises that He will take out our wicked heart and give us a new one, and Jesus says that unless we are generated from above, we cannot see or enter the kingdom of God (Ezk 36:26; Jn 3:3–7). The works of the flesh continue to be contrary to God's will, and Paul commands us all to put that flesh to death—not the physical death of our biology, but the contrary disposition of sin that dwells in our flesh (Col 3:5ff.). Thus we have seen that Jesus is speaking literally. Once we have taken time to realize what the cause of sin is and what it means to cut something off, the passage is perfectly clear.

Q 9:47–50 How come Jesus mentions physical traits in reference to heaven? Elsewhere the Bible says we are made perfect in heaven.

I can't think of a text that says we will have perfect bodies in heaven. There are texts that say we will have our body restored at the resurrection on the last day, but the resurrected body of Jesus retained the signs of His wounds from being crucified (1 Co 15:42–44; Lk 24:36–43). Heaven, like hell, is a temporary place for souls to be until the end of the world, the resurrection, and the creation of the new heaven and earth (Heb 11:13–16; 2Pt 3:13; Rv 20:14–21:1). The key in this text is the conditional language Jesus uses. If it were true that your hand or foot caused you to sin, it would be better to go to heaven maimed than to have all your limbs and go to hell—even though you don't take a body with you to heaven or hell. The truth, as discussed in Mk 9:42–50 above, is that no part of our human physiology is the cause of our sin, but sin itself has corrupted our entire person, like yeast affects the whole lump of dough (see question and answer at Mk 8:15). What Jesus is teaching us to cut off are those desires that move us to wickedness, which is even harder to do than cutting off one of our limbs (Col 3:5–10; Rm 8:13).

Q **9:49 What does this verse mean? Is this one of the texts where the Roman Catholic Church gets the idea of purgatory?**

Both salt and fire have to do with purification. Salt also has to do with creating thirst, like the Law that leads us to Christ (Rm 5:20; Gal 3:24). Fire also has to do with power, like Baptism with the Holy Spirit and fire on Pentecost (Ac 2). Everyone must pass through the judgment of the Law ("seasoned with fire"); Christ has already made this passage for all people so that only those who steadfastly and adamantly insist on their own ability to fulfill the Law will meet the fire of judgment on the last day (Mt 25:31–46; Jn 5:28–29; Gal 2:16). "For everyone will be salted with fire" suggests that God's judgment is not fooled by hypocrisy or pretense, as Jesus plainly demonstrated in Mt 23:13–36. The offering (sacrifice) of Ananias and Sapphira was seasoned with the salt of Peter's discerning questions and bore awe-inspiring results (Ac 5:1–11).

The idea for purgatory developed as a proposed remedy for the reassertion of salvation by works of the Law. Since there is no way to have peace or hope of heaven under the burden of the Law, the idea was developed that a special place existed where people who believed but failed to keep the Law perfectly could go until the Law was satisfied.

Q **9:50 What does the salt represent?**

Salt has properties that parallel the Law in general. Jesus said that we are the salt of the earth, but if we lose our saltiness, how can we be made salty again? We are good for nothing except to be thrown on the ground and trampled underfoot (Mt 5:13). Salt enhances flavor, makes thirsty, and purifies. Disciples of Jesus have this same effect on people: we speak the truth clearly and with precision (flavor); we communicate the Word of God that is truth, light, and grace to forgive and regenerate; the Law of God makes a person thirst for the righteousness that God provides in Christ and for the forgiveness of sins (1Co 14:6–9; Jn 4:7ff.; Php 3:7–12). Have you noticed that the world, in general, does not seem to be very "thirsty" for the Word of God because the hypocrisy and inarticulate condition of what claims to be Christian has given it little reason to be so (Ezk 36:22; Rm 2:23–24)? Having salt in ourselves means to be purified of dishonesty, vanity, and self-delusion by a life in the Word, the way saltwater purifies what is soaked in it. If we have salt—the Word—in us, we will be at peace with one another because we will be more critical of ourselves than others, we will serve others rather than seeking control of them, and we will love others because we are aware of how our life depends on the love of God (Mt 7:1–5; Ruth; Lk 7:40–47).

Q 10:1–12 Under what conditions is divorce permitted?

There are three causes for divorce that are permissible, though reconciliation remains ideal when possible. The first cause is adultery (Mt 19:9). The other two causes are abuse and abandonment: here a spouse is either forced to leave to avoid abuse or is left (1Co 7:12–16). In all three cases a divorce does not break the marriage but only recognizes that the marriage has been and remains broken.

Q 10:7–9 Why does only the man have to leave his mom and dad and not the woman?

Adam was created to be responsible for the care and well-being of Eve. You may note that Adam is not only created first but that he is instructed by God and names the animals before it is clear that a wife must be created for him (Gn 2:7–24). God said it was not good for man to be alone; therefore, He would make a helper to remain before him (2:18). It was not good for man to be alone because being made in the image of God meant that Adam was to give His life for the care and well-being of another—but there was no other. The woman would be man's helper in two ways: she would be the object of his care, and she would carry and bear children, for whom the man would also bear responsibility. The woman would remain before the man—obviously, since it was not good for the man to be alone and they must be together if he is to be responsible for her. Thus, to mature as a man is to become capable of bearing responsibility for others, demonstrated by leaving the care of one's own parents. A woman, in contrast, was made to be provided for and thus remains under the care and protection of her father (or other male relatives) until a man demonstrates the ability and commitment to take her as a wife. See more about this in 1Co 11 and 1Th 4.

Q 10:11–12 Why is it wrong to marry twice? If a man is divorced by his wife, is he allowed to remarry, or is that adultery? Is it true that if civil law said you could have ten wives, you could have ten wives?

Remarrying depends on why the first marriage was dissolved. The question and answer at Mk 10:7–9 above describes permissible causes for divorce. Nevertheless, some care must be taken not to impose prohibitions or condemnation where God has not. We seek reconciliation of spouses and the preservation of marriage when possible. When the past cannot be repaired and people cannot be reconciled, we must begin where people are, absolving the penitent and counseling them forward according to the Word of God. For example, Paul says, "But if the unbelieving partner separates, let it be so. In such cases the brother or a sister is not enslaved. God has called you to peace" (1Co 7:15). Remarriage is only wrong if there is no biblical justification for the divorce, which means in the eyes of God the marriage still exists.

Paul taught that we are to obey the governing authorities, but what a government allows is not the same as what it requires, nor does this make it permissible by God. Our own government has legalized many things that God forbids: abortion, fornication, and homosexuality, for example. Creation reveals God's design for man and woman in marriage; God created the first man and one woman to be his wife, just as Christ has only one Bride, the Church (Eph 5:31–33). Examples of polygamy in the Bible reveal two truths. One, a man can be responsible for more than one woman at a time, but a woman cannot be submissive to more than one man (no more than the Church could be in communion with more than one God; Mt 6:24). Two, polygamy is a human attempt to make the best of a bad situation in a fallen world (1Sm 25:23–42; Is 4:1; 1Co 11:3).

Q **10:12 Why can a woman divorce here but not according to Jesus' explanation in Mt 19?**

Jewish women were not allowed to divorce their husbands. Since Matthew was writing to Jews, there was no need for him to include what Jesus said about women's rights according to Roman law. Mark, on the other hand, was writing to a mainly Gentile audience. Under Roman law,

women had the same legal rights as men in regard to divorce, so it was important that Jesus' words regarding this were included.

Q **10:13–16 Why do the disciples send the children away from Jesus?**

This text says that the disciples "rebuked" those who brought children to Jesus. Jesus shows how serious this action of rebuke is as He rebukes demons and commands them to be silent and come out (Mk 1:25) and as He rebukes wind and wave (4:39). When Jesus described how He would suffer, die, and rise, Peter rebuked Him; then Jesus rebuked Peter (8:32–33). The disciples rebuke people because they share a typical misunderstanding of what power and glory are all about. Like people of all times and places, the disciples think that Jesus is too important to be bothered with common people and their common problems. Soon after the disciples rebuked people bringing children, they also rebuked a blind man who was calling to Jesus for mercy (10:48). Paul helps us understand how God's power and glory compare to human opinions about the same in 1Co 1:18–31. Both Hannah and Mary sang about how the Lord brings low the proud but raises the lowly (1Sm 2:3–8; Lk 50–54). Fallen human nature, having lost communion with God, is left on its own to try to establish its own sense of worth. This means people look for ways to see others as less important so they appear more important. Jesus Himself confronted this dangerous and wicked opinion the night He was betrayed by washing the disciple's feet (Jn 13). Honesty about our utter dependence on God leads us to see that the poor and lowly do not depend on God more than we do but are simply more honest about it because they have no way of attempting to deceive.

● ● ● ● ● ● ● ● ● ● ● ● ● ● ● ● ● ● ● ●

Q 10:17–31 Is Jesus giving us Law, Gospel, or both?

First, let's define the terms. *Law* means "what is required" and leads to judgment. *Gospel* means "what is provided" and flows from grace. Second, there is Law in this exchange only because the young man insists on justifying himself. Notice the contradiction in the man's question, "What must I do to inherit eternal life?" We cannot make ourselves heirs to an inheritance. An inheritance can only be given to us by our Creator when He makes us a child of our parents. Since the man is determined to justify himself by means of the Law, Jesus shows him how absolute and comprehensive are the demands of the Law. Did you notice that Jesus did not repeat the Ninth and Tenth Commandments about covetousness? Jesus waits to deal with those until after the young man claims to have kept all the commandments Jesus named—even though we all know that is not possible for anyone except Jesus (Jas 2:10). Third, notice something that is always true in the Bible: God always precedes and follows the Law with His grace and promises—otherwise the Law would always be the end of us. Even though the man was clear-ly hypocritical or self-deceived in claiming to have kept the Law, still Jesus, "looking at him, loved him." Jesus responds to the man's claim to perfection with a simple task that exposes the man's bondage to covetousness ("go, sell all that you have and give to the poor"). This task is followed by a promise, "and you will have treasure in heaven." Fourth, notice that Jesus did not condemn the man but gave him an invitation. It was the man's own dishonesty and misuse of the Law that kept him from knowing the life he claimed to seek with Christ (Jn 3:18–21). Finally, notice that Jesus' patience with, love for, and wise dialogue with the man is entirely a gift. God would rightly have been offended and angry at the impudence and arrogance of such an approach to Him. Jesus gives a gentle warning about this when He responds to the man, "Why do you call Me good?"

● ● ● ● ● ● ● ● ● ● ● ● ● ● ● ● ● ● ● ●

Q 10:18 Jesus asked the rich man, "Why do you call Me good? No one is good except God alone." Why would Jesus ask a question like that, especially of a person who appears to recognize Jesus as the Messiah? Is it that Jesus wants this man to really think about what he is saying, or is it that Jesus feels that this man may confess Jesus' goodness with his lips but deny Him in his heart?

Remember that Jesus needs to provide instruction for His disciples, a crowd, and everyone who lives afterwards. These things happened as examples for us and were written for our benefit (1Co 10:6, 11; 1Pt 1:12). Jesus asked, as He always does, a great diagnostic question. Why did the man call Jesus good? Was he flattering Jesus to gain favor? Was he revealing how consumed he was with legalism? Did he want to confess that Jesus was truly God? The record that Jesus "looking at him, loved him" suggests that it was not flattery, but the fact that Jesus' responds with this question argues that it was not because he was confessing that Jesus was God. Thus it seems likely that Jesus wants the man to consider how consumed with legalism he is and what consequences that brings (see Mk 17–31 above; see also Ac 15:5–12; Gal 2:16; 3:1–9).

● ● ● ● ● ● ● ● ● ● ● ● ● ● ● ● ● ● ●

Q **10:23 Is it really more difficult to get into heaven the more wealthy you are?**

Yes, though in the next few verses Jesus makes it clear that it is impossible for anyone to be saved by his or her own efforts. Think of salvation as floating in the water. God provides the properties of water and human physiology and the breath that makes us float—effortlessly. This is all God's doing, which we may enjoy and learn from. What happens if we think we need to collect possessions and keep them? Even the clothes we wear would be heavy enough in water to take us under, but ever since the fall, human nature has been determined to hide from the truth behind clothing and possessions. Anything we would claim to possess would weigh us down, and we would need to make an effort to tread

water in order to compensate for the extra weight. So a wealthy person, weighed down with many riches, would find it impossible to stay above water—even though God still provides for that if only the person would let go of what weighs him or her down. Elsewhere, Jesus discusses how we cannot serve two masters (either God or wealth; Mt 6:24) and Paul reveals that the "love of money is a root of all kinds of evils" (1Tm 6:10).

● ● ● ● ● ● ● ● ● ● ● ● ● ● ● ● ● ● ●

Q **10:28–31 Are these verses really saying we should give up our family to show our faith in following God?**

In these verses, Jesus is not saying what must be given up but what God provides for people who have already made sacrifices to serve Him. Jesus taught not only that we must be willing to forsake family but even that we must "hate" our family if we are going to be His disciple (Lk 14:26). There are two reasons for Jesus' teaching. First, there can be no gods before the one, true, living God. The First Commandment is first because without it nothing else can be right. And if we don't have God first and always, we cannot have anything else anyway. With God first, all else follows (Ps 37:4; Mt 6:33), but without God, there is nothing at all (Mk 4:25). Second, we must always distinguish between what is essential and what is indicative of the essential. We have soul and body, but only the soul is essential. We are immaterial or spiritual, and we are physical. Our soul is eternal, but our bodies are bound in time. If we serve what is material, nonessential, and temporary, we will lose both that and the spiritual, eternal life we sacrificed for these things (Mk 8:36; Lk 12:15–21). Eli the priest indulged the material life of his sons and in so doing lost them body and soul (1Sm 2:29; 3:12–14). Thus, when Jesus says we must "hate" our own family, He means that we cannot sacrifice anything for the human nature of our physical family if we are going to follow Jesus. Jesus' own family did not believe in Him, taunted Him, and even tried to silence Him (Jn 7:2–5; Mk 3:21). Jesus always served God above all and in so doing protected the lives of all people, soul and body (Jn 2:4; Gal 1:9–10).

Q **10:32 Why were the disciples astonished?**

This verse says that the people were not only astonished (or amazed) but also afraid. Certainly the teaching that precedes (v. 31) would be frightening to a person who didn't understand that we are composed of body and soul, material and eternal life (see 10:28–31 above). Matthew records more teaching of Jesus that took place between Mk 10:31 and 10:32, which could also cause amazement (20:1–16). Fallen human nature cannot begin to fathom God's love or His wisdom or His strength, all of which are necessary if we are to be saved (Is 55; Rm 11:33–35; 1Co 15:51–57). Mark is the only Gospel writer who uses this word for "amazed." We may understand more of what caused it by checking the other two places it occurs: Mk 1:27 and 10:24.

Q **10:37 Did James and John realize what they were requesting of Jesus in this verse? Were they referring to life on earth or eternal life? Why would one want to sit on the left or "bad" side?**

In v. 38, Jesus says, "You do not know what you are asking." James and John were referring to life in heaven, as they specify "in Your glory." Left isn't necessarily or always bad. In theological language, the "right-hand kingdom" has to do with spiritual matters and the "left-hand kingdom" has to do with civil or temporal affairs. It is possible that James and John wanted to occupy the next level of glory and authority, which would include all things. James and John are not alone in this desire and misunderstanding of what glory is or the path to it. The disciples often had discussions about who was the greatest among them (Lk 9:46; 22:24–26). Paul exposed the error of worldly thinking about power and authority in 1Co 1:18–31. *Glory* means to do what no one else can or would do (Rm 5:7–11). The glory of God is not His power to control others but His nature, which is love, and His power to love absolutely by giving His own life as fulfillment of the Law in our place. Fallen human nature is powerful and weak at the same time. We are vain and proud yet worried and fearful. We want the privileges that are proper for those who are glorious but we reject and even despise the self-sacrifice that demonstrates the glory of a person. Real glory is both selfless and unconcerned with privilege; God rewards this with the honor that is due (Php 2:5–11).

155

Q 10:39 What does Jesus mean when He says, "The cup that I drink you will drink, and with the baptism with which I am baptized, you will be baptized"?

A "cup" has to do with events that you are destined for. Jesus prayed in the Garden of Gethsemane that the Father would take His cup from Him (Mk 14:36) and later that night rebuked Peter, saying, "Shall I not drink the cup that the Father has given me?" (Jn 18:11). God's revelation to John describes the cup of God's wrath and judgment that the wicked unbelievers will soon drink (Rv 14:10; 16:19). *Baptism* means to be entirely united with someone or something, as the children of Israel were with Moses once they crossed the Red Sea (1Co 10:1ff.). When Jesus talks about the cup He will drink or the baptism He is about to be baptized with, He is referring to fulfilling all that the prophets promised about the Savior and enduring all the condemnation that the Law requires for the disobedient (Is 53:1–13; Mt 26:54).

Q 11:1–11 What is the significance of palm branches on Palm Sunday?

Palm branches, like coats, were readily available to spread before Jesus to honor Him as He entered Jerusalem. An interesting, further possibility has to do with Jesus being the remedy for the fall of Adam and Eve. When Adam and Eve rebelled against God, they covered themselves with fig leaves and hid from God. God gave physical witness to His promise to send a Savior by making them clothing of animal skins. Innocent animals lost their lives to cover the shame of Adam and Eve, just as Jesus, the Lamb of God, would take away the sin of the world and thus provide a covering for all. Might there be a relationship between the people's willingness to lay down the leaves of palm trees and their own clothing as God's covering for their sin was entering their city?

Q 11:4 What does the colt that has never been ridden symbolize?

There was a prophecy about this in the Old Testament (Zec 9:9), but the question about why remains. It is not odd that the colt was there or tied. The fact that those standing by it let it go with the apostles according to Jesus' word demonstrates God's control over all things. By entering Jerusalem mounted on a colt, Jesus was revealing both of His natures at once (see Mk 10:37 above for more about glory and humility). By riding into Jerusalem, Jesus showed that He was an authority, even though powerful men usually rode upon powerful horses. By riding on a donkey's colt, Jesus showed His humility: God had become man in order to make Himself accessible to us, to the lowly and outcast, and to children. We sing the song of the people that day as the Lord's Supper begins because there the Lord again takes up humble means by which He comes to us (bread and wine, His body and blood).

The colt never having been ridden is

consistent with Old Testament teachings that we give the first and best back to God to show appreciation and to give thanks (Nu 19:2; 1Sm 6:7; Hg 1:2–9; Mal 1:8).

● ● ● ● ● ● ● ● ● ● ● ● ● ● ● ● ● ●

Q 11:8 Why were people waiting for Christ as He entered the city?

It is possible that word had circulated that Jesus was coming, though we have no text that suggests this. Nevertheless, the roads that lead into Jerusalem were busy and already crowded. Once people recognized Jesus and began to shout praises to Him, others would have quickly noticed and joined in. Compare this with what happened at Pentecost (Ac 2:5, 41).

● ● ● ● ● ● ● ● ● ● ● ● ● ● ● ● ● ●

Q 11:9–10 Who is the messenger that Jesus is sending?

If you are referring to "He who comes in the name of the Lord," it is Jesus Himself, prophesied by Zechariah (9:9) and in the Psalms (118:26). Coming "in the name of the Lord" means to come according to the Word of the Lord; Jesus came just as all the prophets had said and He is the Word of God itself (Jn 1:1–3, 14).

● ● ● ● ● ● ● ● ● ● ● ● ● ● ● ● ● ●

Q 11:12–14 It sounds like Jesus is crabby. Whenever I hear this, I get the image that Jesus is human, not perfect.

Mark's Gospel has a reputation for making Jesus sound frustrated, angry, and even "crabby." Mark alone records that Jesus was angry when He healed the man with the withered hand (3:5). Mark omits the exception that Jesus makes when speaking about giving a sign to this adulterous generation (8:12). At the end of the Gospel, Mark records Jesus rebuking His apostles for their unbelief and hardness of heart (16:14).

Jesus is fully human, but this does not mean His anger makes Him imperfect. The Old Testament is full of references to God's anger against Israel; that anger, like the anger of Jesus here, is justified. Consider what God does with His anger, how He takes it out on His own Son so that He might be gracious and patient with us, as Jesus also displays.

● ● ● ● ● ● ● ● ● ● ● ● ● ● ● ● ● ●

Q 11:13 Why would Jesus not have known that there was no fruit on the tree but just leaves? Did Jesus make the fig tree whither for teaching purposes only? Why did Jesus kill the fig tree?

Here it is worth taking the time to compare Matthew, Mark, and Luke's account of this narrative (Mt 21:18–27; Mk 11:12–33; Lk 20:1–8). We have seen many times in the past that God asks questions for the purpose of drawing attention and teaching (Gn 3:9; Mk 2:8; 5:30). Certainly Jesus, according to His divine nature, knew there were no figs on the tree. Even according to His human nature, He would have known there would be no figs, for Mark is careful to include the comment that "for it was not the season for figs" (Mk 11:13). So the answer is "yes," Jesus made the tree wither and killed it for teaching purposes, but what is there in all of history that is not for teaching purposes (1Co 10:6, 11)? In fact, it is the inability of fallen human nature to learn or retain what it learns from history that makes history repeat itself (Jer 8:4–9; Mk 8:16–22; 2Pt 2:22). Though only Adam rebelled against God in the first place, all mankind fell in His fall, and all creation was subject to bondage under sin, all so that we might come to the knowledge of the truth and life everlasting (Rm 5:12ff.; 8:20–25; Jn 3:9–12). The whole ministry of Jesus and human failure to grasp it was about to climax in the arrest, false condemnation, and crucifixion of the Creator of the universe, but who was ready to bear fruit to God in faithfulness at this singular time (Mt 23:37; Mk 1:15; 13:33)? The fig tree provides a powerful witness to the consequences of being unprepared, whether we think it is the season or not. This is why Paul commands pastors to "be ready in season and out of season" (2Tm 4:2) and Peter warns us, as Jesus did, to be sober and ever vigilant (1Pt 5:8; Mk 13:33–37). This is also why the wise virgins brought oil with them, so that their lamps would not go out (Mt 25:1–13). The good news is that the Lord has given us His Word and Spirit, inexhaustible and ever available to us in the Holy Bible (Jn 6:63; 8:31–32; Rm 10:17).

● ● ● ● ● ● ● ● ● ● ● ● ● ● ● ● ● ●

Q 11:15–19 Were the priests abusing their office by letting vendors sell goods in the temple?

Yes, and Jesus condemns them for it:

"But you have made it a den of robbers" (Mk 11:17). For a more complete look at the abuses of the religious leaders, see Mt 23:1–36.

● ● ● ● ● ● ● ● ● ● ● ● ● ● ● ● ● ●

Q 11:18 Why were they so afraid of Jesus?

According to this verse, the religious leaders feared Jesus because all the people were amazed at His teaching, because He taught as one having authority (Mk 1:22). The chief priests and Pharisees provide more insight to their fear after Jesus raised Lazarus from the dead: "If we let Him go on like this, everyone will believe in Him, and the Romans will come and take away both our place and our nation" (Jn 11:48). The religious leaders feared Jesus because they thought He might provoke a rebellion that would bring a devastating Roman response. The religious leaders also feared Jesus because He was liberating the people from the power of these leaders, undermining their source of income and status. Surprisingly, the religious leaders did not seem to fear Jesus for the power He displayed, perhaps because He always and only used it for good rather than harm (Lk 4:28–30; 22:50–53; Jn 11:45–53; 18:4–6).

● ● ● ● ● ● ● ● ● ● ● ● ● ● ● ● ● ●

Q 11:23 Does this mean a person can make a mountain go into the sea?

Please see response to Mk 4:30–34 above.

Q 11:24 Should we ask God in prayer for more things than we already do?

This verse doesn't include mention of quantity but of variety: "whatever you ask." Fulfillment of our prayers depends, according to this verse, on believing. Here we must be careful to understand what the Bible means by "believe." First, the English words "believe," "faith," and "trust," are all translating the same Greek word *pistis*. Paul teaches that faith comes by hearing the Word (Rm 10:17). Jesus and Peter make clear that faith is God's work in us (Jn 6:29; 1Pt 1:5). John's Gospel provides clarification of this verse as Jesus says that whatever we ask in His name the Father will do—understanding that to ask "in His name" means to ask according to His Word. Notice the logic: whatever we ask in faith God will grant, but faith and the prayers of faith are generated and defined by the Word. Since the Word expresses God's will, He will certainly grant what we ask.

Q 11:28–12:12 Could you explain the verse "the stone that the builders rejected"?

Ever since the fall of Adam, human beings have tried to take the place of God, especially in remaking His creation in our own image. Early man wanted to build his own way to heaven, literally, which God saw as ridiculous (Gn 11:1–9). King David wanted to build a house for God, and Peter wanted to make shelters for Jesus, Moses, and Elijah; both were mistaken in wanting

to do so (2Sm 7:4ff.; Mt 17:4–5). In ancient times, the chief cornerstone was the first to be placed. This stone was cut and laid with extreme care because it would determine the lines for the rest of the building—this stone had to be perfect. Jesus is perfect and, as the Word of God, defines the perfect life. Having Christ as the cornerstone, like having Him as the foundation of our life, requires us to conform our life to His design rather than building our own design, quick and easy on the sand (Mt 7:24–27). Still, people insist on building lives, and sometimes buildings, according to their own designs and contrary to God's. As people construct their lives, like a person builds a building, they may come across Christ, the One who defines and orients our building so it will be good and endure. Fallen human nature rejects Him because He doesn't "fit" our design (Mt 24:1–2; Eph 2:20–22). This is why Jesus describes Himself and His Word as a stone that breaks us if we fall on it but that crushes us if it falls on us. If we break, God rebuilds us in the image of Christ according to His eternal and perfect design. If we insist on constructing a life of our own design, the truth will eventually fall on us and crush us to powder (Lk 20:18).

Q 11:33 Why would Jesus not tell the chief priests and the elders from whom He got the authority to do these things?

Jesus warned about casting pearls before swine or giving what is holy to the dogs, which means He wasn't going to share the truth with those who were entirely opposed to the truth (Mt 7:6). Jesus did give them a chance to hear the truth by asking them a simple question about the authority of John the Baptist. By this question, Jesus left the religious leaders to condemn themselves. The religious leaders didn't want to admit that John's authority was from God (heaven) because that would condemn their rejection of John. They didn't want to say John's authority was from man because then they would lose their control of the people—so they refused to be honest. Their refusal to be honest means they are opposed to the truth. This is why Jesus won't dishonor the truth by sharing it with them.

• • • • • • • • • • • • • • • • • • • •

Q 12:1–12 Why did the evicted tenants think that by killing the landowner's son they would get his inheritance?

First of all, the tenants had not been evicted. The landowner was simply trying to collect the part of the harvest he was due. Consider how little God expects of us in a tithe, when He is the source of all that we have and all that we are! Second, there is no making sense of the tenants' plan (I almost called it logic, but it is clearly not). How in the world would killing an heir make the murderers entitled to the inheritance? Now comes the hard part: this is exactly what humanity thinks in regard to God. God has created and sustains all things. We are utterly dependent on Him for our very breath and heartbeat. He sends His Word to us and sent His Son to confirm and fulfill that

Word. What did people do? We put Him to death. Even people who claim to love God put Him to death, in effect, by refusing to listen to His Word or those who would bring that Word to them. There is no making sense of a creature at war with his Creator. Jesus' description here is proven true as He and the apostles take the kingdom of heaven to the Gentiles (Ac 8:1ff.). His Word here is also proven true by the religious leader's response: "And they were seeking to arrest Him" (Mk 12:12). What a gift that God adopts us by grace and regenerates us as His very own children (Gal 4:4–5; Jn 1:12–13; 3:3–7; 1Jn 3:1ff.).

• • • • • • • • • • • • • • • • • • • •

Q 12:12 If the teachers of the law and the elders know that Jesus is speaking about them in this parable, why would they want to make the parable true in real life?

Good question—why indeed? We know that the wages of sin is death (Rm 6:21, 23), so why do we keep on sinning? There is no making sense of the creature in rebellion against the Creator, especially when creation was "very good" (Gn 1:31; Jer 8:7; Mt 23:37). God did warn Adam that in the day he contradicted God's design he would die, and we have been dying ever since (Gn 2:17). Jesus says that if we remain in His Word, we will know the truth and the truth will make us free (Jn 8:31). Jesus says that we should seek Him and His kingdom first and everything else will follow (Mt 6:33; Ps 37:4). Our fallen human nature keeps us from living according to the truth and grace of God (Jn 3:18–21). God's nature is persistent to intervene and save us from ourselves (Mt 18:10–14).

● ● ● ● ● ● ● ● ● ● ● ● ● ● ● ● ● ●

Q **12:17 Is Jesus saying we should praise others besides Him?**

Let's begin with the particular language of the verse. Jesus is saying that we should pay taxes to Caesar with the means Caesar gives us: coins. Paul taught that we should give to each person what is due (Rm 13:7). King Herod once tried to accept the praise that is due God alone and died as a consequence (Ac 12:21–24). On this occasion, Jesus is making a critical distinction between things that are essential to our life and person and things that are external and trivial by comparison. Our life does not consist in the abundance of possessions (Lk 12:15; Php 3:7–11). So we are free to give temporal and material things to those who require them of us (Mt 5:38ff.; Php 2:5–10). Our life is provided for us by God and is inexhaustible—the realization of this in our lives forever is all that God seeks (Mi 6:6–8; Ps 116:12–13; Gal 5:1).

● ● ● ● ● ● ● ● ● ● ● ● ● ● ● ● ● ●

Q **12:18–19 If they didn't believe in the resurrection, why did the Sadducees consider Jesus to be a teacher?**

The Sadducees call Jesus "teacher" out of professional courtesy, just like someone calls a judge "your honor," even if they think he is the worst scoundrel ever. Hypocrisy, lies, and pretense—all things that are the opposite of truth and honesty—are characteristics of humanity since the fall of Adam. Jesus checked the pretense of the man who called Him good (Mk 10:18). The Bible warns against flattery because it is fundamentally dishonest and never a service to the truth (Pr 26:28; Rm 16:18; Jude 16). On the other hand, the Jewish religious leaders knew very well that Jesus was the Messiah and the Son of God (Jn 3:2; 11:45ff.). What can be done for fallen human nature that lives in the face of truth but continues to despise it (Rm 1:18–31)? The whole history of God saving man is a powerful and hopeful answer to this question (Mt 9:9–13; Lk 15:11–32; Ac 9:1–20).

● ● ● ● ● ● ● ● ● ● ● ● ● ● ● ● ● ●

Q **12:29–30 Why does Mark record that Jesus responded to this question with the *shema*, but Matthew doesn't make that clear?**

Mt 22:34–40 records the same account as this (Mk 12:28–34). It is possible that Matthew records less of what Jesus said on this occasion because his audience, mainly Jewish, would have recognized what Jesus was referring to. Mark records more conversation between the scribe and Jesus, which might have been helpful to a non-Jewish audience. This is a very unusual exchange for Mark's Gospel since it has such a positive tone and outcome.

● ● ● ● ● ● ● ● ● ● ● ● ● ● ● ● ● ● ●

Q 12:28–34 Why did no one dare to ask any more questions?

On the one hand, the religious leaders rarely engaged Jesus with an honest question. They were hypocrites who only pretended to ask Jesus questions, hoping that by testing Him they could find a cause to justify rejecting Him (Mt 19:3; Mk 8:11; 10:2; 12:15). On the other hand, people recognized that Jesus taught and answered questions with authority (Mk 1:22, 27). Jesus' power was demonstrated over and over again in miracles (Jn 10:19–21; 12:9–11, 17–19). Jesus' own disciples became afraid to ask Him questions (Mk 9:32; Lk 9:45).

● ● ● ● ● ● ● ● ● ● ● ● ● ● ● ● ● ● ●

Q 12:29 If this is the most important law, do we break that time every time we sin?

Whoever fails to keep any one part of the Law fails in all parts (Jas 2:10). Isaiah said that "all our righteous deeds are like a polluted garment" (Is 64:6). Moses described fallen human nature in this way: "every intention of the thoughts of his heart was only evil continually" (Gn 6:5). Thus, every part of every human nature is affected by the fall of Adam, which means we are in rebellion against the First Commandment above all the rest (Mk 7:20–23; Rm 3:10–20; Gal 5:19–21). The condition of our human nature is what makes the death of it necessary if we are to be free of it. The love of God is what regenerates us in the image of Christ, so that we trust in His perfect

obedience to the whole Law and so that we do as He did (Jn 8:42; 1Jn 3:9).

● ● ● ● ● ● ● ● ● ● ● ● ● ● ● ● ● ● ●

Q 12:38–40 How did the teachers of the law get to be so corrupt?

You probably know the saying "power corrupts and absolute power corrupts absolutely." Fallen human nature is full of corruption and is always looking for a way to satisfy its appetites (Gn 6:5; Mk 7:2–23). Since the teachers of the law had risen to a place where there was no authority above them, the corruption of their fallen human nature was left unchecked (consider the story of Eli's sons as well as the tragic history of King David's family [1Sm 2:12–17, 27–29; 2Sm 11:1ff.]). This is why Jesus warns His apostles not to consider themselves lords over the people but to understand that they are agents of Christ and must be faithful to Him (Mk 10:42–45; Lk 12:42–47; 1Pt 5:1–4).

● ● ● ● ● ● ● ● ● ● ● ● ● ● ● ● ● ● ●

Q 12:41–44 Why did the widow offer all that she had and the rich just threw in large amounts of something?

Anytime a person abandons God for money, no amount of money is ever enough (Mt 6:24, 33–34). Paul warned that the love of money is the root of all kinds of evil (1Tm 6:10). Apart from God, the more material things people have, the more they are sure they need more and can't do without anything they have (Lk 16:19ff.; Jas 4:1–4; 1Jn 1:15–17; Pr 1:19). On the other hand, the widow clearly exhibits no concern for her physical well-being. She believed that if she sought God first, and His righteousness, all other things would be added to her (Mt 6:33). Communion with God through a life in His Word convinces us of the providence of God that knows no bounds (Rm 8:32; 1Co 3:21). God provides for all at all times, especially for those who have no particular way of being provided for (1Ki 17:8–16; 2Ki 4:1–7). God makes many particular promises to widows and provides many examples of the fulfillment of those promises (Ex 22:22; Dt 10:18; Ps 68:5; Jer 49:11; Lk 4:24–26; 7:11–15).

● ●

Q 13:3–23 Are wars, earthquakes, abortion, and the like just signs of growing pains, or is it close to the end of the age according to Scripture? What is the desecration of the Most Holy Place?

First, notice that Jesus says there will be wars and rumors of war "but the end is not yet" (Mk 13:7). Jesus says there will be earthquakes and famines but "these are but the beginning of the birth pains" (13:8). Second, Jesus says the Gospel must first be preached to all nations (13:10) but there is disagreement about whether this has been fulfilled or not. One can argue that the Gospel has already made its way to every nation centuries ago. Others argue that there are still thousands of languages that the Bible has not been translated into, but this is not exactly what Jesus said. I suspect we will have to wait to know which argument

is right on this matter. Third, Jesus quotes Daniel's warning about the "abomination of desolation" (13:14; Dn 11:31; 12:11). The first time in history that looked like a fulfillment of this prophecy was around 164 BC when Antiochus Epiphanes IV made pagan sacrifices to Zeus in the temple. Here was a physical abomination in the physical temple, but it was only indicative of the fulfillment of the prophecy since the world did not end soon after. I would like to suggest that neither the abomination that causes desolation nor the place where it ought not sit are physical places. Our bodies are temples of the Holy Spirit, which come to us through the Word (1Co 3:16–17; Jn 6:63; Rm 10:17). The arrogance in human thinking has climaxed in modernism, Rationalism, secular humanism, and the Enlightenment. These movements, having arisen during the 1700s, quickly led to the rejection of the Bible as the truth and as the very Word of God. While there has always been moral degradation and danger as described in vv. 17–19, one may argue that the depths of degradation and the prevalence of it in every nation and among all classes of people make our time look very much like the fulfillment of this prophecy. For other passages that support this application, see 2Th 2:3–12; Rv 20:1–10.

> Is there going to be more than
> one antichrist?

Q 13:5–6 Is there going to be more than one antichrist?

There have been and will continue to be many "antichrists," as 1Jn 2:18 clearly states. Paul explains that Satan and his servants disguise themselves as angels of light (2Co 11:13–15). Paul and John both warn about opposition to Christ that comes from among those who gather and claim to be Christian (Ac 20:30; 1Jn 2:19). Finally, there are as many "antichrists" as there are people of fallen human nature, since in this condition we are not only weak, ungodly, and sinners, but also enemies of Christ (Rm 6–10).

Q 13:8 Can this verse relate to what has happened in our nation?

This verse speaks of nations rising against one another, earthquakes, and famines. These have happened in every nation throughout history. Jesus did say "these are but the beginning of the birth pains." It might be interesting to consider how faithfully and abundantly God's creation sustains life in spite of the fall. We tend to compare our experience with our own notions of a perfect world and see what is missing as the sum. What if we consider what our world would be like without God's providential, protecting, and restorative care? This approach makes one marvel at how much life God provides and how wonderfully He provides it in spite of the fall of man. Our wounds heal. Battlefields are covered in time with grass and beautiful foliage. Famines are followed by times of plenty and feasting. Providence and restoration in nature point to God's greater work of reconciling the world to Himself through the life, death, and resurrection of Jesus (Ps 19; Mt 6:26–33; Rm 1). Great Britain and the United States, once at war with each other, have ever since been the closest of allies. Even more profoundly, Jesus reconciles us with God by His love (2Co 5:14–21).

Q 13:10 How can the Gospel be "proclaimed to all nations"?

There is disagreement about whether this has been fulfilled or not. One can argue that the Gospel has already made its way to every nation centuries ago. Others argue that there are still thousands of languages that the Bible has not been translated into, but this is not exactly what Jesus said. There are several ways by which God reveals Himself to people. First, God reveals Himself to everyone through nature (Ps 19:1–6; Jer 8:4–7; Rm 1:18ff.). What is well-known to people because of nature is what the Bible makes use of in parables and in history (Ps 107:43; Jn 3:8, 12; Rm 1:20; 1Co 10:6–11). Second, God reveals Himself to everyone through the conscience (Rm 2:12–15). Third, Pentecost revealed God's intent for the Gospel to be proclaimed and understood by all people (Ac 2:5–8). What

God did to confirm the nature of the Gospel on Pentecost (the Gospel is for all people and brings salvation with the proclamation of the Word) in an instant, God continues to do through the ages by means of people who apply themselves to the study of language and the communication of the Word to all (Mt 28:18–20; Mk 16:16–20; Rm 1:8; 15:28; Col 1:6). No matter when the end of the world comes, we are devoted to redeeming the time by extending the kingdom of God to everyone, everywhere, as diligently as we are able (Eph 5:16; Mt 5:13–16; 2Co 5:20).

• • • • • • • • • • • • • • • • • • • •

Q 13:14 What is the abomination? Can sinners flee from it?

The relationship between the abomination and the cause of Jesus' warning to flee is understandable. When foreign rulers defiled the temple, there was also persecution and abuses that made life ever so difficult for pregnant and nursing women, whether at the time of Antiochus Epiphanes IV (164 BC) or at the time of Titus (AD 70). God consistently sends warnings for people to flee before the consequences of wickedness fall on them (Gn 19:17–20; Jer 4:6; 48:6). Now consider what happens when foreign rulers defile not only physical locations but also the very hearts and minds of rulers and people in general (Ps 11:2–3; 12:8). Since the Enlightenment has convinced humans that we are the measure of all things, we have seen an ever-rising oppression against life itself and especially the lives of women, children, the helpless, and the elderly. The

only way to flee from the atheistic and antagonistic determination of our world is through the Word of God. God's Word warns us to keep ourselves from the ways of the world and promises to provide us with a life that no one can abuse or take away (Pr 4:15; Jn 6:26–29; Rm 16:17; 1Jn 5:18–21; also see answer at Mk 13:3–23 above).

• • • • • • • • • • • • • • • • • • • •

Q 13:17 Why will it be dreadful for pregnant and nursing mothers?

One of the characteristics of our age is the way it despises human life, especially the lives of unborn children. As long as people accept the Darwinian doctrine that all life is the product of accident, they will see unborn children as accidents and pregnant women as careless impediments to the progress of sophisticated humans. For more about the end times, see Mk 13:14 and 13:3–23 above; for more about the fate of women in the end times, see 1Co 11 and 1Th 4.

• • • • • • • • • • • • • • • • • • • •

Q 13:20 Is Jesus trying to point out that because of the sin in the world, God has shortened our days?

God did shorten the days of human beings in general at the time of the flood (Gn 6:3). In this verse, Jesus is talking about shortening "those days," referring to the last days before the end of the world rather than the particular days of certain people. As we near the end of the world and love grows cold and the forces of evil increase their opposition, it will be more and more difficult to keep the faith (Rm 1:28–32; Eph 6:11–12; 1Tm 4:1–3; Rv 12:17). Jesus expresses concern about this in Lk 18:8: "nevertheless, when the Son of Man comes, will He find faith on earth?" Hezekiah prayed to God to lengthen his days, which turned out to be a mistake (2Ki 20:1–19). Paul said he couldn't decide whether to depart and be with the Lord or to stay longer to keep preaching the Word, though the decision was not his to make (Php 1:19–26). God grants to each a measure of faith and length of days (Ps 139:16; Rm 12:3). We can be at peace, knowing that our time and all time is safely in God's gracious control, and apply ourselves with joy to the course of life He has prepared for us (Mt 25:14–30; 1Co 9:24–26; Eph 2:20).

Q **13:23 What does Jesus mean when He says to be on your guard?**

The word used here means "to see" (*blepo*—132 times in New Testament), though in certain contexts, like this one, it has the sense of "keep watch" or "be alert" (see also Mk 13:33). There is another word that is more focused on the idea of keeping watch or guard (*gragoreo*—22 times in New Testament). This more focused word also occurs in this context in Mk 13:34–37; 14:34–38. As you can see from the references given, "watch" means to look with the eyes, paying very close attention to what is happening because there are many dangers and enemies waiting for an opportunity to attack.

Q **13:30 How would "this generation" be understood?**

There are two ways to understand the word *generation*. In our culture, the term *generation* usually means a group or class of people all born about the same time. For example, the children who were born to couples after World War II were called "the Me generation." A rock band called The Who recorded a hit song titled "Talking about My Generation," in which they contrast all the young people in their age group with their parents' generation and grandparents' generation. In biblical writing, *generation* can refer to the source of a human being's generation—referring to your ancestors, all the way back. When Jesus says, "That which is born of the flesh is flesh" (Jn 3:6), and, "You are from below; I am from above" (Jn 8:23, see also v. 24), and when Paul says, "Flesh and blood cannot inherit the kingdom of God"(1Co 15:50), they are referring to fallen human nature, as generated in conception by our parents. This generation of fallen human nature is in contrast to the regenerate soul, which Jesus and John speak about often (Jn 3:3–7; 1Jn 3:1ff.). In this verse, it is possible that both senses are implied. On the one hand, the people who were adults at this time (that "generation") would not die before Jesus' glory was demonstrated in His sacrificial death, resurrection, and ascension (Lk 24:25–27). On the other hand, fallen human nature would continue to regenerate in this corrupt or fallen state until Jesus returns on Judgment Day.

Only on Judgment Day will Jesus finally put a complete end to all fallen human nature (1Co 15:35–58; Rm 7:24–25).

● ● ● ● ● ● ● ● ● ● ● ● ● ● ● ● ● ● ●

Q **13:32 Jesus' not knowing when the earth will perish implies that He gave up the unlimited use of His divine attributes to be human. Why would He have to do this, and what then makes Him God?**

There are many mysteries related to the person of God. If God is one and inseparable, how can only the Son become man and die, but not God the Father and God the Holy Spirit? In this verse, Jesus appears to be talking about nonhuman creatures: the angels in heaven and the Son (of God rather than of Mary). It sounds more like knowledge of the last day is a prerogative of the Father alone, within the Trinity, rather than something the Son doesn't know because of a limitation He imposed on Himself. The Son of God *is* true God. Many texts in the Bible recognize Him as such, and logic recognizes that a son must be of the same nature as the father (Is 9:6; Jn 5:26; 10:31–39; 1Tm 2:3)

● ● ● ● ● ● ● ● ● ● ● ● ● ● ● ● ● ● ●

Q **14:10 Why did Judas suddenly decide to betray Jesus?**

Mark moves very quickly in his Gospel, preferring action to details. John's Gospel makes clear that Judas had been opposed to Jesus' teaching for some time (12:6). On the day before Palm Sunday, when Jesus was at the home of Lazarus, Martha, and Mary,

Mary's anointing of Jesus with expensive oil moved Judas first to criticism then to betrayal (Jn 12:1–6). In John's account of Maundy Thursday, he adds, "The devil had already put it into the heart of Judas Iscariot, Simon's son, to betray Him" (13:2). These texts suggest that first Judas began to reject the Word of the Lord; then he acted on that rejection by stealing what was in their money box. Once Judas had started to reject the Word of the Lord, he was open to being possessed by the devil, who was looking for an opportunity to destroy Jesus (Mt 12:43–44; Lk 4:13). Thus the disposition of Judas came about over a longer period of time according to a number of particular factors and events, which Mark left to the other Gospel writers to explain.

● ● ● ● ● ● ● ● ● ● ● ● ● ● ● ● ● ● ●

Q **14:21 Why did Jesus make the comment that it "would have been better for that man if he had not been born" since Jesus knew it was part of the plan? It makes it sound as though Judas was horrible and can't be forgiven. Wouldn't it be better for anyone destined to hell not to have been born?**

Like everything Jesus has to say, it is entirely for our benefit and instruction (Jn 6:63; 21:25). There are important indications in the Bible that Judas was not forgiven, but making such a condemnation (judgment) is forbidden for us (see Mt 7:1 and answer there). Psalm 109 has been recognized as a prophecy about Judas Iscariot—look carefully at the language of vv. 7, 12, and

14–19. Jesus makes an important observation when He says it would have been better for Him never to have been born because the tragedy of such determined opposition against God and His grace is the worst of all possible dispositions. Jesus says essentially the same thing when He warns about the sin against the Holy Spirit (Mk 3:28–30). Hebrews speaks in the same grave way about those who despise the grace of God (Heb 6:1–8; 10:26–31). Judas was opposed to and cut himself off from the only remedy there is to death. Yet no one is predestined to hell, for God desires all to be saved and has already redeemed all since Jesus bore away the sins of the world (1Tm 2:4; Jn 3:16). God only predestines people to life everlasting (Rm 8:29–30; Eph 1:4). Consider the significance of the difference between God predestining someone for damnation (which the Bible never even suggests) and God warning that a person's own steadfast, conscious, adamant, determined opposition to God will ultimately bring him or her into a condemnation that cannot be reversed, as there is no salvation apart from Christ, whom such a person is opposed to with all his or her being (Jn 3:16–21; Rm 8:1; Gal 3:1–9). As a person's opposition to grace becomes more determined and vigorous, the only hope for reversing such a course is to increase the clarity and severity of warnings and appeals for repentance, which is just what Jesus is doing here (note the severity of Jesus' language and warnings with the religious leaders at the end of His public ministry [Mt 23]).

● ● ● ● ● ● ● ● ● ● ● ● ● ● ● ● ● ● ●

Q 14:24 Is this fulfilling the sacrifice of the old covenant or the new covenant mentioned in Jer 31, or is this fulfilling both of the covenants?

Jesus fulfilled everything in the Law and the Prophets (Mt 17:1–3; Lk 24:27). However, we need to begin by clarifying terms. One kind of covenant refers to an agreement between parties or a conditional promise. Housing developments require people to agree to keep their properties in a certain way. God made a covenant with Israel through Moses that if they would obey His Commandments, He would protect them and provide the land of Canaan as their home (Dt 11:13–28). (Note: the word *if* occurs in Deuteronomy at least 167 times!) Another kind of covenant or "testament" refers to an unconditional promise and is completely the doing of only one person. God made such a covenant with Adam, Noah, Abraham, and David (Gn 3:15; 9:8–17; 12:1–3; 2Sm 7:12–17). Jeremiah's prophecy contrasts these two covenants. Jeremiah says the Lord will establish a new covenant (unconditional—depending on God alone) that is not like the old one (conditional), which their fathers broke. Jesus is certainly fulfilling all the requirements of sacrifice by offering Himself once for all (Lk 22:15–16; Heb 2:9; 7:27; 9:28; 10:10). The whole Old Testament is provided for in the substitutionary atonement of Christ, and the Means of Grace in the New Testament flow from this (Col 1:13–20). God was, in Christ, reconciling the world to Himself and continues to do so by regenerating us in His image, by feeding us with His body and blood, and by confirming His grace in the Words of Absolution (2Co 5:19; Jn 3:3–7; 6:48–63; 20:19–23).

Q 14:33 Why is it always Peter, James, and John that Jesus takes to secret places with Him?

While the Bible does not provide a direct answer, there are some interesting observations we might make. First, there often seems to be a narrowing or limiting of people involved the closer we come to the things of God. God wanted Israel to be the light of the world, and He created that people through Abraham, Isaac, and Jacob. Jesus had many disciples but called twelve, and from those He selected Peter, James, and John. Second, it is interesting to note that James was executed by Herod in the very early years of the apostolic period (Ac 12), Peter was executed somewhere in the middle (late 60s), and John was the last apostle to die, not until the end of the first century. Do these three, then, indicate the spectrum of apostolic witness? Perhaps in these three men the spectrum of personality is indicated, to show that God makes use of each person's particular strengths and weaknesses for the advancement of His kingdom (1Co 12:12–24).

Q 14:51–52 Who is the naked man? Where did he come from? What is the significance of these two verses?

Authors often leave traces of themselves or clues about their identity in their work. Matthew never refers to himself by his old Hebrew name, Levi (cf. Mt 9:9 with Lk 5:27). John never refers to himself by name at all, but only by a description of God's grace: "the disciple whom Jesus loved" (Jn 21:7). If this feature is true for Mark's Gospel, then we would suspect that Mark is the man who ran away naked in the Garden of Gethsemane. Mark seems to have run away again, as Ac 13:13 records that a disciple named John (also known as Mark, Ac 12:25) abandoned the first missionary journey and went home. Suspicion about Mark "running away" on this occasion is supported by Paul's refusal to take him along on the next missionary journey (Ac 15:38). Much later, Paul gives us reason to believe that Mark had become a faithful disciple and asks that Mark come to him (2Tm 4:11). If we put the pieces of this puzzle together, we might see some significance. Like other Gospel writers, Mark identified himself in a way that is humiliating for him but glorifies the Lord who loved and redeemed him still. Our failures and faithlessness highlight and glorify Jesus (Rm 5:20–21). Like Peter, Mark failed more than once yet was eventually made faithful by the power of God and became a useful servant (Mt 14:30–31; 16:23). When we are tempted to judge ourselves useless because of our failings, not only the Word of God but also the work of God in the lives of people like Mark give us hope (1Co 4:3–4; 1Tm 1:15–16). This is why we are saved by grace rather than works, "in order that the promise may rest on grace and be guaranteed to all his offspring—not only to the adherent of the law but also to the one who shares the faith of Abraham" (Rm 4:16).

● ●

Q 14:53–65 Was the Sanhedrin composed of religious leaders or government officials? If they were government officials, why were they concerned with Jesus being the Son of God?

The Sanhedrin was a group of seventy men plus the high priest who presided. These men came from the priests, nobles, and elders and had authority over every kind of matter—religious, civil, and criminal. The Sanhedrin had its own police, which they used to arrest Jesus and guard the tomb (Jn 18:3; Mt 27:65). They had power to arrest and hold trial but not to execute anyone (Jn 18:31–32). This is interesting to remember when we read the account of their execution of Stephen (Ac 7:54–60).

Jesus' assertion that He was the Son of God was the cause of His condemnation by the Sanhedrin for several reasons. First, Jesus was not what they wanted in a Messiah. They expected Jesus to honor them and give them dominion over both Israel and the Gentiles. They were looking for a king like David, who would give them wealth

and power. Instead, Jesus taught them to love their enemies, humble themselves in the service of others, and confess their sins (Mt 5–7). Second, since Jesus clearly demonstrated in His words and work that He was God, they had to find a way of getting rid of Him. The idea of getting rid of God may seem insane, but it was no more insane than the plan for murdering Lazarus after Jesus raised him from the dead (Jn 12:9–11). But think of it: if they could put Jesus to death, that would prove they were right and Jesus was a liar—because you can't put God to death! What they did not know (because they refused to admit it) is that unless God, as a true man, died in the place of all humankind, no one could be saved (Rm 8:1–4). The devil obviously did not understand this either, otherwise why would he have contributed to Jesus' arrest and crucifixion (Lk 4:13; Jn 13:2). They could only arrest, humiliate, and crucify Him because that was His plan from the beginning of time (Ac 2:22–24; Gn 3:15; Is 53).

● ●

Q 14:63 Did the priest literally tear his clothes or did he just get upset?

He really did tear his clothes because he was very upset. Tearing one's clothes was an outward expression of deep emotion, whether grief or anger (2Sm 3:31; 13:19; Jer 36:24). In some cases, people tore their clothes to appear upset though they didn't care. God warns against this hypocrisy (Jl 2:13).

● ● ● ● ● ● ● ● ● ● ● ● ● ● ● ● ● ● ●

Q **14:64 If the Sanhedrin condemned Jesus, why did He also have to go to Pilate?**

The Sanhedrin did not have authority to execute anyone, since they were governed by the Roman Empire. Once the Sanhedrin concluded that someone was worthy of death according to their law and trial (faulty and deceitful as it was), they had to appeal to the Roman governor for an execution order. This group wanted to execute Paul but was unable to because Paul used a privilege of his Roman citizenship to appeal directly to Caesar (Ac 25:9–11). (See also Mk 14:53–65 above for more about the Sanhedrin.)

● ● ● ● ● ● ● ● ● ● ● ● ● ● ● ● ● ● ●

Q **14:65 Are the men who spit on Jesus damned?**

Spitting on Jesus, while hard to imagine doing, is not the unforgivable sin (Mt 12:31–32). What happens to those men is no different than what happens to anyone else—those in the faith go to the resurrection of life, and those contrary to faith to judgment (Jn 5:28–29). There is reason to believe that some of these did come to faith, as indicated in Lk 23:47.

● ● ● ● ● ● ● ● ● ● ● ● ● ● ● ● ● ● ●

Q **14:66 Did Peter disown Jesus because he was afraid for his life, or was it just unpopular?**

We can hardly imagine a person more popular than Jesus, though few or none of the common people were present during His trial (especially His trial before the Sanhedrin, which took place during the night [Mk 14:2]). Peter was afraid for his life because he was in the neighborhood of the ruling Jews, and they meant harm to anyone who confessed Jesus (Jn 7:45–49; 9:22, 35; 12:9–10). This is not the first time Peter's fear kept him from following Jesus (Mt 14:30), nor would it be the last time (Gal 2:11ff.).

● ● ● ● ● ● ● ● ● ● ● ● ● ● ● ● ● ● ●

Q **15:1 What is the Sanhedrin?**

See Mk 14:53–65 above.

● ● ● ● ● ● ● ● ● ● ● ● ● ● ● ● ● ● ●

Q **15:4 Why did Christ not answer Pilate?**

There are several reasons for Jesus' silence. He is silent in order to fulfill a prophecy in Isaiah: "And like a sheep that before its shearers is silent, so He opened not His mouth" (Is 53:7). Jesus is also silent because He always protects the truth from those who would only despise and reject it (Mt 7:6). When hypocrites came to test Jesus, He asked them questions in return, as this exposed their opposition to the truth (Mk 11:28–33). While not silent, Jesus told parables in order to protect the truth (Lk 8:9–10). During His trial, Jesus was silent for the same reason He did not do many mighty works (Mt 13:58) nor provide a sign on demand (Mk 8:11–12); He refuses to reveal truth and mercy to those who have despised them. Only when the truth is directly challenged did Jesus respond in order to confirm and protect the truth (Jn 19:10).

Q 15:16 How many soldiers were in a Roman troop?

Some suggest that a garrison is similar to a battalion, consisting of three hundred to one thousand men. Another source clarifies that a garrison is a place where men and/or supplies are stationed and does not indicate how many are there. Later, when Paul had to be moved from Jerusalem to Caesarea, the commander ordered 200 soldiers, 70 horsemen, and 200 spearmen to accompany Paul—470 men altogether. Certainly there were more men in the garrison yet, as the commander would not have left himself alone in Jerusalem with no troops.

Q 15:16–20 Did the soldiers typically mock, persecute, and beat prisoners who were to be crucified the way they did Jesus?

I have seen the place in the pavement from this time in Jerusalem where marks were scratched for the game soldiers played in order to mock and abuse prisoners (Jn 19:13). We might suspect that Jesus received worse treatment than normal for the following reasons: (1) Pilate wanted to release Jesus, knowing that He had been handed over because of jealousy (Mk 15:10; Lk 23:20). (2) Pilate hoped that humiliating Jesus publicly would satisfy the crowd so they would abandon their demands for a crucifixion (Lk 23:22; Jn 19:1–6).

Q 15:21 Why does Mark mention Simon, the man who carried the cross?

Luke also includes how Simon was compelled to carry Jesus' cross (Lk 23:36). It is likely that Simon was compelled to carry Jesus' cross because Jesus was too weak (having been beaten) to continue the way to Golgotha. This may also be one of many occasions where Jesus' experience bears out His teaching—Simon did take up Jesus' cross and followed Him (Mk 8:34, Lk 9:23). Just as Simon was made to participate in the suffering of Christ, the New Testament says we do as well (2Co 1:5; Gal 6:2; Php 3:10; Col 1:24; Rv 6:9–11).

Q 15:27–28 Did Jesus save one of the robbers who was crucified with Him?

Jesus saved everyone, even the thief who despised Him to the end (Jn 3:16; Lk 23:39). The other thief, recognizing the truth about himself and about Jesus, demonstrated repentance by rebuking the other criminal and appealing to Jesus for his life (Lk 23:39–43). Jesus confirmed His saving work by assuring the penitent that he would be with Jesus in paradise that very day.

Q **15:32 Why do Mark and Matthew say that both the criminals insulted Jesus, but Luke says only one of the criminals insulted Jesus?**

The four Gospels are important because they provide important details and perspectives like this. John says nothing about the criminals except that one was crucified on either side with Jesus in the middle (Jn 19:18). Matthew and Mark provide narratives that move quickly through descriptions of the various groups who mock Jesus to the moment when Jesus cried, "My God, My God, why have You forsaken Me?" (Mt 27:44–46; Mk 15:32–34). Luke provides many texts that show people in a positive light, in contrast to Mark, who tends to show them in a negative way. Sometime between noon and three in the afternoon, one of the criminals changed his disposition from mocker to penitent. This is not so hard to understand given his circumstances and the powerful witness of Jesus' suffering right next to him.

Q **15:34 Why did God forsake Jesus, and what does that mean? Was that the price of sin?**

The natural consequence of contradicting God's Word and design is death, as God warned Adam in the Garden of Eden (Gn 2:15–17). Paul wrote that the wages of sin is death (Rm 6:23). Adam didn't drop dead as soon as he disobeyed, because death is

Why did God forsake Jesus?

essentially the absence of positive relationship—this is what causes the disintegration of human physiology and society and causes enmity with God. What we call death is named so because it bears similarity to what it really means to be dead. Jesus took the place of every human being under the Law. He did all that the Law requires of a person to live, as demonstrated in Jesus' positive relationships. Jesus suffered all the consequences of failure to keep the Law, climaxing with the absence of any positive relationship with His own Father. Simply put, Jesus traded our rejection for His communion with God the Father (2Co 5:21).

Q **15:34 In this verse it quotes Jesus in Aramaic, and then the Bible translates into English. Why is it shown in Aramaic first?**

Authors of all kinds of written work will quote something in the original language for emphasis. Hearing the exact sound that Jesus made is powerful. Mark quotes what Jesus said when He restored the life of Jairus's daughter (Mk 5:41). John's Gospel also records a few terms and their translation (Jn 1:42; 9:7)

Q **15:35 Why do the people around Jesus think He is calling Elijah when He is dying?**

Elijah is well-known for many things; among them was the raising of the dead boy and his challenge to the prophets of Baal on Mount Carmel (1Ki 17:1–24; 18:21ff.). Perhaps the people, knowing Elijah to be the foremost of the prophets, thought he might come to vindicate Jesus and to raise Him from the cross (if not from the dead).

Q **15:39 Why does the centurion suddenly believe?**

Reading the parallel accounts in Matthew and Luke provides part of the answer. According to Matthew, there was an earthquake that affected the centurion (27:54). According to Mark, it was the way Jesus "breathed His last" (15:39). According to Luke, the centurion confessed that Jesus surely must have been innocent (23:47). We also do well to remember that more than three hours passed during which many words were uttered by Jesus and by those watching, including the conversion of the one thief (Lk 23:40–43). While the centurion's statement may seem sudden, a lot went on and a lot of time passed that the Gospels do not have space to include.

Q **16:1–7 Why did the angel tell the Marys to look and tell both the disciples and Peter? Isn't Peter a disciple?**

There are many texts in Mark's Gospel that give Peter special attention. Mark gave us a hint about his own identity in 14:51 (see question and answer above), and this record of what Jesus said bears witness to the suggestion that Mark was writing for Peter (see also Peter's own reference to a Gospel [2Pt 1:15]). You could understand Jesus to mean that Peter was not a disciple, especially if you have in mind Peter's denial of Jesus. On the other hand, the conjunction "and" could have been intended to verify that Peter was still a disciple. The fact that Peter not only remains among the disciples but is highlighted as a leader in Acts supports the latter.

Q **16:9–20 According to a note in my Bible, early manuscripts didn't contain these verses. If this is so, where did these verses come from and why weren't these included in the earlier manuscripts?**

This is a question of textual criticism, the study of how to determine which manuscripts are most likely telling what was in the original. Actually, there are manuscripts that end at v. 8, others that end at v. 16, and still others at v. 20. If you are really interested in the subject, you can read *The Early Versions of the New Testament: Their Origin, Transmission, and Limitations* by Bruce M. Metzger. For our purposes, consider the following: First, while there are variations among the thousands of manuscripts we have of the New Testament in Greek, none of them affect the message of the New Testament or any teaching. Those who copied manuscripts understood the significance of their work and took great pains to ensure accuracy. Second, consider which is more likely: that later individuals would add material to a Gospel (vv. 9–20) or that, over time, this Gospel in a scroll would suffer from wear and the later verses (outside of the scroll?) would be lost. Either way, there is nothing said in vv. 9–20 that isn't said elsewhere in the New Testament, though it is very helpful to have these verses for the clarity they offer on a couple of subjects.

● ●

Q **16:13–14 Why does Mark exclude the Supper in the Upper Room?**

John records that Jesus appeared to the apostles in the Upper Room on Easter evening and again a week later, but there is no mention of the Lord's Supper (Jn 20:19–29). Jesus broke bread with the men He met on the road to Emmaus and made Himself known to them in doing so, but these were not the apostles nor was it the Upper Room and may have been only bread (Lk 24:35). Thus it does not appear that any of the Gospels record Jesus celebrating the Supper with His apostles in the Upper Room after the resurrection. In any case, Mark's Gospel tends to highlight the faults of many, so we might not be surprised that Mark records Jesus rebuking His apostles for their hard hearts and unbelief rather than celebrating Communion with them.

● ●

Q **16:16 This verse, often cited as a proof-passage, is part of the disputed longer ending. Where else is this stated so clearly? Is Baptism not necessary for salvation? If we have to believe and be baptized to go to heaven, what about the thief on the cross? Are we to assume he was baptized?**

The fact that unbelievers cannot enter the kingdom of heaven is stated clearly and often throughout the Bible (Jn 8:30–59; Rm 11:20; Heb 3:19; 11:6). The necessity of Baptism depends on how the term is being used. Unless a person is "awash" or "immersed" in the Word of God he or she cannot be saved. Jn 3, 4, 6, 8, 10, 15, and 17 all speak volumes about this, along with Rm 10 and Col 3. If we are talking about the physical rite with water that confirms God's promises to an individual, then we recognize it is necessary but not absolutely necessary, and certainly desirable and sought after by anyone who is in the Word (Ac 2:38–42; 8:36–38; 10:34–48). The Word of the Lord worked faith and confirmed salvation to the thief on the cross, in person!

● ●

Q **16:17 Does this verse support the practice of speaking in tongues? When it says, "These signs will accompany those who believe," does it mean all believers or is it a reference to the disciples?**

First of all, to "speak in new tongues" means to speak in different languages. We still use this expression when we talk about a person talking in his or her "native tongue." Speaking in different languages was essential at Pentecost because God wanted to confirm that the Gospel is accomplished for all, comes immediately through the Word to all, and is intended for all. The people who were "from every nation under heaven" (Ac 2:5) could have understood what the apostles were saying if they spoke Greek since it was a universal language. God gave this extraordinary ability during the time of the apostles in order to silence the objections of the Judaizers who claimed that people had to become Jewish first, according to the Law of Moses, and then they could be accepted by the Church (Ac 11, 15). The ability to speak in different languages instantly and to confer that gift on others was also intended to confirm the apostles as having authority to speak and record the Word of God. These verses refer to the apostles only, eleven only here, with Matthias and Paul added later. The apostles were enabled to speak in languages and had the ability to confer that gift when authentication of the Gospel was necessary (Ac 10:44–47; 11:15–18; 15:6–9; 19:1–7). (Note well that Philip did not lay hands on the Ethiopian eunuch nor did that man speak in tongues since no Jews who contradicted the Gospel were there and neither Philip nor the eunuch needed any more confirmation of God's grace than the Word and Baptism already provided.)

● ● ● ● ● ● ● ● ● ● ● ● ● ● ● ● ● ●

Q 16:18 What does Jesus mean when He says "They will pick up serpents with their hands; and if they drink any deadly poison, it will not hurt them?"

Jesus means just what He is saying: apostolic responsibility and authority came with extraordinary protection from harm and the ability to help. Acts records the apostles speaking in languages (tongues), raising the dead, and surviving a snakebite, but not drinking deadly poison (Ac 2:5–11; 20:9–12; 28:3–6). We do well to remember that we have only a very limited record of what the apostles did or what others may have tried to do to them (poison). Since the time of the apostles, it is also interesting that those who claim the apostolic gifts invariably claim the gift of tongues or healing but never raise the dead or drink poison.

Luke

Q **1:1–4 If the Bible is the inspired Word of God, why does Luke mention his research and writing?**

Luke wrote as God directed him (2Tm 3:16). However, God can choose His method or means to accomplish His will. God could create every human being with no means, all by Himself. Instead, God created the material world, formed Adam out of the dust of the ground, made Eve from Adam's rib, and has made new life through their descendants (Ac 17:26). God called the apostles to communicate His Word to future generations and authenticated their eyewitness testimony by the miracles they performed (Mk 16:16–20; Ac 1:4–8; 2Co 12:12; 1Jn 1:1–3). In some cases, the apostles had secretaries who wrote down what the apostle dictated. Mark wrote for Peter; Luke, Tertius, and others wrote for Paul (2Pt 1:12–15; Rm 16:22; 1Co 16:21; Col 4:14). God directed and made use of the experiences, dispositions, abilities, perspectives, and insights of each apostle (and their secretaries) to form the text of the Bible just as He wanted.

Q **1:2 Could "the word" and "ministers" refer to Christ and His servants/disciples, or does "the word" in this case only refer to Scripture?**

It is not possible to separate the written Word of God from the Son of God, who is the Word of God and makes Him known (Jn 1:1–3, 18). However, the Gospel records that Jesus ministered to the apostles more than they to Him, and the context here is focused on the Scriptures rather than the Son of God (Jn 13:5; Mt 17:27).

Q 1:3 Who is Theophilus?

We don't know anything for certain about this man. His name means "friend of God." He would have been a Gentile and of high birth since Luke refers to him as "most excellent."

Q 1:6 How could Zechariah and Elizabeth have kept the Law flawlessly? If they served blamelessly, did they still sin?

Yes, Zechariah and Elizabeth still sinned, as do all people born of flesh and blood who have descended from Adam (Rm 3:10–18; 5:12ff.). This is why it was necessary for God to be the Father of Jesus. The word *blameless* occurs only five times in the New Testament, in every case by Paul. In Php 2:15 and 1Th 3:13, Paul explains that it is God's work in us that makes us blameless. Heb 8:7 points out that the New Testament was required because the Old Testament had no power to produce what it required. Paul reveals in Php 3:6 that a devout Jew would evaluate his life on the basis of how he kept the outward, ceremonial rules of the Old Testament. Obedience to such external practices is what the Jews were demanding of the Gentile converts in Ac 15:5. It may be, in this verse, that Luke is trying to make clear that Zechariah and Elizabeth were not childless as some consequence for their sin

or punishment from God (note how Jesus makes this clarification in Jn 9:2–3).

Q 1:7 Why does God wait until women such as Elizabeth and Sarah have reached an old age to grant them children?

First, especially in these days, it is important to remember that God grants conception to women; conception is not a right, nor a simple biological event that happens independently from God (Gn 30:1–2). Second, children are a means by which God demonstrates the reality of eternal life. When the Sadducees tried to prove to Jesus that there is no life after death, Jesus quoted God's (really His own!) words to Moses from the burning bush: "I am the God of Abraham, of Isaac, and of Jacob" (Ex 3:16). Jesus said this to prove that God is the God of the living and not of the dead (Lk 20:29–38). But at the time God said this to Moses, all three men were dead. So how do they prove eternal life? The answer is in the way Isaac, Jacob, and Jacob's sons by Rachel came to be. Abraham had no children—was too old to have any—so when he died, that would be the end of him. But by giving Abraham a son when he and Sarah were too old, God showed that their life would continue in Isaac. The same is true for Isaac and Rebekah and for Jacob and Rachel (Gn 25:21; 30:1–2). Think about how important and powerful this witness is for people who require physical evidence for what they believe. Apparently God anticipated and understood this need as He demonstrates eternal life, not by dreams or personal experience, but through physical, biological history. Third, granting children to people of old age demonstrates that God does what is impossible for us, especially in the case of salvation (Lk 1:37; 18:25–27). As in the case of the Exodus, Daniel in the lions' den, the three men in the fiery furnace, the incarnation of the Son of God, and most of God's activity in history, God regularly does what is impossible to demonstrate two things: (1) He is God and we are not, and (2) His desire is to save His creation and to give, restore, and protect life.

Q 1:9 What is the purpose and significance of burning incense in the temple of the Lord?

Zechariah was offering incense as prescribed by the Law of Moses (Ex 30:1ff.). The reason for offering incense has to do with the smoke and the smell. Smoke is the evidence of fire just as good works are the evidence of faith (Gn 19:28; Is 30:27; Jn 15:1–7; Jas 2:14–24). The Bible describes the good works of the faithful and their prayers as the smoke of incense (2Co 2:14–16; Rv 8:3–4). Incense made a pleasing aroma in the tabernacle of meeting, where the mercy seat covered the ark holding the Ten Commandments, which the people had broken. As the blood of innocent lambs kept God from seeing the broken laws, so also the incense indicated that God would provide a pleasing aroma and remedy for the horrible odors of death and sin (Gn 8:20–21; Ex 30:34–37; Lv 26:31; Jl 2:20; 2Co 2:15).

Q 1:12 Angels are often portrayed in art and movies as women, but this passage refers to a male angel. Are there other passages in the Bible that refer to male angels?

Angels are never female in biblical revelation. Perhaps people have portrayed angels as women for the same reason women have sought to take over the work of men (Gn 3:16b; 1Tm 2:8–15). Perhaps people think that the care and mercy that many prominent women have shown to others in history suggests that angels, being caring and merciful, would also be female. However, there are no passages that suggest angels are women. On the contrary, angels are always male in the Bible because they bear responsibility for the care and well-being of others, which is what it means to be male. They do not reproduce nor are they involved in the intimate relationships required for raising children (Lk 20:35–36). Angels carry God's message, as did the apostles (Mt 28:9–10, 16–20) and as pastors are charged to do (1Tm 3:1–7). Angels are warriors and protectors (Gn 19:1–22; Mt 26:53–54; Rv 12:7–11).

Q 1:13 Zechariah's wife was barren, but he prayed for a child and was blessed with one. If a couple stops trying to conceive because a doctor tells them that they can't have children, are they relying too

much on man-made technology and losing sight of God's power by not continuing to pray for a child?

Wise and honest physicians are careful to report only what tests and observations indicate and refrain from making conclusions they have no way of knowing. Fallen human nature continually loses sight of God's power and also of His will and purposes for us. Jesus urged and encouraged us to pray on many occasions (Lk 18:1ff.). Leah and Hannah prayed for children, and the Lord granted their petition (Gn 30:17; 1Sm 1:8ff.). On the other hand, Paul prayed to the Lord three times for relief from his thorn in the flesh but was denied since the thorn was essential to Paul's life (2Co 12:7–10).

Q **1:13 Why does the Bible put so much emphasis on names?**

For most of the world's history and to this day in many places, names are very important. We generally fail to recognize the significance of names for at least two reasons. First, we tend to give names for sentimental, romantic, or trendy reasons—often not even knowing what a name means. Second, because we do not speak the language from which the names were derived, we don't hear what people of the past who spoke those languages heard. Adam's name means "earth"; Eve's name means "life." Imagine the conversation each morning when they awoke: "Good morning, Life";

"Good morning, Earth." Naming things appropriately and according to significance helps keep us conscious of significant relationships and matters.

Q **1:15 Why was John never allowed to have wine or any other fermented drink? Can someone be filled with the Holy Spirit without being baptized? Does this verse mean that John was not baptized since he was filled with the Holy Spirit at birth? Did the Holy Spirit not "come upon" all believers before Christ's resurrection?**

The Bible indicates that people with extraordinary responsibilities should never risk being impaired by alcohol (Jgs 13:14; Pr 31:4–7; 1Tm 3:3).

The Holy Spirit is present wherever the Word is present (Jn 6:63; Rm 10:17). John had the Spirit from his mother's womb because of the extraordinary work God would accomplish through John, as prophesied and as God had done in the past through His prophets (Mal 3:1; 4:5–6; 2Ki 2:9–11). Acts records, without exception, that the Holy Spirit was present with the proclamation of the Word, which worked faith. Once faith worked by the Word was evident, Baptism was added to confirm the promises of God's Word to those who believed (Ac 2:32–42; 8:12–13, 35–38; 10:44–47; 19:1–5). There is no record of John being baptized, which is not a surprise since John was inaugurating the Baptism of the New Testament, which was instituted, commanded, and empowered by Jesus Himself (Mt 28:18–20).

There is a difference between the coming of the Holy Spirit whenever the Word of the Lord is present and when a very particular purpose of the Lord is being fulfilled (Jn 6:63; Rm 10:17 compared with Ac 2:1–21). Lk 1:15 reports that John would be filled with the Holy Spirit from his mother's womb—an extraordinary measure of the Holy Spirit since John was coming in the power and Spirit of Elijah (Mal 3:1; 4:5; Lk 1:17). In Lk 1:35, the angel was explaining to Mary how it was that she would conceive a child without a human father: "the Holy Spirit will come upon you, and the power of the Most High will overshadow you; therefore the child to be born will be called holy—the Son of God." In Acts, the expression "come upon" occurs three times, when the Holy Spirit gave believers the ability to speak in languages in order to prove the reality of God's salvation for them, immediate and for all (Ac 8:16; 10:44; 11:15).

● ● ● ● ● ● ● ● ● ● ● ● ● ● ● ● ● ●

Q **1:15 The Angel Gabriel told Zechariah that "[John] will be filled with the Holy Spirit, even from his mother's womb." Elizabeth told Mary that "as soon as the sound of your greetings reached my ears, the baby in my womb leaped for joy" (Lk 1:44). Does this mean that birth is what we commonly refer to as conception and not delivery? Conception is defined in English as a commencement, beginning, or inception. Conversely, delivery is defined in English only as the act of liberation or release.**

This is a matter of clarification. The angel told Zechariah that his son would "be filled with the Holy Spirit, even from his mother's womb." The New Testament uses the term *generated* to refer to conception, though this term includes conception, gestation, and birth. When the New Testament is referring to the delivery or birth of a baby, it uses a word that means only the physical delivery of a baby (*tikto*, seventeen times in the New Testament).

● ● ● ● ● ● ● ● ● ● ● ● ● ● ● ● ● ●

Q **1:17 The angel explained how John would fulfill the prophesy of Mal 4:6 to "turn the hearts of fathers to their children." Does this conflict with Jesus' purpose prophesied in Mi 7:6 and described in Mt 10:34–35: "I have not come to bring peace, but a sword" and "I have come to set a man against his father, and a daughter against her mother"?**

This is confusing and troubling to me.

First, the angels announced to the shepherds that Jesus' birth meant "on earth peace among those with whom [God] is pleased" (Lk 2:14). This is very different than a traditional notion based on a mistranslation, "peace on earth, good will toward men." Jesus did not come to bring peace on the earth, as this is not possible as long as people remain in their fallen human nature (2Ki 9:22; Gal 5:17). Second, by forgiving sins and regenerating our souls into everlasting life, Jesus grants us enduring peace (Jn 14:27; 1Jn 3:20). This is a peace that Christ provides between our regenerate soul and God. God's work in people is what binds us together as the Body of Christ in peace and love, in spite of the tribulation caused by our fallen human nature, the world, and the devil (Mk 9:50; Jn 16:33; 1 Th 3:1–5). Christians realize that the essence of family relationships is a matter of the soul, not the body. All people regenerated by the Holy Spirit have God as their Father and are truly brothers and sisters in time and for all eternity. This relationship is essential and takes priority over physical relationships, especially when our physical family would undermine our faith (Mt 12:46–50; Lk 14:25–33; Rm 2:28–29; Gal 3:27–29).

Q **1:18 Why didn't Zechariah believe what the angel said?**

The apostles of Jesus saw Him do miracles for more than three years and still did not believe what He taught them (Mk 16:14). Israel saw miracles and evidence of God's presence every day for more than forty years and still did not believe (Heb 3:16–19). Paul confirms that fallen human nature has no capacity to believe (1Co 2:14). Zechariah, like every man since Adam except Jesus, proves the devastation of our fallen condition. Zechariah was responsible for teaching people the truth. Zechariah, above all, should have been well acquainted with the history of God giving children to men and women who were too old, since that is Zechariah's own genesis through Abraham, Isaac, and Jacob (see 1:7 above). Since Zechariah would not use his mouth to speak the

truth or a faithful response to that truth (as Mary does in 1:38), Zechariah is rightly made mute.

Q **1:19 Why is Gabriel's name recorded here, but in many other places in the Bible the angels' names are not given? Did they not have names?**

It could be possible, even likely, that every angel has a name and just as likely that the Bible doesn't give them lest people think they can choose favorites, pray to them, and idolize them. What is altogether certain is that angels do not want our attention and demons should not have it (Rv 19:10; 22:8–9; 1Pt 5:8–9).

Q **1:20 Why was Zechariah made mute after he was told that Elizabeth would have a child?**

See answer to second part of Lk 1:18 above.

Q **1:21 Why were people waiting for Zechariah?**

Luke tells us in 1:10 that a multitude of people were praying outside the temple when Zechariah went in at the hour of incense. Since they were there when Zechariah went in and noticed that he did not come out for a long time, it is understandable that they would wait to see what that was about. They were not disappointed.

Q **1:24–27 How much older is John than Jesus?**

Luke records that the angel Gabriel visited Mary in the sixth month of Elizabeth's pregnancy, so John would have been between a little more than six to seven months older than Jesus.

Q **1:24 Was it customary for pregnant women to stay at home for five months before the birth of a child? Why did Elizabeth hide her pregnancy for five months?**

What would Elizabeth's relatives and neighbors think if she told them right away that she was pregnant? Elizabeth mentioned the reproach she endured from people because she had been barren (1:25). Perhaps Elizabeth concluded that there would be less reproach and grief if she was clearly five months pregnant than if she claimed to be pregnant but could not prove it for several months.

Q **1:25 Why was Elizabeth disgraced until her pregnancy?**

God created Eve because Adam needed a "helper fit for him" (Gn 2:18). One of the reasons Adam needed a helper is because he could not "be fruitful and multiply" (Gn 1:22) by himself. Adam called his wife's name "Eve" because "she was the mother of all living" (Gn 3:20). Ever since, women have had a sense that their ability to bear children is their glory; they can do what no

one else can (1Co 11:8–12; 1Tm 2:15). For this reason, some women found a path for cruelty in mocking women who were unable to bear children (Gn 16:5; 29:31; 30:1; 1Sm 1:1–7).

Q **1:26 How did Luke know that Gabriel was an angel? Did he look different than a human?**

Sometimes angels cannot be seen (2Ki 6:15–17). Sometimes angels take the appearance of men (Gn 19:1–3). It appears that angels make themselves known as God directs them and according to the needs of those they serve (Lk 2:8–15; 24:3–7).

Q **1:26–38 Why doesn't this narrative tell about the angel's visit to Joseph?**

Luke is focused on Mary. He recorded Gabriel's visit to her, Mary's visit to Elizabeth, and Mary's genealogy (3:23–38). Besides, Matthew had already recorded the angel's visit to Joseph and Joseph's genealogy (Mt 1:1–17, 20–21).

Q **1:27 If Christ was prophesied to come from the line of David, why does it record that Joseph was from the line of David and not Mary, who was actually the same flesh as Jesus? Why does the genealogy go from Jesus to Adam instead of Adam to Jesus? Is there a reason that Luke starts the genealogy of Jesus with Adam and not Abraham?**

Both Joseph and Mary were descendants of David. Mt 1 records Joseph's genealogy, and Lk 3 records Mary's. Notice in 3:23 that Luke makes clear that people supposed Jesus was from Joseph, but Heli was Mary's father. Matthew is concerned with the responsibility of men under the Law, especially regarding the two men to whom God made powerful and particular promises: Abraham and David. Luke, the physician, is interested in biology, focusing on the virgin birth of Jesus and tracing His human nature all the way back to Adam. Paul will expound on the relationship between Jesus and Adam in Rm 5:12–21.

Q 1:28 Was Mary's family of great faith?

We don't know much about Mary's family except what her genealogy in Lk 3 reveals. Certainly they were given a lot to believe: Elizabeth's pregnancy with John, Mary's conception of Jesus by the Holy Spirit, Mary's travel to visit Elizabeth, and Joseph and Mary's journey to Bethlehem in her ninth month.

Q 1:34 Did Mary realize that she was the one to help fulfill the Law and what the prophets said?

It is hard to know how much of what was happening Mary realized. On the one hand, Mary demonstrated faith when she answered the angel, saying "Let it be to me according to your word" (Lk 1:37). Joseph must have shared with Mary the various revelations God had provided him (Mt 1:18–25; 2:13–14, 19–23). On the other hand, Mary seems to have lost memory of or clarity about Jesus during the course of His life (Lk 2:41–51; Jn 2:1–5; Mk 3:21, 31–34).

Q 1:35 Did the Holy Spirit not "come upon" all believers before Christ's birth? What does this statement mean here?

There is a difference between the coming of the Holy Spirit whenever the Word of the Lord is present and when a very particular purpose of the Lord is being fulfilled (Jn 6:63; Rm 10:17 compared with Ac 2:1–21). Lk 1:15 reports that John would be filled with the Holy Spirit from his mother's womb—an extraordinary measure of the Holy Spirit since John was coming in the power and Spirit of Elijah (Mal 3:1; 4:5; Lk 1:17). In Lk 1:35 the angel was explaining to Mary how it was that she would conceive a child without a human father: "The Holy Spirit will come upon you, and the power of the Most High will overshadow you; therefore, the child to be born will be called holy—the Son of God." In Acts, the expression "fall on" (similar to "come upon" here) occurs three times, when the Holy Spirit gave believers the ability to speak in languages in order to prove the reality of God's salvation for them, immediate and for all (Ac 8:16; 10:44; 11:15).

Q **1:36 Did John the Baptist and Jesus minister together, or did they work separately?**

At the beginning of Jesus' public ministry, they crossed paths, but I know no texts that indicate Jesus and John working together (Jn 1:29–36; Lk 3:15–20; Mk 1:14–15). John prepared people for Jesus to begin His public ministry, baptized Jesus, was imprisoned by Herod, and was executed. As John said of Jesus, "He must increase, but I must decrease" (Jn 3:40; see also 3:22–4:3).

Q **1:45 How is Mary's questioning different than Zechariah's? Why did God punish Zechariah but answer Mary when they asked the same question?**

The first part of both questions seems to be an identical "How can this be?" and invites a comparison. However, the situation of the person who asks and the reason for asking are quite different. Zechariah serves as a priest; as such he is to be a leader in the faith. Zechariah must have known the history of Abraham and Sarah since that is every Israelite's origin and claim to the promises of God. So, how is it that a descendant of Isaac who was born to Abraham and Sarah in their extreme old age, a Levite, a priest, a teacher of Israel—how is it that such a man expresses his doubt in a question that challenges what the angel has announced? Mary is a young virgin, betrothed to Joseph. When the angel tells Mary she will conceive a child,

did it make sense for her to ask how this would be? Would she conceive by Joseph or some other way? Never before has a virgin conceived, nor would this ever happen again. Mary asked for clarification from a believing heart while Zechariah, who knew better, asked in doubt. God did not punish Zechariah but disciplined him, giving him a powerful experience by which he might honestly compare his own failure to believe with God's faithfulness to provide. We would do well to notice that both received answers and God blessed both according to His will and promises. Sometimes we will be like Mary, sometimes like Zechariah. We depend upon God and live because God always acts according to His gracious, loving nature as He fulfills all His promises to us.

Q **1:46–56 What is the significance of Mary's song as part of Luke's Gospel? Why isn't it included in Matthew or Mark?**

Luke records the lives of many people that the other Gospels do not, especially at the beginning of Jesus' life. While Matthew is concerned with responding to the opposition of Judaism and Mark is eager to show the Gospel at work in Jesus' public ministry, Luke takes time to give us a more full account of miraculous births and the recognition of their significance by people of that time. Luke devotes two long chapters to the time in Jesus' life that John and Mark spend no time on; Matthew's first two chapters record the events surrounding Jesus' birth and early childhood more than the early life of Jesus Himself. Mary's song has a general significance, like those of Elizabeth, Zechariah, Simeon, and Anna. All of these people were inspired to express thanks and praise to God for His gracious and miraculous works that accomplish our salvation. Mary's song is of particular importance because it is very much like Hannah's song in the Old Testament (1Sm 2:1–10). The two songs have their origin in miraculous conceptions (Mary's being completely unique, of course) and express fundamental truths about who God saves and who God opposes and why (see 1Co 1:18–31 for a remarkable articulation of the same).

● ● ● ● ● ● ● ● ● ● ● ● ● ● ● ● ● ●

Q 1:59 Who were "they"?

"They" refers to the people who came in order to perform and/or be witnesses to the circumcision of John (parallel to the people who would be invited to a Christian Baptism).

● ● ● ● ● ● ● ● ● ● ● ● ● ● ● ● ● ●

Q 1:66 Did John the Baptist's parents know how important he was going to be for Jesus' coming?

We cannot know what people know unless they tell us, but the narratives about and words and songs of Elizabeth, Mary, and Zechariah all indicate that they knew much about John's purpose and the coming of the long-awaited Savior through the Virgin Mary. Promises made to Abraham (Gn 12), to David (2Sm 7), and through Malachi (chs. 3–4) seem to have been well-known

among the children of Israel. Genealogy was important, even necessary to prove at times, and there had been four hundred years of silence since Malachi prophesied, so that gave this prophecy prominence in people's consciousness (Ne 7:5; Mt 12:23; Mk 9:11–13; Mal 4:5).

● ● ● ● ● ● ● ● ● ● ● ● ● ● ● ● ● ●

Q 1:67–80 Why do we use Zechariah's prophecy in our liturgy?

We use this section in our liturgy for the same reason the entire liturgy is composed of biblical texts, arranged in such a way to move us through Confession and Absolution, the Word, prayers, and Holy Communion. This section is focused on the fulfillment of God's promises in sending the Savior. This canticle is a fitting response to the readings and meditation in the service of Matins, where it is found in the hymnal.

● ● ● ● ● ● ● ● ● ● ● ● ● ● ● ● ● ●

Q 1:80 Why did John go into the desert?

Mark's Gospel quotes a prophecy from Is 40:3: "The voice of one crying in the wilderness: 'Prepare the way of the Lord, make His paths straight'" (Mk 1:3). The desert or wilderness is indicative of life in a fallen world. John went into the wilderness to restore life, to bring living water where there had only been death (Ps 107:35). Israel's wandering in the desert and Jesus' victory over every temptation while He was in the wilderness are both indicative of our life in the world. Israel behaved as we do, but Jesus lived as we should (Ex 13:18; Lk 4:1–13).

Elijah, David, the prophets, and God's people in Old Testament times all found refuge, safety, and providence from God in the wilderness, as did the people who followed Jesus there (1Ki 19:4–7; 1Sm 23:15; Heb 11:38; Mt 15:33; Ac 8:26; Rv 12:6).

Q 2:1–20 Why is Luke's account of Jesus' birth so much more thorough than the other Gospels?

Matthew wrote the first Gospel (about AD 50) in response to the Jewish religious establishment. Matthew focused on proving that Jesus was the Christ, in perfect fulfillment of Old Testament prophecy. Mark wrote the next Gospel (about AD 55) for a mostly Gentile audience. Since Matthew had already written about the birth of Jesus and because the Old Testament prophecies were mostly unknown to them, Mark starts with the public ministry of Jesus, where we get to see what it means to be the Christ. Luke, writing for Paul, produced the third Gospel (about AD 60) and took time to give a little more background. Luke, the physician, was interested in the miraculous work of God, especially in the birth of John to parents who were too old and in the virgin birth of Jesus. Luke also demonstrated continuity between Old and New Testaments by beginning where Malachi left off. John wrote the fourth Gospel (about AD 99) as a remedy for the hypocrisy that was, once again, infecting the "people of God," just as it had in the Old Testament (see notes on John's Gospel for more on this).

Q 2:4–5 This passage says that Mary is pledged to be married to Joseph, but where is it recorded that they actually got married?

Joseph and Mary were always husband and wife from the time we hear about them in the Gospels. In Old Testament times, betrothal or engagement was irreversible. Joseph had declared in public that he would be a husband to Mary. Mary's family and Mary had consented; that made them married. Joseph and Mary most likely established a home together soon after Mary conceived in order to protect her reputation, as Joseph was concerned about this (Mt 1:19–20). Joseph and Mary were not intimate sexually until after Jesus was born (Mt 1:24–25).

Q 2:5–21 Why is the Christmas story usually read from Luke instead of another Gospel?

Mark does not provide a Christmas story. Matthew, Luke, and John each record the incarnation of the Son of God with a particular focus. Some Christian churches that follow a series of lessons for the Church calendar that have been established since ancient times use a different Gospel each year for three years. Luke's Gospel is probably more well-known because it offers more detail about the birth narrative itself. For example, the shepherds came to see the baby Jesus right away, but the Wise Men in

Matthew's account would not have come for at least forty days or more after Jesus' birth.

● ● ● ● ● ● ● ● ● ● ● ● ● ● ● ● ● ● ●

Q **2:6–7 This says that Mary gave birth to her firstborn. Did she have other children?**

Yes. Mt 1:25 makes it clear that Joseph remained celibate while Mary was pregnant with Jesus but afterwards consummated their marriage. Matthew's Gospel also records that it was common knowledge that Joseph and Mary had children after the birth of Jesus, as they mention Jesus' brothers by name and that He had sisters (Mt 13:55–56). The letters of James and Jude were written by two of these "half-brothers" (Gal 1:19; Jas 1:1; Jude 1).

● ● ● ● ● ● ● ● ● ● ● ● ● ● ● ● ● ● ●

Q **2:19 This description of Mary occurs also in Lk 2:51. What is its significance? What does it mean?**

There are several interesting features to this phrase about Mary. First, the phrases are not identical. Lk 2:19 says that Mary "treasured up [*sumballo*] all these things, pondering [*suntereo*] them in her heart." Luke 2:51 says that Mary "treasured up [*dia-tereo*] these things in her heart." The word "pondering" is used only by Luke and means to "cast things together" in order to figure something out (Lk 14:31; 20:14; Ac 4:15; 17:18; 18:27). The word translated "treasured up" in 2:51 is also used by Luke only (Ac 15:29 is the only other occur-

rence). The word translated "treasured up" in this verse means to keep in the sense of protect and to not allow something to get away (Mt 9:17; Mk 6:20). Mary did not dismiss, ignore, nor forget what was revealed to her in various ways about her Son. Mary kept these things in mind and continued to "throw them together" in her mind in order to grasp their significance. John offers some insight to Mary's consideration in the account of the wedding at Cana (Jn 2:1–5).

● ● ● ● ● ● ● ● ● ● ● ● ● ● ● ● ● ● ●

Q **2:21–24 How does the circumcision of Jesus fit in the chronology with the flight to Egypt?**

Jesus was circumcised eight days after He was born and named that day, according to custom and with the name commanded by God. After thirty-two more days, Joseph and Mary would have taken Jesus the four and a half miles to Jerusalem to offer the required sacrifice for a firstborn son (Lv 12:1–8). This must have taken place before the Wise Men visited Jerusalem and then Bethlehem. Herod had all male children two years old or younger executed when he realized the Wise Men would not be coming back to tell him where Jesus was (Mt 2:16). Joseph, Mary, and Jesus departed for Egypt almost immediately after the Wise Men's visit, sometime before Jesus' second birthday.

Q **2:22 How long did purification take and what did it entail?**

Lv 12:1–8 describes the purification law. It involved allowing for time to pass after giving birth for a woman's physiology to return to normal and to ensure there was no more bleeding (Lv 15:19–26). Once her forty days for a male child or eighty for a female had passed, then she, her husband, and the baby would take a lamb or pigeon or turtledove to the priest to offer as a sacrifice; the priest would offer the sacrifice, and the woman would be clean.

Q **2:25 What is the consolation of Israel?**

The word translated "consolation" here occurs eleven times in the Old Testament. Sometimes this comfort is part of a general description of God's care for His people; God's mercy holds us up when our feet slip, and in our anxieties His comforts delight our souls (Ps 94:18–19). Isaiah is a book full of prophecies about the coming Savior, and in that context God speaks about restoring comfort to His people (Is 57:18; 66:11). Hosea describes how God will rescue His people and, in so doing, will have no consolation to offer death or the grave (Hos 13:14). Simeon was waiting for God to fulfill His many promises by sending His Son who would bear away the sins of the world and reunite people with their loving, wise, and almighty God.

Can women be pastors?

Q **2:27 Where did this custom originate?**

The custom of offering a sacrifice as a substitute for the firstborn male child has its origins in the Passover in Egypt (Ex 12:1–28; 13:1–2).

Q **2:34–35 Did Simeon and Anna think that Jesus was going to raise up Israel and make it greater, or did they understand that this child would be the Savior for all believers and glory would be brought to the people of Israel that way?**

No fallen human nature or thinking ever thinks as God thinks or understands what He is doing (Is 55; 1Co 1:18–2:14). Jesus' own apostles failed to understand the work of Jesus, though He explained it so many times before and even after His crucifixion (Mt 16:21–23; Lk 24:25–27). Until the day Jesus returns in judgment, there will always be people who try to turn the Christian character of loving, sacrificial service into self-indulgence and self-glorification (Mt 24:15–28; Mk 9:33–37; 10:35–45; 1Tm 6:3–5; 20–21; 2Tm 4:1–5).

Q **2:36–38 What is the significance of the prophetess Anna? Does this mean that women can be pastors?**

Anna is among a number of people we

meet only through Luke's Gospel. Her husband died early in her marriage, and she lived alone and in the temple with much fasting the rest of her life. She is one of the many people who were looking for and awaiting the fulfillment of God's promises to send a Savior. She recognized that Jesus, the long-awaited Savior promised by God for so many centuries, had finally come. Jesus was the remedy for death, loneliness, and hunger.

Anna was a prophetess, as was Deborah in the Old Testament and the daughters of Philip in Acts (Jgs 4:4ff.; Ac 21:9). Note carefully that none of these women were priests, nor were they apostles or pastors. God calls all people to bear witness to the truth, to love others, and to be ambassadors for Christ wherever the course of their life leads them (Mt 5:14; Jn 15:12; 2Co 5:14–21). The public ministry bears hardships, challenges, and responsibilities that God intends men to bear and women to be protected from (1Co 11:1–16; 1Tm 2:8–15; Jas 3:1ff.). The idea that public ministry is the only work that matters or that it matters more than the constant witness of every Christian according to their calling in life is wrong and gives the mistaken impression that men are given more important work than women.

Q 2:38–39 Why isn't the flight into Egypt mentioned?

The flight to Egypt, according to Mt 2, would have taken place between vv. 38 and 39. Notice that in v. 39, Luke says plainly that the holy family returned to Galilee, but they had not lived there since they traveled to Bethlehem according to the emperor's decree. For more on this chronology, see Lk 2:21–24 above.

Q 2:39–52 Why didn't Luke record much about Jesus' childhood?

Luke is the only Gospel that records anything at all about Jesus' childhood. The New Testament says very little about many things, including Jesus' family, the families of the apostles, what happened to the apostles after Jesus' ascension, what became of Joseph, and what heaven is like. The Gospels focus on demonstrating who Jesus was and what that meant, for His life and for ours. Luke's inclusion of a little information about Jesus' childhood serves this same purpose as it demonstrates that Jesus is true God and that He is a perfect man, fulfilling the Law perfectly on behalf of all people.

Q 2:41–52 Why was it not a sin of not honoring His parents when Jesus stayed in the temple? Why was it okay for Jesus to not tell his parents where he was going?

Jesus' childhood gives us some unique insights regarding the Law, especially the Fourth Commandment in this case. First, there is no evidence that Jesus disobeyed or disrespected His parents. It's not as though Joseph and Mary told Jesus to come along and He refused. Second, weren't Joseph and Mary responsible for knowing where their twelve-year-old son was? Third, Joseph and Mary had a gift and a challenge in raising Jesus. Jesus was a gift in that He was perfect: no sickness, no trouble getting Him to do chores or His homework, no trouble ever about anything. Jesus was a challenge because He was the Son of God, which meant that Joseph and Mary would need to remember that He had the will of God, His Father, to accomplish at every moment and in every detail. This is the question that Jesus raises with Joseph and Mary, "Why were you looking for Me? Did you not know that I must be in My Father's house?" This is not disrespect, cynicism, or sass. Jesus is asking a question of fundamental importance. About eighteen years after this, Mary will again display some misunderstanding about Jesus' purpose at the wedding of Cana, and Jesus' response to her will surprise many people (Jn 2:1–5). Finally, if you knew your child was the incarnate Son of God, would you have cause to worry?

• •

Q **2:43 Why didn't Jesus tell His parents He was staying behind? Why did it take so long for Jesus' parents to notice that He was gone?**

We have no authoritative texts that would provide answers to these.

Luke records that Joseph and Mary traveled to Jerusalem in a "group." Luke specifies that Joseph and Mary, "suppos-ing Him to be in the group," went a day's journey before realizing He was not with them (Lk 2:43–44). One day's journey is not such a long time. What is more remarkable is that it took them three days to find Jesus once they returned to Jerusalem. Jesus Himself registered surprise at this (Lk 2:49).

• •

Q **2:48 If Mary knew that Jesus was conceived by the Holy Spirit, why did she call Joseph Jesus' father when she told Jesus they had been looking for Him? How much understanding did Jesus' family have of who He was and what His purpose was?**

Mary's reference to Joseph as father is not necessarily any different than references to stepfathers that omit the word *step*. The divine nature of Jesus seems to have faded in the consciousness of Joseph and Mary (see Lk 2:43 above). Later on, Jesus' family not only questioned His sanity but even taunted Him in disbelief (Mk 3:21; Jn 7:3–5).

• •

Q **2:49 Why did Jesus respond this way to His parents? Didn't He know that they would be leaving and/or wondering where He was?**

Jesus responded this way because it was the right thing to do, in perfect harmony with the will of His Father (Jn 4:34). Jesus must have known everything about His family and their thoughts according to His divine nature but may have chosen not to according to His human nature (Php 2:5–11). Jesus' activity here is important to remind Joseph and Mary and all subsequent generations that we are the ones to learn from Jesus, not He from us. Jesus always stays focused on what matters most and always employs what does not in the service of what does matter most. We depend on His faithfulness, and we benefit from learning His way (Col 3:1ff.; 2Tm 2:11–13).

● ● ● ● ● ● ● ● ● ● ● ● ● ● ● ● ● ● ●

Q 2:49 Why don't Mary and Joseph understand why Jesus must be in His Father's house?

Fallen human nature is quick to take gifts for granted and just as quick to judge challenges as intolerable. Would we be surprised if Joseph and Mary, over time, took Jesus' perfection for granted? God deals with each of us as a perfect, loving Father and orders all things to work for our good—and still we find fault, question, and disbelieve (Heb 12:1–17).

● ● ● ● ● ● ● ● ● ● ● ● ● ● ● ● ● ● ●

Q 2:52 Adolescents struggle with many different changes. Even though Jesus was perfect, would He have struggled as an adolescent as well? Why did Jesus the Son of God have to grow in favor with God? Wasn't He already? Jesus is God and God is all-knowing, so how was He able to grow in wisdom?

We cannot separate the two natures in Christ, but we can distinguish them. According to His divine nature, Jesus is fully God, omniscient, omnipotent, and omnipresent. Terms like "adolescent" and "grow" are incompatible with God. On the other hand, Jesus is fully human and lives in that human nature in order to fulfill all that the Law requires of all people in every time and place. Jesus did grow and develop; He learned and demonstrated His perfect obedience moment by moment—thus growing in wisdom, stature, and favor with God and people. "Adolescence" is a relatively recent phenomenon, the product of modern, Western culture that has abandoned what is essential to life and abandoned relationships for what is artificial and trivial. In any case, it is essential for our salvation and peace of mind that Jesus lived every moment of our lives for us and succeeded in every challenge on our behalf so that we might be justified by His grace before God (Jn 1:29; 16:14; 2Co 5:21). Please see Martin Chemnitz's *Two Natures in Christ* for a full and reliable treatment on this subject.

● ● ● ● ● ● ● ● ● ● ● ● ● ● ● ● ● ● ●

Q 3:3–7 John tells us that there needs to be repentance with Baptism. Why then do Lutherans baptize babies, who can't understand what is happening?

In this section, John commands the people to bear fruits that are consistent with repentance. (John and Jesus both commanded repentance and Baptism, John in Mt 3:2 and Jesus in Mk 1:15.) What is repentance and how is it accomplished? Repentance means simply to turn but occurs in various forms: to change one's mind, to change what one cares about, and to change one's heart.

Ezk 18 provides a thorough and clear explanation of repentance. Repentance is a turning and change that we cannot bring about on our own; we would not think of it nor would we want to if we did (Rm 5:6–11; Eph 2:1–9). Whether adult or child, repentance is the work of God through His Word and Spirit, though we do well to consider which is more difficult to turn, a child or an adult? Baptism means a washing or immersion, first and most significantly in the Word of God. Every Baptism recorded in the Bible takes place after the living water of God's Word has flooded the place (1Pt 3:18–21). The ceremony of Baptism, the application of water in the name of God, is a confirmation of the Word of God that grants grace and works regeneration. The ceremony of Baptism is to the activity of God's Word as birth is to conception and nutrition for a human being. Baptism is not so much about understanding as it is about admitting our inability to understand and renouncing our own thoughts and opinions that are contrary to God's Word and will. The question is not why we baptize children but why we baptize adults before immersion in the Word of God has restored them to the faith of a child (Mt 18:1–4; Ac 2:38–42).

● ● ● ● ● ● ● ● ● ● ● ● ● ● ● ● ● ● ●

Q 3:7 John talks to the people as if he knows they will not properly follow God's will. Why does he continue to baptize them?

Interestingly, the Gospels do not say that John baptized the people he warned in such severe terms. Matthew's account of this same time makes clear that John was talking to the Pharisees and Sadducees (Mt 3:7–12), the same group that Jesus speaks a final warning to in Mt 23. Later on, Luke leaves no doubt that these religious leaders were not baptized by John because they had rejected the counsel of God (Lk 7:29–30). It was the tax collectors, sinners, and soldiers who showed the fruit that is consistent with repentance in their questions of John; these were the ones in whom God had worked repentance and faith, which was then confirmed by Baptism with water (3:10–18).

● ● ● ● ● ● ● ● ● ● ● ● ● ● ● ● ● ● ●

Q 3:7–9 Why does John become so angry with the crowds who want to be baptized? Is it a warning?

John's anger is not against the crowds in general but against hypocrites, in this case the Pharisees and Sadducees, as Matthew's Gospel (3:7–12) and a later comment by Luke (7:30) make clear. Hypocrisy makes God and His servants angry because it is such a deadly and subversive disposition. Hypocrisy not only destroys the life of the hypocrite, but also draws others along into the same deadly course of lies (Mt 23; Gal 2:11–21). The appropriateness of John's anger toward hypocrisy is affirmed by the consequences of the hypocrisy of Ananias and Sapphira (Ac 5:1–11).

Q **3:8 Does God consider the "children of Abraham" to be *anyone* who is faithful and believes?**

Yes, although we might want to say "everyone" rather than "anyone" who is faithful and believes. Abraham had two kinds of children. Ishmael was born by typical biological means (though even these means depend on the blessing and will of God). God rejected Ishmael because he was not the child that God had promised. Ishmael was flesh born of flesh descended from Adam, fallen and accursed. The children of Abraham that God had in mind would be generated by His promises and would, therefore, live forever. The ceremony of Baptism confirms that the essence of a person, the soul, has been regenerated by God's Word and Spirit and is, like Isaac, a child of God's promise (Gn 12:1–3; Jn 1:11–13; 3:1–7; Rm 2:28–29; Gal 3:7).

Q **3:8 What does John mean when he says, "For I tell you, God is able from these stones to raise up children for Abraham"?**

There are several interesting possibilities for the significance of what John says here. In the first place, John could very well be referring to the "deadness" of Sarah's womb. To put it bluntly, Sarah's reproductive organs were like stones (Rm 4:19–20). Second, John could simply be pointing to the power of God, and God certainly could make people from stones if He chose to (Mt

19:26). Finally, John could be exposing the spiritual peril that these religious leaders were in, since it sounds as if it would be more likely or easier for God to make children of Abraham from stones than from these hard-hearted hypocrites (Mt 12:31–32; Heb 6:1–8; 10:26–31).

Q **3:16 What does it mean when John the Baptist says, "He will baptize you with the Holy Spirit and fire"? What does the fire represent?**

The most obvious explanation for John's prophecy is found at Pentecost, when the apostles were filled with the Holy Spirit and tongues of fire appeared on their heads (Ac 2). However, John spoke these words to the multitude, not just the apostles. So, remember that "baptize" is a Greek, not an English, word, that means "to wash or immerse." John's work was to prepare the way for Jesus, who would immerse the people in the Word, and His Word is inseparable from the Holy Spirit (Jn 6:63). Jesus also immersed the people in the truth, by the clarity with which He explained and applied the Law and by His perception and the way He exposed all things to the light (Mt 5–7; 23; Mk 12:15; Jn 3:18–22).

Q **3:19–20 Why did Herod put John in prison?**

Herod put John in prison because John rebuked Herod concerning Herodias, his brother Philip's wife (3:19). Mark's Gospel provides the greatest detail (Mk 6:17–20). Simply put, Herodias divorced her husband, Philip, in order to marry Herod. This was contrary to God's Law, which made them both adulterers. Herod imprisoned John in order to silence him, yet Herod feared John and even protected and listened to him.

• • • • • • • • • • • • • • • • • • •

Q 3:21 Why did Jesus have John baptize Him? Why was Jesus baptized at age thirty?

John expressed this same question when he said that he should be baptized by Jesus. Jesus explained that it was necessary "to fulfill all righteousness" (Mt 3:15). As a human being, Jesus was living His life on behalf of all people of all times and places, from conception through death. Everything the Law requires of us Jesus did, including being baptized. There is no moment, activity, or expectation of our life that Jesus did not accomplish for us. If Jesus had not done all things for us, how would we ever have any peace or confidence of salvation since we would always be wondering if we failed to fulfill the one or two requirements that are required of us on our own? By God's grace, wisdom, and love, Jesus has fulfilled the Law for us in every way and makes that life ours as He binds us in communion with Himself through His Word and Spirit (2Co 5:21; Rm 8:1).

Jesus began His public ministry at age thirty. In order to provide confirmation of that public ministry, Jesus was baptized, God the Father spoke His approval from heaven, and the Holy Spirit came upon and remained with Jesus. I know of no authoritative source that explains why Jesus began His public ministry at age thirty. Perhaps this is as young as Jesus could have been if He expected people to take Him seriously as He taught, preached, and did miracles (Jn 8:57).

• • • • • • • • • • • • • • • • • • •

Q 3:23–38 Do we base the age of the world somewhat by the genealogy in Luke? Do we look at how many people are in the line and then life spans to try to predict the world's age?

No. The genealogy before Abraham in Luke appears to draw on the genealogies in Gn 5:1–32 (Adam to Noah) and Gn 11:10–26 (Shem to Abraham). These list descendants and years of age when someone "begot/fathered/brought forth" the next person in the genealogy. Some have attempted to take the date of Abraham and simply add on these years to determine the age of the world. That won't quite work either. Here's why:

We know that some genealogies in the Bible are selective—they skip generations. This can be demonstrated in the case of Mt 1. Matthew skips some generations (compared to the genealogy in 1Ch 3:17–19) in order to get his 14–14–14 scheme. Ezra's genealogy (Ezr 7:1–6a) skips over six generations between Azariah and Meraioth (see 1Ch 5:33–36).

The genealogy of David at Ru 4:18–22 is another example. It has exactly ten generations and Boaz is seventh. It appears that this is a selective genealogy. Salmon married Rahab around 1400 BC. David was born in 1039 BC. This makes four generations to David, for an average of one generation about every ninety years—hardly possible that each man was waiting until he was ninety to have a son (even if we're not talking firstborn sons). In the other direction, Perez was born c. 1877 BC. This makes five generations to Salmon in about 477 years—or about 95 years per generation—even more improbable. The numbers get smaller if one assumes the late date for the exodus (c. 1270) and a short (215 year) sojourn in Egypt, but not good enough: 48 years per generation from Salmon to David; 51 years per generation Perez to Salmon. The reality is that there is—on average—about 22–28 years per generation over long periods of time. Clearly the genealogy of David was designed to make Boaz number seven, thereby honoring him, and David becomes number seven, thereby honoring him.

"Turning back to Genesis, it should be noted that there are exactly ten generations from Adam to Noah (with Enoch number seven) in Gn 5 and ten generations from Shem to Abraham. These look suspiciously like selective genealogies. If they are selective, then the formula 'when X had lived xx years, he begot/brought forth Y' would mean 'when X was xx years old, he had a son, and some generations down the line it led to Y.' These may or may not be selec-

tive genealogies in Genesis, but I know of no argument that is decisive one way or the other. The most we can say is that the earth is no younger than the sum of the years in these two genealogies added to the date of Abram's birth (2166 BC). [2166 + 1556 + 390 = 3712 BC]." (This part of the answer provided by Andrew Steinmann, Professor of Theology and Hebrew, Concordia University Chicago.)

• •

Q **3:23–38 Why does the Bible have so many long genealogies to show a person's lineage?**

God anticipated contradictions to His Word that would come in the course of time, including the argument that the Bible is all invented and not historical in nature. The list of names is necessary to demonstrate that real human history and relationships were recorded in the Bible. In some cases, as in Matthew's genealogy of Jesus, little details of importance are included that also ground the genealogy in history.

• •

Q **3:22–28 Why does Luke begin the genealogy with Jesus' apparent earthly father, then end with His heavenly Father? Is there any meaning behind the fact that when Matthew gives the genealogy of Jesus, he starts with Abraham and ends with Jesus, while Luke begins with Jesus and ends with Adam?**

Please see notes on Matthew's genealogy. In this genealogy, Luke is bearing witness to the natures of Jesus and both are critical, His divine nature and His human nature. Jesus IS the Son of God on both accounts. Jesus is the Son of God, begotten of the Father from all eternity, and as such can represent all humankind and fulfill everything that the Law requires for all people. Jesus is also true man, the second Adam, descended from Adam who was, himself, a son of God since God created him. V. 23 confirms two important truths at the same time: (a) Jesus was not of the seed of Joseph but of Heli, Mary's father, who was a descendant of David just the same, and (b) Jesus was born of the Virgin Mary, God Himself being His Father. Everywhere you look and in any way you look, Jesus is both God and man, our Redeemer and Savior, fully, for all, and forever.

- - - - - - - - - - - - - - - - - - -

Q 3:23 Why are there no women in the genealogy?

The reason the Bible concentrates on men is because Adam was responsible for the fall and the Son of God took responsibility for correcting that fall and providing the means of restoration and life everlasting (Rm 5:12–21; Heb 10:10ff.).

- - - - - - - - - - - - - - - - - - -

Q 3:38 Why is Adam considered the Son of God if he wasn't born but created?

The term "father" is intended to describe the relationship between a man and his child or children. I'm not sure that term is necessarily restricted to men who produce children by natural, biological means. Since there was no man before Adam to be his father and since God created Adam, how else would we think about God's relationship with Adam?

- - - - - - - - - - - - - - - - - - -

Q 4:1–13 When, chronologically, did the temptation happen?

Mark's Gospel says that "immediately" after Jesus' Baptism, the Holy Spirit drove Him into the wilderness (Mk 1:12). Then again, almost everything in Mark happens immediately after the previous event. After Jesus' Baptism, Matthew says "then" the Holy Spirit led Him into the wilderness; Luke says "and" Jesus returned "and" was led by the Holy Spirit into the wilderness (Mt 4:1; Lk 4:1). While some time might have passed between the Baptism of Jesus and the temptations, there is no record of any time or activity taking place in between. On the other hand, it makes sense that immediately after Jesus was revealed in public and was beginning His public ministry He would confront the devil. Just as the devil came quickly to ruin Adam and Eve's life in paradise, so the Holy Spirit leads Jesus quickly from God's word of approval to a justification and proof of that approval; Jesus would overcome the devil where Adam failed.

- - - - - - - - - - - - - - - - - - -

Q 4:1 Why did Jesus have to go through temptation in the desert? Didn't the devil know it was impossible to tempt

Jesus? When Jesus was tempted by the devil was He actually capable of sinning, or could He physically not sin because He is God?

Jesus had to be tempted with every temptation by the devil in order to succeed where we fail. From conception through death, Jesus lives a perfect life in the place of every human being (Heb 2:9; 4:14–10). The devil clearly does not know many things, especially the mind, nature, and way of God (Jn 8:43–47). If the devil understood God, why would he have moved Judas to betray Jesus so that the crucifixion and the devil's own defeat would be sealed? The devil, suffering from the insanity of self-deception and thinking he could be what he is not, fails to understand anything but simply goes about trying to destroy whatever belongs to God and is good. God shows us this work of the devil so we have a way of knowing the difference between the devil's ways and God's. The devil is completely incapable of understanding that God makes all things work together for good to those who love Him (Rm 8:28). Jesus was and wasn't capable of being tempted because of His two natures. Inasmuch as Jesus was truly a man, he was as capable of being tempted as any other human being (Heb 2:17–18; 4:15). However, since Jesus is also true God and His human nature is inseparable from His divine, He could never, ever, fail to overcome every temptation (Jas 1:13–14). God's work of salvation is not a gamble or a contest that leaves us biting our nails in suspense. Jesus is the Lamb of God who was slain and has been God from the founda-tion of the world; God has always known His good and gracious will and just how He would accomplish it all for our life and salvation (Rv 12:5–10).

• • • • • • • • • • • • • • • • • • • •

Q 4:2 What is the importance of the number 40? Is there a close connection between the Israelites wandering in the wilderness for forty years and Jesus' temptation in the desert for forty days?

Consider the occurrences of the number *40* in biblical history. God made it rain for forty days and nights when He flooded the earth (Gn 7:12). Moses was on Mount Sinai with God forty days (Ex 24:18). The spies of Israel spent forty days spying out the land of Canaan (Nu 13:25). Israel wandered forty years in the wilderness, one year for each day the spies were in the land (Nu 14:34). God gave Israel into the hands of the Philistines for forty years because of their rebellion (Jgs 13:1). David ruled as king over Israel for forty years (1Ki 2:11). Certainly Jesus was reliving the life of Israel in the wilderness, keeping the Law perfectly in place of their failure. The number *4* has to do with things of the world, as in four corners of the world or four points on a compass. The number *10* has to do with the Law, which reveals what must be done if we are to live. Thus it may also be that the number *40* indicates "all that the law requires of us while we live in this world." By this reckoning, Jesus was in the desert on behalf of every human being, living out the course of our lives for us perfectly and overcoming every temptation to the contrary. Notice the significance of Luke's observation that "when the devil had ended every temptation" he departed.

• • • • • • • • • • • • • • • • • • •

Q 4:3 Why didn't Jesus turn on Satan when Satan was trying to tempt Him in the desert? Satan knows many things, but is he like us and can only see up until the present time?

Satan, or the devil, is not an independent being. God can terminate the existence of the devil any time He wants; Jesus, the Son of God, has this power as well. But terminating the devil would not redeem us from the curse of the Law that we fail to keep, because we continually give in to temptation. By assaulting Jesus with every temptation, Satan actually served God's way of redeeming us from the curse of the Law. Since Jesus, as true God and man, was living on behalf of all people, His keeping of the Law perfectly in the face of every temptation provided atonement for our failure. His righteousness is ours.

The Bible tells us relatively little about the devil. He is a fallen angel, a deceiver, a liar, and a murderer (Lk 10:18; Jude 6; Jn 8:44; Rv 12:9).

• • • • • • • • • • • • • • • • • • •

Q 4:4 When He says, "Man shall not live by bread alone," does Jesus have more meaning than the bread of this world?

First, let's define our terms. If "life" means "to be in positive relationship," then we can understand why cessation of physiological function is called "death," even though the person continues to exist according to his or her essential soul. This also makes sense of how people can be "dead" even while they are alive in this world or at least "as good as dead." In a similar way, what we know as "bread" has this name because it is a little bit like the Word of God, which is absolutely essential and provides super-abundantly for our lives (Jn 6:48–58). With terms defined thus, Jesus' statement is easy to understand. Man and woman, whose bodies are not their essence but only an extension or material extension of their souls, do not live by the bread made of grain, but depend absolutely on the Word of God (Jn 4:31–34). Consider how one of Jesus' natures is the Word of God Himself; does this explain how a true human being could go forty days and nights without food and water?

• • • • • • • • • • • • • • • • • • •

Q 4:6 How can the devil say "all this authority and their glory" had been given to him and expect Jesus to believe the devil has more authority than God?

Clearly the devil has no idea about how useless his opposition to God is, in any case. How could the devil be so foolish as to rebel against God in the first place? How can a dependent creature rebel against God, and why would he want to rebel against the only

God, who is all-loving by nature? Jesus possessed all authority and was never in doubt, nor was anyone who paid attention to His Words and deeds (Mt 7:29; Lk 4:36; Jn 10:18). The temptations of the devil against Jesus are bound to sound foolish to us, yet those very temptations are indicative of the means by which the devil overcomes the world. Most people will do almost anything to satisfy their appetites. They will sell their souls for the riches and kingdoms of this world even though it is obvious that aging and death prevent them from owning anything. They will, in selfish lack of purpose, gamble with their lives for no good purpose. We need Jesus to resist the devil's ways perfectly for us; we need to see that Jesus did it and how He did it; we need to see the folly of the devil's lies so that we are better prepared to resist temptations when they come upon us (1Co 10:13; Jas 4:1–7).

Q 4:13 What does "opportune time" mean?

Luke makes very clear that, over a period of forty days and nights, the devil exhausted himself and his means of overcoming Jesus, all with no success. The Word of God cannot be broken or overcome, and since the human nature of Jesus is inseparable from the Son/Word of God, Jesus is unconquerable. The only means the devil can see for destroying Jesus is through another human being, one who is vulnerable to temptation. The devil found that person in Judas Iscariot, who was a deceiver, and thief, and a liar (Jn 12:4–6). John describes the devil's possession of Judas about the time of the Last Supper (Jn 13:2). The "opportune time" that Luke is referring to was the devil's possessing of Judas so that he could lead those opposed to Jesus to the Garden of Gethsemane and arrest Him.

Q 4:14 What is the difference between the fullness of the Spirit in 4:1 and the power of the Spirit in 4:14?

There are several places in the New Testament where "power of the Spirit" occurs, but none of them speak about a change from being filled to having the power of the Spirit (Ac 1:8; Rm 1:4; 15:13, 19; Eph 3:16; 1Th 1:5; Heb 2:4). Heb 5:8–9 appears to speak to this directly: "Although He was a Son, He learned obedience through what He suffered. And being made perfect, He became the source of eternal salvation to all who obey Him." According to His divine nature, Jesus is one God with the Father and the Holy Spirit, Spirit-filled, powerful, and all-knowing. Therefore, these verses must be referring to Jesus' human nature. The human nature of Jesus was filled with the Holy Spirit, and Jesus confirmed the full use of that power through His perfect obedience to God and resisting of the devil in the wilderness.

Q **4:16–29 Why do the people marvel at Jesus' words in v. 21 but then respond in anger in v. 28? Did they not realize He was the Christ?**

Jesus began with the most wonderful words anyone could hope for: He was the fulfillment of all the promises of God. What Jesus said after that is explained by the reaction of the people to His identity. The key is in the term "marveled" in 4:22. We tend to assume that "marveling" is a good thing, but it is not necessarily. In this case, the people marvel in a negative way, as evident from what they said, "Is not this Joseph's son?" A similar response of the people recorded in Mt 13:55–58 exposes the people's negative disposition: "And they took offense at Him. . . . And He did not do many mighty works there, because of their unbelief." As soon as Jesus recognized the contrary disposition of the people, He responded with the truth about that disposition, in order to lead them in repentance from it. The history of these people's ancestors testifies to their rebellion and the sad consequences of it. Rather than learn from the humble and faithful Gentiles in the past and present, the Jews attacked Jesus and intended to kill Him. To the humble and honest, both Law and Gospel are helpful and received with gratitude. For the vain and self-righteous, neither the Law nor the Gospel is of any benefit (Mt 8:5–13; 9:17; 15:21–28).

Q **4:21 What is meant by this verse?**

The quote from Isaiah is a prophecy about the Son of God who would become a man and save all people from sin, death, and the devil. Jesus said this in the synagogue right after He was baptized and returned from the temptations in the wilderness. Jesus is beginning the public ministry that the Isaiah text is describing. So, it makes perfect sense for Jesus to say, on that very day as He began to preach the Gospel to the poor and deliverance to the captives, "Today this Scripture has been fulfilled in your hearing."

Q **4:24 Why isn't a prophet accepted in his own hometown?**

Jesus recites this saying as though it were well-known and well established. There seems to be plenty of history, both well-known and private, that affirms this observation. I have been a pastor for twenty-seven years with an earned doctorate for the past thirteen of those years, yet no one in my family has ever asked me a theological question.

Q **4:23–28 Why not heal those of your own town? Is it because they are unbelieving in the power?**

Jesus was always happy to heal those who came to Him for help (Mt 8:1–3). The problem in His hometown is that these people were more interested in making judgments about Jesus than realizing the salvation He brought (Mt 13:55–58; Ac 13:46).

. . . .

Q 4:24 Why did Jesus antagonize these people?

Equity or justice is a fundamental part of God's nature; He responds to people and situations in the most appropriate way (Ezk 18:25–32). When people seek help from God, they find the help they sought (Mt 7:7–11; 11:28; 2Tm 2:13). When Jesus recognized that the people in the synagogue were dishonest about their own nature and refused to recognize Jesus' nature, He addressed the truth to that problem. Notice how the people condemned themselves. If the people had been honest, they would have sought and enjoyed Jesus' help, just like Naaman the Syrian and the widow of Zarephath. Instead, these people persisted in the lie their ancestors tried to live, and they would therefore suffer apart from the grace of God. It was the people who did the rejecting, not Jesus; it was they who attempted to kill Jesus even while He came to save them (Lk 13:34–35).

. . . .

Q 4:29 Why were the Jews so mad at Jesus that they wanted to kill Him, one of their own?

The Jews were angry because Jesus exposed the fact that they were just as faithless as their ancestors who lived in the days of Elijah and Elisha. Their faithlessness is proven by the fact that God was present to help but helped Gentiles, whom the Jews despised. This is the same disposition that possessed the Judaizers who opposed and persecuted Paul in Jerusalem and during his missionary work (Ac 13:46–51; 22:21–22). God's own chosen people were the ones in history who stoned the prophets and persecuted messengers God sent (Lk 13:34–35; 20:1–20; Jn 19:14–16). People who claimed to be God's chosen and favored were the ones who eventually succeeded in forcing Jesus' crucifixion, asking for a murderer and rebel to be released to them instead (Mt 27:15–26). Even after Christ, it would be people from within the Church who would make the most trouble for it (Ac 20:30; 2Tm 4:3–4). Any person who recognizes their utter dependence on God will hold fast to Him, no matter how damning the truth is, because in Christ alone is the remedy for that damnation (Mt 13:11–13; Jn 6:67–69; 1Co 1:18–31).

. . . .

Q 4:31 If Jesus preached with authority, wouldn't that turn a lot of people away? Why can't the people of Nazareth see that Jesus was the fulfillment of prophesies?

Perhaps teaching with authority attracts as many people as it turns away (Mk 12:37). The problem with authority began in the rebellion of the devil, then the fall of Adam, and then Eve—like dominoes. To this day, most human beings who cannot add one inch to their height or make one hair on their heads white or black continue to insist they have a free will (Mt 5:36; 6:27; Jn 8:31–47). Anyone who knows the truth about our dependence on God welcomes God's authority, teaching, and salvation (Mt 18:3ff.). Anyone who refuses the truth refuses the very source of his or her life and necessarily dies (Jn 3:18–20; 8:24).

• • • • • • • • • • • • • • • • • • • •

Q 4:38–39 In Mark, Jesus calls Simon (Mk 1:16–17), and then He heals Simon's mother-in-law (Mk 1:29–31). However, in Luke, the order is reversed: first the mother-in-law is healed (Lk 4:38–39), and then Jesus calls Simon (Lk 5:1–11). In what order did these events occur? How do we deal with issues like this when harmonizing the Gospels?

The problem in question is a matter of assuming that the men Jesus called to follow Him did so without ever returning to their homes or families. John's Gospel reveals that some of the disciples Jesus called had already been in contact with John the Baptizer (Jn 1:35–51). After Jesus' Baptism and temptations in the wilderness, Jesus began to call men to be His disciples, as related in Mk 1. Perhaps at the end of each day or for parts of days, the disciples would return to their families and work, at least until Jesus called twelve of these disciples, named them apostles, and commissioned them to take the Gospel to others (Mt 10:1–15). Note that after Jesus' resurrection, Jesus finds Peter back on the Sea of Galilee fishing and

calls him yet again (Jn 21:1–18). Most, if not all of the time, apparent contradictions between the Gospels come from assuming that Gospels are reporting the same events, as if Jesus only did or said things once. In fact, the Gospels give a very full account of Jesus' life by recording similar activity of Jesus that happened more than once, at different times and places. For example, Mt 6 is very much like Lk 11, but the Matthew account took place at the beginning of Jesus' ministry in Galilee while the Luke account took place at the end of Jesus' ministry in Judea.

• • • • • • • • • • • • • • • • • • • •

Q 4:41 How can Luke write that the demons said that Jesus was the Son of God when in the next sentence he says Jesus wouldn't let the demons speak? How could he know what they said?

This is a matter of sequence, verb tense, and translation. The imperfect tense of the verb "to come out" in this verse suggests that as the demons "began" to come or as they were "continually" coming out they were crying out, that is to say, they were saying (legonta) to Jesus that He was the Christ. As this took place, Jesus kept on rebuking them in order to prevent them from "speaking this in public" (lalein), that is, to prevent them from saying this to anyone else.

• • • • • • • • • • • • • • • • • • • •

Q 4:42 Did Jesus need to be alone because He was overwhelmed?

This text does not given any indication

of why Jesus went to a deserted place. There is one text that says the crowds kept Jesus so busy that there was no time even to eat (Mk 3:20) and another that suggests Jesus was exhausted from His work among the people (Mk 4:38). Being fully God, Jesus did not do things out of necessity but out of purpose, according to His love for the Father and for us (Jn 14:31). On the other hand, Jesus commanded His disciples on one occasion at least to come away by themselves to rest (Mk 6:31).

Q 5:1 What is Lake Gennesaret?

This is one of the many names by which the Sea of Galilee is known (also as Kinneret and Tiberias).

Q 5:11, 28 If the men left everything and followed Him, what happened to their families?

First, we have reason to believe that these men did have families, as Paul made reference in 1Co 9:5. We also know that the disciples returned to their homes and families from time to time (see Lk 4:38–39 above). After Jesus rose from the dead and showed Himself to the apostles on Easter evening and the following Sunday, we find the apostles back in Galilee fishing on the sea (Jn 21:1ff.). While Jesus spoke about leaving home and family, this does not necessarily mean the apostles did not go out from and return to their homes and families periodically (Mk 10:28–30; Lk 14:26).

Paul lists care for one's family as a requirement for pastors and condemns men who abandon care of their families, which also suggests that the apostles with families continued to provide for them (1Tm 3:4–5; 5:8).

Q 5:14 Why didn't Jesus want the healed leper to tell anyone what He did?

Jesus' feeding of the five thousand reveals that fallen human nature completely misses the point of miracles. Jesus' miracles prove that He is true God and true man, the Savior of the world. However, fallen human beings don't want God to save them from the world but to give them more of it (Jn 6:15, 23). Miracles don't bring anyone to faith, as any number of accounts show (Lk 17:17; Jn 11:45–50; 12:37). Miracles demonstrate the authority and authenticity of a messenger of God and did this for the prophets (Dt 13:1–5; 18:15–22), the apostles (Mk 16:16–20), and above all, Jesus (Jn 3:2; 7:31).

Q 5:17 Wasn't the power of healing *always* present in Jesus? How could it leave Him?

Part of this answer has to do with translation. Luke wrote that the "power of the Lord was with Him to heal." This statement has to do with the nature of the Lord's power rather than the presence or absence of it. Part of the answer may also have to do with the two natures in Christ. Jesus possessed all power according to His divine nature, which communicated that power to His human nature (Jn 5:27). There were also occasions when Jesus refrained from doing miracles, not because He lacked the power, but in order to protect His grace from being despised by unbelievers (Mt 7:6; 13:58; 21:23–27).

• • • • • • • • • • • • • • • • • • • •

Q **5:20–26 Is sickness a possible outcome of sin? Or is the healing of the sick only symbolic of the future judgment?**

Sickness in general is a consequence of the fall in general; the failing of our human nature is a consequence and indication of the failing of our soul in relationship to God's Law (Gn 2:17; 3:22; Rm 6:23). Note carefully that death is a consequence, not a punishment. Punishment comes only for those who despise the grace of God in Jesus Christ (Ps 103:1–3, 11–12; Mt 12:31–32). While sickness is a general consequence for sin in general, God still directs these consequences for good (Jn 9:1–5; Rm 8:28). On the other hand, there is often a specific relationship between cause and effect. Too much alcohol results in a hangover and in time, cirrhosis of the liver; smoking ruins your lungs; overeating leads to increased risk of heart attack; sexual immorality results in venereal diseases. Jesus reveals the relationship between the soul and body, sin and sickness, in his response to the paralytic. Notice that Jesus, when He sees the faith of these men, responds by forgiving his sins. Also notice that neither the paralytic nor his friends are disappointed or upset. Clearly it was forgiveness that these men came for. It

Is sickness an outcome of sin?

was only because the Jewish religious leaders challenged Jesus' authority to forgive that He healed the man (Jas 5:13–16). Miracles do not create faith but rather confirm the truth about Jesus, who is the only worthy object of faith (Jn 6:26–29). The Word of God regenerates our soul, making it perfect and everlasting, and this has positive effects on our human nature (Jn 1:11–13; 3:1–7; 1Jn 3:9). However, the fallen state of our human nature cannot be corrected unless it dies and is then resurrected, also in perfect, everlasting condition (Rm 6:7; 1Co 15:35–55). Both sickness and healing are witnesses to the truth; the wages of sin is death, but the gift of God is eternal life (Rm 6:23). Jesus demonstrates the truth in His words, activity, and life. Jesus proves God's gracious will to save us by forgiving our sins and proves that the forgiveness is real through the miracles of Jesus and His apostles. This witness is still present with us as the health of human nature continues to decline, yet God still works healing in our bodies and still promises us deliverance rather than punishment in our death (Ps 23; Jn 11).

• • • • • • • • • • • • • • • • • • • •

Q **5:23 What does He mean when He says, "Which is easier, to say, 'Your sins are forgiven you,' or to say, 'Rise and walk'"?**

The paralytic, the men who brought him, and Jesus were all concerned with sin since this is the real cause of what is really problematic. Jesus forgave the man's sins, but the Jewish religious leaders objected that Jesus did not possess such authority. How should Jesus demonstrate His authority? From a human perspective, we might say it is just as easy to say "your sins are forgiven" as it is to say "rise and walk." From a human perspective, it is actually easier to *say* a person's sins are forgiven than to heal a person. However, in reality it is much more difficult to forgive than to heal, and both are beyond the capacity of any human being (otherwise we would surely forgive and heal all!). Jesus demonstrates His authority to do what cannot be seen by affecting what can be seen, but not accomplished, by anyone else. Jesus proves the reality of eternal life and His will to restore this to us by raising the dead and by giving children to those whose ability to reproduce is dead (Lk 20:27–38).

●　●　●　●　●　●　●　●　●　●　●　●　●　●　●　●　●

Q 5:27 Why did Jesus chose Levi to follow Him?

Certainly Jesus had reasons for each of the apostles He chose. Levi, known as Matthew, was a tax collector who demonstrated the deepest gratitude and greatest appreciation for Jesus' love in his life and in the Gospel he wrote.

●　●　●　●　●　●　●　●　●　●　●　●　●　●　●　●　●

Q 5:36–39 What does this parable mean?

Jesus is offering an example from everyday life and common sense that shows why the Jewish religious leaders cannot benefit from God's salvation, now present in His own person. There are two problems with trying to make a patch for an old garment out of new cloth. First, when you wash the patched garment, the patch will shrink and make a new tear. Second, the patch will not match the old garment (it will be bright, but the old is faded and worn). The Jewish religious leaders were determined to make the Law of Moses the only means of salvation. The Law of Moses was old (1,400 years old by that time) and the curse of the Law on everyone who failed to keep all of the Law perfectly was also old (everyone was worn out from the burden of the Law [Gal 3:10; Jas 2:10]). Trying to add, patch, or "tack on" the Gospel to the Law won't work. As long as a person is determined to try to justify himself by keeping the Law, the Gospel is like a patch that tears away, leaving a bigger hole; it exposes an even greater failure to keep the Law (Gal 5:2–4). Besides, the two don't match. The Law reveals what God demands, which we can never fulfill; the Gospel reveals what God has given in order to fulfill all for us. For more, see questions and answers on Mt 9:14–17.

●　●　●　●　●　●　●　●　●　●　●　●　●　●　●　●　●

Q 5:39 The wine skin analogy has an additional verse. How does that affect our interpretation of the passage?

This additional verse underscores the problem of human nature preferring Law to Gospel, even though the Law brings condemnation. This is no surprise, since the appetite, tastes, and preferences of fallen human nature are self-destructive, physically and spiritually (Rm 1:18–31). It takes a soul, regenerated by the Word and Spirit of God, to recognize and appreciate the Gospel (1Co 2:14; Php 3:7–12).

• • • • • • • • • • • • • • • • • • • •

Q 6:20–26 Why does Luke's account of the Sermon on the Mount differ from Matthew's? Why are the Beatitudes different from Mt 5? Why does Luke include the woes after the blessings and Matthew does not?

These accounts look similar because Jesus is teaching a similar lesson, just like Jesus cleansed the temple on several occasions, fed multitudes of people on several occasions, and healed and raised the dead on more than one occasion. These accounts are different because Matthew records what Jesus taught in Galilee at the beginning of His public ministry, and Luke records what Jesus taught in Judea at the end of His public ministry. We cannot know for certain why the Gospel writers include or exclude different material, but it is possible that Luke includes the "woes" at this place because he did not include the longer "woe section" that is recorded in Mt 23.

• • • • • • • • • • • • • • • • • • • •

Q 6:24–26 Does Jesus really mean that being rich and full is bad, or is He proclaiming these words only to those who misuse their high positions?

Jesus clarified the problem with riches in Mt 6:19–24. Paul says it is the love of money, not money itself, which is the root of all kinds of evil (1Tm 6:10). James also explains the trouble with fallen human nature and riches (Jas 1:9–11; 4:1–6; 5:1–6). Later in this Gospel, Luke records Jesus recounting the history of Lazarus and a rich man. The problem with the rich man is just what you suggest. He used his riches to indulge his fallen human nature and refused even to let the crumbs from his table provide for the beggar who lied at his gate (Lk 16:19–31).

• • • • • • • • • • • • • • • • • • • •

Q 6:28 In a practical day-to-day sense, what did Jesus mean by telling us to turn the other cheek?

First of all, since the fall, there is a problem with one person trying to take advantage of another, as the saying goes, "Do unto others *before* they can do unto you." This is also known as the "law of the jungle." Second, even if a person doesn't intend to be mean, a selfish sense of justice leads us to misapply the Old Testament law about "eye for eye, tooth for tooth" (Ex 21:24). These laws were not established to justify revenge but to prevent the need for it. Civil authorities were responsible to enforce this law of equity in order to prevent individuals from taking up their own case (Mt 5:38ff.). Third, if we are honest about our own guilt under the Law, we would never feel offended, nor would we ever claim that we are experiencing worse than we deserve under the Law (Rm 3:10–20). Fourth, God has redeemed us from the curse of the Law, regenerated our soul, and given us eternal life, an eternal life that cannot ever be taken away and that, in fact, thrives especially in the face of challenges (Rm 8:1ff.; 2Co 1:7–9; 4:1–5:21; 12:7–10; Php 1:12–18). With this kind of life, humility about ourselves, and confidence in the life God gives us, we are free to always do what is best for the other person. If someone does us wrong, we think first of taking the log out of our own eye before trying to remove the speck from theirs (Lk 6:41–42). Next we think of how to love this person as Christ loves us (Jn 15:12–13). Finally, we apply ourselves to the work of helping the other person come to repentance, the love of God, and loving others as he or she is loved by God (Gal 6:1; Jas 5:19–20; Col 3:1–17).

• • • • • • • • • • • • • • • • • •

Q 6:37 How can someone not judge?

The solution comes in understanding the semantic domain of different words. The word *judge* has different uses, and we have particular words that say what we mean with less ambiguity. For example, a physician makes judgments about a person's health, but we normally call that a *diagnosis*. Athletic competitions employ referees to make judgments, but we usually refer to them as *calls*. Judges make decisions based on the law and evidence or on a jury's conclusion, and we call this *judgment*, but in fact it may be a condemnation. The Bible clearly and consistently reminds us of our responsibility to speak the truth to one another, as a physician makes diagnoses (Lv 19:17; Eph 4:15; 1Co 5:1–13). The Bible, just as clearly and consistently, forbids us from

condemning others (Dt 32:35; Mt 5:22; Rm 2:1–24). Jesus offered a practical method to keep us from condemning while making us more effective at diagnosis when He said we should take the log out of our own eye so that we can see clearly to take the speck out of the eye of another (Lk 6:41–42).

• • • • • • • • • • • • • • • • • •

Q 6:37 This verse talks about forgiving. In the Lord's Prayer we pray, "Forgive us our trespasses as we forgive those who trespass against us." If our forgiveness is not based on us, why is it stated like this?

God is love, and He is truthful and just. His creation is established and exists because of these dynamics. The truth is that we don't deserve to be forgiven, but we have been forgiven because He loves us. The truth is that God's love and forgiveness regenerate us in His image so that we love and forgive as well (see 6:28 above). There is justice in our loving and forgiving others just as we are loved and forgiven. A person who refuses to love and forgive others while asking God for love and forgiveness is despising God's grace, is a hypocrite, and is worse than an unbeliever (Mt 18:21–35; Heb 6:1–8). God's nature is to save and restore; He has done and He is doing just that. On Judgment Day, those people who are condemned under the Law will have no choice but to admit they are only condemned because they condemned others and, by playing the hypocrite, condemned themselves.

Q 6:38 What "measure" is Jesus talking about in this verse?

The "measure" is whatever kind of activity or disposition we have in mind. Jesus said that a person who lives by the sword will die by the sword (Mt 26:52). The Fifth Commandment forbids murder, not killing. The Old Testament provided plenty of details about how to deal with someone who killed another by accident or someone who had responsibility for executing judgment on a murderer (Ex 21:14; Nu 35:11, 15, 19–27; Dt 19:4–12). On the one hand, Jesus tells us not to resist an enemy (Mt 5:38ff.), yet Paul says that the civil governments (police and army) and men on behalf of their families have responsibility to provide protection (Rm 13:1–7; 1Co 11:3; Eph 5:25). What appears at first to be a contradiction actually makes perfect sense in God's economy. As living creatures made in the image of God, we live our lives on behalf of others, just as Jesus demonstrated for us in His life. We do not act on our own behalf but trust in the Lord to care for and protect us, and He has done so by giving us a life that can never be taken away. At the same time, this means that we do not hesitate to sacrifice our lives on behalf of those who cannot protect themselves, just as God does for us. We would prevent evildoers from harming others and bringing guilt upon themselves—by law, police action, or war, if necessary. As agents of God's care according to our calling, we protect others from the harm evildoers would bring upon them. We are never

the aggressors, always the defenders; never for ourselves, always for others.

If Jesus knows all, why was He surprised?

Q 7:9 If Jesus knows all, why was He surprised at what happened?

Knowing about something does not necessarily eliminate the emotion of amazement. We know about re-creative powers in nature, the magnificence of mountains and oceans—yet we are no less amazed when observing these time after time. Jesus is also fully human in His nature and from that perspective could also be amazed. The word translated "amazed" (*thaomadzo*) has to do with seeing something that gives you reason to pause, take notice, and be impressed in some way (not necessarily surprised). Jesus marvels at many different points during His ministry at the unbelief of people: a man whose boy was plagued (Mk 9:24), the apostles about food (Mk 8:17–21), an almost universal absence of faith near the end of time (Lk 18:8). Jesus explained in the parable of the sower why faith is lacking, in His own people and in everyone else (Mk 4:14–19). This is why Jesus explains to Nicodemus that unless a person is regenerated by God through God's Word and Spirit, he or she cannot see or enter the kingdom of heaven (Jn 3:3–8). Jesus also has a very lengthy discussion with the crowds He fed on the subject of faith and unbelief, which is recorded in Jn 6:26–68. With so much un-belief all around, is it any wonder that Jesus marveled at the faith of the centurion?

Q **7:12 Why was the body being removed from the town?**

Israel is a country that is mostly rock. Therefore, they dug caves in the rock, usu-ally making places for three bodies and a fourth place for a box where bones were placed. After a body decomposed, the bones were put in the box and a space was avail-able again for the next burial. There was no place for digging tombs inside a city, so they found suitable locations outside the city. This is where they were taking the body of the young man.

Q **7:14 Did the people hold the people Jesus healed or raised from the dead with higher or more respect because Jesus healed and saved them?**

There is no indication that I know of in the Bible that people who were healed by Jesus or raised from the dead were treated differently afterwards. What seems more likely is that people forgot about those peo-ple Jesus healed and raised from the dead, just like Jesus' own mother seemed to have forgotten the miraculous nature of His birth (see questions and answers on 2:48ff. above).

Q **7:15 The dead man was raised. Where did his soul go? Did he have to come back from heaven?**

This young man's soul would have been in the same place as Jairus's daughter's soul and that of Lazarus (Mk 5:35–43; Jn 11:38–44). The account of Lazarus and the rich man, along with Jesus' words to the thief on the cross, indicate that their souls were in heaven until God restored their souls to their body when Jesus raised them (Lk 16:19–26; 13:42–43).

Q **7:18 Why did he choose to call only two? Why not more or less? Are John's disciples similar to Jesus' disciples? Why did He send two of His disciples instead of going Himself?**

John most likely sent more than one disciple for safety's sake. John sent only two because more than that would not be need-ed. John's disciples were supposed to be-come disciples of Jesus, but apparently some were too attached to John (Jn 1:19–36; 3:22–30; Ac 19:1–10). John could not go to Jesus because John was in prison (Lk 3:19–20).

Q **7:20 Why does John question if Jesus is the Messiah?**

John had been put in prison by Herod (Lk 3:19–20). John knew Jesus was the promised Savior, since that was why God sent John and that was John's message to the people (Jn 1:6–8, 19–36). Is it possible that John was wondering, "If Jesus IS the promised Savior, why doesn't He rescue me from this prison of Herod's?" I suspect that people of all ages who believe that Jesus is the Savior also have their doubts when trials come (Mk 4:35–41; Lk 24:21ff.). We find two kinds of encouragements from knowing this about John. First, if we feel bad about doubting who Jesus is (and we should feel bad about that), we must know that doubting is part of our fallen nature and we will not be free of it as long as we are in this flesh (1Co 2:14). Second, we benefit from the response of Jesus, just as John would have. Any time we have questions about who Jesus is and what He has come to do, we have the whole of the biblical witness to remind, inspire, and regenerate us. We have God's witness in nature and reason as well (Ps 19:1–3; Mt 6:25–34; Rm 1:20–21; 8:32).

Q 7:28 What is meant by this verse?

Jesus is speaking to the contrast between our body and our soul. Every human being ever born has descended from Adam and has a fallen human nature, just like his. Among all such people, John was the greatest of the prophets (the most devout and true to his purpose). But John, according to the flesh, is still human, has failings, and died (see 7:20 above). Notice how Jesus specified "born of women." Contrast this with regenerate souls, generated by the Word and Spirit of God (Jn 1:11–13; 3:1–7; 1Jn 3:9). According to the new person or regenerate soul, we are innocent and perfect, so that even the least among such is greater than John according to his fallen human nature.

Q 7:32 What does Jesus mean in this verse?

Jesus is responding to the classic case of people who simply cannot be pleased. The Jewish religious leaders rejected John the Baptizer, accusing him of having a demon because his diet was so austere (7:33). These same religious authorities turned around and rejected Jesus for the opposite reasons. Jesus ate what everyone else did and drank wine as they did, so the authorities accused Him of being a glutton and an alcoholic (7:34). Therefore Jesus compares these men to children in a marketplace who will neither dance for joy nor weep in mourning.

Q 7:35 Why is wisdom referred to in the feminine form?

The pronoun is feminine only because the rules of grammar require pronouns to match the gender of the word they refer to. In both Hebrew and Greek, the word for wisdom is feminine, but this has nothing to do with gender in the sense of human sexuality. Jesus IS the wisdom of God, as described in Pr 8:12–36. The gender of words is a matter of language, not of essence.

Q **7:36–38 Why did they invite Jesus to dinner? What is the significance of the washing and anointing of Jesus' feet?**

The text doesn't say why, but most, if not all, of Jesus' other encounters with the Pharisees suggest it was to test and find fault with Him (Mt 16:1; 19:3; 22:18). In v. 44 and in Jn 13, Jesus explains that the washing of feet is a simple but important practice among people who walk everywhere in sandals and so have need to wash their feet. Washing another person's feet was a very simple yet profound act of service. On another occasion Jesus said that by anointing Him with oil, Mary had prepared Jesus' body for burial (Jn 12:7). It appears that the washing of feet and anointing with oil have to do with human care and kindness, indicative of love for another but not symbolic.

Q **7:36–50 Why did Simon the Pharisee not want the woman to go near Jesus?**

The word *Pharisee* is based on a Hebrew word that means to "separate." The Pharisees believed that in order to be a righteous person before God, you must be pure. Being pure meant having nothing to do with people, things, or activities that would make a person unclean (Mt 23:25–33). Simon would never want a "sinful" woman to touch him and cannot understand why Jesus is allowing it. Simon does not understand that what defiles or makes a person unclean comes from within, from the heart (Mk 7:1–23). Simon cannot know the grace

of God because he refused to admit his own corruption, failure, and need for that grace—as Jesus went on to explain to Simon (Lk 7:47).

Q **7:37 What is an alabaster jar?**

Alabaster is a rock that is found in the Middle East. The stone is soft enough to be carved and hollowed out in order to make vessels. Real alabaster is translucent; if you put a light in the jar, the jar will light up.

Q **8:1–3 How did the women in Lk 8:1–3 provide for Jesus and His disciples?**

V. 3 says that these women provided for Jesus from their possessions or belongings. This is most likely referring to food that the women had in their homes, since Jesus did not carrry about or care for any possessions. It is possible, though I think unlikely, that the women sold possessions from time to time in order to buy food or give Jesus money for food (Ac 2:44–45; Lk 18:22; 1Ki 17:8–16).

Q **8:2 What was the relationship between Jesus and Mary Magdalene?**

The answer to this question depends on identifying Mary Magdalene. If the "other Mary" mentioned in Mt 28:1 is the sister of Lazarus and Martha, then we know almost nothing about the relationship between she and Jesus. On the other hand, there is evidence that Mary Magdalene is the sister of Lazarus and Martha. First, consider all the occasions where Mary Magdalene is mentioned in the Gospels (Mt 27:56, 61; 28:1; Mk 15:40, 47; 16:1, 9; Lk 8:2; 24:10; Jn 19:25; 20:1, 18). Note her prominent place in all four Gospel narratives. Second, note the occasions when a woman washed Jesus' feet with her tears, wiped them with her hair, and anointed them (Lk 7:37–50; Jn 11:2; 12:3). The two references in John make it clear that Mary, the sister of Lazarus and Martha, was unmistakably that woman who washed and anointed Jesus' feet. She is called a sinner in Lk 7:37 and absolved by Jesus in 7:50. The relationship between a sinner who is honest about her condition and Jesus who truly has saved her is evident here and also in Lk 10:38–42, where Mary cannot be torn away from listening to Jesus.

● ● ● ● ● ● ● ● ● ● ● ● ● ● ● ● ● ● ● ●

Q 8:10 Why does Jesus say, "So that 'seeing they may not see, and hearing they may not understand'"? Why wouldn't He help them to understand what He was talking about? Why does Jesus tell parables, knowing that some people will not understand His message?

Consider the Old Testament prophecy that Jesus quotes and which He is fulfilling, "Go and tell this people: 'Keep on hearing, but do not understand; keep on seeing, but do not perceive.' Make the heart of this people dull, and their ears heavy, and blind their eyes; lest they see with their eyes, and hear with their ears, and understand with their heart, and turn and be healed" (Is 6:9–10).

The Word of the Lord is a sharp, two-edged sword (Heb 4:12). For people who come to the Lord in honesty about their need, the Word of the Lord is clear and comforting. If you are the lost sheep, the lost coin, or the prodigal son, you see yourself right away and realize the Lord's will and persistence in redeeming you. For people who come to the Lord in hypocrisy and deceit, the Word of the Lord is sealed to them and seals their judgment (Jn 8:43; Rm 10:1–4; 2Co 3:14–15). Jesus tells parables to keep what is holy from "the dogs" and from being trampled underfoot by "swine;" that is, parables are a ready feast to those who are hungry but remain treasure buried in a place despised by those who are full of themselves (Pr 27:7; Mt 7:6; Lk 1:46–55; see also notes on the Fifth Petition of the Lord's Prayer above at Lk 6:37).

● ● ● ● ● ● ● ● ● ● ● ● ● ● ● ● ● ● ● ●

Q 8:18 What does Jesus mean when He says, "Therefore consider carefully how you listen"?

Perhaps this proverb will help: "The discerning sets his face toward wisdom, but the eyes of a fool are on the ends of the earth" (Pr 17:24). If we listen as people who realize we don't live by bread alone but by every word that proceeds from the mouth of the Lord (Lk 4:4), then we will listen carefully and gather in and keep every word that Jesus says (Mk 7:26–29). If we listen as people who think we are self-made and provide for ourselves, we will find out too late just how empty and alone we are (Lk 13:34–35; 16:19–31).

Q 8:20–21 Why doesn't Jesus admit having a mother and siblings? Does Jesus not differentiate between family as we think of it and those who put God's Word into practice?

Jesus sees things as they are in truth (Jn 7:24; 8:40–46; 18:37). What does physical descent and genetic relationship mean if the essence of the relationship is not about the soul, love, and eternity? Why is Jesus' physical family outside the house? As we can see throughout history with Ishmael and Isaac, Esau and Jacob, Saul and David, what matters are the promises of God that regenerate us into an eternal family that lives in love and is focused on what matters (Mt 9:9–17; Ac 2:37–47; Gal 2:11–21; 3:7–9; Jas 2:14–24).

Q 8:28 How does the demon-possessed man recognize Jesus and know of His power without having previously seen Him?

It was the demons within the man, not the man himself, who recognized Jesus and cried out. All creation appears to recognize God, even as He is, in the person of Jesus Christ, with the exception of arrogant, self-deceived human beings (Mk 1:13; 4:41; Rv 4:6–11; Lk 23:34–48).

Q 8:32 Why did the demons want to enter the pigs, and why did Jesus give them permission to do so?

There are several reasons for the demons' plea. First, they are fearful of being tormented by Jesus. This is evident in the question, "I beg You, do not torment me" (8:29). We really have no record of what God has said to the devil or his demons, but they clearly have knowledge of the doom that awaits them at the end. Rv 12:12 tells us that the devil is enraged because he knows that his time is short. Rv 19 and 20 also describe how the harlot, the beasts, the dragon, and even death and Hades will be thrown into the lake of fire. Second, demons apparently hate to be without a host. In Mt 12:43–45, Jesus explains how demons who have been cast out wander through waterless places, seeking rest but finding none. Perhaps the demons realize that Jesus, as He was physically present in that place, would never allow the demons to possess any living soul, but He might at least let them find a home in the herd of swine. Third, don't miss the fact that demonic forces cannot do anything without the consent of God. Our world is not "dualistic," meaning there are competing forces of good and evil, no one knowing which will prevail. The created universe is God's creation, and there is only one living God who is the only one who has knowledge and control of all things. Fourth, while the demons seem to know some things (like who Jesus is), they don't know when or what exactly God is going to do. Finally, a general note on demon possession: According to Mt 12:43–45, demons can and do inhabit empty houses, meaning human souls that are not already filled with the Spirit of God. Jn

6:63 makes clear that our source for God's Spirit is His Word. Thus Jesus said, "If you abide in My Word, you are truly My disciples, and you will know the truth, and the truth will set you free" (Jn 8:31–32).

Q **8:39 Why did God not want people to tell others about His healing earlier, but in Luke He tells the man whom the demons left, "Return to your home, and declare how much God has done for you"?**

Location and population are very important in Jesus' ministry. For example, Matthew spends most of his Gospel recording Jesus' ministry in Galilee (north), while Luke moves very quickly to Jesus' later ministry in Judea (south). When Jesus is in the populated cities of Galilee (Capernaum, Nazareth) and Judea (Jerusalem, Bethany), news travels fast and crowds confuse the significance of that news. Jesus restricts news about Himself in these Jewish, urban areas because that news turns into a kind of popularity that is contrary to Jesus' purpose (see Mk 1:44 above). The man who was healed in this narrative lived near the northeastern shore of the Sea of Galilee, an area that was relatively remote and inhabited by many non-Jewish people. Since this area was remote and the people there non-Jewish, it makes sense that Jesus would direct the man now healed and faithful to stay and be a witness to Jesus there.

Q **8:43–48 For questions on this section, please see Mt 9:20–22.**

Q **8:53–55 How many people in the Bible were raised from the dead?**

Including Jesus but not the many who rose on Good Friday, there were eight: the widow's son raised by Elijah (1Ki 17:17ff.); the Shunammite woman's son that Elisha raised (2Ki 4:27ff.); the man who was laid in Elisha's grave (2Ki 13:20ff.); the son of the widow of Nain (Lk 7:11ff.); Jairus's daughter (Lk 8:49ff.); Lazarus (Jn 11:38ff.); and the young man who fell from the window while Paul taught all night (Ac 20:9ff.). As mentioned, there were also the many people who came from their graves when Jesus died on the cross (Mt 27:50–53) and Jesus Himself.

Q **8:55–56 Why did Jesus raise people from the dead?**

Jesus did all His miracles for the same reasons: to prove that He was God and to prove what God's intent is for us. Why would Jesus feed, heal, raise the dead, and forgive sins unless it was His will that we should live and not die? Raising the dead is the ultimate proof of Jesus' divine nature and of life everlasting. God always confirms the truth with at least two witnesses (Gn 41:32). God's promises are one witness; healing and resurrection from the dead are a second. The seasons, sunrise, and procreation also bear witness to eternal life (Mt 22:29–33). God could take us to heaven and show us around while we live, but then we or others might suppose it was all a dream. Therefore Jesus raised the dead and Himself rose to verify the Scriptures and to provide incontrovertible evidence of life everlasting (1Th 15:1–58).

· · · · · · · · · · · · · · · · · · ·

Q 8:56 Why did Jesus order Jairus's family to not tell anyone what He had done by raising his daughter from the dead?

When Jesus was in the populated cities of Galilee (Capernaum, Nazareth) and Judea (Jerusalem, Bethany) news traveled fast and crowds confused the significance of that news. Jesus restricts news about Himself in these Jewish, urban areas because that news turns into a kind of popularity that is contrary to Jesus' purpose (see Mk 1:44 above). Note also from vv. 49 and 53 what kind of people He is dealing with. Jesus is always careful to protect the wonder and magnificence of God's grace from people who despise it (Mt 7:6).

· · · · · · · · · · · · · · · · · · ·

Q 9:1 Why did Jesus send out twelve disciples instead of a different number?

Lk 10:1ff records Jesus sending out seventy disciples at one time. The twelve that Jesus sent out on this occasion were given special responsibilities and means of authenticating them as apostles of God: "and [Jesus] gave them power and authority over all demons and to cure diseases . . . On their

return the apostles told Him all that they had done" (Lk 9:1, 10). The number *12* has to do with the people of God (God [3] works to make people from the world His own again [× 4]). Just as there were twelve tribes of Israel in the Old Testament (actually thirteen), so there were also twelve apostles in the New Testament (actually thirteen), and Rv 4:10 describes twenty-four elders (twelve from each testament, Old and New).

· · · · · · · · · · · · · · · · · · ·

Q 9:1–2 How and why would Jesus give the power to heal to His disciples?

No one has a life and nothing has existence unless the Lord gives it (Heb 1:3; Jn 3:27). God gives whatever is necessary and best for His creation according to His will (Jas 1:17–18). How Jesus gives this power and authority is the same as the "how" of everything else He does: with a word (Mt 8:16; Mk 4:39–41). The reason Jesus gave the power to heal to His disciples was to authenticate them, just as the miracles performed by Jesus authenticated Him (Mk 2:5–12; Jn 3:2; 7:31). Once more, before Jesus ascended into heaven, He gave His apostles authority to do miracles in order to authenticate the Word they spoke and wrote on behalf of God (Mk 16:16–20; Ac 1:8; 2Pt 1:16–21).

· · · · · · · · · · · · · · · · · · ·

Q 9:5 Why should they shake the dust off of their feet when they leave town?

Shaking dust off your feet is the opposite of sharing a meal together. Sharing a meal is a public witness to communion between people, which is why the Bible provides cautions about whom we eat with (1Co 10:14–11:34). By contrast, shaking the dust off of your feet makes a public witness that we have no communion with or responsibility for people who reject God's truth and grace—not even for the dust of their ground.

• • • • • • • • • • • • • • • • • • •

Q 9:14 Did Jesus feed five thousand men or people?

Matthew's Gospel is more clear, saying "five thousand men, besides women and children" (Mt 14:21). Therefore some estimate that Jesus fed between twenty and thirty thousand people on this occasion.

• • • • • • • • • • • • • • • • • • •

Q 9:18–19 Why do some members of the crowds believe that Jesus is either John the Baptist or Elijah?

God made many different promises about a Savior during the Old Testament: He would be the Seed of the woman and of Abraham (Gn 3:15; 12:3); He would be a prophet, like Moses (Dt 18:15); He would put David's Son upon the throne forever (2Sm 7:12–17). God also promised to send His messenger to prepare the way in the power and spirit of Elijah (Mal 4:5). People did not have the Bible to check on their own but relied on what the religious leaders taught and oral traditions that were passed down from generation to generation and from one person to another. This

What does it mean to take up your cross?

circumstance produced some uncertainty about who would be coming to save Israel and what that salvation would look like. People were uncertain about who John the Baptizer was (Jn 1:19–28) and who Jesus was (Mt 16:13–17; 27:11). Herod heard reports about what Jesus was doing. Luke records that Herod wondered who Jesus might be since he had put John the Baptizer to death (Lk 9:9). Mark records that Herod thought Jesus was John the Baptizer who had been raised from the dead and therefore had power to do miracles (Mk 6:16). To this day people continue to ignore or contradict Jesus' own word about who He is, as well as the witness that conscience, reason, and nature provide about Him (2Pt 1:16ff.).

• • • • • • • • • • • • • • • • • • •

Q 9:23 What does it mean to take up your cross?

Criminals were made to carry the cross they would be hung upon from the place of judgment to the place of crucifixion. A cross in Roman law meant that you were being put to shame publicly for what you had done (Lk 23:35–36; Heb 6:6). Hanging according to Old Testament law also meant you were being put to shame, dying under the curse of the Law (Gal 3:10). Carrying a cross bears some similarity to being under a yoke, and Jesus has invited all people to find relief in bearing His yoke (Mt 11:28–30). Taking up one's cross and following Jesus has to do with bearing responsibility for others under the Law, being honest about ourselves, and following the course of life that Jesus commands (Gal 6:2; Jn 13:1–17).

. . . .

Q 9:28 What is the significance of "about eight days after"?

God began creation on the day we know as Sunday. We know this because the Jewish Sabbath is Saturday and that was the seventh day after God began His work (Gn 1). Jesus entered Jerusalem for the last time on a Sunday, was crucified on Friday, and rose on the following Sunday, eight days later. The Christian Church of antiquity, therefore, associated the number 8 with the resurrection of Jesus and His resurrection with the promise of eternal life and new creation (Rm 6:4–5; 1Co 15:50ff.). Many baptismal fonts, baptisteries, Communion rails, church buildings, and religious symbols are octagonal as a reminder of everlasting life.

. . . .

Q 9:33 What purpose would shelters serve?

No purpose whatsoever, except that dignitaries were often provided with shelters at least from sun and heat (Jnh 4:5–8). The real value of what Peter said is in exposing the folly and misdirection of fallen human nature. Luke offers the editorial comment that Peter did not know what he was saying. Note carefully that God's voice from heaven interrupts Peter's building plans to say, "This is My Son, My Chosen One; listen to Him" (Lk 9:35). Jesus had taught that He had no home or kingdom in this fallen, material world (Lk 9:58; Jn 8:36). Abraham lived in tents his whole life because he knew he was a stranger here and was looking for his eternal home (Heb 11:13–16). Fallen human nature seeks control and is selfish and materialistic (Jas 4:1–4). David was the best of Israel's kings, yet he insisted on making buildings for a kingdom that did not endure. David built a temple of stone to replace the tabernacle, and Israel had nothing but trouble because they thought they had God in the temple like a genie in a bottle (1Sm 4:2–11). Though Peter may have had the best intentions, he was repeating the error of fallen human nature, as if God could be contained and therefore made to serve our desires (2Sm 7:1–11). The early Christian Church met in people's homes and used their resources to provide for those who served the Word and for people in need (Ac 2:44–47; 7:1–4; 1Co 9:1–18). It is sad but not surprising that the fallen human nature of people who claim a Christian faith would continue to build temples of stone rather than listen steadfastly to the Lord (consider the contrast between Martha and Mary [Lk 10:38–42]). Not only has the visible Christian Church ignored the lesson of the transfiguration, but it also seems to forget that Jesus said that "one's life does not consist in the abundance of his possessions" (Lk 12:15) and that Paul forbids Christians to be debtors (Rm 13:8).

Q **9:36 Why didn't Peter, John, and James tell anyone what they had seen?**

The simple answer is because Jesus commanded them not to tell anyone until He had risen from the dead (Mk 9:9). As far as we know, they kept it all to themselves until Pentecost. Both Peter and John make reference to this experience in their letters (2Pt 1:17–18; 1Jn 1:1–2). The transfiguration took place shortly before Jesus entered Jerusalem on Palm Sunday and then was crucified. I suspect Jesus commanded them to keep silent about the transfiguration because there was already enough evidence of Jesus' divine nature and that nature was the target of increasing hostility from the Jewish religious leaders (Jn 8:42–59; 11:46–54; Mk 11:15–18).

Q **9:41 Why does Jesus say, "O faithless and twisted generation, how long am I to be with you and bear with you?"**

Jesus was expressing exasperation at the unbelief and perversity of the people all around Him—especially at the inability of His disciples to help others after three years. Jesus, according to His human nature, sighed, groaned, and was amazed at the weak and contrary disposition of people (Mk 8:12; Jn 11:38; Mk 6:6). No matter how often, how clearly, or how profoundly Jesus demonstrated His power and His love, fallen human beings continue to miss the point completely and, in so doing, lose the life God so freely gives (Jn 6:15; 24–66; Rm 1:18–31).

Q **9:48 What does welcoming a child have to do with spiritual greatness?**

Welcoming children is an indication of a person's sense of priorities. What might we learn from people who have no interest in children or despise them? The same apostles who were arguing about which of them was the greatest also tried to turn away the women who were bringing their children to Jesus to have them blessed (Mk 10:13–16). Paul addresses this same problem with the Corinthians (1Co 1:18–31). Anyone who doesn't recognize that children are the reason for the lives of the adults who precede them have no purpose for life except for selfish, material, and fleeting things.

Q **9:49 Why does the passage about a man driving out demons follow the passage about the little children?**

Luke is reporting on many different things Jesus did and said in a very small space. Notice the subjects he has covered in this chapter: sending the apostles, their activity and return, feeding the five thousand, Peter's confession of Jesus' divinity, the transfiguration, healing a demoniac, prediction of Jesus' death, a dispute over who is greatest, Jesus' journey to Jerusalem, and teaching on discipleship. Luke is not as concerned about the circumstances between events and teaching as he is in reporting as much significant information as he can in as few pages.

● ● ● ● ● ● ● ● ● ● ● ● ● ● ● ● ● ● ●

Q 9:49 Who was the unidentified man?

I don't know of any authoritative text that identifies this man. Perhaps it is better that he not be identified so that Jesus' teaching can have universal application; "the one who is not against you is for you" (Lk 9:50). Interestingly, on another occasion, Jesus makes a complementary declaration: "Whoever is not with Me is against Me, and whoever does not gather with Me scatters" (Mt 12:30).

● ● ● ● ● ● ● ● ● ● ● ● ● ● ● ● ● ● ●

Q 9:54 Why do the disciples ask if they should make fire from heaven consume the people? Do they already have the power to do so?

Jesus gave the twelve disciples power when He sent them out as apostles (Lk 9:1–6, 10). James and John ask if Jesus wants them to destroy the city because the people there did not receive Jesus. This is the reaction of fallen human nature that misunderstands the nature of real power and authority; as Jesus explained, "The Son of Man came not to destroy people's lives but to save them" (Lk 9:55 [in some manuscripts]). James and John apparently had tempers besides, since Jesus named them "Sons of Thunder" (Mk 3:17).

● ● ● ● ● ● ● ● ● ● ● ● ● ● ● ● ● ● ●

Q 9:59–60 What does Jesus mean when He says, "Leave the dead to bury their own dead"?

Jesus is using the term "dead" in two ways. He is telling the young man to let people who are "spiritually dead" take care of matters where NO LIFE is concerned, meaning the burying of "dead" human corpses. Jesus' intent may be compared to the practice of "triage" in medicine. This practice was developed in war as a response to emergency situations. Wounded people are separated into three groups: those who clearly cannot be saved, those who are injured but in little danger of dying, and those who will surely die unless treated immediately. Jesus wants His disciples to focus their attention on the people who might be helped if we spent time with them now. His words certainly raise questions about Christian funeral practices. At the time of the death of a loved one, Christians maintain their focus on life, being conscious of the time as an opportunity to make a clear and compelling witness to all concerned.

There are people who are spiritually dead and have no hope of salvation, but we are in no position to make such a judgment (Mt 7:1). Rather, we look for the fields that are white for harvest (Jn 4:35), serving as ambassadors for Christ (2Co 5:14–21) to those who are hungry for the Word (1Pt 3:15).

Q 9:61–62 Is Jesus requesting that He at all times be the most important thing in our lives?

Jesus teaches us to have no other gods and to put nothing before God in plenty of places (Dt 6:4ff.; Mk 12:28–30). In this particular case, Jesus is focused on discipleship and the faithlessness of fallen human nature. It is easy to say we will follow Jesus wherever He goes, but no one did (Lk 9:57–58; 22:33–34; Mk 14:50). People say they will follow Jesus but continue to find other things to do instead (Lk 9:59–60; 8:7, 14; 1Ki 19:19–21; Jn 6:60–66; Mt 19:16–22). Finally, there is the problem of putting your hand to the plow and looking back. In order to plow straight, a person must keep his or her eyes straight ahead all the time. If a person begins to plow and looks back, the furrows will go all over the place and the work will have to be redone. Second, a person who looks back suggests longing for what was left behind, like Lot's wife who turned into a pillar of salt (Gn 19:26) or like Peter who asked to walk on the water to Jesus but then sank because he paid more attention to the wind and waves than to Jesus' Word (Mt 14:28–31).

Q 10:1 Did the seventy-two travel with Jesus and the disciples? Were some of the seventy-two women?

Apparently there were disciples besides the twelve apostles who followed Jesus regularly. We have two other glimpses of them: after the feeding of the five thousand (Jn 6:60–67) and after Jesus' ascension (Ac 1:15). I know of no text that says none of these were women, but they probably were not for at least two reasons. First, men bore responsibility for spiritual leadership, especially in public (Ac 1:16; 1Co 11:4ff.; 1Tm 2:12). Second, moving about in public was often unsafe, especially for women (though one wonders how Mary made the journey from Galilee to see Elizabeth [Lk 1:39]).

Q 10:19 Why are snakes and scorpions referred to as bad creations?

Many hate snakes because that was the form Satan took when he deceived Eve in the Garden of Eden (Gn 3:1), and God did curse the serpent accordingly (Gn 3:14). However, I suspect the real cause for biblical references is that snakes and scorpions are very deadly and the more so because they are silent and usually hidden; in other words, like the devil, they sneak up on you (Gn 49:17; Nu 21:6; Dt 8:15; 2Co 11:3; Rv 9:10).

Q 10:27–28 Why does Jesus give Law to the teacher of the law? Why not Gospel?

Jesus answered the question that the lawyer asked. Notice that the lawyer said, "What shall I do to inherit eternal life?" (Lk 10:25). Did the lawyer not know that there is nothing a person can do to become an heir? The lawyer plainly wants to justify himself on the basis of the Law, so Jesus gives a simple answer to a simple question. If you want to justify yourself, then you must keep the Law (Gal 3:10). When the lawyer sought to justify himself by the Law with a trick, Jesus told a parable that exposed that trick. The Law of God is a description of how reality works. Therefore, any attempt to outsmart the Law must fail. As long as the lawyer is determined to justify himself, he is at the same time despising and rejecting the justification that God has freely provided in Jesus (Mt 25:31–46). The tragedy of self-righteousness is lamented by Paul in Rm 10:1–3 and warned about in Gal 3:10–17.

Q 10:33 Why was there so much hatred between Jews and Samaritans? Why did God choose a Samaritan to help the man on the side of the road?

The root of hatred is the fall of man, the loss of God's image and communion with Him. A deep sense of emptiness, guilt, and need in the absence of God makes people search for an excuse to make themselves look better by making others look worse, to have more by taking what belongs to others. This is at the core of the Jewish hatred of Samaritans. In particular, the Jews despised the Samaritans because the Samaritans had intermarried with foreigners and adopted foreign customs (Ezr 9:1–14). Some Jews feared that tolerating such mingling with non-Jews was the reason God had not yet restored Israel to the glory, power, and riches it enjoyed under King David (Ne 13:23–27). At the same time, these Jews missed the fact that God's relationship with Abraham was based on God's gracious promises, not Abraham's righteousness (Rm 4:1ff.). God has always accepted all people who were honest about their dependence upon Him, as the genealogy of Abraham and King David prove, as witnessed by God's love and redemption for the whole world, and as argued by Paul (Mt 1:2–6; Jn 3:16; Ac 17:22–31).

Jesus used the example of a Samaritan in this parable to emphasize what the Law means by the word "neighbor." In order to justify themselves, the Jews made adjustments in their thinking about and teaching of the Law. They had accepted the notion that the Law actually taught that we should love our friends and hate our enemies (Mt 5:43–48). Notice that Jesus increases the force of His teaching by making the Samaritan the one who did the loving. It is one thing to provide care for a person you think is beneath you but quite another thing for the one who is despised to take pity on and provide care for those who despise him. Jesus was despised and forsaken, mocked, beaten and crucified by the people who should have had the most reason to welcome and honor Him (Jn 1:11–13; Lk 23:34–39).

Q 10:40 Could Martha's way of showing love be preparing food and serving?

Yes, certainly. Jesus never suggested that Martha failed to love. The problem with Martha is she has inverted priorities. If we try to serve the Lord while He is teaching, we are neither serving Him nor being served by Him. Jesus' response to Martha is parallel to God the Father's response to Peter when he wanted to build shelters on the Mount of Transfiguration (Lk 9:33–36). The other problem with Martha is that she is bothered by Mary not helping her. If we love the Lord and love the gifts and work He has given us to do, why are we upset when others don't have the gifts or work that we do? Shouldn't we rather feel sorry for people who do not know the joy and fulfillment of meaningful labor (Mt 20:1–16)? Serving others in love is quickly converted to works-righteousness and self-pity by fallen human nature. It is better to spend our time listening to Jesus first; then good works will be the fruit of faith rather than weeds that choke faith out (Jn 15:1–7).

Q 11:2–4 Luke's account of the Lord's Prayer ends with "and lead us not into temptation." Why is the Lord's Prayer we say different than what is in the Bible?

Some manuscripts of Luke's Gospel include the Seventh Petition and others do not. Matthew's record of Jesus teaching this prayer during the Sermon on the Mount includes the Seventh Petition, but some manuscripts do not include the conclusion, "For Thine is the kingdom and the power and the glory, forever and ever, amen." Certainly the petition is authentic, since Jesus' own prayer on Maundy Thursday evening includes a parallel thought, "I do not ask that You take them out of the world, but that You keep them from the evil one" (Jn 17:15).

Q 11:27–28 Why does Luke include this narrative in his Gospel?

Luke includes narratives about many people we do not meet in the other Gospels, many of whom are women, like Elizabeth, Anna, the widow of Nain, Martha, and this woman. Luke the physician also seems to pay attention to details that have to do with Jesus' human nature. The cry of the woman provided Jesus with an opportunity to speak to the subject of blessedness, redirecting our attention from our physical, temporal life to our spiritual and eternal life.

Q 11:27–28 When the woman was praising Jesus' mother, why did Jesus redirect her praise?

As was the case with Mary and Martha, people tend to reverse cause and effect. The wonder and honor for Mary to be the mother of Jesus is incomparable and beyond words. Nevertheless, it is not her womb or the breasts that nursed Jesus that provide absolute and enduring blessedness. Rather it is the Son of God in her womb. The Son of God became man to reconcile us with God, and His ways and words made God known to us (Jn 1:18). The person who is regenerated by the Word of God keeps on hearing and continues to cling to it is blessed now and for all eternity (Jn 8:31–32; 10:27–28; 15:1–7; 1Pt 1:3–9).

. . . .

Q **11:31 What does Jesus mean when he mentions the Queen of the South?**

The "Queen of the South" is another name for the Queen of Sheba, which is the same as Ethiopia. You can read about her visit to Solomon in 1Ki 10:1–10. Jesus' use of this queen as an example of faith parallels His use of Naaman the Syrian and the widow of Zarephath in Lk 4:25–27.

. . . .

Q **11:44 Why does Jesus tell the religious leaders they are like unmarked graves?**

Just as unmarked graves hide dead people's bones from the people who stand upon them, so also the hypocrisy of the religious leaders hides their spiritual deadness from the people who interact with them. Matthew records a very clear statement of Jesus on this subject: "Woe to you, scribes and Pharisees, hypocrites! For you are like whitewashed tombs, which outwardly appear beautiful, but within are full of

dead people's bones and all uncleanness" (Mt 23:27).

. . . .

Q **11:47 What does this passage mean, "Woe to you! For you build the tombs of the prophets, whom your fathers killed"?**

Jesus explains what He means in the next verse: "You are witnesses and you consent to the deeds of your fathers, for they killed them, and you build their tombs." Building tombs for the prophets only served to draw more attention to the fact that they had been killed by the fathers of these men, and we know that the apple does not fall far from the tree (Lk 11:53–54; 19:47).

. . . .

Q **11:50–51 Why are the teachers of the law being held responsible for killing all the prophets?**

The key is in the location of the guilt, "this generation." When Jesus says "this generation," He does not mean the men who were adults to whom He is speaking but fallen human nature. This is what the Mosaic Law is addressing when it says, "Visiting the iniquity of the fathers on the children to the third and the fourth generation of those who hate Me" (Ex 20:5; Nu 14:18; Dt 5:9). The problem is not that God is holding children responsible for the sins of their predecessors but that the descendants hate God, His messengers, and His Son, just as their predecessors did (Dt 24:16).

Q **12:6 What is the significance of five sparrows being sold for two pennies?**

The point Jesus is making comes in the next verse, "Fear not; you are of more value than many sparrows." Jesus is making a comparison from the lesser to the greater. If God never forgets the life of a single sparrow, how could He and why would He ever forget to look after our well-being? Paul expressed it in the opposite way: "He who did not spare His own Son but gave Him up for us all, how will He not also with Him graciously give us all things?" (Rm 8:32).

Q **12:10 What is the difference between speaking against the Son of Man and blaspheming against the Holy Spirit?**

Mark adds an editorial comment that answers this question. Mark says that Jesus gave this warning because the religious leaders had said, "He has an unclean spirit" (3:30). If you think and say that Jesus has an unclean spirit, then you are despising the very Spirit of Jesus that communicates forgiveness to you and works the effects of it in your life (Jn 6:63). A person might blaspheme God or Jesus and still be brought to repentance and the forgiveness of sins, as was the case with Saul/Paul (1Tm 1:13–16).

Q **12:13–21 Does this mean we should not plan for the future? Is it bad to look forward to or plan retirement?**

Begin with the main point that Jesus

is making: "One's life does not consist in the abundance of his possessions." There can be no question about the truth of this statement; the whole of human history and personal experience confirm it. So why do people insist on contradicting this fact? Fallen human nature lives in panic, like a drowning person, and thinks accumulating materials is the only way to keep one's head above water—but all these materials sink as well. Jesus taught this same lesson at length and with clarity in Mt 6:24–34. The question is not about planning but about what we are planning for and why. Making plans to store up material things in order to serve our selfish nature is a mistake; the material things will not satisfy, nor can we keep them or live very long to enjoy them (Ecclesiastes is all about this!). Planning to remain in the Word each day and doing so reveals to us the purpose of our life and God's abundant providence for the same (Jn 8:31–32; 15:1–7; Ezk 36:24–28). Planning to use our life to discover how God would love others through us is a plan that cannot fail (Jas 1:5).

Q **12:35–36 How can we constantly be ready?**

Half of the answer comes from fear of the consequences of not being ready. Jesus provides terrifying descriptions of what happens to those who are unprepared for His coming (Mt 7:21–23; 25:10–13; Lk 20:9–18). The fear of the Lord is the beginning of wisdom, and our fallen human nature will not respond to anything else

(Pr 1:7; Rm 6). The other half of the answer comes from intense anticipation and eagerness for the coming of the Redeemer. The faithful servant who loved his master watched and waited so that he could receive his master with joy upon the master's return (Lk 12:37–38; 19:13–17; Mt 25:21–23; Php 1:19–26; 1Jn 3:1ff.).

Q **12:48 Is this referring to people in the world who never get a chance to hear God's Word? If so, will people go to hell then?**

We know that God does not deal with us in this life according to our iniquities (Ps 103:10). We also know that He takes ignorance into account (1Tm 1:13). He who believes and is baptized shall be saved (Mk 16:16), and faith comes from hearing and hearing from the Word of God (Rm 10:17). We also know that the mercy of the Lord is upon those who fear Him (Lk 1:50) and that children are the model of faith (Mt 18:3). We know that God has provided a witness to Himself in nature, in every person's conscience, and in reason (Rm 1:18–20; 2:15; 6:21). We know that God desires all men to be saved and that He has redeemed all through Jesus Christ (Jn 3:16; 1Tm 2:4; 2Co 5:19). These things we know for certain and leave the rest to the grace and wisdom of God.

Q **12:50 Why does Jesus say He has a "baptism" to undergo?**

The word *baptism* is Greek and means to be "washed," "awash," or "immersed in" or "to pass through" something. Paul said that Israel was "baptized into Moses" in the Red Sea (1Co 10:2), meaning that they were irrevocably joined to Moses by making that passage through the water—though no water touched them! Jesus was washed with water in a Baptism by John at the beginning of His public ministry (Lk 3:1ff.). At this time in Jesus' life, it was time to complete His work of redemption. This meant that He would bear all the sins of all people of all time under the condemnation of the Law and suffer an eternity of suffering in our place; that is to say, Jesus was immersed in the Law or passed through all the righteous judgment of God (2Co 5:21; Heb 2:14–18).

Q **12:51–53 Why does Jesus say He wishes to bring division among people, especially families, instead of peace?**

Jesus does bring peace, but not like the peace the world offers (Jn 14:27). Jesus makes people a family by regenerating them with His Word and Spirit; this family has a profound and everlasting peace (Ac 2:41–47). It is not possible to make peace among people of fallen human nature; in fact, we cannot even have peace between our regenerate soul and our body (Gal 5:17; Jas 4:1ff.). The world and the devil are also at war with those who are called by and follow Jesus

(Lk 21:12–19; Eph 2:1–8; Rv 12:10–17). We, following Jesus, seek only the peace that is real, substantive, and enduring, the peace that exists among those redeemed who are in communion with each other and with God (Php 3:5–7; Col 3:12–17).

● ● ● ● ● ● ● ● ● ● ● ● ● ● ● ● ● ● ●

Q 13:1 Why are people still making sacrifices, and why did Pilate mingle the Galileans' blood with the sacrifices?

The Jews in Jerusalem continued to offer the sacrifices prescribed in the Law of Moses, just as Joseph and Mary did after Jesus' birth (Lk 2:22–24). Every so often, a Roman ruler tried to impress the population with his power by an act of audacity. Antiochus Epiphanes IV made pagan sacrifices in the temple, which set off the Jewish rebellion of 164 BC. Pilate made a similar attempt at exalting his own power by mixing the blood of some executed Galileans with the sacrifices of the temple (for more on Pilate, this occasion, and the political trouble he made for himself, please see Paul Maier's book *Pontius Pilate*).

● ● ● ● ● ● ● ● ● ● ● ● ● ● ● ● ● ● ●

Q 13:3–5 Jesus says here to repent. We know you have to repent and be baptized to be saved, but how can a baby repent of his or her sins before being baptized?

Repentance is not something we do but something that God works in us. Repentance, like faith, is the product of God's Word and Spirit in our lives—usually aided by circumstances, conscience, and reason (Lk 3:4–14; Ac 2:36–43; Rm 1:18–20; 2:12–15; 6:20–23). You will notice in the references just noted that the commands to repent and believe are set within the context of preaching that accomplishes what is commanded. Repentance is, above all, a turning away from thinking too much of oneself. Faith is, similarly, honesty about our dependence on God. This is why Jesus points to children and infants as the standard of, not an exception to, repentance and faith (Mt 18:3, 6, 10, 14; 19:14; 1Co 1:18–31).

● ● ● ● ● ● ● ● ● ● ● ● ● ● ● ● ● ● ●

Q 13:6–9 What does the parable of the fig tree mean?

The parable of the fig keeper is making several points. First, the parable exposes the fact that the children of Israel had continually failed to bear fruit in spite of all the advantages and opportunities God had given them. He brought them out of Egypt, gave them food and water in the wilderness, gave them a land flowing with milk and honey, protected them from their enemies, and gave them every other conceivable blessing—yet they insisted on doing what was right in their own eyes, adopting the ways of the nations around them, and "whoring" after other gods (Ps 106 is a good summary, otherwise consider Ex 32:1ff.; Jgs 2:10–11; Ezk 16:1ff.). Second, God the Father is the vineyard owner who has given the Israelites plenty of time and cause to bear fruit, but they refuse. God made His complaint long before through the prophet Isaiah (Is 5:1ff.) and by Jesus in a similar parable where the Israelites are renters rather than a fig tree in the vineyard (Lk 20:9ff.). Third, Jesus is the gardener who intercedes for the fig tree. God had been patient all through history, over and over again restoring Israel to the Promised Land and the fortunes of His promises, only to see them rebel and despise Him. The public ministry of Jesus is like that extra year of time the gardener is granted in order to work with the plant to see if it produces fruit. Jesus makes a profound fulfillment of this prophecy on the Monday of Holy Week when He cursed a tree because it had no fruit (Mt 21:18–19; Mk 11:20–21; 2Tm 4:2). The parable has application to every person's life. God gives us life in the world and provides all that we need to thrive in faith. Our fallen human nature refuses to return to God the fruit (thanks, glory, good works, faith, etc.) that He is due. Jesus intercedes for us and sends His servants into our lives to cultivate and make us faithful and fruitful. We do well to remember that while we have a faithful and effective Savior in Jesus Christ, a time of judgment will come, which we will not survive without faith and the fruits of faith that God works in us (Jn 15:1ff.).

Q 13:10–17 Is performing a miracle actually work?

On the one hand, Jesus makes the argument that even if healing someone is work, the religious leaders did work on the Sabbath as well, if it was important (Lk 13:15). On the other hand, Jesus saw healing as rest, because by healing He was relieving people from the hardships of their infirmities (Mt 12:1–8; Mk 3:1–5). Adam and Eve lived in complete rest from the Law, but Adam threw it away in order to pretend he could be in control of his life. Fallen human nature always wants to turn gifts into obligations and grace into Law. God gave the Sabbath as a gift—a time to realize (by not working) that God is the giver of your whole life. Jesus, who bore the burden of the Law for everyone, demonstrated God's will to restore us to a life where the Law supports us in a life of grace (Lk 7:20–23; Rm 8:1; Gal 5:1).

Q 13:14 Why would the ruler care what Jesus did on the Sabbath?

Good question! No matter what day of the week it was, what would you be interested in if you saw a man really heal another person? Here is the insanity and self-destructive nature of self-righteousness; such a nature is so committed to the lie that it can keep the Law and thus earn God's grace that it opposes, despises, and hates the truth of God's saving grace that is active before its very eyes! Peter and Paul exposed this insanity in their words and writing (Ac 15:6–12; Gal 1:6–9; 3:1–14; 5:3–4). A similar example of this insanity can be seen when the Pharisees come to Jesus in order to prove that they are within the Law when they divorce their wives (Mt 19:1ff.). Wouldn't it make more sense to ask Jesus for wisdom and grace in order to preserve their marriages? Yet another example is found in the religious leaders' reaction to news that Jesus had raised Lazarus from the dead. They concluded that they would have to kill Jesus and Lazarus both (Jn 11:46–50; 12:10).

- - - - - - - - - - - - - - - - - -

Q 13:17 Why do the religious leaders keep testing Jesus when they always end up losing or being humiliated?

What else is there for these religious leaders to do? Their pride, greed, and self-righteousness won't allow them to be honest about their utter dependence on the grace of God in general or His redemption through Jesus Christ in particular. The only way they can justify their rejection of Him is to find a way to overcome Him. They tried to kill Him by throwing Him off a cliff, but then He just wasn't there and they failed (Lk 4:28–30). On another occasion they tried to stone Jesus and failed at this as well (Jn 10:31–39). According to Jesus, those who oppose Jesus still refuse to be honest about their lives, even after death, and rather than seek His mercy, they argue with Him (Mt 25:31–40; Lk 16:30). Ps 50:15–23 and Jer 8:4–9 both record laments about this contradictory and self-destructive determination of fallen humans.

> Why do the religious leaders keep testing Jesus?

- - - - - - - - - - - - - - - - - -

Q 13:18 Is the kingdom of God the same as the kingdom of heaven? Is it Jesus?

Yes. Mt 19:23 is a parallel account to Lk 18:24, but Matthew recorded Jesus saying the "kingdom of heaven," and Luke recorded the "kingdom of God." The term "kingdom of God" occurs only five times in Matthew, fourteen times in Mark, thirty-two times in Luke, and twice in John. Only Matthew records Jesus using the term "kingdom of heaven" (thirty-two times). The Gospel of Mark reveals clearly that Jesus is the kingdom of God and heaven in the flesh, as he recorded Jesus saying, "The time is fulfilled, and the kingdom of God is at hand" (Mk 1:15). Having said this, Jesus called His disciples, taught, and healed—evidence that with Jesus came the kingdom of God, the beginning of the restoration of God's creation.

- - - - - - - - - - - - - - - - - -

Q 13:21 Is there any correlation between this verse and the feast of unleavened bread?

There is a correlation, but it is made by Paul rather than Jesus. The feast of unleavened bread was a reminder that God brought Israel out of Egypt by signs and wonders—and very suddenly. Israel was to be ready to travel like sojourners who do not use yeast, because they had no time to wait for their dough to rise. Unleavened, in this case, has to do with knowing that we are strangers passing through a very hostile world (Lk 9:57–58; Heb 11:13–16; 1Pt 1:2). In quite a different context, Jesus refers to the leavening property of yeast in both a positive and negative way. On the one hand, Jesus compares the kingdom of God to yeast, which begins in a very small way but gradually affects the whole lump of dough; God intends this to be a good thing (Mt 28:19–20). The Word and kingdom of God eventually affect everyone, whether they like it or not (Lk 19:14; Rv 18:9–19). On the other hand, Jesus says we should beware of the leaven, or teaching, of the Jewish religious leaders because it infects people so (Lk 12:1). Paul uses leaven as an example of the infectious nature of sin (1Co 5:6–8). In this place, Paul compares the property of yeast to ferment and make dough rise to the arrogance, vanity, and deceit of fallen human nature. At the same time, Paul compares the honesty and simple dependence of faith with unleavened bread—just flour and water; no "nothingness" pretending to be something.

Q 13:23–30 Why does Jesus not answer the people's question directly?

Jesus speaks in parables in order to protect the Gospel from those who despise it (Mt 7:6). At the same time, parables are powerful and memorable to people who are honest about their dependence on God, because they use the witness of God's creation, which is universal and common to human experience. A person who is humble is also fearful, knowing that there are many forces at work in the world that are above and beyond his or her control. This awareness makes such a person very sensitive to language like "when once the master of the house has risen and shut the door." The person who is honest and humble would not want to take any chances or gamble with being outside the house when that time comes. Such a fear leads a person to stay with the master and in the house in order that such a frightening and sad situation would never be possible (Jn 10:27–28).

Q 13:24 Does this verse mean that there will be people who try to get into heaven, who genuinely have repented and believe, but won't be able to? If so, how will any of us get in?

The narrowness of the door has to do with two things. One, there is no other way than Christ because He is the way, the truth, and the life; He alone has provided redemption for the whole world (Jn 14:6; Ac 4:12). When Peter says, "There is salvation in no one else," and Paul says, "Not that there is another [gospel]," they are not being arrogant but accurate (Ac 4:12; Gal 1:6–7). Two, there is no other way through Christ than by faith, which is honesty about our dependence upon Him and humility about ourselves. Honesty about dependence and humility is what makes children the standard and measure of those who are saved (Mt 18:3). Here, then, is something very interesting about the Gospel, especially in comparison with all other religious systems.

The Gospel of Jesus Christ is universal; Jesus took away the sins of the world and, in so doing, redeemed all people of all time (2Co 5:19). This means no one is condemned for being a sinner but only for being an unbeliever, that is, for despising, renouncing, rejecting, and living in contradiction to the truth. The Gospel only becomes particular or exclusive when a person excludes himself by taking a conscious, proud, contrary disposition; if you contradict what God says about your salvation, then you have lost that salvation (Ac 13:45–46; 15:1–11; 18:5–6; Gal 3:10–17; 5:3–4).

Therefore, the problem is that people throw away the salvation of God in Christ Jesus in order to assert themselves, their own ego, and their own works (Rm 10:1–3). Only God knows who and how many will realize the redemption He has accomplished for us. We can find great encouragement in knowing that God makes all things work together for our good and that through circumstances that human pride fears most, like the process of aging and dying, God restores people to the humility and honest dependence of children (2Co 12:7–10; Jas 5:11; 1Pt 1:3–9).

- - - - - - - - - - - - - - - - - - - -

Q **13:30 What does this passage mean? Who's first? Who's last?**

God is love. Jesus demonstrated that love by making Himself a man, then a servant to all, then a sacrifice on behalf of all by dying the worst, most humiliating and painful death there is. God is not much for people who serve themselves or put themselves first, even if they are believers. On one occasion, Jesus noticed how people chose the best places for themselves at a feast and warned against doing so. Jesus taught and demonstrated that we are free to take the lowest places and be servant to others and, in so doing, discover what life really consists of (Lk 14:7–14; Jn 13:3–17). This is consistent with God's character and will; those who would put themselves first and have others serve them are not good to themselves or others. Those who put others first and serve others realize the content of life and increase the significance of their own life by giving it away to others. So, Jesus said, "Whoever would save his life will lose it, but whoever loses his life for My sake will save it" (Lk 9:24).

- - - - - - - - - - - - - - - - - - - -

Q **13:31–32 Weren't all of the Pharisees opposed to Jesus? Why did these Pharisees try to protect Christ from Herod? Why does Jesus call Herod a fox?**

The only Jewish religious leaders who showed a positive disposition toward Jesus were Nicodemus and Joseph of Arimathea (Jn 7:50–52; 19:38). Otherwise the Pharisees seem very consistent in their opposition to Jesus. In this case, they are hoping that suggesting that Herod is a threat will make Jesus flee. Only after Jesus' resurrection are there more Pharisees, and even then they had trouble accepting Jesus' teaching (Ac 15:5). Jesus calls Herod a "fox" because foxes have always provided an example of deadly cunning and stealth (Ezk 13:4–7).

Q **13:33 Why did Jesus say no prophet could die outside Jerusalem?**

Jesus makes His reason for saying this clear in the next verse, "Jerusalem, the city that kills the prophets and stones those who are sent to it!" Jerusalem was the center of political and religious power at this time. Since that concentration of power was opposed to God's Word and will, this was the most deadly place for a prophet of God to be (Lk 20:1–20; Jn 7).

Q **14:1 Why do the Pharisees continually invite Christ to dinner if they see Him as a threat?**

This verse suggests the answer: "They were watching Him carefully." They were, of course, watching Jesus to see if they could find an excuse to reject Him or a cause to have Him arrested. They may also have invited Jesus to dinner for the same reasons they used to go out to see John the Baptizer: to see what the man is all about, to make sure they weren't missing something, to look devout and religious to the people, and to find cause to renounce (Jn 1:19–27; Mt 3:5–12).

Q **14:2 What is dropsy? Was Jesus looking for trouble by healing on the Sabbath?**

"Dropsy" is an old term for the swelling of soft tissue due to the retention of water and is a consequence of congestive heart failure. Jesus is the true light that came

into the world (Jn 1:9). Jesus did not purpose to cause trouble, and He was not the cause of the trouble. Jesus very simply went about doing exactly what God had promised through the prophets since the fall of Adam; Jesus was restoring God's creation to life. The trouble was caused by those who preferred darkness to light and death to life (Jn 3:18–21). All the faithful people who follow Jesus will also have trouble—again, not because we cause it, but because the devil and those who serve him oppose what is good (Mt 10:16–39; 1Th 3:1–5). We don't look for trouble, nor do we fear it when it comes (Jn 16:33).

Q **14:7–14 When Jesus speaks in parables, such as in Lk 14, should we consider them to be Law to follow, or are these simply reinforcing points of His ministry?**

The parable includes imperatives or commands, which are Law. The parables, including the Law within them, reinforce Jesus' ministry, and His ministry reinforces what He teaches in the parables (Jn 13:1–17). However, the Law is not given as if we were able to redeem our lives by keeping them. Jesus provides Law that points the way by which we might make the most of the life He has redeemed for us (Eph 5:15–17).

Q 14:10–11 By taking the lowest place, aren't you exalting yourself in your humbleness?

It is often possible to deceive oneself and others; it is never possible to deceive God. When Jesus teaches us how to live, He does not mean that we should "act" as He instructs us but that we should "be" as He instructs. When the branch is connected to the vine and well pruned, the branch bears real fruit (Jn 15:1–7). A bad tree cannot bear good fruit; neither can a good tree bear bad fruit (Mt 7:18). Taking the lowest place is the opposite of taking the highest place in every way. Jesus warns us against exalting ourselves because such exaltation is based on our desire rather than on truth. Jesus urges us to be honest about our condition as fallen human beings who are weak, ungodly, sinners, and enemies of God (Rm 5:6–10). In this condition, as a child with honesty about our dependence, God is able to raise us up as His own children, as children who are free to serve others because we are not worried about our identity or future (Jn 13:3; Gal 5:1–2).

Q 14:11 How many times does Jesus quote the Old Testament, as He does in this verse?

This is a number nearly impossible to calculate, though many suggest or even argue a certain number. The whole Old Testament is the Word of God, and Jesus Christ is the fulfillment of that Word, so in a sense, we could say "all of it"! What is more important than how many times is what Jesus said on each occasion and the significance it has for our lives.

Q 14:12–14 Are we not supposed to spend time with friends? This "law" seems very harsh.

Any fallen human nature that is selfish and vain will find the Word of the Lord harsh. On the other hand, a soul regenerated in the image of Christ by the Word of God sees love and wisdom in Jesus' instruction. Jesus is not forbidding us from spending time with friends. Jesus is trying to get us to think beyond ourselves, to realize new things and more about the life He gives us by sharing it with new people, especially people who have no one else to care for them (Heb 13:2).

Q 14:14 What is the resurrection of the righteous?

There is one resurrection of the dead at the end of the world on Judgment Day, yet there has already been a resurrection, that of Jesus Christ on the third day. People who are joined to Christ by a life in the Word have, by virtue of that union, already passed with Christ through judgment and death and rose with Christ in His resurrection (Rm 6). This is what Jesus means by the resurrection of the righteous (Mt 25:31–32, 46; Jn 15:3; 16:14–15; Rm 8:1). People who die in their contradiction and opposition to the grace of God in Christ and in their own determination to justify themselves will be resurrected to judgment and condemnation (Jn 5:29).

• • • • • • • • • • • • • • • • • • • •

Q 14:15–24 Is there a correlation between this parable and the "wedding feast" in heaven? If so, doesn't this somehow contradict the parable of the wages, where all the workers get a denarius? What is the purpose of this parable?

This parable is related to the "wedding feast," but remember that this feast has already started with the resurrection of Jesus Christ from the dead. There are two reasons the parable doesn't contradict the parable of the workers who receive a denarius each. First, the denarius is indicative of the life God gives us (talents, resources, abilities, and especially His Spirit). This includes material things, but whether material or spiritual, all resources are applied in service of the everlasting life and kingdom of God. Second, the parable of the workers is making a different point. Interestingly, the person who buried his talent in the ground is the same person who would make excuses for refusing to come to the feast. The good worker who is a faithful steward of the talents God gives recognizes a feast as the opportunity to celebrate the good that God has worked through the talents He gives to the people He has redeemed.

The purpose of this parable, common to Luke's Gospel, is to contrast the ways of two different groups of people: those who considered themselves the "in crowd" on the basis of race and religious pride and those who were made to feel like the "outsiders" because they were not "pure-blooded" Jews and had not submitted to the yoke of any particular religious sect. Can you guess who is who in the parable? Consider the excuses made. Who buys property without looking at it first? And if you have already bought it, it's not going anywhere, so why do you have to go look at it now? Who buys animals without testing them? And, again, if you already bought the oxen, they can wait to be tested. The last is the most preposterous. What man in his right mind would miss the chance to take his new wife to a banquet? I am sorry to report that over the fifteen years I was a parish pastor, these are exactly the kinds of excuses that people made.

On the other hand, there are plenty of people who are not so full of themselves and who do not have the means to acquire the things of this world to be full of. These people were ready and eager to respond to the invitation. Don't miss the gracious nature of the master, made clear in two key phrases: "Come, for all things are ready" and "Still there was room." Jesus makes clear that our life is provided in abundance by God. Salvation and life is not a matter of us making one for ourselves but of realizing the presence of the life God has already prepared for us (Eph 2:8–10). Jesus also makes clear that God desires all to be saved and come to the knowledge of the truth—to the banquet. There is always room so that no one is left out. The only people not at the banquet are those who refused to come.

Q **14:24 This verse makes it sound like the Gentiles were only included because the Jews rejected the invitation. Would Gentiles not have been invited had the Jews believed?**

With parables, it is essential to keep in mind the point that is being made. The same people who put themselves first at dinners (14:7–11) and who only invite people who can invite them back (vv. 12–14) don't have time for the feast God has prepared. God has always had all people in mind from the very beginning. God's first promise to Abraham said, "In you all the families of the earth shall be blessed" (Gn 12:3). If you check a concordance for the word *Gentiles* or *Nations* in the Old Testament, you will see that all through the history of Israel, God continued to make known that they were to be His special people on behalf of the nations, not instead of or in opposition to the nations. Jesus makes this point over and over again in the Gospels (remember Jesus' first day in the synagogue [Lk 4]?). What the history of Israel proves is that flesh and blood cannot inherit the kingdom of God (1Co 15:50). There are no people who have a genetic advantage with God (Rm 3:10–18). Honesty about our condition is the only advantage a person can have, for such honesty readily receives the grace of God and clings to it, as the poor, maimed, lame, and blind in the parable make evident.

Why is there a cost of discipleship?

Q **14:25–35 Why is there a cost of discipleship?**

The word *disciple* means to be a follower and includes the notion of *discipline*, which is to be in control of yourself for a particular purpose. Our fallen human nature is opposed to Christ, though it is willing to fake discipleship if that serves its own selfish, self-defeating purposes (Lk 22:48; Ac 5:1–11). Therefore, Jesus is advancing the truth against our self-delusion. First, know that to follow Jesus really is to endure what He did, including the crucifying of our human nature (Col 3:5ff.). Second, Jesus encourages honesty that will bring about our hasty surrender to God. If we are not able to establish and preserve our own life, why not surrender at once to God, whose only desire is to save our life and restore it?

Q **14:26 Why does Luke use the word "hate" here? Why do I have to hate those I love in order to be a disciple of Jesus?**

The word "hate," used here, means the opposite of "love." If "love" means "to sacrifice everything for" then "hate" means "to sacrifice nothing for." Remember the ever-essential distinction between body and soul, our physical nature that descends from our biological family and our regenerate soul that is generated by the Word of God (Jn 3:11–13). Jesus has already spoken about the division He would cause within biological families and the necessity of following Him above all (Lk 12:49–53). Think of it like this. If you were with your family on a plane and the cabin lost pressure so that it became necessary for you to put those little oxygen masks on, but your family members were afraid to, would you leave yours off because they left theirs off? Or would you put yours on because without oxygen you couldn't be a help to them? And if your family refused your help, would you refuse to help others? We are thinking of the essence of people, their souls, for without that, what significance is a temporary, physical relationship? It is the communion of souls in God's everlasting kingdom that gives meaning to our physical life and the relationships we have with one another. This is why Jesus says if we are going to sacrifice everything for the fallen human nature of our biological family, we cannot follow where He leads us or live by the teaching He provides.

- -

Q 14:27 What does Jesus mean when He says "bear his own cross and come after me"? Is it referring to sanctification?

Sanctification has to do with becoming what God has already declared us to be or realizing who we are as souls regenerated in the image of Christ. Jesus took up a cross because that was God's will for Him—though it was not easy. God has good works prepared for each of us to accomplish, and these will inevitably involve difficulties for us as well (Eph 2:10; 1 Th 3:1–5). Taking up our cross means living in complete honesty and honestly fulfilling the responsibilities we have to love God above all things and to lay down our lives for love of neighbor (Mt 11:28–30; Jn 13:3–17). This is sanctification (Rm 6; 1 Th 4).

- -

Q 14:33 Is Jesus telling us to literally give up everything? If we're supposed to give everything, how much should we keep to sustain our existence?

As is often the case, the meaning of the word used here is critical. The word translated "give up" only occurs six times in the New Testament. Both Jesus (Mk 6:46) and Paul (Ac 18:21) leave people but then return to them again. Jesus is not saying that in order to follow Him we can't own anything. Jesus is saying that if we would follow Him, nothing can own us. We use the word "possession," but in reality we are the ones possessed by material things (Mt 6:24). If there is something in your life you could not leave in order to follow where Christ leads, then that thing has become your god and a poor god it is. Acts gives clear indication that people sold possessions that were not needed but also kept those things which were of service, like a home to live in and for the church to meet in (Ac 2:44–47; 4:32–37; 10:1ff.; 21:1ff.).

Q **14:34–35 What does this passage mean?**

Jesus is asking us to think about what happens if something loses the essence of what it is. If salt isn't salty, then what is its purpose? It isn't good for anything. Can you make it salty again? Apparently not. Human beings were made in the image of God to reflect His glory among one another (Mt 5:13–16; 1Co 11:7). If a person refuses to be that light by following Christ (the way the moon gets its light from following the sun), how can that person ever be restored to life eternal with God (Mt 12:32; Heb 6:1–8)? Certain things in life are all or nothing. If a person is unwilling to leave everything he or she owns when necessary, that person cannot follow Jesus. People who refuse to follow Jesus, like saltless salt, will be thrown away (Mt 13:47–50; 25:41–46; Rv 20:11–15).

Q **Why is the salt metaphor placed where it is in each Gospel? How does it relate to the material around it?**

In Matthew's Gospel, this parable of salt comes in the middle of the Sermon on the Mount, in which Jesus is focused on the substance of the Christian life and exposes the fraud and hypocrisy of the religious leaders. Lk 14:34–35, like Mk 9:50, is part of a large section of Jesus' teaching in Judea at the end of His public ministry and is parallel to the Sermon on the Mount, which took place in Galilee at the beginning of Jesus' ministry. The context of Mark and Luke also are focused on what it means to be a disciple of Jesus.

Q **15:1 Why is the word "sinners" in quotation marks in some translations?**

The quotation marks were an editorial decision made by the translators. They wanted the reader to understand that when Luke identified this group as "sinners," it was not because they were sinners while no one else was; Luke wanted us to understand that the other group, the religious leaders, looked down on these people and called them "sinners," as if they, themselves, were not. Jesus addresses this dishonest arrogance of the rulers in Lk 18:9–14.

Q **15:1–32 Why are all parables restated in all three Gospels?**

The short answer is because God wants certain lessons emphasized by having them repeated. The long answer is that the parables are not all repeated in all three or four Gospels (Mark does not include the parable of the lost sheep, but John records Jesus speaking at length about Shepherd and sheep in Jn 10). Some Gospels have some parables and some have others; sometimes the Gospels are recording the same parable being told on the same occasion, but sometimes they are different occasions and the parables have little variations. The parable of the wedding banquet is similar but not identical to the parable of the feast (Mt 22:1–14; Lk 14:15–24). The variety gives us a more complete perspective, like four views of the same object.

● ● ● ● ● ● ● ● ● ● ● ● ● ● ● ● ● ● ● ●

Q 15:3–7 I have heard that if a shepherd lost his sheep, he would break the sheep's legs so the sheep couldn't run off again. Does Christ "break our legs" with tragedy so we can't run away from Him?

I have heard that story about breaking a sheep's legs as well. It is true that God disciplines those He loves with challenges and hardships in order to keep us near (Jb 42:10–11; Ps 78:34–35; 119:67; 2Co 12:7–10; Jas 5:11). However, the idea of God "breaking our legs" so we "couldn't run off again" is contrary to God's nature and the Gospel itself. The Christian Church or Body of Christ is not composed of people who have been physically prevented from leaving, as if it were a tyrannical dictatorship (if Communist nations are so wonderful, why are the citizens forbidden and prevented from leaving?). It is also important to remember the point of the parable. Jesus is not talking about how He keeps the sheep from leaving. The parable of the prodigal sons that follows suggests that He does not prevent anyone from leaving. The point of this parable is that the Good Shepherd searches *until* He finds the sheep that is lost.

● ● ● ● ● ● ● ● ● ● ● ● ● ● ● ● ● ● ● ●

Q 15:3 Why would you go after one sheep and not stay with the other ninety-nine?

You have grasped the beauty of this parable. What shepherd in his right mind would abandon ninety-nine sheep in order to look for one that is lost? That depends on the ninety-nine and on the Shepherd. Remember the audience, made explicit by Luke in vv. 1–2? The Pharisees and scribes are the ninety-nine who, as Jesus says in v. 7, need no repentance. Of course they do need repentance, but their pride and dishonesty prevent them from admitting it, as you can see from the parable of the Pharisee and publican, Lk 18:9–14. The reason this Good Shepherd leaves the ninety-nine is because though they are near, they are so lost spiritually that they cannot be recovered (Mt 12:30–32; Ac 13:46; Heb 6:4–8). As Jesus instructed His apostles to shake the dust off their feet when rejected by a household or town and move on, so He Himself spends His time seeking the lost that *can* be found (Mt 10:11–15, 23; Ac 13:46). Those who contend that they are not lost continue to be lost in their pride and dishonesty. Those who know they are lost are not lost for long since the calling of the Good Shepherd affects them immediately (Lk 3:7–14; Ac 2:37–47).

● ● ● ● ● ● ● ● ● ● ● ● ● ● ● ● ● ● ● ●

Q 15:4 Are we the lost sheep or the ninety-nine? If we are the ninety-nine, can we switch roles?

If you think of yourself as one of the ninety-nine, you are lost and in danger of being so forever. If you see yourself as the one who is lost, you are already found as you contemplate the Gospel of the Lord who has found you with His Word and Spirit, which will gather you to His flock as His own. Certainly we hope that the ninety-nine who think they have no need of repentance will realize this is not true, repent, and be honest about their dependence on Jesus Christ (Rm 10:1–3). Certainly we need to be careful as the ones who have been found that we do not drift away again or become proud like the ninety-nine (Heb 2:1ff.; Rm 11:1ff.).

Q 15:7 Who is so righteous that they do not need to repent?

Jesus is. This statement of Jesus is the key to understanding the question He asks at the beginning, which makes no sense: "What man of you, having a hundred sheep, if he lost one of them, does not leave the ninety-nine in the open country, and go after the one that is lost?" The answer to this question is the same as to yours: no one. Jesus is comparing the two groups of people who came out to see Him; "Tax collectors and sinners were all drawing near to hear Him," while "the Pharisees and the scribes grumbled" against Jesus. Jesus exposes the hypocrisy of the ninety-nine, who claim they are not lost and have no need of repentance, in the parable of the Pharisee and publican (Lk 18:9–14). For more on this, see the questions preceding this, beginning at Lk 15:1.

Q 15:8 Why is the lost coin parable about a woman, not a man?

There are several possible reasons why this parable is about a woman and not about a man. First, Jesus may be speaking about a woman just so women don't begin to think that these parables do not apply to them. Second, men carried their money in a bag, and if they lost some, it would more likely take place outside the house (Pr 7:19–20). Women (at least some women, I am told) wore their coins tied together around their heads. Therefore a woman would know immediately if she was missing one. Third, women cared about these coins because they were her security for the future, in case her husband died (their equivalent to an insurance policy or retirement account). Fourth, while the parable about the lost sheep contrasts the ninety-nine sheep with the one, the smaller ratio between the nine coins and the one lost coin highlights the concern of the woman and her persistence in looking for it. In all three of these parables, the diligence and concern of the seeker for the lost is paramount (especially as we consider our Seeker of the lost), as Jesus made evident in the previous chapter in the parable of the feast (Lk 14:15–24).

Q 15:11–32 Who does the lost son represent, and who does the son who is always there represent?

Jesus is comparing those people who know and are made to know that they are sinners and worthy of God's judgment with those people who make others feel unworthy while they consider themselves sinless and worthy of God's favor on their own merits. Luke began this chapter by contrasting these two groups: "the tax collectors and sinners" and "the Pharisees and the scribes." Jesus returns to this contrast with the example of the Pharisee and the publican in Lk 18:9–14.

. . . .

Q 15:13–24 What is the prodigal son searching for? Filling a spiritual void? Why did the father throw a big party for the son after he took his money and blew it? Why does he get rewarded for doing something wrong?

The prodigal son is searching for the same thing every human nature is searching for since the fall of Adam: absolute fulfillment. Since God is the only absolute and we have lost our communion with Him, we have an infinite void to fill. Since we feel our human nature so acutely, we assume that the solution for the void we feel is to be found in physical experiences and material things. Notice that the younger son was not satisfied, and when he has spent all, "no one gave him anything." This is an important fact about a world full of people who are all trying to fill the same infinite void with the same finite amount of material things. The human soul is even more empty than the body since the fall. You can see how much less a finite number of material things would be able to fill that void. The father made a

big celebration for the son because what he cares about is his relationship with the son, not with material things that aren't alive and don't endure. The best answer for why the father makes the celebration comes from the father himself (Lk 15:32). The younger son is not being rewarded for what he had done. What you are seeing is the contrast between God and creation, repentance and impenitence. When the younger son left home, he "joined himself" first with material things in creation that appeal to the appetites of the flesh. This is impenitence. But there is no life in these things; rather, they take our life. When the son was as good as dead, he realized that the least important person in his father's house has so much more than he did in the world. Notice the honesty of the younger son's penitence as he maintains his confession of sin, even though the father has already greeted him with open arms. God fills the empty, but the rich He sends empty away (1Sm 2:5; Lk 1:1:53; Jas 4:4). The reward for the younger son's self-indulgence was hunger in a place where no one gave him anything. The father's grace and celebration was a reward for the repentance and faith that the father himself had produced in the son (Lk 15:17; Rm 10:17).

. . . .

Q 15:16 How is the question "Why would you work for someone who doesn't pay you?" in relation to "no one gave him anything" parallel to life for us out of Christ?

I'm not sure what this has to do with life for us out of Christ. What Jesus makes evident by describing such a situation for the younger son is that the world has very few "winners." In other words, if you look at people's lives in the world, they spend a lifetime working and maybe accumulate some things, and then they die and take nothing with them to the grave. Isn't that like working for nothing? God asked that very question through the prophet Isaiah: "Why do you spend your money for that which is not bread, and your labor for that which does not satisfy?" (Is 55:2). Jesus said to the crowds who followed Him after He fed them in the wilderness, "Do not work for the food that perishes, but for the food that endures to everlasting life, which the Son of Man will give to you" (Jn 6:27). So, there is a contrast rather than a parallel; you can spend your whole life working for what the world has to offer and end up with nothing, or you can spend your whole life realizing what God is giving constantly and then move on to eternity in paradise. There is no choice to make. The younger son figured this out; the elder son couldn't realize this though he was living in the midst of it.

• •

Q 15:25–32 Didn't the older son have a right to be mad? He was faithful to his father, and his unfaithful brother, who had left them, was being honored when he got home, and the older son was pretty much ignored. Was the faithful son in the wrong for expecting the father to celebrate for him also, because doesn't God reward all

equally? Why wouldn't the father give anything to the son who was good and obeyed?

Two corrections need to be made regarding the wording of these questions. First, where does it say the older son was faithful? Notice that it is the older son himself, and no one else, who makes the claim that he had "never transgressed" his father's commandment at any time. This older son is the religious leaders who appeared to be righteous but in fact were hypocrites (Mt 23). This son is not faithful but self-righteous, dishonest, hypocritical, and hateful. The older son was neither good nor obedient. If he was a good, faithful, and obedient son, he would have gone to search for his younger brother or at least been watching and waiting with the father. Remember how Jesus precedes this parable with two parables about searching for the lost, which is what Jesus Himself was doing (Lk 5:31–32). Second, the older son had not because he asked not (Jas 4:3). The father prevents mistaken sympathy for the older son when he says, "Son, you are always with me, and all that is mine is yours." The older son's complaint exactly parallels the way Jewish religious leaders changed the Sabbath rest God gave into an endless set of obligations that made the Sabbath the most miserable day of the week (Mt 12:1–8). Even after Jesus' resurrection from the dead and ascension, the religious leaders still steadfastly refused to celebrate and enjoy the bounty and liberty that Jesus has granted all through His Word and Spirit (Ac 2:13; 4:1–22; 5:17ff.; 11:1–18; 15:1–12).

Q 16:1–8 What is the meaning of the parable of the shrewd manager?

The key to understanding the parable of the unjust steward, as it is with all the parables, is to identify the key elements correctly. Let's try a few different associations and see what we learn. What if the master is a merchant and the steward is a clerk? Would the merchant commend the steward for reducing people's debts? I doubt it. What if the master were the head of the Red Cross and the steward was responsible for distributing relief supplies to people after a natural disaster? If the steward had been keeping all the goods but then found out that the Red Cross head was coming to check, would the steward be happy? Would the head of the Red Cross commend the steward for at least beginning to distribute the goods? Now for real life. The Master is God. We are the stewards. We have all kinds of records of what other people owe our Master. The Master receives a report that we have been wasting His goods (stop here and see if Mt 18:23–35 supports this suggestion). What are the Master's goods, or what is God's greatest good? Would you say His mercy or grace or forgiveness? When the Master finds out that the steward has been forgiving debts, now does it make sense that the steward was commended? Therefore, if the Master's will is to give good gifts and to forgive debts, isn't the dishonesty of the steward only what was going on before he found out he would lose his job? Did the steward lose his job in the end? Why would the master dismiss the steward after commending him? These things are certain; God is our Master who gives everything to everyone and whose greatest good is forgiving debts (Jas 1:17–21; Mi 7:18). We are the dishonest stewards who love to hold people under debt but who also fear God's judgment and so repent and forgive (Gn 50:15–21). We are commended by God when we apply His Word and forgiveness to the lives of others (compare Lk 12:42–46 to Mt 23:1–4, 13).

Q 16:9 Why does Jesus tell us to "make friends for yourself by means of unrighteous wealth"? Are we to do as the dishonest steward did?

A related lesson from the parable has to do with how fallen human nature chooses material things over human life. Another reason the master commends the steward is because he finally used the master's goods for something besides holding debt on paper. God did not create the material world so that we could have a means of holding people in the bondage of debt. This is why God established the Years of Jubilee in the Old Testament, when land returned to its original owners (or their families) and all debts were canceled (Lv 25; 27). How different the world and history would be if we always used worldly things in order to make friends!

When Adam disobeyed God, he traded the Creator for the creation. Paul refers to this deadly mistake in Rm 1:25ff. Over time, human beings have continued to be more and more materialistic until, in our time, many argue that there is no soul or anything immaterial to us. Therefore, modern man is more materialistic than ever, especially since our life here is short and then it's over. In this condition, we trade everything for unrighteous wealth because more wealth means more stuff and more stuff means more life faster. But this kind of commitment is opposed to love of others and friendship. Jesus is the Creator and all creation is His, yet He had nothing and said there was no place for Him to lay His head (Lk 9:58). The Lord Jesus loved the whole world and reconciled it with God the Father by spending it all, even emptying Himself completely (Php 2:5ff.). The result was His resurrection from the dead and a living hope for us (1Pt 1:3–9). Since God has given us a life in Christ that is eternal and cannot fail, we are free to use it all in the service of our relationships with others, especially in order to bring others back into communion with God.

Q 16:13 Is it bad to like money and what money gets you, even if you want to use it to give your family a good life?

Will money give your family a good life? The answer depends on how we define "family" and "good life." What has Jesus taught so far in Luke's Gospel about family

and life? Family is a communion of souls regenerated by the Word and Spirit of God (Jn 1:11–13; 3:1–7). Life has to do with positive, enduring relationships. Proverbs, Ecclesiastes, many texts in the New Testament, and many examples in history argue that one's family will have a better life with less rather than more money (Pr 15:17; Ec 4:13; 5:12; Lk 12:13–15; 15:25–30). Jesus said, "Where your treasure is, there your heart will be also" (Mt 6:21). If the souls and eternal life of our loved ones are our treasure, then we will have a good life whether there is more or less money. As long as we think money is a solution or the path to a solution, love of money will overpower us, and there will be no good life for our family, not now or in eternity (1Tm 6:10; Ec 2:1–11).

Q 16:17 What did Jesus mean when He said, "It is easier for heaven . . . than for one dot of the Law to become void?"

Part of your question has to do with translation. Jesus said, "And it is easier for heaven and earth to pass away than for one title of the law to fail" (author's translation). A "title" is a very small stroke of the pen that distinguishes the Hebrew letter *D* from *R*. The Law of God is a description of truth and reality. This is why not even the smallest part of one letter of the Law can fail. Throughout history and even more so today, people try to convince themselves that truth or reality can be "cheated." But spiritual realities are as invariable as physical realities, and they are interrelated so that no cheating ever

Is it bad to like money?

succeeds. People who seek to cheat the Law are only cheating themselves out of the substance of life. People who are cheated discover that God makes that work for good; the false condemnation and crucifixion of Jesus is the best example of this truth.

• • • • • • • • • • • • • • • • • • • •

Q 16:18 Why is 16:18 placed between talks of dishonesty and Lazarus and the rich man? I don't understand completely how divorce and remarriage is adultery. Are there certain circumstances of divorce in which this applies, or does it apply in all divorce-remarriage situations? Could you please explain the second half of this verse? I don't understand why it is committing adultery to marry a divorced woman if a man divorced her and it was not her fault.

This is a very curious placement. On the other hand, Jesus is responding to the derision of the Pharisees who were lovers of money, beginning in 16:14. Jesus appears to be mentioning a number of issues that the Pharisees are guilty of but refuse to admit; they justify themselves (v. 15), people are pressing into the kingdom (v. 16), there is no escaping the Law (v. 17), there is no divorcing your wife (v. 18), then a parable about the rich man who exemplifies the Pharisees. The inclusion of the law about divorce does make sense as Matthew's Gospel reveals this was as significant a problem among the Pharisees, as was the love of money (Mt 19:1ff.).

First, Jesus deals with men who divorce their wives and—or perhaps in order to—marry another. This is adultery. Second, Jesus is still dealing with men who get married, this time regarding men who marry women who are divorced. My suspicion here is that these women sought a divorce or were divorced because they were pursuing a relationship with another man. This was the case with Herod and his wife. Herodias was married to Herod's brother Philip but divorced him in order to marry Herod, which John condemned (Lk 3:19). The law of divorce was established in order to protect women who were divorced by their husbands, not in order to make them guilty of adultery (Mt 19:8–10). The only good reason a man would have for divorcing his wife at this time in history would have been for committing adultery. If that were the reason, then any man who married her would be committing adultery with her. If a woman was divorced by her husband because he was committing adultery (or if he abandoned her or if she left because of abuse), she would be an "innocent" party and free to remarry (1Co 7:1–16).

• • • • • • • • • • • • • • • • • • • •

Q 16:19 Is this the same Lazarus who was raised from the dead? If so, how did he become poor? Wasn't Lazarus a friend of Jesus?

This is not the same Lazarus. The Lazarus that Jesus raised from the dead had a home and two sisters to look after him. This Lazarus died and remained in paradise with Abraham.

Q 16:19–31 Does this prove there is no purgatory?

It is very hard to prove that something does not exist. However, this passage offers no indication of purgatory. On the contrary, this passage is evidence that when our human natures dies, our souls continue and find themselves immediately in either hell or heaven. Jesus' words to the thief on the cross are further evidence of the soul going immediately to heaven (Lk 23:43).

Q 16:23–25 Will we talk between heaven and hell?

Reading the Bible requires us to distinguish between language that is descriptive and that which is prescriptive. Jesus said, "Love your enemies" (Lk 6:27). We recognize that imperative as universal right away; we are all supposed to love our enemies. Paul commanded Timothy to bring his cloak. This is an imperative but clearly not for us to worry about. There must be a way to communicate between heaven and hell because Abraham was doing it with the rich man. However, there is no indication that this a common occurrence nor that just anyone can do so. It is also interesting to consider that heaven was still paradise for Abraham, even though he had to carry on this conversation and deal with a stubborn and ignorant rich man.

Q 17:1 Is this verse basically damning everyone because sin is going to come through us no matter what?

There is a big difference between committing a sin and causing someone else to commit a sin (Mt 18:6–10; Rm 1:32). There is an even bigger difference between sinning and causing someone to despise the remedy God has provided for that in Christ (Mt 23:4, 13–15). Jesus is not damning those who sin—that is what He came to redeem us from (Jn 12:47). Jesus is not talking about sin or sinners here; He is talking about those who put "stumbling blocks" in front of others (*skandalon* in Greek). The serious nature of causing another person to stumble is made clear in Mt 13:41; 18:7; Rm 14:13.

Q 17:4 Are we supposed to forgive those who don't ask us for forgiveness?

Yes. God has forgiven all sins in Christ, and we are ambassadors of that grace. We are not at liberty to decide whether we will ever forgive or withhold forgiveness (Gn 50:19). In reality, we don't forgive or retain sins. What we do is confirm that a penitent person's sins have been forgiven or warn an impenitent person that such a disposition binds him or her in his or her sins (Mt 18:18; Heb 2:1ff.).

Q **17:5 How did the apostles expect Jesus to increase their faith?**

Maybe they expected Jesus to simply say the Word, as He did when He forgave sins or healed or fed multitudes. Maybe they just expected it to happen because they asked, as Elisha did before Elijah departed (2Ki 2:9). You may notice that Jesus' response reveals that faith is not a matter of quantity. Faith is not like the deception of wealth, where people think the more they have the more they can do. Faith is honesty about dependence; it is the realization of all that God has already provided for us.

Q **17:5–6 No one can say to a tree, "Be uprooted and planted in the sea." But Jesus says this can be done if you have faith as small as a mustard seed. Does that mean we don't have faith or we don't have enough faith?**

Anyone could tell a tree to be uprooted and planted in the sea, but the tree might not obey. Such a tree would most certainly obey if Jesus commanded it to move (Mk 4:41). Of course, faith might inform us that there would be no purpose to having a tree move. Faith would direct us to the will of God, and whatever we ask according to His will, He will accomplish (Jn 14:13–14; Jas 1:5–8). If we have faith, which is to be honest about our dependence on God, we would remain in the Word in order to know how God provides for our dependence on Him, and in so doing we would know His will, and His own Spirit would direct our prayers.

Q **17:11–19 What happened to the other nine lepers? Did they continue to go to the priests healed or did they revert back to their original forms? When Jesus said, "Your faith has made you well," was He talking of the sin in the leper (since the others were also healed without the same faith)?**

There is no reason to believe that the nine lepers who were healed became leprous again because they were ungrateful; God does not deal with us according to our iniquities, and He is good to all so that His kindness might lead people to repentance (Ps 103:10; Rm 2:4). The healing of the nine ungrateful lepers would, if they persist in that disposition, be one of many factors that justify their condemnation on the Day of Judgment (Rm 1:21–22). The expression "made you well" does not do justice to the Greek it translates. In our culture, "made you well" sounds like biological healing. The Word in Greek (*sodzo*) is the word for "saved," which includes physical healing but is much more comprehensive than that. The nine lepers may have found relief for their leprosy, but that would be of very little help against the rest of the challenges they face as fallen human beings. The Samaritan who returned found in Jesus not only healing for His body but, more important, healing for His soul.

Q 17:20–21 In what way is the kingdom of God in the Pharisees?

The Greek makes clear that the "you" is plural, not singular. The kingdom of God was in the midst of, or among, the Pharisees literally, in the person of Jesus Christ (compare Mk 1:15). The kingdom of God or heaven, is the restoration of God's creation to what He created in the first place and intended it to be. Jesus demonstrated that He embodied this kingdom by healing the sick, raising the dead, and forgiving sins (Lk 7:19–22). Interestingly, not everyone who surrounded Jesus realized the benefits of this kingdom, only those who were honest about dependence (Mk 5:25–34).

Q 17:34–37 What is the "rapture," and is Jesus talking about that in these verses?

The word *rapture* occurred in an old English translation in 1Th 4:17–18: "Then we who are alive, who are left, will be caught up together ["raptured"] with them in the clouds to meet the Lord in the air, and so we will always be with the Lord. Therefore, encourage one another with these words." This place in Luke and the passage in 1 Thessalonians is what the idea of the rapture and "left behind" is based on, though the idea itself is a human invention. There will be only one return of Christ on Judgment Day (1Co 15:50–54). The idea of a second chance comes from fallen man's rejection of the Gospel and assertion of self, combined with a conscience that argues our failure to keep the whole Law without imperfection. The rapture is one of many means invented by the human mind to provide a way to be saved for people who don't appear to be saved now. The "rapture" idea says that real believers will be taken up into the clouds to be with Jesus, and everyone else will be "left behind." Those who are left behind now have time to come to their senses and apply themselves to obedience to God so they will not be lost the next time Jesus comes in judgment. Notice that right after Paul talks about the faithful being joined to the Lord, he urges us to comfort one another with these words. But the idea of being "left behind" is not a comfort but a threat. All religious systems except Christianity include some means of second chance. Christianity, as the Bible teaches it, doesn't need a second chance because the redemption of Christ is perfect and complete.

Q 17:37 What is meant by "Where the corpse is, there the vultures will gather"?

Jesus is using a common saying that means there is no mistaking certain events. When you see vultures circling in the sky or gathered on the ground in one place, you know for certain that there is a dead body in that place (or soon to be dead). When Jesus returns on Judgment Day, at the end of the world, there will be no mistaking or escaping it. Rather than wondering about where or when, a prudent person would consider how to be prepared always to meet the Lord's coming. Jesus told parables to this effect in Mt 25:13–29; Lk 12:35–40.

● ●

Q **18:8 What does this verse mean?**

Jesus has been speaking about God's disposition to those who cry out to Him for help. If a judge who doesn't care for God or man grants justice for a widow because of her continual appeals, how much more will the living God act and do so quickly for those who are honest about their dependence and seek His aid (Ps 10:18; 68:5)? Now that Jesus is thinking about faithful widows who never give up crying for help and others who seek God's help for their helplessness, He wonders if any such people will still be here when Jesus comes on Judgment Day. Jesus speaks to this subject in another way when He says, "If those days [last days] had not been cut short, no human being would be saved" (Mt 24:22).

● ●

Q **18:15–17 Why were the people rebuked for bringing their children to see and be touched by Jesus? Does this relate to why we baptize infants?**

People wanted Jesus to touch their children because "touch" indicated favor and the communication of authority or power to the one being touched (Mt 8:3; Mk 5:27–31; Lk 22:51). Touch can also mean the communicating of forces that have a negative result, so the New Testament prohibits such (1Co 7:1; Col 2:21). Jesus says very clearly

that children are the standard of faith and that the kingdom of heaven belongs to them; therefore, if a person does not repent and become as a child, he or she cannot be saved (Mt 18:3, 6, 10, 14; 19:14). Yes, we baptize in order to confirm the promises of God, which the Christian life is immersed in, with a physical sign. We baptize infants because they exemplify the truth that God is the one who saves those who cannot save themselves.

● ●

Q **18:17 Why do we always tell kids to grow up? Shouldn't we tell adults to act like children?**

Usually, adults tell kids to grow up because they are acting childishly (1Co 13:11). "Childish" has to do with a fallen human nature that is old enough to assert itself in selfishness and fits over petty matters but not old enough to repress those impulses for the sake of getting along socially. On the other hand, we take seriously Jesus' warning that unless we repent and become as children, we cannot enter the kingdom of heaven. Most important to remember is that we cannot make ourselves repent nor make ourselves a child again by our own efforts. We depend, like children, on the power of God in His Word to bring us back to the simplicity and honesty that realizes the grace of God in His kingdom.

Q **18:19 Why would Jesus deny being called good?**

Jesus did not deny that He was good; He asked the ruler a very important question, "Why do you call Me good?" If the ruler was calling Jesus "good" because he knew Jesus was God in the flesh, wouldn't that ruler be ashamed of his question about inheriting eternal life on the basis of his good works? How or why would a fallen human being even begin to bring up the subject of our petty and few good works to the Son of God who set aside His divine prerogatives in order to die in humiliation in our place (Php 2:5–11; 3:7–14)? If the ruler was calling Jesus "good" in order to flatter Him and thus gain a favorable answer, then what would he answer Jesus? Certainly flattering another person in order to obtain selfish desires is not good.

Q **18:34 Why and how didn't the disciples know? Wouldn't He want them to understand? Why would Jesus tell His disciples about His death if they won't understand it and the meaning of what He said is hidden from them?**

The verse says that the saying (all that Jesus had said about His suffering, death, and resurrection) "was hidden" from the disciples. The expression "was hidden" means that what Jesus said became hidden to them in the past and remained hidden even now. It is likely that this hiddenness came from the disciples' loss of the childlike disposition that Jesus says is necessary if we are to enter His kingdom. Paul says that Jesus Christ crucified is a stumbling block to Jews and folly to Greeks (see answers to questions at 1Co 1:23). It would not be until after Jesus resurrection, indeed, not until after Pentecost and later that the disciples actually began to grasp the truth about our fallen human condition and how God redeemed us in the life of His Son (Mk 16:14; Lk 24:21ff.; Ac 1:4–11; Gal 2:11–21; Ac 15:1–12). Jesus told His disciples about His death for the same reason He says and does everything in the Bible: for our benefit. Jesus is the truth and speaks the truth, whether anyone gets it or not. But His Word does not return void, and sooner or later, as the Lord wills, His Word breaks our hard hearts and then regenerates us in His image so we do realize what He has done and begin to live in appreciation of that (Is 55; Rm 3:19–26; Php 3:7–14).

Q **18:39 Why would people tell the blind man to be quiet if he wanted to talk to Jesus? They should know that Jesus would heal him if all the stories were told before He got there.**

People are curious, aren't they? People were trying to silence the blind man for the same reason the disciples rebuked mothers who were bringing their children to Jesus (Lk 18:15–17), for the same reason Jairus's household sent word that he shouldn't bother Jesus as it was too late (Lk 8:49), and for the same reason the religious leaders complained about people coming to be healed on the Sabbath (Lk 13:14); fallen human nature has no idea about the nature of God or His will, nor do we seem to be aware of being our own worst enemies. Consider the insanity of the religious leaders who get serious about killing both Jesus and Lazarus because Jesus had raised him from the dead (Jn 11:45–50; 12:9–11). Fallen human nature, having lost the sense of inherent worth God gave us and having lost the love for others that is the essence of life, thinks that important people don't want to be bothered by the people who need them most (Mt 9:12). The people who surrounded Jesus failed to realize who Jesus was or what He was about. If they had realized what Jesus was all about, they would have benefited themselves and sought every means of bringing the life of Jesus to others (Jn 4:10–29; Mt 23:13).

● ● ● ● ● ● ● ● ● ● ● ● ● ● ● ● ● ● ● ●

Q 19:1–10 Why does Zacchaeus climb a tree? What caused Zacchaeus to welcome Jesus and to instantly give to the poor and stop cheating? Doesn't salvation come at birth? Why did Jesus have to stay at Zacchaeus's house? Why is this the only Gospel that mentions Zacchaeus?

The answer to these questions is found when we consider why Zacchaeus climbed the tree (v. 4). Luke told us in the verse before that Zacchaeus wanted to see Jesus, but why? The verse before that (v. 2) tells us; Zacchaeus was "a chief tax collector and was rich." We know from many other occasions that tax collectors were despised. They are often mentioned in tandem with the word "sinners," as if to say there are two kinds of people who are so bad that no one should have anything to do with them: "tax collectors and sinners" (Lk 5:30; 15:1). The Romans despised Jewish tax collectors because they weren't Roman and were getting rich by overcharging their own people (Lk 3:13). The Jews despised Jewish tax collectors because they overcharged them and were willing to work for the Romans. More than that, Jewish religious leaders impressed upon tax collectors the notion that there was no redemption for their life, no way for them to be loved or saved by God; neither would any other person besides another tax collector or sinner befriend them. Now, word about Jesus comes along. People talked about how Jesus called Levi (Matthew), a tax collector. Jesus not only befriended him but also called him to be His disciple. Jesus was healing, feeding, forgiving, accepting, and loving lepers and Samaritans and every other person who was rejected by most. This is the Word that inspired Zacchaeus to want to see Jesus and even to climb a tree. When Jesus confirmed all that Zacchaeus had heard about Him by commanding him to come down from the tree and expressing the necessity of staying at Zacchaeus's home, what else was Zacchaeus to do? Jesus had effectively raised Zacchaeus from the dead, which is the gift that moved Zacchaeus to give away most, if not all, of what he had gained on his own, which was no gain at all. Paul has a similar story (Ac 9:1–22; Php 3:7–14).

Each Gospel has a particular audience and focus, even though the content is still essentially the same. Matthew was writing in response to the opposition of the Jewish religious leaders in Palestine; Mark was writing for a mostly Gentile audience outside of Palestine. Luke is intrigued by many people we have not met in the other Gospels, like Zechariah and Elizabeth, Simeon and Anna, Martha and Mary, Lazarus and the rich man, and so forth. Remember that Luke would have known of Matthew's and Mark's Gospels, so he had some freedom to include history that they had not in order to give us a more complete picture of the Gospel.

● ● ● ● ● ● ● ● ● ● ● ● ● ● ● ● ● ● ●

Q 19:5–8 Why did Jesus want to speak with Zacchaeus?

Jesus is the creator of Zacchaeus's conscience that led him to repentance. Jesus is the origin of the reports that inspired the faith that moved Zacchaeus to seek Jesus. The Bible teaches that whoever believes in Jesus will not be disappointed or ashamed (Rm 9:33; 10:11). Jesus sought Zacchaeus for the same reason He seeks us all: in order to reunite us with God and restore our life (Jn 6:40).

● ● ● ● ● ● ● ● ● ● ● ● ● ● ● ● ● ● ●

Q 19:7 Why does everyone call certain people "sinners"? They are sinners too.

If the religious leaders listen to the Law and their own conscience, they would have to admit that they are condemned by the Law and could only be saved by the grace of God. But that admission would be the end of their pride and of their justification for taking their means of living from the people they condemn. Rather than be honest about their condition, they tell themselves that they deserve God's favor and the power and wealth they squeeze out of the people because they are so much more holy than the people. This is why the same religious leaders hated and utterly rejected Jesus, because He demonstrated what real power, wealth, and holiness looks like. Jesus, the Son of God, emptied Himself and made Himself servant of all. The Bible speaks in many places about considering other people better than ourselves (Lk 6:41–42; Php 2:3ff.).

● ● ● ● ● ● ● ● ● ● ● ● ● ● ● ● ● ● ●

Q 19:9 When Jesus said, "Today salvation has come to this house," was He talking about more people than Zacchaeus?

It is possible that there were other members of the household of Zacchaeus who realized the salvation of Jesus on that same day, but Luke does not mention anyone else. Jesus uses the expression "this house" and immediately explains in reference to Zacchaeus alone, "because he also is a son of Abraham." In other instances where others are included in a household, there is mention of this (Ac 10:24; 16:34—note the word "household" in 16:34; this is the only occurrence of this particular word in the New Testament).

Q 19:11–27 How does this parable speak to the kingdom of God not appearing immediately? What was the purpose of this parable?

There are two ways in which Jesus' response deals with their thinking that the kingdom of God would come immediately. First, the parable of the minas makes clear that there is work to be done between that time and when our Master returns (v. 13). Second, the parable makes clear that there is a problem with the disposition of the people. Thinking that the Kingdom will appear raises the question of our relationship to that Kingdom; are we a part of that Kingdom or will we be executed (v. 27)?

The purpose of the parable, as explained in v. 11, was to respond to people's anticipation that the kingdom of God was coming immediately. The description of the people in v. 14, the servant in v. 23, and the judgment of the master in v. 27 exposes the problem with the thinking of the people there.

Q 19:13 What is a mina? In the story of the "minas," why was the third servant's mina given to the first servant, who had the most and not the second, who had only five minas?

One mina is worth $30,958.20 in current dollars (sixty minas = one talent or $1,857,492.00 in current dollars). The third servant's mina was given to the first servant because the first servant had demonstrated the best stewardship (his original mina gained ten more). Jesus says that to the one who has, more will be given, thus we would expect the steward with the most to receive the most (Lk 19:26).

Q 19:14 Why does it matter if his subjects did not want him to be king if he became king anyway?

The people's rejection of their king matters in two ways: (1) what will they miss by not having this king, and (2) what will they miss or suffer from having another? In the very next chapter, Luke records Jesus telling the parable of the vineyard, which a man established and then let out to renters. These renters did not pay the rent and killed the owner's son. This parable is a parallel to the one in question. The significance of rejecting the king is made clear by the renter's rejection of the owner's son, whom they cast out of the vineyard and killed (Lk 20:9–19). Notice how the conclusion of each parable is the same for these who reject God (Lk 19:27, 20:16–19). The Jews at the trial of Jesus shouted that they preferred to have a murderer/rebel released to them and that they had no king but Caesar (Lk 23:18–19; Jn 19:15). Israel rejected God as their leader during the Exodus and again during the time of Samuel with devastating consequences (Ex 32; 1Sm 8). Fallen human nature's rejection of God and the significance of this is best seen at its origin, when Adam rejected God in favor of himself, Eve, and the devil (Gn 3:1–15).

Q **19:20–24 Why was the king so hard on his servant who did not increase his money?**

The king is not being hard on the servant but responding to the servant according to the servant's own disposition. Notice that the servant made no positive effort at all to be a good steward of the king's mina nor did he allow anyone else, like the banks, to be good stewards of that mina on his behalf (v. 23). The servant clearly shares the negative disposition of the other citizens who sent a delegation to reject the king (vv. 14 and 21). The king did not criticize or condemn the second servant who had gained only half as much as the first servant. Nor would the king have condemned this servant if he had only tried or let someone else try on his behalf. This servant didn't look for help or mercy but accused the king of being what he was himself, an austere man who wanted to collect what he did not deposit and reap what he did not sow. How many people in history and in the world today accuse God of being hard and austere while ignoring the universal significance of God's redemption of the world through the sacrifice of His own Son?

Q **19:26 It says that the man who has will be given more and the man that does not have, what he has is taken away. I don't understand.**

The key is not in having more or little (or nothing) but in a person's disposition toward life and toward God. The widow put in the last two pennies she had, yet Jesus said she put in more than all the other people who contributed a little from their wealth (Lk 21:1–4). There was a man whom the Lord blessed with a great harvest, so great that the man pulled down his barns to build bigger ones, but the man had nothing because he died that night (Lk 12:15–21). The history of Lazarus and the rich man is also helpful in answering your questions (Lk 16:19–31). Lazarus has nothing by worldly standards but is wealthy in his hope and expectation for God to bless him for the faith he has. The rich man has nothing but his worldly wealth and the appetite for it that made him so selfish, and in his death, even that little bit of worldly wealth is taken away. Rich or poor in material things, the person who looks to God in hope and faith produced by His Word will be given more and more (Rm 8:28). Rich or poor, the person who despises the Giver of all good things and fails to appreciate that all we are and have is given by God has nothing even now and will suffer indescribable want and emptiness in eternity (Mt 22:11–13).

Q 19:26–27 This sounds like it contradicts what we have read every other time. What is Jesus referring to? After the bulk of the parable of the ten minas is told, the king says, "As for these enemies of mine, who did not want me to reign over them, bring them here and slaughter them before me." I don't really see how this fits into the parable.

Jesus often exposes a troubled cause for the words and deeds of people: the rich young ruler (Lk 19:18–23), the lawyer asking about his neighbor (10:25–37), the man who wanted Jesus to make his brother divide the inheritance (Lk 12:13–15), James and John and their mother (Mt 20:20–23), the crowds that had been fed (Jn 6:27–66), even Mary (Jn 2:2–3). Paul must have realized this trouble with our nature as he expressed indecision about wanting to die or live on (Php 1:19–26). The same attitude that makes a good steward makes a person ready for the kingdom of God to come (Ac 2:37–47). The selfish and vain attitude that makes a poor steward also reveals that such a person is woefully unprepared for judgment (Mt 25:31–46).

Q 19:28–44 To my understanding, I have associated the "triumphal entry" with "loud hosannas." Does Luke not record the "hosannas," or did I lose that in the English transition?

Matthew, Mark, and John all record the singing of "hosannas" when Jesus entered Jerusalem on Palm Sunday. Interestingly, perhaps here for the first time, Luke's Gospel takes on a negative tone, with Jesus weeping over Jerusalem and prophesying a grim future for her (Lk 19:41–44).

Q 19:30 Why did it matter that the colt had never been ridden?

There are two possibilities that I can think of for why it matters that the colt had not been ridden on. First, riding on a donkey instead of a horse and, even more so, on the colt of a donkey is consistent with Jesus being humble rather than proud (Is 53:1–7), approachable rather than terrifying (Is 42:1–4). One of the reasons the Son of God took on human nature was so He might come to us directly and physically be in the midst of us (Heb 12:18–24). Second, it is important and appropriate to give to the Lord the first and best of what He provides to us (Ex 13:15; 23:16; Mal 1:8ff.). Think of what it would mean if we gave the Lord something used? Thus, the donkey upon which no one has ridden is appropriate for the Son of God, and the lowliness of the animal is consistent with the Lord's gracious will to humble Himself that He might save us (Php 2:5–11).

Q 19:40 What does Jesus mean when He says "if these [disciples] were silent, the very stones would cry out"?

We take words in the simplest and most clear meaning unless forced to do otherwise. If with God nothing is impossible, then it would seem that if the people did not cry out the truth about Jesus, then the rocks would. I suspect the point Jesus is trying to make is that the energy and anticipation inspired by Jesus' coming to Jerusalem to complete our redemption is so great and powerful that nothing could hold it back, not even the inanimate nature of a rock. You may recall that John the Baptizer said God could raise up children of Abraham from stones (Lk 3:8). Peter and Paul refer to believers as living stones, set together by God to form His house (Eph 2:19–22; 1Pt 2:4–9).

● ● ● ● ● ● ● ● ● ● ● ● ● ● ● ● ● ● ●

Q 19:47–48 How were the chief priests and teachers of the law trying to kill Jesus? Is this a foreshadowing of Judas's betrayal, or were the priests and teachers trying long before that?

The chief priests and teachers of the law hoped to find some fault in Jesus by which they could disgrace Him before the people and, if possible, condemn Him to death (Mt 16:1; 19:3; 22:18; 23:35; 26:59; Jn 8:6). Religious leaders tried to kill Jesus from the very beginning of His public ministry at the synagogue in Nazareth (Lk 4:28–29). The religious leaders intended to stone Jesus after His "Good Shepherd" discourse (Jn 10:31–39). After Jesus raised Lazarus from the dead, they became even more determined to kill Jesus somehow (Jn 11:45–50).

● ● ● ● ● ● ● ● ● ● ● ● ● ● ● ● ● ● ●

Q 20:1–2 Why were Jesus and His authority constantly questioned? Wasn't word spread about Him to the proper people?

Jesus' authority was questioned for two reasons. One, no one ever taught with authority like Jesus did (Lk 4:36–37). Two, fallen human nature, especially that of the religious leaders, wants to be its own authority so it may be selfish and then justify itself (Jgs 17:6). If you combine these two, you see why the people who wanted to answer to no one but themselves were so determined to find a way to reject the One to whom all people must give account (Lk 19:11–27).

● ● ● ● ● ● ● ● ● ● ● ● ● ● ● ● ● ● ●

Q 20:3–4 Can you further explain these verses?

The Pharisees were desperate for a means of rejecting Jesus. They could not deny that Jesus was doing miraculous signs (Jn 11), and they could not defeat His teaching. They are grasping at straws by challenging His authority with two ridiculous questions (v. 2). Jesus, always the faithful teacher, exposes their error so that they might repent, though they refuse. The Pharisees were powerful and numerous, but their power depended on the support of the people (in contrast to the political and military power of the Romans and the religious authority of the Sadducees). John also exposed the hypocrisy and wicked nature of the Pharisees (Mt 3), but they could do nothing about it because of the large crowds of people that came out to John and revered him *highly* as a prophet (Lk 3). Jesus often asks hypocrites questions that would force them to honesty (Mt 12:1–12; Mk 10:17–18). If they claim disregard for John because he was not from God, the people will revolt. If they admit that John was from God, why didn't they believe John's witness to Jesus? Sadly, rather than admit the truth and benefit, the Pharisees refuse to answer. Contrast a wicked hatred of the light of truth (Jn 3:18ff.) with the practice of the faithful walking in the light constantly (1Jn 1:7; Ps 119:105; Col 3:16).

• • • • • • • • • • • • • • • • • • • •

Q **20:6 Why did the Pharisees think they would be stoned? What does the fact that the people were persuaded have to do with anything?**

If you are committed to the truth, if you love God above all things and your neighbor as yourself, what people are persuaded of still matters a lot. If you truly serve the Lord and the truth, then you care whether people are persuaded by the truth or by lies. If you are against the Lord and the truth, you care—but for very bad reasons. The Pharisees know that their authority does not come from serving God or the people ("Pharisees" are not a group ordained by God). Neither do the Pharisees have civil authority, like the Roman governors or Herod. Therefore, the Pharisees' power depended on the popular support of the people, and since the people were convinced that John was a prophet from God, the Pharisees had to be careful not to contradict that position.

• • • • • • • • • • • • • • • • • • • •

Q **20:9–19 How could the murderous tenants possibly think the vineyard would become theirs if they killed the heir? Would not justice and the heir's living father prevent this?**

God is the vineyard owner. He is the only God, Creator, Sustainer, and Owner of all things, even of each breath and heartbeat of every living creature. So, in the first place, how is it that human beings who depend on God for their very existence and who are blessed by God with a wonderful life and abundance refuse to return the first fruits (rent) of that abundance to God? The prophet Haggai laments this folly (Hg 1:3–9). Ananias and Sapphira dropped dead for trying to lie about returning first fruits to God (Ac 5:1–11). In the second place, how can people beat and mistreat the messengers God sends and think there will be no consequences for this? Yet people who claim to be Christian have rejected and abused God's messengers and His Word ever since the time of Christ. You are right in your observation, which is the third point: how in the world would killing the heir make the vineyard yours, and how would you ever escape the vengeance of the owner? But here we are, in an age when most people offer God no service, thanks, or acknowledgment. Most people abuse His creation, patience, and grace while acting as if they were self-made in their vanity, pride, and selfishness. This is not evidence that there is no God. This is evidence of the insanity of created beings and the incomparable patience and grace of God (Rm 2:4; 2Pt 3:1–9). Refusing, rejecting, and even just ignoring the Word of God is practically the same as putting His messengers and Son to death (Heb 6:1–8; 10:26–31). This is the sort of clear, terrifying truth that our fallen human nature requires in order to be turned in repentance so that the grace of God, communicated by His Word and Spirit, can regenerate us and work a faithful, fruitful, and honest life in us.

● ● ● ● ● ● ● ● ● ● ● ● ● ● ● ● ● ● ● ●

Q 20:17 What is "the cornerstone" and what is its meaning?

Jesus said that the stone that the builders rejected had become the "head of the corner." This "head of the corner" stone was the first stone laid in the construction of a building. Stones used for construction during this time were milled with amazing accuracy and fit together tightly without mortar. I visited the Temple Mount in Jerusalem and saw huge limestone blocks stacked to make a wall; you could not slide a piece of paper between the stones. Since the stones of a building fit together so precisely, if the head cornerstone was not perfect, the whole building would be distorted very

quickly as that misorientation sent each consecutive stone further out of line. Therefore, the chief or head cornerstone had to be perfect. Contrast this with the religious leaders who had corrupted the Word of God by adding their own laws, compromising God's Law, and rejecting His grace. There is no way to construct anything from a perfect cornerstone followed by other stones so badly out of square. Rather than admit their imperfection and welcome Jesus' remaking them as living, perfect stones, the religious leaders were determined to reject this perfect cornerstone, thinking that without a standard of perfection no one could see their imperfections. But the crucifixion of Jesus only makes the folly of rejecting the chief cornerstone more obvious. Jesus is the cornerstone who oriented the rest of the building to perfection (Eph 2:20–22; 1Pt 2:4–5).

● ● ● ● ● ● ● ● ● ● ● ● ● ● ● ● ● ● ● ●

Q 20:18 Is this verse referring to sinners falling to hell?

Think of "fall[ing] on that stone" like falling down when you trip over something. Gravity and the hardness of the ground tell us that we made a mistake; it hurts when we fall. Whenever we contradict the Law of God, whether in physical nature or in spiritual reality, there are consequences. But falling on the Law of the Lord, that is to say, knowing the truth about our failure to keep the Law, breaks us in order to serve God's gracious work of raising us up (1Sm 2:6–8; Ps 51:8, 17; Is 61:1). On the other hand, a person who would refuse the truth about himself or herself in relation to the Law (falling on the stone) still must reckon with the stone, only now the stone is on top of instead of beneath him or her. This is the argument and warning that both Peter and Paul make so vigorously (Ac 15:7–10; Gal 2:11–16; 5:4). If a person denies his or her failing to keep the Law, that person also rejects the work of Christ to redeem us from the Law and thus insists in pride and dishonesty that he or she can uphold the Law on his or her own. In this way, the verse is referring to sinners falling to hell, because without Christ, the burden and curse of the Law, like the heaviest of stones, bears down upon us until justice is done and we are in hell.

Q 20:35 While marriages will not take place in heaven, will existing marriages still be intact? Or will we not know families in heaven?

The account of Lazarus and the rich man indicates that we retain our identity in eternity (Lk 16:23). John said that we don't really know what we will be like after death and resurrection except that we will be like Jesus after He rose from the dead (1Jn 3:2). I suspect that one of the things that makes paradise what it is has to do with the absence of any selfishness and self-interest, especially regarding our relationships with one another. While I may recognize my parents, spouse, and children, I would never dream of claiming them as "mine" but

would be glad to spend eternity with them, while thanking God for them.

Q 20:39 Why did the Pharisees side with Jesus and against the Sadducees when they disliked Jesus so much and wanted to catch Him doing something wrong?

The text says it was some of the "scribes" that spoke, and while they admitted that Jesus spoke well, they were far from submitting to Him as their Lord and Savior. Since scribes, Pharisees, Sadducees, Herodians, Zealots and other groups were all competing against each other for respect, power, and disciples, any of these groups would be glad when Jesus put another group to shame.

Q 21:5–8 Have any of the things that Jesus said would bring about the end of the age already happened? And if they have, what does this mean especially in terms of today's society?

The stones of the temple that these verses refer to were torn apart by the Roman armies in AD 70, barely forty years after Jesus said so. The signs of the end Jesus makes reference to have been experienced in every generation since He described them. However, a more complete fulfillment of the signs is experienced as generations pass and the end of the world approaches. For more on this subject, see questions and answers at Mt 24:1–35 and Mk 13:1–23.

Q 21:1–4 Jesus says that the better person is the one who gives all, but what if you are given something? Should you give it away right after?

Giving is no good unless it is a product of faith in the providence of God (Rm 14:23; Heb 11:6). A Christian recognizes and finds both peace and joy in the fact that all we are and have belongs to God (1Co 4:7). Faith and love motivates a Christian to be a good steward of all that we are and have, whether we give money away or decide how to use it in service of God's kingdom ourselves (Lk 12:41–44; 1Co 4:1; Ac 2:40–47; 5:1–11). Whether someone gives you something or you find it or you receive wages from labor, the grace of God puts us at liberty to use or allow others to use what is in our care for the best possible results (1Co 7:29–31).

Q 21:3 Why does Jesus call out the widow?

Jesus is the absolute teacher, perfectly effective, because He never misses an opportunity to show us as well as explain to us the truth (Jn 14:6). Jesus noticed a contrast between the stewardship of people who brought offerings to the temple and brought it to our attention. Fallen human nature has a habit of judging, or misjudging, in haste and on the basis of appearances (Jn 7:24). Fallen human nature is impressed with large gifts, but those gifts often come as a very small portion of what a person has, which he or she is keeping for himself or herself. Where is the faith or love in that? On the other hand, the widow who put in hardly anything put in everything. It was of no significance to anyone watching except the Lord who created in her the faith that knows where life comes from. It comes from God through people rather than through money. Rich people put in a lot and it seems like a lot to them and they expect to be recognized for it, a lot. The poor widow put in a small amount because it was a small thing to her to put in all she had, since the Son of God had given Himself completely for her (Rm 8:32).

Q 21:4 Why does Jesus make it sound like giving wealth to charities is a bad thing?

Neither wealth nor giving are condemned by Jesus. What Jesus condemns is pretense, hypocrisy, dishonesty, greed, and selfishness (Mk 7:20–23). Where does wealth come from anyway, and why would a person seek to retain it (Lk 12:13–21)? Some people inherit wealth. If it is inherited and not earned, it should be all the easier to share with others who haven't earned it either. If the wealth was earned, we might ask how it is that one person's labor has accumulated so much more wealth than someone else's. The Bible has nothing bad to say about people enjoying the fruits of their labor (provided they have remembered to thank God with the first of those fruits, 2Tm 2:6; 1Co 9:7–14). However, wealth is gained by charging too much for what is sold or paying too little to those who produce what is sold or both, and what is gained by doing so anyway? People who have the ability to manage people and affairs so that they might become wealthy have a responsibility and opportunity to use such God-given ability to bring others along in their abilities and standard of living as well. If one's life does not consist in the abundance of possessions (and every person who has ever died proves this true), then what is the point of wealth? If man (and woman) lives by every word that proceeds from the mouth of God, then we have an inexhaustible source of incomparable wealth that we are completely free to spend our lives sharing with others (Pr 13:7; Lk 12:15; Mt 4:4; Gal 5:1; Php 3:7–14).

• • • • • • • • • • • • • • • • • • • •

Q **21:6 What does it mean that stone would be thrown down, yet no stone would be left?**

When the Roman army came, less than forty years after Jesus said this (AD 70), they destroyed Jerusalem. The temple was torn apart to the very last stone for at least two reasons. First, the Romans wanted to make clear the utter defeat of Israel and its God, for in these times the defeat of a nation and its god(s) were inseparable in the minds of people. Second, there was gold on the walls of the temple, and when it was burned, the molten gold made its way between the stones. Therefore every stone was taken apart in order to recover the gold that was there. The most important message here is the reorientation of the disciples' thinking. They are impressed with stones hewn and assembled by men that make buildings that are hollow, but these are unable to maintain themselves against support or give life to those within. Jesus is "opposite" these buildings on the Mount of Olives. He is the living stone, a rock of refuge, a mighty fortress hewn from a mountain without hands (Dn 2:34, a reference to the virgin birth of Jesus), the very source of life and unconquerable as His ministry, death, and resurrection demonstrate. Please note humankind's preoccupation with building and God's consistent warning and rebuke (2Sm 7:1–17; Mt 17:4–5).

• • • • • • • • • • • • • • • • • • • •

Q **21:10 Why do Christians who are excited for Jesus' second coming also protest war? War must happen before Jesus comes again, so why are these Christians so hypercritical?**

I am not at all sure about the relationship between people who are eager for Jesus' return and those who protest war. There are good and bad reasons for both. Some people want Jesus to hurry and oppose war for selfish reasons. Others might long for Jesus to come precisely because it would be the end of wars among people. We do well to always ask people to explain what they are for or against and why, so that we might understand them truthfully, learn, and perhaps find an opportunity to bear witness to the truth ourselves (Jas 1:19; 1Pt 3:15).

Q **21:12–13 Is it possible to look at these verses as a metaphor or correlation to present times?**

Yes. Regarding correlation, there are still plenty of Christians who are physically persecuted, just like people were in the first century. What Jesus says isn't so much metaphor as indicative of other kinds of persecution that are more subtle. In countries that claim religious tolerance, Christianity is still discriminated against, and many who advocate the truth lose their jobs or are ostracized because these truths also happen to be advanced in the Bible.

Q **21:14 Why should we not worry about how to defend ourselves?**

Jesus answers this question in the very next verse: "for I will give you a mouth and wisdom, which none of your adversaries will be able to withstand or contradict." Compare what Jesus said with Peter's imperative that you be "always . . . prepared to make a defense to anyone who asks you for a reason for the hope that is in you" (1Pt 3:15). Are we to be prepared or not? Pr 16:1 solves the apparent contradiction: "The plans of the heart belong to man, but the answer of the tongue is from the LORD." Jesus said that His disciples would remain in His Word, and that by doing so, they would know the truth and the truth would make them free (Jn 8:31). In this passage, Jesus is distinguishing between being prepared by maintaining a life in the Word and worrying about exactly what to say, as if we were all alone at such times. The Lord is near and promises to bring the right words to mind.

Q **21:18–19 Is this a prediction of the end times? Will we be raptured?**

This is a prediction of the end times, though, to a certain extent, everyone experiences end times in their own lifetime (see Lk 21:5–8 above). We will not be raptured before all these things take place, though; the Lord knows how and when to deliver each of His people at the proper time (2Pt 2:9). For more on the rapture, see questions and answers at 1Th 4:17.

Q **21:20 With all the violence and wars surrounding Jerusalem, could these times be what Jesus was talking about?**

As long as this world endures, there will be the signs that Jesus described. All creation groans under the effects of Adam's rebellion against God, so there will be "natural" disasters like earthquakes, hail, and floods (Rm 8:20–23). Fallen human nature is greedy and proud, so there will always be wars, rumors of wars, and violence (Jas 4:1–4). Certainly people in AD 70 saw a partial fulfillment of Jesus' words when the Roman army did surround Jerusalem. Jerusalem has been surrounded many other times in history by Muslim armies and by Crusader armies, for example. Beware of taking too physical a focus, as Jesus' words may be pointing us to a spiritual situation

(Gal 4:21–31). As the city of Jerusalem was surrounded and destroyed by the Roman army in AD 70, so also near the end of time the people who belong to the kingdom of God (spiritual Jerusalem) will be surrounded by all kinds of forces that mean to destroy truth and faith. We can easily see this in our day where the popular claim and disposition is that there is no such thing as truth, and faith in the truth has been traded for people's selfish devotion to their own appetites (2Tm 4:1–5).

Q **21:23 "Alas for women who are pregnant and for those who are nursing infants in those days!" Is there some particular relationship between women and the terrible events described? Is He just saying it is hard to escape?**

The same forces of the devil, world, and human beings that oppose God also prey on those least able to defend themselves, like women, especially pregnant women, and children (Jer 23:1–2; Am 2:6–7). It was harder for pregnant women and women with infants to flee Jerusalem than it was for anyone else as the Roman army approached in AD 70. In our time, life is even more difficult for pregnant women and women with small children, since they are so often the product of irresponsible and selfish sexual self-indulgence, the target of the abortion industry, or despised as if they were stupid, useless, or a burden to society. (Consider, for example, Margaret Sanger [1879–1966] and the history of Planned Parenthood.)

Q **21:26 Why would Jesus let people die of fright in anticipation of what was coming for the world?**

Why would Jesus let anyone die of anything? How do you convince people of the truth when they think they know better and refuse rational argument and clear witnesses? The means left is to let people experience the truth for themselves. We live in a time when people claim to be self-made and insist that they have a free will. How then can such people have hearts that fail them? Faith has to do with honesty about dependence, our dependence on God in particular. If we are honest about our dependence on God, we find in God the source of our life, physical and spiritual, in time and in eternity. In honesty we learn the truth about our fallen human nature and the truth about God's love for us in Christ who redeemed us and restores our life. Facing their own inability is the last means of bringing people who deny the truth into the truth while there is still time for them to be saved.

Q **21:28 What does it mean to lift up our heads at this time? Shouldn't our heads already be up?**

Jesus is talking about lifting up your head because you are looking up into the sky for the Lord to come (Ps 121). Your head may not be up because you "look carefully then how you walk" (Eph 5:15) or because you "mind your own affairs" (1Th 4:11). Our heads may not be up because we are grieved by the state of affairs in this world (Ps 42:5, 11) or because we have become distracted with our life in this world (Col 3:1ff.).

Q 21:29–33 Although this verse is a short story about the fig tree, what inner meaning does it have?

The example of the fig tree has just one meaning: a fig tree gives you indication of when summer is coming. In the same way, when we see the things happen that Jesus describes in the previous verses, we know that Jesus is about to return. Please note that the end of the world for all people and all time is not as important as the end of the world for each person, which takes place when he or she dies (Lk 12:16–21; 35–40). Doesn't it seem odd that people are preoccupied with the end of the world for everyone while giving little thought to living today as if it were their last?

Q 21:31–32 How is it that Jesus tells the disciples that when they see the signs they will know that the kingdom of God is near and at the same time that this generation will not pass away until all these things have happened?

There are two possible solutions. First, there would be a partial fulfillment of the signs Jesus described during the first century, while people of that generation were still living. Second, the expression "this generation" may be referring to fallen humanity as a whole, which would mean, "There will still be fallen human beings in the world when all these signs have been fulfilled." Both of these possibilities might be true as well.

Q 21:33 How can heaven pass away if we spend eternity there?

Like many words, "heaven" has more than one reference. Sometimes "heaven" has to do with the kingdom of God, eternity, and paradise (Lk 10:9; compare Mt 5:3 with Lk 6:20; Lk 22:42–43). Sometimes "heaven" is referring to the sky above (Gn 1:9; Rv 5:13). Paradise, or the kingdom of heaven/God, is not a physical place but a relationship of communion with God. The whole of creation will be destroyed at the end of time and replaced with a new creation where all people will live in paradise with God and each other forever (Rv 21:1; 2Pt 3:11–13).

Q 21:36 Should we be praying every day about the last days?

We are supposed to pray all the time anyway (Eph 6:18; Php 4:6). What Jesus said was "stay awake at all times, praying that you may have strength to escape all these things that are going to take place, and to stand before the Son of Man." The only imperative in the verse is "to stay awake" or remain watchful. Everything else in the verse flows from this state of watchfulness.

Part of watching has to do with praying that we may have the strength to escape, either physically when we flee as Jesus directs us to or, finally, when we die (Mt 10:23; Lk 21:21; Rv 16:15).

Q **22:3 How can Satan enter Judas? Why was Judas chosen for this role?**

Satan would have entered Judas the same way that any of the demons possessed any of the people we read about in the Gospels. Judas Iscariot became a betrayer because he acted like an apostle but in his heart rejected and despised what Jesus taught (Jn 12:4–6). There is a difference between being a sinner and being possessed. All human nature inherited from Adam (that's all of us except Jesus) is corrupted with sin (Rm 5:12). But only those people who are without the Holy Spirit can be possessed by a demonic spirit (Lk 11:24–26). Satan's purpose in possessing Judas was to betray Jesus so that Jesus would be arrested and executed. Satan literally possessed Judas in his body, mind, and soul and, therefore, in his actions. Different Gospel writers have different concerns and give different perspectives. What would be the use of four identical Gospels? I suspect Luke includes the note about Judas being possessed because Luke is interested in the way unusual things come to pass, like the conceptions of John the Baptizer and Jesus. I'm not sure whether Judas would have been a different person after Satan entered him since he was already opposed to Jesus and was already a

hypocrite in pretending to follow and serve Jesus. For more on Judas, see Ps 109:16–20.

Q **22:3 Why is Judas called Iscariot?**

Iscariot was the family name of Judas. Luke mentions that Iscariot was Judas's surname, and John mentions that Judas's father's first name was Simon (Jn 12:4). He is called by two names for the sake of clarity and historicity, the same way a court of law makes people state their full names.

Q **22:6 As bad as Judas was in what he did, didn't God want to save him too? Did Satan leave him when he felt remorse, and did he go to hell because he committed suicide even though he felt remorse?**

God desires all to be saved and come to the knowledge of the truth (1Tm 2:4). Jesus bore away the sins of the world and reconciled the whole world to God (Jn 1:29; 2Co 5:19). This means that Jesus saved Judas from his sins, just like Jesus saved everyone else. I'm not sure we can know whether Satan still possessed Judas when he felt remorse or when he committed suicide. Paul does distinguish between worldly grief and godly grief (2Co 7:9–11). Jesus warns us not to pass judgment on people, but I know of no texts in the Bible that suggest anything but eternal condemnation for Judas (Ps 9:17; 109; 1Pt 2:7–8). We must be careful not to pass judgment on anyone, whether we think they were good or evil, but especially careful not to condemn anyone, as this is not our place or our desire, nor can we possibly know what is only known to God (Mt 7:1). Suicide is sometimes an act of defiance against God but not always; nor is suicide the "unforgivable sin" (Mt 12:31–32). Both Saul and David felt remorse, but Saul was without the Spirit and Word of God, while David felt this because of the Word and Spirit of God (1Sm 15:10–26; 2 Sm 12:1–13; Ps 32; 51). The same comparison can be made between Judas Iscariot and Peter or Saul/Paul (Lk 22:31–34; 23:54–62; Ac 9:1–22).

• • • • • • • • • • • • • • • • • • • •

Q **22:3 If salvation was won on the cross and resurrection, why would Satan enter Judas and prompt him to betray Jesus? Isn't the cross the last place Satan wants to see Jesus? If Jesus' death was all part of God's plan for us, why was Satan involved? Was it a partnership and God used Satan to fill Judas?**

Luther called the devil "God's ape," because the devil could copy but never understand what God was doing. Mel Gibson's movie *The Passion of the Christ* was mistaken when it portrayed the devil tempting Jesus to escape arrest and execution. No one and nothing that opposes God can even begin to fathom or have the slightest clue about what God is doing in His wisdom, grace, and love. God makes all things work together for good to those who love Him, who are called according to His purpose (Rm 8:28). This means that there is no such thing as the problem of evil. This means

that all opposition to God is self-defeating on two levels. First, those who oppose God do so to their own destruction, since He is the Creator and Origin of our life. Second, those who oppose God can only serve His good purposes, even by their opposition, as the whole of biblical history reveals. God could not have been in partnership with Satan or Judas as God is good and all things evil are the opposite of or absence of God. Because God is good, wise, gracious, loving, and mighty, He makes even that which would oppose Him and His purposes work for good.

• • • • • • • • • • • • • • • • • • • •

Q **22:4 Why did Judas go to discuss betraying Jesus in the first place? Did they ask him to come?**

John's Gospel reveals two important facts about Judas. First, Judas was already opposed to Jesus and playing the hypocrite by pretending to follow and listen. Second, Judas's constant rejection of Jesus' teaching left him without the Spirit that accompanies the Word; therefore, Judas was subject to possession by the devil (Jn 12:4–6).

• • • • • • • • • • • • • • • • • • • •

Q **22:5 Why didn't they just go get Jesus?**

The religious leaders had been plotting to arrest Jesus for some time but found it impossible because of the crowds of people. On one occasion, the religious leaders sent men to arrest Jesus, but they didn't because they were so impressed with Jesus' teaching (Jn 7:44–49). So, they were at a loss for how to capture Jesus and execute Him without causing a riot among the people or bringing themselves under Roman prosecution (Mt 26:5).

Q 22:7 What is the day of unleavened bread?

The Day of Unleavened Bread is part of the Passover commemoration (Ex 12:14–20; Lv 23:4–8). This day is the beginning of a whole week when the Israelites refrained from eating anything with leaven in it in order to remember how they were to be ready to leave Egypt in haste (Ex 12:11, 39; 13:6–10).

Q 22:7–38 Did the disciples actually realize the meaning and importance of the Last Supper?

No. On several occasions, the disciples express their lack of understanding; at other times Jesus makes note of the same (Lk 2:50; 9:45; Jn 16:12–13). It would not be until Pentecost and even some time afterward that the apostles would have a more complete understanding of the significance of all that Jesus taught (Ac 1:4–11; 10:1–11:18). Paul said that we are incapable of knowing fully what God intends for us until we are taken to God (1Co 13:9–12).

Q 22:10 Did the house owner know in advance they were coming, or did they show up and God inspired him to let them in?

The text does not appear to provide an answer for your question. There are plenty of examples in the Bible where God did make people aware in advance that someone would come with a certain request (Ac 10:1–16). On the other hand, there is no reason why God could not or would not have inspired the man to comply with His will at that moment.

Q 22:15 Why is Jesus so eager to eat Passover?

Since Jesus is the Lamb of God, promised to be slain from the foundation of the world, we might expect that He had always been eager to fulfill His love for us in His sacrifice in our place. Though God commanded the sacrificial system in the Old Testament, He also says He desires mercy and not sacrifice (Mt 9:13; 12:7). Consider how fourteen hundred years of people sacrificing animals that are God's creation might affect the Creator, especially since many of those sacrificing despised the importance of sacrifices or complied only as hypocrites (Is 1:10–17; Mal 1:6–2:9; Jn 2:13–18). Therefore, I suspect the eager desire of Jesus to eat this Passover was so He might put an end to the slaughter of innocent animals and accomplish, once and for all, the redemption of the whole world (2Co 5:19; Heb 9:24–28).

Q 22:15–16 Is Jesus' death and resurrection the fulfillment of the Passover?

Yes, in fact, what Jesus would accomplish between the moment He said this and three p.m. the next day when He said, "It is finished," was applied in that very moment. Jesus said He would not eat the Passover anymore until it was fulfilled, and then He ate it. Luke's Gospel is very helpful in making clear that the Passover, indeed, the whole sacrificial system, was fulfilled and thus ended as Jesus shifted from Passover to the Lord's Supper.

Q 22:16 Is this literal? At the end of times, will Christ lead us in Communion? Some churches don't use unleavened bread, is this wrong?

Any text should be taken in the most simple and literal way unless something directs or forces us to do otherwise. Jesus is speaking literally. As Jesus was speaking and eating the Passover meal, He was also fulfilling it and marking the end of that and the whole sacrificial system. I'm not sure what you mean by "lead us in Communion." During our life in this time and place, we have communion with Christ as He is present in His Word, His Spirit is always communicated to us in that Word, and we remain in that Word and let it dwell among us richly (Jn 6:63; 8:31–32; Col 3:16). When we die or at the end of the world, we will be completely united with Christ (1Co 13:9–12; 1Th 4:17). Unleavened bread is used because that is all that was available when Jesus instituted the Lord's Supper (during the Feast of Unleavened Bread). We might also want to use unleavened bread because it is an indication of the humble, honest, and substantive nature of the Gospel—in contrast with hypocrisy, pretense, and vanity (1Co 5:8; Lk 12:1). But Jesus gives no mandate that the bread must be unleavened, and it would be contrary to the Gospel, which this meal confirms, to burden consciences with laws about what kind of bread when Christ has not.

Q 22:17, 20 Why does Jesus use two cups during the Lord's Supper?

The first cup was part of the Passover meal; the second cup replaced the first forever as Christ was giving us His very blood for the forgiveness of sins, for all time and eternity. You may read about the Passover meal on any number of websites if you search the subject.

Q 22:18 Why did Christ say He wasn't going to drink wine again until the kingdom of God came? Is it because Christ will join us in a heavenly Communion after Judgment Day?

Jesus can't be referring to heaven after Judgment Day because in the very next moment He drank wine from the cup with His apostles (Lk 22:20). Jesus said He wouldn't drink wine until the kingdom of God came—and then He drank wine to show that His kingdom had come, now, as He was about to complete His redemption of all the world.

Q 22:21 Why didn't any of the others attempt to stop Judas?

The other apostles did not attempt to stop Judas because they did not know what he was doing nor did they understand what Jesus was saying to him (Jn 13:21–30).

Q 22:24 Did the dispute over who was greatest arise in the Upper Room or did it occur later?

This dispute appears to have taken place in the Upper Room since Luke does not record a change of location until v. 39, when Jesus and the Eleven went to the Mount of Olives.

Q 22:29 What is the kingdom that Jesus is giving the disciples?

Jesus said that the kingdom of heaven was within His disciples (Lk 17:21). Heaven, in this context, is not a place but a circumstance or situation of communion with God. Jesus brought the kingdom of God/heaven in His own person and demonstrated the nature of that kingdom by healing the sick, raising the dead, feeding the hungry, and forgiving sins (Is 61:1–3; Mk 1:14–34). Jesus provided this kingdom to His disciples during His ministry and then gave them au-

thority to convey the kingdom to others in His name (Mk 16:16–20; 1Co 11:23ff.).

Q 22:31 What does "sift you like wheat" mean? Can Satan demand that of God, and why did Jesus adhere to his demand?

To "sift" someone like wheat would mean to put a person through circumstances that reduce them to dust. Since Peter was quick to make claims for himself, he was a natural target for the devil, who succeeds when we fail (22:33–34). Satan didn't demand anything from God, as he surely cannot, but Satan asked for Peter, somewhat like he did with Job (Jb 1:9–12; 2:4–7). Jesus did not adhere to Satan's request but interceded for Peter, which kept Peter from failing altogether and ending up like Judas.

Q 22:31–32 I have always been taught that God gave us prayer for our benefit, to keep us reminded of where we are with Him; if this is true, then why did Jesus need to pray?

Jesus is the Son of God and fully a human being. Can you imagine a perfect Father and a perfect Son not communicating with each other all the time?

Q 22:31–34 Why does Jesus refer to Peter sometimes as Simon and sometimes as Peter?

I don't think the Bible offers an answer to this question. The only explanation

I can offer has to do with why Jesus called him Peter in the first place (Mt 16:16–18). Perhaps on this occasion, since Peter isn't being very "rocklike," Jesus reverts to Peter's given name, Simon.

● ● ● ● ● ● ● ● ● ● ● ● ● ● ● ● ● ● ● ●

Q 22:34 What is the significance of the rooster crowing?

The crowing of the rooster gives an indication of the time. Jesus was arrested on Maundy Thursday evening and tried through the night at the high priest's house, and then the rooster crowed. Not long after that, Luke says, "when day came," the council met, and after that they led Jesus to Pilate. The crowing of the rooster indicates that day is dawning, when the light comes and reveals the world as it is. Just when Peter denies Jesus for the third time, fulfilling the truth that Jesus prophesied about him, the rooster crowed as if to say, "So, Peter, the light has revealed the truth."

● ● ● ● ● ● ● ● ● ● ● ● ● ● ● ● ● ● ● ●

Q 22:36 Why does Jesus tell His disciples to buy swords?

Jesus was speaking with indicative language; we know this from His exasperated response to Peter, "It is enough" (v. 38). Jesus' quotation of Is 53:12 was His way of indicating that the going was about to get tough. While Jesus was with them, during the three years of His public ministry, Jesus was able to keep the challenges and conflicts presented by the opposition to a minimum. During this time the disciples wanted for

nothing, as Jesus was always there with them. But now Jesus was about to submit Himself to all the forces of opposition; He would be arrested, falsely accused, beaten, falsely condemned, and crucified. During this time the disciples would have to resume responsibility for providing for themselves and defending themselves—mainly on a spiritual level.

● ● ● ● ● ● ● ● ● ● ● ● ● ● ● ● ● ● ● ●

Q 22:39 Why is the Mount of Olives mentioned so much during Holy Week, and why does Jesus always go there?

The Mount of Olives is just across the Kidron Valley to the east of Jerusalem, which allows for a great view of the city (Mk 13:1–3). Jesus stayed with friends who lived in Bethany, which is near the south end of the Mount of Olives (Mt 21:17; Lk 19:29). The Garden of Gethsemane is on the western base of the Mount of Olives, where Jesus used to go often to pray (Mt 26:36; Jn 18:1–2). During Holy Week, the Mount of Olives is mentioned a lot because Jesus passed that way each day as He came and went from the city.

● ● ● ● ● ● ● ● ● ● ● ● ● ● ● ● ● ● ● ●

Q 22:39–46 Jesus was praying to God about what was going to happen to Him. Being that Jesus is human even though He's God's Son, was Jesus scared or nervous about what He was going to endure?

The New Testament teaches that perfect love casts out fear and forbids worry

(1Jn 4:18; Php 4:6). Since Jesus is God and God is love, He would not have been fearful or nervous. However, as true God He surely knew what He would be enduring, and as true man He would rightly be distressed about this (Jn 12:27).

Q 22:42 What does it mean when Jesus asks His Father to take the cup from Him? How do we know what Jesus prayed at Gethsemane?

The "cup" describes the experiences of life that a person is destined for; the cup is your life and the content of the cup is the contents of your life (Ps 75:8; 116:13; Mt 20:22–23; Jn 18:1–2). We only know as much of Jesus' prayer as the Gospels reveal (Mt 26:39, 42; Lk 22:42). Jn 17 gives an extensive view of the content of Jesus' prayer in the Upper Room, and though this was before Gethsemane, it still gives insight into what was on Jesus' mind.

Q 22:43 Why did Jesus need help from angels?

The text does not say that Jesus needed this help, only that the angel came and strengthened Him. The next verse gives a very small window into the trial Jesus endured: "and being in an agony He prayed more earnestly; and His sweat became like great drops of blood falling down to the ground." I think it is impossible for us to begin to understand the dynamics with-

in the Trinity or what Jesus went through, even though He was true God and truly man.

Q 22:44 Was Christ really sweating blood, or is that simply a metaphor?

This is actually a *simile*; Jesus' "sweat became like great drops of blood falling down to the ground." As in the previous question and answer, how can we possibly grasp the struggle and trial that Jesus endured, except in a small way by simile?

Q 22:45 Why were they in grief? Why were the disciples exhausted with sorrow? Why does Luke think the disciples' sleeping is significant?

The sleep of the disciples is significant because it shows the weakness and unresponsiveness of fallen human nature to impending trouble. Jesus stressed the importance, indeed, the necessity of watchfulness in parables and in plain warnings (Mk 13:32–37; Lk 12:38; 21:36). Fallen human nature tends to be awake when it should be sleeping and sleeping when it should be awake, aware of what it should ignore and ignorant of what it should be aware of (Rm 7:7–21; Pr 7). The expression "sleeping for sorrow" or "sleeping from grief" is peculiar. Years of pastoral counseling has taught me that grieving, being sorrowful, being nervous, or just about any other intense emotional state is very fatiguing; perhaps this is what Luke the physician is describing.

●●●●●●●●●●●●●●●●●●●

Q **22:48 Why did Judas betray Jesus with a kiss?**

Pr 27:6 says, "Profuse are the kisses of an enemy." Judas Iscariot is above all things the hypocrite, and to mark someone you are betraying with a kiss is the ultimate act of hypocrisy (Ps 41:9). We can also recognize a contrast here. Jesus IS the Word of God; all of His actions and every word from His mouth is truth. The mouth of fallen human nature is quite the opposite, deceiving with words and kisses (the whole history of lies in human communication and sexual perversion demonstrate this). We tend to favor people who give us what we want and tell us what we want to hear while avoiding people who would give us what we need and tell us the truth. This occasion in Jesus' life is a reminder to beware of those who flatter our vanity and be appreciative of those who cultivate our soul (Pr 17:10; 20:30; 26:28; 28:23; 29:5).

●●●●●●●●●●●●●●●●●●●

Q **22:50 How did the disciple only cut off an ear?**

It was only Peter who cut off an ear (Jn 18:10–11). How this happened is a puzzle. The only suggestion I would make is this: when Peter drew his sword (Jn 18:10), servants of the high priest and soldiers would have tried to take hold of him to keep Peter from using the sword effectively. In that

Why did Judas betray Jesus with a kiss?

struggle to control the sword, the blade passed close enough to Malchus's head so that it took off his ear.

●●●●●●●●●●●●●●●●●●●

Q **22:51 Is this the only Gospel in which the man's ear gets healed? Why did the guards and servants still arrest Jesus even after He performed a miracle?**

This is the only Gospel that records the healing of Malchus's ear; not surprising that a physician would want to record this. The fact that the guards and servants still arrest Jesus is remarkable, but no more remarkable than the religious leaders' determination to kill Jesus, who feeds multitudes, heals the sick, and raises the dead (Jn 11:45–53). Many people had second thoughts about Jesus but hid them for fear of the religious leaders (Jn 3:1–2; 7:12–13; Lk 22:54–62). On the other hand, many people paid no attention to what Jesus was teaching them or the significance of miracles He worked for them (Jn 6:15, 25ff.; Lk 17:11–19; Ex 32:1–10).

●●●●●●●●●●●●●●●●●●●

Q **22:53 Why did they choose to arrest Jesus in the garden instead of earlier?**

The religious leaders would have arrested and executed Jesus anywhere and anytime but did not because they feared the crowd (Mt 26:3–5). The garden was away from the crowds, a solitary place where they could arrest Jesus without anyone knowing about it (Lk 22:3–6).

· · · · · · · · · · · · · · · · · · ·

Q **22:62 Why doesn't Peter kill himself after he denies Jesus?**

The difference between Peter and Judas Iscariot is not the magnitude of their sin against Jesus but their relationship with the Word. Judas Iscariot rejected the Word and teaching of Christ, evident in his practice of stealing while still pretending to be an apostle (Jn 12:4–6). If a person rejects the Word, then that person has no Spirit of God in him or her. This makes him or her open to possession by the devil, who is always determined to destroy (Mt 12:43–45; Jn 8:44). Peter thought too much of himself and was quick to assert abilities he did not possess, but the Word and Spirit of the Lord was still with him, and Jesus made clear to Peter that he would recover from this failure (Lk 22:31–32). Saul and David in the Old Testament, like Judas and Peter in the New Testament, are examples of the difference between sinning against Christ and sinning against the Holy Spirit, who conveys and confirms the grace of God to the fallen (Lk 12:8–12).

· · · · · · · · · · · · · · · · · · ·

Q **22:63–71 In the other Gospels, there were moments where Annas or Caiaphas question Jesus. In Luke, instead**

the Sanhedrin questions him. Why did Luke not include the questioning by Annas or Caiaphas?

The similarities between the Gospels exist because they are recording the same history. The differences between the Gospels exist because the Holy Spirit and the particularities of the Gospel and its writer directed the addition or omission of certain accounts or details. John's Gospel tells us what happened first; Jesus was taken to the home of Annas, who was the father-in-law of Caiaphas, the high priest. When Annas was done, he sent Jesus to the home of Caiaphas (Jn 18:13–24; Mt 26:62; Mk 14:60). Next, at the home of Caiaphas, chief priests, elders, scribes, and the whole council accused Jesus (Mt 27:1–2; Mk 15:1). Finally, Caiaphas sent Jesus from his home to Pilate early in the morning (Jn 18:28).

· · · · · · · · · · · · · · · · · · ·

Q **22:63–65 Why did the guards beat Jesus so badly? Did they do the beating or were other people coming through and striking Jesus?**

Fallen human nature is just plain cruel; that's one reason (Gn 6:5, 11). Pride, vanity, power, and arrogance tend to make people hold outsiders in contempt, and the ability to beat them makes the abusers seem justified, for surely if this man should not be beaten, He or His disciples or God would come to His aid (Mt 27:39–44). This is late in the night or very early in the morning, and the group is limited to the religious leaders and their servants. I doubt that random people were there or that they randomly came up to Jesus and hit Him.

Q 23:4 Why do people always associate Pilate with evil if he tried to save Jesus?

People might assume Pilate was evil because he is mentioned in the creeds, "Crucified under Pontius Pilate." They might remember that Pilate had commanded some acts of cruelty that were a cause for concern in Rome and made Pilate concerned about how he would be seen in handling the problem with Jesus (Lk 13:1–2). Maybe people feel like it was not enough at all for Pilate to wash his hands before the crowd and claim he was innocent (Mt 27:24). Some might condemn Pilate for failing to respond to the warning of his wife (Mt 27:19). People might think Pilate is evil because he ordered Jesus to be beaten, though one can argue that Pilate had that done hoping the crowd would be satisfied and agree to Jesus' release (Lk 23:16). Pilate hoped to use the custom of releasing a prisoner on behalf of Jesus, but the religious leaders prevented that by stirring up the crowd to shout for Barabbas to be released and Jesus crucified (Mt 27:17–18). Whatever is the case with Pilate, we might consider what an exceedingly difficult position he was in as the religious leaders put pressure on him to condemn Jesus according to their demands.

Q 23:6–12 If Pilate and Herod were not friends, why could Herod stay so close to him?

In Jerusalem there was a palace area, surrounded by high walls and fortifications, more like a palace fortress. Inside that fortress there were two living areas opposite each other with a reflecting pool in between. The governor of the region lived in one, and Herod, since he was "king," stayed in the other palace when he was in the city.

Q 23:6–24 Pilate and Herod claimed they didn't want to crucify Jesus. Why did they do it?

Both Pilate and Herod had a fine line to walk. If they did not enforce Roman law and execute the desires of the Emperor, they would lose their positions or be exiled or worse. On the other hand, if the people were not happy, they would complain to higher Roman authorities, and if the people rioted, Rome would conclude that Pilate and Herod were incapable of controlling the people. Neither Pilate nor Herod cared that much about a single Jewish man; both of them were concerned about giving the people what they wanted as long as it kept the peace.

Q 23:7 Which Herod is this?

There are four different men referred to as Herod in the Gospels and Acts. The first Herod was visited by the Wise Men and had the baby boys in Bethlehem executed (Mt 2). The second Herod executed John the Baptist and saw Jesus in this verse. The third Herod executed the apostle James but died soon after (Ac 12). The fourth Herod listened to Paul make a defense for the Gospel (Ac 25). For details on the dynasty and genealogy of Herod, please consult a text or article on the subject, as it is fairly complicated.

Q **23:12 How did the death of Jesus change Herod and Pilate's relationship? Why does Luke include that Herod and Pilate became friends?**

In the past, Herod and Pilate had been enemies because they were both rulers of the same region. Herod had the title "king of Judea," but this was inherited and somewhat a formality (like the royal family in England). Pontius Pilate ruled the region by authority and appointment of the emperor, but this was still an appointment and could be easily be revoked. Pilate and Herod became friends on this occasion because Pilate showed Herod the courtesy of deferring to his rule and judgment (vv. 7–8). We might consider if it is significant that even during His trial and even among pagan, civil rulers, Jesus was still making peace.

Q **23:13–16 Are Herod and Pilate arguing after they had become friends?**

If they did argue after this occasion, it is not recorded here. In these verses, Pilate is arguing with the Jewish religious leaders that Jesus should be released because both he and Herod found no fault in Him. Pilate is appealing to Herod's agreement with his desire to release Jesus.

Q **23:15 Why didn't Herod find fault in Jesus—He was claiming to be "king" anyways?**

It was actually this Herod's father who couldn't stand the thought of someone else being king of the Jews (Mt 2). Herod heard many things about Jesus and even supposed that Jesus was John the Baptizer raised from the dead (Mt 14:1–2). There are at least two reasons why Herod doesn't find fault. One, when Jesus doesn't respond to any of the challenges, Herod may have thought they had the wrong man. Two, when Jesus refused to answer, Herod definitely thought the man before him was no one to waste any time with. Treating Jesus with contempt and mocking Him would surely not be possible, they would think, if Jesus were an important or powerful person.

Q **23:17 Where is v. 17 in ch. 23?**

V. 17 is a parenthetical or editorial statement and says, "Now he was obliged to release one man to them at the feast." Some ancient manuscripts include and others exclude this verse. Depending on which manuscripts a particular English translation uses, this verse may be missing. Either way, the verse is only confirming a practice of the governor that is mentioned elsewhere (Mt 27:15; Mk 15:6). There is no disagreement in the New Testament about this practice of releasing a prisoner.

• • • • • • • • • • • • • • • • • •

Q **23:21 Were the Jews who shouted "Crucify Him" the same ones who praised Jesus on Palm Sunday, or was this a different crowd entirely?**

We cannot say for certain that this crowd was different from the crowd who praised Jesus on Palm Sunday; crowds can be fickle (Lk 4:22, 28–29; Jn 6:15, 60, 66). There are two reasons for suspecting this was not the same crowd. First, this trial took place early in the morning within the city, rather than later in the day near the entrance to the city, where different people would be found. Second, there are indications in the text that this crowd was made up of religious rulers and others who were already opposed to Jesus and present during Jesus' trial before the high priest during the early morning hours (Mt 26:59; 17:1, 12).

• • • • • • • • • • • • • • • • • •

Q **23:22 Why are two others led with Him to be crucified?**

The short answer is because there were two other criminals due for crucifixion that day. The longer answer has two parts: (a) to fulfill a prophecy in Isaiah that the Savior would be "numbered with the transgressors" (Is 53:12) and (b) to provide a contrast and a witness to the power of the Gospel. While both other men who were crucified

began mocking Jesus (Mt 27:44), later one of these bandits came to repentance and faith in Jesus, demonstrated in his rebuke of the other criminal, his simple plea to Jesus, and Jesus' gracious response, "Today you will be with Me in Paradise" (Lk 23:39–43). We learn from the criminal who was saved that it is never too late to be saved, that salvation is realized immediately, and that the soul is always alive, going from here right away to heaven or hell. (The history of Lazarus and the rich man is evidence for the same, Lk 16:9–31.)

• • • • • • • • • • • • • • • • • •

Q **23:26 Why tell about Simon of Cyrene?**

Mark also includes how Simon was compelled to carry Jesus' cross (Mk 15:21). It is likely that Simon was compelled to carry Jesus' cross because Jesus was too weak (having been beaten) to continue the way to Golgotha. This may also be one of many occasions where Jesus' experience bears out His teaching—Simon did take up Jesus' cross and follow Him (Mk 8:34, Lk 9:23). As Simon was made to participate in the suffering of Christ, so we also participate in His suffering, according to the New Testament (2Co 1:5; Gal 6:2; Php 3:10; Col 1:24; Rv 6:9–11).

• • • • • • • • • • • • • • • • • •

Q **23:30 "They will begin to say to the mountains, 'Fall on us,' and to the hills, 'Cover us.'" What are the mountains and hills?**

Jesus is quoting Hos 10:8, where that prophet tells the wicked people of Israel about the judgment that is coming upon them. When the armies of Assyria came, the Israelites would be in such desperation and despair that they would cry out for the mountains and hills to cover them. This same cry for something to hide beneath is repeated by the wicked as they face Judgment Day in Rv 6:15–16. The people who were observing Jesus' crucifixion would experience what He was warning about in about forty years when the Roman army surrounded and destroyed Jerusalem (AD 70).

- -

Q 23:40–44 Is this the only Gospel where the robbers who were being crucified next to Jesus talked to Him?

Both Matthew and Mark record the two criminals taunting Jesus (Mt 27.44; Mk 15:32; Lk 23:39). Only Luke records that one of the criminals repented and was saved.

- -

Q 23:42–43 Are we to assume the thief has been baptized prior to his crucifixion? It sounds like this passage is saying we can still get to heaven without Baptism.

The thief could have been baptized previously, but we have no reason to suspect he was. The sacrament of Baptism saves because the Word and promises of God joined with the water save. Baptism is an extraordinary gift of God, providing the additional confirmation of grace through the application of the physical element, water. But where there is no opportunity to apply the sacrament, the Word of God remains effective and saves. Jesus' conversations recorded in the Gospel of John make clear that it is the Word of God that we must be immersed or awash in since it is the Word and Spirit of God that regenerates us, thus making us children of God who endure forever, just like the Word that regenerated us (Jn 1:11–12; 3:1–7; 4:1–26; 6:27–66; 8:31–32; 10:27–28; 15:1–7). The ceremony of Baptism, like the Lord's Supper, includes a physical sign with the Word in order to confirm that the promises of God have applied and still apply to the individual. Notice that the visible, physical body and voice of Jesus was with the thief all the way until he entered paradise that very day.

- -

Q 23:43 What does Jesus mean when He uses the word "Paradise"? How can this be if Jesus must descend to hell and then return to earth and then finally ascend to heaven?

First, there cannot be any contradiction in what Jesus or the Bible says. Second, paradise is a state of being more than a physical place. Language about hell being below and heaven being above is used to give us a reference for understanding. When Jesus ascended into heaven, how far up did He go before arriving (and where is "up" once you leave the earth as a reference point)? The moment that the body of Jesus or the thief or any other faithful person dies, the soul experiences paradise immediately (Lk 16:22–23). Third, Jesus did not descend into hell in order to suffer there. Jesus endured all condemnation for all sin on the cross; therefore, He declared at His death, "It is finished" (Jn 19:30). Jesus was still in the state of paradise when He descended into hell, like victors in war celebrate as they parade through the capital of their enemy. The presence of Jesus in paradise was not altered by His descent into hell, His bodily resurrection, or His bodily ascension.

Q **23:44 How could the sun have stopped shining for three hours and not scare everyone into going indoors?**

This verse does not say that the sun stopped shining, unless you have an English translation that has taken some real liberties here. Luke recorded that there was darkness over the land from noon until three in the afternoon, and this has some relationship to the sun "failing" or "being darkened," depending on how we understand the grammar, how we translate, and which manuscript tradition we use. Certainly God has and can make it dark when He wants, so dark you can't see anything (Ex 10:21–22; 14:19–20). I have seen many a Good Friday dark with thick clouds. Whether by thick cloud cover or by some other extraordinary means, preventing the sun from shining would not be a problem for the Creator. If people were not scared into going indoors, perhaps this is an argument for thick cloud

cover, noticeable and making a point, but not completely beyond human experience? For further discussion of this, see *From Abraham to Paul: A Biblical Chronology* by Andrew E. Steinmann.

Q **23:44–49 When Jesus dies, the curtain is torn in two and there is darkness over the land. I have heard it said that the dead also rose. Is there anything stated like this in the Bible?**

Mt 27:51–53 records what you are referring to as follows: "And behold, the curtain of the temple was torn in two, from top to bottom. And the earth shook, and the rocks were split. The tombs also were opened. And many bodies of the saints who had fallen asleep were raised, and coming out of the tombs after His resurrection they went into the holy city and appeared to many."

Q **23:47 Why doesn't Luke say "truly this was the Son of God" as Matthew and Mark do?**

The similarities between the Gospels exist because they are recording the same history. The differences between the Gospels exist because the Holy Spirit and the particularities of the Gospel and its writer directed the addition or omission of certain accounts or details. As you mention, both Matthew and Mark record the centurion declaring that Jesus was the Son of God, which was a point to emphasize for the Jews of Jerusalem and for the Gentiles of the world who would deny or at least question it (Mt 27:54; Mk 15:39). With two Gospels already confirming the statement of the centurion, Luke wanted to include something else the centurion said, "Certainly this man was innocent!" It is just as important to us that Jesus is a true man who kept the Law for us perfectly as it is to know that He is true God who kept the Law for all of us for all time (Rm 5:12–21; 2Co 5:21; Heb 2:9).

Q 23:48 When the witnesses of the crucifixion beat their breasts, was it to signify sorrow?

If the proclamation of the centurion sets the tone, these people beat their breasts for grief. The only other occurrence of this word for "beat" with this word for "breast" occurs in Lk 18:13, where the penitent tax collector beats his breast from grief.

Q 23:50–53 Who was the Joseph that buried Christ?

Luke tells us he was a member of the council and a good man, he had not consented to their actions in condemning Jesus, he was from Arimathea, he was waiting for the kingdom of God, and he went to Pilate and asked for the body of Jesus. Matthew adds that he was rich and that the new tomb in which he laid Jesus was his own (Mt 27:57, 60). John adds that Joseph was a disciple of Jesus secretly, for fear of the Jews (Jn 19:38).

Q 24:1 How come the resurrection accounts all seem to differ in who came first?

The similarities between the Gospels exist because they are recording the same history. The differences between the Gospels exist because the Holy Spirit and the particularities of the Gospel and its writer directed the addition or omission of certain accounts or details. In fact, if you put the four Gospel accounts next to each other they are very close. First, Mary and friends came to the tomb early in the morning, then Mary ran to tell the disciples, then Peter and John ran to the tomb, and then Mary returned to the tomb where Jesus met her (Mt 28:1ff.; Mk 16:1ff.; Lk 24:1ff.; Jn 20:1ff.).

Q 24:4–8 Why does it say here that there are two men and in the other Gospels it says one man?

Consider what we learn if we compare the Gospel accounts in the order they were written. Matthew said an angel came down, rolled away the stone, and then sat upon it (Mt 28:2). Five years later, Mark added that when the women looked in the tomb they saw a young man who spoke to them (Mk 16:5). Five years after that, Luke wrote that the women looked in the tomb and saw two men who spoke to them (Lk 24:4). Almost forty years after Luke wrote the Gospel, John skipped any mention of other women or entering the tomb or angels, but simply records that Mary saw the open tomb and ran to tell the disciples (Jn 20:1–2).

Q 24:10 What is the significance of Joanna?

She is a witness to the resurrection of Jesus, just like the other women. Luke mentioned that she was the wife of a steward of Herod (Lk 8:3).

Q 24:16 Why didn't they recognize Jesus?

The text says, "Their eyes were kept from recognizing Him." The text does not say whether it was lack of faith that kept them from seeing or whether it was Jesus who kept them from seeing so that He could have the conversation they needed.

Q 24:19 Was the assumption of many of Jesus' followers that He was first a prophet?

Everyone recognized Jesus as a rabbi because He had disciples and taught (Jn 1:38). Many recognized Jesus as a prophet because He spoke the truth in public and because He predicted the future (Mt 16:14; 21:11). Still others thought that "The Prophet" that Moses had prophesied about was going to be a different person than the Messiah—and thought Jesus was this prophet (Dt 18:15; Jn 1:21).

Q 24:22 What is meant by, "Moreover, some women of our company amazed us?"

Cleopas was referring to the report of Mary that she and other women went to the tomb, that they found the stone rolled away and the body of Jesus missing, and that angels had spoken with them about His resurrection from the dead (Lk 24:23; see also Mk 16:11).

Q 24:31 Why does He not stay with them?

At this time, Jesus did not stay because He was returning to Jerusalem in order to appear to the eleven disciples who were gathered together (Lk 24:33–36). I don't know of any text that reports Jesus staying anywhere with anyone for long. Perhaps this has something to do with being risen from the dead; He doesn't need a place to stay but appears to His followers when and where He will in order to benefit them. After Pentecost, the apostles will speak and write the Word of the Lord so that it can be with us all at all times (Jn 14:26; 20:30–31).

Q 24:45 Did Jesus' followers know in advance that He was coming, or did He show up and God inspired them to let Him in?

This question sounds like it is about Jesus coming into the midst of the disciples who met behind locked doors (Jn 20:19,

26). The apostles did not open the doors for Jesus; He simply appeared in the midst of them. V. 45 refers to Jesus opening the understanding of the apostles so they might comprehend the Scriptures. Jesus is God, and Jesus is the one who made it possible for them to believe, as is the case for all of us (1Co 2:14; Rm 10:17).

John

Q **1:1–2 Is this proof of the Trinity?**

Yes, along with Gn 1:1–3, 26; Mt 28:19; and 1Jn 5:7.

Q **1:1–7 What sets John apart from the other Gospels? Why do we study him last? (Note: In my New Testament class, we study the books by author and date of writing; thus, John is studied last.)**

Our course looks at the Gospel of John last because it was the last book of the New Testament to be written. While John's Gospel does report the life of Jesus in chronological order, the existence of the other three Gospels allows John to focus on topics and especially significant occasions. For example, John begins the Gospel with creation and ends with promises of life everlasting; thus, John's Gospel includes everything. John focuses on topics such as regeneration (ch. 3), living water (ch. 4), the bread of life (ch. 6), the Good Shepherd (ch. 10), vines and branches (ch. 15), Maundy Thursday evening (chs. 13–17), and the High Priestly Prayer (ch. 17).

Q **1:4–9 Is it significant that the word *light* appears seven times in this section?**

There are many physical realities that God created in order to teach the truth about Himself and His relationship with us; therefore, many terms occur with greater frequency in John's Gospel than anywhere else. The word *remain* occurs 118

281

times in the New Testament—40 of those are in this Gospel. John records Jesus' focus on concepts such as living water, living bread, shepherds, vines, light, and love.

Q 1:5 What does it mean that "the darkness has not overcome" the light?

The word translated "overcome" is also translated as "understood" or "comprehended." While the exact meaning of this word is difficult to know, the idea is that the darkness neither understands nor is able to overcome the light—the light referring to Jesus Christ, the way, the truth, and the life (Jn 14:6).

Q 1:26 Why does John say, "Among you stands one," when Jesus is not yet there?

John does not mean that Jesus is "right there between those two people." Rather, John is saying that the promised Messiah has come, the Son of God in the flesh. He lives and moves and "stands" among you. Jesus was an adult at this time, only six months younger than John the Baptist (Lk 1:24–26). Jesus had also already been baptized by John, which means He had already overcome the devil's temptations in the wilderness and begun His public ministry (notice the past tense John uses of Jesus' Baptism in 1:30–34).

Q 2:1–11 What is the significance of Jesus turning water into wine?

Any time water becomes wine, it is only because of God's creation; grapes are the means by which water takes on the other properties necessary to become wine. Jesus changed water into wine because He is God, loving and omnipotent. The miracles that Jesus did verify His person (true God) and His teaching (God provides for His creation in every way, especially for our redemption). Jesus provides for this wedding in Cana as one of many indications that even the smallest of human affairs are not beneath His care.

Q 2:3–10 It says that they usually bring out the cheaper wine after they've had too much to drink, so if they're "drunk" then why do they need more wine?

Why does anyone need more food or wine or material things than necessary for health and life (Lk 12:1–15)? Human nature was created by God to be in communion with God, who is infinite. Fallen human nature seeks to replace an infinite God with His finite creation, which cannot be done (Rm 1:20–32). People get drunk because there is more of their lives from which they want to escape than for which to remain fully conscious; they are trying to forget rather than celebrate and remember.

Q **2:3–4 Jesus appears to talk harshly to His mother, calling her "woman." Why would He do this, and what was Mary asking for?**

Mary was not asking her Son for more wine in order to relieve the shortage at the wedding. Mary was addressing the Son of God with a relatively trivial matter of human convenience. Since Mary spoke to God, God answered her appropriately with the term "woman" and the question "What does this have to do with Me?" This lesson brings into focus the purpose of prayer and the issue of our will in contrast to God's. Nevertheless, God is love and demonstrates His patience and kindness by producing an abundance of the very best wine (Is 25:6–8). Jesus indicates His proper work of redeeming us from every form of shame and embarrassment due to our failure, even small failures having to do with a shortage of wine. Jesus indicates His nature as the Bridegroom of His Bride, the Church, and points forward to the continual feast of the Gospel, the Lord's Supper, and His eternal kingdom (Mt 22:1–13; Eph 5:25–32; Rv 19:7–9).

Q **2:6 Why did Jesus need ceremonial washing?**

At this point, John is simply explaining why there was so much water so close at hand. The Bible records real history, meaning that God works in real history, using the elements and circumstances that are

Why did Jesus need ceremonial washing?

present. Jesus did not need any ceremonial washing, but He might have observed this custom as an obedient member of His community (Lk 2:51–52).

Q **2:23 Did the people believe in Jesus only because of the miracles He was performing?**

Miracles do not create or sustain faith, as the whole history of God's miraculous activity among people proves (Lk 16:27–31). The purpose of miracles is to authenticate the truth and those who truly serve as messengers of God's truth (Mk 16:17–20; Jn 21:25; 2Pt 1:16–21; 1Jn 1:1–7).

Q **3:1–8 To whom is John writing? What does the Greek say in these verses, particularly the phrase "born again"?**

The Greek text does not use the phrase "born again." The word *born* in the New Testament always means a physical birth of a baby (Mt 1:21). The word John uses here in the Greek text is "begotten," which refers to conception but includes the whole process of human procreation, including birth. The word translated "again" actually means "from above." This term, like "begotten," includes doing something again, but the point is doing it in a completely different way—in

283

this case, because God is the one doing the begetting, rather than man. The fact is, unless the Word of God regenerates or begets us from above, we have no spiritual or enduring life. John is writing to everyone who would ever live.

Q 3:8 What is the "wind" that blows wherever it wishes? Why does Jesus compare people "born of the Spirit" to wind?

The Hebrew and Greek word for "wind" also means "breath" and "spirit." The Holy Spirit comes with the Word and produces what God's Word describes, including our regeneration. We can hear the Holy Spirit by means of the Word ("its sound"), but the Spirit of God is invisible and mysterious, as God and much of His creation is, though still the most powerful of forces. We don't know when God will begin His work of regeneration in a person or when God will complete that work, but wherever the Word of God is active, we know God's Spirit and regenerate souls are there (Is 55).

Q 3:9–12 Does Nicodemus understand? Are we as humans capable of understanding completely the Word of God?

None of us would be prudent in claiming that we completely understand what God communicates to us (1Co 8:2–3; 13:12; Jb 40:1–42:6). There is reason to believe that Nicodemus did understand some of what Jesus taught, since he demonstrates

devotion to Jesus at the end of the Gospel (Jn 7:50; 19:39).

Q 3:16 I see this verse in many places, especially on signs at sporting events. Why do people choose this verse to share?

People like this verse because it is short and clear. This verse declares plainly that God loves the world, that He gave His only Son to save it, and that we are saved through faith. Unfortunately, fallen human nature wants to change faith into something we do in order to save ourselves.

Q 3:25–36 Is John explaining that it is okay for another man to baptize?

The other man that the disciples of John are referring to is Jesus. John is urging his disciples to remember that their commitment should be to the Christ for whom John came to prepare the way. John is the friend of the Bridegroom; Jesus is the Bridegroom. You may note that despite these efforts, there continued to be men who insisted on idolizing John rather than following the Lord Himself (Mt 9:14; Ac 19:1–6).

Q 3:29 If Jesus is the Bridegroom, would John the Baptist be the best man?

Jesus is the Bridegroom, John is the friend, and all believers as a group are the Bride. Like a best man, John was a witness to Christ.

Q **3:31 Why does John repeat himself?**

Most of the time, repetition is intended to promote learning and memory and to provide emphasis (Php 3:1).

Q **4:17–18 Why does Jesus say she has no husband but five husbands? Why is that important?**

The woman said that she had no husband, meaning not at the moment. Jesus demonstrates His divine nature by exposing that she has already had five husbands and is now in an immoral relationship with another man. The woman, like all fallen human nature, is trying desperately to avoid the truth, as if doing so would make for her the life she longs for (Jn 3:19–20). Jesus demonstrates that His interest in the truth is in order that He might provide the remedy for our fallen condition—as the woman comes to realize (1Jn 1:8–9).

Q **5:15 Did the lame man tell others about Jesus because he thought it was the right thing to do?**

The man told the Jews that it was Jesus who healed him because he wanted it to be Jesus' fault that he, the man, broke the Sabbath (vv. 10–11). Contrast this with the blind man's defense of Jesus in Jn 9:1–41. Not everyone talks about Jesus for the right reasons (Php 1:15).

Why do we praise God?

Q **5:41 Jesus said that He does not "receive glory from people." Why, then, do we sing and praise God?**

Jesus said that He does not receive "glory" from men (not "honor" or "praise" as some translations mistakenly say). Jesus means that the incomparable and magnificent truth about Him *is* the truth because He *is* the Son of God. This glory is vastly different from the glory that people try to produce for themselves by impressing the ignorant (Jn 5:44; Ac 8:9–24; 13:8–11; 19:11–19). *Glory* means to be or do what no one else can or would do. Notice how it is correct that all the glory belongs to God (Gal 1:5; 2Tm 4:18). *Praise* means to report or describe the wonderful things that God has done for our life and salvation (notice how this does glorify God, but we benefit from being reminded of His acts for us as we recount those acts to each other; see Ps 78:4).

Q **6:1–31 Why didn't these followers of Jesus react to the miracle of the bread? They forgot the next day? They ask what signs will be given so that they can believe. But what about all the miracles Jesus has already done? How did they miss those?**

Immediately after Jesus fed them, the people wanted to make Him king by force (Jn 6:15). The people reacted the next morning by seeking Jesus out and wondering how He had crossed the sea without a boat (Jn 6:22–25). Finally, when Jesus asked them why they seek bread that perishes, they turned against Him (Jn 6:30–31, 52, 60, 66). Opposing God and refusing to recognize the truth make it impossible to remember what we should (Rm 1:20–32).

Miracles do not create faith. Miracles authenticate the person and teaching of the one doing them, as with Jesus and the apostles. This authentication tells us where to find the truth and Spirit of God that do create and sustain faith.

· ·

Q 6:16–21 Why doesn't John mention the fact that Peter tried to walk on water after Jesus did?

Matthew is the only Gospel that records Peter walking on the water and then sinking because of unbelief (Mt 14:23–33). Luke does not record this narrative at all. Mark and John record Jesus walking on the water but not Peter (Mk 6:45–52; Jn 6:15–21). It is likely that Matthew's account of Peter's failure is informative and, for Peter, humiliating enough.

· ·

Q 6:44 Does this verse refer to the elect?

This verse is about how a person is saved rather than who is saved. Predestination tells us that anyone who is drawn to the Father is so because God has predestined him or her (Rm 8:29–30). This verse ex-

plains that it is impossible for fallen human nature to come to God; other passages report why this is so (Rm 5:6–10; Eph 2:1–3).

· ·

Q 6:53–58 Is this referring to the Lord's Supper?

This is referring to the communion of God and a person who remains in God's Word (Jn 8:31–32; 15:1–7). The Word of God joined with a physical element is what makes a Sacrament. These words of Christ are the basis and source of the Lord's Supper since the very body and blood of Jesus are communicated to us in the Word always, as well as in the Lord's Supper with bread and wine.

· ·

Q 6:64 What does this verse have to say about predestination? It sounds a lot like double predestination.

There is a fundamental difference between foreknowledge and predestination. The Bible never talks about predestination except in positive terms; God predestines those who will be saved (Rm 8:29–30; Eph 1:3–5). It would seem logically impossible for an omniscient God to be ignorant of anything that would ever be, but God's foreknowledge of our lives does not determine the choices He makes, except to redeem us all (Mt 13:44; Jn 3:16; 2Co 5:19).

Q 7:30 Why could no one touch Jesus?

John's Gospel emphasizes the fact that God alone is in control of His creation so that all things are ordered as the redemptive work of Christ requires them to be (Rm 8:28). John uses the word *hour* twenty-five times, drawing our attention to the climax of Jesus' redemptive work in His arrest, trial, and crucifixion (Jn 12:27). No one can do anything unless God wants them to (Jn 6:44; 19:11; Dn 4:35).

Q 7:53–8:11 My Bible notes that these verses were not in the earliest manuscripts. Why are they included now?

There are more than ten thousand ancient manuscripts of the Greek New Testament. While many of the manuscripts that appear to be the oldest do not include this passage, so many other reliable manuscripts do include it that the translators of other English versions of the Bible considered it authentic and included it. Notice that this section does not teach anything or make any point that is not made in many other places (Lk 10:40–41).

Q 8:3–11 Why was this woman set up to be caught?

Bearing false witness against another person is such a problem for fallen human beings that God devoted one of the Ten Commandments to it. The whole history of the world is full of examples where an un-suspecting person is exposed to judgment and death so that those who are wicked might create a means to escape rejection or condemnation (2Sm 11:14–17; Dn 6:1–24; Jn 12:9–11). Fallen, selfish, proud human nature is deluded in thinking that being better than others (especially by making false witness against them) is a substitute for being perfect (Mt 5:17–48; Lk 18:9–14; Rm 2:1–24; 1Co 1:10–31).

> What can set us free?

Q 8:31–32 What is the truth, exactly, that can set us free?

Truth is the accurate description and understanding of reality, the way things really are. All truth sets us free from ignorance, mistaken notions, or vain contradiction that would undermine our lives. The truth is, for example, that our lives are entirely dependent on God, who provides for us superabundantly (Mt 6:24–34). The truth is that being honest about our dependence on God keeps us aware of all the good He does for us in all circumstances, especially the most difficult; therefore, we can be free of worry or fear (Rm 8:28; Is 55:1–11). The truth is that God has designed us for life and prepared a life for us. This life is obtained by giving ours in the service of others. This life of giving is possible because we are loved. God's beloved people live to give away what God has already given to us rather than living to get something we lack (Eph 2:8–10; Jn 13:3–17; 1Jn 4:19).

Q 8:48 Why did the Jews state Jesus was demon-possessed and a Samaritan?

Whenever anyone realizes he is wrong and in danger of being humiliated for advocating what is wrong so adamantly, the only possible means of escaping humiliation, in his mind, is to hurl insults (Jn 9:24–34; Ac 21:26–22:24).

Q 9:1–38 Why did Jesus heal the blind man in ch. 9, but not say, "Sin no more"? Was this man righteous already?

Jesus told the lame man and the woman caught in adultery to "sin no more" because the trouble they experienced was a direct, immediate, unmistakable, and lasting result of a particular action (Jn 5:14; 8:11). The blind man was not without sin, but his blindness was not a result of any mistake on his part, nor was the man contending any self-righteousness (Jn 9:1–3, 29–38).

Q 10:17 Is the reason God loves Christ because He sacrifices Himself? What about God's unconditional love?

This word for *love* means "to sacrifice everything for the object of that love." The relationship between the persons of the Trinity is bound to have a different nature than the relationship between God and us. God did sacrifice everything for the sake of His Son. God the Father not only sacrificed His Son but also condemned and punished Him in our stead (Is 53:10–12). The Father

sacrificed His own comfort and joy in communion with the Son in order that the Son might do what is God's nature—to love and redeem us (Jn 12:23–33; 13:27–32).

Q 11:2 Is this Mary Magdalene?

Yes, confirmed by the following passages: Lk 7:36–50; 10:38–42; Jn 8:3–11; 11:2; 12:1–8; 20:1–18.

Q 11:14–17 Where did Lazarus's soul go for four days?

Lazarus would have been in heaven, which suggests that Jesus may have wept at the thought of bringing him back by raising his body from the dead (Jn 11:35; Lk 16:19–31; 23:39–43). See Jn 11:35 below.

Q 11:16 What does Thomas mean when he says to the disciples, "Let us also go, that we may die with him"?

The simplest explanation is that Thomas thought Jesus was going to die somehow and join Lazarus—a path that Thomas wanted to follow Jesus upon (Mt 14:28–30; 20:22; Mk 14:29–31).

Q 11:35 Why does Jesus cry at Lazarus's death?

Jesus was not weeping because Lazarus was dead, since Jesus knew that Lazarus was in heaven. Jesus wept because of the unbelief of the people, which is what made it necessary for Jesus to bring Lazarus back from heaven by raising his body (Jn 11:21, 32–33, 37–38). I don't know of any text that explains the special relationship between Jesus and Lazarus.

Q 11:45–57 Didn't the council hold enough sway that they could just take Jesus by force?

People had tried to take Jesus by force already and failed (Lk 4:28–30; Jn 8:59). The council was also afraid of arresting Jesus in public because He was popular with the people (Mt 26:3–5). A third reason why the council could not take Jesus by force is because Jesus, not men, is the one in control of all things (Jn 7:30; 18:4–9).

Q 12:25 What does Jesus mean in this verse?

Understanding what the Bible says depends on remembering our composition as human beings, made in the image of God. If we are one dimensional, only the person we feed and dress, then nothing in the Bible makes sense. On the other hand, if we remember that our physical nature is only the "tent" within which our essential nature (our soul) dwells, then what Jesus said here makes perfect sense (2Co 4:1–5:21; Gal 5:16–26). Aware of this, consider an enhanced translation: "He who sacrifices everything for the desires of his flesh in this material world will lose his eternal soul and its life forever, but he who sacrifices nothing for the desires of his flesh in this material world will keep his eternal soul for eternal life."

Q 12:39–40 If the Jews could not believe, how could they be held accountable?

The passage from Isaiah expresses the judgment of God against those who refused to believe by stubbornly opposing so many witnesses to the truth for so long that now it has become impossible for them to be otherwise. Severe threats like these are the last and most powerful means by which a person determined to self-destruct might be turned back into the way of life (Heb 6:4–8; 10:26–31).

Q 13:2 Why does the devil prompt Judas?

Ever since the devil failed to overcome Jesus with temptation, he has been looking for another way to destroy the Savior (Lk 4:13). The hypocrisy of Judas revealed to the devil that there was no Spirit of God in Judas's soul; therefore, Judas was completely vulnerable to being inspired by the devil to betray Jesus (Jn 12:4–6; Mt 12:43–45). Jesus, as the Son of God, had always known that Judas would betray Him, as is evident in the psalms (109:1–20).

Why does Jesus cry at Lazarus's death?

Q 13:4 Why did Jesus take off His outer clothing?

Clothes were hard to come by in these times and means of washing them were scarce, so men usually took off their outer clothing when they worked (Jn 21:7).

Q 13:5 Why would Jesus wash the disciples' feet?

Jesus explains why He washed their feet in vv. 12–17. When Jesus spoke of washing the disciples, He meant that unless they were regenerated by Him and immersed in His Word and Spirit, they would be apart from Him (Jn 3:1–7; 8:31–32; 15:1–7; 1Jn 1:7). Jesus redeemed the whole world, not just those who were positively disposed toward Him; otherwise what would we do if we found ourselves with a negative disposition, even for a moment? Jesus redeemed everyone, and His washing of the disciples' feet and communing with them demonstrates His universal love and atoning work (Lk 22:21–22; Rm 5:6–10).

Q 13:10 What is the meaning of this passage?

Jesus is exposing the difference between physical and spiritual cleanliness. Just as a person who has bathed need only wash his feet after walking somewhere, so also a person immersed in the Word and regenerated by the Spirit has been redeemed and may be at peace under the ready application of the forgiveness Christ has supplied (Jn 15:1–7; 1Jn 1:8–9).

Q 13:18 What does Jesus mean when He says, "He who ate My bread has lifted his heel against Me"?

Jesus was quoting a psalm that described the nature of betrayal; a person close to Him would be His most vicious opponent (Ps 41:9; Lk 22:48). Psalm 41 prophesied the betrayal of Judas in particular.

Q 13:18–30 Why didn't the disciples understand what Jesus said to Judas?

When you know the whole story, it is easier to see what was developing when you look back along the way. Who had ever been in such a circumstance before, by which to have any understanding of what was going on? The disciples had trouble understanding Jesus most of the time. The idea that Jesus would not only allow but direct the timing of His own betrayal was surely incomprehensible to them (Mt 16:6–12; Mk 4:13; Lk 9:45; Jn 3:10; 8:27; 10:6; 12:16).

Q 13:26–27 Do you think the other disciples believed Jesus when he said Judas was going to betray Him?

Verse 28 reports that the disciples did not know what Jesus was talking about.

Q **13:27 Why did Jesus tell Judas to do what he was about to do quickly?**

The word "quickly" is not primarily about speed but about accomplishing something right away without distraction or delay because it is important (Mt 28:7; Lk 15:22; Jas 1:19). The time for Jesus to endure the full force of His condemnation in our place was upon Him, and He wanted it to be fulfilled, just as His Word had always promised (Jn 12:27; 13:1).

Q **13:33 What is Jesus saying in this verse?**

Where Jesus is about to go is through the condemnation of all humankind for all sins of all time under the Law and wrath of God in our place (Is 53:3–11). No one could or would take this path except the Son of God who is also the Son of Man (Mk 14:27–31, 38).

Q **14:1–8 Why doesn't it seem like the disciples understand Jesus, even after all His preaching?**

Please see answer at 13:18–30 above.

Q **14:6 What about other religions that believe their way is the only way?**

Every other religion teaches that each person is responsible to save himself or herself, more or less. As long as even the smallest fraction of our salvation depends on us,

> ## Why didn't the disciples understand what Jesus said to Judas?

our hope is lost. The only way for us to live and not die is to have our lives redeemed by God Himself, which is why Jesus' statement is not proud but the simple truth (Gal 1:6–7; Rm 4:16).

Q **14:15 What does this mean?**

Jesus is stating a fact: "Any time a person is of a nature to sacrifice everything for the sake of Christ, he or she will definitely hold on to what He has commanded." Notice the expression "keep" or "hold on to" rather than "obey." Holding on to the Word—that is, remaining in the Word—is what produces obedience to God (1Co 15:10). Remember that the foremost of all Jesus' commands is that we remain in His Word (Dt 6:4–9; Jn 8:31–32).

Q **15:7 Is it true that we can have whatever we want?**

Please note carefully the condition stated at the beginning of the verse: "If you abide in Me, and My words abide in you." The Word of God regenerates us in the image of Christ and gives us the same mind and will as Christ (Php 2:5). Remaining in His Word means that Christ also remains in us and informs our prayers so that they are always consistent with what God means to give or accomplish anyway.

Q 15:18 What is meant by "the world"?

When Jesus refers to "the world," He means all of the people who are of the world and contrary to Him, His goodwill, and His gracious kingdom (Jn 8:43–47; 10:26–27; Eph 2:1–3).

Q 16:8 What does the word *convict* mean in this verse?

The word *convict* means to demonstrate or prove that something is true of someone—incontrovertibly.

Q 16:23–28 Is Jesus saying that whatever we pray for will be given to us?

Jesus is talking about prayer here (see also Jn 15:7 above). Notice in v. 23 the all-important condition "in My name." The expression "in My name" means "according to the Word of God and all that it teaches us about the nature and will of God." Thus, it makes perfect sense that if we ask anything because the Spirit of God inspires us to seek it, God is surely going to respond positively.

Q 17:1–26 Why would Jesus pray? Why do we recite the Lord's Prayer in church instead of this prayer?

Why would Jesus pray?

Jesus prayed often, just as any son might communicate often with his father. The timing of this prayer is significant because it gives us insight into the mind of Christ when He faced the full force of what it meant to redeem the world. One of the ways we can have and keep the mind of Christ, as Paul urges us to do, is to keep this prayer of Jesus in our consciousness (Php 2:5–11). If you read this prayer carefully, you will notice that it is an expanded version of the prayer Jesus taught His disciples (Mt 6:9–13). Why we don't pray this in church is probably an extension of why we don't pray it daily in our own lives or do much of anything else the Bible plainly advocates for our good. But we could begin to change that, starting right now.

Q 17:5 What does Jesus mean by this request?

Jesus, when He said this, had entered the sequence of events that would climax in His crucifixion the next day. *Glory* means to do what no one else could or would do. Jesus is asking God, His Father, now to accomplish the extraordinary and unparalleled redemption of the whole world—an accomplishment that was made possible because Jesus is true God and possessed this nature and ability from eternity.

Q 17:12 Who is "the son of destruction"?

"The son of destruction" or "the son of perdition" is referring to Judas Iscariot (see

Ps 109). Judas certainly acts against Christ, as many did and still do; but he is not likely the "antichrist" predicted in other places in the New Testament (2Th 2:1–12; 1Jn 2:18–19; Rv 13:1–10).

● ● ● ● ● ● ● ● ● ● ● ● ● ● ● ● ● ● ●

Q **18:1–11 Why doesn't John mention anything about Judas betraying Jesus with a kiss?**

Anytime any Gospel writer does not mention something another did, it is bound to be for the same reason: a Gospel already mentioned it. The Gospels of Matthew, Mark, and Luke had been around for decades when John wrote his, which means he had plenty of time to consider what needed to be repeated and what needed to be included for the sake of emphasis. John's Gospel records more of the interaction between Jesus and those who came to arrest Him—further demonstration of the divine nature of Jesus, the insanity of those who would arrest Him, and His constant care for those who trust in Him.

● ● ● ● ● ● ● ● ● ● ● ● ● ● ● ● ● ● ●

Q **18:5–6 Why was John the only one to record the men falling backward? Why did the soldiers draw back and fall to the ground?**

John's first letter and Gospel are very concentrated on proving the divine nature of Jesus (Jn 1:1–3; 1Jn 1:1–2). John highlights not only the divinity of Jesus but also the ridiculousness of those who thought they were arresting Him. He also high-lights the care of Jesus for His followers as He directs His assailants to let the apostles go free. The physics of why the assailants of Jesus fell down would be a matter of speculation. What we do know is that they fell down when Jesus declared the truth of His identity, "I AM" (the name of the Lord, a form of the verb "to be" in Hebrew; Ex 3:14).

● ● ● ● ● ● ● ● ● ● ● ● ● ● ● ● ● ● ●

Q **18:11 What does Jesus mean by "shall I not drink the cup" when He responds to Simon Peter's cutting off of someone's ear during the arrest?**

The "cup" that Jesus is about to drink refers to the condemnation of the Law, which He endured in place of all people (2Co 5:21; Mt 20:23; 26:39). Peter drew his sword and used it as if he could use force to prevent Jesus from being arrested and crucified—which would have prevented the very work of Jesus that provided forgiveness for all of Peter's failings.

● ● ● ● ● ● ● ● ● ● ● ● ● ● ● ● ● ● ●

Q **18:13 Who was Annas that he could judge Jesus? What legal authority did he have?**

According to Lk 3:2 and Ac 4:6, Annas and Caiaphas shared the high priesthood. Annas had no legal authority to have anyone executed, but he could have a person condemned for religious reasons and then request (or demand) that the Romans execute the person so condemned (Jn 18:28–32).

Q **18:38 Why is this passage recorded only in the Gospel of John?**

Each of the Gospels contains unique material, which is how they give us a more complete picture of the life of Jesus. John's Gospel provides a focus on several key concepts, truth being one of them. The word *truth* occurs twenty-eight times in the Gospel of John but only three times in the other Gospels combined (Jn 1:14, 17; 4:23; 8:32; 14:6, 17; 17:17; cf. Mt 22:16; Mk 5:33; Lk 4:25).

Q **19:1 Why does Pilate have Jesus flogged if he sees no reason for a charge?**

Pilate was hoping that the beating and humiliation of Jesus would satisfy the jealousy of the Jews so they would let Pilate release Him (Mt 27:18; Lk 23:13–23; Jn 18:38–39; 19:6, 12–16).

Q **19:18 Why were there two others crucified with Jesus?**

Two others were crucified with Jesus because they were due to be executed on that day. This fulfilled a prophecy that said the Savior would be executed with criminals, as if Jesus were actually a criminal Himself (Is 53:9; 2Co 5:21). The crucifixion between these two criminals highlights the fact that Jesus is Immanuel ("God with us") and reveals the difference between the impenitent and the penitent in relation to the substitutionary work of Christ on behalf of both (Lk 23:39–43).

Q **19:26–27 How could relatives of Jesus not believe that He is the Son of God?**

All fallen human nature is incapable of believing the truth about God (1Co 2:14). Jesus once mentioned the old saying that "a prophet is not without honor except in his hometown and in his own household" (Mt 13:57; see also Lk 4:24). Jesus' family always struggled to accept His true nature, as do people throughout the world and time (Mk 3:21; Jn 7:5; Ps 69:8; Mi 7:6).

Q **19:27 Why did Jesus give care of his mother to John? Did Jesus care for her before He was crucified?**

Besides being the Son of God who sustains the lives of all people, Jesus was the eldest son of Mary and did bear responsibility for her. The magnitude of Jesus' love and responsibility is demonstrated by the fact that even in His agony and last hours, He was aware of and attentive to the well-being of His mother.

Q **20:14 Why didn't Mary Magdalene recognize Jesus when she saw Him?**

Jesus was capable of and sometimes did hide Himself from people (Lk 4:30; 24:16). Jesus was an average-looking man (Is 53:2) and the reality of His resurrection from the dead was so foreign to these people that their sorrow, disappointment, and unbelief kept them from recognizing Jesus (Jn 21:1–14; Ac 12:12–16).

. . . .

Q 21:15–17 What is the significance of Jesus asking Simon Peter this question three times?

Things that have to do with God tend to come three at a time (Is 6:3; Mt 28:19; 1Jn 5:6–8). English translations do not indicate that Jesus and Peter were using different words for "love." Jesus asked Peter if Peter would lay down his life for Jesus. Peter answered that Jesus knew Peter was His friend. This exchange was repeated. The third time Jesus asked Peter if Peter was His friend. Peter was grieved, not only because asking a third time would bring back memories of the denial but also because Jesus seems to question whether Peter even loves Jesus enough to be a friend. Jesus is stressing that our ability to love or befriend is not what our life or the lives of others depend on. Communicating the truth and grace of God through His Word (feeding and tending the sheep) is what our lives depend on and is as dependable as Jesus' resurrection from the dead (1Pt 1:3).

. . . .

Q 21:20 Who is the disciple whom Jesus loved? Why is Peter concerned with what will happen to John?

This is John the apostle, the brother of James and a son of Zebedee (Mt. 10:2). John

Who is the disciple whom Jesus loved?

refers to himself this way because he is confessing that the significance of his identity comes from Jesus' love for him, not from anything within himself. Judas had already taken his own life at this time. Jesus had just told Peter that he would die by execution (Jn 21:18–19). Naturally, Peter wants to know what will happen to John. Jesus reminds Peter that God's will for other people is His concern, not ours.

. . . .

Q 21:25 Why didn't John record the account of Jesus' ascension?

The simplest answer is because the Holy Spirit did not want him to. A second reason is because the other Gospels already include that account. A reason with greater explanation would be that John wanted to leave us thinking about the last words he wrote. When we think about the coming and going of Jesus and our own comings and goings, we often fall prey to comparing our lives with others and wondering why God does this or that for them. We do well to stay focused on our own relationship with Christ, which the Word of God abundantly provides for, as this last verse emphasizes.

Acts

Q **1:1 Who is Theophilus, and why does Luke choose to address his Gospel and this letter to him? Is the "first book" the Gospel of Luke?**

The name *Theophilus* is Greek and means "friend of God." Some people theorize that Luke made up this name so that anyone who desired to be a friend of God would understand that this writing was meant for him or her. Others believe that Theophilus was a real man who was of some importance since Luke addressed him with a title of respect, "most excellent" (Lk 1:3). I don't know of any evidence that would suggest more than this. There is no reason to think that this Theophilus is a different person than the one for whom Luke wrote the Gospel. Yes, the "first book" does refer to the Gospel of Luke.

Q **1:3 What kind of proof did Jesus show to convince others that He was alive? Why does Jesus stay with the disciples for forty days?**

Jesus appeared to the disciples for forty days for two reasons. First, this is consistent with many other occasions in history that had to do with life under the Law in this world: days of rain that fell on Noah and his ark; spies in Canaan; years wandering in the wilderness; days Jesus was tempted in the desert. Second, as in the other cases just mentioned, these are enough days to provide the many infallible proofs of Jesus' resurrection to which He is referring. Infallible proofs of Jesus' resurrection include appearing to many different people and numbers of people on different occasions (Jn 20:19–31; 1Co 15:3–8); His invitation that the apostles touch the place of the nail wounds in His

> ## What is the significance of Pentecost?

hands and spear piercing in His side; eating with them; and directing them to a miraculous catch of fish (Lk 24:36–43; Jn 21:4–14).

• •

Q 1:5 What is the significance of Pentecost and the Holy Spirit coming to the apostles? I thought that because they are believers they already had the Spirit breathed into them. When it's written about Baptism with water and the Holy Spirit, are the people who were first baptized with water now being baptized a second time to receive the Holy Spirit?

Remember that the word *baptism* is Greek and means "to wash, be awash, or be immersed by or in something," not necessarily water. For example, the best way to learn language is by "immersion." Paul wrote that the children of Israel "were baptized into Moses" in the exodus event (1Co 10:2). People who were "baptized" by John were washed in water and awash in his teaching as often as they went out to hear him. In this verse, Jesus is not suggesting that the apostles be baptized again, repeating John's Baptism in the Jordan. Jesus is saying that after ten days the apostles would be immersed in the Holy Spirit according to the promise from God the Father, that they would receive power when the Holy Spirit

came upon them (Ac 1:8; 2:1–21). This special coming of the Holy Spirit to the apostles was witnessed by the appearance of flames over their heads and their ability to speak in the native languages of all the many Jewish visitors in Jerusalem, just as Jesus had promised after His resurrection (Mk 16:16–20; Ac 2:2–11).

After Pentecost, the Holy Spirit "fell on" different people when the apostles laid their hands on them, in order to prove that God's grace saved all people and saved them immediately, apart from the Law of Moses (Ac 8:14–23; 10:44–48; 11:15–18; 15:1–10). The only time anyone was rebaptized or baptized a second time in water was in the case where the water baptism applied was not according to Christ's command but by those who rejected Christ (Ac 19:1–6). In fact, these men were baptized only once, and then Paul laid his hands on them and the Holy Spirit fell on them as evidence of the authenticity of the Baptism Paul provided. Christian Baptism is essentially concerned with a life immersed in the Word of God (Jn 3:1–7; 8:31–32; Rm 2:42; 10:17; Col 3:16). The ceremony of Baptism with water was given by the Lord as a physical means to confirm the promises that God applies to us in His Word (Mt 28:19–20; 1Pt 3:21).

• •

Q 1:7 What other New Testament books talk about the ascension? Why does Jesus say He doesn't know when He will come back?

Mark 16:19–20; Lk 24:44–53; Jn 21:15–25; and Gal 1:11–2:21 all report what took place during this time. If Jesus meant that He did not know when the end of the world would be according to His human nature, we might not be surprised. However, since Jesus refers to God as "the Father," it sounds as though He is speaking according to His divine nature. The Trinity is a mystery, and this is one of the mysterious features of it. What is no surprise or mystery is that Jesus is focused on saving the lives of all who live in the world while there is time to do so (Ac 1:8; Jn 3:17).

Q **1:8 Sometimes it is difficult to tell if the Spirit is truly moving us, due to our human nature. What are some baby steps to take to help us better listen to the Spirit?**

Your expression "baby steps" is a good one, since Jesus said, "Unless you turn and become like children, you will never enter the kingdom of heaven" (Mt 18:3). There are two ways we can know if the Spirit of God is moving us. First, we know the Spirit is moving us by our relationship with the Word (Ezk 36:24–27; Jn 6:63; 2Tm 3:16–17). Second, we know the Spirit is moving us if our thoughts, words, and deeds are in harmony with what the Bible teaches (Mt 7:15–20; Jas 2:14–26; 1Jn 1:7; 2:4). Jesus refers to both cause and effect in the Christian life in the example of the vine and branches (Jn 15:1–7).

Q **1:10–11 Were the men in white robes angels?**

Yes, these men were angels, sent as God's messengers. Remember that *angel* is a Greek word, not English. Messengers of God often appear to people as men, though not all texts include that added description. Three men visited Abraham—one of them was the Son of God and the other two were "angels" (Gn 18:1–21). Mark records that a young man in white was present at the tomb after Jesus rose (Mk 16:5); Matthew and John both report an angel or angels in white (Mt 28:2–3; Jn 20:12). The appearance in white robes could be perceived as a type of uniform, similar to how we sometimes talk about the police or police officers as "men in blue."

Q **1:12 What does "a Sabbath day's journey" mean? What is the distance between the Mount of Olives and Jerusalem?**

A Sabbath day's journey is 3,637 feet or about two-thirds of a mile. The Mount of Olives is just to the east of Jerusalem, separated by the Kidron Valley. I have walked this distance, and depending on where you start on the Mount of Olives, it could be a quarter-mile to a half-mile walk.

Q 1:18 Did Judas purchase the field himself? Why doesn't Acts state that Judas hung himself, as the other Gospels did?

Judas returned the money to the chief priests, who then purchased the field. Both accounts are correct inasmuch as it was the money of Judas that was used to purchase the field. Similarly, Mt 27:5 says Judas hung himself, while Ac 1:18 says Judas fell "headlong [and] burst open." Again, the two accounts are supplementary, not contradictory. While attempting to take his own life by hanging, the limb of the tree or the rope that Judas was using broke, and Judas fell so that he burst open and died. There are many reasons for knowing how Judas Iscariot died. One is a warning about what becomes of a person who despises and rejects the Word of God while playing the hypocrite (Ac 5:1–11). Another reason is to reveal a contrast between the Lord, who was "hung" on a tree in order to save the world, and Judas, who hung himself on a tree because he refused what Christ had done (Mt 27:3–10; Ac 1:18–19).

Q 1:20 Doesn't Peter take this Scripture entirely out of context? In that psalm, David is talking about the people against him at that time. If Judas's place isn't supposed to be filled according to the first verse quoted, then why is it filled? The two verses Peter quotes seem to contradict each other.

There are various theories about how to apply prophetic language. Some argue that there is no such thing as prophecy; people described events of their own time and these only appear to be fulfilled in a later time. Others argue the opposite: the prophetic words spoken by the prophet only appear to be fulfilled in the prophet's time but are genuinely fulfilled much later at the time of Christ. I would like to suggest that prophecy has only one proper fulfillment, but that events in history, like the words of the prophecy themselves, are indicative of what is to come—just as nature provides examples of spiritual realities (Ps 19; Rm 1:20). In this case, where Pss 69 and 109 are quoted, I don't know of any particular application these verses would have had in the life of David, though every government in history seems to have had traitors and usurpers within. The first verse quoted (Ps 69:25) says that Judas's home will be desolate, while the second verse quoted (Ps 109:8) says that his office or place (as an apostle) will be given to another, which turned out to be Matthias (Ac 1:26).

Q 1:23–26 Isn't "casting lots" taking matters into their own hands and considered equal to gambling?

Casting lots was an ancient method for settling disputes or seeking the Lord's decision when there was no other way (Lv 16:8; Jsh 18:6, 8; Ne 11:1). The Lord gave priests a particular kind of lot to cast called "urim and thummim" (Nu 27:21). The practice of those churches that call their pastors is based on this passage in Acts and on the passage that records the sending of Paul and Barnabas on the first missionary journey (Ac 13:1–3). The casting of lots was practiced in order to prevent people from taking matters into their own hands and was not like gambling. Having an assembly of congregational members who vote on which man to call as pastor is intended to allow for the Holy Spirit's activity among those who vote, but this practice is subject to manipulation by people if they are intent on doing so. Gambling is a risk one takes for the sake of personal, material gain. Casting lots was practiced as a means of discerning the Lord's will when trying to determine which of two apparently equal candidates should be called.

Q 1:25 Did Judas really go to hell? Did he have faith?

Jesus warned us not to judge others (Mt 7:1). This verse, along with Pss 69:27–28 and 109:17–18, gives very clear evidence that Judas Iscariot died without faith, mercy, or the righteousness of Christ.

Q 1:26 Who is Matthias?

Matthias was one of the many other people who had followed Jesus and had been with Jesus all during the time of His public ministry (Ac 1:21–23).

> What does the word *Pentecost* mean?

Q 2:1 What does the word *Pentecost* mean? Was Pentecost celebrated by Jews, or was the one in Acts the first one and purely a Christian holiday?

The word *Pentecost* is Greek and means "the fiftieth [day]." There was a festival in the Old Testament called Pentecost that celebrated the beginning of harvest, when people brought offerings of the firstfruits (Lv 23:9–21). Luke records that there were so many Jews present in Jerusalem from every nation under heaven because they had come to celebrate the feast of Pentecost. The joyful reception of the Gospel by these people on this day is a demonstration of the firstfruits of the redemption accomplished by Christ and served as an indication of God's intent expressed in the command of Jesus to His disciples (Mt 28:18–20; Mk 16:16–20; Ac 1:8).

Q 2:2 What is meant by "a mighty rushing wind"?

The Greek word for this wind occurs only here in the New Testament, but in the Greek translation of the Old Testament this word occurs five times. In Ex 14:21, it refers to the strong wind that the Lord sent to separate the waters of the Red Sea. Perhaps Luke chose this unusual word in order to make a connection between Pentecost and the exodus. This word also occurs in Ps 48:7; Is 11:15; 58:6; and 59:19.

• • • • • • • • • • • • • • • • • • • •

Q 2:3–4 Are the "tongues as of fire" literal fire? What does it mean to be filled with the Holy Spirit?

Luke wrote that there appeared tongues "as of" or "like" fire, so they looked like fire but were not actually fire. If the tongues were real fire, Luke could have said simply "tongues of fire." I don't know how anyone but the apostles could describe what being filled with the Holy Spirit feels like, but the text describes how they acted. The apostles, who had been meeting behind locked doors for fear of the Jews, now began to speak boldly and in public, and they would continue to do so even when it meant beatings, imprisonment, and finally execution (Jn 20:19; Ac 4:1–22; 5:17–41; 2Pt 1:13–14; 2Tm 4:6–8). Any Christian might have a sense of what the disciples experienced when you find yourself doing or saying something according to the Word and will of God that you never would have on your own (1Co 12:3; 15:10).

• • • • • • • • • • • • • • • • • • • •

Q 2:4 Is there any significance in the fact that this event of speaking in tongues occurred at Pentecost? Is it possible to start speaking in tongues without previously knowing the language?

The creation bears witness to the creator (Ps 19; Rm 1:20). The feast of Pentecost or

"firstfruits" of the harvest celebrated God's gracious providence in giving the crops that supply our food. These crops, given by the grace of God, are indicative of or point to a more important gift of God: the regenerate soul that will be harvested at the end of the world and brought into God's storehouse (Mt 9:37–38). The powerful coming of the Holy Spirit on Pentecost provides cause for a greater celebration—a celebration of God's redemption of all humankind in Jesus, and the first gathering in or harvest of people who realize what He has done for them. The special manifestation of the Holy Spirit in the speaking in different languages made two essential points about the work of Christ. First, the Gospel of Jesus is accomplished and effects salvation immediately in people who hear the Word. Second, the Gospel of Jesus is accomplished for all people. God's gift of the ability to speak, immediately, in the languages of all these people is unmistakable evidence for God's universal redemption of all nations. All things are possible with God (Mt 19:26). If God confused the languages of people in a moment at Babel, certainly He can grant the reversal of that confusion by making the apostles able to speak in the native language of others in an instant, without previously knowing the language (Gn 11:6–9; Ac 2:8–13).

• • • • • • • • • • • • • • • • • • • •

Q 2:4 If the apostles had faith, they would already have had the Holy Spirit, right?

Jesus must have had perfect faith and

the Holy Spirit when He was baptized in the Jordan River by John, yet the Holy Spirit descended and remained upon Him in order to demonstrate His presence with Christ (Lk 3:21–22). The apostles must have had the Holy Spirit before Pentecost, yet on this occasion the Holy Spirit takes the apostles to a new level of faithfulness and service according to the promise of God the Father and according to the demands of the mission that Jesus had given them (Ac 1:4–5; 2:16–21; Mt 10:1–4; for more on this subject, see Ac 1:5 above).

● ● ● ● ● ● ● ● ● ● ● ● ● ● ● ● ● ● ● ●

Q 2:6 Why does the Holy Spirit give people ability to speak native tongues?

The Jewish religious leaders had long forgotten that God loves all people and had separated Israel to be a light to the nations (Gn 12:1–3; Lk 2:32). Before and after Jesus' ministry, these religious leaders forced upon everyone the idea that God loved only Jews who obeyed the rules they had set in place in addition to the Law of Moses (Mt 5:21–48; Ac 15:1–10; Gal 2:11–21; 5:1–4). People typically assume that the apostles spoke in the native languages of the people so that those people could understand what they were saying. However, the people present were devout Jews (as evidenced from Luke's account and their presence in Jerusalem for the feast of Pentecost). All these people would have spoken and understood Greek and perhaps even Aramaic and Hebrew. If the religious leaders were right, we would

have expected the Holy Spirit to make the apostles speak in Hebrew only. However, the opposite occurred. By the special working of God, the apostles spoke in the various languages of the nations from which these visitors had come. How could God say more clearly or powerfully that He had, in Christ, reconciled the world to Himself and that this reconciliation was communicated and applied to people immediately in the proclamation of His Word? Notice that this event and one similar to it is the argument of the apostles that always prevails when the religious leaders try to impose their traditions and laws, which can only condemn us (Ac 8:4–17; 10:1–11:18; 15:1–12).

● ● ● ● ● ● ● ● ● ● ● ● ● ● ● ● ● ● ● ●

Q 2:9–11 How many different languages did these apostles have to speak?

Depending on how you count the nations named, they might have spoken in fifteen or more languages. Please note that they did not "have to" speak in these languages but were enabled to by the Holy Spirit as evidence that the Gospel is communicated immediately by the Word and that the Gospel is for all.

● ● ● ● ● ● ● ● ● ● ● ● ● ● ● ● ● ● ● ●

Q 2:11 What exactly does "Jews and proselytes" mean?

A proselyte is a person who was not born into a religion but converted to it, especially when the religion is taught as though it depended on physical genealogy.

Luke is telling us that there were many people present who were not ethnic Jews; they were born from different nationalities but had submitted to circumcision and the Law of Moses, according to the teaching of the religious leaders at that time.

• • • • • • • • • • • • • • • • • •

Q **2:13 Why do the others think they are drunk?**

Those who mocked said the apostles were drunk for two reasons. First, they could not understand what the apostles were saying, so they concluded that they were simply mumbling, as would a drunken person. Second, they were so convinced that God cared only for the Jews that they could not imagine that God would want to speak His Word directly to the nations in their languages. Interestingly, there are people who claim to speak in tongues but upon examination are simply making up sounds that are no language at all. Those who make these claims miss the point—they are trying to confirm their own faith rather than confirming the universal nature of the Gospel itself, which was the point at Pentecost.

• • • • • • • • • • • • • • • • • •

Q **2:14 Why would anyone listen to Peter after he denied Christ?**

We may suppose that relatively few people were in the courtyard of the high priest in the middle of the night when Peter denied Jesus three times. Perhaps some of these people were the ones who accused the apostles of being drunk. A great number of

people that day, about three thousand, had just come to Jerusalem for Pentecost and would not have known about Peter's denial. In fact, the people were listening to the Holy Spirit, not Peter (Ac 2:37–39). Even the Jews who wanted to kill Stephen and Paul listened to most of what they had to say (Ac 7:1–54; 22:1–22).

• • • • • • • • • • • • • • • • • •

Q **2:17 If God pours His Spirit on all people, wouldn't they believe then?**

You have your finger on a very great mystery. We know that God reconciled the whole world to Himself in Christ (2Co 5:21). We know that God desires all to be saved and come to the knowledge of the truth (1Tm 2:4). We know that God has commanded His people to declare the Gospel to all people and that God has given the witness of creation and the conscience to all people (Mk 16:16; Ps 19; Rm 1:20; 2:15). Why, then, some people steadfastly refuse to believe the truth is a question that seems to defy explanation. For more on this subject, see questions and answers in Rm 9–11.

• • • • • • • • • • • • • • • • • •

Q **2:19 What is the purpose of signs? Do people still speak in tongues?**

The purpose of signs is to provide physical evidence that authenticates the Word of God as truth. How can we know immaterial or spiritual things without physical indications of the same? God created a physical universe in order to bear witness to Himself and to spiritual truths; this is why the parables are effective (Ps 19; Rm 1:20; Ex 4:1–9; 1Ki 18:20–40). Jesus said, explicitly, that He gave His apostles the ability to do signs so that we would know they spoke the truth, on His behalf, with authority (Mk 16:16–20; 1Th 2:13; 2Tm 3:16; 2Pt 1:19–21). God can certainly give anyone any ability He wants at any time. However, the particular purpose of the special manifestations of the Holy Spirit through the apostles was fulfilled as the Gospel was confirmed as the apostles spoke and then wrote it down. People do still have gifts from God in language and in the healing arts, but not with the immediacy that we see in Acts. While time, effort, and at least some natural ability are necessary to work with language or medicine, these are no substitute for special gifts that God gives or the love of God that inspires people to study and apply their gifts for the benefit of others.

● ● ● ● ● ● ● ● ● ● ● ● ● ● ● ● ● ● ● ●

Q **2:34 What is the important about the "right hand"?**

The right side has to do with the things that properly belong to someone or to their work, and it includes the idea of having a second person to execute that authority. Jesus' place at the right hand of God is unparalleled: He is the only-begotten Son of God, the wisdom of God, the incarnate Son of Man and Redeemer of the world (Php 2:5–11).

● ● ● ● ● ● ● ● ● ● ● ● ● ● ● ● ● ● ● ●

Q **2:38–39 Concerning Baptism, isn't this more of a traditional practice? Concerning baptizing children, if you are forcing a Baptism on someone, how is that a good thing? Doesn't it need to be willful? How can Baptism give forgiveness of sins?**

There are two aspects of Christian Baptism, and neither of them have to do with tradition. In the most proper and fundamental sense of the term, Christian Baptism has to do with a life immersed in the Word of God. Notice how this is evident in Jesus' final command to the apostles in Matthew (28:19–20): "Go therefore and make disciples of all nations, baptizing them in the name of the Father and of the Son and of the Holy Spirit, teaching them to observe all that I have commanded you." The relationship of the believer with the Word is essential (Jn 3:1–7; 6:63; 8:31–32; 15:1–7; Rm 10:17; Col 3:16). The other aspect of Baptism is a physical confirmation of this life in the Word. The ceremony of Baptism is a moment in time when we see the words and promises of God applied with a physical means in order to assure everyone that the person baptized has been joined with Christ (Rm 6:1–11; 8:1; 1Pt 3:18–21). The sacrifice of animals ended because the one, single, eternal, and universal sacrifice of Christ, of which sacrifices were indicative, had been accomplished (Heb 10:1–12). The rite of Baptism, like birth, takes place only once in a person's life, but that birth and the life that preceded and follows depends completely on the presence of the Word of God in that life.

Baptizing infants is no more a matter of forcing than conceiving or giving birth to a child. Conceiving a child and giving birth is a good thing; so is all the other care parents provide for the health and well-being of their children. Bringing a child up from conception in the truth and grace of God is even more important than the physical care, for what good is caring for the body of a person if you leave their soul to die apart from the Word? Jesus points to children as the model of faith precisely because as children they did not yet possess the willfulness of a more mature adult. The will of fallen man is contrary to God and does not recognize the things of God; therefore, that will must be silenced, drowned, crushed, and put to death so that God can bring forth a regenerated soul through His grace and Holy Spirit (Rm 5:6–11; 6:1–23; 1Co 2:14; Mt 18:3).

Baptism forgives sins because the Word conveys the forgiveness of sins. Baptism, as explained above, is in the first place a life awash or immersed in the Word of God. This Word of God is what makes Baptism with water significant, including the confirmation that sins have been forgiven because the one immersed in the Word of God is joined with Christ and therefore is without condemnation (Rm 8:1; 1Jn 3–5).

Q 2:41 In some translations, the text says "those who accepted his word." I am always cautious about using the word "accept" in reference to faith because of the works-righteousness implications.

The challenge for understanding the truth about our salvation is not in the term "accept" but in failing to understand what makes that acceptance happen. Fallen human nature never accepts the grace of God, since it is completely corrupt and contrary to God to the day it dies (Mk 7:20–23; Rm 5:6–11; 1Co 2:14). The fact that these people accepted the Word gladly is based on the Law, which puts to death fallen human nature, and the Gospel, which regenerates the soul. John says this very clearly in ch. 1 of his Gospel: "He came to His own, and His own people did not receive Him. But to all who did receive Him, who believed in His name, He gave the right to become children of God, who were born, not of blood nor of the will of the flesh nor of the will of man, but of God" (vv. 11–13). You see that John works backward from effect to cause. Who receives (or accepts) Christ? The one who believes in Him. How does a person come to believe in Him? Only a person who has been generated by the Father through the Word and Spirit of God can believe in Christ.

Q 2:41 When those three thousand returned home, did they have their own churches?

There were no churches for them to go back to as we think of churches today. However, they would have gone back to their synagogues, friends, and families and shared what they had learned, just as the apostles did (Ac 3:1–10; 5:12–16; 17:1–9). These early believers did not build places that were only used for worship services but realized that their whole life was used in service to God, and worship was held as they gathered in one another's homes (2:46).

Q 2:44 When this says they had everything in common, does that refer to the beliefs they held?

It was not just the beliefs they held, though the truth and grace of God was the foundation for all the rest. These people also recognized that all they were and had was a stewardship from God, to whom all things belong. Verse 45 makes clear that they did sell the possessions they did not need in order to provide for those who did not have what was needed. Acts 4:32–5:11 helps fill out the picture of how these first Christians lived. Paul gives helpful explanations of the Christian disposition toward material things in 1Co 7:29–31 and Php 3:7–14.

Q 2:46 Does this refer to partaking of Communion in homes?

Yes, the early Christians understood that the Christian Church was neither a building nor even an organization of people, but the very Body of Christ. They lived in the Word and sought to communicate that Word to the world around them. They gathered, in particular, on Sundays (the day of the Lord's resurrection) to celebrate the resurrection of Jesus and to receive Him in visible form with bread and wine (1Co 11:17–34).

Q 2:47 Who are "the people"? Were they just Jews or a large crowd of all kinds of people?

The "people" would have been anyone and everyone who lived in the neighborhood of Jerusalem: Jews, Greeks, Romans, and anyone else who happened to live there.

Q 3:1 What were the other disciples doing after Jesus' death and resurrection?

There are some traditions about the activities of some of the other apostles, such as the one that says Thomas traveled east to India. Acts 8 records the activity of Philip. Like the Gospels, Acts can only record so much material and is focused on Peter, John, and Paul because their activity is indicative and exemplary of the rest. We can be fairly certain that the other disciples were off "[making] disciples of all nations" as the Lord had commanded them (Mt 28:19).

Q 3:1 What is the significance of the time in the healing of the lame beggar?

Biblical literature regularly includes plenty of detail that argues for its historicity.

For example, Luke provides the names of civil and religious authorities at the time Jesus began His public ministry (Lk 3:1–2). The time of day has nothing to do with the apostles' ability to heal the lame man, but it has everything to do with the fact that what Luke reports did take place in a real place at a real time.

Q 3:2 Why were the temple gates named, and what is the significance of this?

Everything gets a name sooner or later; this is part of being able to describe something to someone or direct them to it with clarity. We even have multiple names for some things, such as particular highways in cities. In biblical times more than today, names were more logically related to the thing named. For example, Jacob named the place where he had the dream about the ladder "House of God" (*Bethel* in Hebrew; Gn 28:19). The gate was most likely named Beautiful because it was, and Luke uses that name so that everyone could place this event.

Q 3:5 Why does he simply expect to receive something?

The beggar was likely used to receiving one of two responses from people who passed him by: they would ignore him, or they would give him something. Since attention was exchanged between Peter, John, and the beggar, and since Peter command-ed the beggar to "look at us," these two men appeared to be the type who wanted to help the beggar rather than ignore him.

Q 3:6 Why does Peter perform miracles? Why didn't Jesus heal this man?

Jesus healed people just about everywhere He went (Mt 8:1–17). The purpose of healing and performing miracles was not so much for the relief of the individual, though this mattered, but in order to authenticate Jesus as the Son of God and twelve of His disciples as apostles who carried His authority to declare truth and grace. If Jesus didn't heal someone, it would have been because the opportunity to do so did not present itself. This does not change the fact that the healings that Jesus did perform pointed to His redemption of the whole world, which provides absolute and eternal healing of body and soul. Peter and the other apostles performed miracles as evidence for their authority to act and speak on behalf of Jesus (Mk 16:16–20; Gal 1:1–10).

When Jesus gave His apostles authority to heal, He commanded them: "Heal the sick. . . . You received without paying; give without pay" (Mt 10:8). Jesus didn't heal or interact with people only if they asked (Mt 9:9–13; Lk 19:1–10). The beggar was actually spending all his time asking for help, and when he gave Peter his attention as commanded, faith was evident.

Must all Christians suffer?

Q 3:22–23 Do people today still have the gift of prophecy?

Let's begin by distinguishing what is meant by *prophecy*. Prophecy can mean (1) speaking in public, (2) declaring what is known only to another person, (3) predicting the future, or (4) all of the above. Certainly God still gives the gift of public speaking to men He wants to serve in the public ministry (though congregations are not always careful to require this gift in the men they call). The Word of God enables those who would serve in the public ministry (2Tm 3:16–17). The Word also gives us some ability to know what is in another person's heart and to discern their thoughts (Mk 7:20–23; Lk 6:45; Heb 4:12). The Bible gives many indications of what we might expect in the future, in a general way (Mt 24:3–51; 1Th 3:1–5; 1Pt 3:3–9; Jas 1:2–4). I don't know of any reason to believe or what purpose would be served by a person who claimed to have prophetic powers like the prophets of old and Jesus. On the other hand, the New Testament warns us to beware of those who claim to be prophets (Mt 24:4–5; 2Co 11:12–15; 1Jn 4:1).

Q 4:1–22 Is it necessary to suffer for the sake of the Gospel? Must all Christians suffer?

Yes, and here is why. The devil, the world, and fallen human nature are all opposed to God (Eph 2:1–3; Rm 5:6–10). Since the vicarious atonement of Jesus took away the devil's ability to accuse us before God, the only harm the devil can do is to keep people from realizing what Christ has done for them and the life He would readily restore to them (Rv 12:7–17; Heb 2:14–15). If the devil convinces the world to oppose God, truth, and grace, then the world will necessarily be opposed to anyone who seeks to bear witness to or be an extension of God's truth and grace (Mt 10:24–25; Jn 15:20–25; 1Th 3:1–5). A second reason the Bible gives for suffering has to do with helping the believer recognize and overcome his or her own fallen human nature. It is easy to forget that our fallen human nature is not the essence of who we are. Realizing the weakness and contrary disposition of this nature makes us thankful for trials by which God disables that nature so that our regenerate soul can live and thrive (Rm 5:3–5; 2Co 4:1–5:21; 12:7–10; 1Pt 1:3–9; Jas 1:2–3).

Q 4:3 Why were Peter and John jailed?

First, the previous verse says that the religious leaders were "greatly annoyed because they were teaching the people and proclaiming in Jesus the resurrection from the dead" (v. 2). You may recall that the Sadducees did not believe in a resurrection of the dead (Lk 20:27). In response to news of Jesus' resurrection, the chief priests paid the guards to say that Jesus' disciples stole

His body (Mt 28:11–15). Even the Gentile crowd in Athens could not endure the subject of the resurrection of the dead (Ac 17:32). The second reason for putting the apostles in jail had to do with the hour being late. There was no time to hold a council or trial, but the religious leaders didn't want to allow the apostles to continue teaching, so they put them in jail overnight. Notice this contrast: Jesus is the truth and taught truth, and it was the truth itself that exposed lies. Those who oppose Jesus and the truth cannot overcome the truth with argument, so they always try to silence the truth by binding it or burying it, along with those who would advance it (Jn 8:40).

• • • • • • • • • • • • • • • • • • •

Q **4:8–22 In an age of great miracles and displays of God's power, why is it so hard for the Jewish rulers to believe the apostles?**

Jesus answered this question when He said, "Woe to you Pharisees! For you love the best seat in the synagogues and greetings in the marketplaces" (Lk 11:43). The word translated "love" in this verse means "to sacrifice everything for the sake of." The problem is not that the miracles were unconvincing; the religious leaders knew that Jesus was the Son of God and that He was fulfilling all the Old Testament promises of God (Jn 3:2; 11:45–53; Mt 27:18). The religious leaders, like the Israelites in Egypt, were held captive, not by a foreign people but by their own idols and lusts. The religious leaders of Jesus' day had power and

wealth because they controlled the people with the law and guilt. Jesus set the people free from these religious leaders and the lies they taught. The silversmiths in Ephesus wanted to murder Paul and his companions for the same reason: the truth they taught undermined the silversmiths' power and wealth (Ac 19:24–26). "The love of money is a root of all kinds of evils. It is through this craving that some have wandered away from the faith and pierced themselves with many pangs" (1 Tm 6:10).

• • • • • • • • • • • • • • • • • • •

Q **4:10 Many times in Acts we read the phrase "Jesus Christ of Nazareth, whom you crucified, whom God raised from the dead." Was this a prominent point Peter used to preach the message of Christ? Why does Peter say, "Whom you crucified"?**

The question of "who crucified Jesus" is an interesting one. Roman soldiers crucified Jesus, if we are talking about who actually did the nailing, but they were only following orders. Pontius Pilate crucified Jesus, but that was only because the religious leaders demanded it. The religious leaders crucified Jesus because they so utterly and bitterly opposed the truth and grace of God incarnate in Christ—some of these were in the crowd at Pentecost and were present again on this occasion. The devil crucified Jesus, since he worked through Judas Iscariot so that Jesus could be arrested. The devil, of course, in opposing God is his own worst enemy; the crucifixion of Jesus, which he assumed would put an end to Him, actually put an end to the devil's power to use the Law to condemn people before God (Jb 1:6–11; 2:1–5; Rv 12:7–11). We crucified Jesus, since Jesus took our place upon the cross (2Co 5:21). Ultimately, it was God who crucified Jesus, since He always acts according to His nature, which is love, and substituting His Son for us was the only way to save us (Is 53:10–12). Responsibility for sin, which Jesus bore upon the cross, is a prominent theme all through the New Testament, because a person cannot realize the salvation Christ has accomplished until he or she accepts the truth about our need for that salvation (1Jn 1:8–9).

Q 4:18–21 Why did the rulers and elders not want Peter and John to speak of Christ?

The rulers could not tolerate the Gospel of Christ for the same reason they could not tolerate Christ Himself: they knew that the truth and grace of God in Christ would set people free from bondage under the Law. Holding people in that bondage was how the rulers gained their power and wealth (Jn 11:45–53; see also Ac 4:3 above).

Q 4:22 What does the man's age have to do with his healing?

The man's age is important because he had been lame from his mother's womb (Ac 3:2). The fact that he had never, ever walked made the fact of this miracle in-

disputable and added to the wonder of it. Jesus healed a man who was blind from his mother's womb and endured similar opposition from the religious leaders (Jn 9).

Q 4:36–37 Why does Luke include these verses?

There are a few possible reasons. First, Luke emphasizes the power of the Gospel not only with general statements about what people did but also with particular examples. This is similar to the way the Gospels not only describe how Jesus healed everyone but also include particular examples (Mt 8:1–15; 8:16). Second, Luke is introducing Barnabas, whom we will meet later as he travels on the first missionary journey with Paul. Luke introduces Paul in just a few verses, then follows Philip before returning to Paul at the beginning of the next chapter (Ac 8:1–9:1). Third, the particular example of Barnabas after the description of Christian stewardship in general heightens the contrast we experience with the narrative of Ananias and Sapphira that follows.

Q 5:1 Is this the same Ananias as in the story of Saul's conversion to Christianity?

This cannot be the same Ananias that visited Saul after his conversion, because this Ananias died and the other was still living and in Damascus some time later (Ac 9:10–17). Note how there is a Lazarus who sat outside the rich man's gate and died, and there is the Lazarus who was brother to Mary and Martha; he died too, but Jesus raised him from the dead (Lk 10:38–42; 16:19–31; Jn 11:1–44).

Q 5:1–11 What point is made by Ananias and Sapphira dying so suddenly?

At the beginning of the Old Testament and at the beginning of the New Testament, God seems to do things "king-size" so there is no mistaking what is happening and what God means to teach us. People still die from lying to God, from greed, covetousness, and self-deception—it just doesn't happen all at once (Rm 6:23). The ability of the apostles to speak in the native languages of the people present at Pentecost made an essential point that could not be disputed. The death of Ananias and Sapphira made an equally essential point. The problem with this couple is not that they could not bring themselves to give all of the proceeds from the sale of a property to the church; Peter made this point (Ac 5:4). The problem was that they wanted to look like they were being as faithful as other believers while they were not—similar to Judas Iscariot stealing what was in the money box while pretending to care about the poor (Jn 12:1–6). Jesus is the truth, and faith has to do with honesty about dependence. Truth and honesty, as the foundation of all things, are essential for life. Without truth, like Ananias and Sapphira, there is nothing but lies and death (Jn 8:44).

Q 5:2 What does it mean by "his [Ananias's] wife's knowledge"?

The fact that Ananias executed this lie with his wife's full knowledge is important for at least two reasons. First, if Sapphira knew about this, then it also means she could have and should have opposed Ananias or at least dissented from what he did. It is one thing to make a mistake alone, in a weak moment. It is another thing to have time to think about what you are doing and for other people to agree with a lie. Second, Sapphira had a chance to regain her life by answering Peter's question honestly—the same chance to reclaim honesty and life that Peter gave Ananias. She knew very well what Ananias had done and not only consented but also would have perpetuated the lie; however, lies always bring death—first, spiritual death, then in every other way.

Q 5:3 How did Peter know that Ananias was being dishonest?

One of the gifts of the Spirit is discernment (Php 1:9). Jesus knew when people were coming to Him in hypocrisy, and it looks as though He included that ability with the others He gave His apostles (Mt 9:4; Jn 6:61; Mk 16:16–20).

Q 5:5 Did the Holy Spirit kill Ananias and Sapphira?

Scripture says plainly that "the LORD kills and brings to life" (1Sm 2:6). There are plenty of examples in the Bible of God killing someone, such as the first two sons of Judah (Gn 38:7, 10). But perhaps we should look at what happened here more carefully, since the text does not say God killed them. The Holy Spirit is the breath of God and the life maker (Gn 2:7; Jn 6:63). Selling a property only to pretend that you are giving the whole proceeds to the Church is a lie and hypocrisy that requires the rejection of the Spirit (Mt 6:24). Notice how the text words the death of Ananias and Sapphira—they each fell down and *breathed their last*. If you don't have the breath or Spirit of God, you're dead.

Q 5:5–10 Why did those who were dishonest die? Why weren't they given a chance to repent?

Ananias and Sapphira died because they rejected the Word and Spirit of God in favor of love of money, covetousness, greed, and, worst of all, hypocrisy. In fact, they did have a chance to repent when Peter asked them about the property; even as Peter responded to their lie, they might have had a change of heart and found mercy (compare the example of David with Nathan, 2Sm 12:1–13). Life depends on honesty, which is why the dishonest necessarily die.

Q 5:18 Are there still apostles today?

There were only, ever, thirteen apostles. To be an apostle you have to have been appointed by Jesus Himself, and those He

Are there still apostles today?

appointed had to have been with Him from the time He was baptized by John until His ascension (Ac 1:21–22; 8:18–24; Eph 4:11).

Q 5:28 Why are they so scared of being accused of crucifying Jesus?

The religious leaders, having rejected the grace of God promised in the Old Testament and present in the life and teaching of Christ, were consumed with defending themselves against guilt. If there is no grace of God and we are all judged on our works, then guilt is damning and without remedy. This is why the religious leaders changed the intent of God's Law in the Old Testament, invented and added their own laws, and continually pointed out the failures of others (Mt 5:21–48; 23:13–36; Lk 18:9–14; Jn 9:34). The crucifixion of Jesus was especially difficult to justify, since everyone knew that Jesus was a righteous man, and the rulers themselves knew that they had condemned Him on the basis of lies and nonsense (Mt 26:59–65).

Q 6:3 What is the significance of having twelve apostles and then adding seven more?

The seven men who were set apart here were not apostles but simply men who would look after the physical matters of distributing help to those in need. One of the reasons for doing this was to protect the authority and responsibility that the apostles, alone, were bearing: to communicate the very Word of God (v. 2). The same idea is still true today: faithful pastors and congregations realize that the pastor should be focused on the study and teaching of the Word and leave the other matters of congregational activity to the faithful (1Tm 4:13–16; 2Tm 2:4; 3:16–17).

Q 7:11 To whom was Stephen referring when he consistently stated "our fathers"?

Stephen is referring to the "patriarchs" (v. 9), who are described as the sons of Jacob, the son of Isaac, the son of Abraham (v. 8). In vv. 17–45, Stephen is referring to the adult male descendants of the sons of Jacob who lived in Egypt at the time of the exodus. In vv. 51–53, Stephen is referring to all the male descendants of the sons of Jacob during the rest of the Old Testament period to the very time that Stephen was speaking. For most of its history, the children of Israel have missed what it means to be a child of Abraham. Abraham's descendants are not born according to the flesh, as Isaac was, but are generated by the Word of God (Jn 1:11–13; 8:30–42; Rm 2:28–29; Gal 3:7; 4:21–31).

Q 7:52 Why don't the disciples realize that the Jews killing Jesus was ultimately a good thing?

There is no doubt that the disciples knew that the crucifixion of Jesus meant redemption for the whole world (2Co 5:14–21). The problem Stephen is addressing is the hard-hearted impenitence that remained in these religious leaders, especially after Jesus had risen from the dead. This determination to oppose the truth, redemption, grace, and Spirit of God in Christ is exactly what Jesus is warning about when He discusses the one sin that cannot ever be forgiven (Mt 12:31–32; Heb 6:4–8; 10:26–30). Remember what a difference there is between God making our mistakes work for good and our disposition toward the mistakes we make. God can certainly save a person who is murdered and even make the family of such a person forgiving toward the murderer, but that does not make murder a good thing.

Q 7:58 Why did the people lay their clothes at the feet of Saul?

Clothes were few and hard to come by in biblical times. (Remember how the soldiers cast lots to see who would get Jesus' clothes? But who would want them unless they were so very hard to come by? See Lk 23:34.) Cleaning clothes was also difficult to do. Thus, the men who were going to stone Stephen to death took off their outer garments in order to keep them clean. Note how this is indicative of the hypocrisy of their life: they appear to be very righteous on the outside, but inwardly they are full of jealousy and murder (Mt 23:25–33).

● ● ● ● ● ● ● ● ● ● ● ● ● ● ● ● ● ●

Q 7:60 Did Stephen really fall asleep, or did he actually die?

The expression "fall asleep" can be very confusing in the New Testament unless we understand human nature and define our terms. For example, death has to do with the absence of positive relationships—this is why a nonfunctioning human body is called "dead." But a human soul is eternal and lives on, experiencing life in positive relationships or death in the absence of them (Lk 16:19–31). Therefore, an unbeliever is dead, even if his body is alive; a believer is alive, even if his body is dead (Jn 11:25–26). This is why Jesus and others refer to a believer who has died as "sleeping," since like the body when it sleeps, the person is still alive (Lk 8:50–56; Jn 11:11–14; 1Co 15:50–58).

● ● ● ● ● ● ● ● ● ● ● ● ● ● ● ● ● ●

Q 8–12 Is there any specific reason why Ac 8–12 focuses on a number of individual persons?

The whole Bible is made up of teachings and examples of the significance of those teachings in the lives of individuals. The Gospel of John moves from a focus on Jesus' mother to Nicodemus to the woman at the well to a lame man and so forth. Acts can be outlined according to the record of opposition that presented itself against the Gospel, from the religious leaders in Jerusalem (Ac 2–4) to hypocrites within the Church (Ananias and Sapphira, ch. 5) to the selfish within the Church (Ac 6) and back to the religious authorities against Stephen (Ac 7).

● ● ● ● ● ● ● ● ● ● ● ● ● ● ● ● ● ●

Q 8:1–3 What kept the apostles in Jerusalem? Why does the author introduce Saul in ch. 8 and then not mention him again until ch. 9?

Luke does a marvelous job of showing us, more than telling us, what is going on. In this case, Luke gives a glimpse of Saul and then spends the rest of the chapter showing what makes Saul furious: God's grace freely and immediately given to the nations. If you skip Ac 8:4–40, you can pick up the narrative at 9:1; however, you wouldn't get the same sense of Saul's fury without knowing how the Gospel just keeps spreading to people who, Saul and the other religious leaders were convinced, could not be loved by God. Please note how Matthew takes a similar approach by describing how Jesus healed three people in succession, each one more despised than the previous in the mind of the religious leaders (Mt 8:1–34). Luke accomplished the same purpose in his Gospel by recording Jesus' reference to foreigners receiving the grace of God in the Old Testament (Lk 4:24–30). Saul is the Jonah of the New Testament!

Q 8:1 Why was everyone except the apostles scattered?

Jesus told the apostles that they would be His witnesses in Jerusalem, Judea, Samaria, and to the ends of the earth (Ac 1:8). In time, some of the apostles did begin to travel to different lands. Acts records the movement of Philip and the missionary journeys of Paul. Peter ended up in Rome, while John spent time in Ephesus and on Patmos. Tradition says Thomas traveled east as far as India. For a long time after Christ's ascension, it was important that the apostles remain together in order to maintain unity in teaching and in responding to challenges to the Gospel (Ac 11:1–18; 15:1–31; Gal 1:18–10).

Q 8:3 Were the children also put in prison?

The text does not say the children were put in prison. They likely would have fled to other family or neighbors or, perhaps, just been left to make their own way.

Q 8:7 Is it through the Word that these people were healed? If so, can people today also be healed through the Word?

It was through the Word that these people were healed, but that Word came by way of apostles who had been given particular authority to do miracles as evidence that they spoke the truth with authority from Christ (Mk 16:16–20). Remember that the physical healing was not the main goal; the main goal was to confirm that the Gospel of Jesus Christ restores us to eternal life and gives us the promise of a resurrected body. People who were healed would become sick again and eventually die in the body. The healing by Jesus and the apostles provided evidence that the Word of God that promised to regenerate our soul and give us eternal life was real. The evidence comes by way of a partial experience of regeneration in healing, exorcism, or by the resurrection of a dead person. God still heals us all the time. God still provides people who are gifted in the healing arts and sciences. God still provides comprehensive and eternal healing by way of His grace communicated in the Word.

Q 8:4–8 Should we assume that the people who were preached to were saved and believed in Jesus Christ and His resurrection?

Luke regularly makes comments about the effectiveness of the Word. In Ac 4:4, Luke describes how many, but not all, of those who heard the Word believed. In other places, Luke reports on the effectiveness of the Word of the Lord but does not say everyone believed (Ac 6:7; 12:24; 13:48–49; 19:20). We can be sure that the Word of the Lord does not return void but is living, powerful, and effective in bringing people to faith according to God's will (Is 55; Heb 4:12; Rm 10:17; Jn 8:31–32). There will always be people who reject the truth. As many rejected Jesus, others will reject His Word as well (Jn 1:11–13; 15:20; Lk 14:15–24; Ac 13:46).

● ● ● ● ● ● ● ● ● ● ● ● ● ● ● ● ● ● ●

Q 8:9–11 What types of magic did Simon do?

Some translations say Simon practiced "sorcery"; others say "magic." Paul and Barnabas met a man named Elymas who was called a sorcerer in Paphos. Paul called Elymas an "enemy of all righteousness, full of all deceit and villainy" (Ac 13:10). Paul's description suggests that sorcerers or magicians who are able to impress people with their magic are able to do so by the power of the devil to perform lying signs and wonders and to deceive (Ex 7:11, 22; 8:7, 18–19; Mt 24:24; 2Co 11:13–15; Rv 13:11–14).

● ● ● ● ● ● ● ● ● ● ● ● ● ● ● ● ● ● ●

Q 8:12, 17 Do you receive the Holy Spirit during Baptism? How does that work?

See questions and answer at 1:5.

● ● ● ● ● ● ● ● ● ● ● ● ● ● ● ● ● ● ●

Q 8:14–16 How can there be a Baptism without the Holy Spirit? Can only the apostles baptize?

Baptism is essentially a life immersed in the Word of God, which is inspired by God, and therefore the Holy Spirit is always present with it (Jn 6:63; 1Th 2:13; 2Tm 3:16). The ceremony of Baptism in which water is added to the Word is given in order to provide physical confirmation of the application of the promises of God to a particular indi-

vidual (2Co 1:21–22; Eph 1:13; 1Pt 3:21). The "falling" or "coming" of the Holy Spirit upon people happens in extraordinary circumstances, where indisputable evidence is needed for the fact that the grace of God saves all and saves immediately through the Word. This "falling" or "coming" of the Holy Spirit comes by the laying on of the apostles' hands and usually manifests itself by speaking in different languages, as was the case on Pentecost (Ac 2:1–21; 15:1–10). The Holy Spirit is there all the way through, providing greater levels of physical evidence as required to authenticate the truth of the Gospel.

● ● ● ● ● ● ● ● ● ● ● ● ● ● ● ● ● ● ●

Q 8:14 Why were Peter and John sent?

The text says the apostles sent them when they heard that Samaria had received the Word of God. The apostles wanted to make certain for themselves and for everyone else that the Samaritans had, indeed, received the Gospel and so were genuinely part of the one Christian Church.

● ● ● ● ● ● ● ● ● ● ● ● ● ● ● ● ● ● ●

Q 8:17 How is it that people were baptized and believed but hadn't received the Holy Spirit?

First, remember that the purpose of miraculous signs and wonders is to provide evidence that the apostles speak with authority from God, that the Word of God is powerful, that God's grace is communicated through that Word immediately and for all. Any time the truth and grace of God is challenged, God provides evidence that overcomes that opposition. You may note that Philip understands that the grace of God is for all, as he eagerly takes it to Samaria and to an Ethiopian and to a region along the coast that was part of Philistia (Azotus). Peter and John came to confirm the truth of God's gracious redemption of all people by granting a sign among the Samaritan believers. Second, notice that Luke is careful to say that the Holy Spirit had "not yet fallen" (v. 16) on them, and then how the Holy Spirit came upon them through the laying on of the apostles' hands. The Holy Spirit came upon Jesus at His Baptism as a witness to the reality that already existed (Lk 3:22). The Holy Spirit came upon the apostles at Pentecost as a witness to the authority Christ had given to them (Ac 2:1–21). The Holy Spirit is always present with the Word (Jn 6:63). Everywhere there are people present who oppose the Gospel, you will find the laying on of the apostles' hands that brings this special manifestation of the Holy Spirit ("falling on them") as evidence that cannot be disputed (Ac 10:44–47; 15:8–9; 19:6).

• • • • • • • • • • • • • • • • • • • •

Q 8:18 How could Simon see that the Spirit was given at the laying on of the apostles' hands?

This is a simple matter of observation. When Peter and John laid their hands on the Samaritan believers, the falling or coming of the Holy Spirit upon them was apparent with physical evidence, usually speaking in different languages. On Pentecost, the apostles spoke in the native languages of the devout Jews who came for the feast of Pentecost in Jerusalem. Speaking to the crowds in their native languages emphasized and demonstrated that the grace of God in Christ was intended for all people. As the Gospel came to others outside of Jerusalem, and Jews in Jerusalem wanted to deny this working of the Gospel, it was important that the Holy Spirit prove the regeneration of these "outsiders" by granting them the same special gift of language that the apostles received. On these occasions, I suspect the Holy Spirit made the foreigners able to speak in Hebrew, since this would be miraculous indeed and the Jews could not claim that this was no language at all (Ac 10:44–47; 11:1–18; 15:1–10).

• • • • • • • • • • • • • • • • • • • •

Q 8:20–23 Peter told Simon that you couldn't buy the gift of God with money. Is it wrong for churches continually to build and acquire fancy things for appearance?

The reader should know that my first answer to this question began with an attempt to argue that what Simon did and what churches do are quite different. As I worked out that argument, I changed my mind. What Simon wanted is quite similar to what you are describing about churches. Simon wanted to be able to communicate the Holy Spirit to others in an extraordinary way, as the apostles did, but Simon wanted to do this for selfish reasons: to have power and importance among the people. It is possible that Simon would have been glad for the people who would be helped by the coming of the Holy Spirit through his hands, just as churches hope that larger and fancier buildings will impress the faith on people for their benefit. Peter's response is similar to God's response when Peter wanted to build shelters for Jesus, Moses, and Elijah at the transfiguration. You may have noticed that the first Christians were disposing of extra possessions and properties in order to provide for the poor and in order to live in simplicity rather than building new properties that would take away resources from the poor and complicate their lives with material concerns (Ac 2:42–47; 4:32–37). No one can make himself an apostle, and no structure of human invention can save. There is great peril in trying to take over God's will and way with our designs and personal interests, as Peter warned Simon so severely (1Sm 15:10–31; 2Sm 7:1–17; Mt 17:4–5; Lk 12:15–21; Ac 8:20–24; 1Tm 6:5–10).

Q 8:22 If Simon prayed and truly confessed, is there any doubt that God would forgive him?

In fact, God has already forgiven all in Christ Jesus. The question is whether a person will realize the benefits of what God has done. Realizing the grace of God in the forgiveness of sins cannot happen when a person is still opposed to God's Word and will, that is to say, impenitent. John assures us that "if we confess our sins, [God] is faithful and just to forgive us our sins and to cleanse us from all unrighteousness" (1Jn 1:9). Luke already informed us that Simon believed, was baptized, and continued with Philip. Simon also seems genuinely terrified by Peter's condemnation of him. Perhaps Luke leaves us with only this much information so that we keep Simon on our mind as a caution.

Q 8:24–25 Was Simon converted to Christianity after he asked Philip to pray for him? Did Peter and John pray for Simon at all?

I don't know of any authoritative text that refers to Simon after this occasion. I suspect Peter and John remembered Simon in their prayers, since praying for those who are weak and fail in temptation is something Jesus did for them (Lk 22:31–32).

Q 8:27 What is a eunuch? Why was the Ethiopian eunuch in Gaza?

A eunuch is a man who is castrated; his testicles have been removed in order to prevent sexual activity. Male servants in harems were castrated so that their master could trust them. This Ethiopian eunuch was in Gaza on his way from Jerusalem back to Ethiopia (Ac 8:27–28). He had come to Jerusalem to worship because he was very devoted, as witnessed by his possession of a copy of Isaiah, his reading of it, and his desire to know how to understand the text (Ac 8:28, 31–34).

Q 8:28 How did this man have access to the Book of Isaiah?

Isaiah wrote around 750 BC. The complete Old Testament had existed for more than four hundred years by the time Philip met the Ethiopian. Luke tells us that this Ethiopian had great authority and was in charge of all the treasury of Candace, the queen of Ethiopia. Luke's description, along with the fact that the man possessed a copy of the Book of Isaiah, suggests that he knew finances and was probably well paid himself. Having a chariot and liberty to travel to Jerusalem in order to worship also suggests great authority, though he is not the first Ethiopian to visit Jerusalem (1Ki 10:1–13).

Q 8:29 Why did the Spirit tell Philip to join the chariot of the Ethiopian?

The Spirit wanted to provide the Ethiopian with answers to his questions and with the preaching of Jesus, which the apostle Philip was able to provide (v. 35). Luke wanted, apparently, to follow Matthew's pattern of providing three extraordinary examples of people whom God intended His grace to embrace (see Mt 8:1–15). Telling Philip to "go over and join" the chariot let Philip know that he was to spend some time with the man, as he did.

Q 8:36 Doesn't this passage seem to go against infant Baptism? Why wasn't the Holy Spirit mentioned at the eunuch's Baptism?

If a person cannot enter the kingdom unless he repent and become like a child, how can anything go against infant Baptism (Mt 18:3)? Modern humanity assumes that children must become adults in order to have faith, but the opposite is true: adults must become like children if they would have faith (1Co 2:14; Jn 3:1–7; Rm 10:17). The Ethiopian eunuch—in childlike simplicity, devotion, and curiosity—had been to Jerusalem to worship and was reading the Word during his journey home. There is no laying on of Philip's hands and no special manifestation of the Holy Spirit because there is no one around who challenges the efficacy of the Gospel or God's desire to bring everyone back into communion with Himself. Only Philip and the Ethiopian are there, and they already believe.

Q 8:37 Did the Ethiopian know he must be baptized because of the Good News given him by Philip?

To some degree, it is likely that everyone in every place and time has associated washing in water with greater kinds of cleansing than just physical. There were many kinds of cleansing rites in the Old Testament, with which the Ethiopian would have been familiar from reading it (Ex 30:18–21; Lv 13:6–58; Ezk 16:4, 9). In particular, he would have known these verses from Isaiah: "Wash yourselves; make yourselves clean; remove the evil of your deeds from before

My eyes; cease to do evil" (1:16); and "when the Lord shall have washed away the filth of the daughters of Zion and cleansed the bloodstains of Jerusalem from its midst by a spirit of judgment and by a spirit of burning" (4:4). The fact that John came baptizing in the Jordan gives further evidence to the familiarity of this practice in religious thought (Lk 3:3–14).

. . . .

Q 8:39–40 Why did God take Philip away from the Church and the eunuch?

God took Philip from the eunuch to Azotus for the same reason Jesus would leave a person or village after He had cared for them: other people need care too. The Ethiopian was a very capable man, already reading the Bible, now baptized and well informed. He would do just fine on his own and surely share the Gospel with those around him. God moves Philip the way He did for the same reason God did and still does all kinds of extraordinary things: to keep us mindful that He is God, that He does the impossible all the time, that He cares for people and does extraordinary things to save and care for us. God is the inexhaustible source of interest and a living hope (Eph 3:20; 1Pt 1:3–9). God did not take Philip away from the Church but expanded the Church through Philip. The Church is not a building or a place; the Church is the Body of Christ, the union of people regenerated by the Word and will of God who remain in that Word and the devoted life it inspires (1Co 1:2; Eph 2:19–22). God

moved Philip from Gaza to Azotus, which is on the coast of the Mediterranean, some distance south of Caesarea. Sometime after this, Philip must have made his way north and settled in Caesarea, where we meet him next (Ac 21:8–9).

. . . .

Q 9:1–2, 15 Why exactly would God choose Saul, who persecuted Him so much, to be used as His "instrument"?

Paul answers this question himself: "But I received mercy for this reason, that in me, as the foremost, Jesus Christ might display His perfect patience as an example to those who were to believe in Him for eternal life" (1Tm 1:16). Paul had many gifts from God, but they had been pointed in the wrong direction. Now, Paul's energy, learning, and determination would be in the service of His Savior instead of in opposition to Him (Ac 9:20–22). Every person has a life prepared by God and has been given gifts in order to fulfill that life (Ps 139; Eph 2:10). As God's creation, we do not have to make a life for ourselves in competition with everyone else; rather, we have the joy, excitement, and anticipation of discovering the life God has for us (Php 3:7–14).

. . . .

Q 9:1–19 Does Luke ever tell us that God changed Saul's name to Paul?

The only mention of Paul's name change comes in Ac 13:9. Perhaps it is not God who changed the name, but He provided the regeneration and salvation that made a name change appropriate. We see a similar case with Levi the tax collector, who never referred to himself by that name after Jesus called him (Mt 9:9; Lk 5:27).

• • • • • • • • • • • • • • • • • • •

Q 9:1 What does it mean that Saul was "still breathing threats"?

Luke introduced Saul at the end of ch. 7 and the beginning of ch. 8. If you skip from Ac 8:3 to 9:1, the narrative flows just fine. Luke "interrupts" what he barely started about Saul so that we could see clearly the essence of the Gospel of Jesus Christ that made Saul crazy. When Luke writes that Saul was "still" breathing threats and violence, he wants you to picture Saul growing more and more furious against the rapid and gracious movement of the Gospel to the nations whom Saul had been taught to despise. For more on this, please see Ac 8:1–3 above.

• • • • • • • • • • • • • • • • • • •

Q 9:2 Why did the Jews in question go as far as Damascus to persecute Christians?

We don't know how many other Jews there might have been who were intent on exterminating Christians, but this narrative only speaks to one Jew who went so far: Saul. Saul's consent to the stoning of Stephen, his persecution of the Church and wreaking havoc on it, and his breathing of threats and murder against the disciples of the Lord all suggest that he was determined to stop the Christian faith before it spread any farther than it had. Damascus is quite a distance to travel just to destroy Christians, but Saul must have thought it was necessary if he were going to stamp out the Gospel.

• • • • • • • • • • • • • • • • • • •

Q 9:3–19 Did Saul not doubt after all those things happened to him? Did he accept Jesus Christ as his Savior right after he heard the voice?

As far as I know, Saul did not express any doubts about the truth after his conversion, but that doesn't mean he didn't have any. Fallen human nature does not believe or accept the things of God and will always be subject to some doubt (1Co 2:14). The New Testament does not use the expression "accept Jesus Christ as a personal Savior" anywhere. God worked faith in Saul just as He does in everyone else: through His Word and Sacraments. God Himself preached the Law to Saul; it worked fear and repentance, evident in Saul's not eating or drinking for three days (Ac 9:9). God sent Ananias to proclaim the Gospel to Saul and baptize him as confirmation of his regeneration and of the forgiveness of sins. Everyone was saved when Jesus said from the cross, "It is finished." Conversion is a process of realization, as the Law continues to quiet our fallen human nature and as the Gospel feeds and strengthens our soul. Only when we leave our fallen human nature behind are we fully "converted" (1Co 13:12; 2Co 5:1–8).

Do miracles still happen today?

Q **9:4–6 Do miracles like the one described here still happen today?**

Anything is possible, especially with God. God can certainly intervene and repeat any of the wonders or miracles He has done in the past, as recorded in the Bible. It is also true that God did the things recorded in order to authenticate and verify His Word (Mk 16:19–20). We know God's messengers and His Son, we know God's Word, and we know the condition of our human nature through the history of His miraculous workings. However, the devil also does signs and wonders in order to deceive, so it is critical that we base our faith and confidence on the Word and not on claims of special experiences (2Co 11:13–15; Rv 13:11–15).

Q **9:5 Was Saul familiar with Jesus' life before his conversion?**

I don't know how Saul could be so violently opposed to Jesus unless he knew about Him, even if he only knew what the religious elders told him. Consider what must have been going through Saul's mind when the Lord met him on the road, knocked him to the ground, then asked why he was persecuting Him. Saul must have been hoping and praying that somehow he had not been wrong, that he had not made a deadly, eternal mistake. So Saul asked the obvious and critical question and received the answer he dreaded. However, this was the best possible answer: Saul, who had never known

mercy, was encountering mercy for the first time. The Lord Jesus had already endured the persecution of the religious authorities, bitter sufferings, and crucifixion precisely to redeem the world so opposed to Him. Saul, the incomparable zealot for the Law he could never fulfill, was completely turned around by the incarnate Son of God, who alone is incomparable and whose love for us can be enjoyed but never fully comprehended (Rm 11:33; Php 3:7–14).

Q **9:7 Was Saul the only person who understood what God said?**

Yes, everyone with Saul saw the light and what was happening to Saul and heard sound, but only Saul heard the words that God was saying to him.

Q **9:9 Is there significance to Saul's being blind and not eating for three days?**

All consequences of the fall, in general, give some indication of our condition since the fall. Spiritually speaking, we are lame, blind, deaf, mute, and dead. Since Saul refused to see Christ as He plainly revealed Himself in the Scriptures and during His ministry, Christ revealed Himself to Saul according to His nature as the Son of God, which was blinding. Saul had three days to think about his past and how blind he had been. Saul had three days to consider what just punishment God would execute against Saul, who not only persecuted His Son but also those who believed in Him. The fact that Saul neither ate nor drank seems appropriate for a man who is waiting for God's judgment. What made Saul so angry and opposed to Christ and His teaching before this is exactly what saved Saul's life, just as it saves us all. The three days that passed while Saul didn't eat or drink is not surprising. Anything regarding God in the Bible tends to come in threes (Is 6:3; Rv 1:4). Hosea prophesied that God would heal us and raise us up on the third day, and so He did in Christ (Hos 6:1–2). The time lapse from the vision on the road until Ananias announced God's grace to Saul is further evidence to the fact that Saul had now been incorporated into or joined with Christ (Rm 8:1).

- -

Q **9:18 What was in Saul's eyes?**

According to Luke, "something like scales" fell from Saul's eyes. What we can know from this text is that there was physical evidence of God's appearance to Saul, both in his blindness and then in whatever it was that fell from his eyes as Ananias proclaimed the grace of God to him.

- -

Q **9:20 Was it by Saul's own ability or power that he returned so quickly and effectively to the synagogue as an apostle of Christ?**

Saul was a young, up-and-coming Pharisee (Ac 22:3; Php 3:4–6). Saul was well acquainted with the synagogue, and it is understandable that he would return to the place where the truth about Jesus was needed most (Ac 17:2).

- -

Q **9:22 How did Saul prove that Jesus is the Christ? Who are the Grecian Jews?**

Grecian Jews were people who were Greek by birth but had converted to Judaism. Saul "baffled" or "confounded" the Jews by proving that Jesus was the Christ, and he did this on the basis of the Old Testament writings. The word translated as "baffled" or "confounded" occurs only in Acts, five times. In all five cases it has to do with a crowd of people not knowing what to think and therefore having nothing definitive to say. This is what the truth does: it stops the noise of lies. The religious leaders wanted to think of the Christ as a physical warrior king, like David, who would not only recapture the power and wealth of Israel but who also would recognize and reward these religious leaders for their extra-special character. Instead, they got the Suffering Servant of Ps 22 and Is 53. The Gospel of Matthew offers a great example of what Saul would have been doing, as he frequently notes how Jesus fulfilled the Old Testament (Mt 1:22–23; 2:15, 17–18, 23; 8:16–17; 10:35; 12:7–8; 13:34–35; 21:4–5, 42; 26:31; 27:14, 35, 46).

Q 9:31 How can this verse claim that the Church on earth had peace when the Romans were trying to imprison or kill the Christians?

Let's begin with a translation that makes the grammar of this verse more clear: "Then the gatherings of believers [churches] throughout Judea, Galilee, and Samaria began to have [or continuously had] peace because they were being built up; that is to say, they were going in the fear of the Lord and being multiplied by the encouragement of the Holy Spirit" (author's translation). Luke is not suggesting that the Christians had peace from the Jewish religious leaders or from the Roman Empire. Luke is saying that the believers, in communion with one another, had peace because of the Lord's presence with and promises to them. This is the same peace that Jesus granted His apostles (Jn 14:27; 16:33; 20:19–26).

Q 9:41–42 What was the motivation or reason for healing Tabitha? She was a believer, but also an old woman, so wasn't it her time to die?

It must not have been her time to die, since God raised her through Peter's ministry. The friends of Tabitha wanted her to be alive again to end their grief and so that she might continue doing those good works that these friends were reporting to Peter. Peter raised her from the dead for the same reason Jesus raised Lazarus: as irrefutable evidence for the power of the Word, for

God's will that we should live and not die, and to authenticate Jesus and His apostles as those who faithfully communicated the truth.

Q 10:1–48 What is the significance of the story of Peter and Cornelius? Why did Cornelius have to go get Simon (Peter)?

The story of Peter and Cornelius is important for two reasons. First, Luke has been providing us with examples of the Gospel working its way out of Jerusalem and Judea and Samaria toward the ends of the earth (Ac 1:8). Philip had brought the Gospel to Samaria, then to an Ethiopian eunuch, then to Azotus and the Mediterranean coast (ch 8). Now that Luke has reported what happened to Paul (ch 9), he returns where we left off, to the outward movement of the Gospel on the coast in Caesarea. Second, Luke has recorded in Acts the history of opposition to the Gospel of Jesus Christ. This chapter reveals how deeply rooted that opposition is in fallen human nature and serves as the occasion for the first Jerusalem Council, where the issue is brought into the open and resolved (though it will have to be resolved again in ch 15).

Cornelius did not "have to" get Simon. Simon Peter was going to be an answer to Cornelius's prayers. Luke and the angel in the vision tell us that Cornelius was a devout man who feared God, prayed, and gave to the poor. Think of how pleased God must have been to be able to send an apostle to Cornelius, an apostle who could make clear to him that all of God's promises in the Old Testament were fulfilled in Christ and that he was, therefore, forgiven and accepted by God. We know how important this was to Cornelius because he wasted no time sending for Peter. Moreover, when Peter arrived, Cornelius had already gathered his relatives and close friends in order to have them also hear what God's apostle had to say.

Q 10:1 What was the "Italian Cohort"?

Cohorts, or regiments, were made up of six "centuries," each century being composed of one hundred men and commanded by a centurion. This regiment, apparently, consisted of men who were not only Roman citizens but were also born in Rome. An Augustinian regiment is mentioned in Ac 27:1.

Q 10:9–43 What is the significance of the number three in this section?

The sheet full of animals came down and a voice from heaven spoke to Peter three times (10:16); three men from Cornelius came to the house where Peter was staying (10:19); Peter reports how Jesus rose from the dead on the third day (10:40). As mentioned above in Ac 9:9, things having to do with God tend to come in threes. The sheet came from God, as did the voice that commanded Peter and then corrected him. The Son of God died and rose from the dead on the third day, as Hosea had prophesied (Hos 6:2). The three men were on an errand that originated with God's command to

Cornelius, and it was three men who visited Abraham on their way to Sodom and Gomorrah (one man was the Son of God and the other two were angels, Gn 18:1–19:1).

Q 10:9–16 Please explain the significance of this vision. Is this passage about "clean and unclean animals" an example of Jesus fulfilling the Law for us?

First, we need to be clear about the law. The covenant that God made with Israel through Moses after the exodus included many kinds of laws. There was moral Law (Ten Commandments), civil law (for example, the prohibition against moving landmarks), and ceremonial law (especially laws concerning sacrifices). Ceremonial laws had to do with special days and what to do on them, sickness and what to do about it, circumcision, and what you could or could not eat. Jesus was the fulfillment of the Law. He fulfilled the moral Law in order to redeem us from our sins against it (Rm 8:1–4; 10:4), but these laws are always in effect. There were civil consequences for breaking civil laws; you could go to jail or be required to make restitution, but you wouldn't necessarily be eternally condemned. The ceremonial laws all pointed forward to God's promise to send a Savior. Jesus made this point over and over again during His public ministry (Mt 5:17; Jn 10:11). Now that Jesus had come, there was no more need to be concerned about circumcision or issues having to do with being clean or unclean.

Second, we need to understand that

fallen human nature wants to satisfy its own desires and at the same time claim it is innocent of any wrongdoing. This is what produces self-righteousness. It is difficult—indeed, impossible—for a person to justify himself on the basis of the moral law (though many try, Lk 10:25–37; 18:9–14, 18–27). It is easier to convince yourself and others that you are holy on the basis of the ceremonial law: washing, resting, and watching what you eat (Mt 12:1–8; Mk 7:1–23). The religious leaders refused to accept Jesus' teaching about the Law and about grace because it meant they would have to confess that they were sinners and they would have to embrace everyone else as fellow sinners, but all redeemed by the grace of God. This would mean humiliation and loss of power and wealth.

Third, Peter is a very powerful example of how determined our human nature is to argue against the truth. Peter had been with Jesus during His whole public ministry. Peter had many personal experiences in which he could not justify himself, though he tried (Mt 14:28–31; 16:13–23; 17:4–5; Lk 22:31–34, 54–62; Jn 21:15–19). Even after Pentecost and several trials before the religious leaders, Peter himself was still clinging to the Law of Moses as if it would justify him or make him better than someone else: "By no means, Lord; for I have never eaten anything that is common or unclean" (v. 14). Notice how this sounds like the older brother of the prodigal son (Lk 15:25–32). Even after this incident with the sheet and voice from heaven, Peter's experience in

Why was it unclean or impure to eat animals?

Cornelius's house, and Peter's defense of the Gospel before the first Jerusalem Council, Peter still relapsed into the hypocrisy of self-righteousness (Gal 2:11–21).

Therefore, the significance of this vision can hardly be overestimated. This vision confirms, yet again, that the Law of Moses had been misapplied by religious leaders and certainly was not applicable after Christ. This vision confirms how inseparable self-righteousness and hypocrisy are from fallen human nature. This vision confirms the patience and love of God, by which He brings Peter along and provides the Gospel to the household and friends of Cornelius. All people of all times share Peter's fallen human nature and need the grace of God that taught him and that was evident in God's working on behalf of those who were made to feel outcast (Lk 7:36–50).

• • • • • • • • • • • • • • • • • • •

Q 10:13–14 Why was it unclean or impure to eat animals?

There are different arguments made to explain the laws about clean and unclean animals. Some argue that God was forbidding foods that were perilous for people in these times to eat because they lacked the sanitary conditions, refrigeration, and cooking methods necessary to eat such things safely. Others argue that God was using diet as another means of separating His people from the nations around them. Perhaps both are correct.

● ● ● ● ● ● ● ● ● ● ● ● ● ● ● ● ● ● ● ●

Q **10:15 Is God here getting rid of His rule of clean or kosher foods that He gave to the Jews?**

Actually, Jesus did that years before this, as recorded in Mk 7:18–19. Jesus also gives us reason to believe that the spirit or intent of the law was what mattered and was ignored by the religious leaders of Israel (Mt 12:1–14).

● ● ● ● ● ● ● ● ● ● ● ● ● ● ● ● ● ● ● ●

Q **10:16 Is there any significance in the number three in Peter's vision, since it appeared to him three times?**

Please see Ac 10:9–43 above.

● ● ● ● ● ● ● ● ● ● ● ● ● ● ● ● ● ● ● ●

Q **10:22 What are the duties of a centurion?**

A centurion has command of one hundred men (a "century"). See also notes on Ac 10:1–48 and 10:1 above.

● ● ● ● ● ● ● ● ● ● ● ● ● ● ● ● ● ● ● ●

Q **10:23 Why did Peter invite the men into his house to be his guest?**

For most of the world's history, hospitality was very common because there were no motels for travelers or credit cards with which to pay the bill. People traveled and sought lodging where they could (Gn 19:1–3; Jgs 19:16–21; Lk 2:4–7). Besides the normal customs of hospitality, the Holy Spirit had told Peter that he was to go with these men, but it was already midafternoon, which meant they would need to stay overnight and leave the next morning.

● ● ● ● ● ● ● ● ● ● ● ● ● ● ● ● ● ● ● ●

Q **10:28 This verse explains the significance of Peter's vision, but why were animals and a sheet coming down used in his vision?**

Please see Ac 10:9–16 above.

● ● ● ● ● ● ● ● ● ● ● ● ● ● ● ● ● ● ● ●

Q **10:35 Does one have to keep the Ten Commandments, or is it enough simply to believe in Jesus?**

The Ten Commandments articulate the moral Law. Failure to keep the Law means death (Rm 6:23; Gal 3:10; Jas 2:10). You must keep the Law in order to live, but no one can; therefore, God provided a substitute in His Son, Jesus Christ. Belief in Jesus means that a person depends on the grace of God in Jesus, who kept the Law for all people and on that basis has forgiven all sins (Eph 2:8–9). Please note that belief in Jesus is a product of God's Word and Spirit working in us (Jn 6:63; Rm 10:17).

● ● ● ● ● ● ● ● ● ● ● ● ● ● ● ● ● ● ● ●

Q **10:45 Were only the circumcised amazed?**

The word translated "amazed" occurs seventeen times in the New Testament. This appears to be the only time it is used of circumcised men, who are astonished that the gift of the Holy Spirit was poured out on Gentiles.

· · · · · · · · · · · · · · · · · ·

Q **10:46–48 Can you receive the Holy Spirit without being baptized?**

The Holy Spirit is always present with the Word of God (Is 55:10–11; Jn 6:63; Heb 4:12). Thinking of the Rite of Baptism apart from a life in the Word is like imagining a birth without a pregnancy or a life of care afterward. The Word of God is the living water that creates the Christian and is what the Christian life is immersed (baptized) in (Jn 8:31–32; 15:1–7). The ceremony of Baptism is effective and significant because the water is joined or connected with the Word according to the command of God (Mt 28:19–20; Mk 16:16; Ti 3:4–5; 1Pt 3:21).

· · · · · · · · · · · · · · · · · ·

Q **10:46 Why did they speak in tongues?**

Speaking in different languages immediately (tongues) is an external sign that authenticates God's Word and work (Mk 16:19–20). On the day of Pentecost, the apostles' ability to speak in the native languages of the devout Jews who were visiting Jerusalem demonstrated that these men were inspired by God to speak on His behalf and that God's Word communicates His grace in bringing salvation to all. The fact that God had redeemed all people by grace in Jesus Christ apart from the works of the Law continued to be opposed and assaulted by religious leaders in Israel (Ac 4:18;

5:17–18, 28; 11:1–3; 15:5). Jews who came with Peter to Cornelius's house, though they believed that Jesus was the Christ, still did not accept that God saves all immediately through the Word. These men were convinced and could not deny that Cornelius and his family had been saved, since God gave these Gentiles the ability to speak in languages, probably Hebrew, just as He had done for the apostles on Pentecost (Ac 15:8–10). Please see notes on Ac 2:4, 9–11; and 8:14–16, 18 for more on speaking in tongues.

· · · · · · · · · · · · · · · · · ·

Q **11:2 Why was Peter criticized for following the teachings of Christ?**

Many religious leaders were so opposed to Christ that they caused Him to be crucified even though He had proven He was the Son of God, raised the dead, healed the sick, fed the hungry, and fulfilled every other prophecy of the Old Testament (Jn 11:45–54; Ac 2:22–36). Some of the religious leaders did at least accept that Jesus was the Christ, the Son of God and promised Savior (Ac 15:5). However, these religious leaders still contended that a person had to keep the Law of Moses before he or she could be accepted by God. Thus, they continued to argue that a person must save himself by keeping the Law, which Paul and Peter both responded to vigorously (Ac 11:1–18; 15:1–11; Gal 2:11–21; 3:10–14). The whole point of the Book of Jonah is to expose the bitter resentment of fallen human nature against God's gracious will and ways (Jnh 1:1–4:11).

> How did Christians
> receive their name?

Q 11:26 How did Christians receive their name in Antioch?

To begin with, people were known simply as disciples of Jesus (Mt 27:57, 64; Jn 18:17). After Jesus' ascension, some people referred to the disciples of Jesus as followers of "the Way" (Ac 9:2; 24:14). Luke does not offer any details about how or why the disciples of Jesus began to be called "Christians" in Antioch, though such naming is common, as in "Americans" and "Australians."

Q 11:28 Who is Agabus? Is he from Antioch?

Luke tells us in the previous verse that Agabus was one of the prophets who came up to Antioch from Jerusalem. Agabus appears again in Ac 21:10–11. The Gospel of Luke and Acts are full of accounts in which we meet someone briefly and never know much about them.

Q 12:8–11 It states they (Peter and the angel) passed through guards. Does this mean the angel and Peter were invisible?

Jesus passed through a crowd that had seized Him and meant to throw Him off a cliff (Lk 4:28–30). Jesus met disciples on the road to Emmaus but kept Himself from being recognized (Lk 24:13–27). In that account, Luke says that the disciples' "eyes were kept from recognizing Him" (v. 16). In theory, Peter and the angel could have been invisible. However, if we consider what we know from Luke, it seems more likely that the eyes of the guards were kept from seeing.

Q 12:13–15 Why did they not believe it was Peter at the door?

They did not believe it was Peter at the door because they knew Peter had been imprisoned by Herod (Ac 12:3–4). Perhaps someone knew how heavy a guard Peter was under. People may have known that if prisoners escaped, the guards would be executed, which Herod did (12:19; 27:42–43). People couldn't believe that Jesus had risen from the dead, and they had trouble believing Peter could have been freed from Herod's prison (Mk 16:11, 14).

Q 12:23 Did worms actually eat Herod? Was his death to be an example to all unbelievers?

Luke does not mean that Herod was eaten by earthworms. Luke is referring to some kind of parasite that would eat a person from the inside. Everything recorded in the Bible is to provide examples for us (Jn 13:15; 1Co 10:6, 11). Herod's death is a particularly powerful example of the way fallen human nature makes claims for itself that it cannot begin to sustain. If Herod were a god, certainly he could overcome or even be immune from a small parasite.

● ● ● ● ● ● ● ● ● ● ● ● ● ● ● ● ● ●

Q 13:9 How and why did Saul's name change to Paul?

In the history of Christianity it is not uncommon for people to change their names or to take a new name when baptized. The apostle Matthew's name was Levi before Jesus called him, but Matthew never refers to himself as Levi. We only know this from Luke's Gospel (Mt 9:9; Lk 5:27). Perhaps people meant to follow the example of God, who changed Abram's name to Abraham, Sarai's name to Sarah, and Jacob's name to Israel because of His promises and grace toward them (Gn 17:5, 15; 32:28).

● ● ● ● ● ● ● ● ● ● ● ● ● ● ● ● ● ●

Q 13:13 Why did John desert Paul and Barnabas?

Luke tells us that John's surname was Mark (Ac 12:25). Luke also tells us that Paul insisted that they should not take John Mark with them on the second missionary journey because of "one who had withdrawn from them in Pamphylia and had not gone with them to the work" (Ac 15:38). We suspect this is the same Mark who wrote the Gospel for Peter and identified himself very cryptically in his account of Jesus' arrest in the Garden of Gethsemane (2Pt 1:15; Mk 14:51–52). Gospel writers identify themselves in interesting ways, always by the inclusion of something unique, as is this account of the young man who ran away

when Jesus was arrested. The running away during the arrest of Jesus and again during the first missionary journey suggests this is the same young man and that he runs from fear. Happily, it appears that in time Mark became strong in the faith and even became very useful to Paul (Ac 15:39; 2Tm 4:11).

● ● ● ● ● ● ● ● ● ● ● ● ● ● ● ● ● ●

Q 13:41 What does this verse from Habakkuk mean?

Ac 13:40 records that Paul was warning the Jews in the synagogue to beware that they did not bring themselves under the condemnation of the prophets, as recorded in Hab 1:5. A more precise translation helps make the prophets' and Paul's point clear: "Look, you despisers, marvel and perish because I, Myself, am working a work in your days, a work that you will surely not believe even if someone declared it to you" (author's translation). The passage means that some people are so stubborn that they will not believe the truth, no matter what. The Epistle to the Hebrews makes severe warnings about this kind of stubborn hard-heartedness, referring to Israel after the exodus as an example (Heb 3:12–4:12). David and Paul also warn against ignoring the constant and marvelous witness of creation (Ps 19; Rm 1:18–31).

● ● ● ● ● ● ● ● ● ● ● ● ● ● ● ● ● ●

Q 14:12 Why were Paul and Barnabas called gods?

In Greek mythology and subsequently in Roman thought, there was a lot of interaction between the gods and human beings. The Roman emperors thought they were a god incarnate, hence Caesar "Augustus." Herod liked the idea too, as we have seen in Ac 12:20–25. People may have called Paul and Barnabas gods as flattery or out of fear or just in case it were true; after all, God had come down in the likeness of men!

• • • • • • • • • • • • • • • • • • • •

Q 14:19–20 After being stoned, how does Paul have the physical strength to leave the next day with Barnabas?

These apostles were a tough bunch—remember how Jesus gave Simon the name "Rocky" ("Peter" in Greek)? It is possible that the stones grazed but did not hit Paul straight on, knocking Paul to the ground and satisfying his opponents that he had been executed. And there is always the possibility of divine intervention. If Jesus, the prophets, and the apostles all healed the sick and raised the dead, certainly God could grant Paul some mighty healing on this occasion.

• • • • • • • • • • • • • • • • • • • •

Q 15:1–12 Why was there a controversy about Moses' teaching?

The controversy over Moses' teaching has to do with different kinds of laws and

> Why was circumcision so important?

how they still affect us. First, regarding different kinds of laws: Through Moses, God informed the Jews about the moral, civil, and ceremonial law. The moral Law is articulated in the Ten Commandments and is always in force because it describes necessary relationships in God's creation. The civil law instructs people on how to best get along together—you wouldn't have to keep it, but why wouldn't you want to? The ceremonial law pointed to the promised Savior, Jesus Christ, the Son of God and Son of David.

Second, how do these laws affect us? Since Jesus fulfilled the ceremonial law, it is no longer applicable, binding, or in force (Mk 7:14–19; Lk 22:14–20; Rm 10:4). Paul warns that anyone who wants to be bound by any single part of that law, or who binds others, is bound to keep it all and will find himself condemned by it (Gal 2:11–21; 5:3–4). While the moral Law is always in effect, Christ has redeemed us from eternal condemnation under that Law by taking our place (Rm 8:1–11; 2Co 5:14–21; Gal 3:10–14).

This controversy is about the old man inasmuch as the old man (our fallen human nature) always wants to justify itself even while it disobeys the Law (see Malachi; Mt 15:1–14). The new man, regenerated and nourished by the promises and Spirit of God, lives in obedience to the Law and holds the flesh in repentance and forgiveness (1Jn 1:8–9; 3:8–9). Christians keep the moral and civil law out of love for God and neighbor because of God's love already given to us in Christ (Jn 14:19–31; Rm 12:1–21).

Q 15:1 Why was circumcision so important to some people?

Fallen human nature wants to justify itself, but this is impossible in respect to the moral Law, that is, the Ten Commandments (Rm 3:9–20; Gal 2:16). Therefore, people like to act like outward, ceremonial activity is what really matters (Mt 23:2–24). Circumcision is a physical work that happens only once and that anyone can get right. Therefore, if you think what matters most to God is circumcision, then you would demand that everyone be circumcised (like you) or remain condemned (by you).

James urged the sending of a letter that instructed the Gentile believers "to abstain from the things polluted by idols, and from sexual immorality, and from what has been strangled, and from blood" (Ac 15:20). James did not urge this because he still wanted to impose just a little of the Law of Moses. James instructed the Gentiles to stay away from these things because they all had to do with cult worship, and if Jews thought a Gentile still had anything to do with idolatrous practices, especially in public, there could be no positive relationship between Gentile and Jew. James's urging is similar to Paul's command that we consider the weaker brother, lest we cause him to stumble (Rm 14:1–15:4).

Q 15:2, 6–7, 13 How is it that Peter, Paul, Barnabas, and James are all in the same place?

Paul and Barnabas had been missionary companions since Barnabas sought Paul out and took him to Antioch (Ac 11:25; 13:2–14:28). These two were chosen to represent the faithful of Antioch at the meeting in Jerusalem (15:2). Peter and James were centered in Jerusalem, partly so they could be ready to handle disputes such as this.

Q 15:5 Why do Pharisees think circumcision is so important?

Please see Ac 15:1; 11:2; and 10:9–16 above.

Q 15:8 How does God give the Holy Spirit?

At any time, to anyone, God gives His Spirit in the Word (Jn 6:63; Rm 10:17). During the time of the apostles, the Holy Spirit "fell" or "came upon" people through the laying on of the apostle's hands in order to authenticate the Gospel, the apostles who taught it, and the people who were saved by it (see also Ac 8:14–16; 19:6).

Q 15:10 How are they testing God by "placing a yoke" on others that no one can bear?

A yoke is a wooden beam, carved to fit over the neck, that joins animals such as oxen to each other and to the burden to be pulled. Any significant and enduring burden could be referred to as a yoke (2Co 6:14;

1Tm 6:1). Jesus took our place under the burden of the Law so that we would not be crushed under its condemnation and punishment (Mt 8:17; Lk 23:13–25; 2Co 5:21). Testing God has to do with refusing what He offers graciously (Is 6:10–14). God had released all people from the condemnation of the Law by His love through the life of His Son. People who want to impose the Law on others to gain power and wealth while robbing others of the grace of God are under the most severe condemnation of God (Mt 18:6–10, 23–35; 23:1–39; Gal 5:1–15).

- -

Q **15:13 James was killed in ch. 12, so who is the James referred to in this verse?**

The apostle James, brother of John, was killed by Herod in ch. 12 (Ac 12:2; Mt 4:21; Ac 1:13). The James mentioned in this verse is the half-brother of Jesus and author of the Epistle that bears his name (Mt 13:55; Gal 1:19; 2:9, 12; Jas 1:1; Jude 1).

- -

Q **15:16 What happened to the "tent of David"?**

A tabernacle is a tent made of animal skins. In the Old Testament, the tabernacle was a tent of skins made according to God's design in which God would come to meet His people and be among them (Ex 36:14; 40:35). John describes the incarnation of the Son of God as such: "And the Word became flesh and [tabernacled] among us" (Jn

1:14). This means that just as the tabernacle of animal skins was a covering for the place God filled in order to be among His people, so now the Son of God had filled a human nature that descended from David's line (Mt 1:1–18; Rm 1:1–4). The "fallen" tent of David refers to Israel's loss of independence and the fact that it had been a long time since a descendant of David served as king (2Sm 7:1–29; Is 11:1–16; Ac 13:21–41).

- -

Q **15:20 What is "things polluted by idols"? If they had decided that Gentiles do not need to obey the same laws as the Jews, then why do they write to give them more rules?**

Things "polluted by idols" means items, especially food, that had been offered as a sacrifice to an idol in a cult temple (Rm 14:1–23; 1Co 10:18–23). While the apostles clearly taught that we are justified by grace apart from the works of the Law, they also knew that our freedom from the Law is given so that we serve others in love, not so that we might indulge the appetites of our flesh from which Jesus has now saved us. The apostles are also concerned that no Christian should continue in practices that would cause divisions or that would cause others to be tempted to act against their conscience. James is instructing the Gentile believers to stay away from the overt worship of idols as well as the idolatry that comes out of the heart and defiles a person and causes others to fall into sin. Note how the Jewish believers need to recognize that ceremonial, outward matters don't matter anymore while the Gentile believers need to be careful of outward conduct that does matter because it affects others (Rm 13:8).

Q 15:22 Why is Judas referred to as Barsabbas?

After Jesus was betrayed, would you want the name "Judas"? If this is the Barsabbas mentioned in Ac 1:23, he has lots of names, including Joseph and Justus. Luke includes this information as evidence of the historical accuracy of what he is writing to us (2Pt 1:16; 1Jn 1:1–3).

Q 15:24 Didn't the apostles know whom they were sending?

The Bible often talks about false prophets and those who claim to speak with authority (Dt 13:1–5; Jer 23:1; Mt 7:15; Ac 13:6–11; 2Pt 2:1). There were men who claimed to be disciples of John the Baptist who refused to follow Christ and were confusing people (Ac 19:1–7). The apostle John laments the antichrists who "went out from us, but they were not of us" (1Jn 2:19). The some who "have gone out from us" were neither sent nor authorized, but went out on their own initiative, with their own teaching, for their own purposes. Only a very few church bodies follow the example in Acts and require public servants of the Word to meet biblical standards of qualification and to be called by the Church (Ac 13:2; 1Tm 3:1–7).

Q 15:32 What is meant here by the word "prophets"?

The word "prophet" has a range of meanings. The essence of the word has to do with speaking out (Ex 7:1). In the Old Testament, prophets of God spoke the Word of God, including descriptions of what would take place in the future (Dt 18:22). God gave the prophets the ability to do signs and wonders in order to authenticate them, just as He did with the apostles (Ex 4:1–9; 1Ki 18:20–46; Jas 5:17–18; Mk 16:19–20). In the New Testament, we still find references to prophets, and these prophets are still inspired to describe what will happen in the future (Ac 21:10–11). Judas and Silas are described as the kind of prophets who speak out in public but do not do signs or tell the future. Like the apostles, the prophets who did signs and told the future came to an end with this generation (Eph 4:11).

Q 15:36–41 Why couldn't Paul and Barnabas solve the disagreement in love? Was it Mark or John who deserted in Pamphylia?

Anytime something isn't settled in love it is because of fallen human nature. Clearly all things can be settled in love, since God is love and settles everything. I'm not sure that this wasn't settled in love. No doubt Paul and Barnabas continued to love each other, and they loved Mark, but this did not change their differences over what to do with him. Barnabas wanted to give Mark another chance just as Barnabas was willing to trust that Saul (Paul) had really been converted (Ac 11:25). There is plenty of work to do according to God's will and in the service of others in this wide world so that people who have honest differences about physical and temporal decisions can go their own ways without hard feelings. As time passed, Mark must have improved, and Paul came to think of him differently, as Paul's mention of Mark in 2Tm 4:11 reveals. See Ac 13:13 above for more about this.

⋅ ⋅

Q **16:1–3 Why would it be easier to talk to Jews if Paul circumcised Timothy? Why did they circumcise Timothy but not Titus? What is the current Christian's view on circumcision and why?**

Circumcision was a physical confirmation of the promises that God made to Abraham (Gn 17:7–14). Jacob's sons spoke as though they could not intermarry or have other dealings with people who were uncircumcised, though they said this in order to deceive their neighbors (Gn 34:13–17). God instructed the people of Israel through Moses that strangers could join them in the Passover as long as they were circumcised (Ex 12:48–49). Fallen human nature turned the confirmation of God's promises and communion into an obligation that a person must fulfill in order to justify himself before God and to be allowed to interact with the Jews (Ac 11:3; Gal 2:11–16).

Paul circumcised Timothy for the same reason James wrote to the Gentiles that they should keep away from practices associated with idol worship (Ac 15:13–21). Neither James nor Paul was imposing an obligation of the Old Testament or of the Law on people. They were only removing a cause for concern or contention that would prevent them from sharing the Gospel with Jews (Ac 21:27–31; 22:21–23). Luke makes clear that Paul circumcised Timothy because the Jews in that area knew his father was Greek and therefore was unlikely to have been circumcised (16:3). Paul did not circumcise Titus because no one would have known to make an issue of it, and those who knew did not see circumcision as an issue any longer (Gal 2:1–9). The apostles did not encourage or demand circumcision. All the Old Testament ceremonial laws were fulfilled by Jesus. Circumcision was replaced by Baptism, just as the shedding of blood of animal sacrifices was replaced by the single eternal sacrifice of Christ (Mt 28:19–20; Heb 8:1–10:18). Christians are free to be circumcised or not as long as they have not thought of being justified thereby (Gal 5:3–6; 1Co 4:4; Rm 14:1–23). Jesus embodied and taught that love moves us to give all we have for the benefit of others, but we can never give away the truth or grace of God, for then we would be of no benefit to anyone (Mt 5:38–48; Rm 13:8; 1Co 6:12; 9:19–23; 10:23–24).

Q **16:1–5 Why is the story of Timothy joining Paul significant to the Book of Acts?**

History is all about people. It is important that the early apostles, pastors, and missionaries had travel companions, just as Jesus sent out the disciples two by two (Lk 10:1; Ec 4:12). It is also helpful to have some history of Timothy when we read Paul's letters to him.

Q **16:6 Why doesn't Luke tell us what means the Holy Spirit used to forbid Paul and Silas from traveling to different countries?**

This is a curious passage. Perhaps Luke does not want the reader to be distracted with special manifestations of the Holy Spirit. The focus is clearly on God's will that Paul travel to Macedonia (Ac 16:9–10) as quickly as possible. The point is not about where the Holy Spirit didn't want Paul to go, but where He did want Paul to go and to go right away. Interestingly, at the end of the third missionary journey, the Holy Spirit had trouble getting Paul to follow directions (Ac 20:22–23; 21:4, 11–14).

Q **16:7–10 How and why did the Spirit not allow Paul to enter Asia?**

Just the same as v. 6, Luke simply says the Holy Spirit forbade ("did not allow" is the same thing) Paul and company from entering Bythinia. As explained above, the Holy Spirit wants Paul to go to Macedonia right away without being delayed or diverted by other people in other places.

Q **16:13–16 Why is there no mention of men at the "place of prayer"?**

Luke does not say they went there in order to find the men. Nor does Luke say there were no men there, though if there were it seems likely Luke would tell us. When Paul wants to engage the men, he usually went to the synagogue or marketplace (Ac 17:1–2, 17). Maybe Paul was looking for a break from the inevitable argument and necessity of defense that speaking with men in the synagogue brought about (9:20–22; 13:42–47; 14:19–20; 15:2).

Q **16:14–15 Why do some hear the message, but their hearts aren't opened?**

We cannot look directly at God, nor can we fathom His wisdom, grace, or timing. We know that God desires all "to be saved and to come to the knowledge of the truth" (1Tm 2:4). We know that God did redeem the whole world in Christ (Jn 3:16; 2Co 5:19). We know that only God can work repentance and faith in a person (Jn 1:11–13; 1Pt 1:3–9). All human beings possess a human nature that opposes God (Rm 5:6–11). Why some people sustain their opposition and others are turned in repentance and regenerated by the Word is a mystery.

● ● ● ● ● ● ● ● ● ● ● ● ● ● ● ● ● ● ●

Q 16:14 What is the significance of Lydia, "a seller of purple goods"?

There are two key words that tell us about Lydia: "purple" and "seller." Purple was a color hard to come by, therefore reserved for aristocrats and rulers, and very expensive. Lydia was a seller in purple cloth, which means she was of some wealth. This suggestion is verified by the fact that she had lodging for Paul and his companions (Ac 16:15).

● ● ● ● ● ● ● ● ● ● ● ● ● ● ● ● ● ● ●

Q 16:15 Why was Lydia's whole household baptized after she responded to the Good News?

The ceremony of Baptism with water joins a physical element to the Word and command of God in order to confirm that God applied His promises to a person. The Christian lives awash in the Word of God that regenerates that person and forgives his sins; the water of Baptism makes that life in the Word evident (Mt 28:19–20; Jn 1:11–13; 3:1–7; Ti 3:4–5; 1Pt 3:21). Lydia's whole household was baptized because they had all been immersed in the Word and thus had the promises of God applied to them, as the baptismal rite confirmed (2Co 1:21–22; Eph 1:13).

● ● ● ● ● ● ● ● ● ● ● ● ● ● ● ● ● ● ●

Q 16:16–19 How did they react to this fortune-teller? Were there a lot of demonic possessions in these times?

Luke says the fortune-teller cried out after them for many days before Paul was so annoyed that he cast out the demon (v. 18). Luke does not tell us more than this. There seem to have been many demonic possessions like this in these times, as the Gospels record Jesus healing many demoniacs, and Acts records the apostles doing the same (Mk 1:32; 5:18; 7:25; Ac 8:7; 19:11–20).

● ● ● ● ● ● ● ● ● ● ● ● ● ● ● ● ● ● ●

Q 16:16 Was the slave girl's ability to predict the future the work of God or of the devil? Does the devil have the ability to tell the future?

The Bible describes our body as a temple of the Holy Spirit (1Co 6:19). If our body is not inhabited by the Holy Spirit, then it is open to, if not possessed by, demonic spirits (Mt 12:43–45). If the spirit in the slave girl was of God, it would not have been annoying or bound in the service of greedy masters; nor would Paul have cast it out. God has granted the devil and his demons that ability to do lying signs and wonders (2Co 11:13–15). If the devil knows anything about the future, it would be only as God granted. The devil seems not to know the future, for if he had known what the crucifixion of Jesus would accomplish, why would he have facilitated it?

● ● ● ● ● ● ● ● ● ● ● ● ● ● ● ● ● ● ●

Q 16:17 Why would a demon help spread the Gospel? If the demon was doing that, why would Paul want to silence it?

The demon isn't spreading the Gospel but only identifying Paul and his companions. I suspect demons are bound to bear witness to the truth of God when God's messengers are near them, as Paul said about the resurrected Jesus: "At the name of Jesus every knee should bow, in heaven and on earth and under the earth, and every tongue confess that Jesus Christ is Lord" (Php 2:9–11).

How would a person know when to believe what a demon says and when not to? There are at least two reasons why Jesus and Paul forbid demons to speak. First, demons are all about destroying lives by deceiving people, so it is unfitting for them to speak the truth about God. If a demon-possessed person were telling the truth, how would you know? If a demon were lying about Jesus or Paul, why would they allow that? Second, the truth is powerful, and demons seem to be bound by Jesus, who is the Truth, and by apostles because they are messengers of the Truth. The demons want to keep talking but are bound in the presence of truth to speak the truth, but God does not want them to speak at all, for reasons described above.

● ● ● ● ● ● ● ● ● ● ● ● ● ● ● ● ● ● ●

Q 16:18 Why did no one appear to be afraid of Paul when he ordered the spirit out of this girl? Why did it take him so long to address the issue?

Average people do seem to be afraid of those who cast out demons, as a few narratives record (Lk 8:37; Ac 19:17). Some people and some religious leaders are so determined to oppose God and the truth that they cannot understand or recognize what is going on right in front of them (Jn 11:45–53; Rm 1:18–32; 2Co 4:4). What kept the owners of the fortune-teller from understanding is described by Luke in this way: "When her owners saw that their hope of gain was gone" (Ac 16:19). Paul warned Timothy that the love of money is the root of all kinds of evil—one evil would be blindness to what God is showing you (1Tm 6:10). What kind of wisdom, if any, can a person have who rejects the Word of the Lord (Jer 8:9)?

Paul wrote that we should strive to be at peace with others, as much as possible (Rm 12:18). Paul also charges Christians to be careful to submit to the governing authorities (Rm 13:1). Since the slave girl was not breaking any law, it was appropriate for Paul to endure her behavior. Paul took a long time to address the issue because he was trying not to address it at all. I suspect the girl did not tell the future but only gave the illusion of doing so (see notes at 16:16 above). If she could actually tell the future, it would only happen because God granted that ability (1Ki 22:22–23). There was an evil spirit within her for two reasons. First, any person in whom the Holy Spirit does not dwell is an open habitation for demons (Mt 12:43–45). Second, she may have been attractive to demons who would not only deceive people who listened to her but also support the greed and wicked conduct of her masters (Ac 16:19–24).

Q 16:19–24 Why wasn't there a trial?

First, the masters of the slave girl were local men and wealthy, according to Luke (v. 16). This means they were bound to be well-known to the civil authorities. Second, the masters of the slave girl did bring Paul and Silas to the authorities in the market-place but there announced that they were Jews. Only Roman citizens had special protection under Roman law, as Paul makes reference to the next day and after another incident in Jerusalem later (Ac 16:37; 22:24–29). Third, civil authorities were typically nervous about riots and knew that dealing swiftly and publicly with a person or people who created uproar was perhaps the best remedy. You will note that the people seemed to be satisfied after Paul and Silas were beaten and jailed, yet the next day the magistrates commanded the jailer simply to release them.

Q 16:23 Were the people really put in jail with beatings?

Yes. While Roman law was fairly comprehensive, fair, and effective, it was not overly concerned with human rights like modern Western cultures. The law was especially disinterested in the comfort of prisoners. The notion of "innocent until proven guilty" is rather recent and Western.

Q 16:25–30 Did the chains come loose as a result of the earthquake? Did all of the prisoners escape?

Luke does not say that the doors opened or that the chains fell off because of the earthquake; he only says that the foundations of the prison were shaken (v. 25). In Ac 12:10, Luke reports that the iron gate to the city opened for Peter "of its own accord" ("automatically" in Greek). That may be what happened here with the doors and the chains.

We know that none of the prisoners escaped since Paul told the jailer to do no harm to himself because "we are all here" (Ac 16:28). Peter escaped the prison of Herod because Herod intended to execute Peter, and an angel led Peter out. Paul and Silas were in no danger of execution—in fact, they would have been released anyway. The earthquake was an extraordinary confirmation of the power of God in the Gospel that Paul and Silas were singing about and provided the occasion for bringing salvation to the jailer and his family.

Q 16:25 Why did Paul and Silas sing in prison? It always amazes me how the praises were still given to God, even from jail.

Paul taught that we should pray "without ceasing" and pray "at all times" (Rm 1:9; 12:12; Eph 6:18). Paul's struggle with suffering taught him that the most important and enduring lessons about life come through hardships. The best answer to this question comes from Paul himself in 2Co, especially 1:7–9; 4:1–5:21; 12:5–10. When God grants us easy times, we often remember to thank Him, but we tend to focus on what God has given rather than on God. When God exercises or tests us by challenges, we tend to focus on our relationship with God more than anything, which is proper. In hardships, we have opportunity to realize that the regenerate soul and life God has given us not only survives hardships but also actually thrives in the midst of them as we realize that the life God has given us is everlasting and finds fulfillment in sacrificial service to others (Jn 15:13).

Q 16:27 What would happen to a jailer who lost his prisoners? Why did the jailer want to kill himself?

The Romans had a brilliant method of making sure guards kept track of their prisoners: if the prisoner escaped, the guard would take the prisoner's place. The jailer, thinking the prisoners had escaped, would rather have killed himself than to have been subjected to the humiliation, torture, and execution inflicted on him by disappointed officials. There is no indication that the jailer experienced anything but positive effects on this occasion since he had all the prisoners and also had been liberated from sin and death by the grace of God.

Q 16:31 How do we know his whole family believed?

We know that the whole family of the jailer believed because Luke says this in v. 34. If we define "belief" as "honesty about dependence," then what Paul says becomes clear: "Be honest about your dependence on the grace of God in Jesus Christ, and you will realize the benefits of the salvation He has provided for you and your household." Most everything we do in life is a family thing. Marriage is a union, and children expand that union into a family. We live together, and parents devote their lives to raising their children in the way of life, both physical and spiritual. Religion is no more a matter of choice than good nutrition or safety. Our lives depend on the truth and knowing the truth, physically and spiritually. When a husband or wife, father or mother came to the knowledge of the truth, he or she naturally sought to include all the family in the benefits of that truth (1Co 7:12–16; Eph 6:4; Dt 6:4–12).

Q 16:37 Why did Paul insist on being escorted out?

Paul simply wanted the civil authorities to face the error of their actions the previous day. As Paul says, they had "beaten us publicly, uncondemned, men who are Roman citizens, and have thrown us into prison; and do they now throw us out secretly?" Leaving quietly but with the escort of the officials may have had several good results.

First, the officials, like the jailer, might have been impressed at the gracious disposition of Paul and Silas, which may have provided an opportunity to witness. Second, the officials might have learned to be more careful in their treatment of visitors. Third, the officials might have come to respect followers of Christ so that in the future they would be protected rather than persecuted. Paul stresses good relationships with governing authorities in order to protect the Christian faith from slander and persecution (Rm 13:1–10; Col 4:5–6; Ti 2:6–8).

Q **17:4 What is meant by "a few of the leading women"?**

Luke mentions "leading women" in Ac 13:50 as well as here. The word means "first," which suggests these women were leaders, wealthy and influential.

Q **17:5–8 Why did the Romans allow mobs to be part of their justice system (see also Ac 19:23–40)?**

While there were established governments and legal systems at this time in history, common people did not have the representation or the voice or the means of making their voices heard that we enjoy today. The text does not suggest that mobs were part of the justice system, but rebellions and uprisings were common so that authorities had to be careful in responding to them. Remember that Paul and his companions were strangers to these places and taught strange things, so naturally the local authorities are going to assume that the citizens have cause when they react violently against foreigners.

Q **17:5 Were the Jews who became jealous the same Jews who had been converted to Christianity (17:4)? Why were the Jews jealous of Paul and Silas if they believed themselves to be God's chosen people?**

Luke makes a definite distinction between the Jews who were persuaded in v. 4 and the Jews who were "not persuaded" in v. 5. The Jews who were not persuaded became jealous because their followers were leaving them to hear Paul. Jesus and the apostles in Jerusalem were persecuted because of the same kind of jealousy that had the same root: selfish pride (Jn 11:45–50; Ac 5:12–18). These Jews were the chosen people of God, yet they rejected the very blessings that God extended to them as His people, which the prophets, Jesus, and Paul lament (2Ch 12:5–12; Mt 23:37–38; Rm 10:1–3; Heb 3:12–19).

Q **17:11 How did the people of Berea evaluate Paul and Silas's sermons and teachings?**

These people had a great advantage as Luke reports that they had the Old Testament Scriptures. The Bereans responded in the most reasonable and productive of ways, searching the Old Testament to see if what Paul taught about Jesus fulfilling these Scriptures was true. When Paul was with the Jews, he always appealed to their own Scriptures (what we call the Old Testament) to prove that Jesus was the Christ, just as Jesus and the Gospel writers made constant reference to the same (Mt 1:22–23; Lk 4:16–22; Ac 17:2–3; 18:27–28).

Q **17:16–21 Why doesn't Paul just tear down the idols instead of reasoning with the people of Athens?**

There is a time to tear down, and sometimes God instructs His servant to do so (Ec 3:3; Jer 1:10). On the other hand, the incarnation of the Son of God and the ministry of Jesus revealed a Gospel that reaches out to people where they are and calls them to leave behind their former ways (Mt 9:9–13; Jn 8:1–11; 1Co 9:19–22). As an ambassador of Christ and acting on His behalf, Paul begins with something common and commendable (fear of God and religious devotion) and moves forward from there. We are all limited human beings, dependent on forces beyond ourselves for every aspect of our lives. We possess a common reason and the same evidence by which we might consider who sustains our life and how He does so. What is universal and undeniable among all people seems like a very good place to begin a fruitful exploration of our lives, future, and potential.

Q **17:23 What does "unknown god" mean?**

People have always and will always wonder about God, since we depend on Him, live in a world that bears witness to Him, and have a conscience given by Him (Ps 19; Rm 1:18–20; 2:15). Few people have had direct revelation from God or even access to the revelation God has given through the prophets and apostles through the Word (Rm 10:14–17). Therefore, throughout history and all around the world, people have imagined what God might be like. The people of Athens had been told about many different gods but suspected there might be another—perhaps the most powerful of the gods, of whom they were unaware—and did not want to offend this God by failing to acknowledge or sacrifice to Him. In effect, they were saying, "We are limited in our knowledge; if there is another God we do not know, we worship You also."

Q **17:30–31 If the people were unaware of God, what happened when they died? How did God decide who went to heaven before Jesus? Some people, such as Job, were considered righteous, but how? Paul says God will come to judge us and use a man that He appoints, so does this mean a man will be making the decisions, or will God?**

What happens to any particular person when he or she dies only God can know for certain. What we can know is the promises that God made and announced to people before Christ saved them, just as the promises of God fulfilled by Christ save all who come after Him (Gn 15:6; Rm 4:3). We also know that God's mercy is upon those who fear Him, both in Old Testament times and in our day (Ps 103:11, 13, 17; Lk 1:50). Job was considered righteous before God because he trusted in the mercy of God (Jb 1:21–22; 42:1–6, 12; Jas 5:11). Judgment on the Last Day will be made not by any man, but by "the Man" whom God has ordained. The definite article and language of "appointment" confirm that Jesus Christ is this man (Ac 3:20; 10:39–43; Heb 1:2).

Q 17:30 Did God not command people to repent before now?

Through creation itself and through our conscience God has provided all people everywhere with a witness to Himself and to the truth (Jer 8:7; Mt 6:25–33; Rm 1:20; 2:15). However, God has not always sent His messengers to all people everywhere to command repentance and preach the Gospel (Is 65:1; Rm 10:20). The focus of God's redeeming activity kept narrowing over time until it was fulfilled in the birth of Jesus. The ministry of Jesus inaugurated the New Testament, when God would send His messengers to all people in order to call them to repentance and to work faith in them through the Gospel (Mt 28:19; Mk 16:16).

Q 17:34 Does Dionysius have any significance?

This person is not mentioned by name anywhere else in the Bible, but this is true of many others. The inclusion of the names of individuals is important because such detail confirms the historical reliability of Luke's account.

Q 18:3 Did Paul work for money when he helped build tents?

Yes, Paul supported himself at various times by the money he earned making tents (1Co 4:12). Part of being trained as a rabbi was to learn a skill that would allow you to support yourself if you lacked students or followers. Many religious orders follow this practice today, including priests in some Roman Catholic orders.

Q 18:5–11 Why did the Jews reject the reading of Paul about Christ? Did Paul give up on their conversion?

For an explanation of why the Jews rejected Paul's testimony to Christ, please see Ac 18:6 below. There were both Jews and Gentiles at the synagogue; we know this from v. 4 and from other accounts about the synagogues (Ac 13:43; 14:1; 17:12). While Paul sounds as though he is giving up, he remained concerned for the Jewish people and continued to reach out to them at every opportunity (1Co 9:20; Ac 21:18–26). Paul remained ever hopeful that anyone and everyone would be turned from their unbelief and regenerated in the faith by God (Rm 10:1–3; Ac 26:24–32).

• • • • • • • • • • • • • • • • • • • •

Q **18:6 Why were the Jews in such opposition to the Gospel, especially if they knew that there was some truth in what the apostles were saying?**

The first reason for such opposition is common to all people of all times: we don't like to be told we are wrong, especially about what we believe. The second reason has to do with ethnic identity. At various times in history the Jews had been conquerors or conquered oppressors or the oppressed (the books of Samuel and Kings record this history, and most of the prophets speak to it). They had received the promises of God and had been set apart by Him, but they came to see this as placing themselves in opposition to all others rather than as advocates (Rm 3:1–3; 11:1–10). Part of this problem comes from our fallen human nature's preoccupation with material things—a physical nature thinks in physical terms. God did give Abraham physical descendants and a physical land, but those were indicative of the real gift, not the gift itself. The gift of God to Abraham was a regenerate soul, eternal life, and an everlasting, spiritual kingdom (Rm 9:1–8; Gal 3:7; Heb 11:8–16). The third reason has to do with ego, control, and income. The Jews who had control of the synagogues enjoyed and coveted the respect, control, and financial support of the people. The Gospel that Paul preached set people

Why were the Jews in opposition to the Gospel?

free and joined them directly with God through His Word and Spirit. This teaching made such leaders jealous and afraid (Jn 11:45–50). The fourth reason has to do with guilt. These Jewish religious leaders were afraid to hear the Gospel because it meant they had been teaching falsely and opposing God. Rather than consider their error and embrace the redemption and grace of God in Christ, they were determined to justify themselves, which required them to shut their eyes and ears to the truth (Jn 8:30–59; 9:39–41; Ac 5:28; 2Co 3:14–16; Heb 3:12–19). Remembering this about fallen human nature would make a believing person humble and grateful for the repentance and knowledge of the truth.

• • • • • • • • • • • • • • • • • • • •

Q **18:17 Was Sosthenes the Jewish leader who had spearheaded the effort to take Paul to the governor? If not, why was he beaten?**

The only clue we have regarding why Sosthenes was beaten is Luke's note in this verse that he was "the ruler of the synagogue." Perhaps they held him responsible for what went on there. It is also likely that they knew Paul was a Roman citizen and would be protected by Roman law and authorities if they attacked him, while Sosthenes was a Jew and of no concern to

> ## What does it mean to be a disciple?

the proconsul, as the text indicates. It was the Jews in Corinth who opposed the Gospel who rose up against Paul and brought him to the judgment seat, no doubt as a result of their jealousy (Ac 18:6).

Q 18:18 Why is it important that Paul cut his hair?

You may be interested to know that taking such a vow and shaving his head is something Paul was encouraged to do the next time he visited Jerusalem (Ac 21:24). The vow and head shaving was part of the law of a Nazirite (Hebrew for "separate") given in Nu 6:1–21. This law said that a man or woman could separate himself or herself from the daily life and interactions with people in order to focus on spiritual life and union with God. A man would not keep his hair trimmed as usual, but let his hair grow so that people would know he had taken such a vow and would leave him alone. Samson was called by God to be a Nazirite from his mother's womb, so he was to never let his hair be cut (Jgs 13:2–5). At the end of the time of separation, a man would shave his head as a sign of completion of the vow.

Q 18:25 What are the differences between the Baptism of John and the Baptism of Christ?

There is no difference between the Baptism of John and that of Jesus. John was baptizing by the command and Word of the Lord to him, and after John was imprisoned, Jesus' apostles took over that work. If you compare the preaching connected with the Baptism of John as recorded in Mt 3:2 with that of Jesus as recorded in Mk 1:14–15 and of the apostles in Ac 2:38, you will see that they are the same. For more on the Baptism of John, please see Ac 19:2–6 below.

Q 19:1 Who are these disciples? What does it mean to be a disciple?

The word *disciple* means "follower" and "student." You may recognize the similarity with our word *discipline*. A disciple follows a teacher, spending great amounts of time learning from the teacher's words and actions. Many people went out into the wilderness and to the Jordan River to listen to the preaching of John (Lk 3:1–18). When Jesus came, John directed his disciples to follow Jesus, which most did (Jn 1:25–37). Some of John's disciples complained that people were leaving John to follow Jesus, but John explained to them that his purpose was to point to Jesus and direct people to Him (Jn 3:25–29). Apparently, after John was put in prison and even after he was executed, there were disciples who insisted on staying devoted to him, even though he directed them to Jesus. Both Matthew and Luke record the presence and contentious nature of these disciples who claim to be of John but in truth are not, since they rejected his witness to Jesus (Mt 9:14; Lk 5:33; 7:18–23).

● ● ● ● ● ● ● ● ● ● ● ● ● ● ● ● ● ●

Q **19:2–6 Why did the people in Ephesus think that they had received "John's Baptism"?**

Here the challenge is to be clear in the language we use. The Baptism that John performed according to God's command and Word is, in fact, the Baptism of Jesus that John administered (see 18:25 above). Let's call this the Baptism of Jesus by John. John had followers who refused to obey John's witness to Jesus, who continued as a sect and baptized people. These men could not have been real disciples of John because John taught clearly and openly about the Holy Spirit (Jn 1:32–34). Let's call this the false baptism of those who claimed to be disciples of John. The people in Ephesus had come into contact with these men who claimed to be disciples of John and had been baptized by them. This is why they had not heard of the Holy Spirit, and this is why Paul baptized them with the Baptism of Jesus. This is also why Paul provided indisputable evidence of their genuine Baptism and faith by laying on his hands so that the Holy Spirit would fall on them and confirm His presence with the speaking of languages and prophesying.

● ● ● ● ● ● ● ● ● ● ● ● ● ● ● ● ● ●

Q **19:3 Can you explain the two kinds of baptism and why we only have one kind today? Did John's Baptism have the same significance as a Baptism by a pastor today?**

For more on this question see Ac 18:25, 19:1, and 19:2–6 above. The Greek word translated as *baptism* means to "wash" or "be awash" or "be immersed" (Mk 7:3–4). Therefore, on the one hand, there are as many kinds of "baptism" or "washing" as there are things to wash or people to do the washing. On the other hand, there is just one Christian Baptism, which was administered by John on behalf of Jesus and by the apostles and ever after by pastors and Christians on behalf of Jesus and according to His command (Mt 28:19–20; Eph 4:5). When Jesus talked about a baptism of fire, He was referring to the extraordinary experience of the apostles on Pentecost, an experience that confirmed the authority of the apostles as Jesus had promised (Mk 16:16–20). On occasions in which people were present who opposed God's grace toward all in the Gospel, the apostles laid their hands on people so that the Holy Spirit would "fall" on them with the result that their salvation and faith was authenticated by speaking in tongues, just like the apostles (Ac 2:1–21; 8:14–18; 10:44–47; 11:15–16; 15:5–9). Whenever there is no extraordinary challenge to the Word of God, a simple Baptism as performed by John, the apostles, pastors, or Christians is sufficient (Ac 8:26–40; 1Pt 3:21).

Q 19:4 What is a "baptism of repentance"?

The word *repentance* means "to turn" or "to have a change of mind or care" (Ezk 18:25–32; Mt 3:8). Since the command in the New Testament is to "repent and be baptized," the change of mind and care that produces the turning into the way of the Lord comes first, then comes regeneration worked by the Word of God in Baptism, then a life immersed in the Word (Mt 28:19–20; Lk 3:7–14; Ac 2:38; Jn 1:12–13).

Q 19:6 Why was it necessary for Paul to touch someone so that the person could receive the Holy Spirit?

God usually connects a physical indication with what He is doing in spiritual matters. For example, Jesus teaches in parables because He created the world for this purpose (Ps 19; Rm 1:20). While Jesus healed with a Word and sometimes at a great distance from the one being healed, He often placed His hands on a person when healing (compare Mt 8:5–13 with 8:14–15 and 8:16). The laying on of hands offered a physical connection between an apostle and a believer and made unmistakable the source and the destination of God's power at work (Mt 19:13, 15; Mk 16:18; Ac 5:12; 8:18; 9:12, 17).

Q 19:9 Why is the "W" in *Way* capitalized, and to what does "the Way" refer?

The word *Way* is capitalized in translations so the reader understands that this is referring to the very particular teaching that Jesus established in contrast to any number of other "ways" that people promote for religious practice. Jesus said, "I am the way, and the truth, and the life. No one comes to the Father except through Me" (Jn 14:6). Peter confirmed that there is only one way to everlasting life, and Jesus is that Way (Ac 4:12). Paul refers to the Gospel as "the Way" in his defense before Felix and gives an overview of its content before Festus and King Agrippa (Ac 24:14–15; 26:19–23).

Luke does not appear to comment about the time when believers began to use this term "the Way," as he had with the name "Christians" (Ac 11:26). The expression "the Way" may have started after Maundy Thursday evening when Jesus referred to Himself as such or after Peter confessed the same before the Jewish council after Pentecost (Jn 14:6; Ac 4:12).

Q 19:11–12 Does the notion of keeping relics of the saints come from this passage?

Yes, this is one of three passages in the New Testament on which the Roman Catholic Church bases its beliefs about relics (Mk 5:27–29 and Ac 5:15 are the other two). The idea is that the material universe is God's creation, made to serve God's will. God is present at all times and in all places and regularly provides for our life and well-being through physical means, such as air, water, food, sunshine, and clothing. Therefore, it is no surprise that God would do extraordinary acts of healing through the human nature of His Son or through the hands, clothes, or even shadow of His apostles. What is not taught in the Bible is that the bones of these apostles or their clothes possess these extraordinary powers inherently or of themselves. It is the Word of God, His command, His authorization, and His will that provide the power of life, whether every day or in an extraordinary manner (Ac 8:18–24; 19:13–17).

• • • • • • • • • • • • • • • • • •

Q **19:13–16 Why were they beaten? Was it actually an evil spirit?**

Evil spirits or demons are neither pleasant nor passive in nature. Their nature is to destroy (Lk 8:27–33). A cause for the demon's attack would have come from the attempt made by the men to command and cast out the demon. They challenged the demon, and he responded. The text speaks of itinerant Jewish exorcists and seven sons of a Jewish high priest who also cast out demons. How is it possible for them to have cast out demons in the past but not now, when they make reference to Jesus? I wonder if these exorcists were successful in the past only because the devil was willing to give the appearance of success in order to encourage people in the legalism that Judaism taught and to keep them away from the grace of God (Mt 7:22–23; 2Co 11:12–15). Luke makes clear that the Word of the Lord Jesus is of no help unless a person has

been regenerated by it and remains in it (see also Mt 12:43–45; Jn 8:31–32; 15:1–7). These Jewish men tried to use the name of the Lord for their own income and ego but found that impossible, just as did Simon in Ac 8:18–24.

• • • • • • • • • • • • • • • • • •

Q **19:15 Why are some demons cast out and others refuse to leave? How does the evil spirit know Paul?**

Demons are subject to God and to His Word no matter what, as the ministry of Jesus clearly demonstrated (Mt 8:16; 10:8). Apparently demons have power to resist those who believe in Christ but whose faith is weak (Mk 9:17–27). I suspect that the devil and demons are willing to give the appearance of responding to false teachers and unbelievers if this keeps people superstitious and away from truth and the grace of God (2Co 11:12–15). Evil spirits would know Paul because of the Word of the Lord that he not only believes but also proclaims as an apostle. There were only thirteen apostles to whom Christ gave authority to cast out demons, and that authority would bear down on a demon, just as we saw in the ministry of Jesus (Mt 10:8; Mk 16:17; Lk 8:28).

• • • • • • • • • • • • • • • • • •

Q **20:1–6 Why does Luke switch from third person to first person?**

Luke uses the first person plural whenever he is with Paul and included in the action. When Luke is absent from Paul, he refers to Paul and others in the third person.

One of the interesting studies of Acts is to follow Luke's involvement or absence from the narratives.

. . . .

Q **20:7–12 What was God's intention when He let Paul raise Eutychus from the dead? Why kill him in the first place?**

First, God did not kill Eutychus. He died because he chose a poor place to fall asleep. Second, it is not God's will that anyone should die, which is why He instructs us in the Law and why He sacrificed His own Son to redeem us from the curse of the Law and our failure to keep it. Lots of people die every day from all sorts of causes, all of them having to do with contradicting God's design, whether accidentally or intentionally. Second, when a prophet or Jesus or an apostle is present, these circumstances provide opportunity for God to demonstrate His will for us to live and how His Word and Son accomplish this. Third, if God protected us from ourselves and the mistakes we make all the time, how would we ever appreciate what He does? Living, suffering, and dying by the consequences of the decisions we make turns us to God's gracious will and loving redemption of our lives.

. . . .

Q **20:10 Was there ever a time Paul tried unsuccessfully to perform a miracle?**

There is only one occasion in the Bible where a genuine servant of God failed to heal: the disciples could not cast out a demon (Mk 9:18). There was a time that Jesus did not do miracles because of the unbelief of the people in that location (Mt 13:58). Otherwise, they always succeed, sometimes without even trying or being aware of their power to help (Mk 5:27–31; Ac 5:15).

. . . .

Q **20:36–38 Was Paul planning on revisiting the people who hated to see him go? Won't Paul see them in heaven?**

Luke reveals that the people were so sad because Paul had told them that they would not see him again (v. 38). It may be interesting to note that some time before Paul told these people he would not see them again, he had written to the Christians in Rome and Corinth about our inability to make plans or to know the future since God moves us about according to His will (Rm 1:11–13; 2Co 1:17; see also Jas 4:13–16).

Of course Paul will be reunited with them in eternity, and Jesus gave this very comfort to His apostles in Jn 14:1–3. Still, the thought of not seeing Paul again in the flesh in this time caused them grief (Ec 3:4).

. . . .

Q **21:1 Where is "Cos"?**

Cos is an island five miles wide and twenty-five miles long. It is located two and a half miles off the southwest coast of Asia Minor or present-day Turkey.

● ● ● ● ● ● ● ● ● ● ● ● ● ● ● ● ● ● ●

Q 21:4 Why did Paul go to Jerusalem if the Spirit said no? Does the Spirit speak to us like this today?

Paul was stubborn, just like Balaam, whose donkey told him not to go (Nu 22). Although Paul had been frustrated with opposition from his own people, he still seems to have had deep feelings for them and for the customs and ceremonies of his own past (Ac 18:6; Rm 10:1–3). Luke records that Paul was in a hurry to get to Jerusalem in order to be there for the day of Pentecost. The combination of Paul's devotion to Jewish festivals and his fearless disposition apparently made him deaf to the warnings of the Holy Spirit from so many sources (Ac 20:23; 21:11). After Paul was arrested in Jerusalem, he had four years of imprisonment, several sea voyages, and one shipwreck during which he might reconsider his former determination. The lessons for us are fundamental and powerful: (a) Listen carefully to the advice of faithful people. (b) Don't agonize over decisions that were mistaken since God makes all things work together for good. (c) Look for the opportunities that God gives in all times and places to advance His kingdom in the lives of others. Luke used the last seven chapters of Acts to show us how Paul defended the faith on many occasions. Luke wrote the Gospel and Acts while Paul was imprisoned, Paul wrote four letters to churches, and many benefited from his witness, which they may never have known otherwise (Php 1:12–14). He did get a free trip to Rome in the end;

he had wanted to go there for years (Rm 1:9–10).

It is certainly possible for the Holy Spirit to speak directly to anyone at any time He chooses. The challenge for us is to know if a voice is from God or the devil or out of our own desires, since we do not have Jesus in person or any apostle to discern this for us (2Co 11:13–15; 1Th 5:21; 1Jn 4:1). The reason God gave us His Word in written form—proven to be the truth by fulfillment of prophecy, history, archaeology, and reason—is so that we would have a reliable voice from Him against which to measure our thoughts and the thoughts/words of others (Jn 20:31; Dt 13:1–5).

● ● ● ● ● ● ● ● ● ● ● ● ● ● ● ● ● ● ●

Q 21:9 What is the significance of the daughters? Is it okay for the daughters of Philip to prophesy?

Luke included this verse because the Holy Spirit inspired him to and because Luke has a habit of including details about people that support the historicity of his writing (2Tm 3:16; Lk 1:1–4; 3:1–2). While Luke does not say this, it is possible that these four daughters who prophesied also warned Paul not to travel to Jerusalem.

There is no problem with a woman prophesying; there is no suggestion of a problem in this text or in the case of Miriam or Deborah in the Old Testament (Ex 15:20; Jgs 4–5). The restrictions placed on ministry have to do with the public ministry and authority over others, which apply to both men and women (1Co 14:29–40; 1Tm 2:8–3:7). Women are forbidden to bear the responsibility of public ministry and authority because this responsibility belongs to men (Gn 2:15–18; 1Co 11:1–16; Jas 3:1–12).

Q 21:21–24 Why does Paul have to purify himself?

Paul did not have to purify himself. Paul knew very well that the Lord Jesus had fulfilled all the Law regarding all things in order to present us pure and undefiled before God (Gal 3:10–14; Eph 2:8–9; 5:25–27). In fact, Jesus grew up in Nazareth so that He would be called a Nazarene (Mt 2:23; Heb 10:1–10). Paul was willing to join some Jewish believers who had taken the vow of a Nazirite (Hebrew for "separate") in order to convince the Jews that he was still faithful to God (1Co 9:19–21; Nu 6:1–21; Ac 22:3–21).

Q 22:2–21 Why does Paul recount his life before his conversion to Christianity?

Paul recounts his life for the same reason he agreed to participate in the practices of a devout Jew: to demonstrate to those who hated him that he had not become a traitor or turned against his people or God Himself. Paul wants and needs those who hate him to understand what happened to him because they need this conversion in their lives as well (Rm 10:1–3). By telling his own story of conversion, Paul is giving them the information they need without challenging them to an argument (1Co 9:19–20).

Q 22:7 Doesn't Jesus know why Saul is persecuting Him?

Jesus knows very well why Saul was persecuting the faithful people who followed His teaching. God typically asks questions not because He doesn't know something but because we don't. For example, when God asked Adam, "Where are you?" (Gn 3:9), He wasn't wondering about the physical location of Adam. Instead, He was asking where Adam was in terms of his relationship with God; that is, why was Adam hiding from God? This is still a great question for us to ponder. When the women came to the empty tomb on Easter morning, the angel asked them, "Why do you seek the living among the dead?" (Lk 24:5). What makes Jesus' question to Saul significant is not the "why" or the "persecuting" but the "Me," since on this occasion Saul was forced to recognize that Jesus of Nazareth was the Lord God Almighty. Later, in his First Letter to Timothy, Paul answers this question from the Lord: "I had acted ignorantly in unbelief." Good for Paul and for everyone is the additional explanation that Paul provides: "And the grace of our Lord overflowed for me with the faith and love that are in Christ Jesus" (1Tm 1:13–14).

Q 22:8 Why does Saul ask, "Who are You, Lord"?

Saul asked who had appeared to him for clarity and, perhaps, in desperate hope that the one speaking to him so powerfully in this vision was not Jesus, whom Saul was persecuting. Saul's question draws the reader's attention to the stark contrast between Jesus as the gracious Lord of our redemption and the kind of harsh, legalistic lordship that Saul was used to (see Jesus' warning against this in Mk 10:42–45).

Q **22:12 I find it interesting that the man God used to speak to Paul was named Ananias, just as the high priest who ordered the people to strike Paul's mouth was named Ananias. Is there any connection in the name?**

There are three men named Ananias mentioned in Acts. There was Ananias, the husband of Sapphira, who lied about giving and died (5:1–11). There was the Ananias who came to Paul and baptized him (9:10–17; 22:12–16). There was the Ananias who was high priest, ordered Paul to be struck, and presented to the governor the case against Paul (23:2; 24:1). Like the names Joseph, Joshua, James, and Simon, Ananias was apparently common in New Testament times.

Q **22:25–29 Why would the fact that Paul was a Roman citizen prevent him from being arrested and flogged?**

The trouble started when they assumed that Paul was not a Roman citizen, which is understandable if Paul's features suggested he was Jewish. Paul is the one who raised the issue of citizenship, which he did on oc-

casion to make use of the privileges of being a Roman citizen (Ac 16:37; 25:10–11). As a Roman citizen, Paul could be arrested and questioned, but he could not be beaten or otherwise abused until a trial had found him guilty and he was sentenced to punishment. There were four ways to become a Roman citizen: if you were the child of a Roman citizen, if you were born in a Roman province (this is the case with Paul), if you were granted citizenship by the emperor or another official with such authority, or if you purchased citizenship (like the commander in this narrative, v. 28).

Q **23:2 Is Ananias the high priest the same Ananias as before?**

This is the same man who appeared in 22:12 but not the same as the other two men with this name who appeared earlier in Acts (see 22:12 above).

Q **23:3 What does Paul mean when he calls Ananias a "whitewashed wall"?**

Whitewash was a sort of paint made from limestone dust and water. The purpose of whitewash was to make something look nice on the outside that was horrible beneath (Mt 23:27). The term was used of people to condemn them for lying and hypocrisy (Jb 13:4; Ezk 13:11–15). The explanation that Paul gives with the expression agrees with this definition—Paul was pointing out the hypocrisy of the high priest.

Q **23:5 What does Paul mean when he says he did not realize that it was the high priest?**

Paul had been traveling for years and would not have known who was serving as high priest or that the high priest was among the council members who came to seek his execution. Maybe Paul thought a high priest would abstain from such unjust proceedings or at least promote them secretly. The fact that the high priest did come in person to argue for Paul's execution reveals just how desperate he and others were to exterminate the followers of Jesus. Years earlier, the religious leaders also had sought any means to silence Christ (Jn 11:45–53).

Q **23:6 Was Paul a Pharisee at some point in time?**

Paul was a Pharisee, educated and trained in Jerusalem by Gamaliel according to the strictest tradition of the Jews (Ac 5:34; 15:5; 26:5; Php 3:5).

Q **23:9 Why were the Pharisees now sticking up for Paul and coming to his defense?**

There are a few possibilities why the Pharisees now defended Paul. First, these Pharisees may not have known why Paul had been arrested and were not prejudiced against him. Second, even if they didn't agree with Paul, they would rather side with Paul than with the Sadducees. Finally, these men may have been much like Gamaliel himself, who had warned the Jewish religious leaders against opposing the disciples of Jesus (Ac 5:33–39).

Q **23:11 Did Jesus physically appear to Paul when He spoke to and stood next to him?**

A fundamental principle of understanding any communication is to take it in the most simple and literal way unless something forces us to do otherwise. This text is very simple as Luke reports that the Lord (that would be Jesus) stood by Paul (that would be physically, just as He did to the other apostles before His ascension) and spoke to him. Imagine what a difference that would make, especially in contrast to the first time the Lord appeared to Paul (Ac 9:3–9).

Q **23:12–15 Why did the Jews want to kill Paul?**

These Jews want to kill Paul for the very same reason Paul wanted to kill Christians before he met Christ on the road to Damascus (Ac 9). The kind of hatred that drives men to murder is the product of rabid nationalism (Lk 4:22–29; Jn 11:48), religious zeal (Rm 10:2), greed (Jas 4:1–4), and fear of God's judgment for failing to keep the Law (Gal 3:10–12).

Q 23:12 Why did the Jews promise not to eat or drink until Paul was killed?

When religious leaders insist that salvation depends on extraordinary obedience to God, people do extraordinary things. These men were hoping that taking an oath not to eat or drink until they had killed Paul would mean that God would reward them both here and in eternity—even though the Bible expressly condemns such acts of murder (Dt 17:6–7). It would be interesting to know what happened to all these men since the Roman officials moved Paul before they could have the opportunity to murder him.

Q 23:16 Why is there no biblical reference to Paul's family? Did his family disown him when he gave all he had to Christ?

You may very well be right in suspecting that Paul's family disowned him when he became an apostle of Christ (Jn 7:13; 19:38). On the other hand, the Bible is very focused on telling us what we need to know and generally says very little about the families of many prominent people. Paul makes an allusion to never having married and to the fact that Peter had married, but not much more than that (1Co 7:8; 9:5).

Q 23:17 Why does Paul have so much freedom in prison?

The first and most important reason would have to do with Paul's status as a Roman citizen (Ac 22:25–29). It may have been that the commander, Claudius Lysias (see v. 26), recognized that this was a religious dispute among the Jews and had nothing to do with civil crimes that would give him cause to be concerned about Paul.

Q 23:22 Why did the young man tell the commander about the plots against Paul?

The young man was Paul's nephew and went to the commander because Paul directed him to (Ac 23:16–17). Of course, the fundamental reason would have been his concern for Paul's life.

Q 24:2 Who is Felix?

Claudius Lysias, the commander of Roman troops in Jerusalem, rescued Paul from the mob (Ac 21:31–40; 23:26–30). When Claudius learned of the plot to kill Paul, he sent Paul to Caesarea to protect him (22:24–30; 23:19–35). Felix was the governor of the region on behalf of the Roman Empire, which is why he handled Paul's case (23:26; 24:1–27).

Q 24:15 Why is it bad that they believe in a resurrection from the dead?

The resurrection of the dead does seem to be a frightening topic to many, both Jews and Gentiles (Ac 4:2; 17:32). On the other hand, many people in biblical history were overwhelmed with joy to have a loved one who was dead raised to life again (1Ki 17:17–24; Lk 7:12–15; 8:49–56; Jn 11:1–44; Ac 20:8–12).

Q 24:22 (26:3) Weren't Judaism and Christianity uncommon in those days?

The world all around Israel had been dealing with Israel since the time of Moses. The Roman Empire had a fairly intense relationship with Israel since the time of the Maccabean revolt (164 BC) and because Herod and his family had descended, in part, from the Maccabee family. The teachings of Christ, by this time, had been carried into most of the Roman Empire by His apostles and disciples for thirty years. Any Roman official moving to this part of the world would have wanted to make sure he understood, as well as possible, the particular religious commitments and tensions of the people there.

Q 24:27 If Paul and the Jews believed the same thing, why didn't they like him? Why did Festus want to grant a favor to the Jews?

It was actually Felix who did the Jews a favor by leaving Paul in prison. Felix, like any other ruler who was responsible for peace in a foreign land, understood that goodwill with the people was priceless. The religious leaders in Jerusalem did not like Paul for the same reason Paul did not like Christians before his conversion (see Ac 23:12–15 above). Paul has the same background as the Jews; he was schooled in Jerusalem and was as zealous as any of them (22:1–5). The difference with Paul was that he not only believed that Jesus was the promised Messiah of the Old Testament, true God and true man, but believed that God reconciled the whole world to Himself in Jesus (2Co 5:18–21). Paul knew that God loved all people without partiality and that He had forgiven and accepted all people because of Christ. Salvation was accomplished for all, and God brought people to the realization of that salvation immediately through His Word and Spirit (Ac 11:1–18; 15:1–12).

Q 25:11 Why does Paul appeal to Caesar, who was the infamous Nero?

There is an old saying about "jumping from the frying pan into the fire" that might describe Paul on this occasion. On the other hand, this is early in Nero's reign (AD 54–68), so Paul may have had no way of knowing what the emperor would be like. Paul did the best he could with no time to think over his options; if he did not use his privileges as a Roman citizen and appeal to the emperor, he was sure to be ambushed and murdered if he was forced to return to Jerusalem (Ac 23:12–15). Finally, the very best reason for Paul to appeal to Caesar was because the Lord had told him that he would bear witness to Him in Rome (23:11).

Q **25:22 Why is Agrippa so interested in hearing Paul?**

Agrippa, like his fathers before him, probably enjoyed circumstances in which he was made to feel important and could appear in royal form (Ac 12:20–22; 25:23–26).

Q **25:25 Why couldn't Paul's appeal have been reversed?**

The whole sequence of events in Paul's life seems to have two main causes. The first cause has to do with Paul's stubborn insistence on going to Jerusalem, even though the Holy Spirit warned him through many reliable sources not to go (Ac 20:23; 21:4, 11). Contradicting God's Word and His will for us brings many unhappy consequences (Gn 3:16–19; Rm 5:12). The second cause, which may actually be the first, is that God intended for Paul to bear witness to the Gospel in Rome (Ac 23:11). The Lord had also told Ananias that Paul was in for a lot of trouble in his life as an apostle of Jesus Christ (9:15–16). Perhaps Paul's continued imprisonment and journey to Rome was the best way to keep Paul from the plots of the Jews in Jerusalem and to deal with those who had taken a vow to kill Paul (23:14). It may also have been that, in order to keep citizens from abusing this privilege of having the emperor hear your case and to keep other governing forces from preventing it, no one could reverse an appeal to be heard by Caesar; if you appealed to Caesar, you would go to Caesar, as Festus said (25:12). If this was the case, then we must wonder

about Luke's report that Felix was hoping for a bribe, and when it did not come, he left Paul in prison as a favor, as if he could have released him (24:26). What we are left with for certain, as in all cases, is that "for those who love God all things work together for good, for those who are called according to His purpose" (Rm 8:28). Not only did Paul make many powerful witnesses during the four years he was under arrest, but he also wrote letters to the Christians in Ephesus, Philippi, and Colossae and to Philemon (Ac 27:1–28:31; Eph 3:1; Php 1:12–18; Col 4:3, 10; Phm 1).

Q **26:12–18 Why does Luke retell the story of Paul's conversion?**

The short answer is because God wanted him to (1Th 2:13; 2Tm 3:16). The long answer has to do with one of Luke's purposes in recording the Gospel and Acts. Luke is writing an "apology" or a response that defends the truth against people who misrepresent or try to contradict it. Rather than compose a book of Christian doctrine, Luke records both Peter and Paul telling and retelling the story of their conviction of the truth of the Gospel (Ac 9:1–19; 10:9–48; 11:4–17; 13:15–41; 15:7–8; 17:22–31; 22:1–21; 23:6; 24:10–21; 26:1–23; 28:12–20, 25–28).

Q **26:14 What are goads?**

A goad is a long stick with a pointed end used to prod animals—usually beasts of burden that would pull a plow. Saul's determination to threaten and murder everyone who followed Christ was hard on the followers of Christ and hard on Saul—like an ox or donkey kicking at the goad of its master. Saul's persecution of Christians was hard for Christ because the lives of His faithful people are precious in His sight.

• • • • • • • • • • • • • • • • • • •

Q 26:21 Did the Jews really feel that what Paul was saying was so bad they should kill him? Wouldn't they believe that murdering someone would condemn them in God's eyes?

Jesus taught about the terrible consequences of having a hard heart; some of those consequences have to do with being blind and deaf to the truth (Jn 9:40–41). Jesus warned His apostles that the time would come when those who killed them would think they were offering a service to God (Jn 16:2). Saul himself had such a hard heart, which had something to do with his physical blindness for three days after Jesus appeared to him on the road to Damascus (Ac 9:4–9). Later, Paul wrote about the blindness of those who try to justify themselves and reject God's grace in Jesus Christ (2Co 3:14–16). Please see Ac 23:12–15 for more on this subject.

• • • • • • • • • • • • • • • • • • •

Q 26:24 Why did Festus call Paul insane?

You may have noticed that Festus interrupted Paul just after he got to the part about the dead rising. The resurrection of

the dead does seem to be a frightening topic to many, both Jews and Gentiles (Ac 4:2; 17:32). I suspect such strong reactions come partially because a resurrection from the dead is not something we experience and because a resurrection from the dead could involve judgment by an authority or God they do not know (2Co 5:10–11; 1Jn 4:18). For more, see Ac 24:15 above.

• • • • • • • • • • • • • • • • • • •

Q 26:32 Why couldn't Paul have been set free?

Agrippa knows that remaining a prisoner and being taken to Rome to stand trial would be a long and difficult process. This process was longer and more difficult for Paul than Agrippa could have imagined. As to why they couldn't set Paul free, please see Ac 25:25 above.

• • • • • • • • • • • • • • • • • • •

Q 28:4 Why did the viper make the islanders think Paul was a murderer?

People always have and always will struggle to understand what forces are at work behind events. Superstitious people do this in one way, scientists, in another. Either way, we want to know why things happen. Luke suggests that the people had assumptions about divine justice, and why would we assume they are mistaken? Jesus said, "All who take the sword will perish by the sword" (Mt 26:52). Salvation by grace, apart from the works of the Law, does not mean that we won't be judged by our works or that justice is ignored (2Co 5:7–11). God affirmed justice by substituting His Son for us under the condemnation of the Law (Mt 5:17–20; Gal 3:13). Still, relationships between cause and effect remain in this life, and for people who reject and despise the grace of God, the Law remains in full force to affect them for all eternity (Rm 8:1; Gal 5:4). The natives on Malta had a belief that people get what they deserve. They figured the storm and shipwreck were punishment, as did the sailors in Jonah's day (Jnh 1:4–11). When the viper bit Paul and remained fastened to him, it was natural for the people to think as they did: "Though he has escaped from the sea, Justice has not allowed him to live."

Q 28:6 The islanders thought Paul was a god, but Luke doesn't mention Paul telling them they were wrong. Is it safe to assume he did so?

You may do more than assume that Paul corrected their thinking based on a previous occasion. In Lystra, on the first missionary journey, Paul healed a crippled man, and the people responded by claiming that Paul was Hermes and Barnabas was Zeus (Ac 14:8–18). Paul and Barnabas tore their clothes, ran into the crowd, and argued passionately for the truth that there is but one God and He is in heaven. Contrast this response of Paul and Barnabas with Herod, who enjoyed the flattery of the people who claimed he was a god, until he was eaten by worms and died (Ac 12:21–23).

Q 28:26–27 Why would Paul end with these verses from Isaiah?

This kind of response of an apostle or faithful witness to determined unbelief is common in the Bible (Is 6:9–10; Mk 4:12; Ac 7:51–53). Hebrews includes two severe warnings against despising the kingdom of God (Heb 6:4–8; 10:26–31). More important than this warning against rejecting the Word and the grace of God is Luke's conclusion noting how the Word of God cannot be bound: Paul "welcomed all who came to him, proclaiming the kingdom of God and teaching about the Lord Jesus Christ with all boldness and without hindrance" (Ac 28:30–31).

Q 28:30–31 What happened to Paul in Rome after the narrative in Acts ends?

Paul was released in AD 63 and probably returned to Macedonia (Philippi), as he suggests in his letters to the Philippians (2:24) and to Philemon (22). During the next two years, Paul continued to travel around the Aegean, writing his First Letter to Timothy and his Letter to Titus from Corinth. Paul was arrested again in the winter of AD 65/66. He wrote his Second Letter to Timothy from Rome (2Tm 4:6–17) and was martyred there in AD 67.

Romans

● ●

Q **1:5 What exactly is the "obedience of faith"? Does this mean we need to obey the Law in order to have faith?**

Obedience and faith are inseparable, like two sides of the same coin. Faith always produces obedience, and obedience can only flow from faith. The Word of God works faith in us, but that faith is active, like the branch attached to the vine (Rm 10:17; Jn 15:1–7). The Word of God regenerates the soul in the image of Christ and inspires that soul to love others as it has been loved by God in Christ (Ezk 36:24–27; 1Jn 4:19). The obedience that flows from faith eagerly obeys the Ten Commandments and all that love of neighbor would require (Rm 13:8–10). See also question and answer at Rm 2:6.

● ●

Q **1:8–17 When Paul was longing to visit Rome, did he know God wanted him to go there, or was it his free will?**

No one has a free will except God; Paul knew this as well as anyone (Rm 5:6–11; Eph 5:1–3). There was a hint that Paul might travel to Rome in the Lord's direction to Ananias when Paul was first converted (Ac 9:15). During his third missionary journey, Paul seemed convinced that it was necessary for him to travel to Rome, but we are not told why he thought this (Ac 19:21). Paul would not have known at this time that he would be taken to Rome as a prisoner after

What is the obedience of faith?

361

his next visit to Jerusalem. Paul knew that he had been chosen to take the Gospel to the ends of the earth, so he wanted to fulfill his apostolic responsibility with the Christians in Rome and receive help from them to press on to Spain (Gal 2:7; Rm 1:10–12; 15:28). After Paul had been arrested in Jerusalem, the Lord told him directly that he would travel to Rome (Ac 23:11).

Q 1:11 What spiritual gift is Paul talking about?

I doubt that Paul had one particular gift in mind. Rather, Paul meant whatever gift the good Lord saw fit to convey to them through Paul's apostolic ministry. The possible gifts and Paul's preferences are listed by Paul (Rm 12:6–8; 1Co 12:8–10, 28–31; 14:1).

Q 1:14 Why does he classify people as Greek and barbarian?

Categorizing people as Greek or barbarian was an easy way to include all people—"Greek" referred to educated people in civilized nations and "barbarians" referred to everyone else. In v. 13, Paul used the term "Gentile" to distinguish people from those who are Jews, and again, by these two terms, Paul includes everyone.

Q 1:16 Why does it say the Gospel is first for the Jews, then for the Greeks? Does this imply that Greeks are inferior?

Paul is not implying that Greeks are inferior; on the contrary, a big part of Paul's conversion included realizing that God had always loved the Gentiles (Greeks), too, and that they were to be held in high esteem (Gal 2:7–8; Lk 4:24–27). Speaking the Gospel to the Jews first makes sense because they have had the prophetic Scriptures and have been waiting for God to fulfill His promises to their forefathers. Once a Jewish person knew that God had fulfilled all His promises in Jesus Christ, that person would already be equipped, on the basis of knowledge of the Old Testament, to share with others what God had done in the Christ (Ac 1:8; 2:5–11; Rm 3:1–2). While Jesus ministered to Jew and Gentile alike, during His earthly ministry He commanded His disciples to go only to the children of Israel (Mt 10:5–6).

Q 1:17 What is meant by "from faith for faith"?

There is plenty of debate about this question because the Greek prepositions translated as "from" and "for" have such a wide range of meaning. The first step in approaching the question is to be clear about the context. Paul just wrote that the Gospel is the power of God, which is because in the Gospel the righteousness of God is revealed from faith for faith. The question then is about how the righteousness of God is revealed or how it became evident. Second, in what way was the righteousness of God revealed "from faith"? We might suggest that the righteousness of God was revealed from the faith of God's Son, who willingly submitted Himself to the will of the Father and thus provided His righteousness in exchange for our guilt (Heb 2:14–3:2; 2Co 5:21; remember how faith and obedience are related, Rm 1:5). We might add that the righteousness of God was revealed from the faith of those who believed these promises, Abraham being the chief example (Rm 4:1–5; Heb 11:1–12:2). Third, the righteousness of God in Christ is what produces faith and is the object of faith, hence the phrase "for faith." The righteousness of God is revealed in the Gospel, which reports the faith of the Son of God and of those who trusted the promises regarding Him. This report of the faith of those who precede generates the faith of those who follow (Rm 10:17).

Q 1:18 Can God show His wrath in a loving way?

You might say that God's wrath is a function of, or servant of, His love, since the love of God for us is what causes His wrath toward all that would ruin the life He intends us to know. God's wrath would not appear to be loving since wrath is opposition and must present itself thus in order to be effective against our rebellious human nature (Jnh 3:4–9; Heb 3:11; 4:3). God shows such wrath lovingly by providing us with warnings and explanations about His will and way.

Q 1:20 Can we see God's invisible qualities through His nature and His creation? If so, why do we concern ourselves with those who have not heard the Gospel?

There are two kinds of revelation from God: "natural" and "special." Natural revelation is what creation makes evident to everyone in all places and all time (Ps 19). Natural revelation includes the conscience, or the Law, written on our hearts, which is also evident to all people in all places and times (Rm 2:11–15). Special revelation refers to the Bible, the Word of God given through the prophets and apostles, written for us, confirmed and authenticated by the extraordinary works of these biblical authors (Dt 18:21–22; Mk 16:16–20; 1Th 2:13; 2Tm 3:16).

There may indeed be people who understand by way of natural revelation that their life and future depends on God and who fear Him and hope in Him alone, though they do not know anything in particular about Him because they have never had access to the Word (Ps 33:18; 85:9; 103:1, 13, 17; 147:11; Lk 1:50). On the other hand, love and concern for others motivates us to make every effort to reach all people with the Word so that fear of God and hope in Him might become certain and assured (Heb 11:1). A relationship of honesty about our dependence on God can be accomplished by God through circumstances and/or through His Word, though the Word is preferable for the certainty it gives (Mt 18:1–4; Ac 18:25–26; Rm 10:17; 2Pt 1:2–10).

The witness of God's grace, love, and intent that we should live is manifest in almost every aspect of nature, but it is most clearly manifest in the life of His Son, who has taken away the sins of the world, thus having already accomplished the justification of all people. What remains is for us to realize that truth more and more in our lives as we seek to help others realize the full effects of that accomplishment (2Co 5:14–21; Php 3:7–16).

Q 1:22–24 Did God let them become more susceptible to sins because they were worshiping idols?

God does not make anyone do anything that is contrary to His will; on the contrary, God does all things to keep people from contradicting His will as nothing but death can result from doing so. God does not keep people from the means of resisting evil but provides witnesses in nature, in experience, in conscience, in His Word, and through people who serve His Word. Idolatry often leads to sexual immorality because the same appetite for indulging the flesh that motivates idolatry also fuels a desire for selfish sexual gratification (Ex 32:1–7; 1Co 10:7).

Q 1:24–27 Does this passage condemn homosexuality? How should Christians deal with homosexuals?

Yes, the Bible forbids homosexuality, along with every kind of thought, word, or activity that is contrary to life, health, and wellness among people. The term "homo-

sexual" is misleading since it describes the whole person by one particular inclination. The Bible does not make any distinction in how we deal with other people, whether they gossip, hate, commit sexual immorality, or condemn others in self-righteousness (Mk 7:20–23; 7:1; 18:15–18; 23:25–33; Lk 18:9–14).

We love all people, just as we are loved by God, and seek their well-being by bringing them into the truth and grace of God. If a person is contentious in impenitence, we hope and pray and wait for circumstances to change that disposition. If a person is ignorant, we share the truth so he may know it and benefit from it. If a person is penitent, we foster that disposition by sharing a life in the Word that holds our fallen flesh in check and in penitence and inspires our regenerate soul by God's grace and Spirit. The Bible addresses homosexuality under the comprehensive term "sexual immorality" and by a variety of related terms (Gn 9:20–23; 19:4–29; Ex 20:14; 22:16; Lv 19:20; 20:10–21; Nu 5:12–13; Dt 5:18; 22:13–28; Rm 13:9, 14; 1Co 6:9–10; 1Th 4:1–12). For a thorough treatment of this subject, please see Robert Gagnon, *The Bible and Homosexual Practice: Texts and Hermeneutics* (Nashville: Abingdon, 2001).

Q 1:24 What does it mean that "God gave them up"? Is God basically giving them to the world because they loved it so much?

God is love, which means He doesn't make people do things. God is just, which means His Law sustains a universe that supports life and consequences for contradicting this Law. God does a lot of protecting and restoring. When a person despises God's intervention and counsel, what is there to do but leave the person to discover the effects of their actions through experience? People insist on their desires contrary to God's design for life, and when they absolutely refuse to listen to wisdom or reason, God leaves them to the way upon which they insist. The way they insist upon will either teach them to repent or inaugurate the judgment they mock. Yes, God is giving such a person over to what he loves because he will tolerate no other way. When such a person experiences the consequences of his actions, he has no one to blame but himself.

- - - - - - - - - - - - - - - - - - - -

Q **1:25 Do we exchange the truth of God for a lie every time we sin?**

You might say that every sin is the consequence of having exchanged the truth for a lie, and every sin is followed by the temptation to exchange more truth for more lies. What is interesting in this verse is that the Greek word translated as "lie" is preceded by a definite article, "*the* lie," which happens only four times in the New Testament (Jn 8:44; Rm 1:25; Eph 4:25; 2Th 2:11—plus five more times in the Greek Old Testament: Jb 16:8; Ps 5:6; Is 28:15; Dn 8:25; Hos 7:3). Both Jn 8:44 and 2Th 2 connect "the lie" with the devil, who is a liar and a murderer. These two passages, plus our verse here, suggest that "the lie" is that there is or can

be any God except the one true God, since all other lies flow from or are addressed at this primary truth. If you have the true God, then you have the truth and all the life and benefits that the truth sustains. If you have the lie, you have nothing but lies, deception, and death (Rm 1:26–32).

- - - - - - - - - - - - - - - - - - - -

Q **1:26 When it says "their women," is that referring to their wives?**

This section began in v. 18 by identifying men "who by their unrighteousness suppress the truth." The wives and/or women of the families of these men are the ones who have made this exchange, which is referring to homosexuality (see Rm 1:24–27 above).

- - - - - - - - - - - - - - - - - - - -

Q **1:28 Is God giving up on these people? If God allows sin to take its course as a punishment, then how do we determine whether God is allowing judgment on those who believe?**

When people insist on opposing God with sufficient tenacity, God often gives them what they demand for three reasons. First, God gives people over to their own ways so they might learn from the consequences of those ways to repent (exemplified in the life and prophecy of Jonah; see also Lv 26:1–45; Ac 17:26–27). Second, because God is only giving these people over to what they insist upon, there is justice in the consequences of destruction that they bring upon themselves (2Pt 2:12–22). Third, those who contradict God's design, love, and intervention serve as a witness to the truth and a warning to everyone else (Pr 7:27; Mt 11:20–24; Jn 12:37–44; 1Tm 5:20).

Would we say that God is "allowing" judgment or "executing" judgment? God is patient and merciful, leaving us to learn from the consequences of our mistakes rather than punishing us according to our folly. This is a function of both patience and mercy. When God gives a person over to a stubborn insistence on rebellion and contradiction, the hope is still that such a person would realize, by consequence, that his ways are a mistake (Pr 14:12; 16:25; Rm 6:21). God has provided a remedy for all our mistakes by the redemption accomplished in Christ, by regenerating our soul, by the everlasting life conveyed in His Word, and by the promised new creation. All that God does, from first to last, is designed to bring everyone into the realization of His goodness and providence and to keep us from destroying our own life and future (Ezk 18:23; Mt 23:37; Rv 3:19; 9:20–21; 16:9–11).

Q 2:1–3 How do you distinguish between judgment and showing your brother his sin so he may repent?

If you tell someone not to judge, you are not judging that person but commanding him not to do what would make him guilty of judgment (not to mention contradiction and hypocrisy). If you tell a person she is going to hell when she dies because ·she says that to others, then you are judg-

ing someone for judging others. Judgment has a spectrum of meaning, from condemnation to diagnosis. God forbids us from condemning others because we cannot know a person's everlasting destiny and because it is not our place (Mt 18:21–35; Jn 8:1–11). Our place is to bear witness to all that is opposed to life and to draw people away in repentance toward all that is life according to God's will (2Co 5:14–21; Gal 6:1; Jas 5:19–20). In 1Co 5, Paul commands the most effective and only loving course of action for the well-being of the man and for all those who knew of his relationship with his stepmother. Here, Paul forbids the condemnation of others, lest we lose both the one doing the condemning and the one being condemned. The Law, conscience, and consequences already condemn what is contrary to God's design for life; what people need is help realizing the redemption Christ has already provided from that condemnation (Mt 9:9–17; Lk 6:37; Jn 3:17–18).

Q 2:5 How do you store up wrath?

What if we think of God's wrath against all ways that oppose life as a blockade designed to keep people from pursuing deadly activities? A person who continued to push against that blockade would cause the wrath of God to pile up, like a bulldozer pushing dirt as it goes until there is a pile of dirt too big for the bulldozer to push. God is gracious and patient, providing an ordered universe that supports life and, as a result, yields consequences for action that is opposed to life.

The thought of God's mounting wrath is intended to be a barricade large enough to turn our fallen human nature back toward the way of life and the loving, inviting countenance of God in Christ (Lv 26:1–45; Jer 8:4–7; Hos 5:13–6:2; Mt 23:37–39).

Q 2:6 Does this mean our works will affect our judgment from God?

This verse is an exact quotation from Pr 24:12 in the Greek translation of the Old Testament. There are way too many passages that speak about the relationship of judgment and works to ignore them or to try to explain them away (Mi 6:6–8; Mt 25:31–46; 2Co 5:10; Eph 6:8). There is no escaping the fact that only the righteous will be saved (Mt 5:20, 48; 11:11). There is no escaping the fact that there is one and only one way to be righteous, that is, by the grace of God (Rm 3:10–26). The Son of God has taken away in His death all that we do wrong. The Word and Spirit of God apply to us all that Christ did right. The Word and Spirit of God regenerate our inner person or soul so that we actually do what is right (Is 40:1–2; Hos 6:1–2; Jn 3:1–7; 15:1–7; 16:14; 1Jn 3:9). The person who steadfastly denies any fault in himself and steadfastly despises all that Christ has done for him and all that God would do in his life dies under the condemnation of the Law (Jn 3:18–19).

Do our works affect God's judgment?

Q 2:8 It says there will be wrath and anger for self-seeking people. Will these people go to heaven?

In Rm 2:5, Paul explained that this wrath will be executed on Judgment Day (see also Rv 6:16–17). These people will not go to heaven; indeed, they cannot because their insistence on selfishness and their rejection of the truth in favor of unrighteousness yields the absolute opposite of all that heaven is. The wrath and anger (or "rage") of God is the opposite of His kindness: it is the natural experience of a person who is opposed to and moving away from God's kindness. The natural, furious, dreadful, deadly consequences of rebelling against the way of life is the last possible remedy for a fallen human nature determined to self-destruct (Mt 27:44; Lk 23:39–43; Ac 9:1–20).

Q 2:9 Why does Paul continue to write that both positive and negative things from God will come for "the Jew first and also the Greek"? How will tribulation and distress be carried out?

All of the promises and activity of God became concentrated over time until they were fulfilled in Jesus. Now the benefit of the promises, the activity of God, and Jesus were flowing back out to all people in the reverse direction. It makes sense to inform those people who were waiting for the fulfillment first, since they were ready and would carry the message forward to others. It makes sense that those who knew the promises of God but despised them would face the consequences of that folly first, since they have no excuse (see also 1:16 above).

Affliction and distress will be the fate of those who have insisted on their own condemnation on Judgment Day (Rm 2:5; Mt 25:41–46; Rv 16:11).

Q 2:10–11 How can God not show favoritism? Are the Jews favored over the Greeks?

God does not show favoritism; that is, He does not deal more graciously with one person than with another since all are His creation and all have been redeemed by His Son (Jn 3:16). God sustains the life of all people, even those who despise Him (Rm 2:4). God is gracious to all who fear Him, no matter who they are (Ps 34:4–9; Lk 1:50). God does make distinctions when it comes to responsibility and accountability (Lk 12:42–48; 19:11–26; Jas 3:1). The Jews were supposed to be God's ambassadors to the Gentiles (Dt 4:5–8). The Jews had the promises, so it would make sense for them to learn of the fulfillment of those promises first and then serve God by sharing the promises and their fulfillment with others (Rm 9:4–5; Ac 1:8). To the Jews much had been given, so from them much was required (Lk 19:11–26).

Q 2:11 If God doesn't show favoritism, why does He say the Jews are the chosen people?

God chose Abraham and gave him descendants for a few reasons—none of them have to do with favoritism. First, God chose Abraham and his descendants so that people might follow the fulfillment of His promise to send a Savior by the seed of the woman (Gn 3:15; Is 7:14). Second, God demonstrated through these people that fallen human nature cannot produce a Savior nor even begin to fulfill the Law on its own behalf (Mt 1:2–12; 1Co 10:6–12; Heb 3:12–19). Third, through the Jews God demonstrated His patience, grace, and love—upon which all fallen human nature depends (Ex 32:11–14; Rm 9:14–29).

Q 2:12 What is meant by "sinned without the Law"?

Paul provides some clarification of his meaning in vv. 14–24. Generally, the term "law" means "the way things have to be." In this context, Paul is referring to the Law that God gave Israel through Moses. The Gentiles did not have or know the Law as God had given it to Moses in the Ten Commandments or any of the other civil or ceremonial laws in Exodus, Leviticus, Numbers, and Deuteronomy. Nevertheless, all people have the moral Law written on their hearts, which we know as our conscience. Whether you know the Law of Moses because it was taught to you or whether you have never heard of it, breaking the Law has the same negative consequences; the wages of sin is death (Rm 6:23).

Q **2:15 Does every person have a basic knowledge of God or need for Him because of the Law written on every heart?**

Yes. The commonality of moral codes and ethics around the world and throughout time is powerful evidence that the Law is written on human hearts, and consciences are active accordingly. Many people have become convinced that all religions are basically the same because they have almost identical moral codes, for which this passage accounts. Christianity is unique because of the vicarious, universal atonement provided for all in Jesus Christ (Ac 4:12; Gal 1:6–7).

Q **2:16 To what does "according to *my* Gospel" refer?**

Paul made plain in his Letter to the Galatians that there is one, and only one, Gospel (Gal 1:6–7). When Paul says "my Gospel," he is referring to the one and only Gospel of which he has been made a steward and that he proclaims, in contrast to the false apostles and Judaizers who teach and preach against the Gospel (Ac 9:3–20; Rm 1:1–5; 1Co 2:1–5; 9:16; 2Co 11:1–15; Gal 1:1–24).

Q **2:21–24 God's name is blasphemed among the Gentiles because we are sinful and our witness is imperfect. How do we reach those who see us as hypocrites?**

If your witness is moralism but you sin, then you are a hypocrite, and there is no way to change that fact except to obey the Law perfectly; but this is not what Christ or His Word teaches. God's name is glorified when people learn of His love, grace, goodness, and power that accomplished universal redemption in Christ Jesus. Christianity does not teach that we can be perfect; rather, it teaches that we can be honest about our imperfections because God has provided a remedy (Ps 130:3–4; Jn 3:16; Gal 2:15–21). Christians seek a godly life not to justify themselves but because they have already been justified in Christ and seek to share that new life with others. Christians love others from gratitude for the love of God, because the love of God is at work in them, because we have a soul regenerated in the image of Christ, and so that others come to know the same love and life of God with which we have been blessed (Jn 15:1–13; 2Co 5:14–21; Php 3:7–14; 1Jn 4:19).

Q **2:25–29 Why does God require circumcision? Didn't Baptism take the place of circumcision?**

The "Law" in this context is referring to the Law that God gave to the children of Israel through Moses (see 2:12 above). Paul is responding to Jews who believed that by keeping the simple, outward, physical requirements of the Mosaic Law, they would impress God and earn His favor. God commanded circumcision as a physical confirmation of His covenant with Abraham, but fallen human nature reversed that and made it a person's own act that would require God to be favorable (just as some teach that keeping the Commandments makes you a Christian and earns God's favor; Gal 2:14–3:29). Outward pretense of religious activity does not deceive or impress God (Mal 1:1–2:9; Mt 7:21–23; 23:4–39; Jas 1:17–2:26). So, then, circumcision does not commend a man to God; rather, it is the fear of the Lord and honesty about dependence upon Him that brings realization of the grace of God already active and accomplished in Christ (Ps 34:7–9; Lk 1:50).

God did not call the children of Israel in order to reject all other people but so the children of Israel could bear witness to the grace of God by which all people are accepted. The Jews insist on their own condemnation and lead others into judgment whenever they contend that by keeping a few of the physical, outward requirements of the Law they have earned the blessings of God they sought selfishly according to their fallen human nature (1Sm 15:10–26; Hg 1:2–11; Mt 23:13–33). The Jews wanted to claim a special place with God on the basis of physical descent from Abraham, just as the Greeks in Corinth wanted to make a claim to superiority on the basis of their genetics and culture (1Co 1:18–31). Third,

Baptism did take the place of circumcision. While circumcision was an outward confirmation of God's promise to send a Savior who would reverse the curse brought on all by Adam, the Rite of Baptism is a physical confirmation of God's grace that was accomplished in Christ and flows to all who live immersed in His Word (Rm 5:12–21; 8:1–39; Ti 3:4–6; 1Pt 3:18–21).

Q 3:4 What does "Let God be true though every one were a liar" mean?

Fallen human nature prefers to justify itself and condemn others, including God, for what is wrong (Gn 3:12; Ex 32:22–24; Ezk 18:25–29; 33:17–20; Mt 25:44–45). When Paul says, "Let God be true," he means to say, "Let everyone recognize that God is true always and at all times." Fallen human nature lies and murders after the image of the one who instigated the fall and, to make things worse, blames, despises, and rejects the truth that alone can work the remedy (Pr 28:13; Jn 3:18–20; 8:30–51; 1Jn 1:6–9). Christ, the source of truth and life, demonstrated His nature and the way to life by assuming in Himself the guilt of every lie and all the destruction of murder, taking it away in His own death and absolving us of it all in His own resurrection (Jn 1:29; 2Co 5:21). Truth is evident in the life it works, just as lies produce nothing but death (Jn 10:10; Rm 6:21; Lk 18:9–14).

Q **3:9–20 Paul repeats that humans are not perfect. Did the people not understand this idea?**

The volume of truth Paul presents here about the absolute depravity of fallen human nature bears witness to how tenaciously this human nature insists on lying to itself, others, and God about its condition. People claim free will but give not the least indication of having one. Many people who claim the Christian faith insist that they have a free will, even though Jesus exposed such a claim as a lie (Jn 8:31–59). Without exception, even after it is justly condemned, fallen human nature insists it is right and suffering unjustly (Lk 7:31–50; 15:25–32; 16:22–31; 18:9–14; see also Rm 3:4 above). Apart from the Word and Spirit of God, we identify with the physical nature that we feed, clothe, and spend our time trying to satisfy. If that is all we know, then we can understand why this nature is at the same time absolutely greedy and absolutely self-righteous. The only way to end the greed is for God to put the human nature to death and raise up a regenerate soul within us, a soul reunited with God, who is infinite and thus infinitely satisfied (Rm 5:6–6:23). The only way to end the self-righteousness is to show the folly of it in contrast to the genuine, universal, comprehensive, and utterly gracious righteousness provided for all in the life of Christ (2Co 5:14–21; Php 3:7–14; Heb 2:14–15). Jesus is the great physician who healed the sick, raised the dead, and rose Himself to prove it (Mt 9:1–8; Lk 7:11–17). Although He is infinitely great, those who are determined to assert themselves against Him are left to the death upon which they insist (Mt 12:22–34; Lk 13:34–35; Jn 3:18–20; Heb 6:1–8; 10:26–31).

Q **3:20 This verse shows me the need for the Gospel. But what does it say about works-righteousness?**

Works-righteousness is a witness to the arrogance, conceit, vanity, and self-destructive insanity of fallen human nature, which is why it is necessary for death to relieve us of this nature (Lk 15:25–32; Jn 3:18–20; 8:31–59; Gal 3:1–24; 5:2–4; Heb 3:12–4:12; 1Jn 1:6, 8, 10; see above, Rm 3:9–20, for more on this).

Q **3:22 Is Paul's theme here: "the righteousness of God comes through faith in Jesus Christ for all who believe"?**

Yes, remembering that the Law is necessary to lead a person to reject pretensions of self-righteousness and righteousness by works and that the Gospel is necessary to regenerate a soul that lives in the Word and by faith in the living God (Rm 8:1–17; Gal 3:15–21; Php 3:7–14).

Q **3:25 What happened to the people who lived and died before Jesus saved us from our sins?**

We are creatures of time and space, so we recognize a time in history when the Son of God took our nature and our place under the condemnation of the Law in order to free us from sin, death, and the devil (Gal 4:4–5). However, God is not a creature of time or space, so from His perspective all of humanity has always been redeemed and He has and always will deal with us according to His grace in Christ rather than as our sins deserve (Gn 3:15; 12:3; Ps 103:10; Mt 25:34; Heb 4:3; Rv 17:8). People before Christ depended upon the grace of God that would be accomplished in Christ; people who lived after Christ depend on the grace of God already accomplished; for God, this gracious work has always been accomplished (Rm 4:1–8; Heb 1:1–4; 1Pt 1:3–12).

- - - - - - - - - - - - - - - - - - - -

Q 3:29 Does this verse, which says "God is one," contradict the Trinity? How is it possible for God to be three?

We are hardly in a position to make decisions about what is possible or impossible. Human history alone is filled with claims of impossibility and then the refutation of those claims: from flight to navigation to invention to the running of a four-minute mile. When will human nature learn to be a good student rather than a hasty judge? How the Trinity is possible is like many questions we are not equipped to answer—such as how gravity works, why the sun doesn't burn out, or how God actually spoke the universe into existence. What we do know is that God makes abundant witness to the fact that there is just one God and yet that God exists as three persons, distinguishable but inseparable (Dt 6:4; Eph 4:4–6; Mt 28:19).

On the other hand, there are small witnesses to the notion of a Trinity in creation. For example, we live in a three-dimensional universe; I can make three distinct drawings of the same object. Or consider a single fire—we can distinguish between the wood, the heat, and the light (we can even experience each of those three aspects individually or all at once). God is very eager to answer the questions that our minds can handle and for which we really need an answer (Jn 3:1–17; 9:35–38; 20:30–31).

- - - - - - - - - - - - - - - - - - - -

Q 3:31 How does this verse coincide with Jesus teaching that not one letter of the Law would disappear?

Paul is teaching exactly what Jesus taught in the Sermon on the Mount (Mt 5:17). The Jews, like everyone else with a fallen human nature, disregarded the Law in two ways: they diluted the absolute nature of the Law and then claimed to have kept what in fact was condemning them. Fallen human nature does this because it is completely overcome with the delusion that it can and must save itself, like a person who is drowning. Jesus and Paul, as His apostle, restore the Law to our hearts and minds in its absolute nature that condemns us absolutely. But Jesus did not save us by diluting, reducing, or negating the Law; He saved us by fulfilling it. The Law describes that upon which life depends, and Christ provided a fulfillment of all that is required and then imparted that to us (Rm 8:1–5).

Q 4:2 How can Abraham be justified by his works?

Abraham was not justified by his works; Paul is stating a condition contrary to fact. The verse should be understood to mean something like this: "If Abraham were to be justified by works, which he was not, he might have a reason to boast among people but still not before God." The whole point of God's promise of a Savior through a descendant of Abraham (who at the time the promise was made had no son, Gn 12:3) was to prove how it is impossible for us to save ourselves by works—how can you make an heir when your wife is barren and now both of you are too old to have a child? But God does the impossible, and those who are honest about their dependence on Him benefit from His gracious work (Mt 19:25–26). For more on this see Jas 2:14–24.

Q 4:5 What does it mean that "faith is counted as righteousness"?

Justification is a forensic or judicial act; sanctification is a process. Justification declares that a person is righteous; sanctification makes a person righteous. God has declared all sins forgiven in the crucifixion of Jesus, and the Holy Spirit imputes or applies (credits or counts) the life of Christ to us (Jn 16:14; 1:29; 19:30). In the United States, a presidential pardon means a person is free from the condemnation of the law, no matter what. However, if the law was broken and damage done, the broken law and damage remain. God declared all people forgiven because Jesus endured the punishment for the Law broken by everyone and did perfectly all that the Law requires of everyone. Therefore, the Law is satisfied, and the damage is repaired (Rm 5:12–21).

Q 4:6–8 How can people get rid of the feelings of guilt they might have?

It may not be possible or even beneficial for fallen human nature to get rid of its feelings of guilt. Fallen human nature cannot accept or understand what God has graciously done for us in Christ (1Co 2:14). Human nature needs a consciousness of the consequences of its actions or it becomes self-righteous, self-indulgent, and all the more abusive of others (Rm 3:19; Gal 3:24). The only real way to get rid of feelings of guilt is to realize that the essence of our life, who we really are, is the soul that God regenerates in the image of Christ through His Word (Jn 1:12–13; 3:1–7; Ti 3:4–6; 1Jn 3:9). While we recognize and repent of our fallen human nature, we also know that God forgives all our guilt because of Christ, sees us as holy and innocent because of Christ, and sustains in us a regenerate soul that is without guilt (Ezk 18:4–32; Jn 8:1–11; Lk 18:9–14).

Q 4:7 Why does this verse jump back to focusing on Abraham?

This verse is a quote from Ps 32, which was written by David. Paul picks up his discussion of Abraham again in v. 9. Paul is focused on Abraham because he is the basis of the Jewish argument for a privileged status and works-righteousness before God, yet Abraham's life absolutely excludes such an argument. Paul uses David's words in Ps 32 because they so clearly articulate Paul's point about Abraham and all who would be like him in a relationship with God.

• • • • • • • • • • • • • • • • • • • •

Q 4:9–25 Did the Jews not think of Abraham as their father before he was circumcised, since they don't think a Gentile is one of them?

The Jews claim Abraham as their father because they are the physical descendants of Abraham through Isaac, Jacob, and the twelve sons of Jacob. Wanting to justify themselves, the Jews argued that obedience to outward, physical rituals is why God accepted Abraham, circumcision being one of God's requirements that Abraham satisfied (Mt 23:13–33; Jn 7:18–24; Ac 15:5–10). Here is the irony of the Jewish claim: if they want to make claims on God and His material blessings because they are physical descendants of Abraham, then they must acknowledge that Ishmael has the right of the firstborn son. If they want to enjoy the blessings of being claimed by God and the children of His promises to Abraham, then they would recognize that God's grace has given them life and the Old Testament was given to confirm that grace. Material claims and blessings would be of no importance to them (Heb 11:13–16). Faith in God, honesty about dependence on Him, has always been

the basis for a person's relationship with God, regardless of physical descent (Mt 8:1–15; Lk 4:16–30; Heb 3:7–4:12; 11:1–40). All human beings, born of the flesh, are children of Adam and destined to return to the dust as he did (Jn 3:6; 1Co 2:14; 15:50). Only those people who are regenerated by the Spirit are children of God; being generated by the Word of the Lord that endures forever means these must also live forever (Jn 1:11–13; 3:1–7; 1Jn 3:9).

• • • • • • • • • • • • • • • • • • • •

Q 4:10–11 Can we imply through Abraham's faith before circumcision that we all have faith before Baptism?

There is no need to imply that people have faith before Baptism just as Abraham did before circumcision since the baptismal rite is for believers (Mk 16:16; Ac 8:35–38). The idea that Baptism can save a person as an isolated event, where the Word of God is absent, is parallel to the Jews' idea that circumcision makes them children of Abraham (Mt 12:34–35; Lk 3:7–9; Rm 10:1–17).

• • • • • • • • • • • • • • • • • • • •

Q 4:12 What is circumcision?

Circumcision is cutting off the foreskin of the male sexual organ. God gave this physical sign to Abraham in order to confirm that He would, in fact, send His own Son into human flesh through a descendant of Abraham (Gn 3:15; 12:3; Gal 4:4–7). This sign was given to men only because the responsibility for restoring the catastrophe caused by Adam rested upon the Son of

God who had created Adam and all things (Rm 5:12–20). Circumcision was replaced with Baptism for all once the Son of God had come as a man and thus fulfilled all that the Law required to restore life to all (Mt 28:19–20; Mk 16:16; Ac 2:38–42).

• • • • • • • • • • • • • • • • • • •

Q **4:16 Why do people use works to try to enter heaven or to be a Christian? What does it mean that the promise is guaranteed to all Abraham's offspring?**

Fallen human nature is entirely self-ish and self-centered. Fallen human nature cannot see or know anything except what it thinks according to its own, fallen disposition (1Co 2:14). In order to have a sense of hope and salvation, fallen human nature does the only thing it knows how to do—it claims this on its own ability. If there is a law that a self-righteous person has failed to keep, then that person rejects the law as faulty. Fallen human nature wants to use all things to satisfy its own insatiable, carnal appetites and will beg, borrow, or steal whatever it wants and find a way to claim it is good and right in doing so. Selfishness and pride are the death of mankind. When Paul speaks of Abraham's offspring who are "adherents of the Law," he is referring to Jewish people who claim Abraham as their ancestor on the basis of the Law—the laws of physical descent and because they claim to keep the Law of Moses (Jn 8:37–44; Ac 15:5; Gal 3:1–29). The significance of Isaac as the heir of Abraham is that his conception was impossible by human means; Isaac

was a child generated by God's promise (Gn 17:15–21; 18:9–15; 21:1–70. Isaac had two sons, but it was the younger son, Jacob, who received the inheritance according to God's Word and contrary to the law of the first-born (Gn 25:29–34; 27:1–29). The genealogy of Abraham demonstrates that there is no hope for humanity in fallen human nature—only souls regenerated by the Word and Spirit of God can live (Mt 1:1–25; Heb 10:1–18; Jn 1:11–13; 3:1–7).

• • • • • • • • • • • • • • • • • • •

Q **4:24 Is Paul saying that believing is what justifies us?**

There are plenty of biblical texts that connect believing with salvation (Mk 16:16; Jn 3:16; Rm 1:16). Knowing the benefit of being a believer does not tell us how a person becomes a believer. Believing or having faith or trust (all the same word in Greek) is the product of God's Word and Spirit at work in us (Rm 10:17; Jn 6:63; 1Pt 1:5). Believers are saved, but that faith is in the grace of God, which provides the whole content of what is believed, and the Word and Spirit, which regenerate us and work faith in us.

• • • • • • • • • • • • • • • • • • •

Q **5:1 What does "peace" mean in Scripture?**

The word *peace* occurs 227 times in the Old Testament (Greek Old Testament) and 92 times in the New Testament. Peace has the idea of living in a spacious place, free of threat and constriction, not just physically but also mentally and emotionally (Ps 4:8;

What does peace mean?

18:35–36; 31:7–8). The New Testament contrasts peace with war, fear, and restriction (Mt 10:34; Jn 20:19–21, 26; Heb 11:31; Rv 6:4). Peace comes with salvation and is confirmed by healing (Mk 5:34). The peace of God endures and is comprehensive (Jn 14:27; Php 4:7).

Q 5:3–4 How does suffering produce endurance, endurance produce character, and character produce hope? How do we rejoice in our sufferings?

Suffering produces endurance in the very same way that forcing muscles to resist weight makes them stronger and more able to endure (Jas 5:11). Character is something like the results of refining metal. As ore endures the heat of the crucible, what is not genuine and useful is burned away. As we endure suffering, the particular strengths that God has given us become more evident as we use them and apply them in response to the challenges we face. Applying your character (the strengths you have) in response to challenges over and over again builds confidence in your ability to meet the challenges that come. An athlete who has discovered his or her potential enjoys each competition with the confidence of much experience (1Co 9:24–27). Those who speak in public, leaders, physicians, and others who have discovered and then developed

their skills through time and challenge are at peace because of their confidence that each new challenge will not only help them develop further but also allow them to apply their gifts for the good of others. We rejoice in sufferings the way athletes or others do, who recognize the value of the strain their work requires in relation to the good such work produces (2Co 4:1–5:21).

Q 5:6–11 Why is human nature so bad?

Human nature is so bad because there is no bottom to the fall of Adam. In other words, once human nature turned to oppose God, it turned completely, the way a ship turns upside down once it has started to turn over. Consider, on the one hand, the consistency of biblical reports on the complete depravity of the human condition (Gn 6:5; Jgs 2:7–12; Jer 17:9; Mk 7:20–23). Even people who do works that appear good may be doing them for selfish, evil purposes (Is 64:6; Mt 23:23–33). On the other hand, consider how universally and passionately fallen human nature is oriented toward its own destruction in what we think, say, eat, and do. Acting so consistently against our own best interests makes no more sense than Adam throwing away Paradise, but his action is the cause of ours (Rm 5:12). Since all people have descended from Adam, all are without strength, ungodly, sinners, and enemies of God according to our fallen human nature; all of history bears this out. On the other hand, history is full of people whom the Lord worked in and through to accomplish His good purposes, even among those who would not claim to be Christian (Is 45:1–13; Mt 23:1–3; Rm 13:1–7). Christians remain afflicted with and opposed by this fallen human nature but are aided in seeking the way of the Lord by the Word, a regenerate soul animated by the Holy Spirit, and the Christian community (Rm 7:13–25; Col 3:1–16; Heb 10:24–25).

• • • • • • • • • • • • • • • • • • • •

Q **5:7 When Paul refers to "righteous" and "good" people, who is he referring to? Isn't it true that no one is good or righteous until forgiven?**

Paul is explaining the magnitude of God's love for us in the sacrifice of Christ by comparing it to human experience. In human experience there are people who are "righteous" in the sense that they obey the laws (or at least do a good job of pretending to), like the Pharisees (Lk 18:11–12). In human experience there are also "good" people who may not be perfect (righteous), but are kind, helpful, loving, and caring. Now, in human experience, who would sacrifice his life for a "righteous" person? Probably no one, since "righteous" people may appear to keep the law but not in the interest of helping anyone. Maybe, just maybe, from time to time there would be a person who was of such good character that another person would sacrifice himself to save that person—the way a Secret Service agent might use his own body as a shield to protect the president. Think of how rare it is, in human experience, to find a person so

good that another person would give his or her life in exchange. God demonstrates His love for us in giving the life of His only Son in exchange for those who are entirely contrary to Him.

• • • • • • • • • • • • • • • • • • • •

Q **5:8 Why does it say, "While we were still sinners, Christ died for us"? We have always been sinners and always will be.**

According to our fallen human nature, we are always opposed to God, which is why the passing away of this nature is a benefit to us. Paul's point has to do with the grace of God. It is impossible for such fallen human nature to begin to reconcile or ever to reconcile itself to God; God knows this. If God waited for us to do even the smallest thing right, we would never be redeemed. If God wanted to save our lives, He would have to act while we were still His enemies. Since no other condition was possible for us, while we were yet opposed to God by nature, God sent His Son into the world to redeem that nature and to accomplish the promises of grace that regenerate us with a new nature, after the image of Christ.

• • • • • • • • • • • • • • • • • • • •

Q **5:10 If we aren't supposed to have enemies, why were we God's enemies?**

Since the fall of Adam we have not once been a single thing we are supposed to be (Rm 3:10–18). The Bible says we are enemies of God because that is the condition of our human nature (see 5:6–11 above). The solution for this condition is twofold: (1) God uses the Law to incapacitate this nature which is opposed to Him, and (2) God uses the Gospel to generate a new person in us who loves God and our neighbor without fail (Rm 6:5–11; Col 3:1–16; 1Jn 3:9).

Q 5:12–21 Verse 13 says that sin was not taken into account because there was no Law. Why, then, was there death (v. 14)? What is the best way to illustrate this section to those who don't believe Christ is the Savior?

What else can this mean but to distinguish between the natural consequences of sin and the more formal and forensic experience of being condemned by the Law before a righteous God? *Sin* is a term that describes the way fallen human nature is opposed to God's design for creation and contradicts His Word. Such a contrary orientation has physical consequences, which we know as accidents and death (Jn 9:1–3; Rm 6:23). In addition to the simple, physical consequences of sin, there is the moral judgment of God against those who willfully and purposefully insist on and persist in opposing Him (Heb 6:4–6; 10:26–31).

Q 5:14 Is Adam considered the type of the one to come because the pattern of sinful humans follows him until Christ breaks the pattern? What does Paul mean by "those whose sinning was not like the transgression of Adam"?

Adam is considered here in comparison and contrast to Christ, like a negative and positive image. Adam and Christ affect absolutely everyone—Adam brought condemnation; Christ brings redemption.

A person could kill himself by a hundred different means that do not break any laws, but the person would be just as dead. The Law that God gave through Moses exposes the guilt of someone who condemns such a person to death, but even before God described the Law for Moses, people died because their human natures contradict God's design.

Q 5:18 Why should everyone suffer for one man's sin?

Since everyone descends from Adam, everyone has a fallen, contrary human nature just like Adam's. This is a natural, organic consequence, just like having all the other particular traits you received from your parents. Do you find it interesting that people complain violently about the unfairness of inheriting trouble but think nothing of taking all the credit and all that is of material value from their inheritance? While a person might claim that being conceived

Why should everyone suffer for one man's sin?

and born into condemnation inherited from Adam is unfair, so is being justified by the sacrifice of Christ under the Law for all people. God has justified all people in Christ and provided by this means invaluable and eternal life for us. If God has already justified all and provided for a life of redemption, love, and learning under His gracious care and leading, what would be a person's complaint or reason for not benefiting? If a person is condemned because he has renounced, refused, and despised the grace of God, how is that anyone's fault but that person's (Lk 13:34–35; 14:15–24; 15:25–32; 19:11–27; Heb 2:1–4:12)?

Q 5:20 Why would God add Law so that sin would increase?

What is wrong with human beings since the fall of Adam is just as wrong whether or not there is a written law that condemns it, because the consequences of contradicting God's design are the same. The Law was given to make the cause of our trouble more evident and then the solution more evident. Think about medicine, for example. Before the discovery of x-ray technology or CT scans or MRIs, people suffered and died from causes that no one could know. Now we can see what causes people's trouble, and physicians may even see that there is much more wrong than a person ever imagined. Knowing the extent of a problem more clearly and obviously urges us to more intense and immediate action and increases

appreciation for a remedy accomplished. Fallen human nature thinks too highly of itself and too little of that upon which its life depends. God provided a more exact articulation of the Law so we could see more clearly just how catastrophic and deadly the trouble is with the human nature that we inherited from Adam and practice for ourselves. Yet, by the grace of God, no matter how great the troubles, so much greater is the cure; no matter how deadly the infection of sin in us, so much more life-giving is the remedy of God's grace accomplished in Christ and effected in us through His Word and Spirit.

Q 6:1 How do people accept their sin while working to stay away from sin? How would grace increase by continuing to sin?

Paul is combating a typical strategy of fallen human nature, which seeks to satisfy its own selfish appetites while claiming to be righteous. Any person might find his mind suggesting that gratifying some lust would be all right since God has already forgiven all sin. If this were not bad enough, some may even argue that sinning more is good because doing so draws attention to the grace of God, which is to His glory. This is the way of corrupt human nature, and this is what the Christians were being accused of by the opponents of Christianity (Rm 3:8). The folly and self-deception of fallen human nature is pathetic, but active and powerful. Fallen human nature, separated from and opposed to the only source of real and lasting fulfillment (God), is frantic in its desperation to satisfy its desires, even though it knows such self-gratification contrary to God's will for us makes matters worse rather than better, as Paul is about to argue (Rm 6:21). The grace of God is boundless and His love infinite, but how would this truth encourage a person to waste the life God so graciously gives and restores to us? Being forgiven, being granted a regenerate soul, and being animated by the Spirit of God makes a person sensitive to and passionate about avoiding all that undermines our life and seeking all means of making it more effective in order to redeem the time (Jn 15:1–13; Eph 5:15–21; Ezk 36:24–27). People are justified in finding comfort and assurance in the capabilities of modern medicine to promote healing. Challenges and catastrophes have often resulted in new discoveries and even greater effectiveness in the healing arts. But what kind of person would recommend careless or reckless living just so she might experience this health care or challenge its ability?

● ● ● ● ● ● ● ● ● ● ● ● ● ● ● ● ● ● ● ●

Q 6:3 What does being "baptized into [Christ's] death" mean?

Baptism and the verb *baptize* have to do with establishing a relationship by immersing one thing in another. The ceremony of Baptism with water gives physical confirmation and evidence of a person being immersed in the words and promises of God (Ac 2:38–42). Paul spoke of the children of Israel being "baptized into Moses" because they had followed him through the Red Sea (1Co 10:2), which meant that these people were bound to Moses for better or worse depending on whether they obeyed or rebelled against him. When a person remains in the Word, the Word immerses such a person in the life of Christ and brings at least three benefits. First, Baptism gives witness to the fact that God has washed away our sin by His gracious forgiveness on account of Christ (1Pt 3:19–21; 2Ki 5:1–14; Is 1:18; Ac 2:38–39). Second, the Word of God credits us with the whole life of Christ; everything He did and endured is credited to us, including His death. In this way, Christ's vicarious atonement for us is applied to us (Jn 16:14–15; 2Co 5:21). Third, a fallen human nature that is buried (immersed) in the Word of God is forced to recognize that the natural consequence of its desires, thoughts, words, and deeds is death. The death of Christ on the cross is exactly what comes of following the passions of our fallen flesh, and seeing it works repentance (Lk 23:44–48; Jn 3:14–21; Rm 6:20–21; Gal 2:20–3:1).

● ● ● ● ● ● ● ● ● ● ● ● ● ● ● ● ● ● ● ●

Q 6:9 Did death ever have dominion over Christ?

Death had dominion over Jesus Christ only because the Son of God took upon Himself human nature and then submitted that human nature to death in our place (Jn 11:50; Lk 23:18–25; 2Co 5:21; Php 2:5–11). Once Jesus had taken away the cause of death, bearing our sins in His own person, it became impossible for Him to ever die again (Heb 2:9–15).

- - - - - - - - - - - - - - - - - - -

Q 6:10 If our death to sin happened once for all, why do we still sin?

In this verse Paul is talking about the death of Christ upon the cross. Christ died only once because His divine nature made it possible for Him to die in the place of every person who has lived or would ever live while bearing all the guilt there would ever be under the condemnation of the Law. We, according to our fallen human nature, die constantly. We recognize this universal truth in the dying of the cells of our bodies (just as we realize God's gracious will that we should live in cell regeneration). Over time, the constant dying of our human nature becomes a force we cannot survive, and our body dies. Christians are inspired by the Word to put their own selfish, self-defeating desires to death, as Paul is explaining in this chapter.

- - - - - - - - - - - - - - - - - - -

Q 6:12 How can we do what God says if our sinful nature is such a part of us and wants to reign?

Only the Word of God can accomplish in us what we are powerless to do on our own (Ezk 36:24–27; 37:1–17; Rm 5:6–11; Eph 2:1–10). The Law works to weaken, curb, and even control our contrary human nature—even as you are reading this verse in Romans (3:19; Gal 3:24; Lk 20:18). The Gospel strengthens and inspires our regen-

Why do we still sin?

erate soul to be in control so that our whole person is employed in the service of God's mission for us (Jn 6:63; 15:1–7; Rm 12:1–21; 2Co 5:14–20; Heb 2:14–15; 12:1–3).

- - - - - - - - - - - - - - - - - - -

Q 6:13 How does one offer part of his body to sin's power?

Maybe it would be clearer to say "use any of your human nature for purposes of wrongdoing." As soon as you notice that your mind is engaged in thoughts contrary to the will of God, turn those thoughts toward good instead. If your eyes are lustful, if your hands are working evil, if your feet are taking you someplace you should not go, turn those eyes and hands and feet toward activity that demonstrates love for God by service to neighbor (Mt 18:8–9; Rm 12:1–21; Heb 12:12–15).

- - - - - - - - - - - - - - - - - - -

Q 6:18–20 What does it really mean to be a "slave of righteousness"?

To be a slave simply means that you are not independent, especially not independent in regard to your master. Human beings, dependent on God for all things and interdependent with one another, are bound to serve someone or something; servanthood is only a bad thing when the master is bad. Fallen human nature, having separated itself from God, spends all its time serving the passions inflamed by the vast emptiness that only God can fill. These inflamed passions make fallen human nature enslave itself to any and every wicked deception that promises satisfaction but delivers only death (Rm 6:20–21). Christ has redeemed us from this death and, by reuniting us with God, has liberated us from bondage to the passions of the flesh. The love of Christ inspires, orients, and motivates us to bind ourselves or enlist ourselves as slaves to life and love that is the product of righteous conduct (Dt 30:11–20; Ezk 18:23–32; Gal 6:7–8; Jas 3:18). No one but God is free, but God and all masters who serve Him provide the greatest possible liberty for all who are bound to them. Those who presume to be masters in their own right are, in fact, slaves to the devil and serve only death (Jn 8:33–44).

Q 6:18 As Christians, are we slaves to do the will of God?

First, distinguish between our regenerate soul and our fallen human nature. According to our regenerate soul, we are children of God and slaves to no one (Jn 1:12–13; 1Jn 3:1–24; Gal 5:1). Our human nature is fallen and utterly dependent and therefore will always be mastered by someone or something. Those who are dishonest about their dependence, or faithless, are enslaved to the devil, the world, and the desires of their own fallen human nature—though they deny this as vigorously as they serve the passions to which they are enslaved (Eph 2:1–3). Those who are honest about their

dependence, or faithful, realize that there is only one good Master, only one Master who does all things from love, grace, and wisdom for the benefit of those who serve Him (1Ki 19:20–40; Pss 107:1–43; 135:13–18; Mt 6:19–32; Rm 8:28; Heb 12:1–11).

Q 6:19–23 If we are slaves of God, can we escape death and have eternal life?

It's true that all people die (with the exception of Enoch and Elijah). There is no other explanation for death than what is provided in Scripture and universal human experience—the consequences of contradicting God's design for life in nature is death. However, Paul has been contrasting our mortal flesh (6:12) with the new life God has given us by regeneration through Christ, His Word, and His Spirit (6:4). This new life or regenerate soul, being generated by the Word of the Lord that endures forever, endures forever also (Jn 11:25–26). This new life is without guilt and innocent, perfectly oriented to keep God's will, and inspired by the Word to faithfulness (Jn 8:31; 1Jn 3:1–3, 6–7, 8–9).

Q 6:19 What does "I am speaking in human terms" mean?

Paul means that he is going to restrict himself to means of expression that any human being could understand, since human perception is so dull after the fall (Mt 15:16; 16:6–12; Jn 3:4–12; 1Co 2:14).

Q 6:21 What benefits do we reap?

Paul says that the end or consequences of the things of which we are ashamed is death. Sin, in general, destroys the life God intended us to know and, in particular, destroys the relationships we have with people, which are essential to life. Idolatry means the death of our relationship with God just as adultery means the death of our relationship with our spouse. Alcoholism is death for the liver; sexual depravity brings disease as a consequence.

Q 6:22 How can we be slaves and free?

Our fallen human nature remains bound in sin until it returns to the dust; our regenerate soul is bound to God who gave us this new life through His Word and Spirit (Lk 9:24; 17:33; Gal 5:16–25; 6:3–17).

Q 6:23 As a Christian, isn't death a good thing since we enter the kingdom of God?

This verse isn't speaking about good or bad but about cause and effect. Fallen human nature insists that having its own way, contrary to God, is the best way to have the most life, but this is the deception of the devil (Gn 3:1–24; Pr 16:25; Jn 8:44). Sin is bad—that's why the result is death. In contrast to working for our own destruction, God gives us eternal life, which is the product of His Word and Spirit working in us (Ezk 36:24–27; Jn 6:26–29).

Q 7:1 In my translation of the Bible, it states that the Law has authority over man, but why does Paul then address laws that women are to follow instead of addressing men as well?

The word translated "man" in your Bible is *anthropos*, the Greek word for human beings in contrast to other living things (Greek has particular words for "male" and "female"). Paul wrote that the Law has power over human beings as long as they are alive.

Q 7:3 If a woman remarries after divorcing because of religious reasons, and her husband is still alive, is she still called an adulteress?

There are a few exceptions to the law against divorce. According to Jesus, if one spouse commits sexual immorality, the marriage has been broken and the other spouse is free (Mt 19:9). Paul explained that a spouse who abandons the other or who forces the other to leave also sets the "innocent" spouse free (see questions and answers at 1Co 7:12–15). If the woman divorced in order to protect her eternal salvation and communion with God in His Church, then she is free to marry another Christian (1Co 7:39; 2Co 6:14).

Q 7:4 Is this verse a metaphor?

This verse is full of indicative language, whether or not "metaphor" is the best way of describing it. For example, "death" means the "absence of relationship." When Paul says we "have died to the Law," he is explaining that the Law has no more effect upon us than it does on a dead person, and we are no more terrified of it than a dead person would be. The expression "through the body of Christ" refers to the literal history of the death of Christ under the Law in the place of all people. By taking our place under the condemnation of the Law, Christ fulfilled the Law and at the same time released us from our bondage to it so that He might bind us to Himself through the love He has for us and through the regenerating work of His Spirit.

• •

Q 7:5 How does the Law cause us to sin even more?

The Law arouses the passions of sin in at least two ways. First, the Law is like a bright light that reveals everything in unmistakable clarity and detail. A microscope or slow-motion video replay exposes trouble and errors in vast proportions. Second, the lust of fallen human nature is inflamed whenever something is forbidden and its pride responds to the Law with vicious defiance. Fallen human nature likes the Law in diluted form because it can be manipulated and actually used to satisfy the passions of the flesh (Gn 3:1–6; Mt 5:17–48; 19:1–26; 23:3–33). The purpose and power of the Law as God has given it is to incapacitate our fallen human nature so that God's grace and Spirit can regenerate in us a new per-

son who can manage the flesh for the better rather than the worst (Mt 4:1–11; Rm 3:19; 6:4, 11–13; Php 2:5–11; Jas 4:7).

• •

Q 7:7 Is this passage saying that the Law is sin?

Any law will do what Paul is describing here because the purpose of a law is to state what is required and what is forbidden. In this verse, Paul uses the definite article—"the Law"—because he is referring to the Law that God gave through Moses. Paul does ask the question, "Is the Law sin?" Paul asks this question because fallen human nature seeks to shift the blame away from itself (Gn 3:12–13). Fallen human nature wants to argue like this: "If it is the Law that brings awareness of sin, then sin is caused by the Law." Such an argument is like saying physicians and diagnostic equipment cause illness because they diagnosis it. The Law is good and necessary if we are to live and enjoy this life in a stable universe. It is inevitable that the same laws that tell us what is required to live also forbid and reveal the consequences for breaking these laws.

• •

Q 7:8–13 Can you please explain these confusing verses?

Some help may come from reading responses to questions on vv. 5, 7, and 8 above. Help for understanding might also come from using the parallel of the human body and the practice of medicine. Many people steadfastly avoid physicians because they don't want to find out that they are sick. Many people prefer to treat themselves with drugs that give relief for symptoms but leave the illness to become more serious over time until it is untreatable. When Paul says he was alive once without the Law, he is referring to his life as a Pharisee, in which self-righteousness depends on ignoring the Law or replacing it with rules that are easier to keep (compare what Paul says about himself in Php 3:6 with what Jesus says in Mt 5:17–48; 23:14–24; Lk 18:9–14, 18–23). Paul considered himself blameless until the Lord destroyed his self-delusion with the bright light of the truth about what the Law requires and what the Gospel has provided (Jn 3:16–20; Ac 9:3–20; Php 3:7–14). The Lord put to death Paul's fallen human nature under the Law and then raised him up as a regenerate soul that lived by the love of God and for the love of others (1Tm 1:5–16).

Q **7:8 Would there be sin if we had no Law?**

Sin only has power when it moves a person to oppose the Law; there is no such thing as speeding if there is no speed limit. Paul is also basing this on v. 5, where he talks about the way our fallen human nature is aroused and inflamed by the Law because it is bound in rebellion against God (Jn 8:33–44; Rm 5:6–11; Eph 2:1–3). When a person is in union with Christ, that person shares in the death of Christ under the Law and is regenerated by the Holy Spirit in the image of the risen Christ (Rm 6:4; 8:1–11).

Such a person is free from the curse of the Law, having died under the Law with Christ. Such a person lives by the grace of God for the love of others (2Co 5:14–21; Gal 5:1–4, 13; Php 3:7–14; 1Jn 3:9; 4:19).

Q **7:9–12 How can one be apart from the Law when original sin is present in all of us?**

You are correct in suspecting that no one can be apart from the Law, and Paul already made this clear (Rm 2:12–14). When Paul says he was alive apart from the Law, he does not mean that there was no Law but that he considered himself very much alive (righteous) because in his mind he had displaced the Law of God with his own standard (see also Rm 7:8 above).

Q **7:14–20 Doesn't it seem like Paul is making excuses for his sin?**

No one making excuses speaks with such grief over his sin or calls himself a "wretched man" (v. 24). Paul is expressing the struggle of the regenerate soul against fallen human nature (Gal 5:16–25; Col 3:1–17). When he sounds as though sin is not his fault, it is because there is an essential difference between the poison of original sin that dwells in our fallen human nature, fallen human nature itself, and the regenerate soul. When Paul rejects and condemns himself for breaking rather than keeping the Law, he is speaking from the consciousness of his regenerate soul about his fallen human nature or flesh. If Paul was not, in essence, a regenerate soul, he would neither be able to nor be interested in having this honest and godly disposition toward his own sin. When someone has cancer, the cancer is his, though he may speak of it as if it were a foreign and unwelcome substance. Cancer is a foreign and unwelcome substance indeed, and deadly, though my body is producing it. I am at fault though I did not choose to be at fault. When physicians and treatment eradicate the cancer, it is necessary that they distinguish between the cancer and the rest of me that is supposed to live. A person cured of cancer realizes that the cure was not the product of any decision he made nor an act of his will but was provided for him by those who care for him, just as God cares for us all and saves us by His Word (Rm 7:25–8:11).

● ● ● ● ● ● ● ● ● ● ● ● ● ● ● ● ● ● ●

Q 7:15 Does this verse prove that there is no such thing as free will?

Yes, this verse and many others, not to mention constant and universal human experience; if we have a free will, why do we have regrets about our decisions or actions (Jn 8:33–44; Rm 5:6–11; Eph 2:1–3)?

● ● ● ● ● ● ● ● ● ● ● ● ● ● ● ● ● ● ●

Q 7:17, 20 What are some analogies we can use to help people understand the control sin can have in a person's life?

One example can be found in sickness and medicine (see Rm 7:14–20 above). Another powerful example is addiction. If human beings had free will, there would be no such thing as addiction. Alcoholism, smoking, drug abuse, and gambling are all common and well-known forms of addiction; these people act against their own lives, lying to loved ones and caregivers in order to protect the addiction, yet are passionate, clever, and vigorous in their pursuit of the addiction. Such a person is and isn't in control at the same time. All people struggle with addictions or what is nearly an addiction of one kind or another. (Work, tech toys, selfishness, and self-righteousness can be addictions.) While we may feel sympathy for a person who struggles with addiction, we may also have to impose restraints on such a person or execute justice for her own good. Why does anyone do anything against his own life or against his relationships with other people? We have inherited this self-destructive orientation from Adam. God has provided forgiveness for this and the remedy of a regenerate soul, animated by God's Spirit and oriented toward love, life, and all things good.

● ● ● ● ● ● ● ● ● ● ● ● ● ● ● ● ● ● ●

Q 8:1 What does it mean to be "in Christ" and to "not walk according to the flesh"?

Paul has explained that we die to sin (Rm 6:10), to the Law (7:4; Gal 2:19), to the elemental spirits (Col 2:20), and to the Lord (Rm 14:8), but not to ourselves (Rm 14:7). "Death" or "dying" has to do with the end of a relationship. When we are united with Christ through the activity of God's Word and Spirit, His death becomes ours so that neither sin nor the Law have any power to condemn us. The Word and Spirit also regenerate us spiritually so that we are oriented and inspired to live and love as God intends us to; this is why the elemental spirits have no power over us. No one can sever himself from God Almighty, which is why Paul says we cannot die to ourselves— that is, we cannot simply "check out" or free ourselves from God and everyone else (Ps 10:13; 2Pt 3:1–7; Rv 9:6). Whether we live or die we are the Lord's, because apart from Christ, God's Law still has power to condemn, and with Christ the death of our fallen human nature releases us to complete and unobstructed union with Christ (1Co 15:35–58; Php 1:19–26).

> ## What does it mean to be "in Christ"?

- - - - - - - - - - - - - - - - -

Q 8:11 Is this referring to the resurrection at the end of times?

The Holy Spirit who raised Jesus from the dead will certainly raise us up at the Last Day (1Co 15:35–58). However, in this context Paul is talking about the restoration of life even while we are in this time and in this fallen human nature. Paul explained earlier that once we have been baptized into Christ, the regenerate soul within begins to control the whole person so that our human nature, though contrary, is employed by God for the love of others in obedience to His will (Rm 6:1–22; 2Co 5:14–21; Gal 5:16–25; Col 3:1–17; Jer 31:31–34; 1Jn 2:20–27).

- - - - - - - - - - - - - - - - -

Q 8:15 What does Paul mean by "you have received the Spirit of adoption as sons"? Does it simply mean that we have received the Spirit through Christ?

Paul is comparing the effect of the Law with the work of the Holy Spirit. The Law reveals and even strengthens the bondage of fallen human nature to sin, as Paul explained in 7:5–11. The Holy Spirit regenerates us by the Word of God, and therefore we are children of God and have His Spirit dwelling in us (Jn 1:12–13; 3:1–7; 1Jn 3:1–24). The Spirit comes to us from Christ, through the Word of God, and unites us with Christ (Jn 6:63; 14:26; 8:31–32). The Holy Spirit regenerates us in the image of Christ to a life that freely and passionately loves others as we are loved (Rm 8:29; Col 3:10; 1Jn 4:19).

- - - - - - - - - - - - - - - - -

Q 8:17 Is Paul talking about certain suffering?

I'm not sure Paul has a specific kind of suffering in mind, though he might be focused on the kind of suffering Christians endure for the sake of the truth and grace of God (Lk 6:22–23; Mt 10:16–39; 2Co 4:8–9; Heb 11:33–40).

> ## Has God only chosen some to be saved?

according to the inner person (Jn 16:14; Rm 8:1; 1Jn 3:9). We do not pray to saints because there is one Mediator between God and people: Christ Jesus (1Tm 2:5).

- -

Q 8:22 What are the visible signs that all creation is groaning with pain?

Creation may indeed be groaning in pain; however, in this verse Paul says that all creation groans. My friends in the music department tell me that the sounds of nature are in minor keys, which make them sound sad. Visible signs of creation groaning would be things such as animals killed by cars and left to rot; vegetation that is trying to grow through cracks in concrete or asphalt; weeds that have taken over an empty lot—or the empty lot itself; abandoned neighborhoods with rotted buildings that are falling down. Bodies of water or skies full of pollution would be other examples. People who visit those few places where nature seems still untouched by fallen human beings tend to be awestruck by the beauty and magnificence of God's creation.

- -

Q 8:27 Does this verse indicate that we should pray to saints?

Notice that it is the Spirit who makes intercession "*for* the saints." The term "saints" refers to Christians, who are called "saints" or "holy ones" because Christ has redeemed us from sin, clothed us with His righteousness, and regenerated us to be holy

- -

Q 8:28–29 Does this passage mean God has only chosen some to be saved?

The Bible teaches clearly and in many places that God has prepared the life we are to live ahead of time (Ps 139:16; Jer 1:4–5; Eph 2:10). Life is not about making one for ourselves but rather discovering the one God has prepared and gives to us (Mt 6:25–33). The root of *predestination*—"destine"—has to do with what is determined by God to happen in and through a person's life to fulfill a particular purpose (Lk 22:22; Ac 2:23). The word *predestined* occurs six times in the New Testament and means that this destiny or purpose has been determined by God from the beginning (Ac 4:28; Rm 8:29–30; 1Co 2:7; Eph 1:5, 11). God not only desires all to be saved (1Tm 2:4) but also has already redeemed everyone in the life of His Son (Jn 3:16; 2Co 5:19). Everyone who actually realizes this salvation does so according to God's calling and predestination (Jn 1:11–13; 3:1–7; 6:44; 15:16; Ti 3:3–8). Those who die apart from the salvation accomplished by Christ do so contrary to God's will by their own insistence (Rm 1:18–32; 3:9–19; Jn 3:18–19). Perhaps the following approach to this question will help: If we give the one who contends he has free will his way, then he cannot blame

God if he ends up condemned, since he insists that his life is the product of choices he freely makes. If we, in honesty and humility, make no claims for free will, then universal atonement is effective, and there is no condemnation about which to complain.

Q 8:31 Why are there so many evil people in our world committing crimes against us?

People commit crimes for the same reason we all sin: this is the orientation of human nature since the fall (Gn 6:5; Rm 3:9–19). The wisdom and power of God is demonstrated in the fact that God makes all things work together for our good, as Paul explained in v. 28. Through suffering, our fallen human nature learns invaluable and eternal lessons about itself and the consequences of opposing God's design for life (Rm 5:1–5; 2Co 4:1–5:21; 1Pt 1:3–9; Jas 1:2–11). On the other hand, we gain consciousness of and begin to realize the potential of our regenerate soul as we have cause to love our enemies (Jb 1:1–2:10; Jas 5:11; Mt 5:10–12, 38–48; Ac 5:41; 1Th 3:1–5; 1Jn 5:18). Consider what would happen if God began to eradicate evil in the world as many wish He would. Sooner or later, wouldn't God also have to destroy many people I care about? Wouldn't God have to destroy me? God is patient, not willing that any should perish (Mt 13:24–30; 2Pt 3:9).

Q 8:37 What does Paul mean when he says we are "more than conquerors"?

This is the only place where this Greek word (*hypernikao*) occurs in the Bible. The prefix "hyper-" intensifies the root word, meaning that the victory is absolute or complete. This is the case because the resurrection of Jesus Christ proves that He succeeded in taking away the sin of the world and, by doing so, saved us all from the power of sin, death, and the devil (Heb 2:14–15). There is no undoing the redemption that Christ has accomplished for all.

Q 8:38–39 If nothing can separate us from the love of God, why do some people reject Him?

All fallen human nature is opposed to God (Jn 8:33–44; Rm 5:6–11; 1Co 2:14; 15:50). This is why the only remedy for our fallen human nature is for it to return to the dust from which it came (Gn 3:19). Only a soul regenerated by the Word and Spirit of God is oriented toward union with and obedience to God (Jn 1:11–13; 3:1–7; 15:7; 1Jn 3:9). Why some people succeed in opposing God's work of regeneration so that there is nothing to them except what opposes God is a mystery (Jer 8:4–7; Ezk 18:23, 30–32; Lk 13:34–35; Rm 1:18–20).

Q 9:1 Why does Paul say in this verse, "I am not lying"?

This is one of several places in the Bible that respond to accusations or anticipate objections (Jn 8:13–18; Rm 3:8; 2Co 10:8–11; 2Pt 1:16–21; 1Jn 1–3).

Q 9:3–4 Why does Paul feel he should be cursed and cut off from Christ and his fellow brothers?

The word *cursed* means to be cut off. Paul taught that a person could only be connected with accursedness if he was without the Holy Spirit or if his teachings were contrary to the one and only true Gospel (1Co 12:3; 16:22; Gal 6:8–9, 3:10, 13). Paul is expressing the magnitude of his concern for Israel by saying he could wish that he were (but would never dare to be) cut off from Christ, if that would mean salvation for them (Rm 10:1–3). Such a desire is not surprising for a follower of Jesus since His love moved Him to take our place under the curse of the Law (Is 53:8; 2Co 5:21; Heb 2:9).

Q 9:8 Who are the "children of the promise"?

When Abraham and Sarah were much too old to have a child (besides Sarah's barrenness), God caused Sarah to conceive Isaac. By granting Abraham and Sarah a child when it was impossible for them to have one, God was demonstrating how He saves people who cannot save themselves (Mt 19:25–26; 1Co 1:31; Eph 2:8–9). First came God's promise, then came the children of God generated by that promise. However, fallen human nature wants to reverse the order, as if we could produce life on our own, and because of that, claim special favor with God. There is a world of difference between people who are born of natural, physiological means and a soul regenerated by the Word and Spirit of God (Jn 3:1–6; 6:62–63; 1Co 2:14; 15:50; Gal 4:21–31).

Q 9:9 What does this verse mean?

Paul was making a distinction between children that are conceived according to the laws of nature and Isaac, who was conceived by the Word of God when conception for Sarah was impossible. When God said these words to Abraham, Sarah was ninety years old and Abraham was ninety-nine, yet she conceived just as the Lord had said (Gn 18:10; Rm 4:19; Heb 11:11–12).

Q 9:10 What is Paul's point regarding Isaac?

Paul is demonstrating from history the power and certainty of God's Word (9:6). Isaac and Rebekah were unable to conceive a child, just as Abraham and Sarah (and Jacob and Rachel, Gn 25:21; 30:1–2). Children are conceived according to the Word of the Lord to a life that has been prepared for them according to the will of the Lord.

• •

Q 9:13–15 Does God hate Esau? Aren't we, as Christians, not supposed to hate others? Who is God taking pity on in this text and why?

God hates what is evil and commands us to do the same (Rm 12:9). Evil is what opposes our relationship with God and all that makes for life and love. Christians are to love others, especially our enemies (Mt 5:44).

God has taken pity on all people and has demonstrated this in the sacrifice of His own Son on behalf of all people (Jn 3:16; 2Co 5:21). Pride makes a person despise and resist God's pity. Honesty about the condition and limitations of our fallen human nature makes us humble; God takes pity on those who are humble and fear Him (1Sm 2:4–8; Mt 11:28–30; Lk 1:50; Jas 4:1–7; 1Pt 5:5–6).

• •

Q 9:15 Does this mean that God looks for those who demonstrate mercy to others?

God *is* love, and there is no injustice with Him (1Jn 4:16; Ps 7:11). God demonstrated His love and justice by making His Son a substitute for every human being under the Law (Jn 3:16; 2Co 5:21). Paul's point, which he stresses in the next verse, is that our life and salvation is not something we earn for ourselves but entirely a matter of God's gracious disposition. You cannot earn mercy or deserve compassion.

• •

Q 9:18 Why does God harden hearts? Doesn't God want to have mercy on all of us?

God has had mercy on all, loves all, and has redeemed all people in the life of His Son who died in place of all people. God only hardens people when that is the inescapable consequence of their opposition to Him. When a person is determined to pursue death, contrary to God's will, God stands in the way to turn that person into the way of life (Ezk 18:23–32). When a person responds by increasing the intensity of his opposition against God and the way to life, such a person becomes hard of heart. The hardening of his heart is the product of God standing in the way of this person's self-destruction, but the fault is with the person who refuses to be corrected (Rm 1:20–32; 1Pt 2:8). The record of hard-hearted people and the severe warnings against this are an important antidote to the cantankerous disposition of fallen human nature. On the other hand, we may never assume that a person's heart has been hardened beyond recovery (Mt 7:1; Ac 9:13–16).

• •

Q 9:22–23 Why are some people "vessels of wrath" while some are "vessels of mercy"? Doesn't God love us all and desire us to be saved?

God has had mercy on all, loves all, and has redeemed all people in the life of His Son who died in place of all people (see previous three questions and answers). Approaching a text that generates these kinds of questions requires the identification of truths that guide our thinking. First, Paul is making an argument about the nature of and proper relationship between God and man. God is sovereign and certainly has authority to act according to His will (Rm 9:20–21; Jnh 4:9–11; Mt 20:1–16). Man is a contingent being, yet since the fall man is arrogant, egocentric, and contentious, asserting pretended authority against real authority.

Second, Paul is making an argument with conditional language, reflected in the majority of English translations (more than fifteen of them): "What if . . ." This is the kind of severe, sovereign language that is necessary for bringing fallen human nature to honesty about its condition (Rm 3:19; Jn 8:33–44; Jb 38:1–42:6; Jas 5:11).

Third, notice the word *patience* or *long-suffering* in v. 22. One feature of God's patience is that it establishes, incontrovertibly, the fact that any given person's condemnation is the product of his or her own insistence (Ps 10:13; Jn 3:18–20; Rm 1:20–32; 1Tm 1:5–7; 2Pt 2:12–22. See also Rm 9:18 above).

Fourth, notice that in regard to "vessels of wrath," Paul uses the word *prepared* (the Greek word *katartidzo* occurs thirteen times in the New Testament) in contrast with the word "prepared ahead of time" (*prohetoimadzo* occurs only here and in Eph 2:10). The Bible speaks of predestination only in positive terms, never in negative.

The preparation of vessels of wrath is the product of wicked, hard-hearted people, who are determined to oppose God to the end. Vessels of mercy, by contrast, are not so by any activity or merit of their own since they have been chosen ahead of time for salvation—just as Paul had argued that Abraham could not have been favored by God for keeping the Law since the Law was not given until long after Abraham was dead (Rm 4:1–11; 1Co 1:18–31; Eph 2:8–10).

Fifth, a solution to the theoretical questions generated by these verses comes in the application of them. Does a certain person wonder if he or she is a vessel of wrath or mercy? Let such a person remain in the Word, as the Word and Spirit of God fill us with mercy even as they regenerate us as vessels of mercy (Lk 10:38–42; Jn 1:121–13; 3:1–7; 8:31–32; 1Tm 1:12–17). Is a person fearful that he or she has been predestined as a vessel of wrath? Such a thing is never suggested in the Bible, and, again, a life in the Word proves that it is impossible for this person to be such a vessel. Is a person arrogant, cantankerous, contentious, and unrelenting in his or her opposition to God's mercy and redemption? Let such a person consider what the inevitable consequence of such opposition will be since this is one of the few means left that might prevent such self-determination from succeeding to the person's own demise.

Q 9:25 Why would He call them His people if they weren't and call her His beloved if she wasn't?

God does not show favoritism, as all people are His creation, all have been redeemed by His Son, and all are the object of the Holy Spirit's intent to regenerate. Paul is quoting Hosea, who was speaking to the people of Israel, who had come to assume that they had a privileged status with God because of their physical genealogy. Israel thought, and still does think, of itself as "God's people" by birthright, and all other people are "not God's people" (the Hebrew word *goyim*, Lk 4:24–30; Ac 10:1–48). The power and grace of God are completely foreign to fallen human nature. God creates out of nothing (Gn 1:1–13; 1Co 1:28). God chooses, as examples, those who seem least likely to be important to Him by human standards to show that honesty about dependence on Him is what matters rather than pretensions, as if we did not depend completely on Him (Mt 18:14; 1Co 1:18–31).

Q 9:30–32 If the Israelites are not saved, why did God call them the chosen people?

Answering this question depends on how we define *Israelite*. If *Israelite* refers to the physical descendants of Jacob, then many of them are not saved, as Paul laments (Rm 10:1–3; Heb 3:12–19). However, this is the same for all physical descendants of Adam, since "that which is born of the flesh is flesh" and "flesh and blood cannot inherit the kingdom of God" (Jn 3:6; 1Co 15:50). On the other hand, if *Israelite* means a spiritual person, regenerated by the Word of God, the way Isaac and Jacob were conceived, then all of Israel is saved (Rm 2:28–29; Gal 3:5–9). While God called all of Israel out of Egypt, only the children and two of the adult men entered the Promised Land (Nu 14:26–32). This history is indicative of all humanity; it has never been birth order or physical descent that mattered, since we are all descended from fallen Adam (Ac 17:26–31). What matters are the words and promises of God that regenerate us as His own children (Mt 8:5–13; 15:21–28; Jn 1:11–13; 3:1–7; 10:28–29; 15:1–7; 1Pt 1:3–9).

Q 9:31 What does it mean that Israel pursued "a law that would lead to righteousness," but did not "succeed in reaching that law"?

The Law knows nothing of grace or mercy. The Law knows only how things must be with no exceptions; the regularity of the universe and all life depends on this fact. If a person is determined to make his own life (present and eternal) depend on keeping the Law without fail, he will absolutely fail (Is 64:6; Rm 7:18). The purpose of recording the Law, of making specific laws for Israel, and for recording the history of humanity is to provide overwhelming, incontrovertible proof that fallen human beings are absolutely incapable of meeting the requirements of the Law (Rm 3:20; 6:23; 7:9). Paul provides further explanation himself in Rm 10:1–17.

Q 9:32–33 Is the reason we trip over rocks and stumble because we doubt God?

It is unlikely that Paul is talking about doubt. Doubt is a weakness, but "stumbling" and "offense" (v. 33) are describing active, aggressive opposition to God's work in Christ, as can be seen among the religious leaders in Jesus' time or the Judaizers in the time of the apostles (Lk 4:16–30; Jn 6:61; 1Pt 2:7–8; Ac 15:1–11; Gal 2:11–16).

Q 9:33 Is it saying that Zion is a stone and a rock?

Zion is the name of the hill (or a very small mountain) upon which Jerusalem is built (2Sm 5:7; Ps 48:11–12; Heb 12:22). The stone or rock that God places there is Christ, the Rock of our salvation—a "rock" because He is the truth and wisdom of God that never changes and cannot be overcome (Pr 8:12–35; Jn 14:6; 1Co 10:4). When Jesus came to Jerusalem on Palm Sunday and for the rest of that week, God was "setting" Him in that place where He would fulfill all of God's promises to save us and where His atonement and resurrection for us would remain an accomplished, irreversible foundation for all who believe (Mt 16:16–20; Rm 1:16–17).

Q 10:1–3 Why don't the Jews believe that Jesus is the Savior? Did Genesis speak of our freedom of choice?

The Jews who refuse to believe in Jesus cannot do so because He is a stumbling block to them (Lk 20:17–19; Rm 9:32–33; 1Pt 2:8). Jesus is a stumbling block to anyone who thinks that the Savior will come as a reward for good works or genetic superiority (1Co 1:18–24). Jesus saved all people by taking their place under the Law and, having done so, was crucified as an insurrectionist and murderer (Mk 15:6–15; Gal 4:4; Php 2:5–11). If Jesus took the place of every person under the Law and that condemned Him to an accursed death, then every person must be guilty of eternal condemnation under the Law, from which Jesus redeemed us. But a vain, proud, and self-righteous person refuses to admit he is guilty before the Law and therefore rejects Jesus, as did the religious leaders of Jesus' time (Lk 4:23–30).

There is a profound difference between freedom to choose and a variety of choices. Adam and Eve were able to make choices as choices were available to them, but they lacked the wisdom and power to make only good choices (they were bound by their limitations). Since the fall of Adam and Eve, we suffer from even greater limitations, which is why we depend on God to make good decisions for us and to teach us what good choices are (Jn 15:16; 2Tm 12–13; Dt 30:19–20).

Q 10:1 What is the condition of the Israelites? Does that mean that as of "now" they aren't saved?

Paul makes very clear that anyone, whether Israelite or Gentile, who seeks to establish his own righteousness in opposition to what God has accomplished in Christ is not saved (Gal 3:10; 5:4). While Christ did take away the sins of the world and in so doing saved all people, a person who insists on rejecting this justification in order to establish his own brings the condemnation of the Law back upon himself (Mt 12:31–32; Heb 6:4–6; 10:26–31).

Q 10:3–4 What happens to those who believe in God but not Christ?

First, it is not for us to judge what happens to people after they die (Mt 7:1). Second, there is a substantial difference between being ignorant and being contentious (Jn 9:35–41; Ac 7:51–58; 28:17–31). Third, people who claim to believe in God but reject Christ put themselves back under the curse of the Law that Christ has saved them from (Gal 3:10; 5:4). The Law is nothing under which we want to be burdened, whether living or dead.

Q 10:7 What does it mean to "bring Christ up"?

Paul explains that the righteousness that comes by faith does not talk about what it does. When Paul makes the analogy of descending into the abyss, he stops to clarify that he is referring to the notion of bringing Christ up from the dead. Proud and self-righteous people refuse to accept that our life depends on what God does for us, not what we do for Him (Ac 17:23–27; 2Sm 7:1–11).

Q 10:9 How do you know if you believe "in your heart"? How does Paul understand "confess" and "believe"? Is it a work that I can do or an action produced by faith?

The conditional statement beginning with "if" is simple and clear: the truth is, if you believe in your heart and confess with your mouth the Lord Jesus, you will be saved. Now the question is, how does a person come by such a heart and such a mouth? We know that the heart with which we are conceived is deceitful, desperately wicked, and the source of everything wicked (Gn 6:5; Jer 17:9; Mk 7:20–23). We know that our mouths and tongues are a world of iniquity (Jas 3:1–12). Therefore, if we are to be a person who believes and confesses Christ, we must have a new heart and a new mouth, which only the Lord Himself can provide (Ezk 36:24–27; 1Co 12:3). Faith itself is God's work, depending on His power and His working in us through His Word and Spirit (1Pt 1:5; Jn 6:29, 63; Rm 10:17).

● ● ● ● ● ● ● ● ● ● ● ● ● ● ● ● ● ● ●

Q **10:11 Aren't Christians being persecuted and put to shame?**

Think about the difference between being ashamed in time or eternity, before people or before God. While the enemies of God try to shame the faithful, they will be put to shame in the end (Pss 6:10; 25:2–3). Peter wrote that the good conduct of the faithful will reverse the intent of those who would shame us and bring shame on them instead (1Pt 3:16). David wrote that the Lord protects from shame those who seek refuge in Him, and Luke records Jesus doing exactly that for a woman who came to Him for healing (Ps 13; Lk 13:10–17).

● ● ● ● ● ● ● ● ● ● ● ● ● ● ● ● ● ● ●

Q **10:12 If the same Lord is "Lord of all," and the Jews believe in this Lord, why aren't they saved?**

Jews and Gentiles have the same Creator, the same Savior, and the same means of salvation (Ac 10:34–35; 17:26–28; Gal 3:26–29; Eph 4:4–6). No matter who you are, if you insist on rejecting the redemption of Christ in order to be judged according to your own life, under the Law you will be condemned (Jn 3:18–20; Rm 3:12; Gal 3:10–12; 5:4).

● ● ● ● ● ● ● ● ● ● ● ● ● ● ● ● ● ● ●

Q **10:13 If we do nothing to receive salvation, why does Paul say (quoting Joel) that "everyone who calls on the name**

of the Lord will be saved"? What does this passage say regarding denominations and other issues that divide the church?

Thanks to God, the true Church, the Body of Christ, is one and can never be divided or separated from its Head (Mt 16:18; Jn 10:28–29; Rm 8:38–39; Eph 4:4–6). Calling on the name of the Lord is not at all the same as calling "Lord, Lord." The "name of the Lord" is the Word of God (Jn 1:1, 14). Calling on the name of the Lord means remembering and relying upon that Word of the Lord (Gn 4:26; 12:8; 13:4; 26:25; 1Ki 18:24; Ps 116:4, 13, 17; Mt 28:19–20). Calling Jesus "Lord" when you don't believe He is your Lord is hypocrisy, which the light of truth always exposes (Mt 3:7–12; 7:21–23; 23:13–38). How would it be possible for the Lord Jesus not to know a person who remains in His Word (Jn 8:31–32)? It is impossible to believe in God but not to call on His name since His Word is what regenerates us and works faith in our hearts (Jn 1:12–13; 6:63; Rm 10:17; Jas 1:18; 1Pt 1:3–9).

Issues that divide people into denominations must be significant, or there would not be a division. Denominations may be known by their faithfulness to or their variance from the fundamental teachings of the Bible. The only way to know if a denomination is committed to the truth or to error is by searching the Word and comparing the teaching of that denomination (or church) to the Word (Ac 17:11; Rm 16:17–20; 1Co 11:19; 2Co 13:5; 1Jn 4:1).

What happens to those who have not heard the Gospel?

Q 10:14 What happens to those who have not heard the Gospel?

Only God knows what happens to anyone in the end. We have tremendous promises and assurances that a person who remains in the Word has everlasting life (Jn 6:63; 8:31–32; 10:28–29; 11:25–26; 15:1–7; 1Pt 1:3–9; 1Jn 3:1–24). In addition to these promises, the Bible reminds us that God has given a witness to Himself through nature and that His mercy remains upon those who fear Him (Ps 19:1–4; Ac 17:24–32; Rm 1:20; 2:15; 1Sm 2:6–8; Lk 1:50; Mt 18:3; 1Co 1:26–31). We hope for God's mercy to rest upon all while we work diligently to bring clarity about and assurance of that mercy to all as soon as possible (Mt 28:19–20; Mk 16:16; Rm 1:11).

Q 11:1–7 Why does God continue to love and save Israel even when they continue to disobey?

If God ever stopped loving and saving those who disobey, who could be saved (Gn 6:5; Is 64:6; Mt 19:25–26; Lk 15:11–32; Rm 5:6–11)? Whether God's love saves someone in the end is a matter of the greatest concern (Lk 13:34; see also the whole Book of Hebrews, especially 2:1–3).

Q 11:5 What exactly is the "remnant" of Israel?

Elijah once thought he was the only faithful person left. Contrary to appearances, God had kept a remnant of Israel for Himself, seven thousand Israelites who were still faithful (1Ki 19:18). During the time of Isaiah, it looked as though all of Israel had turned away from God again, but God promised that He would still keep in the faith a remnant of the descendants of Israel (Is 10:20–22). You might think of all those who are saved as God's remnant from all people, but the New Testament does not speak about us in this way. The New Testament does talk about uniting the faithful people from among the Jews and the Gentiles into one under the Lord Jesus (Jn 10:14–16; Eph 2:14–18). All people who are saved are so by God's election, apart from any merit or worthiness of their own (see Jn 15:16; Rm 8:28–30; Eph 1:3–14).

Q 11:6 What is Paul attempting to clarify in this verse?

Paul is trying to make clear that grace and payment for works are absolute opposites, as he was arguing in ch. 4 and throughout his Letter to the Galatians. Fallen human nature is so proud and vain that it never stops trying to take credit for what only God can do (Ac 12:20–23; Ps 10:3–11; Ex 5:2). Grace is completely undeserved; payment for works is entirely deserved.

Q 11:7 Does God actively harden people's hearts and destine them for damnation? If the "elect" includes all people Jesus died to save, why does this not include Israel?

God does not predestine, elect, or choose anyone for damnation (Ezk 18:30–32). On the contrary, God wills us to live, commands what makes for life, and forbids what takes away life (Gn 2:16–17; Dt 30:19–20; Ezk 16:6). The hardening of hearts is a product of man's activity in opposition to God and God's activity that would save man from the consequences of that opposition (Lv 26:1–46). All people were redeemed in Christ (Jn 3:16; 2Co 5:19; 1Tm 2:4). Everyone who realizes the benefits of this redemption does so because of God's election or predestination. Those who do not realize the benefits of redemption do not because of their own stubborn opposition to the grace of God in Christ. This sounds like a logical inconsistency, but many realities of our universe are not logically consistent though they are real just the same (for more on hardening, please see Rm 9:18 above).

Many of the physical descendants of Abraham rejected the Word of God and its promises by claiming that they possessed God's favor by natural rights and/or by the merit of their life (Rm 10:1–3; Gal 3:7–14; 5:4). These people wanted to obtain physical wealth and special privileges with God but failed to do so because the Law did not commend but condemned them.

Q 11:9–10 Is David addressing all sinners in these verses?

This quotation comes from a messianic psalm (Ps 69:22–23), which means that David's life and thoughts foreshadow what Jesus Christ would experience. In the first place, David is speaking about his enemies in his time. As a prophecy, David is speaking about the enemies of Christ during His ministry. In the end, all people who remain resolute and tenacious in their opposition to Christ in any time and place make these words apply to themselves.

Q 11:11 Did God want the Jews to be envious of the Gentiles?

That is exactly what Paul is saying. Sometimes you can get a person to change his or her mind or disposition toward something by giving it to someone else. Sometimes an unappreciative boyfriend or girlfriend will realize what could be lost when his or her beloved is pursued by someone else. The Jews expected privileges from God even while they despised Him and His love. God's gracious love for the Gentiles was intended to snap Israel out of its contrary disposition. The Book of Jonah is entirely about this method of God for dealing with the problem of Israel's lack of obedience.

Q 11:16–24 What is the significance of the "dough offered as firstfruits"? Is there a connection here to the tree of life in Revelation?

Many places in Paul's Letter to the Romans reveal that he was trying to improve relationships between Jewish and Gentile Christians (2:1, 17). Paul has made it clear that both Jews and Gentiles are made of fallen human nature and are equally condemned under the Law (3:9–20; 5:6–11). Now Paul is reminding the Gentiles that there was a value or benefit that God gave the Jews, even if many of them despised it (3:1–2; 11:1–6). Next, remember to distinguish between the physical descendants of Abraham and the spiritual descendants (2:28–29; Gal 4:21–31). Also remember that the term translated "holy" means to be "set apart" rather than "without sin." Paul is, therefore, saying that the Word of God is the leaven in the dough and the seed from which the tree has grown. The Word of God is what has produced faithful descendants of Abraham, and these have passed on that Word of God so that it would work faith among the Gentiles (2Ki 5:1–3). Thus the same Word of God that generated and regenerated the children of Israel would work the same regeneration for the Gentiles. As the first lump of dough is leavened by the yeast, so will all the rest of the dough be leavened; as the roots of a tree are faithful, so will the branches that grow from those roots (Mt 7:18; Jn 1:11–13; 3:1–7).

The tree of life, mentioned in Genesis and in Revelation, is the Word of God, the fountain and source of all life (Gn 2:9; 3:22; Jn 1:1–4; 4:13–14; 6:63; Rv 2:7; 22:2, 17, 19).

Q 11:21 Is it biblical to anticipate future unknown hardships that will keep us from being too content where we are (i.e., "Things are going really well now; I have a feeling something bad will happen soon")?

I'm not sure there is such a thing as being too content, but our human nature is very much prone to selfish materialism, "entitlement thinking," and complacency. Like the seasons and the Sabbath, God provides times of challenge and times of rest (Gn 2:2–3; Dt 5:12–15; Ec 3:1–7; Mk 6:31). Knowing that our human nature and our regenerate soul are contrary to each other makes it important to remember that the comfort our bodies crave and the discomfort they fear may be the very best circumstance for us as faithful people (2Co 4:1–5:14; 12:7–10). During times of rest and blessings, Christians appreciate God's generosity and kindness; during times of challenge, Christians appreciate God's diligence in drawing us near to Him and training us in the ways of everlasting life (Heb 12:1–17; 1Pt 1:3–9). This perspective makes sense of Paul's command that we give thanks to God at all times (1Th 5:18).

Q **11:22 God will show sternness and cut people off, but how can those people come back to Him?**

The purpose of excommunication is to make the peril of unbelief unmistakably clear (Lv 26:14–45; Mt 18:7–9, 15–18; 1Co 5:4–5). The human nature must be put to death first if there is to be the regeneration of our soul (Jn 3:1–7; 12:24; Rm 6:2–4; Col 3:5–10). The challenge is not for God to raise the dead or to give life where there was none but to convince human arrogance that it is dead apart from God (Ps 14:1; Is 29:13–16; Gn 2:7; Ezk 37:1–14; Rm 4:17; 1Co 1:28–30). Bringing people back to God is simple; the real problem is getting them to admit that they are without Him (Lk 18:9–14; Jn 8:31–44).

Q **11:25 What does the "hardening" mean? Why does the "fullness of the Gentiles" have to come first? Does that time refer to the end of time?**

God desires that all be saved, and He makes all things work together for good for those who love Him (1Tm 2:4; Rm 8:28). God made clear the peril of fallen human nature through the obstinate, murderous, and insane disposition of those who should have been most welcoming of the Messiah (Lk 4:16–30; 14:15–24; 20:1–18; Jn 1:11). "Hardening" has to do with God's patience, waiting until a person has refused every possible means or opportunity to come to the truth and be saved by God's grace (1Pt

2:7–8; 2Pt 2:9; Jude 5; Heb 2:1–4; 3:12–19). Paul is referring to the end of the world and affirms that it will not come until the Gospel has reached all people and brought all whom God has chosen into His kingdom.

Q **11:26 When Paul says "all Israel will be saved," does he mean the Jewish people or the Church?**

Remember that the "children of Israel" never had to do with physical descendants of Abraham, Isaac, and Jacob (Gn 15:1–6; 16:1–6; 21:8–14; Gal 4:21–31). Any faithful person is so because the same Word of God that generated Isaac and Jacob has regenerated that person as a child of God, regardless of his or her physical lineage (Ex 12:19; 48–49; Mt 8:5–12; 21:28–31; Mk 7:26–29; Lk 4:25–27; Rv 7:9–14).

Q **11:28–32 Do these verses indicate that people who do not believe in the Gospel will be saved?**

It is impossible to be saved without faith since dishonesty about dependence on God leaves a person to contend for his own life under the Law while despising the grace of God in Christ (Lk 18:27; Rm 14:23; Heb 6:4; 11:6). The disobedience of Israel, recorded in biblical history, demonstrates the miserable condition of human nature and our absolute dependence on God's grace. God's rejection of the physical people of Israel as a just response to their rejection of Him meant that the ministry of the Gospel would turn to the Gentiles (Lk 14:15–24; Ac 18:5–6; 28:24–28).

How else would our enemies or the enemies of God have hope unless we loved them, and how could we be saved unless God loved us while we were still His enemies (Lk 23:34; Rm 5:6–11)? Thus Jesus commanded us to love our enemies (Lk 6:22, 27–36).

• • • • • • • • • • • • • • • • • • • •

Q 11:30–31 How can one receive mercy because another has been disobedient?

Consider the example of an emergency room physician who has two groups of people to provide care for: one group is from his own neighborhood and able to pay for his services; the other group consists of strangers who cannot pay. Who would you expect the physician to treat first? However, what if the first group refused treatment, cursed, and reviled the physician? Wouldn't such a physician then turn his attention to the other group who were eager for his care, though they were clearly undeserving? For more see Rm 11:28–32 above.

• • • • • • • • • • • • • • • • • • • •

Q 11:32 What does it mean that God "has consigned all to disobedience"?

A primary and deadly feature of fallen human nature is its insistence that it is neither fallen nor in danger of death (Lk 18:18–27; Gal 3:1–6). The word translated "prison" in some English translations has more to do with the idea of confinement than with a physical building that serves as a jail. The very laws of nature that God established to provide for our lives also take away our life when we oppose and contradict them. By creating the world in this way and by adding His written revelation to nature, God has given overwhelming proof of our fallen condition and absolute need for His gracious redemption. God binds all human nature under the Law so that He might, having disabled that contrary human nature, raise us up as a new creation that lives in harmonious dependence on Him (Ps 78:34; Lk 9:24; 2Co 1:7–9).

• • • • • • • • • • • • • • • • • • • •

Q 12:1 What does he mean by "living sacrifice"? Is this saying that living a life that is pleasing to God is like nonstop worship?

Let's begin with a more careful translation: "I beseech you, therefore, brothers, by the mercies of God, to present your bodies as a living sacrifice, holy and acceptable to God, which is your reasonable service." Our human nature was created by God as an instrument by which we care for one another on behalf of God. Since the fall, our human nature is subject to dying and death because it is fundamentally selfish. God gives us a new, eternal life when His Word regenerates our soul. We have two reasons to use our bodies, sacrificially, for the service of God and others. First, though our bodies are passing away, we can at least make that passing mean something significant and helpful. Second, since the essence of our life is an eternal soul, serving cannot take away our life but can only enhance it. Paul makes this appeal on the basis of the mercy of God in contrast with the demands of the Law, which stops every mouth and condemns every sinner but is incapable of producing any real love in us or through us (Rm 3:19–20; 7:8–11; 8:3).

Employing our lives in the service of others is a reasonable service for several reasons. First, using human nature for the good of others, especially their eternal good, gives value, significance, and purpose to our lives. Second, if we do not present our bodies as servants of God, then we will end up using them to serve the devil, thus ruining our own lives and doing no good to those around us. Third, doing good for others produces multiple benefits since the one serving realizes the good of loving another, the one loved is helped, and both are now in a better position to love others so that they may do the same. Fourth, our service to others is oriented toward the soul and eternity, even as we care for the body. Caring for an eternal soul means working to convey benefits that are everlasting. This kind of service (significant, loving, eternal) is the only kind that makes sense and therefore is reasonable. Yes, living a life of service is not only nonstop, but it is the most pleasing kind of worship (1Sm 15:22; Mi 6:6–8; Mt 12:1–8).

Q 12:2 How can we be transformed by the "renewal of [our] mind"? How are we able to test and approve of God's will?

You may not be surprised to hear that we cannot change ourselves. Jesus spoke to the bondage of our human nature since the fall, and Paul describes us as weak, ungodly, sinful, and enemies of God (Jn 8:33–44; Rm 5:6–11). Paul admonishes us here to see that God works through His Word and His Means of Grace to change our minds and lives. The renewing of our minds is produced by the Word and Spirit regenerating us (Jn 6:63; Rm 10:17).

We test in order to discern and/or to confirm what the will of the Lord is, but we do not approve His will since that is not our place. We test all things, especially ourselves, by comparing them to the clear, eternal Word of God, including the corroborating witnesses of nature, conscience, and logic to which the Word points (Ac 17:11; 2Co 13:5; Ps 19:1–3; Rm 1:20; 2:15; 6:20–21). The problem with just believing that His will is what is best for us comes in recognizing and agreeing upon what really is best for us, body and soul, in time and eternity. Our thinking is much too bound up in sin, corruptible, materialistic, and shortsighted to be reliable. This is why Jesus describes the wise person as one who hears God's Word and keeps that Word with him. Keeping the Word of God with us is what makes us like the man who built his house on the rock (Mt 7:24–27).

How can we identify our spiritual gifts?

Q **12:3 Does this verse sometimes explain why murderers and other bad people are saved?**

All people are bad because of the fall of Adam, and all are murderers, according to our fallen heart (Rm 3:10–19; Mk 7:20–23; Mt 5:21–22). This verse does remind us that anything good in us or about us is a gift of God (1Co 4:7; Jas 1:16–18).

Q **12:6 How can we identify our spiritual gifts?**

All depends on remaining in the Word (Jn 8:31–32; 15:1–7). The Word provides wisdom to know where our strengths are, perception to know where we might use them, and inspiration to respond to opportunities for their use provided by God (Ezk 36:24–27). Some people are so obsessed with discovering what their spiritual gift might be that they ignore the need for their gifts that is right in front of them (Lk 10:30–33).

Q **12:9 If we are to "abhor what is evil," does this mean I should actively hate everybody whom I do not like?**

I know of no place in the Bible that says we are to hate our enemies. The Jews had been teaching this, but Jesus renounced them (Mt 5:43–48). By contrast, it is our own fallen human nature and the fallen human nature of our family members that we are called upon to hate (Lk 14:26).

Q **12:17 Why should we be careful to do what is "honorable in the sight of all" if God is the only one who judges us? Wouldn't our current war be replacing evil for evil?**

Doing what is "honorable in the sight of all" is yet another means of testing to know what is genuinely good. Above we considered the Word as of first importance for knowing truth and goodness, then nature, then our conscience, and finally logic (see Rm 12:2 above). What is good and right has the force of inspiring recognition by everyone (or at least exposing the wicked folly of someone who would try to speak against it; 1Pt 2:12).

A just war, like capital punishment, is not about returning evil for evil. The Bible consistently forbids people who would take up their own cause (Mt 5:38–42). Capital punishment is about maintaining justice (Rm 13:1–7). War is about protecting the helpless from aggressors (Is 1:17). At every point we follow the Gospel rather than what the world would have us do (Ac 4:17–20; Rm 12:2).

Q **12:18 How much should we give up to live at peace?**

The answer depends on what we are talking about. Martin Luther observed that love suffers all things, but faith suffers nothing. There cannot be any real peace where false teaching is allowed, so we make no compromises with the fundamental teachings of the Word (Jer 6:14; Rm 16:17; 2Jn 10–11). Regarding hardships that others would impose upon us, we suffer everything for the sake of affirming the life and witness of our Lord (Mt 5:38–48; Heb 12:1–3). Regarding those who are determined to abuse those who cannot defend themselves, we suffer all things to defend the defenseless (Is 1:17). God has established governments to keep the peace in a material world (Rm 13:1–7). God has given us His Word and wisdom so that we might keep real and lasting peace in the spiritual world (2Co 10:3–6).

Q **12:19 How does God, in His wrath, intend to "avenge" and "repay"?**

God already avenged His wrath and repaid evildoers for their ways by substituting His own Son for all of us (Is 53:10; 2Co 5:21). On Judgment Day, those who never repented of despising and rejecting God's grace in Christ will receive the full extent of God's wrath toward those who disobey the Law and who despise His redemption from the Law in Christ (Mt 25:41–46; Lk 16:19–31; Heb 10:26–31).

Q **12:20 It says to feed your enemies and quench their thirst. It then says we will heap burning coals on his head. Doesn't this contradict itself?**

There is a difference between the purpose and motivation of what we are commanded to do and the intended consequence for others. We are commanded to love our enemies because that is the right thing to do: this is how God has loved us, and this is the only means by which our enemies might ever know love (Rm 5:10; 1Jn 4:18–19). The effect of such love on an enemy is like having hot coals heaped on his head—that is to say, the impact of love upon a person who would be our enemy is as powerful and inescapable as having hot coals on his head.

Q **13:1 Are all authorities established by God? What about authorities such as Adolf Hitler, Joseph Stalin, or Saddam Hussein?**

The language of this text is simple and clear: there is no authority except from God. Besides this clear language, reason suggests that this must be the case, otherwise God would not be God. Confusion about or repulsion at this thought comes from human nature's refusal to accept the consequences of rebellion against God or what our redemption from the fall requires. Did God not subject His only-begotten Son, wholly loving and innocent, to the ravages of religious and civil authorities who abused and crucified Him? Why should we think that we deserve better or that our heavenly Father was not accomplishing something for our good through these means (Jn 11:48–50; Rm 8:28; 2Co 1:7–9; 4:17; Heb 12:3–11)? Is it wrong for God to give people what they demand when they despise and renounce His good governance? In the Old Testament, Israel wanted to be like the nations, so God gave them over to the governance of other nations—so they, and we, might know the difference (Ex 16:2–4; 1Sm 8:4–9; 1Co 10:6, 11).

• • • • • • • • • • • • • • • • • • • •

Q 13:2 Should we submit to authorities even if they are in the wrong? Do we have to obey them when they go against God?

Four teachings of the New Testament provide the basis for this answer. First, it is imperative to remember that our bodies, like the physical world around us, are to be used in service of God's everlasting kingdom, not the other way around. We can afford to sacrifice all things physical for the sake of the Gospel because the Gospel provides for all things needful without limit (Lk 9:24–25; Php 3:7–14). Second, Jesus speaks at length about enduring abuses as part of the Christian disposition of love (Mt 5:38–45; Heb 12:1–2; Jas 1:2). Third, Jesus commanded those who would follow Him to be watchful and to flee before trouble came upon them (Mt 10:23; 24:15–44). Fourth, while a person may endure personal abuse for the sake of love, we are also called to

prevent the abuse of the helpless; in both cases, we suffer abuse ourselves for the sake of another (Is 1:17; Rm 12:1).

Rather than speak of rebellion or revolution against authorities, it might be more helpful to speak in terms of submission and fidelity, though this is always first to God and then to men. The apostles defied the command of the religious authorities in Jerusalem, explaining, "We must obey God rather than men" (Ac 5:29; see also Ac 4:19–20). Interestingly, like Jesus, the apostles endured abuses joyfully and respectfully even as they were faithful to God rather than human authorities who were faithless (Jn 18:19–23; Ac 16:16–40; 23:1–5). Therefore, a person's first choice would be to flee a nation that is abusive and contrary to its God-given purpose (this would be true of a child fleeing an abusive parent, a woman fleeing an abusive husband, Christians fleeing a faithless pastor, or citizens fleeing an evil state; 1Co 7:3–15). If unable to flee, it seems that a number of people might gather to defend the defenseless in opposition to authorities who are opposed to God and His intent for them. Such a group could constitute a new body politic, which would have authority to recognize a leader and authorize the armed defense of those who need such a defense.

Q **13:4 Does this support the right for capital punishment? Is there a limit to this punishment in God's eyes?**

This verse supports the responsibility, not the right, for capital punishment according to the Law. God has set limits on all punishment, except that which comes to the wicked who die in their sin (Mt 25:46; Mk 9:42–48). Capital punishment may only be executed against someone who has been duly convicted of a capital crime (Gn 9:5; Ex 21:12–14). Executing a person for a capital crime means death, not a slap on the hand.

Q **13:8 Is it really possible to owe no one anything? How is love a debt?**

Imagine what happens when we begin to set aside what the Bible plainly says because we think it is unreasonable or impossible. Jesus commanded us to be perfect, as our heavenly Father is (Mt 5:48). Jesus also commanded us to love our enemies (Mt 5:44). Should we disregard these commands because they are impossible for us, or shall we keep them, recognize their wisdom, and orient our whole life toward achieving them? If we have debt, it is for one of two reasons: either we want more things—and we want them faster than God is giving them—or too few people have too much

and refuse to use what God has allowed them for the well-being of others. We are no less likely to break this commandment than any of the others, yet we have everything to gain from obeying it.

It is possible to owe no one anything but love, though it depends on living in close communion with God, which is the remedy for our materialistic ways. We are to love God above all things, our neighbor as ourselves, and nothing else, as these would bind us in debts that have no value (Lk 10:25–37).

Q **14:1 How do we know which opinions not to argue over?**

There are many matters of life in this world that the Bible neither commands nor forbids, and people are welcome to their opinions and preferences. There are many other matters that the Bible speaks to in plain language and that are not open to dispute. However, in this verse Paul is forbidding us from receiving a weak brother into arguments as this would only confuse or frustrate someone who is inexperienced in sifting through arguments or patiently enduring what is required to resolve them. Medical students on rotations or first-year residents would not be invited to participate in arguments between experienced physicians in hot disagreement.

How is love a debt?

● ● ● ● ● ● ● ● ● ● ● ● ● ● ● ● ● ● ●

Q 14:14–18 What does this passage about food say to us today?

The Jews had received laws about their diet from God through Moses, and though Jesus had brought dietary law to an end, many people could not overcome the force of these laws (Lv 11; Mk 7:1–19). Among the Gentiles there was also the practice of selling food that had been offered to idols in temples. Some people thought that eating this food would mean they had participated in idolatry (1Co 8:4–13). Here Paul is urging Christians to be considerate of the struggles of other people rather than their own appetites. It is a good thing to have faith that leaves your conscience unburdened, but that is no excuse for laying a burden on the conscience of another person (Php 2:4).

● ● ● ● ● ● ● ● ● ● ● ● ● ● ● ● ● ● ●

Q 14:22–23 Should we adjust our behavior and lifestyle so that we don't offend others?

Correct. The Christian faith does not tolerate for one moment a person who is trying to overthrow the Gospel by imposing rules as if we had to keep them to save ourselves (Ac 15:1–19; Gal 1:6–10; 2:3–21). On the other hand, Christian love means we will sacrifice anything to protect and foster faith in others (1Co 9:19–27; Php 3:7–14).

1 Corinthians

Q **1:1 Who is Sosthenes?**

The only other place Sosthenes is mentioned in the New Testament is in Ac 18:17, where he is described as the ruler of the synagogue in Corinth. When the Jews were frustrated in their attempts to have Paul condemned by the proconsul, Gallio, they seized Sosthenes and beat him before the judgment seat of Gallio, who took no notice (Ac 18:12–17).

Q **1:7 What spiritual gift is Paul mentioning? Do you have to ask for spiritual gifts?**

Paul began this section by thanking God for enriching the Corinthians in everything through the grace of Christ Jesus. This enrichment was conveyed to them through the Word ("testimony about Christ," 1:6), which was confirmed in them. The result is that they were not lacking in any gift as they awaited the revelation of the Lord Jesus Christ. Paul wrote this to a congregation of believers rather than to an individual. Therefore, while the congregation is lacking in no gift, this does not mean that each individual has all the gifts. On the contrary, Paul will come back to this subject in this letter and in subsequent letters, explaining how God determines what each person's work is and providing the gift(s) necessary to fulfill that work (1Co 12:1–31; Rm 12:3–8; Eph 2:10; 4:1–16). Paul urged the Corinthians earnestly to desire the best gifts (1Co 12:31). Paul went on to explain that prophecy or communicating the Word of God faithfully

> ## Has there always been division in the Church?

to others, according to their need, was the very best of gifts and that we should pursue it (1Co 14:1).

As Paul said, the source of all good gifts, including spiritual gifts, is the Word, and the Bible consistently commands us to remain in that Word (Dt 6:4–9; Is 55:1–13; Lk 10:38–42; Jn 8:31–32; 15:1–7; Rm 10:17; Col 3:16; 1Tm 4:11–16). The Word will motivate us and give us the words to communicate as each occasion requires (Pr 16:1; Mt 10:19; 1Pt 3:15).

● ●

Q 1:10–17 Paul admonishes that there should be no divisions in the church, but today we see many divisions in congregations and church leadership. What can we do? Has there always been division in the Church?

Fallen human nature and congregations of fallen human beings don't have the right attitude and will never listen to what God says (Jer 17:9). No matter how biblical or Christian a person intends to be, as long as we have this fallen human nature we will fail to live as God desires and commands (Is 64:6; Rm 7:14–21; 1Jn 1:8–9). No matter how much we might welcome unity and even work for it, we cannot bring about unity by our desire for it, nor can we force it. Unity—real, substantive, meaningful unity—is the product of God's Word at work in us, bring-ing us to honesty about the truth and regenerating us as His own children (1 Jn 1:7–10; 2:18–19; Php 1:27–2:5). Jesus, Paul, and the history of humanity demonstrate that there must be divisions (Gen 4:3–8; 1 Ki 12:1–18; Lk 12:51–53; 1Co 11:19). Both the Old and New Testament require us to separate from people or groups who oppose the truth and grace of God (Lv 20:24–26; Ezr 10:1–3; Rm 16:17; 1Co 5:7–13; 2Jn 10).

There were no denominations in Paul's time as we know them today. However, there were different Jewish sects (Sadducees, Pharisees, Herodians, Zealots) and different groups of people competing with one another in the same congregations (Lk 10:35–41; 1Co 1:12–22; Jas 2:1–9). Denominations exist because people have a greater commitment to their own opinions than they do to the truth (Jgs 21:25; Pr 26:16; Is 53:6; Jn 8:33–44). Churches don't listen to biblical teaching about unity because they are made up of people with fallen human natures. If you inquire, you may learn that churches don't listen to many other things that the Bible has to say, such as "One's life does not consist in the abundance of his possessions" (Lk 12:15) or "Owe no one anything, except to love each other" (Rm 13:8).

Regardless of times, places, or external associations or differences, the true Christian Church, the Body of Christ, is and will always be one (Mt 16:18; Jn 10:16; Eph 4:4–6). Honesty, truth, and Christian love do not seek to pretend or claim that there is unity where there is none (Jer 6:14; Mt 7:21–27; Lk 4:21–30; 22:48; Jn 1:11–13).

The Christian mission is to bear witness to the truth and grace of God out of love for all people because God has loved us. True unity can only be the fruit of the truth and grace of God (1Jn 1:7).

● ● ● ● ● ● ● ● ● ● ● ● ● ● ● ● ● ● ● ●

Q 1:10 How are we to be perfectly united when people have different ideas about everything?

God gives great liberty within a structure that exists to support, promote, and protect life (Gal 5:1, 13). Adam and Eve could eat of any of the trees of the garden (who knows how many there were?) and were only forbidden to eat of one. So much of what we think our lives are about can be decided upon by us and doesn't affect our unity (Rm 14:1–15:6). Unity begins with the Word that reveals the truth (1Jn 1:7). Rebellion against the truth inescapably sets us in opposition to each other, and thus divisions are endless. We become united when the Law works repentance from our rebellion against the truth and when the Gospel regenerates us in the image of Christ and with the mind of Christ (Jgs 21:25; Lk 11:23; Php 1:27–5).

● ● ● ● ● ● ● ● ● ● ● ● ● ● ● ● ● ● ● ●

Q 1:11–13 Shouldn't these people understand Baptism before they are baptized? Why would they think they are baptized in Paul's name?

The more time we have with the Word of God—or, I should say, the more time the Word of God has with us—the better (Rm 10:17). We also want to teach and know as much as we can about what God is doing for us and in us through His Sacraments (Baptism, Lord's Supper, Absolution) before we receive them (1Co 11:27–32). On the other hand, it is not our human nature or our mind that apprehends or understands what God is doing for us in the Sacraments (1Co 2:14; Is 55:8–9). God's Word generates a new person in us, a soul that knows and clings to the grace of God in Word and Sacrament (1Jn 2:20, 28). God's way and gifts are not complicated but simple; it is not the simple who have trouble grasping God's blessings, but the complexity and skepticism of human pride, as Paul goes on to address (1 Co 1:18–31; Mt 18:3; Jn 3:1–7).

To be baptized in the "name" of someone or something meant to be immersed in and connected with that thing (1Co 10:2). People thought they were being baptized into the teaching of Paul, as if Paul's teaching was the product of his own thinking. This is why Paul takes such pains to make sure we understand that his teaching is not his own but has been given to him by God as a stewardship (1Co 2:1–5; 11:23; Gal 1:1–2:10).

● ● ● ● ● ● ● ● ● ● ● ● ● ● ● ● ● ● ● ●

Q 1:12–13 Who is Apollos? Who is Cephas? Did the different divisions have different doctrinal beliefs? What is meant by asking if Christ is divided?

Cephas is the Aramaic form of Peter's name (Jn 1:42). Apollos was a Jew from Alexandria who came to Ephesus having already become a disciple of Christ. In

411

Ephesus, Apollos received the teaching of Christ more accurately from Aquila and Priscilla (Ac 18:24; 19:1). Apollos became a faithful Christian teacher and partner of Paul (1Co 3:6; 16:12; Ti 3:13). Some argue that Apollos was the author of Hebrews.

It is impossible to know if these different groups in Corinth also claimed different doctrinal beliefs. Since Peter, Paul, and Apollos all taught what Jesus taught, we might think they did not. On the other hand, the various Jewish sects all claimed to follow Moses but clearly did not. See Ac 19:2–6 for a discussion of men who claimed to be disciples of John the Baptist but, in fact, could not have been.

Paul is trying to prove the absurdity of claiming to be Christian while claiming to be superior to other Christians. It is no more possible for the believers who make up the Body of Christ to be divided than it is to divide the actual, physical body of Christ Himself. Paul will come back to this argument in ch. 12. Regardless of how obvious it is that Jesus is one and cannot be divided, those who follow Him still possess a fallen human nature that is proud and selfish. Jesus had to rebuke this egocentric, proud, competitive force in His own disciples more than once (Mt 18:1–3; 20:20–28). The people in Corinth were no different; they were in competition with one another, yet all claimed to be Christian. The prayer of Jesus on the night He was betrayed reveals the threat of division and the way of unity (Jn 17:1–26).

Q 1:12 In light of this passage, why do some acknowledge themselves by their denomination instead of simply as a Christian?

Let's begin with clarity and accuracy. People tend to claim association with a group in order to share an identity and to find protection in that group. No matter what name or group a person might claim, it would take time and thoughtful questions to find out what a person truly believes. For example, some Lutherans claim that name because, like Luther, their first commitment is to the Bible as the primary source of truth. Others claim to be Lutheran because they believe in rebelling against the establishment, which is actually a misrepresentation of Luther's efforts to reform the Roman Church. It might be more helpful to figure out why any particular person wants to claim a name and why anyone cares if he or she does so. If we are concerned about the lives of other people, and we know that our lives depend on the truth, then we have the best of foundations for conversation about witnesses to the truth, their reliability, and their content (Ac 17:10–32; Jas 1:19; 1Jn 1:1–9).

Q 1:13–17 Why is Paul glad he didn't baptize these people? Were some of these people worshiping Paul because he baptized them?

When Paul did baptize someone, it was to confirm the grace and promises of God to that person with the physical means of water added to the Word, according to the command of the Lord (Mt 28:19–20; Mk 16:16; Ac 16:25–34; 1Pt 3:21). Paul would say that he was not sent to baptize for the same reason that Jesus did not physically baptize anyone (Jn 4:2). If Jesus had performed the Rite of Baptism on some, those people might well have claimed that they had something that others did not—just as the people of Corinth were making claims about their special history with Peter or Paul or Apollos. Jesus baptized no one, yet Jesus baptizes everyone because He *is* the Word of God, and it is the Word, joined by water, that makes the Rite of Baptism effective.

Paul didn't want to create a following for himself; he had renounced that approach to life at his conversion (Php 3:7–14). Paul was in this world to communicate the Word of God to people so that they might be saved (1Co 2:1–4; 2Co 5:14–21). Paul isn't glad because he didn't baptize anyone. He is only glad that because he didn't baptize very many people, it would be difficult for people to form a cult around him.

If people abandon or ignore the Word of God because they think the ceremony of Baptism is all we need, then Baptism must receive less emphasis and the Word of God more (Mt 12:43–44; 23:16–24; Jn 3:1–7). Without the Word of God there is no Baptism, and apart from a life in the Word the blessings of Baptism are abandoned and unrealized (Jn 15:1–7). We have no record that anyone was worshiping Paul because he baptized them, though some people in Corinth thought their relationship with Paul made them superior to others. There was a time when people did try to worship Paul; he had a difficult time putting a stop to it, and after he did, they stoned him (Ac 14:8–20).

• • • • • • • • • • • • • • • • • •

Q 1:14 Who were Crispus and Gaius?

Crispus was the ruler of the synagogue in Corinth (Ac 18:8). There is more than one Gaius in the New Testament. One Gaius was a Macedonian (northern Greece) who traveled with Paul (19:29). Another was from Derbe, in Asia Minor (Turkey; 20:4). Yet another Gaius, the one Paul is referring to here, lived in Corinth (Rm 16:23). Finally, John the apostle wrote his third letter to a man named Gaius (3Jn 1).

• • • • • • • • • • • • • • • • • •

Q 1:19 How does God plan to "destroy the wisdom of the wise"? Why will God frustrate people who are intelligent when He made people that way?

God did destroy the wisdom of the wise in the crucifixion of His own Son. In Isaiah's prophecy, which Paul quotes here, the "wise" people are not those with wisdom from God, but people who think that by their own clever thoughts they have destroyed God (Ps 14:1–6; 53:1–3). This is how God overcame them. People are worldly because they are materialistic; they believe that there is only the material world and our life in it and that life is passing quickly. This material and temporary view makes them absolutely selfish and driven by the desires of their flesh. To satisfy those desires as fully and as quickly as possible, such people must take what they want from others in defiance of God's will. When God sent His Son into the world, the worldly-wise were convinced that they could be rid of His teaching by humiliating Him and that they could be rid of His power by putting Him to death (Lk 20:9–19; 23:35; Mt 27:62–66; 28:11–15). Jesus demonstrated His wisdom and victory in His resurrection from the dead. The worldly-wise lose their own lives by taking from others and then lose all life in eternal death (Rm 6:19–21). Their wisdom dies with them. Jesus, the very wisdom of God, gave His life to others according to the Word and will of God and then rose to live and reign forever. Like Jesus Himself, His wisdom endures forever and gives eternal life to all generated by it (Jn 1:112–13; 11:25–26; 14:1–7).

God gives human beings abilities to use for life in the fullest sense of the word, which means life in the service of others (2Co 5:15). We have arms that can help a person who needs care, but we can also use our arms to harm a person and put them in need of care. Intelligence works the same way; it can be the best of servants or the worst of masters. God makes all things good, and fallen human nature in contradiction of God's design destroys all things. God grants us the opportunity to learn about His goodness and our inabilities so that we come to love and trust in Him rather than in ourselves (2Co 1:7–9).

Q **1:21 What does Paul mean when he says, "It pleased God through the folly of what we preach to save those who believe?"**

The way of the world is the way of fallen human nature. Fallen human nature has a short life and is, therefore, very selfish and very anxious about getting its way before time runs out. This is why the wisdom of the world says, "Get all you can, as fast as you can, any way you can," or, in contemporary language, "It's all about you." The wisdom of the world says that having power allows you to get what you want by taking it from others. What will such a person and such a world think when God Almighty makes Himself a man who gives His life for others, even for those who despise Him? But this is real power, and this is real love—so powerful that it can regenerate us and inspire us to follow the same path (Rm 1:16).

Q **1:22 If the "Jews demand signs and Greeks seek wisdom," why demand anything?**

You have a good insight, one that Job and any other honest human being would share (Jb 40:3–5; Rm 9:20). The problem with demanding miraculous signs is that such demands are the product of a contradictory and rebellious human nature that refuses the signs even when they are given (1Co 2:14; Heb 3:7–19). Forty years of bread from heaven and water from rocks didn't seem to help Israel at all (Ps 106). Jesus had just finished feeding the five thousand and crossing the Sea of Galilee on foot, yet the unbelieving Jews demanded a sign of Him as if the previous day had never happened (Jn 6:30). Greeks seek wisdom, which is a noble pursuit (Pr 4:5; 19:20). The problem with seeking wisdom comes from a foolish human nature that does not seek genuine wisdom but worldly wisdom that is folly dressed up to appeal to our appetites (Pr 9:13–18). While we are in no position to make demands, God does urge us to ask for and to seek His wisdom, truth, grace, and life (Jas 1:5–8; Mt 7:7–11; Jn 16:23–27).

. . . .

Q 1:23–24 Why does Paul use the terms "Greek" and "Gentile"?

Paul refers to "Greeks" (*Hellenes* in Greek) in 1:22 and 1:24. He refers to "Gentiles" (*Ethnes* in Greek) in 1:23. From a strictly material sense, all people who have not descended from Jacob are Gentiles or "the nations." All Greeks are part of "the nations," but the world is full of people who are not Greek. Paul is writing to the people of a Greek city, so it makes sense to refer specifically to them. On the other hand, what Paul says applies to people all around the world, so he also refers to the same people (those who seek wisdom) as "the nations."

. . . .

Q 1:23 How is Christ's crucifixion a stumbling block to Jews?

Before reading this answer, it would help to read Gal 3:10–14 (actually all of

> ## How is Christ's crucifixion a stumbling block to Jews?

Galatians would help). First, fallen human nature is not only selfish but also proud and self-righteous. Second, God gave the Law to show us our fallen nature clearly in order to bring us to the solution He has provided by grace in Christ (Rm 3:19–28; Gal 3:24). Third, the Jews believed that God had promised and would send them a Savior, the Christ (Gn 12:3). Fourth, here comes the trouble: Jesus came and demonstrated that He was the promised Savior, the Christ, but He did not reward the Jews for their righteousness by making them rule over the Gentiles and giving them the wealth of the nations. Instead, the Savior exposed their failure to keep the Law and their hypocrisy. Then the Savior, having taken their place under the Law, suffered humiliation, crucifixion, and death. Now, if the Savior saved the Jews by taking their place, by accepting what was rightfully theirs under the Law, then it was the Jews who should have been crucified. Being crucified means that you failed to keep the Law, but the Jews had argued that they did keep the Law. This is the stumbling block.

Jewish or not, selfish, self-righteous, greedy, and proud human nature cannot recognize Jesus as the Savior because that would mean admitting that we deserve all that He suffered. Recognizing that Jesus is the Christ means that He came to save us from ourselves, not from others. Jesus as the Christ means that we deserve the condemnation of the Law, yet God graciously forgave us all and substituted His own Son for us out of love. This means humility for us and a life of love and service to others. All this is the stumbling block that Jesus was for the Jews in His day and is still for all proud, selfish people today.

Q 1:25 Does God have weaknesses?

God has no weaknesses, nor is there any foolishness about Him, unless you consider Him according to human standards. Many people despise Christianity because they think it is for the weak: people who always depend on God for help and are unable to defend or care for themselves. By worldly standards, Christ did display weakness when He let Himself be betrayed, arrested, and tried without defending Himself and then crucified while being taunted by His adversaries. Did Christ have the power to come down from the cross? Of course (Mt 27:39–42). What requires more power: to execute physical vengeance on your oppressors or to endure the condemnation they deserve in order to provide for their redemption? Which is more foolish: to sacrifice your soul, the essence of your life, and eternity for the sake of brief, material gratification or to use our physical life in this world to serve the souls of all for all eternity? This is what Paul means by the weakness and foolishness of God.

Q 1:26 Is faith easier for those who have little money and little power?

In a way, faith is the easiest thing ever because faith is simply honesty about our dependence on God. Faith is realizing that God provides for your life in every way, from sunshine to the food you eat to your next heartbeat. What could be easier than knowing that you are provided for? The problem is that fallen human nature, contrary to God and the truth, wants to create its own image and make its own life. Such determination against the truth makes us dishonest with ourselves and about ourselves. Dishonesty is the hardest thing; as Sir Walter Scott said, "Oh, what a tangled web we weave when first we practice to deceive." Jesus points to children as the model of faith because their fallen human nature has not yet developed its determination to complicate living (Mt 18:3). Nicodemus and the crowds of adults could not understand the simple truths Jesus was telling them because their own limited thinking was in the way (Jn 3:1–7; 6:26–68; 8:31–47). Jesus not only pointed to children as the model of faith but also invites us and moves us to join them by the working of His Word and Spirit (Mt 11:28–30; Ti 3:4–5).

Q 1:27 What is the meaning of "But God chose what is foolish in the world to shame the wise"?

When Paul says "wise" and "mighty," he is referring to wise and mighty things by the world's standards. A person who uses all his life and makes himself poor in order to help others is considered a fool by the "intelligent" people of this material world. Infants enjoy the closest thing to peace we might know this side of heaven, but the world despises them because they cannot dominate others in order to have their own way. God has chosen those who are foolish and weak by worldly standards in order to expose the shame of those who claim to be wise and powerful. Where is the wisdom and power of the worldly person when the time of death comes? Physical strength cannot prevent dementia. Worldly wisdom cannot recapture youth nor stop the disintegration of the body toward death. But those who are not and cannot be dishonest about their utter dependence on God find in life and death that God provides for them, loves them, saves them, and gives them everlasting life. Now who is wise or foolish, mighty or weak? Please refer to questions and answers on 1Co 1:19–26 above for background to this answer.

. . . .

Q 1:28 What are the "things that are not"?

Good question, since the only possibilities would have to be absent from a list of things that are. In this context, the "things that are" have to do with things that the world covets: worldly wisdom, physical strength, pride, wealth, power—the ability to gratify the desires of a proud, selfish, self-righteous

human nature. Paul has mentioned some of the things that take us in the direction of what is not: foolishness, weakness, base things, and things despised. Is it possible that what Paul means by the "things that are not" have to do with the fulfillment of God's promises, especially in granting a regenerate soul through the hearing of His Word and Spirit? Our lives as children of God "are not" until His Word regenerates us (Jn 1:11–12; 3:1–7). This inner man or new man is the essence of who we are, but it is spiritual and disinterested in the vanities of the world—which is why worldly people despise the notion. Paul is a tremendous example of both sides, before and after his conversion. He gives clear articulation of the contrast between the things that are and are not in Php 3:3–14.

. . . .

Q 2:1–4 Do people try to be too persuasive with words of human wisdom rather than relying on the power of God's Word when witnessing? Shouldn't we simply pray and hope that the Holy Spirit will do something?

Some people try too hard to witness, as if all depended on their efforts; others don't try at all, as if their efforts did not matter at all. The truth is in between. First, conversion is work only God can do, yet He does this, normally, through His Word and people who speak that Word on His behalf (Mt 28:19–20; Ac 1:8; 1Co 3:5–7; 2Co 5:14–21). Second, God's Word is always effective and never returns void (Is 55). Third, as long as people refuse to hear the truth about their condition under the Law, they will not hear any truth—no matter how eloquently or persuasively we convey it (Lk 16:27–31). Fourth, the truth is powerful and has the power to redeem the most vicious of adversaries; Paul is the perfect example (Ac 9:1–20). Fifth, often the process of conversion and regeneration takes time; Peter is the perfect example (Mt 14:25–31; 16:21–23; Lk 5:8; 9:32; 22:33–61; Ac 10:14–15; Gal 2:11–21). Sometimes time is needed because it allows the witness of nature to bring a person to honesty about his condition and need for God's redemption in Christ (Pss 19:1–3; 106:40–47; 119:67; Hos 6:1–3; Rm 1:18–2:4). The only way for us to be faithful ambassadors for Christ and effective witnesses is for us to remain in the Word so that we might be fruitful children of God, ready to make a defense, quick to listen, slow to anger, slow to speak, and prepared to offer the truth in love (Pr 16:1; 1Pt 3:15; Jas 1:19; Jn 15:1–7; Eph 4:15).

Q 2:1–2 Is Paul saying he set aside his knowledge in other areas in order to focus on proclaiming the Gospel?

Yes, that is one way of saying it. Paul knows that our time is short and the work is great (Lk 10:2; Eph 5:15–16). Therefore, Paul is very focused on communicating to the people that which they need to know most: the Gospel of Jesus Christ. Paul's statement suggests an added concern—that it is the crucified Christ that is preached.

Many Jewish leaders were willing to accept (as it was undeniable) that Jesus was the Christ that God had promised all through the Old Testament, but they wanted to make Him into a new Moses or a second Lawgiver (Ac 15:5). Jesus is not simply another authority who shows by His life what the Law rightly demands of us. Paul argues vigorously against this notion (Rm 4:1–16; Gal 3:1–25). Jesus, the Christ of God, was crucified in order to take the place of all people under the foundation of the Law. This is love, and this shows the way to life. Love for others because of God's love for us, serving in order to give what we have rather than to get what we have not, using our physical life in this time for the sake of our essential, spiritual life for all time—these make up the very core and substance of Christianity.

Q 2:3 Why does Paul say to the Corinthians that he came to them "in weakness and in fear"?

Paul's conversion is the first time we see him afraid—so afraid he did not eat or drink for three days, and rightly so (Ac 9:3–9). Paul had some kind of ailment that may also have made him weak (2Co 12:7–10). Paul suffered abuse in many ways and at many times; he may have suffered both fear and weakness as a result of these trials, though his confidence in God's providence only deepened as a result (2Co 11:23–33; Ac 27:20–25).

Q 2:4 Wasn't Paul a good speaker? Do you think that being a good public speaker is a prerequisite for becoming a pastor?

Paul is not saying that he was not good at speaking or that he was boring (see 2:1–2 above), though he was probably not a great public speaker (cf. 2Co 10:10). On the other hand, as an apostle who faithfully communicated the truth, he was very effective (Ac 9:20–22). Paul is pointing out a contrast between his speaking and that of others. Paul is speaking in public because God called him to do this. His speaking is entirely in service of the message—to accurately communicate the truth. The truth is the key. Other speakers take up this work in their own interest, in order to gain power and influence over the people to whom they speak. They are neither concerned with the truth nor with the lives (especially not the eternal life of the soul) of those who hear them. The truth is of no concern for these people, only their own interests (1Tm 4:1–3).

If "good public speaking" means effective teaching, then it is a necessary ability for one who would serve in the public ministry (1Tm 3:2 lists the qualification as "able to teach"). However, good public speaking that serves a person's ego instead of the truth and grace of God is a very harmful and dangerous thing (Mt 23:11; Ac 24:1–9; 2Co 11:3; Col 2:4–8; 1Tm 6:3–5; 2Tm 2:16–17; 4:2–4).

Q 2:7 Is God's "secret wisdom" faith? It seems like when you have faith, things just make sense.

More precisely, Paul wrote: "But we speak the wisdom of God in a mystery that has been hidden, which God foreordained before the ages for our glory." Jesus spoke of the mystery of the kingdom of God (Mt 13:11; Mk 4:11; Lk 8:10). Paul speaks in several places about this mystery having to do with bringing the Gentiles into communion with God (Rm 11:25; Eph 3:3–9; Col 1:27). Paul speaks of the resurrection of the dead as a mystery also (1Co 15:51). The clearest articulation of the fundamental content of the mystery is revealed in Paul's Letter to Timothy (1Tm 3:16): "Great . . . is the mystery of godliness: [Christ] was manifested in the flesh, vindicated by the Spirit, seen by angels, proclaimed among the nations, believed on in the world, taken up in glory."

If faith means "honesty about dependence," then coming to faith does make sense of things because it is obvious that we are utterly dependent on God, who has reconciled the world to Himself through the life of Jesus. Who would have, in their wildest dreams, even begun to imagine that God, being love and trinity, would provide for the correction and restoration of all things through the life, sacrifice, and resurrection of His own Son? This is exactly what Isaiah said, which Paul quotes in 1Co 2:9 (Is 64:4; see also 1Co 3:20).

Q 2:8 Wouldn't they still have crucified Jesus even if they understood? Wasn't it necessary for the "Lord of glory" to be crucified?

Would you cry out for Jesus to be crucified if you knew He was the Son of God? There are two questions to distinguish here. First, if a person knew who Jesus was, would he or she crucify Him? Saying yes is unthinkable, yet this is what people do who make themselves guilty of the unforgivable sin (Heb 6:4–8; 10:26–31; Mt 12:31–32). Second, will there always be people who do not understand? It appears that the answer is yes. No human nature can understand what God is doing in Christ—this is why Paul calls it a "secret wisdom" in the previous verse (v. 7). Some people succeed in resisting and opposing the truth so that God's Word and grace never do create a regenerate soul that understands who Jesus is (2Co 3:14–16; Ac 7:51–59; 28:23–28).

Q 2:10–15 Why are they so strong about the Spirit?

The Corinthians seemed to be strong about most things, for better or worse. They were in competition with one another, boasted of adultery, took one another to court, and became drunk before Communion services—to name just a few problems. No surprise, then, that they might misunderstand things having to do with the Spirit. On the other hand, Paul spent more time addressing matters of the Spirit in his letters to the Galatians and Ephesians than in 1 Corinthians ("spirit" occurs 40 times in the 16 chapters of 1 Corinthians but 18 times in Galatians and 14 times in Ephesians, which each have only 6 chapters). The Holy Spirit is the person of the Godhead who affects our life according to the Word and will of God. If Christians are competing with one another, it is no surprise that they would focus more on the Spirit and/or make more claims about the Spirit in their lives than in the lives of other Christians.

Q 2:10 How does the Spirit search inside of God? What exactly does "the depths" of God mean?

Is it possible that our spirit searches within us, in a small way, as God's Spirit searches His thoughts (Rm 8:27)? The "depths" of God would be those things least accessible, even impossible to know (Rm 11:33). God allowed Moses to see Him from behind because no one can see God and live (Ex 33:18–23). John explained that the incarnate Son of God, Jesus Christ, has made God known to us (Jn 1:18). Paul uses the word *depths* in his Letter to the Ephesians, explaining that the fullness of God and His depths are revealed to us in the love of Christ for us (Eph 3:17–19; see also 1Co 2:7 above).

Q 2:11–15 Paul says we all have the same spirit, but later he says that the man without the spirit does not accept

the things that come from the spirit of God. How can we all have the spirit yet not accept the things of the spirit?

When Paul says "we," he is referring to believers: people who have been regenerated by the Holy Spirit and are sustained by that Spirit in the faith (Jn 6:63; Rm 10:17; 1Pt 1:5). The soul regenerated by the Word and Spirit of God is naturally oriented toward and understands the things of God. A person without a regenerate soul or apart from the Word and Spirit of God will still have his or her own spirit, or the spirit of the world or of the devil—but this makes such a person even more incapable of receiving the things of the Spirit (Mt 12:43–44; Rm 5:6–11; Eph 2:1–3). It is not up to anyone to do anything in spiritual matters since we have no means or will of our own to do so. God brings us into the world through the family and would keep us in the community of those who remain in the Word, because it is the Word and Spirit alone that convey His grace and accomplish His will in us (Pr 16:1; Gal 6:1; Php 2:13; Jas 5:16, 19–20).

· ·

Q 2:12 Why is there so little that we understand about God?

First, John explained that anyone who has been anointed by God knows all things (1Jn 2:20, 27). Our regenerate soul may know all things, but it lives inside a fallen human nature that is not only ignorant of but also contrary to the things of God (1Co 2:14; Jn 8:43–45; Rm 7:5–6, 16–21; Gal

> ## What does it mean to have the mind of Christ?

5:16–18). Second, Paul speaks of knowing the "things freely given to us by God." The New Testament provides plenty of information about what God has given us in Christ. The problem is that we spend so little time in the New Testament and our fallen human nature is so contrary that it is hard for our regenerate soul to become evident in our consciousness or heard in our thoughts. This is why Jesus equates discipleship with remaining in the Word and Paul speaks of letting the Word dwell in us in abundance (Jn 8:31–32; Col 3:16).

· ·

Q 2:16 What does it mean to have the mind of Christ?

Paul wrote this letter to a congregation of people who suffered from the perilous combination of being very mistaken and very assertive at the same time (1Co 1:11; 5:1–2; 6:1). Human nature with this sort of disposition is more devoted to its own thoughts than to the truth, asserting that its claims are the truth and that God thinks accordingly (Dt 18:19–20; Ezk 13:8–23). Paul is asking the reader to consider whether he or she knows the things that God knows. Furthermore, Paul challenges those readers who thought they knew more than God and were, thus, in a position to teach God how things are (Jb 38:1–4; 40:1–7). Second, Paul's first reference is to the mind of the Lord.

Paul contrasts this with the mind of Christ. While Jesus Christ is the Lord Himself, He is also true man and the means by which the Lord God has determined to make Himself known to us. Jesus said that the Holy Spirit would take what was His and declare it to us (Jn 16:14). Paul told the Philippians that they had this mind, and John said the same to his readers (Php 2:5; 1Jn 2:20, 27). The mind of Christ is not deep and complicated, but simple in its devotion to God and love for others (Jn 15:9–13; Rm 10:6–14). Christ is devoted to loving God the Father above all things and others according to the will of God. He does this perfectly as the fruit of the Word and a perfect faith. This is the mind of Christ that we have and seek to realize more and more during the course of our life in this world (Php 3:7–16).

- - - - - - - - - - - - - - - - - - -

Q 3:1–4 How does Paul want to bring the Corinthians out of their worldly beliefs? Why does Paul say they are acting as "people of the flesh"?

Paul would bring them out of their worldly beliefs in the very same way all correction and progress in the faith takes place: by applying the truth and grace of God (Jer 1:10; Hos 6:1–3). Paul begins with tearing down and demolishing the desires and opinions of our fallen human nature. He does this using Law and logic. The Law condemns these people for being "of the flesh." Logic condemns them for ignoring the fact that "neither he who plants nor he who waters is anything, but only God who gives

the growth" (v. 7). Paul follows the condemnation of the Law with news of the grace of God that regenerates, reorients, and inspires loving service toward others: "You are God's field, God's building" (v. 9); and "No one can lay a foundation other than that which is laid, which is Jesus Christ" (v. 11).

Paul says that they were acting as "people of the flesh" because they were determined to serve their fallen human nature, pride, and selfishness, just like people of the world who don't know better and who have no hope (cf. 1:21–25). Paul lists jealousy and strife as particular problems (see Mk 7:20–23; Gal 5:19–21; Col 3:5–9 for a more complete description of the works of the flesh).

- - - - - - - - - - - - - - - - - - -

Q 3:1 How can we be spiritually mature?

Spiritual maturity comes from the combination of a life in the Word and having experiences in which that Word is applied to the challenges we face in our life. Experience with challenges apart from the Word leaves us to succeed or fail by our own abilities, which tends to lead us to pride or discouragement. Reading the Bible while avoiding the challenges it equips us to face prevents us from realizing the power and potential of the Word in our lives. The Word gives us wisdom and motivation to serve. The challenges of serving give us opportunity to realize a life in the Word and point us back to the Word for the strength, encouragement, and wisdom to embrace the challenges we still face or are yet to engage (Ps 119:50, 67, 71, 75, 92, 107, 153).

• • • • • • • • • • • • • • • • • • •

Q 3:2–3 Does the strife talked about relate to the quarreling that goes on today?

The jealousy and strife that Paul talks about do certainly go on today, as certainly as we are all still possessed by a fallen human nature that is inherently jealous and competitive (Lk 7:20–23; Gal 5:19–21). In fact, every problem that the Bible reveals—from the failure of Adam to the godlessness of people described in Revelation—still goes on today and will continue until Judgment Day comes, when all fallen human flesh is finally destroyed and we are raised with perfect bodies (1Co 35–57; 2Co 4:16–5:6).

• • • • • • • • • • • • • • • • • • •

Q 3:4 How important are the differences in denominations?

The differences among denominations are of critical significance historically—significant enough to cause division among people who all claim to serve the same God on the basis of the Bible. In our time, the differences remain significant but are not as important, since most people do not know or realize the fundamental teachings of the denomination they claim or what difference they make. Few people know or care if their personal beliefs match the public, stated teachings of their denomination. The most significant difference among denominations and religions is the matter of how we are saved: either God saves us or we save ourselves. In this respect, there are only two religions. Only orthodox, biblical Christianity teaches that God alone saves us. He accomplished our redemption in His Son, and He affects that redemption in our lives by the work of His Word and Spirit. There are as many variations and particular teachings among those who believe we save ourselves as there are people who believe it. All "Christian" denominations speak of the grace of God and saving work of Christ, but when you investigate further, you will find they teach that no matter what Christ did, you are not saved until you do what God requires of you, whether that is confessing your sins adequately, obeying the teaching of your church, making a decision or commitment to God, making yourself believe, or living a life that argues for your predestination by God. The most significant issue with denominations is not their differences but their commitment to the individual's opinions rather than to the truth. The truth is universal and singular; common devotion to the truth is what makes us members of the Body of Christ (1Jn 1:7).

• • • • • • • • • • • • • • • • • • •

Q 3:6–9 From God's view, what would you call that man who plants the seed and waters it?

Jesus calls such a man "faithful" (Mt 24:25; 25:21–23; Lk 12:42; 16:10–12).

Q 3:8 How will he be rewarded?

The word translated "reward" can also mean "payment" or "compensation that is due" (Mt 20:8; Rm 4:4; 1Tm 5:18). Matthew's Gospel records Jesus' use of this word much more than the other three Gospels. Jesus taught that we should rejoice when we are reviled and persecuted because our reward "is great in heaven" (Mt 5:12). Jesus asked what reward we have for loving those who love us in return, in contrast to the reward that comes from loving our enemies (5:46). He said that people who did good works only to be seen by people already had their reward—the attention to their ego and the satisfaction of their pride (6:2, 5, 16). At the end of a work day, the owner of a vineyard would call the workers and give them their due (20:8). A reward or wage has a direct relationship with the work that is done. If you plant a field or bring in the harvest, then you have earned a comparable part of the fruit. What's more, if you act graciously toward another, if you love your enemy or give to someone who cannot give in return, your reward is even greater—the reward being the incomparable experience of loving because you are loved by God, giving because God has already given to you, and in a small but significant way knowing what it is to live in God's image as one who deals graciously with others (Lk 14:7–14).

Q 3:10–15 Does this mean that as Christians we start off with Christ, then

what we do to spread the Gospel is shown in how much effort, time, and/or money we spend on it?

This is not what Paul means, and as often as we fail to grasp his intent, our work does go up in smoke. The history of the world is one big example of fallen human nature trying to build a world of its own design, by its own labor (or, what's worse, by forcing others to labor), then fighting over it while that world is either destroyed by the fight or disintegrates on its own. Paul urges us as Christians to make "the best use of the time, because the days are evil" (Eph 5:16). Paul says we have wasted enough time in material, selfish pursuits that never benefit anyone (Rm 6:21; 1Pt 4:3). How, then, can we have a life that is made up of that which endures and cannot be destroyed? Paul wrote that we are being built into the Body of Christ, the Church, of which Jesus is the cornerstone and the apostles and prophets are the foundation (Eph 2:19–22). Peter wrote of this same construction, calling us "living stones" (1Pt 2:5). As Christians, our work is the same as Christ's. We mean to build upon the foundation of Christ and His prophets and apostles (2Co 5:19–21). As careful as we might want to be, according to our fallen human nature in a materialistic world we will no doubt build with the materials Paul lists; but even the gold perishes when tested by fire (1Pt 1:3–9). The Word of the Lord is what endures forever (Is 40:8). The Word of the Lord has given us a regenerate soul that lives forever, and the Lord has given us the mission of communicating that Word to others so that they may also be regenerated by it (Dt 6:4ff; Eph 6:4; Col 3:16).

• • • • • • • • • • • • • • • • • •

Q 3:13–14 What does fire have to do with each person's work?

Ultimately, "the Day" and "fire" have to do with the end of the world and judgment (Lk 12:49; 2Pt 3:10–13). However, during the course of our life in this world both the light of day and fire reveal things for what they are (Mal 3:1–3; Jn 11:9–11). The Word of the Lord is both light and fire that exposes and works to purify all during the course of our life (Jn 3:17–21; 1Pt 1:3–7; 2:9–10). Paul is speaking to every aspect of our life and our honesty (or lack of honesty) about dependence (faith), which affects all that we think, do, and say.

• • • • • • • • • • • • • • • • • •

Q 3:14 Are there levels in heaven?

I know of only one place where the Bible speaks of levels in heaven. Paul said that he was "caught up to the third heaven," where God provided revelation for him (2Co 12:2–7). However, this text offers no indication of what the "third heaven" or any other level means. Could it be that the first level is our sky, the next the solar system, and the third something outside of physical space? The New Testament makes some mention of greater or lesser rewards for our life in the body, but not in terms of a higher or lower place in heaven (Mt 5:12; 6:23; Lk 12:44–48). An important feature of God's

Are there levels in heaven?

grace and justice is that the more a person does good works in order to gain a better place in heaven, the further away such an approach is taking that person. The person who is motivated by the love and grace of God already revealed and accomplished in Jesus Christ remains focused on extending that love and grace to others without thought of reward (Mt 25:31–46).

• • • • • • • • • • • • • • • • • •

Q 3:15 Are pastors who teach what is false or conduct themselves contrary to God's will still saved though they went through the fire? Why is the person who teaches false doctrine saved?

First of all, those who teach false doctrine are described and addressed in much more severe language than Paul is using here (Jer 23:1–2; Mt 18:6–9; 23:1–33; Gal 1:6–9; Jas 3:1). Second, bad pastors may still be saved after passing through the fire of judgment for the same reason anyone else might: by the grace of God. Third, we are all equally contrary to God according to our fallen human nature and build a life of junk accordingly (Rm 5:6–11; Hg 1:2–11). Only the Word of God can generate a new person within us and repentance in our old man (Rm 1:16–17; 10:17). According to the new person or regenerate soul, we build a life according to God's Word and with God's Word. Since the Word of the Lord endures forever (Is 40:8), the faith and relationships that the Word produces must also endure forever (Lk 21:33; 1Pt 1:25). To the extent our old nature asserts itself against our regenerate soul, what we work at in our lives may be compared to gold, silver, precious stones, wood, hay, or straw (not unlike the story of the three little pigs). Some things we do, being very nearly what God would have us do and very nearly what His Word directs, are precious and valuable, like gold (but gold still perishes, 1Pt 1:7). Other things we do, as they are less according to the Word and will of God, are less and less significant, valuable, or durable—like silver, precious stones, and wood. Even hay has some value, at least as feed for cattle or horses. Straw is nearly useless, but not entirely. Regardless of how we use our time, God distinguishes between the believing soul and that person's human nature and folly (Pss 103:14; 130:3–4). What we have made of our lives that is not of His Word and His work will perish in time or on Judgment Day, but the work of His Word in us and through us will endure forever (Mt 25:34–40; Rv 14:13).

● ● ● ● ● ● ● ● ● ● ● ● ● ● ● ● ● ● ● ●

Q 3:16–17 Is eating unhealthily destroying the temple? What does this verse have to say about the death penalty?

It's not the unhealthy eating itself or any other activity that undermines our health that is the problem as much as the source of motivation to do so. Unhealthy activity can be changed, and many of its effects can be reversed, but there is no cure for a fallen human nature left to itself (Jer 8:4–9;

Rm 3:10–18; 6:23). Having a regenerate soul does not change the condition of our fallen human nature, though it does begin to turn its ways back to what God intended for it, which is good for our bodies and good for the people we serve (Dn 1:8–21). When thinking about human behavior, it is essential that we distinguish between body and soul, the condition of those natures, the dynamics between them, and how they are affected by the world and the Word. Without the Word and Spirit of God, no good will come to either body or soul. With the Word of God, good must come, even if the course of life for a person is so very troubled (Rm 8:28).

Paul's thought here flows from the stern language of Jesus against someone who destroys the work of God in general and the redemptive work of God in particular (Mt 18:6–9; Gal 1:6–9). There have been particular times when the fury of the Lord against those who abuse others was unleashed, and God Himself destroyed those who sought to destroy (Gn 18:20–21; 19:23–26; 38:6–10). We all make mistakes and by carelessness do harm to others, which we depend on the grace of God in Christ to forgive (Jas 3:1–2; 5:16). The death penalty is a matter of civil equity. Justice requires that a person who murders another (kills an innocent person with premeditation) must forfeit his own life. Only those authorized to execute civil justice are permitted to make such a judgment, and only based on the testimony of two or more witnesses (Rm 13:1–5; Dt 19:15). The family of the one murdered is protected by keeping them from seeking revenge. The community is helped by learning to fear the consequences for actions and by realizing protection from evildoers. Even the one who is guilty of a capital crime is helped toward repentance by the clear witness of justice faithfully conducted (Lv 19:17–18).

• • • • • • • • • • • • • • • • • • •

Q 3:17 What counts as destroying? Is it physical or spiritual?

If someone destroys God's work, especially His work in creating and redeeming human beings, God will destroy that person (Mt 18:6–9). This destruction of God's work in a human life includes the physical and spiritual (1Co 15:33; 2Co 7:2; 11:3; Eph 4:22; 2Pt 2:12; Jude 10; Rv 19:2).

• • • • • • • • • • • • • • • • • • •

Q 3:19 What is meant by this verse, especially "He catches the wise in their craftiness"?

There are two parts to this answer. The first part has to do with the meaning of "craftiness"; the second part has to do with how God catches the wise in this craftiness. First, "crafty" is not a good thing. The devil deceived Eve with his craftiness and continues to deceive people who are unsuspecting or immature (2Co 11:3; Eph 4:14). The religious leaders who opposed Jesus tried to use crafty means to find a way to condemn Jesus (Lk 20:23). Paul said that the true servants of the Word have rejected all false ways, including the deceptive (crafty) ways of men

(cf. 2Co 4:2). Second, God does not catch them "in" their craftiness but "by means of" their own crafty ways. In other words, God leaves people who are determined to reject the truth in favor of deception to suffer from their own deceptive ways (Rm 1:22–32). Shakespeare provides many examples of the worldly-wise being caught in their craftiness; a poem by Sir Walter Scott gave expression to the dynamic thusly: "Oh, what a tangled web we weave when first we practice to deceive." The more a person lies, the harder it is to keep the lies from being discovered. Every contradiction and force of opposition to God's design has negative consequences. Those with enough pride and conceit to mock those consequences will be caught in them and will have no one to blame but themselves.

• • • • • • • • • • • • • • • • • • •

Q 3:21 It says not to boast, but in a way aren't the disciples boasting about their position with God?

According to the Gospel accounts, each time the disciples made an attempt at glorifying themselves, they failed (Mk 10:35–45; Mt 14:28–31; 16:21–23; Lk 22:31–34, 54–62; Gal 2:11–16). The apostles were more likely to "boast" of their tribulation—that God considered them worthy to suffer for the mission Jesus had given them (Ac 5:28–42; Rm 8:18; 1Co 4:6–16; 2Co 3:4–6; Php 3:3–11).

• • • • • • • • • • • • • • • • • • • •

Q 4:3–5 Shouldn't we judge ourselves so we can confess what we have done wrong? What does Paul mean by "I am not aware of anything against myself"?

The word *judge* has a range of meaning from "condemnation" to "diagnosis." Jesus forbids us to judge others (Mt 7:1). In this case, He means that we are not to condemn others since that kind of judgment belongs only to God; we cannot know what the future holds for a person, and our purpose is to help people out of condemnation. On the other hand, Jesus taught that if our brother sins, we should speak with him about this so that sin would not be his ruin—this is diagnosis (Mt 18:15–18; Lv 19:17; 1Co 5:1–13; Gal 2:11–14). We apply these same principles to ourselves. We should never condemn ourselves, since God has redeemed us from the curse of the Law and its everlasting judgment (Rm 8:1). We must be steadfast in keeping the Law near so that it may work for us, against our contrary and disoriented human nature (Rm 3:19; Gal 3:24; 1Jn 1:7–9). As long as we are in this body, we depend on the Law to make accurate diagnosis for our fallen human nature so that we might repent and hold fast to the promises of God's forgiveness in Christ (Ezk 18:1–32; Mt 5:17–48; Gal 5:16–26). While Paul does not say here that we will never know all the sins we have committed, reason suggests and the Bible confirms that we could never know all our sin (Pss 19:13; 90:8; Is 64:6; Mt 5:23–26).

Paul does not speak about a clear conscience in this passage, though he does mention it in 2Tm 1:3. There are only three ways to have a clear conscience. A perfect, sinless person would have a clear conscience. Jesus alone can claim this. A perfectly hypocritical person could claim a clear conscience, adding hypocrisy and deceit to a seared conscience (Mt 23:1–36; 1Tm 1:19; 4:2). Paul claims a clear conscience on the basis of God's redemptive activity. Paul's conscience is clear because he lives in the grace of God that transferred all his guilt to Christ and the innocence of Christ to him (Jn 16:14; Rm 8:1; 2Co 5:21). Furthermore, Paul's conscience is clear because he lives in repentance and faith, always agreeing with the truth of the Law against his fallen human nature, always depending on the forgiveness of sins, living in obedience to God according to the new man by the working of God's Word and Spirit (Rm 7:1–8:11; 1Jn 3:9).

• • • • • • • • • • • • • • • • • • • •

Q 4:4 Paul says he is without errors (Ac 23:1). What does this mean, especially when he calls himself the "chief of sinners" (see 1Tm 1:15)?

Paul did not say he was without errors. Paul said, "I am not aware of anything against myself" (1Co 4:4). The reason for Paul's clear conscience is explained above in 4:3–5. Notice also that Paul says immediately, "But I am not thereby acquitted." Paul knows nothing against himself because he stands firmly in the grace of God communicated by the Word and Spirit of God in the Gospel (Rm 1:16–17; 8:1; Gal 2:15–21). Being a sinner and being condemned for one's sins are two different things. In fact, the more we are aware of our sins the more firmly we cling to the grace and promises of God that have put away that sin (Mt 25:31–46; Lk 7:47; Ps 51). In Ac 23:1, Paul claimed to be blameless regarding the Law as a response to the Jewish religious leaders. Paul did not say he was without sin but that he had kept every particular law of the Pharisees. He renounced the legal system of the Pharisees because it had taken the place of God's Law and because it was such a powerful means of self-righteousness and hypocrisy (Mt 23:1–36; Php 3:7–14).

• • • • • • • • • • • • • • • • • • • •

Q 4:7 What does this verse mean?

Paul is still responding to the problem of pride and competition among the Corinthians. To help them toward honesty and the truth, Paul asks a great question: "What or who makes you different?" The point is that someone or something makes these people compare themselves to one another as if they had something of their own to commend them before God. Paul addresses the problem of pride with a second question: "What do you have that you did not receive?" The answer, of course, is nothing. Paul concludes with a third question: "Why do you boast as if you did not receive it?" Remembering that we are dependent beings—completely dependent on God and the means God provides to support our

life—is absolutely humbling. But humility keeps us from being careless with the life and means God gives and keeps us connected and near the source of our life (compare the life of Samson with that of Jesus: Judges 13:1–16:31; Jn 8:1–59).

• • • • • • • • • • • • • • • • • • • •

Q 4:9–10 Is Paul being sarcastic here? If so, since this letter is inspired by God, why would sarcasm be considered a sin?

Sarcasm is not necessarily a sin. Like many other things, sarcasm would be a sin if it is an expression of hatred rather than love. Jesus gave a serious warning about what we say, as did Paul, Peter, and James (Mt 12:33–37; Eph 4:15, 25–31; 1Pt 3:8–15; Jas 3:1–12). Now we need to determine whether there is sarcasm in this passage. First, reliable interpretation requires us to understand words as they present themselves to us, unless we are forced to take them otherwise. Second, these two verses are interesting because Paul's communication in all of v. 9 and in the last third of v. 10 is straightforward. The apostles had been displayed as men condemned to death, had been made a spectacle to the world, and were dishonored. Third, is it possible to understand the first two thirds of v. 10 as literal speech? Paul said that the apostles were fools and weak on account of Christ. From the world's perspective, even from the Corinthians' perspective, wasn't this true? Paul began the letter by contrasting the world's measure of wisdom and strength with God's (see questions on 1Co 1:18–29 above). By making such bold and clear statements according to the Corinthian perspective, Paul is pressing them to evaluate that perspective. Who is really wise or foolish, weak or strong? The apostles sacrifice themselves for the sake of others, especially their enemies, as Christ did. Is this foolish or wise? The apostles do not impose their authority on others but use it to serve, as Christ did. Is this weakness or genuine power? Finally, whether we call Paul's language sarcasm or not, he is bearing witness to the truth for the sake of the Corinthians according to the direction of the Holy Spirit.

● ● ● ● ● ● ● ● ● ● ● ● ● ● ● ● ● ●

Q 4:10 What does "fools for Christ's sake" mean? How is it that the Christians in Corinth were strong and honored while the apostles were not?

Paul is making this description from the world's perspective. The wisdom of the world teaches a person to sacrifice others in order to protect one's own life and to satisfy one's own desires. Using everyone and everything around you to satisfy the appetites of a failing human nature makes sense to any person who knows only that material nature. Using your whole life and all your resources in the service of others, especially your enemies, can only be foolishness from such a perspective.

Some of the Christians in Corinth may have been strong because God gave them strong bodies and minds. Others may have followed the ways of the world for making oneself strong in order to exercise power over others. Some Christians in Corinth were honored because they honored themselves and dishonored others (1Co 1:10–12, 18–30; 6:1–4; 12:12–26; Gal 6:12–14). Although the apostles were given authority and inspiration to speak and write the Word of God and to authenticate that Word with miracles, they were still men who struggled with the weaknesses of fallen human nature (Gal 4:13–14; 2Co 12:7–10). Besides their own weaknesses, the apostles were perpetually assaulted by enemies of the Gospel and enemies of the truth (Ac 4:1–22; 5:12–41; 7:54–60; 9:15–16; 11:1–3; 12:1–3; 16:16–23). Fallen human nature, the world, and the devil know how to seek power and honor for themselves—that is an essential part of the fall (Nu 16:1–49; 1Ki 21:1–16; Jude 6; Rv 11:9–10; 13:11–17; 18:9–19).

● ● ● ● ● ● ● ● ● ● ● ● ● ● ● ● ● ●

Q 4:12 What physical labor did Paul have to do?

As part of their training, rabbis were taught a trade so that they could support themselves if and when necessary. Paul was a tent maker (Ac 18:1–3).

● ● ● ● ● ● ● ● ● ● ● ● ● ● ● ● ● ●

Q 4:15 Wouldn't God become their Father through the Gospel?

God is the Creator of all things and Father of us all. Nevertheless, since God created the first living creatures on the fifth day, He has perpetuated His creative work through the living creatures already made (Gn 1:21–28). Jesus taught that we should call no one "Father" except God, yet we still refer to our "biological" father by this name (Mt 23:9). Paul makes clear by the phrase "in Christ" that his role as a spiritual father is only as an instrument or means by which God regenerates people to be His own children in the faith. God has provided civil and spiritual authorities to guard the lives of children on behalf of and in cooperation with parents (Rm 13:1–7; Eph 4:11–15).

Q **4:16 Many times Paul encourages the church of Corinth to be just like him. Shouldn't he be pointing to Christ instead of to himself?**

Like Paul's use of "father" language, here again he is referring to himself as an agent of Christ or the means by which Christ conveys Himself to people (1Co 3:5–7). Remember, these Christians did not have a Bible nor had they known Jesus. The only way they can know how to follow Christ is by listening to the Word of Christ from Paul and by following his example.

Q **4:17 Was Timothy Paul's actual son?**

Timothy's father was a Greek, so it could not have been Paul (Ac 16:1–3). Paul gives the impression that he never married or had children when he speaks to that subject later in this letter (1Co 7:1–7, 32). When Paul refers to Timothy as his child, notice how Paul clarifies what he means by saying "in the Lord." Paul became a father to Timothy as he raised him in the "discipline

Why do people seem to ignore problems?

and instruction of the Lord" (Eph 6:4). Paul already gave indication of such relationships in v. 15: "For I became your father in Christ Jesus through the Gospel."

Q **5:1–12 How should congregation members handle sin today? Why do people seem to ignore problems?**

If there is a specific sin of which only a few people are aware, those people should follow the directions given by Jesus in Mt 18:15–18. If there is a specific sin such as the one Paul responded to in this chapter, of which everyone is not only aware but also proud, then the members of that congregation need to follow Paul's example here (see Gal 2:11–14; Ti 3:10 for further examples). The pastor and/or leaders of such a congregation should call the congregation together and publicly seek confession and repentance from the guilty person(s). If confession and repentance are forthcoming, then absolution is declared, and the matter is resolved (2Co 2:6–11). If the person is impenitent, then the pastor or leaders need to make clear that such a person is excommunicated from the congregation until he or she does repent. Explanation needs to be made to make sure everyone present understands that a person who refuses the Word that would work repentance and insists on leading a life contrary to the Word has no part in the Body of Christ and is in danger of being lost eternally (Mt 12:31–32; Rm 1:18–32). Such people (and the congregation) also need to know that we excommunicate only as a last resort and that we continue to pray for and remain eager to respond to their change of heart (Lk 15:12–24). Clarity regarding the goal of reconciliation is as important as clarity regarding the purpose of excommunication: love for the eternal soul of one of us who is lost.

● ● ● ● ● ● ● ● ● ● ● ● ● ● ● ● ● ● ● ●

Q **5:1 Why does Paul wait until ch. 5 to address these problems, especially since he said in ch. 1 that he always thanked God for the Corinthians and their faith?**

Like Genesis in the Old Testament and Matthew in the New Testament, the Bible usually begins with the good news before turning to the bad. Even Paul's Letter to the Galatians begins with encouraging language (Gal 1:1–5). It is essential that we never forget the context of grace, love, and redemption accomplished in Christ, which is the foundation from which we seek to redeem people (2Co 5:14–21). Paul begins the First Letter to the Corinthians by dealing with a problem that affects most, if not all, the people there. After addressing the more general and underlying problems at Corinth, Paul responds to more particular problems.

● ● ● ● ● ● ● ● ● ● ● ● ● ● ● ● ● ● ● ●

Q **5:2 Why were the Corinthians proud of immorality?**

Why are human beings proud at all? The truth about our absolute dependence on God and our constant failures because of our fallen human nature argue that we should be, at all times, humble (Rm 5:6–11; 1Co 4:7; consider taking time to look at all the passages in which Paul uses the word *boast*). What we lost in the fall is what makes our fallen human nature boast. In the fall, we lost communion with God and clarity about His image in which we were made. Apart from God, fallen human nature is left to and determined to create its own image and support that with its own works—but these are misguided and pathetic. Pride is the vain attempt to convince ourselves and others that we are worthy of life and all that we selfishly want for our own life. Pride may also serve as a disguise for shame that follows self-indulgence.

Our fallen human nature has many selfish, self-destructive appetites; sexual gratification is one of them. The Corinthians boasted about the sexual immorality of their members because it made them sound more progressive than others and because by accepting one form of immorality they were justifying all forms, including the forms of which any one of them might be guilty. Approving of immoral behavior is also so much easier than trying to do something constructive about it. Physicians would have a very easy life if they just declared all forms of sickness and injury to be perfectly natural and therefore healthy, but we would know better. In the clear light of truth, the Corinthian pride in immorality is exposed as shameful carelessness toward those who have fallen into such immorality and the damnable practice of setting a stumbling block of temptation in front of the weak (Mt 18:6–9). Competing for what is supposed to be a progressive image, pride, self-righteousness, self-indulgence, carelessness, and laziness are all reasons for being proud of what should make us ashamed and repentant.

• • • • • • • • • • • • • • • • • • • •

Q **5:3 Why did Paul give himself the ability to pass judgment and to be placed on the same level of importance as Jesus?**

One part of this answer has to do with the authority of an apostle. Jesus said to those He sent: "The one who hears you hears Me, and the one who rejects you rejects Me" (Lk 10:16). Paul echoed this statement of Jesus when he wrote: "When you received the word of God, which you heard from us, you accepted it not as the word of men but as what it really is, the word of God, which is at work in you believers" (1 Th 2:13). Paul is not acting independently, nor is he free to do as he sees fit (Lv 19:17; Ezk 33:1–9; Lk 15:4–10; 2 Tm 4:1–5). Paul is not speaking of himself or for himself; Paul is acting on behalf of God, with full authority. A second part of the answer has to do with the language of judgment (see notes on Mt 7:1).

In this case, when Paul says that he has "already pronounced judgment," he does not mean eternal condemnation. Paul means that he has already concluded or made a determination about the case and what must be done. Paul did not follow the process outlined in Mt 18:15–18 because this was not a private sin. There was no question about the reality of the sin because everyone knew about it, and not only did they know, but they also were boasting about it. The sexual immorality, and the indulgence of the flesh that produces it, was threatening to infect the Corinthians like an epidemic. The only way to prevent an epidemic and save the life of those primarily infected is to isolate them and to treat them with the most powerful means available. You can see that Paul does not have eternal condemnation in mind because he expresses his purpose for the man who had his father's wife: "that his spirit may be saved in the day of the Lord" (v. 5). A third part of this answer has to do with the assembled congregation. Because everyone in the congregation knew about this sexual immorality and many boasted about it, everyone would be affected by what happens next. If nothing happened or if a response were slow or indefinite, more— maybe all—people would have been encouraged to give in to their own temptations and desires of the flesh. Everyone needed to see the intense danger and inherent destructiveness of this immorality in order to be protected from falling because of it. Please refer to other questions related to this passage for further explanation.

Q 5:4 Does this verse relate to birth or Baptism?

The "name of the Lord Jesus" refers to the Word of God that makes known to us God's nature and will. Paul is instructing the Corinthians that they should assemble as a group, and then, according to the Word of God and in the Spirit of God that the Word conveys, they should excommunicate this man (Mt 18:18–20; Jn 6:63).

Q 5:4–5 By delivering someone over to Satan, are we judging ourselves as superior?

Paul is instructing the Corinthians to care for their own spiritual life and for that of the man in question. Regarding judgment, please see 5:3 above.

Q 5:5 How can a man be delivered to Satan but then saved on the day of the Lord? Does this mean that you shouldn't keep trying to save the life of an unrepentant sinner?

Notice the distinction Paul makes between the man's "flesh" and his "spirit." The man who had his father's wife was not just guilty of sexual immorality. He was sinning with no repentance, and the congregation was carried along with him, boasting about this practice. The problem was serious and widespread, making it necessary to respond immediately and with everyone present. Delivering this man "to Satan for the destruction of the flesh" is referring to excommunication (Ex 30:33; 31:14; Nu 5:2–3; 15:30–31; Mt 18:17–18). An impenitent person reveals by his impenitence that he is already bound in his sin (Rm 6:16). The congregation, by publicly excommunicating such a man, is not making something happen that was not already the case; rather, it is making the case evident. If the Word had not been effective in bringing the man to realize his rebellion, then action was required. The public excommunication of the man was also necessary for the congregation itself, since their acceptance of and boasting about this sexual immorality required as firm and clear a condemnation as the man received.

Within the Body of Christ, through a life in the Word, we are protected from the ways and assaults of the devil (Mt 12:43–45; Lk 23:31–32; Eph 6:11; Rv 12:7–11). Yet a person may reject the Word of the Lord though still pretend to be part of the Body of Christ—deceiving himself with hypocrisy and threatening to infect others with the same deadly impenitence and hypocrisy (Jn 12:4–6; 13:2; Ac 5:1–11; Rm 1:18–32). Outside the Word of God and the Christian community there is nothing for a person but the devil and all his works and all his ways. Excommunication makes a person's impenitence and spiritual desperation evident and unmistakable, while there is yet time for the person to come to his senses and repent (Ezk 18:19–32; Lk 15:11–24).

Paul ends this verse with a clear articulation of the goal of excommunication: "that his spirit may be saved in the day of the Lord" (v. 5). This man must have been rejecting the Word of the Lord since he continued to be active in the congregation while he continued to practice sexual immorality contrary to the Word, his own life, and the lives of others. The only way left to turn him from this path of destruction was to make the reality of this sin perfectly clear. If a person does not like or is terrified by excommunication from the Christian congregation in this life, he would certainly not want to experience excommunication from God for all eternity. The experience of such a human nature under the Law has the power to put that human nature to death so that the Word and Spirit of God once again have opportunity to regenerate and revive the man's soul, which is exactly what happened (2Co 2:6–11).

We never give up on a person until he or she has passed away and is thus beyond our care. We never stop seeking the salvation and redemption of a person, no matter what. However, a person's relationship to the Word affects how we relate to the individual: we embrace those who receive the Word; we bear witness to the absence of communion when a person is opposed to and despises the Word. We are the same as physicians and surgeons who must protect the community from those who could infect others with their disease. We seek to protect the one who is ill from himself by distinguishing between healthy and diseased tissue and by separating the one from the other (Mt 9:12–13; 18:7–9; Rm 6:1–14; Gal 5:24; 6:14). Love does not indulge the impenitence of another person nor one's own. Love seeks truth at all times and to impress the truth upon others, for truth is the only way to know the grace of God and our immense need for and dependence upon it (Lv 19:17).

● ●

Q 5:6–8 Why does Paul use this analogy, and what does it mean?

There are two features of yeast to which Paul is comparing the Corinthians. First, boasting is like the result of yeast on bread: puffed up and hollow. Second, yeast works its way through all the dough so that no part of it escapes the effects. The pride of people that gives rise to boasting and competitiveness is like yeast: it produces people who are hollow, and it affects (or should I say "infects") everyone in the congregation (Jude 12–13; Gal 2:13).

Paul uses the analogy of bread because it is accurate. Analogies work, like parables, because God created the material world as one of two witnesses to the truth (Ps 19; Rm 1:18–21). Unleavened bread is like the faithful, honest Christian: all of the same substance all the way through. The word *integrity* refers to this (Pr 10:9; Ti 2:7). Leavened bread, like those who boast, looks large and solid but is really empty and hollow (Mt 23:27–28).

Q 5:9–11 How can we tell who should really leave the Church?

Only those who remain in the Word and are thus kept in repentance and regenerated by the Spirit—only these are truly members of the Body of Christ. If this communion of people is what we are talking about, then the person who is and lives contrary to this would be put out (1Jn 2:19). If some members of the Christian community found themselves in a place with people who claimed to be the Body of Christ but clearly were not, then the faithful would depart (Nu 16:23–35; Rm 16:16–17).

Q 5:9 Isn't there a positive way to associate with sexually immoral people rather than not associating with them at all? Couldn't we show them a better way to live?

The Lord has commanded us to be a good example and show the world a better way (Mt 5:13–16; 1Co 12:31; 1Pt 3:15; 1Jn 1:7). Paul explains in v. 10 that excommunication does not apply to people of the world who make no claims of being Christian or a part of our Christian union. You can't excommunicate someone with whom you have yet to be united. Paul's counsel, like that in the rest of the Bible, has to do with truth, honesty, and integrity (Nu 16:23–35; Pr 1:10–19; Eph 5:11). If someone claims to be a member of the Body of Christ while consciously and consistently contradicting

what it means to be Christian, such a person is living a lie and covering the Christian community with the disgrace of his or her own wickedness (Ezk 36:22; Rm 17–24). People who have yet to know the truth and grace of God need us to share it with them. People who have known the truth and grace of God but now despise it need us to show them the consequences of doing so before it is too late (Heb 4:1–7; 6:1–9).

Q 5:10–12 Why can't a person continue to talk to those who are immoral?

You can talk with anyone at any time who does not claim to be a Christian; this is our commission as disciples of Christ (2Co 5:19–21). The Bible forbids us to have anything to do with those who have known the grace and truth of God yet now deny and contradict that with a conscious and deliberately wicked life (Ex 32:25–27; Mt 18:15–18; Gal 2:11–14). There are two reasons for such complete disassociation. First, disassociation or excommunication is necessary to keep the rest of the Body of Christ from being overcome by temptation or confusion, as if Christians were somehow free to engage in whatever wicked behavior they choose (Gal 5:1, 13). Second, since an impenitent person has rejected God, it is essential that such a person realize the consequences of such rejection while there is still time to repent (Heb 4:1–12). If those in the world who represent God continue to interact with one who is impenitent, how will that person ever come to his senses and turn back from the way that leads to everlasting isolation (Lk 15:14–19; 16:19–31)? See 5:9 above for more on this question.

· ·

Q 5:10 What are considered sexual sins?

Sexual sins have to do with the reproductive systems of the body, in contrast to abuses that affect other parts of our nature, such as the nervous system (drug and alcohol abuse). Sexual sins include any thought, word, or activity that is contrary to God's intent and design for all people, male and female. Our bodies are created to be the temple of the Holy Spirit, honored, respected, and protected from abuse (1Co 3:16–17; 6:19–20). Our bodies were designed to serve God's creative activity in bringing new life into the world and then caring for those new lives (Gn 1:28; Mal 2:13–16). Whether we are single or married, bearing children or not, any human activity that is not oriented toward the care of human life is mistaken and detrimental.

· ·

Q 5:11 Doesn't Jesus tell us to love our enemy and not to turn our backs on anyone? Why, then, does this verse tell us not to associate with sexually immoral people?

First, we need to distinguish between love and indulgence (Rm 13:8–14). Love's first choice is always to speak and act in positive ways toward the object of that love, especially when the object of love is one who would be our enemy (Mt 23:37). When such positive expression of love is rejected or abused, the only other means of loving that same person is to make clear the consequences of despising love (Ps 78:34; Ezk 16; 1Co 4:21). Christian love and sacrifice for the good of another could only be misunderstood as opposition by fallen human natures, determined to rebel against God to their own destruction (Ezk 33:12–20; Jnh 3:4–4:11). We are just as loving when we block the way of the wicked as when we take the penitent by the hand to raise him up and lead him toward life.

Second, we need to distinguish between the temporal body and the eternal soul (Gal 5:16–26). What kind of love sacrifices the eternal, spiritual essence of a person in order to indulge the passing and destructive appetites of the flesh? We care for soul and body, yet we recognize that our human nature is fallen and disoriented. What our fallen flesh wants is bad for body and soul, ours and those we affect. What is good for the soul is good for the body also, ours and everyone else's. Abstinence from sexual activity outside of marriage is good for everyone, and there are no negative effects. Seeking to gratify the sexual appetite of fallen human nature disallows the very experience that appetite seeks while working against the well-being of everyone affected.

Third, we need to distinguish between those who claim to be Christian and those people of the world who make no such claims. We have no expectations of people who make no claims about being Christian. We expect fallen human nature to prevail in the absence of the Word. There is no dishonesty about a person who does not pretend to be anything he or she is not. However, Christ is the truth, and no lie has any part in Him. There is no life in lies because life and truth are inseparable. A person who claims to belong to Christ but who contradicts both truth and life in his ways is lying to God, deceiving himself, and undermining the effectiveness that the genuine Body of Christ would have in the world (1Jn 1:6–10).

Fourth, we need to distinguish between the penitent and the impenitent (Lk 10:38–42; 15:11–32; 18:9–116). We are all sinners and will be until God, through death, delivers us from this body of sin. The issue is our disposition toward sin. A life in the Word produces repentance in the body and a regenerate soul that is oriented and inspired toward God. In the absence of the Word, there is only our fallen human nature doing as it will.

Putting this all together, we are determined to love others with the real and everlasting love of God. Real and everlasting love always does what is best and eternal for the whole person, especially for the soul, because the good of the body will always follow. We have everything to do with those who are penitent because repentance keeps us turned toward God and keeps us clinging firmly to His Word and grace. We seek to draw those who are impenitent into repentance and communion with Christ. For those who have never been and do not

claim to know Christ, we do this at all times by an active witness in word and deed (Mt 9:9–17). For those who claim to be in communion with us but who contradict that claim with their life, we seek to bring them back into communion by making the peril of their hypocrisy clear as powerfully and as quickly as possible (Jas 5:19–20).

● ●

Q 5:12 Is Paul saying it's okay to judge those inside the Church?

Jesus forbids us to judge others (Mt 7:1). Yet Jesus commands us to pursue a person who is erring (Mt 18:15–18). The problem is not a matter of contradiction or inconsistency but of understanding the semantic domain of words. When Jesus forbids us to judge, He means judge in the sense of condemn. We are not allowed to condemn because it is not our place, nor can we possibly know who is condemned in the end. When Jesus tells us to pursue an erring brother, He means we are to judge them as a physician who makes a diagnosis and applies treatment (Mt 9:12–13). In this passage, Paul is explaining that it is not our place to judge (in terms of drawing conclusions about) people who are outside the church. To those outside the church we maintain the best possible witness in word and deed, waiting for the Lord to work in them to seek that witness. But for those inside the church, like members of the body, we have a special responsibility to warn when they are erring (Lv 19:17; Mt 18:15–18; Gal 2:11–14). Our diagnoses or judgments are always in the interest of preventing a person from being in danger of the condemnation of God (2Co 5:14–20).

• • • • • • • • • • • • • • • • • • • •

Q **5:13 Should we purge someone from the congregation forever?**

The Christian community puts the person out of their assembly—and has nothing to do with him at any other time—in order to be honest about the breach his impenitence and hypocrisy has already made. To contradict God's Word and will with impenitence while continuing to live in the Christian community is a lie. If the lie goes unexposed, people will begin to accept it as if it were the truth. Putting the impenitent person out makes the truth evident for everyone's benefit. Such a person is put out, as Paul said, in the interest of bringing him back in again, penitent, honest, and faithful.

• • • • • • • • • • • • • • • • • • • •

Q **6:1–8 What if a fellow Christian breaks into your house and you catch him? He is very sorry and says that he is going to change his life. Do you have a responsibility to report this case to the state or civil authorities, or is this just between you and him? What does this passage say about lawsuits?**

Reporting a crime is not like suing someone. Suing someone is completely voluntary, though you may be suing someone in order to prevent others from suffering harm. Certain crimes require you to report them and to turn in the guilty party,

no matter what. Christians are bound to obey such laws for the sake of everyone's well-being, even the well-being of the guilty party (Rm 13:1–8). Being guilty yet avoiding justice is no way to live (Mt 5:23–26; Phm 8–14). Pressing charges for a crime such as the one described in this question is up to the property owner. It is not against the law for you not to report the case, nor is it necessarily against the Bible for you to turn the fellow Christian in to the authorities. You would have to decide which is better for the guilty person, for his future, and for people in his future. If he is genuinely penitent and remains in the Word, he could be of great service to others, like Saul after the Lord converted him (Ac 9:13–15; Eph 4:28). If he is pretending penitence, the justice system may be the very best thing for him (Gal 3:24).

Since nonbelievers do not submit to the Word or the intervention of the Church, God has established civil authorities to serve and protect justice (Rm 13:1–7). In this passage, Paul is talking about "brother suing brother." This means that people who professed and practiced the same Christian faith were suing each other. How could this be wanted or necessary if both were, indeed, Christians? Christians conduct themselves in love and have a process for loving one who is in error without going to the courts (Mt 18:15–18). If we are dealing with people and matters outside the faith, we use the civil systems provided. If we are dealing with people and matters inside the Christian communion, then we use the means God has given us in the faith.

Q **6:1–4 Is this whole passage mocking the judicial system? Should we not have judges?**

This whole passage is not mocking the judicial system at all, though Paul does raise a good question about that system. How just will a system be that consists of fallen human beings? Nevertheless, the civil government is established by God for the good of all, and faithful people might well choose to serve God and love their neighbor by serving in the government. In this passage, Paul is exposing and rebuking one of many instances of hypocrisy in the Corinthian congregation. They claim to be the very best of Christians, even claiming this against one another, yet they are so selfish and materialistic as to sue one another in civil courts. If Christ has set us free of selfish and material concerns, why would we sue another person, especially another Christian (Mt 5:38–48; Php 3:7–14)? If we are selfish and materialistic even though we believe, why would anyone else be attracted to or impressed by this faith (Rm 2:21–24)? The world outside the Christian communion needs government to keep order and protect the helpless. The Christian communion does well to serve the public interest and to show the public that there is still a better way (1Co 12:31–13:13; Lk 3:12–14).

Are people born homosexual?

Q **6:2–3 In this verse, who are "the saints," and why will they be the ones who judge the world? How will humans judge angels?**

"The saints" are believers. We are called saints because God has set us apart and declared us to be innocent because of the vicarious atonement of Christ (1Co 1:2; Rm 8:29–30; 1Jn 3:9). You are correct about judgment, which belongs to God. However, Paul says we will also be judges by virtue of our union with Christ and association with Him (Jn 5:22; Ac 10:42; 1Co 2:15; Rv 7:15; 20:4; Mt 19:28). The judgment itself will not be a matter of argument or decision-making but only of confirming the condemnation that the wicked have already brought upon themselves (Jn 3:18–20; Rm 1:18–32).

Q **6:6 How can we make that judgment on one who is and is not a believer since many will claim to be of one belief?**

Truth or lies about a person's faith are soon made evident in the process of reconciliation provided by Jesus (Mt 5:23–25; 18:15–18). One claiming to be a believer would have to submit to the ministry of the church rather than sue in the civil courts. If this person refused to pursue reconciliation according to Mt 18 and 1Co 6, then he would prove himself to be an unbeliever, in which case the believer being sued could either choose to accept the wrong or to seek the protection of the civil legal system.

Q 6:9–10 Is homosexuality part of our evil human nature? Are people born homosexual?

There likely will never be a conclusion to the debate about whether homosexuality is genetic in origin or a choice, even though reliable research demonstrates that homosexuality is not genetic. (Please see Robert Gagnon, *The Bible and Homosexual Practice: Texts and Hermeneutics* [Nashville: Abingdon, 2001].) However, we may recognize both arguments as being accurate. On the one hand, all people are conceived with a fallen human nature, inherently wicked and opposed to God—so homosexuality, like alcoholism, adultery, and hatred, is a genetic defect in us (Mk 7:20–23; Gal 5:19–21). On the other hand, fallen human nature, bound in sin, is always making choices that are contrary to God and our own life (Rm 5:6–11; 7:13–21). As long as we are in this fallen human nature, we will struggle against its disposition and inclinations and often fail (Rm 7:24–25). Yet the Word of God generates in us a new spirit and regenerate soul (Jn 1:12–13; 3:1–7; 1Jn 3:9). This new person, the essence of who we are, is oriented and inspired to live as God intended us to live, in real love and faith and eternally. It is neither sinful acts nor sin itself but our disposition toward our sin that is the key. A person who consciously and willfully continues to contradict God's design for life will inevitably die; all human nature does (Rm 1:18–32). But a person who has a regenerate soul struggles against the flesh in order to realize the life that God has provided and promised through Christ (Php 3:7–14). Remembering and distinguishing between our two natures and remembering how the Law helps us restrain the flesh while the Gospel empowers the soul is the means of constructively dealing with not only homosexuals but also every human being and the wickedness with which he or she struggles.

Q 6:12 What does the verse mean by "all things are lawful"?

Why would a person want to do anything that would bring him into bondage or be unhelpful? Since Christ has redeemed us from the curse of the Law, the Law no longer has the power to condemn us (Gal 3:13; Rm 7:6; Rv 12:10). In the New Testament, we no longer do or refrain from doing anything because the Law threatens us or to get something we lack. All things are ours in Christ, and because we are regenerated in His image, we are oriented and inspired to be like Him (1Jn 4:9). The question on our minds is how to be helpful and how to protect the liberty Christ has given us from the bondage of sin, death, and the devil (Gal 5:1, 13). Love motivates us to seek always the best for others because Christ has already given us the best of all things in this world and the next (Php 3:7–14).

Is all sin equal?

Q 6:13 What does "food is meant for the stomach and the stomach for food" mean?

Paul says this as part of his argument about how Christians should live. This phrase refers to the witness that God's design in creation makes. God created a material world as a witness to the nonmaterial or spiritual realities that are the essence of life (Jn 6:63; Ps 19:1–3; Rm 1:20). When we conduct ourselves and live our lives according to the "laws of nature" or according to God's intent and design, all is well. Food was created for our stomachs and our stomachs for that food. A healthy diet helps keep our stomach healthy, and a healthy stomach processes food for the good of our life. Our whole body, as Paul goes on to say, was made to serve God and others, not to indulge its own selfish lusts that resulted from the fall (Rm 6:21). When we deny our lust for selfish gratification of the flesh and instead engage our bodies in the service of others, then we realize the experiences we long for and crave without knowing how to fulfill.

Q 6:18 Is all sin equal? This makes it seem as though sexual immorality is the worst.

All sin is equal, or not, depending on the sin we are discussing. First, there is a difference between acts of sin and the sin against the Holy Spirit (Mt 12:31–32; Heb 6:4–8; 10:26–31; 11:6; 1Jn 5:16–17). Refusing the grace that the Holy Spirit communicates leaves a person condemned in his sins (Jn 3:18–20). Second, whoever keeps the whole Law but fails in one point is guilty of all of it (Jas 2:10). This means that there really is no such thing as a person who commits only one sin or one kind of sin. Fallen human nature sins in all that it thinks, does, and says (Is 64:6; Mk 7:20–23; Rm 5:6–11; Eph 2:1–4). Third, there is a difference among sins when considering the victim. Jesus said that hating a person is the same as murder, but any person would rather be hated than dead (Mt 5:21–22). Jesus said lust is the same as adultery; true for the one lusting, but not the same for those who would be hurt by adultery once committed (Mt 5:27–28; Mk 10:11–12). Finally, sexual immorality does have a peculiar feature to it in the way it affects our human nature, though other sins have their destructive effects as well (Rm 1:18–32; 1Th 4:1–8).

Q 6:19 How does this verse apply to piercing or other body art? How can we honor God with our bodies?

Let's begin by referring back to 6:12 where Paul explains that all things are lawful but not all things are helpful. What is helpful about tattoos or body piercings? Second, what is wrong with or lacking in the image of God in which we are created? We are the climax of God's creative work. We might spend our lifetime discovering what that means by loving others as God, in Christ, has loved us. Third, if a person is looking for an image that has substance beneath it and markings that are significant, why not seek the kind Jesus and Paul received (Lk 24:29; Jn 20:24–27; Gal 6:17)? More often than not, the marks of serving others do not come from nails or whips but from the stresses and emotional pain of helping others with their troubles. However, enduring hardship for the sake of others provides fulfillment that has little interest in markings that are only symbolic or the vanity of creating an image for oneself. Finally, a Christian might consider the stewardship of spending money for something that provides so little benefit for so few. Surely the financial support of missions and of those who are genuinely in need would be a better use of money and bring more lasting and significant fulfillment to the giver (Ac 4:32–37).

Q 6:20 What does it mean that we were "bought with a price"?

Paul is referring to the cost of redeeming us, which Jesus paid with His own life (Mt 13:44; 2Pt 2:1). The whole Old Testament points to and describes this redemption. Peter gives a summary of our redemption in Ac 2:22–36. Notice that Paul repeats this phrase in 1Co 7:23. The cost of liberating us spiritually is indicated by the cost of liberating people physically. Well more than 100,000 men died in the U. S. Civil War while fighting for the freedom of those enslaved. More than one million men died in

World War II to keep the world free from the tyranny of German and Japanese dictators. Christ suffered under the Law, suffered an eternity of punishment for all people of all time, in order to free us from condemnation under the Law. This is what Paul means by "bought at a price."

Q 7:1–5 Is Paul saying not to marry? Did any of the disciples marry?

Paul is not saying anything different than Jesus did when His disciples asked if it was better for a man not to marry (Mt 19:10–12). Marriage is God's creation, evident from the very beginning (Gn 1:26–28; 2:4–25). The New Testament continues to honor and revere God's design and intent for marriage (Mt 19:1–6; Eph 5:21–33; Heb 13:4; 1Pt 3:1–7). At the same time, the New Testament recognizes the threats and trouble that the devil, world, and our fallen human nature pose for marriages. Jesus and Paul both remind us that not everyone is able to remain unmarried and sexually pure (Mt 19:11–12; 1Co 7:2). Those who marry will face the challenges of keeping this union between two people with fallen human natures. In time children may add another challenge to this relationship (though in my experience raising children helps unite a couple). Paul is warning that the continual disintegration of the world and its growing antagonism toward Christ and Christianity will make marriage and child-rearing even more difficult (1Co 7:29–31, 35). Think of the situation as a country under attack.

What was it like in France or England during World War II for people who were considering marriage? It's not that anyone thought less of marriage, but the impending threat and need for defense was a force that oriented many people's thinking away from personal relationships and toward the mission at hand.

Paul indicates that all the other apostles, except Barnabas, were married (1 Co 9:5).

● ● ● ● ● ● ● ● ● ● ● ● ● ● ● ● ● ●

Q **7:1 I have seen Paul's words translated as "It is good for a man not to marry" and also "not to touch a woman." Which is correct?**

I have seen three translations of this verse: (1) "not to marry," (2) "not to have sex," and (3) "not to touch a woman." The Greek is very simple and clear: "It is good for a man not to touch a woman." I suspect that translators abandon the simple language of the text because they think it is unreasonable. Apparently some think that men will inevitably touch women and have sex with them, but they could avoid marriage. Others think that men will touch women but might still avoid sex. Paul knew something that has always been true and is still abundantly evident today: there is a powerful dynamic at work when men and women are in physical contact with each other. Paul explains that it is good for a man not to touch a woman because refraining from this prevents the conception of a relationship that may later be regretted.

● ● ● ● ● ● ● ● ● ● ● ● ● ● ● ● ● ●

Q **7:2 Why did God make Eve?**

God made Eve to complete the creation of human beings in His image. There is a relationship of persons within the one true God. The relationship between Adam and Eve parallels the relationship between the Father and the Son and between Christ and man (1Co 11:3). It was not good for Adam to be alone because he had no one for whom to lay down his life and no way to bring other people into the world for whom he also might lay down his life (Gn 2:18). The woman helps the man by "remaining before him," the object of his love and purpose in life. The woman helps the man by her essential role in God's creation of the rest of humankind. As children we learn what it is to be loved by God. As parents we learn what it is to love like God and the joy, purpose, and fulfillment of the relationship love produces.

● ● ● ● ● ● ● ● ● ● ● ● ● ● ● ● ● ●

Q **7:2 It appears as though we are to have one spouse because sexual immorality makes it unsafe otherwise. How, then, could God have instituted marriage, saying the two flesh will become one? How were the Mormons able to twist this to advocate and practice polygamy?**

Everything in creation was affected by the rebellion of Adam (Rm 8:19–22). Fallen human nature is selfish and seeks relationships with others for selfish purposes. But we were created to be selfless, like God, which means selfish activity is always harmful to others and self-defeating for the selfish person. Paul is not saying that marriage makes selfish, self-indulgent sexual pursuits acceptable or good. Paul is saying that human beings still bear the design of God that we should be in union as man and wife and bear children. If a particular person remains affected by the desire for union, he or she can channel that desire into a healthy and productive marriage. The care of a spouse and children is what makes the physical attraction and union selfless and meaningful rather than selfish and meaningless.

Fallen human nature has also produced a world in which lust makes men seek to indulge themselves with more than one woman and to leave other women abandoned. Polygamy, though contrary to God's intent for one man to be in union with one woman, maintains God's intent that women should be provided for and protected by men. There are positive and negative examples of polygamy in the Old Testament, depending on the motives of the man involved (1Sm 25:1–42; 2Sm 12:7–9). It is possible for a man to care for more than one woman, though it is impossible for a woman to be submissive to the care and providence of more than one man (Mt 6:24; Eph 5:22). This is why there are no examples in the Bible of a woman having more than one husband at the same time. It is possible that the Mormons or any particular Mormon has good intentions when taking more than one wife. It is also possible that a particular man, Mormon or otherwise, is indulging his lust

in the taking of many wives. We might do well to consider the differences and similarities between polygamy and promiscuity. Which man is worse, the man who binds himself publicly in marriage to more than one wife, or the man who takes responsibility for no woman but indulges his lust with many?

. . . .

Q 7:3 What are "conjugal rights"? And how does one harness it?

"Conjugal rights" refers to the part of the marriage union where both husband and wife consent to intercourse as an expression of love and in the interest of bearing children. You will note as Paul's discussion continues that some people thought converting to Christianity required celibacy (v. 5). "Harnessing" any of the passions of fallen human nature depends on a force more powerful than those passions. Some people find such power in a cause outside of themselves, such as work, public service, or missionary activities. Christians find self-control as one of the fruits of the Spirit, which depends on our connection with the Word (Gal 5:22–23; Ezk 36:26–27).

. . . .

Q 7:4 What does it mean that the husband has "authority over" his wife's body and vice versa?

Paul already reminded us that we are not our own (1Co 6:19; Rm 14:7–8). The relationship between husband and wife that flows from the image of God cannot make sense apart from love. A husband and wife who are determined to be autonomous have no union. A husband or wife who is determined to control the other is a tyrant and not a spouse. If such a man demands that his wife submit to his desire for sexual gratification, he may find a wife who demands that he keep himself away from her (note how finding fault works the same way, Mt 7:3–5). Only the husband who loves his wife willingly grants her authority over his body so that it will genuinely serve her well-being; and only the wife who submits to such a husband has no fear of submitting her body to the authority of her husband, since his only desire is to love her genuinely.

· · · · · · · · · · · · · · · · · · · ·

Q 7:5 Does this mean not to deprive your spouse of sex unless the feeling is mutual?

Yes, though we should understand that a mutual feeling is determined within the counsel of God and by the activity of His Spirit. In this case Paul is speaking to Christians who believed that Christianity is opposed to physical intimacy between husband and wife. Paul may also be addressing Christians who intended to adopt celibacy as a means of advancing their spiritual life. While the New Testament does teach us to deny the desires of the flesh, faith comes by the presence of the Word rather than the absence of physical activities (Mt 10:38; Jn 6:63; Rm 6:1–14). In fact, it is the regenerate soul enlivened by the Word and Spirit that seeks to employ the body always more completely

and consistently in service to the Lord and to others (1Co 9:23–27; Php 3:7–14). Every natural human activity is undermined and ruined by selfishness. Every natural human activity is realized as God intended when we engage it for the benefit of others.

· · · · · · · · · · · · · · · · · · · ·

Q 7:6 What does "as a concession, not a command" mean exactly?

Fallen human nature has a way of turning gifts into obligations and promises into laws (Mt 9:14–17; 12:1–8; Ac 5:4). Paul was especially sensitive to the danger of imposing law where God had not, since the Law always condemns us (Gal 2:18–21; Rm 14:13–19). Paul remembered how critical it was that he distinguish godly counsel regarding best practices from commandments that remain binding on all people at all times. Paul's acute sense of urgency for the Christian mission made him wish that everyone would abandon every concern of their life except that which would advance the grace of God into the world (Php 3:7–14). I don't command students to attend class, and neither do I forbid them from missing; this is a concession, not a command, because my wish is that all students were as devoted to the course of study as I am—but that devotion cannot be commanded, it can only be inspired.

· · · · · · · · · · · · · · · · · · · ·

Q 7:7 Why does Paul wish all men were single?

Paul is referring not only to being single

but more importantly to the gift of celibacy. Paul's own conversion and subsequent appreciation for the grace of God made him practically desperate to convey that grace of God to the rest of the world. Freedom from the natural attraction to women, interest in marriage, and concern for a family made it possible for Paul to advance the Gospel in ways and places that the responsibilities of a family man would prohibit (Ac 16:18–24; 19:23–30; 21:18–36; 1Co 7:26–31).

● ●

Q 7:8 Why does it say it is good for the unmarried and the widows to remain unmarried? Why can't priests marry?

Paul encourages Christians to keep themselves free of any kind of relationship or endeavor that might compete for the Christian's focus on bringing the Gospel to the nations (Php 3:7–14. For more, see 7:7 above). Priests in the Roman Catholic Church are forbidden to marry in order to keep them devoted entirely to the work of the church. However, Jesus and Paul warn about trying to live a celibate life if you have not been granted this ability by God (Mt 19:10–12; 1Co 7:1–2). Both Jesus and Paul warned us to beware of those who impose laws that God has not given, including forbidding marriage (Mt 23:4; 1Tm 4:1–3).

● ●

Q 7:9 Why would God's Word tell us to marry simply to satisfy our sexual desires? Wouldn't that mean that the focus of that unity was only sex?

Everything in creation was affected by the rebellion of Adam (Rm 8:19–22). Fallen human nature is selfish and seeks relationships with others for selfish purposes. But we were created to be selfless, like God, which means selfish activity is always harmful to others and self-defeating for the selfish person. Paul is not saying that marriage makes selfish, self-indulgent sexual pursuits acceptable or good. Paul is saying that human beings still bear the design of God that we should be in union as man and wife and bear children. If a particular person remains affected by the desire for union, he or she can channel that desire into a healthy and productive marriage. The care of a spouse and children is what makes the physical attraction and union selfless and meaningful rather than selfish and meaningless.

Marriage is the union of a man determined to give his life on behalf of the wife and a woman determined to submit to that love so that together they can convey the love of God to others, especially to children if God grants them. Denying lust or passion is different than channeling it. Some of our desires and some of the desire we have is intended by God. Some of our desires and much of the desire we have is the product of living apart from and in rebellion against God, being selfish, and being materialistic. We make a grave mistake when we try to forbid what God has not forbidden or command what He has not commanded (Mt 5:21–44; 23:1–4; 1Tm 4:1–3). Wisdom and truth urge us to distinguish between healthy, natural desire for a relationship and selfishness and self-indulgence. As long as we are in this fallen human nature we will be affected by its wicked orientation. However, relationships according to God's design and intent are still necessary and possible by the power of God's Word and Spirit in our regenerate souls and by the grace of God that inspires us to forgive each other when we fail. When a person seeks relationships to satisfy selfish, carnal passions there is neither love nor relationship nor satisfaction as a result. When a person seeks to love others as God loves us and as God intends us to love one another, then satisfaction follows for oneself and for others, soul and body.

● ● ● ● ● ● ● ● ● ● ● ● ● ● ● ● ● ● ● ●

Q 7:10–11 Paul says if a wife separates from her husband, she is not free to remarry. Does this apply to men also? What if the wife leaves for a legitimate reason? If you cannot divorce, what kind of separation is it?

What Paul says here in no way contradicts what the Bible says elsewhere about divorce. Divorce is permitted in cases of abandonment, abuse, and adultery. Abandonment is not only when one spouse leaves the other but when one spouse forces the other to leave (Mt 19:3–8; 1Co 7:15). Abuse necessitates the departure of the one abused; therefore, it is included with abandonment. Adultery means the union has already been broken, so a divorce is simply the public recognition of the fact (Mt 19:9). In every case reconciliation is preferable. If

both individuals are genuinely penitent and remain in the Word, reconciliation is entirely possible.

You may notice that in vv. 10–11, Paul is speaking about marriages in which both husband and wife are Christian (notice in vv. 12–16 how Paul shifts to speaking about marriages in which one spouse is Christian and the other is not). Paul is here addressing two potential challenges for Christian marriage. On the one hand, there were Christians who thought marriage was somehow unclean or that it somehow defiled one's life as a Christian. Paul is warning Christians that marriage does not undermine their life as a Christian and divorce will not enhance it. On the other hand, there may have been those who claimed that the grace of God and the forgiveness of Christ gave us the liberty to divorce if we chose to; this is not the case either. Even a Christian husband and Christian wife may experience challenges in their relationship that make them feel a need to divorce or at least to separate. Paul makes clear that divorce is not an option for a Christian couple because the essence of Christianity is reconciliation by the power God provides in His Word and Sacraments. If a Christian couple did separate, Paul is willing to permit that, but only for a time, then they must be together again. Paul already addressed one peril of the physical separation of husband and wife in vv. 2–5. While separation may offer a time of reflection that leads to repentance, it may also provide time and opportunity for fallen human nature to gratify itself with the absence of effort in loving the spouse and in the presence of temptations to adultery. For these reasons Paul warns that a separation must not be long in duration. The little word *or* in v. 11 includes the understanding that what has been cannot remain, as follows: "But if she does [separate from her husband], she should remain unmarried or else be reconciled to her husband." Paul addresses the woman's situation first, understanding that a loving husband should not and would not force a wife to stay with him. On the other hand, there is no excuse for a Christian husband to abandon his Christian wife, which is why Paul forbids it.

• • • • • • • • • • • • • • • • • •

Q 7:10 Why is it that the church today seems to turn a blind eye to divorce?

Fallen human nature is determined to satisfy itself and usually wants to appear just in doing so (Mt 23:14; Jn 9:40–41). Since the church consists of people who all have such a human nature, it is no surprise that, over time, increasing numbers of people wanted divorces yet wanted to retain their status in the church. The fallen human nature of pastors and other leaders, often fearing men rather than God, decided to approve (at least with silence) rather than oppose them in love (Lv 19:17; 2Tm 4:1–5). Speaking in general about sin during worship is much more tidy and less taxing than addressing particular errors with particular people. Few pastors require substantive premarital counseling; few do any counseling at all. Only a life in the Word can produce a

person and then an assembly of people who are inspired by the truth and grace of God to pursue life as He intended it (Jn 8:31–32; Rm 10:17; 12:1–3).

• • • • • • • • • • • • • • • • • •

Q 7:11 Why is there no exception made for divorce being okay?

In this place only, Paul is speaking to the marriage of two Christians. If both are, indeed, Christians, then there is no reason, excuse, or need for divorce because both are committed to the grace and truth of God that is powerful to make them loving and faithful. If one or the other is not indeed Christian, this would become evident during the process of reconciliation, in which case the allowances for divorce would apply (see 7:10–11 above for more on this question).

• • • • • • • • • • • • • • • • • •

Q 7:12–16 This passage gives rules for couples that marry when only one is a believer. If the Bible gives us rules, why do some denominations require that both are the same religion?

In these verses, Paul is speaking to couples who were *already* married when one or the other became Christian. Both the Old and New Testament teach that believers should bind themselves in unions to other believers only, including the bond of marriage (Dt 7:3–4; Ps 106:34–41; 1Co 7:39; 2Co 6:14). Becoming a Christian does not mean we forsake relationships in which we find ourselves already, unless those relationships are contrary to the faith and endanger ours. As Christians, we seek to love faithfully and to serve others as God grants us opportunity, all the while protecting the liberty granted by God that allows us to love and serve freely (Gal 5:1, 13).

. . . .

Q 7:12–15 If a wife is committing adultery and only wants to be with the husband for his money, is this cause for a divorce? Should the husband, who is a believer, stick the marriage out?

A wife who is committing adultery has broken the marriage. If she is determined to continue doing so, she proves herself impenitent and unbelieving. The husband would be right to bear witness to these facts publicly by way of divorce, yet he is not bound to. A believing husband may want to seek all means by which he might continue to love his wife and restore her to faithfulness (this is parallel to the situation between God and faithless Israel to which the prophet Hosea spoke). According to the Law, such a husband is free from the bonds of marriage. According to love, such a husband is free to bind himself to hope for and the well-being of his wayward wife.

. . . .

Q 7:12–14 If the two were one, would an unbelieving spouse go to heaven if the other spouse were a believer? Does this mean a nonbeliever can marry a Christian and be saved? How can we be sanctified through someone other than God?

Verses 12 and 13 are perfectly understandable from a Christian viewpoint. Paul is speaking to people who were already married when they became Christians. What sense would it make for a new Christian to divorce his or her spouse only because she or he was not yet a Christian? The challenge of this passage comes in v. 14, which gives the reason: "For the unbelieving husband is sanctified by his wife, and the unbelieving wife is sanctified by her husband." It is doubtful that Paul means an unbeliever will be saved *only* because of his or her marriage with a Christian. The union of a man and a woman in marriage is powerful in many ways, some of which we may be ignorant. God's declaration that the two become one in marriage suggests a level of connectedness in this relationship that is unparalleled in human experience. Such an intimate, singular, and powerful union between two people would doubtlessly provide the most effective of all circumstances by which the unbeliever would be positively affected by the Word and Spirit of God (Eph 5:25–31; 1Pt 3:1–6). To be "sanctified" means to be set apart. By union with a believer, the unbelieving spouse is being drawn along in the Word and will of God that will surely work faith in his or her heart.

● ● ● ● ● ● ● ● ● ● ● ● ● ● ● ● ● ● ●

Q **7:12 Paul has in parenthesis "I, not the Lord." Is this saying that the rest of ch. 7 is Paul's suggestions, or is it also God's?**

All of the Bible is God's Word, including what Paul has written (Mk 16:15–20; 1 Th 2:13). Paul is making clear that the Lord Jesus, during His ministry, never articulated what Paul was about to say—you won't find these words in the Gospels. Nevertheless, the Lord was speaking through Paul, and what Paul says here is consistent with the rest of the Bible.

● ● ● ● ● ● ● ● ● ● ● ● ● ● ● ● ● ● ●

Q **7:14 Does God always encourage marriage, or is it a product of our flesh? Does God accept children of unchristian parents?**

Marriage is God's creation and institution; therefore, He would always encourage it when and where it is pursued according to His will and design. Flesh is also God's creation and not evil of itself. It is the rebellious and destructive orientation of fallen human nature that is the problem. If we allow the passions of our flesh to rule our lives, we lose our life, body, and soul. If the Word of the Lord regenerates and inspires us, love rules so that we begin to realize true life in our soul as we employ our bodies in service to others (Jn 12:25; Col 3:1–17).

God does not punish children for the sins of their parents, nor parents for the sins of the children (Ezk 18:1–4, 19–20). Like the unbelieving spouse, children with one

believing parent are sanctified, that is, set apart from the rest of the world that lives in the darkness apart from the Word. Paul is saying neither that God despises children of unbelieving parents nor that they cannot be saved if the Word works faith in them. Paul is stressing the significance of a believing husband/father or wife/mother for the presence of the Word she or he brings to the rest of the family.

● ● ● ● ● ● ● ● ● ● ● ● ● ● ● ● ● ● ●

Q **7:13–15 How are children holy? Does this also mean that children would be saved at birth despite original sin?**

The word *holy* in this context does not mean innocent, perfect, or without sin. The word *holy* (or *sanctified*) means "to be set apart." Children born into a family in which at least one parent is a believer are, through the care of that parent, set apart from the world that lives in darkness and opposition to God. Children born to a believing parent are set apart by a life in the Word and the love of that parent who would raise his or her children in the "discipline and instruction" of the Lord (Eph 6:4; Dt 6:4–9; see 1 Co 7:12–14 above for more).

● ● ● ● ● ● ● ● ● ● ● ● ● ● ● ● ● ● ●

Q **7:15 Can a widow remarry? Also, if a virgin marries someone who has had sex, are both committing sexual immorality?**

According to the Law, marriage is a union that endures as long as nothing breaks that union. Adultery, abuse, and abandonment break that union and are, therefore, exceptions to God's prohibition against divorce (see 1Co 7:10–11 above). The death of a spouse also terminates the union and sets the surviving spouse at liberty to remarry if he or she chooses (Rm 7:1–3; 1Co 7:39; 1Tm 5:14).

There is no sexual immorality if a virgin marries one who has been sexually active in the past, as long as that individual has repented of such activity. If previous sin were carried forward with us, it would be impossible to live with one another or before God, since "every intention of the thoughts of the heart" of our fallen human nature is "only evil continually" (Gn 6:5; Is 64:6; Mk 7:20–22; Rm 3:10–19). We do not carry our sins forward with us unless we are impenitent of them and despise the grace of God that has forgiven them (Ps 103:8–12; Jn 8:1–11; 1Tm 1:12–17).

Q 7:17 What if a man believes God is calling him to do something, but he really isn't?

If a person thinks God is calling him or her to do something that is contrary to God's expressed will, big trouble will follow. If the calling has to do with something God has neither commanded nor forbidden, what results is of little or no matter. For example, Paul was determined to go to Jerusalem at the end of the third missionary journey, even though God warned Paul through

many witnesses not to go (Ac 20:22–21:15). Paul's insistence on a path that God had not called him to cost him four years in prison and a shipwreck (Ac 21:20–28:31). Nevertheless, as Paul himself wrote: "For those who love God all things work together for good, for those who are called according to His purpose" (Rm 8:28). Luke wrote the Gospel and Acts during this time, and Paul wrote at least five Epistles besides positively affecting many people along the way (Php 1:12–18; Phm 10). Another example would be a believer who is agonizing over changing jobs. Could it be the case that God doesn't care which job a person might take as long as he or she serves well in that job?

Q 7:18 How did the Jews react to this statement concerning circumcision?

The Gentiles in Corinth (and elsewhere) would no doubt have found great relief in this confirmation that circumcision was not a requirement of the New Testament. It is possible that the more cosmopolitan Jews in Greece would have welcomed the news as well. However, we have plenty of early evidence that many Jews fiercely resented the abandonment of circumcision and persecuted the apostles because of it (Ac 11:1–3; 15:1–29). There are good and bad reasons why circumcision is important. The good reason has to do with recognizing that God commanded circumcision as a physical confirmation of the promises God had made to Abraham and his descendants.

Surely we can sympathize with people who are fearful of abandoning what was once commanded by God, despite all the assurances that God in Christ had given. The bad reason has to do with the external, physical ceremonies that hypocrisy abuses. Circumcision confirmed the promises of God that created faith in Abraham and gave him everlasting life (Mt 22:31–32). Physical descendants of Abraham who despised God and His promises wanted to use circumcision as the basis for demanding the physical blessings of God while rejecting the spiritual and as a reason to despise people who were uncircumcised (Mt 23:13; Heb 3:12–19).

Q **7:25–40 Does Paul truly believe it is best for people to remain unmarried? Is this passage why some people, such as nuns, do not marry?**

There is no reason to suspect that Paul does not truly believe in the counsel he is giving, especially since he was inspired by the Holy Spirit to write this (1Th 2:13; 2Tm 3:16). The reasons Paul gave are good reasons why many people have refrained from pursuing marriage or relationships of other types that would compete with their devotion to the ministry of the Word. Some religious systems, including the Roman Catholic Church, usually do not allow priests and nuns to marry, but forbidding marriage is contrary to what the Bible teaches (Mt 19:10–12; 1Tm 4:1–5).

Q **7:26 What was the "present distress"?**

The word translated as "distress" is better translated as "necessity" (Mt 18:7; Rm 13:5). This term occurs in two places next to the word *affliction*, suggesting that difficulties or challenges are the source of the necessity (2Co 6:4; 1Th 3:7). The most reliable meaning of the word in this verse is supplied by Paul in 1Co 9:16 where Paul equates the preaching of the Gospel with "necessity." The preaching of the Word is necessary because so much of the world is perishing in its absence and the time is passing quickly (Eph 5:15–16; Rm 13:11). This understanding of the term is consistent with what Paul is arguing in this chapter: that devotion to advancing the Word and kingdom of God is more important than the pursuit of personal and romantic relationships (1Co 7:29–35).

Q **7:28 What does Paul mean when he says that those who marry will face "worldly troubles"? How are their problems bigger than those of unmarried people?**

Paul was acutely aware of the constant and very menacing threat our fallen human nature poses for us (Rm 5:6–11; Gal 5:19–21; Eph 2:1–3). If you consider all of the cautions Paul urges against our flesh and the urgency he felt about advancing the kingdom of God, what he says about marriage sounds quite restrained. Whether you are married or unmarried, the Christian faith seeks genuine love only—no hypocrisy, no pretense, no fraud. If you are going to be married, Paul's clarification of what love is and is not becomes all the more critical. The trouble we will have in the flesh is the trouble that our fallen human nature makes for itself and what the human nature of others makes for us (Rm 7:9–24; 1Th 2:1–2; 3:1–3).

In vv. 32–34, Paul explains, in part, why those who are married will have trouble. Our fallen human nature and that of a spouse often assert themselves against what the Lord would have us or our spouse do. Our human nature is often contrary, not only to the will of God but also to our spouse, and that makes the kind of trouble every married couple knows, no matter how devoted each is to the other. Remaining unmarried has its perils also, but the unmarried person is at liberty to follow where the Lord would lead without facing objections or competition for devotion (Mt 6:24).

Q 7:29 What does it mean to live as though you have no wife?

What if living as if you had no wife provided the best life for her? Isn't it the men who live as if there was no life except their own who treat women with such cruelty? Notice that Paul is not treating the subject of marriage in isolation from all other human endeavors. Paul speaks to those who weep, rejoice, and use the things of this world—reminding them all that the form of this world is passing away. What good is a hus-

band who has allowed his wife to displace God as the authority of his life and who has reduced his concerns to things material (Gn 3:16; Mt 6:24; Gal 1:10)? A Christian man who lives as if he had no wife remains at all times devoted to God's intent for his life and focused on the mission of advancing the kingdom of God. Such a man's wife would certainly benefit from such devotion and focus, both as the object of his ministry and as one who would be inspired to join him in the Christian mission (2Co 5:7–21).

Q 7:32–35 How do I know if I have the gift of staying single? Is this why the Catholic Church does not allow their priests to be married? Is Paul against marriage?

You would know if you had the gift of celibacy if you did not struggle with a desire for sexual gratification or to be married or with loneliness. Even if you did struggle with these, the ability to exercise self-control until each struggle is surmounted would be an indication of this gift.

The Roman Catholic Church does base its ban on marriage for priests and nuns on verses such as these, yet such a prohibition is contrary to Jesus' own words (Mt 19:10–12; 1Tm 4:1–3).

Paul is not against marriage. Paul is concerned that people not be distracted from our mission of advancing the kingdom of God. He is also worried about the challenges we create for ourselves when we enter into marriage (it takes significant effort to maintain a healthy, loving marriage) and the challenges the world presses against us when we carry special devotion to our spouse. Paul did not think that married people were unable to serve the Lord, since he mentions that he and Barnabas had a right to marry and that the other apostles did have wives (1Co 9:5–6). Please see questions and answers on 1Co 7:18–29 for more on this subject.

● ● ● ● ● ● ● ● ● ● ● ● ● ● ● ● ● ● ● ●

Q 7:32–35 What about a couple who divorced, then later remarried, this time focusing on Christ? It is wrong for the two people to marry when their faith has been made stronger and the family is healthier than before?

If these individuals remained single between their divorce and remarriage, what they have done sounds very much like the counsel Paul gives to those who separate (1Co 7:10–11). Adultery is an issue only if these people engaged in relationships with others while they were divorced. The New Testament is entirely in favor of people focusing on Christ, being a blessing to each other, and providing for a healthy family (Col 3:1–16).

● ● ● ● ● ● ● ● ● ● ● ● ● ● ● ● ● ● ● ●

Q 7:32–35 Does getting married necessarily change the mind-set from pleasing God to pleasing the world?

Getting married might not change a person's mind-set toward pleasing the world, but it will certainly change it toward pleasing one's spouse, as Paul says. Yet marriage is an institution of God, even after the fall. The proper, godly love of a husband for his wife and the submission of a wife to her husband is according to God's will and must, therefore, be pleasing to Him (Eph 5:21–33; 1Pt 3:1–7). On the other hand, as Paul warns, the fallen human nature of those who are married causes us to experience passions, weakness, fear, carelessness—all of these challenges to the Christian mindset can exert themselves more powerfully in a relationship between husband and wife.

● ● ● ● ● ● ● ● ● ● ● ● ● ● ● ● ● ● ● ●

Q 7:34 Why are married couples divided between pleasing their spouses and the Lord's work? Is the idea that a woman must please her husband meant to be a bad thing here or something that she has to do?

When a person is single, he or she is free of any relationship that would compete with or exert pressure upon his or her devotion to the Christian mission. An unmarried man or woman may pursue education for ministry, travel, and change plans any number of times with little notice because no one else is necessarily affected by his or her activity, except those who are served by it. To be a husband means to accept responsibility for the care and well-being of a wife; to be a wife means to be submissive to and bound up in the life of the husband. The concern of a husband for his wife may mean that he withdraws from serving in ways or means that would take him away from his wife. A woman's care for her husband may equally take her attention away from care for others. The challenges of sustaining a loving marriage between two fallen human natures requires attention, time, and energy that is, therefore, no longer available for advancing the kingdom of God to those who are still without it. I do know of couples who married because of or have come to share an equally intense devotion for the mission of Christianity. They are a wonder and joy to know, but they are also rare.

• • • • • • • • • • • • • • • • • • • •

Q **7:36–37 What does this passage mean? What relationship is Paul referring to here, a man and the woman betrothed to him or a father and his unmarried daughter?**

Paul uses terms here that are ambiguous, which make some readers wonder whether Paul is talking about a man and the woman to whom he is engaged or a father and his daughter. Given the context from the beginning, it makes more sense that Paul is talking about a man and the woman he intended to marry. The situation is something like this: a man who was a Christian or who became a Christian while engaged to marry a woman had thoughts of remaining celibate without withdrawing his commitment to provide for the woman. They would remain engaged but un-united in order to devote themselves more completely to the Christian mission. But the man is having second thoughts, feeling that this is unfair to the woman and wrestling with his own desire to consummate their engagement.

Paul provides advice consistent with the Gospel. The Gospel would not make them do anything. If they are inspired to remain engaged and celibate, great! If they desire to consummate their marriage, that's fine too. Some confusion is caused by the Greek word for "give in marriage" that occurs in v. 38, as if Paul were speaking to a father who was or was not willing to give his daughter in marriage. But Paul has not spoken of the father of a woman at all in this text, and the Greek word translated in some English Bibles as "give in marriage" can be used in place of the word for "to marry."

• • • • • • • • • • • • • • • • • • • •

Q **7:37 What does this mean, that "he will do well"?**

Paul did not say "has done the right thing" but "do well." The nature of Paul's discussion has been a comparison between good and better, not between right and wrong (see v. 38). A man who accepts the responsibility he agreed to when becoming engaged to a woman does well. A man and woman who agree to keep the engagement but to remain celibate in order to devote themselves entirely to the Christian mission do even better.

• • • • • • • • • • • • • • • • • • • •

Q **7:38 In the process of an engagement and marriage, is it still (as it was in Levitical law) appropriate or necessary to ask the father of your heart's desire for her hand in marriage (ask permission), or is it now a matter of freedom?**

I do not know of any particular text or law in the Bible that requires a man to obtain permission from a woman's father before asking her to marry him (though Nu 30:1–15 discusses women taking vows and a father or husband's authority to reverse it). A father's responsibility for the care and well-being of his daughter and the commandment to honor father and mother combined with biblical narratives suggest that a man should not propose marriage to a woman without her father's approval (Gn 2:24; 24:1–58; 29:15–30; Ex 20:12; 34:1–4; Jgs 14:2; Mt 1:18–20).

• •

Q **7:38 God says man should not be alone (see Gn 2:18), but here Paul says the man who does not marry does better. Is God saying that, when you marry, keep your life as devoted to Him as before?**

The fall of Adam changed just about everything in our world and relationships. Before the fall, there was no death or cause for death (Gn 1:29–31). After the fall, everything became subject to death (Gn 2:16–17; 3:1–24). In creation, it was not good for the man to be alone because that meant there was no one for whom man could give his life in love, and there would be no children for whom the couple might give their lives together. There are plenty of people for whom we might live now. There are vast numbers of women who need men to bear responsibility for them and their well-being much more than they need the particular relationship of a husband. There are scores of children who need men and women to care for them because their biological parents are so careless. No marriage is needed for men and women to join forces in the raising of abandoned children in the nurture and admonition of the Lord. Ideally speaking, it is still not good for the man to be alone, because God created us to bear witness to and experience His image through marriage. Given the urgency of the Christian mission, the ideal has changed from the particular (one spouse) to the general (so many people perishing without the Gospel). Certainly God wants those who marry to be just as devoted as before or more devoted to Him and the Christian mission.

• •

Q **7:39 It states: "But if her husband dies, she is free to be married to whom she wishes, only in the Lord." But in vv. 13–14 it says that unbelieving husbands are sanctified through the woman. Could there not be a situation in which both of these things are possible?**

There might be such a situation, but there should not be. In vv. 13–14 Paul is talking to people who already were married when they became Christian. Paul does not want them to break their union when that union holds the greatest potential for bringing the unbelieving spouse into the faith. On the other hand, if someone is single and already a Christian, why would he or she consider forming a union with a person who does not share the faith that is the essence of the soul? In my experience, believers who pursue marriage with an unbeliever with the hope (or sometimes a promise) that he or she will come into the faith are usually disappointed. Once married, an unbeliever often resents the believer's attempts to draw him or her into the faith. If an unbeliever does not or will not come to the faith before marriage, he or she is unlikely to do so after the wedding. Paul is urging us to protect what God has given us by priority. Our union with Him is and remains first because our life and the good we might do anyone else depends on this union. Our union with others may be kept or sought whenever such unions spread rather than restrict the faith.

Q 8:1 What does it mean that knowledge "puffs up"?

Paul is back to the subject of pride and competitiveness, which was such a problem with the Corinthians (1Co 1:10–31). Anyone who is genuinely interested in truth and knowledge of the truth understands that we actually know very little, and even what we think we know is often severely limited or mistaken. This is not to say that there is no truth; truth is the way things really are, and reality is a witness to it. This is not to say that we don't know anything or that what we know is of no use; we benefit from the most

> Why do Jews have such strict dietary laws?

certain of things we know every day. However, the thoughts and opinions we produce in our own minds and the limited experience and research we may have done often make us contend for a level of certainty that is indefensible.

Q 8:5 What does Paul mean by "many 'gods' and many 'lords'"?

The term "gods" is used in the Bible to refer to rulers (Ps 82:6–7; Jn 10:33–36). The term "lord" is used in a similar way—it can refer to the Lord Jesus, or it can refer to a master or ruler of others (Mt 6:24; 22:41–45; Col 4:1). Paul is using both terms to refer to forces at work in creation, of which there are many (Eph 2:2). Still, there is only one God and Lord in the absolute sense as the origin and source of all things and as the one who controls all things according to His will (Dt 6:4; Eph 4:4–6; Heb 1:1–3).

Q 8:8 If food does not commend us to God, then why do Jews have such strict dietary laws?

God called Abraham away from his people in order to create a people who were distinct in their relationship to God (Gn 12:1–3). After the exodus, God provided Israel with a particular calendar, ceremonial system, and dietary restrictions that would help them to be mindful of being called into a special relationship with God. Fallen human nature, being contrary to God yet proud and self-righteous, used these outward rules about diet to claim special privileges from God while contradicting God's will (Is 29:13; Mt 15:7–9). As Jesus said, it is not what goes into a man that defiles him but what comes out (Mk 7:1–23). The particular foods that the Jews eat were never intended to bring them closer to God. God had already done that through His gracious promises to Abraham (Rm 4:1–16; Heb 9:9–15). The particular foods were intended to remind the Jews that God had graciously called them to be a special people through whom the nations would know the truth and grace of God (Gn 12:3; Lk 2:32). Today, only some Jews still observe laws about what they eat, and they do so mostly to preserve their heritage.

• • • • • • • • • • • • • • • • • • • •

Q 8:9–13 Can this passage be applied to a situation in which you are with non-Christians and you adjust your behavior to make them feel more comfortable? For example, I generally avoid R-rated movies. But I would probably go with a group of friends rather than give them the impression that Christians don't have the free will to do what they want. I may comment after the movie on what I didn't like to express my disapproval without making anyone uncomfortable.

Christians do not have the free will to do what they want. Christians are bound in love to owe no one anything except love (Rm 13:8–14). Christians are at liberty to show love to others by being more, not less, careful. We know that no spiritual harm comes from eating or refusing to eat this or that kind of food (Mk 7:14–19; Rm 14:1–23). If we are with people who abstain from seeing any kind of movie at all because of religious conviction, we might refrain with them and have a conversation about the benefits or lack of benefits in doing so. On the other hand, we are not free to join people in activities that are contrary to their well-being and ours (1Co 6:12; Php 4:8–9; 1Pt 4:1–19).

• • • • • • • • • • • • • • • • • • • •

Q 8:10 What does Paul mean when he says "eating in an idol's temple"?

At this time in history, people regularly built temples where they would make various sacrifices to idols. If meat was sacrificed, after the ritual the meat would be eaten in the temple or sold (1Co 10:25–33). Paul is concerned that a Christian who knew that idols are nothing and that food offered to idols has no significance might, by eating such sacrificial food, cause a weaker Christian to fail. A weaker Christian who felt an inner conviction against having anything to do with idols might be tempted to join in such a meal and in so doing act against his or her own conscience.

Q **8:11 When Paul talks about a weak brother destroyed by the knowledge of another brother, could that also be the case for people who claim that their Lutheran faith approves of their careless or inconsiderate behavior?**

What was most Lutheran about Luther was his absolute devotion to and submission to the Word. There is no way a person could be genuinely too devoted to the Word of God because it is that very Word of God that regenerates us and moves us to do God's will (Ezk 36:24–27; Jn 15:1–7). On the other hand, a person could have his own ideas about what it means to be Lutheran, much like the Corinthians who wanted to claim a special relationship with Paul, Apollos, or Peter (1Co 1:10–17). In such cases it is not real knowledge that destroys a weaker brother but the arrogance and vanity of self-righteous opinion that bears down in judgment upon others rather than seeking to build them up (Mt 9:9–13; Lk 18:9–14).

Q **8:13 How can what we eat hurt another person?**

Let's take a different example for the sake of clarity. There is nothing wrong with drinking alcohol, yet many people have been raised to think it is a sin, and many people sin when they drink to excess (alcoholism). Would it not hurt such people if my drinking led them to drink also—one against his conscience and the other to fail

in his ability to drink in moderation (Rm 14:1–15:3)? Something similar to this was true in Paul's time regarding food that had been offered to idols. Some people could not free themselves from the effects of idolatry, even after they had learned that idols were nothing. Eating food offered to idols, especially doing so in the temple of the idol, could be overwhelming to a person who was struggling to be free of idolatry.

Q **9:5 Does "brothers of the Lord" refer to Jesus' real brothers?**

Jesus had half brothers and sisters, children of Mary and Joseph (Mt 12:46; 13:55–56; Mk 6:3). Paul is referring to the half brothers of Jesus: James and Jude.

Q **9:9 What is the meaning of "you shall not muzzle an ox"?**

Paul says that God's word about muzzling oxen was said for the benefit of those who would serve in the ministry (v. 10). What God said about muzzling an ox is true and applicable for those with animals that work. Like all of God's creation, the material world is a means by which God reveals the truth to us (Ps 19:1–3; Rm 1:20). What is right in the treatment of domestic animals that work is just as right in the treatment of people who serve others.

Q 9:14 How should people receive their living from the Gospel?

A person who is called by God to serve full time in ministry to others should be provided for by the people served (Mt 10:5–10; Gal 6:6). God provided for the Levites in the Old Testament by giving them portions of the inheritance of the other tribes and by giving them a tithe from the other tribes (Lv 18:21–28).

Q 9:16 Do all pastors, like Paul, feel a "necessity" to preach?

The imperative to preach the Gospel occurs four times in the New Testament. Jesus commanded the apostles to preach during His ministry and at the end, before He ascended into heaven (Mt 10:7, 27; Mk 16:15). Paul commanded Timothy to preach, which would extend to all pastors like Timothy (2Tm 4:2). So, yes, all pastors are compelled by their call to preach the truth and grace of God faithfully. It is possible that the Word of the Lord itself, like a fire inside the person, makes it necessary for him to speak, but a person should never presume to do so without a valid call (Jer 14:13–15; 20:9; Ac 13:1–3; 1Tm 3:1–7).

Q 9:19 How do you make yourself a "servant to all"?

When Paul says he is "free" from all men, he means that he does not owe them anything, nor is he afraid of them, nor is anyone aside from God able to compel him to do anything (Ac 13:8; Heb 2:14–15). When Paul says he is a "servant" to all, he means that the love of God has inspired him to love all others with his whole life as God grants opportunity (2Co 5:14–15; Php 3:7–14). Paul's opening address to the Galatians allows you to see how this dynamic actually worked in Paul's ministry (Gal 1:6–10).

Q 9:20–22 How could Paul preach to a multicultural group? How could he "become like a Jew"?

Multicultural is a term that has significance for a relatively small part of people's lives. While we may see and hear a lot about culture, ethnic groups, and race, the essence of all human beings is a soul made in the image of God. Every human soul shares the same hope, fear, peril, and promise. Every regenerate soul struggles against the contrary nature of the body, the bodies of others, and all demonic forces as long as it lives in this fallen human nature (Gal 5:16–26; Eph 2:1–10). Just as human physiology is identical from person to person except for the very smallest percentage (less than 0.1 percent), so the souls of people are the same and are ministered to in the same way, with the same Means of Grace, toward the same hope of everlasting life.

You can make yourself like anyone by adopting their particular way of life; it's not asking that much when you remember that in most ways we are still alike. We need fluids, food, clothing, shelter, sleep, purpose, hope—life itself. By identifying myself with others who assume they are different, I bridge a gap that doesn't really exist and provide them with an opportunity to know what I do. For example, a Christian may not struggle with homosexuality but can honestly claim to have the same fallen human nature and contrary heart that homosexuals and every other person since Adam has had (Mk 7:20–23). Do they struggle to find meaning in relationships? So do I. Do they struggle against passions that are selfish and self-defeating? So do I. How can we combine our needs, interests, and abilities in order to realize the redemption that Christ has accomplished for all people? Paul demonstrated the commonality of human beings as he applied the universal atonement of Christ to the universal human condition inherited from Adam (Ac 17:22–34; Rm 5:6–21).

Q 9:27 Why does Paul discipline his body? Why would Paul be disqualified?

Paul understood very well that we cannot have two masters, as Jesus said (Mt 6:24). If we allow our bodies to rule according to their nature since the fall—vain, proud, materialistic, selfish, and self-centered—then we will lose all meaningful relationships and life, both now and eternally. The body was created to be the servant of our soul, and since our bodies are contrary to God's design for our lives, we must "wear them down" (another meaning for the Greek word translated here as *discipline*) and sometimes even give them a "black eye" in

order to keep the hope of eternal life for our soul and a restored body in the resurrection (Rm 6:1–22; Gal 5:16–25; Col 3:1–16).

If we preach the way of truth and life to others, yet serve our fallen human nature, we become hypocrites with seared consciences and dispositions that despise the riches of God's grace toward us (Mt 23:3–33; Ac 5:1–11; 1Tm 6:3–10; Heb 6:1–8). Without God's grace, we are condemned by the Law, and thus we are disqualified from eternal life.

Q 10:2 I was confused by Paul's mention of the cloud and the sea. Why isn't God's Word written in "black and white" with examples and support? Why would people be baptized into Moses?

The Bible is as "black and white" as any text could be because God is the author and knows how to say what He means to the people who need to know what He means (2Pt 1:16–21). God has given us creation and His Word so that we have two witnesses by which we might test and know the truth (Ps 19:1–3; Rm 1:20; Gn 41:32; Dt 17:6; 19:15). If a matter seems gray, I would suggest the solution comes in realizing that looking more closely and carefully provides the clarity we seek, like magnifying photographs in newsprint—all the gray shades are made up of black and white.

The history of the exodus of Israel brings the meaning of Baptism into focus. The Greek word translated as *baptism* means "to wash," "to be awash in," or "to be immersed." Don't think so much about water for a moment but think about relationship. The relationship between a person's body and the Red Sea was indicative of (a physical view into) the relationship that existed between Moses and the people who followed him through that parted water. "Baptized" into Moses means you are "with" Moses, subject to and beneficiary of all that God was doing through Moses. Follow Moses and you'll live in the land of promise. Rebel against Moses and you cast away from yourself all that God had given and would give still (Lv 26:1–46; Dt 30:11–20).

Q 10:4 Did a rock literally follow Moses and his followers?

This is a very curious passage. There is evidence of an ancient Jewish tradition that said a real rock actually followed Israel throughout the wilderness wanderings. Even so, it is doubtful that the Corinthians would know about it. We know that Christ is referred to as the Rock because He is the truth that never changes or moves (Ps 118:22; Mt 7:24–25; Lk 20:17–18). We know that Christ was with Israel all during their sojourn (Ex 13:21; Nu 14:14). We know that God provided Israel with water from a rock on more than one occasion and that Jesus Christ is living water (Ex 17:6; Nu 20:7–8; Jn 4:14; 7:37–38). Is it possible that the combination of truths about the Son of God as living water and a rock and that He led Israel day and night and gave them water from

rocks became this tradition that a rock followed Israel? Time will tell.

Q 10:6 Is Paul saying that the issues with the Israelites happened as an example of what not to do?

Everything that happens in this life happens for the sake of the lives we will know in eternity. Everything that happens in the body is for the sake of the soul. Is it possible that two lives (physical/spiritual) and two lifetimes (temporal/eternal) are necessary for us if we are to have hope? Can you think of a single thing in all of history and human experience that does not have something to teach us—either what to avoid or what to pursue? Jesus was able to teach in parables because all things physical indicate spiritual realities (Mt 13:34). Paul is able to use logical arguments for the same reason (Rm 6:21).

Q 10:8 Who were the 23,000 people who died?

Paul is referring to the event described in Nu 25:1–9. The Israelite men began to commit idolatry to Baal and sexual immorality with the women of Moab. You may notice that the account in Numbers reports that 24,000 died while your English translation of 1 Corinthians says 23,000 died. Interestingly, Jerome changed the number to 24,000 in his Latin translation of 1Co 10:8. A simple explanation for the difference in

Does God allow us to be tempted?

numbers is that Paul is commenting on how many people died "in one day" while Moses reports the whole number of people who died (people were still dying from the plague after the first day).

- - - - - - - - - - - - - - - - - - - -

Q **10:13 Does God allow us to be tempted, therefore causing humans to sin? If God doesn't allow us to be tempted beyond what we can bear, then why do we give in to temptation?**

When Paul says "common to man," he means that no human being can claim that he or she is being tempted in some extraordinary way that no other human being ever has or would experience, as if to use that as an excuse for failing. Jesus, as a true man, endured every temptation successfully on our behalf (Lk 4:1–13; Heb 2:18; 4:15). God limits and directs the temptations that come to us in order to make them, like all things, work together for our good (Rm 8:28). God does not cause anyone to sin but uses the consequences of sin to teach us why He forbids it and to make us stronger in our resolution to repent of sin (Jas 1:12–14).

We continue to fail in the face of temptation for two reasons. First, we fail because this is the orientation of our fallen human nature (Mk 7:20–22; Rm 5:6–11). Second, we fail because we are simply careless about

the threat of temptation and the power of the Word. No one I know puts on the whole armor of God before starting their day (Eph 6:11–20). The devil uses trials and challenges to inflame our fallen human nature against our own well-being and the Word of God. This is why it is called temptation. God uses trials and challenges to drive us more deeply into His Word and to connect us more fully with the life He provides for us. This is why His activity is called testing. Testing, like the refiner's fire, removes what cannot endure so that only the pure is left, desirable and eternal (Jas 1:2–4; 1Pt 1:6–9).

- - - - - - - - - - - - - - - - - - - -

Q **10:14–17 Is Paul saying that Jesus gives us His actual body and blood or do bread and wine only symbolize Jesus?**

Modern people think of and use symbols differently than God does or how people understood symbols in ancient times. Modern use of symbols is artificial and arbitrary, the product of human imagination. There is nothing essential about "stopping" that is bound up in a stop sign. Lightsaber toys don't do anything real except to stop lighting up when the batteries run out. By contrast, what the Bible calls "symbols" and what Jesus chose to join with His Word are essential components of human life. Water and bread are real and really essential for our life—indicating that Jesus is absolutely essential for our life (Jn 4:13–14; 6:48–51). In the Lord's Supper, the Word of God is really present and joins the true body and true blood of Jesus to the bread and the wine. Jesus, in His body and blood, are just as present as the bread and wine that you can see, touch, and taste.

Q 10:14 Was idolatry an overwhelming problem?

Idolatry was and remains the overwhelming problem because fallen human nature makes anything a god except the one, true, living God. The First Commandment forbids having any other gods because everything else that is wrong flows from idolatry. Jesus addressed this in the Sermon on the Mount (Mt 6:24). Paul explained that covetousness was actually idolatry (Col 3:5). In modern times, we may not keep images made of wood or metal to which we bow down, but everyone has something that governs his or her life. If the one, true, living God is not governing a person's life, then something else is—usually something material that appeals to the appetites of our material nature (Pr 9:1–18).

Q 10:16 If one is to not participate in Communion because it is an expression of faith, does this mean the disagreement is between individuals or denominations?

Truth is singular; therefore, everyone who is in the truth is united and bound together in love by the Word. Where there is no real communion, trying to act as though there is only creates confusion and rightly brings the condemnation of hypocrisy. Where communion really exists, it should

be recognized, appreciated, fostered, and enjoyed. Only the Word of God can create real communion because real communion depends on the truth and grace of God (1Jn 1:7). Like the truth, there is only one Body of Christ, one Christian Church (Eph 4:4–6). There are "Christian" denominations because groups of people insist that they hold to the Bible's teaching, yet must be opposed to some scriptural truth because they are opposed to other groups that make the same claim. There is no shortcut to the truth. If communion is wanted, then we must submit to the Word and find what that Word says in comparison to what groups or denominations claim. It takes time for people to study the Word and know for themselves what they believe. The Word alone creates communion among people. The Word alone judges whether communion is real and everlasting. Where it is, we celebrate. Where it is not, we continue to advance the Word so it may come about (2Co 5:14–21).

Q 10:23 What are "all things" that Paul discusses here?

Why would a person want to do anything that is not helpful or does not build up? Since Christ has redeemed us from the curse of the Law, the Law no longer has the power to condemn us (Gal 3:13; Rm 7:6; Rv 12:10). In the New Testament, we no longer do or refrain from doing anything because the Law threatens us or because we want to get something we lack. All things are ours in Christ, and because we are regenerated in His image, we are oriented and inspired to be like Him (1Jn 4:9). The question on our minds is how to be helpful and how to protect the liberty Christ has given us from the bondage of sin, death, and the devil (Gal 5:1, 13). Love motivates us always to seek the best for others because Christ has already given us the best of all things in this world and the next (Php 3:7–14).

• • • • • • • • • • • • • • • • • • •

Q **10:25 Why does Paul say that they can eat anything in the market when God previously said they should not eat unclean animals?**

Paul is not talking about eating clean or unclean animals because Jesus declared all foods clean (Mk 7:2–23, especially v. 19). Paul has been talking about eating what has been sacrificed to idols, and in v. 28 he makes that clear again. On eating meat sacrificed to idols, see 1Co 8:10 above.

• • • • • • • • • • • • • • • • • • •

Q **10:27–30 Why would he be judged by another's conscience?**

Fallen human nature is relentless about imposing its own judgments upon others (Lk 9:54–56). Jesus often defended people against the legalistic inventions that religious leaders used to burden and control others (Mt 9:9–17; 12:1–8; 23:13–33; Mk 7:2–23). Peter and Paul also defended the faith and faithful people against the imposition of the consciences of others (Ac 11:1–18; 15:1–12;

Gal 2:1–6; 4:21–31; 6:11–14). As Christ defended and fulfilled the gracious promises of God in order to justify and deliver all people from their sins, so we must faithfully defend God's grace toward us from people who would force the opinions of their own consciences on us (Gal 5:1, 13). Being careful not to make a weaker believer stumble and act against his or her own conscience is the opposite of indulging a self-righteous person in his attempts to tyrannize others. We endure all things for the sake of loving others according to the truth; we tolerate no one's attempts to oppose the truth and love of God (Mt 5:13–48; Rm 14:1–23).

• • • • • • • • • • • • • • • • • • •

Q **10:27 Does this say we should not eat with unbelievers?**

Quite the contrary; in this verse Paul says we may certainly accept invitations to eat with unbelievers, a position he had stated previously in this letter (see 1Co 5:9–11). The Bible only warns us against eating meals in public with people whose beliefs are contrary to the truth or whose lives and words reveal that they oppose the truth of the Christian Church even though they insist they are part of it (Rm 16:17–18).

• • • • • • • • • • • • • • • • • • •

Q **10:30 Does this say that under the penumbra of thankfulness anything can be eaten, whether offered to idols or not?**

I'm not so sure about a penumbra, but Paul is saying that all things may be eaten if received with thankfulness (1Tm 4:4). Jesus brought to completion Old Testament ceremonial law and released all people from what it required (Mt 12:1–8; Mk 7:6–19; Heb 10:1–18). This truth was confirmed to Peter while he was in Joppa and became an essential part of his evidence for grace and the New Testament against the legalism of the Judaizers (Ac 10:9–16, 34–35; 11:1–18; 15:1–12).

● ● ● ● ● ● ● ● ● ● ● ● ● ● ● ● ● ● ●

Q 10:31 Can we do anything and claim that it was done for the glory of God?

Christianity suffers much misplaced hatred and abuse because so many people since the time of Christ have claimed that their evil thoughts and deeds were done for the glory of God (Jer 14:14; Rm 2:24). Only what is done according to the will of God, clearly revealed in the Word, can be done for the glory of God, and no one can claim any other cause for what is done that is good and right except the glory of God (Jn 15:1–8; 1Co 12:3; 15:10).

● ● ● ● ● ● ● ● ● ● ● ● ● ● ● ● ● ● ●

Q 10:32 When Christians go out drinking, is that "muddying" up people's thoughts on Christians or a good chance to evangelize? How can you prevent everyone from stumbling? Is there a place where a line can be drawn?

There are places and activities that are so contrary to the Word and will of God that a person could hardly claim to be involved for the glory of God or the benefit of others—places and activities that have only evil and wicked intent (Gn 6:5; Pr 7:1–27; 12:26; 1Co 15:33). On the other hand, Christians should be devoted to finding a way to meet those bound in such places and activities so that we might share with them the redemption of Christ (Mt 5:38–42; Ac 17:16–34; 1Co 9:19–23; 2Co 5:14–21; 1Pt 3:15). I suspect it is impossible to live in this fallen human nature and never do or say something that causes another person to stumble. Only the Word and Spirit of God in us can make us so devoted to and focused upon the benefit of others that the trouble we make is minimized (Lv 19:17; Jn 15:1–13; 1Co 6:12; 10:23; 2Co 5:14–15). What we do or don't do, say or don't say is not so much a matter of where we draw a line, but what the likelihood or potential is of doing good or harm—owe no one anything except love (Rm 13:8).

. . . .

Q 10:33 In Gal 1:10, Paul says that his job is not to please people, but in this verse he says he tries to please everybody. How can we understand this?

Let's compare the two readings, translated for accuracy:

1 Corinthians 10:33	Galatians 1:10
Just as I myself in all things I please all, not seeking my own benefit BUT the benefits of others, in order that they may be saved.	. . . for now men am I trying to persuade or God? Or am I seeking to please men? if still men I keep on pleasing, I would not be a servant of Christ.

Key words reveal the difference between Paul's intent in each verse. In both cases, Paul is concerned with the well-being of people. In Corinthians, he warns against hurting others by indulging our own fallen human nature; in Galatians, he warns about hurting others by indulging their fallen human nature. Paul makes clear his purpose in 1 Corinthians with the phrase "that they may be saved." This was his purpose with the Galatians, which is why he refused to please the Judaizers who would have robbed the Galatians of the saving grace of God.

. . . .

Q 11:1–16 These rules ring strongly of Levitical law. Is this a new ceremonial law?

Here we need to clarify the relationship between cause and effect. Many Levitical laws were based on and meant to reflect truths about creation, just as the moral Law is present on tablets of stone in Ex 20 and in the teaching of Jesus in the Gospels (Mt 22:37–39). The proper relationship between men and women according to God's design in creation is an ideal that was evident in some Old Testament laws and would be pursued even more passionately by Christians who for the sake of love would reclaim what was lost in Adam's fall (Gn 3:1–15; Rm 5:12–21).

. . . .

Q 11:2–4 Why do some men feel the need to be mean about their "power" protection of women? In class, we discussed the "support/protect diagram" based off these verses, which shows the family members protecting one another. What would happen if one of them were removed?

Could it be "reconstructed" or would it fall apart?

Genuine power is revealed in self-sacrifice for others rather than in power over them (Jn 13:1–17; Php 2:5–11). If men are ever mean, it is because our hearts and human nature have been entirely corrupted in the fall of Adam (Mk 7:20–22; Rm 5:6–11). The diagram referred to shows that "dominion," in the proper, divine sense of the word, means to support and protect. Jesus is Lord and has dominion over all things because all things came from, are supported by, and depend on Him (Jn 1:3; Col 1:15–18; Heb 1:2–3). God the Father is the head of and therefore supports, protects, and guides the Son. The Son of God does the same for every man, and every man for every woman. I'm not sure it is possible to have any one (support, protection, or guidance) without the others. It seems to me that if one is missing the others would be also.

● ● ● ● ● ● ● ● ● ● ● ● ● ● ● ● ● ● ●

Q **11:3–16 Why would Paul spend time on commands for head covering? Why are women and men commanded to act differently in church?**

First, there is a need, especially in modern times, for integrity that produces consistency in the way we live our lives. You can tell a tree from its fruit (Mt 7:20). What a person is, essentially, is revealed by his or her actions and appearance. Why would a person want to act or appear differently than he or she is essentially unless it were hypocrisy or for the purpose of deception?

Second, our heads do play an essential role in our life. All five of our senses reside in the head, and four of them are found only there. Our thoughts take place in our heads and then move the rest of our bodies. We live "head first," if you will. Similarly, heads of states or armies control the thinking that provides for the well-being of all who follow. For most of the world's history, rulers led people by their own way of living. Only in more recent times have leaders or heads of state retreated to the safety and luxury borne upon the masses of people (note the trouble David brought upon himself, his family, and his people by failing to be where he should have been, 2Sm 11:1–27). Third, "head" means to be responsible for others by way of leadership and support. To have one's head "uncovered" means to bear responsibility in public, to be exposed to threat, harm, and hardship in order to "cover," support, and protect those for whom you are responsible.

Now think in terms of integrity and consistency. Men were created by God to be responsible for the support and protection of women and children. The way short hair exposes a man's head physically and visually is consistent with the way that man exposes his whole person to the perils of life in a fallen world in order to lead, provide for, and protect his family and people. Interestingly, short hair is also a good idea if a man is going to be in combat. Women depend upon and cherish the protection that God provides absolutely and through men as His means. Women live in the support and protection of men who cherish them as the helpers who are to remain before them, for "it is not good that the man should be alone" (Gn 2:18). God has given women long and beautiful hair to indicate at the same time that they are the object of man's love and protected (covered) by man's responsibility for them (Eph 5:21–33).

Men and women do not act differently in church—unless they are not the Church of God at all and/or are hypocrites. Men, women, and children are always the Church, the Body of Christ, and all are enlisted as ambassadors for Christ at all times and in all places (2Co 5:14–21). When the Church becomes visible because it has gathered in public to receive the visible body of Christ (in the Sacrament of the Altar) from the visible representative of Christ (the pastor), then men, women, and children as a group become the Bride of Christ and the pastor is the head—responsible for supporting and protecting that public assembly with the Word (1Tm 2:8–15; Jas 3:1).

● ● ● ● ● ● ● ● ● ● ● ● ● ● ● ● ● ● ● ●

Q **11:3 What would you say to those who would have a major problem with this verse? Shouldn't Christ be the Head of women too?**

If someone had a major problem with this verse, James urges us to be slow to speak, quick to listen, and slow to anger (Jas 1:19). Listening will reveal experiences, fears, and misunderstandings that explain why people would assume they are opposed to the counsel of God. Demonstrating love

for a person by listening carefully eventually allows for an opportunity to share what the Bible actually teaches and why. Biblical teaching resolves problems generated by fallen, rebellious human nature.

All things in creation honor God, the Creator, when they function according to His will and realize the benefits of doing so. God creates all men, in general, to support and protect all women in general. Within that general context of society, women also have a father, perhaps brothers and uncles, certainly male cousins. In other words, every woman has a large number of relatives who bear responsibility for her well-being (Dt 25:5; Ru 4:1–12). Christ is the Head of every person, and women are associated with Christ—as becomes evident if you visualize what Paul is saying as an inverted pyramid. The Head of Christ is God—how can this be otherwise? God is the one and only, true, living God; all things come from and depend upon Him (Jn 1:3; Col 1:15–18). Next, connecting (rather than "coming between") God and humanity is Christ. Christ is the means by which God provides for us (Jn 14:5–11). All people are supported and provided for by God through Christ. Next, serving God through Christ as the means by which Christ provides for women are men. The primary and essential task of the man is to keep the woman connected with Christ by keeping her in the Word (Eph 5:25; Jn 17:6–8, 12). All of this support and providence, from God through Christ through men, is in place so that women may offer their lives as the means by which God creates new lives in the world (1Tm 2:15). By her connection with her husband and the two of them with Christ, children are kept in the grace and love of God (Dt 6:4–9; Eph 6:4).

• • • • • • • • • • • • • • • • • • •

Q 11:4–15 What about those who do not prophesy or speak in tongues?

Not everyone prophesies, and one ought to be careful about doing so (1Co 12:29; Eph 4:11; Jas 3:1; 1Pt 4:11). Speaking in tongues was granted in order to confirm that the apostles were authorized to speak the Word of God and that the Gospel worked immediately to save those who heard and believed (Mk 16:16–20; Ac 8:14–18; 10:44–48; 11:1–18; 15:1–10). All those who do not prophesy or speak in tongues seek to be good stewards of the gifts God has given them, while the Word is provided for them in the Bible and in those who are called to teach (Rm 12:3–8; Gal 6:6; Eph 4:11–16).

• • • • • • • • • • • • • • • • • • •

Q 11:4–10 What does this mean for us today? Are we supposed to keep our heads covered? Didn't Jesus have long hair?

What Paul says here means the very same thing for all people of all times and places because he is addressing the very essence of relationships between men and women and God based on creation (v. 14). We would apply everything the New Testament says to ourselves unless there are clear reasons not to do so. For example, a specific command to a specific person, such as Timothy, would not apply to us; we cannot bring people and things to Paul (2Tm 4:11–13). We understand all things as literal unless something requires us to do otherwise. Parables and apocalyptic (representational) material identifies itself as such (Mt 13:3; Rv 1:10; Ezk 1:1). In this case, Paul is talking about how we might best fulfill and make evident God's will for us according to our gender. What Paul is saying does not have to do with hats or veils because these are superficial inventions of human vanity and carelessness with the Bible. Paul explains in clear language that God has given women their hair as a covering, a very beautiful covering, for their heads, which bears witness to God's intent that they be supported and protected by men (v. 15; see also Eph 5:25–27). This is law, inasmuch as it explains to us the facts of nature and God's design. The fact that God designed women to be beautiful and protected, and men to love and care for them, is Gospel, and only the Gospel can regenerate us to be people who realize and appreciate God's genius in doing so.

Jesus may not have had long hair because men were commanded to keep their hair and beards trimmed, thus we only think He had long hair because that is how artists have portrayed Him (Ezk 44:20). If Jesus did have long hair, it would only have been because He was a Nazirite (Mt 2:23). The law of the Nazirite and history of Absalom both demonstrate that men did not normally have long hair (Nu 6:1–21; Jgs 13:5; 16:17; 2Sm 14:25–26; 18:9–15).

Q **11:5 Doesn't this contradict the idea of men and women being equal in today's society?**

The answer depends on your definition of "equal in today's society." The best case for the equality of men and women is made in the Bible. Creation proves our equality as living beings by recording that the woman was made from the man, as Paul recalls in v. 8. Redemption proves our equality because Christ bore the sins of and redeemed all people on the cross (Jn 3:16). Sanctification proves our equality, as the Holy Spirit makes no distinction between people according to their human nature (Ac 2:17–18; 10:34–35). Paul teaches the equality of men and women as human beings, redeemed and being sanctified (Gal 3:28; Eph 5:21). On the other hand, just as there are physiological similarities among all human beings, there also are significant differences between male and female. These differences were designed by God so that men and women would be complementary to each other and have a relationship that is parallel with God's relationship to us (v. 3). Relationships, according to God's design, are not a matter of equality but a matter of responsibility and purpose. God created men to give their lives on behalf of women so that women might offer their lives in the bearing of children. Together, men and women discover their lives and realize eternal significance as they bear and raise children for eternal life.

Q **11:6 Isn't the external supposed to be less important than the heart? Aren't we set free from the practice of external "Jewish" laws in the Gospel?**

Paul is describing the relationship between men and women on the basis of creation, not Jewish law or any other social or ethnic custom (vv. 14–15). Living with integrity—consistently and gladly demonstrating outwardly what is true of you essentially—is not a matter of law but a gift from God. If people who claim to be Christian do not follow what the Bible teaches about our relationships and conduct, it is because they are ignorant of the teaching, misled by an incompetent or false teacher, or dishonest about their claim. One of the many benefits of our redemption is the opportunity to recapture and realize at least something of what Adam lost for us all in the fall (Eph 5:15–21).

Paul said, "All things are lawful" (1Co 10:23), but that is not all he said. Paul added, "But not all things are helpful" and "not all things build up." Paul is giving instructions to people who intend to live according to God's design and for the benefit of others. How would a person do that? One way we benefit others is by providing a silent but visible witness to God's design. Men wear short hair as one of many indications that they understand their life is bound up in bearing leadership and responsibility for the lives of women. Women wear their hair long as an indication of their appreciation for the beauty God has given them as the object of man's care. Many people think women have stopped covering their heads because they assumed that artificial covers such as hats or veils were what God intended. But the text and nature plainly show that God provides the covering for the woman in her beautiful hair. Women who do not have any hair or long hair because of an illness or treatment for an illness are not in control of their hair; this is not an issue. Long hair, according to the use of this language in the Bible, means to have hair that lays on your neck. If you are a man, you would keep your hair trimmed so it is not on your neck. If you are a woman, you would make sure that your hair was long enough to cover your neck. In both cases, the length of a man's or woman's hair would leave no confusion about gender. A pastor who wears long hair is, at the very least, by ignorance or defiance of a clear, biblical teaching confusing those people for whom he is responsible. If such a pastor disagrees with the teaching, then he should stop pretending to be a servant of it. If such a pastor is ignorant, then he should withdraw from public service until he knows what he should be teaching and how to live accordingly.

• •

Q **11:7 It is hard for me to accept that "woman is the glory of man." Is there a way for us to better understand this?**

Let's start with a definition of *glory*. *Glory* means to do or be what no one else can. Jesus glorifies God by being (Son of God and Son of Man) and doing (redeeming the world) what no one else can (Php 2:5–11). What Jesus is to God the Father, women are to men. This is hard to accept? It was not good for man to be alone because he had no one for whom to lay down his life (love) and no way to be fruitful and multiply (Gn 2:18; 1Co 11:9). God created the woman because she was and could do what no man could: serve as the means by which God would create every other human being and eternal soul who would ever live. Far from hard to accept, this truth is hard to fathom in the wonder and honor it bestowed upon all women.

• •

Q **11:8–9 What does it mean that women were created for men, but men were not created for women?**

Genesis records that God made the man, Adam, first and then said, "It is not good that the man should be alone; I will make him a helper fit for him" (Gn 2:18). Man, made in the image of God, needed the object of his love, and no other animals were suitable, so God made the woman. Man was to be fruitful and multiply but could not do so by himself. This is why Paul says that the woman was made for the man, even though men were made for women inasmuch as men are created by God to care for women on God's behalf.

Q **11:9 Paul uses words strangely, just as Jesus said, "The Sabbath was made for man, not man for the Sabbath" (Mk 2:27). Here it is in regard to man and woman. Is there a connection?**

There are at least two reasons why Paul's language sounds like that of Jesus. First, Paul is writing the Word of God, of which Jesus is actually the author (Jn 14:26; 1Th 2:13; 2Tm 3:16). Second, just as Jesus was, Paul is arguing about the natural and reasonable relationship between things. Man was created before the woman, and both man and woman were created before there was a seventh day to set aside as the day of rest. Nevertheless, we do well to think carefully about what the little word *for* means in these discussions. We are created *for* God as women are created *for* men, but God does not depend on us. Men are *for* all women as God is *for* all people, not because God had no purpose apart from us but because we depend upon Him and He provides for us.

Q **11:10 What is the "symbol of authority" on a woman's head?**

First, authority and responsibility belong together, as we see absolutely with God. God has absolute authority over His creation, which is why He took absolute responsibility for redeeming it (Gn 3:15; Is 53; Jn 3:16). Since God holds men (men in general and husbands in particular) responsible for the well-being of women, it was neces-

sary for men to have authority. No physician would accept responsibility for a patient over whom he had no authority nor would a military commander for his troops. Second, the very nature of the fall was the breaking of this relationship; Adam usurped God's authority, and then the woman usurped the man's (Gn 3:1–7). In many ways it is true that men and the civilizations of men have reserved most authority for themselves, especially legal authority. On the other hand, ever since Eve, history reveals the prevalence and significance of the authority of women (Gn 3:16; Jgs 4:4–14; 2Ki 9:7–37; Est 7:1–10).

In the original text, there is no mention of a "symbol" of authority. Paul's argument is that women should have "authority upon" their heads because women are under the responsibility of the men, just as men have Christ as their head (v. 3). The word *angel* means "messenger" and does not necessarily refer to the heavenly, winged creatures of Bible texts or human imagination. In a way, men are "angels" toward women as they bear responsibility from God for their care, though I doubt this is what Paul means. Biblical texts indicate that angels pay attention to and are affected by the obedience or disobedience of people (Gn 19:15; Ac 12:23; 1Pt 1:12). Is it possible that Paul is cautioning women to be careful not to upset or grieve the men and heavenly beings who watch over them for good by despising their protection?

Q 11:13–15 Is it okay for women to have short hair?

Remember that twice already in this letter Paul has reminded us that "all things are lawful" (1Co 6:12; 10:23). The question for a Christian is not so much about wrong as about helpful. Why would any Christian woman—whether she is a pastor's wife, deaconess, or anyone else—want to ignore or contradict the New Testament? Wouldn't a Christian woman who knows and believes God's wonderful design in creation want to bear witness to that as clearly as possible by every means possible? What are fellow Christians and those outside of Christianity supposed to think when people who claim to be Christian so often and so casually disregard what the Bible clearly teaches as integral to our life and well-being? Many people assume that women no longer cover their heads in church because the practice of women wearing hats has gone out of fashion (though I don't know why—hats are awesome!). However, hats or veils or other superficial and artificial head coverings are not what Paul was speaking of here. God, as the Head of all, has provided what women need to cover their head: their long hair (v. 15). A woman's long hair, like many other beautiful features God has given, inspires us to think about the many aspects of wonder of which she is a steward by God's good graces (Ru 3:8–13; Pr 31:10–31).

Q 11:14 Do men with long hair go against the teachings of the Bible?

Yes, men who have long hair are going against what the Bible teaches. Like women who have short hair, men can have long hair, but why would they want to? Samson had long hair because he was a Nazirite from his mother's womb (Jgs 13:1–5). Absalom had long hair because he was vain, and it was the death of him (2Sm 14:25–26; 18:9–15). If a man wanted to follow Christ and be what God intended in creation, then keeping his hair trimmed as the Bible directs would provide a consistent witness and constant reminder that he is to use the life God has given him for the protection and support of women on behalf of Christ. For more on this see 1Co 11:4–10 above.

Q 11:17–33 If the Bible states that the bread and wine are the body and blood of Christ, then why do Baptists believe otherwise? Why do some churches not offer Communion every Sunday?

Fallen human nature rejects the truth for its own opinions (Ps 50:16–17; Jer 8:9; Rm 5:6–11). Baptists are not the only people who don't believe in the real presence of Jesus' body and blood in the Lord's Supper. In fact, most people, Christian or non-Christian, don't believe in the real presence or other wonders the Bible records. Here is the folly and inconsistency of fallen human nature: people take no time nor do they care to understand what they like or enjoy. How does our heart beat or our respiration work apart from our conscious will? How can television and wireless communication work, and why should it? How can the sun keep shining and not burn out? Why is there gravity? Fallen human nature only makes arguments against realities that threaten to get in the way of its self-gratification. There is no reason and no way to argue a reason against how God's creation might work or how He might choose to work within it because we are in no position to know what is possible or impossible.

There are a variety of reasons why churches do not offer Communion every Sunday. Some churches are unaware that the practice of communing only once a month or once every three months was caused by necessity. When America was being settled, several congregations would be served by a single pastor who would travel by horse—these pastors were called circuit riders. Such pastors traveled from congregation to congregation over a period of weeks and months. So, in fact, the Lord's Supper was celebrated every time the pastor came, but he did not come often. People are often more committed to traditions than to the Word, so they insist on maintaining the infrequency of the Lord's Supper. Others are afraid that having the Lord's Supper every week will diminish its significance. This notion may be true of human activities, but it is totally misplaced here. The Lord's Supper is an extraordinary work of God, and those who seek it are inspired to do so by God. Without the Word, there is no good moti-

vation to receive it. With the Word of God, there is always desire to receive it (Jn 10:28–30; Rm 10:17). Others do not offer Communion very often because they deny the real presence of the Lord's body and blood. Such people claim that the Lord's Supper is only symbolic and therefore of very limited benefit. As a symbol, they would argue that having it less often would make it more special, as discussed above. Others resent the time and/or cost of providing the Lord's Supper, even though no one makes them pay for the elements or stay for this part of the service. All of these reasons for not celebrating the Lord's Supper each Sunday are the product of fallen human nature that opposes what God does, even when the only purpose of God's activity is to give, forgive, and bless (Lk 13:33–35). Fallen human nature invents endless numbers of excuses and arguments for contradicting the Word of God. Only a soul regenerated by the Word and inspired by the Spirit recognizes and seeks what the Lord gives (Jn 1:11–13; 1Co 12:3).

If this answer makes sense, we should have Communion every Sunday and other occasions when the Body gathers in memory of significant events in biblical history. The Lutheran Confessions say, "Masses are celebrated among us every Lord's Day and on the other festivals. The Sacrament is offered to those who wish to use it, after they have been examined and absolved" (Apology of the Augsburg Confession, XXIV 1; from *Concordia: The Lutheran Confessions* [St. Louis: Concordia, 2006]). How often we celebrate and receive Communion does matter. Having too little interest in Communion indicates we are missing the significance of the gift and are in danger of despising it (Heb 10:29). Making rules about how often a person must receive it would be turning a gift into an obligation (Gal 3:13). How often we seek and receive the Lord's Supper would seem to follow naturally (or supernaturally) from the significance of the Sacrament. How often would a person with a fallen human nature like to have physical confirmation of the grace of God and His Spirit that regenerates us? Jesus said, "Do this, as often as you drink it, in remembrance of Me" (v. 25). If we were to be in error, would we want to err on the side of too often or too seldom?

● ● ● ● ● ● ● ● ● ● ● ● ● ● ● ● ● ● ●

Q 11:17–18 How can they hold to the teachings and still do more harm than good in their meetings? What kinds of divisions does Paul mean?

In v. 2, Paul praised the Corinthians because they remember him and "maintain the traditions" he delivered to them. Paul said they "maintain" (literally "have") the traditions, as in "hold as their ideal." Paul did not say that they obey what the Word teaches. There is a big difference between holding onto something and living in perfect obedience to what that something commands. Paul already responded to some of the divisions among the Corinthians in 1:10–31; 6:1–8; and 8:1–13. Paul adds to this list of divisions and factions (v. 19) the division caused by people who have food

and wine yet do not share with those who have not (vv. 21–22). When Christians, the Body of Christ, come together in public so that this Body of believers becomes visible, we would hope to see a Body of believers doing what the body of Jesus did during His ministry. The Body of Christ at all times— but certainly in public—ought to be living in love and service to others. The selfishness and self-indulgence of some who ate and drank too much while others had nothing completely contradicted their purpose and witness. Better to refrain from coming together as the Church at once in public if doing so is the occasion for the mistreatment of those who have little or the judgment of hypocrisy by those who are outside (1Co 6:6–7).

● ● ● ● ● ● ● ● ● ● ● ● ● ● ● ● ● ● ●

Q 11:18 Paul refers to them coming "together as a church." Is he referring to them being the true Body of believers?

Believers of all times and places make up the Body of Christ (1Co 12:27; Eph 4:4–6), but this Body is invisible as people simply live out their calling in the world around them. The phrase "come together" occurs four times in this section (11:17, 18, 20, 33). This section is concentrated on the Lord's Supper. This suggests that the purpose of gathering believers together in one place was for this purpose. However, on the day of the sun (Sunday), at the rising of the sun (morning), the Body of Christ became visible as the believers assembled in one place (as Jesus' body was visible on Easter

Sunday) to receive the visible body and blood of Christ (under the forms of bread and wine) from the visible body of Christ (the pastor). This is to say, the early Christians kept celebrating the redemption of Christ with all the means available to keep that celebration clearly connected with the history from which it flows.

Q 11:19 How do we know if we have God's approval?

We know if we are approved by God if we are the product of His Word and are living according to it (Jn 1:11–13; 3:1–7; 8:31–32; 10:28–30; 15:1–7; 1Jn 1:3–7; 2:19). There is only one true Christian Church, but there are many who falsely claim to be this body. The only reason groups can claim to be "Christian" denominations is because there is no authority among people to require them to demonstrate their fidelity to the Word, nor are there means of resolving disputes between groups with contrary claims. Churches, like the people of which they are made up, tend to believe what they want. This means that there are, in fact, practically as many "churches" as there are people who claim to be members. Christians do not seek to invent or maintain their own beliefs. Christians and the Christians' Church are singularly devoted to the truth as revealed by the one and only true God in His Word and creation (Dt 6:4; Rm 10:1–17; Eph 4:1–16). The only way to know if you have God's approval is to keep on comparing your thinking to what His

Word teaches and to remain in the Word so that His Spirit causes you to walk in His statutes and observe His commandments (Ezk 36:24–27; Jn 8:31–32).

Q 11:20–30 Can Lutherans and Catholics commune together?

The answer to your question depends on the Lutheran church to which you belong; some Lutheran denominations commune Catholics and some do not. What is more important is how to determine whether we should commune in a church of a different faith tradition. The name and essence of what we are talking about should answer our question. Expressing communion by sharing a meal together is appropriate if the communion of those doing so is real. In other words, people who all share the same public confession of faith are maintaining the truth when they give public witness to that in Communion. People who do not share the same faith are guilty of deception, hypocrisy, and even lying by appearing in public to be in communion as a congregation when, in fact, they are not. Real communion can only be created by the Word of God at work regenerating us in His image and bringing "every thought captive to obey Christ" (2Co 10:4–6; 1Jn 1:7; Eph 4:13).

Q 11:20 What does Paul mean when he says they are *not* eating the Lord's Supper?

Paul is exposing a contrast between God's purpose for His faithful people to gather in public and the purpose of those who were selfish. God's purpose for the Church to gather in public is to demonstrate the communion that His love creates among us with the celebration of His Holy Supper. God provided for us freely in His Son so that we are made free to provide for others (Php 3:7–14). The purpose of those who were selfish was to satisfy themselves, to eat as much as they wanted, and to drink until they were drunk while others had nothing (Lk 16:19–31). Paul is telling these selfish people that when *they* come together it is (obviously) not for the Lord's Supper but for a meal of their own devises.

Q 11:21 Why does Paul tell people to wait for each other when they receive Communion?

Paul was most likely not. When they gathered, the early Christians shared a meal in addition to the Lord's Supper. People brought food and wine as they were able. According to this verse and the next, some people were more concerned for their own hunger or thirst for wine than for the other people who were there. These selfish, self-centered people did not wait until the time came for everyone to share the food and wine and eat together.

Q 11:24–25 How do we as Lutherans use this text to justify our specific beliefs on Communion?

Beliefs, faith, and trust can be justified only if they are consistent with the truth. Luther used these verses along with the Gospel records of Jesus' institution of the Lord's Supper to learn what the Lord's Supper truly is (Mt 26:26–28; Mk 15:22–24; Lk 22:14–23). The truth about the Lord's Supper is profound yet uncomplicated, extraordinary yet simple: Jesus gives His real body and real blood with the bread and the wine for the forgiveness of sins according to His Word (Mt 18:3; Jn 3:1–12; 6:51–53). If faith means honesty about dependence, then people with true faith realize their dependence on God, which God provides for abundantly in this Sacrament as in all other aspects of our life. People who refuse the truth insist on being judge of what can or cannot be and contend that they provide for their own lives. In so doing, unbelievers cut themselves off from what God has freely and abundantly provided in His Son (Jn 3:18–21; Heb 6:4–8; 10:26–31). There is no way to justify beliefs that oppose and mean to contradict the truth.

Q 11:26 Why does it say that we will "proclaim the Lord's death" if we have a risen Savior?

The Lord's death was the climax and fulfillment of His work of redemption. Everything God promised from the beginning was fulfilled when Jesus said, "It is finished" (Gn 3:15; Jn 19:30; Lk 24:25–27). Paul has already used the crucifixion of Jesus as an expression that includes everything Jesus accomplished for the world when he said, "I decided to know nothing among you except Jesus Christ and Him crucified" (1Co 2:2). The body of Jesus was given and the blood of Jesus was shed on the cross when He died in our stead so that we would be forgiven (2Co 5:21). Declaring the Word of the Lord and distributing the very body that died on the cross and the very blood that was shed on the cross to those who come to have forgiveness confirmed is a public declaration of the death of the Lord (Heb 2:14–15; 9:24–26; 10:10). The crucifixion of Jesus teaches us *how* our salvation was accomplished; the resurrection of Jesus proves *that* it was accomplished.

● ● ● ● ● ● ● ● ● ● ● ● ● ● ● ● ● ●

Q **11:27 What causes someone to take Communion in an unworthy manner?**

The word *worthy* has to do with two things that match or are suited to each other rather than one thing being "good enough to deserve" another. For example, John the Baptist warned the crowd of hypocrites that came out to him that they should bear fruits "in keeping with repentance" (Lk 3:7–8). John was not telling these people that if they bore enough fruit, then they would become repentant; rather, John was saying they should bear fruit that is consistent with repentance or properly related to repentance. Worthy reception of the Lord's

Supper cannot have anything to do with our being good enough, since the very purpose of the Sacrament is to confirm forgiveness for not being good at all. Our fallen human nature, of itself, cannot receive this Sacrament either, since the natural man does not receive the things of the Spirit (1Co 2:14; Rm 5:6–11). Only a soul regenerated by the Holy Spirit through the Word is "worthy" or of a nature that is a match so that it is capable of and desires to receive what is given in the Lord's Supper. The same Word and Spirit that convey the Lord's body and blood in the Supper create the regenerate soul within us that receives that meal and its benefits. The selfish, vain, self-gratifying behavior of some Corinthians argued that this regenerate soul born of the Word was either dormant or absent, which is why Paul warns them about taking the Sacrament unworthily. You may want to note that the Gospel itself, Baptism, and Absolution are also restricted to those who would receive these worthily (Mt 10:11–15; 1Tm 1:8; Lk 3:7–9; Jn 20:22–23).

● ● ● ● ● ● ● ● ● ● ● ● ● ● ● ● ● ●

Q **11:29 What is the Greek word for "discerning"?**

The Greek word translated as "recognizing" or "discerning" in this verse is *diakrinon*. The root of the word is *krino*, which means "to judge." Thus *diakrino* has to do with being divided in one's judgment or judging accurately between two things. Jesus noted how the religious leaders were able to determine what the weather would be based on signs in the sky (Mt 16:3). Peter affirmed that God does not judge between this person and that person based on external differences (Ac 15:9). When people are divided in their judgments, this word is translated as "doubt" (Mt 21:21; Jas 1:6). In this verse, Paul is exposing the problem of people not judging or recognizing or discerning the difference between the bread and wine that are joined with the body and blood of Christ in Communion and ordinary bread and wine that we consume for our body's sake.

Q 11:30 Does Paul mean "weak and ill" spiritually?

Paul uses three words here to describe those who take Communion unworthily: *weak*, *sick*, and *asleep*. The first word, *asthenes*, occurs twenty-six times in the New Testament, having to do mostly with physical weakness but sometimes hinting at or speaking to spiritual weakness (Mt 25:43 and Ac 5:15 compared with Mt 26:41 and Rm 5:6). The second word, *arrostos*, occurs only five times, all of them having to do with physical illness. The third word, the verb for sleeping, *koimaomai*, occurs eighteen times, having to do with simple, physical sleep or the death of the body (Mt 27:52; 28:13). Those who are without the Word and thus incapable of receiving the Lord's Supper are already weak, sick, and perhaps even dead spiritually (Heb 6:1–8; 10:19–31). This fact plus the common meaning of the three words Paul uses here argues that Paul

is talking about people becoming physically weak or ill or even dying.

Q 11:34 Are there other problems concerning the Lord's Supper among the Corinthians that are written down anywhere else that provide Paul's further direction? What or how does one fill that hunger at home?

In the New Testament there is a remarkable absence of material that speaks to the Lord's Supper. Matthew, Mark, and Luke record the institution of this meal by Jesus, but in very few verses (Mt 26:26–28; Mk 15:22–24; Lk 22:14–23). Paul also recounts what happened at the Jesus' institution (1Co 11:23–25). Hebrews warns of despising the Sacraments along with the Gospel itself (Heb 6:1–8; 10:19–31). It is possible that the New Testament says so little because the matter is rather simple and because Old Testament practice concerning the Passover provided an example and answers to questions that might arise (Ex 12:24–27, 43–49).

Paul simply means to say that if people are going to be too hungry during worship to wait until the meal following, they should eat something at home before they come. Christians are oriented toward the well-being of others. If I eat at home, it is in order to be prepared to serve the best interests of others. If I abstain from eating during worship, it is out of consideration for others who have nothing to eat (Rm 14:7–23).

Q 12:3 Nobody can say "Jesus is Lord" but the Holy Spirit?

Right. Since the fall of Adam, our human nature has no capacity for any positive relationship with God (Gn 6:5; Jer 17:9; Rm 5:6–11; Eph 2:1–3). Only God, through the activity of His Word and Spirit, can regenerate us to be His children who love Him and confess the truth (Jn 1:11–13; 3:1–7; 8:31–32; 15:1–7; 1Jn 3:9).

Q 12:8–10 Are these the only spiritual gifts the Holy Spirit gives us?

The gifts of the Spirit are not exhausted or restricted by this list. Paul mentions other gifts in Rm 12:6–8; Gal 5:22–23; and Col 3:12–17.

Q 12:9 Why is faith listed among the diversities of gifts?

All faith is created by God through the working of His Word and Spirit (Jn 6:29; Rm 10:17; 1Pt 1:5). Even the measure of faith we possess is determined by God (Rm 12:3). Perhaps Paul is referring to the gift of an extraordinary faith, such as that found in Enoch, Noah, Abraham, Job, and Daniel (Gn 5:24; 6:8; 15:6; Job 1:8; Dn 6:10, 18–23; Ezk 14:12–20).

Do people still speak in tongues?

Q 12:10 Do people still speak in tongues and interpret today?

It is possible that speaking in languages and interpreting them is still happening today as in the first century, but how to know if this is the case? In the first century, the Holy Spirit provided the ability to speak in foreign languages immediately in order to confirm the Gospel, to confirm that the Gospel comes to all immediately through the Word, to fulfill Old Testament prophecy, and to confirm that the apostles are authorized by God to communicate His Word (Mk 16:16–20; Lk 10:16; Ac 2:1–21; 8:14–18; 10:44–48; 11:1–18; 15:1–10). Since we have the Word of God established and authenticated in the biblical text, and since the apostles and the circumstances God provided for through them have passed, it seems impossible for speaking in tongues and interpreting to happen just as it had then. However, there are still people who clearly are gifted by God in languages and the interpretation of languages. The gifts of God are still with us, but not with the magnitude and immediacy that was essential after Jesus' resurrection in order to establish the truth and grace of God against all opposition.

Q 12:23 What is meant when Paul says that "we bestow the greater honor" on "those parts of the body that we think less honorable"?

Begin by understanding the parallel between human anatomy and the composition of the Christian Church. Modesty has taught us to cover certain parts of our bodies in order to avoid embarrassment, which is a product of the fall of Adam (Gn 3:7–8, 21). Paul is not saying that parts of the human body are shameful in themselves—quite to the contrary. Paul is arguing that the human body is one unified whole, but parts of our bodies are more protected than others; some need to be covered, even if only to avoid embarrassment by their exposure in our culture. Similarly, all believers make up the single, unified Body of Christ, the Church. We are all the same, generated by the Word of God, yet we are all different, created by God for particular purposes (Rm 12:3; Eph 4:1–11). Some people have a strong faith, yet they need protection, which Jesus provided (Mt 9:9–13; Lk 10:38–42; Jn 8:2–11). Other people have, perhaps, a weaker faith but are called by God to serve Him in very public ways, like Peter (Lk 22:31–34, 54–62; Jn 21:15–22; Ac 10:9–11:18; Gal 2:11–16). As Christians, we openly confess that all we are and have are gifts from God according to His will and good pleasure (Jb 1:21; Jn 15:5; 1Co 4:7). Accordingly, we are careful to respect one another and consider just how necessary each person is by what he or she contributes to the life of the gathering of believers, the Church.

● ● ● ● ● ● ● ● ● ● ● ● ● ● ● ● ● ● ●

Q **12:28 Do those with gifts of healing still exist today? If so, do they perform miracles at the same magnitude of those in biblical times?**

The purpose of miracles in the ministry of Jesus and by the apostles was to confirm who they were and to prove that the promises of God had been fulfilled; this is the New Testament (Jn 10:31–39; Mk 16:16–20). There are still people who are clearly gifted by God in languages and healing. Anyone who has sought healing for a difficult medical problem is likely to know that all physicians are not created equal. The gifts of God are still with us, but not with the magnitude and immediacy that was essential after Jesus' resurrection in order to establish the truth and grace of God against all opposition. See 1Co 12:10 above for more on this question.

● ● ● ● ● ● ● ● ● ● ● ● ● ● ● ● ● ● ●

Q **12:31 What does it mean to "earnestly desire the higher gifts"?**

Sometimes Paul refers back to things about which he has already spoken. At other times, Paul refers to something he is going to talk about next, which is the case here. Paul spends all of ch. 13 and part of ch. 14 on the subject of love. Paul said that faith, hope, and love remain, but the greatest of these is love (1Co 13:13). Paul uses the same superlative expression, *meidzon*, in this verse and in 13:13. Paul does not mean to covet, for covetousness is idolatry and disrespect for God's wisdom in making us as we are (Col 3:5; Rm 9:20–33). Paul is directing all believers to a common virtue that always unites those who pursue it through the very love we pursue and the mutual concern and service it inspires.

Q 13:1–7 Doesn't this love apply only to God's love? Why is it used at weddings?

Agape, the Greek word translated here as "love," means "to give up everything for the object of your love." When fallen human beings love that which is unworthy of love, then death and disaster result (Lk 11:43). God is love—and the source of all love—that works for good (1Jn 4:16, 19). When God loves this way, it is good because we are the object of His love, and His love is the source of life (Jn 1:1–4).

This text is used at weddings because Christians are to love one another, and husbands are supposed to love their wives (Jn 15:9–13; Eph 5:25–27). While our fallen human nature still loves the wrong things, our regenerate soul is determined to love according to God's design for us (2Co 5:14–15; Php 2:5–11; Heb 12:1–3).

Q 13:1–3 Why is love more important than faith, prophesying, or knowledge?

Paul does not use the language of "more important" but does say that among those things that abide, love is the greatest (1Co 8:1; 13:13). Love is the greatest because of the way it directs and controls all other activities. Without love, prophecy and knowledge become the tools of selfishness and pride, which undermine the potential benefit of any good endeavor. Jesus berated the religious leaders for using their call to prophesy and their learning to take advantage of the people God intended them to serve (Mt 23:1–36; Jer 23:1–40).

Q 13:1 What is the Greek word translated as "love" that Paul uses? Why would some people be noisy gongs or clanging cymbals?

The Greek word for love used here is *agape*. This word for love means to "sacrifice everything for the object of that love," as Paul makes clear in Gal 2:20: "the Son of God, who loved me and gave Himself for me." This word for love can be contrasted with the Greek words *philos*, which has to do with friendship (also the root for *kiss*); *storge*, which has to do with family; and *eros*, which has to do with sexuality (but this term does not occur in the Bible). God's purpose in the gift of speaking in tongues—granted to His apostles and those upon whom the apostles laid their hand—was to confirm that the Gospel of Jesus Christ was accomplished, was communicated immediately through the Word, was for all people without distinction, and was declared with authority by the apostles (Mk 16:16–20; Ac 2:1–24; 8:4–18; 10:9—11:18; 15:1–12). In other words, the purpose of speaking in the languages of other, foreign people was to convey the love of God for them, love so great and powerful that it reversed and transcended all that separated people from God and people from one another (Gn 11:1–9). God communicates His love clearly to all because of His love for all.

When people claimed to be speaking in tongues as a matter of pride and competition, as was the case in just about everything occurring among the Corinthians, they were not communicating love at all. People who speak from pride and selfishness, regardless of the words they say, are only making noise that confuses the truth in the minds of those who hear them. Such people are doing what God has always condemned: "This people draw near with their mouth and honor Me with their lips, while their hearts are far from Me" (Is 29:13; Mt 15:7–8). Paul picks up this argument about speaking in tongues without love in the next chapter (1Co 14:6–19).

Q 13:8 If a marriage ends, does this mean the couple never shared loved?

If a marriage fails, it is always because love is lacking. Where love is lacking, marriages are bound to fail. Many human relationships are based on other forces and regulated by rules to which mutual consent is given, like business partnerships, labor contracts, or purchases. A marriage is the union of a man and woman according to the image of God in which they were created (Gn 1:26–27; 2:18–25). Love is not a substance independent of us that can be shared, like an apartment. Love is the determination of a man to love a woman just as God loves us (Eph 5:25–27). The love of the husband for the wife makes the way for her to submit to his care for her (5:22–24).

Q 13:10–12 What is the meaning of vv. 10–12?

Paul is contrasting the constant and everlasting nature of love with temporary things. Although God's love for us is perfect and everlasting, our fallen human nature constantly rebels against it and keeps us from realizing it fully. God uses the course of our life to lead us out of our fallen human natures into the life of a regenerate soul that His Word and Spirit work in us (Jn 1:12–13; 1Jn 3:1; Rm 6:1–23). The love of God revealed in nature and in His Word, the love of God for us in Christ, and the Holy Spirit's work in our lives all work to bring us to maturity, that is, to realize fully the love of God for us when we are reunited with Him apart from the fallen human nature that separates us (1Co 15:50–57).

Q 13:11 Jesus said we should become like children to enter heaven, so why does Paul say to give up childish ways?

The New Testament speaks to us in particular ways, according to our composition. Sometimes a text is speaking to or about our fallen human nature (Rm 3:10–20). Sometimes a text is talking about our regenerate soul (1Jn 3:9). Sometimes a text is speaking to the whole of us (Rm 8:1). When Jesus says you cannot enter the kingdom of heaven unless you repent and become as a child, He is speaking about our human nature (Mt 18:3; 1Co 2:14). In this verse, Paul is speaking about the whole person—fallen human nature and regenerate soul. As Christians, we are determined to give up the ignorance, thinking, and childish things of our fallen human nature. The Word of God works repentance in our human nature while it inspires and orients our regenerate soul so that as a whole person we become more mature and faithful (Heb 12:1–29).

• • • • • • • • • • • • • • • • • • • •

Q 13:13 Why is love greater than faith and hope?

Please see 13:1–3 above.

• • • • • • • • • • • • • • • • • • • •

Q 14:2 Is speaking in tongues real today? Is speaking in tongues similar to praying?

Speaking in tongues is not prevalent throughout Christianity today, but there are church organizations that claim a Christian confession and insist that they speak in tongues. In some cases these churches make speaking in tongues necessary for salvation. I don't know how we could say that speaking in tongues does not or cannot happen today because God could certainly enable people to speak in tongues if He wanted to do so (Eph 4:7). On the other hand, we no longer possess the cause or means of authenticating these claims. The purpose of speaking in tongues was to authenticate the apostles and to demonstrate that the saving grace of God in Christ was for all people and was worked immediately through the Word and Spirit (Mk 16:16–20; Ac 2:1–24;

8:4–18; 10:9–11:18; 15:1–12). We have the authoritative Word of God in the Bible and its witness to the nature of the Gospel, and God's love for all is clear. God does still gift people with language ability, though not as profoundly or as instantaneously as reported in Acts (please see 13:1 above). Neither Christ nor any of His apostles are here to discern for us whether those who claim to speak in tongues are actually doing so. Some studies done by university departments of linguistics report that there was no discernible language in the sounds made by people who claimed to be speaking in tongues.

We might suppose that it is possible for a person to pray in a foreign language he or she had not previously studied, though I don't know what this would have to do with the purpose of speaking in tongues as revealed in Mark and Acts (Mk 16:16–20; Ac 2:1–24; 8:4–18; 10:9–11:18; 15:1–12). Paul speaks about speaking in tongues as prayer, but this is within a chapter in which Paul is cautioning against speaking in tongues, and he may even be speaking sarcastically at times (v. 18).

• • • • • • • • • • • • • • • • • • • •

Q 14:2 What is the purpose of speaking in tongues, especially if you speak the same language as those who are listening? Is Paul in support of speaking in tongues?

In 1Co 13:1 Paul mentioned the languages "of men and of angels," but as we have seen, "angel" does not necessarily mean a heavenly creature, nor does it mean they speak in some language unintelligible to people (see 1Co 6:3). All language has a divine origin because the Son of God is the Word and because God created the multitude of languages at Babel (Gn 11:7). Your question about speaking in tongues when there was already a common language is critical. The majority of people at this time spoke Greek. On Pentecost, the crowd in Jerusalem could easily have understood what Peter had to say if he spoke in Greek. But the point that had to be made irrefutably was that the Gospel was for all people, and what better way to prove that than to give the apostles the ability to speak the Gospel in all the particular languages of the places from which these people had come (Ac 2:5–21). On later occasions, I suspect the converts who spoke in tongues were speaking Hebrew, otherwise the Jews who doubted the Gospel could have claimed that speaking in tongues was deceit (Ac 10:44–11:18; 19:1–9. Note the absence of speaking in tongues with the Ethiopian, because he did not need to be convinced about the nature of the Gospel or God's disposition toward all people, Ac 8:26–39).

Paul is in support of all that serves others and builds up the Christian Church (vv. 3, 4, 5, 12, 26, and 31). Paul wants people to prophesy because this describes the practice of sharing the Word of God with one another (Col 3:16). Paul is opposed to speaking in tongues because it either comes without interpretation or comes for selfish, egocentric reasons or both (13:1; 14:2, 4–19). Please see notes on 14:2 above for more about speaking in tongues.

• •

Q 14:5 Why does Paul rank the gifts of God? Why does he want all from the church in Corinth to prophesy?

Jesus taught that "greatness" had to do with humility and service rather than conceit and selfishness (Lk 22:25–27; Jn 13:2–17). Jesus also taught that His Word was the one thing needful (Lk 10:38–42; Jn 8:31–32). Paul and Peter repeat this teaching in their letters (Php 2:5–11; 1Pt 5:1–4). Love is the greatest among those things that endure because of the way it directs and controls all other activities (1Co 8:1; 13:13). Without love, prophecy and knowledge become the tools of selfishness and pride, which undermine the potential benefit of any good endeavor. Jesus berated the religious leaders for using their call to prophesy and their learning to take advantage of the people God intended them to serve (Mt 23:1–36; Jer 23:1–40). The person who prophesies—that is to say, shares the Word of God with others—is greater than others because sharing the Word provides the grace and Spirit of God by which all other benefits come (Jn 6:63; 15:1–7; Ezk 36:24–27).

Paul did teach that only some were given by God to be prophets (1Co 12:29; Eph 4:11). In those instances, Paul is talking about men who bear extraordinary and public responsibility for representing God, as the prophets did in the Old Testament and as the apostles of Jesus did in the New Testament (Is 6:6–10; Jer 1:4–10; 23:30–32; Ac 8:18–20; 1Tm 3:1–13; Jas 3:1). In this text Paul is using the word *prophesy* in the sense of sharing His Word with one another, as he urges in many other places (Eph 5:18–19; Col 3:16). What is known as the Great Commission was spoken by Jesus only to the eleven apostles, yet Paul says we are all "ambassadors for Christ" and Peter refers to us as a "royal priesthood" (Mt 28:16–20; 2Co 5:20; 1Pt 2:9).

Q 14:12 If we should "strive" to obtain gifts, does that mean God doesn't grant them to us?

You may have noticed that Paul does not speak this way in his other letters or in Acts. Paul is using the language of the Corinthian mind-set and speaking to their competitive spirit. Rather than insist only that the Corinthians be humble servants of one another, Paul tries to direct their energy toward those activities that will build up rather than disintegrate the church. This direction of energy is parallel to what Paul was doing in his counsel to the unmarried (1Co 7:1–9, 25–40).

Q 14:14 Why is my mind unfruitful?

If a person claims he is speaking in tongues but does not know what he is saying, his mind is unfruitful or of no use because it doesn't know what was said. Paul devotes the majority of Rm 6 to the necessity of applying our minds to opposing our fallen human nature and promoting the way of Christ.

Q 14:15 What does it mean by "I will pray with my mind"?

Paul has been talking about a conscious, loving devotion to the well-being of others. At the same time, Paul has been exposing and casting down claims from conceited and competitive people who wanted others to think they were better and closer to God because of extraordinary spiritual experiences that defied explanation (2Co 10:4–6). Later in this chapter, Paul will say, "The spirits of prophets are subject to prophets" (v. 32). Paul is saying that he will (and we should) pray by the inspiration and instruction of the Holy Spirit and with full application of our minds toward the care of others and their needs (Ezk 36:24–27; Jn 16:13).

Q 14:20–21 Why did God previously tell us that to enter the kingdom of heaven we have to become like little children, but now Paul is telling us to stop thinking like children?

First, Paul commands us to stop being "children in thinking." Second, Paul commands us to be small children in what is evil. Third, Paul commands us to be "mature" in thinking. Thus being childlike or mature depends on what we are talking about. According to our fallen human nature, we must repent and become like children; that is, we must make our fallen human nature as incapable, ineffective, and naïve as an infant. On the other hand, regarding our regenerate soul and the Word of God, we are to be mature and capable (Mt 10:16; 18:3; Rm 13:3; 1Pt 3:15). For more on this subject, see 1Co 13:11 above.

. . . .

Q 14:21 When Paul refers to the psalm in this verse, is he saying that God is trying to speak to these people through "strange tongues"? Does it seem to go against the point he is making?

Throughout Old Testament times and now in New Testament times, there is a curious reversal of relationships. Anyone might have expected that God's chosen people, the children of Israel, would have always and faithfully served as God's ambassadors and messengers to the rest of the people in the world who did not know God (Is 9:1; Lk 2:32). However, there are a vast number of examples in which foreigners were actually the ones bearing witness to the children of Israel (Jnh 1–4; Lk 4:24–30). The Jews from foreign countries who were in Jerusalem for Pentecost received the witness of the apostles in the languages of their countries, while the Jews from Jerusalem mocked (Ac 2:11–13). The fact is that people from foreign nations, who had a native language foreign to the Jews, were often witnesses to the truth, yet the Jews still refused to hear (Mt 2:1–16; Ac 13:44–48; 28:23–28).

. . . .

Q 14:22 If speaking in tongues is a gift from God, why does Paul say it is a sign for unbelievers?

Faith, belief, and trust all mean the same thing: honesty about dependence. True believers, in honesty, recognize that all human beings have descended from Adam, all are equally fallen and in need of redemption, and that God loves all and has redeemed all in Christ. True believers, therefore, do not need to be convinced that the Gospel is for all, saves all, and comes to all, even as the Word is proclaimed. The extraordinary witness of speaking in tongues on Pentecost, in Samaria, and in Cornelius's house was necessary to combat the unbelief of self-righteous Jews (Mk 16:16–20; Ac 2:1–24; 8:4–18; 10:9–11:18; 15:1–12). When the apostles spoke in the languages of people from foreign lands, and when foreigners spoke in the language of the Jews, the truth of God's universal love and grace was demonstrated irrefutably. The Corinthians had lost sight of this purpose for speaking in tongues and, as is the case in our day, had begun to claim they were speaking in tongues as a means of promoting their own ego or image in competition with others (1Co 1:10–23). On Pentecost, the Jews visiting Jerusalem understood the languages the apostles were speaking. In Samaria and at Cornelius's house, the Jews understood their own language as these foreigners spoke it. When the Corinthians did what they claimed was speaking in tongues, no one understood—which is why Paul is concerned about people assuming the Corinthians are insane (14:23). Speaking in tongues had served as a sign for people who did not believe the Gospel was for all. Speaking in tongues could also be the Holy

Spirit inspiring the speaker with truth that would expose and convict unbelievers who were present, but only if the speaker or someone else present could translate what had been said in the tongue.

● ● ● ● ● ● ● ● ● ● ● ● ● ● ● ● ● ● ●

Q 14:26–28 Why don't Lutherans speak in tongues (with interpreters, of course)?

Lutherans don't speak in tongues for the same reasons the vast majority of Christianity does not and is not seeking to: (1) the apostles have been authenticated (Mk 16:16–20); (2) the nature of the Gospel as coming immediately through the Word and for all has been demonstrated (Ac 2:1–24; 8:4–18; 10:9–11:18; 15:1–12); and (3) there are no apostles present anymore who could confirm whether claims to speaking in tongues were true or a lie. Those who claim a Christian confession and claim to speak in tongues have no way of knowing that their claim is true nor any certainty about what they are saying. They might as easily be cursing God as praising Him; how are we to know? On the other hand, there are plenty of Lutherans and others who are very gifted in language and who, by steadily applying themselves to this work, are bringing the grace and truth of God to people of various tongues around the world.

Is it wrong for women to be voting members of a church?

● ●

Q 14:34–35 Why does Paul say it is wrong for a woman to inquire about something in church? Is it wrong for women to be voting members of a church?

We must understand what Paul means when he says "in the churches." All believers of all times and all places make up the Body of Christ, which is the Church (1Co 12:12–27; Eph 2:19–22). However, when Paul uses the expression "in the churches," he is referring to believers who have gathered together in public to receive the Lord's Supper (1Co 11:17–33). In this setting, not only the women but also almost everyone is to remain silent because this is the occasion for the pastor or elders to speak publicly and with authority on behalf of Christ (1Co 14:26–33; 1Tm 2:8–3:7; Jas 3:1; 1Pt 4:11). Outside of the particular and public gathering of the church, all members of the Body of Christ seek to make as clear and constant a witness to the truth and grace of God as possible (Lk 10:1–2; Jn 13:35; 2Co 5:14–21; 1Pt 3:15). The difference does not have to do with advancing the Word of God in the hearts and minds of others; all Christians do this through the whole course of their lives and during the course of each day (Dt 6:4–9; Col 3:16). The difference has to do with where Christians advance the Word. When the Body of Christ has become visible by gathering, they receive the body and blood of Christ under the visible forms of bread and wine from the visible form of Christ in the pastor—all are to be silent and listen to him, just as would be appropriate if Christ Himself were with us (Lk 4:16–21; 10:16, 38–42). Asking questions during a Communion service would be disruptive, which is one of the reasons for making sure the pastor can teach faithfully and clearly. Outside of the public gathering of believers for Communion, everyone is free and encouraged to speak and ask questions.

There are at least three problems related to voting within the Christian congregation. The first problem is that people from Western democratic nations seem to think that voting is necessary and indispensable, but this is not the case. The second problem is that the Christian church has become so involved in worldly affairs and so covetous of the ways of the world that there are matters to be decided that the Word does not address. When Peter wanted to build shelters on the Mount of Transfiguration, God the Father interrupted Peter with the command that he listen to Jesus (Mt 17:4–5). If we are strangers and sojourners here, as was Abraham, our father in the faith, why do we insist on constructing buildings for ourselves (Heb 11:8–16; 13:14)? If one's life does not consist in the abundance of possessions, why do Christian congregations spend so much time voting on what to purchase and how much (Lk 12:15)? The third problem has to do with women seeking to exercise authority and control over men while men abandon their responsibilities to care for the women. This subject is discussed in detail in 1Co 11. It will be very helpful—even essential—to re-read 1Co 10:14–11:34 in order to have a broad view and better understanding of the relationship among Communion, worship, and gender relationships. Many of these questions have answers there.

• • • • • • • • • • • • • • • • • • • •

Q **15:5 Why did Paul say that Jesus had appeared to the Twelve when Judas was already dead at this time?**

There are a few ways to resolve this apparent difficulty with the text. One is to recognize that Paul may not have been concerned with using the precise number of apostles actually present. The Bible refers to the twelve tribes of Israel and the twelve apostles, yet in both cases there were actually thirteen. Another related possibility has to do with manuscript transmission. There are manuscripts that have "eleven" rather than "twelve" in this verse. Whether this was the original reading or the result of scribes meaning to make a correction, it reveals that ancient Christians had noticed what you did. I suspect the most likely explanation is that "the twelve" had become a shorthand term for the apostles—perhaps similar to the use of "the three musketeers" even though there actually were four. The presence of the definite article suggests it was a title for the apostolic group rather than a count of the number of disciples who saw Jesus on that particular occasion.

• • • • • • • • • • • • • • • • • • • •

Q **15:8 What does Paul mean when he says he was "untimely born"?**

Some translations say "one born out of due time." What Paul means is that he was not with the other apostles from the beginning (Ac 1:21–22). Paul was converted and called to be an apostle sometime after Jesus' ascension, and he received the revelation of Jesus Christ in an extraordinary way (Ac 9:1–20; Gal 1:11–23; 2Co 12:2–4).

• • • • • • • • • • • • • • • • • • •

Q 15:10 On what does Paul base his claim that he worked harder than all the other apostles?

Probably on the facts. Paul mentions that the other apostles had families with whom they, no doubt, spent time (1Co 9:4–6). Paul was almost always traveling, which is more taxing than working locally. Paul provides a partial account of his hard work in 2Co 11:22–33. The account of Paul's labors and tribulation is hard to beat by anyone's standard, and all this took place before his arrest in Jerusalem, imprisonment, further journeys, second arrest, and execution.

• • • • • • • • • • • • • • • • • • •

Q 15:12 Why did Paul spend so much time explaining the resurrection?

According to this verse, there were some among the Corinthians who argued that there was no such thing as a resurrection from the dead. Opposition to the truth of the resurrection was evident from the Sadducees' interaction with Jesus, from the council that arrested Peter and John after Jesus' resurrection, and from some of those who heard Paul teach on Mars Hill (Mt 22:23–33; Ac 4:1–2; 17:32). In the case of the resurrection from the dead in comparison with other doctrines, such as gender relationships, the problem is not how many different things were being taught but the magnitude of the single subject. Unlike other doctrines, the resurrection is something very few have witnessed, and the thought of an everlasting destiny terrifies most people. Interestingly, God has provided more witnesses to the resurrection than those of which we might be aware. Jesus raised people from the dead as evidence of this truth, but healing itself is a witness to God's ability and desire to restore life. Hibernation of animals, the resurgence of plants in spring, and the sunrise all bear witness to the resurrection (Ps 19:1–3; Rm 1:20).

• • • • • • • • • • • • • • • • • • •

Q 15:29 What does it mean that the Corinthians baptized on behalf of the dead?

Christians do not baptize for the dead. "Baptizing for the dead" is a cult practice in which a living person, often a relative of someone who has already died, is baptized in place of the deceased person so that the soul of the deceased may be saved. Paul is using a cult practice with which the Corinthians are familiar as a response to those who claim that there is no such thing as the resurrection of the dead. Paul wants to know how people of a culture that practices baptism for the dead can object or disbelieve the fact that Jesus did rise from the dead and promises the resurrection of life to all who believe in Him. The Bible clearly teaches that once we are dead there is no changing our situation (Mt 25:1–13; Lk 16:22–31).

Q **15:32 Was this verse written to comfort those believers facing death in the Coliseum? Did Paul really fight wild beasts in Ephesus?**

Sound principles of biblical interpretation direct us to understand passages simply, as they present themselves, unless something forces us to seek another understanding. Paul had been prevented by the Spirit from traveling to Ephesus on his second missionary journey, perhaps because of some danger there (Ac 15:6). Paul did visit Ephesus at the end of that missionary journey and returned there at the beginning of the third missionary journey (18:19–21; 19:1–10). Paul refers to some life-threatening situations that occurred while he was in Asia, which would include Ephesus (2Co 1:8–10). Paul says plainly that he fought with wild beasts at Ephesus. Many scholars remind us that Paul, as a Roman citizen, was not subject to torment or execution by wild animals. In this case, then, "wild beasts" is a reference to those who oppose Paul (Gal 5:15; Php 3:2). Paul's point is that it makes no sense for him to fight for his life if there is nothing in our future for which he should want to live.

Q **15:39 Aren't birds and fish animals? Why do we all not have the same flesh?**

Land animals, birds, and fish were each created according to their own kind (Gn 1:20–31). Birds and fish were created on the fifth day, corresponding to God's creative work in the heavens and the seas. Land animals were created on the sixth day as God developed the land. Classifying creation depends on the level of which we are speaking. If we are comparing animals with plants and minerals, then fish, birds, and animals are all animals. If we are comparing kinds of animals, then we can easily see the differences among sea creatures, flying creatures, and land animals. God gave each different creature the kind of flesh it needs to thrive in its proper environment.

Q **15:45 Who is the "last Adam"?**

All human beings descended from Adam (Gn 2:7–24; Lk 3:23–38; Ac 17:26). All redeemed souls, regenerated by the Spirit of God to be children of God, are descended from Jesus (Jn 1:11–13; 3:1–7; 1Jn 3:1–9). Paul provides a lengthy comparison and contrast between Adam and Christ in Rm 5:12–21.

Q 16:1–4 Did the collection for the saints happen during worship?

In New Testament times, there were no expenses for the Christian church as an entity. People met in one another's homes and brought what was needed for Communion. The offerings that people brought, and the collections that were taken, provided for the physical needs of the poor, those in hardship, or those who devoted all their time to the ministry (Ac 2:42–47; 4:32–37; 6:1–7; Gal 2:10; 6:6; 1Tm 5:3–8; 1Co 9:1–11).

2 Corinthians

Q 1:1 Who are "all the saints who are in the whole of Achaia"?

Achaia is the southern end of present-day Greece, and Corinth was its most important city. The "saints" in this province refers to those who have been "set apart" by the grace of God, who trust in the forgiveness accomplished by Christ, and who have been regenerated by the Word and Spirit and are, therefore, holy.

Q 1:2 Do many churches begin worship with this verse?

Usually worship services begin with the invocation: "In the name of the Father and of the Son and of the Holy Spirit" (Mt 28:19). Many hymnals direct pastors to precede the sermon with these words and to follow the sermon with the words Paul wrote in Php 4:7.

Q 1:3–4 Why does Paul use the word *comfort* so much?

The first answer to this question is easy: because the Holy Spirit directed Paul to (1Th 2:13; 2Tm 3:16). The second answer is not so easy, as Paul does not tell us, in his own words, why he uses this word so much, as you rightly noticed. Paul uses the Greek verb translated as "comfort" more than half of the times it occurs in the New Testament (58 of 109 occurrences) and the noun almost all of the times it occurs (23 of 29 occurrences). Perhaps Paul cared about comforting people because he used to be the reason they needed comfort (Ac 7:57–8:3). Then again, Paul needed plenty of comfort himself for all the trouble he endured (Ac 9:16; 13:50; 16:16–23; 2Co 11:23–33; 12:7–10). Paul is doing for us exactly what he instructs us to do for others: comfort them as we, ourselves, are comforted by God.

Q 1:3 Is there any reason that Paul writes "blessed be the God and Father of our Lord Jesus Christ"? It seems as if Paul likes to relate to Christ as our God and His (and our) Father, contradicting the Trinity.

Paul is not contradicting the Trinity, but he speaks to and about each of the persons of the Trinity as God Himself directs. In Eph 4:4–7, Paul confirms that there is just one God, and yet Paul makes reference to the Father, Son (Lord, Christ), and the Holy Spirit. In this verse Paul begins with the source of all things, God the Father, from whom His only Son was begotten and from whom the Spirit proceeds. Christ has invited us to know and to pray to God our Father, and Paul advanced this teaching (Jn 14:13–17; 16:25–27; Rm 8:15–16). Paul calls the Father "blessed" because He is the one who makes all things come to be according to His will. This blessedness of God moved

> Why does God allow His apostles to suffer?

Him to send His Son into our flesh to suffer in our place that we might be comforted eternally by the work and presence of His Spirit (2Co 1:22; 3:17–18).

Q 1:4 Is the church of Corinth going through tribulations?

The church of Corinth had plenty of trouble of its own making, as Paul revealed in 1 Corinthians. The church in Corinth also had trouble from the outside, because the devil, the world, and human nature never stop opposing God's redemptive work (Ac 18:6, 9–17; Eph 2:1–3; 1Th 1:6; 2:2; 3:1–4).

Q 1:5–11 Why does God allow His apostles to suffer?

Suffering is the result of contradicting God's design and intent in creation; this is why God warned Adam about eating from the tree of the knowledge of good and evil and why God warns against everything else about which He warns us (Gn 2:15–17; Dt 30:19–20). Suffering is, therefore, a simple matter of cause and effect. We depend on all the different dynamics of nature that make it possible to build a house with hammer and nails, yet I suffer terribly if I hit my own thumb instead of the nail. Suffering is made worse when fallen creatures begin to afflict one another with their hatred and rebellion (Gn 6:5–6, 11–13; Mt 23:13–36; Jas 4:1–6). Suffering is made beneficial when God directs and limits it so that it serves to discipline those He loves, as was the case with the apostles, especially Paul (2Co 12:7–10; Heb 12:3–15). Suffering is a necessary means of turning our attention from a fallen, fleeting human nature to a regenerate soul that endures forever by the grace and Spirit of God (2Co 4:7—5:17).

Q 1:5 Does this mean that Jesus puts His pain into us, just as we do to Him?

Paul said, "The sufferings of Christ abound in us." The word *of* in English reflects a variety of particular relationships between words in the Greek text. Paul could mean that the sufferings that Christ suffered are inflicted on us, but this is contrary to Christ's purpose. Christ is the Lamb of God that took away the sin of the world. He bore our sufferings in order to deliver us from them. Paul could mean the sufferings of which Christ is the source, but again this is contrary to His nature and all that the Word says of Him. Paul most likely means the same kind of sufferings that Christ endured (Jn 15:20–21). To be Christian is to have the same disposition of love and service that Christ had and to experience the same response of hatred from the world (Mt 10:16–39). Christ never treats people the way they treat Him, otherwise there would be no hope for any of us (Ps 103:10–11; Lk 11:51–56; Heb 12:1–29; 1Pt 2:21–25).

Q 1:8–11 Suppose hardships keep us from moving and speaking. How does the comfort from God encourage us in this?

This may be a translation problem. Paul did not say "so we can work" for Him but "so that we may be able to comfort those who are in any affliction, with the same comfort with which we ourselves are comforted by God" (v. 4). If the hardship kept us from moving, then God would provide others and other means for us to make our way among people whom we could comfort. If our hardship was the loss of speech, then we could write or use sign language, as many people do. The comfort from God has to do with the contrast between our temporary lives in this world and eternal life, between our physical life in this material world and our regenerate soul in the spiritual kingdom. God's comfort comes from recognizing that just when our selfish, vain human nature thinks we have lost everything, then the life of the soul becomes evident in relationships with others. Not only can't hardships take away our life, but they actually provide the occasions for us to realize more of the eternal, invulnerable life God has given us. Notice how this is precisely the case with Christ. He demonstrated His nature and glory to all as He assumed in Himself their hardships and infirmities (Mt 8:1–17). Just when the devil, world, and fallen human nature thought they had made an utter end of Him, Christ triumphed by taking away the sin of the world and reconciling us to God (Php 2:5–11; 2Co 5:14–15; Heb 2:14–15). A person who has come to realize the fullness of life through hardships is the very best person to help others realize the potential of the hardships they face.

Q **1:8 Who is the "we" to whom Paul refers? What is the "affliction" about which Paul wrote? I thought God wouldn't give us more than we could bear.**

Paul mentions Timothy at the beginning of this letter (v. 1). Luke records that Paul met Aquila and Priscilla in Corinth and worked with them (Ac 18:1–3). Luke mentions Silas, Justus, Crispus, and many Corinthians who believed and were baptized in Corinth as well (18:5–8). Paul may have had any or all of these in mind when he wrote "we."

There is plenty of debate and speculation about the nature of the hardships to which Paul is referring. In Paul's previous letter to the Corinthians, he mentioned fighting with wild beasts at Ephesus (1Co 15:32; please see answers to questions there for more). Later in this letter Paul describes other hardships, such as beatings, shipwrecks, and imprisonments (2Co 11:23–27). When Paul says they "were so utterly burdened beyond our strength that we despaired of life itself," he is talking of the human nature of those who suffered. In the next verse and later in this letter Paul explains how the realization of our disability according to our fallen human nature is necessary if we are to become the spiritual children of God (2Co 1:9; 4:16–5:8).

Q **1:9–10 What happened to them in Asia?**

Please see 2Co 1:8 and 1Co 15:32 above.

Q **1:9 Is the purpose of suffering to allow us not to think too highly of ourselves?**

Absolutely. Fallen human nature insists on thinking too much of itself and blames sufferings for its inabilities. All of history proves this truth and was recorded that we might learn this lesson without needless suffering (Ps 119:50, 67, 71, 75, 92, 107; Pr 22:3; 27:12; 1Pt 1:6–9).

Q **1:13 Why does Paul emphasize that they will "fully understand" what he writes?**

Paul is making the point that his teaching is consistent with all the genuine Christian teaching they have ever previously heard. Inasmuch as the Corinthians have read and have come to understand the Christian faith, Paul believes they will recognize as genuine and understand what he is teaching them as well (Jn 14:26; 16:13).

Q **1:14 Wouldn't God be their first reason to be proud? What is meant by the word *boast*?**

God is obviously and absolutely the source of all legitimate boasting (Rm 3:27–28; 1Co 1:30–31). On the other hand, our ability to boast of God depends on the evidence that is provided by God's work through and among us (Jas 2:18; 1Co 2:4; 4:19). Jesus Christ provides for us the tangible demonstration of His life and activity in our own (Mt 25:31–40).

● ● ● ● ● ● ● ● ● ● ● ● ● ● ● ● ● ● ●

Q 1:15–22 Is Paul saying in this chapter that God always says yes when we are following God's plan and therefore never says no to us when it can benefit us?

I suspect you are correct. Jesus promised that whatever we would ask Him or the Father in His name would be done (Jn 14:13–14; 16:24–27). If we recognize that the phrase "in My name" means "according to My Word," then the relationship between our prayer and God's answer becomes obvious. God's will is that we should live, know the fullness of life, and communicate that life to others (Gn 1:26–31; 2:15–17; Ezk 18:32; Jn 10:7–18; Rm 8:28). Whatever we seek or ask against life, God surely opposes; whatever we ask or seek that is for life God surely provides (Nu 22:20–35; Jas 4:1–6; Mt 7:7–12; Eph 3:14–21).

● ● ● ● ● ● ● ● ● ● ● ● ● ● ● ● ● ● ●

Q 1:16 Why does Paul have to be sent by the Corinthians?

Paul was very conscientious about being responsible for his own needs and expenses (Ac 18:3; 1Co 4:12; Eph 4:28). On the other hand, Paul taught that those who are called to the public ministry should have their expenses provided for by the people whom they serve (1Co 9:1–18; Gal 6:6).

Sometimes Paul made particular references to or appeals for financial support during his ministry and travels (Php 4:15–17; Rm 1:13; 15:24). Paul knows that the Lord provides for all our needs abundantly. Sometimes the Lord provided for Paul through the gifts of faithful people, sometimes by granting Paul an opportunity to work, sometimes through the government (Ac 23:11–35; 25:12).

● ● ● ● ● ● ● ● ● ● ● ● ● ● ● ● ● ● ●

Q 1:17–20 What does he mean by this "yes" and "no"?

The answer to these questions follows from the answer to 1:17 above. When Paul talks about "yes, yes" or "no, no," he is referring to a person's attempt to say he will do something for certain and will certainly not fail. Paul argues against speaking as if we had absolute control and knew with absolute certainty what would happen in our lives. Overstating the certainty of our plans is similar to taking the Lord's name in vain; we are deceiving ourselves and others if we deny the fact that we do not ever know what will be until it has come to pass. Paul contrasts the limited nature of our knowledge and ability with that of God's own knowledge, will, and grace in Christ. The certainty we seek as the foundation of peace and hope in our life, like life itself, comes from God. God made promises to send a Savior for us from the very beginning and fulfilled them all to the smallest detail in the life of His Son, our Lord Jesus Christ (Gn 3:15; 12:3; 2Sm 7:12–17; Is 53:1–12; Mt 1:22–23; 2:15, 17, 23; 4:12–17; Gal 4:4). God always keeps His promises and always speaks the truth (2Tm 2:13; 1Jn 1:9). We find life, hope, peace, and courage as we abandon our own opinions and vanity for the Lord's will and Spirit (Is 55; Rm 6).

● ● ● ● ● ● ● ● ● ● ● ● ● ● ● ● ● ● ●

Q 1:17 Why does Paul question his planning?

Paul questions his own plans only out of humility, as is appropriate (Jas 4:13–15). Paul said that he does not make his plans lightly or without care, yet he understood that the Lord's ways are not our ways, and our plans are often made in ignorance of His (Is 55:8–9; Pr 20:24). Christians seek to discern and follow the will of the Lord for our lives while remembering that our ability to discern and to follow are severely lacking (Mt 26:41; Rm 3:10–17; 7:17–25; 1Co 13:12). Christians remain in the Word, pray for guidance, then remember that the will of the Lord will prevail and that His will toward us is always gracious and effective (Jn 8:31–32; Rm 8:28; Heb 12:3–17; Jas 1:2–6; Jer 29:11).

● ● ● ● ● ● ● ● ● ● ● ● ● ● ● ● ● ● ●

Q 1:20 Can we take all God's promises as our own?

God's promise to Abraham and Sarah was particular; Sarah is the one who conceived a child when she was way too old to do so by natural means (Gn 17:15–16; Rm 4:19). Elijah promised an old woman that she would have a son (2Ki 4:16). Gabriel's message to Mary was particular; she was the only virgin to ever conceive a child (Lk 1:26–38). On the other hand, even promises as particular as these apply to us because they demonstrate the love, grace, and faithfulness of God upon which we depend. Whatever God has done in history to save His people pointed forward to Christ, was fulfilled in Christ, and was recorded and accomplished for our benefit (1Co 10:1–13; 1Pt 1:10–12). I doubt it is possible to find anything in all of history or in the Scriptures that does not apply to us. All things either point to our need for a Savior or point to the Savior Himself (Gal 4:21–31; 1Co 9:9; Heb 2:1–4; Jn 20:30–31).

● ● ● ● ● ● ● ● ● ● ● ● ● ● ● ● ● ● ●

Q 1:21 If it is God who makes us stand firm, is it also God who allows us to fail? Do we really have free will?

Let's begin with a more careful translation: "Now He who has established us with you and anointed us is God." Paul uses the perfect tense to describe the activity of God in regenerating us as His own children, a new creation through the power of His Word and Spirit (Jn 1:12–12; 3:1–7; 2Co 5:17; 1Jn 3:9). The Word and Spirit of God that created this regenerate soul or inner person continue to orient and inspire that soul according to God's will and wisdom. All that we do right and well is the product of this work of God in us (Jn 15:1–7; 1Co 15:10). All that we continue to do badly and wrong is the work of our own, fallen human nature, tempted and led astray further by the world and the devil (Rm 5:6–11; 1Co

2:14; Eph 2:1–3). We do not have a free will, as Jesus and universal human experience makes evident at all times (Jn 8:31–47; Rm 6:15–22). The will we experience and the decisions we make are the results of our two natures in conflict and the forces all around affecting us (Rm 7:13–25; Gal 5:16–26). The presence of the world or the Word in our lives will determine which nature is more dominant and effective in what we think, do, and say (Ezk 36:24–26; Jn 15:1–7; Rm 10:17; 13:14).

Q 1:22 Is this "seal" of ownership set by God on everyone or just on believers?

The Greek verb translated as "to seal" occurs fifteen times in the New Testament. "To seal" means to provide the means by which something is verified or made certain (Mt 27:66; Jn 3:33). This verb occurs eight times in Revelation, where making sure the faithful are recognizable before Judgment Day is a matter of incomparable importance. The noun occurs sixteen times in the New Testament, all of them in Revelation except for three in Paul's letters. Like the verb, the Greek noun translated as "seal" has to do with verifying or making something certain. In this verse, I would suggest that the meaning is provided by the phrase that follows. The *and* in the middle of this verse is "epexegetical" or explanatory—an equal sign rather than a plus sign. Consider the following translation: "Who also sealed us, that is to say, has given us the deposit of the Spirit in our hearts." The Spirit that the Word of God communicates to us does

the sealing and is the seal, as Paul says a bit more clearly in Eph 1:13: "In Him you also, when you heard the Word of truth, the Gospel of your salvation, and believed in Him, were sealed with the promised Holy Spirit." As we have seen very consistently so far, the Word and Spirit are inseparable and actually accomplish what they promise (Jn 6:63).

Q 1:23 Why wouldn't a second visit benefit the Corinthians?

There is no record in Acts of Paul traveling to Corinth between the time he wrote the first and second letter, though some argue that Paul hints at a second visit in the first verse of ch. 2. But 2Co 1:23 seems to say very clearly that Paul did not make such a visit, and ch. 2 makes no sense if Paul had visited. Paul's point is that he stayed away on purpose. Subsequent visits to Corinth by Paul would surely have produced benefits for all. In this passage Paul is still responding to those who claim he has no apostolic authority because he doesn't know what he is or isn't going to do. Paul is explaining that he did not come to Corinth in order to give the Word and Spirit time to work repentance and faith among the people there. Paul sounds as if he were convinced that, had he returned too soon after his first visit, there would have been much conflict and bitter words (2Co 2:1–5). The conflict and bitter words (or severity of Christian discipline) is what Paul wanted to spare the Corinthians, if possible.

Q 1:24 Paul says, "Not that we lord it over your faith." What is he talking about?

Paul has been talking about why he did not come to Corinth, and he will talk about this more in the next chapter. Whether Paul comes or writes, he has powerful and authoritative counsel from God for the Corinthians. Yet Paul's authority as an apostle of Christ is exercised in a manner that is consistent with Christ and the Gospel. Neither Christ nor the New Testament nor the Gospel nor any apostle forces people to obedience (Gal 3:24). The Word and Spirit of God disable the noise and nonsense of our fallen human nature while His wisdom and grace inspire and orient us toward life and love (Jn 3:1–7; 15:1–7; Rm 6:21–23; Php 3:7–14). This is what Paul is stopping here to remind his readers.

Q 2:1–2 Do we know what happened that Paul had such a painful visit to Corinth?

If the "painful" visit was an occasion not recorded in Acts, it is impossible to say what made it painful. If the visit Paul refers to is recorded in Ac 18:1–17, then 1 Corinthians is our best, if not only, source of information. Might we suppose that the many issues that Paul addressed in 1 Corinthians were already issues while he was with them? The necessity of correction on so many subjects with people who were so competitive and self-centered would easily have made the visit painful for Paul, who would have been compelled to do the correcting, and for the people, who would have been subjected to such correction (1Co 1:10–13; 3:1–4).

Q 2:2 What is meant by "who is there to make me glad but the one whom I have pained"?

Paul just explained that he had not returned to visit the Corinthians in person because it would likely have been an occasion for harsh words and much conflict because the people were so far and frequently contrary to God's will in their living. If Paul had visited the Corinthians as they were, the painful nature of necessary discipline would have robbed him of the joy he always hoped for when visiting the faithful (Rm 1:8–13; Eph 1:15–23; Php 1:3–5; 1Th 1:6).

Q 2:5 What is this verse stating? Why does Paul say he will not put it "too severely"?

Paul is simply reminding himself and his readers that he does not wish to exaggerate or overstate the trouble. There seems to be an inverse relationship between the truth of a matter and how much needs to be said about it. Speaking accurately is powerful because accuracy argues for honesty and an honest report of the truth. Exaggeration, like swearing falsely, is the attempt to convince people that something false is true. Paul also wants the Corinthians to keep their focus. The issue here is not a selfish or self-centered one, having to do with what we suffer on behalf of one another. The issue here has to do with faithfully and lovingly correcting the conduct that produces conflict, grief, sorrow, and death.

• • • • • • • • • • • • • • • • • • • •

Q 2:6–11 Is Paul talking about a specific sin here, or is he speaking in general terms?

Paul is writing to the Corinthians about the man who had his father's wife (1Co 5:1–13). By saying "his father's wife," Paul is making clear that the man was committing sexual immorality with his stepmother (Gn 35:22; 2Sm 16:20–22).

• • • • • • • • • • • • • • • • • • • •

Q 2:7 Is this passage showing how public Confession and Absolution before a group should be handled? Since we are forgiven, are we still held accountable? Were the Corinthians supposed to forgive the man and allow him back into the church?

Yes, this passage is an invaluable example of how to handle a very public sin within a Christian congregation. Public sins must be responded to publicly, otherwise people are confused or enticed to do wrong (Ac 11:1–18; 15:1–12; Gal 2:11–16; 1Tm 5:20; Ti 3:9–11). Interestingly, it is Christ who bore responsibility for our actions, having taken our place under the Law (Mt 8:16–17; Jn 11:50; 18:39–40; 2Co 5:21; Gal 4:4–5).

There are consequences for our actions, which seems logical and inescapable. Jesus has redeemed us from the spiritual and eternal consequences of our contradiction to God's will. Jesus directs us to be reconciled with each other in time, to repent of our sins, and to apply ourselves to love and service to others (Ezk 18:30–32; Mt 5:23–24; 18:15–18; Mk 1:14–16; Jn 8:3–11). When a person continues to act against God, the faith, and the neighbor, he or she has strayed from the church and therefore has excommunicated himself or herself. The church responds carefully by recognizing this broken relationship and seeking, through repentance and grace, to draw that person back into communion with the faithful (Lk 15:11–32; Jas 5:19–20; 1Jn 1:5–10). The church doesn't change a person's relationship, but by bearing witness to the truth, the church serves the Lord's will for turning a person from darkness and death into light and life (Jn 3:1–21; Rm 1:18–2:29; 10:1–17; 2Co 5:16–20).

• • • • • • • • • • • • • • • • • • • •

Q 2:8 How are we supposed to reaffirm our love for God as Paul says?

Paul was directing the Corinthians to reaffirm their love toward the man who had his father's wife and was now repentant. The Corinthians would demonstrate their love toward him by confirming the truth of God's redemption in Christ and by applying that redemption to him through Absolution, the Lord's Supper, and the encouragement of fellowship with the faithful. This text is not talking about the rite of confirmation practiced by some denominations (a practice that is not taught in the Bible). While the Greek word translated as *reaffirm* in this text is not the word commonly translated as *confirm* in the New Testament, its purpose would be accomplished by the confirmation provided in the Sacraments. (The word used here, *kuroo*, occurs only here and in Gal 3:15.)

- - - - - - - - - - - - - - - - - - -

Q 2:9 What test is Paul referring to here?

Paul is referring to 1 Corinthians, where he commanded the people to act according to truth and love toward the man who had his father's wife (1Co 5:4–7). Faith is demonstrated in obedience to the Word and will of God (Mt 7:16–20; Jas 2:18–24). By giving them instructions on what to do about this man and what their own disposition toward him should be, Paul was testing their faith (Gn 22:1–14; Ex 15:25; 16:4; 20:20).

- - - - - - - - - - - - - - - - - - -

Q 2:10 Is this saying we have the same power of forgiveness as Christ does?

God forgave all sins when Jesus bore them and suffered condemnation for them in His crucifixion (Jn 1:29; 2Co 5:21). Jesus gave His disciples the responsibility and authority to confirm and assure people of this truth (Mt 18:18; Jn 20:23; Col 3:13; Jas 5:14–20). The Greek makes clear by the use of the perfect tense that sins have already been forgiven and remain forgiven. English translations fail to express this essential fact. Thus we do not decide to forgive, nor do we

make something happen that hasn't already taken place. Christians bear witness to the truth, even as Jesus did. If someone is repentant and seeking God's forgiveness, then it is our responsibility (and joy) to confirm that God has already forgiven sins. God establishes the reality; we help one another realize it is so (Lk 24:13–49; Ac 8:26–38). The Corinthians had trouble orienting their conduct to truth and grace. First, they contradicted the truth by accepting conduct that was inexcusable by a man who was impenitent; then they contradicted truth by refusing to confirm the grace of God to the same man when he had repented. The Corinthians did not need Paul's approval to forgive, but they certainly needed his counsel for doing so faithfully.

- - - - - - - - - - - - - - - - - - -

Q 2:12 Where is Troas? Why does Paul go there?

Troas is more commonly known as Troy, in present-day Turkey, on the eastern coast of the Aegean Sea, south of Istanbul. Paul went there during the second missionary journey. Paul traveled through southern Galatia, then headed northeast to Troy because the Holy Spirit had directed him to go to Macedonia (northern Greece, Ac 16:6–12).

- - - - - - - - - - - - - - - - - - -

Q 2:15–16 What does Paul mean by speaking of aromas and fragrances?

God created us and the world around us so that He could reveal Himself to us

(Ps 19:1–3; Rm 1:20). We see what God shows us (Mt 6:26). We hear what He speaks to us (Jn 10:27). We feel what He offers to us to touch (Jn 20:27). God appeals to our sense of taste (Ps 34:8). In this passage Paul compares the lives of people with what can be smelled (Ps 115:3–8 mentions all five senses and how idolatrous people lose the use of them). When Paul and his companions are with people who despise God, the truth to which Paul bears witness reveals that these people are spiritually dead. When Paul is with people who have been regenerated by the Word and inspired to love God, the Gospel that Paul proclaims to confirm and sustain their faith reveals that these people are alive. God is aware of both, just as we are aware of smells in the air.

● ● ● ● ● ● ● ● ● ● ● ● ● ● ● ● ● ● ● ●

Q **2:17 Paul goes out of his way to say he is not preaching for profit. What would his reaction be to televangelists? What about Christian businesses that sell for profit?**

There is a big difference between preaching the Word and then accepting what people provide and preaching the Word so that people will provide. If we love God above all things and our neighbor as ourselves, then everyone would work for the sake of love and be happy to live on what people provide in gratitude. Since we fail to love as God designed us to, it becomes necessary to promote fairness in our civil relationships. We may still maintain the ideal and a consciousness of serving God as good stewards with our skills and abilities while we name a price for the services given that is fair to the people we serve. Still, this arrangement will not work for certain functions. Judges, law enforcement officers, armed forces, and government leaders would have little hope of serving faithfully and fairly if they were paid by individuals for services rendered. Similarly, pastors cannot work for money nor are they paid by the person or people served because they act on behalf of Christ and must, therefore, always serve faithfully. Ultimately, God is the one who always provides (Gn 1:29; Ex 15:22–16:35; Dt 29:5–6; Mt 6:19–34). God made particular promises to and provisions for those who serve the spiritual needs of others on His behalf (Nu 18:21–32, Mt 10:5–11; 1Co 9:6–18). God provides particular commands for the people to tithe so that those who serve the Lord in this way (and others) would not be neglected (Gal 6:6; Ac 2:42–47; 4:32–37). Paul refused to receive anything from the Corinthians to prevent any confusion about the nature of his relationship to them on behalf of God (1Co 9:14–18; 2Co 11:7–12).

A televangelist could certainly speak the truth, and people could always be helped by hearing the truth. However, there are some particular problems associated with individuals who represent Christ in public but have no call to do so. First, there is the absence of a call. No one is to claim or try to represent Christ in the public ministry unless qualified and called to do so (Jer 23:30–32; Mt 10:5–15; Ac 8:14–24; 13:1–3; 19:11–20; 1Tm 3:1–7; Ti 1:5–9). Second, the "mass" approach to ministry is contrary to

Jesus' own example. Jesus did not raise His voice or cause it to be heard in the streets (Is 42:2). Jesus avoided crowds because they inevitably missed the point of what He was doing and teaching (Mk 5:24; 9:35; Jn 5:13; 6:26–27). Paul's uninvited and unapproved public appearance in the temple cost him four years of imprisonment and trouble (Ac 20:22–23; 21:4–14, 23–36). Third, operating independently and by self-appointment leaves such individuals without a congregation or brother pastors who provide accountability (Gal 2:11–14; Ac 11:1–18; 15:1–12; 18:24–28).

A business cannot be Christian, though it may employ Christians and serve the Christian mission. If this is the case, one might rightly expect such a business to be run on a nonprofit basis, as many hospitals and other genuinely philanthropic services are. Profit can come only from paying workers less than is fair and/or charging customers more than is fair. God condemns both practices (Lv 19:13, 35–36; Amos 8:4–6; Mt 20:1–15; Lk 3:10–14; 19:1–10; Phm 8–16; Rv 18:11–15).

● ● ● ● ● ● ● ● ● ● ● ● ● ● ● ● ● ●

Q 2:17 How can a church worker discuss pay without "working for hire"?

I don't believe it is possible and would argue against doing so. How can those called to serve in public ministry advocate trust in God if they are unwilling or unable to do so themselves? What kind of Christian congregation finds the Word of God inadequate for bringing about not only faith but

also the fruits of faith? If such workers are not provided for, why wouldn't they rather work with their own hands as Paul did, rather than confuse their witness by seeking more money for themselves (Ac 18:1–3)? If a congregation refuses to provide for its pastor, then should he not shake the dust off his feet and move on or consider that he had no call in the first place (Mt 10:11–14)? On the other hand, it is fitting and consistent with the Gospel for those with authority and leaders of congregations to advocate for those who serve so that they need not do so for themselves.

● ● ● ● ● ● ● ● ● ● ● ● ● ● ● ● ● ●

Q 3:1–3 If Christians are their own letter, why does Paul write letters to them?

Paul did not say that Christians were their own letter, but that the Christians of Corinth communicated to others what a letter written by Paul might have, particularly a letter of commendation. How would anyone know that Paul was an authentic apostle of the Lord Jesus? The other apostles in Jerusalem could write a letter of commendation for Paul, but then others would claim that Paul's authority came from the other apostles rather than from Jesus (Gal 1:1–2:10). Paul is explaining that he does not need to defend his apostolic authority or carry letters from others about his authority because the fruits of his labor prove this for him (Mt 7:15–20; Ac 16:16–18; 19:11–12; 20:17–21).

Q **3:3 What does this verse mean?**

At the end of ch. 2 and the beginning of this chapter, Paul talks about genuine servants of the Word in contrast to those who pretend to serve God but are really serving themselves ("peddlers of God's word," 2Co 2:17). In our culture, as in theirs, a person would need letters of recommendation when applying for a job or contracting services. Paul argues that the authenticity of his ministry and of the Word of God he communicates as an apostle is verified not with letters of reference in ink on paper, but with the very lives of people who have been affected by the Gospel (Mt 7:15–23; Gal 6:12–14). In our time we might compare this to evaluating the faithfulness of a pastor, teacher, or parent. Any one of these might boast about what a great pastor, teacher, or parent he or she is. A person may even have received awards and letters of commendation, but a true and irrefutable witness to the faithfulness of a pastor, teacher, or parent would be found in the lives of the people under their care.

Q **3:3 Does this mean that there are people who may not even know what is written on their hearts and still go to heaven?**

I do not know how it would be possible for a person to manifest the presence of God in his or her life by the activity of the Holy Spirit and not know that this was the case. The Holy Spirit and the faith He works come through the Word, which a person is fully conscious of as he or she reads and hears it (Jn 6:63; Ac 10:44–48; Rm 10:17). Taking people over against their will and without their being conscious of this is how the devil and demons work, not the Spirit of God (Mk 5:1–15; 2Co 11:13–15).

Q **3:6 What does Paul refer to as the letter that kills? How can it kill if "the letter" stands for the Word of God?**

This expression of Paul is still in common use today; he is referring to the letter of the Law. You can see this from the context that precedes and follows, where Paul continues to contrast the Law of the covenant given through Moses with the promise of the testament accomplished by Christ (3:3, 7–18). Paul refers to Moses and to tablets of stone, which are unmistakable references to the Law given on Mount Sinai (Ex 19:16–21; 34:1). The Law always kills because it exposes our failures and justifies our condemnation; the promises fulfilled by Christ always save because He gave us His righteousness and took upon Himself our condemnation (Rm 7:1–8:14). The Word of the Lord, in terms of Law, is what sustains nature and makes it function consistently so that it can be studied and so that it can sustain our lives. Negative, deadly consequences for contradicting the Law are universally evident and inescapable (Gn 2:15–17; 4:6–8; Rm 1:27).

Q 3:6 Should the word *testament* be used instead of *covenant*? If so, how does this affect the meaning Paul is trying to convey?

The word used here can mean a will, as in a "last will and testament," or a covenant, as in an agreement between two people. Context indicates how we are to understand the term. In some cases the word *testament* is consistent with the unilateral nature of a promise (Gn 12:1–3). In other cases the word *covenant* is consistent with a bilateral agreement, as in Ex 19:1–8 and Dt 30:15–20.

Q 3:7–11 To what ministry are they referring in the beginning, and to what ministry are they comparing it?

The phrase "carved in letters on stone" identifies the ministry of death. Moses delivered the Law, written on tablets of stone, to the Israelites, and this Law exposed, condemned, and executed them because of their rebellion (Ex 20:2–6; 32:32, 25–29; 1Co 10:1–11). Paul is comparing the ministry of the Law through Moses with the ministry of God's grace in Jesus Christ (Jn 1:17). Just as the Law condemns those who fail to keep it perfectly, so also Christ justifies all by assuming the burden of the Law and its condemnation. Paul describes this contrast in Rm 5:6–21 and throughout the Book of Hebrews.

Q 3:11 Does this verse indicate that the Law is no longer important?

Paul is talking about the ministry of Moses rather than the Law itself. Moses was given the responsibility and authority, under the Law, to bring the Israelites to their Promised Land. The fallen, corrupt human nature of the Israelites made them always rebellious against the Law rather than obedient to it. The ministry of Moses had to pass away because it was a ministry relating to the flesh, which is always passing away because it is always failing (Gal 3:24; Heb 8:1–10:18). The moral Law remains important because it still describes what is right and wrong; disobeying the Law has consequences still. The civil law remains important because it provides wisdom on how to get along with one another. The ceremonial law was fulfilled and, therefore, came to its end with Jesus' life (Mt 5:17–48; Lk 10:25–28; Rm 13:1–14; Mk 7:1–19; Gal 2:3; Ac 15:1–12). The Law remains as a curb against our rebellious nature, as a mirror that shows us ourselves as we really are and as a rule or guide in defense of wicked deceit that would always seek to corrupt the truth (1Co 5:13; Rm 5:66–11; Gn 3:1–5).

Q 3:13–18 What is the "veil" of Moses?

The veil that Paul refers to was a literal veil, a cloth that Moses put over his face after he had come down from the presence of God on Mount Sinai (Ex 34:29–35). Apparently being in the presence of God, something like being in direct sunlight, made the face of Moses shine, which in turn made the Israelites fearful. The direct presence of God and the Law that Moses brought down from God are terrifying to fallen human nature. This is why God provided Moses as an intermediary and wrote the Law on tablets of stone. However, the glow on Moses' face faded in time, and so did the impression of God's presence on the mountain and His Law on the tablets of stone. Fallen human nature can be impressed from time to time and even obedient for a moment, but it quickly and always returns to self-destruction by opposing all that is godly and good. This history of Moses indicates our condition under the Law in order to turn our attention to God's solution in His own Son. The Son of God took upon Himself our nature so that He could deal directly with us and fulfill the Law for us. The restoration of communion between God and people is demonstrated in the incarnation, the life of Jesus, and (in a very focused way related to this text) in the tearing of the curtain in the temple when Jesus died on the cross (Mt 27:51). Note that the Greek word *kalumma* translated here as *veil* is the same word used of many coverings related to the tabernacle, though it is not the same word used for the "veil" in the temple (*katapetasma*) that was torn when Jesus died (see Heb 10:20 for more on this subject).

God veils Himself because in our current, fallen condition we cannot see Him as He is and live (Ex 33:20). Moses veiled his face because the sight of the glory of God

What is the "veil" of Moses?

that was reflected in it terrified the Israelites (Ex 34:30). Fallen human beings put veils over their minds and hearts as if they could hide from God, but in doing so they only succeed in blinding themselves in darkness (Gn 3:7–8; Ps 10:1–13; Jn 3:18–20; Rm 1:18–32).

● ● ● ● ● ● ● ● ● ● ● ● ● ● ● ● ● ● ● ●

Q **3:14 What does it mean that "their minds were hardened"?**

Paul is making a contrast between what he explains about the veil of Moses in v. 13 and the spiritual condition of Israel in v. 14. The Israelites had asked Moses to hide his face from them so they would not have to see the glory of God reflected in it (Ex 33:29–33; Is 7:10–14). The religious leaders of Israel at the time of Christ were equally determined to hide from the glory of God revealed and demonstrated in Jesus (Is 53:1–3; Mt 27:39–44; 28:11–15; Ac 7:51–58; 9:1–6; 26:4–11). Steadfastly refusing to see what God clearly shows us leads, inevitably, to utter and irreversible blindness, darkness, wickedness, and death (Mk 6:52; 8:17; Jn 12:40; Rm 1:20–32; 11:7; Heb 10:26–31; 1Pt 2:7–8).

Q **3:15–16 Does this mean that when they took Moses' words to heart, nothing happened, but when they took Moses' words as the words of the Lord, they were saved?**

Moses gave the Law to Israel, and the Law is our tutor to bring us to Christ (Gal 3:24). The veil that lies over their hearts is self-righteousness. When circumstances or conscience make it impossible to justify ourselves in our own minds, when we are utterly crushed under the demands and condemnation of the Lord, then the Lord removes the veil of self-righteousness and gives us His own righteousness instead (1Sm 2:2–8; Lk 1:50–53; 10:38–42; Jn 4:6–29; Jn 8:2–11, 30–59; 1Co 1:18–31).

Q **3:15 What does "a veil lies over their hearts" mean? Why would it lie over their heart when Moses is being read?**

As explained above, the veil that lies over their hearts is self-righteousness and the darkness of self-deception. It covers their hearts when Moses is read because the Law of Moses is that with which they presume to justify themselves or what they twist in order to approve of their dark ways (Gn 3:1–13; Ex 32:22–24; 1Sm 15:10–26; Mt 23:1–35; Lk 15:1–32; 18:9–14; Rm 10:1–17; Gal 4:21–31).

Q **3:16 Is the word *turns* referring to repentance or acceptance of Christ?**

There are plenty of active verbs with people as the subject in the Bible, not to mention imperatives from God for us to obey. The question is not the meaning of the verbs or commands but how to become a person who does what the verb describes or the imperative commands. Jesus explained that those who receive (or accept) Him are the children of God, who were generated not of blood nor the will of the flesh nor the will of man but by God (Jn 1:12–13). Only the Word of God can so affect our fallen human nature and generate, orient, inspire, and invigorate our soul so that we turn to Christ (Jn 3:1–7; 8:31–32; 15:1–7; Rm 10:17; 1Co 12:3).

Q **3:17 What idea of freedom is being portrayed in this reading?**

Freedom begins with the absence of obligation or necessity (Rm 13:8). Fallen human nature in bondage cannot find satisfaction, no matter how much it takes for itself or how much it takes from others (Ec 5:10, 13; Hg 1:3–9; Jas 4:1–4). God created us for freedom and now has redeemed us to restore freedom from every concern for ourselves. He provides for every need of this body and life (Gn 1:29–30; Mt 6:25–33; Eph 3:20–21). He provides forgiveness of sin, the removal of guilt and condemnation under the Law, and the regeneration of our soul (Gal 5:1; Mt 9:9–17; Lk 10:38–42; Jn 8:2–11;

notice how Jesus speaks for the people who are attacked in these texts!). First, then, freedom begins with being delivered and protected from obligation under the Law and accusation because of the Law (Rm 8:1–11). Second, freedom has a purpose, an orientation that is consistent with itself. We experience and realize the freedom we have as we seek to liberate and bring freedom to others (Jn 15:12–13; 2Co 1:3–4; 5:14–21; Heb 2:14–18).

• • • • • • • • • • • • • • • • • • • •

Q 3:18 Does this verse have anything to do with the pastoral formation?

Because Paul is writing to the Corinthian congregation, he would seem to be including all believers when he says, "We all . . . are being transformed into the same image." This verse does apply to pastoral formation, not because pastors have a different calling than Christians in general but because their calling is so concentrated and public. The Word alone can make someone a disciple, and the Word alone, perhaps in more concentrated form, can make a man fit for the ministry and keep him so (Jn 8:31–32; 1Tm 4:12–16; 2Tm 3:16–17).

• • • • • • • • • • • • • • • • • • • •

Q 4:1 What is meant that we "do not lose heart"?

There is only one Greek word that is translated as "lose heart" in this verse, and it does not contain the word *heart* at all. The expression "lose heart" is an English idiom that means not to become discouraged or

give up. Paul is the only apostle who used this term: once having to do with persistence in prayer, twice having to do with persevering in good works, and three times having to do with enduring trouble (Lk 18:1; Gal 6:9; 2Th 3:13; 2Co 4:1, 16; Eph 3:13, respectively). The Gospel prevents us from becoming discouraged because we know that God makes all things work together for good, that affliction works for us, that trials purify us and build character, and that the life God has given us thrives in precisely those circumstances that the world finds most discouraging (Rm 8:28; 2Co 4:17; 1Pt 1:3–9; Php 2:5–11). All fallen human nature that opposes God dies and returns to the dust, but Jesus rose from the dead, never to die again. What greater antidote for discouragement could anyone have than the resurrection?

• • • • • • • • • • • • • • • • • • • •

Q 4:3–4 If the veil is a symbol of being blind, and these two verses are saying that we should leave the veil for the spiritually blind, how are we to do that?

These verses do not say that we are to do anything at all. These verses are describing the condition of people who despise the grace of God in Christ (Lk 13:34; Ac 7:51–58; 28:23–29). The persistence and determination with which these people resist the truth is what keeps the truth of the Gospel from enlightening them (Mt 23:1–39; Rm 1:20–32).

Q **4:3 What does it mean when it says the Gospel is "veiled"?**

People who are perishing under the condemnation of the Law are doing so because they insist that they either don't need to be saved from this or that they can save themselves (Ac 15:5–10; Gal 3:1–14). The ego and self-righteousness of such people keep them from seeing what God has accomplished for them in Christ (Lk 20:9–18; 1Co 1:18–31). For more on this, see 2Co 3:13–18.

Q **4:4 What is meant by "the god of this world," and why is the Gospel blinded to the unbelievers?**

The "god of this world" is the devil (Eph 2:2; Rv 12:7–17). It is not the Gospel that is blinded, but the unbelievers who are blinded to the Gospel. Unbelievers deny the truth—the truth about their need for salvation and the truth that God has provided that salvation graciously and universally in Christ. Making an idol of oneself and/or of the things of creation robs a person of all their senses (Ps 115:4–8; 1Tm 6:3–10).

Q **4:7 What is the significance of "jars of clay"? Is light the treasure inside?**

Paul uses the expression "jars of clay" as a way to describe our fallen, physical, human nature that is made of the same stuff as the ground (Gn 2:7; 3:19). Paul describes our bodies as "jars" because they are not the essence of who we are but only a container. The "jar of clay" is our physical body or outer person; within that jar dwells what is essentially us, our inner person or soul (Rm 8:5–11; Gal 5:16–25; Col 3:1–17).

According to v. 6, the full description is "the light of the knowledge of the glory of God in the face of Jesus Christ." Part of this treasure, a product of the work of Christ in us, is the "inward man" that Paul mentions in v. 16 and discusses at length in ch. 5. Inside this body ("jar of clay") is a soul regenerated by the Word and Spirit of God that is oriented, inspired, and empowered by the Word and Spirit (light).

Q **4:10 How can we carry around the death of Jesus in our bodies?**

The key to this answer is in the purpose clause: "so that the life of Jesus may also be manifested in our bodies." Jesus used His human nature in the service of others, ultimately sacrificing it completely in order to redeem the world. We are called and inspired by God to do the same. Since God has given us a regenerated soul with eternal life, we are free to carry in our hearts, minds, words, and actions the same sacrificial mind-set that Jesus had (Php 2:5–11). Jesus referred to this "carrying" of His sacrificial way when He said, "Whoever does not bear his own cross and come after Me cannot be My disciple" (Lk 14:27). The "dying of Jesus" includes denial of the desires of the flesh, which the New Testament consistently calls us to do (Lk 9:23; Rm 6:4–17; Col 3:5–16).

Q 4:11–12? Why is death at work in Paul and Timothy but life in those in Corinth?

Paul has been explaining how Christians, who have been granted regenerate souls that live eternally, use their bodies in this life to serve others. We deliver our own bodies to death by denying our will in order to serve the will of God and by denying our own passions and appetites in order to provide for the life and well-being of others (Php 2:5–11). By serving Christ in this way, we also become the target of the devil and the world that seeks to arrest this work of God in and through us (Mt 10:16–39). The sacrifice of Paul and his companions (their dying) brought the Word and Spirit of God to these Corinthians and thus worked life in them, just as the dying of Jesus meant life for those around Him and ultimately for the whole world (Mt 8:16–17; Lk 7:11–17; 2Co 5:21). The "we" in these verses refers to Paul and his companions but ultimately describes all faithful Christians. The "you" in this passage refers to the Corinthians but extends to all people to whom the Gospel is extended.

Q 4:16 What does Paul mean by saying "so we do not lose heart"? Does "being renewed day by day" equate with daily forgiveness?

See v. 1. Notice also that by repeating this phrase here, Paul is "bracketing" the text between vv. 1 and 16. The content within these sixteen verses is the best explanation for what it is to lose heart or not to lose heart and for why Christians do not lose heart.

Yes, we live in or under the forgiveness that Christ accomplished in His crucifixion (Jn 1:29; 19:30). Living in the Word provides constant confirmation of forgiveness and at the same time provides the regeneration of our inner person or new man, as Paul calls it (Is 40:2; Jn 3:1–7; Rm 6:4–11). The water of the flood in Noah's day and of the Red Sea in Moses' day did two things at the same time. Water meant the end of rebellious, fallen human nature while it made a way or lifted to safety those who had been called by and were following the Word of God (1Co 10:1–4; 1Pt 3:18–21; Heb 11:29).

Q 4:17 Is Paul saying that our bodies will be harmed? Why is it sometimes hard to see purpose in our suffering?

Paul did not say our bodies are not harmed—quite the contrary. Whether by accident and illness or by the tribulation imposed by those who hate the Gospel or by the simple fact of aging, our outward man or body is perishing. On the other hand, our inward man is being renewed by the Word of God day by day. A simple yet profound truth revealed by the Word and confirmed in experience is that the weakening and dying of our physical nature serves the strengthening and liveliness of our spiritual nature, our eternal soul (2Co 4:17–18; 12:7–10; 1Pt 1:3–9; Ps 119:50, 67, 71, 75, 92). People who are in good physical health are often unappreciative, vain, greedy, selfish, and arrogant, while they have no interest in spiritual matters, eternal well-being, or devotion to God. People who suffer in the body have cause to consider what is the origin and essence of their life. Such consideration opens the way for the Word and grace of God to show them where life is really found. People who are paralyzed or in accidents have extraordinary opportunities to bear witness to the truth that life resides in the soul, is eternal, and transcends and even thrives in the face of physical difficulties.

One powerful reason why it is hard to see purpose in suffering is when that suffering is the product of damnable human self-indulgence at the expense of those who suffer (Am 2:6–12). Another reason we struggle to see purpose in suffering comes from misplacing and misidentifying our life. If we see our life as essentially physical and the satisfaction of its lust as our purpose (which Darwinism, modernism, rationalism, humanism, and materialism all stress), then we are bound to be confused, frustrated, and even enraged by suffering. If, on the other hand, we see our life as essen-

tially spiritual, residing in the soul, and consisting of relationships with people rather than things, then we understand why a fallen world is so full of misery but, more important, how essential this experience is if we are to live eternally in communion with God and one another and with everlasting contentment. Athletes, laborers, leaders, and many others understand that some suffering is inevitable in the interest of greater goals and good. They see the difference between worthy ideals and the desires of the flesh. They also see the difference between suffering that yields benefits and moves us toward a greater good and suffering that is cruel, useless, and only moves everyone involved toward a worse end.

• •

Q 5:1–10 What does the discussion of the "heavenly dwelling" mean?

Paul is talking about the relationship of and differences between our physical, fallen human nature and our regenerate, spiritual soul. Paul calls our physical nature a "tent" because it is not the essence of who we are but only the place where that essence dwells while we are in this world. (Note how Adam had been formed of the dust of the ground but did not become a living being until the breath [Spirit] of God entered him, Gn 2:7.) Our physical nature is subject to death and burdens us with its rebellious and self-destructive disposition. When Paul speaks of "we" or "us," he is referring to our inner person, the regenerate soul that is perfect and eternal (Jn 1:12–13; 3:1–7; 1Jn 3:9). We look forward to the time when God delivers us from our mortal and sinful flesh. We look forward to being reunited with God and to the resurrection when He will give us new, perfect bodies to match our souls (Php 1:19–26; 1Co 15:50–58; Jn 11:21–26; 14:1–6).

Q 5:1 Does this verse give us proof that when we die we will go to God's heavenly home?

Certainly. Other passages confirm what this passage is saying (Lk 16:19–22; 23:40–43; Jn 14:1–3; Rv 6:9–11; 7:9–17).

Q 5:2 What is meant that we "groan"? Is this our flesh, not our spirit?

This verse makes clear that the "we" that groans is our inward man, the soul regenerated by God's Word and Spirit (Jn 1:112–13; 1Jn 3:9). V. 4 makes this equally clear. The regenerate soul is what lives in the tent of this fallen human nature, repents of the disposition of that nature, resists its desires, and longs to be free of it (Rm 6:4–22; 7:13–25). Our physical or outward person only groans when it cannot satisfy its selfish, materialistic, self-destructive lusts. Our regenerate soul groans when the physical nature has its way because we know that way is destructive to ourselves and to others (Pr 14:12; 2Pt 2:20–22; Heb 2:1–4:1).

Q 5:4 What does it mean that we want to be clothed with our heavenly dwelling so that "what is mortal may be swallowed up by life"?

We recognize that our physical nature is still of God's design and workmanship, even though that nature is poisoned against God (Rm 6:5–11). We do not look forward to a spiritual life only but to the restoration of all creation, spiritual and physical, in harmony with itself and with God (Rm 8:12–39; 1Co 15:1–58; 1Jn 3:2). Since God is going to re-create the heavens and the earth at the end of the world and the resurrection of the dead, it is necessary for those who die before the end to live in paradise with God during the time in between (Lk 16:19–22; 23:40–43; Jn 14:1–3; Rv 6:9–11; 7:9–17).

Q 5:7 What does it mean that our lives are only guided by faith not sight?

Let's begin with a more careful translation: "For we walk through faith, not through sight." Next, consider the significance of the way this expression is formed in Greek. Paul could have used the dative of means, so that we would understand that we walk "by means of faith" rather than "by means of sight." Is it possible that Paul formed the sentence as he did in order to invite a more comprehensive understanding of walking by faith and sight? In other words, perhaps it is not only the means by which we navigate the course of our life but the very course itself that is different for us?

If faith means "honesty about dependence," then Christians walk with a consciousness of the truth, not only the truth about ourselves and God but also the truth about what life consists of and its purpose (Mt 11:28–30). We know from our Lord's life that serving oneself leads only to death, but serving others while we are alive, even to the death, leads to everlasting life for us and those we serve because of the inexhaustible life and grace that the Lord provides us in His Word and Spirit (Mt 23:1–39; Jn 10:17–18; 13:12–17; 15:12–13; 16:13–15; 1Jn 4:19).

Q 5:11 What does this verse mean?

Paul had just reminded the Corinthians that we must all appear before the judgment seat of Christ, where each person receives the just consequences of their deeds (v. 10). Anyone who knows any biblical history has an abundant and clear witness to what happens when those who oppose and despise God are met with His judgment (Gn 6:5–7; Nu 16:24–35; 1Sm 15:10–29; Mt 21:18–19). Since we know the terror of the Lord on the one hand, we are the more appreciative of His gracious redemption in Christ on the other (Gal 1:6–10; 3:1–17). By a life in the Word, Paul and his companions came to repentance, to the assurance of forgiveness, and to possess a regenerate soul that is perfect before God (Rm 4:1–8; 8:1–11; 1Jn 3:9). By a life in the Word we are joined with Christ so that we already have passed through judgment with Him. Those who despise Christ insist on standing

before God on their own merits and making their own defense—which will only serve to condemn them (Mt 22:11–13; 25:31–46; Lk 19:20–27; Heb 4:1–16).

Q 5:12 Why should they "boast" of the apostles?

On occasion, Paul found it necessary to defend his apostolic authority and "commend" himself to his listeners/audience (2Co 1:17–24; Gal 1:1, 11–24; Ac 22:1–21; 26:2–29). At this point in this letter, Paul does not want the reader to misunderstand his intent since he has been using plenty of first person plural pronouns ("we," "us"). Paul wants the reader to understand that he has been communicating the Gospel that no one else knew or had communicated to them; this is what it means to "glory on our behalf." Paul wants the Corinthians to be armed with the genuine Gospel as a ready defense against those who come preaching themselves and teaching a salvation of works under the Law (Gal 1:6–10; 2:1–5; 6:11–15; Ac 8:14–24; 11:1–18; 13:6–12; 15:1–12; 1Pt 3:15; 3Jn 9–11). The truth belongs to God; it is singular; it reveals His glory (what no one else could or would do); and it is always substantive because it describes reality as it is. Lies are infinite and without substance except to expose what opposes God as only doing or saying or thinking what no one else should (Jn 8:30–59; 2Pt 2:1–22).

Why do we continue to sin?

Q 5:13 What is the difference between being "beside ourselves" or being "in our right mind"?

Part of this answer depends on whether "God" and "you" are the object of the action described or the cause of it (dative of advantage or dative of means, respectively). Literally, Paul said that if we are "beside ourselves," it is for God or by God's activity. To be "beside oneself" makes sense if we remember the body/soul distinction in our nature. To be "beside oneself" is a way of saying that the regenerate soul or inward man is dominant and the physical nature or outward man is subdued. This can only be the case by the activity of God, and the purpose of this activity is to serve God's gracious will in love for others, as Paul explains in the next two verses. The second part of the verse says that if we are of "right mind," it is for your benefit. This is the purpose of being "beside oneself." Seeing our life as abundantly provided for by God and invulnerable is what produces the love that moves us to use our life, with all the care that wisdom and thoughtfulness can supply, on behalf of the well-being of others (Jn 15:12–13; 1Jn 4:19; Rm 12:1–21; Eph 4:1–5:21).

Q 5:16 How do we view nonbelievers?

The world—or we might say, worldly people—are materialistic, selfish, and self-centered. Worldly people are consumed with how to satisfy the desires of their human nature because they have a deep sense of emptiness and of impending doom that comes with death. This materialistic worldview makes people frantic to get what they want as quickly and as easily as possible, even as they are concerned about justifying themselves as being righteous in doing so. Taking from others is the quickest way to satisfy the passions and desires of the flesh, and judging people according to material differences is the easiest way to justify such abuse. Christians have been reunited with God through Christ and have been regenerated in the image of Christ. This fullness and eternal, abundant satisfaction inspires us to see people according to the condition of their soul and need for redemption. Christians look past economic status, social place, and nationality; we reject the notion of "race" as absurd (Ac 17:16–32). All human beings are God's creation, descended from one man, Adam, equally in need of redemption and equally redeemed by Christ (Jn 3:16; 2Co 5:19–20). We see people according to their real needs and according to their potential in the wake of Jesus' life, death, and resurrection.

Q 5:17 Why do we continue to sin? Is the devil really that powerful?

It is impossible to understand what the Bible teaches or the experience of our life unless we distinguish between our physical and spiritual nature. According to our fallen, physical, human nature, we are always sinful in all we do and contrary to God until the day that nature dies and returns to the dust (Is 64:6; Jn 3:6; Rm 5:6–11; 1Co 2:14; 15:50). According to our inward man or regenerate soul, we are holy and perfect (1Jn 3:9). It is this inward man or regenerate soul that is in Christ, united through a life in the Word, and therefore a new creation free from condemnation under the Law and freely pursuing the will of God (Jn 8:31–32; Rm 8:1–17; 10:17; Gal 5:16–26; Col 3:1–17).

• • • • • • • • • • • • • • • • • • •

Q **5:20 If indeed we are Christ's ambassadors, would the message not become muddled when ambassadors of other Christian faiths are present? Were Christ's ambassadors the apostles who followed Him?**

The apostles were called to be leaders of all ambassadors for Christ by their example and through the Word of God that they set in print for us. There will always be false ambassadors even as there will be false christs (Mt 24:24; 2Co 11:13–15; 1Jn 2:18–19). This is why Paul commands us to test those who claim to be of God and search the Scriptures to see if what they say is true (Ac 17:11; 1Th 5:21; 1Jn 4:1). False ambassadors and false teaching are not so difficult to recognize because they never affirm or advance the fundamentals: that the Bible is the Word of God and that to be a disciple is to remain in it; that man is utterly fallen and opposed to God since Adam's fall; that God is the Trinity; that God's Son was born of the Virgin Mary; that Jesus Christ redeemed the whole world in His life, crucifixion, and death; that Jesus rose from the dead, which proves the success of His redemption; that God brings about the realization of these truths in the lives of people through the Means of Grace (the Word, Baptism, Holy Communion, and Absolution).

• • • • • • • • • • • • • • • • • • •

Q **6:1 What does it mean to "receive God's grace in vain"?**

The Greek word translated "in vain" occurs eighteen times in the New Testament and means "empty" (Mt 12:3; 1Co 15:14). To receive the grace of God "into emptiness" would mean for no purpose or with no result. For example, Jonah was a paradigm for all of Israel, who had received the grace of God but had no interest in realizing the benefits of that or of passing that grace on to others. Jesus provided the example of unfaithful servants, which clarifies Paul's meaning (Lk 121:42–46; 19:20–26).

• • • • • • • • • • • • • • • • • • •

Q **6:2 To what does "now is the favorable time" refer?**

Paul quotes Isaiah regarding God's response to our need for redemption: "I listened to you . . . in a day of salvation I have helped you." When Paul says "now," he means any time anyone reads this Epistle. Paul meant that the Corinthians should know that God had accomplished and was extending His grace and Spirit to them even as they read these words (Is 55:6–11; Jn 6:63; Rm 10:17). Paul also meant that anyone else who would ever read or hear these words should also realize the salvation accomplished by Christ and communicated in this word (Ac 1:8; 1Pt 1:12). Your question reveals a common mistake among people who share an intense interest in knowing when Judgment Day will come (Mk 13:1–37; Ac 1:6–7). The "end of the world" comes to each person when he or she dies, regardless of when God brings all things to an end on Judgment Day. The end of the world is one place appropriate for a person to think about himself (Jn 21:20–23).

Q 6:3–10 How can we grow closer to having the same attitude as Paul, who physically suffered many things yet was happy throughout it all because of the grace of God?

The answer to your question might well begin with studying how Paul came to be as he was. Paul was well schooled in the Scriptures, was forgiven for his persecution of the people of God, was regenerated by the Gospel, was called to be an apostle, and never ever forgot that the Gospel of Christ alone restored him to life and communion with God (Ac 9:1–22; 22:1–21). It was, I suspect, that God forgave Paul for the evil he inflicted on others that made Paul so willing to endure the evil that others inflicted on him (Lk 7:39–50; Ac 9:16; 22:3; 1Tm 1:12–17). The Law reveals the magnitude of the condemnation we deserve and, in turn, points

to the even greater magnitude of God's grace in redeeming us (Rm 5:12–21; 7:1–25; Gal 3:24). Being more aware of the condition of fallen human nature in ourselves makes us more understanding and compassionate toward those who are still dominated by this contrary and self-destructive nature (Rm 5:6–11). Finally, a life in the Word regenerates us in the image of Christ and gives us His heart and mind that sees people as out of their minds with desperation over the sense they have that their life is passing away (Jer 9:4–7; Php 2:5–11; Heb 12:1–3). God has given us a life that cannot be taken away but, instead, is realized more and more as we apply it to the care of others and give it away to them, especially to those who would oppose us most.

Q 6:3 What does this say about pastors who kick people out of church unfairly?

This says that pastors who kick people out of church unfairly are acting contrary to the apostolic witness and are thus enemies of the Gospel. However, it is impossible for pastors to kick people out of the church. On the one hand, no one can kick anyone out of the Body of Christ, the genuine, invisible Church, because Christ holds close and protects those who are His (Jn 9:1–38; 10:27–30). On the other hand, when pastors bear witness to the fact that a person has rejected the community of faith and Means of Grace, he is not kicking out that person but making clear that such a person has kicked the church, pastor, and God out of his or her life; it is always man who does the rejecting, not Christ (and Christ who does the choosing, not man; Ex 32:1–8; Lk 13:34–35; Jn 15:16). Excommunication is the responsibility of the pastor and the congregation, pursued in love and devotion to all (Lv 19:17; 1Co 5:5). If the offense of an impenitent person who claims to be a part of the church is known publicly, excommunication protects everyone from the deadliness of hypocrisy (Ac 5:1–11; 15:1–12; 1Co 5:1–13; Gal 2:11–17).

● ●

Q 6:7 What are our "weapons of righteousness"?

The weapons or tools of righteousness are all found in the Word, particularly in recognizing how the Law and the Gospel work. First, it is important to know that the Greek word translated as "weapon" is something like a "tool" or an "instrument," including the notion of armor (Rm 6:13; this verse in NKJV translation). Second, Paul connects this word with the term "light" in Rm 13:12, and we know that light has to do with the Word of God (Jn 1:4–5, 9; 3:19; 8:12; 12:46). Third, the "right hand" and "left hand" have to do with one's proper or alien work. God's proper work according to His loving nature is to give life, and He does this through His Word that conveys what He has done for us in Christ and all of His promises to us (Jn 10:7–18; 1Jn 4:7). God's alien work or that which is foreign to His loving nature is that of the Law (Heb 12:1–

24; Jas 5:10–11). In the same way, parents' singular goal is to provide the best possible life for their children (their proper work), yet such parents are compelled to discipline their children (inflicting appropriate but effective discomfort) in order to teach children how to prevent their own fallen human nature from ruining that best possible life (2Co 1:8–9; 4:16–5:15; 12:7–10). The Word of God revealing the Law is the weapon in our left hand that disables and counters the lies of opposition toward God and life; the Word of God revealing the Gospel is the weapon in our right hand that regenerates, heals, and raises the soul to life everlasting (Ne 4:17; Heb 4:12).

● ●

Q 6:8 What is Paul contrasting here?

This verse comes amid a list of contrasts that are all true of disciples of Christ. The contrasts can be true of the same person at the same time because we are composed of two natures: the outward man or physical nature and the inward man or the soul. In this verse Paul notes the contrast between the world's disposition toward Christians and the disposition of those who know the truth. The world dishonors the disciples of Christ, spreads evil reports, and accuses them of deceit (Mt 10:16–25; Lk 6:22–28; Jn 7:11–12; Rm 1:20–32). On the other hand, those who are honest and seek the truth honor Christians for their devotion to the truth, share reports of the good works God accomplishes through His servants, and recognize that the Word of God advanced by Christians is true (Ac 17:11, 16–33; Rm 12:1–21; Php 2:12–16).

⚫ ⚫ ⚫ ⚫ ⚫ ⚫ ⚫ ⚫ ⚫ ⚫ ⚫ ⚫ ⚫ ⚫ ⚫ ⚫ ⚫ ⚫

Q 6:13 Who are Paul's children?

Paul refers to those who were regenerated by the Word of God that he communicated as his children (Gal 4:19; 1Th 2:11; 1Tm 1:18; Ti 1:4; Phm 10; 2Jn 1, 4). However, in this verse Paul does not refer to the Corinthians as his own children; rather, he is describing the manner of speech he is using when communicating with them: "as to children." Jesus was referring to the honesty and dependence of children when He taught that we cannot enter the kingdom of heaven unless we repent and become like them (Mt 18:1–3; Jn 3:1–7). Paul is at times frustrated with those who claim to be Christians because of their "childishness," that is, their preoccupation with selfish, petty interests (1Co 13:11; 14:20; Eph 4:14; 1Tm 1:18; Heb 6:1–8). Paul is speaking in simple, plain terms so that the Corinthians will understand his message, but with this language he is using the Law to put to death this childishness in them and so liberate them from it (1Co 13:11–12).

⚫ ⚫ ⚫ ⚫ ⚫ ⚫ ⚫ ⚫ ⚫ ⚫ ⚫ ⚫ ⚫ ⚫ ⚫ ⚫ ⚫ ⚫

Q 6:14 If we are to be separate from unbelievers, how are we supposed to be witnesses? How can you tell who is an unbeliever?

First, the word *yoke* means an inseparable or nearly inseparable relationship (note how animals yoked together have no ability to change this relationship). The most obvious yoke between people is marriage, though business partnerships, memberships, and even citizenship can assert the pressures of a yoke because they may cause a person to do what he would not otherwise do. Second, we are not supposed to be separate from unbelievers, except in our celebration of Communion (1Co 5:9–13). Living, working, and even playing with unbelievers is not a yoke, but it is similar to the relationship of salt to the earth or light to the world (Mt 5:13–14). God keeps us in this world and keeps us free precisely so we might reach unbelievers with the Word (Mk 16:15; 1Co 9:19–23; 2Co 5:17–20; Gal 5:1, 13; Php 1:21–24). Third, yoking oneself to an unbeliever with the hope of changing that person would be similar to making oneself a slave in hopes of changing the master; it is possible for this hope to be realized, but why serve in bondage rather than in freedom (1Co 7:12–24)? There are a multitude of ways by which we might engage unbelievers productively without being in danger of forfeiting our freedom; friendship is one of them.

The only way to be a believer is through a life in the Word (Jn 8:31–32; Rm 10:17; Col 3:16). Anyone who is a believer cannot help revealing this as the Word bears fruit in his or her life (Mt 7:16–20; Lk 3:7–14; 6:43–49; Ac 2:42; Jas 2:14–26). We cannot know who goes to heaven or hell once they are dead, but we can know a person's disposition to the faith while they are living—though it takes time and care if our perception is to be accurate (Mt 7:1; Jas 1:19).

Q 6:14 How would a Christian deal with being in love with a non-Christian? Is denomination a factor in marriage?

First, this verse does more than imply a warning. This verse forbids us from binding ourselves to unbelievers, and why would we want to do so? Second, there is no such thing as "being in love." Some people are overcome with lust, infatuation, or addiction to self-gratification—but these are the opposite of love. Love is a matter of thoughtful determination to offer one's life for the service and well-being of another (Jn 15:13; Rm 13:8–14; 1Co 13:1–18; Gal 2:20; 1Th 4:1–12). Christians do love all others, especially our enemies, just as Christ loves us (Mt 5:44–48; Jn 13:34–35; 15:12). If a Christian had a romantic interest in an unbeliever, he or she would be careful to make sure that such a passion did not displace genuine love for the other. Any couple would need and would want to come to unity about truth, as all other substantive unity would depend on this. If a couple agrees on the truth, but the individuals claim different denominations or religions, then they would need to research until they found the system or denomination that maintained a public confession of faith that was consistent with their own (Mt 10:32–33; Heb 10:23–25).

Q 6:15 Who is Belial? Is this contradicting Paul's statement about being all things to all people?

Belial is a Hebrew adjective composed of two words: *without* and *value*; thus the meaning is "worthless." This term occurs twenty-seven times in the Hebrew Old Testament but never in the Greek translation of the Old Testament and only here in the New Testament. Some argue that the term is a proper name for one of Satan's demons. However, biblical context indicates that the term is more generic, simply referring to someone who is a worthless person, especially when unbelief is the root. The Greek translation of Pr 6:12, for example, translates this word as "foolish," which means an unbeliever. This Old Testament use is consistent with the context of Paul's argument here.

Paul said he was all things to all people in order that he might save some—but he never bound himself in a yoke nor took part with anyone who was not of the same faith. See 2Co 6:14 for more on the difference between being yoked with someone and being an ambassador to someone.

Q 6:16–17 Why are we supposed to be separate from unbelievers? Aren't we supposed to treat others as we would like to be treated?

To understand Paul, we must distinguish between being in union with someone and simply interacting with someone. The union of a husband and wife is unique, shared by no one else except the two—though these two have interaction with family members, friends, neighbors and even enemies. Paul is warning the Corinthians about uniting themselves with the religious practices of people devoted to idolatry, a subject he addressed at length in his previous letter (1Co 5:1–13; 10:14–11:34). We are here to extend the grace and truth of God to people for their salvation, but we cannot do this when the person is determined to be joined in devotion to what is contrary to God. A physician would not consent to prescribing drugs to a person who would use them only to serve his addiction. A surgeon would not consent to doing surgery in an environment that would infect and therefore kill the patient. We reach out to people as those who share a common human nature, common struggles, and common needs. In sharing this identity we become all things to all people. Doing this is a very different matter than joining people in practices that are destructive and counterproductive. We can hardly help someone into the lifeboat if we are drowning with them in the water. Please see 2Co 6:14 above for more on this subject.

• • • • • • • • • • • • • • • • • •

Q 7:1 Doesn't Christ purify us and make us clean?

On the basis of the promises of God quoted in 6:16, 18, Paul is calling Christians to become what they are. What does that mean? According to our regenerate soul or the inner person, we are already clean, pure, and holy because the Word and Spirit of God have regenerated us (Jn 15:3; Rm 8:1; 1Jn 3:9). But this regenerate soul lives in a fallen human nature that remains contrary to God (Rm 5:6–11; 1Co 2:14). In order to realize the life God would have us lead, it is necessary for the promises of God that regenerate us to also move us to draw our human nature away from all that is contrary to God and to enlist it in the service of all that is God's will (Rm 6:1–22). This work of purification and of drawing us toward the ideal (making all of us what we already are according to the inner person) is God's Word, affected through His Word and Spirit. Nevertheless, it is our regenerate soul that is inspired toward the will of God and our fallen human nature that is affected by the Law (Jn 14:10–12; 1Co 15:10).

• • • • • • • • • • • • • • • • • •

Q 7:8 Which letter is Paul referring to in this verse? Why does Paul not care about causing grief on the part of the person to whom he wrote?

Paul could certainly be referring to 1 Corinthians because almost the whole letter is disciplinary language, intended to turn them in grief to repentance (2Co 1:23–2:5). Some suggest that Paul is referring to a letter that he wrote between 1 Corinthians and this letter, but that is only speculation. The only reason Paul cares about causing grief is when doing so is necessary to lead to repentance, faith, and godliness, as he explains in the rest of this verse and the verse that follows: "For godly grief produces a repentance that leads to salvation without regret" (v. 10).

• •

Q 7:9 What are the people of Corinth doing wrong?

First Corinthians provides a catalog of all they were doing wrong that required repentance: contentiousness (1:10–25), envy (3:3), worldliness (3:18), pride (4:7), sexual immorality (5:1–13), litigation (6:1–8), idolatry (10:14), selfishness and drunkenness (11:21), and lovelessness (13:1–13), for example. It may be that Paul has in mind, chiefly, the problem of sexual immorality addressed in 1Co 5 and 2Co 2:6–11.

• •

Q 7:10 What exactly is "godly grief"? Is this the same as guilt?

Worldly grief is selfish, materialistic, shortsighted, and short-lived. Fallen human nature is only sorry for not getting what it wants or for getting caught trying to get it. Worldly sorrow is sorry about having to be sorry but will pretend as needed to get back to having its way. Godly sorrow is grief over and turning away from all that is contrary to God and life. Godly sorrow produces repentance or the turning of our lives into the ways of salvation, and it is not to be regretted. Being sorry and staying sorry for what has been wrong is a part of making sure we don't repeat our mistakes and bring suffering unnecessarily upon ourselves and others (Heb 2:1–4; 12:1–29; 2Pt 1–22).

Sorrow (*lupe*) is not the same as guilt (*enochos*). Sorrow has to do with regret about what is or has been wrong. Guilt means to come under the effects of the Law (Gn 26:11; Mt 5:21; 1Co 11:27).

• •

Q 8:1–9:15 Do chs. 8–9 refer to the same subject matter? Do you think they were inserted later?

Yes, these two chapters both deal with stewardship. There is no reason to think these verses are not original to the text. Why would a later editor insert material so specific to Paul's occasion, and how would he know to do so? These two chapters are not as redundant as some critics complain, and any redundancy that is present argues against an editor rather than for one (the goal of an editor is to avoid suspicion not produce it).

• •

Q 8:1–7 How can we participate in giving and encourage others to do the same?

Whatever good comes of us is the product of God's Word and Spirit working in us (Jn 15:1–8). If we want to bring out generosity in others, we must first connect them with the generosity of God in Christ and of His Spirit (1Jn 4:10–11, 19). The Word reunites us with God, whose goodness is inexhaustible and who provides us with all that we need in order to provide for others (Jas 1:17–18; 1Co 3:21; Eph 3:20).

● ●

Q 8:3 If money doesn't solve anything, and only makes matters worse, then why should we tithe?

Tithing was a practice instituted in the Old Testament. It was designed to provide for the tribe of Levi, which was devoted to the service of the tabernacle. It also kept the people mindful of the source of all they received and freed the people from worrying about or becoming dedicated to the increase God gave (Lv 27:30–32; Nu 18:1–28; Dt 12:6–7). The New Testament does not teach tithing; it teaches something much more like the Gospel itself. The Old Testament demonstrated that fallen human nature is incapable of returning to God even a fraction of what belongs to Him (Heb 8:7–13; Gal 3:24). The New Testament regenerates people in the image of Christ so that we understand our whole life is provided by God and we realize that life in giving it in loving service to others (Ac 2:42–47). A Christian is not obligated to give anything to anyone because Christ has fulfilled all the obligation of the Law (Rm 10:4; 1Co 6:12; 10:23). On the other hand, a Christian freely employs all that he or she is and has because the life God gives us is realized, enhanced, and increased as we share it (Lk 4:25–26; 19:1–10; 21:1–4; Ac 4:32–5:11). Money doesn't cause or solve problems. Money can provide for people and materials that do good. The love of money is the root of all evil (1Tm 6:10).

● ●

Q 8:5 What did Paul expect from the Macedonian church?

With this statement Paul is drawing attention to the remarkable faith of the Christians in Macedonia. Paul means that the Macedonians did more than he and the other disciples expected, not only providing a gift to send with them for relief of the needy but also, more impressively, giving themselves entirely to the Lord. Paul would mention the faithfulness of the Philippians and their support of him a few years after he wrote this letter to the Corinthians (Php 4:10–20).

● ●

Q 8:8 Is Paul comparing the Corinthians with others based on how much money they give to the Lord?

The Greek word *dokimadzo*, translated here in some translations as "test," is not the same as the word used for God's testing of Abraham or the testing of Jesus in the wilderness (*peiradzo*, Gn 22:1–18; Mt 4:1–11). *Dokimadzo* has to do with determining what is the case in fact, while *peiradzo* has to do with challenges that strengthen or overthrow one's faith, depending on the source of the test/temptation (Jas 1:12–14). Paul makes clear at the beginning of this verse that he is not speaking with them according to a command, though Paul does command us to examine or test ourselves in several other places (1Co 11:28; 2Co 13:5; Gal 6:4; 1Th 5:21; 1Tm 3:10). As long as we are in this fallen human nature, it will be necessary to use the Law as a safeguard against our fallen human nature's rebellious and deceptive ways. Our fallen human nature would like us to believe we are sufficient on our own, apart from the Word and Spirit of God (Ps 14; Jas 4:13–14). Our fallen human nature disregards God's revelation in nature and the Word or twists that revelation to its own purposes (Mt 5:21–42; 15:1–9; Rm 1:20–32; 2Pt 3:16). Paul was observing the Corinthian response to an appeal for relief assistance as a means of examining them in regard to the faith (please see the third question and answer under 6:14 above).

Q 8:9 In what ways was Christ rich?

Jesus Christ is the Son of God, the Lord of all creation; He is absolutely rich, for all things are His (Jn 1:1–3, 14; Rm 1:1–6; 11:36; Heb 1:1–3). We have no indication that the family of Mary or of Joseph were rich (Is 53:2–3; Mt 13:35–36).

Q 8:18–24 Who is the other brother with Titus?

In 2Co 1:1, Paul refers to Timothy as "the brother." This is, because of context, the most likely person. Others suggest that Paul is referring to Luke. I know of no certain answer. The use of "the brother" instead of naming the disciple is similar to John's practice of referring to himself as "the disciple whom Jesus loved" throughout his Gospel. Perhaps Timothy, like John, was concerned

with modesty—as we all do well to be (Rm 12:3).

Q 8:20 What gift are they talking about, and why is it generous?

This is the only occurrence of this word in the New Testament. The word has to do with abundance, sometimes translated as "lavish" (see NKJV).

Q 9:1 What is this "ministry for the saints"?

This "ministering" or "service" to the saints has to do with supplying financial relief to the Christians in Palestine (Ac 2:44–45; 11:27–30 [this gift of relief took place six or seven years before 2Co was written]; Gal 2:10; 2Co 9:12).

Q 9:2 Is it sinful for a man to boast or to be proud of another?

It is a mistake to boast about oneself, since this would be claiming for oneself what belongs to God and serving oneself rather than others (1Co 4:7; Pr 25:14). Boasting that is approved in Scripture has more to do with rejoicing over someone in appreciation and thanks to God than bragging about or flattering someone (Ps 5:11; 32:11; Jer 9:23–24; Rm 5:3, 11; 1Co 1:31). It is absolutely proper to rejoice in the Lord and to tell others His praises (Php 4:4–9; Ps 78:4–8). It is also proper to thank God for

His gifts to people and His work through them as this honors God and encourages the person who seeks to serve Him (1Th 1:2–10; 1Co 14:31).

• • • • • • • • • • • • • • • • • • • •

Q 9:5 When Paul talks about generosity here, is he referring only to money or gifts in general, like talents, etc.?

Paul is referring to a gift of money that would be taken to Jerusalem for relief of the poor (Rm 15:25–27; something like it is reported in Ac 11:27–30). However, Christian generosity includes all our resources, talents, gifts, and abilities, because love sacrifices everything for the sake of others (1Jn 15:13; Ac 4:32–35; Gal 2:20).

• • • • • • • • • • • • • • • • • • • •

Q 9:6 Isn't this verse a bit Law with no room for Gospel?

This verse provides both Law and Gospel. The natural dynamics Paul expresses are indisputable, making his point clearly and powerfully as parabolic references are meant to do. The Law rightly condemns a person who uses what God has given sparingly, for God has given to us in abundance (Mt 18:21–25; Lk 16:1–31; 19:20–26). Any person who contradicts the truth deserves the consequences they despised (Ac 5:1–11). On the other hand, to sow bountifully is an activity that can be provided for only by God, both the will to give generously and the resources to give thusly (Lk 6:38; Php 3:7–11; 1Jn 4:19). Besides giving us what we

are to sow, God provides an abundant harvest that is a joy to those who have sown (Mt 25:31–40; Lk 19:11–19). There is only condemnation here for one whose selfishness and greed make him rightly condemned.

• • • • • • • • • • • • • • • • • • • •

Q 9:7 What does this verse have to say about our purpose of collecting offerings in the church?

A Christian is free to give a tithe (10 percent) of his or her income if inspired to do so, and Old Testament practice lends support to such an approach to giving (please see second question under 8:1–7 above for more on tithing). However, in this verse Paul is not so concerned about the percentage of one's income that is given back as an offering but about the person's disposition toward that giving or reason for giving thus. The Gospel reveals not only what God gives but also how and why God gives. The Gospel converts a soul to this same manner of giving: generously, freely, gladly, thoughtfully, and hopefully. Any kind of giving that is not the product of faith and gratitude is no giving at all (Rm 8:8; Heb 11:6). The New Testament does not require us to do anything but conveys all that God has done for us in Christ and from that fullness inspires us to give all we are and have for the good of others in like manner (Jn 15:1–13; 1Jn 4:19; Ac 2:42–45; 4:32–35). I'm not sure this verse says anything about our purpose in collecting offerings in the church; it says everything about our disposition toward making offerings. The purpose for offerings in the church is more evident in Acts and some of Paul's other Epistles (Ac 2:45; 4:34; 6:1; 11:27–30; 1Co 9:1–13; Gal 6:6; 1Tm 5:1–8).

• • • • • • • • • • • • • • • • • • •

Q 10:1 What is Paul talking about when he says he is "humble" in their presence yet "bold" when away?

Like many people, Paul was timid, lowly, or subdued in person but very bold and powerful when writing to people. Paul is clearer about this in vv. 8–11 (see also 2Co 12:7–13).

• • • • • • • • • • • • • • • • • • •

Q 10:3 Why does my translation have *flesh* instead of *world*? Which is correct?

This verse says, "For though we are walking in the flesh, we do not make war according to the flesh." The ways of the world are the product of the people who make up the world. Perhaps a translation that has "world" instead of "flesh" is trying to say that we do not make war as the world makes war, establishing an absolute contrast between the history of war and the history and way of Christianity.

• • • • • • • • • • • • • • • • • • •

Q 10:4 What are our weapons?

It is interesting to note that Paul does not actually say what the weapons of our warfare are, only what they are not ("of the flesh") and what their effect is ("destroy arguments," v. 5). The effect of the weapons of our warfare suggest that they are arguments themselves, as the apostles so often made in public and in their Gospels and Epistles (Ac 3:11–4:21; 9:17–22; 1Pt 3:15). Paul wrote that we are to enlist our bodies in order to advance the kingdom of God in Word and deed (Rm 6:13). The best description of the weapons of our warfare is found in Eph 6:10–17. Paul describes these items as "the whole armor (weapons) of God" (*panhoplon*).

• • • • • • • • • • • • • • • • • • •

Q 10:6 In order to punish, don't we have to judge first?

Paul's First Letter to the Corinthians made clear what the troubles were, that they were widespread, and that they were well-known (1Co 1:11; 5:1–3; 6:1–6; 11:21). In order to respond to the trouble in the Corinthian church, Paul must first know if they are still in the faith, demonstrated by their disposition to the Word of God and repentance (Jn 8:31–32; Ezk 18:23–32). The word *punish* in your translation is better understood as "avenge" or "restore justice" (Lk 18:3–5). While God forbids us to avenge ourselves, He does call us to restore justice (Rm 12:19; Mi 6:8). Later on in this letter, Paul reminds the Corinthians that when he comes to them next, he will correct whatever is still contrary to faith and the Gospel (13:1–10).

Q **10:11 In general, why does Paul focus so much on boasting?**

Paul responds as circumstances require. When adversaries wanted to undermine the truth and grace of God, Paul contended for truth and grace by boasting about them (1Co 1:31). When adversaries wanted to reject the New Testament by contesting Paul's apostolic authority, it was necessary for him to defend that authority (Gal 1:1–17; 2Co 12:1–5). Apart from such attacks, Paul generally focuses on the grace of God in Christ Jesus (1Co 2:2).

Q **10:12–18 Is Paul being conceited here, or is he crediting God all the time? Are we all to brag in the name of the Lord?**

Paul is not bragging or being conceited. On the contrary, Paul is urging honesty and humility by his own example. Paul refuses to compete with or be like those who commend themselves (v. 12). Paul reminds us that all glory properly belongs to the Lord, so any boasting should be of Him and His gracious, powerful work (v. 18). Paul expressed concern that he not say more for or about himself than was proper for the defense of His apostolic authority in service of the kingdom of God (vv. 13–16). Bragging or boasting about oneself is a mistake because this would be claiming for oneself what belongs to God and serving oneself rather than others (1Co 4:7; Pr 25:14). Boasting that is approved in Scripture has more to do with rejoicing over someone in

appreciation and thanks to God than bragging about or flattering someone (Ps 5:11; 32:11; Jer 9:23–24; Rm 5:3, 11; 1Co 1:31). It is absolutely proper to rejoice in the Lord and to tell others His praises (Php 4:4–9; Ps 78:4–8). It is also proper to thank God for His gifts to people and His work through them because this honors God and encourages the person who seeks to serve Him (1Th 1:2–10; 1Co 14:31).

Q **11:1 Why does Paul say he is foolish?**

There are different words in Hebrew and Greek that are translated as "fool" in English. This word means to act contrary to reason or good sense (Ps 69:5; Pr 5:23; 9:6; 18:2, 13; 19:3). In the New Testament, this word for folly occurs only four times (Mk 7:22; 2Co 11:1, 17, 21). Paul has decided, at this point, to make the same kinds of arguments that the false teachers are making, in order to expose them (Pr 26:4–5). Paul makes plain the folly of these false teachers and the folly of the Corinthians in accepting them in a few particular verses (vv. 4, 12–15, 20). In particular, the folly is that false teachers think they cleverly are gaining a life for themselves by imposing themselves as religious authorities on undiscerning people, but this takes away life rather than gives it. The Corinthians are acting foolishly by accepting these self-acclaimed, self-serving, self-appointed pseudo-authorities and by submitting to their ridiculous claims to authority and manipulation.

Q 11:2 What is "divine jealousy"?

The Greek word translated as "jealousy" in this verse has more to do with "zeal" than with envy (*phthonos*, Mk 15:10). As the case is with many actions (verbs), the activity can be good or bad depending on the subject and purpose of the action. Love is to sacrifice everything for the object of that love (Gal 2:20). God's love gives life; the love of the Pharisees for honor meant death for them (Lk 11:43). If zeal is selfish, only harm comes of it (Ac 5:17; 13:45). Godly zeal or jealousy is a passion of concern for the truth and grace upon which the lives of others depend, especially the lives of the helpless (Jn 2:17; Ps 69:9).

Q 11:5 What is a "super-apostle"? Who would Paul consider to be a "super-apostle"?

The expression "super" apostle is a choice translators made for a Greek term that means "more" or "above" something (the NKJV has "eminent"). If Paul is being sarcastic, then these "super" apostles would be the men with whom Paul is comparing/contrasting himself in this chapter: the false apostles who transform themselves into apostles of Christ but are really ministers of Satan (vv. 13–15). Paul's comparison in 2Co 11:22–12:13 shows that he is the one who bears the signs of authenticity and authority as a genuine apostle of Christ rather than Jews who asserted themselves as authorities for their own selfish interests and contrary to God's will (Jer 23:30–32). On the other hand, if Paul is being serious, then the eminent apostles might be Peter, John, and James, who were more well-known and who were leaders of the church in Jerusalem (Gal 2:9). Jews who opposed Paul's work among the Gentiles may have been arguing that Paul was not really an apostle, as were Peter, John, and James (Ac 13:45, 50; 15:1–13; Gal 1:1, 11–2:10). While Paul admitted that he was late in being called as an apostle and was unworthy to be one, yet as an apostle called by Christ Himself, he was in no way inferior to any other apostle (Rm 16:7; 1Co 9:5; 15:9; 2Co 12:11).

Q 11:8 Why does Paul use the term "robbed" in reference to being paid for preaching the Gospel?

Paul uses the term *robbed* for effect. Paul has taught, as did the Old Testament, that those who are served should provide for the needs of those who do the serving (Gal 6:6; 1Co 9:3–18; Lv 27:30–32; Nu 18:1–28; Dt 12:6–7). Paul wanted people to support his missionary activity, but Corinth was not a mission (Rm 1:13; 15:24). By living on funds provided by other congregations while serving the Corinthians, Paul was using (taking) what rightly belonged to another purpose (missionary) and applying it to the benefit of the Corinthians, thus "robbing" other churches.

● ● ● ● ● ● ● ● ● ● ● ● ● ● ● ● ● ● ● ●

Q **11:12–15 How is Satan able to be disguised as an angel of light as in this verse?**

Satan disguises himself as an "angel of light" when he misuses the Word of God, pretending to serve life when his purpose is only to murder, as he did with Eve, King Saul, Jesus, and Judas (Gn 3:1–5; 1Sm 15:10–26; Lk 4:1–13; Jn 8:44; 12:4–6; 13:2). Many people use the Word of God to take advantage of others and to control them contrary to that very Word (Jn 10:7–8, 11–13; 1Sm 2:12–17; 1Tm 6:3–5; 2Tm 3:1–7; Php 1:15–16; Ac 8:18–23).

● ● ● ● ● ● ● ● ● ● ● ● ● ● ● ● ● ● ●

Q **11:13 As Christians, what should we do with these false prophets?**

Jesus said that the sheep flee because they do not recognize the voice of one who is not the Good Shepherd (Jn 10:5, 8). Jesus also taught that the people should listen to the Word when spoken but should not follow the ways of false teachers (Mt 23:1–36). Paul wrote that we should note those who cause divisions and have nothing to do with them (Rm 16:17–18). John wrote something similar (2Jn 10). Pastors have special responsibility to protect the people from false teaching and should expose the same in public if necessary, as Paul did with Peter's hypocrisy (Gal 2:11–16).

● ● ● ● ● ● ● ● ● ● ● ● ● ● ● ● ● ● ● ●

Q **11:16 What is Paul talking about?**

Paul is making clear that he is not a fool nor would he boast like a fool, except that boasting like a fool seems to be the best way to expose the folly of his adversaries (Pr 26:4–5).

● ● ● ● ● ● ● ● ● ● ● ● ● ● ● ● ● ● ● ●

Q **11:17 Why does Paul say he is talking "as a fool" when he tells the people he is going to boast about his sufferings?**

This Greek word, translated as "fool," means to act contrary to reason or good sense (Ps 69:5; Pr 5:23; 9:6; 18:2, 13; 19:3). There are at least two ways in which Paul's conversation about his suffering is contrary to good sense. As one redeemed by the grace of God, Paul knows better than to claim (boast about) anything except his weaknesses, for all that is good and wonderful in his life is a gift of God (2Co 12:5–10). Remembering what the Lord does for us honors God and at the same time reminds us that our life is safe with Him. As one replying to the folly of his adversaries, Paul is going to use his suffering as evidence that he is more authentically Christian and an apostle than anyone else who would make such claims (Mt 10:16–26; Lk 6:22–26; Ac 9:15–16). Paul's adversaries think that power and authority insulate one from suffering, but Christ demonstrated that power and authority are demonstrated in loving self-sacrifice for the lives of others; this is Paul's apostleship (1Co 1:18–2:5).

Q 11:22–29 Is it right that Paul boasts about his accomplishments in these verses? He seems to put himself as a Christian above everyone else in Corinth.

Please see answer at 11:1 above.

Q 11:23 What is meant by the parentheses?

When Paul says, "I am speaking as a fool," he is making a parenthetical comment; that is to say, Paul is interrupting his explanation to clarify something for us.

Q 11:24 Why did Paul receive "forty lashes less one"?

Paul was beaten on several occasions because people who oppose the truth were trying to put an end to Paul, or at least an end to the effectiveness of his ministry (Ac 16:16–40). When the Jews gave beatings, they inflicted only thirty-nine blows because they did not want to risk miscounting and then be guilty of breaking the law that forbade more than forty blows (Dt 25:3).

Q 12:1–13:14 Paul seems so worried and stressed out in these last two chapters (12–13). Why is that? Why does he repeat himself so much?

Paul tends to deal as methodically as possible first with the big, fundamental matters of doctrine and life; he then addresses all the many smaller issues as he approaches the end of his letter. If Paul sounds worried and stressed out in these last two chapters, it would be the result of the passion for the well-being of the faithful and against the enemies of the truth that has been building throughout the letter.

Q 12:1 Do people still get these visions?

I don't know how we could prove that no one gets visions like those given to Paul, but I also don't know what purpose they would serve. Paul needed authenticity and authority in order to serve God as an apostle; that is why God granted him such visions and revelations. The apostles, in turn, have provided us with the authentic and authoritative Word of God (Mk 16:16–20; 1Th 2:13; 2Tm 3:16). The Word of God is our source of visions and revelations that are not only authentic but also are set in the body of Scripture that interprets and applies them to our lives with certainty.

Q 12:2–6 Is Paul referring to himself as having had this vision?

Paul is talking about himself and the visions and revelation God gave him. Paul speaks of himself in the third person ("I know a man") in order to maintain proper humility, which he has been advocating among the Corinthians (1Co 1:18–31). Paul is distinguishing between what he was according to his own efforts and determination and what God had made of him through his conversion and apostolic call (Rm 7:13–25; note how the apostle John never referred to himself by name in his own Gospel, but as "the disciple whom Jesus loved").

. . . .

Q 12:2 What is the third heaven? Does this verse support the Catholic teaching of purgatory?

Some suggest that the first heaven is the sky (Gn 1:1, 8–9, 20). The second heaven is outer space (Gn 1:14). The third heaven, then, would be paradise, as Paul goes on to say in v. 4. As far as I know, this is the only place the Bible speaks of heavens in numerical order, though some disciples asked Jesus for a place of special honor in heaven, and Jesus once mentioned that there would be different levels of punishment for the unbelieving (Mk 10:35–40; Lk 12:47–48). The Bible says very little about heaven, and I suspect this is to keep human opinion from having too much information about which to form opinions.

Roman Catholic sources I checked did not make any reference to this passage in regard to purgatory. The teaching of purgatory is made necessary by rejecting the universal, vicarious atonement of Christ as redemption for all people of all time. Purgatory was invented as a "second-chance system," that is, a way for believers to complete what they failed to do in order to save themselves while they lived in the body. In part, the Roman Catholic teaching of purgatory depends on an argument that Heb 9:27 and Mt 25:31–32 are describing two

What is the third heaven?

different times of judgment for a person. Augustine's *City of God* is also referred to as supporting the teaching of purgatory (21:13).

. . . .

Q 12:7–8 Isn't being conceited a sin? So why would Satan torment Paul to keep him from being conceited?

Being conceited is a mistake and a sin because conceit is a person taking credit for what belongs to God and denying what belongs to himself. God granted Paul a thorn in the flesh in order to keep him from this mistake.

. . . .

Q 12:7 Did God send Satan to Paul? What was the thorn in Paul's flesh?

Although the devil is entirely devoted to opposing God, he is still God's creation and must serve God's purposes. It was God who raised the question of Job to the devil (Job 1:2; 2:3). It was the Holy Spirit who drove Jesus into the wilderness to be tempted by the devil for forty days and nights (Lk 4:1–13). It was the devil who led Judas to betray Jesus and the Jewish religious leaders to demand His crucifixion—but in all these cases it was the devil who failed and God's grace, wisdom, and power that prevailed. Paul says himself that this messenger

533

of Satan or "thorn in the flesh" was given to him in order to keep him from losing faith by growing conceited. Paul explained previously in this letter that our affliction "is working for us" because realizing the vulnerability of our fallen human nature drives us to the invulnerability and promise of our regenerate soul (1:8–10; 4:7–5:7). No one knows for certain what this "thorn in the flesh" was, though some have suggested it was some problem with his eyes (Gal 4:13–15). The phrase "thorn in the flesh" likely does not mean a literal thorn embedded in Paul's body, but some ailment that bothers Paul constantly, the way a thorn in our flesh would. Paul mentions weakness in his ability to speak and in his physical person, but I suspect that has more to do with Paul's disposition and condition after physical difficulties than it does with his thorn in the flesh (1Co 2:3; 2Co 10:10; 11:30; 12:5). I cannot think of any of the other apostles mentioning that they had a thorn in the flesh, though Peter made plenty of trouble for himself at various times, as did James and John (Mt 14:28–31; 16:22–23; 17:4–5; Lk 22:31–34; 23:54–62; Gal 2:11–16; Mk 10:35–40; Lk 9:53–56; Mk 3:17).

● ● ● ● ● ● ● ● ● ● ● ● ● ● ● ● ● ●

Q 12:9 When did God or Jesus talk to Paul? What is the deeper meaning of this verse? How is power made perfect in weakness?

Presumably, God spoke with Paul in the visions and revelations granted him when he was taken to paradise. In order to serve as an apostle, it was necessary for Paul to have certain knowledge of the Lord Jesus, as the other apostles did (Ac 1:21–22). Fallen human nature is contrary to God in all things (Rm 5:6–11). Therefore, when that human nature is weak, it is less able to resist and oppose the work of God in our regenerate soul (2Co 1:7–9; 4:7–5:21).

● ● ● ● ● ● ● ● ● ● ● ● ● ● ● ● ● ●

Q 12:9–10 If we are content in our weakness, what does this mean for us? Is it a state of mind, or is this an action?

Being content in our weakness is beneficial only if we distinguish between our fallen human nature and our regenerate soul, which is the essence of our person. If we recognize that our fallen human nature is our own worst enemy, then we are grateful and glad when the Lord weakens it, by whatever means (Rm 7:13–25; Gal 5:16–26; Col 3:1–16). Being content is a state of mind, a way of "reckoning" or thinking about things that affects our actions (Rm 6:1–22).

● ● ● ● ● ● ● ● ● ● ● ● ● ● ● ● ● ●

Q 13:1–10 What were the "final warnings"?

This is not the language of the biblical text, but a heading provided by a publisher that is intended to summarize the content that follows. It is common for Epistles to conclude with a sort of "shopping list" of details, cautions, warnings, and encouragements (Rm 16:16–20; Heb 13:1–22; Jas 5:7–20; 1Pt 5:1–10).

• • • • • • • • • • • • • • • • • • • •

Q **13:5 Paul says to examine and to test ourselves. How does a person know if he or she is truly in the faith?**

The word *test* or *examine* means to look for something in comparison to some goal or standard. The test here has to do with being in "the faith." The faith Paul is referring to is the content of the Holy Scriptures, all of which point to or flow from Jesus Christ, the Son of God and Savior of the world (Lk 24:25–27; Rm 1:1–6). We can know if we are in the true faith by two means: what comes in and what comes out. No one can be a disciple or have faith unless he or she remains in the Word (Dt 6:4–9; Jn 8:31–32; Rm 10:17; 1Pt 1:3–9). When someone is in the Word, the Holy Spirit produces the fruits of faith in that person (though the works of the flesh will always be evident to some extent; Mt 7:17–20; Jn 15:1–7; Col 3:1–16; Heb 2:1; Jas 2:14–26).

Galatians

Q 1:3 Does Paul start with a prayer to show the people of the Church what should come first?

This verse is not a prayer but an introduction to and a statement of the purpose of the letter that follows. Paul is writing to the believers in Galatia in order to convey the grace and peace of God to them. You are right about showing the people of the Church what comes first. If the Word of God does not come first, nothing else good will come (Lk 10:38–42; Jn 6:63; 8:31–32; Ac 2:42; Rm 10:17; 1Tm 3:16–17).

Q 1:6 What is the "different gospel" the Galatians were turning to? Does this simply mean that the Galatians were not

believing in Christ as their Savior, or were they confusing the use of God's Law with the Gospel?

Luke gives us a view to this "different gospel" (which is no gospel at all) through the history recorded in Acts. After Peter had visited Cornelius's house, certain Jews in Jerusalem opposed him because he had entered the home of uncircumcised men and eaten with them (11:3). Later, after Paul returned from his first missionary journey, some of the Pharisees who believed that Jesus was the Christ raised this objection: "It is necessary to circumcise them and to order them to keep the law of Moses" (15:5). This "other gospel" may be described as the Law of Moses plus Jesus. In other words, the Jews wanted to keep their idea that God favored them as a race and a nation and

Who led the Galatians astray?

that they earned God's favor by obeying the Law of Moses given in the Old Testament, especially the laws about circumcision, diet, cleanliness, and the calendar (Mt 23:1–33). They concentrated on these physical, external practices because they are easier to keep, rather than the moral law in the Ten Commandments (though the Jews had altered even the moral law in order to claim that they had kept it; Mt 5:21–48). Fallen human nature always tries to justify itself, and in so doing not only fails but also renounces the justification that God freely provided in Christ. Like God Himself, there is one and only one Gospel: God saved us in the life of His Son and brings us into the realization of that salvation through His Word and Spirit (Gal 2:16; Eph 2:8–9).

- - - - - - - - - - - - - - - - - - -

Q **1:7 Who were the people leading the Galatians astray?**

Paul wrote this letter immediately after returning to Antioch from his first missionary journey, which Luke records in Ac 13–14. We know that these people were envious Jews who contradicted Paul and blasphemed in their opposition to him (13:45). They stirred up devout and prominent women along with chief men in the cities in order to raise a persecution against Paul and Barnabas (13:50). In Iconium, the Jews stirred up the Gentiles and poisoned their minds against the brothers, which resulted in a violent attempt to abuse and stone Paul and his companions (14:3, 5). Perhaps the best example of these people is Paul himself before he was converted (8:1–3; 9:1–2).

- - - - - - - - - - - - - - - - - - -

Q **1:8 Doesn't this undermine the other apostles' authority (especially knowing they were meeting over this issue soon)? Paul says even if *he* preached a different gospel than the first, they should not believe him. How can he expect them to trust his words in the first place? Why would an angel of God do this?**

There is one and only one true God: Father, Son, and Holy Spirit. Like God, the truth is singular, but lies are as many as there are people to make them up. There is one and only one Gospel for two reasons. First, there is only one God, which means there is only one source of absolute grace that provides for all things absolutely. Any means that convey grace or provide for us must still admit that really, the source is God (Jas 1:17). Second, by definition, *gospel* means "good news or message." Any message that makes us responsible in any way for our salvation is not good, since we will fail and be lost (Rm 3:10–20; 4:16; Gal 3:10). In this verse, Paul is making an argument based on what I have just explained in the strongest possible terms—because our lives and eternity depend on it. There are plenty of false prophets and apostles, liars and deceivers, not to mention the devil and his demons (all fallen "angels") who spend every moment trying to overcome, corrupt, and ruin the Gospel of our salvation (Mt 23:1–33; Jn 8:44–45; 2Co 11:12–15; Col 2:8; Rv 22:18–19). Paul is not claiming authority for himself or priority over anyone else. Paul is defending truth and grace and the only true God, who is the source of it all. Paul speaks so strongly because the lives of all people are at stake, and he knows that if he were ever to be apart from the grace of God in Christ, he would be eternally condemned (Ac 9:3–19; Gal 2:11–18).

• • • • • • • • • • • • • • • • • • • •

Q **1:8–9 Why does Paul repeat v. 8 in v. 9?**
Paul repeats this language, and would repeat it a million more times if necessary, in order to protect the truth—the truth that only the grace of God, from beginning to end, at all times and in every way, can save us from our own fallen human nature, from others, and from the condemnation of the Law (Rm 3:10–28; Gal 3:10–29; Php 3:1).

• • • • • • • • • • • • • • • • • • • •

Q **1:9 Paul is so harsh toward other Christians. If we are so closed-minded, despite our motivations, won't we make Christianity seem negative to people that we want to bring to Christ?**
Paul is not being harsh toward other Christians or even toward people who are ignorant or disinterested. Paul dedicated himself to becoming like the people he served in order to communicate grace and truth to them (1Co 9:19–23). Paul is being harsh with the same kind of people Jesus was harsh toward: those who knowingly,

consciously, and wickedly seek to destroy with false teaching and lies (Mt 23:1–33; Rm 1:18–32).

Being closed-minded might protect a person from error, but it also keeps out the truth, and if a person knew the truth, a closed mind would keep it in. Being open-minded is problematic because it lets everything in and everything out. I might learn and share the truth, but I am just as likely to learn and share lies. God urges us to be like the Bereans: to search the Scriptures, to test and challenge what we hear in order to discern truth from lies and to discern life and the way of life from death (Dt 18:9–22; Ac 17:10–11; 1Th 5:21; 1Jn 4:1). The constant search for truth in the freedom provided by the grace of God because of love for others is the most positive thing a person could ever do.

• • • • • • • • • • • • • • • • • • • •

Q **1:9 Here Paul talks about the Gospel "you received," so what does this say about decision theology, or how does it relate to decision theology? Is this saying that those who don't agree with a preacher will be condemned?**
The word *received* puts less emphasis on the person, as some see it. Whether we say "accepted" or "received," the solution to the issue comes in asking, who is the person that accepts or receives? How is it that a person is motivated to or wants to accept the Gospel? Jn 1:11–13 makes clear that only a person who has been regenerated by God

can accept the Gospel. Jesus said He chose us; we did not choose Him (Jn 15:16). Paul wrote that we have no capacity to choose for God; on the contrary, our fallen human nature is entirely opposed to God (Rm 5:1–11; 1Co 2:14).

The issue is not about hearer and preacher agreeing, but about public preaching and teaching that is consistent with and faithful to the Gospel. Any person who presumes to argue against and contradict the truth and grace of God is already condemned (Jn 3:18–19; Jas 3:1ff.; 1Pt 4:11). We are warned in several places not to keep company with those who claim to be Christian but who publicly, consciously, and consistently contradict the truth, because doing so would subject us to the effects of lies and confuse others who assume we agree with what is being said (Rm 16:17; 1Co 5:1–13; 2Jn 7–11).

Q **1:11–12 If the Gospel is not for man, whom is it for? How did Paul know what the Gospel was without hearing it from the apostles?**

When Paul says it is "not man's gospel," he means that the Gospel he preached came directly from God. God revealed His truth and grace to Paul during and after his conversion (Ac 9:3–25; Gal 1:15–17; 2Co 12:1–6).

Q **1:13–14 Why does Paul speak as if Judaism was a bad thing?**

The answer to your question has to do with distinguishing between being an Israelite and being Jewish; between being of Abraham's faith and Judaism. God did not call Abraham to separate from his family in order to make him opposed to all people but to make him and his descendants ambassadors of God in the world (Gn 12:1–3; Is 9:1–7; Lk 2:30–32). However, over time, being Jewish took on a nationalistic character. Jews saw themselves and the kingdom of God in a materialistic way rather than a spiritual way. This mind-set has, in part, caused a history of competition between Jews and others for land, wealth, and power (Jn 11:46–50; Rm 2:28–29; Gal 3:7–8; Heb 11:8–22). Abraham believed, like Adam and Eve, that God would send His own Son as a descendant and that this Son would redeem all people from sin and death, so that we would all be reconciled to God by His grace and His grace alone (Jn 8:30–59; Rm 4:1–12; Gal 3:8–14). Judaism is a religion focused on physical rather than spiritual things. Judaism includes a belief that there is something inherently more acceptable to God about Jews according to their physical descent. Judaism focuses on land and physical property as a sign of God's favor. Judaism believes that when people obey the physical, outward laws of circumcision, diet, cleanliness, ceremonies, and festivals, God will be pleased and provide salvation. Note well this "materializing" and displacing salvation by grace with works-righteousness also exists among people who claim to be Christian and in practically any other religion you can name. This world, like our human nature, is fallen and contrary to God (Rm 5:6–11; Jas 4:1ff.). Jesus said His kingdom was not of this world, which is why His disciples did not fight to protect Him (Jn 18:36). Christians pray for God's kingdom to come; that is, we pray that God's Word and Spirit would inspire us to live as Jesus did, as people who love others—especially our enemies—even as we are loved, in order to bring them into God's kingdom of love and grace (Mt 5:38–48).

Q 1:17 What did Paul do in Arabia and Damascus?

Paul was on his way to Damascus to beat up Christians when Jesus appeared to him on the road (Ac 9:1–5). Paul's companions led him into the city, as the Lord commanded, where he stayed until Ananias came and baptized him. Paul immediately preached Jesus in the synagogue, which resulted in a plot by the Jews to kill Paul (vv. 20–25). Paul found out about the plot and escaped to Arabia, where he stayed for a time before returning to Damascus (Gal 1:17–18). Certainly Paul went to Arabia to preach the Gospel. He may also have gone to be free of plots to kill him and allow time for those who made such plans to forget about Paul. It is also possible that during this time, Paul received the revelation he described in 2Co 12:1–6 and Eph 3:1–7.

Q 1:18–2:14 Why does Paul recount his missions to the Galatians? What is he trying to prove?

The Jews who opposed the Gospel of God tried to destroy the Gospel and Paul's ministry of it by claiming that Paul had no authority but was a self-serving, self-appointed teacher who had turned his back on the Mosaic Law in order to gain a personal following among the Gentiles. Notice that as Paul begins this letter, he immediately clarifies how he came to be an apostle and clarifies the Gospel he was preaching (Gal 1:1, 6–11). Paul recounts his history in order to prove two things. First, Paul is proving that God Himself called, appointed, authorized, and taught Paul the Gospel. If Paul's authority is from God, which it plainly is, then there is no excuse for, cause for, or sense in fighting against it (Ac 5:27–39; Gal 1:11–2:2). Second, Paul is defending the Gospel against attempts to corrupt it and oppose it (Gal 2:3–4:31). Paul proves that the Gospel means all people are redeemed and justified by the grace of God in Christ. Paul proves this by pointing out that none of the believing Jews tried to force the Law of Moses on Titus, none of them added anything to what Paul taught or tried to correct anything, and Paul even withstood Peter when his hypocrisy contradicted the Gospel. It is interesting to note that the unbelieving Jews opposed Jesus in the very same ways, trying to undermine His authority and corrupt the truth (Mt 5:17–48; Lk 11:14–20; 20:1–9).

Q 1:24 Is Paul being boastful about his faith?

No, but it's a good question just the same. As in other cases, how the words are translated can be either more clear or less clear. Paul says that the churches in Judea either began to or continually glorified God (imperfect tense). The reason they glorified God is because He had changed Saul into Paul—from persecutor of the faith to preacher and defender of the faith. Paul must have done just what Jesus commanded: let his light shine before men in such a way that they would see his good works yet glorify his Father who is in heaven (Mt 5:16).

Q 2:1 Why did it take 14 years before all the apostles really accepted Paul? Why does Paul have to be taken into the group of apostles? Wasn't he already an apostle?

I don't see where the text suggests that the other apostles didn't accept Paul for 14 years. Paul was authorized and active as an apostle from the time of his conversion. He was busy doing the work of an apostle and keeping away from those who plotted to murder him (Ac 9:15–30). The timing of Paul's visit to Jerusalem, which allowed opportunity to visit with the other apostles, was coincidental to his ministry according to God's plans for him. Paul was an apostle because God made him so. However, Paul was aware that his circumstances were different from the rest, both because he had persecuted the Church and because he had

not been with Jesus during His three and a half years of public ministry (1Co 15:8–10). Paul reveals the authenticity of his apostolic authority in the face of opposition to the Gospel, but he also confesses his unworthiness to those who feel unworthy of God's grace just like Paul (1Tm 1:12–17).

Q 2:2 If Paul had a revelation from God to go preach to the Gentiles, why was he so concerned about hiding his preaching? Was he concerned that he had misinterpreted the revelation?

How certain might an honest person ever be? Paul had been very certain when he was persecuting the Church of God and found out he was sorely mistaken (Ac 8:1–3; 9:1–3; Php 3:4–6). We might imagine that Paul might still be fearful of getting the message wrong, even though he received it directly from God by revelation. Paul was ready to accept any consequences—except eternal condemnation by God—for contradicting His Word and will (Ac 20:18–24). Paul never hid his preaching or teaching, but he was glad for the opportunity to compare what he knew and taught with the other apostles' teaching and know that it was identical.

Q 2:3 Why was Paul emphasizing that Titus was not circumcised?

The Jews who rejected the Gospel and tried to impose the Law of Moses on people argued that Paul had no authority and was not a genuine apostle like those who had been with Jesus. Paul argued, in response, that if we were still required to keep the Law of Moses, why didn't the apostles in Jerusalem require Titus to be circumcised? Certainly if any little part of the Old Testament law was still necessary, it would have been circumcision since that practice started with Abraham; but it was not required, which proved that Jesus had fulfilled all the Law and set the New Testament in place, as Paul describes (Gal 2:4–6).

Q 2:4 What does Paul mean here by "spy out our freedom"? Who were the "false brothers"?

Paul calls them "brothers," so they must believe that Jesus is the Christ. However, they did not believe that Jesus fulfilled the Old Testament and replaced it with the New. These false brethren simply added Jesus to the Old Testament, teaching that in order to be saved, a person still had to obey the Law of Moses (Ac 15:5). These false brothers were "spying" because they did not come in search of truth or grace by which they might be saved. Like the religious leaders who came to Jesus hoping to find a cause to reject Him, these brothers wanted to find a way to regain their control over the apostles and Christians, whom the Gospel had made free (Mt 22:15–46; Gal 6:12–15). Jesus brought the truth to light. The truth includes God's grace toward all; the truth makes a person free from the curse of the

Law—from the deceit of the devil, world, and flesh—and orients us to use our freedom for the liberation of others (Jn 1:1–3; 8:31–32; Gal 5:1–26; Eph 2:1–9).

Q 2:7 Why was Paul's task to preach the Good News to the Gentiles and Peter's task to preach it to the Jews?

Peter's ministry to the Jews and Paul's ministry to the Gentiles were not exclusive of each other. God granted Peter a powerful experience with the Gentile household of Cornelius that demonstrated how the Gospel is meant for all people and that the Word of the Gospel works salvation immediately (Ac 10:1–48). Paul continued to interact with Jews even after he expressed his frustration with them (18:4–7; 21:15–26; 28:17ff.). I suspect that God wanted Peter's ministry to focus on Jews because his apostolic authority was never in question and because his witness to the Gospel was irrefutable (11:1–18; 15:6–12). God wanted Paul's ministry to focus on the Gentiles because his profound experience of God's grace made him so very eager to reach the Gentiles with the Gospel, his Roman citizenship granted him some privileges as he traveled, and he was willing to endure any hardship in the preaching and defense of the Gospel (1Tm 1:12–17; Rm 10:1–17; Ac 16:37–39; 21:37–40; 22:23–29; 1Co 9:19–27; 2Tm 4:6–8).

Q 2:10 Is there biblical/historical evidence to believe that Paul lived an ascetic life?

The New Testament makes no suggestion that Paul lived an ascetic life. Paul says that he knew how to be satisfied and abound and he knew how to do without (Php 4:10–20). Paul spent time in prisons, suffered beatings, and fasted, but he also enjoyed being provided for by the faithful and those to whom he had ministered (Ac 16:25–34; 24:22–23; 2Co 11:22–30). Paul never suggested any advantage to living an ascetic life; in fact, he warned against outward acts of self-sacrifice that are of no use in our struggle against the flesh (1Co 13:1–3; Col 2:20–23). Paul followed Jesus' teaching and example, which made love—genuine love—for others the principle that determines all that we do (Mt 23:23; Jn 15:11–14; Rm 13:8–10; 14:1–23).

Q 2:11–21 Is Peter losing his faith?

It is unlikely that Peter was losing his faith, since he is an apostle and this is after Pentecost. Peter did give in to his human nature, letting fear of certain Jews make him deny by his actions the very Gospel that had saved him from denying and failing the Lord in the past (Mt 14:28–31; Lk 22:31–34; 23:54–62). We all have a human nature that is contrary to the faith (Rm 5:6–11; 1Co 2:14). If we have been regenerated by the Word, we have a soul that is perfectly faith-

ful (1Jn 3:9). Which nature prevails at any given time is a function of how strong one nature or the other is (Rm 6; Gal 5:16–26). Without the Word, our soul languishes and becomes weak (Mt 25:1–13). Remaining in the Word keeps the soul strong (Jn 8:31–32; Rm 8:1ff.; 10:17).

Q 2:11 What was Paul accusing Peter of being wrong about, besides his being afraid of the circumcision group? Did the other disciples also think Peter was wrong?

Peter was guilty of hypocrisy because he had been eating with Gentiles until certain Jews came from Jerusalem, but then he separated himself for fear of these men who still argued that God only accepts those who are circumcised and keep the Law of Moses (Gal 2:12–13). Peter is without excuse for this conduct since he knew and taught that all people are equally condemned by the Law and all people are equally loved and redeemed by God (Rm 3:10–23; Mt 8:1–15; Mk 7:14–23; Lk 4:24–30). Even after God confirmed the Gospel to Peter on Pentecost, through his ministry to Cornelius and through Peter's own defense of the Gospel in Jerusalem, Peter still withdrew from the Gentiles as if they were unclean (Ac 2:1–46; 10:1–48; 11:1–18; Gal 2:12–14). We don't know what other disciples thought, but Paul tells us that Peter's hypocrisy was so powerful that others joined Peter in his hypocrisy, even Barnabas (Gal 2:13). The very heart of the Gospel is that people are still God's creation, made in His image, and that He has redeemed all people through the life, death, and resurrection of Jesus Christ (Jn 3:16; Ac 17:22–31; 2Co 5:19).

● ● ● ● ● ● ● ● ● ● ● ● ● ● ● ● ● ●

Q 2:12 Why were Peter and the other Jews afraid of the Gentiles who belonged to the circumcision group?

It was not Gentiles who belonged to the circumcision group that frightened Peter but Jews who came from Jerusalem. Why did Peter fear them? Why is anyone afraid of anything at all, except God? John wrote that fear exists where there is judgment instead of love (1Jn 4:18). Hebrews says that the fear of death holds people in bondage for their entire life (Heb 2:14–15). Jesus asked repeatedly why people fear for their physical life (Mt 6:25–34; Mk 4:40; 5:39). We are so fearful because in the fall, we lost our communion with the living God and we lost our sense that the soul is the essence of our life, not the body. Men from the circumcision group—like the religious leaders who intimidated the common people, had Jesus executed, and arrested Peter and John—were powerful men. These men had both the desire and the means to do harm, just as Paul had before his conversion (Jn 9:22–34; 19:1–16; Ac 3:13; 4:1–3; 5:17–18, 27–40). There was also a history of competition for priority among the apostles (Mk 9:34). James the half brother of Jesus had become a powerful leader in the Church at Jerusalem (Ac 15:13–21). Perhaps Peter was

afraid that James would become even more powerful unless he won the loyalty of the Jews who argued for circumcision.

Jesus once said that a person who is forgiven much loves much (Lk 7:47). Paul never failed to defend the Gospel because he knew the magnitude of God's forgiveness to him from the time of his conversion (Ac 8:1–3; 9:1–19; Php 3:7–14; 1Tm 1:12–17). Peter, on the other hand, like so many of us, had trouble abandoning his own ego and attempted to justify himself (Lk 22:31–34; Ac 10:14). It was not until after the incident in Antioch, where Paul rebuked Peter in public, and Peter's defense of the Gospel at the Second Jerusalem Council that Peter seems to have overcome his fear of the opposition of men by the love of God for him (Lk 22:31–32; Ac 15:1–12). We know the love of God through His forgiveness (Jer 31:31–34). The love of God is what moves us to love others more than we fear them and so maintain a faithful witness to the truth and grace of God (2Co 5:14–15).

● ● ● ● ● ● ● ● ● ● ● ● ● ● ● ● ● ●

Q 2:14–21 Why did Paul rebuke Peter in front of everybody instead of talking to him privately?

Paul rebuked Peter in front of everyone because everyone had seen and even been carried away in Peter's hypocrisy. In contrast to "private" sins, there was no question about what Peter had done, that it was a terrible transgression, and that others were being affected (or perhaps *infected*) by it.

Paul commanded this same approach to the faithful in Corinth regarding the man who had his father's wife (1Co 5). Notice in that case also that the sin is public and that others were affected by it (v. 2). The practice outlined by Jesus in Mt 18 has to do with "private" sins (vv. 15–18). Private sins are those that no one knows about except the sinner and another person who knows or thinks he knows of this sin. The practice outlined by Jesus has the goal of keeping private sins private, unless the sinner's impenitence forces us to draw the faithful in for help. Jesus' method for dealing with private sins also provides an opportunity for the person who thinks there is a sin when there is not to find out he is wrong before false accusations are made or rumors are started. If the person who has sinned or the one who thinks there is sin but is mistaken refuses to admit this after the first meeting, he might still be corrected and public embarrassment spared during the second meeting with one or two other witnesses. All Christian activity is motivated and directed by genuine love. We seek to protect the lives of others by engaging them privately in private matters and publicly when their errors are in public and affect others.

• • • • • • • • • • • • • • • • • • •

Q 2:15–16 If observing the Jewish laws cannot justify us, why should we still obey the Ten Commandments and the other Old Testament laws?

There are three kinds of law: ceremonial, civil, and moral. None of these laws has the power to justify us, because we lack the ability to keep them (Rm 8:3–4). The ceremonial law (sacrifices, dates, diet, purification, and circumcision) was given to point us toward the coming Savior; it shows us what He would do and what we can never do, simple as it is (Gal 3:24; Heb 8:1–9:15). The civil law shows the way for us to get along together while we live in this world. Failing to keep it may not keep us from paradise in the next life, but it certainly keeps us from paradise in this one. The moral law is expressed in the Ten Commandments. This law cannot justify us any more than the other two can, because we cannot obey it. Jesus redeemed us from the curse of the Law by keeping it perfectly for all and by suffering the consequences of not keeping it. Saving us from condemnation under the Law doesn't mean the Law has no purpose; it still describes God's design for life and warns of all that ruins life; Jesus' life is absolute proof of this. We do not seek to keep the Law in order to justify ourselves but in order to love others even as we are loved by God (Lk 19:1–10; Rm 13:8–10; 1Jn 4:10–21).

• • • • • • • • • • • • • • • • • • •

Q 2:16 Why does Paul say the same thing three times in the same verse? We are justified by faith clearly, so why do some faithless refuse to accept this?

You answered your own question with the word *clearly*. Paul says the same thing three times in this verse but a thousand more times in the rest of his letters because our human nature, until it breathes its last, never, ever submits to the truth that we cannot save ourselves. The whole of human history recorded in the Bible shows how the devil, the world, and fallen human nature never admit that we cannot save ourselves or that God has already saved us by His grace (Jn 8:31–51). The crucifixion of Jesus indicates what horrifying measures human nature will go to in order to silence the truth—even the truth that loves us and redeems us (Jn 19:14–16). Acts records the history of opposition to salvation by grace from outside the Christian community and from inside (3:1–4:23; 8:1–3; 11:1–3; 12:1–4; 13:44–45; 15:1–12). We must keep hearing the truth about our fallen human nature, or we will be overcome with lies (Jn 8:33–47; Rv 12:15–17). We must keep hearing the grace of God so that our faith is strong and keeps us in life everlasting (Jn 8:31–32; Rm 10:17; Php 3:1; Heb 2:1ff.; 1Pt 1:3–9).

Q **2:17–21 How do we know what is right and wrong, and how do we rebuild it?**

When Paul says, "If I rebuild what I tore down," he is referring to the case he had made to justify himself before others and God (Paul's boast about his own flesh recounted). Paul refers to the things he tore down in Php 3:7–14; especially in v. 9 where he describes the "righteousness of [his] own that comes from the law."

Q **2:18–21 Paul says "I" a lot, but who or what is supposed to be the "I"?**

Paul is referring to himself; Paul is the one who would never dream of rebuilding the things he "tore down" or destroyed. Paul is the one who died through the Law in order that he might live to God. We have all been crucified with Christ. Christ now lives in Paul, and God would have Him live in each of us as well.

Q **2:19 What does it mean, "through the law I died to the law"?**

The Law always kills because it always reveals how we have failed to keep it and are, therefore, condemned by it (Rm 8:3; Gal 3:10; Jas 2:10). Paul is saying that once he looked honestly at the Law, he saw that there was no way for him to try to justify his way of life; he abandoned his former way of life as if he were dead (Ac 9:3–19; Php 3:7–14). After his conversion, Paul took up a new life and a new name to bear witness to it. Since Paul had already died under the condemnation of the Law in the vicarious atonement of Jesus and since Paul now had taken the disposition of a dead person toward his previous life of opposition to the grace of God, he was no longer condemned under the Law but lived in the grace and regenerate life that God provided (Rm 7:1–24; 1Co 15:10; Gal 2:20). If all a person has is the fallen human nature inherited from Adam, then there can only be death and condemnation. But if God regenerates our soul in His image, then the putting to death or incapacitation of the flesh by the power of the Law allows the regenerate soul to have dominion according to the way of life (Rm 6; Gal 5:16–25; Col 3:1–17).

Q **2:20 If I have been crucified in Christ, and I no longer live, why do I still have to work to do good things? Wouldn't Christ do all the work for me?**

One of the reasons Jesus was called the "Son of Man" is because He represented and embodied all people of all times and places (Jn 1:29; Rm 8:3–4; 2Co 5:21; Gal 4:4–5). Therefore everyone was crucified with Christ on the cross, and thus the Law was fulfilled. This truth was made evident in the exchange of Jesus for Barabbas (Mt 27:15–22). When Paul said that he had been crucified with Christ, he is referring to his fallen nature having been judged with Christ. The same Word of God that is effective in its condemnation under the Law is also effective in regenerating our lives from above (Jn 1:12–13; Rm 1:16–17; Jas 1:18). Paul still has a fallen human nature, but he has renounced and resists that nature; you hear him doing so when he says, "It is no longer I who live." Paul, like all Christians, now recognizes that the essence of his person, the "real" Paul, is the soul regenerated and animated by the Holy Spirit. We don't live or work or do good things in order to satisfy the Law but in order to provide care for others as a result of the care God provides for us. The Law is satisfied, but our neighbors still need a lot of help (Jn 13:12–17; 1Jn 4:19).

Q **2:20 Is being crucified with Christ the same thing as dying with Christ? Is this referring to Baptism?**

The dying with Christ is not Baptism, but being a Christian means that we are baptized into Christ and all that He is and does (Rm 6:3–4). Christ is the Word of God incarnate (Jn 1:1). Anyone who remains in the Word is thus immersed in Christ so that His life becomes our life, both as God sees us and as we really are more and more (Rm 8:1ff.; Php 2:5ff.; Col 3:16).

Q **2:21 What is he saying when he says, "Christ died for no purpose"? When the Bible states so clearly that we can't get to heaven by our own works, how can people still think they can?**

It is impossible for Christ to have died in vain. Whether anyone ever realizes the benefits of His redemption or not, the redemption itself is the product of His loving nature and an everlasting, accomplished demonstration of His love for all (Rm 5:8). Paul is pointing out the absolute impossibility of righteousness coming through the Law by claiming that if this were so, then Christ died in vain. In other words, if it is true that each person can only be saved and live by doing all that the Law requires by doing this himself or herself, then there is no use or purpose in Christ's death. Some who claim to be Christian teach that Christ did not live and die in our place. They teach that the expression "Christ died for us" only means that He gave us an example of what to do. But an example is still Law and only makes the Law more powerful in its condemnation. If Christ, a true man, obeyed the Law, then what is our excuse? He is all the more righteous in condemning us by the Law for our failure to do what He has already done. The death of Christ as an example only is in vain because it is no help to us. However, Christ did not live and die as an example only, but actually in our place (see 2:20 above). The Law does not care who fulfills it, as long as it is fulfilled. Since Jesus is also true God and eternal, He can fulfill every requirement of the Law for every person of every time and place. This suggests the magnitude of what Jesus meant when He said, "It is finished" (Jn 19:30). The word *finished* that Jesus used is the same word Paul uses when he says, "Christ is the *end* [that is, "finishing"] of the law . . . to everyone who believes" (Rm 10:4, italics added).

Part of the terrible condition of fallen human nature becomes evident when we observe how the clear, constant message of grace in the Bible is ignored, reversed, and inverted by people who are determined to argue that they must and will save themselves (Mt 23:1–33; Lk 10:25–37; 16:14–31; Rm 10:1–3). The danger of everlasting tragedy posed by a human nature that contends for its own righteousness explains why the whole of Scripture addresses it in such severe terms (Is 64:6; Mt 12:24–34; Rm 3:10–20; Heb 6:1–8; 10:26–31). The incapacitation

of fallen human nature by the working of circumstances or by the Word is necessary if we are to realize the truth and benefits of God's gracious activity for us in Christ and in us through His Word and Spirit (Mt 18:3; 1Co 1:18–31; 2Co 12:7–10).

Q 3:1 Who were the Galatians? Was Paul pointing out the devil by saying they had been "bewitched"? When he says, "Christ was publicly portrayed as crucified," is he saying simply that the Gospel was made known to them?

Galatia was an area in the upper center of Asia Minor, in present-day Turkey. Paul visited cities in southern Galatia during his second missionary journey (Ac 16:6). Galatians were Celts or Gauls who immigrated to this area by way of Thrace (the part of Turkey that is on the European continent).

The word translated "bewitched" occurs only here in the New Testament. The word has to do with harming another person by means of words spoken to them. Paul makes clear that the Jews who insisted on legalism meant to do harm by holding people under the Law and keeping them from the grace of God in Christ, which alone can save us from the condemnation of the Law (Gal 1:7; 3:10; 4:9–11; 5:1, 7–12).

Jesus was indeed actually crucified, dead, buried, and raised on the third day. Paul is making the point that these Galatians have no excuse for abandoning salvation

> How do you know whether you have the Spirit?

by grace for works-righteousness. The crucifixion of Jesus demonstrated the penalty of failing to keep the whole Law perfectly, and Paul communicated that history clearly. How could anyone want to trade the grace of God in Jesus Christ for the Law, which only condemns and crushes fallen human nature (Pr 26:11; 2Pt 2:22)?

Q **3:2–3 How do you know whether you have the Spirit or not?**

Not everyone has the Spirit of God. The Spirit of God comes with the Word and according to the Word (Jn 6:63; Jl 2:28–32; Ac 2:1–21). There are two witnesses to a person having the Spirit. The first is one's relationship with the Word. The second is the fruit of the Spirit. A person may be in the Word but always opposed to that Word and, therefore, without any fruits of the Spirit, like Judas Iscariot (Jn 5:39; 12:4–6; Rv 11:7–10). A person may appear to have the fruits of the Spirit but only because he is determined to justify himself by good works (Mt 23:27–28; Lk 10:25–42; 15:25–32; 18:9–14). It is the combination of life in the Word and fruits of the Spirit that bear witness to an authentic faith inspired by the Spirit of God (Mt 7:15–27; Jn 8:31–51; 1Co 12:3; Gal 5:16–26; Col 3:1–16).

Q **3:3 According to this verse, our faith in God is what is important; having His Word and believing it should be foremost. Yet we see church members sometimes being punished for breaking church policy or church rules. How can we reconcile this?**

What is wrong is always the same at the root: the Word and Spirit of God are missing. An answer to this question would depend on what you mean by "church's rules" and "severely punished." Many religious leaders tried to murder Jesus many times during His public ministry, and people who followed Jesus were threatened or cast out of the synagogue (Lk 4:28–30; 9:22–34; 10:31–39; 11:45–50; 19:38; Ac 4:1–21; 5:17–40). Jesus gives very clear instruction on how to love others, whether we are the person who has erred or the person who is trying to correct the person who is erring (Mt 5:21–24; 18:15–35). Paul explained what to do when a person is publicly and persistently contradicting God's Word and will (Rm 16:17–18; 1Co 5:1–13; 2Co 2:6–11).

Q **3:1–14 How is it possible for religions to believe in works of righteousness? How could they possibly reconcile their belief in themselves with this passage that is so clear?**

Fallen human nature's drive to justify itself is a powerful force because it is driven by ego, greed, and fear. Fallen human nature has forgotten that it was made in the image of God, with design, purpose, and incomparable worth. Without a consciousness of this worth, fallen human nature is desperate to prove itself worthy. Competition is one way in which fallen human nature would argue its value; "I may not be perfect, but I'm better than others" (Rm 2:1ff.; 2Co 10:12–18). Fallen human nature is greedy because being separated from God means we suffer from an infinite emptiness. Since we misidentify ourselves as essentially or only physical beings, we look for material things to fill the emptiness. But the emptiness is infinite and no amount of material things will ever begin to take the place of God in our lives (Mt 6:19–34; Lk 12:13–21; 4:1–6; 1Jn 2:15–17). In fact, trying and failing to substitute material things for God only makes the sense of loneliness worse. Finally, fear of impending judgment makes fallen human nature frantic and irrational. Like a drowning person who would drag down anyone coming to help in an effort to get above and out of the water, fallen human nature continually pushes down and under the help God sends (Heb 2:14–15). Thank God for sending His own Son, who was rejected, despised, crucified, and buried, but who rose again and ascended to reign as Savior of all for all eternity.

● ● ● ● ● ● ● ● ● ● ● ● ● ● ● ● ● ● ● ●

Q **3:7 Who are the people who don't believe, but physically do come from the line of Abraham? We are all "Jews" (children of Abraham), but if we are "catholic" because there is only one truth, why do we have many denominations?**

The answer to your question depends, in the first place, on distinguishing between the superficial and the essential. People who are physical descendants of Abraham call themselves "Jews," but physical descent makes them no better than or different from Ishmael or any other descendant of Abraham (Gal 4:21–28). All fallen human nature has descended from Adam and suffers from Adam's fall (Rm 5:12). The physical, fallen human nature is no better off because it descended through Abraham, Isaac, or Jacob; "that which is born of the flesh is flesh" (Jn 3:6). The same thing is true of "Catholics" or anyone else who would claim to be Christian on the basis of an outward, physical association. A person is not necessarily of the one true, universal, and catholic faith just because he or she was born into a Catholic family or physically practices the ceremonies of the church (Mt 7:21–23; 15:7–9; Mk 3:35; Lk 4:24–30). People who genuinely fear God according to their human nature and have been generated from above by the Word of God (as Isaac was) are the genuine children of Abraham, members of the Body of Christ, united in the one holy, catholic, and apostolic faith (Lk 1:50; Jn 8:31–59; Rm 2:28–29; 1Co 1:18–31; Eph 4:4–13; Jas 2:14–23).

There are as many denominations and as many subdivisions within denominations as there are people who possess a fallen yet proud human nature. Turning away from God means turning away from truth, which means a person moves farther away from God and from others at the same time. Only when God regenerates us through His Word and as we remain in that Word are we His disciples in truth and truly of the one true faith (Jn 8:31–32; 14:6; Ac 4:12).

. . . .

Q **3:10–13 Are we cursed, or is it Christ?**

We are both cursed, but we need not remain so. Anyone is cursed who does not keep everything the Law requires. Every unpleasant consequence in our physical world bears witness to this truth. If you eat or drink too much, you feel sick. If you fail to keep yourself upright, then your body will hurt as a result of falling down. This physical witness points to the greater, spiritual, eternal consequences of being opposed to God (Rm 5:6–11). Whoever remains in opposition to God will suffer the curse of the Law for eternity (Rv 21:8). Therefore, the Son of God took upon Himself our nature so that He might take our place under the curse of the Law, as Paul explains here and elsewhere (Jn 11:50; Rm 8:1; 2Co 5:21; Php 2:5–11). Since Christ has borne the curse of the Law for all people and fulfilled it, the only way to be cursed is to put yourself back under the Law, which is the very spiritual suicide that the whole Bible speaks against and exists to prevent (Mt 18:6–9; 23:2–5, 13; Ac 11:1–18; 15:5–10).

. . . .

Q **3:10 Why does Paul rebuke observance of the Law so frequently?**

First, it is not observance of the Law that Paul attacks, but it is forcing the Law on people as an obligation that Paul resists so passionately. Paul resists this forcing of the Law because those who force it are hypocrites and those upon whom it is forced are cursed by it (Ac 15:5–11; Gal 2:11–16; 3:10; 5:3–4). Second, Paul rebukes those who would force the Law on others only as frequently as they force it upon someone. Pride and self-righteousness are powerful forces in the fallen human nature of every person (Mk 7:20–23). A person who is determined to argue that he is better than others will inevitably impose the Law on others in order to make himself look better and others look worse (Mt 12:1–8; Rm 2:1–4). Third, Paul is especially sensitive about how the Law is used because he knows the magnitude of his own guilt under the Law (1Tm 1:12–17). In contrast to Peter, who still tried to claim righteousness according to the Law after all his failures, Paul never, ever lost sight of the fact that his life was restored to him only by the mercies of God through Christ Jesus (Ac 10:14; Rm 7:5–6; Heb 2:1–4; 3:12–4:16).

. . . .

Q **3:10 Everyone who does not continue to follow everything in the Law will be cursed. Is this the same as saying that we want to do good because we are forgiven?**

Jas 2:10 says, "For whoever keeps the whole law but fails in one point has become accountable for all of it." This does not say we want to do good because we are forgiven, though it does explain why that is true. The Law must be kept perfectly, absolutely perfectly, with never any failure, if we are to live by it (Gal 3:12). The wisdom of God and the magnitude of His love become apparent when we learn that Jesus redeemed us from the curse of the Law by taking our place under it (Gal 4:4–5; Rm 8:1–3; 2Co 5:21). The love of God, which we know through our redemption that Christ accomplished, is what regenerates us in His image, inspires us, and moves us to love others (Lk 7:40–50; 1Jn 4:19).

• • • • • • • • • • • • • • • • • • • •

Q 3:12 Are works only meaningful if they are done with faith?

Yes. Heb 11:6 says it is impossible to please God without faith. Rm 14:23 says, "Whatever does not proceed from faith is sin." Works that do not flow from faith may still benefit other people, but they are not meaningful to God because at the root they are still selfish. Faith produces work that does not want anything because God has already provided all. The person in whom God produces the fruits of faith wants only to be a faithful steward of the life, resources, and opportunities that God gives us to love others on His behalf. Bad trees cannot bear good fruit, and good trees cannot bear bad fruit (Mt 7:17–18; Jas 2:14–26).

• • • • • • • • • • • • • • • • • • • •

Q 3:13 Was everyone who was crucified on a cross cursed? How can Christ's crucifixion be considered a curse for us? How can Jesus be a curse when He is not sinful? Why must Christ become a curse in order to save us from a curse?

Anyone who dies by crucifixion or hanging dies a miserable, accursed death. Death by hanging on a tree is indicative of what it means to fail to keep the whole Law. Death in this way takes a long time, causes misery, and subjects the one dying to the contempt, derision, and mocking of people in public (Mt 27:39–44). When Paul says "Christ [became] a curse for us," he does not mean that Christ makes us experience being accursed. Paul is explaining that Christ has become the one accursed *in place of us!* In another place, Paul explains that God made Christ, who knew no sin, to be sin for us (in our place) so that we might become the righteousness of God in Him (2Co 5:21). Anyone can trade places, and the Law does not care who fulfills it, as long as it is fulfilled perfectly. Christ can take our place under the Law because as God, He is infinite and almighty, and as man, He is subject to the Law (Rm 1:1–5; Php 2:5–11). This exchange of Christ for us is described in terms of a lamb bearing the sins of the world and is demonstrated in real life when Barabbas was set free while Jesus was condemned (Jn 1:29; Mt 27:16–26; Is 52:13–53:12).

• • • • • • • • • • • • • • • • • • • •

Q 3:14 We receive the Spirit by having faith, and we have faith by hearing the Word. Does the Spirit give us faith?

Faith does come by hearing and hearing by the Word of God (Rm 10:17). How is it, then, that the Word works faith in us? The Word works faith because it is inseparable from the Holy Spirit (Jn 6:63). The Holy

Spirit is the one who caused the Word to be written (Jn 14:26; 2Tm 3:16). The union of the Spirit of God with the Word of God explains why His Word cannot return void (Is 55:11).

Q 3:15 What does this verse mean?

Paul is using a legal practice among people that is based in God's Law in order to teach us about our salvation. The last will and testament is among the most protected legal instruments because everyone wants assurance that their wishes will be respected after they have died. Therefore, the last will and testament of a person, legally established and witnessed, cannot be changed, and the legal system is bound to enforce it. If this is true for us, how much more so for God, who promised to send His Son to accomplish our salvation and His Spirit to work the realization of that salvation in our lives? God promised salvation by grace in Christ 430 years before there was a Moses and the Law that was given through him. The Law that God gave through Moses could not possibly contradict or undo the salvation God had already promised. Any attempt to use the Law for that purpose would be contrary to the Law itself. Rather, God gave the Law through Moses to serve the Gospel by demonstrating at all times and in every way our inability to save ourselves and our absolute need for God to save us by grace (Mt 5:16–17; Rm 3:19–28; Gal 3:24).

Q 3:15–16, 29 Is the inheritance Paul is talking about the kingdom of heaven and Israel?

The inheritance Paul is talking about is the kingdom of heaven or kingdom of God; they are the same thing (Mt 3:2; Mk 1:15). This is the same as the inheritance of the children of Abraham and Israel, as long as this means people generated by the Word of God (as Isaac was) who seek a spiritual kingdom, rather than physical descendants lusting for a material inheritance (Lk 12:13–15; Jn 8:31–47; 18:36; Heb 11:6–16). The kingdom of heaven and God can be seen in the ministry of Jesus as He restores God's creation by feeding the hungry, healing the sick, raising the dead, forgiving the penitent, and protecting the faithful from all who would tyrannize them (Mt 8:1–17; Jn 8:1–11; 12:7–8).

Q 3:15–25 Is Paul telling the Galatians about Abraham's promise of children to show them about Jesus? What is the law and the promise?

The problem that Paul is addressing is that physical descendants of Abraham tried to claim particular privileges with God and material interests based on their obedience to the law. In this section, Paul is referring to all of the law given through Moses: moral, civil, and ceremonial. Paul is using two witnesses to make the point that children of Abraham are of a spiritual nature, created and sustained by the grace of God alone

(Gn 41:32; Dt 17:6). The first witness has to do with Isaac as evidence of God's grace, power, and will. God gave Abraham and Sarah a son by the power of His own promise, proven by the advanced age and inability of Abraham and Sarah to produce a child by any natural means they possessed (Rm 4:1–5; Heb 11:8–16). God came to Abraham when he was an idolater in a foreign nation, also as evidence of the fact that God was alone responsible for this gracious, life-giving act (Ac 7:1–8). Abraham could not possibly have gained what God gave on the basis of keeping the Law, because the Law had not yet been given. The second witness has to do with the nature of the Law. While the Law describes what makes for life with God and with one another, the Law has no ability to produce what it describes (Rm 8:3). On the contrary, the Law reveals, exposes, and condemns all failures. By exposing our gross inability to live according to God's will, the Law reveals the magnitude of God's grace in promising that He would send His Son as a man, born through a descendant of Abraham. This Son of God and Seed of Abraham would fulfill the Law and forgive all our failure to keep it.

• • • • • • • • • • • • • • • • • • • •

Q **3:17 Is this why Jewish people are stuck in the Law? Are they more concerned with controlling their people, what laws do, than with the actual promise given them? Is it possible for us to understand the timeline of events?**

This verse makes it more difficult to understand why anyone would cling to the law. Fallen human nature is "stuck" in the law because we want to justify ourselves, even though the law actually condemns us. We do have the clever ability of ignoring laws we break and highlighting laws or inventing laws that we can claim to keep (Mt 23). Controlling other people is also a factor. The Gospel requires us to trust in God and His Word to inspire others to life and love. Since we are selfish and impatient, we prefer to use the law to control others, even though at best the law can only work outward obedience (1Jn 3:18).

For dates and details about the timeline of events, please see Dr. Andrew Steinmann's book, *From Abraham to Paul: A Biblical Chronology* (St. Louis: Concordia, 2011).

• • • • • • • • • • • • • • • • • • • •

Q **3:18 Was Israel's original purpose to convert nonbelievers to their religion, or were they exclusive?**

When God first called Abraham and promised a Savior, He included everyone: "In you all the families of the earth shall be blessed" (Gn 12:3). God called Abraham and his descendants out of the nations in order to deliver them from the miserable practices of those people (Lv 11:44–45; 19:2ff.; Ps 105:42–45; 106:8–39; 1Co 5:1–13). God did not separate His people from the nations in order to abandon and oppose them but in order to make a faithful and powerful witness to His truth and grace to the nations through His people (Is 9:1–7;

Lk 2:32). God's people are still called to be holy, to keep away from the ways of the world, and to reach out from within the kingdom of God to those who are still lost (Mt 5:48; Eph 5:8–14; 2Co 5:16–20).

· · · · · · · · · · · · · · · · · · · ·

Q 3:19 What was the purpose of the Law? Did the Law come from angels instead of God?

The answer to the Law's purpose comes in v. 24: "So then, the law was our guardian until Christ came." The expressions "It was added because of transgressions" (v. 19), "the Scripture imprisoned everything under sin" (v. 22), and "we were held captive" (v. 23) all describe the work of the Law. The Law, like a mirror, makes our transgressions clear and evident. The Law provides an insurmountable witness that we are in bondage to sin since we are never able to do what it commands. The Law guards us from deception and self-righteousness so that Christ and His righteousness can save us from its condemnation.

The word *angel* in English has become associated with winged heavenly creatures who serve God's will, but the word *angel* is Greek, not English. The word *angel* means "messenger." Winged heavenly creatures are messengers of God, but they are not the only ones. Prophets, apostles, and Jesus are also messengers of God (*Malachi* means "My messenger"). God gave His Law for the first time ever to Adam, and it was Adam's responsibility to be God's messenger in communicating His command to Eve and to

subsequent generations (Gn 2:16–17). God gave commands to Noah, Abraham, and the prophets (9:1–7; 17:9–14; Is 48:18–20). The major Lawgiver was Moses (Ex 20:1–26). God uses means to accomplish His purposes. He created all things through His Son, the Word (Pr 8:22–31; Jn 1:1–3; Col 1:15–16). Jesus healed with the Word and often added a physical sign like touching the person or applying mud to the eyes of a blind man (Mt 8:3, 16; Mk 8:23; Jn 9:6–7). Jesus used water to confirm His promises to us in Baptism and bread and wine to confirm His grace to us in the Lord's Supper. Jesus gave His Word to His apostles, but He sent the Holy Spirit to remind them of what He said and to write it down for us (Jn 14:26; 2Tm 3:16). There is, then, just *one* mediator between God and human beings: Jesus (1Tm 2:5). There were many messengers of God, authorized and authenticated by God as men who conveyed His Law to us (Ex 4:1–9; Mk 16:16–20).

· · · · · · · · · · · · · · · · · · · ·

Q 3:19–20 Are we to obey every Old Testament law?

There are three kinds of law in the Old Testament: moral, civil, and ceremonial. Ceremonial law was given to the children of Israel in order to remind them of their need for a Savior and God's promises to send one. Jesus fulfilled all of these laws, so they are no longer in effect (Mt 5:17–18; Lk 22:15–20). Civil law was given to help us live well together. As long as we live in a physical world, civil law provides a reliable guide for what is right and wrong. The moral law is expressed in the Ten Commandments. The first three commandments concern our relationship with God; the last seven concern our relationship with people. The moral law is equally binding on all people of all time. However, the redemption from the Law that Christ accomplished includes all the Law. Now we teach and seek to obey the Law not in order to save ourselves but because we are saved; not to get what we lack but to give to others what God has given to us. We know which Law to concern ourselves with because it is repeated by Jesus and the apostles in the New Testament (Lk 10:27–28; Rm 13:8–10).

Q 3:22 What Scripture is Paul referring to in this verse?

Paul is not referring to any passage in particular but to the Old Testament Scriptures that reveal the Law in general. All of Scripture can be divided into two groups: Law and Gospel. The Law tells us what God demands because this is required to live (Lv 18:5; Dt 6:4–12; 30:11–20). The Gospel tells us what God provides because we cannot do what the Law requires (Rm 8:1–4).

Q 3:23–25 It says right here that the Law passed away with Christ, so why do Lutherans place so much emphasis on the Law and Gospel?

Lutherans deal with Law and Gospel because Martin Luther recognized how we

are saved by distinguishing the one from the other. During the early years of his life, Martin Luther thought that "the righteousness of Christ" revealed in the Gospel was describing the perfect life of Christ by which we would all be judged and condemned. He was perfect; we are not (Rm 1:16). However, Luther noticed in Rm 4, which quotes Gn 15 and Ps 32, that the Gospel applies the righteousness of Christ to us as a gift. Some people think the Law is something we can take or leave, but this is not the case. The Law describes how life works, like the laws of nature. Violating these laws brings certain destructive consequences, which is why God warns us not to do so (Dt 30:11–20; Ezk 18:24–32). Some people turn the Gospel into Law, making Absolution, Baptism, and the Lord's Supper commandments that we must obey in order to earn God's favor. Jesus warned of this mistake with the parable of the wineskins (Mt 9:17). The Law shows us our need, and the Gospel conveys to us God's provision for that need in Christ. While the Law can only describe what must be and terrify us with that truth, the Gospel not only describes what is, regarding the grace of God, but actually communicates and grants that grace to us.

Paul did not say that the Law passed away with Christ, though Jesus did fulfill all that the Law demands. What changed with the sacrifice of Christ is that the Law is no longer our tutor or guardian; we are not under the Law anymore (Rm 8:1). Christ restored our proper relationship to the Law, so that it is not over us to condemn but under us to support. The Gospel regenerates us in the image of Christ, gives us His mind, and moves us to love as we are loved (Jn 1:12–13; 3:1–7; Php 2:5–11; 1Jn 4:19). This new man not only keeps the Law but agrees with the Law and uses it in order to keep our old man, or flesh, under control (Rm 6:1–23; 12:1–3; 1Jn 3:9).

· ·

Q 3:25 Does this verse imply that we are no longer under the commands of the Law?

This verse says that we are no longer under the Law as a guardian. Paul gives the reason for this change in the next verse: "For you are all sons of God." We become children of God when His promises (Gospel) regenerate us (Jn 3:1–7; Jas 1:18). As children of God, we no longer need to be forced by the Law or threats of punishment, the way a rebellious child is (Ezk 2:1–7; 12:1–25; Php 3:7–14; 1Jn 3:9; 4:19). As children of God, we are eager to love God and others by the power of His love for us.

· ·

Q 3:26–29 I have heard this passage used to support women's ordination. How does this view affect women's roles in the Church?

Paul is talking about our relationship with the Law throughout this chapter and through ch. 4. Being immersed in the Word covers us with Christ in regard to the Law. As Christ fulfilled all the promises of God, so Christ satisfied all the requirements of the Law for us. According to our regenerate soul, our new or inner man, we are a new creation, holy and innocent before God (Col 3:9–11; 1Jn 3:9). On the one hand, these verses do not change our relationship to one another according to our human nature. We are still born of Jewish or Greek or other parents. Slaves remained in bondage under civil law. Men remain male; women remain female; and though we are one, we are still individuals who struggle to get along. What changes after our regeneration is not our physical nature but the place that nature holds in our lives. As regenerate children of God, our human nature is no longer the selfish master of our life but the humble servant of God and others. On the other hand, being children of God makes us more inclined to learn and follow God's design for us, not less. It is as regenerate children of God that we begin to realize what it is to be male (bearing responsibility for) and female (submitting to), since Christ demonstrated both. He bore responsibility for redeeming the whole world and did so. He submitted perfectly to the will of His Father. As Christ is in relation to His Father and to His creation, so are men and women (1Co 11:3–16; Eph 5:15–6:9).

· ·

Q 3:27 Is it necessary for people to be baptized in order to be saved? If God considers us all equal, then why do we have all different groups?

The answer to your question depends on how we define *baptism*. If you mean the ceremony where water is applied according to God's command, the answer is a qualified no. We know that the ceremony or Sacrament of Baptism is not absolutely necessary from the example of the thief on the cross (Lk 23:40–43) and because we know it is the Word that saves, not the water (Rm 10:17). What is absolutely necessary is a life immersed or awash (baptized) in the Word of God ("living water"; see Jn 3:1–7; 8:31–32; Mt 28:19–20; Rm 10:17; Col 3:16). A life in the Word regenerates us, makes us desire and seek God's confirmation of this regeneration in the Sacrament of Baptism, and teaches us to appreciate that gift (Ac 8:26–39; 10:24–48).

God considers us all the same because we are incorporated into Christ, being regenerated by His Word. Nevertheless, we still have a human nature that is contrary to God, everyone else, and even our own best interests (Rm 5:6–11). When the Word of God is absent, the Spirit of God is also absent, and our fallen human nature fights to satisfy its pride and selfishness. This is what causes divisions and perpetuates different groups, which all claim to be Christian (1Co 1:10–31; Gal 5:15–26).

• •

Q 3:28 If we are all one in Jesus Christ, then why is there still such discrimination? Why is the man's place higher in the Church?

First, as long as we live with fallen human natures, in a fallen world, under assault constantly by the devil, nothing will ever be entirely as it should. Fallen human nature is proud and selfish. Second, discrimination is not necessarily a bad thing. Again, it is pride and selfishness that make people want to climb upon one another, as if that would make a life that matters and endures (Ec 1:1–11; 2:1–11; Jas 4:16–5:6). *Discrimination* in this sense means "to discern between one thing and another," which is helpful and often necessary. Third, Paul provides a great answer to your question as he describes our unity in Christ as a body (1Co 12:1–31). The Corinthians were competing with one another, just as you complain about, and Paul responds with this example. The highest and incomparable place in our union belongs to God, who in Christ is the Head, singular and singularly focused on the will of God. Christ determines the composition of the rest of the body and who will serve which purpose (Eph 2:20–22; 4:16). Fourth, as Paul's reference to the body indicates, different members of a body have different functions, some more visible and some less. The life and work of God's people is the same; we are ambassadors for Christ, every man, woman, and child (2Co 5:20). The difference comes in the role we have in relationship to one another and whether we fulfill that role in public or in private.

People in authority are only "higher" in a fallen world where they use their authority to take their life from the lives of others. According to God's design, to be in authority is to bear responsibility, thus "higher" means taking the lowest place or living to support others (Lk 14:7–35; Php 2:1–11). Speaking in public for Christ is a fearsome

559

responsibility and therefore rests upon men who were created to lay down their lives for the sake of women and children (Jas 3:1ff.; Ezk 33:1–11). Men also bear public responsibility for women so that women have a safe environment in which they may pursue the life God has prepared them for, especially in the bearing of children (Gn 2:18–24; Pr 31:10–31; Eph 5:15–33; 1Tm 2:8–15; 1Pt 3:1–7).

Q 4:1–7 What is the text really saying here?

Paul is describing two changes that are related to each other that make all the difference in the world. The first change is in the middle of this section: God sent His Son to take our place under the Law. By redeeming us, Christ has delivered us from the burden of the Law and the bondage of sin. The second change flows from the first. Without Christ, we were bound under the burden of the Law, and in our ignorance, we wasted our life, thinking we could justify ourselves. Trying to justify ourselves under the Law only exposes our failures more profoundly and insults God, whose grace provided the remedy for our failures in Christ. The coming of Christ in the flesh and the coming of Christ to us in His Word and Spirit changes us from the bondage of a slave and ignorance of a child. Since Christ redeemed us from bondage, God has made us His own children again by adopting us according to our human nature and by regenerating us according to His own (2Pt 1:2–4).

Q 4:1 What form of child is this verse referring to? Does this mean that children are slaves to their parents?

Paul is referring to the law of inheritance and is referring to a child in the normal, literal sense of the word. In v. 3, Paul uses the word *children* to refer to a state of ignorance and inability regarding the faith.

Children are not the same as slaves. Paul makes a comparison only in respect to an inheritance. Until a child comes to the age of maturity, he or she has no more right to an inheritance than a slave, but that is where the similarity ends. A child is completely different from a slave since maturity will come and the inheritance will be claimed. This is not true for a slave.

Q 4:3 What are the "elementary principles" of the world?

The word translated "elementary principles" occurs seven times in the New Testament. In every case, the word has to do with basic elements of God's created universe and the laws that govern those things. We have a chance to see the relationship between God and those elements in the life of Jesus, where He is never subject to or threatened by the basic elements of the world but is in full control of them, making them serve His purposes as is appropriate (Mk 4:35–41; Jn 6:4–21). The basic elements of the world (earth, wind, fire, air, stone) and the laws that govern them were intended by God to serve our lives as we love one another and learn of God in His creation (Ps 19:1–3; Rm 1:18–32). When these basic elements become master and god, then we become slaves with no hope since these created things have no way to free us from the foolishness, idolatry, and selfishness that enslaves us to them (Ex 32:1–6; Nu 11:4–9; Col 2:9–23; Heb 5:12; 2Pt 3:10–12).

● ● ● ● ● ● ● ● ● ● ● ● ● ● ● ● ● ● ● ●

Q 4:8 Are the Galatians Jews or Gentiles?

This verse makes it evident that the people of the churches in the region of Galatia were Gentiles. Paul makes this clear again in 5:2, where he warns them about being circumcised, and again in 6:13, where he speaks about those who are circumcised and how they do not keep the Law.

● ● ● ● ● ● ● ● ● ● ● ● ● ● ● ● ● ● ● ●

Q 4:8–9 Wouldn't this situation with the Galatians demonstrate how people can turn themselves off from the Gospel (2Pt 2:18–21)? Is it irreversible in this case?

Yes, Paul is warning the people of the region of Galatia of the very same thing Peter warns about (see also Mt 12:43–45; Col 2:9–23; Heb 6:1–8; 10:26–31). The question of impossibility is interesting. On the one hand, Scripture talks about the impossibility (or near impossibility) of restoring a person who has known the faith and then rejected it (Mt 12:31–32; Heb 6:4). On the other hand, Jesus said, "With God all things are possible" (Mt 19:26). It is never our place to draw conclusions or judgments about people (Mt 7:1). It is God's intent, I believe, to use the most severe language with those who are turning away or have turned away in order to reverse this most severe of threats (Lv 26:1–45; Ezk 18:24–32).

● ● ● ● ● ● ● ● ● ● ● ● ● ● ● ● ● ● ● ●

Q 4:9 Why does this verse say "now" that you have come to be known by God? Hasn't God always known us?

There are several words and a range of meaning for the word *know* in Hebrew and Greek that are often lost in translation to English. Certainly God knows all things and is conscious of all things all the time. Furthermore, an important part of "knowing" has to do with being connected with what or who you know. Adam "knew" his wife Eve and she conceived a son (Gn 4:1). Professors and teachers who "know" their subject are described this way because they are inseparable from that subject. They have great knowledge about and passion for the subject because they are joined to it. Paul is building a powerful argument in order to keep fallen human nature from falling away from the truth and grace of God. First, Paul appeals to the fact that they had come to know the true and living God, Creator of the universe, and Author of their salvation. How could they abandon that? Then Paul immediately reverses the direction and asks them to think of what it means to know, that is, to be joined together in communion with this very God.

Q 4:10 What was wrong with observing special "days and months and seasons and years"?

The problem with months, seasons, years, and festivals is the same as the problem with the elements of the world (see above, 4:3). None of these things are problems in themselves; they only become problems when people put themselves in bondage to them. For example, God gave the Sabbath as a gift to all people (and even animals). What a great thing to have a day set aside to rest. However, fallen human nature's determination to ignore God and justify itself caused people to make the Sabbath day a burden rather than a blessing (Mt 12:1–14; Mk 3:1–6; Jn 9:1–41). As long as times of the year, festivals, and the elements of creation serve our union with our gracious God, there is no problem with them. Any and every time fallen human nature would seek to enslave us to these things and undermine our union with God, we abandon them in order to protect our union with God alone (Php 3:7–14; Rm 14:1–15:13).

Q 4:12 What does Paul mean when he says that he became like the Galatians?

Paul's purpose after his conversion was to bring as many people as he could into the grace of God, as God had done for him. In order to be more effective in his purpose, Paul was determined to reach as many people as possible by identifying with or becoming like them (1Co 9:16–27). Paul was humble among these people, actually suffering from some kind of ailment while he was there (4:13–16). Paul did not claim to be better than the Galatians as a Jew, nor as a Roman citizen. Paul identified with them as a man who had been rescued from ignorance and self-destruction by the grace of God (1Tm 1:12–17; 1Co 15:8–11).

Q 4:13–14 Is this the Paul that was Saul? What was Paul's illness, and why did it lead him to share the Gospel with the Galatians?

This is the Paul who was Saul (Ac 13:9). No one knows why he was ill or what the illness was. Many speculate, but this is of no help. The only other reference we have to Paul's illness is where he describes a "thorn in the flesh," though we cannot even know for sure if this is the same trouble that bothered him while he was in Galatia (2Co 12:7–10).

Q 4:17 Who is the "they" to whom Paul is referring here?

"They" are the Jews who were usually jealous of Paul, who contradicted the Gospel, who tried to impose the Law on believers, and who claimed to be righteous on the basis of their own life (Ac 11:2–3; 13:45; 14:2; 15:5; 17:5; 21:27–31; Rm 10:1–3; Gal 5:2–4; 6:12–13).

Q **4:19 What are the birth pains Paul says he endures? How could he possibly know what that feels like?**

Obviously Paul would not know what a woman feels when she is delivering a baby, and this is not what he is saying. Paul said he was laboring again to bring the Galatians to birth. Paul had already labored once to bring the Gospel to the people of Galatia so that the Lord might regenerate them and make them His own children (3:1–7; 4:7–9). Unbelieving Jews came after Paul had visited and contradicted the Gospel, imposing on these people the Law of Moses and self-righteousness on the basis of works (3:10–13; 5:2–4; 6:12–13; Rm 10:1–3). Now Paul had to labor all over again to deliver these people back into the kingdom of God's grace in Jesus Christ.

Q **4:20 Why is Paul giving up on the Galatians if he had once already turned them in the right direction?**

Paul is not giving up, though he does express exasperation and doubts about the Galatian people. Anyone can understand the exasperation since Paul has to redo the work he had already accomplished (Heb 6:1–3). The word translated "doubts" or other terms that make it sound like Paul is giving up simply means "uncertainty." Paul is uncertain about them because they were without Christ or the grace of God when he came to them; then they came to the knowledge of the truth about their redemption in Christ; then they turned away from justification by grace through Christ to the works of the Law. This last turning from the knowledge of the truth and grace of God into the lies and deception of human ego and self-righteousness is what made Paul so uncertain, because there is a profound danger in renouncing the faith once we have been incorporated into it (Gal 5:3–4; Mt 12:43–45; Rm 10:1–3; Col 2:9–23; Heb 6:1–8; 10:26–31).

• • • • • • • • • • • • • • • • • • • •

Q 4:21–31 What does it mean when Paul talks about the child of the free woman and the child of the slave woman?

Consider the table below that indicates the comparisons Paul is making. An explanation follows the table.

4:21	Under the Law (3:21)	From the Gospel	
4:22	Hagar—a slave bears Abraham a son	Sarah—a free woman and wife bears Abraham a son	
4:23	Ishmael—conceived according to the laws of nature	Isaac—conceived according to God's promise	
4:24–25	Mt. Sinai = LAW = bondage = Hagar = Mt. Sinai = Jerusalem now and those who are devoted to its religion of self-justification under the law = bondage with her children	Jerusalem above = kingdom of God and heaven and Christ + all who are generated from God's Word	4:26
4:27	Hagar has a husband, like people who claim the Law, but the Law has no ability to bring forth life	Sarah was barren but now has more children than the woman who can have children under the laws of nature	
4:29	Ishmael = born according to laws of nature by activity of human nature—persecuted the one born according to the Word/Spirit of the Lord	Believers = children of promise, like Isaac	4:28
4:30	Cast out the slave woman, Hagar — her son, born under the Law, will not inherit	Only the son born of the promise is the heir and will inherit	
4:31	Believers are NOT slaves born of a slave woman under the law	Believers are children of freedom	

Life as a human being in the physical world is indicative of our spiritual life before God. In the physical, civil world, Sarah was a free woman and wife of Abraham, yet she had no power by the laws of nature to bear a child. It was God and God alone who provided her with a child, even though the law (laws of nature) had demonstrated that she could not. Isaac was generated by the Word of God, promised to Abraham, and born to a free woman. Isaac was free also and the heir of all things that belonged to his father. This is true of us. God generates us through His Word to be His children, free from the obligations, burden, and curse of the Law, and heirs of the kingdom of God. We live the life of love and service that we do because we are children of our Father.

In the physical, civil world, Hagar was a slave, and though she had the ability to produce a child according to the laws of nature, she had no power to make him free or to make him an heir of Abraham's estate. Similarly, as human beings, we are capable of generating children biologically, but we have no ability to make them free, to give them a life that endures forever, or to make them heirs of the kingdom of heaven. Only God can do this, as Abraham and Sarah proved.

Q 4:22 Why is Sarah referred to as "a free woman"? Why not just call her "Sarah"?

Sarah was a free woman in contrast to Hagar, who was a slave in Sarah's home (Gn 16:1–6). The relationship between Sarah and Hagar parallels the relationship between believers, who are free from the curses and obligations of the Law, and unbelievers, who are bound under the Law and in their rebellion against God (Jn 8:31–47).

Q 4:24 If this story of Hagar and Sarah can be interpreted allegorically, what does that say about the interpretation of other Old Testament passages? Why is the covenant from Mount Sinai to Hagar?

One of the keys to reliable interpretation and application is clarity about terms we use. Terms like *allegory, parable, literal, figurative, symbolic,* and *representative* mean different things to different people. All of these terms have something to do with the correspondence or relationship between one thing and another. Let's skip the terminology for a minute and focus on the concept. God created the physical world in order to teach us about Himself and ourselves (Ps 19:1–3; Rm 1:19–20). Jesus made reference to physical realities all the time in order to teach us about things spiritual (Mt 6:19–34; Jn 15:1–7). Relationships that are similar mean that common realities in the physical world are indicative of or are models of more essential, spiritual truths. The creation of Adam and Eve indicates what their relationship should be like with each other, as well as what our relationship should be with God (1Co 11:3–16). Noah's ark and the flood, like the exodus and Red Sea crossing, are indicative of Baptism (1Co 10:1–13; 1Pt 3:18–21). What is important to remember is that there is no empty symbolism or artificial or trivial relationship between Old Testament passages and lifelong significance.

Mount Sinai is a real place, God really gave the Law to Moses there, and that Law really is binding upon all human beings. Hagar was a real woman and was really a slave and really had to run away from Sarah with her son, who was born into slavery. There is nothing trivial or insignificant in all of God's creation. It is fallen man who has invented things artificial and trivial, things which have a hollow symbolism because they lack substance and import (Is 55:1–11; Mt 23:23–24).

• • • • • • • • • • • • • • • • • • • •

Q 4:25 Why are Hagar and her offspring in slavery? Why does Paul turn the story around and indicate that the Jews are actually the ones in slavery with Hagar?

We don't know why Hagar is in slavery. Sometimes people put themselves into slavery in order to avoid starvation; other times, people became slaves when they were captured by others (Gn 47:19; Ex 21:1–6; Lv 25:39–46; 1Sm 30:1–2; Is 4:1). In most cases, children who were born to people while they were slaves became slaves also (Ex 21:1–4). Any Jew who recognized and depended on God's promises to Abraham for salvation would be a genuine child of Abraham, like Isaac, and free (Jn 1:11–13; Rm 2:28–29; Gal 3:7). Any Jew who made claims for himself on the basis of physical descent and on claims that he was keeping the Law of Moses would make himself a slave to the Law and thus be bound by its condemnation (Gal 3:10–11; 5:2–4).

• • • • • • • • • • • • • • • • • • • •

Q 4:27 For whom is this written, and what is the purpose behind it? It doesn't sound very comforting to those who can't have children.

Paul is quoting Is 54:1. You would benefit from reading Is 53–55 to get a sense of what this is about. God is describing the work of redemption that His Son will accomplish and the significance of that work. Paul is writing this for everyone for this reason: like a woman who has no power to conceive children, we have no power to preserve or regenerate our own lives (Ps 49:7–15). Even if we can have children, like Hagar did, we are still bearing children of our own fallen human nature, bound by the Law and bound to die, just as we are (Jn 3:1–12; Rm 5:12–14). We are the barren ones who have no power to live; but God, by His Word, grants us this power to live and generates in us a new person that lives and endures forever (Jn 8:31–32; 11:25–26; 14:6; Gal 5:1; Eph 2:1–10; 1Pt 1:3–9; 1Jn 3:9). This passage and the truth it conveys are of the greatest comfort to those who cannot bear children physically because it reveals the tenuous nature of doing so. What good is it to bear children who are doomed to death under the Law? What really matters is communicating the Word of God so that people are regenerated and become children of God who live freely and eternally (Phm 10; 1Tm 1:18). Abraham and Sarah had no children and no power to produce them, yet God said Abraham's descendants would be more than the stars in heaven or the grains of sand on the shore (Gn 15:5; 22:17). We are among those descendants that God's promises have generated, and since we are generated by the eternal Word of God, we are eternal children and God is our Father. We, in turn, as ambassadors of Christ, bring the Word to the lives of others, that God may also regenerate new life in them (Mt 28:19–10; 1Co 7:12–16; 2Co 5:20; Eph 6:4).

• • • • • • • • • • • • • • • • • • •

Q 4:31 Who are the children of the slave woman?

The key is recognizing who we are, in essence. Ishmael was the child of Hagar. Their relationship is illustrative of all physical procreation: parents who are able to bear children according to the laws of nature can only bring forth children who are also subject to those laws. Parents with fallen human nature and subject to death can only bring forth children in bondage to these same forces (Jn 3:6; 8:33–44; Rm 5:6–11). As children of God, generated by His eternal and perfect Word, we are free from the curse of sin and death under the Law (Jn 1:12–13; 3:1–7; 8:31–32; Col 3:10–17; Heb 2:14–15; 1Jn 3:1–9).

• • • • • • • • • • • • • • • • • • •

Q 5:1 How does God say that there is no law for a Christian? Since Christ has set me free, why am I not free from the old Adam? Why do I still sin?

I don't know of anywhere that God says there is no law for a Christian. Jesus said that He was giving a new command to His disciples, that they love one another as He had loved them (Jn 13:34).

Paul wrote that there is no condemnation for those in Christ Jesus and that love was the fulfillment of the Law (Rm 8:1; 13:8). To understand a Christian's relationship to the Law, we must remember the two natures of a Christian. According to our fallen human nature, the Law is still effective, the wages of sin are still death, and we continue to realize the consequences of our failure to keep the Law—but this is only in respect to our bodies (1Co 15:35–50; 2Co 5:1–4). According to our new person, our soul regenerated by the Word of God, we are perfect and without sin (1Jn 3:9). The Holy Spirit, working through the Word and Sacraments, continually inspires and animates our soul to serve in love even more and even before the Law ever commands us to do so (Rm 6:1–8:17; 12:1–3; Gal 5:16–26; Col 3:1–17). God prophesied by Jeremiah that in the New Testament, God would write the Law on our hearts (Jer 31:31–34). God prophesied by Ezekiel that His Word and Spirit would cause us to walk in His ways and observe His statutes (Ezk 36:24–27).

• • • • • • • • • • • • • • • • • • •

Q 5:1 Is freedom in Christ comparable to free will?

We can always try to make a comparison and see what we learn. Free will, in the proper and absolute sense of the word, would apply only to God since God alone is independent, free of necessity, all knowing, and all powerful (Ps 50:12; Jn 10:18; 19:11; Ac 17:24–25). Freedom in Christ includes freedom from the curse and condemnation of the Law (Gal 3:13; Rm 8:1); freedom of a regenerate soul animated by the Word and Spirit of God to love (Mt 10:8; 1Jn 4:19); and freedom to seek, discover, and live to the fullest the life God has prepared for us (Ps 139:16; Jer 29:11; Ac 20:22–23; 21:4, 11–14, 17–40; Eph 2:8–10).

Q **5:2 Why is circumcision looked upon badly in this verse? I thought circumcision was a sign of a believer.**

God commanded Abraham to circumcise himself and his sons as a physical confirmation of the promise that He would send His Son through a descendant of Abraham (Gn 17:11). Like God's command for the Sabbath, fallen human nature changed it from a gift to an obligation, from a physical indication of justification by God's work by grace to a work man would do in order to justify himself. A believer would know that circumcision was confirmation of God's gracious promises and find assurance of salvation. Only an unbeliever would subject himself to circumcision in order to prove to God that he was obedient to the Law and should, therefore, be accepted by God. Once the promised seed of Abraham had come in the person of Jesus Christ, circumcision gave way to Baptism (Ac 11:1–18; 15:1–12). Circumcision looked forward from Adam through Abraham to Jesus. Baptism flows from all of God's Law and promises fulfilled in Jesus to all people (Mt 28:19–20; Mk 16:16). Justifying oneself by obeying the Law and being justified by grace on account of Jesus Christ are absolute opposites of each other (Rm 4:1–8). People who decided to accept circumcision in order to justify themselves by keeping the Law were, therefore, rejecting the work of Christ in favor of their own work and would be doomed, since the Law cannot justify us (Rm 3:19–20; Gal 2:16; Jas 2:10).

Q **5:6 Why don't Jews baptize people who haven't been circumcised?**

Many Jews did not or could not see that Christ was the point of the Old Testament and fulfilled it (2Co 3:12–16). These Jews accepted that Jesus was the Christ but saw Him as sort of a second Moses, who gave more law for us to keep (Ac 15:5). In their minds, you could not be accepted by Jesus or begin to keep the Commandments He gave unless you first obeyed Moses and kept his law. This is why the coming of the Holy Spirit upon Gentiles who heard the Word was such a shock to the Jews; yet they could not deny the authenticity of this since they spoke in different languages (probably Hebrew), just as the apostles did on Pentecost (Ac 2:1–21; 8:14–18; 10:34–48; 11:17; 15:7–8).

Q **5:11 Paul isn't preaching circumcision, is he?**

No, Paul is not preaching circumcision. While Paul refused to circumcise Titus, he did circumcise Timothy and still felt compelled to observe certain Jewish customs (Gal 2:3–5; Ac 16:3; 20:16; 21:21–26). It is possible that Paul's opponents argued that people should keep the Law of Moses because even Paul still kept it and imposed it on others. Paul is confounding such an argument with the fact that these opponents continually oppose, harass, and persecute Paul; why would they do that if he meant to subject people to the Law just as they had?

Q 5:12 What is meant by this? In what tone is it said?

Paul is angry with those who would impose the Law of Moses upon others, because this would rob them of the grace of God in Christ and force them under the bondage of sin and condemnation. Paul is expressing a desire for justice in this verse. If these Jewish religious leaders are so intent on taking a knife to the flesh of Gentile men, he wishes they would take the knife to themselves (1Ki 17:25–28; Mt 7:2; 26:52; Gal 6:12–13).

Q 5:18 What does this verse mean?

Begin by distinguishing our two natures: a fallen human nature (the flesh or old man) and a regenerate soul (the spirit or new man). If we are led by the Spirit, it can only be due to the presence of God's Word in our life (Jn 6:63; Rm 10:17). The Word and Spirit of God are what cover our old man with the righteousness of Christ, forgive all that is wrong, and generate our new man, which is holy already and therefore not subject to the demands or condemnation of the Law (1Jn 1:7–9; 2:2; 3:9; Rm 8:1–11; Col 3:1–15).

Q 5:21 Does this verse imply that salvation depends on works?

No, of course not; the Bible is absolutely consistent in denying our ability to save ourselves by works and in affirming that God alone saves. Salvation comes by grace alone, but condemnation can only come by the works of the individual, the critical work being self-justification in opposition to the grace of God accomplished in Christ. Even our wicked works and ways cannot condemn us if we live in repentance and faith (Mt 9:12–13; Lk 7:36–50; Jn 8:2–11; 1Jn 1:7–9). The single work that makes all of our other works bring condemnation upon us is the work of unbelief; of dishonesty about our dependence on God and a conscious, willful, determined, relentless insistence that we are just and have earned our own life (Gal 5:3–4; Mt 12:43–45; Rm 10:1–3; Col 2:9–23; Heb 6:1–8; 10:26–31).

Q 5:22 What is the difference between "the fruit of the Spirit" (singular) and "the fruits of the Spirit" (plural)?

The word *fruit* occurs sixty-six times in the New Testament. It occurs in the plural, "fruits," only sixteen of those times, most of these in the Gospels where Jesus says you will know a tree from its fruits (see Mt 7:16–20). My suspicion is that people who use the plural of "fruit" in reference to the work of the Holy Spirit are not aware that the term is only singular or that it matters. Understand that the singular matters in at least two ways. First, translating and speaking accurately always matters; to do otherwise is to promote uncertainty where certainty is the point. Second, the fruit that the Spirit produces in us is singular; it is good (Gn 1:31). There are many virtues and characteristics of goodness, and the expression "fruit of the

Spirit" is typically followed by a list of attributes. Unlike the gifts of the Spirit, which are distributed to people according to God's will, the fruit of the Spirit is given equally and to all who are regenerated and inspired by the Holy Spirit (Rm 12:1–8; 1Co 12:31; Eph 4:1–16).

Q 5:24 If we have crucified our sinful nature, why do we still sin?

Perhaps a phrase from the Apostles' Creed would help: "was crucified, died and was buried." Crucifixion makes a very clear statement of judgment, and death will follow without a doubt, but those crucified take time to die. Early during Jesus' crucifixion, both thieves mocked Him, but in the course of the afternoon, one thief came to honesty and then to faith (Mt 27:44; Lk 23:39–43). When Paul says we have crucified the flesh with its passions and desires, he means that we have recognized these as accursed and have renounced them, the way people recognized the same about someone who was crucified (Gal 3:10–11; see Jn 3:14–16 for more about the significance of crucifixion). While a believer lives in his body in this world, that fallen human nature will continue to oppose God, His Word, and His will (Rm 5:6–11; 1Co 2:14). God has provided atonement for this nature, forgiveness, and a regenerate soul that does not sin but lives as God wills (Rm 3:25; 4:4–8; 1Jn 3:9). A regenerate soul agrees with the law of God and does oppose, renounce, and hold in contempt the fallen human nature that it remains joined to until

death grants a final relief (Rm 6:1–25; 1Co 15:50–58; 2Co 4:1–5:21).

Q 5:25 How can we keep in step with the Spirit in accordance with what Paul says?

Living in or by the Spirit requires one to remain in the Word (Jn 6:63). Remaining in the Word means that the Spirit Himself will keep us in step with the will of God (Ezk 36:24–27; Jn 15:1–7; Rm 10:17). Since our fallen human nature does not receive the things of the Spirit, Paul is also making a point of logic for a believer to use against the opposition of his own human nature (1Co 2:14). The fact is, just as breath is required for us to live biologically, so the breath or Spirit of God is required for us to live essentially (Gn 2:7; Ezk 37:1–14). Our flesh does not believe, but it can understand that without the Spirit of God and the Way provided by Christ, there is no hope or life to be had (Rm 6:1–23).

Q 5:25–26 Paul talks about living in the Spirit. Is Paul saying we need to practice what we teach and not act like hypocrites?

Yes, Paul is saying exactly that—except that no one ever "acts" like a hypocrite. Hypocrisy is the absolute opposite of honesty and truth (Mt 23:13–33). Hypocrisy is what predisposed King Saul and Judas Iscariot to failure from which they could not recover (1Sm 15:10–31; 16:14; 18:12, 17, 21, 25; 28:5–25; Jn 12:4–6; 13:2). Hypocrisy is not something anyone would ever "act like," but rather it consumes the person who is willing to entertain it. We do need to practice what we teach, but we must also remember that practice is the product of the Word and Spirit's work in us. We can only practice the truth if we are remaining in the Word and Spirit of truth (Jn 15:1–7).

- -

Q 6:1 Should we give Law or Gospel first to people?

We might want to consider how the Bible communicates the Word to us. Genesis begins with Gospel, describing God's gift of creation. In Gn 3, God gives the promise of a Savior before He explains the consequences of Adam and Eve's rebellion. God brought Israel out of Egypt before He gave them the Law on Mount Sinai. The gospels begin with the birth of Jesus and His victory over the devil and temptation in the wilderness before recording Jesus' teaching of the Law. Ps 130:3–4 says, "If You, O LORD, should mark iniquities, O Lord, who could stand? But with You there is forgiveness, that You may be feared." Without some certain knowledge of the grace of God, the Law can only drive a person to complete despair or complete contempt. The Law only condemns, and fallen human nature is too selfish and proud to accept this. However, the grace of God in history and active in His Word and Spirit provides a context of hope that regenerates

and raises up a soul, even as it drowns and buries our contrary human nature, just as the waters bore up the ark sheltering believing Noah while they drowned the wicked and disobedient and as the Red Sea made a path for those who followed the promise of God but a tomb for those who opposed God (Gn 6:1–9:1; Ex 14:1–31; 1Co 10:1–12; 1Pt 3:18–21). What we give a person depends on the condition they are in. If a person knows the grace of God but has drifted away or is fighting against His grace, we must make the Law clear in order to incapacitate that fallen human nature (Mt 12:29–31; Heb 2:1–15; 6:1–8; 10:26–31; 2Pt 2:1–22). If a person is already overcome by the Law, then we proclaim the Gospel so that the grace and Spirit of God may regenerate and raise up the new man inside that person (Ezk 37:1–14; Lk 10:38–42; 15:20–32; Jn 8:1–11; 1Tm 1:8–10).

- -

Q 6:1–5 Why does it say in v. 2 to "Bear one another's burdens," but in v. 5, "For each will have to bear his own load"?

The verb is the same in both cases, "to bear." In v. 2, we are commanded to carry each other's burdens. In v. 5, we are reminded that we must each carry our own burden ("load"). These two words for "burden" appear to mean the same thing (cf. Mt 20:12; Ac 15:28; and 2Co 4:17 with Mt 11:30; 23:4; and Lk 11:46). The difference has to do with our relationship toward our neighbor in contrast to our responsibility before

God. Helping others with the burdens they bear in this life is evidence that we know the freedom from the burden of the Law that Christ has provided for us, which Paul just spoke of in 5:1–4 (Jn 13:34; 15:12, 17; 2Co 5:15; Php 2:1–4; 1Jn 4:19). While we are made free to help others in this life, no person can take another's place in judgment before God, except the One who took that place for all (Jn 3:16; Rm 5:12–19; 2Co 5:14, 18–21). The same person who rejects the vicarious atonement of Christ on his behalf will spend his life trying to serve and justify himself and thus has no time or interest in helping others with their burdens.

- - - - - - - - - - - - - - - - - - -

Q 6:2 How can we Christians bear one another's burdens in a nonphysical or materialistic way? What is the "law of Christ"?

The law of Christ is best articulated by Christ Himself: "A new commandment I give to you, that you love one another: just as I have loved you, you also are to love one another" (Jn 13:34). Paul echoes this command of Jesus in Rm 13:8: "Owe no one anything, except to love each other, for the one who loves another has fulfilled the law." Christians bear one another's burdens by

How can we bear one another's burdens?

loving one another in both material and immaterial ways (Rm 12:10–15). We sympathize with people as they endure emotional and psychological hardships (Rm 14:19; Col 3:12; Heb 13:3). We use the material means God has given us to help provide for those who are lacking (Lk 6:38; Ac 2:44–46).

- - - - - - - - - - - - - - - - - - -

Q 6:6 Are the "good things" spiritual or physical?

I don't see any way or reason to limit what Paul means. We know that God intended those who bear spiritual responsibility to teach in the public ministry to receive physical means to live from those who are taught (Mt 10:7–10; 1Co 9:6–14). People are very quick to call upon their pastor when facing spiritual challenges or emotional difficulties, but they rarely even think of the pastor when realizing spiritual or emotional blessings. It would be a great help and encouragement to pastors if people remembered to share equally in all things experienced (1Th 5:12–13; Heb 13:17).

- - - - - - - - - - - - - - - - - - -

Q 6:9 What does it mean that at the proper time, we will reap a harvest?

Human nature tends to do good only as long as it receives good in return. We who know the love of God and how abundantly He provides for us do good because it is God's love working its way out through us (Mt 5:38–48; Lk 6:30–36; 1Co 15:10). The proper time for harvest certainly means the end of the world, when God gives to each according to his works (Mt 25:31–46). It is possible, from time to time, that God allows us to see some results from our labor even now (Mt 19:28–29; Rm 1:13; 1Co 9:11).

Q 6:10 Why would Paul say to do good, especially to those who belong to his family of believers?

Every command and instruction in the Bible is given because we have a fallen human nature that is opposed to God and all things good (Mk 7:20–23; Rm 5:6–11). As Christians, we have a regenerate soul that is already oriented to do good, but our flesh is weak and contrary (1Jn 3:9; Mt 26:41; Rm 7:13–21). Our regenerate soul depends on the Word and Spirit of God to make us strong to do what is good, and it depends on the Law to press our fallen human nature into compliance (Jn 6:63; 15:1–7; Rm 6:1–22; 2Co 5:14–15). Jesus taught us to love everyone, especially our enemies (Mt 5:38–48). If we are, in fact, determined to love our enemies, it would not follow that we love fellow believers less. On the contrary, if we mean to love those who are most opposed to us, we wouldn't want to miss times when we could do good to those who are fellow members of the Body of Christ (Ac 2:44–46; 5:32–35; 6:1–4; Php 4:15–19).

Q 6:11 Why does he point out that he uses large letters to write to them?

I suspect Paul ends this letter as it began, making sure they recognize his authority as an apostle (Gal 1:1, 11–23). Paul wants there to be no question about the origin of this letter or the authority of its content; this is the Word of the Lord (1Th 2:13; 2Tm 3:16).

Q 6:13–14 Why would some Christians brag about being circumcised?

Fallen human nature never changes its disposition, even if a regenerate soul lives within (Jn 3:6). Even after Pentecost, the apostle Peter wanted to claim that he had kept the Law, at least in part (Ac 10:14). Paul warned that people who believed that Jesus was the Christ yet still wanted to justify themselves by the works of the Law were in trouble (2Co 10:12; Gal 3:10–12; 5:1–4). Paul never, ever wanted to argue the merit of his works before God because doing so would place before God the very life of Paul that God has so graciously forgiven (Gal 2:18; Rm 2:17–29; 2Co 12:1–13).

Q 6:17 What does Paul mean when he says, "I bear on my body the marks of Jesus"? Could Paul have been the first case of stigmata?

Paul had suffered physical abuses many times in the course of his mission work, including being beaten with rods (2Co 11:22–27; Ac 16:16–37). I recommend great caution regarding stigmata. Why would God inflict on the most faithful of His people the pain and suffering of crucifixion from which Jesus delivered them (2Co 5:15; Heb 10:11–18)? As we see in the case of Paul and throughout the history of Christianity, there is no need for God to provide the signs of suffering in His people; the world has always been more than eager to do so (Mt 23:31; Heb 11:36–40; Rv 7:10–17).

Ephesians

Q **1:1–14 Is everyone predestined to believe? Why are some chosen and not others? What happens to those who aren't saved?**

Paul's teaching on predestination is most clearly expressed in v. 5, where "having predestined us" (*pro-orisas*) functions as the source of all that flows from Paul's pen. The expression "through Jesus Christ" describes a circumstance that is itself a function of God's preceding choice. God has redeemed all people in the vicarious atonement of Jesus Christ, and those who realize this redemption in the course of their lives do so because God has predestined or elected them to do so. So, how does this predestination relate to the universal atonement? May I suggest that universal atonement and individual election

function together, providing redemption for the individual from two directions. On the one hand, God has redeemed everyone in the person of His Son. On the other hand, a person realizes this redemption by being drawn into and held within the Word of God, which blesses, regenerates, sanctifies, and applies to the one predestined all the myriad benefits of Christ—a choice within a choice. This redemption from two directions provides absolute comfort for the one in the Word and perhaps an explanation for those who struggle with the relationship between God's grace, universal atonement, and election.

What can we say to the person who objects that this conclusion about predestination excludes the notion of human

What happens to those who aren't saved?

freedom and thus makes God responsible for those who are damned? If we give the one who contends he has free will his way, then he cannot blame God if he ends up condemned, since that was what he insisted upon. If we deny free will within the context of humility regarding our nature, then universal atonement is effective and there is no condemnation to complain about; only the contention for freedom of choice puts a person under the consequences of doing so.

Paul is clearly using these initial verses of Ephesians as an introduction to his war against the notion of self and self-assertion. An individual who makes claims for himself would do well to remember that not everyone who exited Egypt entered the Promised Land, nor did all the disciples nor even all of the apostles remain faithful, nor will individuals who make claims for themselves prevail against God (Mt 7:21–23; 25:41–46; Heb 3:12–19).

Perspective and timing may provide another avenue of understanding. From God's perspective, all people are redeemed in Christ and chosen, because Christ is God's chosen one. From our perspective, being "in Christ" is the place to be since everything good, including a sense of God's election, is realized there. How can election be anything less than corporate and individual at the same time, given the nature of God? The individual is elect by God from eternity, yet is so according to the part he or she fulfills within the Body of Christ, in His Word, in His Church, in His kingdom and the work of extending it to others.

While some of Paul's language in Eph 1 could be instrumental (God has blessed us "by means of Christ," v. 3; God bestows grace upon us "by means of the Beloved," v. 6), some of it cannot be (we are saints and faithful "in Christ," v. 1; God chose us "in Him," v. 4). Ultimately, as is the case with the question of election being corporate or individual, the answer to the question of location or means is both: God predestines and effects that predestination by the agency of Christ and by our union with Christ.

According to Eph 1, is election corporate or individual? The answer according to Paul is a resounding yes! Given the nature of God, this might have been expected. As God is omniscient, omnipotent, and omnipresent, so His election is comprehensive. He has predestined us since we are incorporated in His Son, the Son of Man, and all aspects of our life and times are also predestined, individually and exhaustively. For the regenerate, the comfort, faith, and inspiration provided by knowing this is as comprehensive as the election itself. For those who would argue that this is unfair or that they rightly blame God for their condemnation, this biblical teaching precludes their objections since they cannot argue that they were not elect and redeemed with Christ, and so why would they argue, assume, or contend that they are outside of God's good election for them?

⬤ ⬤

Q **1:3 This verse uses past tense, saying Christ "blessed" us. Does God not continuously bless us?**

God does bless us continuously, and He does so because of the redemption He accomplished for us in Christ, once for all (Rm 8:1; 2Co 5:21; Gal 3:5–9).

⬤ ⬤

Q **1:12 What does Paul mean here?**

Glory means to be or do something that no one else is or can do. *Praise* means to declare or recount the wonderful things that someone has done. Anyone who hopes in Christ does so because God has predestined him or her to do so and has inspired that hope through His Word and Spirit (Rm 8:28–39). The fact that God saved us despite ourselves, entirely by His love, wisdom, power, and person, is unparalleled. Our salvation is God's glory, since no one else could or would save us, and the story of our salvation is the praise of that glory.

⬤ ⬤

Q **1:13 Paul writes, "When you *heard* the word of truth, the gospel of your salvation, and believed in Him, [you] were *sealed* with the promised Holy Spirit" (emphasis added). Does that mean you do not need to** have Baptism to be marked as God's child forever, but that belief is enough?

A form of the verb *seal* occurs fifteen times in the New Testament. Matthew uses the term in relation to a physical seal on the tomb, and John writes of the faithful receiving a seal on their foreheads, though this is visionary language (Mt 27:66; Rv 7:3). John uses the term twice in the sense of "verifying" something (Jn 3:33; 6:27). There is a text parallel to this verse in Ephesians where Paul makes it clear that the seal is the granting of the Holy Spirit to us as a deposit (2Co 1:22). The noun *seal* occurs sixteen times, all but three in Revelation. The three occurrences outside of Revelation are all in Paul's writing and have to do with the idea of a spiritual seal rather than a physical seal (Rm 4:11; 1Co 9:2; 2Tm 2:19). The Holy Spirit is the one who seals us in the faith; He is received through the Word, and He is the reason we believe and confess Christ (Jn 6:63; 1Co 12:3).

⬤ ⬤

Q **1:19 What does this power enable us to do?**

Paul is not discussing the power of God with regard to what it makes us able to do, though we might consider that His mighty power is what enables us to do absolutely everything (Jn 15:5). Since we are completely dependent on God, knowing that God's power, might, wisdom, and love for us are infinite gives us hope.

Q 2:1–3 Does this mean that our spirit is alive, and our human flesh is dead in transgressions and sins?

First we need to define *dead*. Death cannot mean the end of our consciousness and experience, since then it wouldn't mean anything. Death means the absence of positive relationships, the opposite of life, which means the presence of positive relationships. Trespasses and sins have to do with contradicting God's design and intent for us. It is contradicting God's design and intent that makes an end of positive relationships and leaves us with only the negative experiences in body, soul, mind, and spirit. After conversion or the regeneration of our soul, our body is still dead in trespasses and sins, but it is no longer the essence of who we are. After conversion, the living, regenerate soul is our essence.

Q 2:2 Why is the devil the prince of the power of the air?

I am not sure we would know that Satan or the devil is being referred to here except by the expression "the spirit that is now at work in the sons of disobedience." The devil was the one who tempted Adam and Eve to disobey, and he continues to prowl about in order to keep people disobedient (Gn 3:1–5; Lk 4:1–13; Jn 8:44; 13:2; Rv 12:9).

Q 2:3 What does Paul mean when he says that we "were by nature children of wrath"?

Notice in the beginning of this verse that Paul refers to himself and his readers as "we." So, anyone who would read this letter is the "we." In addition, anyone who is not reading the letter or claiming a Christian confession would also be included; all have sinned and fallen short of the glory of God (Rm 3:10–20; 5:6–11).

Q 2:6 When Paul speaks of how God raised us up with Christ, it sounds as though we are equal to Christ. Why does Paul use this language?

One of the reasons why Jesus is referred to as the "Son of Man" is because He *is* all people in relation to the Law and God's judgment (2Co 5:21). The truth of Christ taking our place was confirmed by a historical, physical event when Pilate released Barabbas and condemned Jesus to death (Lk 23:18–25). The vicarious or substitutionary life of Christ means that whatever He has done, all people have done with Him. As long as a person is united with Christ by dependence upon Him (faith), that person has the benefits of Christ's work (Rm 8:1). To say that we were raised with Christ and seated *with* Him is not at all the same as saying we are equal to Christ by nature or prerogative. Christ is the Son of God by nature; we are children of God by the regenerating work of the Holy Spirit, who takes what belongs to Christ and makes it ours (Jn 16:14).

. . . .

Q 2:8–9 Why do Catholics believe that you are saved by works, when Paul clearly states, "by grace you have been saved through faith"?

The "catholic faith," by definition, means the one and only true, universal, and Christian faith. This faith teaches only the truth according to the Word of God. The Roman Catholic Church, along with most other denominations and most people regardless of denomination, teaches works-righteousness because this is what fallen but proud human nature asserts. As if our fallen rebellion against God were not bad enough, we are also contrary to the very means by which God would save us from ourselves. We are our own worst enemies, like a drowning person who, in his frantic and desperate attempt to save himself, pulls under and drowns everyone who swims out to help him. This condition of fallen human nature is what makes it necessary to incapacitate rather than simply reform the flesh (Lk 9:24; Rm 3:19; Col 3:5).

. . . .

Q 2:10 If we aren't saved by good works, then why does it say that we were created in Christ Jesus to do good works? If we were created to do good works, what about all the evil things we do? Do we not have a choice in the things we do?

Good works are the effect of our salvation, not the source. God redeemed our lives in the life of His Son, and now God is redeeming our lives by working His will in us. Good works are good because loving our neighbor is the substance of life as God created us to know it. God has prepared all things in advance, including the measure of our faith and the particular good works we will accomplish in the course of our lives (Ps 139:16; Rm 12:3). How could God make all things work together for the good of those who love Him or provide prophecy and fulfillment in Christ if He did not have all things planned in advance? The evil that we do or anyone else does is contrary to God's will, yet even what is contrary to God's will must serve God's purposes (Ac 2:22–24). We make choices all the time, but the choices are the product of all the other forces we are subject to and dependent upon.

. . . .

Q 2:11 Why does it say, "Remember that at one time you [were] Gentiles"?

Paul adds the phrase "in the flesh" to make clear that the Christians in Ephesus were not physical descendants of Abraham, like the people who call themselves Jews. As he did in the Letter to the Romans, Paul cautions the Gentile Christians against thinking too much of themselves and despising the Jews (Rm 11:11–32).

Q **2:12 At one time, were Gentiles excluded from being saved by the covenants of the promise?**

No; those who are honest about their dependence on God and His Word have always enjoyed the benefits of that Word (Ps 117; Lk 4:24–27). On the other hand, the Gentiles did not have the advantage of the Lord being right in the midst of them and communicating to them through a leader, as the Jews had with Moses and the prophets (Rm 3:1–2).

Q **2:14 Isn't there a passage in Scripture that says that Christ came not to abolish the Law, but to fulfill the Law? What is this barrier between Jews and Gentiles?**

Jesus Himself said that He did not come to abolish the Law but to fulfill it (Mt 5:17). The Law was a barrier between Jews and Gentiles because the Gentiles either did not know of the Law or did not consider that they were under any obligation to keep the Law. Living according to the Law of Moses meant that the Jews could not live in communion with the Gentiles (Ac 15:13–21).

Q **2:15 Paul says that Christ made one new man out of two, thus making peace. What does this mean? Does this refer to physical bodies or to our spirits?**

The two men that Paul is referring to are the Gentiles and the Jews (see 2:11). Some

Jews were fearful of Gentiles because they were always a threat to Jewish fidelity toward God (Dt 7:3–4). Other Jews despised the Gentiles, assuming that God had not chosen them because they were not worthy (Dt 7:6–8; Gal 2:15). Some Gentiles resented the Jewish disposition toward them; others might have thought the Mosaic Law unsophisticated or backward (Ac 17:32; 1Co 1:22–25). Christ fulfilled all the Law on behalf of all people. The peculiar laws of the Jews that pointed forward to Christ (sacrifice, diet, calendar, circumcision) were accomplished in Christ and thus came to an end (Ac 10:9–35). The moral law, which fallen human nature manipulates in order to justify itself and condemn others, was also satisfied for us by Christ, leaving no need to set ourselves in opposition to each other (Mt 7:1–5; 18:21–35).

Q **2:16 Does "one body" refer to the body of Christ offered on the cross?**

Grammatically speaking, it is possible for Paul to be saying that Christ reconciled Jews and Gentiles by means of His own body, by which He satisfied the Law, made peace with God, and rose to rule over all; that is, after all, what God did. However, the immediate context suggests that Paul is talking about the way Christ's work unites Jews and Gentiles into one new Body, the Church (Rm 11:17–18; 1Co 12:12–27; Eph 4:1–6).

●●●●●●●●●●●●●●●●●●●

Q 2:19 Is he referring to just Gentiles or to all believers and their relationship to God?

When Paul says "strangers and aliens," he is referring to Gentiles, who in the past had not been in the same relationship with God as the children of Israel (Ac 17:30; Rm 2:14–16). All human nature is foreign to God since the fall, whether Jew or Gentile. The Law of Moses made the fallen condition of that human nature evident by exposing the disobedience and obstinacy of all. Only those generated by God's promises and sustained by His Word were or ever will be citizens, saints, and members of the household of God (Mt 8:5–13; 21:28–32; Lk 4:25–27; Rm 2:28–29; Gal 3:27–29).

●●●●●●●●●●●●●●●●●●●

Q 2:20 What is the meaning of a cornerstone?

There is some debate over Paul's intent with this term; he could mean a cornerstone or a keystone. A cornerstone is essential because it is the basis of the rest of the structure and provides its orientation. In ancient times, cornerstones were more essential to the stability of the structure in contrast to modern buildings, where they are a formality or decoration. A keystone is the final stone that completes an arch and holds it together. If Paul meant a keystone, it had to do with the end times and Christ's return. Is it possible that Paul means to include both ideas, since Christ is the Alpha and Omega, the beginning and the end (Rm 11:36; Rv 22:13)?

●●●●●●●●●●●●●●●●●●●

Q 3:1–7 Why does Paul call himself "a prisoner for Christ Jesus" and a minister of this Gospel?

Paul was a prisoner at this time, having been arrested in Jerusalem and then transferred first to Caesarea and then to Rome, spanning AD 57–61 (Ac 21:15–28:17). Paul calls himself "a prisoner for Christ" because he was arrested, accused, and under assault by the Jews for bearing witness to the truth about Jesus Christ (Ac 22:1–22; Php 1:12–18). Paul calls himself a "minister" (or servant) of the Gospel because he owes his life to the grace of God, which redeemed him through the sacrifice of Christ (1Tm 1:12–17; Php 3:7–14).

●●●●●●●●●●●●●●●●●●●

Q 3:2 What does Paul mean when he mentions the administration of God's grace?

This term (*oikonomia*) occurs only in Paul's letter and the Gospel of Luke (written for Paul). Paul is talking about management, or stewardship, which has to do with looking after the affairs and/or property of another person (see the parable of the unjust steward, Lk 16:2–4). In the New Testament, stewardship is more than a job; it is a trust (1Co 9:17). As an apostle, Paul has been entrusted with the Law and Gospel of God by which he "manages" the flesh and "builds up" the spirit (1Tm 1:4, 8–11).

What is the "mystery of Christ"?

Q 3:4 What is the "mystery of Christ"?

The word *mystery* occurs twenty-eight times in the New Testament. Essentially, the word refers to things that are beyond the human capacity to know or even imagine unless God reveals them. The center of this mystery is the Gospel itself, that God was in Christ reconciling the world to Himself (2Co 5:19; 1Co 2:1). The expression "mystery" occurs with language about the kingdom of heaven (Mt 13:11), the Sacraments (1Co 4:1), Christ and Christ in us (Col 1:27; 1Tm 3:16), faith (1Tm 3:9), end times (1Co 15:51), and the parallel between Christ with the Church and husband with wife (Eph 5:32).

Q 3:10 How is the "wisdom of God" made known to the angels through the Church? Who are the "rulers and authorities in the heavenly places," and why do they need us to show them God's wisdom?

The phrase "rulers and authorities in the heavenly places" refers to the fallen angels who are opposed to God (Eph 6:12; Col 2:10, 15). The redemptive work of Christ demonstrated His absolute power and authority, brought to nothing, and put these opposing powers under His feet (1Co 15:24; Eph 1:21). We make the wisdom of God evident when His grace and power forgive our sins and regenerate us as children of God, holy and blameless (Rm 5:8–11). These rulers and authorities don't need us to show them the wisdom of God so they can believe. Rather, showing them the wisdom of God in Christ confirms that the condemnation of these opposing forces is just (Php 2:5–11).

Q 3:13 How are Paul's sufferings my glory?

Begin with a definition of *glory*: "that which no one else could or would do." Paul is suffering because he is faithfully declaring the Gospel, that God has, in Christ, freely and graciously redeemed all people. Paul's willingness to endure every hardship for the sake of restoring our lives to us shows that the life God would restore to us is incomparable, just as God's love for us in Christ is His glory and incomparable (Php 3:7–14).

Q 3:17 How are we "rooted and grounded in love"?

We are regenerated by the seed of God and grow as fruitful branches because of the Vine, Christ, who supports and provides for us (Mt 7:17–18; Jn 15:1–7; Rm 11:16–21; 1Pt 1:23).

Q 4:1–6 Why is it hard for people to understand there is one true God?

Apart from a life in the Word, people tend to assume that God exists in their own image—"I think God thinks like I think because that is how I think, therefore it must be right." If a person's notion of God is subjective, then another person's different notion of God will be seen as a threat and will feel threatening. Only when the truth of God is known, through His Word and other means of revelation, can a person be at peace with who God is and live in the service of others who may not yet know God as He is. Knowing the one true God inspires us to share the truth of God, and knowing the condition of fallen human nature inspires concern and sympathy that orients us toward patience and hope as we seek to share the truth.

Q 4:1 Why does he refer to himself as "a prisoner for the Lord"? What is the manner in which we should walk?

On the "prisoner for the Lord," see Eph 3:1–7 above.

In a style similar to that found in Proverbs, Paul writes at length about the productive walk of the faithful in contrast to the destructive ways of the lazy (Eph 4:1; 5:1, 8, 15). "The way" in Proverbs becomes "the walk" in Paul, because in Christ's suffering and death, the One who is the Way gives His people the power to walk, guides them on His path, and leads them to His righteous-

ness. In Proverbs, God's Old Testament people were taught that the righteous path belonged to God. There, the path was used to make the promises of God more vivid and to invite readers to faith and the subsequent sanctified walk before God in righteousness and purity.

While "the walk" is also used in Proverbs in passages designed to be a deterrent to sin (first use of the Law), a reading of Proverbs that sees only such passages and ignores the invitation of God to life through Christ, the Wisdom of God, is pointless moralizing. Instead, a comprehensive reading of "the walk" in Proverbs reveals that it prepared God's ancient people for the coming of the Savior by inviting them to believe the Gospel and respond through God's power to enable them to walk the sanctified path of life. Paul expands on the concepts connected to the walk in Proverbs by explaining them in the light of the ministry of Christ to save sinners. Paul assumes that his readers know that the path is Christ Himself. Therefore, to walk in the path is to walk *in Christ*, to walk *in love* as Christ loved them, to walk *in newness of life* that Christians have in their risen Lord, to walk *in good works* that Christ has prepared for them.

While not directly referring to Proverbs, Paul in essence invites his readers to ponder those ancient wisdom sayings as he expounds on what it means to walk in a way that *pleases the Lord*, to walk *properly* or *circumspectly*. Like Proverbs, Paul can speak about the walk in negative terms, employing the first use of the Law. However, also like Proverbs, Paul is not simply moralizing, but constantly understands the difference between the world's walk according to the flesh and the Christian's walk in Christ, the path of life. In the light of Christ, the walk is illuminated, and those who walk on it do so because of the Gospel. This was true already for the walk in Proverbs. Yet with the coming of Christ in the flesh, Paul is able to explain the full implications that were latent in Proverbs' words. For him, the walk is now available to everyone who believes in Christ because we now are more familiar with Jesus, who is Himself the path.

• • • • • • • • • • • • • • • • • • • •

Q 4:3 If an external unity or union is unattainable or wrong because we can't have unity outside of being "connected" spiritually with others, how can we say an external unity with a specific denomination is right and every other external unity is wrong? When is the proper time to "make a break" with a church body?

Rather than defend one particular church body against another, let's speak in ideal terms that can then be applied to specific situations. First, there is only one Christ and thus only one Body of Christ—the true believers of every time and place. Second, a person is either part of the Body of Christ by the regenerating power of God's Word and Spirit or he is not. A person cannot be contrary to the true God and His kingdom yet be united with it at the same time (Mt 6:24; 1Co 10:14–21). Third, what determines outward unity among people or the necessity of breaking off relationships with others depends on the relationship people have with the truth (Rm 16:17–18). Therefore we make every effort to know the truth—the truth about God and the truth about people's relationships with God. We seek the truth so that we may discover unity where it is produced by the Word and celebrate it according to the Word (Jas 1:19–20; Col 3:12–16).

• • • • • • • • • • • • • • • • • • • •

Q 4:5 Why do some denominations baptize people twice, once as an infant and once as an adult?

I don't know of any denominations that perform two baptisms on the same person. Some people believe that we play a part in our own salvation and that faith is our work. These people reject the baptizing of infants and children because according to them, Baptism is a command we obey. They argue that such an act does not count as obedience if the person is not conscious of this. These people will rebaptize a person if he or she was baptized as a child, but they do not themselves baptize a person twice. Others baptize infants and children because they are the model of faith that Jesus points to in the Gospels (Mt 18:1–6, 10, 14; 19:13–14; 1Co 1:18–31). Faith is a work of God and is the only remedy for fallen human nature that becomes ever more contrary to God as it "matures" (1Co 2:14; 1Pt 1:5; Rm 10:17). Some people are rebaptized if their original

Baptism was of uncertain nature (Ac 19:1–7). There is only one Baptism, just as there is only one God. Our task is to make sure that the baptisms we perform are done within the context of the Word and according to the Word. Then the person baptized will have assurance of regeneration and communion with the Body of Christ (Jn 1:11–13; 3:1–7; Ac 2:38–42).

● ●

Q **4:7 Does this verse imply that grace is different for every person?**

Paul provided a more detailed explanation of the way God's grace relates to particular gifts in Rm 12:3–21. God's grace is absolute and universal in dealing with all of His creation (Jn 3:16). To many, God's grace even seems inverted, since He appears to give most to those who deserve it least (Mt 20:1–16; Lk 15:11–32). While God's grace is absolute and abundant for all, God has particular plans for each person and gives grace as needed for each of us to complete His will for us (Jn 3:22–28; 2Co 12:7–10; Eph 2:10; 1Tm 1:12–17).

● ●

Q **4:8 Why did Paul change the wording of Ps 68:18 from "receiving gifts among men" to "gave gifts to" men? What does "led a host of captives" mean?**

First, it is important to remember that Paul is not quoting the psalm but describing what it says; thus he changed the language from first person singular ("you") to third

person singular ("he"). Second, Paul was not only describing what Ps 68:18 says but was explaining its significance by revealing that Christ "received" or "acquired" gifts in order to give them to men (Mt 10:1; Ac 1:4; 2:14–21; Jn 16:13–16).

The phrase some translations render as "led a host of captives" is more accurately translated and easily understood as "He led captivity captive." This means that all the means by which the devil, the world, and our own fallen human nature hold us captive were themselves captured by Christ and thus emptied of their power (Rv 12:7–11). The Law held us captive under guilt and condemnation, but Christ has redeemed us from the curse of the Law (Gal 3:10–14). The world would tempt us to captivity (with addictions, for example), but Christ has overcome and has given us the means of overcoming every temptation (Lk 4:1–13; 1Co 10:13). Our own fallen human nature would hold us bound to selfish, petty desires, but Christ regenerates our souls so that we are a new creation (Rm 6:1–14; Col 3:1–16).

● ●

Q **4:9–10 Why is the victorious descent of Christ into hell only mentioned twice? Why is this in parentheses? Why did Paul include this?**

The Greek word referring to the "lower" parts of the earth occurs only here. However, the verb "to descend" occurs here and in Rm 10:7, which includes a reference to "the abyss." This evidence plus the contrasting statement about Jesus ascending into heaven suggests that Paul is referring to Jesus' descent into hell (see also 1Pt 3:19). Jesus' descent into hell is mentioned three times in the New Testament, which is still not many references. Perhaps the reason for so few references is that Christ wants us to focus on the way of life rather than the place of death.

The original Greek manuscripts did not include parentheses. The parentheses were added by editors of English translations to indicate that these two verses are a thoughtful pause or note of Paul that digresses from his main flow of thought. I suspect that Paul included these thoughts (1) because the Holy Spirit inspired him to do so, and (2) because it is important to remember that Christ, having been crucified and raised, is Lord over all things, including death, the grave, and hell.

• •

Q 4:11 Are there still prophets? How do we deal with church workers working solely for money? If pastors are teachers, then why does this verse say "shepherds [pastors] *and* teachers" (emphasis added)?

On the one hand, one might argue that the time of prophets, like apostles and evangelists, has passed (1Co 13:8; Lk 6:13; Ac 1:21–22). While we no longer have prophets immediately called by God who tell of future things and are granted authority to do signs in order to authenticate their word, all Christians are called to confess Christ before men (Mt 10:32–33).

Every child of God has become so because God has called him or her (1Pt 2:9). A very few individuals receive another, more focused call into public ministry—in ancient times as a prophet, apostle, or evangelist or, since the time of the apostles, as pastors (Jer 1:5; Lk 6:13; Ac 21:8; 1Tm 4:14; Ti 1:5).

No Christian should work for the money, since love of it is the root of all evil (1Tm 6:10). Christians recognize that God provides for us exceedingly abundantly, beyond what we can think or ask (Mt 6:25–34; Eph 3:20). Therefore, Christians do not work to get what they lack or for their own gratification but in order to provide for others as God has provided for us (Lk 12:42–45). Every Christian is an ambassador for Christ and seeks to make disciples as he or she goes about the life God has prepared for him or her (2Co 5:7–21; Mt 28:19–20; Eph 2:10; 1Pt 3:15). Of all Christians, God calls a very few to represent Him in public (1Tm 3:1ff.; Jas 3:1ff.; 1Pt 4:10). Public servants of the Word do this work because God has called them to it, and those who are served provide for them (1Co 9:1–14; Gal 6:6).

Paul uses the expression "shepherds and teachers" to clarify his meaning. The word *pastor* means "to shepherd," but how does a man shepherd the people of God? The word *and* often signals an explanation, something like an equal sign rather than a plus sign. Thus, Paul is saying that God "gave some to be pastors, that is to say, teachers." Jesus was the Good Shepherd whose teaching was and is the means by which He tends His flock (Jn 10).

● ● ● ● ● ● ● ● ● ● ● ● ● ● ● ● ● ● ● ●

Q 4:12 If lay people are to perform the works of service, is there still a line between pastors and laity? What is the Body of Christ, and what defines it?

The "line" between pastors and the rest of the believers is one of "where" rather than "what." All Christians, including pastors, are disciples and ambassadors of Christ (Mt 28:19–20; 2Co 5:14–21). Only a very few Christians are equipped and called to bear the responsibility of doing this work in public (1Co 12:27–31; 1Tm 3:1ff.). The Body of Christ is made up of all people who have been regenerated by the Word and Spirit of God and remain in that Word and Spirit (Lk 8:21; Jn 1:11–13; 3:1–7; 8:31–32; 15:1–7; Ac 2:42).

● ● ● ● ● ● ● ● ● ● ● ● ● ● ● ● ● ● ● ●

Q 4:13 If some are predestined to be God's people, why does Paul say "we all attain to the unity of the faith"?

Many people claim to be God's people but are opposed to clear, essential teachings of the faith; are opposed to those who clearly hold to the true faith; or conduct themselves in a way that is contrary to the faith. Paul is making it clear that just as Christ is one, so is His Body. There is one and only one Body of Christ, and only the Word of God can so affect our fallen human nature and so regenerate and inspire our soul that we actually do reach and realize this unity under Christ, our Head.

● ● ● ● ● ● ● ● ● ● ● ● ● ● ● ● ● ● ● ●

Q 4:14 Why do we not want to be like children but yet have a childlike faith? How do we know for sure that we are no longer children?

First of all, the word in question describes a young child, no longer nursing but not old enough to be disciplined. Second, as in almost every case of applying biblical texts, we must distinguish between our fallen human nature and our soul. Our fallen human nature is contrary to God, which means "maturity" only makes it stronger and more opposed to grace and truth (1Co 2:14). This is why Jesus says unless we repent and become as children, our contradictory nature will keep us from communion with God. Our soul, regenerated by the Holy Spirit, is what must mature if we are to make progress in the faith and be helpful to others. A rebellious young child with a mature, faithful, loving parent has a chance; a weak and helpless child only suffers under the abuses of a rebellious and wicked parent.

We know we are maturing according to our regenerate soul by several means: (1) time spent in the Word, (2) the depth and fruitfulness of the time we spend in the Word, (3) the growing consistency with which we apply and live out what we learn in the Word, (4) a growing devotion to the fundamentals learned in the Word combined with a love and thirst for weightier matters, and (5) a growing focus of attention on serving others rather than ourselves (Mt 7:15–27; Jn 8:31; Php 2:1–11; 3:7–14; Col 3:1–16).

Q 4:17 What is the Gentile's futility of thinking? Is Paul referring to the "new Gentiles," those not following Christ?

Paul was writing to the Christians in Ephesus—some of them would be Jews and some Gentiles (Ac 19:1–10). Some manuscripts do not include the expression "rest of," which limits Paul's warning to the Gentile believers only. If Paul did not include that expression in the original letter, he would mean that neither Jews nor Gentiles should walk any longer in the futility of pagan Gentile thinking (Ps 135:15–18; Rm 14:1–23). The futility of Gentile thinking included the vast spectrum of thoughts and ways that are contrary to God's will and creation (Rm 1:18–32; 1Co 1:18–25; 2Co 10:4–5; Col 2:8). The most futile and deadly of all thinking is that we are independent and in control of our own lives (Ps 2:1ff.; 14:1–6; Gal 3:1–3; 5:1–4; Rv 3:17–18; 18:7–8).

Q 4:18 Does ignorance cause hardening of the heart? Who has hardened their hearts, and what does this mean?

It was not ignorance that caused the hardening but the other way around: "because of the ignorance that is in them, due to their hardness of heart." There appears to be more than one kind of ignorance. There is an ignorance, apparently not caused by a hard heart, which God treats with mercy (Jnh 4:9–11; Ac 17:30; 1Tm 1:12–13). A hard heart is caused by fallen human nature's determination to oppose God (Rm 5:6–11). God provides a remedy for hard hearts through the work of Jesus Christ and His Spirit (Ezk 36:24–27; 2Co 3:14). On the other hand, when a heart becomes hardened by the unrestricted determination of a person to despise, mock, detest, abuse, and oppose the grace of God over and over again, such a heart is evidence of coming judgment (Lk 12:10; Heb 6:4–6; 10:26–31; Mk 3:5; Rm 11:7, 25).

Q 4:26 How does one go about fighting this sin? What anger is not sin?

Your Bible may note that this is a quote from Ps 4:4. That psalm goes on to suggest this remedy: "Ponder in your own hearts on your beds, and be silent. Offer right sacrifices, and put your trust in the LORD" (vv. 4b–5). The meditation suggested includes being slow to speak, quick to listen, and slow to anger because our wrath does not work the righteousness of God (Jas 1:19). The "right sacrifices" might well include rejecting our own ego and vanity because they would have us believe that we are entitled to better things than we are receiving, which is what makes us angry. Trust in the Lord, defined as "honesty about our dependence on Him," complements the "right sacrifices" as it works humility that resists entitlement thinking. Humility reminds us that Jesus endured what we deserved so that God could give us what Jesus had earned (Jn 16:14). Knowing the abundant grace of God upon which our life depends makes us graciously disposed, rather than angry, toward others (Mt 18:23–35). The kind of anger that is not sin is directed toward the devil, world, and other forces at work in fallen human nature that work ruin in people's lives. The Bible makes very clear that the contrary and self-destructive orientation of fallen human nature is distinct from that nature itself and distinct from a regenerate soul (Gal 5:16–18; Col 3:1–16).

● ● ● ● ● ● ● ● ● ● ● ● ● ● ● ● ● ● ●

Q 4:30 What is the meaning and significance of the word *grieve* in this verse? How does one "grieve the Holy Spirit of God" if they have been sealed for the day of redemption?

Grief is an experience of remorse or emotional pain over something that is contrary to what should be (Is 63:8–10; Mk 3:5). God was grieved in His heart by the evil of fallen man before the flood (Gn 6:6). Samuel grieved for King Saul because he realized there was no way to bring him back from his faithlessness (1Sm 15:35). Hopelessness makes a person grieve (1Th 4:13). Having been sealed by the Holy Spirit does not make it impossible for our fallen human nature to take over our life and ruin our faith. On the contrary, it is the fact that a person had known the grace of God and turned to despise it that makes his fall so very grievous (Heb 6:4–8; 10:26–31).

● ● ● ● ● ● ● ● ● ● ● ● ● ● ● ● ● ● ●

Q 5:5 I noticed how strong these words are. Am I correct in assuming that it is not the actions that are the issue but what

is in the person's spirit, the "god" that they are in service of?

Fallen human nature is corrupted with all manner of evil, more than Paul mentions here (Mk 7:20–23). Therefore, no one can inherit the kingdom of God according to the flesh (Jn 3:6; 1Co 2:14; 15:50). If the fallen human nature is the only nature a person possesses, if there is no regenerate soul, then such a person would have no inheritance in the kingdom (Ac 8:21; Heb 6:4–8; 10:26–31). The Psalms remind us that people become like the gods they serve—blind, mute, breathless, and lifeless (Ps 115:4–8).

● ● ● ● ● ● ● ● ● ● ● ● ● ● ● ● ● ● ●

Q 5:7 Does "partners" mean "friends with" or "husband/wife with"?

The word *partner* is broad and could include a spouse. However, in this context, Paul is speaking more generally about the "sons of disobedience," warning believers to keep themselves from sharing in the wickedness and rebellion they practice.

● ● ● ● ● ● ● ● ● ● ● ● ● ● ● ● ● ● ●

Q 5:12–13 Sometimes I struggle with the idea of exposing people's sins through the act of love. Why should I do anything to expose others' sins?

In v. 11, Paul commands us to expose the "unfruitful works of darkness." Love sacrifices all for the sake of the object of that love—in this case, a person's eternal soul. For the sake of a person's eternal soul, we would risk the humiliation of the flesh, though we might seek to protect another from humiliation if we are able. Like physicians in the emergency room who must undress a person, who take X-rays, or who must probe in a tender wound in order to remove foreign objects that cause infections, a servant of Christ exposes the sins of others in order to deliver that person and others affected from the consequences of those sins (Lv 19:17; Rm 13:8–10; Gal 2:11–20; 1Co 5:1–5).

Q 5:16 What does it mean by "the days are evil"? Does this refer to our entire earthly life?

In the Bible, "evil" is different from "wicked." Evil is the opposite of good or the absence of good. Paul recognized that since the time of Adam, evil has been in the world (Rm 5:12). Paul referred to the age he lived in as evil and noted that it is always going from bad to worse (Gal 1:4; 2Tm 3:13). Finally, Paul explained that the love of money is the root of all kinds of evil (1Tm 6:10). As long as the Lord is patient, waiting for sinners to come to repentance, and as long as the devil is the prince of this world, the days of our earthly life will be evil (2Pt 3:9; Eph 6:12). What a blessing to know that God makes all things work together for good to those who love Him, who are called according to His purpose (Rm 8:28).

Q 5:19 Why would we speak to one another that way? Isn't that reserved for God?

People might speak to one another in psalms and hymns and spiritual songs because Paul commands them to. It is more likely that people would speak to one another in this way more naturally as the Word of God they learn by recitation becomes a part of their consciousness and informs or is blended with their words. We do learn our patterns of speech and vocabulary from what we hear and read. While God is the proper subject of psalms and hymns, He urges us to learn and sing them for our sake. The glory of God is the wonderful works that He has done for our benefit.

Q 5:21 Why does my Bible translation say "submitting yourselves one to another in the *fear* of God" (emphasis added)?

This word for "fear" occurs 178 times in the Bible; whether we like it or not, the importance of the term cannot be dismissed. On the other hand, a person's dislike of the word is probably a consequence of misuse in our time rather than any problem inherent in the word itself. The word *fear* means to have an honest and accurate perception of the forces we are subject to and depend upon. A person is right to be afraid of dehydration or starvation. A person is prudent who fears dangerous neighborhoods after dark. More importantly, fear does not exist in isolation, especially not in reference to

What does it mean to submit?

God. While "the fear of the LORD is the beginning of knowledge" (Pr 1:7), the mercy of the Lord is upon those who fear Him (see Lk 1:50).

● ● ● ● ● ● ● ● ● ● ● ● ● ● ● ● ● ●

Q 5:22 What does it mean to "submit"? Does this verse indicate that wives are to treat their husbands like God? Is there anything for which wives don't have to submit to their husbands?

The word *submit* means to be "under orders" and occurs thirty-eight times in the New Testament and twenty-one times in the Old Testament. All of the occurrences in the New Testament are in Luke, Acts, or the Pauline Epistles, except for one time in James and six times in 1 Peter. Luke reported that Jesus was submissive to His parents in all things (2:51) and that evil spirits were submissive to the disciples whom Jesus had sent with His authority (10:17, 20). Paul lamented that the Jews refused to submit to the righteousness given by God freely in Christ (Rm 10:3). Paul commands all Christians to submit to the governing authorities (Rm 13:5). Interestingly, the word *submit* does not occur in the Greek text of Eph 5:22, but is implied as an extension of the previous verse, "submitting to one another out of reverence for Christ."

Notice that the word *submit* in this verse is not a command, but a participle revealing activity flowing from four commands that occur in 5:17–18: "do not be foolish," "understand what the will of the Lord is," "do not get drunk," and "be filled with the Spirit." Paul in no way suggests that women should treat their husbands like God. On the contrary, it is the wife who treats God as God who also knows the fitting way to relate to her husband, submitting "as to the Lord." The wife is free to submit to her husband because his interest in her is the same as Christ's, completely selfless and for her well-being. A woman whose husband is not as Christ would be knows what to do on the basis of 1Pt 3:1–6 and 1Co 7:12–15.

● ● ● ● ● ● ● ● ● ● ● ● ● ● ● ● ● ●

Q 5:22–30 Wives should submit to husbands, and husbands should love their wives like Christ loved the Church. Why shouldn't husbands submit to their wives and wives love their husbands as Christ loved the Church? What is the distinction between Paul's call for wives to submit and husbands to love? How can I use these passages as I prepare for marriage?

Love and submission are complementary, forming a beneficial relationship. Love has to do with providing; submission has to do with receiving what is provided. God the Father is love in the absolute because He is the provider of all things. An infant is submissive because of its natural state. Christ, men, and women both love and submit, depending on the relationship in question (1Co 11:3). Christ submits to the Father, who provides for His life so that He may give that life in love. Men submit to Christ so that they may love their wives. Women submit to their husbands so that they may love their children. Marriage, like every other human relationship, is not a matter of control. All control properly belongs to God, who alone is capable of exercising it well (Rm 8:28; Heb 12:9–10).

· ·

Q **5:23 The husband is the head of the wife like Christ is the Head of man?**

Correct. Christ is, ultimately and absolutely, the Head of all people. Christ has created and redeemed everyone. Christ gives and sustains the lives of all people. A husband has the privilege of loving his wife as an agent or means of Christ, but it is still Christ who is the Head and Provider. Wives are well provided for inasmuch as a husband submits to Christ as his Head.

· ·

Q **5:24 Should wives submit to everything the husband asks, even if the wife doesn't agree with the husband? In the original Greek, does the word translated as "everything" in this verse mean the same thing in English?**

The question of submission brings into clear focus the importance of a woman being very careful about whom she marries. Why would a woman marry a man she is afraid to submit to? Having said that, let's consider the extremes. In theory, a woman could submit to her husband no matter

what, knowing that ultimately she will be taken by God to paradise and that God is with her, especially if she is suffering for her submission; but then, what would be the point of the Word and means that God has provided for her protection? On the other hand, a woman could live in absolute defense of herself, never submitting in any way unless she would have done the very same things on her own; but then, what would be the point of the marriage? As is often the case, the truth rests in between the extremes. First, a woman would want to be more careful about whom she marries than she has ever been about anything in her whole life. Second, once married, a woman would hope to submit to her husband in all things since all things that a godly husband is about would be for her well-being. A godly husband would be concerned with matters of the greatest significance and in doing God's will in them all. He would be less concerned with matters of preference. Rather, he would collaborate with or defer to his wife. Third, if a woman's husband was expecting or would force her to submit to anything contrary to God's will, she would appeal for help and protection from the other men in her life (father, brothers, pastor, elders). She would not only be free to but *encouraged* to liberate herself from an abusive husband according to 1Co 7. Fourth, a woman who would only want to submit to decisions she agrees with would not be submitting at all. Such a woman would either put herself in constant competition for headship of the marriage or require a husband to do the submitting. In either case, the relationship would be altogether contrary to God's design and would realize none of the benefits God intended.

• • • • • • • • • • • • • • • • • • • •

Q **5:28 It says that husbands who love their wives love themselves. But aren't we supposed to hate ourselves because of our sinful nature?**

Making sense of the Bible depends on recognizing that we are not one-dimensional. We have a fallen human nature that we must deny and put off; this is the nature and the life that we are to hate (Lk 14:26; Col 3:5–7). We also have a regenerate soul that is the essence of our life, holds our potential, and endures forever (Jn 1:12–13; 3:1–6; 11:25–26). Christ loves everyone and has redeemed everyone. A significant part of His redemptive work is to liberate us from the corruption of sin that dwells in us (Jn 8:11; 1Co 5:1–13; Lv 19:17). As God loves us, so we love one another. As God loves us but hates the corruption that dwells in us, so husbands love their wives and live to liberate them from that corruption (Eph 5:25–27).

• • • • • • • • • • • • • • • • • • • •

Q **5:31 When does God consider people married: ceremony or consummation?**

If sexual intercourse created a marriage, then there would be no such thing as fornication, but adultery and divorce would be too numerous to count. A man is married to a woman when he makes a public commitment to be her husband. Cohabitation

and sexual intercourse follow and naturally flow from this commitment (Mt 1:18–20). Any sexual activity before such a public commitment (whether in the court or in the Church) is fornication; any sexual activity with another person after that commitment is adultery.

• • • • • • • • • • • • • • • • • • • •

Q **5:32 Paul talks about two becoming one flesh, then says it refers to the Church. Who does the Church leave? Who is her father but God?**

Throughout this section, Paul has been making a comparison between Christ/Church and husband/wife. Paul uses the language of comparison in every single verse from 5:22–29 (vv. 26–27 relate to v. 28). It is Christ who left His prerogatives at the right hand of God in order to become a man and redeem His creation (Php 2:5–11). The reality of love, self-sacrifice, redemption, and union all flow from Christ. From Christ, each husband and wife obtains the regeneration and means to submit and love, thus making a witness to Christ's relationship with us. All of creation and particularly the relationship between husband and wife are, in truth, extensions of and witnesses to the Creator (Ps 19:1–3; Rm 1:20).

Q **5:33 Is there a reason why a wife is not required to love her husband in this section?**

Love and submission are universal in relationships. Christians are called to love one another, especially their enemies (Mt 5:44; Jn 15:12). We are called to submit to one another (Eph 5:21). In particular, husbands are to love their wives as Christ loves the Church, sacrificing everything for the sake of the beloved (Gal 2:20). Women should not lay down their lives on behalf of their husbands; rather, they are to "fear" their husbands, that is, regard with all appreciation and protect the benefits that love provides.

Q **6:1–4 We are commanded to obey our parents. What if we have proof and solid reasoning that their idea(s) are not the best? Do we continue to honor our parents?**

Parents, like husbands, pastors, masters, and governments, all serve God for the welfare of others. If any of these authorities serve poorly, we may still do well to submit to them out of reverence for Christ. On the other hand, if any of these authorities are acting contrary to God's will, then we must obey God rather than men (Ac 5:29; see also Eph 5:22 and 5:22–30).

Q **6:2 Why did Paul say that "honor your father and mother" was "the first**

commandment"? What did he mean by "with a promise"?

Unlike the other commandments, the commandment to obey parents is followed by the particular promise, "that it may be well with you and you may live long upon the earth." That is why Paul calls it "the first commandment with a promise."

Q **6:4 What is meant by "Fathers, do not provoke your children to anger"?**

The word translated "provoke" here occurs only twice in the New Testament. The other occasion is Rm 10:19, which is a quote from Dt 32:21 describing how God will provoke Israel to wrath by a nation without understanding. Provoking someone to wrath has to do with inflaming contrary and negative emotions by forcing a situation upon someone that should not exist or doing something that should not be done (see Mt 18:34, where the simple root form of this verb is used). The second half of this verse suggests that fathers exasperate their children by failing to raise them in the nurture and admonition of the Lord. Heb 12:5–11 describes the nurture and admonition of the Lord: teaching us what we need to know and disciplining us in order to keep us from what is wrong. A father provokes a child to exasperation by punishing him for doing what is right and rewarding him for what is wrong. Fathers do well to remember Jesus' severe warning against causing children to stumble (Mt 18:3–10).

Q **6:5–8 Are these verses condoning slavery? What if the master commands the slave into immoral service? Why does Paul discuss relationships between master and slave when God says you shall not serve two masters?**

Since Adam abandoned his responsibility before God and toward Eve, human beings have been in bondage to sin (Rm 6:16; Eph 2:1–3; Heb 2:15). While our human nature will remain subject to this bondage until it returns to the dust, God liberates our souls through the regenerative work of His Word and Spirit (Jn 1:12–13; 3:1–6). Therefore, if a person's soul is still bound in sin, it makes little difference whether he lives as a slave or not. On the other hand, no one can enslave a person whose soul has been liberated by God. Most slave owners were slaves themselves to the passions of the flesh. Many slaves lived with souls much more liberated than those who sought to master them, as Harriet Beecher Stowe's book *Uncle Tom's Cabin* indicates. We also do well to remember that in biblical history as well as in much of human history, slavery was a means of saving people from poverty, homelessness, and destitution (Dt 15:9–18).

Q **6:8 Does this verse contradict Eph 2:9 by saying we have to do good works to get into heaven?**

Notice that Paul is not talking about getting into heaven in this section. Paul deals with how we are saved at the begin-

ning of his letters. Having clarified how we are saved, Paul moves on to talk about the Christian life (cf. Rm 1–11 with 12–16). Salvation by grace, apart from the works of the Law, means that we do good works in order to share what we have been given rather than to get what we have not. While the Lord is gracious and saves us graciously, He is also just and provides equity (Lk 16:25). Jesus used the word *reward* nine times during the Sermon on the Mount (Mt 5–7). Remember that the measure of our faith, the number of our days, and the good works that we do are all prepared beforehand by God (Rm 12:3; Ps 139:16; Eph 2:10).

Q **6:10–17 What is the significance of each piece of armor What happens if a Christian is missing a part of the armor, such as the sword or the shoes? Will the incomplete armor fail its bearer? How did the concept of the armor of God originate?**

There is significance to each piece of armor, but all the armor comes to us by way of the Word of God. It is possible that a Christian would be missing one or more pieces of armor, yet the Word of God conveys all we need and would supply what is lacking. In ancient times, men "girded" their waists so they would have freedom of movement for a fight. The Word of God reveals the truth, which makes us free and is unconquerable (Jn 1:5; 8:31; Lk 4:1–13). A breastplate protected the vital organs, just as the righteousness of Christ, imputed to us and accomplished in us, protects us from condemnation. The Gospel not only saves us but motivates us to take that Gospel to others (Mt 10:8; Rm 10:14–17; 2Co 5:14–21; Php 3:7–14). If faith is honesty about dependence, then it is easy to see how the shield of faith can quench all the fiery darts of the devil. The fiery darts of the devil have no chance against living water (the Word), in which the Christian is immersed. Since we depend on God and God is absolutely dependable, our shield is impenetrable. The helmet protects the head as the breastplate protects the vital organs. God's salvation of the world is an accomplished fact; Jesus Christ has taken away the sin of the world. This helmet protects our thoughts and liberates us to freely serve others (Heb 2:14–15). Finally, our sword is the Word and Spirit of God that is always effective, disabling, or regenerating, as the nature or situation requires (Heb 4:12).

- - - - - - - - - - - - - - - - - - - -

Q 6:12 Is Paul saying this is all about spiritual warfare, not having to do with the flesh and blood? If that is the case, where is this dark world?

Paul cannot be excluding the struggle against our own flesh since he speaks about that at length (Gal 5:16–25; Col 3:5–11). There are two possibilities for understanding what Paul means here. On the one hand, Paul may be clarifying the magnitude of our struggle, as if to say, "Don't think our struggle is against flesh and blood only; the forces against us are much more powerful and severe than that." On the other hand, Paul

may simply be focused on spiritual warfare, especially in contrast to material battles that people and nations wage over material objects. Paul mentioned our fallen human nature, the forces of this fallen world, and the demonic, spiritual forces in Eph 2:1–3.

- - - - - - - - - - - - - - - - - - - -

Q 6:18 What does it mean to pray "in the Spirit"?

The relationship between the Spirit and prayer can be studied in two ways. First, we may consider the meaning of in. The preposition in is not necessarily talking about location (in that place); it also may convey means ("by"), connection ("with"), or manner ("according to"). Thus, Paul may be saying that Christians are praying "by means of the Spirit" or "with the Spirit" or "according to their spiritual nature." In the Greek translation, there is no definite article with the word spirit in this verse, but this does not mean it is not referring to the Holy Spirit.

In regard to prayer, it seems impossible to separate the work of the Holy Spirit and our spirit. Our spirit is a product of the Holy Spirit's work in us, and part of the Holy Spirit's work is to remain present with us, as the next point will make evident. Second, we may track other texts that speak of the Spirit's work. Paul wrote that "you . . . are not in the flesh but in the Spirit, if in fact the Spirit of God dwells in you" (Rm 8:9). We know that the Spirit of God is present with and communicated by the Word (Jn 6:63; Rm 10:17). We know that the Word and Spirit of God regenerate our soul, give us the mind of Christ, and inspire us to pray according to God's own Word and will (Jn 1:12–13; 3:1–7; 14:13–14; 15:7, 16; 16:23; Php 2:5). When Christians pray, every sense of the preposition "in" is at work; we pray according to the spirit that God's own Spirit has given us, with that spirit, in union with the Holy Spirit, and by means of the Holy Spirit who communicates the Word of God to us and thus teaches us to pray, how to pray, and what to pray.

● ● ● ● ● ● ● ● ● ● ● ● ● ● ● ● ● ● ●

Q 6:19 Paul asks for the people to pray for him. If God takes care of His children, what is the purpose of prayer? Does it really change God's actions or what happens to a person?

God can certainly do anything without us but has chosen to do things with and through us. For example, God made Adam and Eve, but since then creates all people through their offspring. God can speak directly to anyone, but normally speaks to us through His prophets and apostles, now preserved for us in the Bible. Prayer is very obviously for our benefit rather than to inform God or move Him to action. If our prayers are informed and inspired by the Word and Spirit of God (see 6:18 above), then prayer is a means by which our mind, heart, and will are drawn into harmony with God as we recognize His will, marvel at the wisdom of it, and hope to realize the gracious nature of it. If we pray out loud with others, they learn the same through our prayers. Prayer is also a means of main-

taining our care and concern for people when we are unable to do anything else for them, either because their condition is beyond our ability to help or because we are separated by distance.

● ● ● ● ● ● ● ● ● ● ● ● ● ● ● ● ● ● ●

Q 6:21–22 Who is Tychicus? To whom will he be sent?

Tychicus is a "beloved brother," referred to five times in the New Testament (Ac 20:4; Eph 6:21; Col 4:7; 2Tm 4:12; Ti 3:12). Paul is sending him to the Christians in Ephesus, as the reference in Col 4:7 confirms.

Philippians

Q 1:3–4 Who is the "you" to whom Paul is writing?

The "you" is referring to "all the saints in Christ Jesus who are at Philippi," as stated in v. 1. Besides other information about them provided by this letter, we know about Philippi from Ac 16; 20; and 1Th 2:2.

Q 1:12 What has happened to Paul?

Paul was a prisoner either in Caesarea (Ac 23:31–35; 24:22–27) or, more likely, in Rome (28:30–31) when he wrote this letter (Php 1:12–18). The whole story of Paul's imprisonment is recorded by Luke in Ac 20:13–16; 21:1–28:31.

Q 1:13–18 Is Paul in actual prison or still under house arrest? Or are the chains he speaks of metaphorical?

The chains that Paul is talking about are not metaphorical; notice how Paul says metaphorically that the Word of God is not chained (2Tm 2:9). In Caesarea, Paul was kept somewhere in the palace complex (Ac 23:35; 24:23). In Rome, Paul was allowed to have his own apartment, where a soldier guarded him (28:30). While Paul had some liberty and was not in a prison, he must still have worn chains since he refers to them and was still a prisoner.

Q 1:13–14 Do all Christians have chains (so to speak) for Christ? Why did Paul's arrest encourage people to preach the Gospel more?

Chains made of iron keep people from doing what they would like to do, whether good or bad. Fear can keep a human being from doing what is right or what is wrong (Heb 2:14–15; Pr 16:6). When Paul says that "my imprisonment is for Christ" (v. 13), he means that he has been arrested and bound in chains because of the truth he taught about Christ. Any Christian who is forcibly bound by others in order to keep him or her from speaking the truth could also say that his or her chains are in Christ. Paul was not afraid to keep on declaring the truth and grace of God even though he was treated like a criminal, chained, and threatened. This fact is what encouraged others to be bold as well (Ac 4:4:1–31; 5:12–42).

Q 1:15–17 Should we do something about teachers with false motives or leave it to God? Why would people try to upset Paul by preaching the Gospel? How can one preach God's Word appropriately with wrong motives?

A well-respected principle of marketing says that you should never include your competition's product in your advertising because you are paying for people to see what you don't want them to buy. Whether people are for or against the truth, if they are talking about it, then people are hearing it, and the truth, especially divine truth accompanied by the Holy Spirit, works salvation. The New Testament records plenty of severe warnings against false teaching and false teachers (Mt 18:6–9; 23:1–33; Gal 1:6–10). As often as we have authority and means, we would certainly want to correct, remove, or run away from false teachers (Rm 16:17; 3 Jn 9–11; Rv 2:2; Jn 10:5). Paul was in a circumstance, like many of us are or will be, where there was little he could do about people who were speaking against the truth, except to recognize that God makes all things work together for good and uses the energies of the wicked against their own purposes. (Consider God's use of the devil in Job's life and in Jesus' life to accomplish His purposes. See also Rm 8:28; Jas 5:11; Ac 2:22–24; 4:27–28.)

Q 1:18 Does this mean that even if you do not want to be spreading God's Word and you can't do it joyfully, then you should preach anyway?

Our fallen human nature is usually opposed to doing the will of God, so if we waited to feel joyful about doing His will, we might never do it. On the other hand, a regenerate soul well nourished by the Word and Spirit of God rejoices in all the will of God (Ps 1:1–6). If we don't feel joyful, increasing our sense of guilt by imposing the law that we should be joyful only makes matters worse. If we don't feel joyful, then we obviously need to rest in the Word until the Word and Spirit of God revive us and restore joy to us (Ps 51:12–13). In this verse, Paul is referring to people who talk about Christ in pretense, which means they are not sincere or devoted to what they are talking about. These people are either talking about Christ negatively or in order to make themselves more important than the message (1Tm 6:3–5; Ac 19:13–16).

Q **1:21 What is meant by "to live is Christ, and to die is gain"?**

Paul means that to live on in this world, in every way, has to do with Christ. Paul was created and regenerated by Christ (Ac 9). Christ had given and continued to give life to Paul so that Paul would be an extension of Christ to everyone around him (Php 3:7–14; 1Co 2:2; 2Co 5:16–20).

Q **1:22 What does this verse mean?**

Paul was eager, as anyone would be, to leave the trouble of life in this world to realize perfect communion with God in heaven (v. 23b). On the other hand, Paul knew that he had gifts and authority from God that he was to use for the benefit of many, many people. Paul was acutely aware of our world's great need for the truth and grace of God. If Paul was going to live on in this material world in his physical body, he would do as much good in that time as he possibly could; that's what he means by "fruitful labor for me" (cf. Eph 5:15–20; 1Co 15:9–10).

Q **1:22–26 Why does Paul struggle with life and death when he knows that God has put him here for a purpose?**

Our fallen human nature struggles with life in this world because it is physical and selfish; when life is easy, we want more of it, and when life is painful, we want none of it. However, Paul did not say that he was struggling with life and death, but that he was "hard pressed" between the two (v. 23). A regenerate soul within a fallen human nature is hard pressed. As people re-created in the image of Christ, we long to help those in the world around us, even as we long to be perfectly reunited with our Redeemer. This is a positive tension since the anticipation and certainty of our everlasting life with God in paradise inspires us to communicate the truth and grace of God to as many people as possible while we are here so they may also realize the salvation we enjoy.

Q **1:22–24 It speaks of Paul being torn between staying on earth and going to heaven. Does this mean that Paul could decide if he wanted to die or not?**

God alone decides to create a life, and God alone has the authority to remove a person from this world (whether to heaven or hell; 1Sm 2:6–10; Ezk 18:4; Jn 19:11). When Paul says he is "hard pressed" between the two, he is talking about the power of the significance of each place upon his life, not his intent or ability to choose.

Though Paul expresses the question of what he shall choose, he knows that the choice is not his (1Tm 1:12–17). Human beings are far too fickle and shortsighted to be granted authority over the duration of our lives; think of how many times we might have departed for heaven already if allowed to and what we would have missed in our lives if we had done so. Only God knows what good He would accomplish for us and through us according to His love and wisdom (Jb 3:11–13; 38:1–2; 40:1–2; Ps 139:13–18; Eph 2:10).

• • • • • • • • • • • • • • • • • • •

Q 1:23–24 In regard to suicide, what if the person has the mind-set that he or she thinks he or she is being a burden to others? How does a person deal with that mind-set?

We must be very careful here not to say more or less than the Word teaches us. First, as Christians, we know that our mind-sets are very untrustworthy, so we reject our own thoughts for the sake of the truth (Is 55; 2Co 10:4–5). Second, the thought that we are a burden to others and the disposition that flows from it is the *most* burdensome of things. We all depend on one another, and the refusal to consider this is a matter of pride, arrogance, and selfishness. We all need others to care for, and we all need to be cared for. Notice that infants do not have such prideful thoughts about their dependence on others. Therefore, Christ says that unless we repent and become like them, we cannot enter the kingdom of heaven (Mt 18:3; Lk 18:15). For example, aged

grandparents can provide an unparalleled experience for grandchildren to learn in unparalleled ways if given the opportunity to do so. Such elderly people can retain a sense of significance as the object and opportunity for such care. The challenge for human beings is not to create our own significance; this is given to us by God (contrary to evolutionary theory that says we are accidents). The real challenge for human beings is to discover how, in all circumstances, we can realize the life God intends us to know by serving and being served.

• • • • • • • • • • • • • • • • • • •

Q 1:27 Why does Paul find it necessary to act like a moral supervisor in order that he might know that the people are following the Word of God?

The text does not argue that Paul thought of himself as a moral supervisor or that it was a necessity for him. Paul is arguing that the point is not to act a certain way when he is present and a different way in his absence. On the contrary, Paul is asking the Philippians (and every reader of this letter) to consider the fidelity with which Christians are called to live their lives. A Christian life is not one of compromise or blending of preferences between God's will and the desires of the flesh (Rm 6:1–23; 13:8–14). Thus Paul says, "*Only* let your manner of life be worthy of the gospel of Christ" (italics added), explaining further that this means "with one mind striving side by side for the faith of the gospel." Paul goes on, through the rest of this letter, to provide the very means of grace and wisdom from God that gives us such a determination, knowing that the grace of God alone can produce the good fruit that no amount of moral supervision could ever inspire (Gal 2:15–3:14).

● ● ● ● ● ● ● ● ● ● ● ● ● ● ● ● ● ● ●

Q 1:29 Why did Christ want Christians to suffer? Why does it say we are to suffer for Him, when Christ died so that we do not have to suffer?

English translations use various means to translate what Paul describes as the relationship between a Christian and Christ. Literally, Paul says that God has graciously granted us "honesty about our dependence on Christ." Honesty about dependence (faith) brings a person into a realization of all the benefits of Christ's redeeming work during His life and now, through the Word and Spirit, during our lives. Suffering is a product of rebellion against God and a contradiction against His design for us. Fallen human beings bring suffering upon themselves by misusing and abusing God's creation (including our own bodies and minds). Besides this suffering, there is the suffering experienced when we deny our own fallen passions and seek to live contrary to the world and devil—suffering for doing what is right (1Th 1:6; 2:2; 3:1–4; 1Pt 2:18–25). Christ took our place under the suffering of everlasting condemnation and rejection by God in order to save us from that. Christ did not come or die to put an end to the suffering of a fallen world, but in order that we should know that such suffer-

ing is (1) not a matter of God punishing us according to what we deserve (Ps 103:10); (2) important to work everlasting conviction and contentment in us (Rm 6:21); and (3) all directed by God's wisdom so that it works together for good for those who love Him (Rm 8:28; 2Co 4:16–18). Pleasure is often the result of being loved and provided for; suffering is the more substantial and enduring result of loving another.

● ● ● ● ● ● ● ● ● ● ● ● ● ● ● ● ● ● ●

Q 1:29–30 Should we feel guilty if we don't have a lot of struggles?

As Christians, we need not "feel" guilty at all. On the one hand, we are entirely guilty of everything possible (Is 64:6; Mk 7:20–23; Rm 3:10–18; Eph 2:1–3). On the other hand, Christ has redeemed us from this guilt, having become guilty in our stead (2Co 5:21). We are never guilty according to our regenerate soul because this nature, created and sustained by the Word, never sins (1Jn 3:9). Thus we are guilty in one way and not guilty in two ways at the same time (Is 40:2). We might be grateful to God if we don't have a lot of struggles because He is protecting us from them or keeping us from making them for ourselves. We might also rest and prepare ourselves for struggles yet to come, knowing that struggles are not punishments but the consequences of a fallen world, which God directs always and only for our benefit (Rm 8:28; Heb 12:1–15).

Q 2:1 What does Paul mean by "if there is any encouragement in Christ"?

Paul is using a rhetorical and literary means of getting our attention by grossly understating what we know to be true. Paul is pretending to answer the objection or argument of selfish human nature: "Well, you know, I would be like-minded and loving and selfless *if* there were even the smallest reason for doing so" (cf. Is 7:10–14). Not only is there consolation in Christ, but this consolation is also as infinite and magnificent as its source.

Q 2:4 How can we know or determine the line between when one should seek his own well-being and when to seek the well-being of others?

The idea that seeking one's own well-being and that of others are opposed to each other is the work of the devil—a hideous lie (Jn 8:31–47). It is by giving our lives for the sake of others that we realize our lives (Lk 9:24; Php 2:5–11). The real question does not have to do with making sure we don't give too much of our lives away. The real question is, what will the passing away of our human nature mean? Our human nature is passing away—the wages of sin. Most people respond to the fleeting nature of our material life by trying to indulge it as much and as often as they can, but this only increases the rate of decay. Selfish preoccupation with our human nature is what made all the trouble in the first place (Heb 2:14–15). Christ has set us free from the fear of death by enduring it for us. He has given us a regenerate soul in the image of Himself, a soul that lives and thrives as it takes in the fullness of God through the Word and as it gives away that fullness in Word and deed (Jn 12:24–25; Php 3:1–16). Love is the most miraculous of things; the more of it you give away, the more you have (1Ki 17:8–16; Lk 9:10–17).

Q 2:5 Can we ever have the same attitude as Jesus Christ?

If we are regenerated in the image of Christ, we will have the same mind and attitude (1Jn 3:9; 4:1–5; 5:18). The problem is that our regenerate soul with this mind of Christ lives within an entirely contrary fallen human nature. This is why we deny the flesh in order to weaken it and why we remain in the Word in order to strengthen the soul (Lk 14:25–27; Jn 15:1–7; Rm 6:1–7:23). We will experience and display the same attitude of Jesus Christ to the extent that we are connected to the Word as He was (Jn 1:14; 1Jn 1:7).

Can we ever have the same attitude as Jesus Christ?

Q **2:6–11 How do we respond to those who argue the immutability of God, that His nature is unchanging?**

You could always begin by reading Col 2:8. Next you could ask, how would fallen, limited human beings presume to make judgments about what can or cannot be? Categorical negatives ("something cannot be") are impossible to prove or defend. Next, who said that God changed when the Son of God assumed a human nature from the Virgin Mary? Doesn't the Son of God prove that God is love by assuming human nature in order to redeem us from the curse of the Law? The best thing to do when human nature becomes judge rather than student is to ask real questions that human beings are really not equipped to answer (Jb 38:1–42:6; Jn 9:35–41). Once the mouth of man has been stopped, the ears can open to hear the wonders of God's nature that mean life for us (Jn 4:1–42; Ac 9:1–22; Rm 3:19–20).

Q **2:6 How can the verse say that we are equal with God when we are not even close?**

Paul is talking about Christ Jesus only (v. 5). Paul is explaining that since Jesus Christ was, according to His divine nature, true God, He never considered His equality with God as something to cling to selfishly or as if anyone could take it from Him or as if He could somehow lose it. On the contrary, it was because of the fact that Jesus is true God that His loving nature moved Him to empty Himself, even to the point of death on the cross. Knowing that we have an inexhaustible life from God and a regenerate, eternal soul is what moves us to give our lives on behalf of others, just as He did (Jn 13:3–17; 1Jn 4:19).

Q **2:10 Does this verse mean that even the devil and those in hell will worship God someday? What is the purpose of having those in hell who cannot change their destiny worship God?**

"Under the earth" is a reference to those who are in hell (Mt 18:6–9; Lk 16:22–23). While hell may not be a physical place beneath the surface of the earth, the language of being thrown into hell, of passing down into hell from burial, and of lifting one's eyes to look up to those in heaven gives the special impression that hell is below. Yes, this means that the devil and those in hell will kneel before God as a witness to the truth of His nature and work. The reason for rebellious people kneeling before God is not to change their destiny. Rather, their kneeling is a matter of honesty that they finally cannot resist: Jesus Christ is true God, the Savior of all creation, and their damnation is no one's fault but their own (Lk 13:34–35; Rm 1:20–32; 1Pt 3:18–19; Rv 18:2–19).

Q **2:12 How does someone "work out" their salvation?**

Notice that in the next verse, Paul explains: "For it is God who works in you, both to will and to work for His good pleasure." The Christian life is neither passive nor self-sufficient; it is neither fruitless nor saved by its fruit. Paul's admonition to "work out" is a remedy for our fallen, lazy, and apathetic human nature. Paul's explanation, that it is God who works in us, is part of the remedy for fallen human nature that is proud and self-righteous (Jn 15:1–7; Rm 11:17–22).

• • • • • • • • • • • • • • • • • • • •

Q 2:14 Has our church seen this verse or have we crossed it out of the text at some point? Is it possible to do everything without complaining?

There are many plain biblical passages that the visible Christian church is clearly unaware of or consciously ignoring. All things are possible with God (Mt 19:26). Doing all things as the New Testament describes is possible as the Word of God is present to regenerate and inspire us to do the same. Remember, it is not we who uphold the commands (though we apply ourselves to do so) but God who does this work in us (v. 13).

• • • • • • • • • • • • • • • • • • • •

Q 2:15 How can we be pure when we are sinful? What is the purpose of not arguing? In what way does this make us blameless and pure?

We are entirely sinful according to our fallen human nature (Rm 3:10–18; 6:5–11; Eph 2:1–3). We are entirely righteous since the perfect life of Christ covers ours and

He has regenerated our souls to live perfectly before Him (2Co 5:21; 1Jn 3:9; 5:18). Complaining and arguing are evidence of the contamination of sin: selfishness, pride, greed, arrogance, and the like (Mk 7:20–23; Gal 5:19–21; Col 3:5–9; Jas 4:1–4). Love for others that rejects complaint and argument also repels those selfish and hateful desires, which corrupt all that we do.

• • • • • • • • • • • • • • • • • • • •

Q 2:17 What is a drink offering? What is the significance of Paul comparing himself to a drink offering?

Drink offerings are simply the pouring out of a fluid in honor of someone or something. Jacob poured oil on a rock where God appeared to him and made promises to him (Gn 35:14). Drink offerings were part of the sacrificial system in the Law of Moses (Lv 23:13; Nu 28:14). Idolaters poured out precious fluids to their idols also (Jer 19:13). Paul was prepared for execution, if Caesar condemned him. If Paul was executed or even just beaten, his blood would have been poured out for the sake of advancing the truth about God's love for us in Christ (Ac 24:10–21; 26:1–29; Php 1:13).

• • • • • • • • • • • • • • • • • • • •

Q 2:19 Paul seems to have several messengers or workers. How many did he have? Were they always with him?

Paul did have a number of companions and fellow disciples, including Barnabas (Ac 13:1–2), Mark (2Tm 4:11), Silas (Ac 15:22), Timothy (2Tm 4:11), Luke (2Tm 4:11), Titus

(Ti 1:4), Sosthenes (1Co 1:1), Tertius (Rm 16:22), Onesimus (Phm 10), Apollos (1Co 16:12), and Epaphroditus (Php 2:25). A full reading of Acts and the Pauline Epistles reveals that these companions came and went regularly and often.

● ● ● ● ● ● ● ● ● ● ● ● ● ● ● ● ● ●

Q 2:19–30 When Timothy goes to these people, is he taking this letter or is the letter being sent ahead of him?

The text indicates that the Philippians would have received this letter before Paul sent Timothy ("to send Timothy soon").

● ● ● ● ● ● ● ● ● ● ● ● ● ● ● ● ● ●

Q 2:25 Is anything else known about Epaphroditus besides what Paul writes here?

Epaphroditus is only mentioned here and in 4:18. There appears to be no certain knowledge of this disciple apart from these references.

● ● ● ● ● ● ● ● ● ● ● ● ● ● ● ● ● ●

Q 2:29–30 Is Paul condemning the Philippians here?

Paul is referring to Epaphroditus in this section, having left off his notes about Timothy in 2:19–23. Paul uses no language of condemnation here. On the contrary, Paul is focused on the language of commendation, giving the Philippians good reasons for welcoming such a faithful and helpful servant as Epaphroditus.

● ● ● ● ● ● ● ● ● ● ● ● ● ● ● ● ● ●

Q 3:1 Why is Paul talking about outdated laws? Does Paul mean that he will continue to write the same things to them for as long as they didn't follow them?

The fall of Adam made human nature contrary toward God and contradictory. Our souls are regenerated by the Word of God, yet still continue to depend on the Word of God like we depend on the sun in the sky, the air we breathe, the water we drink, and our daily bread. Our contrary, fallen human nature and our regenerate soul depend on the truth and grace of God; this is why Paul does not mind communicating the Word of God as long as he is in the world to do so.

● ● ● ● ● ● ● ● ● ● ● ● ● ● ● ● ● ●

Q 3:2 Why does Paul refer to men as "dogs"? Should we not seek out non-Christians and tell them about the Gospel?

Paul is describing the same, particular kind of people throughout this verse. Dogs were not lovable and loving pets at this time; they were dirty predators, like evil workers, like the Jews who refused the grace of God in Christ and insisted in continuing to mutilate the flesh by requiring circumcision (Ac 11:1–18; 15:5–12; Gal 5:4, 11–12; 6:11–15). We are in the world for the express purpose of seeking out the lost (Mt 28:19–20; 2Co 5:20). We are also called to make a defense before those who disagree with us and a clear, gracious witness to those who would persecute us (1Pt 3:15; Mt 10:16–31). The

Bible reserves very severe language about those who knowingly work to subvert the truth and foster lies to the harm of others, especially people who are simple and naïve (Mt 18:6–14; 23:13–33; Rm 1:20–32; Gal 1:6–11).

• • • • • • • • • • • • • • • • • • • •

Q 3:3 Why does Paul refer to circumcision if it was not necessary once Christ came? What does it mean when it says "we are the circumcision"? Why does Paul go back to referring to "the circumcised" as those who are favored by God? When did we learn that outward practices are worth nothing to God?

Paul had to talk about circumcision because many people refused to believe what the Bible said about its purpose or what Jesus taught about its fulfillment. Sometimes Paul "fights fire with fire," using the language of the opposition against them. In this case, Paul is fighting the superficial and hypocritical claims of those who were circumcised with the deeper, substantive truth that circumcision was instituted to convey. God gave circumcision to Abraham as a physical confirmation of the promises He had made that would save the world. Christians are evidence of the fulfillment of those promises (Rm 2:25–29; 1Co 7:19; Gal 6:15; Eph 2:11).

• • • • • • • • • • • • • • • • • • • •

Q 3:4–6 What does Paul mean when he says he has more reasons to put

confidence in the flesh? We don't want to put confidence in the flesh, do we?

Paul is responding to people who compare themselves with others in order to argue that they give God more reason to accept them than anyone else. Paul will demolish such an argument in two steps. First, Paul argues that he has more reason to boast about his genetic pedigree and works than anyone else, but this will not keep him from dying under the Law. Second, Paul will explain why he considers all that is physical and of his own making to be rubbish in order to know the grace of God conveyed to us through Jesus Christ. If a person wants to compete with others for God's recognition under the Law, there is always someone else more deserving. Yet only one who is perfect can succeed, and that one is Jesus Christ. If a person wants to be just before God and genuinely valuable, this can only come from the Work of God in us (Jn 6:29; Eph 2:10).

• • • • • • • • • • • • • • • • • • • •

Q 3:6 Is Paul persecuting the Church as a Christian? What does Paul think of the Christian Church?

Paul is referring to his former life as a Jewish religious leader, the life that was of his own making before his conversion (Ac 8:1–3; 9:1–2, 13–14; 1Tm 1:13). After his conversion, Paul became part of the foundation of the Church, advanced and defended it against all manner of opposition, and finally was executed for refusing to deny the truth of it (Eph 2:20; 2Co 11:24–28).

Law for our guilt under the Law (Lk 23:13–25; 2Co 5:21).

Q 3:7 What does this mean that a "gain" (or profit) becomes a loss?

When Paul talks about the things of "gain" or "profit," he is referring to material wealth, power, and vanity—all the same things associated with "profit" and "gain" in our materialistic culture. Paul's conversion was the product of the grace and truth of God, which saved Paul from such profit in two ways. First, God, in Christ, had forgiven Paul for all the evil he had done in seeking wealth, power, and vanity. Second, God showed Paul that sacrificing one's eternal soul and relationship with God and all other people is the most absolute and catastrophic of all mistakes. Thus, Paul is explaining the magnitude of God's work; what God has given and shown Paul is so valuable that he considers all the supposed valuables of a fallen, material world to be rubbish (something that should be lost or cast away and that anyone would be glad to be rid of).

Q 3:9 How can righteousness come from the Law?

Paul is describing a righteousness that comes according to the Law, as measured by the Law. This is exactly the righteousness that Jesus accomplished on behalf of all people (Rm 8:1–4; 10:4; Gal 4:4; Jer 23:6). The righteousness that comes by faith still depends on keeping the Law perfectly, but that perfection is accounted to the one who believes (Jn 16:14; Rm 4:1–5). Jesus exchanged His righteousness according to the

Q 3:11 How do we "attain"? I thought we always had the promise of the resurrection through grace.

The promises of God regarding life everlasting and the resurrection of the dead are abundant and clear (Jn 11:25–26; 14:1–4; 1Pt 1:3–9). The expression "if somehow" (translated as "by any means possible" in the ESV) occurs only four times in the New Testament (Ac 27:12; Rm 1:10; 11:14; Php 3:11). In each case, there is an earnest desire to realize some significant good, but modesty and honesty urge a person to express hope rather than making a negative conclusion (Ps 51:11–13; Rm 7:7–25; Jas 4:13–16). As long as we are in this flesh and world with the devil prowling about, we cannot afford to give up our watchfulness as though we were free of threats against us (1Pt 5:8–9). In fact, honesty about our limitations and utter dependence on the grace of God are two of the forces of God that move us toward realization of the resurrection.

Q 3:12–13 Isn't Paul talking about eternal life when he talks about "mak[ing] it [his] own"? Why does he say he doesn't consider himself yet to have "made it [his] own"?

According to our regenerate soul, we have obtained the new life that God promised and provided for in Christ (1Jn 3:9;

5:18). Nevertheless, we will not have fully realized or obtained the new life God is giving us until we "put off" this fallen human nature and then are restored to a perfect physical nature as well (1Co 15:20–58; 2Co 5:1–11). It is a terrible mistake to think that God's saving work for us is uncertain or that it depends on our labor. It is an equally terrible mistake to think that the work of saving us is finished if we are still in the flesh (cf. Gal 1:6–10; 3:1–18 with 5:1–26).

Q **3:14 Why is Paul talking about winning the prize of heaven? Hasn't that already been won for us? Is this works-righteousness?**

The best explanation of this verse is found in the second half of v. 12, "I press on to make it my own, because Christ Jesus has made me His own." Christ Himself commanded us to strive for perfection not in order to justify ourselves but for the sake of realizing a fullness of life sooner than later, of being His agents through love of neighbor, and of redeeming the time (Mt 5:17–7:14; 2Co 5:4–20; Eph 5:15–21). The more singularly we concentrate our lives on realizing the life God has called us to and is restoring us to, the less vulnerable we will be to the opposition of the devil, the world, and our flesh (Eph 6:10–17; 2Pt 3:10–14).

Q **3:15–16 When are we considered "mature" Christians? How do we live up to what is already attained? What have we already attained?**

The word Paul uses here that is translated "mature" most often means "perfect" (Mt 5:48; 1Co 13:10; Eph 4:13; Col 1:28). In a few instances, the term has the sense of maturity, like outgrowing the kinds of childish thinking or petty concerns that keep people from realizing the potential of life (1Co 2:6; 14:20). Being mature has to do with being capable of serious, essential matters of life. According to our regenerate soul, we are already perfect and have already attained life everlasting (Jn 15:3; 1Co 3:21; 4:8; 1Jn 3:9; 5:18). According to our fallen human nature, we are childish and petty until the day we die (1Co 1:10–11; 2:14; 3:1–3; 13:9–11). Maturity, then, comes by a life in the Word that strengthens the soul so it is dominant, overcoming the flesh so it is submissive (Rm 6:8–14).

Q **3:18–19 How will enemies of the cross be destroyed? Is this describing what we see in books and movies such as *Left Behind*?**

Left Behind and other books and films like it are sadly mistaken since they reverse the proper reading of the biblical texts—reading literal texts as figurative and figurative texts as literal (not to mention gross inconsistencies in their interpretation). Notice that Paul describes these people as "enemies of the cross." The cross of Christ was the place where God demonstrated His love for us by making His Son our substitute and where He redeemed us from the curse of the Law (Is 53:4–9; 2Co 5:21). Any person who is an enemy of Christ's redemption must come to destruction, not only for failure to satisfy the Law but also for despising the gift of God in Christ (Mt 12:31–32; Heb 6:4–8; 10:26–31). Such people die while they are in this world because opposition to Christ is opposition to all ways, means, and things that life is made of (Jn 3:16–20). Such people die eternally, having cut themselves off from Christ, the only source of life and light (Gal 1:6–10; 5:4; Rv 18:1–24).

• •

Q **3:19 What does Paul mean when he says, "Their god is their belly"?**

A god is anything that governs our life. Whatever we have time, energy, and money for, especially when we are short of time, money, and energy, is very obviously our god. For most people, the desires of our fallen human nature rule. As our stomach tells us we are hungry and seeks to rule us until it is satisfied, so all the desires of our flesh tempt and nag at us relentlessly until we gratify them. One problem with trying to satisfy the flesh is that it won't stay satisfied, either because we use up what we get or because we quickly become dissatisfied with what we have, always wanting more or other things (1Jn 2:15–17). The only remedy for a stomach that would be god is to deny it in favor of the true God, who satisfies our

soul in such a way that we wish for nothing except what God is already and abundantly giving us (Lk 6:37–38; 11:9–13; Jn 6:26–29).

• •

Q **3:20 Does God allow us to never feel satisfied here on earth in order for us to realize that we belong somewhere else (heaven) and shouldn't get too comfortable here?**

God is absolutely wise, loving, and careful to give us neither more nor less than what serves to provide us with the fullness of life, both now and forever (Heb 12:3–11; Pr 30:7–9; Rm 8:28; Jb 1:21–22; Jas 5:11).

• •

Q **4:2 Who are these women, and why are they arguing?**

These two women are mentioned only here in the New Testament. Paul offers no other information about them except that they disagreed about something. Paul's instructions in ch. 2 suggest that selfish ambition and conceit might have been the problem.

• •

Q **4:3 My translation uses the phrase "yoke fellow" in this verse. What does that mean? How can Paul know for sure whose names are in the Book of Life?**

This is the only place in the New Testament where the phrase "yoke fellow" occurs. Very simply, it means the person who bears the yoke with you, as two animals would, hence the ESV translation "fellow workers." The yoke can be any sort of relationship that is so significant that no person could leave it, any more than an ox could walk away from or shake loose a yoke.

If Paul knows for sure that Clement's name is written in the Book of Life, it could only be due to a revelation from God. For all we know, the Book of Life may be a literal book with names written in it. Whether it is or not, God wants us to know that our salvation is something He accomplishes according to His will, according to His predetermination and foreknowledge, and by His effective working (Rm 8:29–30; Eph 1:3–12; 2:8–10). A person's relationship with the Word, Baptism, Holy Communion, and Absolution all bear witness that a person is in such a state of grace because his or her name is written in the Book of Life (Rm 8:1; 2Co 1:21–22; Eph 1:11–14; Rv 3:5; 13:8; 17:8; 20:12–15; 21:27).

- -

Q 4:7 Is it possible to know God's peace but not be able to understand it?

To begin, consider how many things our daily lives depend upon whether we know about them or not and whether we understand them or not. Since the fall of Adam, human beings understand almost nothing about creation or our lives within it,

though we know much. Next, we must distinguish between knowing *about* something and knowing as in being *inseparably united* with something. God gives us His peace by granting us forgiveness and a regenerate soul that is free from all threats (Jn 14:27; Heb 2:14–15; 1Jn 3:20). While we can understand the peace of God only in part, that does not prevent us from knowing (living in) the benefit of that peace (Jn 20:19–23, 26–29; 1Co 13:8–12; Php 3:7–12).

- -

Q 4:8 How do we help post-modern people, so focused on themselves, to understand this? Do our thoughts need to meet all of these criteria?

The most faithful Christian people I know have regular habits that are contrary to what Paul urges in this verse. Our thoughts do not meet these criteria, but they never will if we ignore them. The value of what Paul commands in this verse is clear and obvious; there are no drawbacks or negative consequences possible for following this ideal. Therefore, we might wonder why people refuse to work toward such a beneficial goal or are so careless about doing so. There is little to be gained by talking about what Paul says in this verse; there is everything to be gained by practicing what it says.

Is it possible to know God's peace?

Q **4:17 If we are saved by grace, not good works, why would we need credit?**

You will notice that Paul is not talking about how we are saved in this part of the letter. Paul is talking about the evidence, or fruit, of faith. Here the clear example of God's creation commends the truth and exposes error. No tree makes itself produce apples so that it can become an apple tree. On the other hand, no apple tree can keep itself from making apples. Making apples is the fruit of the tree that God made and sustains according to His will (Mt 7:17–20). The Philippian Christians have been saved by the grace of God. These Christians, in faith and gratitude, have supported Paul with gifts (Php 4:10). These gifts allowed Paul to concentrate on teaching rather than supporting himself, and these gifts helped provide for his needs while he was a prisoner (Ac 18:3–4; 24:23). Still, Paul says he is not interested in the gifts but in the fruit of the faith of these people, which is evidence of their faith. Just as the blessed ones in judgment are commended for the fruit of their faith, so Paul commends these Philippians (Mt 25:34–40).

Q **4:22 What saints belong to Caesar's household?**

The Gospel is not limited by any human relationship or superficial feature, since all souls are created equally by God, have been redeemed by Christ, and are the object of the Holy Spirit's regenerative work (Ac 17:26; 2Co 5:20; Mt 28:19–20). Members of Caesar's extended family, servants to royal people, soldiers, tax collectors, harlots, foreigners, and lepers were all restored to life and to God by the power of the Word (Php 1:13; Lk 1:1; 3:10–14; Ac 10:1–7; 13:1; Rm 16:11).

Colossians

Q **1:15–20 I know the Trinity is hard to understand, but if God is the Creator, and Jesus is the Son, then did Jesus also create the world?**

In many different places, the Bible records how God the Father, Son, or Holy Spirit are active in a particular way (Lk 3:22; Jn 16:14–15). On the other hand, God is one and cannot be separated as if He were three gods. The Athanasian Creed takes great pains to answer the very question you have asked. The best way to resolve any confusion regarding the truth is to hold the truth as it is clearly recorded in the Bible and resist all temptation to change the truth, so stated, into our own words or to conform it to our own limited thinking (Jb 38:1–42:6; Rv 22:18–19).

Q **1:18 What does it mean when it says Christ is "the firstborn from the dead"?**

Jesus is the first human being to be resurrected from the dead, never to die again. Jesus is the firstborn in many respects, since the incarnation of the Son of God is unique (Lk 2:7; Rm 8:29; Col 1:15; Heb 1:6; Rv 1:5). Believers, regenerated by the Word and Spirit of God, are also called "the firstborn," since we follow the pattern and are regenerated in the way that Christ made for us (Heb 11:23).

Q **1:20 What does "reconcile to Himself all things . . . in heaven" mean?**

We know that the whole of creation was affected by Adam's fall (Rm 8:19–22). God was, in Christ or by means of Christ, reconciling the world to Himself, charging all that was wrong against Christ and declaring us innocent in exchange (2Co 5:19). Notice that Paul excludes from this reconciliation "things below." In Php 2:10, Paul expresses the three realms: heaven, earth, and under the earth. "Things above" must mean the created heavens as part of the universe since the immaterial, heavenly beings that fell with Satan have been cast down to the lower places (2Pt 2:4).

● ● ● ● ● ● ● ● ● ● ● ● ● ● ● ● ● ● ● ●

Q 1:22 If we are holy and blameless in God's sight, does this mean that He no longer sees us as sinful beings?

Yes, no longer sinful for three reasons: (1) the perfect life of Christ covers us (atonement = cover); (2) God regenerates our soul so that it is innocent and perfect (1Jn 3:9); and (3) God imputes the righteousness of Christ to us by the forgiveness of sins (Rm 4:3; Jn 16:14).

● ● ● ● ● ● ● ● ● ● ● ● ● ● ● ● ● ● ● ●

Q 1:23 Here it says that the Gospel is preached to every creature. Do animals have souls and go to heaven?

The Bible does not speak of animals having souls, though they do have "the breath of life" (Gn 1:30; 6:17). All creation was affected by Adam's fall. Creation groans, waiting for redemption (Rm 8:19–22). God certainly cares about His creation, as is evident from a comment regarding cattle in Jonah (4:11) and His command that

Do animals go to heaven?

the Gospel be preached to all creation (Mk 16:15). Perhaps preaching the Gospel to all creation has more to do with a return to taking care of it as we were intended than with declaring the Gospel with words (Gn 2:15; 1Co 7:31). As St. Francis said, "Preach the gospel at all times; if necessary, use words."

● ● ● ● ● ● ● ● ● ● ● ● ● ● ● ● ● ● ● ●

Q 1:24 What does Paul mean in this verse?

Jesus explained to the apostles that their ministry was an extension of His own (Lk 10:16). Jesus also warned that people of the world would abuse them just as they abused Him, even to crucifixion and death (Mt 10:16–18; 21–42). Jesus made a particular reference to the sufferings of Paul when giving instructions to Ananias about Paul's conversion (Ac 9:16). In two of his letters, Paul mentions the suffering he had endured for the sake of the ministry of Christ Jesus (2Co 11:22–33; Php 3:7–14). Since we are the Body of Christ, when one of us suffers, then all suffer (1Co 12:12–27).

● ● ● ● ● ● ● ● ● ● ● ● ● ● ● ● ● ● ● ●

Q 2:1 Is Paul struggling physically or spiritually?

Paul endured endless physical trials in his effort to bring the Gospel to the Gentiles (see Col 1:24 above). Paul also mentions his internal fears and concerns for the spiritual well-being of the people he served with the Gospel (Rm 1:11; 1Co 3:1–3; Gal 1:6–10; 5:7–12). A Christian is concerned for all the things of God, physical and spiritual (1Co 7:29–31). A Christian is bound to struggle in body and soul as he or she bears concerns for all things and enlists the body for the sake of the concerns of the soul.

Q **2:8 Why do some schools, including Christian organizations, require students to take philosophy classes that make no mention of Christ? How do we avoid philosophy?**

Philosophy is "the love of wisdom" or "to be a friend or companion of wisdom," and the Son of God is wisdom itself (Pr 8:12–36). Paul is not warning us against philosophy but against the philosophy of fallen human nature, which he makes evident in the rest of this verse. Paul warned against these basic principles in Rm 1:20–32, noting especially what happens when people worship and serve the creation rather than the Creator. Any school, even though it intends to be Christian, is bound to suffer from the effects of fallen human nature since the institution is staffed by fallen human beings. While we might prefer professors of philosophy who lead us into the truth, we may still benefit from professors who drive us into the truth by challenging or contradicting what is true. Consider how much of the Bible, and the Gospels in particular, records how the truth responds to the challenges of lies and deceit.

Q **2:9 What is *deity*?**

The word *deity* comes from the Latin *dea*, which refers to a god or goddess. In this verse, Paul is explaining that all the fullness of God dwells in Jesus as in a body. The reality of this statement is unfathomable to the human mind, but the benefits of it are real and essential for our salvation: "In Christ God was reconciling the world to Himself" (2Co 5:19).

Q **2:13 (and Eph 2:11) If Paul is trying to convince the people that the Jewish tradition of circumcision isn't necessary, why would he relate uncircumcision with sinful nature?**

The key here is recognizing the significance of flesh and spirit. Circumcision has to do with removing the foreskin of a male reproductive organ. The foreskin is a covering and a breeding place for bacteria. After disobeying God, Adam tried to hide himself—among the trees of the garden, behind a fig leaf, and finally behind Eve (Gn 3:7–12). God promised salvation from the curse of sin to Abraham and gave a physical sign of that promise in circumcision. Thus circumcision was a physical indication of the fact that God had uncovered man's guilt, yet was providing a remedy for that guilt through the seed of the woman (Gn 3:15). The circumcision of the male reproductive organ was to indicate the inward truth that God had uncovered the sin in our hearts and, by faith, was purifying us (Rm 2:25–29). Jesus rebuked the hypocritical notion that outward ceremony could change or conceal a soul that was still corrupt and opposed to God (Mt 5–7; 23). A regenerate soul is not concerned with circumcision of the flesh because it has nothing to hide (1Jn 3:9).

• • • • • • • • • • • • • • • • • •

Q 2:16 How do we not let anyone judge us? How are we to find out what we need to improve on? What is a new moon celebration?

First of all, the Greek word *krino* has a spectrum of meaning, from "condemn" to "judge" to "diagnosis." Jesus forbids us to condemn anyone (Mt 7:1). On the other hand, Paul rebukes the Corinthians for neglecting to diagnose (in the sense of warning or correcting) since this is our responsibility (1Co 6:1–6; Lv 19:17). Second, people are bound to condemn and criticize us, but we are at liberty to honestly consider whether we deserve this criticism so that we might repent, confess, seek absolution, and make amends (2Co 7:8–12; Pr 28:13). Third, if we are condemned or criticized wrongly, we need not take it to heart, as truth and grace uphold and protect us (1Co 4:3–4; Php 3:7–11; Ac 5:40–42).

Numbers 28:11–15 describes the sacrifice to be made at the time of the new moon or the beginning of the month. Observances having to do with the new moon are recorded in 1Sm 20:5, 18, 24; 2Ki 4:22–23. They include feasting and seeking religious instruction. Several Old Testament texts include the new moon with lists of other special days of observance, such as the Sabbath and annual feasts (1Ch 23:30–31; 2Ch 2:4; 8:12–13; Ps 81:3). For more authentic information on the Jewish festivals, see *The Jewish Festivals: A Guide to Their History and Observance* by Hayyim Schauss (Union of Hebrew Congregations, 1938).

• • • • • • • • • • • • • • • • • •

Q 3:11 Why does it say that Christ is all, when we don't believe that Christ is in all things?

If God is omnipresent, then Christ is in all things. However, the omnipresence of God is entirely different from pantheism, which teaches that all things are themselves god. Paul is working to remove the superficial and trivial categories that separate people and inflame divisiveness. All things created are God's creation, and He is present in His creation. All people are God's creation, descended from one man and thus equally fallen and, through Christ, equally redeemed. Paul is working to facilitate the very unity that Christ prayed for, as recorded in Jn 17.

• • • • • • • • • • • • • • • • • •

Q 3:15–17 Are these verses a type of benediction? Is this where the Church got some of its benedictions?

These verses record some of the many benedictions that the Scriptures provide, which the Church has been careful to employ through time (Nu 6:24–26; 2Co 13:14;

Aren't we all slaves to sin?

Php 4:7). Some Bible versions highlight such verses by formatting them differently than the surrounding text. What kind of benediction ("good speaking") could be better than the Lord's own Gospel to us?

Q **3:22 Why is Paul talking about slaves submitting to their masters? Isn't slavery bad? Aren't we all slaves to sin and need to obey God?**

Since Adam abandoned his responsibility before God and toward Eve, human beings have been in bondage to sin (Rm 6:16; Eph 2:1–3; Heb 2:15). While our human nature will remain subject to this bondage until it returns to the dust, God liberates our souls through the regenerative work of His Word and Spirit (Jn 1:12–13; 3:1–6). Therefore, if a person's soul is still bound in sin, it makes little difference whether he lives as a slave or not. On the other hand, no one can enslave a person whose soul has been liberated by God. Most slave owners were slaves themselves to the passions of the flesh. Many slaves lived with souls much more liberated than those who sought to master them, as Harriet Beecher Stowe's book *Uncle Tom's Cabin* suggests. We also do well to remember that in biblical history, as well as in much of human history, slavery was a means of saving people from poverty, homelessness, and destitution (Dt 15:9–18).

Q **4:6 What does it mean when it says we are to "season" our conversations "with salt"?**

Salt purifies and preserves, much like the truth works humility by revealing what is real and exposing what is the product of ego, arrogance, pride, selfishness, and greed (Mk 9:50). To "season" our conversation "with salt" means to test our words before we say them to ensure that they are honest and thus modest and helpful (Eph 4:25–29).

Q **4:11 Is the Justus in this verse a different Jesus?**

Justus is a Latin name and means "just." *Jesus* is the English form of the Greek, pronounced "Yeh-soos," which is a translation of the Hebrew *Yeshua*, which means "salvation is of the Lord."

Q **4:16 What is the letter that was sent to the Laodiceans?**

We don't know any more about that letter than what Paul wrote here. Laodicea was in the same region as Colossae, and Paul intended his letters to be circulated between them. There is no way of knowing what the content of that letter might have been.

Q 4:18 What is the significance of the chains?

Paul was a prisoner either in Caesarea (Ac 23:31–35; 24:22–27) or, more likely, in Rome (Ac 28:30–31) when he wrote this letter (Php 1:12–18).

1 Thessalonians

Q **1:1 Why is Silas referred to as "Silvanus"?**

There is a suggestion that "Silas" is derived from the Hebrew "Saul" and its Aramaic version, "Seila." The name "Silvanus" is the Latin form of "Silas." Silas is referred to by this name always in Acts, but he is called "Silvanus" in 2Co 1:19; 1Th 1:1; 2Th 1:1; and 1Pt 5:12.

Q **1:4 What convinced Paul that these people were chosen by God?**

Jesus said, "You did not choose Me, but I chose you" (Jn 15:16). If anyone is honest about his or her dependence on God, it is because God has chosen that person to be regenerated in the image of Christ (Jn 1:12–13; 3:1–7; Rm 8:28–30, 9:6–29; 1Co 12:3; 1Pt 1:3–9). Since God is omniscient, omnipotent, and omnipresent, His election is comprehensive. He has predestined us since we are incorporated in His Son, the Son of Man, and all aspects of our life and times are also predestined, individually and exhaustively. For the regenerate, the comfort, faith, and inspiration provided by knowing this is as comprehensive as the election itself. For those who would argue that this is unfair or that they rightly blame God for their condemnation, this biblical teaching precludes their objections. They cannot argue that they were not elect and redeemed with Christ, and so why would they argue, assume, or contend that they are outside of God's good election for them?

● ● ● ● ● ● ● ● ● ● ● ● ● ● ● ● ● ●

Q **1:6 What was the opposition faced by Paul and his companions? The word** *imitators* **is unsettling. Was the Thessalonians' imitation of God incorrect because Paul and others were middlemen?**

Paul wrote this letter to the Christians in Thessalonica right after he had first visited that city during his second missionary journey in the spring of AD 51. Ac 17:1–9 records that first visit to Thessalonica, where the Jews who were not persuaded "were jealous, and taking some wicked men of the rabble, they formed a mob, [and] set the city in an uproar" (v. 5). This kind of opposition is described throughout Acts, as the vicious opposition of many Jewish religious leaders was the same from city to city.

The word *imitate* is what the Holy Spirit, through Paul, chose to write. The key to resolving your concern is not with that word but with the focus and specific language in the rest of the verse. First of all, the "and" that comes before "of the Lord" is not adding the Lord to Paul and his companions as equal examples. The "and" is epexegetical, which means it is explaining what proceeds from what follows, something like this: "and you became imitators of us, that is to say, of the Lord." Second, the circumstance of this imitation is very focused. The Thessalonians imitated Christ in the way they endured the affliction that came with receiving the Word. The joy that accompanied the reception of that Word was the product of the Holy Spirit, just as it was with the apostles

after Pentecost (Ac 5:40–42). Paul is not taking anything away from Christ, but is a living witness to people who did not have the Bible to read and learn from (Mt 5:16; Jn 13:15; 2Co 5:18–20).

● ● ● ● ● ● ● ● ● ● ● ● ● ● ● ● ● ●

Q **2:1, 5 Paul constantly repeats the phrases "you know" and "as you know." If the Thessalonians know all this, why is he retelling them?**

Paul answered that very question in his Letter to the Philippians about ten years after this: "To write the same things to you is no trouble to me and is safe for you" (Php 3:1). John wrote something similar near the end of the first century in his first letter (1Jn 2:12–14). The problem with living a Christian life according to what we believe is not that we don't know what is right or wrong. The problem for Christians who struggle against our fallen human nature is to stay conscious of our faith and of what that faith would have us think, say, and do (Rm 6:1–13; 7:7–21). Only the Holy Spirit can regenerate and inspire us to live what we believe, and the Holy Spirit comes to us in the Word (Jn 6:63; 8:31–32).

● ● ● ● ● ● ● ● ● ● ● ● ● ● ● ● ● ●

Q **2:2 Was Paul the only one that was persecuted for being a Christian while doing his ministry? Why were the people insulted in Philippi?**

Every Christian during the first centuries after Christ was likely to suffer

Why would God test us?

persecution, either from the Jews or the Romans or both. James was killed by Herod, and Peter was imprisoned with the same intent (Ac 12). John was exiled to the island of Patmos (Rv 1:9). Jesus explained to His disciples that if the world hated Him, it would hate His followers also (Jn 15:18–20).

Paul is referring to the beating and imprisonment he and his companions suffered because the masters of the girl who told fortunes were angry that Paul had cast out of her the demon that made people think she could tell fortunes (Ac 16:12–40).

● ● ● ● ● ● ● ● ● ● ● ● ● ● ● ● ● ● ● ●

Q **2:4 Are all pastors tested to see if they try to please God rather than men or was that just for the apostles? What is the difference between God testing us and being tempted by Satan? Can both happen in the same situation? Why would God "test our hearts"?**

The devil, the world, and our own fallen human nature are relentless in their opposition to God working in our lives and through us, no matter who we are. It does appear that the more authority or visibility we have, the more severe a target we become for the devil (Jb 1:6–12; 2:1–8; Lk 22:31–34).

God and the devil are at work in the same circumstances but for very different purposes. The essence of a trial or test or temptation is that a person is challenged in a significant way, and that person's response will bear significant consequences. God tested Abraham's faith with the command to sacrifice Isaac, knowing that this was the only way to confirm Abraham's faith that God would provide him with an heir (Gn 22:8; Heb 11:17–18). God's Spirit drove Jesus into the wilderness in order to be tested by the devil for forty days and nights. God's purpose was to provide a perfect response to every test/temptation, which would provide atonement for all our failures, while the devil's purpose was to ruin the work of the Savior. God, in fact, never tempts people to ruin their lives in any way. God does test those He loves in order to confirm them in the faith (1Pt 1:6–7; 2Co 1:8–9, 4:1–5:21, 12:7–10). The devil is always prowling about, seeking whom he may devour (1Pt 5:8; Pr 7:7–27). Our own human nature is full of selfishness, greed, and lust, which create and seek out all sorts of temptations that would surely ruin us now and forever except for the intervention of God, the intercession of Christ, and the sanctifying work of the Holy Spirit in us through the Word and Sacraments.

● ● ● ● ● ● ● ● ● ● ● ● ● ● ● ● ● ● ● ●

Q **2:8 Why does Paul say they shared their lives as well? Does that indicate that church workers are allowed to separate their ministry and their private lives?**

First, the New Testament doesn't speak in terms of "church workers" as we do today.

All Christians were disciples of Christ, remaining steadfastly in the apostles' doctrine, the fellowship, the breaking of bread, and the prayers and seeking to be ambassadors for Christ (Jn 8:31–32; Ac 2:42; 2Co 5:19–21). The first Christians shared everything with one another (Ac 2:44–47). Some Christians, like apostles and pastors, were called to proclaim the Word of God in public settings and were held accountable for doing so faithfully (Ac 20:28; Jas 3:1–2; 1Pt 4:11). Other Christians were given responsibilities for the physical care of the faithful (Ac 6:1–7). I don't think Paul is describing an exception from the normal practice of separating his private life from his ministry. Paul is emphasizing the close, dear relationship he and his companions had formed with the new converts in Thessalonica. Christians live in communion established by God through the Word, but sometimes there is an additional, personal bond that develops as well, as between Jesus and Lazarus and his sisters (Jn 11:5).

Q 2:9 Did Paul have another job in Thessalonica to pay for his own expenses or does that refer to the work of the Kingdom? Why would Paul have to work hard and not be a burden while preaching the Gospel?

Whenever financial support was not present or when receiving such support would have been an issue, Paul took up his skill of tent making in order to earn what he needed to live (Ac 18:3; 1Co 9:6–18). Paul was very careful and sensitive to the fact that Christian giving is only good and acceptable to God when it is the product of faith worked by the Gospel (Ac 4:32–5:11; 2Co 9:1–5). By working to provide for his own needs, Paul provided an example of good stewardship and provided time for believers to begin to give as the fruit of salvation provided rather than as a payment toward salvation that must be earned.

Q 2:10 What did Paul mean in this verse? How does this not sound like good works? Are we not supposed to be humble? How can God be a witness to the righteousness of some men?

You may recall that some of the Jews in Thessalonica, having become jealous, used evil men in the marketplace to put the city into an uproar (Ac 17:1–9). Paul is concerned not only for the spiritual well-being of these new Christians but also for how they might be affected by accusations that Paul and his companions were false teachers, troublemakers, and enemies of God (Ac 24:5–6; 28:22; 1Co 4:11–13). As Luke was doing in the Gospel and Acts, Paul also spends a lot of time in apologetics—writing responses that will present the truth in response to the lies of those who oppose Christ and all who serve Him. Paul does not mention salvation here at all. Paul is pointing out that in Thessalonica, he and his companions were careful to do the very thing Paul advocates for everyone who would claim the name of Christian, as he wrote Titus: "Show yourself in all respects to be a model of good works, and in your teaching show integrity, dignity, and sound speech that cannot be condemned, so that an opponent may be put to shame, having nothing evil to say about us" (Ti 2:7–8).

Paul is talking about civil conduct and wants to confirm the truth of his description of that conduct by calling God as a witness. The idea of calling God as witness is that no one would do this if he were not telling the truth, since God would never hesitate to expose a liar and punish him accordingly, as the Second Commandment warns (Ex 20:7; 1Sm 14:44; 2Sm 3:35; 1Ki 2:23; Ac 5:1–11).

Q 2:12 How can they live lives worthy of God?

Here is an example of the importance of translation. First, Paul wrote that they should "walk," not "live," worthy of God. Second, *worthy* does not mean "to earn" but "to be consistent with" (Lk 3:8). While we live in this world, we have a fallen human nature that always opposes God and His will (Rm 5:6–11). At the same time, we have a regenerate soul that is made in the image of Christ and does God's will (Jn 1:12–13; 3:1–7; 1Jn 3:9). Paul has been explaining that the purpose of His ministry is communicating the Word of God so that it produces a life in us that is consistent with God's will, working repentance and restraint in our human nature while inspiring and strengthening our regenerate soul (Rm 6:1–22).

See also the question and answer found at Eph 4:1.

Q 2:13 How do churches that insist that the whole Bible is not divine deal with verses such as this?

There are several ways to undermine what Paul is stating clearly in this verse. First, some would claim that Paul is overstating the case, either from blind passion or because he wants his words to have added force in people's lives. Second, some would claim that Paul is a product of his time and place; he thought this because he was unenlightened and didn't know any better, like superstitious people. Third, some claim that the Bible does contain the Word of God but it has to be separated from all of the other words of men that surround it. Finally, some argue that the Word of God is present in the overall message of the Bible, that God loves us and wants us to love and accept one another. Notice that all of these responses leave any particular text in the Bible subject to rejection by anyone as they wish, and no text would remain authoritative since we have no authority besides the Bible to tell us which passages are the Word of God and which are not. Jesus, Paul, and Peter anticipated and spoke to these arguments against the truth (Jn 6:63; 10:35; 2Tm 3:16 [notice the expression "*all* scripture" is inspired by God]; 2Pt 1:16–21).

• • • • • • • • • • • • • • • • • • • •

Q 2:13 Why does Paul praise the Thessalonians for accepting the Word at face value, while later he praises the Bereans for studying and double-checking Paul before they accepted it? It sounds like the people accepted the Word of God of their own volition and not that the Holy Spirit led them to accept it.

Anyone might be delighted when a person recognizes that the Bible is the very Word of God, powerful, life-giving, true, eternal, inspired, inerrant, and infallible (Jn 6:63; 1Tm 3:16; Heb 4:12). Only disaster comes from rejecting the truth (Jn 3:18–20; 8:43–47). But Paul does not commend the Thessalonians for accepting the Word as the truth blindly or against all evidence to the contrary. The Word demonstrates that it is the truth constantly and especially in the face of contradiction, as Jesus showed so often in the Gospel (Mt 19:1–9; 22:34–46; Jn 10:31–39). The Bereans were commended by Paul because, unlike the Jews who kept on making trouble for Paul, they wanted to hear and evaluate the Word for themselves. Whether accepting or rejecting, no good comes of doing so without cause and without testing (Dt 18:9–22; 1Th 5:21; 1Jn 4:1). No one can accept anything except what God gives (Jn 3:27). No one can choose God, for our fallen human nature is contrary to Him until we are converted and regenerated (Jn 15:16; 1Co 2:14; 1Pt 1:3–9). No one can say "Jesus is Lord" except by the Holy Spirit (1Co 12:3).

• • • • • • • • • • • • • • • • • • • •

Q 2:15–16 He says that Jews "displease God and oppose all mankind by hindering us from speaking to the Gentiles that they might be saved." Be saved from what?

Paul is talking about being saved from eternal condemnation and from everything else that is contrary to God's will for us to live. The Jews did not please God because they were controlled by their love of money, power, and popularity (Lk 11:43; Jn 11:45–53; 1Tm 6:10). The Jews who rejected Christ and the grace of God could not possibly please God, because without Christ they could only be condemned by the Law before God (Is 64:6; Rm 10:1–3; Gal 5:4; Jas 2:10–13). What makes matters worse is that the Jews not only rejected the truth and grace of God for themselves but also tried to keep others from knowing these. Jesus gives clear witness to His wrath against such opposition in Mt 23:4–39. Acts provides many examples of the effort of the unbelieving Jews to keep people from the truth (Ac 4:1–22; 5:28–40; 11:1–3; 13:44–46; 14:3–6; 15:1–10).

• • • • • • • • • • • • • • • • • • • •

Q 2:17–3:6 Why did Paul want to go to Thessalonica even if he knew and believed they had faith?

Paul returned to the churches of southern Galatia twice in order to make sure they were continuing in the faith and to provide reassurance (Ac 14:21–26; 15:36). Paul knew that the Christians in Rome had faith, yet he wanted to see them in order to strengthen their faith by the use of his apostolic gifts (Rm 1:11–12). Paul wrote to the Christians in Philippi the same things he had taught them because he knew they needed a constant witness to the truth (Php 3:1). Paul was anxious about the faith of the Thessalonians because he knew there were Jews in that city who might continue to oppose and undermine his authority and the truth, just as they had done in southern Galatia (Gal 1:1–23).

Q 2:18 How did Satan stop them from seeing the Thessalonians again? Wouldn't God just defeat Satan so that he could not stop the spreading of the Gospel through the prophets?

Paul does not explain the circumstances by which Satan hindered them from returning. Paul made a similar lament regarding the Romans and the Corinthians, though he does not mention Satan in those cases (Rm 1:11–13; 2Co 1:17). Certainly God could remove Satan and any other obstacle according to His will. Therefore, in this passage, we have a chance to see that even the apostle Paul wrestled with frustrations to his own plans, though in time the Lord revealed to him that all things work together for God to those who love Him, who are called according to His purpose (Rm 8:28; 2Co 12:7–10).

Q 2:19–20 Aren't we supposed to boast in the Lord? If so, why is Paul boasting in the Thessalonians?

You are not the first person to wonder about boasting in something other than the Lord. There are ancient manuscripts that use the Greek word for "rejoicing" rather than "boasting." Still, the overwhelming majority of manuscripts have the word *boasting*. Now what? Let's begin by noticing that Paul doesn't claim this boasting for himself personally, nor does he claim this boasting here in time. Paul asks, "What is *our* hope or joy or crown of boasting . . . at [Jesus'] coming?" (v. 19, italics added). If by "our" Paul means everyone united in opposition to Satan, then he means we share in the boasting of the Lord and His saving work over Satan. This agrees with the time Paul is referring to—not now in this world, but at the end of the world when Christ returns in victory over all who opposed Him. Notice also that Paul is not boasting but speaks of a "crown of boasting." The New Testament speaks often of the crown that God will bestow upon those who remain faithful to the end—faithful, of course, by God's own working in such a person (1Pt 1:5). This crown is described as a crown of life and of glory (2Tm 4:8; Jas 1:12; 1Pt 5:4; Rv 2:10). God makes us His own children, heirs with Christ and in communion with Him. Since Christ will stand victorious over His enemies at the Last Day and boast over them in the lives of those He saved, we will share that boast as well (Rm 8:15–17; 2Tm 2:12).

• • • • • • • • • • • • • • • • • • • •

Q 2:20 Why are the Thessalonians the "glory and joy" of Paul? I thought joy was an emotion we have because of God and humans cannot give us joy.

The word *glory* means "to do or be what no one else can or would." The word *joy* means "to be happy because of your circumstances." Apostles like Paul, pastors, and all disciples of Christ are agents or ambassadors of His Word, which works repentance and regenerates people in the image of Christ (Ac 1:8; 2Co 5:19–21). We recognize that in Christ and through the Means of Grace, God saves His people, something no one else could or would ever do (1Co 1:18–25; 2:9; Eph 3:20–21). We cannot help being joyful as we recognize God's saving work in the lives of people around us (Mt 2:10–11).

• • • • • • • • • • • • • • • • • • • •

Q 3:1–2 Why did only Timothy go back to Thessalonica?

Paul said that he and Silvanus were left in Athens alone and they sent Timothy back to Thessalonica in order to "establish and exhort" them concerning their faith (v. 2). We know Paul was anxious about the faith and well-being of the Thessalonian Christians from 3:5. It is possible that Paul thought he could send Timothy back there because one man alone would not draw attention and because Timothy was half Greek, which would make him even less noticeable (Ac 16:1–3).

• • • • • • • • • • • • • • • • • • • •

Q 3:1 What is the "it" they could no longer bear?

The "it" Paul can't bear has to do with knowing that the Thessalonian Christians are well in the faith. In 2:17, Paul refers to having been "torn away from you" because of the uproar started by jealous Jews who opposed Paul (vv. 17–20). In the verses that follow, Paul expresses concern that "no one be moved by these afflictions" (3:3), referring to the same uproar (3:1–4). In v. 5, Paul describes the "it" in his own words: "I sent to learn about your faith, for fear that somehow the tempter had tempted you and our labor would be in vain."

• • • • • • • • • • • • • • • • • • • •

Q 3:3 What trials were they going through?

Luke describes the trouble they had in Ac 17:1–9, and Paul describes those same events as speaking "to you the gospel of God in the midst of much conflict" (1Th 2:2). The narrative in Acts provides a very consistent portrait of the opposition that came from Jews who refused to believe the truth and, due to jealousy, tried every means possible to destroy the Gospel. They were contentious, they argued, they recruited evil men to create an uproar, they rioted themselves, and they tried to tear Paul to pieces—all because Paul taught that God had, in Christ, freely forgiven all people and now called them all to communion and peace in His Word and Spirit.

Q 3:10 What does Paul mean by sup-plying "what is lacking" in the Thes-salonians' faith? Paul says in 4:9 that the Thessalonians have been taught brotherly love by God. How does Paul know what he needs to teach and what God has already taken care of?

The short answer is that Paul knows be-cause he is an apostle and God makes him know what is necessary. The longer answer has to do with distinguishing between our fallen human nature and our regenerate soul. Once the Word and Spirit of God have regenerated a person's soul, he or she is gen-uinely a new creation, anointed by God in Baptism and knowing all things according to that nature (Jn 1:12–13; 1Jn 2:20, 27; 3:9). This is what Paul means when he says they have been taught by God. The problem is that our human nature, contrary in every way, remains and fights against faith (Rm 5:6–11; 1Co 2:14). A third consideration has to do with completing or filling out the biblical instruction that Paul had started. At this time, individuals did not have Bibles. They only had opportunity sometimes to hear the Word read to them from Scriptures that would circulate (Col 4:16). Paul wants to return to Thessalonica so he can fill out their knowledge of the Word of God.

How can we please God?

Q 4–5 Why does God not offer any Gospel in these chapters? It is all Law.

There are two answers to this ques-tion. First, our fallen human nature, being contrary to God, is so preoccupied with having its way or justifying its contradiction to God that it sees only the Law and misses the Gospel completely. There is Gospel here; for example, "even so, through Jesus, God will bring with Him those who have fallen asleep" (4:14) and "You are all children of light, children of the day" (5:5). The sec-ond reason has to do with the location of this Law within the entire letter. The Law is always preceded and followed by the Gos-pel, because it is the Gospel that allows us to hear the Law and the Gospel at work in us, which responds to the Law and wants to exceed what it commands in love (Ps 130:4; Rm 13:8–10). Rm 12 contains forty-two commands, but Paul does not turn to this kind of direction until he has set the grace of God firmly in place in the preced-ing eleven chapters. All of God's will for us is always surrounded by His grace that for-gives, regenerates, orients, and inspires our life (1Jn 4:19).

Q 4:1–12 Here God talks about people living a good and decent "love" life. If this is the way it has to be and the way God wants it, then why does He allow otherwise? How can we please God in how we live? Does God punish men for all such

sins? Does God have all our sins planned and when we will sin and how we will be punished?

These questions cannot be answered until we distinguish between consequences for actions, discipline, and punishment. First, in a universe that is ordered so that life can be sustained, there must be cause and effect. You can't have gravity without skinning your knee if you trip and fall down on the concrete sidewalk. It is not God's will that you trip; His will is that you walk carefully (Eph 5:15ff.). It is not God's will that anyone should push you down; His will is that you and your neighbor should love one another (Mt 22:37–39). It is not God's will that we should produce hard surfaces that hurt when we fall on them; God created lush, green grass; man covers it with concrete (1Co 7:31; Rm 8:20–22). If we contradict God's design for us in sexual matters, there will be negative consequences, just like any other contradiction of design. Second, God remains in control of His universe and so orders the events of our lives so that they work to discipline us—to teach us toward a better life now and a perfect life for all time (Rm 8:28). God does not violate His own order of creation, nor does He become subject to it as if it now ordered Him. God so orders and directs all the events of our lives so that we mature in wisdom, faith, and love (Heb 12:1–28).

Third, punishment is the final execution of justice since the Law cannot be violated without consequences, both in time and in eternity, between people and between people and God. This is why God sent His Son into our world, to take our nature upon Himself and to take our place under the Law. Christ did perfectly all that the Law requires for all people of all time, and then He suffered all that the condemnation of the Law requires for those who violate it—all in our place. God does not deal with us according to our iniquities because He executed justice against His own Son in our place (Ps 103:10; Is 53; 2Co 5:19–21). Therefore, the only people that suffer punishment are those who insist on being judged by the Law according to their own life and steadfastly refuse, reject, and despise the life that Christ provided for them (Mt 12:31–32; Heb 6:4–8; 10:26:31; 2Pt 2:12–22). God does not plan our sins, but He knows what they will be and so directs our life in combination with others so that good comes of our plans instead of evil (the best study of this reality is Ac 20:17–28:31). The only way to please God in the way we live is to live in Christ. Remaining in His Word keeps us in the forgiveness of sins, keeps us in repentance for all that is going wrong with us according to our fallen human nature, and keeps us filled with His Spirit that regenerates our soul to do God's will freely and intently (Jn 8:31–32; Col 3:1–16; 1Jn 3:1–5:21).

• • • • • • • • • • • • • • • • • • • •

Q 4:3–8 Do these acts of sexual immorality include married couples? Does this mean it is always wrong to have sex for pleasure? If sex shouldn't be necessarily pleasurable, then if your thoughts stray to that purpose, are we wrong and should we stop? Does this also apply to women?

God's will for us to love one another as He loves us applies to everyone at all times (Jn 15:12). For those who are married, love includes physical intimacy with the spouse; for the unmarried, love would keep a person from physical intimacy (1Co 7:1). The problem with pleasure of any kind is not with pleasure itself but when pleasure becomes a selfish master. We are commanded to have no other gods because there is no other than God, and that is the truth. To submit to any other force as if it were a god would be to sacrifice our life for what cannot give life or satisfy. The reason addictions exist is because what a person is addicted to can never satisfy what only the true God can provide. Pleasure from sexual intimacy is of the same nature as pleasure from every other good gift and wonder in God's creation. However, that pleasure becomes addictive, fleeting, elusive, then corrupted when it is what controls our thoughts and actions. Our thoughts will stray as long as we are in this fallen human nature (Rm 5:6–11). If we were to isolate ourselves in some way, our thoughts would only stray in other ways; thus the Internet pornography epidemic (Pr 18:1). The remedy for straying thoughts is a steady life in the Word and Spirit of God

that liberates us from the selfish and self-defeating desires of the flesh (Rm 6:1–23). When the love of God holds us together, then love of others, especially of a spouse, brings pleasures unfathomable and without regret (2Co 5:14ff.). Note carefully that Paul does not condemn passion, but the passion of lust. Paul condemns this because lust, which is by definition the "desire for more," cannot be satisfied. The passion of lust, in its blind determination to find gratification, prevents any possibility of fulfillment because it is selfish. Only the passion of selfless love for another can know the fullness of pleasure that God intended for us (Ps 16:11).

What Paul says here does apply to women, though he was not writing this to women. What Paul says applies to women in two ways. First, if a woman were tempted to pursue what this text forbids, it would apply to them also. Second, this text applies to women because they will benefit from every man who obeys and they will suffer from every man who disobeys. Women do need to know all that God has said to or about men in order to know what they need to beware of or can look forward to.

• • • • • • • • • • • • • • • • • • • •

Q 4:3 What exactly is considered sexual immorality? Would kissing fall under this category? Why can't people be clear about this stuff?

Adultery concerns only those who are married and is included in the terms *sexual immorality* and *fornication*. Sexual immorality or fornication includes every kind of sexual or sexually related activity that is contrary to God's design and intent for us. Kissing, touching, holding hands, even conversation, e-mailing, texting—all of these can fall in this category if it has to do with the selfish self-indulgence of the desires of the flesh, even for spouses within their marriage (Ti 1:15). Love is the key. We can communicate with, touch, and even kiss one another any time love for another is served by so doing (Rm 16:16). People can't be clear about this because they do not remain in the Word, which makes it clear, and because we all still possess a fallen human nature that forever tries to twist or ignore what God says (Jn 3:18–21; 8:43–47). Only the Word and Spirit of God active in a regenerate soul can understand, appreciate, and seek God's intent for us to live in loving service of one another.

Q 4:4 What can I say to someone who has been sexually active and feels terrible about it because of these verses?

The short answer is that you can take someone to 2Co 7:8–10, where Paul explains that the purpose of his letter is to produce godly sorrow that leads to repentance that leads to salvation. Like any healing process, first comes pain, then recovery and health. The long answer is that you can take someone to Gn 1:1 and start with that person at the very beginning, studying God's will and grace in creation, the nature and consequences of our fall, and God's

will and grace again in redemption. Sexual immorality is the focus of only one of Ten Commandments, and we should feel terrible about breaking all of them. The remedy for such feeling is repentance and the grace of God that comes through Christ.

Q 4:4 My translation reads "finding a husband or wife for yourself." Is that a bad translation or is it referring to the dating practices of Christians?

That is a very bad translation in at least two ways. First, Paul is talking to men because that is where the responsibility rests for how relationships develop, either along genuinely loving lines or according to selfish male sexual appetite. Second, Paul is talking about so much more than looking for a husband or wife. Paul is telling men that they need to possess or have control over their reproductive organ rather than letting it possess them. Paul means to exclude from men every motivation that does not love according to God's design, in order to protect women from abuses of every kind. There is an interesting parallel to this verse in 1Co 7:1, where Paul says "it is good for a man not to touch a woman." The word Paul uses is very simple and means "touch." However, some English translations have "it is good for a man not to have sexual relations with a woman," while others say it is good for a man "not to marry." What could be further from the truth, as if anything goes as long as you don't get married or have intercourse? In our era of "sex as recreation," that leaves a lot of open territory that is unhealthy and unhelpful. Everything changes when a man touches a woman, even just a casual touch, which is why Paul warns against it. Men can only know the heights and wonders of real love when they really love women according to God's design, altogether in her best interests.

● ● ● ● ● ● ● ● ● ● ● ● ● ● ● ● ● ● ● ●

Q 4:6 In class, you explained that part of what "defrauding" means has to do with a man preventing his wife from having children. Then, you went to Malachi and discussed a man fulfilling God's design by having children with his wife. What about an infertile couple, or those who do not have kids? Are they not fulfilling God's design?

The love of children and intent to have children is different from having control over this. The love of children is integral to God's design for our lives because they are an indispensable example to us and because in serving them, we have a purpose for our lives that is living and eternal. A couple who want children but are not successful in conceiving are completely different from a couple who are determined not to have children because they despise children and idolize themselves. The adult world that despises children is vain, greedy, selfish, petty, artificial, and worst of all, desperately unfulfilling for those determined to live it. A couple might choose not to have children in order to devote their lives as a couple to caring for children in need. There are many ways for couples who want but cannot have children to care for children, such as foster parenting, adoption, teaching, and mission work. What is most important to remember is that the same disposition that makes a person love and cherish children also makes that person capable of authentically loving others, especially a spouse. In fact, I have heard many a man and woman claim that having a spouse is like raising another kid. What's wrong with that?

● ● ● ● ● ● ● ● ● ● ● ● ● ● ● ● ● ● ● ●

Q 4:6 Does the word *brother* mean more than just the brothers in faith? Does it not also mean sisters, and therefore also a wife?

Interpreting the word *brother* to include both men and women makes it very difficult to make sense of the rest of the passage because it is talking to men, who are the ones that have the vessel that needs to be possessed in sanctification and honor and who had to be warned against defrauding their brothers. If a man took a woman from her father and brothers only to gratify his sexual appetite, he would be defrauding those men by taking her out of the good care of their home only to abuse her (Mal 2:13–16). The Bible is written for all people, and all are called to remain in it, but the Bible also understands and impresses us with the responsibility of adult men, especially husbands and fathers, to pursue the Word, receive the Word, and convey the Word to their families (Gn 2:7–17; 3:9; Rm 5:12–19; Eph 6:4).

Q 4:8 Is this another example of Paul establishing his "credentials" to an earthly Church?

Paul is referencing his credentials to some degree, but that is not his primary purpose. When Paul is arguing his apostolic authority, you know it (Gal 1:1–2:10; 1Co 9:1–18; Php 3:3–7). Here Paul is anticipating arguments from people who want to dismiss what he is saying about the responsibilities of men in particular and of sexual morality in general (1Co 11:16). What Paul is teaching is the truth and flows from God's design in creation. Biblical teaching on gender and relationships is not the product of local customs of particular times but is universal in time and place, just as human physiology is the same everywhere and for all people (1Co 11:1–15; Ac 17:26).

Q 4:9 What would you say to people who consider themselves "perfect" Christians, yet fail to show love to their brothers who don't love according to their standards?

Are you suggesting that these "perfect" Christians fail to meet your standard? Now what? To begin with, rather than saying something to these "perfect" Christians, we would want to submit ourselves to a few important passages. First, we want to be slow to speak, quick to listen, and slow to anger, for the anger of man does not work the righteousness of God (Jas 1:19–20). Second, we would want to be careful that we are not condemning others in our thoughts, words, or disposition (Mt 7:1–2). Third, we would want to take the log out of our own eye before we tell someone else to take the log out of theirs, for it may only be a speck and not a log after all (Mt 7:3–5). Fourth and only at this point, we would want to ask such people to help us understand their disposition toward others who don't meet their standard. What is their standard of love? How does their standard compare with Christ's standard and how He demonstrated that in His ministry to sinners? Do such people refuse to show love to people who fail to meet other standards, like the ones expressed in the other nine commandments (Rm 2:1–3:28)? The path to love begins with recognizing the universal condition of fallen human nature as described in the Word, then repentance that the Word works in us, then regeneration by the Spirit of God, who loves us and loves others through us (Rm 3:10–18; Ezk 18:21–32; Lk 7:36–50; Jn 8:3–11).

Q 4:9–12 These verses speak of mutual charity. Is a part of it saying that one should do charity for others and not expect to get something in return?

Christians love because they are loved by God first (1Jn 4:19). Christians give all they are and have because they have been given all things by God (1Co 3:21–4:2). A Christian life is not and cannot be lived in order to get what it lacks, for it lacks nothing except the experience of giving all on behalf of others, as Christ did for us (Jn 13:3–17).

Doing charity is good because that is what God does. God is gracious and charitable because our lives depend on it and because everyone benefits by true charity, the giver as well as the one given to.

● ● ● ● ● ● ● ● ● ● ● ● ● ● ● ● ● ● ● ●

Q 4:10 Why should we love more?

For as many reasons as there are people, situations, times, and places that need more love. Both Paul and Peter speak in terms of adding one virtue to another (Rm 5:3–5; 12:4–21; 2Pt 1:2–8). Since we are composed of two contrary natures, a fallen human nature that is unloving and a regenerate that is loving, if we are not adding to the strength of the loving soul, the unloving flesh will be taking love away (Rm 6:1–23; Gal 5:16–26; Col 3:1–16).

● ● ● ● ● ● ● ● ● ● ● ● ● ● ● ● ● ● ● ●

Q 4:11–12 We work and toil to support ourselves, yet the Bible tells us that women should let their man support them. Why is that, and why won't some Christian men let their wives stand up on their own two feet?

Every Christian man, after the image of Christ Himself, wants every other person to realize and thrive in the life God has prepared for them (Eph 2:10). You may also consider that this letter, like the rest of the Bible, was directed at men in the first place because God created men to be responsible for the care and well-being of women. Paul is telling the men to work with their own hands rather than expecting others, especially women, to support them. The reason women "work and toil" to support themselves is because men have abandoned their responsibility (Gn 2:7–3:16). The purpose of men is to provide an environment in which women may safely pursue and develop the gifts God has given them, especially as those gifts apply to family and the home (Pr 31; Ti 2:1–8). The question is not about standing on your own two feet but about where you will take that stand. Neither God nor any Christian man would have you take that stand because you have been abandoned to a life of threat and abuse (1Tm 5:8; Mal 2:13–16). God has given the life of His own Son, and Christian men would give their lives in order to see women live theirs to the fullest.

● ● ● ● ● ● ● ● ● ● ● ● ● ● ● ● ● ● ● ●

Q 4:11 How should this apply to our lives? Does this mean we should quit a job in certain circumstances? Why does Paul instruct the Thessalonians to lead a quiet life? Shouldn't they spread the Gospel?

Let's begin with a passage from Isaiah that describes the Christ: "He will not cry aloud or lift up His voice, or make it heard in the street" (42:2). Proverbs says "a soft answer turns away wrath, but a harsh word stirs up anger" (15:1), and James wrote that we should be "quick to hear, slow to speak, slow to anger" (1:19). If we are going to let our light shine in this way, so that others see it and give glory to our Father who is in heaven, we would have to conduct ourselves in a way that did not attract attention to ourselves but to God (Mt 5:16). It is selfish, materialistic, vain, and artificial work that depends on noise to gain a following and support. The substantive work of loving others according to God's design and their need is a very quiet but lasting work because it treats body and soul for real benefits in time and eternity (Jn 4:13–14; Rv 14:13).

Q 4:12 Is it a sin to be dependent on someone?

That depends on who you are. We are all dependent on God, and it is a sin to be dishonest about that. To desire dependence on the devil rather than God is the worst of sins. To depend on others to the extent that you need them is not something you can help and therefore is not a sin. To make others provide for you when you have the ability to provide not only for yourself but also for others is despicable (Eph 5:25–28; 1Tm 5:8).

Q 4:13–18 Why did Paul move from sexual immorality to the end of the world? Does this section support the rapture? What is the new heaven and the new earth?

As Paul nears the conclusion of his letters, he often addresses lots of different subjects one after another, like a shopping list. Luke's record of Jesus' teaching is sometimes like this (see Lk 6). Sometimes Paul is working through a list of questions or issues one after another (1Co 1:11; 5:1; 6:1; 7:1; 8:1). It may also be that once Paul finished addressing ethical issues, his attention

naturally turned to Judgment Day and the end of the world. For questions about the rapture, please see 4:17. For questions about the new heavens and earth, please see 2Pt 3:10–13.

Q 4:13 What does Jesus mean by those who "are asleep"?

Neither life nor death is concerned essentially with our bodies' functioning because the essence of who we are is the soul, and our life is a spiritual one, even when we are having physical experiences. To "live" means to be in a positive relationship with God and others, primarily according to our soul, but this may be accompanied by the body. To "die" means to be in absence of any positive, spiritual relationship. We call an active body "alive" because it is in relationship with others. We call an inactive body "dead" because it cannot be in a relationship. The soul, which is what we are essentially, is always conscious and aware. If we are not in positive relationship with God and others, then we are dead even while we live. On the other hand, if we are in positive relationship with God and others, we are alive no matter what (Jn 11:25–26). Unbelievers, who are in the absence of positive relationship with God, are dead while they live and dead after their bodies die (like Ebenezer Scrooge from Dickens's *A Christmas Carol*). These are dead in a horrible and absolute way because hell is the absence of God. When the body of a believer stops functioning, he or she is described as "asleep" because that body will wake up again at the resurrection on the Last Day. In 1Th 5:6, Paul is using the word *sleep* to describe the state of a body being unaware, like the apostles in the Garden of Gethsemane (Mk 14:32–42). Physical sleep is a way to understand the peril of being unaware of more fundamental, spiritual events.

● ● ● ● ● ● ● ● ● ● ● ● ● ● ● ● ● ● ●

Q 4:13 Does that mean that grieving like the rest of men is wrong or sinful?

Yes, grieving like unbelievers is sinful and a shame since God has taken away our reason to grieve through the life, death, and resurrection of Christ. This does not mean that Christians are not supposed to grieve at all, for many things in a fallen world are very grievous. But we do not grieve as those who have no hope in two ways. Christians know that God, in Christ, has made death the path to life. While we are sad to be separated from loved ones and sad for the human condition that brings death, God has redeemed us and takes us to Himself through death (Jn 14:1–4; Rm 6:4–7; 1Co 15:35–58; 2Co 4:16–7). Christians are free to live for the sake of others, which means we want to make the best possible witness to the world when there is a death (Mt 5:13–16; 1Pt 3:15).

● ● ● ● ● ● ● ● ● ● ● ● ● ● ● ● ● ● ●

Q 4:13 When Jesus was hanging on the cross, He said to the thief, "Today you will be with Me in Paradise" (Lk 23:43). It

seems as though this verse conflicts with His words.

This verse and Jesus' words to the thief on the cross do not conflict. When a person dies in the grace of God, the body ceases but the soul joins Christ in paradise, just as Jesus said. At the end of the world on Judgment Day, God will raise all the dead, give new bodies to the faithful who have been waiting in heaven or still living on earth, and restore them to live forever on a new earth under a new heaven (1Co 15:35–57; 1Jn 3:2; 2Pt 3:10–14). Those who had despised the grace of God and rejected Christ, either in hell or still on the earth, will be cast into the lake of fire forever (Rv 20:11–15; Mt 25:41–46).

● ● ● ● ● ● ● ● ● ● ● ● ● ● ● ● ● ● ●

Q 4:14 Who are those "fallen asleep" in him?

Those who "sleep in Jesus" are people who have a physical body that has ceased but whose souls live on in paradise. These people will be granted a new body in the resurrection of the dead on the Last Day and will live in the new earth, in perfection, forever (1Co 15:35–57; 1Jn 3:2; 2Pt 3:10–14). Please see 4:13 above for more on this question.

● ● ● ● ● ● ● ● ● ● ● ● ● ● ● ● ● ● ●

Q 4:15 What does "by a word from the Lord" mean? How are we to understand the use of the term "we"?

Paul was careful in his writing to distinguish between sayings that the Lord Jesus had given directly to the apostles and sayings of the apostles that were true and inspired by the Holy Spirit, but had not been said by the Lord Himself (1Co 7:10, 12; 1Tm 3:16). In other passages, "we" would refer to Paul and his travel companions, such as Luke, Silas, and Timothy (1Th 1:1). In this case, since Paul is talking about conveying the Word of the Lord, he is referring to himself and the other apostles (Mk 16:16; 1Th 2:13; 2Pt 1:16–21; 1Jn 1:1–4).

• • • • • • • • • • • • • • • • • • • •

Q **4:16–18 Who are "the dead in Christ"? If the dead rise first, are we all left behind then? Is this where many people get the idea of the rapture? Does this mean our souls do not go directly to heaven when we die? How will we be caught up? Will marriage be recognized in this "new heaven"? Will we see the ones that died before us when we all go to the new heaven?**

The "dead in Christ" are all the people who "died" in respect to their human nature but who live on because their souls were regenerated by the Word and Spirit of God. These are all the faithful people from Adam and Eve, Abel and Noah, David and Daniel—everyone who lived and believed in the grace of God. The Bible sometimes refers to these as being "asleep," as Paul does in v. 15. Jesus proved that such are not dead according to their essence, or soul, by raising them from the dead (Mk 5:35–43; Jn 11:1–44; Ac 20:7–12; see 4:14 above for more).

No one gets left behind. Paul describes an order of priority but not of chronology, for the whole resurrection happens in a moment, in a twinkling of the eye (1Co 15:51–52). All people who died according to their human nature but who live on with Christ in paradise in their soul will be resurrected first, then all other believers will rise, and all unbelievers who have already died and gone to hell will be gathered up along with unbelievers who were still "alive" on the earth and will be cast into the lake of fire for all eternity (Rv 20:13–15). There is no reason for God to resurrect the bodies of unbelievers since they will spend eternity in the lake of fire.

This is the passage that people who talk about the rapture claim as their basis. The word *rapture* is based on a French word that was based on the Latin translation of the New Testament. The Latin word translated "rapture" means "to be seized, taken, or kidnapped." The Greek word that Paul used, *harpadzo*, means "to snatch up or carry away." The point is that people will be caught up suddenly into the sky, as most English translations make clear. The teaching that this event is a preliminary Judgment Day with more to follow and a warning to those who are hypocrites or still unbelievers is mistaken for several reasons. First, there is no partial judgment or sequence of judgment days. As Christ came once in His incarnation and died once for all, having borne away the sins of the world, so Christ will come only once more, at the end of the world. The idea that there needs

637

to be time for unbelievers to have a second chance is contrary to the Gospel of Christ, who redeemed all so that no second chances are needed. Second, Paul concludes this passage by saying, "Therefore encourage one another with these words" (v. 18). Paul wanted us to know that no believer will be missed, overlooked, or mistakenly gathered up with the unbelievers (a point that Revelation makes over and over again, cf. 7:3; 9:4). However, the teaching of being left behind that is based on a mistaken notion of rapture is intended to terrify people, contrary to Paul's expressed intent.

I don't think there is any way of knowing how all this takes place, in terms of physical dynamics, except to say that the same God who created and sustains the universe will gather to Himself all of His people and cast away all those who despised Him (Mt 13:44–50). The resurrection itself, as mentioned above, takes place in a moment (1Co 15:51–52). The judgment itself seems to take some time in order that the faithful make clear confession that they have been saved by God's grace and that the unfaithful, even in judgment, argue against the truth and suffer accordingly for all eternity (Mt 25:31–46; Lk 16:19–31). Apparently we will recognize one another, since the rich man recognized both Abraham and Lazarus (Lk 16:23). We will not marry nor be given in marriage in life everlasting, as Jesus made clear in His response to the Sadducees who didn't believe in any resurrection at all (Mt 22:23–33).

● ● ● ● ● ● ● ● ● ● ● ● ● ● ● ● ● ● ● ●

Q **5:1 What does God think about those who are scared by these end times verses?**

We must be careful not to speculate about what God thinks. He has provided the thoughts He wants us to know in His Word and in the life of His Son, Jesus Christ (Is 55:6–13; Jer 29:11; Jn 1:18; 1Co 2:11). Jesus responded to the fears of His apostles about the end on Maundy Thursday evening with powerful words of assurance (Jn 14:1–6). Solomon said, over and over again, that the fear of the Lord is the beginning of wisdom (Pr 1:7). Mary, the mother of Jesus, said that God's mercy is upon those who fear Him (Lk 1:50). Paul anticipated our fear of the coming judgment of God and said, in the preceding verse, that we should comfort, or encourage, one another with the truth about Jesus' return on Judgment Day. A person is aware of doubts and fears because he is honest with himself about the truth. Such honesty is necessary for genuine repentance and the working of the Spirit of God, which regenerates a soul that trusts in God and lives in peace (Ezk 18:24–32; Jn 18:31–32; 20:19–31).

● ● ● ● ● ● ● ● ● ● ● ● ● ● ● ● ● ● ●

Q **5:2 Where did the term "the day of the Lord" come from?**

The prophets used this in the Old Testament, where it refers to God's judgment against all the wicked who oppose His will (Is 2:12; 13:6, 9; Jer 25:33; Ezk 30:3; Jl 3:4 [which is quoted in Ac 2:20]; Am 5:18). In the New Testament, Jesus uses the term to refer to His second coming on Judgment Day (Mt 24:42). Paul and Peter use this expression in the same way Jesus did (1Co 1:8; 5:5; 2Co 1:14; 2Th 2:2; 2Pt 3:8, 10).

. . . .

Q 5:5–8 What is Paul's intent in comparing night and day?

Day has to do with light and night with darkness and the absence of light. Light reveals things for what they are and provides heat and energy for life; thus light is a witness to God as the source of truth and life (Jn 1:1–5). Darkness hides and allows danger to hide; thus darkness is a witness to the effect of lies, cold, and lifelessness (Jn 3:17–21). People are awake, aware, and productive during the day; people are asleep, unaware, and unproductive in the night (Jn 9:4; 11:9–10). Jesus is the Son of God and the light of the world; therefore anyone regenerated by His Word is a son or daughter of light, which means we live in the service of truth and work while there is time for the lives and well-being of others (2Co 5:14–21). Those who are determined to contradict God with their life avoid the truth and any other circumstance that would expose the lies they live and promote (Rm 1:18–32).

. . . .

Q 5:9 If we are not to suffer wrath, why do we suffer from the temptations of sin? What does wrath mean in this context?

God's will has always been that His creation live to the fullest according to His design; this is why He commands what is right and forbids what is wrong (Gn 2:15–17; Dt 30:11–20; Ezk 18:32). Everyone whom God has chosen will never know the wrath of God or even taste death because God provided Jesus as our substitute (Mk 15:6–15; Jn 8:51–52; Ac 3:14–15; 2Co 5:21). There are many causes of suffering in our lives, but none is punishment for our sins as we deserve (Ps 103:10). Temptations can only make us suffer if we give in to them, feel sorry for ourselves at having to resist, or simply miss the point (Mt 4:1–11; Heb 2:10–17; Jas 1:12–15). In this context, "wrath" refers to the wrath of God against everyone and everything that seeks to ruin His creation and the life He intends that creation to know. That wrath will be executed on Judgment Day only against those who despise Christ, who rescued us from that wrath, and only because they insist on provoking God to wrath with their rebellion against life and grace (Lk 14:16–24; Jn 3:34–36).

. . . .

Q 5:10 Is Paul talking of "asleep" in the same context as the previous verses in saying "let us not sleep [sin] as others do" (v. 6)? If so, is he saying even as we are amidst sin or have fallen away (briefly) from God that we're still fine?

Paul is talking to the believers in Thessalonica and includes himself when he says, "whether we are awake or asleep." Being a believer depends entirely on living in communion with Christ through the Word (Jn 8:31–32; Ac 2:42). In the first and most literal sense, Paul is relieving Christians from fear of what might happen to them if He comes while they are sleeping in their beds (Ps 4:8; 127:2). It is possible that Paul also means to include the sense of physical life or death. Whether we are alive in our bodies here in the world or our bodies are in the grave, our regenerate soul is living and well in communion with the Lord. Paul is probably not talking about sleep in the sense of being inattentive or careless, and certainly not morally unconscious, as all of Scripture warns against these (Ps 13:3; 24:33; Mk 14:37–41).

Q 5:15 How does this verse apply to capital punishment?

Capital punishment prohibits one person from returning evil for evil. Only those authorized by God may execute capital punishment, only for capital crimes, and only after confirming on the basis of two or more witnesses that a person deserves capital punishment (Rm 13:1–4; Mt 5:38–48; 18:16; Dt 19:1–20; Heb 10:28). Capital punishment keeps people from being discouraged or enraged by those who commit capital crimes. Rather, we may be sympathetic toward them, pray, and hope that the judgment that came as a result of their action may result in repentance and faith, as it did for the thief on the cross (Lk 23:40–43).

> Are we supposed to spend all our time praying?

Q 5:17 How does someone "pray without ceasing"? Are we supposed to spend all our time praying?

Paul commands that we "pray without ceasing," and this language is simple. You raise a reasonable question, which the principles of biblical interpretation anticipate. How could a person possibly pray without ceasing? What about when we are asleep? How are we to obey the other commands of the New Testament if all we do is pray? These questions require us to consider understanding the text in a different way. To suggest that Paul doesn't really mean literally without ceasing would cause us to question what other commands he is not serious about. No help there. Is it possible that by "prayer," Paul means to include the whole Christian consciousness that is in communion with God? We know that the Holy Spirit intercedes for us in prayer and so does the Lord Jesus (Rm 8:26–27; Heb 7:25). We also know that we have the mind of Christ according to our regenerate soul (Php 2:5). If our thoughts of appreciation toward God, recognition of the wonders of His work and creation, confessions in our own heart and mind, and desires of our heart are all considered forms of prayer, then a Christian who remains in the Word is praying without ceasing since the Spirit of the Lord is always with him (Ps 37:4; Col 3:1–16).

Q **5:19 Is Paul warning against worship that discourages expression of the gifts of the Spirit, or something else? Can the Spirit's power ever be put out?**

The Spirit's power cannot be put out since the Holy Spirit is true God. It is possible for people to blaspheme and grieve the Holy Spirit (Mt 12:31–32; Eph 4:30). The obstinate and contrary disposition of people kept Jesus from doing mighty works in their midst, so the same would be true of the Holy Spirit's work (Mt 13:58). I would not confine Paul's imperative to worship. In this last little flurry of advice and warnings, Paul is addressing the importance of discerning what we should welcome from what we should reject. We can see what "quenching the Spirit" is by observing the religious leaders as they despise, reject, and seek to contradict both Jesus and the apostles throughout the Gospels and Acts.

Q **5:21 What do they mean by "test everything"?**

John wrote that we should test the spirits to see if they are of God (1Jn 4:1). In the Old Testament, God had warned Israel about false prophets and had given them means for testing those who claimed to speak for God. A false prophet would be exposed if his word contradicted the Word God had already given or if what he prophesied did not come true (Dt 13:1–5; 18:20–22). Here, Paul is expanding that thought to include all things that matter in life, but especially ideas, trends, teachings, customs, and practices.

Q **5:23–24 I feel these words are very powerful. Are these words meant for all people or just those who believe in God?**

Paul is directing this blessing to the believers in Thessalonica (1:1), and this kind of blessing is fulfilled by the Lord in everyone who remains in His Word and grace through death into life everlasting. On the other hand, Paul certainly wants this to be true for all people, even as Jesus commanded that the Gospel should be preached to every creature (Mk 16:16; 1Co 9:16–23).

Q **5:26 What does Paul mean by a "holy kiss"?**

A holy kiss, in the first place, would be given for the sake of the other person, not for one's own gratification or in the interest of igniting any sinful passion (1Co 7:1; 1Th 4:5). A holy kiss, in the second place, would be given most likely on the cheek and in public as a demonstration of loving interest and hospitality. This understanding of what a kiss is intended to mean is what made Jesus' betrayal by Judas so hypocritical (Lk 22:48).

2 Thessalonians

Q **1:3 How long after 1 Thessalonians did Paul write the second letter?**

Paul wrote 1 Thessalonians in the spring of AD 51. Paul wrote this second letter in the fall of the same year—six months or so later.

• • • • • • • • • • • • • • • • • •

Q **1:6 Does this verse indicate that God will not only allow bad things to happen to us, but bring them upon us when we "trouble" others? Or is Paul only referring to eternal justice in the form of heaven and hell?**

There are laws of nature that God established in order to support life in His creation. One aspect of the laws of nature has to do with equilibrium or balance, which is related to justice. Isaac Newton observed that for every action, there is an equal and opposite reaction. Jesus said that if you live by the sword, you will die by the sword (Mt 26:52). Our culture recognizes the same truth but says things such as "What goes around comes around." Notice that Paul says "it [is] just" to repay. Therefore, the justice and equity of God and His creation means that a person who troubles others will bring trouble upon himself. God established the Law to teach us the consequences of our errors and faults in this life so we might repent of them and know forgiveness now, without having to suffer eternally for these sins (Gal 3:24). If a person is determined to contradict God's Word and witness in creation, then he will also find eternal consequences for the same (Mt 23:13–36; 25:41–46; Rm 1:18–32; Rv 14:8–13).

• • • • • • • • • • • • • • • • • • • •

Q 1:7 When will Christ be "revealed" as described in this passage?

Paul is talking about the revelation of Jesus Christ on the Last Day or Judgment Day. No one knows when this will be, not even Jesus, but only God the Father (Mk 13:32; Ac 1:6–7).

• • • • • • • • • • • • • • • • • • • •

Q 1:11 It sounds like there is a lot of emphasis on "you" and not God. What is the reason for this?

Paul talks about "you" twice in this verse: once as the object of Paul's prayers and once as the object of God's grace. Paul talks about God in four ways: (1) that God would count you worthy of calling, (2) that God would fulfill His good pleasure, (3) that God acts according to His goodness, and (4) that God accomplished the work of faith and power in our lives. If there is a lot of emphasis on the people to whom a letter is addressed, such as in 1 Peter, it is because they are in distress and need to know how the things of God apply to them. In this case, there is some distress from persecution and confusion about end times, but this verse still seems very focused on God.

• • • • • • • • • • • • • • • • • • • •

Q 2:2 Is this the verse some religious groups believe indicates that the Messiah has not yet come? Paul refers to "the day of the Lord" as Judgment Day. Is this the echo of the phrase "the Day of the Lord" in Joel, for example, or is the phrase about the Messiah and the Judgment Day new?

If there are groups out there who don't believe the Messiah has yet come, this would certainly be a verse to which they could refer. The only religious group I know of that doesn't believe the Messiah has come would be the Jewish people, but they aren't interested in the New Testament. If Paul is talking about the coming of "our Lord Jesus Christ" (v. 1), he can only be referring to His second coming—otherwise no one would know who the Lord Jesus Christ is.

The "day of the Lord" is referring to Judgment Day and is more than an echo from Joel since Peter quotes Joel in his sermon on the day of Pentecost (Ac 2:16–21). Please see 1 Th 5:2 for more on "the day of the Lord."

• • • • • • • • • • • • • • • • • • • •

Q 2:2 Who would be sending word to the church claiming that the "day of the Lord" had already come? Why is there always someone proclaiming the end of the world?

There is no end to the people or teachings that mean to contradict the truth (Rv 12:15–17). The people who were troubling the Christians in Thessalonica may have promoted ideas that would later be known as Gnosticism. The word *Gnosticism* comes from a Greek word for knowledge (*gnosis*). The idea is that the material world all around us isn't real or doesn't matter; what matters is what you think and what goes on in your head. These people pointed to Jesus, who was against materialism. They thought that Jesus' disappearance after He was crucified meant that the Messiah had come and shown the way to a life free of material concerns. They could not see why we should expect the Messiah to come back a second time or why we should hope for a new earth and resurrected body when Jesus had shown us the way to transcend material things. In their minds, the Messiah had come and established His kingdom by way of knowledge—and that was it. They give a whole different meaning to Jesus' exclamation from the cross, "It is finished." However, if the material world is inherently evil or doesn't exist, why did God create it, record its creation, sustain this creation, and most of all, take on human flesh and raise that body from the dead?

Like the religious leaders of Jesus' time, there are always people who want to satisfy their lusts by controlling other people.

Why is there always someone proclaiming the end of the world?

Claiming to have "figured out" when the end of the world will be gets the attention of people who are fearful. Fearful people do not challenge self-appointed religious leaders who make such claims because they assume these leaders know more than they do. Challenging such leaders, fearful people believe, could only result in being humiliated by the vast power and knowledge of such leaders or, even worse, in being shut out of the kingdom of God that is coming so soon (Mt 24:3–36; 2Co 11:13–16; Jude 12–19; 3 Jn 9–11).

Q 2:3–12 Is the "man of lawlessness" Christ revealing the end of the world or is he some type of antichrist? What is the rebellion Paul talks about?

The "man of lawlessness" is not Christ in any way but is exposed by Christ as a threat and as a sign of the end times. This person is not the devil himself since Paul says he comes according to the activity of Satan (v. 9). It seems possible that there will often, if not always, be a person who stands out as fulfilling the description given here, while at the same time there are plenty of other people, philosophies, trends, and movements that are also lawless and opposed to Christ (Jn 8:44–45; Col 2:8; 1Jn 2:18–19). The rebellion that Paul mentions in v. 3 may be recognized to some extent in every generation since Paul wrote this letter, just as John wrote of the Antichrist and of many antichrists. The falling away or rebellion that is unparalleled in history followed the Age of Enlightenment, or Rationalism (see Mk 13:14 and Rv 11:7–10 for more about this).

•••••••••••••••••••••

Q 2:3–4 What distinguishes this antichrist from the many which are talked about in John?

Nothing; Paul and John are talking about the same thing that Jesus warned of in Mk 13:14 (1Jn 2:18–19).

•••••••••••••••••••••

Q 2:4 Is this verse talking about the antichrist?

This is, by definition, a description of the antichrist since this "man of lawlessness" opposes all that God is and does. The antichrist or man of lawlessness not only opposes God but seeks to take God's place. This person (and people with the same determination) work to displace God as the authority over all and to replace His Word and the truth with their own words and deception. This person (these people) takes the glory and honor that belongs to God for himself and holds people under his control for his own gratification (Jn 8:43–44; 2 Co 11:13–21). For more on this, please see related questions at Mk 13:14 and in Revelation.

•••••••••••••••••••••

Q 2:6–7 What or who is holding back the lawless one?

The Son of God is holding back the antichrist/man of lawlessness, and He does so

with His Word. Revelation 20 is a parallel to this account, where an angel binds the dragon with a great chain for a thousand years. This "thousand years" refers to the time from the first coming of Christ, when the Word became flesh and dwelt among us, through most of the time remaining until Christ comes again. Revelation provides yet another view, in this case indicating the Word of God by way of those who communicated His Word (Rv 11:3–7). The Gospels provide witness to many occasions where we can see the Word of God in the person of Jesus "binding" the work of the devil by His sheer presence as the way, truth, and life and by the word of power that proceeded from His mouth (Mk 1:34; 5:6–20; 12:28–40).

•••••••••••••••••••••

Q 2:9–12 Does God give up on people and actively oppose them? What is this delusion that God sends, and why does He send it? Why does it seem like God is trying to trick us in this passage? I thought that He was putting off the day until He came again so that no one would perish and we would all repent, but this sounds like God is going to not try and save us and just get rid of all those who do not believe in Him.

God does not give up on people, because He is love, and the mercy of the Lord is everlasting toward those who fear Him (1Jn 4:8; Ps 103:17). God is opposed to people who are determined to destroy their own lives and the lives of others (Ne 13:2; Jer 21:13; 23:30–32; 50:31; Na 2:13; 3:5). God actively opposes all fallen human nature with the Law in order to keep it in check and eventually, through death, to put an end to that source of opposition (Gn 3:17; Ezk 18:4, 30–32; Rm 3:19). For the faithful, God will raise up a new body on the Last Day that will be in perfect union with God's will for eternity. God actively opposes fallen souls by regenerating them in the image of Christ (Jn 1:12–13; 3:1–7).

If a person is steadfastly determined in body and soul to despise, hate, reject, and resist God's workings for them to live, their condemnation may begin here and now. The signs of condemnation are another powerful witness that they should repent, but if they do not, their impenitence grows even worse as they harden their heart against the love and grace of God (Ex 4:21–23; 7:1–14:30; Rm 1:18–32). The delusion that God sends is what Paul describes in Rm 1 as "gave them up" to their own wicked thoughts (vv. 24, 26, 28). Letting people have their own way when they demonstrate over a long time that they insist on having it so is just, though tragic.

God is patient and long-suffering, not wanting any to perish. This is why the end of the world is so long in coming (2Pt 3:9). At the same time, God is concerned that He not be so patient that the faithful are overwhelmed by the wickedness of those who hate God (Mk 13:20).

God desires all to be saved and come to the knowledge of the truth (1Tm 2:4). God has, in fact, saved everyone of every time and place in the crucifixion of His own Son (Jn 3:16; 2Co 5:21). God works through nature, His Word, the witness of people, circumstances, reason, and our own conscience to bring us to repentance and regeneration (Ps 19:1–3; 119:105; Rm 1:16; Heb 4:12; Jer 35:15; Jnh 1:4–10; Rm 2:11–16; 6:20–21).

- -

Q 2:9 "False signs and wonders" have been around throughout history. Is this all a foreshadowing of the end of the world?

There have been counterfeit miracles, signs, and wonders for as long as there have been the devil, demons, and people who would gladly serve the devil's purposes (Ex 7:11–13, 22–23; Ac 8:9; 13:6–11; 2Co 11:13–15; Rv 13:13–15). One possible indication of the end of the world that would come from these forces of deception has to do with their effectiveness among people as the end of the world draws near (Mk 13:21–23; Rm 1:18–32; 2Tm 4:3–4; Rv 11:7–11). People have always been deceived, but never has so much of the population been deceived, lived in contempt of the Word of God and truth, and been so determined to have it so (Ps 12:8; Lk 21:5–28; Rm 1:32).

- -

Q 2:13 Could this be read as works-righteousness? Doesn't God want all people to be saved?

Works-righteousness is opposed by every word of the Bible, including this verse. Paul explains that God chose us from the beginning and brought the effects of that choice into our lives by the Spirit's work of setting us apart (sanctifying us) and causing us to be honest about our dependence on God (belief). No one is lost because God has not chosen him, for God desires all to be saved and has redeemed all in Christ (Ezk 18:32; 1Tm 2:4; Jn 3:16; 2Co 5:21). If a person is lost, it can only be due to his or her own determined, persistent, conscious, and willful opposition to God's grace in Christ (Jn 3:18–20; Rm 1:18–32). These truths are clearly revealed, endure, and cannot be contradicted. The person who is fearful may take consolation because it is God's will and choice that he or she realize the salvation Christ has accomplished (Mt 11:28–30; 1Pt 1:3–9). Any person who would blame God for not choosing someone would have to explain what makes him or her think God hasn't. Thus, the only person who would suffer under the assumption that he or she is rejected by God would be the person who insists he or she is not chosen, which is not what God has said.

Q 2:15 Was there a problem with the people not standing firm in their faith?

Fallen human nature is opposed to standing firm in the truth and in honesty about our dependence upon it. History provides a powerful and irrefutable witness to this fact (Gn 2:15–3:12; Ex 32:1–8; Jgs 17:6; Mal 1:11–13; Gal 1:6). Paul is especially concerned about the Thessalonians because the Jews who made such trouble that Paul had to leave were likely to cause trouble for those who had come to faith by Paul's ministry (Ac 17:5–9; 1Th 3:1–5). There were others who attempted to cause fear and confusion among the believers, and Paul is concerned about that as well (2Th 1:6–7; 2:1–3). No matter when we live, the devil will always be prowling about seeking whom he may devour; the world will seek to overwhelm us; and our own fallen human nature will be contrary to the truth (Eph 2:1–3; 1Pt 5:8). Therefore it is imperative—and the Bible is full of imperatives—that we be watchful and stand firm in the truth (Ezk 33:1–7; Mt 7:24–27; Lk 12:39–40; Jn 8:31–32; Gal 5:1).

Q 3:6 It says to "keep away" from those not in accord with the apostolic teaching. As Christians, are we not supposed to turn their lives toward God and teach them?

The key is in the word *brother*. On the one hand, we are called to be ambassadors for Christ on behalf of all who do not know Him (2Co 5:20). This is why Paul was determined to be all things to all people, so that he might by all means reach out to all people with the truth and grace of God (1Co 9:19–23). We must associate with unbelievers if they are to hear the Gospel, and we can do so without causing confusion, not as if we approved of a life without God or were in communion with those who do not know Him. On the other hand, if we associate with people who claim to be Christian but openly and consistently contradict God's

Word and will, then we would cause terrible confusion. The seriousness of the matter has to do with hypocrisy. Unbelievers who act as such are not deceiving anyone, nor do they care to. People who pretend to be Christian but are contrary in their thoughts and actions intend to deceive and do great harm to themselves and others (Jn 12:4–6; 13:2). Christianity is about honesty that brings life. Hypocrisy is about dishonesty that works death, which is why it is such a danger and is warned about so severely (Ac 5:1–11; 1Co 5:1–13).

Q **3:7–8 Paul almost sounds as if he is laying a guilt trip on the Thessalonians. What's the point of saying it this way that makes them sound lazy?**

Paul is not comparing himself to or criticizing the Thessalonians. He has already praised them in many ways in both letters (1Th 1:2–3, 7–8; 2:13–14, 19; 4:9; 2Th 1:3–4; 2:13). In these verses, Paul is drawing a contrast between himself and other authentic apostles and servants of the Word on the one hand and false teachers on the other (Gal 6:12; 2Co 11:2–12; Jn 10:10–14). Paul points out that one of the ways you can know a servant of the truth and grace of God is that he is truly a servant, coming only to give, not to take. False teachers try to make themselves authorities over the lives of others so that they can be in control and take what belongs to others for themselves.

Q **3:6–14 This section mentions that it is not good to "eat anyone's bread without paying for it." How does that relate to being a college kid whose parents pay for a lot of your well-being?**

The answer to your question depends on what kind of student you are. If you are still dependent on your parents as a full-time student, then the time you spend in class and in your studies is work, preparing you for a lifetime of service to others. Your lifetime of service in the future is a return on the investment your parents made by providing you the opportunity to study. On the other hand, if you are going to college so that others pay for your life while you throw it away, then this warning of Paul is for you. The heart of the Gospel is that God provides for us absolutely so that we are free to give our lives in the service of others. Pretending to be something we are not—whether that would be as a Christian, church worker, or student—in order to take from others rather than give is a lie that does injury to everyone, but to the liar most of all (Ac 5:1–11).

Q **3:11 What does it mean here that some people were idle?**

The word translated "idleness" or "busybodies" occurs only here in the New Testament. Paul appears to be making a play on words as first he says these people are not *ergadzomenous* (working) but *peri-ergadzomenous* (pretending to work =

"busy bodies" = idle). You can usually tell the difference between people who have real work to do and are really doing it and people who have real work to do but are only pretending to work at it, or who have nothing real to do but try to make what they are doing look real.

. . . .

Q 3:11–13 Are the unemployed undisciplined and sinful for their unemployment?

Like Jesus, we want to always look beneath the surface to see if there is a real problem or no problem (Jn 7:24). There is all the difference in the world between being unemployed and being idle or a busybody. A person may be unemployed for various reasons he or she has no control over, yet that person continues to serve others, working at tasks that need to be done and being good stewards of time and resources until employment comes. Another person may be happy to use unemployment as an excuse to do nothing, even though there is always plenty to do in our world (Mt 20:1–16; 24:42–51; 25:14–46).

. . . .

Q 3:14 Wouldn't refusing to talk to certain church members as Paul commands lead to disunity and factions in the Church? Aren't we supposed to have fellowship among believers?

Genuine fellowship or communion among people is not something we do or make happen; only God can create true communion among people (1Jn 1:7). If we pretend to have fellowship when we do not, we are contradicting the truth to the harm of ourselves and others (Lv 19:17; 1Co 5:1–13; 1Jn 2:4). When Jesus came to Jairus's house, people who insisted they were good and religious were there, making a great show of their grief for his daughter who had died and for the family. But these people making a show were not believers, and Jesus put them out of the house (Mk 5:35–41). We must be careful here so that we don't confuse hypocrisy with being penitent sinners. We don't refuse communion with people who are sinners since that would exclude us all. We do refuse to associate with those who refuse to admit their sin, refuse to admit that what they are actively doing is sin, or refuse to hear the truth about their sin while they still insist that they are Christian (1Jn 1:8–9).

1 Timothy

Q 1:8 How do you keep the Law lawfully or unlawfully?

Paul is talking about how the Law is misused by some who presume to be teachers (1:6–7). Everything that God made is good, but anything can be misused contrary to His will (Rm 1:18–32). A knife can kill when used by an evil person or provide for healing when used by a surgeon. As a knife is good if used medicinally, so the Law is good if it is used lawfully (according to God's intent for it). The purpose of the Law is to reveal the truth that points us to Christ (Gal 3:24).

Q 1:9 How do we know who the righteous and unrighteous are? Don't the righteous and the sinners need the Law too? Isn't this talking about those who have been made righteous because of what God has done for them?

Here we must distinguish between civil and spiritual righteousness, between fallen human nature and a regenerate soul. In civilizations, it is true that the laws are not enacted for good people but for evil ones. A regenerate soul, like a good citizen, does not need the Law because it is already doing what the Law commands (Rm 13:10; 1Jn 3:9). Yet every person has a fallen human nature that needs the Law to serve as a curb, mirror, and rule for life.

Why does Paul tell women not to braid their hair?

Q **1:13 If Paul was a member of the Pharisees, how can he claim to be ignorant of who the Messiah was?**

In this verse, Paul equates ignorance with unbelief. Living according to the passions and blindness of fallen human nature is one thing; knowing what the truth is and then consciously, tenaciously striving to oppose it is quite another (Mt 12:31–32; Jn 9:39–41; Rm 1:18–32; Heb 6:4–8; 10:26–31).

Q **1:20 Is this where we get our model for excommunication? What does Paul mean when he said "Hymenaeus and Alexander, whom I have handed over to Satan"?**

Our model for excommunication comes from Mt 18:15–18 (see also 1Co 5:1–13; 2Co 2:6–8). Paul uses the language of handing someone over to Satan in 1Co 5. When someone refuses to be warned or corrected, it is just and often effective to leave such a person to his or her own determination. If a person is determined to despise God's truth and grace, then such a person is left with the devil and his ways. Notice that Paul refers to the devil as "Satan," which means "accuser." If a person refuses God, who forgives, he is left with Satan, who accuses.

Q **2:8 Why do Lutheran pastors not participate in public prayer services?**

The problem with joining in religious services is that they are in public, which either confuses people about what to believe or leads them to conclude that what a person believes does not matter. In private, day-to-day circumstances, we want to have conversations with others about what we believe and why (Mt 28:19–20; 1Co 5:9–12). In public, we want to be careful to provide a clear witness to the truth by joining for services with others who are committed to the truth just as we are (Rm 16:17–18).

Q **2:9–10 Why does Paul tell women not to braid their hair? Should this still apply in today's society? How do women "adorn themselves with good works"? Should men also dress modestly? Did Paul intend these verses to be followed literally or symbolically?**

The concept behind these verses is essential for applying them to our lives. First, notice that in the previous verse, Paul talks to men who pray "in every place." The concept, based on God's design in creation, is that men are responsible to provide for and protect. Women are provided for and protected so they might do the same in bearing and raising children (Gn 2:7–25; 1Co 11:3). The complement of men engaging the world in public is women who dress modestly in order to keep them protected from the evils that prowl in public. The point, therefore, of what Paul says to women in this verse is that women should not present themselves in public in a way that draws unwanted attention. The attention a Christian woman wants is the same as the attention we all want and depend upon from Christ (Eph 5:25–27). Christian men, like women, want to dress and present themselves in a way that does not attract attention but supports our intent to direct people's attention to God (Mt 5:16).

• •

Q 2:11–12 Do these verses mean that men should be in charge of all organizations, clubs, companies, and so forth? What if a woman won't be quiet? Is there a time when a man should be submissive? How can congregations read this and follow what the Word says, but still have women pastors in good faith?

Men were designed by God to support and protect women. That support and protection provides for women so they might provide for and protect children. Men deal with matters in the world outside the home so women are at liberty to deal with the world inside the home. Activities of men or women that are consistent with this ideal are helpful. Activity contrary to this design brings challenges and difficulties. The Christian Church always remembers that we are not trying to justify ourselves or our conduct, but having been justified by grace, we seek to recapture the design of God for us and the blessings inherent in that design.

If a woman won't be quiet, we would pursue that challenge in the same way that we pursue any other problem, by pursuing the truth and grace of God according to His Word. Everyone except God the Father is submissive in some way (1Co 11:3; Eph 5:21).

Some congregations, like the population in general, treat the Bible as if it were only a record of human thought from old times. Therefore, they embrace what appeals to them and reject or ignore the rest.

• •

Q 2:11–15 What exactly is Paul trying to get across here? He makes it seem as though the women are the only ones to blame for the fall and that their only purpose is childbearing.

The language here can be understood in two ways. One way assumes a negative disposition toward women: they were not first, they were deceived, they can be saved if they have children. Such a disposition yields a misreading of these verses because it betrays an attempt by men to sacrifice the women, as Adam did (Gn 3:12). The other way to read these verses begins with recognizing the relationship that God intended for male and female. Paul's reference to Adam being made first means that Adam bore full responsibility for Eve and for God's creation (Rm 5:12). The woman was deceived because her compassionate instincts make her vulnerable to such, but Adam has no such excuse. Adam knowingly and willfully abandoned his responsibility for Eve in keeping silent even while she was being deceived (1Pt 3:7). Finally, the woman is not saved because she bears children but in spite of the peril childbearing brings. Though the sons of Adam will continually abandon their responsibility for women, exposing them to peril, God has and will always provide for their lives so they may still pursue childbearing without fear (Gn 21:15–21).

Q **2:14 If man is the "head" and Adam was right there with Eve—and also ate the fruit—how can Paul make this argument against all women through Eve?**

Paul's argument clarifies that the responsibility for the fall rests with Adam, not with Eve (see answer to 2:11–15 and Rm 5:12–21).

Q **3:1 What is an "overseer"?**

The words *elder*, *presbyter*, *bishop*, *overseer*, and *teacher* in the New Testament are all referring to the pastor, who is a public, called representative of Christ. Each of these terms has a certain emphasis that describes an aspect of the pastoral office as in feeding, leading, watching over, and protecting (Jn 10:7–14; 21:15–19; Ac 20:28; 1Pt 5:1–4).

Q **3:2 Should a person be considered for the Office of the Holy Ministry if his sinful nature causes him to have problems with certain criteria listed in this verse?**

No person should be considered for the public ministry if there is a question of qualification.

Q **3:4 Does this "manage his own household" apply to wife and kids only or to parents and siblings as well?**

A man who cannot care for his own wife and children as God would have him will be unable to care for a congregation of people as he should. One of the important measures of character is consistency.

Q **3:8 What is the difference between bishops (overseers) and deacons?**

Bishops are pastors. As public representatives of Christ, they must be male. Deacons, like deaconesses, are so focused on Christian service that they are distinguished from other believers, but they do not serve in the public ministry.

Q **3:10 What does Paul mean by saying that deacons must "be tested first"?**

People often mean well, agree to responsibilities, and commit themselves to the same, but fail. Paul is saying that a person should have demonstrated his abilities before being recognized as a deacon.

Q **3:11 Does the word *wives* in this verse refer to deaconesses?**

There is disagreement about the meaning of this verse because the word here could be translated "women" or "wives" (of deacons) or perhaps "women" as the female counterpart of the deacons in v. 8. The point is that Christian women who are very visibly involved in Christian service must have a life that is consistent with the Gospel.

Q **4:1–16 Clearly this chapter was written for Timothy, a young pastor of the Church. Is it okay, then, to draw certain themes and admonishments and apply them to us (especially women)?**

Necessary qualities and activity for one who represents Christ in public are likely good for Christians to practice in our everyday life.

Q **4:1 What are these "deceitful spirits"?**

The devil is the source of deceiving spirits (Jn 8:44; 2Co 11:13–15). People of the world, the media, religious leaders, and any fallen human nature might communicate the deceit of the devil (Ps 12:8; Eph 2:1–3; 6:12; Php 3:2; Col 2:8).

Q **4:11–14 If God called us to these positions, why are the hardest problems church related? What does the phrase "laid their hands on you" mean? What is Timothy's gift?**

The Christian life is difficult because we are trying to live as God would have us live in opposition to the devil, world, and our own flesh (Eph 2:1–3; 1Th 1–5). When someone is going to represent another in public, the investment of authority was made evident by the laying on of hands (Dt 34:9). Paul does not say what the gift is, but it would certainly have to do with those qualities required to serve in the public ministry (1Tm 3:2–4).

Q **5:9 What is the significance of the widows' "enrollment" and the criteria for it?**

The idea of there being an enrollment has to do with an English translation. Paul is saying that a woman should not be considered as one of the widows who are recognized for their piety and need unless she is genuinely so (Lk 2:36–38; Ac 6:1).

Q **5:11–14 Is remarriage wrong? Verse 14 says widows should marry, but v. 12 says this brings judgment on them and they have broken their first pledge.**

See answer to 5:9 regarding devout widows. Paul is explaining that young women, like anyone else who lacks the gift of celibacy, should seek a spouse rather than commit to widowhood and then fail (Mt 19:10–12; 1Co 7:1–40; Jas 4:13–17).

Q **5:20 Does this contradict Matthew's process for rebuking sin privately?**

The process Jesus gave in Mt 18 is for dealing with private sins; thus the need to speak privately first. Here Paul is talking about dealing with public sins, where the sin is obvious and many people are in danger of being affected by it (Jn 2:13–22; 1Co 5:1–8).

Q **5:23 Why does Paul say this?**

Paul suggests that Timothy drink a little wine because the wine will be good for his health. Paul may also be providing a mild correction if Timothy is thinking that drinking only water and no wine would commend him to God (Rm 14:1–23).

Q **5:24 Does this indicate that God sees some sins before others? What is the place of judgment?**

Some sin cannot be hidden and the consequences are immediate, like being sick after drinking too much. Alcoholism is often evident, and the trouble it makes indicates the coming disaster for a person's life. Other sins are subtle or secret, yet the consequences of these will be revealed in time (Mt 10:26; 25:31–46; Lk 16:19–25).

Q **6:7 What does Paul mean here?**

When we are born, we come into the world with no material possessions. When we die and leave this world, we can take nothing with us (though many have tried, like pharaohs and emperors).

2 Timothy

Q **1:9 Does this mean we were saved even before Christ died on the cross?**

Since God is eternal, the redemptive work of Christ has always been accomplished. Since we live in time, it was necessary for the Son of God to become man and accomplish our salvation in history (Heb 4:8; Rv 17:8).

Q **2:11–13 Is it typical for Paul to write sayings? This seems like it belongs in Proverbs.**

The New Testament is full of quotations or allusions to Old Testament texts, including Proverbs, because prophecies were fulfilled and the truth remains constant. If your Bible formats these verses to look like a poem or hymn stanza, it is because the translators suspect it was recited and memorized by the apostolic Christian Church as such.

Q **3:1–9 Weren't the people Paul is talking about here prevalent in his time as well as ours and throughout human history? The godlessness in the last days sounds no different from our world today. Are we in the last days according to these verses?**

You have recognized what Solomon also noted: "There is nothing new under

Why do Christians have to suffer?

the sun" (Ec 1:9). What may be different in our time is the number of people and the intensity with which human beings oppose God and their lives. The warning of these verses was intended to make every generation watchful (Mt 24:32–25:30; 1Pt 5:8–9; 1Jn 2:18).

Q **3:8 Who exactly were Jannes and Jambres?**

These names occur only here in the Bible, but some ancient writings identify them as Pharaoh's magicians, who did oppose Moses (Ex 7:11–12, 22).

Q **3:12 Why do Christians have to suffer in order to live a life pleasing to Christ?**

If you consider that the Christian life in obedience to God is the opposite of fallen human nature, then the persecution of Christians is inevitable. The devil certainly wants to entice, deceive, or beat faithful people into unbelief. The world hates to be reminded of the truth about its error. Even religious leaders who want to displace rather than serve God are always going to persecute those who are faithful to God (Jn 9:13–34; 11:45–53; Ac 4:1–21; 13:44–50; 16:14–23; 17:30–32).

Q **3:15 How can we know the Scripture when we are infants? When it says "which are able," wouldn't that confuse the argument for infant salvation, at least to some extent? Does this verse support infant Baptism and Communion?**

The Word of God is powerful and effective, creating all things, raising the dead, healing the sick, multiplying food, and regenerating the soul (Gn 1:1–31; Is 55:10–11; Jn 6:1–64; 11:43–44). While physical maturity allows a person to read the Bible for himself or herself, it is also that very nature that is opposed to and contradicts the truth (1Co 2:14). Adults are instructed before Baptism to ensure that the Word has regenerated their souls and returned their human disposition to infancy (Mt 18:3; Jn 3:1–17; Heb 3:12–19). It is also a life in the Word and the soul regenerated by the Word that produces a faithful recipient of the Lord's Supper (see Luther's Large Catechism on the Lord's Supper). For more on the ability of infants, see *The Secret Life of the Unborn Child* by Thomas Verny.

Q **3:16 This clearly states what Scripture is and is for. Why do people not believe it?**

People don't believe because fallen human nature is incapable of belief and, in fact, opposes the truth and Word that works regeneration and faith (Jn 8:43; 1Co 2:14). This is why the Law must come first, to stop every mouth and bring every person to the truth about our absolute dependence on Christ (Jn 4:6–30; Rm 3:19).

● ●

Q **4:14 What did Alexander do to Paul?**

Paul was well educated in the Old Testament and was very conscious of God's command to love others and leave judgment and vengeance to Him (Rm 12:19–20). As an apostle of Christ, Paul was also determined to follow Jesus' teaching about love for enemies (Mt 5:43–48). Paul does not say what Alexander did to him, but the narrative of Paul's life in Acts suggests false accusation and the stirring up of opposition in some form (Ac 13:44–50; 14:4–6; 16:16–23; 17:5–9; 19:21–34; 21:26–36).

Titus

Q **1:5 When were Paul and Titus together?**

Luke does not record any occasions when Titus was with Paul, but Paul mentions Titus in respect to Corinth, Macedonia, and Jerusalem (2Co 7:5–6; Gal 2:1).

Q **1:5–9 What's the difference between elders then and elders today?**

There should be no difference between elders of any time. However, contemporary congregations elect men to help the pastor and call them "elders," which is confusing because that is one of the New Testament terms for the pastor, as we see here.

Q **1:6 In regard to elders, how are they meant to be "above reproach" since no one is without sin? Should a pastor step down or be removed if his children are openly disobedient and rebellious? Was it custom for men to take more than one wife, even Christian men? Does this verse also apply to divorced, separated pastors' families as well, or would certain considerations need to be taken?**

By "above reproach," Paul means a person whose life gives no one cause to accuse him of failing in any of the requirements of conduct for a pastor (1Pt 2:12). A pastor should most definitely resign his call if his family is disobedient and rebellious (1Tm 3:4–5). If he will not resign, then he must be removed. Polygamy has been and continues to be practiced in various places around the world. God's design was for one man to be in union with one woman, and pastors should be witnesses to that design in word and life. There are circumstances when a divorced man might remarry and serve as pastor, but care would have to be taken so that his history and circumstances did not cause confusion or encourage careless practices of divorce and remarriage among the people.

● ● ● ● ● ● ● ● ● ● ● ● ● ● ● ● ● ● ●

Q 2:2–4 Why teach the older men and women so they can teach the younger? Why not just teach the young?

Titus, like all pastors, was not there to do all the work of Christian ministry but to equip the people for the work of ministry (Eph 4:12). One of the responsibilities of elders is to pass on the truth. An equally important responsibility is to make sure that each succeeding generation also passes on the truth to the next generation (Eph 6:4; Dt 6:4–6; Ps 78:5–7).

● ● ● ● ● ● ● ● ● ● ● ● ● ● ● ● ● ●

Q 2:3 Why does Paul connect older women and being addicted to wine?

The reason Paul mentions wine as a problem for older women only is a curiosity. He does warn about this in regard to men in Ti 1:7 and 1Tm 3:2. Paul warns about drunkenness in general at Gal 5:21 and Eph 5:18.

Could the roles of men and women be switched?

● ● ● ● ● ● ● ● ● ● ● ● ● ● ● ● ● ● ●

Q 2:4–5 If women are to be the "working at home" (v. 5), are they not to work outside the home? Could the roles of men and women be switched?

The answers to these kinds of questions comes best from returning to the ideal, as Jesus did (Mt 19:3–6). The purpose of man is to support and protect. This means dealing with the world outside the home in order to provide for the world of the home. The woman was created to care and tend for the world of the home in union with the husband. Think of husband and wife being together, the husband facing the world, the wife facing the inner life of the home—yet they are together (Gn 2:15; Pr 31:10–31). What the world calls "progress" has tempted first the man and then the woman out of the home, where they are more vulnerable. For most of history, the place for both man and woman was in the home; why would they want to be elsewhere? In our time, we have inspiration from the Word, imagination, and great liberty to recover the ideal as much as we are able.

Q 2:9 Does this verse imply that slavery is permissible?

Paul said three times that all things are lawful but not necessarily what we want to be content with (1Co 6:12; 10:23). Paul is more concerned about the bondage of body and soul to sin than about a person's physical circumstance (Rm 6:1–21; 1Co 7:21–23). In addition, we might consider that slavery is not an evil in itself but, like so many other things, can be abused and abusive by those who are evil (Eph 6:9; Col 4:1). In the Old Testament, slavery was a way to protect the life of someone who was destitute, and after six years, that slave was to be set free and provided for so he might remain free (Ex 21:1–6; Dt 15:13–14).

Q 3:2 What does it mean "to show perfect courtesy toward all people"?

Truth is essential for all positive relationships. If we are honest with ourselves and others, then we are relieved of the burden of pretending to be what we are not, and others are relieved of all the many troubles caused by pretentiousness. Christian humility flows from the truth, not only about our condition as fallen human beings but also about our ability to serve others because of the way Christ has served us (Jn 13:1–17).

Q 3:4–8 Why do we associate this passage with Baptism since it doesn't mention it overtly?

The expression "washing" in v. 5 suggests that the Sacrament of Baptism is being referred to (though the Greek word *baptidzo* is not used here). Paul is saying that God redeems and sustains our lives graciously by immersing us in His Word—physical evidence of this being provided in the Sacraments (Jn 3:1–7; 6:25–63).

Q 3:5 What is "washing of regeneration"?

A life awash in the Word regenerates the soul to life and holds our fallen human nature under the Law so that it will not be the death of us (Jn 3:1–7; Rm 6:1–22; 1Pt 3:21).

Q 3:9 What controversies are considered foolish? How do you halt these controversies when there is a definite disagreement but it is not an element of salvation?

Notice two important expressions in this verse: "foolish" and "about the law." The term *foolish* has to do with unbelief (Ps 14:1). Why should we spend time and energy arguing about things that don't matter one way or the other? Jesus demonstrated how to prevent arguments about the Law in the Sermon on the Mount (Mt 5–7). Arguments about the Law come from fallen human nature trying to justify itself or condemn others unjustly (Gal 3:10–14; 5:1–26).

● ● ● ● ● ● ● ● ● ● ● ● ● ● ● ● ● ● ● ●

Q **3:10–11 Are divisive people like those discussed here still eligible to function as a part of the Body of Christ? Why would God have us give up someone after only warning them twice?**

"The person who stirs up division" is hurting not just himself or herself but also others—and not just in physical ways but in spiritual ones as well. If a person were doing so ignorantly, one admonition would work repentance. If a person continues after one or two admonitions, that individual is too determined and too serious a threat to be permitted to continue in the fellowship of believers (Jn 2:13–16; 1Co 5:1–8; Rm 16:17–18; 3 Jn 9–12).

Philemon

Q **1–2 If Paul is sending Onesimus back to Philemon, why is he writing to the whole Church? What is the relationship between Philemon and Archippus? What is the purpose of Philemon?**

When Paul wrote this letter to Philemon, he knew that it would have significance for the believers that gathered in Philemon's house and for all other believers in the course of time (1Pt 1:12). The truth and grace of God that direct Paul's counsel to Philemon in this situation can be applied to our lives as well. Archippus is mentioned in Col 4:17, revealing that he was devoted to the ministry of the Word, as Timothy and Titus were. The New Testament only records the fact that both men were devout and faithful Christian leaders in gathering the faithful and advancing the Gospel among them.

The purpose of this Letter to Philemon is a fascinating study. The obvious purpose of the letter was to secure the freedom of Onesimus from Philemon, his legal master/owner. This was apparently accomplished. The enduring purpose of the letter for the Christian community has to do with the proper use of authority, the power of grace, and the conduct of Christians. Paul has authority but does not use it to command what love has readily inspired. Paul relies on the power of God's grace for his own life and now for the good will of Philemon toward Onesimus. Christians do not run away or hide from the law but submit to it in love for others and in the fearlessness that comes from being delivered from the condemnation of it (Gn 3:8–10; Jn 18:4–9; Rm 3:28–31).

● ● ● ● ● ● ● ● ● ● ● ● ● ● ● ● ● ●

Q 8–9 Why does Paul have authority to order Philemon to do something? Why won't Paul command what Christ wants us to do?

Paul might be bold to command Philemon to do what is right on the basis of his authority as an apostle of Christ (Lk 10:16; Heb 13:7). Paul might also be bold to command Philemon to do what is right because Paul was responsible for Philemon's conversion; in this sense Philemon owes his life to Paul (Phm 19). But Paul does not make demands or command Philemon to do anything because that is not the nature of the Gospel. It is the love of God that directs our relationships (2Co 5:14–15). Paul treats others as God has treated him so that others, in turn, treat one another with love and kindness (1Tm 1:12–15; Jn 15:12–13; 1Jn 4:19).

● ● ● ● ● ● ● ● ● ● ● ● ● ● ● ● ● ●

Q 8–21 Who is Onesimus? Why is Paul pleading for him?

Onesimus is mentioned only here and in Col 4:9. Paul describes Onesimus as a faithful and beloved brother who is among the Christians in Colossae. We know from

Who is Onesimus?

this letter that Onesimus was a slave of Philemon who had run away but was then converted to Christianity by Paul.

Paul is pleading for Onesimus for two reasons. First, Paul wants to help both Philemon and Onesimus realize their potential according to the Gospel; Philemon is free to love Onesimus by granting his freedom according to civil law so that Onesimus is free to give the whole of his life for the love of others. Second, Paul is careful to demonstrate Christian faith and love in submission to the civil law. Roman law had something to say about Onesimus. The power of the life God gives us is realized when we submit to rather than circumvent the law (Rm 13:1–16).

● ● ● ● ● ● ● ● ● ● ● ● ● ● ● ● ● ●

Q 9 What is the significance of appealing on the basis of love?

The Christian life is the product of God's love for us in Christ Jesus. This life is in contrast to the Jewish life under the Law of Moses, where people obeyed the law because of threats and punishment (Mt 15:8–9). Law and threats can force outward obedience, but such obedience is never the same as loving care for others that is the substantive and spontaneous product of God's love for us (Lk 7:36–50).

Q 9–10 Paul discusses his imprisonment as "a prisoner . . . for Christ Jesus," but he goes on to mention in v. 23 that there is at least one other fellow prisoner. Was his prison reference literal or metaphorical?

Paul was a literal, physical prisoner in Jerusalem, Caesarea, and then in Rome (Ac 23:10; 24:27; 28:16). After his conversion, Paul was never a prisoner in the metaphorical or spiritual sense because Christ had liberated him from his own guilt and from the fear of men (Ac 9; 1Co 6:12; Php 1:12–14; 2Tm 2:8–10).

Q 10 How did Onesimus become Paul's "child" while Paul was imprisoned?

Onesimus was regenerated by the Spirit through the ministry of Paul; this is why Paul considers Onesimus a son. Biological generation is the means by which God continues to create new lives, but spiritual regeneration is the means by which God re-creates us to be His children and realize a life that endures forever.

Q 11 How is Onesimus useful as stated in Philemon? Did Paul talk about him elsewhere?

Onesimus is mentioned only here and in Col 4:9. Onesimus was a slave of Philemon who had run away, had come into contact with Paul, had been converted by him, and now was returning to Philemon.

Paul does not say what he means by "useful." However, we do know that companions brought things that Paul needed, wrote when he dictated, and were encouraging to him (2Tm 4:9–16; Rm 1:12; 16:22).

Q 12 Why didn't Paul help runaway slaves?

Paul *did* help runaway slaves, in the most profound and enduring way. What does it matter if a slave runs away, only to live in fear of the law and bondage to the flesh (Lk 9:25; Rm 1:20–32; Eph 2:1–3)? The Gospel that Paul communicated to Onesimus relieved him from the bondage of guilt and fear (Heb 2:14–15). The Gospel is not only freedom from the curse of the Law but also freedom to fulfill the Law by fearless and enduring love for others (Rm 13:1–16; Gal 5:1–4, 13–26).

Q 14 Why does Paul say that he doesn't want to do anything without Philemon's consent? Could he get in trouble for having Onesimus with him?

Paul could find himself in trouble for having a runaway slave with him since it would be his obligation under the Mosaic Law and under Roman law to make sure Onesimus was returned to Philemon (Dt 22:1–3; Rm 13:7–8). Paul could have used his apostolic authority to command Philemon to free Onesimus, but such a command would be contrary to the nature of the Gospel which Paul serves (1Co 6:12; Gal 3:1–14). Paul's life depends on the grace of God in Christ. Paul wants nothing to do with lives or relationships that are not the product of the grace of God (Ac 15:1–12; Gal 2:11–21).

● ● ● ● ● ● ● ● ● ● ● ● ● ● ● ● ● ● ●

Q **18 What does he mean by "charge that to my account"? If debt is bad, then why does Paul have an account with Philemon?**

The New Testament forbids debt in the clearest terms (Rm 13:8). In this case, Paul is not talking about borrowing money but about gratitude and appreciation for what one person does for another. We owe God our whole life but give only rebellion. Jesus paid our debt under the Law in order to deliver us from the curse of debt to it (Gal 4:4–7). In a much smaller but similar way, Philemon owes his life to Paul the way Paul owes his whole life to the grace of Christ (Philemon 19; Php 3:7–14; 1Tm 1:12–17; Rm 8:12). Notice how Paul isn't seeking anything for himself but seeks instead for Onesimus (even for Philemon's own spiritual well-being). Debt in the worldly sense is all about selfishness, both of those who lend so they can control others and those who borrow because they are controlled by lust and greed. The only debt Christians know is that of love, which is selflessness. Selflessness always gives and receives in the interest of others.

● ●

Q **19–20 It sounds like Paul is tricking Philemon and guilting him into accepting Onesimus back. Why does Philemon owe Paul his self?**

The expression "to say nothing of" is self-contradictory when misunderstood. The intent of that statement is to make reference to something that is significant and should be recalled, yet is not the basis for resolving the issue at hand. Philemon owes Paul his life in the sense that Philemon knows Christ and eternal salvation because of Paul (just like Paul owes his life to Christ). Philemon's debt to Paul is significant, but it is not the basis upon which Philemon should do what Paul requests. Philemon's gratitude for the life God has given him in Christ is the proper motivation for Philemon setting Onesimus free, and Paul is pointing him to that. Paul's letter to Philemon is an interesting study in how to use Law and Gospel when dealing with human beings who are composed of a fallen human nature and a regenerate soul. Fallen human nature must be managed with the Law (1Co 2:14; 9:19–21). A regenerate soul does not need the Law because it is already eager to love as it has been loved (1Jn 4:19).

● ● ● ● ● ● ● ● ● ● ● ● ● ● ● ● ● ● ● ●

Q 22 It seems rude of Paul to practically demand that Philemon prepare a room for him. Was that socially acceptable back then?

One of the problems with written communication is the potential to be misunderstood. It is possible to read Paul's letter to Philemon as demanding and rude. On the other hand, a closer reading of the text and an understanding of human nature suggests that Paul is communicating in honesty and kindness. Paul refers to Philemon's prayers and his own that God would grant them time together. If Paul was responsible for Philemon's conversion, then it is natural that Philemon would welcome a visit from the apostle, especially knowing that Paul's interaction with others is never selfish (Rm 1:11–15).

Hebrews

Q **1:1–2 God spoke creation into being through His Son. So, would it be safe to say that Jesus was present at the time Genesis records the following: "In the beginning, God created the heavens and the earth"?**

Yes. The Son of God, who became the man Jesus through His conception and birth of the Virgin Mary, is eternal and was present in the beginning and spoke the universe into existence (Gn 1:1–2:3; Pr 8:12–31; Jn 1:1–5).

Q **1:1–3 Does God still send prophets to us to speak to us?**

God could still send prophets if He wanted to, but this is unlikely because the purpose of the prophets has been fulfilled in Christ (Lk 9:28–31; 24:25–27; Rm 1:12; 1Co 13:8; Eph 2:20; 4:11; 2Pt 1:19). The prophets foretold what Christ would do; the apostles recorded what Christ had done. Christians share with others the truth about Christ as revealed in the prophetic and apostolic Word (2Co 5:20; 1Pt 3:15).

● ● ● ● ● ● ● ● ● ● ● ● ● ● ● ● ● ● ●

Q 1:1–4 What's the reason for going lesser to greater (speaking to us through the prophets, but now through His Son)?

In the beginning, God lived in communion with Adam and Eve until Adam destroyed that relationship (Gn 3:8–12). God preserved human life and gave us hope of restoration by providing promises that He would reestablish communion with us through the incarnation of His Son. God spoke to us through prophets because He cannot be joined with that which is contrary to His nature (Gal 3:19–25). God provided prophets so that His Word and promises could work faith and life in all who hoped for reconciliation (Gn 12:3; 2Sm 7:18–29). The time that passed between Adam's rejection of communion with God and the restoration of that communion in Christ was a lesson in the consequences of rebellion. Thinking that we can contradict God's design for us and still keep the blessings of communion with Him is absolute deception (Gn 3:1ff.; 1Sm 8:1–21; Rm 1:20–32). Now that God has come to us in the person of Jesus Christ, restored our communion, and given us His inspired Word so that He can remain with us, we want to be very careful to protect that communion (Jn 1:14; 15:1–7; Col 2:8–19).

● ● ● ● ● ● ● ● ● ● ● ● ● ● ● ● ● ● ●

Q 1:4 Is there a finite number of angels or are there more as time goes on and more people live and die? If all angels are named, then why aren't specific names (other than Michael, Gabriel, and Raphael) mentioned in the Bible? Does Paul have any other references that disprove the theory of Michael as the archangel?

I do not know of any text that suggests that God creates more angels, nor any that say He does not. Similarly, there are no biblical texts that say all angels are named nor any that say they are not. When angels are named in the Bible, it likely has to do with allowing the reader to recognize patterns or parallels in the kind of work that particular angel is tending to. For example, it was Gabriel who told Zechariah that he and Elizabeth would have a son (Lk 1:11–20). Some months later, Gabriel told Mary that she would conceive by the Holy Spirit (vv. 26–38). The name of an angel may also convey a particular character or identity. Gabriel told Zechariah his name after Zechariah challenged the Word of the Lord. Gabriel means "My strength is of God," which may have been intended as both rebuke and warning for Zechariah's skepticism.

There is good reason to believe that the angel Michael ("Who is like God") is actually the Son of God, often referred to with the definite article in the Old Testament (*the* angel of the Lord; Rv 12:7–11; Gn 22:11; Ex 3:2). The angel name "Raphael" only occurs in the Book of Tobit in the Apocrypha. There seems to be little need or use in convincing people of the names of angels. I don't know of any references in Paul or the whole Bible that disprove the suggestion that Michael is an archangel. If he is the Son of God (who is more "like God" than His Son? Jn 14:7–11), then He is the absolute "arch" (ruler) of all angels.

● ● ● ● ● ● ● ● ● ● ● ● ● ● ● ● ● ● ● ●

Q 1:4–14 Why is there such a focus on angels? Why was it necessary for the author to state that Jesus is superior to the angels? Was it a common false belief that Jesus is merely an angel, rather than God?

The answers to all these questions have to do with fallen human nature's desire to hide from God and yet have its way. People would prefer to deal with anyone but God because God cannot be manipulated, while people, kings, and perhaps angels can (1Sm 8:19–20). People also like romantic notions of heroes and extraordinary beings who will come and make their dreams come true (e.g., genie in the lamp, Cinderella's fairy godmother, comic strip superheroes now glorified in films). Not only angels but all of the physical features of the Old Testament are addressed in this letter since people were clinging to their forms while refusing to recognize the substantive fulfillment of them all in Christ. Matthew's Gospel constantly notes Jesus' fulfillment of Old Testament prophecies ("as it is written in the prophet" occurs ten times). Luke's Gospel records Jesus affirming such fulfillment in His own words (Lk 4:21; 24:27). On the other hand, these same people would accept anyone but the Son of God; indeed, anyone who had his own agenda and was self-serving was welcomed (Jn 5:43). But those who know that only God can redeem them will quickly recognize and readily confess that Jesus is the Christ, the Son of the living God and the only means of our salvation (Mt 16:13–16; Mk 10:47; Lk 10:38–42; Jn 9).

● ● ● ● ● ● ● ● ● ● ● ● ● ● ● ● ● ● ● ●

Q 1:5 What does it mean, "I will be to him a father, and he shall be to me a son"?

This part of the verse is a quotation from 2Sm 7:14, where God again articulates His promise to send His own Son into the flesh in order to save us by taking our place under the Law (Gn 3:15; 12:1–3; Gal 4:4). God promised that His own Son would become a man through a descendant of David, so in this way God would become the Father of David's descendant and David's descendant would become God's Son (Mt 1:1–25; Lk 1:26–3:38).

● ● ● ● ● ● ● ● ● ● ● ● ● ● ● ● ● ● ● ●

Q 1:5; 3:7, 13, 15; 4:7; 5:5 Why so much emphasis on "today"? When is "today"?

The word *today* is used in two contexts. The first refers to the incarnation of Christ, "You are My Son, today I have begotten You" (Heb 1:5; 5:5; also Mt 1:18; Lk 1:35). You can imagine the significance of saying "today" in reference to the fulfillment of God's promises that have been established since the fall of Adam and Eve (Gn 3:15).

The second context refers to God's call for people to repent of their contrary and self-destructive ways. There is no time to waste, nothing to decide; the call to turn from the ways of death into the way of life is urgent and immediate (Mk 1:14–15; Rm 13:11; Eph 5:16).

● ● ● ● ● ● ● ● ● ● ● ● ● ● ● ● ● ●

Q 1:5–14 Wasn't it obvious that Jesus was and is superior to angels? Why did the author use all these Old Testament quotes?

The superiority of Jesus to angels was not obvious to everyone. The religious leaders of Jesus' day were willing to admit that Jesus was a messenger (Greek = "angel") of God (Jn 3:2). People in modern times are willing to admit that Jesus was a great teacher. The fact that Jesus *is* true God and true man in one person is unparalleled and impossible for any human to believe apart from the revelation and grace of God (Mt 16:13–17; 1Co 2:14). This letter provides many quotes from the Old Testament that demonstrate the unique character of the Christ and His vast superiority to angels, as vast as the superiority of the Creator over His creation.

● ● ● ● ● ● ● ● ● ● ● ● ● ● ● ● ● ●

Q 1:7 What does this verse mean?

First of all, the point being made is that angels are created beings ("He *makes* His angels," italics added) while Jesus Christ is the Creator (Heb 3:3). Second, the Hebrew word translated "winds" in your Bible means "breath" and "spirit" as well. God makes His angels spirits or spiritual beings. Some of His angels are called "seraphim," which means "to be burning" (Is 6:2, 6; Nu 21:6, 8). The Holy Spirit indicated His presence on Pentecost in tongues of fire (Ac 2:3). God demonstrated His presence to Moses in a burning bush and to Israel during the exodus with a pillar of fire and with a burning fire on Mount Sinai (Ex 3:2; 13:21; 24:17). It might be no surprise to find that messengers of God's Word and will are flaming.

● ● ● ● ● ● ● ● ● ● ● ● ● ● ● ● ● ●

Q 1:10–11 Is this referring to heaven or simply the universe?

Verse 10 mentions the earth; it also mentions "the heavens," which is more likely a reference to the sky above than to the immaterial place where God's throne is, so to speak. Nevertheless, these verses are referring to all of creation, the whole created universe, which God will destroy on the Last Day and then re-create in perfection for all eternity (2Pt 3:12–13).

● ● ● ● ● ● ● ● ● ● ● ● ● ● ● ● ● ●

Q 1:14 Do we all have our own angel watching over or serving us? What are angels?

Angels are a lot like heaven; the Bible tells us enough to know they exist and are important for us, but not much more than that. Maybe God is saving us from knowing enough to think we could have opinions about them. We know that angels were created by God to serve His will for our well-being (Jn 1:3; Heb 1:7). We do well to remember that the word *angel* is Greek and means "messenger." Sometimes "angel" is referring to the Son of God before His incarnation (Gn 16:7; Ex 3:2). Sometimes "angel" is referring to the pastor (messenger) of a congregation (Rv 2:1). Demons and the devil himself are angels who disobeyed God and are now bound under judgment for their rebellion (Jude 6; Rv 12:9). Good angels are faithful to the Lord, praising Him, delivering messages from Him, strengthening those who are in need, defending, and executing judgment on the wicked (Is 6:1–7; Mt 1:20–21; Lk 1:11–20, 26–38; 2:9–15; Mk 1:12–13; Ps 78:49). Faithful angels serve God alone and direct us to do the same (Rv 22:8–9).

What are angels?

Q 2:1 Does this mean we need to pay attention to everything?

You may note that the verse says we must give the more earnest heed to "what we have heard." The things we have heard are the Scriptures, both the warnings of the Law and the promises of the Gospel. Yes, we must pay attention to both.

Q 2:4 Do miracles continue to happen in the present day? Does this mean that some do have more gifts than others? Is everyone given gifts?

Whether or not miracles still happen today depends on two things. First, we need to define what we mean by "miracle." If a miracle is "something that God does all the time but in this case He does it in an instant," then we may think that He is not still doing miracles (all healing is a product of God's design and care; healing someone in an instant is a miracle). Second, we need to consider how little we know of what goes on in our world and in our own life. Is it not possible that God does miracles for us all the time but we are unaware? How many times and in how many ways might God have healed or saved us in an instant, though we are unaware? Everyone *is* a gift of God and has the gifts of God necessary to accomplish the work God has prepared for that person to do (Rm 12:6–8; 1Co 12:1–31; Eph 2:10; 4:7–16). Remember that miracles and gifts do not create faith but verify the truth of the Word, which is what creates faith (Mk 16:16–20).

Q 2:5–8 Who is the man these verses are talking about?

These verses are speaking about "man" in the sense of a human being. These verses are referring to all of us.

Q **2:9 What does Paul mean when he says Jesus "for a little while was made a little lower than the angels"? If God tastes death for us, why is it still painful (physically)?**

In the verses before this, the author is asking us to consider two things. First, that Jesus Christ, as the Son of God, is the Creator and so infinitely greater than His creation (Heb 3:3–4). Second, even though human beings are so much lower than God, lower even than the angels, God has glorified and honored us by setting us over His creation as caretakers. In this verse, our attention turns to Jesus Christ as the Son of Man. According to His human nature, He was made a little lower than the angels and as such, received help from them (see 1:14 above). He was made man so that He could endure the condemnation of the Law and death in our place—and since He is also God, He could suffer as a human being in the place of every human being, thus redeeming the whole world (2Co 5:21).

The answer to your question regarding the taste of death begins with understanding and defining what death is. If death is the absence of positive relationships, then we can see why the cessation of physiological function is called death and how Jesus could taste (endure) death for everyone. Physical death is of limited consequence since our physical nature is fallen, failing, and contrary to our regenerate soul that seeks communion with God and love of neighbor. Though we endure some pain and suffering

in this body, there is no comparison between what we experience and what it is to be completely cut off from God as Jesus was (Ps 22; Mt 27:46). The essence of our nature is the regenerate soul God has worked in us (Jn 3:1–7; 1Jn 3:9). According to this nature, we will never experience death since we are and always will be in a positive relationship with God and others (Lk 16:19–31).

Q **2:10 Why did Jesus have to suffer? What does it mean to be made perfect through suffering?**

The word translated "perfect" means "complete," as in finishing, filling up, or making an end of something. This word occurs twenty-three times in the New Testament, and nine of those are in Hebrews. God brought His Son to the fulfillment of His nature through the process of redeeming His creation. This is fitting because God bears responsibility for all of His creation. Through His own suffering, death, and resurrection, God demonstrates both the consequences of opposing His design and the singularity, necessity, and magnitude of the wonders that flow from His loving, almighty being.

Q **2:13 What does he mean by saying, "I will put my trust in him"?**

First of all, this might seem as if trust were an object and we decide where we will put it. The words *trust*, *faith*, and *believe* all translate the same Greek word. They all have to do with honesty about dependence. Second, these quotes belong to the human nature of Jesus. As a true man, He is perfectly honest about His dependence on God, and because of that, He fulfilled all that the Law requires of us.

• • • • • • • • • • • • • • • • • • •

Q **2:14 If God upholds all things, good and bad, how does the devil hold the power of death? Does this mean Jesus has taken away that power of death through His resurrection?**

No one has any power or ability or life unless God grants it (Jn 3:27; 15:5; 19:11). The devil holds the power of death because of his ability to deceive (Gn 3:4–13). First, the devil deceives people by making them think life can be improved by contradicting God's design rather than by living according to it. Second, the devil also deceives by making people think that there is no remedy for their failure. Third, the devil holds people in bondage by making them afraid to sacrifice their physical life in favor of the spiritual life. Jesus revealed that only those who lose their lives can save them (Lk 17:33). Paul explained how the fallen human nature and its deceived thinking must be drowned in favor of the truth that was made clear by Christ (Rm 6:1–23).

• • • • • • • • • • • • • • • • • • •

Q **2:16 What does this verse mean?**
This verse becomes clear by way of an accurate translation, which might read as follows: "For certainly He does not receive

anything which is of angels but of the seed of Abraham." This verse is still working to make clear that Jesus is not a creation, not an angel or even the best of angels, but entirely beyond them, just as God is above His creation. The incarnation of the Son of God was not to the nature of an angel but to the nature of a genuine human being, in order to take our place under the Law (Gal 4:4–5).

• • • • • • • • • • • • • • • • • • •

Q **2:17 How do you respond to people when they ask why an omnipotent God could not (did not) save the world without having Jesus die?**

The omnipotent God is also omniscient, suggesting that if there were a way to save the world without the death of Jesus (or anyone else), He would have done so. On the other hand, we might wonder what is necessary to live in harmony with one another and God forever. We might wonder if reality and significance can exist without real consequences for what happens. We might ask people what God is saving us from and the nature of that problem. Is it possible that people wonder about God's ways because they accept their own thoughts uncritically while ignorant or careless of God's thoughts (Is 55) and because their focus is on their physical life in a material world rather than on their eternal soul in God's kingdom (Mt 6:19–34)?

Q 2:18 How exactly did Christ suffer when He was tempted?

The word translated "tempted" also can mean "tested" or "to attempt (try) to do something." The word *suffer* has to do with enduring any number of challenges, difficulties, or hardships. We can already see that a person who is being tested/tempted must, by definition, experience challenge/difficulty. In the case of Christ, He suffered unimaginable hardship while He was tempted by the devil since He hadn't had anything to eat or drink for forty days and nights in the wilderness and because the devil assaulted Him with every temptation (Lk 4:1–13). The coming of angels to minister to Jesus after these temptations is additional evidence of the suffering they must have inflicted on Him (Mk 1:13). Besides His time in the wilderness, Jesus was tempted/tried by the religious leaders during His entire public ministry (Mt 16:1; 22:18). The word *tempt* occurs thirty-eight times in the New Testament; fourteen of those are in the Gospels in reference to Jesus. This is further evidence that Jesus was the primary and unparalleled target of temptations that afflicted Him, not only with the burden of resisting them but also with responding to them in loving wisdom and in bearing grief over those who would tempt Him rather than seek the salvation He brought (Lk 13:34–35; Gn 6:6; Mk 3:5; Eph 4:30).

Q 3:1–6 Why would Moses be compared with Christ since there is no one like Christ?

Proud, arrogant, self-righteous people argue that they are righteous on the basis of the Law of Moses (Jn 9:28; 1Co 9:20; Gal 3:1–7). There is no comparison between Christ and Moses, but realizing who Christ is requires us to be honest about our condition, which is humiliating in the absolute and which human nature hates to experience (Jn 5:45–47). We can lie to ourselves about Moses and our ability to keep the Law, but we cannot lie to Christ. This is why Israel always wanted a human leader (1Sm 8:5–22).

Q 3:6 Does the phrase "we hold fast our confidence" imply predestination? This sounds more like we can "choose" to accept or reject Christ.

The Bible contains many conditional "if/then" statements. Conditional statements describe the way reality is but say nothing about who is or isn't capable of meeting the condition. If you can meet the requirements, you can be a Navy SEAL, a surgeon, or a nuclear physicist, but we cannot do so by simply choosing or accepting those jobs. Anyone who holds fast the confidence and boasts in the hope can only do so because God has predestined him or her to do so and has accomplished what He predestined through His means (Rm 8:29–30).

Q **3:7 How does the Holy Spirit say these things?**

The words recorded here are quoted from Ps 95. The Psalms, like the rest of the Bible, were written by men who were moved and directed by the Holy Spirit to produce what we have received (Mt 22:43–45; Ps 110; 2Tm 3:16; 2Pt 1:19–21).

Q **3:11 What does it mean that "they shall not enter My rest"?**

There are many kinds of rest; all of them have to do with enjoying relief from or the absence of strains or attacks of one kind or another. God established a day for rest after His own pattern of resting on the seventh day (Gn 2:2–3). God gave the children of Israel rest from the oppression of the Egyptians, which became a second reason for remembering the Sabbath to keep it holy (Dt 5:15; 1Ki 8:50–51; Jer 11:3–5). The land was to have rest every seven years (Lv 25:2–6). Everyone was to enjoy rest from debt every fiftieth year (the year after seven Sabbath years; Lv 25:10–54). God offered all kinds of physical rest to the Israelites in the Promised Land on the condition that they would remain faithful to Him (Lv 26:2–13; Dt 6:10–11; Jsh 24:8–14). The atonement of Christ gives us rest from the curse of the Law (Gal 3:13–14). Thus, we may think of God's rest in the physical world or spiritual rest in time and eternity. Certainly those who oppose and despise God will never know spiritual rest or eternal life; it is likely that they will not ever really be at rest in this world among their material things or while trying to justify themselves (Lv 26:14–43; Hg 1:3–6).

Q **3:12 Since we still have old Adam in us, how can we not have "an evil, unbelieving heart"?**

The answer to your question is likely bound up in our understanding of "heart." Certainly the muscle that pumps our blood is not the problem, though it is affected by the fall of our nature. In this context, "heart" must refer to what is the heart or essence of our being, the very soul of our being, which is corrupt and contrary by nature (Mt 15:18–20). The Word and Spirit of God replace this fallen, contrary heart with one that is in harmony with God (Ezk 36:24–27). The New Testament speaks of this in terms of regeneration (Jn 3:1–7).

Q **3:13 What is meant by "as long as it is called 'today'"? Why do some translations capitalize "Today"?**

There is no capitalization in the original manuscripts of the New Testament. The capitalization is probably to emphasize the word. This verse anticipates fallen human nature's determination to find a way to disobey, ignore, and circumvent God's good intent for our lives. As long as any given day is still "today," then the time to be penitent and careful is right and the time is now (Lk 12:39–40; 2Pt 3:10).

Can Christians harden their hearts?

Q **3:14 What is the "original confidence"? How can we hold to that due to our doubt and sin?**

Doubt and sin are a problem with fallen human nature but not for the regenerate soul. Fallen human nature is doubtful and contrary to God and cannot be otherwise; thus the necessity of death for this nature if we are to be free and rid of it (Rm 6:1–23; 1Co 2:14). On the other hand, a soul regenerated and sustained by the Word of God is free of doubt and sin (Jn 3:1–7; 1Jn 3:1–8; 5:18). The necessity of "hold[ing] . . . firm to the end" is obvious from considering the contrary; how could a person be saved who is apart from the Word of God that saves? Conditional statements in the Bible report truth and remind us that only God has the means and will to meet those conditions for us and in us (Mt 19:25–26).

The word translated "confidence" in your Bible occurs only five times in the New Testament and has to do with the substance of things (2Co 9:4; 11:17; Heb 1:3; 11:1). The "first," "original," or "initial substance" is the Word. It is the Word that regenerates our soul, the Word that gives us the strength and will to hold firmly, and the Word that is the substance to which we cling (Dt 6:4ff.; 32:47; Rm 10:6–8).

Q **3:15 Can Christians harden their hearts? Why is this repeated here and in 4:7?**

The answer to this question depends on recognizing the composition of a Christian and what sustains the Christian life. Christians are people who have a fallen human nature that has not changed but who also possess a regenerate soul living within and are seeking to live out the life of Christ through that contrary human nature. The fallen human nature of the Christian is just as contrary as ever and just as prone to hard-heartedness, except for the counterforce of a regenerate soul inspired and energized by the Word and Spirit of God. If the fallen human nature of any Christian is allowed to isolate itself from the Word, if it succeeds in seeking its own desires, if it lives in the flood of worldly lust and the deceit of the devil, then it certainly can become hard; Saul and Judas are frightening examples.

The teaching of Hebrews on this subject, the urgent language evident in the word *today*, and the repetition of the warning are provided because a hard heart is such a menacing and catastrophic threat. Yet, such a warning with all the intense severity that the Letter to the Hebrews can muster is a vital part of prevention. Severe warnings under the Law plus the awesome inspiration of the Gospel act as a double remedy for our condition, pushing a contrary human nature back toward God and drawing the regenerate soul upward (Is 40:1–2). The family and communion of saints is another part of prevention; God has and would always keep us surrounded by other faithful people who will keep us warned of the world and inspired by the Word.

● ● ● ● ● ● ● ● ● ● ● ● ● ● ● ● ● ● ●

Q 3:18 I find myself always being tempted. What advice would you give to someone like me, who understands the Word but is always feeling pressured by the issue?

As long as we are in this fallen human nature in this world under the devil's attack, we will face temptation. Recognizing that the desires of our fallen human nature are self-defeating can help expose temptations for what they are (Jas 1:14–15). Recognizing that the temptations of the world are deadly also helps us reject them (1Jn 2:15–17). Jesus demonstrated the means of escape for the temptations of the devil by responding to each temptation with the Word (Mt 4:1ff.; Lk 4:1ff.; 1Co 10:13). Temptations depend on isolating and deceiving a person; therefore the best defense against temptation is a life in the Word in the company of others who are in the Word.

● ● ● ● ● ● ● ● ● ● ● ● ● ● ● ● ● ● ●

Q 4:1–10 Does this talk of "rest" imply life in Christ or eternal life?

God rested after six days of creating, and He established every seventh day for people to do the same (Gn 2:2–3). This rest of God was likely not a matter of physical rest or fatigue but simply the cessation of activity in order to enjoy what had been accomplished. God commanded rest for people in the Old Testament as a way for them to remember that God had provided and is always providing their life for them, so they might reflect upon and appreciate the life God gives (including their labor); and after the exodus, in order to remember that God had delivered them from a life of bondage to foreign powers (Ex 20:8–11; Dt 5:12–15; Jer 11:3–5). The experience of Israel in Egypt is parallel to and indicative of the fallen human condition under the Law (Eph 2:1–3; Heb 2:14–15). The substitutionary atonement of Christ has delivered all people from the curse of the Law and has thus provided us with rest from the burden of the Law every day and forever (Gal 3:10–14). Christians, according to the New Testament, never do anything because they *have* to but always because they are regenerated in the image of Christ and inspired by His Spirit to live and love as He did—all of this within the rest from all the burden of the Law that He provided for us (Ac 4:20; 1Jn 4:4, 19).

● ● ● ● ● ● ● ● ● ● ● ● ● ● ● ● ● ● ●

Q 4:1 Why should we "fear" according to this verse?

The everlasting rest that God has provided from the condemnation of the Law through Jesus Christ has no substitute, yet our fallen human nature is proud and careless. Such a nature needs the fear of everlasting tragedy to keep it from pulling us out of and away from the grace of God in His Word and promises.

Q **4:2 How can you unite the Word with faith? I thought the Word produced faith.**

The word translated "unite" has to do with putting things together; it is used only here and in 1Co 12:24, where it refers to God's composition of the human body (the root occurs three times in the New Testament and refers to something mixed in a cup; Rv 14:10; 18:6). We know that the Word of God is powerful and that it does not return void (Heb 4:12; Is 55:11), so the answer must be in realizing the dynamics of the Word in relation to our nature. The parable of the sower describes how perfectly good seed bears fruit in only one out of four circumstances (Lk 8:5–15). The parable of wine and wineskins reveals that the Word of God is made up of Law and Gospel that interact very differently with fallen human nature or a regenerate soul (Lk 5:37–38). Paul noted the difference between Law and Gospel and noted the necessity of rightly applying each (2Co 3:6; 1Tm 1:8–10). The Law is required to make way in fallen, contrary human nature for the Gospel to regenerate the soul and inspire this soul. This verse is speaking about the promises of God (Gospel) accomplishing no benefit for the Israelites in the desert because they were only of the flesh and always contrary to God, as their history and refusal to enter the Promised Land clearly demonstrated (Heb 3:12–19). These passages of warning in Hebrews are Law that is intended to clear the way through our contrary human nature for the promises of God to regenerate us and successfully convey us into the kingdom of heaven (Heb 4:9–16).

Q **4:3 Is God speaking to the unbeliever?**

God was speaking to the unbelieving Jews who refused to enter the Promised Land as God directed them to (Nu 14:32; Ps 95:11; but read Nu 13:1–14:45 for the whole account). However, those people who refused to enter the Promised Land are indicative of everyone and anyone who refuses the truth of what God freely and readily provides for us. If God makes the universe support our life and makes our hearts beat though we take little thought of it, and if He has sacrificed His own Son to restore our life to us, what would keep us from the continual rest of knowing that He provides for all things in our life (Rm 8:28–32)?

Q **4:6 What happens to people who never have the Gospel preached to them?**

Only God knows His plans and ways (Is 55), and we cannot know whether there is such a person in real life (Mt 7:1). What we *can* know is that God desires all to be saved (1Tm 2:4), that He has actually saved all in the life, death, and resurrection of His Son (Jn 3:16; 2Co 5:19), that God has provided creation as a witness to Himself (Ps 19; Rm 1:20–32), and that He has provided His Word and His people as a further witness to Himself (Mt 5:13–14; Jn 20:30–31; Rm 10:1–17; 2Co 5:20).

• • • • • • • • • • • • • • • • • • • •

Q 4:6–8 How can you compare these passages to those in the Old Testament concerning rest?

These verses are consistent with the Old Testament teaching about rest. God set apart the seventh day because rest is good (Gn 2:2–3). God delivered Israel from their bondage in Egypt in order to give them rest (Ex 20:8–11; Dt 5:15; Jer 11:3–5). The main difference in the New Testament is that every day is restful because Christ has redeemed us from the burden of the Law and gives us a life that we may freely give to others (Gal 3:13–14; Mt 10:8).

• • • • • • • • • • • • • • • • • • • •

Q 4:7 When is "Today"? Is it the Last Day or Judgment Day?

"Today" means just what it says. The person who hears that proclamation or reads it benefits from paying attention to it from that very moment on; why delay? Jesus lamented over Jerusalem because the people there did not realize the time that had come with Jesus' ministry (Lk 13:34–35). Other passages in the Bible that call us to repentance and faith use the urgent expression "now" (2Co 6:1–2).

• • • • • • • • • • • • • • • • • • • •

Q 4:9–11 Is this place/time of rest referring to corporate worship on Sundays? How does one enter God's rest? Is it our work for salvation that we cease to

do when we enter into God's rest? It says, "They shall not enter My rest" (v. 5), but then it says anyone who enters God's rest also rests from his own work (v. 10). How can this be?

The place and time of rest is every time and place since Jesus said, "It is finished." Sundays and corporate worship can be part of this rest, but only if the entire life of the Christian rests in the Words and promises of God (Ac 2:42). When this text urges us to enter that rest, it is doing the same thing that Joshua and Caleb did when they pleaded with Israel to cross the Jordan and inherit the land of milk and honey according to the promises and providence of God (Nu 13:26–14:9). The law that warns and urges is the necessary remedy for fallen human nature that is contrary to God's gracious will: proud, egocentric, and self-righteous—all labor-intensive determinations. The promises of God regenerate and inspire the soul to realize the rest of God's grace and providence by resting in it and loving others because of it.

The references about not entering His rest refer to what God swore in response to the stubborn refusal of Israelites to enter the Promised Land (Heb 3:16–4:5). The people who enter His rest are all who have been regenerated by God's Word and Spirit (Jn 1:11–13; 3:1–7; 6:27–68; 8:32–51).

Q **4:9 Are we still commanded to remember the Sabbath in the same way described in the Bible?**

You may notice that several ways of keeping the Sabbath are recorded in the Bible. God-fearing people would have kept the Sabbath from the beginning since God established the day of rest at the time of creation (Gn 2:2–3). The Sabbath was reasserted in the Ten Commandments given by God through Moses (Ex 20:8–11). The Sabbath was often ignored or changed into a burden by people throughout history (Mt 12:1–14). Since Jesus fulfilled all the Law, every day since He said "It is finished" is a Sabbath, which explains why the Sabbath law does not appear in the New Testament when the Law is rehearsed (Lk 18:18–20; Rm 13:9–10). The Sabbath is kept in the New Testament when we rest from thoughts of self-sufficiency by the Word and Spirit of God, which inspire us to love God and to serve others as good stewards of all He has given us (Php 3:7–14).

Q **4:12 How is the Word of God sharper than any two-edged sword? How can it judge the thoughts and attitudes of the heart? Could the first part of this verse be proof that what is written in the Bible still should be held true today, and that we shouldn't move words around so that they fit in our own time?**

The terms *sharp* and *two-edged* both have to do with the effectiveness of a sword; it cuts in two directions. Similarly, because the Bible is true and clear, it is always effective (Is 55:10–11). Any attempt to change what the Bible says undermines its effectiveness, just as if you said "true is false and false is true." The Bible is effective and clear because God knows His creation, He knows the thoughts and intentions of our hearts, and He knows how to speak to us about them. The Word of God, because it is true, is like a bright light that exposes all things for what they are. But the Bible also has the capacity to work healing by communicating God's grace to us and by regenerating us to be gracious people in His image. The Bible exposes and clarifies the differences between our bodies and our souls, then separates them by inspiring us to abandon fleshly desires for material things in favor of the regenerate soul's desire to love and live in the kingdom of God (Jn 6:27–64; Php 3:7–14).

Q **4:14 What does calling Jesus a "high priest" encompass?**

Calling Jesus a "high priest" has to do with Jesus serving God on our behalf in general and has to do in particular with Him sacrificing Himself on behalf of all people (Heb 5:1–4; 8:3; 9:7). Jesus is our substitute under the Law (2Co 5:21). Jesus is our advocate and intercessor (Jn 17:9; Rm 8:34).

● ● ● ● ● ● ● ● ● ● ● ● ● ● ● ● ● ● ●

Q 4:15 Does God feel all emotions? Does He feel regret and sorrow for others? If Christ has been tempted in every way and gone through all hardships, how is He able to relate with people that are married, since He never was married? If Jesus is God and God cannot be tempted by evil, then how can we say that He was tempted?

Would it make sense to say that God feels all emotions that are not inherently wicked or evil? Perhaps it is best to note the emotions that the Bible ascribes to God and avoid any further speculation. Christ is able to relate to and sympathize with all human experiences for at least three reasons. First, as God, He knows all things, which would include our thoughts and feelings. Second, in the case of marriage, for example, Christ knows more and better than anyone who is married because marriage is His institution, which parallels His own relationship with human beings and with the Father (1Co 11:3). Christ commands husbands to love their wives and knows what it means to do so absolutely since He actually did lay down His life to make us holy and without blemish (Eph 5:25–33). Third, the human nature of Jesus is what makes it possible for Him to be tempted as we are, yet without sin. Jesus was hungry (Lk 4:2) and tired (Jn 4:6). In fact, we might consider that Jesus was more severely tempted than we are because His obedience and perfection would have made the temptations that much more intense by contrast.

● ● ● ● ● ● ● ● ● ● ● ● ● ● ● ● ● ● ●

Q 5:2 Paul says that high priests are supposed to deal with those who are ignorant and going astray. Does this mean only within their church, or are the high priests supposed to reach beyond their congregation?

The ideal High Priest is Christ, and He reached out (and still does) to all. All Christians should be kind and sympathetic with everyone else since we know our own weaknesses; we all should strive to take the log out of our own eye before removing the speck from another (Lk 6:41–42). While pastors are careful to never abandon the people they are called to shepherd, like Christ, they lead the people in drawing others into the fold (Jn 10:16; Eph 4:11–12).

● ● ● ● ● ● ● ● ● ● ● ● ● ● ● ● ● ●

Q 5:3 Why does this verse seem to imply that Jesus sinned?

Notice that v. 1 explains that we are talking about high priests chosen from "among men." At v. 5, the comparison changes from high priests (who were fallen humans) to Christ, the Son of God.

683

Q 5:4 Are only priests/pastors given a call, or do other areas of ministry receive a call from God too? How do we deal with people who take upon themselves the office without a call from God?

Every Christian is called by God, having been predestined by God from the foundation of the world (Rm 8:30). Christians who bear responsibility for and exercise authority over others in public ministry need to be called in order to authenticate them as equipped to serve as called and to insure that they are the persons whom God would have serve in such a way. Christians who are called into public ministry need to know that they have authority to serve and that they are accountable to those who are served and to God (Jn 10:1–5; Ac 13:1–3).

The Bible very consistently says that we should avoid people who are not qualified to teach the Word (Jer 23:1–3; Jn 10:1–5; 2Jn 9–11).

Q 5:5 When did God say this to Jesus, and why did He say in particular, "*Today* I have begotten You" (italics added)?

This declaration occurs first in Ps 2:7 but offers no time reference for when God said so. God the Father may have said this

Are only pastors called by God?

in eternity, since His Son is begotten from eternity (Pr 8:22–31; see also the apocryphal book Wisdom of Ben Sirach 24:1–12). Bibles that provide references may suggest the Father's declaration from heaven at Jesus' Baptism, but the relationship between God the Father and Son did not begin but was rather confirmed at that time (Mt 3:17; Mk 1:11; Lk 3:22).

Q 5:6 What exactly is "the order of Melchizedek"?

The "order" of a priesthood has to do with who founded it and how a person comes to it; for example, Franciscans among Roman Catholics or the tribe of Levi in the Old Testament (Lk 1:5–9). The order of Melchizedek is a puzzle because we have no way of knowing if the Melchizedek described in Genesis is the Son of God appearing as a man or whether the narrative is describing an earthly king, leaving out any mention of his family or origin so that he serves as an example of Christ (Heb 7:3; Gn 14:18–20).

Q 5:8 What is meant by "He learned obedience through what He suffered"?

This passage is talking about the human nature of Jesus, similar to the descriptions about Him being tempted and sympathetic (Heb 2:18; 4:15).

Q **5:12–14 What does the milk symbolize? Do these verses support a "seeker service," where one would begin with milk and move to solid food (regular Sunday worship)?**

"Milk" is defined in v. 12 as "the first principles," meaning the fundamental, simple, basic teachings of the Bible. The Bible argues against "seeker services" since public worship is evidence of the communion of saints, which depends on the communion of the saints being in place already and genuine (1Jn 1:7–9; Jn 4:24; 1Co 10:16–11:34). First we make disciples by immersing people in the Word; then such people join us in the public confession of the truth and grace they have been inspired to hold fast (Mt 28:19–20; Jn 1:12–13; 3:1–7; 8:31).

Q **5:13 Here it sounds as if we shouldn't be like infants. Doesn't this contradict Jesus' earlier commands?**

Jesus did say that unless we repent and become as children, we cannot enter the kingdom of heaven (Mt 18:3). Then Paul complained that the Corinthian people were babes and not mature (1Co 3:1–4). The solution to the apparent contradiction is to remember that we are composed of two natures: body and soul. Unless our human nature is returned to and kept in the honest dependence of infancy, it will assert itself against the truth and grace of God. Unless our regenerate soul is strong and mature, it will be dominated by the works of the flesh (Gal 5:16–26). Jesus described this relationship within us when He said, "Whoever seeks to preserve his life will lose it, but whoever loses his life will keep it" (Lk 17:33); Paul described it by commanding, "Do not be children in your thinking. Be infants in evil, but in your thinking be mature" (1Co 14:20).

Q **5:14 How will we know when we are as mature as God wants us to be?**

We will know we are mature when we see and know God as He intended from the beginning (1Co 13:9–12; 15:50–54).

Q **6:1 What is the "elementary doctrine"? Aren't we supposed to enter the kingdom of God as little children?**

The most likely meaning for "elementary doctrine" is provided in the later part of this verse and in the next verse: repentance, faith, Baptism, laying on of hands, resurrection, and eternal judgment. The idea is not that we abandon these foundational teachings but that we build on that foundation in order to grow up into the fullness of the revelation of God provided through Christ in the Word and His creation (Eph 2:19–22; 4:11–15). Our fallen human nature must repent and become as a child (honest about dependence) while our regenerate soul matures, grows, and becomes more effective according to the will and working of God (Mt 10:16; 11:25; 1Co 13:8–12).

Q **6:2 What is the "laying on of hands"?**

The laying on of hands was and continues to be a public, physical demonstration of something being transferred to a person—usually power, authority, and ability (Ac 8:17–19; 9:12, 17; 1Tm 4:14), but in one instance, guilt (Lv 16:21–22).

Q **6:4–6 Why is it impossible to bring someone back to faith? Does this mean true Christians can't fall away and then come back?**

First, we must remember that it is not for us to make any such judgment; we cannot know if any particular person has fallen to such a catastrophic condition. Second, a warning in such severe language is a necessary part of God's antidote for our fallen, careless, and contrary human nature. The purpose of such a severe warning is to prevent any person from ever being guilty of what it describes. Third, while all things are possible with God, you can see that it is impossible to do anything positive for a person who is determined and constant in his opposition to the grace of God (Mt 19:26; Lk 12:10; 14:34–35; Heb 10:26–31). Fallen human nature is always contrary to God but is broken and repented of by the power of the Word in the regenerate soul of a Christian (Rm 7:7–25). Sometimes the Law in the Word works this contrition in us, sometimes it is the law of nature, or sometimes it is both (Lk 15:11–21; 20:18; Gal 3:24). Hope is always found in God's gracious nature, in the universal vicarious atonement of Christ, and in the powerful activity of God in Word and nature to keep our fallen flesh from being the end of us.

Q **6:4 Is it better to be ignorant of God than to have learned of Him and then turned away?**

Only by comparison is it better to be ignorant of God than to despise Him by turning away (Lk 12:9–10; Heb 10:26–31). Neither condition is good for a person, so we seek to reverse the disposition of those who despise God, and we seek to inform the ignorant (Pr 26:4–5; Rm 10:14–17).

Q **6:6 What does it mean when they say they are crucifying the Son of God all over again and subjecting Him to "contempt," or public disgrace? What does this say for people who leave the Office of Ministry to do a job not even related to ministry? How is it impossible "to restore them again to repentance" when "with God all things are possible"?**

The purpose of executing someone by crucifixion was to make that person's disgrace as public and enduring as possible. The "and" in this verse indicates that "holding Him up to contempt" is an explanation of the preceding "crucifying." The crucifixion of Jesus was clear evidence of the constant, relentless, vicious contempt that motivated those who falsely arrested and condemned

Him. Any time any person follows this pattern of rejection, the impossibility of restoring that person to saving faith is a terrifying possibility (Mt 10:33; Gal 3:10–14; Heb 6:4; 10:26–31).

All things are possible with God, but not all are His will. If a person leaves the public ministry, it may be that he was not capable or genuinely called in the first place. Sometimes it is the faithful man that admits his inability to serve while many unfaithful men continue in public ministry under the pretense of serving. This warning applies to anyone described by it, whether in public ministry or not.

Q **6:7–8 What do these verses mean?**

Remember that Adam was made from the dust of the ground, so we are all similar to the ground in this description; if we bear good fruit we are blessed, but if we produce bad fruit we are cursed (Mt 7:15–20; Lk 8:5–15; Jn 15:1–6).

Q **6:8 Doesn't this verse imply salvation by works? What is "it" and what is the curse?**

This is not implying salvation by works because good works, or the fruit of the Spirit, can only be produced by God (Jn 6:29; 1Co 15:10; Eph 2:8–10). The "it" refers to the ground or, more importantly, to us, and the curse is being cut off from God (Jn 15:1–6; Gal 3:10–14).

Q **6:10 In heaven, how will God reward those who have served Him faithfully? Will the reward be greater for those who have served in a more powerful way?**

Matthew 19:29–30 records Jesus speaking about the reward for those who leave family in order to serve Him. The Bible makes clear that places of particular honor are all determined by God for us, just like the days of our life, the good works we do, and the measure of our faith (Mt 20:20–23; Ps 139:16; Eph 2:10; Rm 12:3). Jesus once mentioned that there would be different levels of punishment for the unbelieving (Mk 10:35–40; Lk 12:47–48). The Bible says very little about heaven, and I suspect this is to keep humans from having too much information to form opinions about.

Q **6:16 What does this say about making oaths, and how does it fit with the command to keep God's name holy?**

This verse is a reference to a common practice among people and not something God wills men to do. Jesus warned against making oaths or promises; James did likewise (Mt 5:33–37; Jas 4:13–17). Adding a reference to God when making assertions about ourselves or the future is strictly forbidden since we would be claiming something we cannot know and the only reason for doing so would be to deceive.

> ## How can all people know God's law?

Q **6:17 What does this mean?**

God is completely reliable, but in order to provide even greater inspiration for faith, He added an oath to His promise.

Q **6:20 What does Melchizedek have to do with Jesus?**

See answer at 5:6.

Q **7:1–4 Was Melchizedek a priest of the true God? Why is Melchizedek "greater" than Abraham?**

Genesis 14:18–20 speaks briefly of Melchizedek. Melchizedek was greater than Abraham either because He was the Son of God or because he was a great, faithful priest of God who prefigured Jesus Christ. See notes at 5:6 for more on Melchizedek.

Q **7:5 Why does the law require descendants of Levi who become priests to collect a tenth from people?**

Serving as priests meant that the Levites did not have time to provide for their own needs by farming or business activities (Nu 18:21–26; 1Co 9:1–10).

Q **7:10 If Melchizedek was a high priest, then why wasn't he of the line of Levi?**

That is the point. If God had given the sacrificial system under Moses in order to save us, then Christ would have to come from the tribe of Levi. Notice that Jesus was not from anyone's firstborn son, not of Abraham, Isaac, or Jacob; nor was He from the priestly family of Levi—showing the impossibility for man to save himself from the condemnation of the Law. Only the Son of God, having taken to Himself a human nature, could fulfill the Law for everyone and so save us from it (Rm 8:1–4; Gal 4:4–5; Heb 8:7–9:15).

Q **8:4 Does this mean that no individual should bear the title of "priest"?**

This verse is making clear the distinction between the incarnate Son of God, Jesus Christ, and all the priests who are born of fallen human beings. Christianity uses terms such as *pastor*, *elder*, and *bishop* because these are the terms used by the New Testament and because the purpose of the priesthood was fulfilled by Jesus once and for all (Heb 7:27; 9:12).

Q **8:6–7 How did God institute an inadequate covenant? What was wrong with it?**

There are two kinds of "testaments" in the Old Testament. One kind of testament is "unilateral," meaning it is one way—from God to us—and it depends entirely on Him. The other kind of testament is "bilateral," meaning God agrees to do certain things as long as we fulfill what is required of us. Fallen human nature is proud and selfish and so unable to keep the law of love, but also unable to be honest about its failure. In order to demonstrate this truth to us over and over again, God provided a testament through Moses where the agreement was inadequate because we cannot ever do what is required of us (Gal 3:10–24). Realizing our inadequacy under the Law is what drives us in honesty and humility to Christ, who fulfilled all the Law for us (Rm 8:1–4).

Q **8:8–13 Is the new covenant the way they learned about Christ's second coming?**

The verses here that speak of a new covenant are quotations from Jer 31:31–34. These verses describe how God promised the Old Testament people that He would provide for our salvation without fail by the first coming of Christ. The second coming of Christ is the fulfillment of all that God has promised and is already providing blessings in the lives of His faithful people.

Q **8:10 So, for those people in the far corners of the earth who haven't heard the Bible, God, or Jesus, how is it that God's Law is on their hearts and minds? How do they "all" know Him? Who exactly did God start this "new" covenant with?**

All people have the Law written on their hearts, even though this promise is looking forward to the extraordinary work of God in regeneration by the Holy Spirit (Rm 2:15; 1Jn 2:20, 27). The Lord had the people at the far corners of the earth in mind when He commanded His apostles to make disciples of all nations (Mt 28:19–20; Mk 16:15–16). Paul was striving to fulfill that intention of the Lord before his own life's end (Rm 10:18). You may also want to remember that God has provided a universal, constant, and powerful witness to Himself in nature and reason, no matter where a person lives (Ps 19:1–4; Rm 1:20; 6:21; Pr 1:1–5).

Q **8:11 Shall we assume there is no need to speak the Word to our neighbor since we can be confident that he already knows the Lord, because the Law is written on his heart?**

The Law is written on the heart, but the Gospel is not. Any honest person can recognize the disaster we bring upon ourselves, but we can only hope that God has provided a solution for this (Rm 10:14). The Word of God is needed for a person to have particular knowledge of Christ and the benefits that knowledge brings (2Pt 1:2–12). The heart that knows the Lord is provided by the Lord through the Word and Sacraments (Ezk 36:24–27; 1Jn 2:20, 27).

Q **9:1 Is this implying that the second covenant doesn't have regulations for worship?**

The covenant with Israel was all Law; if Israel would keep the Law, then God would provide paradise for them. The second covenant is free of the Law for two reasons: 1) because Christ fulfilled all the Law and 2) because the soul regenerated by God is oriented and inspired to love God and neighbor as God intended from the beginning (Rm 10:4; 1Jn 3:9; Is 40:2). You may note that neither Jesus nor the apostles prescribed regulations for worship; rather, they make clear the essence and ideal of worship (Jn 4:24; Ac 2:42). The challenge for worship isn't about regulations but about orientation toward God and the soul rather than human vanity and selfishness.

Q **9:2 What is this "tent" the verse refers to?**

This tent, also known as a "tabernacle," was the place in Old Testament times where God revealed His presence in the midst of Israel (Ex 40:33–37). In New Testament times, the Son of God took on human nature as His "tabernacle," and He has provided His enduring presence in the Holy Bible (Jn 1:14; 2Tm 3:16).

Q **9:4 What is the significance of the gold-covered ark of the covenant?**

Nearly everything inside the tabernacle, and later in the temple built by David, was covered with God to reflect the incomparable presence of the Lord (Ex 25–26). The ark in particular, with the mercy seat above, was the place where God came to meet with Israel (Ex 25:21–22).

Q **9:7 Was the blood from a human or an animal?**

It was real blood from a real animal that had been sacrificed—just as the blood of Jesus was really given and shed in order to save us from the condemnation of the Law. The high priest entered the Most Holy Place (where the ark of the covenant rested) only once a year, on the Day of Atonement (Ex 30:1–10). The text makes clear that even the high priest of Israel was still as guilty under the Law as the people he represented. The high priest needed atonement just as much as any other Israelite or foreigner (Heb 7:25–28).

Q **9:11–15 Does the idea of tabernacle and sacrifices being done away with through Jesus apply in today's churches as well? Many times, focus gets shifted to the external regulations, like order of worship; so how should the Church interpret this** idea of a cleansed conscience so that the focus may be on serving the living God?

Yes, Jesus fulfilled all of the Law in order to save us from its condemnation, and Jesus regenerates us in His image so that we are oriented and inspired to realize a fullness of life by loving others as He loves us (Rm 10:4; Gal 4:4–7; 1Jn 3:9; 4:19). The life of the Church is a product of the love of God for us communicated to us through the Means of Grace (Ac 2:42–45; Jn 4:24). Regulations, orders of worship, and all other aspects of our lives are adopted or rejected on the basis of their consistency with God's Word and thus their effectiveness in advancing His kingdom.

Q 9:11 What is the "greater and more perfect tent (not made by hands . . .)"? What are the "good things"?

The perfect tabernacle made without hands is Jesus (Jn 1:14; note in this verse that the word used for Jesus dwelling among us has the same root as *tabernacle*). The "good things that have come" have to do with the New Testament: having the Word written in our hearts and minds, having the Word and Means of Grace readily available to us, enjoying freedom from the curse of the Law, and most of all, the resurrection from the dead into a new heavens and earth (Jer 31:31–34; Ezk 36:24–27; 1Jn 2:20, 27; Gal 3:13).

Q 9:17 What is meant by "a will takes effect only at death"?

While a person is alive, he retains control of his estate, no matter what is written in his will. On the other hand, once that person dies, his will remains in force, no matter what. The legal will of a person who has died is nearly impossible to contradict or alter.

Q 9:22 Did the people of the Old Testament need shedding of blood for forgiveness because Jesus hadn't died yet?

The people in Old Testament times needed the shedding of blood not for forgiveness, but as a constant reminder of the need for a Messiah who provided forgiveness eternally through God's promises and His redemptive work (Heb 10:4).

Q 9:23 What are "better sacrifices"? If heaven is perfect, why does this verse talk about purifying heavenly things?

"Better sacrifices" have to do with the living sacrifices of people in contrast to the blood of bulls and goats (Heb 10:4–7). The very best and all-sufficient sacrifice was that of Christ. The means and inspiration of presenting our bodies as living sacrifices on behalf of one another flow from His (Heb 7:27; Rm 12:1). The term "heavenly things" does not refer to objects in a physical place far away but to spiritual things in contrast to physical (1Co 15:40, 48–49; Eph 1:3; 3:10; 6:12). Jesus once explained to Nicodemus that unless a person is "born again he cannot see the kingdom of God" (Jn 3:3; see also v. 5). Nicodemus could not understand that Jesus was talking about the essence of our lives as spiritual beings, not just a paradise where the faithful who have passed away reside until the end of this world (v. 10).

Q 9:25 What do Catholics say about this verse?

First of all, distinguish between Roman Catholics, who obligate themselves to the teachings and decrees of the Pope and Roman tradition, and the catholic or "universal" Church, which consists of all of God's people of all times and places. The Roman Catholic Church contradicts this verse by teaching that Jesus is sacrificed again and again every time a priest says the mass: "Christ arranged His religion so that all of us could offer up the most perfect sacrifice. In the Catholic church we actually offer up Jesus Christ Himself—not goats, oxen, or lambs" (*Instructions in the Catholic Faith* [Des Plaines: Fare Inc., 1976], p. 98).

Q 9:27 Why do so many people believe in reincarnation?

Many people believe in reincarnation because that is what they have been taught and because the populations in places where this is taught are large, like India and China. Reincarnation is a popular belief because it relieves the fear of eternal condemnation; you live as many lives as it takes for you to reach paradise. Every religious system except biblical Christianity has a "second chance" component. Non-Christian systems and mistaken versions of Christianity need some way of trying again after you die because your salvation depends on yourself, yet we are incapable of what is necessary to live. The other significant challenge for accepting reincarnation has to do with the reality of it: Is there reincarnation? If reincarnation were real, how would we know? And how would we know how it works? A reincarnation that results in eternal life might just as easily result in eternal death. Genuine Christianity needs no "second chance" component because we have been saved already, and the realization of our salvation is God's work entirely. No amount of "second chances" will change the self-defeating condition of fallen human nature, and no amount of chance can defeat God's saving work in us.

Q 9:28 If we have already received salvation and eternal rest in heaven, why do we wait for salvation when Jesus comes a second time? Won't we already be there? When we die, do we go straight to heaven, or are we waiting for Christ's return?

Salvation actually comes to us in three ways. We are already saved now and realize many benefits of this salvation, but our fallen human nature, our fallen world, and the devil still make trouble (Mk 1:14–28; 1Co 4:8; 1Jn 3:9). We realize relief from all that makes trouble when our human nature passes away and we join God in heaven (Lk 16:22–25; Rv 7:9–17). We realize the fullness of our redemption when God re-creates the heavens and the earth and restores our human nature to us (1Co 15:1–58; 1Jn 3:1–2). The essence of a human being, the soul, is always conscious ("alive," if you will). When the body passes away, the soul goes immediately to heaven or hell (Lk 16:22; 23:42–43).

● ● ● ● ● ● ● ● ● ● ● ● ● ● ● ● ● ● ● ●

Q 10:1–18 Is this speaking of universal justification?

Yes; all people of all times and places were justified when Jesus fulfilled all that the Law required, saying, "It is finished" (Jn 19:30).

● ● ● ● ● ● ● ● ● ● ● ● ● ● ● ● ● ● ● ●

Q 10:1 Why is the Law considered good, since it is supposed to show us our faults? How is the Law a shadow of good things that are coming and not realities themselves? Did God put an end to the sacrificial system in the Old Testament?

The Law is good because it accurately describes reality and what is required to live. Laws provide order that sustains life and necessarily provide the consequences of opposing what life is made of. Our faults are the problem, not the Law that exposes them (Rm 7:7–12). If the Law were not present to

Why is the Law considered good?

expose our faults, how would we recognize them as the source of our trouble? The sacrificial laws are called "a shadow" because they indicated but never accomplished our redemption (Heb 10:11).

The whole Old Testament history and the history of the Jewish people to this day continue to demonstrate that the sacrificial system has no power to justify or give life. But the sacrificial system does remind us that contradicting God's design in creation has real consequences and that nothing short of God Himself could accomplish what was necessary to restore creation (Rm 8:3). God did put an end to the sacrificial system by the incarnation of His Son and His sacrifice (Mt 9:9–13; Lk 22:15–16; Heb 7:27). Some Jews would like to practice the sacrificial system but cannot because they have no Levites to serve as priests, no ownership of the location in Jerusalem where the sacrifices were to be offered, and no temple in which to offer them. Other Jews do not care about offering sacrifices because they see the Old Testament as either legend intended to teach a moral lesson or ancient practices that have given way to more enlightened ways of thinking.

Q **10:4 Why did God command the sacrifice of animals if that practice did not offer forgiveness? If someone did theoretically keep the ceremonial law perfectly, would it take away sin? Why does the author try to argue why Jesus is the Christ? Is it not faith, rather than logic or reason, that saves us?**

First, consider the significance of God saying that He desires mercy, not sacrifice. This means that everything else that God does must be a function of or in the service of His mercy. God's mercy provided the sacrifice of substitutes for us—animals that pointed forward to Jesus. Notice how the substitutionary work of Jesus is made physically evident in the exchange of Jesus for Barabbas (Mt 27:16–26). Jesus did keep the ceremonial law perfectly and did take away sin, but this worked because He also kept all of the Law for all people of all time, which is why He had to be both true God and true man. This is the very point the Letter to the Hebrews is trying to make. Fallen human nature is forever idolizing something less than God in order to seize control and justify itself (Ex 32:1–4; 1Sm 8:4–7). If we consider that faith means "honesty about dependence," then we can see that logic and reason have their place in our salvation. Our fallen human nature is not capable of faith but must be silenced by the clear truth (Jn 3:1–7; Rm 3:19; 1Co 2:14; 15:50). While the truth about Jesus is bringing fallen human nature to honest humility, that same truth is regenerating and inspiring the soul

that lives because of Him (Jn 5:41–47; Ac 15:1–11; Gal 3:1–14). Christ alone saves us, but reason and logic serve this salvation by revealing why and how He did so.

Q **10:8 If God does not desire sacrifices, why does the Old Testament law require them?**

What is the relationship between a requirement and a desire? A general may require soldiers to attack the enemy and command them to do so, but his desire is that they should live, not die. How could God take pleasure in the death of any living thing when He had created a world where nothing died (Gn 1:29–31; 2:16–17; Ezk 18:32; 33:11)? God's institution of the sacrificial system in the Old Testament was a function of His mercy in at least two ways. First, God was mercifully providing the substitution of the life of His own Son for ours, and the animals that died pointed forward to the sacrifice of Christ (Gn 3:15, 21; Is 53:1–12; 2Co 5:21). Second, God would teach mercy by providing a clear witness to the cost of being merciless. We all too easily hide the consequences of our wicked, fallen human nature from ourselves, but the slaughter and blood of innocent animals forced a recognition that our pride and selfishness has constant, real, and deadly effect (Mt 27–48; Rm 2:4; 1Jn 1:8–9).

Q **10:11 Did these Old Testament people under the Law know they were cleansed by the coming Messiah? If not, what was the use of these sacrifices?**

Apart from the biblical narrative, we know little about what these people thought. Hebrews 11:4–40 gives some insights into the understanding of Abel, Abraham, Isaac, Jacob, and others. We might also consider that a God who is all-knowing is able to make His intent in the sacrificial system understood through the sacrifices and the servants of His Word whom He sent to lead the people (Ezr 8:1–9).

Q **10:12–13 What do these verses mean?**

The priest described here is Jesus Christ, whose human nature made it possible for Him to sacrifice His life and whose divine nature assured that He would do this once for all—for all sins of all people of all time and all places. Anyone who opposes God's work in Christ must still serve God's purposes, though in despicable ("footstool," v. 13) rather than honorable ways (Ac 2:22–24; Rm 8:28; 2Co 4:17–18).

Q **10:17–18 How do we know for sure that God will really forgive us and forget about our sins instead of holding onto them and using them to punish us?**

We know by God's Word and deed that He will not punish us according to our sins—there is nothing more certain than God's Word and accomplished deeds (Heb 6:13–18). The Bible is full of texts that express and explain the grace of God, which moves Him to save rather than condemn us, such as Ps 103:10–17 and Eph 2:1–9. The Bible itself is the history of God providing a substitutionary atonement for the sins of all. For example, God provided a ram for Abraham to sacrifice instead of his son Isaac (Gn 22:1–14). The Old Testament sacrificial system was instituted as a constant reminder of God's promise to redeem the whole world by the life of His own Son (Gn 3:15; Is 53:1–12). Jesus' institution of the Lord's Supper and the release of Barabbas bear witness to the fact that He is the everlasting sacrifice on behalf of all (Lk 22:14–20; 23:13–25). Paul preached Jesus Christ "and Him crucified" (1Co 2:2) because God executed all of the force of the Law against His Son in the crucifixion. This is the everlasting answer to your question.

Q **10:17 What is meant by "lawless deeds"?**

The original word (*anomos*) is very simple; it means "to be contrary to or against the law." Simply think of all the ways in which we act against the Ten Commandments.

● ●

Q **10:25 As Christians, are we sinning willfully if we do not go to church every week? Is the importance of "meeting together" only to be encouraged?**

Christians don't "have" to go to church for two reasons. First, because we *are* the Church, and second, because Christian life is a matter of love and gratitude, not obligation (Eph 2:19–22; Rm 10:4–8). Christians remain in the Word (Jn 8:31), which produces fellowship that provides occasion for the Lord's Supper and common prayers (Ac 2:42). The Early Christians met together on the day of the Lord's resurrection (Sunday) at the rising of the sun (morning) as the visible Body of Christ (the Church) to receive the body of Christ (Lord's Supper) from Christ Himself (in the person of the pastor). This public activity of the Church is the product of the Christian's constant life in the Word—just like fruit comes from a living tree with roots constantly in the soil, or like the tip of an iceberg, which depends on the majority of the iceberg, which is hidden from view. Meeting together in public gives Christians a chance to recognize a "like precious faith" and encourage one another (2Pt 1:1; 1Co 14).

● ●

Q **10:26 What about those who hear about Jesus but don't accept His salvation until years later? When we continue to repeat sins, even though penitent, are we willfully sinning? Don't we do this all the time?**

The salvation of God through Jesus' vicarious atonement is accomplished and for all people. Any person who is contrary to the benefits of that salvation suffers from an existence without them, and if a person died in such a state, he would suffer judgment apart from Christ (Mt 25:1–46; Gal 3:1–10). Anytime a person is honest about his dependence on God and remains in the Word, that person immediately begins to realize the benefits of what Christ has done (Ac 2:38–42). Fallen human nature is always contrary to God, no matter how strongly a regenerate, believing soul within wants to do what is right (Rm 7:13–25; 1Co 2:14). Sinning willfully has to do with constant, consistent, conscious, determined, proud, and arrogant opposition to what we clearly know is good and right. There is no salvation for a person in such a condition because there is clearly no active regenerate soul that is clinging to and in communion with the grace of God (see Heb 10:29). Any person who is concerned about being guilty of this sin is likely not guilty of it since the person this verse is speaking about never gives a single thought to what is good and right. Our fallen human nature is always contrary to God and life, but there is an absolute difference between that nature being all there is to a person and that nature being counteracted by a regenerate soul made strong by the Word and Sacraments.

● ●

Q **10:26–31 If we have previously sinned but now have been brought back to the faith, are we still able to receive eternal life?**

This passage does not say it is impossible for such a person to be brought back into the faith and eternal life. However, Heb 6:4–8 and Mt 12:31–32 describe a condition similar or identical and include the warning that it is impossible to restore such a person. We must be careful not to conclude that such is the case with any person, including ourselves, as we cannot know this for certain and would be guilty of the Lord's prohibition against condemning others (Mt 7:1). What we know for certain is that such a condition is to be avoided absolutely and that God is very gracious to have rescued us from it.

● ●

Q **10:28 What is the significance of two or three witnesses? What about those before Moses? What criteria do we have for them?**

The purpose of requiring two or three witnesses was to provide a means of confirming the truth and exposing false witness (Mk 14:55–59; Gn 41:32; Mt 18:20). However, this measure did not always prevent the wicked from agreeing about false testimony before giving it against someone (1Ki 21:4–14; Mt 26:59–61). This practice was likely widespread before the Law was given to Moses as a practice of common sense

and justice. In many cases, the Law that was given to Moses was consistent with practices already upheld (cf. Gn 38:1–26 with Dt 25:5–10).

● ●

Q **10:29 What does it mean to "spurn the Son of God" or to trample "underfoot the Son of God"? How do we make sure that we are not rejecting the Spirit?**

"Outrag[ing] the Spirit" (v. 29) is related to spurning the Son of God and counting the blood of the covenant a common thing. The Holy Spirit comes to us through the Word of God and the Sacraments. When a person ignores or neglects time in the Word for other activities, he or she is trampling the Son of God underfoot; that is to say, he or she is depending on Christ but only using Him as the means to be committed elsewhere. Multitudes of people count the blood of the covenant a common thing as is evident from how infrequently they receive the Lord's Supper. Some churches and church bodies clearly count the very body and blood of Christ as common by how infrequently they offer the Lord's Supper or by their denial that it really is the true body and blood of Christ. Thus, "outraging the Spirit" means rejecting, ignoring, and neglecting the Holy Spirit and essentially telling the Holy Spirit you have no use for Him. The only way to make sure we are not making this mistake is to remain in the Word (Jn 8:31–32; Ac 2:42; Rm 10:17).

Q 10:31 Does this mean that we shouldn't get on God's bad side?

First of all, God doesn't have a bad side, which is very good news for us (1Jn 1:5). Second, trying to live in opposition to the One who is alone God, the creator and author of life, is self-destructive and useless. Third, it must necessarily be fearful to fall into the hands of the living God. The nature of our relationship with God determines whether falling into His hands means disaster or deliverance (Mt 25:31–46; Heb 2:1–4).

Q 10:35 What is this confidence?

The word translated "confidence" in your Bible has to do with certainty about something that cannot be hidden, dismissed, or overcome; it has to do with being obvious, clear, and unmistakable (Mk 8:32; Jn 7:14; 10:24; Eph 3:12; 6:19).

Q 10:36 Is heaven what we have been promised to receive?

Yes, heaven, plus every other gift that God has promised—a body resurrected in perfection, a re-created heaven and earth, no more tears or pain, and life in the presence of God eternally.

Q 10:38 Who is "My righteous one"?

Hebrews is quoting Hab 2:4, "The righteous shall live by his faith." This is talking about those who believe that Jesus has fulfilled the righteous requirements of the Law on behalf of us all (Rm 1:16–17; 10:1–17). The person who "shrinks back" is a person like the one described in Heb 6:4–8; 10:26–31 (see questions and answers there).

Q 11:1–40 What is the point in making this section so long? In this day and age, we are told to learn from our mistakes and the mistakes of others. Should we ignore the mistakes and only focus on the positive?

The point of making this section so long is to drive home the point that Hebrews has been making from the beginning: honesty about dependence on Christ is everything. We have seen many examples of people refusing to be honest about their dependence, and those who are mentioned here for their faith also had times when they failed. The difference isn't that some people are sinners and others are saints; the difference is that some refuse to be honest about their condition while others, in honesty, realize the salvation of Christ because they know they depend entirely on Him—and He is entirely dependable. Learning from our mistakes is an important means of avoiding trouble, but not as important as a life in the Word that confirms forgiveness for our failures and regenerates our soul, which lives according to God's good will (Eph 2:1–10; 1Jn 1:7–9; 3:18).

Q 11:2 Who are "the people of old"?

The word translated here as "people of old" is normally translated as "elder." The term *elder* can mean an older person but is really concerned with wisdom and maturity that does not necessarily come with age. If you read on, you will note that this chapter is talking about wise and mature people from ancient times.

Q 11:3 Does the phrase "by faith" show that faith is not ours but is a gift of God?

The Bible reveals that faith is God's work and a gift to us, no matter how well or badly people translate the text. For example, many translations use the expression that such-and-such a person "put his faith in" something, which makes it sound like faith is a thing and we decide what to do with it. On the contrary, faith or belief or trust (all are the same word in Greek) means to be honest about our dependence on God. This condition is God's work and is described as such in many places, like Jn 6:29 and 1Pt 1:5.

Q 11:5 Since Enoch was a sinner, how is it possible that he was taken to heaven without experiencing death? How could he have pleased God?

This verse provides the explanation that Enoch "pleased God" by faith. The beginning of v. 5 and then v. 6 remind us that only by faith can fallen human beings please God. Paul informed us that God assigns a measure of faith to each person (just as He numbers our days and prepares good works for us; Rm 12:3; Ps 139:16; Eph 2:10). Enoch pleased God because God regenerated him and inspired him to do so—as an inspiration to us and a demonstration of what God does sooner or later for everyone He brings to faith.

Q 11:6 Is faith needed for God to hear your prayers? If a person without faith does something good, will it mean nothing to God?

According to this verse, faith is needed for any and every positive aspect of a relationship with God. If we define faith as "honesty about dependence," then the necessity of faith becomes obvious. While good works are helpful to our neighbor, if they are done in the absence of faith, they are not pleasing to God because such works are done from motivation that still retains an element of selfishness and self-righteousness, no matter how slight (Is 64:6). Even prayers that are not generated by faith are an abomination to God since they refuse the honesty that allows for real communion and communication between God and man (Pr 28:9).

Q 11:7 Is the "reverent fear" that Noah felt fear of God or of the flood?

The word translated as "reverent fear" appears only here in the New Testament but many times in the Old Testament. The word means "to be cautious" because doing so is prudent, given the circumstances. Noah obeyed God because he was honest about his dependence on God. Noah took God's warning of the flood and instructions for the ark seriously and therefore acted upon them.

Q 11:13–14 What does it mean that the people are "seeking a homeland"?

Notice in v. 13 that these people confessed that they were strangers and sojourners on the earth. People who are faithful are so because the Word has regenerated them and inspires them to be people of God's kingdom—spiritual and innocent rather than physical and wicked (Jn 1:11–13; 3:1–7; 8:43–59). Abraham and the others knew that their fallen human nature and this world were passing away, but that God had given them a new, spiritual citizenship in the kingdom of heaven. This is the country they were looking for and looking forward to (1Jn 2:15–17).

Q 11:16 Is this saying that even those who died before Jesus' resurrection are saved merely because of their faith in God's promise? Did God prepare a city because of their faith?

All people of all time have been saved by the substitutionary life of Jesus. He fulfilled all that the Law requires in order to live in body and soul during His life, then He died under the condemnation of the Law for everyone of all time, and then He rose from the dead (Rm 5:6–21; 8:1–5). Faith realizes or obtains the benefits of this salvation because faith is honesty about our dependence on Jesus (Mt 18:3; 1Pt 1:3–5). The city that God has prepared is not about buildings and streets but about harmony between people who live in perfect communion with God and one another (Rv 21:2–22:5).

Q 11:19 It says that Abraham "considered that God was able even to raise him from the dead." Where is proof of that?

The report of how and what Abraham reasoned is likely based on Abraham's immediate obedience to God's command, perhaps oral tradition originating with Abraham himself, but most of all on the inspiration of the Holy Spirit (2Tm 3:16). We might even wonder how anyone could miss the reasonable consideration that God, who created a son through Sarah when this had been impossible, was certainly able to raise such a son from the dead. Which is more difficult, making a human being from parents who could not conceive or raising from the dead a person already conceived (Mk 2:8–11)?

● ● ● ● ● ● ● ● ● ● ● ● ● ● ● ● ● ● ●

Q **11:20 Isaac didn't intentionally bless Esau and Jacob, so how is it an act of faith?**

The expression "by faith" points to what is beyond us, not what is within our ability (Rm 4:1–4; Jn 11:49–52). Isaac blessed his two sons as he did because God was working out history according to His will and for our learning (1Co 10:6, 11). Being moved, inspired, guided, and led according to God's will, Word, and Spirit is what "by faith" means (Ps 47:5; Pr 20:24; Jer 23:10).

● ● ● ● ● ● ● ● ● ● ● ● ● ● ● ● ● ● ●

Q **11:21 What does it mean when Jacob is commended for his faith because he worshiped as he leaned on the top of his staff?**

The part about Jacob leaning on his staff is a historical detail rather than a matter of faith. Faith had to do with Jacob's ability to bless each of his sons according to God's will and foreknowledge, which the rest of the history of Israel reveals. (See 11:20 for more on the meaning of "by faith." See Ac 2:23; Rm 8:28–30; and Eph 2:8–10 for more on God's foreknowledge.)

● ● ● ● ● ● ● ● ● ● ● ● ● ● ● ● ● ● ●

Q **11:27 Didn't Moses flee out of fear because he was a murderer?**

Moses did flee Egypt after he killed an Egyptian because he was afraid of Pharaoh (Ex 2:11–15). This passage is talking about Moses after he returned to Egypt in order to lead Israel out of bondage to the Promised Land. At that time, Moses had no fear of Pharaoh (Ex 10:27–29).

● ● ● ● ● ● ● ● ● ● ● ● ● ● ● ● ● ● ●

Q **11:32 How does Jephthah, who made a tragic vow (Jgs 11), fit into this chapter of the faithful?**

Who is there in biblical history that did not suffer the consequences of a fallen human nature that was contrary to faith (1Co 2:14)? Adam, the patriarchs, the judges, the prophets, and the kings all bore witness to what the Savior would be but could not save even their own lives because of their failures (Heb 5:1–4; 7:23–28). The Son of God became a man in order to do perfectly and accomplish all that we fail to do—and this He did for us, so we might live in spite of our failures, through faith (Rm 8:1–11).

● ● ● ● ● ● ● ● ● ● ● ● ● ● ● ● ● ● ●

Q **11:35 What is meant by "rise again to a better life"?**

Many people were raised from the dead in biblical times, but they all died again later in their lives (1Ki 17:17–24; Jn 11:38–44). The resurrection referred to in this verse is the one that comes at the end of the world, when we will have received a perfect body for all eternity (1Co 15:35–58).

Q **11:40 Does this verse apply to life before or after death?**

This verse applies to both, but ultimately to life after death. All during our life, God is fulfilling promises to us—giving us life, forgiving us, regenerating our soul, raising us up again and again from trouble, failure, and disappointment. But we never know the fullness of the life He has for us or of His promises until death delivers us from this fallen human nature and the resurrection and re-creation is completed by God (1Co 13:12; 15:20–58; Rv 21:2–22:5).

Q **12:1–2 Why is the analogy of the race used? Why do we keep all our possessions so close? Why don't churches help us cast them off?**

The footrace analogy is used because a runner has a singular purpose, refuses to be encumbered or distracted, and must endure. None of us would be materialistic if we had to carry what we call "our own" with us as we ran. We are possessive and materialistic because our human nature is physical and seeks its life from physical things, even though they are always passing away (Is 55:1–3; Jn 6:27; 1Jn 2:15–17). Human nature apart from God is like a drowning person, climbing up on anything and everything in order to escape the process of sinking. Churches, as physical, human institutions, are just as materialistic as the people that organize and promote them. The only real remedy for human nature is a regenerate soul, raised continually to life by the Word and Spirit of God.

Q **12:1 What is the great "cloud of witnesses"? Do all these "witnesses" need to be Christians?**

The great "cloud of witnesses" are the people referred to throughout Heb 11. Consider that a cloud is living (moving) water in a visible form; so also people of faith are visible evidence of the living water of God's Word at work in them (Jn 4:1–42). These witnesses couldn't be anything but Christians since the Spirit of God that regenerated and led them did so by faith in the promised Christ (1Co 12:3).

Q **12:4 What does this verse mean or imply?**

Many people do not care to struggle against sin at all. People who do struggle with sin often feel sorry for themselves, as if denying the fallen passions of the flesh constituted serious suffering, in contrast to the real suffering of genuinely faithful people, recounted in Heb 11. What our human nature dreads, our regenerate soul rejoices in (and vice versa; Rm 7:14–21; 2Co 12:1–10).

Q **12:5 How does God discipline us?**

Paul provides a marvelous account of how God disciplines us (Ac 8:1–24:31; 2Co 12:1–10; see also remarks of Paul throughout his letters). Generally speaking, God disciplines us in a way that parallels the way coaches train athletes: God strains our fallen human nature, then gives it rest in order to make it serve while continually inspiring and regenerating our soul.

Q 12:8–9 Why do the fathers not discipline their sons?

Human fathers fail to discipline their sons for the same reason everyone continually fails to do what promotes life according to God's design. In particular, fathers fail to discipline their sons either because they don't care enough (lazy), because they are afraid to do so (selfish), or because they don't know how (ignorant). (See 1Sm 2:12, 29; 2Sm 13:1–19:6.)

Q 12:13 What does this verse mean?

This verse is making a comparison between a leg that is lame and a person who is struggling to do what is right. Wisdom instructs a person who is lame to bind up that leg so that it will not be dislocated but rather heal. Similarly, we need to wrap ourselves with the Word and grace of God so that our fallen human nature does not dislocate our relationship with God and others. The wisdom of God keeps us from stumbling, which would make our condition worse. The grace of God promotes healing and strengthens our ability to live in the love of God and communicate that love to others in word and deed.

Q 12:14 Is this passage saying that war is wrong? Doesn't this verse sound like works-righteousness?

There are many significant differences between reasons for waging war; some are godly and some are ungodly. God holds civil government responsible to fight against oppressors on behalf of the people (Rm 13:1–4). War is not for individuals to wage, nor for nations to instigate in self-interest. Spiritual warfare is an entirely different matter (2Co 10:3–6). This verse does not say that we can make ourselves righteous or that God expects us to do so. The Law requires a person to keep it in order to live (Mt 5:20; Gal 3:11–14). The Gospel explains how Christ fulfilled the requirements of the Law and so has already justified all.

Q 12:16 Why is Esau's godlessness equated with selling his birthright for a meal?

Esau's godlessness is not equated with that action, but his godlessness is evident by the fact that he thought so little of his birthright ("despised" it, Gn 25:34) that he sold it for a bowl of stew (v. 32). Are we not doing something similar whenever we trade time with the Word of God for time with the fallen world (Is 55:1–3; Jn 6:26–67; Heb 2:1–4)?

Q 12:18–25 What is Paul referring to when he talks about a mountain that cannot be touched? Why is God called a consuming fire, as this seems to relate Him to Satan?

When God had brought Israel out of Egypt, He met with Moses at Mount Sinai. God commanded and warned the people to keep their distance, lest they die (Ex 19:17–24). Mount Sinai is where God dictated the Law to Moses, the Law that always exposes our failure (Ex 20:1–17; Mt 5:17–48; Jas 2:10–11). Mount Zion, or Calvary, is where the incarnate Son of God came to be with people and to redeem them from the curse of the Law (Gn 22:5–14; Mt 1:23; Gal 3:10–14; 4:4–5).

God is, among other things, a consuming fire. The Word of God thrives in, endures, and protects us from fire (Dn 3:19–25; Rm 8:1). The sun was created by God as a witness to one aspect of His nature (Gn 1:14–19; Jn 1:4–5; Ps 19:1–3). Since God is almighty and always righteous, He is a fire that burns eternally and consumes everything that is not righteous (1Jn 1:5–10). God is also love, which is both why and how He redeemed us from the condemnation of the Law (4:8; Jn 3:16). Satan is not the source of fire nor fire itself; Satan is condemned to the judgment of fire (Rv 20:10).

Q 12:27 What can and cannot be shaken by the Lord's voice?

This verse says that things that are made can be shaken. The only thing that is not made is God Himself (Pr 8:22–31; Jn 1:3). If we are regenerated by the Word of God, then we can endure and not be shaken (Mt 7:24–27; Ps 62:6; 2Th 2:2).

Q 13:2 What does it mean to "show hospitality to strangers"? How have some entertained "angels"?

The word *angel* is Greek, meaning "messenger." The text speaks of entertaining "angels unawares." The word *angel* occurs 463 times in the Bible. A messenger can be a divine creature that does what God commands or a human being that does the same (Gn 19:1; Mt 4:11; Rv 1:20–3:14). The most obvious example of what this verse is talking about is Gn 18:1–19. In this account, the Lord visited Abraham in the form of a man, having two angels with Him who were also in human form. However, the text indicates that Abraham was aware of the nature of his visitors. There are many other accounts of the Lord or angels visiting people and accounts of people showing hospitality, but not to angels and not unaware (Jgs 13:3–23; 1Ki 17:8–16). Jesus explained that anytime we care for another person, it is the same as if we were caring for Him (Mt 10:40–42; 25:31–46). So the point of this passage is that Christians help anyone as often as we are able because we are God's agents in this world and because we never know who or how God has determined that we should help other agents of His activity among us (Gal 6:10).

Q 13:3 Why should we treat prisoners as if we were in prison with them and the mistreated as if we were suffering?

This passage is not talking to those who hold prisoners about how to treat them, though mistreating prisoners is certainly contrary to God's will (as is mistreating anyone at any time). This passage urges us to remember people who are prisoners (especially those wrongfully imprisoned, like Paul; Ac 21:26–28:31) and who are mistreated (2Co 4:8–10). The word *sympathy* is Greek, meaning "to suffer with" someone. Sympathy reminds us to treat others as we would want to be treated (Mt 7:12). God's providence for each of us means that we are free from selfish concerns to apply our lives for the care of others (Lk 10:25–37). There is nothing better for us than to realize what it means to be made in the image of God by providing for others. There is nothing more extraordinary than living a life that appreciates how God provides for us through others (Php 4:11–13).

Q 13:9–10 How does this relate to Holy Communion?

The Lord's Supper certainly comes to mind with these verses since the Christian Church has had altars in the sanctuary for so many centuries and because the Lord's Supper is served from that altar. However, Jesus did not institute the Lord's Supper in a church or on an altar but in the upper room of a man's home. This verse means to review the contrast that has been made throughout Hebrews between the Old and New Testaments. Some people rejected Christ Jesus because they refused to give up their efforts to justify themselves, as if making animal sacrifices could accomplish this (Rm 10:1–2; Heb 10:4). Our "altar" is the whole New Testament, accomplished by Jesus and conveyed to us through His Word, Spirit, and Sacraments. Those who would justify themselves cannot realize the benefits of God's gifts as long as they oppose them (Gal 3:1–29).

Q 13:17 Do you think church meetings and classroom situations would be helped by this verse if people considered how their following affects the leader's abilities?

All of the verses in the Bible help because they communicate the grace and wisdom of God. Certainly leaders and followers would benefit from cooperation. However, a passage that calls followers to obedience makes passages that call leaders to accountability all the more important (Jer 23:1–6; Mt 18:6–9; 1Pt 5:2–4).

Q 13:24 Was Italy a country when Paul wrote this letter?

Italy was a country when Paul wrote this letter (as was Spain, Rm 15:24). However, Italy was not unified as a nation but was composed of city-states with centers like Milan, Florence, Venice, Rome, and Naples.

James

Q 1:1 Who was James referring to when he says, "To the twelve tribes in the Dispersion"? If James was writing the letter to the "twelve tribes in the Dispersion," then where did he send the letter? Was there only one copy or were there multiple copies? Does it ever indicate the names of any of the twelve tribes that James is writing to?

James is using the phrase "twelve tribes" to refer to Christian believers, that is, the real children of Abraham (Gn 12:3; Rm 2:28–29). Many believers had already been scattered (dispersed) because of persecution. His letter would have been read first in Jerusalem but then circulated as believers traveled and could take it with them.

We do not know how soon manuscripts began to be copied after the original letter was written. The oldest manuscripts of James we posses date from the third century. James does not name the tribes, since he is referring to Christians.

Q 1:1 Why does James not introduce himself as Jesus' brother?

James does not provide an answer for this question, but it could be humility. James refers to himself as a "servant" of God and of the Lord Jesus Christ, which bears witness to the fact of his relationship with God. It is for Christ to say that James is His brother (Heb 2:11). Similarly, John never refers to himself by name in the Gospel but only as "the disciple whom Jesus loved"; that is to say, everything in John's life depends on this one thing, that God deals graciously with him and gives him a life because of Jesus' love for him.

● ● ● ● ● ● ● ● ● ● ● ● ● ● ● ● ● ● ● ●

Q 1:2–3 How is faith tested?

First, let's define faith so: dependence and our honesty in *honestly acknowledging* what we depend on. With this understanding, we can see the different ways that faith is tested. For example, many people are convinced that their life depends on money and are severely tested when circumstances threaten their income or reduce their wealth. On the other hand, family trouble or personal illness can also test that dependence, bringing a person to realize that what they really depend on is God and relationships with their family. People are convinced that their life depends on all sorts of other things or circumstances that have nothing to do with God (like having everything *my* way), and a fallen and competitive world is always threatening. Other people want to live in honest awareness of their dependence on God, but the devil, world, and fallen human nature are always working to drive them from that honesty. God will always work to expose what is false and deadly in order to make us aware of our dependence on Him for life abundant and eternal. The devil will always work to punish us for an honest awareness of our dependence on God; he will cultivate that relationship in

How is faith tested?

order to lead us to dependence on anyone or anything that cannot support us so that we die (Jn 8:31–59).

● ● ● ● ● ● ● ● ● ● ● ● ● ● ● ● ● ● ● ●

Q 1:2–4 Could the "tests" of faith be minor and of no importance?

On the one hand, we could rightly see the testing we encounter as minor in comparison with the terrible and often long-lasting troubles that some people endure through oppression, persecution, poverty, illness, or disaster. On the other hand, no testing is minor as long as it has the potential to drive us from the truth. History indicates that many people become acutely aware of the truth and their dependence on God, as they can only hope for Him to save. This is the origin of most of the psalms and many of the hymns, poems, and works of art we appreciate best. History also demonstrates that in the absence of testing, people become dishonest about what their life depends on and come to ruin (Ps 78). Failure to recognize this fact is what makes people contend that there is "the problem of evil." There is, of course, no problem of evil— only the problem of people who want to do evil while experiencing only good.

● ● ● ● ● ● ● ● ● ● ● ● ● ● ● ● ● ● ● ●

Q 1:2–8 What happens to those who lose their drive to persevere?

Only God knows what finally happens to anyone. We may know a few things about such people in time. One, any person can lose their drive to endure or determination to thrive in this world, no matter how impossible that might seem for some. Two, losing one's drive can have a spiritual cause or a physical cause, so it is essential to take some time and care in seeking the root of the problem. Three, God "knows our frame; He remembers that we are dust" (Ps 103:14), so we must be careful not to make a person's salvation depend on their drive to persevere. Four, we are not independent of God or one another. God has absolutely surrounded us with witnesses to this fact in nature and in His Word. We are also dependent upon one another, which is why we enter the world by way of parents and family and make our way through this world in the communion of saints (Heb 10:23–25). Therefore, the best answer to this question might be that people who lose their drive to persevere will be surrounded by care from the faithful and at least protected if not restored by the Word of God communicated to them in abundance (cf. Gal 6:1ff.; Col 3:12–17).

● ● ● ● ● ● ● ● ● ● ● ● ● ● ● ● ● ● ● ●

Q 1:5–6 God gives generously to those who ask "without reproach"; yet if you doubt, you won't receive. Since all men doubt, how is anything accomplished through prayer?

Part of the answer comes with knowing that several different Greek words are translated as "doubt" in English translations. The word here, *diakrino*, means to hold two judgments or opinions at the same time. This is more of a determination to maintain an opinion contrary to the truth rather than a struggle to cast off one's fear and simply believe (Mk 5:36). The father who sought help for his son is a good example of the struggle to belief (Mk 9:4–29). The other part of the answer comes in Jas 1:8, where "doubt" is more carefully defined as being "double-minded"—literally, "two-souled" or with two "psyches." On the one hand, James is saying that there is no reluctance or limitation in God's generosity toward those who seek Him and His will for them. On the other hand, God is no fool, nor is He mocked. No one who willingly holds opinions and a will contrary to God can "get what they want" by pretending to be genuine in their approach to God (Mt 7:21–29). This is the kind of hypocrisy that is condemned everywhere in the Bible.

As long as we possess a fallen human nature, we will doubt (1Co 2:14). On the other hand, every soul regenerated by the Word and Spirit of God is inspired to pray and knows what to pray, including prayers that seek forgiveness and help for our doubtful ways (Jn 14–16).

Q 1:5 What does "wisdom" specifically mean?

The Son of God *is* wisdom (Pr 8:12–36). Knowledge of the wisdom of God urges us to what is good and warns us away from what is bad (Pr 9). True faith is the awareness of our dependence on the wisdom of God and consequently our desire to live wisely (Eph 5:15–21). Wisdom is the truth about the way that everything works in order to provide life (Jn 14:6).

Q 1:9–10 What does God mean when He inspired James to write that those who are humble should take pride in their humiliation? Why is it always assumed that the rich are bad people?

The word translated "humiliation" (v. 10) refers to God's activity of raising up the lowly (Mt 23:12; 1Pt 5:6). James is talking about the life God gives us as His children, not a high position of any trivial human measure. Similarly, the rich can glory in their humiliation because God only empties them of their pride and ego so that He can make way for the true riches of His mercy and love (Php 3:4–14).

It is not *always* assumed that the rich are bad people. Both Abraham and Job were wealthy but not bad people. Second, rich people are *often* bad because "the love of money is a root of all kinds of evils" (1Tm 6:10). Jesus warned that we cannot serve both God and riches, making it clear that riches have the power to hold us in bondage (Mt 6:24). Finally, consider the examples of Solomon (1Ki 10:14ff.) and the rich man (Lk 16:19–31) as well as the warnings from Dt 6:10–15 and 1Jn 2:15–17.

Q 1:10–11 Is it always wrong to be wealthy? What if God has blessed you?

It is not wrong, but it is perilous, as James explains in v. 11. Wealth, like anything that provides an advantage to our ego and selfish inclinations, is perilous. Great intelligence, great strength, great beauty, and every other form of greatness by human standards fuels a fallen human nature that already wants to think too much of itself, too little of others, and not about God at all. Paul recognized this and explained his own life in 2Co 12:7–10. Jesus points out this truth as He refers to children as the standard of faith (Mt 18:3); Paul does the same thing as he contrasts the proud with the weak (1Co 1:18–31). God blesses everyone in one way or another. The key is to be a steward who administers those blessings on God's behalf for the benefit of others (Lk 12:42–46). Jesus is the absolute and unfailing steward of all He is according to both His divine and human natures. His stewardship created the world, then redeemed it, and even now sanctifies it. The real challenge for fallen human beings is not to get blessings but to be free and faithful in giving them away for the life and well-being of others.

Q 1:10 Why do we place so much emphasis on wealth and power when, in the end, it does not matter to God?

The short answer is because of the fall of Adam (Rm 5:12). The longer answer has to do with appetite and helplessness. Human beings seek wealth because we are trying to fill an infinite void, the void that was created when Adam destroyed our union with God. But no amount of material things or experiences can even begin to fill the emptiness of a soul without God. On the contrary, abundance often intensifies the realization of emptiness. Human beings seek power in order to convince ourselves that we are not powerless and that God is not God. The idea is that if we can control what happens in our life now and live in abundance and comfort, then we should be able to live just the same in the next world. If there is no life after death, at least we had the most enjoyable life possible while we could. Jesus was the only person who ever cared about what mattered to God absolutely, without fail, and on behalf of us all. Only a soul regenerated by Him and animated by the Holy Spirit through the Word knows real fulfillment and is, therefore, free to care about others, which is what matters to God.

Q 1:12 This verse sounds very works-oriented to me. What does James mean in this passage? How can you be both blessed for withstanding a trial and sinful to be having one? Doesn't a trial come somewhat from temptation?

The solution to this kind of question comes with a second question: what makes a person stand the test and persevere? As we are of ourselves, we not only fail to do what is right, but we are also determined to do what is wrong (Rm 3:10–18; 5:6–10). The only way a person can even want to do the right thing, especially in the face of testing, is by the activity of God in that person. As the saying goes, "good works are God's works" (see Jn 6:29; 1Co 15:10; 1Pt 1:5).

The answer regarding being both blessed and sinful comes in clarifying biblical language. There are two different Greek words that are translated "blessed" in English translations. The word used here, *makarios*, means "to be happy in spite of your circumstances because of what lies ahead." Note the sense this makes in this context: we are happy not because we face trials but because we know that God will sustain us through all trials and make us stronger and more faithful accordingly (Jas 5:11; 1Pt 1:6–7). There is also a difference between the trials that God directs to us in our lives and the temptation we bring upon ourselves. God uses trials to discipline us as a loving Father (Heb 12). God uses the trials others impose or that we impose upon ourselves for good (Rm 8:28). There will always be sin in all that we do as long as we are in this fallen human nature, but God has put away that sin and does not deal with us according to it (Ps 103:10–14).

Q 1:13–14 Is the Greek word for temptation the same word used in the Lord's Prayer in Matthew? If God cannot be tempted by evil, why was Jesus tempted in the desert by Satan? Doesn't God test our faith?

The same word is used in the original text when God tested Abraham (Gn 22:1); when the Holy Spirit drove Jesus into the wilderness to be tempted by the devil (Mt 4:1); in the Lord's Prayer where Jesus teaches us to say, "and lead us not into temptation"; and in Jas 1:13–14, where James says that God tempts no one. In this case, the problem is not that different original words are being translated with the same English word but that the same original word is translated into different English words in order to clarify the intent of the subject. God and the devil are at work in the same circumstances, but for very different purposes.

The essence of a trial or test or temptation is that a person is challenged in a significant way and that that person's response will bear significant consequences. God tested Abraham's faith with the command to sacrifice Isaac, knowing that this was the only way to confirm Abraham's faith that God would provide him with an heir (Gn 22:8; Heb 11:17–18). God's Spirit drove Jesus into the wilderness in order to be tested by the devil for forty days and nights. God's purpose was to provide a perfect response to every test/temptation, which would provide atonement for all our failures, while the devil's purpose was to ruin the work of the Savior. The Sixth Petition is very curious because English translations make it sound as if Jesus is teaching us to pray that God would not do something that He never does. The solution here comes in knowing two things. First, the word translated "lead" actually means "bear." Second, we need to remember that God sustains or "bears" the life of everyone, even when we are putting ourselves in danger of ruining our own salvation. Knowing the self-destructive, contrary disposition of our human nature, Jesus provides a petition that reminds us that it would be better for God to let us die than for Him to sustain our physical life while we follow temptation to the ruin of our eternal soul.

Finally, James is making a contrast between the purposes of God, the devil, and our own fallen nature in regard to challenges that come. God, in fact, never tempts people to ruin their lives in any way. God does test those He loves in order to confirm them in the faith (1Pt 1:6–7; 2Co 1:8–9; 4:1–5:21; 12:7–10). The devil is always prowling about, seeking whom he may devour (1Pt 5:8; Pr 7:7–27). Our own human nature is full of selfishness, greed, and lust, which create and seek out all sorts of temptations that would surely ruin us now and forever except for the intervention of God, the intercession of Christ, and the sanctifying work of the Holy Spirit in us through the Word and Sacraments. See also question and answer at 1Pt 4:12.

Q 1:14–15 Is it sinful to desire to commit a sin?

Yes; in fact, Jesus makes a point of exposing desire as the more serious cause or root of sinful actions (Mt 5:21–30; see also 1Th 4:3–5; Jas 4:1ff.). Sinful desire blasphemes God because it is fallen human nature claiming that what God wills and provides for us is either wrong or inadequate (Gn 3:1ff.; Ex 32:1–6; 1Sm 8:5–9; Jer 8:4–7; Rm 6:15–21). The cure for sin is Christ—by way of His atoning sacrifice that provides forgiveness for us and by His Spirit that regenerates us to know His will and seek what He desires (Ps 37:4; Mt 6:33; Ti 3:4–6; Php 3:7–14).

Q 1:18 What is God's will? Why were we given the "firstfruits"?

God expresses His will for us in a number of places and ways; ultimately, His will is that we live in fullness of life eternally (Jn 20:31). The Ten Commandments forbid what would undermine life (Ex 20:3–17). Jesus condensed the Ten Commandments into two and stated them positively: "Love the Lord your God with all your heart and with all your soul and with all your mind. . . . You shall love your neighbor as yourself" (Mt 22:37, 39). It is God's will that we should live in the fullest sense of the word that moved Him to regenerate us in the image of His Son (Jn 1:11–13; Ti 3:4–7).

James writes that we are the "firstfruits of His creatures." Paul wrote that Jesus was the firstfruits of those risen from the dead (1Co 15:20, 23) and that we receive the firstfruits of the Spirit (Rm 8:23). God has been in the process of redeeming His creation ever since the fall. The incarnation of the Son of God, His vicarious atonement, and His resurrection from the dead accomplished this redemption, and the resurrected body of Jesus proves the reality of God's promises to re-create all things (1Jn 3:1–2). God's Word provides us with a regenerate soul that, following Christ, is the firstfruits of His re-creative work (Jn 3:1–6; 5:24–29; 1Jn 3:9; 4:7; 5:1, 4). At the end of the world, when the heavens and earth are destroyed with fire, we will endure and enjoy eternally the new heavens and earth, for we have been regenerated by the Word of the Lord, and that Word endures forever (Mt 24:35; 2Pt 3:13).

Q 1:19–20 If the righteous life would be without anger, then why does it say "slow to anger"?

Verse 20 actually says, "For the anger of man does not produce the righteousness of God." The Bible does warn about anger (Ps 4:4), and self-control is one of the fruits of the Holy Spirit (Gal 5:23), but James is speaking more specifically here. James is talking about being angry toward another person, especially when we have not listened to what he or she has to say. Such anger has at least three problems: it is selfish, it is often mistaken, and it negates any genuine Christian concern that might be shown for the other person. While we are in this body, we will be prone to anger. James is providing help against that inclination by way of command and explanation.

Q 1:19 What does this mean?

This means exactly what it says, and there are plenty of proverbs that say the same; for example: "If one gives an answer before he hears it, it is his folly and shame" (Pr 18:13); "Do you see a man who is hasty in his words? There is more hope for a fool than for him" (29:20); "Whoever is slow to anger has great understanding, but he who has a hasty temper exalts folly" (14:29; see also 16:32; 22:24; 29:11). Being quick to speak but slow to listen and quick to anger is a product of a fallen human nature—selfish, determined in ignorant opinions, all too hasty to condemn others while defending itself. Think how often our relationships are troubled needlessly by hasty words and a failure to listen, and think how many relationships are ruined by the same. Yet by the grace of God, we have all received infinitely more and better than we deserve, and God protects our life so we are free to look to the interests of others. Those who are still apart from God need our help, not our condemnation or anger—that will come all too soon to those who remain in their stubborn unbelief. Therefore, we are quick to listen in order to discover what word of God to advance in the life of another to bring them well within God's redemption.

Q 1:25 What if you believe but don't act?

There is no such thing as believing but not acting accordingly. As the saying goes, "Faith alone saves, but faith is never alone." The word *believe* is essentially about dependence and an honest admission of dependence. If a person knows that he or she depends upon God and His Word, then God and that Word move this person to act accordingly. To say you believe something yet not act accordingly is to be dishonest about what you depend on. Thus people might say, "I believe in God," or, "I believe in Jesus as my Savior," but their actions might argue the contrary—that they really believe in satisfying themselves above all things. God loves everyone and has proven that by redeeming everyone through the life of Christ, but God is clearly opposed to the dishonest and hypocritical because they are acting against Him, against their neighbor, and against themselves all at the same time (Mt 7:15–20; Lk 13:6–9; Jn 15:1ff.).

Q 1:26 Today there is a split between religion and spirituality. How can I help show the sameness of the two?

Let's begin with definitions of key terms. *Religion* may be defined as "what governs." Everyone does certain things "religiously," and we use that term because it recognizes a regularity of action produced by a significant force. However, people are often dishonest with themselves and others about their religion or "what governs" their life. For example, if you ask people what they believe, then ask them what they always have time, money, and energy for (especially when they have no time, money, or energy), their answers will not match. Yet the answer to the second question is clearly their "religion," since it is what controls their life.

Spirituality is not a word that occurs in the Bible, and in modern times it seems to be a word invented to immunize the individual from religious criticism, insulate from challenges, and elevate as a more enlightened human being. On the other hand, one might sympathize with the use of this term by those who want to claim a spiritual aspect of life but do not want to be associated with all the evil that has been done through history while claiming religion as justification. The Bible teaches that every human being is spiritual and has an eternal soul and a physical nature. James demonstrates the connection between religion and spirituality by checking the continuity between words and actions. Thus, a person's spirituality and what they do religiously are both a product of their religion; the key is to discover what is really governing the person. If God is governing through His Word and Spirit, then a person is regenerated and inspired to think, speak, and do as Christ did and commands. In the absence of God's influence, fallen human nature will attempt substitutes of various names—none of which can satisfy nor endure honest inquiry.

Q 1:27 Is James equating "religion" with an individual's pity?

Following the explanation to the previous question, "religion" has to do with what governs a person. Many people claim religion as a means of justifying selfishness, greed, hatred, and a host of other evils. James is contrasting that misuse of the term *religion* with the simple fact that true religion, or being governed by God, results in concern for others, especially those least able to care for themselves. The truth is that God provides super-abundantly for us because of His great love for us and because He wants us to be free and able to care for others on His behalf. In our time, "pity" has more to do with sentiment than action. James is writing to expose words and pretense that are of no use to anyone. Pure and undefiled religion produced by God is evident in pure and undefiled love for others.

Q 2:1–4 Should we be giving attention to those who need help learning the Word without showing favoritism?

Certainly favoritism infects every area of human activity because we are fallen, faithless, and selfish. We are always looking for people and circumstances that can benefit us (Lk 14:7–14), and people who claim to be Christian are no exception. On the other hand, James is not talking so much about those with ability to understand the Bible as he is about people who are wealthy or powerful or both. We like to think we are loving, godly people, yet we are selfish and weak, so we prefer to claim love for people who have the most to give and require the least from us in return. Godly love is revealed in the face of challenges, when we love our enemy as only God's Spirit could enable us to do. In this way, God is glorified, we grow in our dependence upon God, and those most difficult to love are loved (Mt 5:43–48; Ac 9:10–18; 1Co 15:9–11).

∙ ∙ ∙ ∙ ∙ ∙ ∙ ∙ ∙ ∙ ∙ ∙ ∙ ∙ ∙ ∙ ∙ ∙ ∙ ∙

Q 2:2–4 Is James saying that a person is justified by what he does and not by faith alone?

We are not and cannot be saved by what we do; all human experience, biblical history, and biblical instruction make this absolutely clear (Mt 19:25–26; Rm 5:6–10; Eph 2:1–10). However, the word *justified* has two aspects. On one hand, "justified" can refer to the *means* of salvation—in our case, by God's grace, the atoning life of Christ, and the sanctifying work of the Holy Spirit. On the other hand, "justified" can refer to the *evidence* of salvation. Like the fruit of a tree, our life demonstrates whether we are saved, both in view of our connection with the means of salvation and in view of the good works produced by those means (Mt 7:15–20; 25:1–13, 31–46).

∙ ∙ ∙ ∙ ∙ ∙ ∙ ∙ ∙ ∙ ∙ ∙ ∙ ∙ ∙ ∙ ∙ ∙ ∙ ∙

Q 2:5–7 Isn't it possible to be rich and keep God's Word?

There is particular language in this text that explains the kind of rich person or the

> ## Why did God make people rich or poor?

conduct of a rich person that is at issue. For example, in v. 6, James speaks of oppression, especially through the courts; in v. 7, he mentions their blasphemy. The problem with the rich is that their riches want to be god, and this is a god that is oppressive, blasphemous, and potentially all consuming.

∙ ∙ ∙ ∙ ∙ ∙ ∙ ∙ ∙ ∙ ∙ ∙ ∙ ∙ ∙ ∙ ∙ ∙ ∙ ∙

Q 2:5 Why did God make people rich or poor? Why not all the same?

God does all things for the same reasons: because of His nature to love and because of our need for life. Sometimes, God makes a person rich or poor as a test, as in the case of Solomon or Job. Other times, God makes a person rich or poor as a judgment (1Sm 1:7–9; Lk 1:52–53). In other cases, it is not God who is making rich or poor but the activity or inactivity of people (Gn 4:7; 1Co 9:7–9; 2Tm 2:6). God blesses people with wealth of various kinds in a bountiful life that brings pleasure but also the temptation to love riches rather than God (Mt 6:24; 1Tm 6:10). God also blesses people with times of hardship and want, which can work a great number of benefits but can also tempt a person to unbelief (2Co 4:7–11; 12:7–10).

● ●

Q 2:10 Does this mean that if you break one law, you break "all" the Commandments?

Yes. This is because any one particular sin has a source, and that source is opposed to all the Commandments. Jesus exposes this source in Mk 7:21–23, and Paul describes the universal, contrary nature of our fallen flesh in Rm 5:7–9. Dishonesty and hypocrisy are bound up in our fallen flesh, which explains the need for James to write this. We would like to think that if we did sin, it would only be in one particular and small way, like the Pharisee of Lk 18:11–14. The truth is that all our best deeds, according to our fallen human nature, are corrupt and defiled (Is 64:6). This absolute corruption of our human nature, which corrupts all that we do, requires a substitute on the one hand and a putting off of that nature on the other. God has provided absolutely for all. The Son of God became true man in order to do all things perfectly from conception to death in our place *and* to suffer the consequences of all our failures for all our life; He has regenerated us in His image *and* relieves us of our fallen human nature by forgiving our sins, by providing for the death of our human nature, *and* by promising to raise us from the dead with incorruptible bodies for life everlasting (Rm 5:12–21; 2Co 5:21; 1Co 15:47–53; Ti 3:4–6; 1Jn 3:9).

● ●

Q 2:12 What judgment is James talking about?

The expression "law of liberty" is used only here and in 1:25. For true believers, judgment was accomplished in Jesus' crucifixion, so for us, Judgment Day is a confirmation of God's work in us rather than condemnation under the Law (Rm 8:1; Jn 5:24, 29; Mt 25:31–46). Matthew 25:14–30 may be exactly what James is talking about since each of the servants was freely given a talent or talents to work with and the talent itself did the work. There has always been a temptation to think of judgment or righteousness in terms of what we don't do ("I didn't do anything wrong") while ignoring what we ought to have done (the films *Babette's Feast* and *Chocolat* address this theme). Paul's use of the term *freedom* in Gal 2:4; 5:1; and 5:13 may also help. Paul confirms that we have been restored to freedom from the condemnation of the Law by the mercies of God in Christ, but while in the flesh we must be careful to use that freedom according to God's intent. Being faithful stewards of the gifts God has provided is very different from being expected to earn one's own justification without any gifts at all.

● ●

Q 2:14–26 Where is the balance between the contradictions of "good deeds do not get one to heaven" and "without good deeds, faith means nothing"?

Faith connects a person to Christ, who lived the perfect life of faith and works, imputes that to us, and works in us to live the same way. In Christ, we have perfect faith and works. Any good work and all genuinely good works point back to the cause of those works, which is the faith that God works in a person. Both faith and works are a gift from God, as James wrote in 1:17–18.

• • • • • • • • • • • • • • • • • • • •

Q 2:14–17 If you don't do works to accompany your faith, will God not accept your faith? Is your faith then void because you haven't done any works, even though you still believe in Jesus Christ?

We must begin by understanding that the Greek New Testament has only one word for "faith," which is translated into English as "faith," "believe," or "trust." All three English words have the same meaning, though few people are aware of this and few can articulate the meaning. *Faith* means "dependence upon." True faith means depending on God, which is accompanied by awareness and ready articulation of the truth (Rm 10). All other claims to faith may reflect what a person is devoted to submitting to, even though everyone depends on God whether or not they know or admit this. True faith is God's work and therefore absolutely acceptable to Him. False notions or claims to faith are not accepted by God because they are contrary to the truth and life and, therefore, contrary to Him. Faith cannot be voided by works because true faith always produces genuinely good works. The absence of good works or works that are not genuine can only give evidence of a false faith.

• • • • • • • • • • • • • • • • • • • •

Q 2:14–15 If we are saved by grace alone, why do we need deeds? Why would we be judged by our works?

We are saved by grace but judged by works; the Bible is clear and consistent about this (Gal 2:16; 2Co 5:10). The difference has to do with "causes" in contrast to "evidence." If we are talking about what causes salvation, good works, or anything else that is good and according to God's will, then God alone is the cause of such (Jn 6:29; 15:5). But how do we know with certain and tangible means that we are saved, especially before Judgment Day when it would be too late to make amends? Here is the key: the good works that provide the indisputable evidence of faith are provided by God in three ways. First, God imputes to us the perfect life of Christ so that our life before God under judgment is not just pretty good, but absolutely perfect (Rm 8:1; 2Co 5:21). Second, God forgives all that we have ever done that is not absolutely perfect (Ps 103:12; Is 1:18). Third, the Word of God that creates faith also produces a life and works that are consistent with that faith (Jn 15:1–7; 2Co 5:7). Notice carefully that faithful people do not focus on or rely on their works to save them, but on the grace of God (Lk 18:13–14; Mt 25:31–46).

> ## What does it mean to have faith without works?

Q **2:14 What does it mean to have faith without works?**

Claiming to have faith is among the easiest things for fallen human nature to do, with the worst possible eternal results. Consider Jesus' warning in Mt 7:13–23 or the desperate plea of the rich man from the torments of hell (Lk 16:23–31). The word *hypocrite* occurs seventeen times in the New Testament—thirteen times in Matthew, once in Mark, and three times in Luke. Hypocrisy may be thought of as absolute dishonesty—dishonesty with God, with everyone else, and with oneself, in public and in private. This dishonesty is so detrimental that God has provided at least three means of detecting it. First, faith is the product of God through the Means of Grace (Rm 10:17; 1Co 12:3). Therefore, if we have no constant life in God's Word, we cannot have faith (Jn 15:1–7). Second, faith is always productive. Good works are those which the Word of God commands, describes, and effects through us. If we claim to have faith but have no works, that claim is at least mistaken if not a conscious lie. This is what James is getting at. Third, God has set us in families and the community of believers so that we have the perspective of many other people on our life (Mt 18:15–18; Lv 19:17). Besides these means of detection, God has granted the most powerful of forces to draw us into honesty and keep us there: redemption. Honesty about our condition and our life takes place within the context of God's gracious activity to redeem, forgive, regenerate, and fulfill all His promises toward us.

Q **2:18 If demons believe, what is the difference between believing and faith?**

The difference is not between believing, having faith, or trusting, as all three English words mean the same thing (see Jas 2:14–17 above). Demons depend on God for their very existence, as everyone and everything else does (Heb 1:3). However, there is an absolute difference between knowing that you depend on God for your existence and seeking His will for yourself and others. This is the difference between saying "God does exist" but opposing Him in all things and saying "God does exist" and seeking the communion and life that He would restore to us through His Son. Admitting a fact is one thing; a person's disposition to that fact is another. Acts 15:5 reports that there were a group of Pharisees who believed that Jesus was the Son of God but they still opposed the salvation He freely provides. Being aware that something exists is not the same as being connected to that thing. You can know all about food and still starve to death. God wants us to know about Him and to live in communion with Him (2Pt 1:2–8).

Q 2:19–24 Is this another area where attitude is highlighted, that is, that good works flow out of an attitude of love and respect and show that we are justified?

You could use the word *attitude*, though I think the term *disposition* is better because it includes the whole person. Believing the truth about God but opposing Him with your whole person is of no benefit (Rm 1:18–31; Pr 28:9; Mk 5:7). Believing the truth about God and living in communion with Him means that His Word is continually with us to regenerate us in His image and to produce the life that He wills for us (Jn 8:31; Eph 5:7–10; Ezk 36:24–27). The very Word of God that creates genuine faith inspires us to stay connected to that Word and is active in us to bear good fruit (Jn 15:1–7).

Q 2:20 Is faith without deeds dead?

Indeed, faith does not need our works, but depends solely on God's work through His Word and Spirit (Jn 6:29; Rm 10:17; 1Pt 1:5). Yet it is just as certain that this faith always produces fruit or good works and is never without them (Mt 7:17; 25:34–40; 1Co 15:10). James is trying to keep people from the disaster of thinking that knowing about God is the same as living in Him, just as Jesus was doing in the Sermon on the Mount (Mt 5–7, especially 7:21–23).

Q 2:24 Is there a difference between being saved and being justified?

Yes, there is a difference in how those two words may be used. The word *saved* is confined to the act of saving itself, in which the object is passive. Notice how the expression "save yourself" makes no sense. The word *justified* can refer to that saving act itself or it can refer to the evidence that the saving act has taken place. When the Bible says we are justified by grace through faith apart from the works of the Law, it is talking about *how* that salvation is accomplished. When James says we are justified by works and not by faith alone, he is talking about the evidence that proves that our salvation has been accomplished. Think of it like the difference between making a fruit tree and proving that a tree is such. Only God can make a fruit tree; yet, without any fruit, someone might well argue that it is no fruit tree at all. But if a tree is loaded with apples or has even one apple, it is inarguably an apple tree. Only God can save, and only one saved by God can do genuinely good works. Genuinely good works can only be the fruit of salvation and only God can save.

Q 2:24 How can you keep people from taking this verse out of context when we take similar verses, such as Eph 2:8–9, by themselves?

As soon as anyone would use a verse, another will rightly ask what the context is and if the use is consistent with that context. In Ephesians, Paul is responding to the contention of fallen human ego that we can save ourselves. James is responding to the contention of a deceitful human ego that we can have faith and still live selfishly. Paul uses the word *saved* but James uses the word *justified* in the sense of "proven to be just."

. . . .

Q 2:26 Does this mean that if I don't do good deeds, my faith is dead?

Yes. We are always "alive" inasmuch as we all have an eternal soul (Lk 20:38; Rv 9:6). A more helpful definition of life might be "positive relationship" and of death, "absence of positive relationship." A body without breath (the Greek word *pneuma* means breath, wind, and spirit) is dead, that is to say, unable to be in any positive relationship, witnessed by its return to dust. Like a body, a faith without works is no faith at all; it is not in any positive relationship and, in fact, does not exist.

. . . .

Q 3:1 Why is James discouraging people from becoming teachers? How does God prepare pastors?

Peter issues the same warning in 1Pt 4:11, and John issues one in Rv 22:18–19.

How do we keep from saying negative things?

God gives this warning because of the authority that teachers possess over those who hear them, especially those more vulnerable to deceit (Jer 23; Mt 18:6). The term *teacher* refers to a pastor and is one of many terms used interchangeably in the New Testament for the Office of Public Ministry (*elder*, *bishop*, and *shepherd* are all words used for pastor). The first reason for discouraging people from entering the Office of Public Ministry is provided by James in this verse and those that follow; pastors will receive a stricter judgment, which is all the more daunting since we all stumble in many things, especially in our speech. The second reason has to do with our words and the authority they carry because of the office, the power that authority has to corrupt, and the vulnerability of faithful people who want to submit in humility to God's servants. This is why the texts from 1Pt 4 and Rv 22 say, in essence, if a person opens his mouth on behalf of God in public, then it must be the Word of God that comes forth from it. We also do well to remember that the vast majority of Christian life and education is accomplished in private and in our homes, wherever our life takes us (Mt 28:19–20; Eph 6:4; Dt 6:4ff.).

. . . .

Q 3:8 If no man can tame the tongue, how do we keep from cursing and saying negative things?

God provides several remedies for the wicked tongue of fallen man. For example, God gave the law "so that every mouth may be stopped" (Rm 3:19). James expressed that law at the beginning of this chapter with a warning (Jas 3:1–12). God touched Isaiah's mouth with a coal from the altar. God regenerates us by His Spirit through His Word so that we have the mind of Christ and speak His words for the benefit of others (Php 2:5; 1Pt 4:11; Eph 5:19).

Q 3:13–18 If someone of faith is wise, should they admit they are wise (trust) or deny it (humility)?

Wisdom is related to but different from trust. Trust is dependence; we depend on God for all things, and genuine faith recognizes this, while false faith lives in dependence on what is not God and therefore fails. Wisdom is to know what is the right thing to do and when and how to do it. The fear of the Lord is the beginning of wisdom because it reveals how aware a person is of his or her dependence on God. Depending on God moves us to listen to Him through His Word, which is where we learn what the right thing to do is, and the means by which God's Spirit inspires us to act accordingly. A wise person would probably neither admit nor deny that he or she is wise. Instead, the wise person would confess to a fear of the Lord and a sincere desire for wisdom. To deny having wisdom would be dishonest for such a person; such false humility is hypocrisy, which James warned about in v. 17.

Q 3:13–17 Is James talking about both godly wisdom and earthly wisdom?

Yes, James speaks of earthly first, then godly. In v. 15, James calls earthly wisdom "unspiritual" and "demonic." In v. 17, James describes the wisdom that is from above, which means it is from God (1:17).

Q 3:13 Why is James talking about works when grace is what saves us?

James is not writing to people who don't know how to be saved or who are challenging the fact that we can only be saved by grace. James is writing to people who claim that they are saved by grace but whose lives contradict that claim. For example, many people argue that we save ourselves by obeying the Law (Ac 11; 15; Gal 3; Eph 5; Rm 10). Any response to such a contention would necessarily argue that we are saved by grace apart from works of the Law. On the other hand, how would you respond to those who say they can do as they please because they are saved by grace? How to become an apple tree is one thing; only God can create an apple tree. How to prove a tree is an apple tree is another; the most obvious way to prove that is to look for the apples. Notice this combination of issues in Jesus' parable of the farmer and a fruitless tree. The tree is judged on the absence of fruit, but the tree can do nothing for itself; it takes a servant to intercede for and act on behalf of the tree to give it hope (Lk 13:6–9).

Q **3:14 How are we supposed to build self-esteem if we can't take any credit for what we've done? If we have free will, can't we take credit for the good we do?**

First we might clarify whether the "self" in "self-esteem" is referring to the inherent value of a person or the value that a person constructs for himself or herself. In view of our creation, redemption, and all that God would accomplish through us, we are priceless. If a person rejects this in favor of evolution and/or atheism, there is little hope of building self-esteem since we are the product of accidents and will cause many ourselves. Second, why do we need to take credit for anything we do? If all things are ours because God has declared them to us (1Co 3:21–23; 2Co 5:21), then all that is left for us is to be good stewards—that is, we are free to simply enjoy being of service to others (Mt 25:14–29). Third, we do not have a free will—far from it. According to our fallen human nature we are weak, ungodly, sinful, and enemies of God (Rm 5). We are dead in trespasses and sins, yet we walk in them according to the course of this world and the control of the devil (Eph 2). On the other hand, according to our regenerate soul, we act according to God's will because our new man is oriented so (Php 2:5) and because His Spirit moves us so. God creates us, redeems us, and sanctifies us. God works His will in our lives, which does good for others, and we are blessed with the experience, memory, and relationship that results.

Q **3:16 How do you control jealousy?**

The answer to this question has to do with God's nature and ours. God saves us, even from envy, disorder, and evil practice; we cannot save ourselves. God provides the Law (stern warnings, examples of negative consequences, parables) in order to curb our fallen human nature (1Sm 25:37; 2Sm 12:7; Rm 7:9). God also provides His Spirit, which regenerates our soul in His image and produces the fruit of the Spirit, which includes self-control, love (which excludes selfishness), and kindness (Gal 5:22–23; 1Co 13). As mentioned above in Jas 3:14, God provides fullness in our lives that is an antidote to envy and the like. Each human being is fashioned by God Himself (Ps 139) to accomplish good works that God has prepared (Eph 2:10), which flow from a faith that God has assigned (Rm 12:3). If we are children of God and all that is His is ours, how could we possibly be envious of another or spend our life in anything but faithful stewardship for the good of others (Jn 16:13–15)?

Q **4:1 How should quarrels within a church be dealt with?**

All matters, inside and outside the church, should be dealt with according to the counsel of God. When quarrels arise, we first want to stop the quarreling. We do so by being slow to speak, slow to anger, and quick to listen (Jas 1:19). Next, we want to examine the matter for what it is, exposing wicked causes, seeking repentance and absolution, and advancing good causes for the benefit of everyone (Php 1:27–2:4; Mt 18:15–18; 1Co 6:1–12). It helps to distinguish between the initial matter (e.g., "Should we paint the church red or blue?" or "Should we get rid of the pastor or keep him?") and the deeper matter, which actually turns initial matters into conflicts. If we can remember who we are, what our purpose is, and how the Lord provides for that purpose, the "what" and "how" of our daily lives becomes much simpler (Lk 12:13–15; Col 3:1–17).

⬤ ⬤ ⬤ ⬤ ⬤ ⬤ ⬤ ⬤ ⬤ ⬤ ⬤ ⬤ ⬤ ⬤ ⬤ ⬤ ⬤

Q 4:3 James says that God may not give us something because of our motives. What does He consider to be a good motive?

James warns against asking for what we would "spend . . . on [our] passions." This is similar to Paul's warning about the passions of lust (1Th 4:5) and John's warning about lust (1Jn 2:15–17). God is not willing to give us those things that fallen human nature seeks to its own and everyone else's destruction (Gal 5:17; Jas 4:1). A good motive, then, would be any interest in the well-being of others, because taking good care of others is the best way to take good care of ourselves (Eph 5:28b). This well-being begins with our eternal soul, which is provided for by the Spirit of God, and works out through our bodies. This is why Jesus says, "If you remain in My word, you are truly My disciples, and you will know the truth, and the

truth will set you free" (Jn 8:31–32). His Word supplies us with His Spirit and His Spirit regenerates and makes a life for us (Jn 6:63). His Word also inspires us to pray according to His will and with the words He Himself has taught us (Jn 14:13–14).

⬤ ⬤ ⬤ ⬤ ⬤ ⬤ ⬤ ⬤ ⬤ ⬤ ⬤ ⬤ ⬤ ⬤ ⬤ ⬤ ⬤

Q 4:4 What does God mean when He says that if you are a friend of the world, you become an enemy of God? So should we not love anything of this world (e.g., football, cookies, cars, etc.)?

Jesus warned that we cannot serve God and riches and that where our treasure is, there our heart would be also (Mt 5:21–24). Paul warns that "the love of money is a root of all kinds of evils. It is through this craving that some have wandered away from the faith and pierced themselves with many pangs" (1Tm 6:10). Notice that both Jesus and Paul provide explanations for their warnings, having to do with the deadly and destructive nature of love for the things of this world. The trouble has to do with a combination of factors. First, we were created to live in communion with God, but that constant communion was lost in the fall. In the absence or even limited presence of God in our lives, our fallen nature seeks to fill this infinite void with finite, material things. Finite, material things can never begin to compensate for the loss of God; yet rather than seek God, our fallen nature simply tries to gain more material things to put in the void. This is why lust cannot be satisfied. Lust, which is the desire for more, cannot be satisfied because once it obtains its desire, it looks ahead to what might be next. Second, we never actually possess material things; they possess us. Being "friends" with football or cookies or cars inevitably makes us the servant of these with negative effects for us and those who should be served by us.

. . . .

Q **4:5 Isn't jealousy sinful?**

Jealousy in itself must not be sinful because "the LORD your God [is] a jealous God" (Dt 5:9). The key to understanding is to distinguish the essence of an action from the subject and the subject's motives in that action (see the case of temptation in Jas 1:13–14). *Envy* means to have an intense concern for something. In God's case, this intense concern is for what is properly His, motivated by love, for our well-being. In our case, this intense concern is for what is not ours at all, motivated by greed or lust, for what works against our life. God's Spirit envies intensely because we were created to be inhabited by that Spirit, and only by that Spirit can we live.

. . . .

Q **4:7 Isn't it true that the harder you try to resist the devil, the harder he tries to overcome you with temptation? Since we**

are sinners and cannot truly resist the devil, is it impossible for us to force the devil to flee from us?

I suspect the key here is the phrase "resist the devil." If a person in his or her own vanity and self-righteousness attempted to resist the devil by his or her own ability, the devil would try harder because such a person's ability would run out and/or be overcome at some point. On the other hand, to resist the devil with the Word and Spirit of God is to bring into your life all the power and judgment of God against the devil. Remember how the Lord defeated "every temptation" of the devil (Lk 4:13) and how the demons were bound in fear of judgment whenever the Lord was near (Mt 8:28–34; Mk 1:34). Though we are sinners according to our flesh or fallen human nature, God has given us a regenerate soul that not only can but is determined to resist the devil. Besides the Spirit of the Lord that is made available to us without limit in the Word, that same Word of God provides wisdom, guidance, and encouragement to resist the devil. Consider this: what will the devil do if he knows that a person has a strong life in the Word of God and that temptations only drive that person more deeply and more often into the Word? Close, daily relationships between believers also help since one person is not so easily overcome in the company of many faithful people (Ec 4:12; Gal 6:1–3).

Is it impossible for us to resist the devil?

Q **4:8 Does God not come to people who do not come close to Him? Is there hope for those who do not come to Jesus on their own?**

Be careful here to note the positive imperative of James without any negative language or judgment. James is encouraging those who have already been brought near to God through His Word and servants of that Word. It is impossible for anyone to come to God on their own since before conversion, we are utterly opposed to God (Jn 3:18ff.; 14:6; 15:4; 16; Rm 5:6–10; Eph 2:1–6). God did come near to those not close to Him, absolutely, in His incarnation, in the person of Jesus Christ (Jn 1:11–13; 2Co 5:21). God continues to come near to those far from Him through the people He has already brought near to Himself (Mt 10:1–42; 28:19–20; 2Co 5:14–20). At the same time, God warns us about sustaining relationships or communion with those who reject the Word of the Lord and the repentance and faith it would work (1Co 5:9–13), though faithful people have historically interceded for those who would go far from God (Gn 18:20–33; Ex 32:11–35; 13:6–9). God desires every human being to draw near to Him (1Tm 2:4). God demonstrates His love and power in bringing near those who appear most opposed, like Saul/Paul (Ac 8–9). God will not draw near to those who reject the truth but pretend faithfulness in hypocrisy (Pr 28:9; Mt 23; 25:41–46).

Q **4:9 Why does James want us to change our feelings?**

Here it is essential to look back and recognize the kind of person James is addressing with this imperative. James has been addressing the person who is proud, double-minded, devoted to the things of this world, self-indulgent, murderous, and covetous (Jas 4:1–8). James uses such intense and anxious language because such a person, who also was or at least claimed to be faithful, is in great danger of securing eternal condemnation for himself or herself (Heb 6:4–6; 10:26–31).

Q **4:11–12 I know and understand the premise that only God can judge, but it seems futile to tell people not to judge others. How do we reconcile the whole judicial system or the typical human response to any stranger? I naturally do not like some people, so am I judging them?**

Look carefully at the language of James. He forbids us to "speak evil" of one another (v. 11). Perhaps this is parallel to what Jesus said in Mt 7:1: "Judge not, that you be not judged." Jesus continues in the next verse by providing the reason for this prohibition: "For with the judgment you pronounce you will be judged, and with the measure you use it will be measured to you" (v. 2). Since God says He will deal with us as we deal with others (remember the Fifth Petition of the Lord's Prayer), it makes sense to refrain from saying anything about another person that we would not want said about us, especially before God. It is also important to know that Jesus does not forbid us from speaking the truth to another in love, even if this takes the form of a severe warning (Lv 19:17; 1Co 5:1–6:11). Jesus forbids us from condemning others, and He does so for at least three reasons. First, only God has the authority to judge. Second, only God knows the truth about a person—the whole truth. Third, our task is to live and act on behalf of others, not against them. We know that the Law condemns and that those who live and die outside of Christ remain condemned (Jn 3:18ff.; Rm 8:1). The appropriate disposition for us toward others is the same disposition we depend on from Christ: compassion, intercession, encouragement, and warning. If we stop thinking about ourselves, we can realize two benefits. First, we think more about Christ for us (which is inexhaustible in wonder) and about others who need Christ just like we do. Second, caring about Christ and others shifts our thinking to things essential (what's on the inside) and draws our thoughts away from what is irrelevant (what's on the outside). God is judge and judges flawlessly. Like Christ, we are physicians, not making judgments but diagnosing the trouble we see in order to apply the remedies provided by God in His Word.

● ● ● ● ● ● ● ● ● ● ● ● ● ● ● ● ● ● ●

Q 4:12 What do we do if someone does judge us?

We do have a command to love our enemies and pray for those who persecute us and spitefully use us (Lk 6:27–28). We also might examine ourselves, as we also have a command to do that, to see if there isn't a log in our own eye in the judging department (1Co 2:15; 4:3–4; 11:28, 35; 2Co 13:5; Mt 7:1–5). Once this has all been done, we might also talk with such a person about their practice of judging, not because we are so affected, but for their own well-being (Eph 4:15; 1Co 4:3; Mt 18:15–18).

● ● ● ● ● ● ● ● ● ● ● ● ● ● ● ● ● ● ●

Q 4:13–16 Planning for life is essential! How are we expected to balance faith in God's action and our own ambitions?

James says, "You do not know what tomorrow will bring. What is your life? For you are a mist that appears for a little time and then vanishes" (4:14). The problem here is not that a person wants to plan in order to be faithful, responsible, or prudent. The problem is an attitude that claims we are in control of our lives rather than God, that we are self-sufficient and fully able to do just as and whatever we please (2Co 3:5). Pride and selfishness is rebellion against God and neighbor at the same time; this is what James is concerned with.

● ● ● ● ● ● ● ● ● ● ● ● ● ● ● ● ● ● ●

Q 4:17 How does one find time to do all the good we are expected to do?

Ah, the problem of time is a hard one. Wise King Solomon suggests in Ecclesiastes that we try too hard to do too many things that don't matter in the end. Is it possible that the good we know to do takes a lot less time than the things we think we need to do? Perhaps, then, the problem is not one of time. Why would God expect us to accomplish more good in our life than there is time for, since our times are in His hands (Ps 31:15; 139:16; Eph 2:10)? According to our fallen human nature, we never do the good we know, for even our righteous deeds are as filthy rags (Is 64:6). On the other hand, according to our regenerate soul, we always do what is right (1Jn 3:9). Our whole person, by faith, lives in the forgiveness that Christ accomplished (Rm 8:1) and claims the righteous life of Christ, which the Holy Spirit provides to us (Jn 16:15; 2Co 5:21).

Q **5:1–6 Why would he warn the rich? Is James encouraging the rich to have concern and fear? Aren't we supposed to give our worries to God?**

James is warning the rich because of the trouble that serving riches makes for a person (note vv. 2–3 and Mt 6:24); but even more important, James is warning the rich because it is so very difficult to rescue a person from greed, covetousness, the love of money, and indulgence of the flesh (Mt 19:16–22; Pr 15:27; 28:25; Ps 10:3).

Q **5:1 When James talks about wealthy people weeping because their riches are gone, is he referring to when they die and their riches don't go with them?**

The history of Lazarus and the rich man (Lk 16:19–31) supports your suspicion. Revelation also describes the bitter lament of the greedy (18:3–20).

Q **5:3 To whom was James referring in this verse?**

James 5:1 identifies the "rich" as those testified against here. It is the rich who will have their flesh eaten by the corrosion of their gold and silver.

Q **5:7 How does this deal with drought and famine?**

Here James is talking about being patient as we seek to follow God's will in a world and with a fallen human nature that is opposed. All through biblical history the faithful have cried out to God for deliverance—and sooner rather than later (Ps 13:1; 38:22). Farmers also must be patient, waiting for their seed to sprout and their crop to mature after the early and late rains. Famines and droughts, on the other hand, are evidence of creation affected by the fall and are indicative of the human condition in absence of the Word of God. Why should anyone expect the nature of God's creation to function perfectly according to our standard when we don't? How can God remind us of our utter dependence upon His Word and the grace it conveys (living bread and living water; Jn 4 and 7) except by giving us an indicative experience in our material life? The Bible deals with droughts and famines the way it deals with all the hardships and consequences of rebellion against God: He remains a loving and gracious Father who makes all things work together for good (Rm 8:28), disciplines us perfectly as a Father (Heb 12), and is the author of every good and perfect gift (Jas 1), including the gift of life that not only transcends but even thrives by His Spirit in the most desperate of challenges (Ex 15:5ff.; Dn 3:14ff.).

● ●

Q 5:8–12 When there is a great deal of suffering, it is hard to look to God for guidance when we are so busy assigning blame. How can we remember to turn to God?

The key to suffering is to recognize our composition as human beings and to realize when and where we are living. First, we are made in the image of God. Among other things, this suggests that we are composed of body, soul, and spirit. Since the fall, the Spirit of God was lost and our body and soul are perishing in rejection of God (Rm 5:6–10). After conversion, when God regenerates our soul by the power of His Word and restores His Spirit to us, we live in a constant battle with ourselves (Gal 5:17). Now comes the fascinating consequence: because our body and soul are in opposi-

tion, when one suffers, the other thrives, just as Paul describes in 2Co 12:10: "For when I am weak, then I am strong." On the other hand, when our fallen human nature has its way, our soul suffers, as you see in the case of Ananias and Sapphira (Ac 5). Second, we are not yet in heaven and misunderstand everything if we try to make this place and this time paradise for this fallen human nature. While God is exceedingly gracious in the abundance of joy, beauty, and love that we experience even now, to make our human appetite for material comforts our god in this world is a catastrophic mistake for several reasons: our human nature cannot be satisfied with material things (that's why there is so much greed and addiction); trying to satisfy ourselves means we lose the essence of joy, beauty, and life in the love of others; and trying to satisfy ourselves with material things puts us in competition with all other selfish, vain, greedy human beings, most of whom are more powerful and able to compete than we are. Once we realize who we are and where we are, the consistency and clarity with which the Bible speaks to us becomes evident and all of the Bible is a comfort. (See also 2Co 1; 4–5; and 12.)

● ●

Q 5:12 What does it mean to not swear?

First of all, distinguish between swearing and cursing. Cursing is forbidden because only God has the right to condemn (Mt 7:1), because we are called to love our neighbor and even our enemy rather than curse (Lk 6:28) and perhaps because cursing

How can we remember to turn to God?

is associated with witchcraft and demonic practices. Swearing refers to claiming the certainty of something on the basis of something most reliable—in this case, God. God forbids this because the truth verifies itself and because lies would always want to make claims on God only to deceive and ruin.

Any text should be taken in its most literal and simple meaning unless something forces us to understand it in another way. James here forbids us to try to use God's name to convince someone that something is true. James says we ought not to swear "so that you may not fall under condemnation." This is only one of many places in the Bible that threaten judgment against many different acts. The purpose of the Law is to make clear what works undermine life and to point us to Christ, who restores life. Pride and greed motivate swearing, while the providence of Christ and truth work humility in us. As long as we possess a fallen human nature, we will break the prohibitions of the Law, but as long as we are in the Word, the Spirit will work repentance, forgiveness, and regeneration. The severity of the Law is necessary if it is to be effective against the desires of the flesh, and the atoning work of Christ is absolute and universal in its remedy against judgment.

Q 5:14 How are people anointed with oil?

Anointing someone with oil is a rather simple matter of pouring a little oil on a person's head (Ex 29:7; 30:25; Ru 3:3; 2Sm 12:20; Ps 89:20). While anointing with oil is not a sacrament, such as Baptism and the Lord's Supper, the physical element helps confirm that the words and promises of God are present and active in the life of the individual.

Q 5:15 What, then, can we say to those who have lost loved ones to sickness? Is this talking about the spiritually sick?

First of all, notice that the issue of sin is distinct from—though related to—the problem of sickness. Sin is a sickness of our fallen human nature that causes all kinds of illness of body, soul, and relationship. Sometimes there is an obvious, unquestionable connection between cause and effect, as in drunkenness and hangover. In other cases, there doesn't seem to be any particular relationship, as between bearing false witness and coming down with a cold (but who knows?). In any case, God does not deal with us according to our iniquities; He disciplines and teaches us for our benefit, all through the consequences of our fallenness (Heb 12; 2Co 12; Rm 8:28). However, we will misunderstand God's work in our lives if we fail to distinguish our fallen human nature from the regenerate soul His Word and Spirit work in us.

This brings us to the phrase "save the one who is sick." Consider what happens when we look beneath human physiology and the sicknesses that affect the soul and cause rebellion against God. What good is it to save the body from a physical illness in time if doing so leaves the soul lost for eternity (Lk 9:25; 16:19–31; 17:11–19; Heb 3:12–4:1)? It may be important that a person recover from a physical ailment in order to spend more time in the body learning and serving in this life. It may be that the time has come for a person to be delivered from his or her contrary human nature and from this "valley of the shadow of death." God makes all things work for good to those who love Him, who are called according to His purpose (Rm 8:28ff.). The working of God for our good includes physical health or illness always in service of our enduring spiritual life and our relationship to the lives of others.

James could be including the spiritually sick, since the Word, anointing with oil, and absolution certainly provide the remedy (though anointing with oil is not a sacrament). However, the context suggests that he is talking about physical ailments. Consider how the majority of people who sought Jesus out did so in search of physical healing or help, which Jesus addresses at length in Jn 6.

• • • • • • • • • • • • • • • • • • • •

Q 5:16–18 Will God listen to the prayers of a humble Christian more so than the prayers of an unbeliever? Are the prayers of a pastor more potent than the prayers of a "baby Christian"? What difference is there in the effectiveness of prayer if you are righteous or not?

Proverbs 28:9 says, "If one turns away his ear from hearing the law, even his prayer is an abomination." God even forbade Jeremiah from praying for Israel because they were so contrary to God in their thoughts, words, and life (Jer 7:16; 11:14; 14:11). Pr 1:20–32 provides a powerful narrative and warning to those who would be determined in their wicked rebellion and then expect God to answer them when they need help for the consequences of such a life.

On the other hand, the Bible says that God will not despise a broken and contrite spirit (Ps 51:17) and that His mercy is on those who fear Him (Lk 1:50). It is important to remember that God's silence toward the wicked and His severe words about their pretentions in prayer are meant to bring them to honest repentance, so that they do begin to listen to His Word and are thus inspired to the plea of genuine humility that the Lord so graciously and eagerly awaits (Ezk 18; Lk 15:11–32; 18:9–14).

It may seem more likely that a baby's prayer would be more potent, since pastors are adults and adults seem to have the most trouble with God (Mt 18:1–4). Certainly the idea that adults in general and pastors in particular make prayers that are more effective because they are more sophisticated is renounced soundly by God all through the Bible (Mk 10:13–16). On the other hand, inasmuch as a pastor is a product of the Word (2Tm 3:16–17) and has learned how to pray and what to pray for according to the Word, his prayer might indeed be more potent than a child's (1Co 13:11), especially for other people who may be listening to that prayer and growing or declining in faith because of it. Finally, all power rests with God and flows from Him. If a prayer is potent, it is because the Lord has inspired the person with His Word, which produces good fruit (Mt 7:17; Jn 15:1–7). Let us also not forget that the Son of God and the Holy Spirit remain to intercede for us (Heb 7:25; Rm 8:26).

If you are self-righteous, then your prayer would be at least ineffective, or perhaps even an abomination to God (Lk 18:9–14; Pr 28:9). If you are righteous because God has worked repentance and regeneration in your life, then your prayer would be absolutely and always effective, according to Jesus' own words in Jn 14:13, 14, 26; 15:15; 16:23, 24, 26. The Word of God works the right disposition in us (contrite and broken), turns our attention to the solution that God wills to provide, and gives us the language and motivation for the prayer itself ("if you ask anything according to My name [that is, according to Jesus' Word], I will do it").

Q 5:16 Can prayer cause the forgiveness of sins for others?

Only God can *cause* the forgiveness of sins, and He has accomplished this absolutely, completely, and universally in the life, death, and resurrection of His Son. We have both authority and responsibility to confirm this truth for people who are penitent and seek God's grace (Mt 18:18ff.; Jn 20:22–23; 2Co 5:21). Psychological studies seem to agree that unresolved conflict and/or guilt

have a very detrimental effect on human health.

Q 5:17 Why doesn't prayer always heal?

As mentioned above, we need to remember the relationship between our body and soul, our life in this world and in eternity. Like God, the Christians are concerned with making sure the soul is healed for all eternity, which includes the regeneration of our body to perfection in the resurrection at the Last Day. People who are preoccupied with the body risk losing body and soul, now and forever.

Q 5:19–20 It says that we are able to bring those who strayed from the faith back, yet we are told that no one can bring someone to faith because God is the only one who can do this; is there a contradiction here? Is the sinner James refers to a believer or a non-believer, or does it apply to both?

Consider how consistently we make ourselves the subject of action ("I believe . . .") or the possessors of objects ("my . . .") when, in fact, God gives us our ability (Jn 6:29; 1Pt 1:5) and all things (1Co 7:29–31; Jas 1:17). God is the mover and source of all things, yet He uses His creation to accomplish His will. James is describing the work of intercessors and ambassadors, which Jesus and Paul also describe (Mt 5:43–45; Gal 6:1ff.; 2Co 5:20).

The Bible talks about people who have come to sin in such a way that they cannot be restored. All but two of the 603,550 adult men whom Moses led out of Egypt died in the wilderness because of their unbelief (Nu 14:26–38; Heb 3:12–19). God forbade Jeremiah to pray for Israel because of their rebellion (Jer 7:16). John also wrote that we are not to pray for those who are entirely, consciously, and always opposed to God in every way (1Jn 5:16–17; Mt 12:32; Heb 10:26–31). On the other hand, Jesus forbids anyone from condemning someone as a sinner who cannot be reconciled to God (Mt 7:1). The language in Nu 14; Jer 7; Mt 12; 1Jn 5; and Heb 10 is so intense and severe in order to keep anyone from being such a person and falling under such condemnation. Therefore, our task is not to make judgments about belief or unbelief but rather to communicate the Word and will of God to people as their disposition requires. Jesus outlines the process of caring for an erring brother in Mt 18:15ff. Paul gives a similar admonition in Gal 6:1: "If anyone is caught in any transgression, you who are spiritual should restore him in a spirit of gentleness. Keep watch on yourself lest you too be tempted."

● ● ● ● ● ● ● ● ● ● ● ● ● ● ● ● ●

Q **5:20 Is there scriptural evidence for a baby being filled with the Spirit before Baptism (John the Baptist is the only one I can think of)? Aren't we born sinful, as enemies of God?**

David says very clearly that we are sinners from conception (Ps 51:5). Jesus says that our hearts are full of all that defiles us (Mk 7:14–20). However, Jesus also says that unless we repent and become as children, we cannot enter the kingdom of heaven (Mt 18:3, 10, 14). Paul said that Timothy had known the Holy Scriptures from infancy (2Tm 3:15). (Note that the word used here is "infancy," not just "childhood." "Infancy" is from conception until a child is weaned. Consider John the Baptist leaping in his mother's womb for joy.) Fallen human nature is always sinful and at enmity with God, regardless of age (Rm 5:6–10). Indeed, the Word and Spirit of God are the most powerful of all forces, and they are the only remedy for our fallen condition. The Bible also teaches that children are not the exception but the best example of the condition for human nature if it is to be positively affected by the Gospel (1Co 1:18–31). The purpose of the Law is to bring arrogant, self-asserting, self-deceptive human nature back to the honesty of the helplessness of its condition (Mt 18:3). Every person is filled with the Spirit before Baptism, for it is immersion in the Word of God that Baptism with water confirms and bears witness to (Lk 3:7–18; Ac 2:37–42; 8:30–39; 10:44–48). The Law puts to death (i.e., incapacitates or makes "infant-like") our contrary human nature, while the Gospel raises us up (that is, regenerates our soul) and inspires with the orientation and means to live as God intends (Rm 6).

1 Peter

Q 1:1–2 (2:9–10) Peter calls Christians "chosen" and "elect." Does this indicate predestination? What does "according to the foreknowledge of God" mean?

The terms *chosen* and *predestined* are related but not identical. Predestination tells us that the choices God makes are made ahead of time. Indeed, since God is eternal and infinite, His decisions would always have been made, as Paul said, "before the foundation of the world" (Eph 1:4). Before we spend any time thinking about why some are not saved, we do well to remember that Jesus has forbidden us from making that kind of judgment about people in general and anyone in particular (Mt 7:1).

Why some are chosen and not others is a mystery that has the potential to distract us from what we do know: God "desires all people to be saved and to come to the knowledge of the truth" (1Tm 2:4); God has redeemed everyone in Jesus (Jn 3:16); people are saved by God's activity alone (Eph 2:8–9); and people are condemned by their own stubborn insistence alone (Jn 3:19). God certainly knows who believes since He is the one who creates and sustains faith in us (Rm 10:17; 1Pt 1:5). For more on predestination and election, see Rm 8:29; 9:14–33; and Eph 1:4–5.

Q 1:1 Why does Peter address specific places in this verse, rather than all believers? If the apostles were preaching in Asia, why aren't other religions, such as Buddhism, mentioned?

Peter is referring to regions that made up the landmass of present-day Turkey. These regions are mentioned because believers in the first century had been "scattered" or "dispersed" there because of persecution from Jewish religious powers and Roman political forces. While Peter wrote this letter to these people at that time, what he says is applicable to all people everywhere, as is the case with the rest of the Bible. The prophets spoke to the people of their day but understood that the message was for us as well (1Pt 1:12). Paul wrote to the Colossians but clearly intended the Word for everyone (Col 4:16).

There is a tradition that says the apostle Thomas took the Gospel east, perhaps as far as India. If this is so, it would certainly be very interesting if there was an account of what happened, as we have in Acts. The "Asia" that Peter refers to is the southwestern corner of present-day Turkey, where Ephesus is located. Paul's first attempt to go there was forbidden by the Holy Spirit (Ac 16:6). On the third missionary journey, Paul did travel there (Ac 19:1ff.).

Q 1:2 What does the sprinkling of blood mean? Why does Peter speak as if the reader has already done these things?

Let me begin with a very careful translation: "by the work of the Holy Spirit which sets you apart for obedience and the sprinkling of the blood of Jesus Christ." There are three parts to this section of the verse. First, Peter makes clear, as he will very consistently, that our salvation is God's work; the Holy Spirit sets us apart to realize the benefits of God's grace in Jesus Christ. Second, the Holy Spirit sets us apart for obedience in two ways: (1) The Holy Spirit takes the obedience of Christ and applies it to us (Jn 16:14; 2Co 5:21). (2) The Holy Spirit also regenerates us in the image of Christ and inspires us to actual obedience in our life (Ezk 36:25–27; Rm 1:5; 1Jn 3:9). Third, the "sprinkling with [Jesus'] blood" is referring to atonement. In the Old Testament, the blood of a lamb was sprinkled on the Mercy Seat atop the ark of the covenant and on the people. God said that our life is in the blood and that the lamb is innocent and without blemish. God was showing the people how an innocent life could cover the commandments we had broken; not that the blood of a lamb could do this, but the blood of the lamb pointed to the Lamb of God who provided forgiveness for all by giving His life in our place (Heb 10:4; 1Jn 2:2; 4:10; 1Pt 4:8). Notice then, that the Holy Spirit sets us apart to be given the righteousness of Christ, to actually become righteous, and to have our sins covered.

● ● ● ● ● ● ● ● ● ● ● ● ● ● ● ● ● ● ● ●

Q 1:3–4 Is the new birth Peter speaks of Baptism and daily gifts? Why does it say they are kept in heaven for us? Doesn't God give us new birth daily?

For a discussion of the "new birth," see the answer below at 1:3. God has generated us from above into a living hope. That living hope is for life everlasting in paradise, after we are raised from the dead with bodies restored and perfect. This hope and inheritance of life everlasting in perfection is what has been kept in heaven for the faithful, where thieves cannot break in and steal and neither moth nor rust can destroy (Lk 12:32–33). God blesses us with this life even now through His Word, the Sacraments, and daily blessings without number, but we know the good of it all only in part as long as we struggle in this corrupt human nature (2Co 5:1–6).

● ● ● ● ● ● ● ● ● ● ● ● ● ● ● ● ● ● ● ●

Q 1:3 If one word can be changed in the Bible just because the editors thought it would sound better, how do we know other parts have not been changed?

This question was the result of a discussion in class about translation. Some English translations use the phrase "born again" for the Greek, which actually says, "generated from above." The Greek word for "born" occurs seventeen times in the New Testament, all of them referring to a literal, physical birth (Lk 2:7). The Greek word here means "generated" or "begotten" in the sense of conceived and includes the beginning of life, including birth. The point of this word, however, is not the physical passage of a person from womb to world, but the origin of this person—from where and whom did this life come? The Greek word translated "again" actually means "from above," which includes the idea of "again" but means more, as in the expression "let's take it again from the top." A director or conductor who says this doesn't mean we should just repeat what we just did, rather, the phrase means we need to start all over again, from the very beginning. Jesus makes this point with Nicodemus when He says, "That which is generated of the flesh is flesh, and that which is generated of the Spirit is spirit" (Jn 3:6, author's translation). Thus, the original Greek phrase "generated from above" does affect birth and is talking about doing something again but is concerned with the origins that precede birth and prevent a simple repetition of what has already been (Jn 3:4).

Anyone who cannot study the Greek text of the New Testament faces significant challenges in knowing what changes have been made in the translation process and what the original text means to convey. Many church bodies require their pastors to learn biblical Greek so they can answer these kinds of questions. Many people look up and compare different English translations in an attempt to be more certain about what a text says, though doing so is no guarantee that the favorite, chosen, or most popular translation is accurate. The best safeguard of the meaning of the biblical text

Why do some people reject faith?

is the breadth of the text itself—the Bible interprets itself and often provides definitions (2Pt 1:20–21; Gal 1:20; Heb 11:1). Context, historical narrative, and cross-references all help us toward certainty about the intended meaning of biblical texts. Jesus said, "If you abide in My word, . . . you will know the truth, and the truth will set you free" (Jn 8:31–32). The emphasis is on the word *abide* or *remain*. There is no substitute, no matter how many languages a person knows, for remaining in the Word until what it intends to say becomes apparent (Gn 32:24–26; 2Pt 1:19).

• • • • • • • • • • • • • • • • • • • •

Q 1:5 Is this a reference to faith as something God does rather than us? This verse talks about people being shielded by God's power in the faith. Why do some people reject faith?

Here are just a few examples where Scripture discussions faith as God's work: Eph 2:8–9; Jn 6:29; Rm 10:17; 1Co 4:7.

Rejection of the faith (or apostasy) is a disposition of all fallen human nature (Gn 6:5; Mk 7:21–23; 1Co 2:14). Besides the contrary disposition of fallen human nature, the world and the devil labor relentlessly in constant schemes to overthrow a person's faith (Eph 2:1–3; 1Pt 5:8; 1Jn 2:15–17; Rv 12:17).

The power of God, which regenerates us, makes us faithful, and fuels faith, is provided in His Word (Jn 6:63; Rm 10:17). Having warned about the danger our faith is always in, Paul urges us to put on the full armor of God, which we do by reading the Word. But how many heed Paul's warning (Eph 6:11–18)? The Word is to faith like oil is to a lamp, so why did half of the virgins bring no oil (Mt 25:1–13)? We know that fallen human nature, the world, and the devil are all opposed to faith. We know that God desires all to be saved and that God is the one who works salvation in the life of the saved (Jn 1:11–13; 1Tm 2:4). We know that some people who have been made faithful are careless about abandoning the Word, which sustains faith and protects us while in the faith (Jn 8:31–33; Lk 12:39). We know that some people not only lose the faith from absence of the Word, but actually become opposed to the faith, despise it, and fight against it (Heb 6:1–8; 10:26–31).

• • • • • • • • • • • • • • • • • • • •

Q 1:6–7 I have often heard that by doing good works and suffering greatly you will prove your worth to reach heaven. Could these verses be confirming that?

James and John asked to sit at Jesus' right and left hands. Jesus told them they had no idea what they were asking for (Mk 10:35–45). A young man tried to prove his worth to Jesus and found it impossible (Mk 10:17–22). Paul laments for the people of Israel because they have a zeal for God but reject the righteousness He provides by faith in order to assert their own good works, thus many of them are not going to reach heaven at all (Rm 10:1–5). Peter and Paul both argued vehemently that it is impossible to save ourselves by works of the law (Ac 15:6–12; Gal 2:16). Some might still argue that doing good works allows you to obtain a better place in heaven. This idea suffers from at least three problems. First, Paul said that the measure of our faith, which is the only possible source of good works, is assigned to us by God (Rm 12:3; 14:23). Second, how can heaven be paradise if some have it better than others? Finally, Jesus warned in severe terms that we ought not to think our good works or sufferings have any merit before God (Lk 17:6–10). Who we are, what we do, and the eternity we receive are all a gift of God's good will (Jas 1:18; Ps 139:16; Rm 12:3; Eph 2:10). The challenge for us is not to make something of ourselves but to realize, appreciate, and enjoy what God has prepared for us from the foundation of the world.

• • • • • • • • • • • • • • • • • •

Q **1:6 Why do Christians seem to have or advertise so much trouble in their lives? Are all of the trials referred to a result of persecution?**

The next verse provides a first and positive answer: "that the tested genuineness of your faith . . . may be found to result in praise and glory and honor at the revelation of Jesus Christ." When our lives are easy, we tend to take that for granted or take credit for it and forget that God is the provider.

> Why do Christians seem to have so much trouble?

Trials require our human nature to be honest about our dependence on God and His grace. This honesty about dependence is faith, which keeps us connected firmly to the words and promises of God upon which our life depends (Ps 78:34). Paul sums it up well: "when I am weak [according to the flesh] then I am strong [according to the Spirit]" (2Co 12:10). As we age and death approaches, the durability of the faith God gives us (tested and enduring over and over again) gives more and more assurance that death is only a shadow for us as we pass from this life to paradise (Ps 23; Php 3:1–12).

Second, Paul explains that believers should not be "moved by these afflictions. For you yourselves know that we are destined for this" (1Th 3:3). When describing the ways of fallen humanity, we talk about trends, movements, revolutions, and "going with the flow." What experience should we expect if we are heading the opposite direction, if we are "swimming upstream" so to speak? While Christians are opposed to no one but are devoted to love, advocating for life in a culture of death may well seem like opposition. But it is the self-destructive conduct and disintegration we are opposed to because we are advocating for the person's life, temporal and eternal.

Paul describes the forces that are against us in Eph 2:1–3: the world, the devil, and our flesh. Consider the particular features and dynamics of each force. The world will be opposed to Christians because they resist lust for material things, which is how the world gains power and wealth (Ne 13:15–19; Jn 11:48; Jas 4:1–4; Rv 18:11–15). Jesus warned that the cares of this world and the deceitfulness of riches choke the Word (Mt 13:22). Nehemiah had to order the gates of the city to be closed to prevent foreigners from having market on the Sabbath (Ne 13:15–19). Paul was thrown into prison by the masters of a slave woman because he cast a demon out of a woman who was a fortune teller (Ac 16:14–19). The silversmiths in Ephesus started a riot because they feared that Paul would ruin their business of making idols (Ac 19:23–41).

The devil opposes Christians because that is the only thing left for him to do. From the fall of Adam until Christ, the devil might have thought he could forever accuse people before God (Jb 1:6–12; 2:1–6). When Jesus took away the sin of the world, the possibility of accusing anyone of any sin was taken away as well—nailed to the cross (Col 2:13–15). When Jesus cried, "It is finished" (Jn 19:39), the devil was cast down from heaven forever (Rv 12:7–11). Since the devil can no longer argue for people to be condemned before God, the only way left for him to do harm is by turning people against the grace of God (Mt 13:24–30, 36–43; Rv 12:17; 18:4–8:). This is why Jesus and the apostles are so urgent in their warnings to be alert and armed against the devil and

his deceptions (Lk 12:37–40; 2Co 2:10–11; Eph 6:10–17).

Our fallen human nature is weak, ungodly, sinful, and at enmity against God (Rm 5:6–10). Though we are so limited by our dependence on forces outside of us, we still fancy the idea that we are in control, masters of our own destinies, even god (1Sm 8:19; Job 38:1ff.; Ac 12:21–25; Jas 4:13–17). A soul regenerated by God in the image of Christ is necessarily in conflict with such a fallen human nature and will remain so until this human nature returns to the ground from which it was made (2Co 4:16–5:17; Gal 5:17).

Q 1:10–12 Is Peter talking about the old prophets (Isaiah, Jeremiah) speaking about the time people are living in?

Peter is talking about the prophets of the Old Testament, from Elijah to Malachi. These prophets kept on trying to figure out at what time and in what way God would fulfill His promises but could not (just like people since Christ have tried to predict the end of the world). God did reveal to these prophets that they were conveying the Word of the Lord for the benefit of people for ages to come. King David understood that God's promise to establish his offspring as an everlasting king would not happen for a long time (about a thousand years as it turned out; 2Sm 7:19). Certainly Isaiah would have been waiting to hear that a virgin conceived, but this would come about many centuries later (Is 7:14; Lk 1:26–38).

Q 1:12 Why do the angels long to look upon things? Can't they already see them?

What the angels long to look into are not material things you can see with your eyes. The Gospel is what the angels long to look into. Paul calls the Gospel a mystery (Rm 16:25). In 1Co 2:7–8, Paul describes this mystery as the hidden wisdom of God, ordained before the ages, which no one knew; then, in v. 9, he quotes Is 64:4: "What no eye has seen, nor ear heard, nor the heart of man imagined, what God has prepared for those who love Him." Finally, in Php 3:7–11, Paul talks about abandoning everything else that exists for the excellence of the knowledge of Christ Jesus, "that I may know Him and the power of His resurrection, and may share His sufferings" (v. 10). On the basis of texts like these, I suggest that angels can only long to look into these things because they don't know what it is to be redeemed (just as we don't know what it is to live perfectly according to God's will at all times).

Note: the word translated "to look" really means to stoop down in order to see something and only occurs five times in the New Testament. In the Gospels, this word describes what Peter and Mary did when they came to the empty tomb (Lk 24:12; Jn 20:5, 11). James uses it in regard to the perfect law of liberty (Jas 1:25). The angels knew Jesus was not in the empty tomb and even questioned the apostles about coming to the tomb at all ("Why do you seek the living among the dead?" [Lk 24:6]). Thus, it is apparent that the angels cannot stoop to look into the wonder of Christ's crucifixion and resurrection on our behalf—redemption that provides us with the perfect law of liberty by God's grace (Mk 16:5–6; Lk 24:7). There is a difference between knowing what Jesus is doing and pondering that He has done it for you (Rm 8:31–39; Eph 3:18).

Q 1:15–16 Due to our sinful nature that surrounds us, how can we be holy like God?

Jesus also gave this command (Mt 5:48). Is it possible that this imperative from God is like the imperatives at creation: "Let there be light" (Gn 1:3)? If this were the case, the imperative itself would produce what it commands. What we know for certain is that God has provided for our perfection. First, God has provided Christ as a covering of righteousness for our lives, like the Mercy Seat that covered the ark of the covenant (1Jn 2:2; 4:10). Second, God has forgiven all that has been, is, or ever will be wrong with us (Ps 103:11–12). Third, God regenerates our soul in the image of Christ and this regenerate soul, animated by the Word and Spirit of God, always does what is right (Ezk 36:27; 3:9). As long as we are in the flesh, as a whole person we will be far from perfection, as Paul laments (Rm 7:13–21). But the triple remedy of God means that we are in fact, by God's grace, at all times perfect before the Law until He re-creates our bodies in perfection as well (Rm 7:24–25; 1Co 15:50–54).

• • • • • • • • • • • • • • • • • •

Q 1:17 What does this verse mean? Why should we live as strangers since God judges our work impartially? What does He mean by work?

Let's begin with clarity. Peter says God judges "impartially," meaning "without bias" (rather than "partially," which means only part gets judged). Peter is reminding readers that the only true God, whom we call Father, has a nature we must be aware of. What is the nature of God? Among other things, God judges with perfect fairness or impartially. If we are children of this Father, then we need to live during our journey through this life in this world in fear. As long as we are in this fallen human nature, fear is necessary as a restraint. Our flesh does not obey God, nor does it receive or keep matters of faith (1Co 2:14). Only fear sustained by the Law can provide any significant restraint to our human nature, which is weak, ungodly, sinful, and an enemy of God (Rm 5:6–10). God judges our whole life and all that we think, do, and say (Mt 20–48; 12:36). If we are in Christ by faith (honesty about dependence generated by the Word, Rm 10:1–17) then His life, thoughts, deeds, and words are ours and we are perfect (Rm 8:1; 2Co 5:21; Mt 25:31–40). Notice how on Judgment Day there is a resurrection to life and a resurrection to condemnation (Jn 5:29). We are saved by grace but judged by works—genuinely good works being evidence of faith. Those who steadfastly reject the atoning work of Christ demand to be judged on their own life apart from Christ, which is entirely wicked (Gn 6:5; Is 64:6). Those who are in Christ have already endured judgment and condemnation with Him and so pass immediately to the resurrection of life.

• • • • • • • • • • • • • • • • • •

Q 1:21 "Through Him are believers in God"—is "Him" Christ or the Holy Spirit? Does this mean that before Christ people couldn't have confident faith?

The nearest referent for the pronoun "Him" is Christ who shed His blood (v. 19), who was foreordained but manifest by His incarnation (v. 20). This is the One through whom we believe in God. While the Son of God became physically manifest as the Christ in the person of Jesus, born of the Virgin Mary, He is God and has always existed. The Son, who is the Word of God, created faith in people before the incarnation and it is the same Son of God, now also Son of Man, who creates faith through the Word ever after (faith of Eve: Gn 3:15, 4:1; faith of Abraham: Gn 12:1–3; faith of David: Ps 51; 2Sm 12:23). Confidence or strength of faith may be a function of the measure of faith God has assigned (Rm 12:3) or a function of the presence or absence of the Word (Col 3:16; Jn 15:1–3; Eph 6:11–17).

• • • • • • • • • • • • • • • • • •

Q 1:22 Why is he talking about purifying ourselves?

Hypocrisy, self-righteousness, and self-deception are perhaps the most significant threat to our eternal life. The whole Bible

consistently refers to honesty or genuineness ("in truth"), in contrast to the peril
and catastrophe of fraud and pretense (Mal
1:10–13; Ac 5:1–11). Be careful to remember that no matter what good we are doing,
God is the source and cause of it. In 1:2, Peter explained how obedience is the work of
the Holy Spirit (see question and answer at
1:2 above).

Q 1:24 Why is Peter using an analogy of grass and flowers?

Human nature since the fall of Adam
is like grass and flowers because of its short
duration and fragile condition. Grass with-
ers under the bright sun, especially when
there is no rain (Jn 4:13–14). Flowers fade,
especially when they are cut (Jn 15:6). Peter
is speaking about the differences between
our human nature and our regenerate soul.
Our human nature since the fall returns to
the dust from which it came, just like Adam's. On the other hand, our regenerate soul
endures forever, just like the Word of the
Lord that generated and sustains it.

Q 2:4–10 What is this section about?

All of God's creation provides insight
into our lives as Christians (Ps 19:1–3). Jesus is referred to often as a "rock" of refuge
and strength (Ps 18:2; Mt 7:24–25). Jesus
is described as a stone that was cut out of
a mountain without hands that became
a great mountain and filled the earth (Dn
2:34–35). This is describing the incarnation
of the Son of God by the virgin birth ("cut
out by no human hand"), His redemption,
and the bearing of the Gospel into all the
world ("became a great mountain and filled
the whole earth"). Jesus says that He is a rock
that can either support the penitent sinner
or crush the hard-hearted and impenitent
(Lk 20:17–18). Paul described Jesus as the
cornerstone, the apostles and prophets as
foundations, and all believers as the material that makes up the Church (Eph 2:19–22).
Stone or rock is enduring, like the Word of
God (Mt 24:35; Jn 10:35; 19:36). Jesus is the
author, source, and giver of life, so He is a
living version of many things: stones, water,
and bread (1Co 10:4; Jn 4:10; 6:51). Those
who are regenerated by His Word are therefore also enduring and stable yet living, active, and productive (Rm 12:1).

Q 2:7 What does Peter mean when he says, "The stone that the builders rejected has become the cornerstone"? Is he talking about the Word?

Jesus and the Word of God are one and
the same (Jn 1:1, 14). Fallen human beings
are determined to build a life of their own
design, contrary to God's design and will.
Whenever fallen humans are made aware
of the cornerstone or capstone, they reject it
because it doesn't "fit." For more on Jesus as
the cornerstone, see Mk 11:28–12:12.

● ●

Q **2:8 I do not understand how Christ is "a stone of stumbling, and a rock of offense." Does this mean God destined for us to stumble? Does God predestine people to hell? Are the ones who sin appointed to sin?**

This verse is explained nicely by Paul in 1Co 1:18–25. To stumble means to be unable to follow the path that Jesus would lead us on. Pride and selfishness of fallen human nature is what makes us stumble over Christ. Our efforts to recapture the honor of being made in the glory of God makes us proud, and pride makes us think we must be served rather than serve. Jesus provided this lesson in the entirety of His teaching and life, yet how many, even among those who claim to be Christian, live by His teaching (Jn 13:3–17)? Our efforts to fill the space in our lives where God should be make us selfish, and selfishness makes us think that life consists of getting what we want. Jesus emptied Himself of His prerogatives as the Son of God, humbled Himself to become a man, and then humbled Himself further in service to His enemies, even to a cursed death by crucifixion. How many people really believe that our life is realized in giving to others rather than getting for ourselves (Mk 12:41–44; Lk 6:38; 12:15)?

God does not predestine anyone to hell. We know this because He not only says He desires all to be saved but has in fact saved all by taking away the sins of the world (1Tm 2:4; Jn 3:16). Peter is describing a particular consequence to a particular disposition: "they disobey the word." If the

Word is the means by which God applies the saving work of Christ to our lives, refusing that Word leaves a person opposed to and without the benefits it conveys (Rm 10:1–3). Why some people are determined to despise, resist, and oppose truth and grace to their dying breath is something we cannot fathom (Rm 9:14–29).

● ●

Q **2:9–10 Is the author relating Old and New Testament thought or objective justification versus subjective justification thought?**

Yes. The Old Testament demonstrated the need for and pointed forward to the New Testament. The Old Testament revealed God's promises to save and the human condition that depends on God alone. God chose the descendants of Abraham and Sarah that were generated in spite of impossible conditions (Gn 17:1–19; Rm 4:1–25). God chose the tribe of Levi to mediate between God and the rest of Abraham's children. In the New Testament, Christ is the perfect child of God and perfect mediator, making atonement for all and reconciling us all to God through the forgiveness of our sins. This work of Christ once and for all, for all people, is "objective" justification (being declared just or innocent before God). Subjective justification is the application of that work of Christ in an individual's life. Think of objective justification as *reality* and subjective justification as *realization*. The Word of God regenerates us in the image of Christ; thus we become the chosen people and royal priesthood. We continue and extend the work of Christ by bringing His Word to others so they also might know they have been reconciled to God and realize the blessings of this reality.

• • • • • • • • • • • • • • • • • • •

Q 2:9 Why do some denominations still have priests? I thought we didn't need priests anymore because Jesus was the ultimate sacrifice.

Why some religious bodies return to the laws, ways, and names of Old Testament times is a mystery, except for the fact that fallen human nature seems determined to bring destruction on itself (Gal 3:1ff.; 2Pt 2:22). Jesus warned that we should call no one Father except God, but some ministers insist on being called this (Mt 23:9). Jesus warned against making promises but people who claim to be Christians still do (Mt 5:34–37). On the other hand, Peter did say we are a "royal priesthood" (1Pt 2:9). By "priesthood," Peter means to describe the nature of Christian life; we advocate for others, especially our enemies; we extend the kingdom of God to others by word and deed; we are devoted to helping others realize the reconciliation that Christ has secured for all (Mt 5:44; 2Co 5:21).

• • • • • • • • • • • • • • • • • • •

Q 2:11 Why does Peter call his readers "sojourners" and "exiles"?

Peter began this letter by addressing the "pilgrims" of the Diaspora (a Greek word meaning to "spread," as in the spores of plants). Those regenerated in the image of God must be strangers and aliens here since Christ Himself was not received by His own people nor could He find a place to rest His head (Jn 1:11; Lk 9:58). Our human nature, passed through all generations to us from Adam, is made of the dust of the earth and is sinful, materialistic, and destined to return to the dust from which it came. Our regenerate soul, created and sustained by the eternal Word of God, is only passing through this place and time. We have much to do as ambassadors of Christ while here, but this is not our home, nor do we seek one here (Heb 11:13–16; Php 3:7–14). God has prepared an eternal dwelling place for us in heaven with Him; therefore, we are free to be wise stewards here, using all He gives for the love of others (Jn 14:1–4; Gal 5:1; Lk 12:42–46; 2Co 5:14–15).

• • • • • • • • • • • • • • • • • • •

Q 2:12 What is "the day of visitation"? In what ways will nonbelievers be able to "glorify God"?

Jesus used this word when He foretold the coming destruction of Jerusalem by the Romans in AD 70, which is indicative of Judgment Day for the whole world (Lk 19:44). On Judgment Day, God will be recognized as gracious, true, and faithful in all things and to all people. No one will accuse God of wrong, especially not those who opposed Him all their lives. Peter is reminding and urging the faithful to serve the truth of God by their honorable conduct. Notice that Peter contrasts how unbelievers will speak of the faithful as evildoers now with how they must in the end be honest and give God glory for the good He worked through the lives of His people.

Faith or honesty about our dependence is a reality that infants and helpless people affirm (Lk 18:15–16; 1Co 1:18–31). Only the most arrogant and perverse people try to deny what the Word and all of creation make so clear, and a consequence of their insistence on deception is being bound by it (Ps 19:1–3; Rm 1:18–31). On Judgment Day, when God's immediate and physical appearance comes with the destruction by fire of all things material, no one will be able to deny the truth or lie to anyone else about it (2Pt 3:10–13; Rv 18:1–24; Mt 10:26; 1Co 4:5). Paul explained that every knee will bow and every tongue confess that Jesus Christ is Lord (Php 2:10–11). For all those who lived in honesty about their dependence on God, Judgment Day has already passed in Christ's crucifixion, which makes the Last Day one of relief and the beginning of eternal bliss (Jn 5:29; Mt 25:31–46; Rv 7:9–17; 21:1ff.).

. . . .

Q 2:13 How much should we submit to authorities? What about as we contemplate war? Should men submit to an elected woman official?

First, God commands that we have no other gods before Him (Ex 20:3). Peter applied and obeyed this commandment when he told the Jewish authorities, "We must obey God rather than men" (Ac 5:29). Paul explained that we obey authorities, whether civil governments, religious leaders, or our parents, because they act on behalf of God for our welfare (Rm 13:1–7). When an authority opposes God, then we are opposed to them—though we are careful to exercise this opposition according to God's will (Mt 5:38–48; here be careful, as those with responsibility for others would not be right to leave those whom they care for by simply surrendering their lives to an enemy).

Second, when a nation goes to war, the citizens must consider the cause of war and conduct of the military. It might be necessary for citizens to leave their country. It might be possible for citizens to help their own country and the enemy by different forms of service, as one might do with the Red Cross.

Third, relations between men and women according to God's design promote life and well-being for all. Christians strive to live consistently with God's will and provide the best possible witness to the world around us. However, the condition of the world we live in is confused, entrenched, and hostile. It seems impossible to live by the letter of the law regarding male and female relationships, so we do the best we can to live according to God's design, to make a strong, clear witness, and to draw others toward God's way (Col 4:5).

Q 2:15 Does Peter mean "damned" when he says "foolish"?

The term *fool* in the Bible means an unbeliever, which is why Jesus forbids us from calling anyone a fool, though people might act foolishly (Jb 2:10; Ps 14:10; Mt 5:22; 7:1). Foolish people are subject to the thinking (or lack of thinking) of unbelief or a lack of honesty about our dependence, which explains their ignorance. Good conduct, because it is genuinely good, is a powerful witness, especially against anyone determined to undermine the truth (Mt 5:16).

Q 2:16 What exactly is "free" referring to?

As children of God, redeemed from the condemnation of the Law, provided for by His bountiful goodness, and regenerated by His eternal Word, we are absolutely free from all harm (Jn 11:25–26). In fact, not only is it impossible for us to die, but all things must work for our good according to God's direction (Rm 8:28; 2Co 4:17–18). While we may experience easy times of comfort or difficult times of challenge, there is no such thing as a bad day for a Christian (Job). Thus free from fear of death, we respond to opportunities to apply our lives for the greatest benefit to others (Heb 2:14–15; 2Co 5:14–15). Living on behalf of God and for love of others keeps us from the folly of trading our freedom for the appetites of our fallen human nature that would bring us back into bondage (1Co 6:12; 10:23; Gal 5:1). Consider how effective Paul was in all circumstances, even while imprisoned (Ac 16:25–34; Php 1:12–18). This is why Paul commands that we give thanks to God in *all* times, not in spite of difficulties but especially because we know that challenges are opportunities that God makes work for us (1Th 5:18).

Q 2:17 How can you honor both God and authorities?

We fear, love, and honor God when we give the fear, love, and honor due to those who act in His service for our good (Jn 5:23; Rm 13:1–7; Eph 6:1–3; 1Th 5:12–13).

Q 2:18 Is there any limit elsewhere in the Scriptures to how much a slave must submit?

There is no limit on suffering for a slave or free person (Mt 5:38–48; Jn 15:13; Php 2:5–8). We deserve to suffer as Christ did, but will not because He suffered in our place. If God delivered us from suffering and death through the sacrifice of His Son, we can surely trust Him to watch over our life and deliver us from suffering according to what is best for us (Heb 12:1–11; 2Co 4:1–18). On the other hand, we need not endure suffering unnecessarily and we are urged to avoid it when possible, just as slaves are urged to gain their freedom if they can (Mt 10:23; 1Co 7:20–23).

• •

Q **2:18 How did the Church view this verse and others like it during the times of slavery? Is it right to refer to us as servants or slaves? The term *slaves* or *servants* does not really show our freedom through Christ. Is Peter condoning slavery?**

The usual term for "slave" occurs 126 times in the New Testament. The term used in this verse occurs only 4 times in the New Testament and is a little more specific, suggesting a slave that serves in the house. Whether speaking of slavery universally or of some form in particular, God is absolutely against slavery. God forbade Adam from eating of the tree of the knowledge of good and evil in order to protect Adam's freedom and prevent slavery (Gn 2:17). Now that human nature is in a fallen condition, weak, ungodly, sinful, and opposed to God, it is in bondage until the day it dies (Rm 5:6–10; 6:7). The question since the fall, therefore, is not whether human beings will be slave or free, but who will be our master and what does that master want with us (1Ki 18:21; Mt 6:24). The devil, the world, and our own sinful nature are hard, relentless masters, and though they claim to offer life, there is only death (Rm 1:18–31; 6:20–21; Eph 2:1–3). God is Master of all since all things depend on Him, but His will is only that we live and thrive (Jn 10:10; 15:11).

Slavery has been around practically since the fall, but not always of the despicable type that we are so familiar with from early American history. Throughout history there have been people whose dire straits left them no alternative but to offer their lives in exchange for food and shelter, and there have been masters who cared for slaves as they did for their own family members (even in early American history). Good relationships between master and servant reflect good relations between the individuals and their common, absolute Master (Dt 15:12–18; Philemon). While few people in the world may be called "slaves" today, many people are hardly better off than slaves though they are called employees and receive a paycheck. Perhaps we may summarize the subject of slavery as follows:

1. There are different types of slavery: spiritual, physical, mental, emotional. Addictions of any sort are all forms of slavery. As long as a person is possessed by a fallen human nature, he or she will be in bondage. If a person is in bondage spiritually, his or her whole life is one of slavery that is tragic during life and in death (Rm 6:16).

2. There is honesty and deception involved with slavery. God is our Master, but according to His nature His dominion is one of love and providence. Any other master is forbidden by God because they are liars and murderers (Jn 8:44). There is no benefit in calling slavery or bondage "employment."

3. Like our Lord Jesus Christ, we seek to liberate people absolutely, body and soul. We seek to liberate whenever and as often as there is need and we have opportunity; personally with family,

neighbors, friends, and co-workers; collectively as citizens of a nation; globally, even if that requires war. Most of all, we never forget that the body can never really be liberated unless the soul is liberated by the truth and grace of God.

● ● ● ● ● ● ● ● ● ● ● ● ● ● ● ● ● ● ●

Q 2:19–25 How much pain and suffering should you be willing to put up with? Why does God allow people to suffer unjustly in His name? Why do some suffer more than others?

How much pain and unjust suffering did Jesus endure on behalf of each one of us? Until a person accepts this truth, there can be no progress in answering the rest of the questions. We will never suffer what would be just, nor will our suffering even begin to compare with what Jesus endured because He tasted death for all (Jn 8:52; Heb 2:9). Therefore, God does not deal with us according to our iniquity (Ps 103:10). God disciplines us in the course of our life, but only as love prescribes for our good (Heb 12:4–11). God knows what is best for us, makes all things work for good, and sets limits on what we must endure (Rm 8:26; 1Co 10:13; 2Co 4:17). God directs the course of life (a) so that we can recognize His wisdom, power, and grace, (b) in order to make our human nature serve our regenerate soul, (c) in order to make the experiences in time serve perfection for all eternity, and (d) to prove that the judgment of those who relentlessly opposed Him is just (Dn 3:8–30; 6:1–28; Rm 8:18). The hardest part of this passage to confess is that we rarely suffer unjustly. The most wonderful part of this passage is that Jesus was our substitute, that He alone suffered unjustly, that God has delivered us from real suffering, puts limits on suffering, uses suffering for our benefit, and promises to relieve us of suffering for all eternity, each at the right time.

● ● ● ● ● ● ● ● ● ● ● ● ● ● ● ● ● ● ●

Q 2:20–24 Why can't we stand up for ourselves?

Here is a mystery and aspect of the genius of God. First, we are essentially a soul, not a body; we are eternal, not temporary. This means that we are free to use our human nature in time for the eternal welfare of the souls of others. Jesus demonstrated this absolutely (Php 2:5–11). Second, fallen human nature is opposed to God, neighbor, and the life of the individual. After conversion, a person's regenerated soul and his or her fallen human nature are opposed to each other (Gal 5:17). Third, the loss of life (we lose God, we lose our neighbor, and we lose our own life) comes from making others suffer so that we can satisfy ourselves. The recovery of life (being restored to God and neighbor and realizing our own true life) comes from using our human nature in the service of others, no matter how much suffering that requires (Lk 9:24–25). Note: God controls and sets limits on the suffering people endure. He provides the ultimate remedy through death, when the soul is released from the troubles of the body in paradise and at the end, resurrected in a perfect body in a new earth. (See also 1Pt 1:6 and 1:6–7 above.).

• • • • • • • • • • • • • • • • • • • •

Q **2:21 As a Christian, where do you draw the line between enduring suffering and sticking up for yourself?**

Actually, we leave the line drawing to God. Since God is Judge, Father, and Redeemer, we need not fear for our life (Ps 18:43, 48; 68:5). As people regenerated in the image of Christ, generated and sustained by His Word and Spirit, and devoted to following His way, we order all our thinking according to love of God above all things and for our neighbor as ourselves. On the one hand, Jesus says we should not resist an evil person (Mt 5:38–48). On the other hand, He authorizes parents, civil authorities, and spiritual authorities to arrest evil—to protect the helpless from evil and to protect the evildoer even from himself or herself (Rm 13:1–8; Eph 6:1–3; Heb 13:17). So we consider how to best apply our lives for the good of others for the greatest good for the longest time. If we are left with no alternatives, we still have God watching over. If we must protect our own life in order to protect others, then so we must. If we have opportunity, we protect our life even while we are using it for the good of others. We always follow that path that promotes and protects life, giving priority to the eternal soul and then to the temporal body as we are able.

• •

Q **3:1–7 What does it mean for a wife to submit to her husband? Does this mean that wives are sinning against God by becoming independent and not submissive? Why do people today have such a hard time accepting the places that God made for men and women?**

Everyone except God must be submissive in a significant number of ways since we are dependent creatures. We submit to our need for air, water, food, shelter, clothing, sleep, and more. Since the fall, we submit to even more forces from without and within, all working against our lives—self-gratification, pride, selfishness, greed, passion, lust, and more. As discussed in reference to slavery above (2:18), the question isn't whether we will submit; the question is to whom and to what end. The word translated "be subject to" or "submit" occurs thirty-eight times in the New Testament and reveals the spectrum of who submits to whom as follows:

Romans 8:7—The mind of fallen human nature cannot submit to the Law of God;

Luke 2:51—Jesus submitted to Joseph and Mary;

Luke 10:17—Demons to the Word of the Lord;

Romans 8:20—Creation to futility;

Romans 13:1—Every soul to the governing authorities;

1 Corinthians 15:27–28—All things to Christ;

Ephesians 5:21—Everyone to one another;

Titus 2:9—Servants to their masters;

1 Peter 5:5—Young men to their elders.

The Son of God in the person of Jesus Christ is the finest example of submission, as He expresses in His own words: "For I have come down from heaven, not to do My own will but the will of Him who sent Me" (Jn 6:38; see also 4:34; 5:19, 30; 18:11). Jesus makes clear that rebellion against God's design for life is deadly, but submission to the Word and will of God brings life. Jesus also demonstrates that godly submission does not undermine value nor does it endanger a person's life. We learn about submission by watching and listening to Jesus.

No one is independent except God; everyone submits except God.

People cannot accept their places because of fear. In the fall of Adam, all humanity lost its connection with God. This means the loss of certainty about our inherent worth, our purpose, and God's providence for us. When men and women feel they must, or when their egos make them think they can be their own gods, how can they not become greedy, arrogant, dishonest, tyrannical, and contrary to design? Men generally despise responsibility and the care of others which God designed us for. Women generally seek control and

> ## What does it mean for a wife to submit to her husband?

abandon the bearing and raising of children (Gn 3:16–19; see 1Co 11 and Eph 5 for more on this subject).

● ● ● ● ● ● ● ● ● ● ● ● ● ● ● ● ● ●

Q 3:1–7 Is this section full of laws or just guidelines for a happy marriage?

Paul is using imperative language (commands) which applies the Law to our lives. Every law of God is a guideline for a happy life because it explains God's design in creation (Dt 5:16; Ps 19; Gal 3:12). There are always positive consequences for living in harmony with God's design and always negative consequences for contradicting God's design: cause and effect, trial and error—we live and learn this way all the time (Rm 6:15–23). Though Christ has redeemed us from the curse of the Law, there are still two perils to beware of. First, though we may not risk eternal condemnation for contradicting the Law, we may certainly make life accursed for ourselves and for others by doing so; and why would we want to (1Co 6:12; 10:23)? Second, a persistent, conscious disregard for the Law and contradictory disposition suggests there is a soul within that despises God's Word and grace. This disposition is in deep jeopardy of eternal condemnation (Heb 6:4–8; 10:26–31).

Q 3:1–3 Doesn't God want us to marry only Christians?

The Bible does clearly teach that we should be careful who we enter any kind of communion with, especially marriage (Dt 7:3; 2Co 6:14–15). In this passage, as in 1Co 7, the New Testament speaks to people who were already married when they came to faith. Now that a husband or wife has come to faith, must he or she end the marriage? Certainly not—unless the unbelieving spouse is antagonistic to the faith (1Co 7:12–16).

Q 3:1–2 If women are supposed to be submissive to their husbands, how are they role models to believe in God? Could a wife's behavior really win her husband over to God without words?

Submissiveness produced by love and faith is completely different than submissiveness produced by tyranny and fear. Jesus provides the perfect example, as He submits to the whole will of the Father yet is clearly free in His words and actions—unlike everyone else (Jn 13:1–17). Submission from love and faith has an energy, purpose, and devotion that tyranny and fear drive out of a person. When a person is humble yet excellent in some kind of service to others, people notice and wonder, "How can that person be so capable and yet serve with such humility?"

No one can make anyone else believe; this is a fundamental characteristic of the Gospel. Only the Holy Spirit, working through the Word, can regenerate a soul and sustain it with faith. However, every Christian is an ambassador for Christ, and every Christian can be a powerful witness to an unbeliever by providing a life in the Word (1Co 7:12–16; 2Co 5:20; Eph 5:25–27).

With God, all things are possible (Mt 19:26). It is never the words of husband, wife, or neighbor that "win" another person, but the Word of the Lord (Rm 1:16; 10:17). Indeed, it is an overabundance of words without deeds that turn people away from the Gospel (Rm 2:17–24; Jas 2:14–18). Note: the submissiveness and silence of a wife is in respect to a husband who loves and cares for his wife, though he is an unbeliever. The Bible does not encourage, let alone insist, that women subject themselves to abuse; rather, they are to seek refuge and let others (especially decent men) advocate for and protect them.

Q 3:3 Why do women today cover themselves in jewelry when the Bible says it is not appropriate?

Why do women or men cover themselves in this way at all? Adam and Eve covered themselves in order to hide because they were ashamed; does this have to do with covering shame or hiding something (Gn 3:7–8)? The faith and stewardship of the early Christians most likely inspired them to use their resources for more important things than vanity (Ac 2:42–46). Few women had wealth or liberty to adorn themselves in opulence; it is likely that faithful women did not want to be associated with women of such selfish and worldly interests (2Ki 9:30–37; Jas 2:1–6; Rv 17:1–6). As with all imperatives from God, it is essential to remember their purpose. Christian men and women seek to be good stewards and ambassadors. We consider how our use of resources and the way we present ourselves helps promote or detract from the Gospel. All things are lawful for us, but not all things are helpful, nor do we want to be brought into subjection to any (1Co 6:12; 10:23–24). We don't agonize about our choices as if we lived under the Law, but neither are we careless about how we present ourselves to the world. Drawing attention to ourselves because we are unkempt or in rags is no better than drawing attention because we are overly adorned (Mt 6:16–20; 23:5–7).

Q 3:4 When Peter says women should have a "quiet spirit," is he referring to their demeanor?

Jesus said, "For out of the abundance of the heart the mouth speaks" (Mt 12:34). If we accept the truth about our fallen human nature, we are at peace because we know our whole life is better than we deserve. If we know the truth about God's grace toward us, we are at peace because we know that our life is imperishable, undefiled, and kept in heaven for us (1Pt 1:3–6). The inner peace that God establishes by truth and grace is the source of a quiet spirit and demeanor (Pr 16:33; 29:11). The word translated "quiet" occurs only here and in 1Ti 2:2, where Paul urges us to pray for leaders who protect peace so we may lead a quiet and peaceable life. Another form of this word occurs in Ac 22:2; 2Th 3:12; and 1Tm 2:11–12, where it means to be silent. The verb form of this word occurs in Lk 14:4; 23:56; Ac 11:18; 21:14; and 1Th 4:11, where it means to not speak, though in Lk 23:56 it is used to describe rest on the Sabbath and in 1Th 4:11 it describes an uncontentious life.

Q 3:6 Should a woman submit to her husband if he is wrong? Is a man supposed to obey his wife in the same matter? Sarah called Abraham her master; is that something we should follow in this present day?

What happens when anyone is wrong? There are consequences. How concerned should we be about people being wrong? That depends on how serious the consequences are. If a husband, father, pastor, or government official would cause us to sin, we must obey God rather than men (Ac 5:29). Jesus submitted Himself to the hardships of constant service to those in need and to execution by those who were wrong to hate Him—then He was exalted to the right hand of God, and the world was reconciled. Ephesians 5:21 says we all submit to one another in the fear of God; this submission means that husbands love and wives submit to that love. For all the matters of a relationship that fall between "entirely according to God's will" and "entirely opposed to God's will," a wife would want to consider which is more important: her witness of faith or enforcing her opinion. In regard to what Sarah called Abraham, I don't know if we can recover the customs of people in Abraham's time or in Peter's. The point is that the way we speak to one another be consistent with our relationship to one another. Neither speech nor actions are of much use if they are a matter of hypocrisy. How would a wife in a given time and place bear witness to her submission to and appreciation of her husband's love and care for her?

● ● ● ● ● ● ● ● ● ● ● ● ● ● ● ● ● ● ● ●

Q 3:7 How can prayers be hindered? Why are women considered the "weaker vessel"? How do Christians deal with the issue of women's rights?

Any time a person consciously and consistently mistreats another, that person's prayers will be hindered, as the proverb says: "If one turns away his ear from hearing the law, even his prayer is an abomination" (Pr 28:9). Since a husband loves his wife on God's behalf, his conduct is especially important.

Women are the "weaker vessel" for two reasons. First, think of weaker as having to do with delicacy. Think of the delicacy and intricacies of women that make them capable of bearing and raising children. Many things in our world are considered precious for a beauty that is fragile, like fine artwork or butterfly wings. Second, a woman's need for a man is real, like an infant's need for its mother. God created Adam and instructed him in the Law before there was Eve (Gn 2:7, 15–17). Eve was created to remain before Adam and help him by being the object of his love and by bearing children for both of them to love (2:18). Eve depended on Adam to love and protect her life, especially by maintaining the truth. Notice that the devil, the deceiver, attacked the woman and succeeded with his deception because Adam failed to protect her according to the Word of the Lord (3:1–8). Eve admits she was deceived (3:13). Adam was not deceived at all but knew he was abandoning his responsibility for the woman and abandoned it again when he blamed Eve for the failure (3:12). The Son of God became true man in order to correct the failure of Adam and all men (Rm 5:12–21). Notice how Jesus always maintains the truth, especially in defense of the helpless, and how He bears all burdens and failings Himself (Mt 8:17; 22:29ff.; Jn 8:3–11). Paul confirms this understanding of gender and of the fall: "For Adam was formed first, then Eve; and Adam was not deceived, but the woman was deceived and became a transgressor. Yet she will be saved through childbearing—if they continue in faith and love and holiness, with self-control" (1Tm 2:13–15).

Rights depend on laws. According to the Law, we have no rights because we have rebelled against the Law. This is why Paul uses the term *slave* for sinners (Rm 6:16). Another problem with thinking in terms of "rights" is that the conversation is typically selfish and combative; this person would assert his or her rights in opposition to another. Given the reality and nature of God's creation, perhaps it would be more honest and helpful to speak of value. Women have inherent value, as do unborn children, animals, and all of God's creation. Christians, on the one hand, deplore and oppose the mistreatment of women. Christians, especially Christian men, lay down their lives for the well-being of all women in general and of their wives in particular. Christian men and women together might work to recognize the truth that movements expose, as well as the deceit that they promote. For example, Christians oppose abortion because it does harm to everyone and despises the value inherent in abstinence, sexual intimacy, marriage, human life, women, men, and our society in general, which loses the value of the one aborted.

NOTE: Several of the following questions reflect the thoughts of students following the September 11, 2001, terrorist attacks.

Q **3:9 With all that is happening in the world, it seems no one is listening to this verse. Weren't the atrocities against the Early Church worse than the terrorist attack, and didn't they follow this teaching?**

Which verse in the Bible is anyone listening to? Jesus and Peter weren't the only ones who taught peace; Muhammad, Gandhi, and Nelson Mandela also taught peace. No matter what the truth is or who is trying

to teach it, fallen human nature is in rebellion and determined to work destruction (Jn 8:42–47).

Yes, the Christians in the early centuries after Christ and even during the Reformation period suffered horrible cruelties and death, and they did follow this teaching. It is interesting and sad to note how history is full of faithful people who blessed those who persecuted them and also full of people who claimed that the atrocities they inflicted upon others were in obedience to the faith.

Q **Does this require that we do not seek justice for this week's terrorist events?**

As the children of God, Christians live in the image of and according to the Word of the Lord. We turn the other cheek, we love our enemies, and we bless those who persecute us (Mt 5:38–48). However, we do all this in love, actively and consciously seeking opportunity at all times and in all places to advance the Gospel, just as Jesus did before Pilate and Paul did before the Roman guards and others (Jn 18:28–19:12; Ac 16:25–34; Php 1:12–18). Furthermore, as citizens, we respond according to our calling, whether firefighters, paramedics, or law enforcement officers. If we are authorized by our government to protect against injustice and prosecute criminals, then we must be faithful in that service on behalf of all, but especially the innocent and helpless.

Q 3:13 Why does it sound as though Christians will rarely be harmed for doing good when many Christians past and present have been persecuted?

The Bible reveals that all people have two lives and two lifetimes. One life is physical and bound by time; the other life is spiritual and eternal. This composition allows us to learn, understand, and have the benefit of experiences without suffering consequences eternally or spiritually. Human beings, since the fall and apart from faith, forget, ignore, and even despise things spiritual—the soul and eternity. A fallen world sees our physical life in time as all that matters, which is why there is so much of selfishness and the conflict it produces (Jas 4:1–6).

Q 3:15 How can we always have an answer to everyone who asks about our faith?

This is an interesting verse, especially if we recall that Jesus said, "When they deliver you over, do not be anxious how you are to speak or what you are to say, for what you are to say will be given to you in that hour" (Mt 10:19). Jesus commands us not to worry about what to say, but Peter tells us to always be ready to give a defense. Is this a contradiction? Proverbs 16:1 provides the answer:

"The plans of the heart belong to man, but the answer of the tongue is from the LORD." Jesus did say that His disciples remain in His Word and thus they know the truth, and truth makes us free (Jn 8:31). If we are His disciples, we will remain in His Word; this is the preparation of the heart. The Word of God in us produces hope, and when people ask us about that hope, the Holy Spirit will bring to our minds and mouths the words God would have us say. Thus we are neither inactive nor worried.

Q 3:17 Does God will us to suffer?

What does it mean to be God if He does not direct all things according to His wisdom and love? All natural consequences to actions are so because of God's design in creation. Note carefully: the very dynamics our lives depend on will take our life if we are careless with them or contradict them. Even certain vitamins become toxic if we take too much of them. God disciplines people through hardships (Ps 78:34; Heb 12:5–11). The devil, world, and even our fallen human nature afflict us in order to destroy us. Happily, God uses even these forces for our benefit (Job; Rm 8:28; 2Co 12:7–1). For more on suffering, see 1Pt 2:18–25.

Does God will us to suffer?

Q **3:19 Who or what were the spirits in prison, and where is this prison located? Is Christ the one proclaiming? Is this the only verse from which we get the statement "and He descended into hell" in the Apostles' Creed?**

The "spirits in prison" describe the souls of people who died in unbelief (Mk 9:43–48; Rv 20:13). After Jesus said, "It is finished" (Jn 19:30), and died, He descended into hell to demonstrate that the Word of God preached from Adam until Jesus was true, that He had fulfilled all that it promised, and that God had loved and redeemed His creation. Jesus' ability to descend into hell and rise again demonstrated that He conquered death and held absolute power over life and death (Ac 2:24, 31). This prison is hell, which is a temporary place of punishment until Judgment Day when it and those in it are cast into the lake of fire for eternity (Rv 20:14–15). This verse and Ac 2:31 are the only passages I know of that support the language of the Creed about Jesus descending into hell.

Q **3:20 What does he mean that only eight people were saved? When did Baptism begin? Is the great flood compared to Baptism anywhere else in the Bible?**

God commanded Noah to build an ark in which he, his wife, and his three sons and their wives (eight people; plus two of each kind of animal) could be preserved during the flood that covered the whole earth. The ark would not have saved Noah from the violent and self-destructing world around him if not for the water that bore it up to safety and destroyed the wicked (Gn 6:5–8; 11–21).

Ceremonies of washing with water, like Baptism, have been in use since Old Testament times. It was customary for people to wash their feet when entering the dwelling of another person (Gn 18:4). Priests washed themselves and their clothes before serving in the tabernacle (Ex 19:10). Elisha commanded Naaman the leper to wash in the Jordan in order to be healed (2Ki 5:10). David prayed that God would wash him from his iniquity (Ps 51:2). Isaiah and Ezekiel both talked about washing that took away sin and provided for regeneration (Is 1:16; Ezk 36:25–27). Mark records the Jewish religious leaders' many forms of washing, which reveals the way washing rituals were perpetuated and expanded over the Old Testament period (Mk 7:1–4). John made clear four particular features of his Baptism work: (1) It was not his Baptism, but God's work effected by his hands; (2) this was a Baptism of repentance for the forgiveness of sins; (3) Baptism confirmed the grace of God and the beginning of a new life; and (4) John refused to baptize hypocrites who came only in pretense (Lk 3:7–14).

This is the only place I know of in the New Testament that compares the flood to Baptism. However, Paul compares the crossing of the Red Sea with Baptism, which indicates that in every way, water bears witness to the essential nature and work of the Word of God (1Co 10:1–2; Jn 4:7–24). Whenever we seek the cleansing and refreshing effects of water, we receive an extra benefit if we consider how the Word of God does the same even more profoundly (Jn 3:12).

. . . .

Q 3:21 How does this verse fit with our belief of Baptism?

This verse in Peter is the origin and substance of the our belief in Baptism, as are all the other biblical texts about Baptism. We understand that Baptism with water reveals and confirms a life immersed in the Word of God (the living water) that saves (Jn 3:1–7; Ac 2:38–42; 8:30–39; 10:44–47; 16:32–34). If you are immersed in the Word of God, you will seek and cherish the application and confirmation of God's promises in the water of Baptism. Anyone who thinks nothing of Baptism with water must also think nothing of the Word of God that teaches us about it, commands it, and makes it effective.

. . . .

Q 3:21 Does Baptism represent us being saved by having the flood destroy the evil?

I prefer the term *indicate* rather than *represent* or *symbolize* because water really is essential to our life, restores life, cleanses, and more. Water in our physical world and life is indicative of the Word in all of our life, especially the life of the soul. Paul makes clear that in Baptism, our fallen human nature, contrary to God and self-destructive,

is incapacitated by drowning. If we held a person under the water until he or she died, we would see that the water will keep the person from ever sinning again, but it is not water that we are to be immersed in. If we are immersed in the Word of God, the living water, then the Law overcomes our contrary human nature while the Gospel regenerates and animates the soul.

. . . .

Q 4:1 Peter writes about suffering a lot. Is he writing to persecuted Christians? If I've suffered physically, does this mean I will no longer sin?

Peter does write about suffering a lot because he was writing to persecuted Christians (see 1:1). Jesus and Paul also spoke about suffering, and much of the Old Testament is a history of the persecution and suffering of the faithful (Mt 5:11, 44; 1Th 3:1–5; 1Ki 19:10). As long as we have a fallen human nature, it will oppose God (Is 64:6; Gal 5:17). Jesus commanded His followers to deny themselves (Mt 16:24–25). Paul commanded that we should make no provision for the flesh to gratify its desires (Rm 13:14). Yes, Jesus commands us to be perfect, and James warns that whoever keeps the whole Law but fails in one point is guilty of all of it (Mt 5:48; Jas 2:10). Is it possible, then, that while we cannot be perfect in this sinful flesh, suffering in the flesh has a way of incapacitating or limiting ("has ceased") the sinful activity of the flesh? This is likely what Peter means to say (see Paul saying something similar in 2Co 12:7–10).

Q 4:3 Will alcoholics, drug addicts, adulterers, and the like go to hell for what they've done?

Since Jesus took away the sins of the world, the Law no longer has the power to condemn (Jn 1:29; Jn 12:10–11). No one goes to hell for what they have done. People go to hell for despising what Jesus has done (Mt 12:31–32; 13:15; Jn 3:18–19). Condemnation does not come from drinking too much or from drug addictions or by committing adultery. Condemnation comes from loving and being devoted to these as if they were God while despising God and rejecting the redemption of Christ and the Means of Grace vigorously and steadfastly (Rm 8:1).

Q 4:4–6 Who exactly was Peter writing this letter to?

The term *they* is referring to the "Gentiles," whose will it is to walk in "sensuality, passions, drunkenness, orgies, drinking parties, and lawless idolatry" (v. 3). The recipients or audience of this letter are described in 1:1.

Q 4:5–6 When God said He will judge both the living and the dead, does this mean that the dead have not gone to heaven and not already been judged? Or are they judged twice?

One judgment came when Jesus was crucified. God judged Jesus in place of everyone in the whole world for all time (Is 53:4–12; 2Co 5:21). Therefore, everyone who is in Christ has already experienced Judgment Day with Christ (Rm 6:5; 8:1). The only other judgment day possible is for those who refuse Christ's substitutionary work and insist on arguing their own righteousness (Mt 25:44; Rm 10:1–3; Gal 5:3). You can see how sad it is for people to have already passed through judgment by Christ's suffering and death only to be condemned for rejecting Christ's work. Regarding the timing and sequence of judgment, please see the answer to 4:5 below.

Q 4:5 On the Last Day, will one immediately go to heaven or hell, or will there be a chance to talk to God first about your sins?

The transition on the Last Day is not to heaven or hell but to the new heavens and earth or to the lake of fire (2Pt 3:13; Rv 20:13–14). Before the Last Day, each person goes directly to hell or heaven when their body dies (Lk 16:19–24; 23:40–43).

There are several descriptions of what will happen on the Last Day. While more than one passage speaks about everyone giving an account of what they have done, either good or bad, Jesus distinguished between the resurrection of condemnation for unbelievers and the resurrection to life for believers (Mt 12:35–36; 2Co 5:10; Jn 5:29). Jesus' description of Judgment Day does not describe people giving an account but only their response to what God says to them (Mt 25:31–46). Both wicked and good people responded to God, and God answers them, but His answer appears to be the end of the conversation. God's revelation to John reports that people will be judged according to what is written in books, which are their deeds, and for the faithful because their names were written in the Book of Life (Rv 20:12–15). The parable of the wedding banquet describes a person who met judgment from God on that day and was struck speechless (Mt 22:12).

Q 4:6 Is Peter really talking about the dead in this verse?

The "dead" can refer to at least two groups of people. If Peter is referring to the "spirits in prison" in 3:19, then these dead are the souls of people who not only died but died in unbelief. Peter may also be referring to people who are alive physically but dead spiritually because of unbelief (Mt 8:22; Eph 2:1–2; notice that the "dead" in these verses walk!).

Q 4:7 How would Peter know the end of all things is near?

Peter said that the end of things was at hand for the benefit of everyone who would ever read this letter for two reasons. First, Peter was well aware that he was writing the Word of God for all generations that would come after him, including the generation that would be alive when Jesus returned on the Last Day (1Pt 1:12). Second, the end of

all things for each individual is always at hand, for none of us knows when we will die (Lk 12:16–20). What difference does the timing of the end of the world make for the multitudes of people who will live and die before it comes? Each generation should see a fulfillment of Jesus' prophecy about the end times even if the fulfillment is not complete. An acute awareness of the trouble in the world due to the devil, the world, and fallen human nature keeps the faithful alert and ready to meet challenges both to the faith and to the Lord in whom they believe (Mt 24:33–25:13; see also answers to questions at Mk 13:1ff.).

Q 4:8 How does love cover "a multitude of sins"?

The Greek word for love used here is *agape* and means "to sacrifice everything for the sake of something" (see Gal 2:20). The love of God moved His Son to take our nature and live a perfect life in our place in order to provide a covering for us (Rm 3:25; 1Jn 2:2; 4:10). This covering is what allows God to deal with us kindly instead of in judgment according to our iniquities (Ps 103:10). The righteous life of Christ is what God clothes us with so that while we are in the flesh, our sin is not exposed to His righteous judgment (Gn 3:21; Ps 32:1; Ezk 16:8ff.; Gal 3:27). As ambassadors of Christ who love because God first loved us, we extend the love of God by covering others with the life of Christ and dealing with them kindly, just as God deals with us (2Co 5:20; 1Jn 4:19; Col 3:13). There-fore, it is only the person who despises and continually "throws off" the cover of God's grace in Jesus' righteousness whose sin is exposed, because he insists on having it so (Mt 12:31–32; Rm 1:18–32; Rv 3:17–18).

Q 4:12 Since James says God doesn't tempt anyone (Jas 1:3), why is Peter writing about trials "to test you"?

The Greek word translated "tempt" in Jas 1:13 is the same word used when God "tested" Abraham (Gn 22:1) and in this verse in 1 Peter. Peter doesn't say who is responsible for the test, Genesis says it is God, and James says it is not God but our own desires. What are we to make of this? The key is in recognizing that different subjects may be doing the same activity for very different reasons. For example, one word for "love" in the New Testament means to "sacrifice everything for the sake of the object of that love" (as in Gal 2:20). God loves the world, and Pharisees love the best seats at feasts, but for very different reasons and with very different consequences (Jn 3:16; Lk 11:43). God wanted His Son to die on the cross and so did Caiaphas, but for completely different reasons (Jn 11:50). God limits, directs, and even at times makes difficulties in our lives in order to refine us, the way precious metals are made pure (1Pt 1:6–7; Jas 5:11). The devil makes difficulties only in order to destroy (Jn 8:44; 10:10; Rv 12:17). See also question and answer at Jas 1:13–14.

Q 4:14 How, if you are insulted for the name of Christ, can you be blessed?

Peter provides the answer immediately, indicated by the word *because* followed by "the Spirit of glory and of God rests upon you." But there is more. Both Hebrew and Greek have two different words that are translated as "blessed" in English. One word (*barach* in Hebrew and *eulogetos* in Greek) means "to become what God intends" (Gn 1:28; 1Co 10:16). The other word, used here, means "to be happy despite your circumstances because of what lies ahead" (Mal 3:12, 15; Mt 5:3–11). You cannot be insulted for Christ unless you are in Christ. If you are in Christ, then you are laying down your life in service to others, just as Jesus did (Jn 13:35). If you are laying down your life like Christ, then you share in His glory ("to do what no one else can or would do") and God will, in time, raise you up as He did His only Son (Jn 14:12; 15:20; Php 2:5–11).

Q 4:15 Why are meddlers included on a list with murderers, thieves, and other criminals?

This is the only place in the Bible where this word occurs. The word is built on the root for the word *overseer*, which suggests that "meddling" has to do with asserting ourselves where the responsibility and authority belong to someone else. Paul warned about the same, saying "Who are you to pass judgment on the servant of another?" (Rm 14:4). Jesus forbids us from judging others (Mt 7:1). Paul commanded that people "mind your own affairs" (literally "to do the things that are their own," 1Th 4:11; see also 2Th 3:11). In some ways, meddlers are worse than all the rest because they create and perpetuate trouble among people who would otherwise be peaceable.

• • • • • • • • • • • • • • • • • • •

Q **4:17 What does it mean to "obey the gospel?"**

The word translated "do not obey" actually means "to oppose persuasion." (Paul uses the expression in Rm 1:5, rightly translated as "obedience of faith." Please see question and answer there for an explanation.) Peter asks a good question: on Judgment Day, what will become of people who are opposed to being persuaded of the truth of God's love, providence, and redemption freely accomplished in Jesus Christ? When they are condemned under the Law, they will not be able to complain that God is unfair, because God redeemed them from the curse of the Law (Gal 3:1–14). They won't be able to complain that they didn't know because it was the knowledge of the truth that they so steadfastly and vigorously opposed (Mt 12:31–32; Ac 7:51–53; Rm 1:18–31; 10:1–3).

• • • • • • • • • • • • • • • • • • •

Q **4:18 How is it hard for the righteous to be saved?**

Here is an interesting question of translation and interpretation. Peter is quoting Pr 11:31, and his quote matches the Greek translation of the Old Testament exactly. The original Hebrew text is simple to understand: "If the righteous will be repaid on the earth, how much more the wicked and sinner?" In a fallen world where all people are wicked and sinners, it is very hard for a person who does what is right to receive the fair results of that labor. On the other hand, there are endless consequences for wicked and sinful behavior—both natural consequences and those provided by people who return evil for evil or who do wrong to others for no reason at all. If it is only by God's intervention, diligence, and justice that a person who does what is right receives the benefit of doing so despite all wicked opposition, certainly it will be an easy thing for God to execute His righteous judgment against the wicked and leave them to the consequences of their own wickedness (Gn 50:19–21; 2Ch 20:22–23; Rm 1:27). We can make sense of the Greek if we recognize that the Greek word translated "saved" includes smaller matters of help during life in this world, like healing or being provided with justice (1Ki 17:8–16; 17–24; Mt 8:25; Lk 18:3–7).

• • • • • • • • • • • • • • • • • • •

Q **4:19 What kind of suffering is being discussed here?**

Peter is talking about the suffering of penitent believers, suffering that is the product of a fallen nature in general or that is imposed by others unfairly. Contrast this with the particular kind of suffering that a person may bring upon himself or herself as a consequence of a particular rebellion against God.

God clearly revealed His will that no one should suffer by creating a world that was "very good" and instructing humans on how to keep it that way (Gn 1:31; 2:7–9, 15–25). People brought suffering into the world, yet God graciously makes even that serve our good (Rm 8:28; 2Co 4:17–18). People who are penitent believers suffer only according to God's will, since He does not deal with us according to our iniquities (Ps 103:10). People who suffer because they knowingly, willfully, and persistently oppose God's will bring this upon themselves, contrary to God's will that all things work together for our good (Ezk 18:23–32; Mt 23:37).

Q **5:1–4 How can Peter appeal as a "fellow elder?" Is Peter talking about pastors here when he says "elders"? Is this why we have elders in the church?**

Elder is a term that is essentially about responsibility. Elders are men who are capable of being responsible for others by strength of character, education, and experience. Elders are devoted and reliable because of the Lord's Spirit in them (Ac 6:3; Ti 3:5–9). Peter has additional authority like the other apostles to be Christ's witness to the world, but as such he still retains the qualities of an elder.

Yes, Peter is talking about pastors, though he is using the term *elder*. The terms *elder, bishop, pastor,* and *teacher* are used interchangeably in the New Testament (Ac 20:28; Eph 4:11; 1Tm 5:17). Notice how Peter uses "elder" in v. 1 and pastor or "shepherd" in v. 2. There are many reasons for having elders. The first and most important reason is a product of creation. Just as children need parents, so, too, people in general need leaders and teachers to protect and equip them properly. Through parents, civil rulers, and pastors, God intends to provide strong and faithful care for the vulnerable and inexperienced by the strong and experienced (Ti 1:5–11; 2:1).

Q **5:2 What are "overseers" responsible for? It says here to shepherd not because you must, but because you are willing—is this the calling?**

Jesus says an overseer or shepherd gives his life for the sheep, calls them by name, leads them, and protects them (Jn 10:1–14). Paul says that pastors equip the saints for the work of ministry and must be able to teach, correct those in opposition gently, preach the Word, convince, rebuke, exhort, and anoint the sick and pray over them (Eph 4:11–15; 2Tm 2:24–26; 4:1–2; Jas 5:14). This is a calling rather than something a person volunteers for or asserts himself as. Just as Jesus designated twelve of His disciples to be apostles, authenticated them, and gave them authority, so He still calls and gives authority to those who serve in the public ministry and bear responsibility for souls (Jn 10; Ac 20:28). All believers are ambassadors for

Christ, but only those qualified and called by God through the congregation can represent Christ in the public ministry (2Co 5:20; 1Tm 3:1ff.).

Q 5:6–11 Does Peter's prayer serve a literary purpose?

I am not sure about a literary purpose, but this verse does serve a practical and divine purpose. Peter is writing to believers who are being persecuted. Persecuted people need to know that suffering is inevitable for those who follow Christ. Suffering does not come because God is unable or unwilling to help or because they are being punished for sin (see 1Pt 1:6; 2:21; 3:14 above). Notice how Peter follows his prayer by saying that God does "restore, confirm, strengthen, and establish" (v. 10) us after suffering, with recognition that glory and dominion belong to God. *Glory* means "to be and do what no one else can be or would do." *Dominion*, in the proper, divine sense of the word, means "to bear responsibility for" (like an inverted pyramid). The glory of God is His wisdom and genius in making our suffering work for us, refining us, strengthening our union with Him, and confirming that our faith is true. The dominion of God means He rules over all and makes all things work for His purposes. What marvelous yet succinct assurance to anyone who struggles with questions and doubts during difficult times.

Q 5:10 Has God called all people to eternal life?

God desires all people to be saved and come to the knowledge of the truth (1Tm 2:4). God has redeemed all people and forgiven all sins in Jesus Christ (Jn 3:16). God calls everyone to repent and believe through the preaching of His Word (Ac 17:30). God has chosen us to be saved in Christ, before the foundation of the world (Eph 1:3–4). God has called and blessed all people with eternal life in Jesus Christ. Why some people insist on despising this gift is a mystery.

Q 5:12 Who is Silvanus?

Silvanus is Latin for Silas, which is Greek, possibly for Saul, which is Aramaic and Hebrew. This man is mentioned by the name Silas twelve times in the New Testament, all of them in Acts. He traveled with Paul and was imprisoned with him in Philippi (Ac 16:19–24). He is mentioned by the name Silvanus four times in the New Testament (2Co 1:19; 1Th 1:1, 2Th 1:1; and here in 1Pt 5:12).

Q 5:13 Who is this "she who is at Babylon" Peter talks about? Why does Peter refer to Mark as his "son"?

The "she" Peter is referring to is the Church, the Bride of Christ, the one Church consisting of all the faithful—but in this case, the faithful who are in Rome. Rome is sometimes called Babylon because of its opposition to the people of God, the way Babylon was in the Old Testament. Babylon is mentioned as a witness to Israel's unfaithfulness four times in Mt 1 and once in Ac 7. Babylon is mentioned six times in Revelation as the home of opposition to God and persecution of His people.

Peter is referring to Mark as his son in the faith, just as Paul and John also refer to particular believers as their children (1Co 4:17; 3Jn 4).

• • • • • • • • • • • • • • • • • • • •

Q **5:14 Is the kiss of love similar to the kiss of peace that was part of the Church's liturgy and symbolized the reconciliation they had among one another (before receiving the Lord's Supper)?**

I'm not sure if the kiss Peter is referring to was part of the Church's liturgy as a formality, but it certainly is urged as a normal practice among the faithful as they encountered one another. In contrast to the kiss of betrayal that Judas gave Jesus, a kiss between believers is not symbolic but an actual expression of love and communion (Lk 22:48; Gn 29:11; Ac 20:37; Rm 16:16).

2 Peter

Q 1:1 Why does Peter introduce himself as "Simon" or "Simeon"?

Peter's first name was Simon. Jesus gave him the name Peter (Greek for "rock") in Lk 6:14. The distinction between Peter's given name, Simon, and the name Jesus gave him, Peter, is evident in Ac 10:5; 11:13. Jesus reveals an interesting contrast between the natural character of Simon, which is more like shifting sand than rock, and His Word, which is absolute and eternal truth (Mt 16:16–18). The New Testament reveals the change in Simon's character from sand like to rock like—from sinking in fear (Mt 14:28–31), contradicting the truth (Mt 16:21–23), denial (Mt 26:69–75), and hypocrisy (Gal 2:11–16) to a clear, fearless witness and defense of the truth even to martyrdom (Ac 2:14–39; 5:29; 11:4–18; 15:7–12; Jn 21:18–19; 2Pt 1:15).

The way Peter names himself is not explained, though we know at least two things about the apostles that give us a little insight. First, the apostles seem to shift over time from concerns about maintaining the authority God gave them as apostles to greater humility about who they are. Over time, Paul described himself as an apostle from God (Gal 1:1), the least of the apostles (1Co 15:9), a sinner (Rm 5:8), and chief of sinners (1Tm 1:15). Second, how each apostle referred to himself reflected his faith and bore witness to his gratitude for the grace of God in redeeming his life. Matthew never refers to himself as Levi, for Levi was a despised and rejected tax collector with no hope. John only refers to himself as "the disciple whom Jesus loved," since the gracious love of Jesus for John is the essential element of his life.

• • • • • • • • • • • • • • • • • • • •

Q 1:2 What is the knowledge that Peter is talking about in this verse?

The knowledge Peter is talking about is both from the Lord and about the Lord. The more we know about the Lord, the more He communicates His wisdom and Spirit to us through the Word, the more grace we receive, and the more peace we experience. Besides the Scriptures, God has provided creation as a witness to Himself (Ps 1:1–4; Rm 1:18–21), written His Law on our hearts (Rm 2:15), and given us reasoning as servants (not masters) that recognizes truth (Rm 6:21). Jeremiah seems to include all of these witnesses in one of his prophecies to Israel (Jer 8:4–9).

• • • • • • • • • • • • • • • • • • • •

Q 1:3 What does Peter mean when he says "godliness"? Can we even compare ourselves to being like God? How do we make sure we are called?

We are descendants of Adam and Eve, who were made in the image of God, so there must be some comparison, even after the fall. The word translated "godliness" occurs fifteen times in the New Testament, never in the Gospels, perhaps because Jesus *is* godliness. Paul calls godliness a mystery

and equates it with Jesus' incarnation and the Gospel (1Tm 3:16). In the same letter, Paul describes the words of our Lord Jesus Christ as "teaching that accords with godliness" (1Tm 6:3). The term occurs four times in 2 Peter, which suggests that believers were abandoning the Word of God and so also losing a manner of living that bears the image of Christ (Heb 2:1ff.). According to our fallen human nature, we are as contrary to God as anyone could be (Rm 5:6–10; Eph 2:1–3). But according to our regenerate soul, we are, in fact, the children of God (Jn 1:12–13; 1Jn 3:8).

For a discussion of "calling," please see answer to questions at 2Pt 1:10.

• • • • • • • • • • • • • • • • • • • •

Q 1:5–7 Why is love the last thing to be added?

Peter isn't adding love as the last thing, but building toward the highest of all virtues with the virtues that produce genuine and enduring love. Paul spends all of 1Co 13 describing love. He concludes the chapter by saying that of faith, hope, and love, "love" is the greatest. God is love (1Jn 4:8). Love is the goal and principle for the Christian life (Mk 12:29–31; Rm 13:8). Love is the product of the virtues that precede it.

• • • • • • • • • • • • • • • • • • • •

Q 1:7 What is the difference between Christian affection and love?

The word translated "Christian affection" or "brotherly affection" is the combination of the Greek word for "brother" and "love of a friend" (*philos*). The word translated "love" here is *agape* and means "to lay down one's life for the object of that love" (see Gal 2:20).

● ● ● ● ● ● ● ● ● ● ● ● ● ● ● ● ● ● ●

Q 1:10–11 Peter says, "If you practice these qualities you will never fall. For in this way there will be richly provided for you an entrance into the eternal kingdom." This sounds a lot like being saved by our merit.

The things "you do"—upon which all depends, according to this passage—refers to making your calling and election sure. Making your calling and election sure is a product of the sequence that Peter described in 1:5–8: being diligent to add love to brotherly friendship to godliness to perseverance to self-control to knowledge. The knowledge that provides all these virtues is the knowledge of the Lord, which He brings to us through those who precede us in the faith (Mk 16:16–20; Rm 10:14–17; Eph 6:4). The Bible is exceedingly clear, abundant, and consistent in its testimony that all that we are and have and will become and all that is good is a gift of God and His work in us (Jas 1:17–18; Eph 2:8–10). However, the life we live as a product of God's work in us bears witness to His work in us; you know a tree from its fruit (Mt 7:17–20; Jn 15:1–7;

Jas 2:14–24). No matter what is said about a person or what a person may say about himself or herself, we still must ask, "And how did this come about?" The answer to that question is always "by God's gracious will and work." We are saved by grace but judged by works, but the works themselves are also God's gracious work in us (Jn 3:27; 1Co 4:7).

● ● ● ● ● ● ● ● ● ● ● ● ● ● ● ● ● ● ●

Q 1:10 How can we be sure of our calling? How and why will we not fail? Has everyone been called/elected?

The idea here is to confirm what is true by recognizing and experiencing the benefits of it every day. Our calling and election are determined by God, just like the measure of our faith, the course of our life, and the number of our days (1Pt 1:2; Rm 12:3; Eph 2:10; Ps 139:16). If we remain in His Word, we will know the truth, including the truth about our calling and election. If we know the truth, the truth will make us free from fear about not being among the called. If we remain in the Word, as a branch remains in the vine, then God will also bear fruit through us, which is further evidence of His gracious activity in our lives (Jn 8:31; 15:1–7; 1Co 15:10). God wants all to be saved and has redeemed all in the life of Christ (1Tm 2:4; Jn 3:16). God has given us His Word and the Sacraments in order to provide limitless assurance of His relationship to us. However much assurance a person might need, the Word and Sacraments are available, powerful, and more abundant than that need.

How can we be sure of our calling?

If we remain in the Word so that God's grace can produce faith and the fruits of faith as confirmation, then such a relationship with the Word and Spirit of God make it impossible for us to fail. According to our fallen human nature, of course, we do nothing but fail. But according to the regenerate soul, we are more than conquerors through Jesus Christ (1Jn 3:20; Rm 8:37–39). For more on predestination, see 1Pt 1:2; Eph 1:4–5; and Rm 8:29–9:33.

● ● ● ● ● ● ● ● ● ● ● ● ● ● ● ● ● ● ●

Q 1:12–15 When Peter writes, "To stir you up by way of reminder," does he mean that we should read or memorize Scripture daily?

Peter says three times in four verses that he will provide a reminder for us. Peter provided two reminders already in Mark and 1 Peter; now he is providing a third (2Pt 3:1). The word translated "stir up" occurs in the Gospels in the account of a storm at sea. The water was "stirred up" by the wind, and the disciples, being terrified, roused Jesus from His sleep so He might save them. Jesus, having been roused, did just that (Mk 4:39; Lk 8:24; Jn 6:18). Peter means exactly what you suggest: that we should read the Bible daily and memorize it. Jesus was clearer by saying we are to remain in the Word (Jn 8:31) just as He had directed Moses to teach the Israelites (Dt 6:4ff.). Paul said we should let the Word of the Lord dwell among us richly and that we should surround ourselves with it (Col 3:16; Eph 6:10–17).

● ● ● ● ● ● ● ● ● ● ● ● ● ● ● ● ● ● ●

Q 1:15 Does Peter know exactly how he is going to die?

I'm not sure we can know if Peter knew exactly how he would die since he has not told us. However, John recorded what Jesus said to Peter regarding his death, and the history of persecution against Christians would have given Peter a pretty good idea of what to expect (Jn 21:18–19; 1Pt 4:12ff.).

● ● ● ● ● ● ● ● ● ● ● ● ● ● ● ● ● ● ●

Q 1:16–18 What do these verses mean? The section refers to "we." Is Peter referring to himself and the disciples? Were people accusing the disciples of making up the events they recounted?

Peter is referring to himself and the other apostles; you can see this clearly in v. 17 when Peter refers to the transfiguration (Mk 9:2–8). You may recall that after Jesus rose from the dead, the Jewish elders paid the soldiers to say that the disciples had come and stolen the body. Note how Matthew says, "And this story has been spread among the Jews to this day" (approximately AD 50; Mt 28:11–15). The accusation that the content of the Bible never took place but is "cleverly devised myths" has continued ever since. In the last three hundred years, the truth of what the Bible records has been attacked so intensely that we may suggest the majority of people living do not believe it. Yet here is Peter, by his own circumstances and by the Spirit of God, anticipating claims that the Bible is not true. Peter explains that he and the other apostles were eyewitnesses of the events reported, just as courts record the testimony of witnesses and scientists record their observations. Paul adds to the weight of Peter's argument by recording the number of occasions and people to whom Jesus showed Himself after He rose from the dead (1Co 15:3–8). The testimony of the apostles is even more reliable because it was given in the face of endless and widespread threats, from the Jewish leaders as well as from the Romans (Ac 4:1–20; 16:22–23. See also any history on the persecution of the Early Christian Church).

• • • • • • • • • • • • • • • • • • •

Q **1:19 What does it mean when Peter talks about the day dawning and the morning star rising in our hearts?**

Consider how darkness tends to mean not only the inability to see but also cold, danger, lifelessness, and opposition to God. The "morning star" is the star that makes it impossible for us to see all the other stars once it rises in the morning: the sun. In the dark, we cannot know what is around us or where we are. As dawn approaches, we begin to see the outlines of shapes, but we still do not see things as they are. Many hunting accidents occur when there is enough light to see an object but not enough to know it is a person rather than a deer. Many people spend some time reading the Bible but soon lose interest, complaining that they didn't get anything out of it (Mk 4:14–15ff.). Reading the Bible only a little is like trying to see things when there is just a little light before dawn. Peter is urging us all to continue to

read, meditate, discuss, and reread the Bible until the light of God's truth is clearly evident. This relationship to the Word is parallel to Jacob's wrestling with the Son of God. Jacob refused to let the Son of God go after wrestling all night until the Son of God blessed him (Gn 32:24–31).

• • • • • • • • • • • • • • • • • • •

Q **1:20 What is meant by this verse? Was there already a Bible in circulation? Won't we always have different interpretations of the Bible?**

"No prophecy of Scripture comes from someone's own interpretation" asserts that the message of the Bible intended by God can be known with certainty and that every other interpretation can be recognized as mistaken. At the time Peter wrote this letter, the Old Testament cannon had been established for more than four hundred years and most of the New Testament was written. Peter explains that the Bible is not of any individual's own interpretation because it is not the work of human authors who struggle to make themselves understood. The Bible is what "men spoke from God as they were carried along by the Holy Spirit" (v. 21). Surely God is capable of communicating to us by means that are clear, a message that can be verified. The breadth of Scripture, the languages, the cross-references, and the witness of nature all work together to provide certainty. For example, some argue that the Bible does not teach that the Son of God is truly God. John 1:1 and 1:14 teach very clearly that Jesus *is* the Son of God and true God in very simple language. Some still argue against established rules of biblical Greek. Now what can be done? What happens when we compare Ps 23 with Jn 10? Psalm 23 says, "The Lord is my Shepherd," and Jesus in Jn 10 says, "*I am* the good shepherd" (emphasis added). Jesus' assertion is unmistakable, and we have the reaction of the educated Jewish religious leaders as confirmation. They wanted to stone Jesus to death because, they argued, He was clearly asserting that He was God (Jn 10:30–33).

The Bible is to be understood literally, which includes listening to how it tells us to understand it. We understand every text in the Bible as it presents itself, in the most plain and obvious sense, unless something compels us to do otherwise. People who fail to do this, who approach the Bible as figurative, typically end up interpreting literal language as figurative and figurative as literal. For example, many insist that the 144,000 people in Rv 7 and the thousand years mentioned in Rv 20 are exact numbers to be taken literally. Yet these same individuals argue that the locusts with tails like scorpions are attack helicopters. John tells us when he is seeing a vision. Familiarity with the language, history, and teaching of the clear passages of the Bible make the import of his visions understandable. The problem with biblical interpretation is not that the intended meaning cannot be known. The problem is that people are unwilling or unable to take the time to test assertions against all that may be known about a text.

Q **1:21 How good was Peter's knowledge of prophecy? Is Peter saying that he believed the Holy Spirit spoke through him when wrote this? Were the prophets of the Old Testament filled with the Holy Spirit? What does "carried along by the Holy Spirit" mean?**

Peter knew as much as Jesus taught him, as the Holy Spirit brought to his memory, and as Pentecost enabled him to know (Jn 14:26; Ac 1:4–5; 2:1ff.). Yes, Peter knew that it was the Holy Spirit who was communicating God's Word through him (Mk 16:16–20; Ac 1:8). The prophets of the Old Testament were filled with the Holy Spirit, spoke, and wrote as God directed them (Mt 22:43; Ac 4:25). The translation "carried along by the Holy Spirit" is accurate, and the language is simple. What being carried along by the Holy Spirit means exactly is a mystery. It must have something to do with the breath of God, which is His Spirit at work in the prophet or apostle (2Tm 3:16; Jn 14:26). It includes the process of God putting His words in their mouths or pens (1Th 2:13; Ex 4:15–16; Jer 5:14).

Q **2:1 How can one recognize a false teacher?**

Recognizing false teachers is difficult, in spite of the fact that God has revealed Himself so clearly (Ps 19:1–3; Rm 1:18ff.; 2:15; Jn 3:2). False teachers may be difficult to recognize if they disguise themselves as "angels of light" or "wolves in sheep's clothing"

(2Co 11:14–15; Mt 7:15; Ac 20:29). False teachers not only come from outside but also rise up from within the midst of the faithful (Ac 20:30; 1Jn 2:18–19). According to many warnings in the Bible, we recognize them in two ways: (1) by their teaching, which contradicts the authenticated Word of God that we already possess; and (2) by their fruits (Dt 13:1–5; Mt 7:15–18).

● ● ● ● ● ● ● ● ● ● ● ● ● ● ● ● ● ● ●

Q **2:2 What happens to someone if they accidentally teach something contrary to the Bible?**

First, we must distinguish between a person who is teaching in public and a person who is simply having a conversation. We all make mistakes in what we think, do, and say (Jas 3:2). But the person who teaches in public has a special responsibility to communicate the truth on behalf of God (Jas 3:1; 1Pt 4:11). Second, there is an important difference between consciously contradicting the truth and making a mistake in ignorance. Paul claims that he received grace from God because he acted in ignorance before his conversion (1Tm 1:12–14). Apollos had already been teaching when Priscilla and Aquilla took him aside and "explained to him the way of God more accurately" (Ac 18:24–26). On the other hand, God's wrath burns hot against those who presume to teach others, knowing that they are teaching lies (Jer 23:1, 25–32; Mt 23:1–36; Rm 1:32; 2:17–24).

As long as we are in this fallen human nature, we will fail and there will be accidents, but one who has responsibility to teach the truth in public must make every effort at all times to make sure to teach the truth.

● ● ● ● ● ● ● ● ● ● ● ● ● ● ● ● ● ● ●

Q **2:3 Is Peter referring to a specific group of people or just sinners as a whole?**

Peter is referring to the false teachers who secretly introduce destructive heresies, who deny the Lord, and who are carnal, greedy, and exploiters. Peter is not referring to a specific group or the average sinner. Peter is talking about people who consciously, willfully, purposefully, and relentlessly work to contradict the truth to their own destruction and the destruction of others.

● ● ● ● ● ● ● ● ● ● ● ● ● ● ● ● ● ● ●

Q **2:4 Do angels sin just as humans do? When did God send fallen angels to hell, and are they still there? Is Satan only being held in hell until Judgment Day? Would that not have been the time when the world became sinful? Does that mean that not all demons/evil spirits have free reign over the earth until Judgment Day?**

If we define "sin" as "contradicting God's design," then yes, angels sin as humans do. However, it is hard for us to know what angels think or why or how they behave as they do. We simply don't know much about them, and there is no benefit in speculating. The fall of the angels must have taken place between the sixth day of creation when God looked at all He created and said it was "very good" (Gn 1:31) and that time when the devil tempted Eve in the garden (Gn 3:1ff.). The devil or Satan and all the fallen angels/demons are held in hell until Judgment Day, though we ought not to think of hell as a location so much as living with no positive relationships, not with God or with anyone else. The devil and demons move about like predators, and before the crucifixion, the devil even went before God in heaven to make accusations (Mt 12:43–45; 1Pt 5:8; Job 1:6–12; Rv 12:7–17).

The devil and demons are powerful, but not free (Mk 5:1–14; 9:17–29). They seem to know that their time is short and how to make the most of that time by spreading lies, deception, murder, and death (Jn 8:44).

● ● ● ● ● ● ● ● ● ● ● ● ● ● ● ● ● ● ●

Q **2:6 Why haven't the ungodly places on earth been destroyed like Sodom and Gomorrah?**

Part of this answer is provided in the verse itself, as Peter explained that the destruction of Sodom and Gomorrah was an example for all the rest. Examples are not given as exceptions to nature but as heightened or intensified cases by which we might have greater appreciation for the significance of our own lives. Jesus washed only the apostles' feet, as an example (Jn 13:1–17). The flood in Noah's time and the exodus from Egypt were indicative of universal human experience in our struggle with bondage to sin and of the means by which God restores liberty (Gn 6; Ex 12–14; 1Co 10:1ff.; 1Pt 3:18–21). The visible coming of the Holy Spirit on Pentecost and the speaking in various languages demonstrated that the Gospel comes immediately through the Word and that it was accomplished for all, a truth that motivates mission work to this day (Ac 2). The other part of the answer is supplied by Jesus in His parable of wheat and tares (Mt 13:24–30). If God were to destroy all the ungodly places on the earth, what would be left? In fact, when the time appointed by God has come, He will destroy the whole earth (2Pt 3:10). In the meantime, we are concerned with saving lives according to the example and command of Jesus; we leave the judgment to God (Lk 9:54–55; Jn 12:47).

● ● ● ● ● ● ● ● ● ● ● ● ● ● ● ● ● ● ●

Q **2:13 Is it okay for a Christian to go to a wild college party?**

That would depend on what "wild" means. Paul said that all things are lawful but not all things build up, nor did he want to be brought into bondage to any (1Co 6:12; 10:23). Christians base their decisions about how to live on love rather than the Law, though the substance of the Law is to love God above all things and one's neighbor as oneself (Mk 12:30–31). Paul said that the whole Law is fulfilled in this one expression, "love your neighbor as yourself" (Rm 13:8–10). Therefore, if you can be of positive, enduring service to other people at the party, be there for them. If you are going for selfish reasons or are likely to be overcome by selfish, self-defeating ways at a wild college party, then it would be better to stay away.

Q 2:14–18 Why does Peter put such emphasis on sexual sins in this book?

Sexual sin is parallel to idolatry and is the root of practically every other problem you can think of (Hos 3:1). As people divorce themselves from God by embracing what opposes Him, so also people divorce themselves from a spouse or from virginity in order to embrace the passions of the flesh, which are self-defeating rather than loving. In every case, the Bible prohibits that which is opposed to our life, in the fullest sense of the word. Sexual sins affect body and soul, those people involved, and countless other people (Rm 1:18–31).

Q 2:15 Who is Balaam?

Balaam's history is found in Nu 22–24 and is worth reading before continuing with this answer. Balaam of Beor is what we might call a "freelance" or "independent" religious leader, force, or mystic (Nu 22:5–7). Whether by God's working or the devil's, there are always human beings who serve as agents of these opposing forces, one way or the other. There is reason to suppose Balaam's ability and effectiveness were supplied by the devil since he finds his intent overwhelmed by God's intervention (22:12; 22:20–35). Peter confirms this suspicion by his reference to Balaam here (see also Jude 11; Rv 2:14). As Jesus demonstrated in the Gospels, there are no forces genuinely independent of God; but such forces are not only dependent on Him but also subject to

Him and unwittingly used by God to serve His good purposes (2Co 4:17).

Q 2:20–22 Does this apply to Christians who are struggling with a sin that continues to plague them? Why would it be better if a person would never hear about Christ if he turns away? Isn't it better to know about Christ so it may be easier to turn back?

The key word in your question is "struggling." In these verses, Peter makes the same kind of severe warning we heard Jesus make in Mk 3:28–29 and Paul make in Heb 6:1–8; 10:26–31. Paul exposes the peril of knowingly, consciously, willfully, and continuously advocating for lies and perversity in opposition to the truth (Rm 1:18–31). It is better for a person never to have heard of Christ because God distinguishes between people who oppose Him deliberately and those who are simply mistaken due to ignorance (1Tm 1:12–14). We might be tempted to think that it would help to know Christ because His gracious disposition would encourage repentance, but the Word of the Lord indicates that the fallen human nature that has known Christ and then turns away could only have done so because it despises the gracious disposition of Christ.

All people share the same fundamental, significant features. All fallen human nature is opposed to God and contrary to Him, but not all fallen human nature is indulged and allowed to rule as in the case of the impenitent. Nevertheless, fallen human nature is a threat as long as we live in it, and these warnings with examples from history are provided as a powerful defense (Heb 2:1ff.; 1Co 10:1–13).

● ● ● ● ● ● ● ● ● ● ● ● ● ● ● ● ● ● ● ●

Q 2:21 Is this verse saying that it would have been better for sinners to have never known God at all than to know Him and then reject Him?

Correct. Jesus spoke about the difference between acting against God in ignorance and acting in full consciousness and understanding (Lk 12:47–48). Paul refers to ignorance in his own case as the reason he found mercy from God (1Tm 1:12–14). Jesus demonstrated endless patience with and sympathy for the weak (Mk 9:21–25; Jn 8:3–11). On the other hand, Jesus issues the most severe of warnings against religious leaders who know the truth but despise it and, worse, undermine it in the lives of others (Mt 18:6–9; 23:13–36; Jn 9:30–41). In Rm 1 and in Hebrews, Paul warns against conscious, willful, and persistent opposition to the truth (Rm 1:18–31; Heb 6:4–8; 10:26–31).

● ● ● ● ● ● ● ● ● ● ● ● ● ● ● ● ● ● ●

Q 2:22 Why does a dog return to its vomit? Where is the quote from?

This quote is from Pr 26:11. Many claim there is no way to know for certain why dogs do this; others suggest explanations having to do with a dog's ready appetite, concern for wasting food, and instincts for removing traces of their activity that predators

could smell. The point is that just as returning to one's vomit is repulsive to us (even unthinkable), so also Christians would find it repulsive to repeat their mistakes, while a fool (unbeliever) would have no concern for this at all.

● ● ● ● ● ● ● ● ● ● ● ● ● ● ● ● ● ● ● ●

Q 3:1 Why does Peter write two letters warning people of the coming of the Lord? What does Peter mean by "sincere mind"?

I'm not sure there is a book of the Bible or even a chapter that does not include some kind of warning, either explicit or implied. Peter had a heightened sense of concern about the coming of the Lord because his own death was imminent (2Pt 1:14).

The word Peter uses in the phrase "sincere mind," translated in some Bibles as "wholesome," occurs only five times in the New Testament (in two forms). It is the combination of the words for sunlight and judgment, meaning something like "judged by the sunlight." The idea has something to do with clarity or purity, being able to see clearly, and seeing the clarity or impurities in something by holding it up to the sunlight. Thus the idea has to do with purity as in a life and thinking singularly devoted to God and including or tolerating nothing to the contrary (see 1Co 5:8; 2Co 1:12; 2:17; Php 1:10; 2Pt 3:1). Fallen human nature is like a pitcher of water mixed and clouded by impurities and longing for more impurity. A soul regenerated by the Word of God is pure and, by the power of God's Word and Spirit, seeks to live in that purity, even though the human nature is impure.

• • • • • • • • • • • • • • • • • • •

Q 3:3 What is a scoffer? Don't we already have scoffers among us? Will the scoffers be Christians as well as non-Christians?

A "scoffer" or "mocker" is a person who lives according to his own desires, despising any wisdom, knowledge, or insight from any authoritative sources (this word occurs only here and in Jude 18). Scoffers pay no attention to authorities and will even ridicule or taunt an authority with verbal abuse (Mt 2:17; 27:31). Yes, all fallen human nature scoffs and mocks at authority since that was the nature of the fall; Adam mocked God and His instruction by disobeying. Christians are bound to scoff and mock since we all possess a fallen human nature bound to do so. However, Christians are penitent, so we do not willfully, consciously, and persistently go on mocking as if this were not something to repent of.

• • • • • • • • • • • • • • • • • • •

Q 3:8 Since God created time, how is His timetable any different than ours?

What Peter says about God and time makes sense. God is infinite, all-knowing, and all-powerful; therefore, God can pay attention to every detail and aspect of every moment of time with as much care as if we had a thousand years to devote to that one moment. On the other hand, all things are known to God already and He doesn't change; therefore, a thousand years have no more effect on God than a day has on us. There is much debate about God's relationship with time, but a few things seem obvious. First, God is neither bound by time nor incapable of acting in time. Second, time is more likely a function of change than the other way around. The change in light, seasons, our thirst, hunger, and fatigue all give us a sense of the passage of time. But God is without change and without any necessity, as He depends on no one and nothing outside Himself.

• • • • • • • • • • • • • • • • • • •

Q 3:8 Could this imply the world took longer than six days to create?

Absolutely not. There is a distinct difference between God explaining His relationship to time (which makes sense) and God explaining how our universe came about. The president of the United States can travel whenever and wherever he wishes, but his staff is bound by the schedule he provides. In addition, if the timing of creation is not literal, none of the Scripture based on that timing makes sense. For example, God says that since He made the world and everything in it in six days and rested on the seventh, we should do the same. If *day* in Genesis means "an indefinitely long period of time," what happens to the Law? How are we to make sense of this command: "For six indefinitely long periods of time you shall work, but on the seventh indefinitely long period of time you shall rest, for the Lord created the heavens and the earth in six indefinitely long periods of time and on the seventh indefinitely long period of time He rested"?

• • • • • • • • • • • • • • • • • • • •

Q 3:9 How patient is God? Does this verse say anything about Judgment Day? Is God going to wait for everyone to know, love, and have faith in Him first?

God's patience is infinite, just as He Himself is. When God acts, it is not because He has lost His patience but because He always knows and does what is best for all, always, at just the right time (Gn 18:22–33; Ps 78:26–35; Heb 12:3–15).

This verse is talking about Judgment Day, whether that means the day of any particular person's death or the end of the world. Individuals pray for deliverance for themselves and for all (Ps 3:7; Rv 22:20). The word translated "patient" or "longsuffering" in this verse explains how and why God waits. On the one hand, God waits in order to allow time for His Word and workings to bring a person to repentance and faith. On the other hand, God waits in order to make it evident that those who are saved are so by His gracious activity alone and that those who are lost are so because of their own stubborn, obstinate contradiction of truth and contempt for God's grace (Ex 4:21–23; Lk 13:34–35). Apparently God cannot wait indefinitely due to the overall decline and growing faithlessness of the world, as Jesus laments, "Nevertheless, when the Son of Man comes, will He find faith on earth?" (Lk 18:7–8).

How patient is God?

• • • • • • • • • • • • • • • • • • • •

Q 3:10 Is the earth going to be destroyed by fire or is this a metaphor for earthly desires and practices being destroyed in hell? Considering this verse, why do people attempt to predict the end of the world? Is the "heaven" it talks about the heaven where the throne of God is or the heaven where the stars and planets are?

Defensible standards for interpretation argue that we must take any text in its most simple and literal sense unless something forces us to do otherwise. The earth is going to be destroyed by fire; Peter makes this even clearer in v. 12, and there is nothing compelling us to think otherwise. Hell itself is temporary and will be cast into the lake of fire on Judgment Day (Rv 20:14). People try to predict the end of the world for the same reason we try to do all the other things the Bible says we cannot: our inability to rightly handle the knowledge of good and evil. People try to predict the end of the world in order to convince others that they possess the authority of God Himself, even though Jesus, who is God Himself, said even He didn't know the Last Day (Mt 24:36). People try to predict the end of the world in order to gain control over the lives and possessions of those who are vulnerable and deceived (1Tm 6:3–5). The "heavens" refers to the space where plants, stars, and other created things exist. All of God's material creation will be destroyed in order to be rid for all eternity of the corruption it suffers due to the fall of Adam (Rm 8:20–22). The place of God's throne is not physical but a matter of His omniscience, omnipotence, omnipresence, and omnibenevolence by which He has created, redeemed, and sustains our lives.

● ● ● ● ● ● ● ● ● ● ● ● ● ● ● ● ● ● ●

Q **3:10–13 How does Peter know all these details?**

Peter knew what Jesus revealed to him and wrote what he did by the power and inspiration of the Holy Spirit (Jn 1:18; 14:25–26; 1Th 2:13; 2Tm 3:16; 2Pt 1:16–21; 1Jn 1:1–3).

● ● ● ● ● ● ● ● ● ● ● ● ● ● ● ● ● ● ●

Q **3:12 Is Peter saying we can "hasten" the coming of the Day of the Lord by what we do?**

It would appear that Peter is saying exactly this, so what are we to make of it? There are at least two ways to understand Peter's writing. First, the Bible does indicate that the Day of the Lord will not come until the Gospel has reached all people and been spread to the ends of the earth (Mk 13:10). This explains, in part, why Paul was so eager and determined to take the Word of God to the ends of the earth (Rm 15:28; Eph 3:8). Since the last times are accompanied by many trials and hardships, it is natural that the apostle wants to shorten those last times by taking the Gospel to all as quickly as possible (Mk 13:14–27). Second, since

the Gospel does convey the very kingdom of God to the one who hears, bringing the Word of the Lord to people is effectively bringing the Day of the Lord (Mk 1:14–15; Jn 3:16–18; Rm 8:1). In a way very similar to what Paul experienced, we want the Lord to come soon but we also want time to bring the Word of the Lord to those who have not heard or still have not believed (Php 1:23–24).

● ● ● ● ● ● ● ● ● ● ● ● ● ● ● ● ● ● ●

Q **3:12 Peter writes that when the Day of the Lord comes, the heavens will disappear and the earth will burn. How are we supposed to know we're doing the right things to be saved from this?**

God has provided several witnesses by which we might know the truth: His Word, nature, our conscience, and reason (Rm 1:16–2:16). The most important thing to know is that God does the saving and has already accomplished our salvation in the redeeming work of His Son, Jesus Christ. All people were saved when Jesus took away the sins of the world (Jn 1:29; Mt 8:17; Jn 19:30; Rv 12:7–11). God's gracious work of keeping us within the blessing of this accomplishment is the second, critical factor (Rm 8:1; 1Co 1:30; Eph 2:8–9; 1Pt 1:3–9). No other teaching or religious system is nearly so well attested by its authoritative text (the Bible), by archaeology, by external historical witnesses, or by universal human experience. While many religions teach good morals, none even dream of God as He is—as He loves us, sent His only Son to redeem us, and works regeneration in our lives even now through His Holy Spirit (Gal 1:1–7).

Q **3:13 What is the "new earth" that Peter says will come after the world ends?**

That remains to be seen, literally. One might suspect that the new earth would be like the Garden of Eden. John describes paradise, but his language is more indicative than precise (Rv 21:9–22:5).

Q **3:14 Why does Peter tell us we must be spotless and blameless on the Day of Judgment when he knows that we will fall short? Why would we be "at peace" when the earth is destroyed?**

Paul said that the work of Christ for us is to present us without spot or blemish (Eph 5:27). Christ does this in three ways: by covering us with His own life and righteousness, by forgiving all that is wrong with us, and by working a righteous life in us (Jer 33:16; Gal 3:27; Ps 103:11–12; Is 40:2; Mt 25:31–40; Jn 15:3; 2Co 5:21).

Peter says that we are looking forward to new heavens and a new earth (v. 13). God delights in His good creation and in the lives of His people (Ezk 18:23). Though Adam brought death into the world and we continue to bring death and destruction upon ourselves, God continues to show His wisdom and grace by making all this work for us (Rm 8:28; 2Co 4:17).

Q **3:15 What does it mean to "count the patience of our Lord as salvation"?**

If God were not patient, who could be saved (Ps 130:3–4)? The patience of the Lord means salvation, for He waits for His Word and ways to bring us to repentance and faith in the course of our lives (Rm 2:4; 9:22; 1Tm 1:16; Jas 5:10; Heb 6:12). In the days of Noah, the patience of God waited for the ark to be completed, just as God waited for the fullness of time (or just the right time) to send His Son into the world to accomplish our salvation (1Pt 3:20; Gal 4:4). The other occurrences of this noun in the New Testament are in lists of the characteristics of God's people, who apply these characteristics toward the salvation of those who are not yet in the faith (2Co 6:6; Gal 5:22; Eph 4:2; Col 1:11; 3:12; 2Tm 3:10; 4:2).

Q **3:16 Why does Peter warn us about Paul's letters being hard to understand?**

The history of disagreement over what Paul intended to say and teach in his letters explains Peter's warning. What exactly Peter is referring to in Paul's letters may vary with each person who finds one thing easy to understand but another difficult. Another principle of biblical interpretation applies here: difficult passages are to be understood in light of the simple and plain passages.

• • • • • • • • • • • • • • • • • • •

Q 3:17 What, exactly, is meant by "lawless people"?

The word translated "lawless" occurs only here and in 2Pt 2:7. It is the negation of a word that means "law" or "custom," meaning "against or opposed to the laws or customs."

• • • • • • • • • • • • • • • • • • •

Q 3:18 Is Peter referring to growing in grace as though we have the ability to receive and achieve more grace or rather that our person grows while residing in the grace of our Lord and Savior Jesus Christ?

Think of the grace and knowledge of the Lord as a place of abundant resources. Peter is urging us to live our lives both within and by means of the grace and knowledge of the Lord. Thus Peter ends this letter where he started (2Pt 1:2–8). We can only be as gracious and knowledgeable as the Word of the Lord makes us, as Jesus said, "Apart from Me you can do nothing" (Jn 15:4–5).

1 John

Q **1:1–3 Why does John use the perfect verb tense so much ("we have heard")? Is it to emphasize the action of these things?**

The predominant verb tense in these verses—"perfect"—stresses that the action is accomplished and enduring. John is using this tense so that people don't miss the eternal and irreversible results of God's redemption through Jesus Christ. Jesus' own expression from the cross, "It is finished" (Jn 19:30), is in the perfect tense (in the original Greek text), and John is drawing our attention to this. God redeemed all people of all time and every place in the life of Jesus; this fact is permanent. The only question that remains is whether people will realize the benefits of this reality (Rv 12:7–17).

Q **1:1 If this is written by John, why does he use "we"?**

The "we" refers to the apostles, who were eyewitnesses of everything that Jesus said and did during His ministry and after His resurrection (Ac 1:15–22; 1Co 15:3–7; 2Pt 1:16–19).

Q **1:3–7 What, exactly, does "fellowship" mean here? Is it similar to the way we use it today to discuss church relations?**

The Greek word *koinonia* means "to be joined together" or "connectedness." The issue today is not about the meaning of the word but about how it comes about. People today assume or contend that fellowship is something that we can produce by our own external efforts because we want it to be so (like taking Communion together even though we don't believe the same things); you cannot produce a cause by simulating the effect. Verse 7 makes clear that only a continual walk together in the truth can provide true fellowship; the Word always produces the good effect (Is 55:8–11; Mt 7:17).

Q 1:5–10 What is meant exactly by walking in the darkness? How do you stay walking in the light?

Think first about literally walking in the darkness. The darker it is, the harder it is to know what is around you and where you are going. Walking in the darkness would make a person believe that no one else could see him or her (the way children hide by covering their eyes). Now, think of darkness as the opposite of God, truth, honesty, and goodness. A person who walks in the darkness thinks, speaks, and lives in every way contrary to God's design for life and thinks no one will discover this. But even if no one else did know, such a life is futile, unproductive, and self-destructive. The only way to keep walking in the light is to keep reading the Word, testing for truth and honesty, remembering and applying that truth, and staying in close connection with others who are doing the same. As long as any part of our body remains connected to the body, it benefits from the life that is in the blood (1Co 12:11–27).

Q 1:7 What does it mean by "He [Jesus] is in the light"; isn't Jesus the light itself?

If we consider Jesus' human nature, then John is saying that we should remain in the light (truth and honesty) as Jesus did. If we consider Jesus according to His divine nature, then the point is the same—just as the Son of God is the light and must, therefore, always be in it, so we should always walk in the light and never be apart from it. Consider the danger and folly of setting a lesser ideal.

Q 1:8–9 Why are these verses part of our liturgy? Can you please explain the full meaning of these verses a little more?

Human nature, since the fall, seeks deceit rather than truth (Jn 3:19–20). John is trying to deliver us from such deceit by showing us clearly the folly of certain contentions. We use these verses at the beginning of our worship for two reasons. First, if we are not going to be honest with ourselves and about ourselves, there is no point in continuing with the worship. Second, worship begins with Confession and Absolution so that we receive confirmation of God's remedy for our failure right from the start.

Q 2:1 Why does he say, "*if* anyone does sin?" We all sin.

First, God does not change the standard of life, since life depends on what the standard describes. This is why Jesus said, "You therefore must be perfect, as your heavenly Father is perfect" (Mt 5:48). Second, John will go on to say very clearly that those who are generated by God do not sin and cannot sin (1Jn 3:9). But that regenerate soul lives within a fallen human nature that does nothing but sin in thought, word, and deed (Is 64:6). Therefore, John is echoing Jesus' imperative that we be innocent, but he is also quick to remind us of God's remedy for our failure as long as we are in the flesh (Rm 7:13–25). Third, there is a difference between the sins of someone penitent and struggling and the sins of someone who is doing so consciously and intentionally (Ezk 18:21–32; Gal 5:16–25).

Q 2:4 Isn't everyone a liar?

Fallen human nature is, above all things, deceitful and desperately wicked (Jer 17:9). There is a difference between being a liar (you do nothing but tell lies), telling lies intentionally and without regret, and telling lies though you resist and repent of doing so. John is concerned with the first two categories because apart from repentance, there is neither faith nor salvation (Lk 3:7–9).

Q 2:7 John speaks of an old command which we have had from the beginning—what does this verse mean?

Fallen human nature loves novelty—things that are new just because they are new. John is offering evidence that what he

has to say is the truth not because it is new but because it has always been and will always remain the truth (permanence is one of the characteristics of truth). Notice that Jesus did not do away with the Old Testament but fulfilled it; while He established the New Testament, this was promised and prophesied since the beginning (Mt 5:17; Jn 5:19–21).

Q 2:9 In 2:9 and 4:20, John exclaims that if one hates his brother and says he loves God, he is a liar. Why did John say the same thing two times in two chapters?

Repetition is an important method of teaching. Repetition indicates significance and the necessity of a powerful response to some problem (Php 3:1). John speaks to the problem of love and hatred almost constantly throughout this letter and the Gospel of John (*love* occurs fifty-two times in 1 John and fifty-seven times in the Gospel; *hate* occurs eight times in 1 John and twenty times in the Gospel).

Q 2:10–11 Can a person be in the light and hate a brother and know that it is wrong and work on a change of heart?

Fallen human nature is always contrary to the will of God. This means that a person with a regenerate soul that is walking in the light will still think, speak, and do wrong. However, a person walking in the light is repentant—sorry for, opposed to, and wanting to overcome the works of the flesh (Gal 5:16–25). A person who is not in the light might also come to know what he is doing is wrong and have a change of heart since this is God's will and God's work through ordinary means (we are His ambassadors for this very purpose) and extraordinary means (Paul's conversion on the road to Damascus, Ac 9).

. . . .

Q 2:12–14 Why doesn't John address women in this passage? Is there a reason why John was more poetical in these verses?

One essential element of man being created in God's image is responsibility. As God is responsible for all of His creation and as the Son redeemed all creation, so God wills every man to grow up into this work of supporting and protecting women and children (1Co 11:3; Eph 5:19–6:4). This section has a very interesting structure, whether a person considers it poetic or not. Notice how John speaks to each of the three groups twice: children, young men, and fathers. John says something different to the children each time, repeats something and adds something to the young men, and only repeats what he said to the fathers.

. . . .

Q 2:15–17 How do we live in this world but not of it? Are we not to love one another if our human nature is of this world? What about our family? How do we find existence in a world we hate?

Jesus taught that a person who did not hate his or her family and life could not be His disciple (Lk 14:26). Understanding this verse depends on knowing what the words mean. For example, the word for "love" used in this verse means "to sacrifice everything for." The word *hate* means "to sacrifice nothing for." It would be a tragic mistake to sacrifice everything for a fallen world and fallen human nature that are passing away and contrary to God's will. Hope is realized in loving the soul of a person that God can regenerate through His Word and Spirit. Such a regenerate soul—the essence of a person—endures and awaits God's new heaven and earth and is the only thing worth sacrificing everything for (Heb 12:1–3).

. . . .

Q 2:18 How can we tell who the antichrists are? How can there be more than one? Wouldn't the human nature in all of us be considered an antichrist according to these verses? How do we know who to trust and who not to, even in our congregations? Couldn't even our pastors be antichrists, and then what should we do about it?

The way to know about the Antichrist is to know Christ Himself. The Word of God became flesh, both in the person of Jesus Christ and in the Scriptures, so that we would have a certain, enduring, unchanging means of knowing the truth and discerning error. Fallen human nature, like fallen angels, is contrary to Christ (Rm 5:8–10). When a religious leader is completely devoted to contradicting all that Christ did and said in order to destroy rather than save, then he or she certainly qualifies as an antichrist in a more significant way. It may be that "the Antichrist" has more to do with false teaching/religion as a whole than with one particular person.

● ● ● ● ● ● ● ● ● ● ● ● ● ● ● ● ● ● ● ●

Q 2:19 Who is he talking about going out from there?

In order to be a hypocrite or deceiver, someone must appear to belong (Mt 23:1–7; 2Co 11:13–15). Notice that John contrasts "went out from" with "continued with." The essential and enduring factor in determining our relationship with God is our relationship with the Word (Jn 8:31–32; 15:1–7; Ac 2:42).

● ● ● ● ● ● ● ● ● ● ● ● ● ● ● ● ● ● ● ●

Q 2:20, 27 What does anointing from the Holy One mean? How can he say we know all things? I know that I always want to keep learning, so why does this verse say you don't need anyone to teach you?

"Anointed" is English for "Christ." Jesus was anointed at His Baptism (Is 61:1; Mt 3:16). The ceremony of Baptism provides physical evidence for and confirmation of all that the Word of God does for us as we remain in it (Ac 2:38–42; 2Co 1:21–22; Eph 1:13–14). The Word regenerates our soul, which brings many extraordinary benefits, including knowledge of all things and holiness (Jn 3:1–7; 1Jn 3:9; Jer 31:31–34). The reason we don't think or feel like this is because our regenerate soul lives within a fallen

and contrary human nature. This problem is made even worse because we tend to live in and for our human nature while leaving our regenerate soul to grow weak and languish from having so little contact with the Word (Is 55:1–13; Jn 6:24–69).

● ● ● ● ● ● ● ● ● ● ● ● ● ● ● ● ● ● ● ●

Q 2:22 What is the difference between this antichrist and the Antichrist discussed in Revelation?

No difference; they are the same (see also 2Th 2:1–12).

● ● ● ● ● ● ● ● ● ● ● ● ● ● ● ● ● ● ● ●

Q 3:1–3 Is this one of the verses to show that the kingdom of heaven is for little children because they are pure?

The most significant part of being a child of God is the genetic relationship; if the Word of God regenerates us, then we are genuinely His children (Jn 1:11–13; 1Jn 3:9). Nevertheless, being a child of God includes all the characteristics of childhood that Jesus held up as examples for the faithful (Mt 18:3–5, 14; 19:13–14).

● ● ● ● ● ● ● ● ● ● ● ● ● ● ● ● ● ● ● ●

Q 3:1 What does he mean by "the world does not know us"?

The word *recognize* or *know* in this context has to do with realizing the significance of something. People, in general, clearly did not know the significance of Jesus Christ (Jn 6:24–66; 1Co 2:8). If we are disciples of Christ, we can expect the world to treat us just as it treated Him (Jn 15:18–19).

Q 3:2 What does John mean by we shall "be like Him"?

There are two important parts of this verse that suggest answers to your question. First, the Gospels provide us with an extraordinary witness to Jesus, including what He was like after His resurrection. We know that Jesus had a resurrected body, that He could eat and be touched, and that He retained the scars of His crucifixion (Lk 24:36–43). Second, John says that we will be like Him "because we shall see Him as He is." Paul says something like this in 1Co 13:12; 15:3–8, 12–58. Thus, we will also have real, physical bodies and gladly and naturally live as God intended forever.

Q 3:4–6 How should I take John's statement that no one who is in Christ keeps sinning? I know I am in Christ, yet I keep sinning. Paul says the same in Rm 7:20–25. Because we sin, does that mean we don't know God?

We always need to distinguish between fallen human nature and a regenerate soul (Gal 5:16–25). Even after conversion, our fallen human nature never does what is truly good and never believes (Is 64:6; 1Co 2:14). But according to John, our regenerate soul never sins and knows all things (1Jn 2:20, 25; 5:18). The existence of and enmity between these two natures in us explains what Jesus meant when He spoke of losing our life to save it and Paul's complaint about not doing what he willed (Lk 9:24; Rm 7:13–25).

Q 3:7 What does John mean when he says "whoever practices righteousness is righteous"? This sounds like works-righteousness.

John is trying to expose and correct the problem of hypocrisy. John already warned that a person who said he had no sin was a liar and made God a liar by claiming so (1Jn 1:8–10). In this verse, John is responding to the claim that we can do whatever we want that is contrary to God's will without reservation or repentance and still be righteous. John's statement is not about how a person could ever be righteous or be saved when he is not. John states a fact: the person who does right is righteous. If we cannot do right in all things as we are, then we can only be right because God forgives what is wrong, imputes to us the actual, perfect, righteous life of Christ, and regenerates our soul so that it wills and does what is right as well (Ps 32:1–2; 103:11–12; Jn 16:14; 1Co 1:30; 2Co 5:21).

Q 3:8–9 What happens if someone keeps on sinning but was born of God? Why would all the sins be forgiven if sinning keeps happening?

Fallen human nature always struggles against a regenerate soul and vice versa (Gal 5:16–25). What determines which nature dominates and prevails has to do with which nature is empowered: the flesh by feeding its lust for the world (things that are passing away) or the regenerate soul by a life in the Word (which endures forever, Jn 8:31–32; 10:27–28; 15:1–7; Rm 10:17). As long as we are in this flesh, we will be sinning. When John says "keep on sinning," he means a person who consciously, intentionally keeps doing what is wrong with no regrets or repentance (Mt 12:31–32; Heb 6:4–6; 10:26–31).

Q 3:10 What does this verse mean?

The Bible intends to provide clarity and help in discernment. Anyone can assert that they are righteous, and many people were, though their lives raised suspicions to the contrary. John provides a simple measure and explanation. Any person who genuinely does what is right does so because God has generated and so enabled that person (Is 64:6; 1Co 15:10; 1Jn 4:19). Anyone who is not doing what is right or laying down his or her life for a brother or sister is not of God but of the devil. Note that the phrase "children of God" is referring to a regenerate soul. Such a person is still doing what is wrong according to his or her human nature but is doing so penitently and with a desire to do always and only what is right. A person without a regenerate soul cannot do what is right or love because such a person persists in and insists on refusing God (Ezk 18:21–29).

Q 3:15 Is it true that anyone "who hates his brother is a murderer"?

Jesus taught that evil intent in the heart makes us just as guilty before God as evil deeds (Mt 5:21–48). This teaching is necessary to expose the lie of hypocrisy—that the appearance of being righteous can make us righteous even if we are evil beneath (Mt 23:25–33). The deeds we have done, like the words we have said and thoughts we have had, are not what condemn us. Our disposition toward sin is what matters. An impenitent heart rejects the grace of God to forgive and regenerate. A penitent heart clings to God's forgiveness and is inspired by the Spirit to do what is right in thought, word, and deed (Mt 7:17–20).

Q 3:21 Is John talking about true faith and commitment to God?

John is making a simple statement of fact, describing one of the many benefits of the grace of God. Any time a person has a heart that does not condemn him or her, that person is at peace and at ease when thinking about being in the presence of God. These things—a heart that does not condemn us, peace, and ease before God—are all products of the grace of God working in us through His Word and Spirit (Ps 32:1–2; 103:11–12; Jn 16:14; Rm 8:1–4).

Q **3:23–24 Why does love mean we live by what God commands?**

There is a simple chemistry with God. God loves us and has commanded us to love one another. Anyone who claims to love God but ignores His command to love others is a liar and self-condemned (Lk 10:25–37; 1Jn 2:10–11). Love is what all the other commands of God are trying to accomplish (Rm 13:8–10).

Q **4:1 What does testing spirits have to do with false prophets? How do you test the spirits?**

The Holy Spirit inspires prophets so they can speak the truth (1Co 12:3; 2Pt 1:16–21). The devil and demonic spirits inspire false prophets to deceive and lie (Jn 8:44; 2Co 11:13–15). John is reminding us to look past the person who is speaking in order to determine what kind of spirit is at work in him or her (Dt 18:20–22).

Q **4:16 If God is love, why do some Christians not act lovingly?**

There is a big difference between God, who is love, and Christians, who are neither God nor free from a fallen and hateful human nature. Any Christian's ability to love depends entirely on the presence of God's Word and Spirit within him or her (1Jn 4:19; Jn 8:31; 15:1–7).

Q **4:17–21 Were there people who claimed to be Christian in order to appear "good"?**

While there is some evidence that some people thought highly of Christians, most people in most times have been suspicious, antagonistic, or hostile (Lk 2:52; Jn 16:2; Ac 2:47; 21:28–30; 28:22; 1Co 4:9–14).

Q **5:3 How can John say that God's "commandments are not burdensome"?**

John does not mean to say that the Commandments of God are not difficult; in fact, they are so difficult that none of us can begin to keep them perfectly. But difficult is different than burdensome. The endless laws and criticisms of the Pharisees were burdensome because they were the inventions of men and were about pretending self-righteousness rather than genuine love of neighbor (Mt 23:14–24; Lk 10:25–37; Rm 13:8–10). The commands of God reflect His design in creation; this means that following His commands is what we were created for and is what makes for life (Php 2:5–11).

Q **5:4 Does God pick those who will be born of Him?**

The word is actually "generated," which includes birth but begins with conception. Yes, God chose before the world was created those who would be so generated (Rm 8:29–30; Eph 1:4–5; see questions on these passages for more about election and predestination).

Q 5:10 What about if someone has never heard the Word of God?

God has provided more witnesses to Himself than just the Word. God created the universe as a second witness to the truth, gave us reason as a third, and has written His Law on our hearts as a fourth (Ps 19:1–3; Rm 1:20–32; 2:15; 6:21; 1Jn 2:15–17). Anyone willing to be honest about the facts of our lives would realize our utter dependence on God and hope in His mercy (Ps 33:18; Lk 1:50).

God has redeemed everyone in the life of His Son, Jesus Christ, the Lamb of God who bore away the sins of the world. God desires all to be saved, that is, to realize the full benefit of Christ's work by coming to the knowledge of the truth (Jn 8:31–32). The Word of God is the very best and unparalleled witness to that truth, inspired by the Holy Spirit and effective, which is why believers all devote their lives to proclaiming the Good News in every place at every time (Is 55; Mt 28:18–20; Mk 16:16; Rm 1:1–17).

Q 5:15 Couldn't this be interpreted to mean that our prayers will be answered the way we want them to be?

This verse follows and is interpreted by the verse before it, "If we ask anything according to His will He hears us." The only way to have confidence that God hears our prayers is by a life in the Word that inspires and informs such confidence. That same Word of God regenerates our soul and turns our thoughts to God's will, which means life for us and through us for others. God certainly grants all such petitions, for they are His own work in us and His own will for us.

Q 5:16–17 What is a sin that does not lead to death, and what is John's point in discussing it? What about Rm 6:23: "The wages of sin is death"?

The wages of sin is death, as Paul states; this is why all human nature returns to the dust. There is also the death of the soul that is impenitent, contrary, and unceasingly opposed to God (Mt 12:3–32; Heb 6:4–6; 10:26–31). God commanded Jeremiah that he should not pray for such people (Jer 7:16; 11:14; 14:11). This is the most severe of warnings and the gravest of conditions to be in. Yet Jesus also forbids that we condemn others (Mt 7:1). It is not for us to conclude that a person has committed such a sin, but we are to be warned and warn others so that we are not guilty of persistent, unrelenting opposition to God—for then where would our help come from?

Q 5:21 Why does this letter close with "keep yourselves from idols"?

Ending with these few, pointed words of warning certainly gets our attention, which was likely John's intent. All of the Commandments relate to one another, and the root of all disobedience is idolatry (loving self or things more than God). What fallen human being doesn't suffer from idolatry?

2 John

Q **1 Who are "the elect lady and her children"?**

No one is certain about this reference. Some argue that John is speaking about a particular woman in a particular place, perhaps Ephesus. However, most scholars suspect that John is referring to the Christian Church, the Bride of Christ (Jn 3:29; Rv 18:23; 19:7; 21:2, 9; 22:17).

Q **7 Is John talking about Jews or all nonbelievers? Why did some say Jesus did not come in the flesh? Is anyone who does not acknowledge Christ a part of the Antichrist?**

John is talking about anyone who denies that Jesus Christ came in the flesh; this was a lie that John took pains to respond to in his first epistle. People deny that the Son of God came in the person of Jesus Christ for at least two reasons. First, fallen human nature is generally contrary to the truth. Second, people realize that if God did come in the flesh and accomplish all of His promises, then there is no excuse for disobeying His call to obedience and faith. Fallen human nature pretends, at all costs, to be its own god, even though this is so obviously not the case.

• • • • • • • • • • • • • • • • • • •

Q 8 The phrase "that you may not lose what we have worked for" sounds as though it's in terms of the Law. Why is it that way?

Our fallen human nature does not understand the things of the Spirit (1Co 2:14). Yet, our fallen human nature is always with us. God provides the Law for us after conversion as a means of dealing with the contrary nature of the flesh (2Pt 1:12–15).

• • • • • • • • • • • • • • • • • • •

Q 12 Why does John conclude with saying that he has more to write but instead hopes to see them face-to-face?

Writing materials were not easy to come by in the first century and, as in our day, writing allows for misunderstanding by the reader(s). Therefore, John wants these people to know that he does have more to say and that he hopes to do so face-to-face.

• • • • • • • • • • • • • • • • • • •

Q 13 Who are "the children of your elect sister"?

Elect is a term reserved for the children of God (Eph 1:3–6). God brings His Word to us and regenerates us through the ministry of His Bride, the Church (2Co 5:14–20). Individual congregations that make up the Bride/Body of Christ might be thought of as sisters.

3 John

Q 9 Is this the first instance in the Bible where we see the Christian Church dividing?

Fallen human nature, the world, and the devil are full of deceit. As long as this fallen world endures, fallen human nature will pretend to be part of the Christian Church and, in so doing, will divide it (Gn 25:23; 1Ki 16:21; Jn 6:60–66; Ac 14:4; 1Co 1:10–17). The first recorded instance of the visible Christian Church being divided is in Ac 6 over the unfair distribution of charity. A more serious division is evident in Ac 11 and 15, where the apostles must contend for the truth of salvation by grace.

Q 11 Does this mean that our flesh side is not of God, but we could still be of God spiritually?

Correct. As Jesus said, "That which is born of the flesh is flesh, and that which is born of the Spirit is spirit" (Jn 3:6).

While our flesh or human nature is still God's creation, it is thoroughly corrupted by Adam's disobedience and is contrary to God's will and design for us. For this reason, God regenerates our soul and inspires us with His Spirit, so we are in fact and indeed children of God.

Q 12 What is "the truth" that speaks well of Demetrius?

Since Demetrius was very faithful about speaking the truth, the truth itself would verify that he was faithful and true (Lk 7:35).

Jude

Q 3–4 Why does this section seem so harsh?

The rest of this letter describes the various threats to the spiritual well-being of Christians. If the tone seems harsh, it is because those who received this letter were not taking those threats seriously; carelessness can be just as deadly as a mistake (1Co 5:1–13; Gal 1:6–10; 3:1–9; 1Jn 2:18–23; 3Jn 9–10).

Q 8 Why are sinners referred to as people "relying on their dreams"?

Jude means "dreamers" in the sense of displacing the truth with ideas and opinions of their own invention, not in the sense of hope.

Q 9 Why would Michael be arguing with the devil over Moses' body? Wasn't it God's?

All things are God's. God created a physical universe with time and consequences and means of accomplishing things so that we would have a way of learning what makes or destroys life. No doubt the devil wanted to abuse or dishonor the body of Moses, as this is often the last act of violence that an opponent can accomplish (1Sm 31:8–13). The success of Michael's intervention was always certain but still needed to be accomplished, just as Jesus really suffered and died, even though death could not hold Him (Ac 2:24).

Q 11 Who is Korah?

Korah was the great grandson of Levi (Levi, Kohath, Izhar, Korah). The history of Korah and his rebellion against Moses is recorded in Nu 16:1–49.

Q 12 Please explain this verse.

The "love feasts" refer to the Lord's Supper. Paul describes what this verse is referring to in great detail in 1Co 11:17–34. In summary, the Lord's Supper is a public demonstration of God's love for us and our love for one another in contrast with abuse and inconsideration that flows from selfishness.

Q 14 Where does this prophecy of Enoch come from? Who is Enoch?

Enoch, as this texts notes, was the seventh generation from Adam (Gn 5:1–24; Lk 3:37–38).

Q 17–19 What does this say about people who divide the Church today?

This notes that some people will be mockers who walk according to their own, ungodly lusts. Such people are unlikely to divide a church because they don't have anything to do with it (except to mock it). The true, invisible Church, the Body of Christ, cannot be divided. When the visible Church is divided, it always has to do with people trying to assert their own ways in opposition to God's (1Co 1:10–31; 5:1–6:11).

Q 18 What is a scoffer?

A "scoffer" is someone who thinks very little of someone or something and makes that clear by mocking. The word occurs only here and in 2Pt 3:3.

Revelation

Q **1:1–20 What is the difference between the angels in v. 1 and v. 20?**

The key to understanding has to do with knowing that "angel" is a Greek word, not an English one. The word means "messenger," but in v. 1 it refers to the heavenly beings and in v. 20 it refers to the pastor of each church.

Q **1:3 Obviously John didn't see the end of the world in his lifetime; was this written as a warning to always be prepared?**

If you think about it, every person sees the end of the world when he or she dies. Yes, everything written in the Bible is for our benefit, including prophecies about the end times that help us stay watchful and urge us to be energetic in outreach (Mt 24:36–25:30; 1Pt 5:8–9).

Q **1:4 What are the seven spirits of God? What is the significance of the number 7? Why is John writing to seven churches in the province of Asia, these in particular?**

The Spirit of God is the Holy Spirit, but described with seven characteristics (Is 11:2). The number 7 has to do with God's creation; God is Trinity (3), His creation is described in fours (four directions of the compass), and those numbers together make seven, as in the number of days God used to create and rest (Gn 1:1–2:3). John describes letters to seven churches because these will be indicative of all the churches of every time and place. By writing to seven churches, the reader would understand that there is nothing that ever happens in a church that is not addressed here and that God has no directions for the Church that are not included here.

Q 1:5 Why does it say Christ was the first one to come back from the dead when Lazarus was actually the first?

Lazarus was raised by Jesus but after a time died again. "Firstborn of the dead" means raised with an eternal body, never to die again (1Co 15:1–58; Heb 7:23–24; 9:27–28; 1Jn 3:2; Rv 20:6).

Q 1:7 Why would we "wail on account of Him"?

Those who are wailing are the "tribes of the earth," an expression that refers to people who have not been converted or re-generated ("born of God" [1Jn 3:9; 5:18]). People who are of this world are opposed to God and hate the realization that they thought too much of themselves and too little of Him (Jn 1:11–13; 3:6; 1Co 15:50; Rv 18:1–24).

Q 1:9–20 When does this happen? If this is Jesus, why doesn't John recognize Him and refer to Him by name? Where is Patmos?

John wrote this book around AD 95. John did recognize Jesus and described Him here in language that reveals His character: pure (white), omniscient (eyes like flames of fire), strong (bronze), royal (sash or band), like the Son of Man (Dn 3:25; Jn 5:27; 6:27).

Patmos is located off the southwest coast of present-day Turkey.

Q 1:10 What is meant by "I was in the Spirit"?

John probably means that he was in a state of consciousness where God could reveal to him everything He intended John to know and communicate. The preposition "in" can also mean "with," that is to say, the Holy Spirit was with him to reveal God's Word (Jn 16:13).

Q 1:13 Who is the "son of man?"

Jesus is the Son of Man (Mt 8:20). This term for Jesus occurs at least eighty-six times in the New Testament.

Q 1:16 Why did the man in John's vision have a sharp double-edged sword coming out of his mouth? Does the double-edged sword represent God's Word?

All of the descriptive language used by John is already present in the rest of the Bible and is familiar to anyone who spends a lot of time in the Word. Hebrews 4:12 describes the Word of God as a sharp two-edged sword that discerns the thoughts and intents of the heart. Jesus Christ is the Word of God and always speaks the Word of God (Jn 1:1, 14; 8:38; 14:10).

• • • • • • • • • • • • • • • • • • • •

Q **1:18 Does this mean that Jesus is the one who will lock the gates of hell? Why is Christ holding the keys to death and hades?**

When Adam disobeyed God, all human beings became bound in sin (Rm 5:1–21). Since Jesus is the one who liberated us from sin by His vicarious atonement, He alone has the power to open or close the kingdom of heaven and to lock or unlock the gates of hell. (Mt 16:19; 18:18; Mk 2:5–12; Lk 23:42–43; Heb 2:14–15).

• • • • • • • • • • • • • • • • • • • •

Q **1:20 What exactly does this verse mean, and what is the significance of the lampstands?**

See the answer to the question in 1:4. The churches are described as lampstands because we are the light of the world (Mt 5:14–16).

• • • • • • • • • • • • • • • • • • • •

Q **2:1, 8, 12, 18 What is meant by the seven stars? Who is "the angel of the church?"**

The seven stars are "the angels of the seven churches" (Rv 1:20). The "angel" of each church is the pastor (see Rv 1:1–20). See the following Bible passages that speak to pastors and churches: Jn 10:1–10; Ac 20:17–28; Ti 1:5–9; 1Tm 3:1–13; 1Pt 5:1–5;

Why would Jesus hate anyone?

Eph 4:11–15; 1Th 5:12–13; Heb 13:17; 1Co 4:1–2.

• • • • • • • • • • • • • • • • • • • •

Q **2:4 What does this verse mean? Who or what is "the love you had at first"?**

"The love you had at first" is likely referring to the Christian's love of sharing the truth and grace of God. (Notice how often this sharing of truth and grace happened, even when it was forbidden [Mk 7:36; 10:46–49; Jn 9:1–34; Lk 2:20; 8:38–39; Ac 4:13–31].)

• • • • • • • • • • • • • • • • • • • •

Q **2:5 What is the significance of the removal of a lampstand? What does God mean when He says, "Remember therefore from where you have fallen"?**

If a lampstand indicates a church, then the removal of a lampstand means rejection by God (1Co 5:4–7). The place from which these people have fallen is related to their first love (v. 4). These Christians, once converted, were faithful and loved to advance the faith among others, but now they had become more concerned with judging false teaching than with advancing the truth.

• • • • • • • • • • • • • • • • • • • •

Q **2:6 Who are the Nicolaitans? Why would Jesus hate anyone or anything?**

The Nicolaitans were followers of a man named Nicolas who taught a form of

Gnosticism. Gnosticism is the belief that life and all that really matters takes place in the mind (*gnoos*) and the material world does not matter. The word *hate* is the opposite of love. To hate means to give up nothing for the sake of what is hated because it is contrary to life in the fullest sense of the word. Jesus taught that we cannot be His disciples unless we hate our family and our own life (Lk 14:26). Jesus doesn't mean that we should mistreat or do wrong but that we must be careful not to sacrifice things spiritual, eternal, and life-giving for the sake of our fallen human nature or the fallen human nature of others (Lk 9:24).

* * *

Q **2:10 Why does he specify that they will be in tribulation for ten days?**

Understanding any text begins with taking what it says in the most simple, straightforward way. In this case, Jesus tells them they will be in prison ten days because He knows this in advance—there being no particular significance to the number of days. When there is significance for the number ten (as in the Ten Commandments), it has to do with what is required to live or realize life during our time in this world.

* * *

Q **2:11 Does this mean that we will go to purgatory before going to heaven? What is the second death?**

The first death has to do with our physical body; the second death is the eternal condemnation and punishment of an unregenerate soul (Rv 20:6, 14; 21:8). The Bible teaches against any and every idea that we can do what the Law requires to save ourselves, whether in this life or after we die (Gal 1:6–10; 3:1–14). Purgatory is the invention of people who do not know of the grace of God in Christ but do know that they cannot fulfill what the Law requires in this life (Lk 16:19–29).

* * *

Q **2:16 What is the sword of His mouth?**

The sword is indicative of the Word of God that comes out of His mouth. Hebrews 4:12 describes the Word of God as "sharper than any two-edged sword," discerning the thoughts and intents of the heart. Jesus Christ *is* the Word of God and always speaks the Word of God (Jn 1:1, 14; 8:38; 14:10).

* * *

Q **2:17 What is the hidden manna and the white stone?**

Manna is what God gave Israel to eat each day while they wandered forty years in the wilderness (Ex 16:31). The hidden part of the manna has to do with how God provides for our lives, especially through the redemptive work and Word of Jesus (Jn 6:1–69; Rm 8:32). A white stone was used in ancient times as an indication of a judgment of innocence for a person who had been accused and was on trial. Notice that what is hidden about the manna is the same as what declares us innocent: Jesus Christ our Redeemer (Jn 16:14; 1Co 2:8;

Gal 2:14; 1Pt 3:21). Consider the relationship between this verse and the language of a wedding garment (white = purity) provided for those attending the banquet (bread = providence) in Mt 22:8–13.

Q 2:20–23 What is the problem with what Jezebel preaches?

Jezebel was the wicked wife of Ahab in the Old Testament (1Ki 16:30–21:26). Jezebel taught Israel to be idolatrous and contrary to God in every way imaginable (and some unimaginable). She had the prophets of God executed and a neighbor falsely accused and executed so that Ahab could have his property. Notice how Jezebel opposed all that is right in the spiritual kingdom and the physical world.

Q 2:24 What are "the deep things of Satan"?

These people probably meant incantations and other means of deception by which they could exercise control over people. Whether people actually know the deep things of Satan or not, certainly we are better off being ignorant of them.

Q 3:1 What are the seven spirits of God?
See answer at 1:4.

Q 3:7 What is the door that no one can shut? If it is heaven, why is it opened with the key of David?

Jesus is, in fact, the key of David. Jesus is the descendant of David who made an entrance to heaven for us (Jn 14:6). The key of David is referred to in Is 22:22. For more on the significance of keys, see notes at Rv 1:18.

Q 3:16 What is meant by the terms *cold*, *hot*, and *lukewarm*?

A person who is cold has no life in the Word of God and wants no life in it; cold indicates being contrary to something. A person who is hot is inspired by a vibrant and constant life in the Word (Jn 8:31–32; Jer 20:9). A person who is lukewarm is neither for nor against anything except his or her own selfish intentions.

Q 3:20 This verse is a little confusing; it makes it sound as if we choose to let God into our lives.

There are plenty of verses in the Bible that speak of making a choice, just as there are conditional sentences (Jsh 24:15; Rm 10:9). Conditions and choices explain the facts of relationships but give no information about how or who is able to make such choices or meet such conditions. The very words of such verses and the words surrounding them are the means by which God's Law incapacitates our contrary human nature and regenerates and inspires our soul to love and obedience (Rm 10:8, 17; 1Pt 1:5; Ezk 36:24–27).

- -

Q 4:3 What are jasper and carnelian?

Jasper and carnelian are precious stones (gems). Precious metals and stones are used throughout Revelation in order to convey a sense of beauty and value for God Himself and for His kingdom (Rv 1:13–15; 21:9–21). These precious stones also remind the reader of the breastplate that the high priest wore in the Old Testament (Ex 28:21–29).

- -

Q 4:4 What is the significance of the number 24? Why is it repeated twice?

There were twelve tribes of Israel in the Old Testament (actually thirteen) and twelve apostles (actually thirteen) in the New Testament. The number 2 has to do with certainty, which the narrative about Pharaoh's dreams makes evident (Gn 41:32). Therefore, the number of thrones and elders indicates that all the people of God from the time before and after the first coming of Christ are surely present with God.

- -

Q 4:6 Why is there so much imagery in this chapter? Do the four living creatures represent the four Gospels?

Most of Revelation is full of imagery that is intended to connect the reader's thoughts with biblical history and with the significance of God and His kingdom. They say a picture is worth a thousand words, and images are pictures of a sort. People from ancient times have identified each one of these living creatures with one of the four Gospels, but that is not why they appear in Revelation. All of God's creation is present before His throne, animals and faithful people. Each of these four living creatures is indicative of a type of living being on land or in the air: human beings, domestic animals, wild animals, and birds (Gn 1:20–30).

- -

Q 4:6–8 Were these creatures angels? Why are the creatures covered with eyes?

These creatures are never referred to as angels and do none of the work that God gives angels to do. These creatures are indicative of all of nature, where God is present and active. The creatures are covered with eyes to remind the reader that God sees and is aware of all that is taking place in His creation.

Why is there so much imagery in this chapter?

> ## What do horses represent?

Q 4:10 Who are the twenty-four elders, and why do they have crowns?

We don't know the particular identity of these elders, but we understand that they are indicative of the people of God from Old and New Testament times (see Rv 4:4 above, also Mt 20:20–23; 1Co 6:2). They are wearing crowns because God had promised this and because crowns indicate royalty and authority (Ps 8:5; 103:4; Pr 4:9; 14:24; 2Tm 4:8; Jas 1:12).

Q 5:1 What is a seal? Is there any significance to the number 7?

A seal was wax melted onto the place where a scroll or document overlapped, then imprinted with some kind of symbol that authenticated the document and protected the contents (Rm 4:11; 2Co 1:21). A seal could also be used to identify ownership. Regarding the number 7, please see Rv 1:4 above.

Q 5:6 Who is the Lamb? Who are the "seven spirits"? Why did he have seven horns and seven eyes?

The Lamb is Christ (Is 53:7; Jn 1:29). The seven spirits refer to the Holy Spirit (see 1:4 above). The number 7 has to do with God's activity in His created universe. Horns have to do with power (1Ki 22:11; Ps 74:5–11). Eyes have to do with seeing. Jesus Christ is the sacrifice that was offered instead of all people; He is almighty (horns) and omniscient (eyes).

Q 5:8 What do the "four living creatures" symbolize?

Each of these four living creatures is indicative of a type of living being on land or in the air: human beings, domestic animals, wild animals, and birds (Gn 1:20–30).

Q 6:1–12 What do the seals and horses represent?

Horses have to do with power or powerful forces (Jb 39:19). Seals have to do with providing proof that something is authentic and true—and with protecting the contents that make it so (Rm 4:11; 2Co 1:21). A seal could also be used to identify ownership. What will surely take place has been sealed or made unknowable to us, but now the Lord Jesus is revealing what will take place between His first and second coming (that is, the New Testament period).

Q 6:2 Who is the rider of the white horse?

Jesus is the one who is pure (white; Ps 18:26; 1Jn 3:2–3) and who has conquered all (Jn 16:33).

Q 6:5–6 What power was the third horse given?

It was given the power to strike the world with famine—that's why grain was so expensive. A denarius was a day's wages.

Q 6:6 Why not damage the oil and the wine?

Wheat, barley, oil, and wine are mentioned in 2Ch 2:15 as part of what Solomon provided to Hiram, King of Tyre, in exchange for help with building the temple. Rehoboam, Solomon's son, fortified cities with "food, oil, and wine" (2Ch 11:11). The Good Samaritan (Jesus in real life), treated the injured man with oil and wine (Lk 10:34). There is no explanation that I am aware of for the famine to strike grain but not oil and wine.

Q 6:7–8 Why were there only four living creatures associated with the seven scrolls and not seven creatures?

There are only four living creatures, one for each main group of living creatures that live on land or above the land: human beings, tame animals, wild animals, and birds. The first four seals each reveal a different color horse, having to do with some powerful force: Christ, war, famine, and death. One of each of the four living creatures calls forth one horse/powerful force.

Q 6:8 Who or what is "Hades," and why does he follow "Death"? Is this referring to the mythological god Hades?

Hades is otherwise known as hell, a place where those condemned suffer (Lk 16:23–28). Hades or hell has existed ever since the fall produced people who would suffer eternal condemnation for their wicked impenitence. Hades comes after or follows death for those who insist on rejecting God, just as life and comfort "follows" for those who live in God's Word and grace (Rv 7:13–17; 14:12–13). This place in history and reality predates Greek mythology, though Greek mythology may have obtained its ideas about hades by way of interaction with the Hebrew people.

Q 6:9–11 Who are the "souls of those who had been slain"?

We don't know who these people are by name, except for those reported in Heb 11:37–38. Ever since Cain murdered his brother Abel, faithful people have been slain by the wicked (Gn 4:3–10; 1Ki 18:4; 21:14; Ac 12:1–3).

Q 7:1–8 What is the significance of the 144,000 who were sealed? Is this really the exact number of those who are sealed? If this is not literal, why do they mention a specific number instead of just saying multitudes that no one can count?

The significance of the seal has been

discussed above at 5:1 and 6:1–12. The number of the saints indicates all the people whom God has certainly saved as His own by fulfilling what the Law requires for them (10 [Law] to 3rd power [God] = 1,000 and 12 [people of God] to 2nd power [certainty] = 144,000). Notice that John clearly shows that this number is indicative rather than an actual count of the people in v. 9 where he goes on to describe these people as a "great multitude that no one could number." The number of 144,000 is shorthand for the great multitude from all nations, tribes, peoples, and tongues who stand before Christ, having been redeemed (clothed in white) and rejoicing to be with Him (palm branches in their hands, Mt 21:8–11).

Q 7:4 Why do the Jehovah's Witnesses claim that only 144,000 people will be saved?

Like many who misread and misunderstand the Bible, the Jehovah's Witnesses are inconsistent in their interpretation of biblical language. For example, they argue that the 144,000 are the actual, literal number of God's people but ignore v. 9, which describes them literally as being beyond number, and they ignore Rv 14:3–5 that further describes the 144,000 as Jewish, male, and virgin.

Q 7:5–8 Was the tribe of Dan left out because of idolatry?

All of the tribes of Israel were idolatrous at one time or another. Even Solomon built

temples for idols (1Ki 11:4–7). The whole Bible uses several means to make sure we don't misunderstand the text, especially the indicative or symbolic language. While we think of the tribes of Israel and the number of apostles both as twelve, there were actually thirteen of each. This list of tribes is followed immediately by a description of them as innumerable and from every tribe, nation, people, and language (v. 9). You have noticed that the tribe of Dan is missing, but the tribe of Ephraim is not mentioned either. The tribe of Joseph is mentioned, but so is Manasseh, who came from Joseph—though Ephraim also came from Joseph. Being a child of Israel was never about physical descent but rather about having been generated by the Word and promises of God (Rm 2:28–29; Gal 3:7–9).

Q 7:14 When and where is the great tribulation?

Jesus spoke of great tribulation in Mt 24:9–44. Jesus' prophecy was fulfilled in part when Jerusalem was destroyed by the Romans in AD 70. Yet every generation of Christians has experienced tribulation and seen in their times the signs that Jesus described—this is to be expected in a fallen and hostile world and serves to keep Christians watchful (1Th 1:6; 2:2; 3:1–5; 2Pt 3:1–13). The most likely fulfillment of what Jesus described to date would be the Age of Enlightenment or Rationalism, which displaced God as the authority over His creation in favor of human intellect and personal desire (the "abomination of desolation standing where he ought not" [Mk 13:14]).

Q 8:1 Why is there silence following the seventh seal?

The first two visions (6:1–8:1 and 8:2–11:19) are partial views of the New Testament period (from the first until the second and final coming of Christ). They speak of damaging fourths (6:8) or thirds (8:12) in contrast to the following five visions that speak in terms of completeness (12:10; 15:1; 19:2, 20; 20:10). The silence at the end of the first vision gives readers pause to consider the vision just revealed and to transition to the next (Gn 24:21; Dt 27:9; Jb 4:16–19; Ps 62:1, 5).

Q 8:2 What is the significance of the seven angels and seven trumpets?

Each of the seven visions that provide deeper and deeper views of what will take place between the first and second/final coming of Christ has seven parts, seven having to do with God's activity in His creation (3 + 4). "Angels" are messengers of God, either heavenly beings, as in this case, or pastors. Trumpets have to do with communicating clearly and effectively (Ezk 33:3–6; 1Co 14:8).

> Why do the angels bring blood?

Q 8:6–13 Why is a third of everything changed? What is so significant about a third?

Part of the significance of thirds has to do with understanding that this second of seven visions is providing a partial view of what will take place between the first and second/final coming of Christ. Is it possible that thirds are indicative of events in the world that are the inverse of God's will (three turned upside down)? If so, then it is also possible that fourths are indicative of events that are contrary to the natural laws that God created (four turned upside down).

Q 8:6 How should we interpret and understand the events of the seven trumpets?

The seven parts of this second vision are parallel to the seven parts of each of the seven visions of the time from the first until the second/last coming of Christ (Rv 6:1–21:1). There will be physical troubles parallel to and indicative of the more substantial and catastrophic spiritual troubles in the world (see Mt 24:9–44).

Q 8:7–9 Why do the angels bring blood?

Blood has to do with life. It is what provides for life according to God's design or what ends life when the blood is shed, contrary to God's will. The blood came mixed with fire and hail. Destruction from cold and heat comes in a measure consistent with the guilt of people upon the earth and gives a partial indication of the devastation of the earth due to the fall of mankind (the shedding of blood in murder [cold] or hatred [heat] causes humans to make war and, historically, this has meant a devastation of the landscape and a stripping of the land; Jgs 6:4; Ezk 14:15).

Q **9:1–2 Is this metaphorical or can hell be unlocked with a "key" (star)?**

Stars are angels (Rv 1:20; 12:2–17; Jude 6). The devil was cast down from heaven and has the means of murder and lies by which to open the way to hell for everyone who does not remain in the Word and grace of God (Is 14:12–14; Jn 8:31–47; Mt 12:43–45; 2Co 11:13–15). Keys are simply means of manipulating what binds or looses (Mt 16:19).

Q **9:5 What is the significance of five months of torture instead of death?**

The number 5 has to do with blessings or curses (Is 3:24; Jer 33:11). Death means the absence of positive relationships, which is why we call the cessation of physiological function in the body (or the function of anything) "death." People who insist on rebelling against God and His will for their life will suffer the consequences of such rebellion and, in this suffering, will wish to die physically in order to escape the pain, but they will be unable to do so (Lk 16:22–26; Rv 2:11; 9:6; 20:6, 14; 21:8).

Q **9:20–21 Does this mean that non-believers who died in the past have less of a chance for repentance since they weren't around to see the plagues?**

God desires all to be saved, has in fact saved all through the vicarious atonement of Christ, and provides means of revelation that all might repent and believe (1Tm 2:4; 2Co 5:19; Rm 1:20–32; 2:11–16). The point of this lesson is that fallen, rebellious human nature is not converted by signs and wonders, which history demonstrates and the Gospels record (Lk 16:27–31; Heb 3:7–4:13).

Q **10:9–11 Why does John eat the scroll? What is the relevance of this? Why did the scroll make his stomach bitter?**

John ate the scroll because God told him to. Eating the scroll is parallel to the effect that the Word of God has on us. The Word of God is easy to talk about but not so easy to do—easy to agree with on the outside but very hard for a contrary human nature to swallow (Is 29:13; Mt 15:8; Jn 6:26, 60; Jas 2:14–19).

Q **11:1–14 Who are the two witnesses? What do they represent?**

Verse 6 makes clear that one witness is Elijah (no rain falls [1Ki 17:1; Jas 5:17–18]) and the other is Moses (turn water into blood [Ex 7:14–18]). These two witnesses indicate all of God's Word to us, Moses

> ## Why does God use specific amounts of time?

indicating the Law and Elijah the promises of God (Ex 20:1–17; Mal 4:5; Mt 17:1–13; Lk 24:27).

- - - - - - - - - - - - - - - - - -

Q 11:3 Why does God use such specific amounts of time (1,260 days)?

God uses specific amounts for clarity and reference. There are four main directions on the compass, seven days in a week, and ten commandments. God provides order in His creation because order supports life.

You may have noticed that 1,260 days is the same as 42 months or 3½ years. If 7 indicates the fullness of time (as in 7 days in a week), then 7 also indicates the whole of time, from creation to re-creation (Gn 2:1–3; 2Pt 3:11–13). The first coming of Jesus indicates the half-way point in history; thus the time between the first and second/last coming of Jesus would be referred to as 3½.

- - - - - - - - - - - - - - - - - -

Q 11:8 Where was our Lord crucified?

The Lord Jesus Christ was crucified in Jerusalem. However, the physical location of the cross upon which Jesus was crucified is not as important as the place in the hearts and minds of the people who crucified Him (Heb 6:4–6; 10:26–31). Sodom and Egypt were both known not only for their evil and

wickedness but even more so for their obstinate, vicious refusal to repent in the face of all the warnings and invitations to life that God provided for them (Gn 18:16–19:28; Ex 6:1–14:28). This stubborn rejection of Christ is what crucified Jesus in Jerusalem and in the hearts of anyone who similarly despises Him (1Co 1:23; Gal 6:14).

- - - - - - - - - - - - - - - - - -

Q 11:9–11 Is there anything significant about the 3½ days?

There was a time of four hundred years at the end of the Old Testament period, between the prophecies of Malachi and the coming of John the Baptist, when there was no Word from God. So also, for a relatively brief time (3½ days compared to 3½ years [see 11:3]) at the end of the New Testament period, there will be few people who recognize the Word of God for what it is (Rv 12:17; 20:3; Lk 18:8).

- - - - - - - - - - - - - - - - - -

Q 11:9 Why were the bodies being gazed at and not buried?

This narrative parallels the description in ch. 20 of the devil being released for a short time (Rv 20:3). If the two witnesses indicate the Word of God, then we can see how this vision anticipated what has happened in the last three hundred years—people still have Bibles, but the Bible's witness has been slain in the sense that few people recognize it as the Word of God. Multitudes of academic scholars still make their livings by writing and teaching about the Bible, but what they write and teach is that the Bible is all deception and invention. Worse than that, these scholars rejoice with each other over how they have put the Word of God to death, and they even give each other honors for how cleverly they have done so. People look at the Bible in order to mock or criticize it rather than simply ignoring it because doing so makes them think they are right to do so. Many people mocked Jesus at His crucifixion because they thought His lack of response meant He could not be the almighty God (Lk 23:35–37).

Q 11:11 Could this be used to support the idea of a nonimmediate transfer to the afterlife?

No, the continuous, uninterrupted consciousness of the soul is evident in Lk 16:22 and 23:42–43.

Q 11:14 What are the "woes"?

The first woe has to do with the torments experienced by wicked unbelievers (Rv 9:12). The second woe has to do with the great earthquake (11:13). The third and final woe is the end of the world (11:15; see later visions in Revelation for more detail about why the end of the world is so woeful to the wicked, 18:1–24; 2Pt 3:1–13).

Q 11:15–19 Does this refer to the rapture?

This refers to Judgment Day, which is the same day that is described in 1Th 4:13–

18 and Mt 24:29–25:46. There is no partial Judgment Day between the first and second/final coming of Christ.

Q 11:16 Who are the twenty-four elders?

See Rv 4:10.

Q 12:1–6 Do the woman and the dragon have anything to do with astrological signs? Do astrologers give names to signs based on the Bible?

God tells us plainly that creation bears witness to Him and that He made the stars for signs and seasons (Gn 1:14–19; Ps 19:1–3; Rm 1:20–23). Astrology, in contrast to astronomy, is the misuse of God's creation as a means of knowing what we cannot know or attempting to manipulate what we cannot control. I doubt that astrologers make any use of the Bible at all.

Q 12:1–5 Who is the woman and what does she represent? Is the son Jesus Christ?

The woman is indicative of all the people of God—and especially Eve and Mary—who were part of His promise to send His own Son through the seed of the woman in order to be the Savior of the world (Gn 3:15; Lk 3:23–38). The dragon is the devil, also recognized as the serpent from the Garden of Eden (Rv 12:9; Gn 3:1–14; Jn 8:44). The Son whom the woman gave birth to was Jesus Christ. The devil tried to destroy Jesus at His birth by means of Herod's jealousy (Mt 2:1–18). The description of the sun, moon, and twelve stars echoes the dream of Joseph about himself and his family (Gn 37:9–10). The people of God have always been surrounded by His promises, supported by His prophets, and encouraged by the generation of children, which were a constant reminder that God is the author of life and restores it in the face of impossibility (Ex 14:19–20; Is 40:1–5; Gn 15:1–5; Mt 22:23–33).

- - - - - - - - - - - - - - - - - - - -

Q **12:3–12 Did the devil reside with God in heaven until Jesus died on the cross, and if so, why? Was Jesus' death on the cross God's method of banishing Satan?**

The Book of Job reveals that the devil wanders to and fro upon the earth but comes, from time to time, before God in order to accuse people (the name *Satan* means "the accuser" [Jb 1:6–12; 2:1–7; 1Pt 5:8]). The promises of God, which would be fulfilled by Christ, prevented the devil's accusations from bringing condemnation upon believers until Christ, in time and space, bore away the sins of the world and so permanently removed the devil's means of accusing anyone of anything (Rv 12:7–11). The devil cannot undo the universal, vicarious atonement of Christ (2Co 5:19–21). All that is left for the devil is to keep people from realizing the benefits of redemption by deceiving them into thinking that they have not been justified but need to and are able to justify themselves (Rv 12:17; 2Co 11:13–15; Gal 5:4; Mt 22:11–14; 25:1–46).

- - - - - - - - - - - - - - - - - - - -

Q **12:3 Why would the devil have seven heads when that number is usually associated with God and signifies completeness?**

The devil has not just seven heads but ten horns and seven crowns on his heads. There are a few ways of understanding what this language indicates. First of all, the devil is still and always will be a creation of God and must, therefore, necessarily serve God's purposes (3 [of God] + 4 [created] = 7). Second, "heads" have to do with authorities and "seven" has to do with time, meaning the devil works through worldly authorities over the course of time. This relates to the "horns" and "crowns." "Ten" has to do with the Law, "horns" have to do with power, and "crowns" have to do with political position. These three features indicate that the devil would exercise power through the law processed by human authorities like governments and legal systems. Consider how political authorities and courts have made it their business in recent decades to oppose and limit the free exercise of Christianity.

- - - - - - - - - - - - - - - - - - - -

Q **12:4 What is the significance of the dragon sweeping the stars out of the sky?**

When the devil turned to oppose God and fell from communion with Him, apparently he did not fall alone. The devil corrupted other angels who became demons, in opposition to God (2Co 11:13–15; Is 14:12–15).

Q 12:6 What is the significance of 1,260 days? Why does John use 1,260 days to refer to the woman but 42 months to refer to the beast when they are both equal to 3½ years? There has been a lot more time than just 3½ years in between Christ's first coming and His future second coming.

You may have noticed that 1,260 days is the same as 42 months and 3½ years. If 7 indicates the fullness of time (as in 7 days in a week), then 7 also indicates the whole of time, from creation to re-creation (Gn 2:1–3; 2Pt 3:11–13). The first coming of Jesus indicates the halfway point in history (conceptually, not mathematically); thus the time between the first and second/last coming of Jesus would be referred to as 3½.

Q 12:7 How can there be war in heaven? I thought heaven was supposed to be perfect without the battles of life.

Heaven can refer to paradise, but it can also refer to the place where God resides (which is what makes it paradise; 1Ki 22:19). The war that broke out in heaven was not the kind of enormous, populated, and bloody battle scene we think of but more the fundamental conflict between God and the devil, who was determined to oppose Him (futile as that had to be).

Q 12:9 If Satan can't accuse people after Jesus died on the cross, does that mean he could do so before Jesus took away the sins of the world?

We know from the history of Job that Satan was able to and did accuse people before God (Jb 1:6–12; 2:1–7). Once Jesus had taken away the sins of the world, there was no longer any guilt for Satan to accuse people of. Nevertheless, the final judgment of the devil does not come until the end of the world, so until that time, he makes war with those who seek to live in the kingdom of God (Rv 12:17; 1Pt 5:8).

Q 12:14 What does this verse mean? What does "time, and times, and half a time" mean?

"Two" has to do with certainty. "Wings" have to do with protection and escape (Ex 19:4; Ru 2:12; Mt 23:37). "Eagle" has to do with power (2Sm 1:23; Ps 103:5; Is 40:31). If the woman is indicative of all the faithful people of God from creation to the first coming of Christ, then God is making clear that these people, who hoped in His promises, are and remain safe from the devil's assaults (1Jn 5:18; Rv 6:10–11).

Time (1) + times (2) + half time (½) = 3½. See 12:6 above for more about this time.

• • • • • • • • • • • • • • • • • • • •

Q 13:1 How can the Left Behind series be wrong when many of the things it says are right here in Revelation? Who or what is the beast coming out of the sea? What do the blasphemous names on each head mean?

Many people misunderstand and misinterpret biblical texts because they treat literal language as if it were figurative and figurative (indicative) language as if it were literal or some inconsistent combination thereof. The beast is indicative of any person or group of people who pretend to be Christ in order to deceive and mislead people (antichrists; see 1Jn 2:18–19; 2Co 11:13–15). All of the features of this beast are counterfeits of the Christ, including the blasphemous names (Mk 13:14–29).

• • • • • • • • • • • • • • • • • • • •

Q 13:3 Why does the beast have a mortal wound that is healed?

If this beast is the Antichrist, then everything about this beast is going to be a counterfeit of Christ. Therefore, just as Christ retained the marks of His crucifixion after His resurrection from the dead, so this beast was mortally wounded, but that wound was healed (Lk 24:38–39). What was the wound? Perhaps the wound has to do with Christ having taken away the sin of the world and restoring/confirming the truth and grace of God (Mk 1:23–27; Mt 5:17–48; Rv 12:7–16). The beast seems to have recovered from this wound in as much as those forces that oppose Christ still bind people

in their sins and continue to oppose God by contradicting the truth and tempting people to abandon grace and eternity for materialism and time in this world (Ac 20:28–30; Rv 12:17; 2Co 11:13–15).

• • • • • • • • • • • • • • • • • • • •

Q 13:5 Why was the beast given a second mouth to blaspheme God? Is this merely to tempt us or to see how "good" we are?

The first mouth, like a lion (v. 2) indicated that this beast tries to sound like Jesus, the lion of Judah, whose mouth speaks with power (Jer 25:36–38; Mt 7:29; 9:6–8; Mk 1:27). This verse is not interested in us simply thinking the beast has a second mouth; rather, we should realize the mouth it has is not only like a lion (threatening; counterfeiting real power and authority) but also making claims for itself that are only true of the Son of God, Jesus Christ (Jn 10:30–39; Mk 13:14, 21–23; Ac 13:6–12; 3Jn 9–11). The mouth was given to the beast by the dragon (the devil) in order to provide a means of deception (Jn 8:44). The mouth does test us—not to see how good we are, but to remind us of the absolute necessity of remaining in the Word so that we know the difference between the truth of God and the deception of the devil (Jn 10:1–29; 1Jn 4:1–3).

• • • • • • • • • • • • • • • • • • • •

Q 13:11–12 Who or what is the beast that comes out of the earth?

This beast that comes from the land is the "anti-spirit," or the product of the devil that is intended to counterfeit the work of the Holy Spirit. Notice how the description of this beast's work parallels the relationship between the Holy Spirit and Christ (Mk 16:16–20; Jn 6:63; 16:13–15; Rm 10:17; 1Co 12:3). This beast comes from the earth, suggesting that this source of deception comes from human institutions (governments and business created in a physical world, from the physical world, concerned with life in this physical world; Rv 17:2; 18:3, 9, 11, 23) in contrast with religious institutions (counterfeiting Christ, who is living water).

• • • • • • • • • • • • • • • • • • • •

Q 13:12 Why do they refer to the wound being healed again?

Jesus did defeat the devil absolutely in His life, death, and resurrection (Rv 12:7–11). However, the devil still works to take away or keep people from the benefits of Christ's redemption by deceiving them into misbelief (Rv 12:17; 20:1–3; 2Co 11:13–15; 1Pt 5:8). Repetition is usually for emphasis.

• • • • • • • • • • • • • • • • • • • •

Q 13:16 What does the mark of the beast on the right hand or forehead refer to?

The "right hand" indicates a person's proper work. Connect the notion of one's proper work with restrictions and hindrances placed in the way of goodness by the fallen world. Notice how in our time especially and in our culture, almost anything is permitted and protected except the truth (Ps 12:8). The mark on the hand indicates the opposite of the marks on Jesus' hands

What does 666 mean?

and feet; rather than love and self-sacrifice, people today bear the marks of compromise and capitulation. The mark on the forehead sounds like a counterfeit of the seal of God that is on the forehead of believers (2Co 1:21–22; Eph 1:13; Rv 7:3). If Christians have the Word of God in their hands and on their minds, then unbelievers have the work of the devil on their hands and in their minds—lies and murder rather than truth and life (Jn 8:31–44).

• • • • • • • • • • • • • • • • • • • •

Q 13:18 What does 666 mean?

We have already seen how the number 7 is associated with God's activity in His creation (God as 3 + creation as 4 = 7; Rv 1:4). The devil wants to be God but is not, the first beast wants to be Christ but is not, the second beast wants to be the Holy Spirit but is not; in each case, the opposition to God falls short, thus 666.

• • • • • • • • • • • • • • • • • • • •

Q 14:1–5 Where exactly is Mount Zion? What is the significance of the number 144,000? If the 144,000 are really a great multitude that can't be numbered, why does it only refer to them as the 144,000 in this chapter?

Mount Zion is where Jerusalem is built and is indicative of the place where our redemption to God was accomplished by Christ, the place of our salvation (Ps 9:11–14; Jn 12:15; Gal 4:26). For a discussion of the number 144,000, see the answer at 7:1–8.

Q 14:8 Do you think the Western world of materialism is Babylon the great?

Ever since the fall, all human beings and the cultures they create have been fundamentally materialistic because this is what a material body relates to. I can't think of a place, Western or Eastern, that is not a world of materialism (see Rv 18:9–16).

Q 14:9–10 What do these verses mean?

To worship the beast means to consciously, constantly, and obstinately oppose all that God is and does, especially through the Savior, Jesus Christ (Mt 12:31–32; Heb 6:4–8; 10:26–31). These people will experience the absence of God since that is what they insisted on; they will experience the wine of His wrath rather than the living water of His grace (Mt 25:31–46; Jn 4:1–26).

Q 14:13 Who is this speaking?

The apostle John heard the voice. The voice was that of the Holy Spirit.

Q 14:14 Why does he say, "Like a son of man"? If it wasn't the Son of Man, who was it?

In Greek, the word for "like" does not necessarily mean something only similar but can mean the thing itself (consider the description of Jesus in Php 2:5–7). The Book of Daniel records one "like a son of the gods" walking about in the fiery furnace, but we understand this to be the actual Son of God (Dn 3:25).

Q 14:16 Is this the rapture?

If you are thinking that the rapture is an event before the end of the world where only believers are caught up to heaven, then no, since the Bible teaches no such thing. If you recognize that the rapture is part of the singular event of Judgment Day, then yes, this is describing Judgment Day (Mt 24:36–42; 1Co 15:50–52).

Q 15:1 Are these plagues symbolic of the plagues in Exodus? What does it mean when it says that with them God's wrath is finished?

Use of the term *plague* is surely meant to remind the reader of God's redemption of Israel in the exodus. However, only the second and third plagues, which turned water to blood, are parallel to the ones in Egypt (Ex 7:17–21). In contrast to the first two visions where destruction was partial (thirds, fourths), in this vision the destruction is total, and the whole vision ends with the words Jesus spoke from the cross, "It is finished" (Rv 16:17; Jn 19:30). This vision may describe the plagues as completing the wrath of God because the judgment of those forces that brought God's wrath upon the earth (the harlot, the two beasts, and finally the dragon) follow immediately.

Q **15:5 Is it significant that the tabernacle is open?**

The tabernacle is not opened so that the faithful can be there with God, nor is the verb in the perfect tense, which would mean it was opened and would stay open, so I suspect there is no significance except to reveal the origin of the plagues. The language of openness having to do with salvation does occur in Jn 1:51; Heb 10:20; and 2Pt 1:11.

Q **15:8 It sounds as if the seven plagues did not harm or affect anyone (except those marked by the devil, according to ch. 16) because no one was allowed in the temple. Is this correct?**

There was smoke in the temple that kept anyone from entering while the plagues were being executed by the angels. Like the plagues in Egypt, only unbelievers bring such judgment upon themselves.

Q **16:7 What is the significance of the altar, and how could it speak?**

It was the voice of an angel that responded from the altar ("the voice of another," referring to the angel in v. 5). The altar is indicative of the means by which Christ redeemed the world. He sacrificed Himself in stark contrast to the destructive selfishness of fallen human beings (1Co 1:17 – 2:2).

Q **16:12 What is the significance of the Euphrates River?**

The Euphrates River marked the border between the Middle East and the East. It was from the Euphrates that the Babylonians came and took Judah captive in 587 BC (2Ki 24:1–25:28).

Q **16:13 Who is the false prophet?**

Given the list of enemies (dragon, beast, false prophet), the third would most likely be the second beast, the anti-spirit (Rv 12:3; 13:1–10, 11–17; 1Ki 22:19–25).

Q **16:16 What does Armageddon mean? What is this place?**

Armageddon is a Hebrew word meaning "Mount" ("Har") "Megiddo." Mount Carmel is, perhaps, the best known mountain near the plain of Megiddo, where Elijah tested the prophets of Baal (1Ki 18:17–40).

Q 16:18 What is the significance of the lightning, thunder, and earthquake in this verse?

"Light" from lightning has to do with clarity of vision; Jesus is the light of the world and exposes all things for what they are (Jn 3:19–20; Ex 19:16). Lightning and sound indicate the presence of God. "Sound" and "thunder" have to do with clarity of hearing; no more closing one's ears or arguing about interpretations (Ezk 1:22–24; Jn 12:28–29). "Earthquakes" have to do with the world bearing witness to the power of God, especially His power to correct what is wrong and as a reminder not to trade the Creator for creation (Is 29:6; Jer 23:19; Ezk 3:12; Mt 24:7; 27:54; 28:2; Ac 16:26; Rm 1:20–32).

Q 16:19 What is the "great city?"

The "great city" is mentioned by name as this verse continues: "God remembered Babylon the great, to make her drain the cup of the wine of the fury of His wrath." Be careful not to restrict your thinking as if one physical city is meant. Rather, the great city of Babylon has to do with all that fallen, contrary human beings construct for their own selfish and vain purposes (Gn 11:3–9; Rv 18:2–8).

Q 17:3 What does the woman sitting on the scarlet beast represent?

According to v. 5, this woman is Babylon or the "anti-church." If you read the description of her in vv. 4–6 and 18:1–24, you will notice how in every way she is the opposite of the virgin Bride of Christ, which is the Christian Church. She is sitting on the beast, which is indicative of the governments and institutions of fallen mankind, just as governments and institutions of mankind have and still do support false religion.

Q 17:5 Is this verse a metaphor, or did the woman really have an inscription on her forehead?

Most language in Revelation is indicative, that is, physical descriptions that point to or highlight spiritual realities. The woman has an inscription on her forehead because she is a counterfeit of the faithful people who are sealed on their foreheads (Rv 7:3; 9:4). The seal on the forehead indicates what is true and will remain true about the one sealed and the thinking of that one. Those who oppose Christ may pretend to be faithful but will always be opposed to what is godly and good (Mt 23:1–39; Jude 5–13).

Q **17:6 What does it mean that the woman was drunk with the blood of the saints?**

The woman represents the anti-church, which is the opposite of Christianity and opposes Christians. The people and organizations that attempt to counterfeit Christianity intoxicate themselves with the destruction of the lives of innocent people, especially Christians (saints). Consider the way people who claim to be religious advocate and even demand abortion, euthanasia, sexual promiscuity, and general moral decline (Jn 11:46–53; 18:22–23; Hab 1:2–4; Ex 32:1–6; Mal 1:1–2:17; 1Co 1:10–13; 5:1–6:8).

Q **18:1–24 What is Babylon, and why was it used in this vision?**

Revelation is full of contrasts between what is true and what is false and counterfeit. The harlot is the opposite, the counterfeit, of the true Christian Church and referred to as Babylon (Rv 17:5). If Jerusalem is the city of God, the place where faithful people live, then Babylon indicates the communities, religions, and institutions of people who mean to deceive and destroy under the pretense of godliness (3:12; 21:2, 10; Ps 87).

What is Babylon?

Q **19:5 Why do we still fall short of praising God even though we are told to praise Him throughout the Bible?**

Ever since Adam disobeyed God, human nature always falls short of everything God commands (Gn 6:5; Is 64:6; Rm 5:6–10).

Q **19:7–10 What is the wedding of the Lamb?**

The wedding of the Lamb refers to the coming together and permanent union of Christ and all those who have been regenerated and sustained in the faith by His Word (Mt 22:1–14; Jn 3:29; 2Co 11:2; Eph 5:25–27; Is 61:10; 62:4–5).

Q **19:13 Why is the rider of the white horse wearing a robe that is dipped in blood?**

The rider is Jesus Christ, and the robe that is properly His comes from having given (immersed) all His life (blood) in order to redeem all the world (Mt 26:28; 27:25; Jn 6:51; Ac 20:28; Rm 3:25; 1Jn 1:7; Jn 6:51).

Why do people try to predict the Last Day?

Q **19:19 Where did the demons come from to help Satan in the battle of heaven?**

The devil brought other angels with him when he fell; these became demons (Jude 6; Rv 12:4).

Q **19:20 Is the false prophet the Antichrist? If so, is the Antichrist the pope?**

The false prophet is the anti-spirit; the beast is the Antichrist (see Rv 13:11–12). Anyone or any position that opposes Christ by claiming to speak His Word while actually speaking what is contrary to His Word is "antichrist" by definition (Mk 13:14; 2Th 2:3–4; 1Jn 2:18–22).

Q **20:1–10 Can angels get hurt when they are fighting?**

There is no evidence I know of that angels or demons are hurt since they are all subject to God's will and God seems always to dispense with them immediately and decisively (Mt 8:28–32; Ac 16:16–18; Rv 12:7–8).

Q **20:2–7 Why do people try to predict the Last Day? What is the symbolism of the thousand years in each of these verses?**

People want to know the Last Day for the same reason they want to know so many things: curiosity, fear, advantage, or selfishness. Fallen human nature wants to know the Last Day so it can continue to do what is contrary to God's will but then repent at the last moment and so gain heaven (Mt 24:45–51; Mk 13:3–37). One thousand years indicates the time that will pass in order for all that God has commanded according to the Law to be fulfilled (10 [law] to the 3rd [God] power). Elsewhere in Revelation (11:2–3; 12:6, 14), this period of time is described as 1,260 days, 42 months, or 3½ years. This is the period of time from the first coming of Christ until just before His return. The devil was bound during this time because the Word of God was recognized by the world as the truth communicated and confirmed by God. When the world generally renounced the Word of God as truth, the devil became unhindered in his activity to deceive, lie, and murder without restraint.

Q **20:3 Why is Satan released?**

The devil is released so that he can go forth and deceive people, as stated expressly in v. 8. This time of deceiving is part of the just judgment against people who refuse the truth in favor of lies even though they had been warned (Jn 3:19–20; Rm 1:20–32; Mt 21:33–46).

Q **20:4 Have we already been given the mark of the beast?**

The mark of the beast cannot be given to those who belong to the Lord, since we are already sealed with the Holy Spirit (see Rv 7:3). The mark of the beast indicates a way of acting (hands) and thinking (head) deluded by and consistent with the destructive ways of the devil (Rm 1:20–32; 1Tm 4:1–2).

Q **20:5–6 Can you explain the first and second deaths and the first and second resurrections?**

The first death refers to our body in time. The second death is eternal separation from God in the lake of fire (Rv 20:14). The first resurrection is that of Jesus Christ and all who are joined in it with Him by faith. Anyone who is joined with Christ has already passed through judgment, which is why the second death has no power over us (Rm 8:1). The second resurrection comes at the end of the world when everyone rises; the faithful rise to life everlasting, and the unfaithful rise to judgment (Jn 5:24–29).

Q **20:11–15 What does this passage mean?**

This passage describes Judgment Day. Everyone must appear before the judgment seat of Christ and then live eternally in paradise or suffer everlasting punishment (Mt 25:31–46).

Q **20:12 I thought we were saved by believing in the crucifixion and resurrection of Jesus Christ. Why, then, does this say that the dead were judged according to their works?**

We are saved by grace but judged by works (Mt 25:31–46; Jn 5:29; 2Co 5:10). How is it that some people have good works and no guilt? These people are covered with the righteous life of Christ (His good works are credited to us), regenerated by the Spirit (so we do genuinely good works), and forgiven (no evil deeds to be condemned for; Rm 8:1; Jn 16:14; 1Jn 1:7; 3:9).

Q **20:15 I thought Revelation was a prophecy, but sometimes we discuss the events in this book as if they already happened. How does that work?**

Remember that John recorded these revelations at the end of the first century. We have almost two thousand years of fulfillment since John wrote. Revelation describes the period of time from the first to the second coming of Christ. The signs of the end times have been seen, at least in part, by people from every generation since Jesus ascended into heaven—which serves to keep us all watchful (1Pt 4:7). However, the absolute fulfillment of all that John saw is still coming (obviously, since the world has not ended).

Q 21:1 Why should the first heaven pass away?

Heaven is primarily a reference to the sky and space above the earth (Gn 1:6–9). All of God's first physical creation will be destroyed to assure that nothing from the first creation that was affected by the fall of man will remain in eternity (Rm 8:19–23; 2Pt 3:10–13).

Q 21:10–21 The city of God seems very full of material items from earth (gold, pearls). Are these metaphors?

Most of the descriptive language in Revelation refers to God's physical creation in order to indicate truth about spiritual realities, which is why God created a material world (Ps 19:1–3; Rm 1:20). Precious metals and stones indicate beauty, value, durability, and parallels with Old Testament history (remember all the precious stones and metals used for the priesthood and tabernacle [Ex 25:1–28:43]).

Q 21:16 What does "stadia" mean?

A stadia is about 600 feet or 200 meters. The physical measurement is not as significant as the number of stadia: 12,000. This number indicates that the city is the work of God that provides habitation for all of those who are His people (10 [law] to the 3rd power [God] times 12 [people of God] = 12,000).

Q 21:27 If God already knows who is going to spend eternity with Him, then what is the point of being here?

First, consider what it would mean if God did not know something; how could He be God? How could we have any peace or confidence unless we know that we depend completely on God, who knows all? God has redeemed everyone in the life of Jesus Christ (Rm 5:6–21). Second, experience is what life is made of, whether we know what will be experienced ahead of time or not. Sometimes we like to have new experiences and are excited because they are unknown. However, most of the time we enjoy something especially because we know what the experience will be; a favorite drink or meal, restful sleep, beauty in nature, or truth.

Perhaps the greatest of all experiences is sharing God's Word with people and observing the multitude of blessings that His Word brings.

Q 22:1 What is the "water of life?"

The Son/Word of God is the water of life (Jn 4:1–26).

Q 22:11 Why would we let these people keep on sinning?

At this point in Revelation, the current time, rather than the future, is being addressed. These words are a warning to the wicked and an encouragement to the faithful. The wicked oppose God and assure themselves that they have power to defy God because He only warns them, He does not destroy them all at once. What else can be said to a person who despises warnings except "just keep it up and see what happens"? On the other hand, faithful people can be discouraged when they see the wicked renounce God day after day. Therefore, God also urges the faithful to continue on the path of faithfulness because they also will, no doubt, see what happens. Justice requires fair warning or patience first, but then follows the necessary outcome of contradicting or obeying God's design in creation (Mt 23:32; 1Th 2:16).

● ● ● ● ● ● ● ● ● ● ● ● ● ● ● ● ● ● ● ●

Q 22:18–19 Does this refer to adding/ removing words from the entire Bible or just the Book of Revelation? How do you defend against Mormon views?

This warning is against adding or removing anything from the entire Bible. Such a warning is consistent with the whole history of revelation, during which God was faithful to authenticate His Word and His servants were careful to test for authenticity (Dt 13:1–18; Mk 16:16–20; 1Jn 4:1). The history of the Bible and its contents provides an enduring and clear witness by which we might know whether other words or writings are from God or not. The Book of Mormon, like many others, comes long after the canon of the Bible was closed and is not of the same character as the biblical books. Any person or group of people that attempts to add new texts to the Bible or remove/reject biblical texts are the subject(s) of this dire warning.

Index